International Management

International Management

Second Edition

David H. Holt
James Madison University (retired)

Karen W. Wigginton
James Madison University

Australia · Canada · Mexico · Singapore · Spain · United Kingdom · United States

International Management, Second Edition

David H. Holt, Karren W. Wigginton

Publisher
Mike Roche

Acquisitions Editor
Tracy Morse

Market Strategist
Beverly Dunn

Developmental Editor
C.J. Jasieniecki

Project Manager
Andrea Archer

For more information
contact South-Western,
5191 Natorp Boulevard,
Mason, Ohio, 45040.
Or you can visit our internet site
at: http://www.swcollege.com

For permission to use material from
this text or product, contact us by
Tel (800) 730-2214
Fax (800) 730-2215
http://www.thomsonrights.com

Library of Congress Control
Number: 2001090953

ISBN: 0-03-031962-5

DEDICATION

To my wife, Judith K. Holt, a companion in world travel
and respected professor in her own right

Thank you for years of love and quiet endurance

To my husband, David S. Wigginton

Thank you for your love, patience, and support

PREFACE

Management is about people working in organizations, and international management is about people from many cultures working together, competing against one another, or trying to cope with one another's differences. Consequently, this book is about people from many walks of life, from affluent countries and from struggling regions, who are part of a global society. With that said, no book will adequately represent world events, but in this revised edition, we have tried to represent a broad spectrum of worldwide business and culture. The book is about people, values, and cultures, and although the structure of a textbook requires specific attention to topics such as international trade or corporate strategy, the human side of enterprise and its cultural antecedents are woven into presentations wherever possible.

International Management was written as an upper-division text with sufficient comprehensive treatment and case selection for use at the MBA level. It was written primarily for business students who would have had foundation courses in management, organizational behavior, and economics. The text is not intended to replace "principles" course materials, and consequently many fundamental terms and concepts cited may not be developed in order to avoid unnecessary replication. This should not be detrimental to students from other disciplines who might be taking an international management course or pursuing graduate studies.

The authors' objectives for this textbook were simply to provide a human relations approach to managing internationally, and to emphasize the wonderful differences among peoples of the world that make an international career rewarding. The joy and challenge of working in a global environment are both exhilarating and educational. Each thing that we learn abroad enriches our understanding of home. Each foreign experience opens new ideas for us about how to better our own society. Each person we meet from another culture is a learning experience in cultural values. Each encounter makes life a little bit more rewarding. As managers, we become more capable both at home and abroad through trade and commerce that, indeed, is what much of history is about. We hope that we can convey these values to students and inspire them to pursue international management careers.

Features and Structure

There are five Parts to the text, each with several chapters that focus on a theme. Part One includes chapters that address fundamental issues of international business and management. We introduce management concepts, provide a global view to the environment of international business, emphasize the history of commerce and future directions of international business, and provide a framework for ethical conduct in management. These issues are all interrelated and represent a summary of a vast amount of information on globalization and trends in international management. They constitute a foundation for the remainder of the text.

Part Two is devoted to strategic management and international competition. It presents the theories and concepts of global strategy, organizational structure, methods of competing internationally, and trends in global alliances. The chapters build on one another to address core strategies, how companies organize to pursue those strategies, and how managers implement strategies through international expansion and foreign alliances.

Part Three focuses on cultural aspects of international business, and the chapters could easily form the basis for a separate textbook. Culture is so important that it could have been emphasized at the beginning of this book and, indeed, early chapters were accentuated by cultural considerations. With that said, Part Three is the heart of the text that addresses contrasting world cultures, intercultural communication, and the challenges of negotiating and managing in foreign cultures. With more than 200 nations and many more societies and communities with their own unique human histories, we offer at best a selective view of cross-cultural concepts.

Part Four extends cross-cultural themes to examine human resource management. The first chapter in this section deals with international labor relations. This is a bridge chapter that builds on cultural communications and intercultural negotiations, and it is important for managers who must work with employees in other countries. We devote one chapter to the special challenges of expatriate management—the act of going abroad, managing in a foreign environment, and also returning home. We devote a third chapter specifically to human resource development, and this includes domestic and foreign training and development for managers and employees.

Part Five is concerned with leadership. The primary focus is on motivation in a cross-cultural environment and managing in a multicultural environment. Cultural diversity plays a significant role in leadership, and it is addressed in conjunction with prominent theories of leadership behavior. We conclude with a chapter on team development and how international management careers are likely to change during the early years of this new millennium. As we wrote the final words of the final section, it became increasingly apparent that we had not said enough about people, cultures, organizations, strategies, human relations, or any aspect of interpersonal relations that really capture of the nature of international management. Perhaps that is an impossible task, but we hope that we have provided an imaginative foundation on which students can build a rewarding future in the field.

Cases, Exercises, and Illustrations

Each chapter begins with a real company or individual profile of an international manager, and each chapter has at least one internal boxed illustration of a real person or incident to enhance the presentations. At the end of each chapter, there are two brief cases that were purposely kept short for in-class use. There are several experiential exercises included for each chapter, and in most instances, they have been class-tested by the author or colleagues in the United States, Europe, and China. Many of the exercises are structured for small group work so that students can be challenged to work as teams, either in class or through external assignments. Indeed, many of the exercises can be expanded into term paper assignments. Review questions vary in their intensity and some require students to offer their own insights and defend positions. They are meant to be "reviews" in the true sense of the word, not test materials. We have provided a structured test bank to serve examination purposes.

All cases are real. Very few hide names or disguise companies except when information would be too sensitive or embarrassing for the people involved. Most cases in the revised edition have been class-tested or used in professional development seminars in Central and Eastern Europe, Southeast Asia, and Latin America. The Part-ending cases integrate concepts around the themes of each grouping of chapters. These are difficult to use in class, but they are useful for supplemental assignments or student presentations, particularly at the graduate level.

Supplements

Anyone teaching a course in international management faces significant limitations in being able to bring alive theories and concepts presented in a text medium. Consequently, we have provided a supplemental package of materials for traditional instructional methods, including a detailed instructor's manual, test bank, and set of transparency masters. We also have included recommended materials to enhance the classroom experience, including videos, interactive resources, and research assistance. The test bank includes multiple choice, short essay, and true-false questions. Research materials include Internet resources and Web sites that students can access for more thorough insights on international companies, foreign events, and international management. A brief list of potential term papers and research cases is also provided, and within the instructor's materials, there are more extensive bibliographies that have been very helpful for graduate students and topical research.

Acknowledgments

The revised edition of *International Management* has greatly benefited from colleagues, contributors, and reviewers who have often spent tedious hours helping us improve both form and content of the textbook. Unfortunately, there was extremely interesting information and many recommendations that could not be accommodated within the space limitations of the book. Writing and editing the manuscript was a perplexing challenge of how to retain crucial information and maintain necessary brevity, yet not fall into a trap of superficiality. The result is a text somewhat longer than many professors would wish to see, yet one with sufficient choices for selecting topics of interest when a comprehensive use of the textbook is impossible. Still, there are many topics, issues, examples, and cases that could have been included. Indeed, perhaps only a third of all reviewers' recommendations have been addressed, and no more than a quarter of case materials and examples provided by contributors have been utilized.

With that said, we are extremely grateful to our colleagues, to our reviewers, and those contributors who are profiled in the textbook. We are equally grateful for those who have assisted us with tedious editing and to the publisher's enthusiastic team members who have helped with design, illustrations, and production of the final product, including Tracy Morse, acquisitions editor; CJ Jasieniecki, developmental editor; and Andrea Archer, project manager.

We also express our thanks to Lewis J. Bernstein, Vice President of Global Sesame Street Productions, and Benjamin Lehmann, Assistant to the Vice President of Global Sesame Street Productions, for their help with the Sesame Street case in Chapter 8.

CONTRIBUTORS AND REVIEWERS TO THE SECOND EDITION Jenet S. Adams, Kennesaw State University; Sam Black, Caterpillar Corporation; William Boyd, President of Transprint USA; Dharma deSilva, Wichita State University; David J. C. Forsyth, University of the South Pacific, Fiji; Macierj Gajewski, Partner Uniglob, Warsaw, Poland; Richard Hirschler, World Bank; Sean D. Holt, Vice President of Finance, Equalfooting.com; Hung Sui-yip, Zhongshan University, PRC; Armands Jurjevs, Insurance Institute of Riga, Latvia; Sue Kenworthy, George Washington University; Jon Lindborg, USAID, American Embassy, Jordan; Roger Nibler, Lingnan University, Hong Kong; Richard Peregoy, University of Dallas; Moksevi Prelis, CEO DFCC, Colombo, Sri Lanka; Pho Ba Quan, Board Director, Shangri-La Hotel and

Resorts International; John Robertson, President Robertson Marketing Group; John Schermerhorn, Ohio University; Robert Terpstra, University of Macau; Marion White, James Madison University; and Leslie Wright, Managing Director, Westminster Portfolio Services, Thailand. Special thanks to Susan Leshnower of Midland College for her tireless work on the accompanying ancillary, and to Douglas McCabe of Georgetown University for his contributions to the textbook website, <www.harcourt-college.com/management/holt>.

REVIEWERS OF THE FIRST EDITION Rice P. York, Belhaven College; Jim Davis, University of Notre Dame; Marion White, James Madison University; Carolan McLarney, Illinois State University; Sully Taylor, Portland State University; Mary Lou Lockerby, College of DuPage; Claudio Milman, Western Michigan University; Kevin B. Lauder; Gyula T. Vasdag, Michigan State University; Jitendra Mishra, Grand Valley State University; Prashant Kale, University of Pennsylvania; Ernesto M. Reza, California State University—San Bernardino; J. Michael Geringer, San Luis Obispo; Phil Hall, St. Ambrose University; John A. Kilpatrick, Idaho State University; and Amit Shah, Frostburg State University.

Not least of all, we are very appreciative of our families who have supported us and who had the patience to understand the commitment we faced in preparing this manuscript. We are blessed with loving and caring families who are as much a part of this script as the authors themselves.

David H. Holt
James Madison University (retired)
Strategic Consultant to USAID

Karen W. Wigginton
James Madison University

Brief Contents

CONTENTS

PART TWO:
STRATEGY AND GLOBAL ORGANIZATION   165

PART THREE:
SPANNING BORDERS FOR CROSS-CULTURAL MANAGEMENT   281

PART FOUR:
HUMAN RESOURCES IN THE GLOBAL CONTEXT   403

Chapter 15: Leadership in the Global Context   579

Chapter 16: International Teams: The Emerging Management Challenge   617

THE GLOBAL IMPERATIVE

CHAPTER ONE

INTERNATIONAL MANAGEMENT: A GLOBAL PERSPECTIVE

CHAPTER OBJECTIVES

Define the terms *international management, international business*, and *global business*, and explain key concepts for transnational organizations.

Explore the historic foundations of global business activities and recent changes in world trade relationships.

Describe the nature of international organizations and multinational corporations, and show how these institutions are changing.

Specify the fundamental characteristics and roles of international managers.

Examine future challenges for managers in a global economy.

Akio Morita and Jack Welch were destined to become internationally acclaimed icons of management, each following very different lives on opposite sides of the world. Morita founded Sony Corporation soon after the end of World War II, and launched a portfolio of innovative products that led to a global transformation of audio and visual electronics.[1] Welch became CEO of General Electric in 1980, and set about to revolutionize one of the largest and oldest American companies. Under his visionary leadership, GE embraced world markets in high-tech, information-led products and services while rapidly shedding its consumer electronic commodities and the company's staid image of an old-line domestic manufacturer.[2]

Sony's story is that of founder Akio Morita, who as a young naval officer at the end of World War II refused to commit ritual suicide by hara-kiri when Japan surrendered. He saw no value to his family or nation in his death. This did not endear him to his compatriots; yet he was the eldest son of the Morita family, and his return home was welcomed. He was slated to become the fifteenth-generation *Kyuzaemon*, or head of the family, and subsequently to inherit and manage the Moritas' 300-year-old sake distilling business. Instead, he passed this inheritance to his younger brother and set off to create an electronics business that he envisioned as a platform for internationally marketed products. He purposely studied western management techniques, established friendships and business alliances in the United States and Europe, and championed new management ideas and western concepts among his Japanese colleagues. When Jack Welch came to power at GE, Morita had firmly entrenched his audio innovations in American and European markets. These were led by the Sony Walkman and the first viable videocassette recorder (VCR), known as the Beta Max system.

Paralleling GE's early years under Welch—characterized by Welch as an era of "reinvention"—Morita launched American-made products from Sony's California plant, entered the entertainment business with dozens of new commercial and consumer electronics products, and introduced high-definition video and television equipment. He later acquired Hollywood recording and film production studios. By 1990 Sony had leading globally branded products in 160 countries, with production facilities and foreign alliances in 83 nations. Ironically, Morita's most exciting project—the Beta Max VCR system—was one of his greatest failures. The introduction of Sony's VCR system instantly made the industries of handheld movie cameras, 8mm film, and existing video projection technology obsolete. Ironically, Morita could not compete against another Japanese corporation, giant Mitsushita Electronics Inc. (MEI), which penetrated Sony's American markets with its own VCR technology. MEI soon established VHS as the industry standard on a global scale.

Until his death in 1998, Akio Morita was the embodiment of innovative Japanese electronics and the emblematic persona of an international manager capable of adapting to foreign cultures. He honored Japanese cultural traditions, yet he embraced western business values and encouraged his managers, both at home and abroad, to adapt to global commerce. To those ends, he was somewhat of an enigma to other Japanese business leaders. He was also an enigma to Americans, particularly management scholars who touted him as an example of so-called Japanese management acumen. Morita rejected such notoriety, instead claiming modestly only to have been a student of sound management techniques and able to accommodate constructive practices of insightful leaders such as Jack Welch.

On the eve of his retirement as the year 2001 began, Jack Welch was considered to be a revolutionary manager with a gift of inspired leadership. During two brief decades, Welch had redefined GE as a global company with few holdover products or practices from the old General Electric. Indeed, GE had become a major force in postindustrialized America and consistently atop the leaderboard as the nation's best-managed company. Welch, like Morita, endured years of controversy, often being called reactionary (or worse), and was strongly criticized during his early years as CEO for "tearing apart" one of the cornerstones of corporate America. Indeed, he was reactionary, calling for a "revolution in management thinking" when he became CEO in 1980. Welch began by burning the company's policy manuals that preached traditional industrial management. He flattened the company, thus eliminating two entire levels of management. Welch also pervasively delegated authority thereby decentralizing decision-making and streamlining operations. Within the first several years of his tenure, he sold off 71 businesses—many of those having been foundation commodity divisions of the old bureaucracy—and generated 118 new business divisions through acquisitions and joint ventures. More than half of the new divisions were alliances with foreign corporations, and Welch brought into GE an entire new cadre of multicultural managers with international experience.

Welch pursued two goals that have become the cornerstones of GE progress. First, to build a company on value—value to customers and stockholders through products and services of the highest quality with the greatest profit potential. Second, to establish a world-class organization capable of making every business that the company pursued No. 1 or No. 2 in its industry. Incidentally, he wasn't crazy about these just being No. 2. He did not want a larger corporation, but one with larger interests at the cutting edge of technologies positioned to compete in a borderless world of commerce.

Like Morita, Welch encouraged innovative thinking and challenged managers to adapt the best practices from wherever in the world they might be found. Before it became popular to "benchmark" (to adapt the most successful techniques found in other organizations), Welch positioned GE to instigate effective asset management from Toyota, to emulate market intelligence practices from Wal-Mart, and to introduce product management systems from Procter & Gamble. His team-management philosophy built on Volvo's integrated work groups, and he sought greater worker participation in managerial decisions, reflecting the more successful aspects of Japanese consensus decision-making behavior.

Welch also set GE on its ears with his often audacious changes in management expectations. Through so-called workout sessions, Welch encouraged open communications among managers and workers, much like town meetings. He instituted rigorous personnel evaluation systems that candidly gave credit when due, and just as rapidly vetted the organization of underperforming managers. Much of Jack Welch's genius was in his ability not only to embrace change without being hamstrung by prevailing corporate practices but also to adapt to the realities of global competition. He tore down cultural barriers and promoted a multifaceted international corporation without artificial ethnic and political boundaries.

Akio Morita and Jack Welch were responsible for pervasive changes in management practices in their respective countries, and they influenced an entire generation of managers who have collectively become part of a global community. Both men faced and overcame many of the same cultural barriers that had handcuffed a previous generation caught up in nationalistic traditions. Both men, each in their own realms of influence, broke away from an age of industrial isolation to pursue global strategies. Both redefined corporate governance and responsibility for managing across cultures in an age of rapid and pervasive organizational transition.

THE ROOTS OF INTERNATIONAL MANAGEMENT

When astronaut Neil Armstrong first stepped on the moon barely a quarter of a century ago, one of the most intriguing sights was a view of Earth, transmitted live on television to more than a billion earthbound viewers. Here was a bluish global orb with bright tints and patterned hues of oceans, mountains, and clouds that represented planetary life as one consolidated entity. From that distant view, there were no social or political distinctions. Boundaries between countries within Europe and the Americas were not apparent, and even continents were outlined rather abstractly. Such a view is almost metaphoric of changes that have since occurred to redefine global business and international relations. Today, global corporations are secular organizations that in many ways capture the image shared from space by early astronauts. Managers of these globally integrated companies are part of a strategic vision that defies limits of time, space, national boundaries, languages, customs, and ideologies. They are part of worldwide networks of economic activity, often part of companies with revenues that exceed the gross national product (GNP) of many of the world's sovereign nations.

Today, many international managers deal with earth-spanning technologies. They have products that can be made almost anywhere and sold almost everywhere. Nike's branded shoes are as well known by school children on the side streets of Jakarta as they are by Wall Street joggers. Coca-Cola's ads can reach billions of people at the same instant in 160 countries. Visa bank cards are as welcome in South Africa as they are in London, Chicago, or Tokyo. People in Moscow, Beijing, Tel Aviv, and Toronto plug into CD players and listen to international music stars with little regard for national origin or ethnicity. Although relatively few companies are truly "global" with unbounded interests, many are part of expanding global networks. *Globalization* is a fashionable word, but it is also a vision rooted in the evolution of Earth's societies.[3]

Within this grand vision we are still earthbound, and in most instances, still of one society or another with daily priorities of work and careers. Consequently, this book is more about the practical aspects of living and working in a more partitioned environment, yet the advent of globalization cannot be denied. As American firms reach out to the world, companies from other nations come to America—making the United States the single largest target for foreign direct investment and the primary market for the world's merchandise. Indeed, European companies now have matched America's pace of global investment. Combined with Japan, they account for nearly half the world's total annual direct foreign investment. On a global scale, the rate of direct foreign investment has more than tripled the rate of total global output of goods and services during the past two decades. Although Japanese companies entered the new millennium focused on economic recovery after a decade of internal monetary problems, European companies continued to expand their foreign investments. In 1998 and early 1999, EU corporations spent close to $300 billion, buying into U.S. companies or making entire acquisitions. This was nearly 10 times the annual European investment activity in prior years, and EU analysts expect a similar high level of sustained foreign investment through 2005.[4]

Foreign investments today are rarely simple trade arrangements. They are often large and complicated transactions involving multi-country operations, joint ventures, strategic alliances, and subsidiaries that span borders and cultures. Many are global endeavors that have outgrown their national identities, and to the discomfort of many observers, the sheer breadth and power of these organizations often eclipse the capabilities of many sovereign nations. Australian delegates to the World Economic Forum in 2000 pointed nervously to the fact that the 10 largest multinationals each had annual sales larger than Australia's gross tax revenues. Indeed, the world's 1,000 largest companies account for nearly 80 percent of world industrial output.[5] Such clout demands capable management and accountability for effective and ethical organizations, a fact not lost on protesters who brought an agenda of concerns to the public during the World Economic Forum in Switzerland. Similar demonstrations at the Seattle World Trade Organization conference on the eve of the millennium underscored the public's concern about potentially excessive power of global enterprises.[6]

Defining International Organizations

The terms *globalization* and *global managers* have become popular expressions in international business. They suggest a universal involvement in worldwide business and lend an air of adventure to management, but they are not synonymous with *international activities*. An extraordinary number of companies are involved in international trade and investment, yet relatively few are truly global enterprises. The distinction between being "international" and competing as a global company is important. Commercial enterprises have been involved with international trade, investment, and—to no small extent—colonialization for centuries. However, the emergence of companies with global interests is a recent phenomenon.

An *international* firm conducts business outside the home country and may have significant foreign investments, but it is not necessarily a *global enterprise*. A **global organization** is characterized by having integrated systems of international operations and management that bind the company together as an interdependent endeavor.[7] The definition alone, however, does not capture the essence of a global company. Unfortunately, the idea of a global company is rather abstract; yet an enterprise with pervasive international interests, foreign alliances, world markets, and a multicultural organization is clearly much different from those that merely export, import, or have limited foreign investments. The global company has extensive interests that transcend national borders and political institutions, and its managers work among people from diverse cultures with different languages, religions, customs, and values.

At the outset, this chapter also draws a distinction between two other terms used to describe international business enterprises: the *transnational corporation* and the *multinational corporation*. The term **transnational corporation (TNC)** has been widely used by the United Nations since the early 1980s to describe a "globally integrated" organization, which is a multinational, yet distinct in its expansive interests, its pervasive markets and transactions, and its interdependent management systems. The UN defines the transnational corporation as:

> an enterprise (a) comprising entities in two or more countries, regardless of the legal form and fields of activity of those entities, (b) which operates under a system of decision making permitting coherent policies and a common strategy through one or more decision-making centers, (c) in which the entities are so linked, by ownership or otherwise, that one or more of them may be able to exercise a significant influence over the activities of the others, and, in particular, to share knowledge, resources, and responsibilities with others.[8]

The **multinational corporation (MNC)** is a company with significant direct foreign investment in at least one foreign nation other than its home country, and it has actual management responsibility for those foreign operations. This often suggests that the MNC has foreign markets, but that is not always the case. Some companies obtain resources for importation from overseas operations (e.g., those in mining, petroleum extraction, and forestry industries), and others manufacture products in foreign locations for export to other countries, markets in the host country, or reimportation to the home country. Despite the variations in foreign activities, all multinationals retain management responsibility for their foreign assets and activities.

This familiar description characterizes an international organization, but the term *multinational* is often used indiscriminately to refer to any company with international interests. Such an all-inclusive term fails to distinguish among various types of international enterprises, such as those that are primarily exporters, those that essentially import products or resources, and those that fulfill agency roles (traders, brokers, and expediters). Many of these are not multinational organizations—even though they may be very large—unless they also satisfy the criteria of having invested directly in foreign facilities and being accountable for managing those foreign assets.

The criteria for a transnational corporation, as defined by the UN, takes the concept of a multinational corporation to a higher level of complexity. All TNCs are multinationals, but the TNC has a global reach with integrated activities, interdependent shared resources, and intricate networks of management decision-making systems. Some scholars argue that the differences are semantic, but most adamantly defend boundaries between different categories of international companies.[9]

The term *multinational corporation* is used often throughout the book because most international enterprises that concern international management fit this description. Only a few of the very largest corporations qualify as transnational enterprises; yet when appropriate, this distinction will be made. The book also avoids using either term in referring to smaller organizations that have limited foreign investment, or to those that have no clear management responsibilities for their foreign operations.

Defining International Management

International managers have different roles in the various types of enterprises that "do business" in the international arena. In addition, an *international manager* differs from someone *involved in international business*. The purpose of this book is to introduce concepts and practices related to managing in the international arena, not to address international business, which involves trade, finance, marketing, and economics of cross-border commerce.

International management is concerned with ownership and management of assets and operations that go beyond one's home country. The fundamental responsibilities for planning, organizing, leading, and controlling remain intact, but they become more complicated and challenging as organizations become part of multicultural environments. In contrast, **international business** is a comprehensive concept that includes trade, finance, selling to, or buying from companies in other nations, and the political economics of international business relations.[10] International business and management are described in Figure 1.1. The terms can be differentiated, for example, by understanding that people can be involved in international business without ever leaving home. They might be sitting at desks in New York or Tokyo, trading foreign currencies, conducting financial services, or selling computers to clients in Saudi Arabia; but they are not involved in managing foreign operations. Other people in New York or Tokyo may be managing operations owned by companies headquartered in London or Munich. They are international managers, often foreigners in the context of where they work.

It is not necessary that international managers work outside their own countries. They may be employed by foreign enterprises located near their homes, or they may

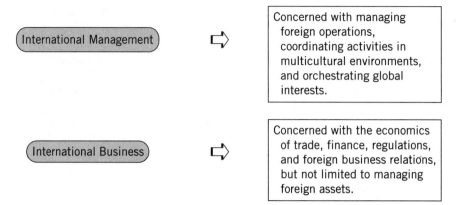

FIGURE 1.1
International Management versus International Business

be part of an international team that works both at home or abroad on periodic projects. For example, Americans and Japanese work together at Sony Corporation in California, and at Honda's plant in Ohio. Europeans and Americans jointly build BMWs in North Carolina, and an international team of Americans with French connections is found in Bic's plant in Virginia. These people are involved in international management as surely as a Chinese manager working for one of Citigroup's banks in Hong Kong or an Italian manager at IBM's facilities in Rome.[11]

A manager's success in these circumstances rests partially on individual qualifications, such as language skills or technical knowledge. But more important, it requires an appreciation that other cultures have unique contributions to make to management thought. A **global manager** takes an even broader perspective, becoming involved with people throughout the world and synthesizing their talents to surmount national and political frontiers through an integrated transnational corporation.

International managers who participate only modestly in foreign activities, just like those who fulfill global responsibilities, must gain an understanding of their own culture and subsequently learn about other cultures and the values of those with whom they work. Consequently, much of this book is concerned with cultural issues. This is so important that an entire discipline of **cross-cultural management** has emerged to explore similarities and differences among nations, examine how people differ in their values and behavior, and address challenges of managing in a multicultural environment.[12] As a prelude to studying international and cross-cultural management, this introductory chapter more closely examines the historic precedents of international business and managerial roles.

THE HISTORY OF INTERNATIONAL BUSINESS

Although globalization will be a vital concern to managers in the new millennium, it is only the latest stage in a long history of international business. Indeed, space development may create some form of "cosmic" management to antiquate the concept of global management, but that is unlikely to affect the importance of daily commerce and trade. People from almost every culture on every continent have participated in international commerce, and organizations have evolved throughout history to reflect emerging social and technological realities.

In early times, small groups of adventurers roved among villages bartering goods. Somewhat later, caravans plied the African sands and Asian silk routes. Early seagoing ships exploited navigational innovations to spread the influence of trading companies. Indeed, entire cities such as Venice developed to serve the needs of such trade. European mercantile companies emerged during the Renaissance, sending ships and colonial adventurers far and wide. The Americas were colonized by European traders seeking treasures from the New World for their home markets.

The Industrial Revolution redefined relationships among the colonial powers and accelerated trade throughout their empires, reaching exotic places such as the "Spice Islands" (also known as Ceylon and now the modern state of Sri Lanka). Hong Kong, Singapore, and Shanghai became international commerce centers, and Japan opened its doors to the West. Dutch and Portuguese traders, even though they came from small countries, were among the foremost to establish foreign enterprises in Africa, South America, and Asia. During the nineteenth century, immigration and economic displacement brought many Europeans and their technologies to their colonies and to the Americas. In turn, America created breakthrough innovations in electric power, communications, mineral extraction, petroleum engineering, and many other fields, and these developments found their way to Europe and Asia.

Emergence of American Influence in International Trade

European colonial strength peaked on the eve of World War I, but as kingdoms fell through war or revolution, economic prosperity built on colonial empires was replaced by widespread depressions. Most European nations drew into themselves, and their far-flung territories became political and economic battlegrounds rather than colonial trading partners. Before World War I began, Europe enjoyed a sense of affluence and notoriety associated with international commerce. That reputation was not fully justified, just as the reputation of the United States as isolationist was in error.

Europe taken as a whole certainly accounted for a large majority of world trade activities, yet the United States had more large industrial companies whose combined gross income exceeded those of rivals in the United Kingdom, France, or Germany.[13] Leading American companies also generated higher aggregate foreign sales volume than their European competitors in the petroleum, electric machinery, automotive products, and telephone and telegraph industries. At that time, these industries represented four of the five leading sectors of industrial activity; the fifth was mining, primarily for coal.

American influence gained international recognition only after World War I, when foreign trade intensified, yet companies such as Standard Oil had been exporting heavily to Europe since 1885, with long-standing exploration, refining, and transport facilities in the Far East, Middle East, and parts of Africa. Standard Oil derived nearly 70 percent of its business from foreign sales until domestic antitrust legislation forced the old company to sell its domestic and foreign interests to separately owned corporations. General Electric, Western Electric, General Motors (GM), AT&T, and the predecessors of Mobil Oil, United Technologies, and several other notable companies had already become well entrenched in Europe and parts of Asia and South America.[14]

America emerged from World War I with strong industrial, financial, and technological resources, while the leading European nations were in economic shambles.

The rest of the world needed things that America could supply. Consequently, American multinationals spearheaded foreign redevelopment. They were not called "multinationals" (a word coined in the 1950s), nor did they speak of having "strategic alliances" (a term that is common now but came into use during the late 1970s). They just began to have a significant overseas presence. GM purchased Vauxhall in England, acquired Adam Opel Motors in Germany, and opened assembly plants in Brazil during the 1920s. GM also expanded exports into 29 countries on three continents.[15] AT&T invested in several European manufacturing facilities, and created a joint equity company in Belgium to establish a European center for continental telephone and telegraph services prior to World War II. During that era, several major petroleum consortia were created for drilling and refining in Asia and the Middle East, and America's consumer products distributed by companies such as Coca-Cola and Procter & Gamble became leading brands in nearly every market they entered.[16] Citibank opened the first American bank in China during the 1920s, followed closely by Wells Fargo with banking and shipping interests. Before the depression years, Pan American Airlines had established the "China Clippers," seaplanes that linked Hong Kong, Shanghai, Guam, and other Pacific territories to the United States.[17] By 1939, IBM had gone international, and foreign sales accounted for more than one-eighth of the company's revenues and one-sixth of its profits.[18]

Of course, many European firms made strong postwar recoveries, and they also expanded internationally, overcoming even greater economic obstacles than those that inhibited U.S. companies. From its base in the Netherlands, Royal Dutch Shell bought European subsidiaries and established new, autonomous divisions such as Shell U.S., making it a major international petroleum company. Nestlé, the giant Swiss chocolate company, quickly became the world leader in powdered drinks and packaged foods. The Dutch electronics firm, Philips, was on its way to becoming one of the world's most diversified and successful electric appliance and electronic components companies. Bayer and Siemens, both well-established German firms, were rising from the war ashes to quickly penetrate other European and North American markets. There were many other successful examples, but World War II shattered Europe, and the postwar period once again witnessed a rapid and sustained growth of American multinationals. Europe's leading industries reemerged with the help of war-related industrial technology and, in particular, America's huge excess production capacity. International demand for nearly everything from soap to steel far exceeded foreign supply capabilities, and many foreign countries searched desperately for infrastructural capabilities and financial resources required to rebuild their industries.

A huge post–World War II gap in demand and supply provided ample opportunities for exporting both goods and services. In a classic example of Adam Smith's model, need in much of the world fueled strong demand, and the United States enjoyed a comparative advantage in manufacturing capacity, technology, human resources, and financial resources. For nearly three decades, U.S. firms remained dominant in international trade and foreign investment. During that time Europe and Asia (Japan in particular) rapidly reconstructed, often through cooperative alliances with the United States and other nations, but also through international development agencies that provided funding and access to international markets.

The cold war, and subsequent conflicts in Korea, the Middle East, and Southeast Asia, also played a significant role in keeping demand high. In most instances, those conflicts brought together armed forces of many nations who either countered the so-called Soviet threat (e.g., NATO) or fought together in the field (e.g., the Korean conflict and the Vietnam War). Consequently, there was an equally important diffusion of international technology and a pervasive growth in trade and direct foreign investment.

In 1974, however, U.S. and European expansion suddenly slowed. During the next few years, a sustained period of "stagflation" plagued national economies with double-digit inflation, high unemployment, and a quagmire of political difficulties.[19] European economies suffered greater problems than those encountered in the United States, but Asian economies were growing at a tremendous pace. Japan and smaller economies of South Korea, Taiwan, Hong Kong, and Singapore were rapidly expanding through aggressive trade policies, setting the stage for a power shift in global trade.

The Rise of Japan and the Asian Dragons

Japanese firms quickly began to penetrate U.S. markets during the 1970s. By the early 1980s, they were well entrenched in American and European automotive and consumer electronics sectors. They also became the prominent force in Pan-Pacific development. Meanwhile, U.S. and European industries seemed to be stalled. Consequently, the onslaught of Japanese products was not entirely welcomed in the West, because money and jobs seemed to flow toward Japanese companies that could offer less expensive products with better performance capabilities. In 1970, 49 of the world's 50 largest global corporations were European or American (Toyota had just made the list in 1969); but by 1975, Toyota, Hitachi, Mitsubishi Heavy Industry, and Nippon Kokan were among the top 50; 16 American firms dropped from the list. By 1980, only 24 U.S. companies remained in the top 50, shrinking to 17 by 1989. The Japanese improved with 12 companies among the top 50 by 1980, four of those in the top quadrant. Japanese banks, unnoticed during the 1970s, accounted for eight of the top 10 global banking corporations by 1989.[20]

Japanese automotive industries remained strong well into the 1990s with increased direct foreign investment, but consumer electronics soon evolved into microelectronics with pervasive changes in information technology. The Japanese were

Asia's Businessman of the Year, Dr. Keiji Tachikawa, is president of NTT DoCoMo—Japan's largest corporation, with a market cap of more than $225 billion, and one of the world's three largest mobile telephone companies. Tachikawa transformed NTT DoCoMo into a global network of alliances in the United States, the Netherlands, Sweden, and Finland and launched the world's first third-generation wireless on-line communications system, called *i-mode*, with full cellular Internet access. In a communications industry marked by mergers and hostile takeovers, Tachikawa has relied on cooperative investments and constructive alliances, creating a multinational enterprise with extraordinary growth but maintaining corporate autonomy among its global partners. Today the company has more mobile subscribers than traditional telephone customers, and it is adding more than 80,000 subscriptions each month to an international nonvoice data communications network.

well prepared for these changes, and through their large and somewhat feudal organizations called *keiretsu*, they penetrated regional Asian and North American markets with computer components, chips, and a wide range of products using chip technology. The **keiretsu** (pronounced roughly as key-reit-soo) is a conglomerate with vertically integrated systems of manufacturers, trading subsidiaries, contractors, and networks of suppliers, financial institutions, and political connections.[21] The keiretsu are based on feudal systems of families and personal associations, and they have been criticized as behaving like giant cartels. These conglomerate groups have an unusual capacity for collectively leveraging assets and reallocating resources to subsequently take advantage of market or technological changes. For example, microchips developed in the United States gave birth to computer and information technology, but Japanese companies adapted microelectronics to audio and video entertainment media. They also established new industries for electronic toys, mobile communications, and robotics. Sony was unusual as an independent company that succeeded in this industry, but Hitachi, Matsushita Electric Industries, and Mitsui & Company were powerful keiretsu capable of achieving huge scale economies in a wide range of diversified industries. Specifically, Hitachi used microchips in small appliances, electronic instruments, and navigation systems. MEI, as noted in the opening scenario of Sony's founder Akio Morita, set world standards after introducing VHS systems and video recording applications. Mitsui spearheaded use of microelectronics for industrial robots, production control equipment, and its own lines of video equipment, televisions, and small appliances. Far more chips have been made for rice cookers and small appliances than for the total computer industry; and in the chip industry, where scale economies are crucial, the Japanese outpaced world markets.[22]

The Japanese growth record is well documented, but from an international perspective there are two crucial points. First, the keiretsu organization could mobilize its internal group resources rapidly to target both industrial output and high-potential markets, and second, the keiretsu were based on core *trading companies* that had been historically involved in international trade. These trading companies were initially created following the Meji Restoration in the 1880s as a pervasive Japanese effort to penetrate foreign markets. Japan's government orchestrated the formation of trading groups based on alliances called **zaibatsu** (pronounced zah-e-baaht-soo). These family-dominated holding companies wielded extraordinary power, much like earlier seventeenth- and eighteenth-century feudal clans. Although organized for commerce, the zaibatsu were able to direct enormous resources into Japan's war efforts. During World War II, they significantly influenced Japan's political policies. At the end of the war, U.S. occupation forces outlawed zaibatsu and disbanded many of the cartels' holdings, yet the core trading companies remained intact. In effect, the zaibatsu survived their official dissolution as their legacies carried forward to the commercial keiretsu. Consequently, resource-poor Japan has benefited from their keiretsu trading conglomerates to expand rapidly into world markets.[23]

A similar transformation occurred in South Korea, where Japanese industries spearheaded Korean growth through subcontracting and joint alliances. Although political relations have been strained between the two countries, Korea enjoyed rapid industrial development, fueled in part by supplying parts and components to Japan. Korea also established a system of international trade conglomerates known as *chaebols*. The **chaebol** (pronounced roughly as shaw-a-bowl) is the counterpart to the Japanese keiretsu. It is a large, vertically integrated conglomerate with a core trading company that often has interlocking equity ownership by families and associations. Most Korean chaebols, like the Japanese keiretsu, have a history of feudal clan connections; in fact, the Chinese characters and meanings for chaebol and zaibatsu are identical.[24]

Although Japan led the way and South Korea soon followed, the entire Asian region was rapidly changing. The *four dragons* of Asia (also called the four tigers)—South Korea, Taiwan, Hong Kong, and Singapore—all became regional trade powers. Their economies suffered temporary setbacks during the Asian banking and political crises that rocked Japan, Thailand, and Indonesia during the late 1990s; yet today, they are again among the world's fastest growing economies. Their influence on world commerce far exceeds their relatively small population bases and resource-poor environments.[25]

Korea grew by focusing on product-driven manufacturing, such as automotive parts and machine tools. Korean companies also integrated forward to capture major positions in world markets for microwave ovens, televisions, computers, and other consumer electronics. In contrast, Taiwan chose to target major industry segments focused almost entirely on export potential of products using microelectronic technology. Taiwan's success is a testament to niche marketing; its companies quickly became the low-end clone masters of the microcomputer world, then captured markets in microswitching devices, computer peripherals, and network components. They mastered the art of avoiding direct confrontations with world powers in high-end markets, quietly emerging as world leaders in low-cost microelectronics.[26]

Hong Kong, a British colony until 1996, has nearly seven million people crowded into a small area with no natural resources. Before becoming a semiautonomous "administrative region" of China, Hong Kong was the leading exporter of fashion garments, toys, household products, and glassware. Although most of these products are no longer manufactured in Hong Kong as costs and wage rates have reached world standards, Hong Kong is the conduit through which much of East Asian products flow. Indeed, it is still the leading Asian exporter for garments, toys, and fabricated household products. Hong Kong also is the financial center, distribution port, and primary trade center for much of East Asia's trade with the West. The territory's banking system channels substantial foreign investment into the People's Republic of China, and redirects much of China's direct investment abroad.[27] It enjoys wealth, a number of leading companies with global interests, and a standard of living for its citizens that ranks fifth in the world.[28]

What Hong Kong is to East Asia, Singapore is to Southeast Asia. It is the financial and physical distribution trade center for petroleum products, textiles, agricultural products, electronics, and consumer goods that flow from Southeast Asian nations to Middle Eastern and European markets. Singapore built its economy on strategic alliances with western multinationals and European affiliates. As a city-state of less than four million people, it is known as a corporate center in Asia for many European firms. Like Hong Kong, Singapore has a strong economy with an excellent commercial infrastructure.[29]

The Role of International Trade Organizations

Trade development in Asia, and more recently in Central and Eastern Europe, has been substantially enhanced through international trade organizations. These geopolitical organizations have played major roles in generating free trade and regulating trade disparities. The first major effort to establish a multinational trade organization was the 1947 General Agreement on Tariffs and Trade (GATT). This agreement established a representative body of delegates from signatory nations who established regulations for tariff duties under a mandate to reduce trade restrictions, ultimately to encourage free trade among member nations through ethical multilateral agreements.

A glittering view of Hong Kong from the island's "peak" across the harbor to Kowloon and beyond to mainland China. More than 200 high-rise buildings, two among the world's tallest, dominate the commercial and financial district. This is the heart of Hong Kong, Asia's busiest port and East Asia's wealthiest investment center. It was recently returned to China as a Special Administrative Region after 150 years of British rule, but remains autonomous. The city has seven world-class universities, more than 100 commercial banks, and 27,000 multinational corporations registered from 83 different nations. Hong Kong is home to nearly 7 million people, with the third-highest per-capita income in the world.

GATT agreements have been periodically negotiated among nearly a hundred member nations and associated countries. In 1994, the World Trade Organization (WTO) was created through GATT as a conduit for dispute arbitration and a trade-monitoring agency. GATT, together with world organizations such as the International Monetary Fund (IMF), International Labor Organization (ILO), Organization for Economic Cooperation and Development (OECD), World Bank, and International Finance Corporation (IFC), has redefined the economic and financial climate of global trade.[30]

These organizations, operating in cooperation with international regulatory systems such as the World Court, set the stage for major political realignments. For example, the European Community (EC) evolved from the Treaty of Rome, originally signed in 1957 by eight nations that shared a common objective to unify independent European states under one borderless trade federation. A parallel system, known as the European Free Trade Association (EFTA), evolved among seven non-EC European nations. Membership in the EC has expanded to 15 nations following ratification of the Maastricht Treaty in 1993; today the EC is known as the European Union (EU). Both the EU and EFTA have further expansion opportunities, and they are participants in many bilateral trade agreements with nonmember nations in Eastern Europe, the Baltic and Balkan states, and the Middle East. Table 1.1 illustrates the most recent profile of EU and EFTA nations.[31]

Meanwhile, the United States and Canada established the Canada–U.S. Free Trade Agreement in 1987 to systematically eliminate tariffs and trade restrictions between the two countries by the end of the century. Subsequent to that agreement, the North American Free Trade Association (NAFTA) was enacted to include Mexico (and conceivably others in due time) as a trading bloc with minimum trade restrictions.[32] Although NAFTA has had the spotlight, the World Bank treats Latin America and the Caribbean (LAC) as a regional economic zone with as many as 200 different interregional trade agreements; many involve both the United States and Canada in bilateral and multilateral trade treaties.[33] For example, the Canada–Chile Free Trade Agreement, enacted January 2000, immediately affected agricultural,

TABLE 1.1

MEMBERS OF THE EU AND EFTA, ESTIMATED FOR THE YEAR 2000

European Union (EU)			European Free Trade Association (EFTA)		
Country	GDP ($bn)	Population (million)	Country	GDP ($bn)	Population (million)
Austria	247.9	8.1	Austria*	247.9	8.1
Belgium	255.8	10.2	Denmark*	182.3	5.3
Denmark	182.3	5.3	Finland*	137.0	5.1
Finland	137.0	5.1	Iceland	51.9	0.2
France	1,603.3	59.1	Norway	168.8	4.0
Germany	2,314.3	82.1	Sweden*	327.4	9.1
Greece	72.9	9.9	Switzerland	323.1	7.1
Ireland	75.1	3.8			
Italy	1,246.0	58.4			
Luxembourg	17.1	0.4			
The Netherlands	423.7	15.8			
Portugal	102.3	10.0			
Spain	628.2	39.1			
Sweden	327.4	9.1			
United Kingdom	1,411.6	59.2			
Totals	$9,044.9	375.6		$1,256.1	34.4

*Primary EFTA nations, recently joined EU following national referenda. Norway remains a candidate for the EU, but voters rejected membership. Turkey has petitioned for membership and several East/Central European nations are under consideration.

Source: *The 2000 World Development Indicators* (Washington, D.C.: World Bank, 2000); CD-ROM, Population Projection Series and Economic Timeseries Tables.

textile, and plastics industries through elimination or reduction of tariffs. By 2007, bilateral trade between these two countries is expected to accelerate from a current $25 million annually to more than $500 million.[34] Other examples and international development in Latin America are addressed later in the book, in several different chapters.

A more complicated system of agreements has emerged in Asia, as shown in Table 1.2. The Association of Southeast Nations (ASEAN) initially joined the six member nations of Brunei, Indonesia, Malaysia, the Philippines, Singapore, and Thailand together as a regional free-trade zone. This group may soon include Vietnam. In concert with ASEAN, APEC (Asia-Pacific Economic Cooperation) was created in 1993 to include the ASEAN nations and China, Japan, South Korea, Australia, New Zealand, Hong Kong, Taiwan, Canada, and the United States. This unusual amalgamation of often-contentious trade partners has established a forum for delegates to address interregional trade and investment issues. The forum, now in its infancy, is known as the East Asia Economic Caucus. A primary goal of the caucus is to create a trade zone with reduced trade barriers and more stable trade relations through a Greater East Asia Coprosperity Sphere.[35]

In 1995, the World Bank identified 62 multilateral associations and 287 cooperative agreements ranging from major European, North American, and Asian initiatives

TABLE 1.2

MEMBER NATIONS OF ASEAN AND APEC, ESTIMATED GDP AND POPULATION IN 2000

Association of Southeast Asian Nations (ASEAN)			Asia-Pacific Economic Cooperation (APEC)		
Country	GDP ($ billions)	Population (millions)	Country	GDP ($ billions)	Population (millions)
Brunei	7.6	315	Australia	419.7	19,100
Indonesia	215.0	216,400	Brunei	7.6	325
Malaysia	108.9	23,100	Canada	664.1	31,100
The Philippines	96.9	78,300	Chile	77.3	15,200
Singapore	106.8	3,300	China (PRC)	902.0	1,260,000
Thailand	177.2	61,900	Hong Kong	171.5	6,900
			Indonesia	215.0	216,400
			Japan	4,841.7	126,500
			Malaysia	108.9	23,100
			Mexico	460.5	99,000
			New Zealand	65.8	3,750
			Papua New Guinea	5.8	4,800
			The Philippines	96.9	78,300
			Singapore	106.8	3,300
			South Korea	491.9	47,000
			Taiwan	321.6	21,000
			Thailand	177.2	61,900
			United States	8,286.8	272,800
Totals	$712.4	381,305		$17,421.1	2,280,775

Source: *The 2000 World Development Indicators* (Washington, D.C.: World Bank, 2000); CD-ROM Population Projection Series and Economic Timeseries Tables.

to trade pacts in Latin America, Africa, the Middle East, Eastern Europe, and the Indian subcontinent. Nearly half of these came into existence after 1992, and all but a few were negotiated between 1987 and 1995. By 2000, the World Bank listed 88 multilateral associations and 493 cooperative agreements, indicating an extraordinary expansion of trade pacts and cross-border alliances. The pattern of these alliances suggests major global trading blocs in Asia, North America, and Europe, with many smaller regional and bilateral alliances elsewhere.[36] These alliances are explained in more detail in Chapter 2, but for the moment they help to emphasize that the roles of international managers span world affairs, international alliances, regulatory practices with regional and global commerce, and concern for ever-changing trends in world business.

INTERNATIONAL ORGANIZATIONS

The study of international management requires an understanding of the structure of international organizations. The way a company defines its reporting relationships and managerial responsibilities determines its *organization*, and the common, prevailing image of an organization resembles a giant pyramid. Typically, one person is at the apex of power, followed by successively lower levels of managers with relatively less authority and more narrowly defined roles. At the bottom, of course, is a large pool of labor. We have this hierarchical structure rooted in our minds, and it is easy to extrapolate, thinking that international companies will be the same, perhaps only with more extensive relationships in the pyramid of authority.

Broadly speaking, all organizations have hierarchical systems with a pyramid of authority, but international organizations cannot be described so simply. The stereotypical pyramid suggests a unified company with well-defined reporting relationships and symmetry, yet most international companies have complicated associations and alliances with multiple divisions on several continents. They may have hundreds of operating divisions with multifaceted purposes, and their activities are often interdependent. Ownership can also be complex, bringing together private and government interests, holding companies, joint ventures, and networks of subsidiaries. Their organizational charts (if they exist) might resemble spider webs, but even then global activities are changing so rapidly that a company's organization can be a fluid mosaic of relationships.

A simplified illustration of the Colgate-Palmolive organization is shown in Figure 1.2. The company has its global headquarters in New York, and appears on paper to have six major geographic divisions reporting to New York from locations in the United States, Europe, the Middle East, Japan, Southeast Asia, and South America. In reality, Colgate-Palmolive's divisions in Asia are nearly autonomous companies with subsidiaries that develop new products, manufacture, and market regionally.

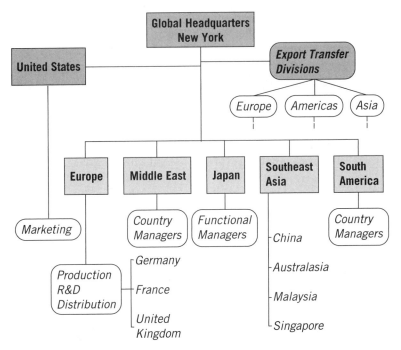

FIGURE 1.2
Colgate-Palmolive Company—A Global View

Sources: Adapted from Colgate-Palmolive Company <http://www.colgate.com/Tour> websites: "What We Are," "Investor Relations," "Colgate History" [cited 8 September 2000].

Meanwhile the company's European center remains intact, but management responsibilities have been systematically "unbundled" since 1994. Marketing for globally branded products shifted to New York, while regional marketing and distribution responsibilities—including production, R&D, financial controls, and logistics—were relocated to facilities in Germany, France, and the United Kingdom. The company subsequently created *export transfer* divisions among its Asian groups that manufacture bulk materials for repackaging in local markets on three continents.[37] The authority structure in Colgate-Palmolive seems, on the surface, to be chaotic. It certainly cannot be described through traditional block diagrams, and trying to devise an organizational chart would be futile because once produced, it would be obsolete in a company where interrelated responsibilities are continuously changing. Many multinational companies find themselves in similar circumstances, unable to explain the fluid nature of corporate relationships for more than an instant of time.

Trends toward Change and Reorganization

Multinational companies vary tremendously in their size and complexity, and most successful enterprises are constantly evolving. One structure may be appropriate at one stage in the firm's development, but totally inadequate in another. Even for those with some sense of organizational stability, changes in technology, markets, economics, and methods of work often force companies to reorganize. Peter Drucker, one of the more prolific writers on management, has had a knack for recognizing the need for change before it is apparent to others. In the 1960s, he predicted a resurgence of entrepreneurship and innovation as driving forces that would affect the success of companies in the 1970s and 1980s. During the 1970s, Drucker emphasized the productivity challenge and the need for American firms to compete with the Japanese through leaner and meaner organizations. In the 1980s, he predicted that transborder management systems would replace the domestically centered model of enterprise; with that change, he suggested, international cultures would become "seamless" with respect to management behavior. The corporation of the future, he said, would no longer be identified with one nation or bounded by artificial political mandates. He attributed many of these changes to rapid technological development that have been easily adapted worldwide, to information technology and telecommunications that are immune to political or social differences, and to international monetary flows where money and securities can be instantaneously repositioned almost anywhere in the world.[38]

Asked his opinion about how business might change by the year 2000, Drucker said in 1989: "Business will undergo more and more radical restructuring in the 1990s than at any time since the modern corporate organization first evolved in the 1920s. . . . Knowledge will replace physical effort as the driving force of productivity . . . and organizations will become self-empowered international enterprises."[39] Drucker's predictions quickly became reality. Between 1990 and 1995, approximately 75 percent of all the Fortune 500 U.S. corporations reported major reorganizations, and 44 of the world's 50 largest multinational corporations had launched efforts to "reengineer" their management systems.[40] The term *reengineering* was coined to suggest major restructuring of an organization and redefinition of the fundamental philosophy of how work is accomplished. It was a topic of several best-selling books, and came to be associated with well-managed companies that intentionally redefined their organizations.

At the cusp of the new millenium, reengineering as a business concept had run its course. Yet many companies such as GE, Motorola, AT&T, Ford, ICI (U.K.), British

Petroleum, and Philips (Netherlands) had consciously downsized by introducing a philosophy of transnational corporations based on information systems. During that same brief period, the "dot-com" era emerged, which has now evolved into the so-called *new economy*. The advent of global and instantaneous communications, together with web-based commerce, has effectively redefined every major corporation's structural processes. Business-to-business marketing, distribution, and materials sourcing, financial transactions, and information networking have become virtually *seamless*, as Drucker predicted. Although the new economy is an embryonic concept, e-commerce has left none of the Fortune 500 or the Global 100 corporations untouched. In the post-2000 wave of change, business analysts predict that by 2005 or soon thereafter, the world's leading companies will make "E" such a core part of their businesses that the difference between E and everything else will be nonexistent.[41]

Bruce Elbert, Vice President of Hughes Space and Communications International, reinforced Drucker's predictions in 1999 by illustrating that all but a small minority of the world's 1,000 leading multinational companies had come to rely on satellite communications for "instant infrastructure." Phone lines, faxes, and "snail mail" had become obsolete in his view, replaced by interactive communications and similar decision-making processes that defied gravity. Specifically, company communications (and the authority channels for information and decision-making) were no longer earthbound, thereby changing the fundamental structure of management relationships in global organizations.[42] Many of the larger companies involved in this transition have had impressive productivity and profitability gains—with fewer facilities and employees, yet a broader scope of world commerce. In contrast, many other companies have grown dramatically by having greater capacity to manage an expanding base of world assets. These include, for example, Compaq, MCI/WorldCom, Federal Express, Asea Brown Boveri (ABB), Dell Computers, SmithKline Beecham, Oracle Corporation, and Johnson & Johnson.[43] How these companies have changed, and how they currently structure their organizations, are topics addressed in Part Two on strategic management and organizational design. The point to emphasize here is that the way organizations and their management structures were perceived several years ago is no longer valid today. Moreover, that perception will certainly change again through social and technological transformations in the very near future.

Trade and the Rise of Multinational Corporations

The fundamental process of *trade* remains at the heart of international commerce. **Trading companies** involved in exporting, importing, brokerage, and distribution play roles even more important today than those of the past, as international exchange and transportation systems have simplified and reduced the cost of international transactions. However, the means of trade and the nature of trading organizations have changed dramatically during the past several decades.

A few tribes on remote islands and from jungle enclaves still engage in barefoot barter, and caravans still climb the Kyber Pass; but most trade is conducted through world trade fairs, on-line electronic contracting, and information-based procurement systems. Physical goods are transported through huge containerized shipping systems or rapidly flown to destinations. Even perishable food products can be shipped almost anywhere in the world with little danger of spoilage. Further, details of financial transactions flash through computerized account systems with little need for hard currency.

Until recently, trade depended largely on colonial settlements of territorial trade missions. Indeed, Canada and the United States were colonized to benefit European trade. The last of the colonial settlements became history as the British Colony of Hong Kong and the Portuguese enclave of Macau were returned to China in 1996 and 1999 respectively. Although Britain, France, and the United States have a few political alliances with territorial economies, the new millennium began without formal European or American colonial interests abroad for the first time in nearly 600 years. Yet colonial influence remains in the laws, customs, trading organizations, and investments that European companies created. Similar transformations have occurred among the Indian Ocean nations, African countries, and recently in Pan-American and Latin states. Trade organizations often reflect these colonial antecedents, with structures based on European precedents, often with European investments and managers and doing business in European markets. North American trade connections have evolved simply because the United States has offered the most affluent available markets for foreign goods. In contrast, Japan has followed trading patterns to acquire natural resources that the country lacks. Therefore, Japan has aggressively pursued trade and foreign investment to secure needed inputs, as well as to exploit market opportunities.

Today, colonies are no longer needed to provide an infrastructure for trade. Indeed, trade requires no more than a single broker equipped with a mobile telephone and a laptop computer, although transactions often involve large subsidiaries of global firms operating integrated telecommunications, financial, and physical distribution systems. Organizations, and their structures, are no longer geographically constrained—or explained—by their national origins. Most do not "manage" foreign operations, but rather "deal in" foreign markets. In contrast to multinational corporations (MNCs), trading companies seldom undertake foreign investments, or at best they accept modest exposure through overseas offices, avoiding the complications of foreign ownership. Larger traders may form contractual associations, but management and legal ownership remains entirely separate for both the home company and any foreign affiliates.

When a trading firm establishes a foreign system of management to oversee foreign investments, it becomes an MNC as defined earlier. Unfortunately, that definition says little about the nature of an MNC's organization; Exxon Corporation and a Florida citrus broker with an office in Jamaica both qualify as MNCs. Observers tend to think of multinational corporations as companies with *significant* foreign operations and management responsibilities in one or more foreign countries. This explanation is rather broad, yet it differentiates the concept of an MNC from that of a trading company, as shown in Figure 1.3.

Many MNCs assign professional *expatriate* managers to run these overseas operations. An *expatriate* is a native of a country other than the one in which he or she is assigned, typically after working for the parent company at its home office. The MNC also may rely on host-country managers, particularly if the mother company has created foreign subsidiaries through acquisitions or joint alliances. A foreign operation may define a separate unit within the parent company's hierarchy, much like a domestic division, with authority defined according to the parent's organizational structure. The expatriate or host-country manager may report to a division executive who either works within the headquarters management group or reports directly to headquarters. However, this scenario blurs many variations in reporting structures, and a block diagram cannot reveal the autonomy (or lack of it) vested in managers for controlling local operations.[44]

The nature of the industry in which a company competes often influences management structures. Specifically, many merchandising and service industries require

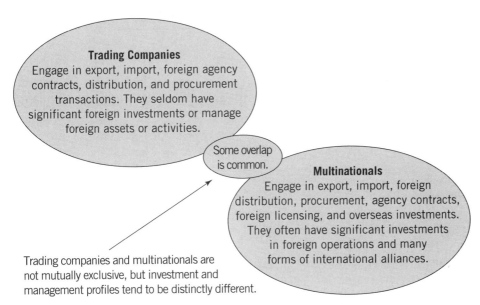

FIGURE 1.3
Trading Companies in Contrast with Multinationals

local control over their products and services to satisfy specific demands of an immediate customer base. These firms cannot efficiently manufacture products in one country for worldwide distribution, nor can they control global services from centralized headquarters. For example, Coca-Cola bottlers are local or regional distributors with substantial local autonomy for processing inventory, supplying retailers, and marketing against local competitors. Most other food and beverage companies serve distinctly local client groups and compete within limited sectors of local industries. Enterprises such as commercial banks, advertising companies, and engineering firms compete by offering exceptional personal services, so they often configure their organizations to address local customer needs. Consequently, these often are insular operations under a corporate umbrella with independent strategies related to specific markets. Companies such as these are called **multilocal corporations** to emphasize their identities as loose associations of multiple foreign operations, each independent of others, usually with local management.[45] These forms of enterprise are discussed thoroughly in later chapters on strategy, human resource management, and leadership.

Transnational Organizations—An Overview

As noted earlier, a transnational company manages *global* investments and fulfills worldwide management responsibilities. It may maintain a legal base in one nation (e.g., a corporate charter registering it as a U.S. company), yet its primary operations could be headquartered anywhere in the world. A holding company may incorporate component companies listed as individual public companies in Europe, North America, and the Far East. Royal Dutch Shell is one of many corporations with securities listed on world stock exchanges, and it has maintained foreign operations and

TABLE 1.3

TOP 10 GLOBAL COMPANIES IN REVENUES AND PROFIT

Rank	Company	National Origin	Revenues ($billion)	Company	National Origin	Profits ($billion)
1	General Motors	United States	$176.6	General Electric	United States	$10.7
2	Wal-Mart Stores	United States	166.8	Citigroup	United States	9.9
3	Exxon Mobil	United States	163.8	Royal Dutch/Shell	Netherlands/ United Kingdom	8.6
4	Ford Motor	United States	162.5	SBC Communications	United States	8.2
5	DaimlerChrysler	United States	159.9	Exxon Mobil	United States	7.9
6	Mitsui	Japan	118.5	Bank of America	United States	7.8
7	Mitsubishi	Japan	117.8	Microsoft	United States	7.8
8	Toyota Motors	Japan	115.7	Intl. Business Machines	United States	7.7
9	General Electric	United States	111.6	E. I. du Pont de Nemours	United States	7.6
10	Itochu	Japan	109.1	Philip Morris	United States	7.3

Source: "The Global 500," *Fortune Database* <www.fortune.com/fortune/global500> [cited 8 September 2000].

international investment for so long that its national identity is seldom an issue. Table 1.3 summarizes the 10 largest global companies, ranked according to revenues and profits. Most are widely recognized with rather obvious national origins, yet all of these companies earn most of their revenues and profits from foreign markets.

The TNC is not necessarily managed by so-called *home country executives*, nor are its worldwide operations managed by any particular staff. In addition, technology and people flow among operations with a broad-based integration of products and services.[46] On the other hand, some major companies with transnational characteristics also maintain strong national identities among their foreign subsidiaries. For example, Procter & Gamble's plant in Guangzhou (also known as Canton) in the People's Republic of China is codirected by a Chinese manager and a P&G expatriate from Australia. The marketing director, British by birth, was formerly stationed in Japan. Managers of human resources and training come from the United States and Canada, and several engineers worked previously in European facilities. Most young managers at P&G Guangzhou are Chinese, and the facility is half owned by Chinese interests in a joint venture. The products that the company sells in China are entirely manufactured there. Nevertheless, because of P&G's strong brand images, customers consider P&G Guangzhou as an American company. Managers and employees view it as a Chinese company with multicultural responsibilities, and P&G's corporate management see the enterprise as one of many linkages in its transnational organization.[47]

This introductory section suggests a pattern of transition for many international organizations, but there is no comprehensive model that defines the multinational enterprise. Trading companies, usually small operations with limited markets, often expand through exports or foreign alliances. At some point, many trading companies invest in foreign operations, becoming multinationals when they assume management responsibilities for foreign activities. As these firms grow, they become extensive multinationals with global interests. Eventually, a major multinational may become a globally integrated transnational corporation with networks of interdependent worldwide activities. However, not all trading companies become multinationals, and only a small percentage of those aspire to become transnational corporations. Only a few of the largest international companies ever develop transnational characteristics. Many multinationals are simply constrained by the nature of their multilocal industries, and others are content with limited international exposure. Consequently, international managers play substantially different roles in their organizations, depending on the nature and size of operations, the industries in which their companies compete, and the prerogatives of senior executives.

ROLES OF INTERNATIONAL MANAGERS

International managers cannot rely on so-called *universal* principles of management to guide their behavior, primarily due to cultural constraints. The core concepts in management were developed on western (mainly Anglo-American) phenomena, and other societies differ so vividly in their cultures and ideologies that these concepts seldom have universal applicability. In addition, international managers often interact with several cultures at once; that is, their integrated enterprises have diverse, multicultural organizations. Consequently, a presumption of managing activities abroad according to western-Anglo concepts is precarious. Behavior and managerial decisions are situational.

In leadership parlance, we would say that international managers must accept *contingent* roles. The concept of contingency leadership, although widely accepted, does not capture the full richness of international management roles. It suggests that managers armed with one set of expectations or one style of leadership can, when confronted with new circumstances, turn to an alternative set of expectations with an optional style that works better. The astute manager may therefore have several "contingency" models tucked away, so that when "A" fails, "B" or "C" gets the nod.[48] International management is far more intriguing, and effective role behavior is far more complicated, than conceptual models of contingency leadership presented in most management textbooks.

Emphasis on Adaptability

The term *adaptability* may be an improvement over *contingency* to indicate that managers must modify behavior in response to unique circumstances. The pervasive message of this book is that managers must become adaptable. They must develop a foundation of management capabilities within their own cultural perspective, but be prepared for differences that they will face in other cultures. Therefore, the fundamental role of an international manager is to become an adaptable, integrating persona in a multidimensional world.

That may sound very fuzzy, perhaps of little value to someone trying to define an international career path, yet it has very real implications. For example, most business students are in well-defined programs such as marketing, accounting, information systems, and so on. These majors have *specialist* orientations that focus attention on carefully compartmentalized skills, which is perfectly consistent with corporate recruitment and career expectations that have defined industrial societies. This is particularly true in North America and much of Europe, and consequently individuals identify themselves within an organizational hierarchy and explain their responsibilities within their specializations. In many other regions of the world, and increasingly in western enterprises that operate globally, specialist orientations are becoming less common. In

Japan, it is common to hear students say that they are "studying commerce" or "preparing to work in engineering." In Britain, students are likely to say they are "sitting for degrees in economics" or "on programs" of science or social science. These statements reflect rather general orientations, and in most instances graduates enter the workforce without specific career expectations. European companies such as Unilever often look beyond explicit qualifications in an effort to recruit managers who demonstrate diversified interests and have the ability to work with multicultural groups.[49] Japanese recruiters have emphasized personal qualities such as a sense of loyalty or an aptitude for participation; university grades and performance are important as measures of intelligence, but a recruit's specific field of study is not highly correlated with selection decisions.[50]

When companies consider managers for international positions, the candidates' abilities to adapt outweigh other considerations. More specifically, an expatriate must have the capacity to be part of a diverse team, to tolerate uncertainty, and to accommodate a wide spectrum of interests beyond performance qualifications.[51] Research has shown that unlike practices in American firms, where managers are selected and trained with an emphasis on technological factors, selection and training among many European and Japanese firms emphasize sociological factors.[52] Differences in role expectations, therefore, can be better understood by examining *technological* and *sociological* perspectives.

Technological and Sociological Perspectives

From a technological viewpoint, an organization reflects the sum total of its equipment, processes, knowledge base, and conversion systems. This orientation makes sense when explaining how an auto manufacturer works or how a bank does business. Within the technological system, managerial roles are defined by job responsibilities, which are technical descriptions, assignments, and authority for decisions specific to job contexts. Industrialized countries in the Americas, Europe, Asia, and the Middle East have developed technological systems with many similarities, including patterns of comparable *specialized* jobs and roles.

On closer inspection, cross-cultural researchers have found important differences in role behavior, even among people with very similar technical qualifications. For example, design engineers in a Japanese auto plant may have backgrounds and educational qualifications identical to those of design engineers in an American plant, yet the cultural work environment strongly influences different patterns of behavior. The Japanese engineers are more likely to work in a *kanban* system of highly integrated processes that defines role behavior within a group of technicians who accept broad accountability for the group and for interaction with other groups. **Kanban** literally means "moving card," and it refers to a control device within a continuous stream of inventory. Today, the term suggests a fully integrated production system with carefully orchestrated and interrelated job responsibilities extending throughout an organization. In contrast, American firms tend to favor departmental systems with process technology based on coordinated series of isolated activities. In effect, the American engineers are buffered or "uncoupled" from other parts of the system, with an emphasis on individual accountability. American job responsibilities, and to a substantial degree role expectations, are defined narrowly within the individual's specialized field. Thus, sociological processes within an organization crucially influence role expectations, and the social system of an organization captures the nuances, customs, and expectations of the culture in which it operates.

The example suggests that an American engineer working in Japan, or a Japanese engineer working in the United States, must make considerable adaptations in behavior to work effectively in respective foreign systems. That principle may seem obvious, given the extreme differences between the United States and Japan, but comparable scenarios create far greater challenges in countries with Islamic laws, those with Hindu cultures, or in Africa, where tribal affiliations dictate role relationships.

Major differences can also separate even geographically close and culturally similar countries. For example, French managers tend to define their positions and roles based on social factors. These include family reputations, education, prestige of schools attended, and political affiliations. In contrast, German managers tend to define their positions and roles based on technical skills, job credentials, and seniority within their organizations. Consequently, French and German managers may display remarkable differences in motives, decisions, and behavior. Even within a country, individuals exhibit significant differences, such as the variations in the languages and customs of French-speaking and English-speaking Canadians.

Managers from countries that have sharp contrasts in social systems tend to show greater tolerance than American managers do, so they can often adapt more readily to international assignments. Europeans, in particular, benefit from this advantage due to the proximity of their cultures, even though they maintain their individuality. Americans and Japanese seldom have had similar exposure to cultural diversity and often find it difficult to cope in multicultural environments.[53]

The Expatriate and Generic Roles

An **expatriate** manager encounters the problem of adaptability even more acutely than others because expatriates clearly do not belong to the cultures in which they find themselves. They seldom ever feel *acculturated* in the sense of becoming members of foreign societies, even if they have lived overseas for many years. Many British expatriates have lived in Hong Kong since arriving as youths, and some have stayed to retire, yet they still remain isolated from the predominant Chinese society. They tend to maintain their close identity as Scots or Welsh or Londoners, but they never become "Hong Kong people," as locals call themselves.[54]

Except in rare instances, expatriates seldom gain full acceptance in their foreign societies. They remain outsiders, constantly proving themselves worthy of respect by local workers. Expatriates usually remain highly visible when working abroad, and their actions and behavior are subject to quick criticism. Some escape this stigma when home and host cultures are similar (e.g., Canada and the United States); but ethnic differences are quite apparent elsewhere, and when something goes wrong, ethnicity often becomes a reason for placing blame. On the other side of that coin, expatriates show equal difficulty accepting local customs, and vivid differences continue to distinguish their own values from those of their employees. Ethnic biases or stereotypes too often become pretexts for explanations, mistakes, or misunderstandings among host-country employees.[55]

Regardless of the culture or the position of an expatriate, generic management roles of planning, organizing, leading, and controlling are similar worldwide. Responsibilities within each category of activity, however, change substantially in a global environment. Several chapters address these generic roles, noting the lack of universal principles, as discussed earlier. These discussions will address how managers plan foreign strategies and organize international operations. Organizing presents

GLOBAL VIEWPOINT

New Meaning for an Expatriate's Life

Twelve years ago a young Canadian, Bryan McAlister, arrived in Spain to take up his first management post as a corporate trainer for his American employer. He spoke Spanish, but once in Spain, he found that his language abilities were far from the fluency required. Nevertheless he learned quickly, worked well with local employees, and came to be respected, despite many mistakes.

Initially, he complained of the beer and disliked local wine. He found bathing facilities terribly inadequate by home standards, and his habit of talking business at lunch irritated his Spanish colleagues, who preferred to talk about soccer or simply to relax. McAlister was criticized for smothering his food in ketchup (which, he was told, insulted a restaurant or hostess), and he failed to appreciate bullfights. He dated a local girl, and they were eventually married even though he failed to present himself properly to her father—a slip in protocol for which he was never fully forgiven.

Professionally, McAlister adjusted well; and after nearly six years in Spain, he considered himself "accepted" and "resident." He and his wife began a family and had two girls, born two years apart. McAlister was promoted to a senior post in the company's Madrid office. Despite a comfortable life, he had always assumed that he would return to Canada. Too often, he complained of local conditions and customs, regularly speaking to his wife of the advantages of living in Canada. His criticisms did not always sit well with her or with McAlister's colleagues.

Suddenly, the company's Spanish division was sold, and McAlister was called home. At a farewell dinner, his staff gave him a present with the message that roughly translated to "Good wishes to the nice visiting Canadian." He discovered with surprise that his years in Spain were little more than an interlude. He had never really been accepted locally, and now that he was going home, he wondered what awaited him there. His family was apprehensive about leaving Spain. What were they leaving behind? His wife was in tears as she boarded the plane to leave, and after a few months in the winter conditions of Toronto, she returned to Spain.

McAlister worked for some time in a Canadian advertising agency, but he found everything as awkward at home as he had in Spain when he first arrived. He also brought home to Canada some behavior that reflected his years abroad. For example, he avoided business talk and took long lunches, preferred casual chats with clients in meetings when they seemed anxious to "cut to the chase," and was criticized by colleagues for his overly laid-back work habits. When he talked with family or friends about Europe, they seemed disinterested or bored. Consequently, McAlister felt that he was not fitting in, and his employer soon suggested that he find another job.

During several months of job searching, McAlister felt more and more out of place. A return to Spain to briefly visit his family revealed an interesting sense of familiarity, and he soon found a new position at a Spanish subsidiary of a British clothing manufacturer. Today, he considers himself simultaneously an international citizen and a patriotic Canadian. He sees his career as that of a permanent expatriate pursuing exciting opportunities in southern Europe.

Source: Adapted from an unpublished student paper: Ian McAlister, "Why Go Overseas? Why Not? And Who Cares Anyway?" James Madison University, July 1995.

substantial challenges for staffing foreign operations, creating harmonious multicultural organizations, and implementing new work processes. This book examines leadership more extensively than other functions of management because behavioral adaptation proves so important in foreign assignments. Chapters on expatriate management, human resource management, motivation, and leadership focus on these sensitive topics. Controlling as a facet of management role behavior runs like a continuing thread through the fabric of these discussions, because managers in foreign assignments encounter tremendous constraints on what they can do and how they can influence performance.

The concept of *cultural adaptability* underscores this entire presentation on international management, and the core of the book consists of chapters on culture, intercultural communications, and international negotiations. Culture is a pervasive theme throughout the text, with a prominent influence on each topic explored. Successful international managers shed their parochial assumptions about how the world should be and adapt to circumstances that determine how the world is. This principle applies equally to recent graduates just launching careers as well as to seasoned executives in global enterprises. They discover more about themselves and about how to live in a tremendously complicated international environment, and those who can develop the characteristics of cultural adaptability will be in high demand. In a broad survey of global companies, the National Foreign Trade Council found that the demand for expatriate managers will increase substantially into the new millenium. Most executives in the survey said that they were paying very close attention to graduation lists of schools specializing in international programs, such as the American Graduate School of International Management in Glendale, Arizona. The survey also revealed that more than 60 percent of companies, including small and mid-sized enterprises, are developing expatriate training programs.[56]

FUTURE EXPECTATIONS AND CHALLENGES

The most important challenge facing international managers is to effectively position their organizations in a rapidly changing global economy. For many large multinationals, this may require a major shift in emphasis, toward transnational management and away from merely being a multidomestic corporation with foreign outposts. Not all companies are ready to make this transition, and not all industries dictate a pattern of global competition.

Harvard professor Michael E. Porter, arguably the best-known scholar of global strategy, emphasizes that many companies compete essentially in local markets.[57] They operate domestically to generate their particular goods and services, but they begin to manage worldwide interests when dealing with collections of domestic enterprises, such as retailing, consumer finance, caustic chemicals, and insurance. This chapter earlier referred to these sorts of companies as *multilocal* enterprises. Retailers, for example, serve very specific local markets; consumer finance companies lend to select groups of clients, usually under regulation by state, provincial, or national laws; caustic chemicals cannot be safely distributed over long distances; the terms of insurance products depend on statutes of a nation or state. These, and similar industries, dictate *localization*.

At the other extreme, certain industries dictate *globalization*. Production of commercial aircraft, microelectronics products, automobiles, textiles, telecommunications, optics, and base metals are examples. Companies cannot compete in these industries within the confines of domestic markets. Their products tend to be universal, they face global price competition, and buyers are not seriously restricted by local mandates. Aircraft and semiconductor products, for example, no longer need national identities, nor can they be isolated in markets with arbitrary boundaries. Until a few years ago, only a few industries compelled companies to establish global operations, most of them limited to natural resource extraction and fossil fuels. Today, makers of athletic shoes, denim jeans, watches, eyeglasses, and many other products compete globally, as do companies in the aircraft and semiconductor industries.

This chapter has emphasized, in broad terms, the differences in management roles for multilocal and global businesses. It has also marked a definite trend toward globalization that requires a transition in management away from a provincial view of competitive behavior and toward a holistic perspective on globally integrated commerce. Management literature refers to this transition as the **globalization/localization imperative.**[58] The term suggests that, although a company must "go global" to compete effectively, it must tailor its operations to local conditions to maintain its individual market characteristics. In summary, managers must *adapt* to the demands of world enterprise and to cultural characteristics among the world's societies.

The following chapters will explore the global-local dilemma in more depth, addressing many other challenges facing international managers in the new millennium. As Peter Drucker said, "Management has emerged as the decisive factor of production. It is management on which competitive position has to be based."[59] He points out that other factors of production—land, labor, and capital—have become substantially neutralized as competitive advantages. Specifically, global companies with widespread holdings can rapidly redeploy assets, thereby reducing the importance of physical properties. These companies can also reposition operations to take advantage of world labor markets and recruit globally for specialized talent; labor is at best only a temporary factor that differentiates competition. Money is fluid and it can be rapidly mobilized, particularly with global communications and electronic transaction systems. Consequently, the human leadership factor makes the difference, and perhaps it has always been the most important consideration.

REVIEW QUESTIONS

1. What does the term *globalization* mean, and what effect is this trend having on international competition?
2. How can you distinguish *international business* from *international management?* Can someone work in international business without becoming an international manager? Explain.
3. What is the most common description of a *multinational corporation?*
4. How would management of a *transnational corporation* differ from practices in a *multinational corporation?*
5. What important developments occurred in Europe in the eighteenth and nineteenth centuries to accelerate international commerce, and what developments are currently influencing European commerce?
6. How have Japanese firms emerged as major international competitors, and what significant changes have occurred to determine their approach to international business?
7. Explain the meaning of the term *multilocal* organizations. How would you describe a manager's role in a multilocal foreign subsidiary versus a global enterprise?
8. What critical considerations demand attention from international managers working abroad? Explain in terms of cultural adaptation, technical skills, and organizational skills.

GLOSSARY OF KEY TERMS

Chaebol   A large Korean trading company based on family associations and encompassing vertically integrated systems of contractors, subsidiaries, suppliers, and political and financial interests.

Cross-cultural management   The process of managing company interests across national boundaries and often among diverse cultures.

Expatriate   A parent-company employee assigned to a foreign position or working and residing in a foreign environment.

Global manager   An international manager capable of synthesizing talents among managers on a worldwide basis, transcending political and national frontiers through an integrated transnational corporation.

Global organization   An enterprise characterized by integrated systems of international operations and management that bind the company together as an interdependent endeavor.

Globalization/localization imperative   The perceived requirement that a company go global in pursuit of worldwide integration to achieve its objectives while at the same time developing capabilities to compete as a local enterprise within distinct markets or niches.

International business   The field of trade, financial, economic relations, and other activities, some of which may not require management or direct investments in foreign assets.

International management   Responsibilities beyond foreign trade and business relationships in companies with assets and operations outside their home countries.

Kanban   Literally a "moving card," and a label in Japan for an entire philosophy of fully integrated corporate operations and interdependent management systems.

Keiretsu   A Japanese conglomerate, often controlled through prominent families or associations, made up of widely networked, vertically integrated systems that include trading subsidiaries, suppliers, contractors, and financial institutions, reinforced by political connections.

Multilocal corporation   An enterprise composed of multiple foreign operations, each independent relative to others and usually managed locally and competing in a narrowly defined market.

Multinational corporation (MNC)   A company with direct investments in one or more foreign subsidiary interests with management responsibilities for foreign operations.

Trading company   An organization ranging in size from a one-person agency to a major corporation that engages primarily in international exporting, importing, brokerage, sourcing, or distribution.

Transnational corporation (TNC)   A globally integrated company with many interrelated systems of activities, alliances, and relationships through which it seeks to achieve optimal performance through a seamless organization network without regard to national or political boundaries.

Zaibatsu   A form of Japanese group enterprise based on feudal family associations and clanlike allegiances with extraordinary influence on commerce, political policies, and social development.

EXERCISES

1. Through the library, Internet, or industry publications, identify two multinational companies that you can contrast as having "multidomestic" or "globally integrated" operations. How do they differ in their products or services, their customers, and their organizations? Discuss how you believe management responsibilities will differ for each company in relation to home-based managers who are responsible for coordinating foreign interests, and in relation to managers of foreign subsidiaries.

2. Interview a foreign manager who is employed locally as an "expatriate," and a local manager who has worked overseas as an expatriate. Ask them what their greatest difficulties were in their "foreign roles" and in adjusting to unfamiliar cultures. What important lessons have they learned from managing in a country foreign to their own? What obstacles did they have to overcome to be effective? What recommendations would they make to a young graduate interested in global business?

MERCEDES IN THE NEW MILLENNIUM

Mercedes unveiled its award-winning CLK Coupe in Detroit in March 1997 as a "world car" manufactured in Europe, but the result of design and component manufacturing activities in 19 other countries. A year later, the Mercedes M-Class sports utility van set new production records in its Tuscaloosa, Alabama, plant, becoming that state's eighth-largest employer. Meanwhile, the company's Freightliner truck division, formerly a domestically owned U.S. company, became the third-largest North American competitor in its field. By 1999, Daimler-Benz AG—the German parent corporation of Mercedes—was directly employing more than 90,000 U.S. workers in automotive, heavy truck, railroad, space, and aircraft component manufacturing facilities. In addition, the company held joint venture agreements with other U.S., Swiss, Swedish, and German interests, including a consortium of American suppliers with procurement contracts to European Airbus. The company's American assets alone placed Daimler-Benz among the top 25 corporations on the *Fortune 500* list. But that represented only the tip of the iceberg.

Daimler-Benz merged with Chrysler Corporation on the eve of the new millennium to become DaimlerChrysler, ranked in 2000 as the fifth-largest company in the world on the *Fortune Global 500* list. Today it ranks sixth in world assets, twelfth in profits, and eighteenth in employment. By the end of 2001, the Mercedes M-Class division in Alabama is expected to be the fifth largest employer in the state, and its third largest exporter. Indeed, the U.S. auto division plans to invest more than $600 million to double production of the M-Class SUV, immediately adding more than 2,000 new jobs. Currently, the Mercedes SUV assembles 80,000 vehicles annually, which are marketed in 135 countries.

On a world scale, Mercedes automobiles are manufactured in 34 countries and sold in more than 200 countries. The parent company DaimlerChrysler maintains joint corporate offices in Michigan and Stuttgart, Germany, with regional executive groups in 60 other countries, including design engineering centers in Japan and India, and a global communications center in Ireland. The company's chairman, Jurgen E. Schrempp, is a principal sponsor of the Trans Atlantic Business Dialogue, a forum that mobilizes North American and European business to promote free trade. The company also sponsors one of America's largest intercultural exchange programs. During the last decade, the company has reached more than one million American teenagers with educational projects and cultural exchange sponsorships to bring together American and German youngsters. Today, that program extends to the company's South American and Asian operations.

These extraordinary changes have transformed the staid old German automaker into one of the world's leading international corporations. Most of these changes occurred within a brief decade of corporate restructuring, yet they began in earnest when Schrempp launched plans for the Alabama Mercedes plant in 1993. The Alabama plant is only one part of Schrempp's plan to remodel DaimlerChrysler as a "world company," not German, European, or American. The M-Class Mercedes, for example, is a German-engineered car, yet it was essentially designed through technological R&D centers in Palo Alto, California, Portland, Oregon, Shanghai, PRC, and Bangalore, India. At the same time, the company is building a new class of smaller cars called the A-Class, and the "Smart Car," both designed for city commuters and being initially marketed in Europe and Asia. DaimlerChrysler also has equity interests in Japanese and Scandinavian automotive manufacturing, and it has comanufacturing agreements with Korea's Ssangyong Motor Company.

In Schrempp's view, DaimlerChrysler has retained the best of its core German technology and American ingenuity, but the company is rapidly becoming a global transnational enterprise through alliances, distribution agreements, and consortia. Although the company has been historically considered a "very German" company, Schrempp says that it is being completely restructured to respond to the reality of global commerce.

He emphasizes that nearly all major industries and services are entering an era of regionalism; markets, alliances, capital movement, and social systems themselves are being redefined through the European

Union, NAFTA, ASEAN, and APEC. Competition for resources and markets is intensifying as more and more corporations scour the world for lower-cost areas in which to relocate production and for the opportunity to network optimal cross-border systems. To keep up with fast-paced global economic change, Schrempp says, business leaders must benchmark their operations against the best in the world, in efficiency, in quality, and in financial performance.

Most important, however, management must accept the challenge of an international community where there is no room for parochialism. Managers must learn to be global citizens, not Germans, Americans, or Brazilians; yet in this great transformation, they must honor their cultural identities and the richness of their histories. Schrempp's 13-member executive board, the body that effectively coordinates the company's strategic business groups, represents eight different nationalities; DaimlerChrysler's regional executives represent 32 different ethnic groups on four continents. Becoming global, in Schrempp's view, is not about worldwide assets or activities, and it is not about organizational alliances. It is about people, and the transformation to a global company involves a fundamental change in management thought and behavior.

QUESTIONS

1. DaimlerChrysler's chairman characterizes the company as a developing transnational global organization. Do you agree, or would you describe the company differently? Explain how you view the corporation.
2. How would you explain the rationale by which Mercedes Benz is locating assembly plants and activities to places such as Mexico, Brazil, and India? What advantages does the company have in these facilities?
3. Why would Mercedes invest in a major new U.S. manufacturing facility for a top-line automobile? What problems would you anticipate when the firm brings together German and American managers with local American workers in a U.S. plant?

BIBLIOGRAPHY

DaimlerChrysler website: "History, Chairman's Comments, News Releases, and Global Operations" <www.daimlerchrysler.com> [cited 28 August 2000].

Justin Martin. "Mercedes: Made in Alabama." *Fortune*, 7 July 1997, 150–158.

Brandon Mitchener. "Mercedes's Werner Resigns as Chairman: Executive Felt Left out of Operations in Wake of Big Restructuring." *Wall Street Journal*, 17 January 1997, p. A10.

Jurgen E. Schrempp. "Thriving on Global Economic Changes: A European View." *Vital Speeches of the Day* 63, no. 10 (March 1997): 306–309.

CASE 1.2

SINGAPORE: PRAGMATISM PREVAILS

Once a remote colony tied loosely to Europe through British rule, Singapore has become a model city-state in Southeast Asia. It rivals Hong Kong as the busiest seaport in the world, eclipsing London, New York, and Rotterdam, and it serves as a major air transport and passenger hub for the Pacific Rim. With a population of barely three million, including foreign residents and contract workers, Singapore has compiled a record of nearly 8 percent annual growth spanning two decades. Even during the 1998 Asian economic crisis, as other regional economies suffered negative growth and near financial collapse, Singapore's GDP slid to barely a half-percent growth, yet remained positive. By the end of 1999, growth in GDP had reached 5.4 percent, and targeted 8.4 percent for year 2000. The government is relatively debt free with a strong balance of payments, and the country as a whole enjoys little or no inflation, pleasing an affluent population with one of the world's highest per-capita GNPs. This country, small in both size and population, has few natural resources and only a short history as a nation. Still, it handles more trade in statistical terms than the combined countries of the entire Indian subcontinent.

Singapore achieved self-governance in 1959, and it became an independent nation in 1965. At that time, the per-capita income was barely more than U.S. $400 per year, unemployment was nearly 25 percent, and most of its citizens had achieved only marginal literacy. Indeed, it was an underdeveloped, resource-poor country, emerging from the remnants of a crumbling colonial era. Its first prime minister, Lee Kuan Yew, held power until he voluntarily stepped aside into a "senior minister's" role in 1989. He sought to create a democratic state based on a strong constitutional government and profound respect for free enterprise. In effect, however, the country has become a one-party socialist system, with only a weak second party contending for power without substantially different views from the ruling People's Action Party.

In a political sense, Singapore is a paradox. It maintains democratic government to the extent that citizens vote to confirm the party's policies and people. Mr. Lee describes his economy as one operated by a "visible hand" in which government participates actively in commerce, infrastructure development, and more than 500 different strategic alliances with private-sector and foreign interests. Government officials call the shots on social policies, and they can impose rigorous commands. The country is relatively drug free, due largely to uncompromising enforcement of the death penalty for drug trafficking. Streets are almost squeaky clean because the government imposes strict laws against littering. Someone caught dropping trash or a cigarette butt on the street, for example, can be sentenced to a clean-up squad—along with fellow offenders attired in vests noting their infractions—and required to pick up trash in the most public places and before TV cameras. The government also enforces public dress codes and widespread bans on smoking and chewing gum.

Such micromanagement of daily activities can irritate some, but most Singaporeans enthusiastically support Mr. Lee's brand of government intervention. During the early 1960s he publicly announced the goal of making Singapore a private-enterprise economy open to foreign investment, but he pledged to avoid all foreign assistance or borrowing. To become successful, he said, Singaporeans would have to save and invest at record levels, and government would encourage this thrift through very low taxes, including no capital gains or tax on income from savings. In effect, the country taxes income between 15.0 and 17.5 percent. Corporations pay taxes at similar rates, and the law allows significant reductions for foreign

investments that generate employment and revenue for the nation. Singapore's per-capita savings rate averages nearly 40 percent—four times higher than that of most nations—and it remains a self-financed, strongly invested country. The country established the National University of Singapore and then aligned it in joint ventures with MIT and several other notable institutions to rapidly develop scientific, engineering, and business education programs at both undergraduate and graduate levels. Education at the lower levels became compulsory and free, transforming Singapore in less than three decades into one of the premier Asian centers of technological education, with a highly skilled workforce and a literate population.

During his tenure, Lee Kuan Yew founded an administration known for its incorruptibility and efficiency, yet his international reputation is that of a benevolent dictator. He tolerates little criticism and denies the relevance of any economic philosophy to Singapore. "Being pragmatic is important," he recently quipped, and he continued, quoting from an old adage, "It is not the color of the cat that is important. What is important is whether it will catch mice." Consequently, Mr. Lee avoids labels such as *Keynesian, Marxist, Maoist, Socialist, Capitalist*—or any other "ist"—and simply says, "you pay your own way, and government must protect your opportunity to do so." High-ranking officials and wealthy Singaporeans were mildly criticized in the press recently for receiving favorable treatment such as priority choices in luxury housing, favorable financing, large discounts on major purchases, and free or honorary club memberships. Mr. Lee's response in a public speech was: "Come on! Grow up people! Those with power and money enjoy those benefits. Those that succeed reap rewards. We will all share alike in public benefits, education, security, human rights, and an ethical society, but stop being silly—life is a matter of inequalities, and if you want more, achieve more."

In a public forum in 1996, Mr. Lee pleaded with Singaporeans to preserve the "wealthy and honest but authoritarian society" he had been instrumental in creating. He reproached the nation for becoming complacent and criticized those who would seek democracy as practiced elsewhere. "Western style democracy as practiced in Taiwan or India," he said, "may make for an enjoyable election campaign but I am not sure we need that in Singapore." He also criticized entrenched communist societies, saying that a nation cannot succeed without private enterprise and a free-market economy, yet he expressed concern that many developing societies would disintegrate under democratic rule because people have no knowledge of self-determination.

Unfortunately, many foreign managers come to Singapore or other Southeast Asian economies with the notion that they will democratize the workplace. Indeed, some hope to change these communities to fit their ideals of business behavior. Such efforts fail because the participants cannot accept value differences. In Mr. Lee's view, international managers must set aside personal ideologies and accept local priorities; they must accept his pragmatism. Yet that does not mean that local people should remain barricaded behind their customs; they too can learn, and pragmatism demands that they also adapt.

QUESTIONS

1. Assume that you were posted to a western multinational's office in Singapore, and living there forced you to adapt to local cultural conditions and work expectations. What problems would you envision for your personal adjustment to the commercial environment in Singapore?

2. Singapore's political and social policies often seem odd to foreigners, who have difficulty reconciling a "wide open" free-market economy with apparently tight control through the government's "visible hand" philosophy. Describe the economic difficulties of living in such a country, as well as the potential advantages for a competitive multinational firm.

3. Mr. Lee strongly emphasizes pragmatism and carefully avoids political stereotypes of his government. In your view, what do these positions imply for an international manager who works in Singapore with local employees, and what do they imply for employees who work for foreign companies?

BIBLIOGRAPHY

Clad, James. *Behind the Myth: Business, Money, and Power in Southeast Asia.* London: Unwin Hyman, 1989, 125–145.

Lee Kuan Yew. "America in Asia, the Lee Strategy." *South China Morning Post,* 6 June 1996, p. 15.

Lim Chong-Yah. "Government and Development: The Case of Singapore." In Tzong-biau Lin and Chyau Tuan (eds.), *The Asian NIEs: Success and Challenge.* Hong Kong: Lo Fung Learned Society, 1993, 147–178.

"Sustain Miracle, Entreats Founder." *South China Morning Post,* 9 June 1996, p. 7.

East Asia Recovery and Beyond. Washington, D.C.: The World Bank, 2000, 4–6.

CHAPTER 2

THE INTERNATIONAL BUSINESS ENVIRONMENT

CHAPTER OBJECTIVES

Describe the global business environment, and outline the evolution of regional trading blocs.

Review changes taking place in developing countries that influence international managers and their organizations.

Discuss recent social and economic changes and their effects on international commerce.

Detail the implications for international commerce of domestic growth and development.

Explain how technological developments influence patterns of world trade and development.

Highlight the specific forces of privatization and workforce diversity, which have dramatically influenced international management practices.

List the implications of global changes and trends for international managers.

Taiwan-born Paul Liao describes himself as a world citizen and global thinker. He is an ethnic Chinese, an American citizen, and an engineer whose company, KCM Inc., has worked in more than 30 countries on projects ranging from a village fish farm to a multibillion-dollar water infrastructure system.[1] KCM provides international engineering consulting services with more than 200 engineers, architects, and applied scientists. From its Seattle headquarters with views of the bustling port area and Puget Sound, KCM oversees a number of foreign subsidiaries and alliances. In one notable alliance between KCM and the Taiwanese government, Liao acts as special adviser on a $22 billion water and sewage systems infrastructure project that includes plans for a Ministry of Education, the National Museum of Marine Biology, and Taipei's mass transit system. KCM is also responsible for Seattle's urban sanitation system. Under Liao's leadership, the firm has engineered air and water projects, aquariums, aquaculture systems, highways, bridges, and public buildings.

Paul Liao came to the United States in the early 1960s after graduating from a Taiwanese university with a degree in environmental engineering. He earned a master's degree in bioengineering at Oklahoma State University and later a doctorate at the University of Washington. Initially, Liao planned to learn American technology and then return to Taiwan, but he took a job with a small U.S. partnership called Kramer, Chin and Mayo in Seattle. The company evolved to become KCM, and Liao rose to the office of chief executive officer.

In one of his early projects in 1978, Liao worked in mainland China on a project to help improve the country's commercial fish-farming industry. Fish and shrimp farms are common in the hundreds of coastal villages of China, yet because of antiquated methods, controlled shrimp farms generated a total annual yield of less than 2,000 tons in 1978. Liao's team created an integrated aquaculture system for shrimp production, from breeding to final processing for export. They designed the first hatchery in China, brought in scientists to formulate shrimp food and manufacture bulk nutrients, designed machines for processing, and trained villagers in export marketing. The project was a first in China, and by 1990, the coastal shrimp-farming industry was producing more than 200,000 tons of shrimp for export to markets in Japan, Canada, and the United States. In 1978, annual family income from a village fish farm was less than $200; the same family enterprise earned more than $5,000 a year in 2000.

KCM has produced similar results in many other ways through projects in Southeast Asia, the Middle East, South America, and Eastern Europe. The company's employees and associates represent more than 50 ethnic groups, and half of the permanent staff in Seattle are minorities, including Asians and Native Americans. Together, they speak more than 30 languages, yet nearly all are U.S. or Canadian citizens. Liao says simply that no one in the company is anything in particular—all are just different individuals with interests in world development. He is admired in mainland China and Taiwan for introducing new American technologies to those economies, but Liao describes his contribution as helping to transfer knowledge of systems that assist people to become self-reliant.

If a single trait has made KCM and Paul Liao successful, it has been the ability to adapt to other cultures and to bring them appropriate technologies rather than just transplanting state-of-the-art technology that might work in America but fail elsewhere. For example, the rural Chinese fishing villages where KCM worked during the 1980s could not operate computer-controlled, integrated fish-farm systems. Although the computerized systems might have produced excellent results, Liao created mechanical systems that matched the capabilities and resources of the villages. His foreign crews brought with them operational plans for the hardware and engineering requirements, but education and management at the local level also helped to determine the project's success. Paul Liao concludes that managers today must think globally but operate pragmatically overseas, always remaining sensitive to cultural differences.

A GLOBAL VIEW

As a new century unfolds, global competition is accelerating with new economic developments throughout the world. More change in international activities is taking place more rapidly than at any other time in history. Just as the calendar expired on the twentieth century, European investments in the United States eclipsed America's investments abroad for the first time in more than 100 years. European companies put close to $300 billion into American firms in 1999 alone, tripling investments in 1998 and dwarfing previous years. Nevertheless, American firms continued to invest heavily in Europe, including Ford's recent purchase of Sweden's hallmark auto company, Volvo.[2] Today, companies with substantial resources have many opportunities for efficient redeployment of their assets, and global companies can often choose where to invest and how to compete advantageously. The strength of the U.S. consumer market, however, has drawn foreign interests, and the depth of America's capital markets has been the primary engine of growth for many multinational organizations. Other affluent nations with well-developed economies also are very attractive for international expansion, and they have the means for substantial foreign investment. Unfortunately, most of the world's economies are less fortunate and far less attractive. Some are just emerging from repressive ideological systems, and some are incapable of sustained economic development or trade.

Within this framework, companies of many nationalities are expanding their international investments. Some are simply exporting, others are establishing foreign facilities, and some of the largest enterprises are becoming global companies with integrated technology with world-brand products and services. In nearly all instances, these companies are searching for opportunities among promising transition economies where social changes promise accelerated growth of free enterprise. These trends mean a greater need for international managers who must work in more complex, multinational management systems.

SOCIAL AND ECONOMIC CHANGES

Worldwide, trade has grown over the past two decades at an annual rate of 8.4 percent, with an estimated annual increase to 11.8 by 2005. Meanwhile, the average annual rate of change for world GNP has barely nudged 0.9 percent. In real terms, more than two-thirds of the world's increased economic activity during the past two decades has occurred through trade, and while some countries participated in this growth, many others experienced no growth. Some suffered economic decline.[3] Most of those with no growth (or deteriorating economies) are **less-developed countries (LDCs)** that lack social and economic infrastructure capable of sustained development. In contrast, **developing economies (DEs)** have demonstrated capabilities for growth supported by appropriate social and economic systems.

Some countries are involved in political transitions or conflicts that are economically devastating. Setting aside the humanitarian costs of a decade of wars in the

Balkan states, the countries that now remain from the former Yugoslavia together with their immediate neighbors are unlikely to regain positive economic momentum for many years. Indeed, Bosnia-Herzegovina was only barely emerging from a destitute postwar situation in 1999 when Serbian forces under Belgrade command sought to eradicate the ethnic Albanians of its Kosovo region. Macedonia subsequently felt the brunt of refugees and major disruptions to its regional economic development efforts. Bulgaria, Slovenia, and to some extent Hungary and Croatia had to embrace refugee problems, regional trade quagmires, and distortions in international trade and development.[4]

Meanwhile, even high-income peaceful countries with relatively stable governments suffer unexpected economic reversals. This is evidenced by Japan's continuing difficulties with capital markets and monetary policies, and with Sweden's controversial fiscal policies and repressive social structure of tax-based benefits. International investors have been cautious about opportunities in Japan and Sweden for several years, and even domestic capital in both countries has been channeled outward to more lucrative foreign opportunities.[5] Social, economic, and political changes substantially influence the relative risk of international investments, which in turn have rapid and often devastating effects on a country's trade. Consequently, a country's gross national product suffers together with its ability to compete in world markets. Selected indicators of world GNP and trade data are shown in Table 2.1 as a basis for further discussion.

Several growth patterns emerge from this data.[6] First, per-capita GNP for the high-income economies more than doubled the world average since 1980, and per-capita GNP for the low-income economies (including China and India) more than tripled the world rate for the same period. Also notice that without China and India, the remaining low-income economies suffered a substantial net loss. The middle-income nations also suffered a net loss. Put another way, the affluent nations have become even wealthier while less-fortunate nations have systematically become poorer. Although not shown in Table 2.1, China has had the highest average per-capita GNP rate of growth among the low-income societies—7.8 percent. India averaged 2.9 percent during the same period. Because of their huge populations, these two countries skewed the data and obscured the true picture of *negative* growth in countries such as Rwanda, Azerbaijan, Armenia, Nicaragua, the Congo, and nearly 20 others. The highest growth rates occurred among Asian nations that were considered to be underdeveloped until recently, although the 1997–1998 Asian financial crisis temporarily set back Thailand, Malaysia, and Indonesia. Notable gains were reported for Mexico, Jamaica, the Philippines, Sri Lanka, Ireland, and Portugal.

International managers find several more interesting trends in the trade data of Table 2.1. First, with the exception of the high-income economies, the rest of the world experienced a dramatic increase in both exports and imports between 1980 and the end of the millennium. World Bank research showed that China experienced the highest rate of change in exports (average annual 14.7 percent increase) and the highest rate of change in imports (24.6 percent). Poland recently registered a 3.9 percent increase in exports and a 26.5 percent increase in imports to pace Eastern Europe, but these economies are not very stable, and periods of successful expansion cannot always be sustained. Also, there are several paradoxes. The transition Baltic states of Latvia, Estonia, and Lithuania, together with 14 Latin American countries, experienced increased trade resulting in positive trade balances, yet GDP in most of these nations remained dormant or was negative due to domestic inflation or political problems. The one consistent theme is that nearly all high-income economies of North America and Western Europe have experienced a moderation of imports (they continue to increase

TABLE 2.1

SELECTED INDICATORS BY REGION FOR WORLD ECONOMIES

Regions by Income[c] (number of economies)	GNP per Capita (dollars/annual percent change)[a]		Exports and Imports of Merchandise (annual percent change)[b]			
			Exports		Imports	
	Dollars 1998	Percent Change 1980–1998	1980–1989	1990–1998	1980–89	1990–1998
Low-income (51)	$ 520	2.1%	3.8%	9.2%	1.6%	12.5%
Low-income (49) (excludes China and India)	380	−5.9	1.0	1.1	0.9	−2.0
Middle-income (57)	2,950	−1.1	0.9	2.2	1.0	1.1
High-income (25)	25,570	1.2	5.0	4.9	6.1	4.6
World total (133)	4,890	0.1	4.0	5.7	3.8	8.7

[a]GNP is U.S. dollars normalized for exchange rates, and GNP percentage change is weighted average based on population.

[b]Exports and Imports are weighted averages and normalized to 1998 U.S. dollars by country GNP deflators.

[c]The World Bank tracks a total of 209 economies, including those of sovereign nations, territories, and semiautonomous dependencies. Its longitudinal studies exclude data on 76 of the smallest economies and those whose governments choose not to provide data (e.g., Cuba, Iraq, Monaco, Tonga, Sudan, etc.). The study lacks complete data for some of the remaining 133 for the entire range of years. (It includes data from the republics of the former Soviet Union and countries in Central and Eastern Europe for varying periods between 3 and 13 years; data for several African and Middle Eastern countries span varying periods between 1 and 5 years.)

Sources: Compiled from *World Development Report 1999/2000*, CD-ROM (Washington, D.C.: World Bank, 2000), Statistical Index Tables, updated September 2000 from <http://www.worldbank.org/html/extdr/data>.

imports but at lower rates of change relative to exports). Consequently, they have reduced their monetary outflows and improved their trade balances, further strengthening their ability to sustain increased foreign investments.

Unbalanced Trade Development

The economic data summarized in the previous section also reveals a somewhat uncomfortable trend in regional development. The income disparities noted there suggest potential social problems for many relatively small world economies that have not yet emerged as competitive trading nations. In addition, many firms that have begun to expand their international interests seem clustered within several regions. Specifically, the economies of Central and Eastern Europe are struggling with internal transition problems (inflation, political unrest, backward financial infrastructures, and domestic redevelopment), yet their private-sector enterprises are also rapidly expanding trade ties with Western Europe. Some of these companies have established effective trade alliances with U.S. and Canadian companies through the help of government foreign-assistance programs, but the monetary value of their trade with Western Europe is approximately 12 times greater than their trade with North American partners. Foreign investment in Central and Eastern Europe by Western European firms is currently about 14 times greater than that invested by North American interests.

A similar pattern has been observed for emerging economies in Southeast Asia, where regional investment and trade eclipse trade with North American and European partners by four times. The Association of Southeast Asian Nations (ASEAN) and Asia-Pacific Economic Cooperation (APEC) treaties have fostered multilateral trade agreements that are consolidating international activity in the Asia-Pacific region. Similar clusters have emerged through trade alliances such as the North American Free Trade Agreement and EU initiatives that may extend membership to several Central and Eastern European nations. These developments have led some observers to suggest that international business is not becoming *global* in the sense of integrated world trade and investment, but *regionally insular* with selective pockets of trade and investment.[7]

Two important points emerge from these cluster patterns. First, domestic policy issues are becoming less important than economic development among low- and middle-income nations, and national economic priorities are becoming subservient to market demands of regional business. Second, globalization and intraregional expansion are creating international commercial alliances that transcend parochial political interests. The result is a growing number of interrelated enterprises without national identities or borders. In addition, regional trade blocs compete with other regional clusters, creating new patterns of world commerce.[8]

Regional Trading Blocs—The Triad

The concept of regional trading power began to emerge in the mid-1980s, and it strengthened after the reformations of 1989 and 1990 in the former Soviet bloc. Chapter 1 mentioned this trend as part of worldwide changes in economic development. Regional trading power does not, however, imply isolation but a regional consolidation of preferential trade alliances. The United States and Japan, key economies in two distinct regions, continue to maintain strong international alliances; but within their regions there are trade agreements that favor select member nations. France, Germany, and the United Kingdom have forged multilateral agreements among themselves under the EU, yet they are keenly aware of relative imbalances among themselves and other European nations. Trade issues, currency differentials, and bilateral sparring take place continuously everywhere, but within each of several regions, a distinct sense of proximity translates to closer commercial interests.

Regional development has fostered the concept of a world **triad** comprised of three powerful trade regions. Each region encompasses proprietary markets within their spheres of influence, creating far-reaching implications for the balance of world power.[9] The pattern of *triad influence* emerged in 1986 when the EU passed the Single European Act (SEA). In effect, EU member nations made a commitment to unify European markets by the end of 1992, and then to transform Europe into a single-currency trade region by 1999.

World leaders outside Europe immediately became concerned that the EU would become a closed system. Their concern was that a *Fortress Europe* would evolve among EU member nations with protected trade restrictions, tariffs, banking regulations, and licensing requirements that could insulate the region from outside competition. European companies would subsequently have a tremendous advantage within the region. Indeed, many of these fears have become reality in what is today a combined EU-EFTA trade bloc stretching from the Arctic Circle to the Mediterranean Ocean. Within this regional bloc, there are approximately 400 million consumers.[10] Further expansion of European trade agreements to include nonmember Central and Eastern European economies would create a consumer market exceeding 540 million people

FIGURE 2.1
Consolidation in Europe—Toward a Unified Market

Shading indicates EU member countries and associated states, EFTA affiliates, and current Central and Eastern European candidates for EU membership.

with nearly 24 percent of world GNP.[11] Eleven of these nonmember countries are positioned as candidate members to the EU, ranging from Cypress to Poland and the new Baltic States. The Treaty of Nice 2000, which unifies regional defense cooperation, will further strengthen the European region. The treaty takes effect at the end of 2001, at about the same time the EU will vote on membership for several Central European nations.[12] Figure 2.1 emphasizes this consolidation; shading indicates countries that are EU members or associates, EFTA affiliates, and Central and Eastern European states under consideration for EU membership.

The second triad region is North America. The United States, Canada, and Mexico constitute the core members of this trade bloc, but its sphere of influence extends to most of the 23 Latin American and Caribbean nations. The United States, Canada, and Mexico, with 360 million consumers, generate more than $6 trillion in total annual output. Consequently, the North American market is only marginally smaller than the European bloc, but it represents slightly larger productive capacity. Excluding contributions by Latin American nations, North America represents nearly 29 percent of world GNP. If trade liberalization continues, Brazil, Argentina, and Chile could, in due course, become formal members of the North American Trade Agreement (NAFTA), thereby swelling consumer ranks to nearly 500 million and GNP share to 32 percent.[13]

In the third triad region, Asia, Japan is clearly the leading economy and most influential force. Unlike Europe or North America, however, Asian trade agreements do not reflect a move toward consolidation. Most regional countries are insular, often competing fiercely with one another. Nevertheless, the nations of ASEAN and APEC share a strong sense of regional identity, with several exceptions. Australia and New Zealand are indeed important economies within the region, but both countries also have strong ethnic and economic ties to the British Commonwealth. Also, as noted in Chapter 1, Canada, Mexico, and the United States are members of APEC, and although they have significant interests in the Pacific, these countries lack ethnic ties and geographic proximity to Asian markets. If the region is defined by APEC nations (excluding the United States, Canada, and Mexico), there are more than 1.5 million consumers generating 28 percent of world GNP. Further exempting China, the combined market has slightly less than 300 million consumers with 18 percent of world GNP.[14]

Compared to Europe and North America, the Asian bloc seems to be a weak third region, but China and Indonesia (with the largest and fifth-largest populations in the world) have extraordinary resources and trade potential, despite recent economic setbacks in Southeast Asia. There is even more to this scenario; Vietnam is pursuing regional trade linkages, and Brunei, a country that is not well known outside the Pacific region, may be the wealthiest nation on Earth in per-capita assets. The Sultan of Brunei is the world's wealthiest person, but since he is an absolute monarch, it is difficult to distinguish his fortunes from those of his nation. With that said, Brunei's petroleum resources and projected offshore reserves rival those of Saudi Arabia.[15]

Continental Africa and the Middle East

Although the three regions that form the triad collectively account for nearly two-thirds of world economic activity, they account for less than a quarter of the world's nations. Those countries that comprise the rest of the world differ substantially in their economic development. Figure 2.2 provides examples of contrasting data for selected economies. These nations do not constitute a region like those in Europe, but managers need to recognize clusters where significant trade and foreign investment occurs.

North African countries—those of the sub-Saharan region, western coast, and southern Africa—may be loosely called African, but they differ substantially in anthropological, political, and economic characteristics.[16] Somalia, for example, is destitute, yet South Africa is well developed with a vibrant economy and strong private-sector enterprise.[17] Several neighbors of South Africa are in turmoil and barely able to maintain subsistence-level economies, yet many coastal nations with European colonial histories have government and financial infrastructures capable of attracting trade and foreign investment. Central and coastal regions also have a number of economic coalitions, but the members are more often on the verge of economic and even armed

FIGURE 2.2
GNP Growth
in Selected African
and Middle Eastern
Countries

Note: Data normalized to
1998; GNP is used for better
data measurement methods
and reliable estimates for
preliminary data in 2000.
Source: *World Development
Indicators 2000*, CD-ROM
(Washington, D.C.: World
Bank, 2000), Data Series,
GNP & Growth Statistics.

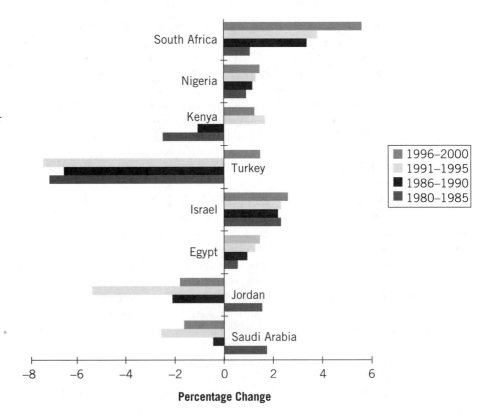

conflict.[18] North African countries have a heritage linked to the Arab world, yet these multicultural societies combine notable ethnic mixes from southern Europe and the Mediterranean. Israel adds another diverse element to the regional jigsaw puzzle. Therefore, it is illogical to consider African countries, or even regions within Africa, under one label.

It would also be a mistake to think of Africa as a continent of "less-developed" countries. Many African societies are indeed less developed—some even destitute—but there are strong economies anchored in the extreme north and south geographic regions. The relatively better developed countries in the north are more closely aligned with Middle East interests. Several are members of the Arab League, but these are political alliances rather than trade forums, and even then, relationships are tenuous. Iraq, Iran, Saudi Arabia, Egypt, Syria, Jordan, the United Arab Emirates, Kuwait, Oman, and several others have major ideological differences as evidenced by the 1991 Gulf War. The proximity of Turkey and Israel to both the Arab states and to Mediterranean Europe complicates political and trade relations for both countries, yet the Middle Eastern nations depend on similar regional and European markets. These countries also have significant interests in the Gulf and Indian Ocean regions.[19]

The Indian Subcontinent and Gulf

The United Nations and World Bank define the Indian Subcontinent and Gulf as a region composed of India, Pakistan, Sri Lanka, Bangladesh, the Maldives, and several others stretching down the Indian Ocean to Madagascar. India is the world's largest democracy and second-largest country next to China in population. Although smaller than China, India has a greater arable land mass, a significant financial infrastructure with confederated banking, and considerable resources.[20] India's trade expansion trails only that of China's in continental Asia. Unfortunately, India ranks poorly on the *Index of Economic Freedom* (118 among 148 countries), a measurement created by the Heritage Foundation and published annually to indicate a nation's proclivity for free trade and international investment.[21] According to this index, a "relatively free" nation is one with little government intervention in trade, a favorable regulatory environment, control over property rights and black-market activities, taxation and monetary policies conducive to economic trade and development, and "equitable" wage and price structures. India does not rank well on any of these criteria, yet the country has improved noticeably during the past five years. Not long ago, India was ranked very close to the bottom along with North Korea and Myanmar (formerly Burma). Heading into the new millennium, government corruption has been reduced and legislative control over trade and commerce has improved; yet India has not resolved serious gaps in wages and social welfare benefits that create a repressed economy for a majority of its population.[22]

In contrast, India's strong neighbor, Pakistan, maintains well-developed regional trade alliances, an industrial base, and a promising economy, but it has repressive trade restrictions and ideological disparities that are unattractive to North America and Europe. Political and military skirmishes with India have also prompted temporary trade restraints imposed against Pakistan by the United States and its European allies. In 1999, India suffered a military coup that has temporarily crippled economic progress. Another of India's neighbors, the island nation of Sri Lanka to the south, may become one of the region's future star performers. The country recently shed four decades of communist control and is embarking on a free-market economy positioned for export development. It is world renowned for its Ceylon teas, exotic spices, and exquisite gemstones. A nation of slightly more than 15 million people, Sri Lanka has excellent deep-water ports and air transport capabilities, located strategically midway between the heart of Southeast Asia and the Middle East. Although troubled by civil war, the country has established a commercial infrastructure that is attractive to foreign investment. It currently ranks 27th on the Index of Economic Freedom, a position shared with Sweden and Norway.

The Indian Subcontinent and Gulf region enjoys strong connections to the Arab world and the Persian Gulf states, and its principal countries conduct regular trade throughout Southeast Asia. Although the region lacks cooperative trade associations (indeed, the individual countries often have rather strained relations), the composite potential of the Gulf, Indian Ocean, and Southeast Asia could match growth in China and East Asia.[23] Many American companies, such as General Electric, have substantial investments in the region. GE chairman Jack Welch, who believes the next "economic miracle" will occur in India, recently said, "We see India, with the intellectual capability of the people, as the most cost-competitive country in the whole array of global business."[24] Carrier Corporation has a half-billion-dollar investment in India, and an automotive industry has emerged through production lines developed by Ford, Peugeot, and Mercedes. Sri Lanka offers the physical trappings of a paradise nation with pristine beaches and breathtaking mountains dotted by huge tea plantations, yet the country also has attracted more than 2,000 international companies since 1990, including IBM, Caterpillar, NEC, Coca-Cola, Bayer, and Unilever.[25]

Latin America

South America and the Latin countries of Central America and the Caribbean share a geographic identity within the hemisphere, and many have similar colonial histories, but they are quite different from one another.[26] Figure 2.3 contrasts four Latin

FIGURE 2.3
GDP Growth for Selected Latin American Countries

Note: Data is normalized to 1998, but implicit GDP deflators for Brazil and Argentina between 1983 and 1991 are approximations due to several changes in methods of measurement.
Source: *World Development Indicators 2000*, CD-ROM (Washington, D.C.: World Bank, 2000), Data Series, Income & Growth Statistics.

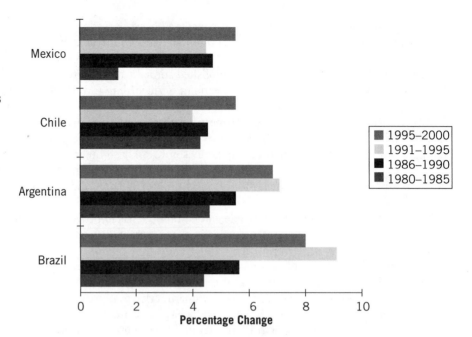

economies that all have strong trade profiles and expanding economies. Of course, Mexico is a member of NAFTA, but the remaining three countries are considered good candidates for NAFTA membership. Each country, however, has had recent political and economic setbacks.

Mexico has not yet fully recovered from three years of political scandals and a prolonged banking crisis. Even so, the country reduced inflation and liberalized trade. A new government in 2000 settled many internal political disputes, and the nation's commercial tax policies were reformed. Lower corporate taxes coupled with improved wage and price controls have helped Mexico regain a high profile in the region, with significant North American investments. It also has attracted European alliances through incentive programs and regulatory changes. Although Mexico is viewed as a politically risky place to do business, it is relatively stable compared to Panama, Colombia, and the warring equatorial nations.[27]

In contrast to Mexico, Brazil has always nurtured strong European trade connections that evolved from its colonial link with Portugal. The country has expanded this activity through major trade missions in Asia and long-standing trade pacts with the United States. Compared to other Latin countries, Brazil has seen a much higher rate of change in per-capita income, with a respectable 10-year average annual increase of approximately 6.5 percent. However, the data obscure the fact that Brazil's economic base and income levels remain far below those of Mexico, Chile, and Argentina. Although its rich natural resources attract trade in the form of foreign procurement, the country has had a checkered economic record. Business there suffers from high inflation and unstable monetary policies, which raise the risk of international trade and foreign investment. Several major political reform movements over the past two decades have produced only mixed results; some of these reforms have stalled economic growth, while others have overheated the economy. Inconsistent tax policies and instability in the workforce have caused problems for international companies. Consequently, foreign enterprises find the Brazilian environment somewhat puzzling and only moderately attractive for expansion.[28]

Argentina was the fourth-richest country in the world in the 1930s, and when World War II erupted, Argentina had a living standard equal to that of the United States and much of Europe. During the war, however, Argentina created tremendous trade barriers and strident social policies that led to a postwar period of extreme isolationism. The country maintained this posture until 1990, when political reforms began to reverse the half-century era of repressed foreign relations. During that half-century, Argentina went into a deep decline and lost its trade advantages. Government was considered extremely corrupt, and foreign interests were threatened during the 1950s and 1960s with arbitrary expropriation of assets. Corruption, a topic addressed in Chapter 3 on ethics, is still a serious problem for many commercial enterprises, but Argentina has resolved many of its problems and is again beginning to attract foreign investments. Argentina has not been able to increase exports significantly, but it has reduced imports dramatically through improved domestic industrial development and major international alliances. These include joint ventures and comanufacturing agreements with major corporations such as Glaxo-Wellcome, Coca-Cola, Bristol-Myers Squibb, IBM, Ford, GM, and British Petroleum. It has the lowest adult illiteracy rate in South America (4 percent compared to 13 percent in Mexico), and resurgent domestic growth has produced a per-capita GNP above $8,000 (double that of Mexico and nearly four times greater than Brazil).[29]

Chile is cited by the World Bank and the United Nations as the best example of economic success in Latin America. During the early 1980s, the country transformed its economy into a democratic society through broad-based political reforms.[30] A long history of protectionism abruptly gave way to low tariffs and reduced export and import barriers. Corporate taxes on earnings fell to 15 percent, and a new hands-off government regulatory policy encouraged growth in a market economy. In addition, centralized government functions were privatized, including a model program of social security that is entirely private and investment based. Although Chile has not yet achieved the income levels of Argentina or Mexico, it has become a member of the high-middle-income group of nations with a 10-year record of export increase at an annual rate of nearly 10 percent. The country has also attracted major international companies and more than a dozen U.S. universities that sponsor joint programs in business and commercial education in Chile.[31]

These four examples of Latin nations do not capture the rich diversity of the region's 28 economies (including Caribbean countries and two dependencies). Several Latin countries are still struggling to achieve agricultural reforms, some are politically explosive, and a few are controversial for their lack of control over illegal drugs and weapons contraband. Still others, such as Costa Rica, are quiet, peaceful havens with reasonably stable trade relations that provide comfortable standards of living. In many Latin countries, the priorities of agrarian self-sufficiency outweigh priorities of commercial development. Countries such as Paraguay, for example, find it difficult to shift resources away from subsistence activities toward industry or trade.[32] These less-developed countries (LDCs) are often dependent on foreign assistance aid programs, but they cannot attract foreign investment necessary for sustained growth.

In contrast to the LDCs, Latin countries with recent records of economic growth, such as Peru, have attracted new foreign investments that promise a sustained period of development. North American, European, and Asian multinationals are noticeably involved in the developing economics of Latin America with extensive mining, forestry, and agricultural investments. Also during the past few years, major alliances have been established in Argentina, Chile, and Peru for offshore manufacturing and infrastructure development of roads, water systems, and power stations. These involve companies such as Ford, GM, PepsiCo, DaimlerChrysler, IBM, Compaq, Toshiba,

ABB, Philips, Shell, and Deutsche Morgan Grenfell. A number of regional trade treaties and economic cooperation pacts have emerged, including South America's version of a common-market accord, called the *Mercosur*. These measures have encouraged economic trade development throughout the Americas, but they have also attracted European and Asian investors that have accelerated trade.[33]

Central and Eastern Europe—The Former Soviet Bloc

The countries that once comprised the Soviet bloc present a complicated picture. The former Soviet Union, when it was intact, was a controlled amalgamation of 15 states. Following the 1991 coup there has been a major realignment, sometimes peaceful but also sometimes violent, as in the case of the ongoing Chechnyan conflict. Russia is a core country of the Commonwealth of Independent States (CIS), which consists of 11 separate states. To the south, Georgia proclaimed itself an independent republic, and Ukraine has regained independent statehood. To the west, the three Baltic states of Estonia, Latvia, and Lithuania are now sovereign nations.[34] Russia considers Georgia as the twelfth member of the CIS, but Georgia has been ruled through a separatist government since 1993. Civil strife in Chechnya continues between the ethnic minority in that region and Russia. Other nations—such as Azerbaijan, Uzbekistan, Kazakhstan, and Turkmenistan—were part of the Soviet bloc and effectively under Soviet rule, but they are now sovereign nations with distinct cultural identities that are genealogically closely related to Islamic South-Asia. They also are relatively small, underdeveloped, and politically unstable.[35]

The Soviet bloc sphere of influence also included East Germany, Poland, and other Central and Eastern European nations. East and West Germany have, of course, been reunified, and this process weakened Germany's short-term economic growth as the country directed its resources inwardly to help solidify the enlarged state. Germany has focused on improving conditions in the east, tackling massive redevelopment efforts and creating private-sector employment. However, Germany has remained influential as an economic power, and its trade and foreign investment have paced continental Europe. The sudden addition of underutilized labor following reunification fueled unemployment, and Germany now faces a delicate problem with immigrants from Eastern Europe who have fled their own troubled countries to take advantage of more abundant, higher-paying jobs there. Although Germany is not part of the Central and Eastern European region (CEE), it is perhaps the most influential western power there—with substantial investments, comanufacturing, extensive trade liaisons, financial interests, and major export markets among the CEE transition economies. Indeed, German is spoken as a third language after a country's native tongue and Russian in most of the Baltic and Balkan countries, and Germany's deutsch mark is the most common exchange currency. Germany's reputation for high standards of productivity, along with its technology development in heavy industries, electronics, chemicals, and pharmaceuticals, have resulted in significant expansion into CEE countries through joint ventures and equity alliances.[36]

The strength of Germany's influence is not entirely comforting to leaders of other European countries, who fear a "deutsch-mark-dominated continental Europe" if the European Monetary Union (EMU) does not establish a pervasive backing for the new European currency (the *ecu*).[37] The **ecu** is the cyberspace reserve currency of the signatory nations under the EMU; it is not yet minted, but serves as an electronic exchange currency for trade and account balances. Currently, only 11 countries of the 15-member European Union and two CEE nations have officially ratified membership in the EMU. Nevertheless, transactions denominated in the European currency

Cobblestones mark a path once part of the Berlin Wall that separated East and West Berlin, isolating the eighteenth-century fortress that had been the Reichstag (capital) under Adolf Hilter. Today the Reichstag is restored. Although once a symbol of horror, it now serves as a symbol of hope for the unified Germany.

are common in Britain (not a member of the EMU accord), Switzerland (neither an EU nor EMU country), and Scandinavian countries (where the EMU failed to achieve ratification). Meanwhile, the German deutsch mark remains the second reserve currency in Europe and the most prominent exchange currency in the emerging nations of Central and Eastern Europe. Entering the 21st century, Germany subsequently retained its competitive posture for international trade and investment.[38]

In the northeast corridor of Europe bordering Russia, the nations of Poland, Latvia, Lithuania, and Estonia form a rim of countries stretching from Germany through the Baltic region. Poland is better positioned than most for economic growth and has had good success as the first Eastern bloc country to break away from Soviet influence. Poland also is a large country relative to other Central and Eastern European nations; it has nearly 40 million people, substantial natural resources, and an established industrial infrastructure. The Baltic states are extremely small with city-size national populations, and although they have unique histories and cultures, they are not dramatically different in their ideologies or ethnic backgrounds. Poland and the Baltic states have been trading partners for centuries, and often allies both politically and economically during the nineteenth century. Poland was once a European power, and the nation is comfortable with German or Western European business methods. In contrast, the Baltic states are more aligned with their Scandinavian neighbors than with Western Europe, and therefore international alliances and trade gravitate toward this north Atlantic subregion.

Central and Eastern Europe also includes Hungary, the Czech Republic, Slovenia, the Slovak Federal Republic, Romania, and Bulgaria. Albania, and to some extent Bulgaria, are identified with the Balkans as border economies to Yugoslavia. After the collapse of Yugoslavia, the Balkans now include Croatia, Macedonia, Bosnia-Herzegovina, Republika Srpska, and the core of Serbia that retained the name Yugoslavia. Countries in this broad eastern region have unique cultures and peoples with quite different political and economic systems. Albania, Croatia, and the southern area of Bulgaria identify with Mediterranean rather than European cultures. Many Bulgarians, for example, have Greek roots; others have a lineage with the Turkish Ottomans; and in the north and east, people have Slavic or Germanic origins. Romanians represent an intercultural mix of migrating tribes and Latin influence dating to the Roman era. In contrast, the Czechs, Slovaks, Slovenians, and Hungarians have maintained individual cultural identities, which subsequently led to national consolidation when the Soviet bloc disintegrated. Other nations were less fortunate; in the case of Yugoslavia, political collapse resulted in devastating internal strife. Economically, the Czechs, Slovaks, Slovenians, and Hungarians recovered rapidly, established trade relations with Western Europe, and revitalized their industrial bases, but most others have languished.[39] These economic dichotomies are illustrated for selected countries in Figure 2.4.

Social and Economic Change in Perspective

More than two-thirds of the world's nations have gone unmentioned in the previous presentation on regional development. Also, the selective overview has introduced only general characteristics of economic changes and trade relationships. It is beyond the scope of this book to address issues of nations throughout the world. However, there are many considerations concerning social and ideological changes that go beyond those described here—and many of them are important to international managers, who often work in transition economies. This book tries to address

FIGURE 2.4
GDP Growth for Selected Central and Eastern European Countries
Note: Baltic states include composite data for Estonia, Latvia, and Lithuania. GDP is normalized by GDP deflators; but there is discontinuous data for years prior to 1989, with estimates only for Poland, while the former Soviet bloc as a region selectively reported income for economic zones.
Sources: *World Development Indicators 2000*, CD-ROM (Washington, D.C.: World Bank, 2000), Data Series, Income & Growth Statistics; *World Development Report 1996* (New York: Oxford University Press, 1996), World Bank Data, Tables 1, 3.

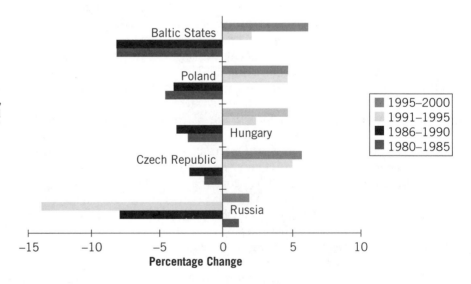

issues such as cultural evolution, sociological trends, ideological changes, and technological development in appropriate chapters. However, the remaining sections of this chapter provide a theoretical framework for exploring these topics, together with some necessary insights into ideological and technological advancements.

NEW GROWTH THEORY AND IDEOLOGY

Nearly every affluent nation has been economically successful through sustained international trade and substantial foreign investment. Successful developing nations have likewise accomplished strong economic growth, primarily through trade and their ability to court foreign investments. In nearly every instance, sustained economic growth has been accompanied by political shifts away from isolationist policies and socialist ideologies toward open trade and market capitalism. Consequently, there is a strong correlation between economic prosperity and the combined elements of trade and investment. This is the fundamental doctrine of *New Growth theory*, which is described momentarily.

There is an underpinning assumption of New Growth theory that private enterprise development in a free-market economy is essential for growth to occur. Even in China, the world's primary stronghold of communism, growth has occurred almost entirely through private enterprise development and expanded trade. Indeed, China was economically stagnant before its leaders announced an open-door policy emphasizing modernization based on rapid expansion into world trade. That occurred in late 1979, when private enterprise in China consisted of scattered village cooperatives, small shops, and a few independent vendors who collectively contributed barely 1 percent to the country's gross domestic income. By 1990, private enterprise consisted of more than 5 million independently owned business organizations that contributed 11 percent to gross domestic income. By 2000, private enterprise had grown further to more than 9.5 million companies representing 31 percent of China's gross domestic product. Private enterprise also accounted for approximately 73 percent of the total economic growth, and all but 3 percent of the remaining growth came through expanded international alliances as a result of direct foreign investment. Although China has not abandoned its communist ideology, it has introduced significant market mechanisms and encouraged rapid growth of private enterprise supported by capitalist institutions, including securities exchanges and commercial banking.[40]

Destitute economies, and those with little or no growth, are riddled by internal strife or trapped by resource-poor subsistence environments. Examples include Rwanda, Afghanistan, Somalia, and Bosnia-Herzegovina. Some countries have languished despite essential conditions for growth—resources and human capabilities for development—either because they remain closed socialist societies or they have not completed the transition from a communist legacy or an extremist centralized government. Examples include Albania, Romania, Myanmar (Burma), North Korea, Iraq, Haiti, Libya, and Syria. Although this is not the place to present political arguments for comparative ideologies, economic growth has proved to depend heavily on private enterprise with commensurate development in foreign trade and investment.

New Growth theory encompasses the economic and sociopolitical mandates noted earlier. The theory is based on a mathematical system of equations first introduced by Paul Romer in 1983, but expanded through more than 50 global economic studies, including work by 1995 Nobel Prize Laureate Robert Lucas.[41] This research emphasizes six keys to economic growth, summarized in Figure 2.5. First, a country

FIGURE 2.5
New Growth Theory and
International Development

Source: Adapted from Kim R. Holmes,
Bryan T. Johnson, and Melanie
Kirkpatrick, *1997 Index of Economic
Freedom* (New York: Dow Jones and
Company, 1997), 4–6.

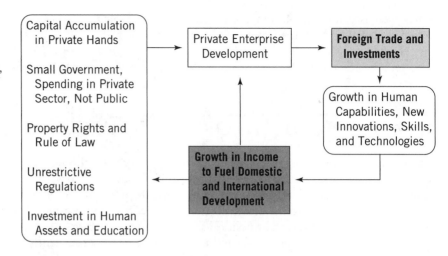

must accumulate physical and financial capital through a widely shared domestic per-capita income. This capital base represents excess capacity in productive enterprise that the country can leverage for growth. Second, the government must remain small because government spending consumes scarce resources, which distorts economic investment. Private-sector spending rather than government intervention increases incentives for individual and corporate growth. Third, an open economy with foreign trade and investment supports essential diffusion of new technology, vigorous competition that results in continuous improvements, and rapid accumulation of capital. In effect, the capital accumulation-investment-trade cycle feeds on itself and creates inertia for growth, increasing returns for long-term growth. Fourth, property rights and the rule of law must maintain incentives to invest. Without these rights and a secure political environment, individuals and firms hesitate to invest. Fifth, government must minimize regulations on business, and in particular wage and price controls. In an ideal state, mandated wage and price controls ensure income and profits only at the absolute lowest common denominator. By eliminating opportunities to profit from labor, production, or trade based on differentials of value, these controls destroy incentives to innovate or to grow. Sixth, development requires a sustained investment in human capital—education, skills, and technological capabilities. In autocratic or socialist regimes, education and training institutions mainly serve the ends of social justice, but they are incapable of responding to individual needs for personal growth.

The New Growth theorists present convincing arguments that growth is defined by increasing net income, generated through private enterprise and unrestrained by excessive government spending or regulation. Net income provides a basis for investment, and private enterprise rewards those who are innovative and productive. These benefits enhance trade and foreign investment, which in turn expand wealth for investment at an accelerated pace. In addition, trade and foreign investment rapidly diffuse technology and incite competition, which together drive nations toward even higher levels of economic activity. Strong domestic institutions for education and career choices improve mobility of human resources and provide unrestricted incentives for innovation and entrepreneurial risk-taking.

New Growth theory presents many implications for international management, foreign trade, increased foreign investment through subsidiaries or global alliances, and multicultural cooperation. Continuing rapid development in many world economies will create strong and growing demand for international managers who can earnestly participate in social and economic change. Those who look at international careers as a temporary adventure—a foreign safari—are unlikely to be part of that environment. Companies that earnestly seek long-term foreign alliances rather than exploitative opportunities will likely be the industry leaders in multinational business. If foreign trade and investment do indeed feed on themselves to generate capital ever more rapidly, then increasing returns and sustainable profits will continually enhance incomes of the leading trade nations, their people, and their multinational corporations.

TECHNOLOGICAL ADVANCEMENTS

An important theme of the New Growth model stresses the crucial role of *technological innovation* in both domestic growth and international development. Equally important, the theory emphasizes that innovations created through private enterprise result in opportunities for wealth accumulation, thus further motivating individuals and companies to risk new ideas and business ventures. The model's core element, however, focuses on the process by which foreign trade and investment diffuse technology and create an upward cycle of new income and productive capacity. This aspect of the model is not really new. It was a recurrent theme in Adam Smith's work more than two centuries earlier, when he explained the wealth of nations as a reflection of comparative advantage.[42] Technology, in Smith's theoretical framework, included the combined factors of production that created added value to commerce and generated profits. He also emphasized that comparative advantage would exist only until the technology was diffused through a competitive assimilation of knowledge.

Technology and International Competition

The Industrial Revolution was the result of commercialization of science. Successful nations were those able to translate science into useful technology and in turn to fuel their economies from wealth created by innovations. The same is true today. Technological innovation is concerned with research and development and the creativity of inspired entrepreneurs. **Innovation** is the useful adaptation of science or knowledge. This process may include *invention of new products or processes*, but it need not extend that far. **Invention** is the creation of something entirely new. Consequently, relatively few people or companies invent new things, but many are able to adapt scientific knowledge to generate wealth by *application and commercialization*.[43]

Neither invention nor innovation occur in isolation; they seldom remain proprietary to one nation or company, but instead become commonplace through international exchange relationships. For example, the Bessemer steel-smelting process that revolutionized metal industries in the nineteenth century was a give-and-take process of incremental improvements in mining, smelting, and engineering in Britain, Germany, France, and the United States over a 50-year period. Exports, international shipbuilding, rail development, and infrastuctural demand (such as the famous nineteenth-century bridges in Europe and the Eiffel Tower) drove steelmakers to create new methods that would outperform their competitors. As steel technology improved, temporary supremacy in the industry shuffled back and forth across the Atlantic until the Bessemer process became the industry standard. The United States became the dominant steelmaking nation using this process, which provided the materials and engineering required for early twentieth-century wonders such as the Empire State Building and the Golden Gate Bridge.

Major scientific inventions (or discoveries) do occur, but they do not remain proprietary for long. Electricity emerged as a source of power from research in theoretical physics during the 1830s by British and German (then Prussian) researchers. Electricity as a useful science was relatively dormant for decades, until other European researchers introduced concepts of electromagnetic induction and radio waves. These ideas slipped into early commercial innovations, such as telegraphic transmission, but electricity as a revolutionary power source emerged only after Edison invented the light bulb in America. Indeed, Edison did not "invent" in the sense of creating new scientific knowledge, but brought together existing technologies of an incandescent lamp, a wire filament, and the flow of electricity in a vapor tube. However, his bulb was not the crucial innovation. Commercial use of electricity required "systems" for power generation, ways to distribute power, and applications for electricity other than light bulbs. Even light bulbs had to have lamps, insulated wire, plugs, and household outlets. Literally thousands of new innovations had to be developed, ranging from power engineering systems to home appliances. The process is the same today with commercial applications of the transistor, microchip, fiber optics, information systems, and laser technology.

The innovation process and international competitiveness are two determinants of a nation's fundamental wealth, and many multinational companies are strategically positioned to pursue competitive advantage through innovation. Patterns of innovation, however, differ substantially among the world's societies. For example, Japan has focused on process technology, and through national policy mandates has purposely targeted industries such as automobiles, steel, telecommunications, and microelectronics. Japan has not actively pursued innovations in aerospace, chemicals, or agriculture. In contrast, Germany has historically spearheaded innovations in chemicals, pharmaceuticals, automotive engineering, medical instrumentation, and machine tooling. Italy has established a reputation as world leader in textiles, stone and masonry, and leathers. Sweden excels in hydroelectric power engineering. France has also been at the cutting edge for tactical weaponry, including aeronautical engineering. The United States and Britain have pursued eclectic interests, but the size of the United States and the combined effect of markets and resources have vaulted American companies into every industrial sector. Differences in national priorities and technological profiles can be assessed by comparing R&D expenditures, emphasis on education of scientists and engineers, and sector-specific applications of innovations. Table 2.2 summarizes these data.

Although the six countries in Table 2.2 are among the world's most affluent nations, they provide several stark contrasts in R&D capabilities.[44] The United States, Japan, and Germany have almost identical allocations to R&D as a percentage of total GNP. The absolute size of GNP in each country is different, but per-capita GNP is quite similar. Consequently the United States has a major advantage; but in relative terms the resources committed to R&D are actually much stronger in Germany, where fewer industries engage in more intensive research and development. With half the population of the United States, Japan's R&D budgets are approximately twice those in the United States. France, the U.K., and Italy have far fewer resources in R&D, and with populations half the size of Japan, one-quarter of the United States, and smaller than Germany, these nations appear to be at a technological disadvantage.

Private R&D indicates the percentage of all resource allocations; the remaining portion is almost entirely government-funded research or grants to universities for theoretical research. Japan and Germany have a significantly higher level of privately funded R&D than elsewhere. More than half of the U.S. effort is linked to government contracts (mainly defense applications and educational grants). France and Italy

TABLE 2.2

CONTRASTS IN RESEARCH AND DEVELOPMENT FOR SELECTED COUNTRIES

	United States	Japan	Germany	France	United Kingdom	Italy
R&D expenditures as a percentage of total GNP	3.1	2.0	2.9	2.3	2.2	1.2
Private R&D as a percentage of total R&D	51.4	78.4	62.5	40.1	49.8	41.3
Business-related R&D as a percentage of total R&D	77.5	68.2	74.1	52.8	69.0	55.2
Scientists and engineers as a percentage of total population	0.34	0.49	0.27	0.21	0.24	0.12

Source: Compiled from *Development Co-operation*, CD-ROM Beyond 20/20 Version (Paris: Organisation for Economic Cooperation and Development, 1998), Table of Economic Statistics.

also have significant research sponsored by government agencies, which reflects a socialist approach to government control. Business-related R&D, however, can be misleading. If an American aerospace company has a government contract for new fighter aircraft, that is "business related" because it generates income in the private sector. In Japan, the same contract would not be considered business related. Definitions vary in each country, but the general pattern of a relatively strong focus on business applications in the United States and Germany are symptomatic differences in government intervention programs and social priorities. Also important is the human resource index for scientists and engineers. Because this is a percentage of the total population, it is a direct indicator of the investment in human resource research capabilities. Japan has a comparably large percentage of technical graduates, and most of these people work in Japanese industry. The United States has a significantly lower percentage of technical graduates, and less than half of them work in industrial R&D. Germany's low percentage hides a strong education system of technical apprenticeship and private-sector training. The other three countries are noticeably lagging behind in human resource capacity.

All industrialized countries must be concerned to a certain degree with research and development; however, most countries also have focused on selected sectors in which to compete. Table 2.3 is a summary of six countries and nine leading export sectors. The countries with large positive coefficients are among the leaders in the industries listed. The relatively lower (or negative) coefficients of other countries do not always mean that those countries lack strong industries. Countries such as Australia, Sweden, and Switzerland lead in industries not listed in the exhibit. With that said, notice that Germany leads in four sectors, the United States in three, and Japan in two. If a tenth sector of Motor Vehicles were included, the United States would lead, Japan would be second, and Germany a close third; but this category (although one of the largest) has been disaggregated due to global integration of component suppliers that cloud definitions of *country of origin*. The relative strengths point out advantages for international companies that seek foreign alliances or markets. For example, Japan and Germany have distinct advantages in automotive engineering, and although the data does not reveal what those advantages are, we can sense the quality of innovative

TABLE 2.3

RELATIVE ADVANTAGES BY MAJOR INDUSTRY SECTOR FOR SELECTED COUNTRIES

	United States	Japan	Germany	France	United Kingdom	Italy
Air frames and aerospace	3.1[a]	−1.9	0.1	2.4[b]	1.8	−0.8
Pharmaceuticals	1.6[b]	−0.4	2.1[a]	0.1	1.5	−0.9
Chemicals and chemical engineering	2.1[b]	1.1	2.2[a]	−0.9	0.9	−1.7
Coal and petroleum	2.9[a]	−0.9	1.1	0.8	1.8[b]	−0.9
Mechanical engineering	−0.2	3.1[b]	3.3[a]	−0.7	−0.2	−0.4
Automotive engineering	1.6	2.9[b]	3.1[a]	−1.1	−0.1	1.4
Electronics and microelectronics	2.2[b]	3.3[a]	1.8	−0.2	0.5	−0.1
Food products and technology	2.2[a]	−0.5	−0.4	1.4[b]	0.3	0.6
Scientific and medical instruments	2.3[b]	−0.2	3.1[a]	0.8	0.9	−0.1

[a]Leading in industry

[b]Strong relative advantage in industry

Note: Negative numbers indicate relative weakness compared to 29 OECD nations studied. Values between +0.4 and −0.4 imply insignificant differences; countries competing in these sectors may have neither distinct advantages nor distinct disadvantages.

Source: *International Trade By Commodities Statistics*, CD-ROM 1998 Version (Paris: Organisation for Economic Cooperation and Development, 1999), Long-Term Sector Competitiveness Tables.

high-end design and engine technology that has made German cars famous. We also are aware of the process technology and quality advantages of production models in Japan. Consequently, automakers from other countries would look to Germany or Japan for alliances to tap into this expertise. This is precisely how Ford and General Motors entered the European markets prior to World War II.[45] A further well-known example is New United Motor Manufacturing (NUMMI), a joint venture between Toyota and General Motors that in 1983 brought together Toyota's superior process engineering technologies and GM's market power to create a unified plant in California to engineer and manufacture the Geo Prizm.[46]

Smaller countries do not have to compete with larger ones for broad-based technologies. Many simply become niche players with focused strength in one or two industrial sectors. Italy, for example, has a very strong presence in unusual sports cars and high-performance engineering. The Fiat's less-exotic line is positioned for exports to European and Asian niche markets. Italy also is renowned for marble and stonework, industrial designs, and fashions. Most countries tend to specialize, and in doing so attract foreign capital or compete successfully in foreign niches. Market competition plays an important role in deciding upon industrial priorities, but there are few places where markets are unrestricted. Hong Kong and Singapore, even though they are among the leading economies with free-market systems, severely restrict imported automobiles though heavy customs duties (up to 150 percent or more for luxury models).[47] These custom duties are levied for social reasons, such as restricting traffic congestion, but all countries have rather extensive lists of protective quotas and custom duties. Regional trade alliances and WTO mandates are reducing many of these restrictions, yet when possible, nations erect barriers to protect their industrial technology or domestic markets.[48]

Restrictive trade and investment regulations influence where multinational companies will engage in foreign commerce, but many location decisions are based on host-country technology capabilities. For example, Ford consolidated R&D in its German-based European design engineering center, and this unit serves Ford interests worldwide for production engineering technology.[49] In contrast, Philips Electronics, while home based in the Netherlands, localizes design engineering in more than 40 international subsidiaries where electrical appliances and instrumentation can be customized for individual markets. Ericsson, one of Sweden's leading industries with global markets for wireless telecommunications, favors regional joint alliances with strategically located R&D facilities that serve a network of integrated manufacturing subsidiaries.[50] Ultimately, multinational companies strive to find the most effective combination of appropriate technology and cost efficiency, but an overriding concern is how to manage worldwide interests. Information technology has helped to integrate communications and to bring often-diverse interests together.

Effects of Information Technology

It is nearly impossible to overstate the effects of information technology on business during the past few years, and if recent changes are any indication of the future, the so-called new economy and the "dot.com" revolution will be relics by the year 2010. Indeed, change is occurring so rapidly that anything presented here is in danger of being obsolete before the book is published. Consequently, what follows is a general approach to information as a management resource.

In the lexicon of business, **information technology (IT)** is the science of creating and using information resources, and from a management perspective, information is a crucial resource in its own right. Business leaders have subsequently come to regard IT as a strategic dimension of organizational development that brings together the engineering of systems with management of those systems.[51] As a strategic resource, IT has redefined many industries and changed the fundamental processes of how business is accomplished.

For example, the airlines industry became global through information systems that instantly linked worldwide reservations among hundreds of competing airlines and thousands of travel agents. American Airlines created the SABRE system that is currently the most comprehensive reservation network. The benefits of SABRE changed the competitive philosophy of American Airlines. This vast information network can provide reports and controls on worldwide seating, load factors, optimization systems, and pricing. With this type of information, the airlines can rapidly reallocate resources, alter routes, shift staffing assignments, and much more, thus optimizing a global system of interrelated activities. American Airlines became the flagship of international carriers during a period of deregulation that attracted hundreds of low-cost airlines. Most of those companies disappeared because they lacked the information technology to provide the same services as American and other major airlines.[52]

Information technology functions as a strategic resource in four ways. In its least strategic sense, it promotes efficiency through office automation and accounting procedures. IT becomes more strategically important in developing new process technology, such as computer-aided design systems and automated factory controls. At a higher level, IT supports strategic management decisions and competitive analysis. Ultimately, the technology itself becomes the business in firms such as Microsoft, Intel, and Oracle. Although most people equate IT with computers, many industries employ information technology well beyond computational hardware. These include global financial services, securities investments, commodity markets, video entertainment media, all facets of E-commerce, and logistical dissemination of virtually every type of communication.

International companies have invested heavily in IT, which has the unique benefit of immediately linking together global systems of corporate staff and their activities. The ultimate aim of global companies is to achieve *transnational systems integration*. This is accomplished through a process called a **transnational management support system (TMSS)**.[53] An example from Dow Chemical, a global company with manufacturing and sales in 42 countries, demonstrates how TMSS works. Dow monitors demand for its products through computer-linked feedback in its wholesaling function, and it monitors production capacity and scheduling in every foreign operation. Recently, Dow noticed a drop in demand for industrial solvents in Europe with a commensurate upswing in North America. The TMSS instantly recorded this change and recommended shifting resources from a German plant to a U.S. plant with idle capacity. Dow's system projected cost savings and schedules for production changes, allowing a rapid response by the company. Shifts of this kind have occurred regularly as the TMSS fine-tunes global procurement of materials, allocates manufacturing, maximizes resource distribution, and optimizes the corporation's total process system. Managers still make the decisions—TMSS is not an autopilot—but they do so from extremely well informed positions armed with timely reports and accurate analyses of their options. More interesting is that the demand for these systems by giant companies such as Dow Corning, Johnson & Johnson, Ford, and many others has given birth to an entirely new industry itself, reaching global proportions. This industry is composed of the integrated hardware/software systems companies that provide the TMSS networks and expertise to the business world. A sample of companies in this industry include Lucent Technologies, SAP (AG) of Germany, Oracle, and dozens of less well known enterprises such as Luminate, QualComm, and InNet Solutions.[54]

Information technology also can present problems without diligent management. Companies can easily obtain hardware, for example, but effective use of it presents a greater challenge. Computers by themselves mystify many executives, and automation threatens workers who fear losing their jobs to inanimate systems. Managers must remain sensitive to people and conditions to avoid the mistake of introducing inappropriate technology in the wrong manner or in the wrong place. For example, international managers may routinely work with computers at their home offices, but in many developing countries, there is no reliable electricity supply to support computer systems. A 1999 World Bank study on poverty points out that while most people in the developed world take for granted the availability of telephones, nearly 60 percent of the human race has never used a telephone. The lesson here is that many people who go abroad to work will face harsh realities about the technical and social environments in which they find themselves.[55] *Optimal technology* at home may be a complicated IT system, but overseas it may be a mechanical typewriter.[56]

Some countries and their people are anxious to accept new systems, yet others are unable to adapt to technology. This difference becomes apparent in the comparison of Internet capabilities in various countries shown in Figure 2.6. Obviously, significant problems curtail implementation of network systems in transition economies such as Poland, yet Finland has outperformed the United States. Among the affluent countries (representing about 12 percent of the world population) there are approximately 115 Internet users per 1,000 people, yet among the low-income and low-middle-income nations (representing 57 percent of world population), there are barely 100

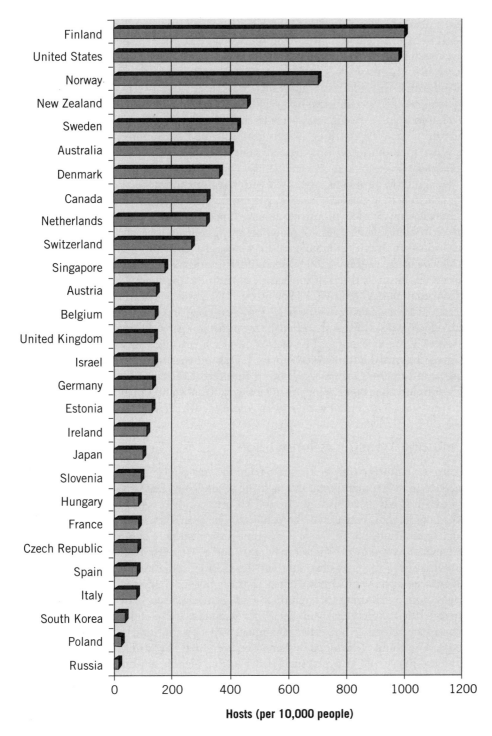

FIGURE 2.6
Internet Hosts in Selected Countries

Source: *World Development Indicators 2000*, CD-ROM (Washington, D.C.: World Bank, 2000), Table 5.11, The Information Age.

Internet users *per million* people; also, these users are almost entirely within government agencies or large corporations.

Part of the explanation for these disparities clearly rests with relative technical capabilities, and part of the explanation for such polarized differences rests with culture.

Japanese managers, for example, prefer face-to-face meetings and group communications, so even with technology at hand there is a general reluctance by many mature Japanese managers to communicate by e-mail or to use the Internet. Even greater ironies exist in countries such as Guatemala, where foreign aid workers recently tried to introduce on-line education programs and simple educational software to Mayan villagers in an effort to improve basic skills and literacy. The aid volunteers provided the technology and expertise at no cost to the villagers, but Mayan families refused to participate, feeling that their cultural traditions would be compromised. The aid volunteers had to limit their efforts to rural classrooms equipped with no more than chalk and blackboards.[57]

Managing the problems associated with advances in information technology has created entirely new global industries. Electronic Data Systems Corporation (EDS) is one of the leading services industries designed specifically to solve information-related business problems. EDS does not manufacture systems, sell hardware, or create commercial software. It creates bundles of IT services specifically for corporate clients on a worldwide basis. This is a $100 billion industry with major companies competing for corporate IT business through specialized consulting divisions. These companies include, for example, AT&T, MCI-WorldCom, IBM, and Accenture; yet some unlikely competitors have also entered the field. Hughes Space and Communications International, which evolved from the Hughes Aircraft Company, has repositioned its core business to address corporate IT systems development together with IT services for managing diversified international offices.[58] This industry is concerned with appropriate use of information technology, but on an international scale, it is also involved in how best to introduce technology to societies with substantially different capabilities. In this sense, it is concerned with *technology transfer*, which is addressed next.

Technology Transfer as Innovation

The term **technology transfer** has two common meanings. The first is the *conversion* of knowledge into something useful, and the second is the *introduction of existing technology* to a less advanced society through an international venture.[59] In the first instance, a company is concerned about how to create marketable products or services through innovation, but the second meaning suggests that a company seeks to profit from established products or services by introducing them to fresh foreign markets.

International managers working in developing economies focus primarily on profit-making opportunities for their company's products or services, or on cost advantages of manufacturing through their foreign subsidiaries. When Procter & Gamble entered the China market in 1988, for example, the company introduced Zest hand soap and Head & Shoulders Shampoo, two new and unusual products for the Chinese. The company avoided higher-priced products that would have been a strain on Chinese household budgets, such as disposable diapers or sanitary napkins.[60] But with simple hand soaps and shampoos, P&G created an unusual profile of U.S. branded items that gave it an image and market advantage over competitors.

Companies throughout the world follow this model, and home-country governments often encourage this strategy as a means of improving trade balances and domestic development. Procter & Gamble is perhaps the world leader in consumer marketing, and it was built on a unique line of soaps and detergents strongly positioned in domestic markets. P&G's foreign expansion required strategic selection of products considered quite ordinary by U.S. consumers, yet they were unique to P&G's foreign consumers. Colgate-Palmolive has been equally successful by introducing a wide range of hygiene products to developing countries in Latin America, Asia, and Eastern

Europe. More importantly, when these companies establish foreign production systems or new distribution networks, they bring to the host country new process technologies. These may be old or common by western standards, yet in many instances, the transfer of process technologies represents *new and productive knowledge* to the host country. Consequently, many host governments court multinationals, offering substantial incentives to companies that can bring with them new industrial technologies that the nation is lacking.

Managing Technology Transfer

When a company goes overseas, even with a simple product such as a bar of soap, it must take along all the knowledge and innovation required to produce and market that product. The company brings management know-how, marketing skills, promotional insights, packaging and distribution experience, and brand management savvy. Local employees and managers join the firm and undergo training in these areas, eventually managing the foreign business themselves. When the firm also manufactures its product overseas, it introduces product design and process technologies to the host country. It may take steps to safeguard some proprietary information against patent or copyright infringement, but production or service delivery cannot occur without a significant transfer of knowledge about materials, process engineering, manufacturing, packaging, handling, and logistics. If the company sets up a foreign subsidiary or joint venture, then it also brings administration, finance, and accounting methods to that environment.

On a global scale, these considerations take on far more pervasive significance. Managers face difficult tasks in leadership and strategic management as companies redefine the scope of their operations and redesign their organizations. The "technology" of management itself undergoes transformation as global managers begin to *integrate the functions of management.*[61] Rather than "disintegrating" processes, or breaking them down for mass production (as implied by Taylorism and functional specialization), global enterprises today work to "reintegrate" systems to encourage cross-functional cooperation. R&D, engineering, marketing, manufacturing, process management, and information resources are coming together. Each no longer stands apart, isolated in its own department, to the degree implied by conventional knowledge, and decisions are no longer isolated within closely defined functional specializations typical of an industrial society.[62] Consequently, the very nature of foreign expansion and commensurate transfer of managerial processes can accelerate the pace of integration throughout the organization. In a sense, the "world as a tribal village" expresses a main theme of the evolution that occurs through enhanced global organizations.

NEW CHALLENGES FOR INTERNATIONAL MANAGERS

Managers are often blindsided by unexpected incidents. These may seem to be unimportant at the time, yet they often have extraordinary consequences. For example, a trade dispute over bananas that began in 1996 between the United States and the European Union has accelerated into retaliatory sanctions and harsh rivalries affecting hundreds of companies and products. In 1999, the WTO ruled in favor of the U.S. claimants, which brought European diplomats and governments on both sides of the Atlantic into the fray. Hundreds of companies and international executives are now involved in a perplexing incident that has aptly been called the "banana war." (See the

Global Viewpoint feature for more details).[63] The point is that managers are constantly facing new challenges in international business, and that environment is becoming more complicated by foreign politics, shifts in power, waves of corporate mergers, and enormous changes in global markets.

CEE countries present new challenges for managers working in the transition economies that have emerged from the yoke of Soviet ideology. These countries are driving hard to become free-market economies with modern states based on private enterprise. Multinational companies have subsequently found attractive markets in the CEE, and substantial foreign investment there has resulted in more than 20,000 expatriate Americans working in these transition economies. Unfortunately, many people in these countries are accustomed to a centrally planned economy and cannot easily adapt to the realities of a free-enterprise system. Consequently, the move toward self-determined growth has often resulted in economic chaos. Unemployment, depression, deprivation, and the ill effects of inflation have plagued many people, even when their national economies have shown positive signs of sustained growth. These conditions are ripe for civil unrest, which has occurred to some extent in nearly all transition economies, but instigated bloody revolts in Romania, Albania, and the former Yugoslavia. Problems of transition to market economies also occur among the Gulf states, Southeast Asian nations, and African countries. These circumstances require skillful behavior and sensitivity to perplexing issues in unfamiliar cultures by international managers responsible for foreign operations.

The Rise of Market Economies

Changing from a centrally planned economy to one that is market driven is substantially fueled by an increase in trade and capital investment. National leaders recognize that domestic growth requires private enterprise and a solid industrial base to succeed in their objectives. Therefore, even nations steeped in socialist ideology encourage private-sector development and improved trade relations. China is the obvious example, where domestic enterprise development and an open-door policy generated substantial foreign investment and expended trade. In two brief decades, China has reversed generations of isolationism, and while not abandoning its Communist political agenda, it has established a large favorable trade balance, accumulated currency reserves, and established investment linkages with major western firms.

Malaysia is another case in point. When the Uruguay Round of Multilateral Trade negotiations began in 1986, Malaysia was a substantially closed market with high import tariffs and protectionist regulations. Between 1986 and 1996, in 10 short years, the country reduced tariffs by approximately 65 percent, eliminated quotas on 79 percent of its total imports, and added nearly 7,000 items to its import-export profile of trade. These items range from high-tech machinery to consumer goods such as snack foods. The result was a general rise in national income, an improved standard of living, vast improvements in roads, water systems, and telecommunications, and a significant reduction of *net* imports. Even though Malaysia suffered during the height of the Asian crisis in 1998, the economy began to rebound in 1999 after political and banking reforms were implemented. The nation is expected to have sustained growth through 2005, with nearly a quarter of annual GDP derived from new multinational alliances.[64]

An expansion strategy such as Malaysia's is based on developing domestic enterprises capable of rapidly expending the nation's exports, but this strategy also systematically reduces dependence on imports. This is called an **import substitution strategy**.[65] Such a strategy often focuses on technology transfer through enhanced foreign

THE U.S. BANANA WAR WITH EUROPE

The so-called "banana war" between the United States and the European Union has accentuated regional tension between the two triad powers and triggered trade disputes over more than 80 categories of products that flow between Europe and America. The problem began in late 1996 when the American company, Chiquita, with the backing of the U.S. State Department, filed a claim against the EU for illegal restraint of trade in bananas imported to Europe. Diplomats became involved on both sides of the Atlantic, and after nearly three years of prolonged hearings and six rulings that upheld U.S. claims, the WTO condemned the EU for unfair trade practices. The core issue was that the EU favored vegetable and fruit products imported from former European colonies in the Caribbean by providing preferential quotas and low (or exempt) tariffs to their Latin exporters. When Chiquita filed charges, singling out bananas, a substantial list of claims surfaced concerning other products that were crippling imports to Europe from U.S. companies.

Ironically, the 1999 WTO ruling apparently did little to change EU practices, and the U.S. State Department became involved, charging European authorities with failing to comply with WTO mandates. The U.S. authorities also retaliated against the EU to bring pressure on governments to comply with WTO rulings. This involved U.S. sanctions equivalent to 100-percent duties on a broad range of European goods exported to the United States. European diplomats then re-ignited a festering debate over hormone-treated beef, a problem that began with the outbreak of mad cow disease in the early 1990s. This led to agricultural embargoes of American beef, which is commonly raised on hormone-supplemented feeds. American beef exporters were outraged and pressed the State Department to retaliate more strongly with more pervasive bans on EU products unless the beef embargo was lifted.

The debates and WTO hearings have created a domino effect. For example, Britain escalated its trade restrictions, banning genetically modified foods such as vegetables exported by Monsanto. Then EU authorities instated a regulation that required U.S. aircraft to be modified with "hush kit" mufflers or lose airport landing privileges throughout the region. The United States immediately retaliated with threats to deny landing rights for British and French Concordes in the United States, and the State Department further tightened U.S. quotas on imported steel. The disputes now involve 15 European countries and 12 American and Caribbean nations, which collectively address products and trade regulations affecting more than $100 billion in annual trade. Successful resolution of the disputes is not expected for several years. Although more than 90 percent of all trade between the United States and Europe remains unaffected, ripples from the disputes affect hundreds of companies on both sides of the Atlantic. Managers in the steel and aircraft industries, for example, are asking how their companies were pulled into a global fray that began with a skirmish over bananas.

Sources: Lionel Barber, "What's the Beef?" *Europe*, May 1999, 8–9. Also see Robert J. Guttman, "Charlene Barshefsky, U.S. Trade Representative: An Interview on the WTO and the EU's Banana Import Policy," *Europe*, May 1999, 11–13.

alliances, and a country must aggressively court multinational investments to help develop local industries. In Malaysia, for example, there was no industrial foundation for motor vehicle production 20 years ago. All vehicles, trucks, vans, and cars had to be imported. By forming joint alliances with foreign companies such as Nissan and Ford, the country established its own assembly plants with a workforce educated in western technologies. The foreign alliances initially created huge capital outflows and trade imbalances for Malaysia, but as its industries solidified, Malaysia's automotive firms became profitable exporters serving Singapore and neighboring nations. More importantly, the country acquired a new level of sustainable technology, enhanced its education systems, and created new job opportunities.[66]

One of the most interesting dimensions of working in an emerging economy involves human resource development. Few developing economies have the management expertise required for domestic or foreign business, and fewer still have management capabilities. These situations open the way for international management education as well as basic skill development in business disciplines. In Singapore, for example, MIT has a joint program for graduate business education with Singapore's National University, which is one of Asia's foremost educational institutions. In Bangkok, the University of Pennsylvania is among more than 30 leading North American and European universities with business and executive development programs. Virtually all the top 100 American business schools have foreign interests in Eastern Europe, the Middle East, or Southeast Asia; most have programs in all three regions.[67] Major American universities also have programs in Latin America, some dating back to the 1920s, but more recently, smaller state and private universities have introduced international business programs throughout South America.[68]

Privatization

Managing newly privatized companies in developing economies is another interesting challenge for expatriates working abroad. **Privatization** is the process of converting government-owned organizations into privately owned and independently managed enterprises.[69] Often the change in ownership results from multinational companies buying these foreign companies or forming alliances, bringing their own management teams to the new enterprise. The emphasis on building market-based economies has accelerated privatization in many countries. Under communist regimes, the state or its collectives held ownership control over all productive assets. However, even in democratic societies, public ownership or significant regulatory control is common. These often include government postal services, utilities, transportation, airport, and port facilities. In Europe they may include steel, petroleum, automotive, telecommunications, fuel coal and oil, and the defense industries. Privatization has occurred in many of these sectors in Britain, Sweden, the Netherlands, France, and even the United States. However, compared to privatization in former Soviet bloc countries, western practices are generally mild forms of deregulation or shifts toward private funding. These options are summarized in Figure 2.7.

The least controversial method of privatization is to deregulate public assets, thereby creating quasipublic or fully private organizations. This was President Ronald Reagan's approach to reduce federal involvement in airlines, postal services, utility companies, and telecommunications. The British, under Prime Minister Margaret Thatcher, spun off most of the industries that were formally under government control or those that had been protected by government subsidies. British Petroleum (BP), British Leyland, British Airlines, and British Steel were restructured as competitive, privately managed organizations.[70] Some, such as the British Airport Authority (BAA), became quasipublic in the sense of joint responsibilities for airport development and port management, but today BAA competes as an entirely private company. It not only operates Heathrow and other U.K. airports but also develops and operates air transport and cargo facilities in 34 other countries. BAA could not have had international activities or invested jointly in foreign operations as a government-owned agency.[71] British Leyland, the giant automaker, was broken up and its major divisions sold. Ford subsequently purchased the Jaguar division, including British factories and worldwide distribution centers, and Daimler merged with the German Mercedes

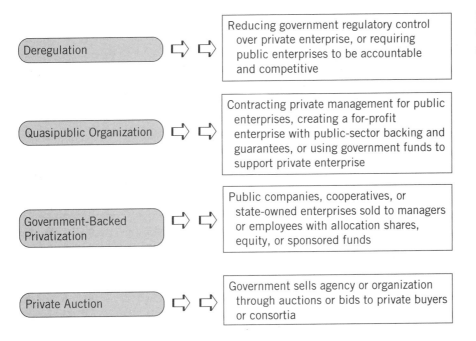

FIGURE 2.7
Conceptual Modes
of Privatization

Benz group to become DaimlerBenz, which later merged with Chrysler to become DaimlerChrysler.

In Germany unification required substantial privatization of the former East German sector, which included holdings that ranged from small village hotels to the largest steel plants. German leaders met this challenge through a mass privatization program under a special agency called the *Treuhand* (officially, *Treuhandanstalt*).[72] Between 1990 and 1994, the Treuhand helped privatize more than 14,000 East German companies, liquidated nearly 3,000 that were not economically viable, and created roughly 1.5 million jobs. The Treuhand met its objectives and subsequently shut down as a privatization agency, but it continued to assist the new owners and entrepreneurs through a consortium of banks, advisors, and foreign investors.[73]

Privatization in the former Soviet bloc countries has concentrated on converting military and defense assets into private industries. For example, the world's largest military complex for tanks and munitions was in the city of Cheyabinsk, deep in the heart of Russia's Ural Mountains.[74] The city of nearly six million people was devoted almost entirely to the defense industry, and the military tank complex employed 30,000 people. In 1992 the complex was mandated to "go private" as part of President Boris Yeltsin's program to convert 130,000 Russian manufacturers into privately held companies. Yeltsin envisioned a massive conversion to joint-stock companies managed by employee-management teams. The military complex began by issuing stock claims to every employee as pledge rights to shares at the end of the conversion period, when government would cut off support. Managers, once employed as part of the state bureaucracy, suddenly became company employees. They immediately stopped making tanks and began making farm tractors and mining equipment. In addition to the converted tank facilities, the company subdivided into nine other divisions, with products ranging from kitchen utensils to industrial machine tools. Within two years it had contracted with Fiat in Italy to manufacture car parts, and it had created a joint venture with a Shanghai consortium to manufacture office furniture. It also developed trade links with German, Swedish, and Danish companies. However, the sudden transformation was difficult for company employees. The new company could employ only 15,000 people, about half of its original workforce, and only its exported products were profitable. Poorly trained managers knew little about marketing, employees felt disillusioned at the loss of protection from state-provided entitlements, and neither employees nor managers were enthusiastic about owning a company with questionable profit potential. Most felt they would have been better off under the old Soviet system.[75]

Other countries have had better success than Russia with privatization. The Czech Republic has done extremely well by bringing in western management teams, establishing new production and marketing techniques, and creating university business centers in concert with mass privatization to help new ventures become competitive. The Czech Republic has built its privatization efforts on the strength of exportable products while improving domestic operations that reduce imports, and as a rule, it has been more selective in allowing companies to issue private stock. Hungary, Poland, Slovenia, Latvia, Lithuania, and Estonia have privatized successfully through various forms of public auction, stock certificates, and employee buyouts. These states have transformed a majority of formerly government-owned industries into competitive private-enterprise companies, with public stock listings on exchanges and extensive alliances with foreign companies. Research on privatization has found that companies succeed most often under foreign management or in managerial partnerships between expatriates and host-country managers. The outsiders become conduits for knowledge, helping to manage the transition in a way that promotes development of management skills in the host companies. Privatization has flourished in the transition economies. However, when managers of state-owned enterprises simply take over newly privatized firms, the results are generally less favorable.[76]

During the crucial period of mass privatization between 1992 and 1996, there were nearly 32,000 "interventions" for privatization assistance in Eastern Europe and the CIS republics. These included consulting and management education, direct investments, joint venture development, and cross-cultural management assignments. The combined effect of these interventions amounted to an estimated $440 billion in new economic activity.[77] In addition, western governments provided an estimated $86 billion in direct foreign aid for private-sector development, generating more than 7,200 new export products targeted for European and North American markets. By 1999, more than 82,000 expatriate western managers were working in Central and Eastern Europe under multinational contracts.[78]

Global Workforce Diversity

Dissolution of international borders and rapid expansion of global companies throughout the world have greatly affected the composition of business organizations. Today corporate boards of directors often reflect a diversified membership, with individuals drawn from many different nations and backgrounds. Only a few years ago these corporate boards were dominated by home-country directors. For example, after somewhat reluctantly appointing its first non-American director in 1990, IBM has subsequently added foreign directors from international subsidiaries and appointed external directors from Europe and Asia. American companies have seldom included foreign members on their boards, but it is common practice among Europe's leading multinationals. Shell Oil, Unilever, Fiat, Bayer, and Alcatel all have internationally diversified boards.[79] At the other extreme, Japanese firms rarely admit directors from beyond their immediate industrial groups, let alone foreign nationals, to their boards. Sony has been one of the few exceptions. Its founder and CEO, Akio Morita, included foreign external directors during the early 1980s. Before he retired, Morita established positions for both American and European directors on an executive committee. However, most Japanese companies avoid foreign representation, carefully protecting the homogeneity of senior management.[80]

As multinational companies become more diversified in their foreign interests, ethnic diversity becomes more apparent down through lower ranks. As these managers earn promotions or move through the organization in new assignments, higher levels in management become more diversified. This is particularly notable among senior executives from regional overseas divisions. Today, the top 100 U.S. multinationals report that approximately 30 percent of their senior managers are foreign nationals. European multinationals are estimated to have nearly double that number, approximately 59 percent, but Japanese multinationals have fewer than 2 percent non-Japanese in senior posts.[81]

At the workforce level, multinational companies obviously employ local people and have widely diversified organizations. However, within these foreign enclaves, ethnic diversity presents unusual challenges. For instance, German companies not only employ former East German citizens but also have workers from Eastern Europe and border Baltic and Balkan states. The "soft borders" of EU countries also have resulted in a transient flow of workers, ranging from North Africans who favor France to Turks and Romanians who favor Germany. Spanish workers frequently cross into Germany and France, where wages are much higher, and the entire European region has witnessed a surge of "guest workers." Many of these come on their own accord, but companies throughout Western Europe often recruit temporary low-wage workers or transients. European migration has subsequently changed the composition of many communities, and the mixing of nationalities has created sensitive labor-management issues.[82] (Labor management and human relations are addressed in separate chapters.) Meanwhile, the emerging Central European and Baltic states have attracted a huge number of Western Europeans and Americans. Ukraine has actively sought companies such as IBM, GE, and PepsiCo which, together with nearly 300 other U.S. companies, account for nearly 5,000 non-Ukrainian employees in their plants.[83]

Diversity is also rapidly increasing in North America as the effects of NAFTA soften the U.S.–Canadian border, adding a flow of people between the two countries. Even greater changes in Mexico have attracted more than 400 U.S. companies that have established Mexican facilities since 1993. This expansion complements about 2,300 American enterprise investments that predated 1993, plus approximately 430 European operations established in Mexico since 1990. Most of these foreign facilities are manufacturing sites with local labor under the direction of expatriate technicians and managers. Still, bilateral agreements have also established training programs in the United States for a large number of Mexican technicians. The southwestern United States hosted a significant multicultural population before NAFTA, but in the aftermath of trade liberalization, Mexico is only one of many Latin American nations that have seen more integrated operations and multinational interests.[84]

Workforce diversity has increased further as more women join the ranks of international managers. Each year, the number of women employed in foreign locations grows, and these workers are well educated and skilled at jobs needed in expanding trade environments. Nancy Adler, a well-known scholar of cross-cultural management, has documented an increasing number of American and Canadian women going overseas as expatriate managers, and most are finding greater success there than they enjoyed at home. Adler's research suggests that gender issues are secondary to performance expectations, and although many foreign societies do not easily accept women in management roles, multinationals offer women rewarding career opportunities.[85] At the shop-floor level, women hold many skilled jobs, and they fill more tedious data-input and microelectronics assembly jobs than men do. This trend is increasing in the Southeast Asian states of Malaysia and Indonesia, where companies such as Compaq, Ford, Siemens, Hoechst, and Unilever, among many others, have launched major expansion programs. It is also apparent in Eastern Europe where a combination of foreign government assistance programs and western alliances have increased skills training and employment programs for women nearly fivefold since 1990.[86]

THE CONTEXT OF MANAGEMENT— A SUMMARY

As a closing comment, bear in mind that the role of an international manager is not categorically defined, nor can any amount of analysis reduce it to simple principles often found in management texts. In time, there will be no distinction between principles of management and international management; all managers will be cast in global roles or be part of a worldwide society of business activities. Recalling Peter Drucker's prophecy of rapid evolution toward a norm of global management introduced in Chapter 1, the pervasive changes taking place worldwide suggest that managers must make the mental transition to a global view or go the way of the dinosaurs.

These introductory chapters intend to puncture the image of management as a domestic and parochial concept and to emphasize the opportunities for international managers capable of thinking in global terms. Recall the opening profile of Paul Liao, a Taiwan-born engineer who came to America to study and ended up heading a company that now operates in more than 30 countries, with a staff of international scientists and engineers representing more than 50 ethnic groups and cultures. Liao urged that a manager should "think globally and adapt pragmatically as a world citizen," and his example illustrates not only this philosophy but also the essence of international management.

The next two chapters examine problems of political risk and business ethics. These foundation concepts complement the introductory chapter and this presentation on the environment of international business.

REVIEW QUESTIONS

1. Describe how trading blocs have developed, and list the characteristics of the triad of global competition.
2. Explain how disparities in economic growth occur. Why do some countries experience very rapid development while others languish?
3. Describe social and economic changes taking place in Central and Eastern Europe. What new challenges do these changes present for international managers?
4. Detail growth and trade patterns in Latin America, and explain how a developing country can position itself for more rapid growth.
5. Define and contrast the terms *less-developed country* and *developing economy*. In your answer, cite examples from the Indian Subcontinent to illustrate the differences.
6. Describe New Growth theory, and explain how high-growth Asian countries have implicitly followed the model in their successful development.

7. What constitutes technology, and what role does technology play in international management?
8. How has information technology transformed global companies and affected the management process?
9. Describe how privatization occurs, and explain why it is important to emerging economies.
10. Why is diversity important to multinational corporations, and what challenges complicate managing culturally diverse workforces?

GLOSSARY OF KEY TERMS

Developing economy (DE)   A country with at least the beginnings of economic systems and sustainable infrastructure needed to support growth and attract private-sector development.

Ecu   New European currency for trade and commerce transactions used primarily as an accounting medium under the European Monetary Union.

Import substitution strategy   A development strategy based on nurturing domestic private enterprise to provide goods and services that have been, or are currently, imported.

Information technology (IT)   The science of creating and using information resources commonly associated with computational applications, communications, and data storage and retrieval processes.

Innovation   The useful adaptation of science or knowledge that converts inventions or concepts into valuable applications.

Invention   The creation of entirely new knowledge, devices, or processes.

Less-developed country (LDC)   A nation without economic systems and infrastructure capable of self-sustained growth.

New Growth theory   The assertion that international trade by private industry relatively free of government intervention allows a country to accumulate wealth and continue to grow, expand technology, and improve human resource capabilities. Growth begets growth, with continuously increasing returns.

Privatization   The conversion of state-owned or politically controlled enterprises into privately held companies responsible for profits and losses in competitive environments.

Technology transfer   The process of either converting knowledge into a useful product or introducing existing technology to a less advanced society through some form of international venture.

Transnational management support system (TMSS)   A global information system that provides fully integrated communications and information technology to network globally diffused companies with diversified international operations.

Triad   In global business jargon, the concept of three regional trading blocs—Europe, Asia, and North America.

EXERCISES

1. Select a developed country within one of the triad power blocs other than your home nation, and develop a profile of its economic environment. Cover the topics of growth potential, employment, social or political trends that could affect business, and other relevant factors that would briefly describe the advantages or disadvantages of doing business there. If possible, speak with a student or manager from that country, and ask for personal insights about the environment of business, living conditions, and benefits of that society.
2. Identify a less-developed country and a developing economy. If possible, choose countries from the same region, and contrast their strengths and weaknesses in economic development, stability, foreign exchange, trade relationships, and potential for international development either by pursing new exports or attracting foreign investments.
3. Many news stories report on trade negotiations between nations and on business activities in developing countries. For example, media reports have covered controversies over trade relations between the United States and China, complications of NAFTA involving Canada, the United States, and Mexico, and unresolved issues in Europe arising from EU

membership and relationships with former Eastern bloc nations. Choose a situation that interests you, and summarize the main issues. Try to look at the problems from both sides, and then consider how they affect a company from one nation doing business in the other. What challenges do you perceive for an expatriate working in this environment?

SMITHKLINE BEECHAM PLC

As the 21st century unfolds, American and European executives are reflecting on two decades of political and economic changes that pervasively changed international business. These executives are concerned about how unprepared they were for changes in global competition that began to escalate rapidly during the 1980s, followed by the sudden disintegration of the former Soviet Union in 1989 and subsequent reemergence of 23 transition economies. Putting aside political and economic upheaval that occurred elsewhere, the commercial and political maps of Europe and southern Asia were substantially redefined. Major trade agreements proliferated on several continents; not least of all, there were daily headlines about the coming "Fortress Europe" that might emerge with European monetary and economic unification. Many business leaders expected devastating consequences for American multinationals that were generally at a disadvantage in Europe and in a very weak position to compete in trade with the transition economies.

Fortress Europe did not occur. Instead, American firms became widely involved in European alliances that resulted in huge new markets for U.S. firms in Europe and equally enormous market opportunities for Europeans in North America. Trade did not crumble; instead, it accelerated throughout the 1990s. Although 1989 was a year of extraordinary change—a benchmark year for the Soviet demise, the end to the Berlin Wall, and dramatic anticommunist demonstrations in China—it was relatively calm compared to the decade that followed. There were bloody coups in several nations, years of "ethnic cleansing" in Bosnia, the Kosovo region of Yugoslavia, near-economic collapse in Southeast Asian countries, and wars in the Gulf states, the Caucuses, and northern Africa. From a business viewpoint, events were just as unnerving. Prior to 1989, fewer than a hundred international mergers were registered between European and North American companies; corporations were more concerned with competition in their home countries. Midway through the decade, in 1995 alone, there were more than 1,500 mergers or acquisitions among major international companies; between 1996 and

1999, that number doubled. In addition, approximately 800 entirely new ventures emerged in Central and Eastern Europe through privatization, involving international companies from France, Germany, Britain, Italy, and the United States.

Although many of the new multinational alliances have struggled, most have enjoyed huge success, and all of them have been changed by the experience. One of those, SmithKline Beecham PLC, is typical of the success stories of cross-Atlantic business. Today the company is among the most respected multinational enterprises in both the United States and Europe. The company is the result of a quiet merger in 1989—one of those deals that seldom gets more than a nod on back-page news. Before the merger, SmithKline Beckman Corp. was a $1-billion-a-year U.S. pharmaceutical firm headquartered in Philadelphia, with diversified interests in human health care products, over-the-counter drugs, beauty aids, animal nutrient supplements, chemical additives, and a dozen other product lines, none of which were particularly well known. The company had sold into international markets in Europe, Asia, and South America for several decades through export offices and marketing agreements, but it was basically a stodgy organization with hierarchical management, homegrown executives, and functional separation of activities. It sold American products overseas and serviced foreign accounts through a predominately American expatriate management system. Meanwhile, Beecham Group PLC of London was an equally stodgy British firm earning about $1 billion annually selling ethical pharmaceutical products, animal health care lines, and an undistinguished array of cosmetics and home care products. Neither company was positioned to compete well beyond their home markets, except perhaps against one another.

With the threat of Fortress Europe looming large in 1989, SmithKline attempted to acquire Beecham as a way of getting a foot planted in Europe. Beecham firmly rejected the acquisition offer, but company executives recognized the wisdom of horizontally amalgamating the product lines of the two competitors. The negotiating executives found themselves agreeing to a merger, and a new SmithKline Beecham (SB) emerged. The result was a new multi-national Anglo-American corporation with marketing muscle to compete among the top five industrial leaders on both sides of the Atlantic. Old facilities were closed, research and development was combined, entirely new marketing systems were developed, and more than a third of both companies' product lines were sold or terminated. Animal health products and nutrients, for example, were abandoned, and marginal cosmetics lines were sold.

Management restructuring followed a complete corporate relocation to Britain, where the firm's world headquarters were established, and between 1990 and 1997, nearly all senior division managers and the executive staff were replaced. Many of those who had engineered the merger were eligible for retirement, and many more retired slightly ahead of schedule. They were replaced by well-seasoned international managers with strong histories of foreign assignments and notable positions in their respective fields in the United States, Britain, Germany, Sweden, Canada, and France. The company executive core was transformed into a global team with no particular national identity. Indeed, the company no longer described itself as American, British, or even European, but as a world organization. The stodgy management structures have long since disappeared, and functional departments and divisions exist only as a convenience. Instead, employees work in transnational teams serving Asia, Europe, and North America. Division presidents oversee U.S. health care products and British chemicals, for example, and a dozen division executives focus on regional markets or product sectors in Central and Eastern Europe, the Middle East, and Asia.

With a decade of exceptional performance, sales grew fivefold to more than $9.5 billion by 1999, yet SmithKline Beecham was still not among the giants. It had, however, become one of the top 10 most respected multinational corporations in Europe, where credit is given to a unique blend of American and British management talent tempered by a cosmopolitan world outlook on global development. In a recent management survey of Europe's largest 250 multinational companies, SmithKline Beecham was ranked seventh for long-term market potential, fourth in research and development acumen, and third in corporate value (a financial stability measurement). The company was noted as among the top five for its ability

to attract and retain quality employees, and for its track record in corporate ethics as a multicultural employer. As the last millennium came to an end, industry analysts on both sides of the Atlantic believed that SmithKline Beecham was uniquely positioned for rapid expansion within the European Union as well as throughout Central and Eastern Europe. Indeed, the company had negotiated more than 30 alliances in the emerging countries for joint manufacturing and distribution of ethical drugs and human health care products. SmithKline Beecham also concluded a major acquisition of Sterling Drugs in the United States, quickly adding 10 percent to its North American market share, and opening new opportunities to expand into Latin America.

SmithKline Beecham executives—comprising one of the best cross-functional international management teams in the industry—were still apprehensive as the year 2000 unfolded. They reflected on lack of foresight in the 1980s when neither they, nor most of their industrial colleagues, envisioned the political and economic changes that had occurred. At best, they only "sensed" correctly that companies would no longer remain isolated behind political boundaries. Ironically, their success led to yet another surprise in early 2000, when the four largest pharmaceutical companies in the world almost simultaneously targeted SmithKline Beecham for acquisition. Within three months, the company had concluded negotiations with Glaxo-Wellcome for a cooperative merger, and by September 2000, the newly combined company was poised to become the world's largest integrated global chemical-pharmaceutical enterprise. At that point, the executive strategists began asking what would be in store for them over the next decade. Will China awaken and Asia become the battleground for new markets? Will NAFTA expand, opening Latin America's emerging economies to more intense competition? What new challenges will test the corporation in the new century?

QUESTIONS

1. Based on information about development in Central and Eastern Europe, and about changes that are shaping commerce in the CIS and its sister republics, what opportunities and risks do you foresee for this corporation?

2. Political and economic changes in Latin America have not generated headlines like those for Europe

or Asia, yet the region has undergone dramatic changes. Put yourself in the position of an executive with SmithKline Beecham as its merger with Glaxo-Wellcome was concluded, and evaluate the potential for expansion within the Americas.

3. After the initial merger of SmithKline and Beecham companies, what transition problems do you think the new company faced in bringing together corporate cultures from the United States and Great Britain? How do you think executive roles changed in that process? Glaxo-Wellcome, also an Anglo-American multinational with diverse executive talent from German and Scandinavian divisions, adds a more complex dimension to management. What managerial problems or advantages would you envision for the newly merged corporation?

BIBLIOGRAPHY

Barnard, Bruce. "Cross-Continental Convergences." *Europe*, September 2000, 32–34.

du Bois, Martin. "World Business; Together but Equal: Binational Mergers Look Great on Paper; but They Often Run into Problems." *Asian Wall Street Journal*, 30 September 1996, p. S8.

Fedor, Kenneth J., and William B. Werther Jr. "Making Sense of Cultural Factors in International Alliances." *Organizational Dynamics* 23, no. 4 (1995): 33–48.

Merriden, Trevor. "Companies to Emulate in the UK." *Management Today*, December 1996, 32–44.

"JP Garnier Appointed Chief Operating Officer of SmithKline Beecham; Key Step in Healthcare Integration." SmithKline Beecham PLC, *Newsline*, 2 October 1995, pp. 1–2.

CASE 2.2

ARGENTINA AT THE CROSSROADS

Once among the world's 10 wealthiest countries, Argentina suffered a prolonged recession after World War II that resulted in further decades of economic decline. Today, however, Argentina is mounting a serious bid to regain its position in the global community. During the imperial period a century ago, Argentina was the leading supplier of beef, wool, grain, and minerals to Britain, with an enclave of European investors, colonial companies, and traders from the heart of the continent. Argentina's capital rivaled the sophistication of Vienna and Paris with fine arts, an exceptional opera house, theaters, museums, and universities. City streets were crowded with cars, electric lights lit homes when New Yorkers still squinted in gaslight, and commuters enjoyed public tramways and motorized streetcars when most of the world's city dwellers still relied on horsedrawn transportation.

When World War II erupted, Argentina was the major strategic port for food and materials in the Americas, yet the country was strong enough economically and militarily to maintain neutrality. After the war, however, the country suddenly became isolated as North America and Europe concentrated on massive industrial recovery, while the miracle growth in Asia bypassed it. Because of its wartime neutrality, the country also became a refuge for fleeing Nazi officials, many of Europe's common criminals, and even many shadowy characters from America's depression-era underworld. Politically, Argentina was pigeonholed and cut off from mainstream commerce.

Argentina answered these problems by creating a "statist" government led by General Juan Peron and his legendary wife, Evita. Peron ran Argentina as a populist caudillo from 1946 to 1955, and he returned to power briefly in the 1970s. He created what was called a "Switzerland of America" with a state-centered power system that tightly held the country's economic controls. Under Peron, all essential industry was owned or controlled through the state. The government participated in an all-embracing partnership with labor in which widespread unions provided political muscle and, at times, almost paramilitary strength to enforce government policies; in return, the government provided extraordinary benefits. Union workers in Argentina were among the world's highest-paid industrial workers, often benefiting from subsidized housing and birth-to-death welfare benefits. All citizens enjoyed free education, health care, food entitlements, and even holiday favors such as seaside chalets.

Early in Peron's reign, this utopian society seemed to work well, as major new foreign investment flowed into Argentina. The vast pampas produced sufficient beef and grains to meet the needs of a hungry Europe, and American bankers rapidly poured money into the country to pay for exports and gain access to the high returns of resource-rich mineral exports and shipping trade. But Argentina lacked the industrial base to sustain such an idealistic welfare state, and those in power became extremely wealthy at the expense of the general population. Society polarized as vast numbers of unskilled and disenfranchised citizens lived in abject poverty. Peron's miracle collapsed, leaving in its wake an inefficient and unmanageable state-controlled economic system. The education system could not deliver on its promise of free schooling to more than a small part of the population, the health system was woefully inadequate, and the industrial infrastructure, which had relied on foreign money, degenerated quickly when investors withdrew.

For nearly 40 years and two generations, Argentina languished. Inflation brought astronomical price increases, and people survived through corruption, handouts, illicit trade with the country's neighbors, and barter. The government maintained civil order only through harsh police terrorism, and the country's legal system did not function effectively. A foreign company could not protect its investments, nor its patents or intellectual property, and alliances with Argentine firms lacked any legal enforcement systems. Consequently, few multinationals ventured into the country or even risked export trade agreements.

During the late 1980s, however, Argentina began to recover. It had slowly built up fundamental infrastructure, and austerity measures had begun to bring inflation and foreign debt under control. Currency revisions and economic developments were aimed at solidifying the country's resources and creating a viable export community. By 1990, Argentina had brought inflation under control and had set in motion a commercial legal system that attracted foreign investors. By the end of 1994, it was among the strongest growth economies of Latin America with a stable, fully convertible currency that was pegged to the U.S. dollar. Unfortunately, much of this and other Latin American prosperity was linked to new initiatives under NAFTA and the resulting growth in Mexico and Brazil. When the Mexican peso collapsed and the fragile Brazilian economy plummeted into recession, most of South America followed. Argentina's hard-gained progress was met by skepticism among foreign investors, who believed the country was once again on the brink of economic disaster.

Unlike many of its neighbors, however, Argentina quickly regained its markets, held inflation intact, and fought through a devastating currency crisis. In 1996 the country recorded a 7.4 percent growth rate and even faster expansion in per-capita GNP, approaching 8 percent. A democratic government replaced the statist paternalism of the past, began to privatize a major part of the public sector, and implemented a system of taxation that encouraged private enterprise. With many eyes intent on Mexico and NAFTA, Argentina helped to lead a consortium of South American countries into the Mercosur agreement that established the equivalent of a Latin American common market. Member countries drastically reduced import and export restrictions, and Argentina reduced all of its import tariffs and quotas. Domestic companies no longer received major state subsidies; instead, governments encouraged them to expand into foreign markets through tax incentives and trade assistance.

By 1999, Argentina was exporting 28 percent of its industrial output. Although trade with Brazil represented nearly 5 percent of the GNP, Argentina's privatized airlines, automotive industry, metals, major mining interests, and commercial banking attracted investments from major foreign companies, including Chrysler Corporation, GE, Fidelity Investments, and Bristol-Myers Squibb Company. CitiCorp (now CitiGroup), American Express, and other major bankers quietly brought into Argentina more than $2 billion in new capital. The mining industry, which had barely produced $30 million for export in 1990, capped $3.2 billion in 1999. U.S. investors alone sank more than $3.5 billion into alliances with enterprises in Argentina by 1997, with another $1.1 billion under registration for 1998 and nearly $1 billion earmarked through early 2000. Argentina's emerging stock market recorded 28 percent annual growth following the 1995 economic jolt, although, like many nations, the equity markets seesawed in 1999 and early 2000.

Argentina's leaders characterize the country as "an Asian transformation with Swiss-like humanism." Translated, political leaders describe a model of free-market enterprise not unlike that in Singapore or Hong Kong, yet they share Switzerland's values for human welfare benefits of health, education, and community support to be maintained by public-sector administration. Time will tell whether they have set a feasible goal. Certainly, the government is rushing to privatize industrial companies, banking, and services. The country still has a long way to go to become a free-market economy, but privatization has rapidly brought in new technology and major infrastructure development through international alliances. Unfortunately, foreign investors streamlined companies to attain acceptable profit levels, generating more unemployment and a backlash by the country's labor leaders. Argentina faces 17.5 percent unemployment, mainly among workers with low skills and little education. Rural farms and small businesses have given way at an accelerating pace to large-scale, efficient agricultural systems, and a disgruntled urban population resents the reductions in government giveaways and welfare programs. Health care and education problems have not yet been adequately addressed; commercial corruption, coupled with questionable enforcement capabilities to protect investment and intellectual interests, discourages many foreign investors.

QUESTIONS

1. Argentina seems to have reached a critical decision point between development that emulates European models of state-supported commerce, with substantial nationalized industries and social welfare systems, and Asian models of minimalization, with almost entirely market-driven commercial development and trade. Contrast these general approaches to development, and argue a case for Argentina.

2. Does Argentina seem like a viable host country for multinational investment? What advantages and disadvantages would you envision for a major MNC doing business there?

3. If you were a manager employed by a foreign multinational company working in Argentina, what problems would most concern you for managing the workforce, generating profits, and maintaining growth?

BIBLIOGRAPHY

"Argentina: Invisible Hands." *The Economist*, 2 September 2000, pp. 33–34.

"Emerging Market Indicators." *The Economist*, 2 September 2000, p. 98.

"Mercuosur Becalmed." *The Economist*, 11 December 1999, p. 34.

"The Americas: Argentina's Lopsided Recovery." *The Economist*, 14 June 1997, pp. 63–64.

Friedland, Jonathan. "Peron's Legacy: As Argentine Economy Booms, Workers Fret They'll Be Left Behind." *Wall Street Journal*, 25 June 25 1997, pp. A1, A14.

Moffett, Mark, Paul B. Caroll, and Jonathan Friedland. "As the Crunch Eases, Latin Economies Stay for Free-Market Path." *Wall Street Journal*, 12 May 1995, pp. A1, A7.

GOVERNMENT RELATIONS AND POLITICAL RISK

CHAPTER OBJECTIVES

Describe how multinational corporations interface with host-country governments, and demonstrate the importance of establishing effective business-government relations.

Explain how countries differ in their fundamental legal, political, and regulatory systems.

Identify methods of government intervention that can threaten a multinational enterprise.

Illustrate the risks to a company of different types of political and social events, including chance incidents such as terrorism.

Detail the process of political risk assessment and the methods that international managers apply to make informed decisions about foreign investments.

Define the two mainstream concepts of defensive and integrative strategies through which multinational firms manage risk in foreign operations.

CHAPTER 3

Douglas N. Daft became the tenth chairman and CEO of Coca-Cola Company in April 2000, succeeding two controversial chief executives and two turbulent decades of change.[1] Roberto C. Goizueta, the first person to head the company who was not a descendant of the founders, was also the first ethnic Hispanic to hold the executive office at one of America's largest and most esteemed corporations. Under his leadership, Coca-Cola grew at a meteoric rate, its stock price rising 3,500 percent between 1986 and 1997, when Goizueta died of cancer. During this era, the company nearly doubled its product line to include 230 soft-drink and fruit beverages, sold through its global network of bottlers and distributors in 201 countries.

Goizueta and Coca-Cola also experienced more than a few crises. Early on, India attempted to gain access to Coke's highly guarded formula for its syrup. In what was called a blatant form of political blackmail, Indian officials and investors wanted trade secrets in return for Coca-Cola's licensing rights to bottle and market in India. Goizueta stood his ground, and Coke withdrew from India until agreements could be reached without corruption or political avarice. Then so-called cola wars erupted between Coca-Cola and Pepsi-Cola distributors in Latin America. Local owners licensed under both companies competed fiercely for market share, in often-dangerous confrontations. In Argentina alone, both companies suffered huge losses not only from legitimate competitive costs but also from questionable events that seemed to spread to Brazil, Mexico, and other Latin countries. Both companies lost facilities due to suspected arson and terrorist raids, had trucks hijacked, staff threatened, and several executives targeted for kidnapping and ransom. Goizueta personally intervened to protect assets and staff. He established a corporate crisis team responsible for rapid-response problem-solving in high-risk countries, and hired security services based in the United States and in each foreign country to protect its people, provide security for assets, and to evacuate employees in extreme situations.

Before Goizueta's successor took the reigns, Coca-Cola had launched China trade, been rejected, then reinitiated business under a system of agreements. The company had faced more than two dozen armed terrorist situations involving its foreign operations. In Europe, Coca-Cola was charged with poisoning its drinks, but found innocent of the charges after investigations proved that Coke bottles were being used by pirate companies to fill with their own mixtures. Pirating by renegade bottlers penetrated the company's revenues in several Asian and Latin countries, and corrupt foreign government officials had regularly sought payoffs from Coke's locally owned franchises. The company had also been rebuffed by European regulators who feared Coke's dominance would threaten domestic soft-drink bottlers. This closely followed the European contamination scare, which cut deeply into overseas sales, squashed several expansion agreements, and depressed company investors.

In 1997, M. Douglas Ivester became CEO and chairman of Coca-Cola's board of directors. Ivester was expected to stabilize the company's financial markets and bring back a more traditional approach to management, with less aggressive foreign expansion and less risk-taking. Ivester was a logical choice as the company's chief financial executive; he had made a career in finance and accounting and was an intense manager with very clear objectives. He was very successful at reengineering the financial structure of Coca-Cola and rationalizing some of the company's marginal markets and product lines. He also had achieved some notoriety in international business as the person under Goizueta who had pushed the company into the former Soviet arena of Eastern Europe, negotiating deals in Iron Curtain countries during the years just before the Soviet collapse. Indeed, it was Ivester who personally drove a truckload of sodas into East Germany as the Berlin Wall was literally being torn down.

Unfortunately, Ivester was not tuned into international business, and having ventured overseas only rarely, he knew little about foreign cultures or the realities of managing foreign operations. His career was almost entirely focused on corporate finance, and he took a rather autocratic stance toward managing international operations. His handling of the European contamination issue—a problem inherited from Goizueta—was called combative, and he further fueled dissent among the company's overseas managers during a confrontation and messy racial discrimination suit against Coca-Cola. Consequently, when the Asian crisis ignited with riots in Indonesia and bank failures in Thailand, Ivester was unable to resolve foreign security issues or to react constructively to the emergencies. The company's Asia Pacific Group, together with contracted security firms, responded with local protection for Coca-Cola employees, initiated a safety-net action plan for facilities and assets in Jakarta and Bangkok, and in several instances, evacuated company personnel from dangerous riot areas.[2] Unlike Goizueta, who often flew to the scene during company crises, Ivester remained at the Atlanta headquarters. Unlike Goizueta, who often intervened directly with foreign governments and in many instances had developed close relationships with many diplomats, Ivester remained aloof. In the aftermath of the Asian crisis, Coca-Cola found itself with a large number of destitute Asian partners and licensed bottlers who were victims of financial chaos or bankrupt by lost assets and failed currencies. The corporation's major investors and Wall Street analysts voiced grave concerns about Coca-Cola's leadership, its ability to meet global competition, and its foreign risk profile.

Invester's tenure as chief executive at Coca-Cola came to an abrupt end with his announcement in December 1999 that he would retire early. During a brief transition period, the company quietly replaced five senior executives under Invester, and he officially stepped down to retire in April 2000. His successor was Douglas N. Daft, the President of Coca-Cola's Asia Pacific Group. Daft was a man who had spent his entire career in the field, often in the company's most controversial foreign markets. Daft was responsible for opening markets from Australia to China, and for rebuilding the Indonesian market and restructuring the company's operations in Jakarta and Bangkok. He had built the Japanese market under the mentorship of Goizueta, and had been the key executive during the disputes in India. On the eve of his appointment to Coca-Cola's chairmanship, Daft had worked 31 years with the company, narrowly escaped kidnapping in South America during the cola war crisis, and lived through the Tianamen Square riots in China during 1989.

Daft is characterized as someone who builds relationships rather than someone who directs a company, and he has established a strong network of credible associations within the company and with foreign interests. Such alliances, in his view, have been instrumental in reducing the risks of foreign business—more so than security forces, and far better than legal maneuvers or retaliatory behavior. Daft has yet to make his mark on Coca-Cola as its CEO, but at age 56, still young as a chief executive, he is expected to bring long-term stability to the company. A native Australian with global management experience and a reputation as having spearheaded the company's most profitable markets in Japan and China, Daft also seems to have the requisite talent to respond effectively to the inevitable challenges a company will face in foreign markets.

THE INTERFACE OF POLITICS AND BUSINESS

Globalization and the expanding presence of transnational corporations foreshadow a world where politics will be secondary to commercial inertia. To some extent, governments must accept subservient roles to global economic priorities, and politicians cannot ignore the importance of international business to their national development plans. Indeed, governments and politicians often find themselves swept up in the economics of transnational business. Like multinational corporations, they must accept the challenges of forging global business relations. National priorities, home-country politics, and local economic development no longer escape the influences of the seamless world of international commerce.

Disintegration of the Soviet state and subsequent reform movements in Central and Eastern Europe attest to the priorities of global economics over indigenous ideologies. But ironically, government and political institutions have not become less important to world commerce. Instead, politicians must accept a broader role in regional and global competition, orchestrate their own national interests with those of other nations, and protect their own economies against encroachment or deterioration.

From a corporate perspective, global integration requires managers to be well informed about foreign politics and legal mandates. A company must be concerned with where it locates, how it positions its operations, and the extent to which it is exposed to risks by operating in a foreign country. At the local level, international managers must comply with host-country laws, be adept at dealing with foreign regulations, and understand the political priorities of host governments. Corporate managers also must understand the relationship between the company's home-country government and host-country governments. For example, a U.S. corporation with business in China may be threatened by a U.S. government trade sanction against China for perceived human rights violations. Whether the company has good trade relations in China is of little consequence if home-country policy initiatives suddenly disrupt its activities. In these and many other situations, multinational corporations can be caught up in circumstances beyond their control. International managers often can do little to prevent the difficulties that they face, yet they must recognize the risks of doing business abroad in order to make effective plans and decisions.

Country Risks and Political Risks

Every multinational corporation has, by definition, chosen to operate in certain foreign countries. Perhaps the decision to go overseas has been coincidental with trade, or perhaps with an opportunistic venture; but before the decision is made, managers attempt to assess the risks involved. The risks associated with foreign business are called either *country risk* or *political risk*. The two terms imply slightly different meanings, but they are not mutually exclusive. **Country risk** includes the uncertainty associated with government continuity, regional politics that can affect the country, ineffective legal and regulatory systems, currency instability or lack of convertibility, and home-host country relations. The term often appears in diplomatic communications, such as official advisory notices to businesses or cautions to foreign travelers. **Political risk** is associated specifically with the commercial interests of companies involved in trade or international investments. It refers to the probabilities that political decisions, civil disruptions, social problems, monetary problems, or trade issues will affect the business environment such that companies will be exposed to financial or material

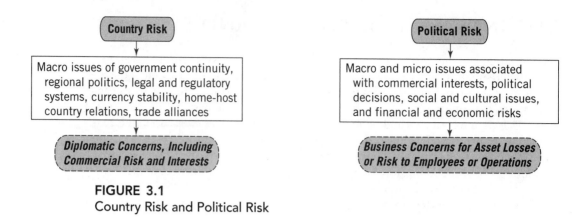

FIGURE 3.1
Country Risk and Political Risk

losses.[3] Diplomats and business executives look at many of the same variables when assessing country or political risks, but a multinational corporation must focus on specific risks such as expropriation of its foreign assets, physical and intellectual security, trade restrictions, labor relations, procurement systems, licensing, costs of trade, and transactional difficulties such as constraints on profit repatriation and convertibility of currency.[4] These points are summarized in Figure 3.1.

Another way of looking at county risk is that it is primarily concerned with macro issues, such as relationships between the home and host countries. Other elements of country risk include international treaties, ideological differences, and host-country economic and social systems. More recently, acute problems have surfaced, such as terrorist activities. They can occur almost anywhere, but there is a higher probability of terrorism in certain countries, such as Colombia and Peru. Armed clashes within transition economies, such as Yugoslavia's Kosovo region, or between countries, such as Iraq's sudden invasion of Kuwait, often catch foreign companies off guard. In many instances, however, managers who stay abreast of published country risk reports often can be prepared for such dangers. Problems that arise because of ideological differences are more difficult to forecast, yet these differences create a general risk profile that must be accommodated in a company's foreign operation plans. An American company doing business in China, for example, has a far greater country risk than when doing business in Britain, because the ideological differences between America and China influence virtually everything from trade agreements to daily transactions.

Political risk also has a macro component, since a company's relationship with the host government and differences in cultural values or social systems produce important influences on a firm's success. However, political risk is more often associated with micro considerations, such as specific trade restrictions, potential government interference with a subsidiary's operations, or particular regulatory constraints. For example, an American company in China faces a macro political risk due to unpredictable government policies as well as micro risks associated with China's inability to enforce intellectual property rights. Country and political risk are influenced by host-country relations with other societies and by a company's activities in other countries. For example, an American company with business interests in Israel may not be welcome in neighboring Arab states, or vice versa; companies doing business in Taiwan often find themselves at a disadvantage in the People's Republic of China because of political tensions between Taiwan and mainland China.

Management and Foreign Relations

Many events that influence country and political risk are beyond a company's control. Other difficulties depend on relationships between its managers and representatives of the host-country government. As discussed later, patterns emerge in these relationships that can moderate risk exposure, but circumstances become more complicated when a multinational corporation operates in many different countries, some potentially at odds with one another. Consequently, managers must establish relationships with a number of foreign constituents and keep themselves well informed about their own government's foreign relations.

This chapter explores differences in political and legal systems among selected countries, and contrasts differences in business systems that influence international management decisions. The chapter also addresses relationships between government and corporate interests, and presents a framework for understanding both country and political risk. Several methods of assessing political risk are compared, and the chapter concludes by presenting some methods that successful companies employ to cope with these risks.

POLITICAL AND LEGAL SYSTEMS

All governments have some role in business through their legal systems and regulatory codes. In some countries government actively intervenes in business interests, while in other countries government maintains a hands-off policy toward private enterprise. This often reflects differences in political ideologies, such as the polar extremes of communist and capitalist societies. But even when nations' ideologies are similar, the extent of government intervention can be significantly different.

In Sweden and Japan, for example, government involvement in business is a virtue. There is no perceived conflict of interest in either country for corporations and government ministries to jointly determine industrial policy, regulate wages rates, or leverage private loans with government funds.[5] In both countries, the state is involved in private enterprise to the extent of influencing strategic decisions and industrial development, yet these are not communist ideologies where government owns or controls the means of production. In contrast, the United States and Canada view government in counterpoint to business interests. Public-sector interests and national security aside, North Americans generally prefer to be insulated against government intervention. These contrasts and other issues concerning government relationships with business will be addressed for selected countries in later sections, but a society's cultural foundations often determine variations in government intervention. The following section introduces culture as a prerequisite to later discussions on contrasting models of government intervention in business.

A Cultural Perspective of Foreign Systems

Culture is the collective value system that evolves from an accumulation of social behavior and historic patterns of beliefs and customs. Cultural values determine how people in a society relate to one another. Although cultural issues are emphasized in later chapters, it is important to stress here that collective human values strongly determine social systems. For example, dictatorial systems survive only when people in those countries are accustomed to authoritarian rule and are willing to accept it. They may find it difficult to accept a democratic form of government, just as Americans would find it difficult to accept an autocracy. An ethnic caste system, such as in India, or a government based on religious fundamentalism, as in Saudi Arabia, would be unacceptable in many other countries. Britain's parliamentary system is not fully understood by Americans, and the venerated position of a monarchy in Japan seems archaic to outsiders.

Several Middle Eastern and Southeast Asian countries have absolute monarchies in which sultans, kings, or other royalty rule the countries. These include, for example, Brunei, Thailand, Oman, Bhutan, Jordan, Saudi Arabia, and the United Arab Emirates. Their governments are molded by traditions of royalty or by religious codes, and substantial control rests with members of ruling classes rather than in constitutional systems. In most instances, these systems fit within the value systems of the people ruled.[6]

Culture also molds expectations for political leadership and government responsibilities in regulating businesses. In Mexico, government authorities are expected to paternalistically control resources and national business systems such as banks, trade unions, and entire industries.[7] In Japan, government is expected to set industrial policy and to regulate industrial development on behalf of the country's general welfare.[8] In Sweden and several other Nordic states, collectivist values permeate expectations, and citizens assume that the responsibilities of government include everyone's welfare. A culture that places little value on individual rights will generally place high value on collective security. The individual is less important than the group, and the group is subservient to government, which in turn embodies the nation as a whole. In Confucian social philosophy, for example, political leaders are the trustees of human welfare.[9] Consequently, in a collectivist society, government initiatives—such as nationally legislated wage rates—are not viewed as inappropriate interventions into business affairs but as responsible initiatives by government to protect people's rights.

Cultural considerations for international management are extremely complex. Foreign politics, social systems, legal systems, and business behavior cannot be explained apart from a country's cultural antecedents. More important, every society differs from all others in its cultural heritage. Significant cultural differences distinguish even apparently quite similar societies, such as the United States and Canada. International managers must therefore accommodate behavior patterns in foreign subsidiaries that often run counter to their personal value systems.

Contrasts between Government Roles in Business Activities

Government systems in five countries are presented here as representative of leading nations with multinational corporations and a history of foreign investment. Japan, Germany, France, the United Kingdom, and the United States hardly represent the full spectrum of western systems, let alone others, yet they provide a basis for understanding several critical differences between leading economies in three major regions.[10]

Japan

Under its postwar constitutional government, Japan has created a parliamentary process. Two major bureaus are specifically designed to guide industrial policy and to regulate business activities: the **Ministry of International Trade and Industry**

(MITI) and the **Ministry of Finance (MOF)**. Both bureaus are headed by senior career civil servants, not elected politicians or appointees. MITI is responsible for overall guidance of Japan's domestic and international industrial development, and the scope of its activities include industrial subsidies, joint regulation of commerce with industrial management groups, and social initiatives for employment, technology, and trade. It has an influential role in decisions relating to foreign assistance, trade treaties, and export-import regulations.

No bureau similar to MITI exists in the United States, or indeed, in most other countries. The Ministry of Finance, however, may be even more powerful than MITI. Japan's MOF is legally responsible for financial management of the nation's central government, monetary reserves, and foreign currency. The ministry also manages Japan's Export-Import Bank and the Japan Development Bank. Consequently, MOF wields extensive control over direct allocations of development and industry funds, loan approvals, and government guarantees. It is, in fact, the economic policy center for the country.

Both MITI and MOF retain policy powers to negotiate with foreign interests, approve foreign investments, determine importation and customs policies, and intervene in industrial disputes. They can influence the formation of business enterprises, and they can sway the behavior of Japan's leading industrialists and financiers through employer organizations and national industry associations convened under their governmental authority. Both MITI and MOF are accustomed to exercising supremacy over politicians. They recognize no direct accountability to Japan's parliament but act as semiautonomous civil bureaus. MITI and MOF senior career officers almost invariably retire in their fifties and serve on the boards of private industrial firms. In some instances they accept appointments to senior company positions, where they fulfill roles as industrial diplomats, acting as liaisons with their former government bureaus. This unusual arrangement further tightens bonds between private companies and the two government bureaus. An American might view this arrangement as a blatant conflict of interest, even collusion, but the Japanese regard it as an essential process of harmonizing national interests.[11]

Germany

The strong parliamentary system in Germany turns out pervasive legislative initiatives that affect business. The authority in this system is eclipsed, however, by powerful associations and cooperative liaisons between top ministries and business leaders. German banks have been characterized as the country's "quarterbacks of all business systems" because they hold positions on government decision-making committees. Through their alliances with national employer associations and industry consortia, banks often maintain substantial equity positions in major German businesses.[12] Indeed, the banks have decision-making influence in almost all major international alliances involving German companies. National industrial unions also wield political power with formal representation on company boards and membership in local and national government associations. German business associations are also well represented on government decision-making bodies. In a very real sense, business is part of government.

The German associations cannot define national policies; but as powerful special interest groups, the banking associations, unions, employer federations, and industry consortia have extraordinary influence on commercial regulation. As in Japan, these groups can directly influence trade policies, in effect guiding national agendas for domestic and international business. Unlike Japan, government is far more decentralized in Germany, where there are no official ministries like MITI and MOF with equivalent power. Foreign companies operating in Germany do not have to deal with similar powerful ministries, but they must be responsive to regional and local governments that have significant authority to control business-related taxes, employment, and commerce.

France

The French government is dominated by a well-respected, relatively autonomous bureaucracy that is characterized as a strange mix of authoritarianism and social democracy. Government is literally charged with "being a reflection of the general will . . . a will that is superior to that of any business or individual interest."[13] This underpinning theme is the basis for socialism, as practiced in France, under a democratically elected government, yet government itself is given exceptional control in what is called the French *l'etat*. This concept is described as "an almost metaphysical notion of a unified authority of society."[14] The bureaucracy is controlled through a select group of well-insulated civil servants called the Grand Corps, under a centralized system of administration headed by the Director du Tresor in the Ministry of Finance. This core group has official control over capital markets, credit allocation, public-enterprise policy, and financial intermediation for private companies. The Grand Corps draws its members exclusively from graduates of the nation's two elite educational institutions, which in turn are exclusive in their selection of students. These are the Ecole Nationale d'Administration and the Polytechnique.

The primary role of France's government in business is described as primarily *faire*—direct state action to regulate, fund, and administer commerce—and its secondary role is *faire faire*—the incitement by government to guide commerce in appropriate ways. The famous doctrine of *laissez faire*—or freedom to act unfettered by government—reflects a general philosophy that people accept only to the extent that business interests serve the "general will," or the best interests, of society. Observers of French policy suggest that the "general will" has been permeated by a desire to keep France "uncontaminated by the world," and toward this end, the state has acted in partnership with business to pursue French interests while shielding them from foreign competition.[15] The French are not isolationist—far from it—but industrial policy and international competition on French soil cannot be explained apart from the Grand Corps and the French bureaucracy.

United Kingdom

The cultural antecedents of Britain and other Anglo societies are distinctly different from those in Japan, Germany, or France. Individualism and the concepts of capitalism, private property, and self-directed enterprise have been deeply rooted in British industrial development. Therefore, government relies on a parliamentary system that wields rather blunt policy instruments to influence the economy. Direct intervention in business affairs occurs, but not in the same fashion as in France, Germany, or Japan. Britain relies on macroeconomic policy tools, such as taxation, monetary controls, fiscal spending, and parliamentary regulations. It lacks the interwoven government and industry associations that exist in Germany or Japan, and it has no equivalent to the French Grand Corps.

With a strong history of labor union involvement in political parties and grassroots social welfare, the country has purposely avoided developing an industrial aristocracy. Its royalty and titled gentry do not necessarily involve themselves in commerce or seek responsibility for public policy. Perhaps the most influential special interest group in Britain is the Trades Union Council (TUC), an instrumental force in the country's Labour Party. The TUC, however, does not participate directly in government or cooperate with industrial associations (as in both Japan and Germany). Instead, the TUC acts as a countervailing force to balance the influence of capitalist and management. Consequently, Britain has an adversarial business environment comprised of working-class interests, capitalist ownership of industry and private enterprise, and representative government. The government tends to favor social programs and general welfare initiatives, but it avoids direct intervention in business.

United States

The U.S. government stays as far away from business interests as possible, and business leaders generally would prefer even greater distance. Domestic and international economic interests are addressed through a disparate group of departments and agencies, including those in Commerce, the State Department, the Treasury, the Department of Agriculture, and through the White House, the office of the U.S. Trade Representative, and offices of Management and Budget. A presidential Council of Economic Advisors combined with a number of congressional committees act almost independently, and often in direct opposition to one another. As a result, the United States has had little success in trying to generate a national industrial policy with coordinated programs of international development.

The United States has no counterpart to Japan's centralized bureaus, to France's Grand Corps or its elite ministries, or to Germany's highly coordinated business-union-banking-government system. Unlike the British systems, the U.S. government has not been substantially influenced by consolidated trade union power, nor by social welfare mandates that would foster nationalized industries. Trade missions, however, often include trade union officials and business executives. Also from time to time, presidential advisors are drawn from private industry, but almost all government intervention in business is concerned with foreign aid and political objectives. Consequently, American business interests have little support by government to collectively compete as a nation or to protect U.S. interests abroad. The United States competes on the sum total of individual initiatives with little direct government guidance or subsidization.

Trade treaties and government initiatives such as NAFTA certainly have major implications for trade and foreign investment, and government influences business through monetary policies, taxation, and fiscal spending, but these are macro considerations. Individual companies must sort out their own business affairs under broad-based umbrella policies. Nevertheless, the U.S. State Department provides extensive business support services, such as country-specific commercial guidelines that provide important tools for assessing political risks, and it maintains perhaps the most extensive commercial advisory services anywhere in the world.[16] U.S. diplomats also will quickly intervene with foreign governments or international organizations like the WTO to protect American trade interests, such as the ongoing disputes over EU sanctions against American exports of genetically enhanced beef.[17]

Implications for International Managers

The structure of a foreign government and its role in commerce determines how a company fits into the social and political fabric of that nation. In Britain and the United States, where government and business interests are more sharply differentiated than in other countries, a multinational enterprise might compete with little regard for formal government relations. In Japan, France, or Germany, however, a multinational company may subordinate its business interests to social priorities, thus becoming a participant in political and social institutions. Alternatively, it may remain aloof and become isolated from the networks that often determine business success or failure. A wholly owned Japanese subsidiary of an American company, for example, would not join in Japan's national industrial development effort unless it could become affiliated in some way with a Japanese organization. Without this affiliation, the U.S. company would lack access to resources, finances, markets, or government support on which domestic companies rely. Even with globally branded products such as IBM or Coca-Cola, managers would find themselves at a competitive disadvantage.

These activities are only marginally less important in Germany, where employer associations, unions, and government ministries work together through strong interconnections. Unlike Japan, Germany has a broader ethnic base and greater regional integration through the European Union. Links to outside societies help non-European multinational companies to operate in Germany and other EU countries, but the fundamental social and cultural characteristics of each country remain intact. Foreign managers cannot automatically bring their companies into the German industrial community or compete with the same government cooperation that domestic competitors receive. France presents greater barriers than Germany, including a rather obvious sense of nationalism that is reinforced by government officials who control commercial and industrial policy. Without proper connections, or some justification for encouragement by the French government, a foreign multinational operates as something of a social and political orphan.

Great Britain's more disaggregated industrial base has prevented the formation of a core government-business network of relationships. Therefore, foreign multinationals feel less pressed to develop sensitive government connections, as they must in Japan or Germany. Without domination by a bureaucratic elite, Britain's government also offers a more open system of international commerce than in France. International managers therefore concern themselves with the legal and regulatory framework of doing business in Britain more than with building network relationships with special interest groups or government officials. The U.S. market poses the fewest problems for foreign multinationals, which can easily invest in the country, compete much like domestic companies, gain access to financial and labor resources with few constraints, and devote little attention to preferential government intervention. If anything, foreign companies will enjoy advantages through support from state or local industrial incentive programs.

Contrasts between these large, well-developed countries illustrate how the structure of government and cultural expectations can influence multinational management. Even sharper contrasts prove more difficult to understand between nations in Africa, Latin America, and Southeast Asia, where practices vary due to a wide diversity in stages of economic development. Many countries have not yet established a **rule of law,** so those currently in power largely determine government's role in business. This situation, called the **rule of man,** often results in frail commercial regulations, unpredictable economic policies, and trade agreements subject to the prerogatives of political leaders.

BUSINESS-GOVERNMENT RELATIONS

International managers must be able to cope with problems such as detrimental policies or political uncertainties inherent in "rule of man" situations. Being prepared to respond to these problems requires a frame of reference—or an appropriate model—for understanding how to manage a company's foreign assets. This section looks more closely at models of business-government relations, examining specific aspects of political risk that a company can face in its foreign operations.

A Framework for Business-Government Relations

Managers gauge political risk according to subjective measures of the likelihood of something going wrong in trade relations or operations of a foreign subsidiary as a result of host-country political, economic, or social circumstances. As described later in the chapter, formal methods of assessing risks can also be applied, but they all begin with a framework for understanding business-government relationships. This framework must reflect the risks associated with four sets of relationships, as summarized in Table 3.1 and described in the following paragraphs.

Host-Government and Organizational Relations

When managers consider political risk, they implicitly think about business in a specific country and relationships with the host government. These relationships may include government investment in the enterprise, government support or incentives for the multinational business, or contractual obligations with the government. Contracts often specify local procurement of government-owned materials or resources. Host governments might also court foreign investment through favorable import-export agreements, negotiated reductions in customs duties, or special tax exemptions. Host government relationships also may be tenuous as political leaders impose regulatory control of foreign subsidiaries or create legal constraints on foreign-owned enterprises.

The most troublesome concerns of multinationals are politically motivated regulations and trade sanctions. Whenever new political leaders come to power, there is a sense of apprehension among foreign multinationals about changes in foreign policy that could threaten their operations. Of course, new political leadership often means

TABLE 3.1

BUSINESS AND GOVERNMENT RELATIONSHIPS—FOUR VIEWPOINTS

Relations Between	Concerns of International Managers
Host government and corporation	Political instability, currency convertibility, danger of government intervention or expropriation, regulations, security, property rights, export-import control, taxes, etc.
Home government and corporation	Home-imposed sanctions, treaty constraints, domestic laws applicable overseas, control over export-import licenses, taxation, currency restrictions, etc.
Home government and host government	Ideological differences to strain relations, embargoes, boycotts, trade treaties, sanctions, licensing, home or host pressure on business for political ends
Host government and other governments	Secondary influences of relations between host and third countries, regional treaties or trade restrictions, re-export of sensitive products, ideological pressures, etc.

new opportunities for international business, such as favorable trade policies or improved commercial regulations. More often than not, new government administrations make changes resulting in both threats and opportunities that require careful assessment by multinational managers, who then implement new plans to reduce potential risks or to benefit from new opportunities. This is a central theme of a later chapter on international business strategy. It is important here to recognize that cordial relationships between host governments and multinationals not only provide a cushion against potential threats, but can also influence political leaders to introduce beneficial changes while avoiding detrimental policies.

It is more common to think of risk in terms of foreign operations located in developing countries, where governments are often unstable and economic policies are uncertain. The sudden jolts to international business relations during the recent Asian crisis attest to this, and the volatility in both Eastern European and Latin American politics emphasize the fragility of many host governments. Political leaders in all nations, however, are capable of foreign policy initiatives that at times can seem almost arbitrary, and in many instances disrupt international business. One common tactic is to impose trade sanctions against other nations. These usually are politically motivated decisions with little concern for business needs. For example, between 1997 and 1999, the U.S. government enforced specific political sanctions or import penalties against 35 nations, affecting nearly $4 trillion in world trade. The Foreign Trade Council, a consortium of 560 leading U.S. companies, expressed alarm to Congress over unilateral restrictions against Indonesia, Burma, China, and Japan. The restrictions were designed to blatantly embarrass foreign powers and coerce them to accept U.S. viewpoints on issues ranging from human rights to democracy. Trade sanctions and excessive duties also were imposed on European goods imported to the United States, in retaliation for EU-imposed bans on U.S. hormone-treated beef food products sold in Europe. Subsequent to the U.S. sanctions in Asia, companies such as Monsanto and Boeing have lost huge foreign government contracts and faced severely declining market share in Asia. Several billion dollars in trade is affected by diplomatic rivalries between the United States and Europe, and these debates are expected to run well into the new century.[18] Regardless of the underpinning ethical issues, imposed sanctions are intervention tactics that embroil multinational managers in diplomatic complications with foreign governments that threaten their ability to compete effectively.[19]

Home-Government Relations with Multinational Companies

All companies are registered in a particular country, usually the home country of origin, and they are legally responsible for complying with commercial codes and laws of that country. In addition, a home country's political agenda often includes rather specific policy guidelines for foreign relations, which may prohibit exports of certain products to protect national security. Multinational corporations cannot ignore preferences of their home-country governments, and they must comply with formal constraints imposed by government on international commerce. These constraints include boycotts, embargoes, trade sanctions, and mandates for particular terms in negotiated foreign trade agreements. The home government also can intervene in business through controls such as import and export licensing, regulation of foreign exchange, rulings on mergers or acquisitions, and investigations of questionable ethical behavior.

Managers must comply with their home-country laws—regardless of other countries in which they operate—but foreign laws take precedence for the corporation's subsidiary activities. Consequently, a company may find itself facing several entirely different and conflicting situations. Compliance with home-country regulations or political mandates may put the corporation in violation of foreign laws, or perhaps increase the risk of foreign political intervention in the firm's overseas operations. These issues are particularly acute for ethical issues involving methods of managing foreign assets and what constitutes legal conduct in commerce. Indeed, the topic of business ethics is so important that Chapter 4 is entirely devoted to addressing ethics and social responsibility in some detail.

Host-Government and Home-Government Relations

Political and diplomatic relations between two countries often determine the relative risk of doing business in one country rather than another. Obviously, good relations reduce risks and encourage trade by private companies, but rapidly changing circumstances can suddenly magnify risks. During the early 1970s, for example, most western companies considered Iran a safe haven in the turbulent Middle East. U.S.–Iranian relations had long remained very stable and friendly, and many American companies had developed significant investments in Iran. In 1979, however, a revolution deposed the Shah of Iran and installed an extremist religious regime. The safe haven was suddenly transformed into a nightmare of anti-western purges. Rioters took American hostages and held them in grim cells for more than a year, several U.S. and European businessmen were killed, and the government confiscated all foreign business assets.

Of course, sudden political changes that alter relationships between home and host governments can also be very beneficial. The collapse of Soviet power and the fall of the Berlin Wall abruptly ended the cold war, thus creating favorable opportunities for international investments and trade in formerly hostile markets. During the brief decade following these events, more than a trillion dollars in new trade and investment has occurred between western companies and the transition economies of Central and Eastern Europe.[20]

Host-Country External Relations

Every foreign government maintains social and economic ties with other countries. These relationships may differ substantially from those between the host and home countries. A multinational must therefore monitor and analyze the host country's external relations. In 1996, for example, a U.S. subsidiary located in Malaysia made metal casings for sale locally and for export. This arrangement seemed innocent enough until UN forces in Bosnia-Herzegovina discovered war materials and mine casings imprinted with the U.S. company's name. Evidently, the Muslim government of Malaysia had purchased materials in Kuala Lumpur and converted them for military use by Muslim defenders of Bosnia. In another example, a U.S. trade mission to China in 1995 discovered that U.S. electronics components exported to that country were finding their way into missile systems sold to Pakistan; strained relations between Pakistan and India led to threats of expulsion against U.S. companies with subsidiaries in India. The Indo-Pakistan conflict has subsequently become more sensitive with both India and Pakistan capable of nuclear weapons, and both with substantial U.S. trade and investment interests. Both countries have threatened U.S. companies with expulsion or sanctions if they have any business with the other. These concerns were among the issues that prompted President Bill Clinton to personally visit India and Pakistan's leaders in March 2000, hoping to defuse the potential for economic and actual warfare in the Asian subcontinent.[21]

Benefits and Liabilities of Multinational Investments

From the viewpoint of a foreign host country, investments by multinational companies provide many benefits, but foreign companies can also generate liabilities for the host nation. International managers must be keenly aware of how their company's presence is perceived in order to understand the risks they face by investing in foreign facilities.

To a host nation, the fundamental benefit of multinational investment is economic growth through new infusions of foreign capital to underwrite subsidiary operations that create jobs and increase taxable income. In studies of more than 160 countries, the United Nations found a high correlation between the rate of foreign capital formation and a country's domestic growth rate. This is not limited to developing countries, but exists in all economies. For example, capital formation in Singapore averages nearly 35 percent per annum from multinational investments, and the United Kingdom relies on foreign infusions for about 12 percent of its annual capital formation. Even in the United States, foreign investment accounts for nearly 7 percent of capital formation. In contrast, 82 countries in the UN study that were unable to sustain substantial growth or suffered declining economies had attracted little or no foreign capital.[22]

In addition to creating new employment opportunities and infusing capital into a foreign economy, multinational enterprises bring with them new technology, actual equipment and processes, and knowledge that enhances human resource capabilities. These benefits have a multiplier effect in less-developed economies of stimulating domestic productivity. A substantial level of multinational interests also has a secondary effect on a nation's infrastructure, such as improved educational systems, roads, power generation systems, water resources, and industrial logistics. Higher levels of domestic income result in a commensurate increase in consumer demand, and enhanced taxable revenues fund vital social welfare programs. Meanwhile, the foreign subsidiary benefits either through profitable operations or local activities that support the parent company's integrated business systems. Consequently, well-founded foreign investment is a win-win situation.

On the downside, foreign activities can be disruptive to host countries. The presence of multinational corporations (MNCs) often threatens indigenous industry or leads to antagonism by host-country competitors, who are unable to match the strength and resources of foreign enterprises.[23] In many instances, local industries simply cannot compete with powerful multinationals. If government has attracted the MNC through economic incentives, local industries may be at a competitive disadvantage engineered by their own government. Indeed, the presence of a major foreign enterprise may preempt local development by indigenous companies. Whether the multinational generates benefits or creates liabilities depends to some degree on why it has invested in the host country. There are three primary reasons for overseas investments, as described next. They are to pursue new resources, develop new markets, or seek cost efficiencies.

Effects of MNC Pursuit of Resources

Companies in search of resources are often involved in oil exploration or mineral extraction in less-developed countries, but many other resources are pursued by multinationals in affluent countries. For example, Ford and GM have major investments in German subsidiaries to gain access to automotive engineering technology. IBM, Intel, and Motorola are among leading companies with subsidiaries in Japan to specifically pursue research and development in semiconductor technology. Japanese companies have similar interests in the United States, often underwriting university research programs or working with American alliances to tap into U.S. innovations. In other instances, companies go abroad to gain access to skilled labor that may be in short supply at home, or they establish offices in international financial centers such as London, Hong Kong, and New York to solidify their positions in world equity markets.

These multinational interests may benefit both the enterprise and the host country, but they can also create difficulties. For example, exported natural resources such as crude oil may enhance host-country income, but they also deplete that country's reserves and pose a long-term threat to sustainable development. A foreign company pursuing research and development (R&D) interests may find that although the host country welcomes its capital contributions, at the same time it resents the company's attempts to gather industrial intelligence. In extreme cases, the foreign company's activities can be viewed as industrial espionage.

Effects of MNC Pursuit of Markets

A company's expansion into a new foreign market may trigger an imbalance at the outset, through increased imports that do not initially generate offsetting benefits of investment, income, or technology for the host country. Unless the multinational forms domestic alliances or invests in foreign subsidiaries, the benefit-cost equation may result in a net outflow for the host country. On one hand, foreign consumers may welcome new goods and services; but on the other hand, they may deplore the currency imbalance that results as profits are repatriated to the multinational's home country. This concern is a pervasive issue in trade negotiations, particularly between Japan and the United States, which seek to limit foreign competition without stifling the benefits of foreign investment. Multinationals therefore feel pulled toward new markets by consumer demand, yet are viewed with apprehension in the host country. In many instances, the imbalances caused by foreign-market expansion prompt governments to enact protectionist regulations or to impose restrictions on profit repatriation.

Effects of MNC Pursuing Cost Efficiencies

The most common reason for global expansion has been to seek cost efficiencies achieved through relatively low labor rates, less expensive material resources, or better leverage of capital assets. Offshore manufacturing or foreign distribution centers are common in developing countries, where affluent countries have shifted operations to low-cost locations. This has been one attraction of cross-border operations between U.S. and Mexican alliances, and although both sides may benefit, relationships can be tenuous. Specifically, low-cost labor may result in new jobs and increased domestic income, but the company's presence may be viewed as exploitative. At home, the shift of operations to offshore facilities can result in domestic job losses that incite labor retaliation or political initiatives to discourage an outflow of domestic capital. Trade restraints on re-importation of foreign-made products by multinationals are not unusual, and currency restrictions can be imposed to cripple repatriation of profits.

Power Politics by MNCs

In any of the foreign investment scenarios just noted, there is potential for conflict that can grow to crisis proportions if the MNC tries to manipulate government or to take advantage of its competitive advantages. While some multinationals may intercede in host-country activities, most try to keep local affairs at a distance. For example, it would be difficult if not impossible for an energy company to move its operations to another country due to resource availability. Therefore, it is likely more beneficial for this type of multinational to focus on building long-term relationships with the country as a whole and avoid involvement in local issues.

In some instances, companies are merely caught up in local events by their sheer size and notoriety. For example, several years ago, IBM was accused of unfair competition and malicious marketing tactics in France. The company became a target of new legislation that redefined "local content" requirements in such a way to selectively exclude IBM products from mainstream French markets.[24] Although IBM has addressed the problem by repositioning itself in Europe with French alliances, the American and French governments continue to disagree over international business issues ranging from competition in Africa to reciprocal business affairs in Paris and New York. Multinational companies never know exactly how they will be affected by American and French bickering, which *The Economist* has described as "squabbling in public like children."[25]

GOVERNMENT INTERVENTION

Governments compete among themselves to attract foreign investment, offering attractive incentives to foreign companies that thrust them into interventionist roles. Their efforts to create domestic commercial environments conducive to multinational interests amount to a direct and positive form of intervention, but as governments expand their commercial activities, they also tend to expand regulatory influence over foreign enterprises. The initial benefits of government-sponsored incentives often evaporate, and foreign subsidiaries may subsequently find themselves in unpleasant circumstances. In extreme cases, some have been expelled from the countries they entered at government invitation.

Intervention is not always a direct and obvious activity. It often builds through subtle regulations and controls that proliferate as a government becomes more bureaucratic. Therefore, analysts can separate intervention into direct attempts to control multinational activities and indirect measures of influencing business decisions through pressure by government agencies. Local intervention initiatives also can have ramifications for a multinational corporation's related operations in other countries. Consequently, a multinational seldom views host-country operations in isolation. More often, a firm's foreign subsidiaries represent *platforms* for supporting a broader range of activities in several different countries.

Global Platforms and Host-Country Intervention

The comparative benefits of locating in one particular country or another are important considerations, but multinational managers rarely make location decisions based on specific comparative advantages. Instead, they are concerned with how foreign subsidiaries fit into the corporation's world network of activities, and in particular, how operations in specific countries can create *global platforms* for industry competition. Michael Porter explained a **global platform** in the following way:

> A country is a desirable global platform in an industry if it provides an environment yielding firms domiciled in that country an advantage in competing globally in that particular industry. . . . An essential element of this definition is that it hinges on success outside the country, and not merely country conditions that allow firms to successfully manage domestic competition.[26]

The concept of a global platform has two particular implications. First, a particular government cannot lure foreign investment solely on the merits of its domestic markets or cost advantages. Instead, it must provide the MNC a place from which to compete effectively within its global industry. Second, the MNC is likely to combine selling goods and services domestically with export sales in other markets where the host country may have competing interests. This overlap can threaten relations between the host-country government and those of neighboring countries. In either situation, a host government's intervention strategies affect more than its own interests, and they sometimes conflict with the intentions of competing nations with similar interests. Such competition between governments can lead to bitter disputes and charges of "beggaring thy neighbor."

Consider the following example. During the early 1980s, the French government set out to overhaul the country's entire telecommunications industry. As part of this effort, it set up a bidding environment with favorable incentives for a joint venture with a foreign telecommunications MNC. The three final bidders included major companies from Sweden, Germany, and the United States. Based on cost and technological capabilities, the obvious choice was the American firm, AT&T. However, the Germans felt that a dominant position for AT&T in France would threaten the entire European market, and they lobbied other nations to pressure France not to consider the American bid. Meanwhile, the French hesitated to accept AT&T's offer on political grounds. The Americans resented Germany's political intervention as well as the French government's political overtones, and in the end, France selected the Swedish bid. This was not the best business option, but an alliance with the Swedish company avoided further political controversy.[27]

The Risks of Direct Intervention

Political risk is most often concerned with the probability that foreign governments will intervene in a multinational's operations. The multinational is specifically concerned with loss of control over host-country activities. This intervention can be extreme, such as outright confiscation of company assets; but more often, it is a subtle form of intervention such as regulatory constraints on material procurement, government controls on licenses, and restrictions on trade permits. At the extreme end of the spectrum, intervention constitutes a direct threat to the company's ownership, its assets, property rights, and perhaps also physical security of employees. At the subtle end of the spectrum, intervention constitutes loss of some control over operational decisions. Figure 3.2 suggests how these forms of intervention occur.

The risk of government intervention becomes more pronounced when government is not stable, and rules and regulations can be arbitrarily changed by politicians. Risks are also high when the economic environment is so unpredictable that significant changes can trigger government intervention. For example, between 1960 and 1979, 22 new governments came to power in Africa, Asia, and the Middle East as existing governments were overthrown or colonial authorities ousted. In Iran, Cuba, Laos, and Vietnam, a total of 1,535 North American and European multinationals had substantially all their foreign assets expropriated. During that same period, the World Bank reported that 76 national governments implemented more than 500 political initiatives against MNCs, resulting in substantial state control over foreign assets.[28] However, since 1979, there have been relatively few incidents of expropriation or outright confiscation. New international laws and the transparency of world news coverage have helped to deter flagrant seizure of business assets, but government seizures still threaten multinational companies, as described in the following paragraphs.

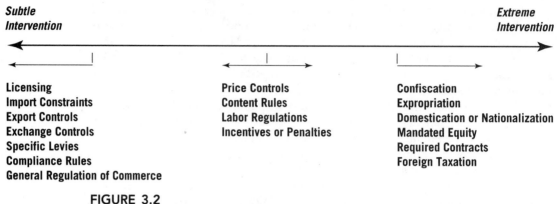

FIGURE 3.2
A Spectrum of Intervention

Confiscation

Outright confiscation occurs when a government simply takes over a company's assets and expels foreign managers. Confiscation may follow a war, coup, or a change in ideology that prompts a sudden edict to obliterate foreign interests from the country. It may be directed at all foreign assets, such as when Burma's military leaders literally closed its borders after World War II, or it may be directed at specific nationalities, such as Cuba's unilateral expulsion of American firms and seizure of their holdings after Fidel Castro came to power. The company loses everything in confiscation, and in many cases the expatriate managers are not always able to escape unharmed. There is no negotiation, no effort by government to reimburse the company for its losses, and no apology.

Expropriation

A government can appear to confiscate a foreign-owned property, and the effect is the same; but **expropriation** has a specific meaning in international law. The expropriated company has the right to fair compensation from the host government for its losses, and in most instances, the takeover is not hostile. There is no presumption of physical threat to property or life, but it is a unilateral mandate of government to nationalize ownership of the company or the industry in which an MNC operates. Expropriation can lead to unpleasant conflicts, but governments usually attempt to negotiate the ownership transfer, and in many instances, the company may retain partial minority ownership. Fair compensation is part of sanctioned expropriation, although payment may never be fully realized.

Expropriation always carries the risk that a company will lose its entire foreign asset base, but this is much different than outright confiscation. The mining industry in Bolivia, forestry in Brazil, electric utilities and banking industries in Argentina, Mexico, Turkey, and Zimbabwe were nationalized, thereby ousting foreign interests. In nearly every instance, government expropriation resulted from a sense of *ethnona-tional* security rather than political upheaval. The threat of expropriation, however, is greater when there is an ideological shift toward socialization of private enterprise.[29]

Domestication

A less severe form of expropriation normally occurs in nationalization policies. Britain's post–World War II government imposed ownership controls over its auto industry and major petrochemical holdings by becoming jointly involved with management and asset ownership. Unlike expropriation, the concept of domestication commingles public and private rights. The United States has followed a similar model through public regulatory agencies and government investment programs for public utilities such as the Tennessee Valley Authority. U.S. port facilities are often an extension of local or federal authority, and tax-supported housing and urban development programs are funded and managed much like quasipublic companies. The United States has no record of expropriation or domestication of foreign enterprises, but the government has exerted financial and management controls through regulation of industries such as mining, commercial air transport, financial intermediation, securities markets, and telecommunications. Some of these have been recently deregulated (e.g., those affecting telecommunications and air transport); yet from a multinational perspective, these regulatory systems have the same effect as excluding foreign ownership—except in rare instances when foreign-owned enterprises are involved in a majority-owned American alliance.

Legal and Regulatory Intervention

Regulation in its purest sense is direct government intervention to control a company's operations without holding direct investment in the company. Management of the company presumably remains in private hands, but this is not always the case. For example, Japan's National Development Bank emerged from the postwar redevelopment period as a private subsidiary of Mitsui Corporation, yet government funds were allocated to the bank for development loans. The Japanese government subsequently exercised authority over bank loan activities, effectively guiding the bank's primary investment strategies. This form of intervention occurs as a regulatory activity in Britain, Germany, Sweden, and many Southeast Asian societies such as Singapore and Malaysia, but it is rare in North America. However, even if government has no stake in the business enterprise, it can exert tremendous pressure on management decisions through regulatory controls described in the following paragraphs.[30]

Exchange Controls

Governments levy specific quotas, taxes, importation rules, and penalties on certain products or companies in an effort to protect domestic industries. France has had a history of severe restrictions on Japanese consumer electronics, such as microwave ovens, VCRs, and audio systems. Japan is notorious for restricting automotive components and parts, and although contrary to popular belief, car imports are not severely restricted. Japan effectively protects its industry by stifling imported parts and components. The United States has been relatively successful in protecting the computer industry by listing all foreign-made computers as *strategic materials*. A strategic material under U.S. customs classifications can be almost anything vital to the economy, so by defining computers as strategic, the United States could conceivably eliminate imported computer systems. In any event, stiff quotas and import duties are imposed to protect American industries.

Content Controls

Governments mandate **local-content rules** requiring that certain percentages of parts, costs, or manufacture of finished products be attributed to the host country. The percentages are usually based on a formula of the total value-added costs (material, capital, and labor) that comprise the finished product. Therefore, for a product to qualify as being "made in the USA" or "made in Japan," it must conform to U.S. or Japanese content rules for that type of product. For example, an automobile currently assembled in France must have more than 50 percent of all parts and components, including labor contribution, of French origin. A car that meets the content rules will be considered "domestic" and exempt from import regulations or tariffs. A car that cannot meet the specifications will be subject to foreign import restrictions and duties.

Content rules are continually being revised and renegotiated through trade treaties, domestic commercial regulations, and regional commercial codes such as those under consideration by the EU and NAFTA. Content rules also apply to specific products or services, such as individual models of automobiles, and to categories of products, such as home appliances. Consequently, "made in" any country can have a wide variety of meanings, and it is not always clear how imported components or raw materials are classified for their country of origin. A subtle change in content definitions can have serious implications. For example, in Mexico no foreign company can employ more than 20 percent non-Mexican workers.[31] This is a form of "local content" that addresses a political priority of social employment protection. In Sweden, labor unions (which are almost universally extensions of government) have centralized agreements for using members only in production of automotive, aerospace, pharmaceutical, and electronics products. Union membership, however, is governed by residency requirements, and this effectively excludes foreign workers. Consequently, Sweden is able to control labor content and reinforce its political agenda of social welfare.[32]

Price Controls

Nearly every country exercises some form of price control over critical goods and services. Food, health care, social services, domestic materials, forestry products, port utilization, airline fares, and many other products and services have some degree of pricing control. International companies often face blatant price discrimination with differentially higher prices for products that are purchased locally. Governments are able to justify differentials on nationalistic grounds, and they reinforce their regulatory controls through popular appeals. This is interesting because a country like China can attract foreign investment through incentives, but then regain advantages for domestic industries—either by mandating price premiums for domestic resources purchased by foreign companies or by subsidizing domestic companies, thereby giving them a cost advantage. In China, a foreigner is legally charged a premium for everything from a local taxi fare to electric utilities. When a foreign company is mandated to buy local materials (usually through a state-owned procurement system), there is no effort to hide the premium. In fact, premiums are often publicized, and price controls are commonly used as political weapons or negotiation levers. Governments can also limit prices charged for products or services, and therefore control marketing and profitability.[33]

Risks from Chance—The Uncertainty Factor

Wars, revolutions, paralyzing national strikes, disruptive social movements, and many other events threaten a company's foreign operations. Michael Porter identified these as **chance factors** that affect a company's ability to compete. He included chance economic factors, unpredictable natural disasters, and unforeseen technological developments that could act for or against an international enterprise.[34] These are partially captured in the concept of *country risk* defined earlier, and home governments try to monitor foreign events in order to advise their multinational companies of potential problems.

During the past several years, political terrorism has become a major concern. Some acts of terrorism have been almost random, such as aircraft bombings and indiscriminate shootings at airports, public markets, and sporting events; but for the most part, terrorists have targeted foreign companies and business executives where they can ransom their captives for money, arms, or actions (such as the release of imprisoned terrorists or political prisoners). Today extortion and terrorist activities affecting multinationals are most prevalent in Latin America, somewhat less pronounced in Europe and the Middle East, and relatively minor in Asia and Africa; yet it seems that no country is free from terrorism.[35] Kidnapping and extortion have become the primary risks that concern foreigners—particularly high-profile expatriates and their families, who have become targets of political extremists.

Terrorism clearly is exacerbated in areas of political instability as well as in countries, such as Colombia, where drug-related violence is not effectively policed. Often, these situations are beyond the control of host governments or the multinational corporations, but as described later, companies do have ways to protect their people and foreign assets. With that said, few companies have seriously prepared their overseas managers for terrorist threats. The hostage crisis in Peru, for example, illustrates the relative naiveté of companies about terrorist activities. A Peruvian paramilitary group took 72 Japanese expatriates hostage on December 17, 1996. The group raided the Japanese ambassador's residence following an embassy party where more than 600 international dignitaries had been guests earlier that evening. The guerrillas were selective in taking hostage key Japanese executives while avoiding diplomats and

Taxi drivers in New York and Chicago face some risky situations with late-night fares, but nothing on the scale of danger in many Latin countries. In Nicaragua, muggings, robberies, drug-related violence, and terrorist attacks on foreigners who risk hiring a cab have forced taxi drivers to arm themselves. The latest weapon of choice is a handheld mortar that cabbies can use to stop almost anything short of an armored tank.

high-profile foreigners from other major countries where retaliatory action might be invited. The Japanese and their families were held as ransom for the release of hundreds of imprisoned guerillas, and it was not until well into 1997 that Peruvian commandos tunneled into the residence and freed the hostages.[36] Spokesmen from Toshiba, Hitachi, and several other firms with managers being held hostage admitted at the time that they were unprepared for these situations. Meanwhile, the Japanese Foreign Office in Tokyo initiated corporate training programs to prepare managers for potential terrorist activities in foreign assignments. Since this incident, 27 countries, including the United States, have revised foreign policy procedures in an effort to improve protection for expatriates from terrorist activities.[37]

POLITICAL RISK ASSESSMENT

Assessing political risk may be one of the oldest fields of international studies. Statesmen, military strategists, and merchants have tried to assess political risk since scattered tribes of people first coalesced into trading communities, but these efforts have always relied on intuition more than on scientific inquiry. These evaluations have always focused on a question implied by the earlier definition of *political risk:* What are the possibilities of losses (of whatever kind) as a result of political, economic, or social circumstances in a foreign environment? The answer usually contrasts one country with another: Country A is more risky than Country B but less so than Country C. Also, because it is concerned with what might happen, the answer involves extensive guesswork.[38]

The issues examined earlier for government relations and country risk provide a framework for assessing political risk, yet there are more specific factors to consider for every company with foreign assets. Consequently there are many different profiles of political risk, and although there is no ideal model for assessing risks, multinationals tend to rely on one or more of three main approaches. These are described as intuitive, advisory, and analytical methods of political risk assessment.

The Intuitive Approach

Whether a company applies formal, sophisticated means of assessment or relies entirely on individual judgments, managers ultimately rate the risk of doing business abroad based on their personal perceptions. Conditions that seem risky to one person may represent an opportunity for another. One viewpoint may prompt managers to react with caution to conditions that incite others to rush headlong into new markets. Risk is a subjective measure of expectations. Consequently, many companies rely on the judgments and opinions of senior executives to rate political risk. A common practice today is to engage in some form of structured dialogue among company executives and their foreign managers. Companies may also rely on outside consultants to formulate organizational profiles of potential risks. Such a dialogue raises the categorical questions of risk described earlier, including concerns for political stability, government intervention, regulatory controls, home- and host-country relations, currency factors, labor issues, economic policies, and technological factors. Other concerns may include ideological considerations, social and cultural profiles, and evidence of terrorist activities.

With so many issues to consider, a company often begins with executive brainstorming to identify risk factors most important to the company. The process then continues to evaluate those risks for specific markets. This analysis may result in a

GLOBAL VIEWPOINT

COMMERCIAL TERRORISM—THE NEW PRIORITY

As developing countries expand their business sectors and income gaps widen, commerce-related crimes and violence increase. In many of the developing world's major cities, criminal acts have created a special form of international terrorism in which disenfranchised individuals and groups target the beneficiaries of development and those who have been instrumental in generating growth. Of course, not all of these countries have erupted in violence, but during the past five years, Buenos Aires, the Argentine capital, has seen a tenfold increase in kidnappings, a threefold increase in muggings, and a doubling of extortion schemes. Half of the victims of those crimes have been wealthy Argentines, a third have been foreign business executives or their families, and many others have been highly visible foreign visitors.

Similar problems have plagued other growing economies in cities such as Santiago, Lima, Mexico City, Jakarta, and Manila. Other Latin American countries, such as Colombia, must contend with drug-related kidnapping and extortion plots. The Middle East adds yet another dimension to this activity, with zealous religious fundamentalists using terrorist tactics to press for money, arms, or freedom for imprisoned comrades. In addition, unexplained attacks, bombings, and other terrorist activities have targeted embassies, government buildings, or busy subway stations throughout the world.

International managers are easy targets for many of these crimes. Perpetrators see foreigners backed by companies with deep pockets and pragmatic reasons to bend to their demands and avoid publicity. Of course, random terrorism does not necessarily target foreigners or businesspeople, and drug traffickers and religious and ethnic groups fight their own brands of limited warfare without much regard for foreign business interests. Nevertheless, foreign residents, many of them international managers, face desperate situations in many areas of the world.

More than 800 kidnappings took place in Mexico during 1999, and although this number was down slightly from previous years, muggings in Mexico City increased by one-third in 1999 over 1998, which also had been up by nearly 50 percent from prior years. In both types of crimes, nearly eight out of ten victims were businesspeople and their families, and roughly half were foreigners. Most of the victims suffered attacks in their cars while traveling between work or school and home, and criminals tracked a few to social or recreational events.

Foreigners cannot lock themselves away, and their routine activities put them at risk on the home turf of local extremists. However, multinationals have not sat by and idly waited for local law enforcement agencies to protect their people. Expensive armored cars find a lively market in Mexico, and Executive Armoring Corporation in San Antonio has rushed to convert enough Mercedes models to meet Mexican demand. Services of U.S.-based security companies are also in high demand. For example, Pinkerton Business Risks International has a standing contract to protect U.S. State Department personnel in overseas assignments with services such as security training, personal bodyguard protection, electronics securities measures, and safe transport routing. Kroll Associates, a Virginia-based company, specializes in executive training and risk-intervention intelligence. The Kroll company also has a worldwide telecommunications network to intercept corporate distress issues or to detect overseas dangers. In moments, Kroll personnel can be dispatched to intercede in crisis situations.

Vance International, another Virginia security firm, contracts with multinationals to provide door-to-door protection for expatriate staff and their families, often escorting children to school in high-risk areas such as Mexico City or Moscow. Vance specialists take charge of traveling executives arriving at the Mexico City airport, meeting them with preplanned itineraries, chauffeuring them in armored cars, handpicking restaurants, arranging hotels and 24-hour security service, advising guests on appropriate behavior, and supplying bodyguards and surveillance for meetings and conferences.

Hoping to bring commercial terrorism under control, Mexican authorities themselves have established a special law enforcement group under the command of a military general. In Argentina, special squads of trained agents are assigned to protect high-profile companies and executives. With drug-related terrorism becoming much more pronounced in Latin America, the U.S. government has joined with Latin governments to establish international anti-terrorist forces and drug enforcement squads. These paramilitary organizations can mount raids and engage in combat, but they also provide extensive training and advisory services to high-profile business leaders, politicians, and visitors to Latin countries such as Colombia.

The problem is just beginning to emerge in Central and Eastern Europe, as rapid expansion of foreign alliances has led to internal power struggles and development of organized crime groups in major cities. The real danger to foreign executives in these situations became apparent when a sniper gunned down American entrepreneur Paul Tatum in Moscow in November 1996. Tatum, a native of Oklahoma, was among the first western businessmen to enter Russia during Mikhail Gorbachev's reform era. He was shot while leaving the luxurious Radisson Hotel, a gem of western engineering and the result of his dream to build a flagship facility to launch a world-class hospitality industry in Moscow. Since this incident more than 300 persons in Moscow have been killed by bombings, often blamed on Chechnyan rebels—though many are the result of attacks on foreign commercial centers. Unfortunately, the Tatum killing is only one of several thousand professional killings of

prominent people in Moscow during the past several years. At least 560 of those were recorded as contract assassinations, many targeting Russian executives with western business alliances.

Commercial terrorism results in selective acts aimed squarely at business interests. The extraordinary growth of trade and international alliances guarantees that risks will continue and expand for foreign and domestic managers in strategic positions. Multinational managers, however, can do much to help themselves and their employees with the cooperation of special security companies and the U.S. State Department's Overseas Security Advisory Council, which is specifically responsible for providing information and measures to help prevent terrorism against American commercial interests abroad.

Sources: Mel Mandell, "Avoiding Overseas Crises: Nothing Beats Being Prepared," *World Trade*, October 1999, 44–45; "The Assault on Democratic Society in Colombia," *The Economist*, 18 March 2000; Erin Arvedlund, "Murder in Moscow," *Fortune*, 3 March 1997, 129–134; Mel Mandell, "Safer Traveling," *World Trade*, December 1999, 48–51; and Elizabeth Malkin, "Bang! Bang! Welcome to Mexico," *Business Week*, 14 October 1996, p. 56.

---

simple conclusion that a country is too risky for trade or foreign investment, or it may separate several countries into those considered good opportunities and others considered poor opportunities. In considering new markets or choices for entry modes (e.g., export offices, joint ventures, or more substantial investments such as wholly owned subsidiaries), multinational corporations tend to rank candidate nations through risk-preference strategies that match types of foreign investment strategies with management perceptions of acceptable levels of risk exposure.[39]

As part of the decision-making process, companies such as General Electric, Xerox, Chase Manhattan Bank, Exxon, and IBM, to name a few, assign letter grades or rank scores to each country in which they operate.[40] Each year, the companies grade their foreign activities as well as potential foreign markets in categories of low-to-high risk exposure. For example, in a given year, GE may rate Britain and Canada as equally low risks in the "A" category, while rating Japan and Germany as slightly higher risks in the "B" category, and Colombia and Zaire as unacceptable risks in the "Z" category. Each year, the company's dialogue will result in a reconfiguration of country rankings. Currency difficulties in Japan or strained trade negotiations may drop the country to a "C" category; unemployment in Germany may reduce its rating; economic development in Chile may raise its ranking. GE and other multinationals annually assess more than 150 countries and territories.[41]

Although most companies rely on some form of internal fact-finding process, the process of **intuitive risk assessment** has several limitations. First, although foreign managers are the best source of local information, they rarely understand the company's operations beyond their own activities. When a company evaluates risk, it must not only form a broad concept of how individual operations fit into the firm's global platform for business but also address risks of a particular country. Second, local managers tend to be well informed about operating priorities, but they can seldom provide full information about political and economic affairs. Third, local managers often have vested interests in their host-country activities that prompt them to accentuate good news while avoiding pessimistic issues. Companies such as Exxon protect against these biases by supplementing the opinions of overseas managers with assessments of risks compiled by internal planning staff, who evaluate regional circumstances and the corporation's global network of activities. Independent assessments from corporate planning staff and local managers are then reconciled by an executive committee for a more comprehensive picture of the company's risk exposure.[42] These methods often require extensive analytical work to supplement intuition, yet country rankings still boil down to executive judgments about where to compete and how much risk exposure to accept.

The Advisory Approach

Few multinational corporations rely entirely on intuitive methods to assess risk. Instead, they also employ **advisory risk assessment.** Most turn to published risk-rating services, consulting reports, and government advisory services that provide a tremendous amount of data on foreign affairs. The U.S. State Department, for example, publishes a *country guide* for nearly every nation and territory in the world. These are updated regularly and supplemented by monthly "advisories" distributed through embassies and foreign office commercial sections. The State Department and several other U.S. agencies provide statistical indexes on economic development and analyses of social and political events. Except in special periodic reports, countries are not rank-ordered for political risk; therefore, multinational corporations must interpret the research in applying it to their own use.

The Overseas Private Investment Corporation (OPIC) also provides advisory services to U.S. businesses, and the Foreign Credit Insurance Association (FCIA) publishes risk-adjusted country trade and investment profiles. OPIC and FCIA provide fee-based services, but they also offer publicly accessible data related to foreign trade. Both organizations are concerned with underwriting U.S. business contracts or providing insurance for companies operating abroad, so their information is often focused on financial criteria such as currency transfers, payment records, banking, investment profiles, and transaction risks.[43]

Companies can avoid the difficulties of interpreting government data by subscribing to risk advisory services or contracting consultants for specific reports tailored to the company's needs. One of the largest data services is provided by *Euromoney*, which regularly publishes an index of Country Risk Ratings based on six primary criteria. The criteria include analytical indicators of economic performance and country political risk, and debt indicators that score each country on national debt, default records, credit ratings, and access to international finance. The result is a *Euromoney* numerical rank-order list of approximately 170 countries and territories. The lowest possible risk (a perfect score) would earn a country 100 points, and the highest possible risk would result in a score of 0. No country has scored perfectly, but the United States, Switzerland, Luxembourg, Singapore, and the Netherlands consistently fall in the top 10, with ratings that exceed 95 on the 0-to-100 scale. At the other extreme, Cuba, Iraq, North Korea, and Somalia consistently hug the lower limits, each scoring under 20 points. The relative risk ratings change each month and can be tracked over time to illustrate trends. For example, when a country like Chile moves steadily up the scale, or a country like Mexico makes huge upturns and then equally drastic plunges in its ratings, companies can learn a great deal more about foreign opportunities than by considering an absolute rating determined at one point in time.[44] Strictly speaking, the *Euromoney* index is an analytical tool, but it is offered as an advisory publication and used primarily for trend analysis.

The Economist also publishes country ratings through its "International Country Risk Guide," which is based on regional studies by its global research units.[45] In addition, the Organization for Economic Cooperation and Development (OECD) and the World Bank periodically publish reports on selected countries and regional development trends. Public agencies and private consulting organizations also publish regional studies, such as the "Latin American Special Reports," the "ASEAN Annual Guide to Trade," and the Asia-Pacific Institute "Studies of Risk-Adjusted Foreign Investments." Companies can contract for private reports prepared specifically for their own purposes through PriceWaterhouseCooper, Accenture (formerly Andersen Consulting), Political Risk Services, Chase Econometrics, and Dataquest, among others. Most of these services measure political risk in similar economic and financial terms, but their methods differ substantially. Some rely on a few variables and expert respondents to rate risks, while others generate econometric models on as many as 200 variables.[46]

The Analytical Approach

Advisory services base their reports on sophisticated **analytical risk assessment** techniques, but many global companies generate their own systems for analyzing political risk. These proprietary studies reflect a company's efforts to quantify information generated through in-house fact-finding methods. For example, GE has created a weighted index of factors that decision makers use in conjunction with reports from the firm's own foreign managers to generate a numerical score for political risk in each of the company's international activities. As noted earlier, Exxon uses several panels of experts and its managers to generate priority lists of political risk factors; it then rates countries on these criteria through survey techniques to develop composite probability tables for country risk throughout the world. Most companies do not create their own forecasting models, but contract with companies such as DRI and Dataquest to prepare these studies and advise them on the global effects of specific industry trends.

Studies of political risk-forecasting methods have not been able to conclude which approach provides consistently superior results. Consequently, there is little credibility in the field for any particular means of assessing political risk.[47] With that said, researchers at the American Graduate School of International Business and the American University joined forces to make a direct comparison of three mainstream assessment techniques. These are reviewed next, according to the organizations that created them: *The Economist, Business Environment Risk Intelligence,* and *Political Risk Services.*[48]

The Economist Approach

The system created by *The Economist* ranks a country's risk based on a 100-point scale in which a high score indicates high risk. This study evaluates risk in three broad categories, assigning points to each based on specific variable scores. The first category, "Economic Variables," can contribute a maximum of 33 points based on the values of six variables. The second category, "Political Variables," adds a maximum of 50 points

TABLE 3.2

THE ECONOMIST APPROACH TO RISK ANALYSIS

Three categories of economic, political, and social risk include a total of 16 variables scored by experts. A high score indicates a high risk, with a maximum of 100 possible points. Each variable carries different weights. Suggested variables in each category are briefly described below by *The Economist*.

Economic Variables (total 33 points)
1. *Falling GDP per Person*—declining growth or economic stagnation
2. *High Inflation*—erosion of buying power and standard of living
3. *Capital Flight*—outflow of capital resources required to development
4. *High and Rising Foreign Debt*—increased reliance on foreign assistance
5. *Decline in Food Production*—deterioration of fundamental human welfare
6. *Raw Materials as a Percent of Exports*—depletion of non-renewable assets

Political Variables (total 50 points)
1. *Bad Neighbors*—regional tensions, immediate threats to nation or its people
2. *Authoritarianism*—lack of democracy or totalitarian form of governance
3. *Staleness*—complacency in governance, detached leadership
4. *Illegitimacy*—an imposed governance versus uncoerced acceptance
5. *Generals in Power*—instability of civil authority and lack of legal institutions
6. *War/Armed Insurrection*—risk of war, civil unrest, presence of internal tension

Social Variables (total 17 points)
1. *Urbanization Pace*—too rapid, chaotic, danger of crime and loss of control
2. *Islamic Fundamentalism*—religious fervor lacking in other religions, threat to foreigners
3. *Corruption*—uncontrolled corruption that distorts the economy or social stability
4. *Ethnic Tension*—social tensions that convolute society and polarize communities

Sources: Adapted from "Countries in Trouble," *The Economist*, 20 December 1986, pp. 25–28, and from Llewellyn D. Howell and Brad Chaddick, "Models of Political Risk for Foreign Investment and Trade: An Assessment of Three Approaches," *Columbia Journal of World Business* 29, no. 3 (1994): 70–83.

based on six more variables. The third, "Social Variables," can contribute a maximum of 17 points through scores on four variables. The model is relatively simple to use, and observers like the practicality of the variables, as summarized in Table 3.2.

In using the model, a company would query a panel of experts on a particular country and assign risk values to each variable in each of the three categories. *The Economist* recommends maximum risk scores for each variable and a justification for each item. For example, one of the easiest variables to explain is "Inflation," whereby the actual rate of change in consumer prices is observed for a country. If panel members find inflation to be excessively high, they would assign a risk score of four or five points (zero would imply no risk and low inflation). Under the category of political factors, the variable "War/Armed Insurrection" is considered the most serious threat and carries a maximum of 20 points. Consequently, a country at war or struggling under a tenuous cease-fire agreement, such as Bosnia-Herzegovina, would justify a full 20-point risk rating; while Switzerland, which has been free of civil strife and remained neutral during devastating world wars, would rate the minimum, near zero. For a third example, the variable "Corruption" in the "Social Variables" category has a maximum risk rating of 6. An extremely corrupt society would rate either 5 or 6 points in this category, and an ethically clean society would be rated near zero. *The Economist* justifies corruption as a risk factor because of distortion in economic or business activities that result from bribery, black-market questions, or unethical politicians.

Scores can change substantially, depending on when the panel does its assessment. In addition, risk profiles can be generated for a number of countries to provide comparative ratings. Researchers who evaluated the model tested data for a sample of 36 countries and correlated scores with events in those countries during a five-year period. They found that the model generally reflected information most often required for decisions relating to foreign investments, but the researchers expressed concern about potential controversies associated with several variables. For instance, the model treats the variable "Authoritarianism" as a negative indicator for political stability (e.g., it assumes that a more authoritarian government would achieve less stability). Critics note that history does not entirely support this assumption. Several well-established monarchies have prevailed for generations in the Middle East and Southeast Asia with few difficulties. Therefore, it could be argued that many cultures find authoritarianism beneficial to their economic development. Consistent interpretations therefore require careful justification and a consensus about what the ratings mean.

Business Environmental Risk Intelligence (BERI) Model

The BERI assessment is called the *Political Risk Index (PRI)*, and it is based on a composite score from ratings by global experts on 10 variables. Between 70 and 100 experts are queried on each of the 10 variables in three categories. The PRI is clearly focused on political issues, yet it includes some information on social issues. The information and rating index is provided to subscribers in a confidential report that can include additional advisory services or consultant recommendations. A brief summary of the 10 variables is shown in Table 3.3.

When the PRI was introduced in 1978, it rated 48 selected countries on four continents, and it was specifically directed to help U.S. multinationals assess risks of loss due to political or government activities. Today, an expanded PRI includes data for approximately 100 countries, and it is marketed to clients in North America and Europe. The PRI is based on an assigned score between 0 (maximum risk) and 7 (no risk) for each of 10 variables. This generates a scale between 0 and 70 points. But unlike *The Economist* model, which associates high values with high risks, the PRI correlates high values with low risks. The PRI also allows respondents to assign bonus points to eight variables (excluding the "symptoms" issues), allowing a total bonus-adjusted index to reach as high as 100 points for a given country.

PRI assessments are provided as proprietary information to subscribers who need to analyze current conditions or generate 5- and 10-year business forecasts. BERI also provides a detailed description of forecasted conditions with justifications for its ratings, so that clients can impute their own meanings to the risk ratings. The company also suggests ranges of results as guidelines for relative risks. A country that scores between 70 and 100 points offers a very stable, low-risk environment for foreign investment. A country that scores between 55 and 69 points appears moderately risky, with some difficulties in daily business operations and questionable government stability. A country scoring between 40 and 54 would be a relatively high risk, and a score of 39 or below would represent an unacceptable environment for foreign investment.

Researchers who compared these systems found that the PRI was marginally better than *The Economist* model for predicting losses, yet there was not a huge difference in the reliability of the two methods.[49] The strength of the PRI is that it focuses intensely on a few political factors and relies on a carefully selected group of experts who

TABLE 3.3

COMPONENTS AND RATINGS FOR THE POLITICAL RISK INDEX (PRI)

The PRI is a proprietary assessment model of Business Environmental Risk Intelligence, a company that provides client forecasts of foreign business risks. The index is based on 10 criteria in three categories, each criterion having a maximum rating of 7 points. Bonus points can be awarded as indicated for a maximum rating of 100 points, indicating the least degree of risk; riskier countries will be rated with low score totals.

Internal Causes of Political Risk (7 points each, maximum 42 points)
  1. Fractionalization of the political spectrum and the power of these factions
  2. Fractionalization by language, ethnic and/or religious groups and the power of these factions
  3. Restrictive (coercive) measures required to retain power
  4. Mentality—xenophobia, nationalism, corruption, nepotism, or willingness to compromise
  5. Social conditions, including population density and wealth distribution
  6. Organization and strength of forces for a radical left government

External Causes of Political Risk (7 points each, maximum 14 points)
  7. Dependence on and/or importance to hostile major power
  8. Negative influences of regional political forces

Symptoms of Political Risk (7 points each, maximum 14 points)
  9. Societal conflict involving demonstrations, strikes, and street violence
  10. Instability as perceived by non-constitutional changes, assassinations, and guerrilla wars

Total raw score maximum 70 points. Bonus points can be awarded to any criterion 1–8 for a maximum total rating score of 100 points.

Source: Adapted from Llewellyn D. Howell and Brad Chaddick, "Models of Political Risk for Foreign Investment and Trade: An Assessment of Three Approaches," *Columbia Journal of World Business* 29, no. 3 (1994): 70–81.

can consistently apply the same criteria in their judgments. The weakness of the PRI is that it does not address broader social and cultural issues, and it does not include economic or financial data that could be important for investment decisions.

Political Risk Services Index (PRS)

The PRS assessment provides a proprietary report to corporate subscribers with expert commentary about the countries studied.[50] It is based on *probabilities* of losses due to political risk, rather than an absolute scaled index as used in other models. PRS provides 18-month and 5-year political risk forecasts for as many as 100 countries. A corporate subscriber would also receive a monthly report tailored for that company's industry. The PRS index is based on evaluations from more than 250 specialists in the United States and abroad who are selected from diverse backgrounds in academic, business, and government positions. The final index reflects probabilities of loss classified into 12 categories, described in Table 3.4.

The 12 categories of risk represent "risk attributes" that are derived from more detailed variables on each item. Therefore, the PRS is a very complicated forecasting model that brings together expert opinions from a large number of respondents on lists of issues, which are then factored into the categories and assigned probabilities

TABLE 3.4

INDICATORS AND RATING SYSTEM IN THE POLITICAL RISK SERVICES (PRS) INDEX

The PRS is a proprietary assessment service that rates foreign business risk for a current (18-month) period, 5-year period, or 10-year period. The 12 indicators are scored separately to generate probabilities for each criterion and a total forecast of the probability of a major loss by a foreign business for the forecast period.

1. *Political Turmoil Probability*—civil strife or political or social activities in opposition to law or accepted social norms
2. *Equity Restrictions*—imposition of investment regulations, forced equity holdings or intervention by government
3. *Personnel/Procurement Interference*—government intervention to restrict hiring and procurement with respect to the foreign company, ethnic groups, or other special interests
4. *Taxation Discrimination*—preferential taxes, or premiums, that are not subject to formal adjudication processes or to constituted commercial codes
5. *Repatriation Restrictions*—restrictions on currency flows and convertibility of funds, either to restrict profit repatriation or to control financial accountability to host country
6. *Exchange Controls*—intervention to limit transaction management of currencies or assets
7. *Tariff Imposition*—new or unanticipated tariffs that affect trade or create add-on costs
8. *Non-Tariff Barrier Imposition*—restrictions that affect physical movement or transactions for products, components, or services
9. *Payment Delays*—inability to collect or to enforce payment on activities and obligations
10. *Fiscal/Monetary Expansion*—distorting effects of monetary or fiscal policies that disrupt business or affect currency stability, markets, costs, and operations
11. *Labor Cost Expansion*—intervention that results in expanded labor costs, higher-cost local utilization, or distortions in labor relations and benefits
12. *International Borrowing Liability*—requirements for attracting or using international debt or preferred underwriting as directed by host-country political interests

Source: Adapted from William D. Coplin and Michael K. O'Leary, *Introduction to Political Risk Analysis* (Croton-on-Hudson, N.Y.: Policy Studies Associates, 1983), 40–41, and Llewellyn D. Howell and Brad Chaddick, "Models of Political Risk for Foreign Investment and Trade: An Assessment of Three Approaches," *Columbia Journal of World Business* 29, no. 3 (1994): 70–81.

based on statistical forecasting techniques. The model also projects probable changes in future governments and potential influence from political factions. Probabilities associated with individual variables include arguments for factors that are most influential for calculating high or low ratings, and descriptions that accompany reports provide managers with guidelines for adjusting their risk estimates. Although the results are often highly speculative, the PRS index provides a consolidated projection for each country.

Comparative research on the three models suggests that the PRS model outperforms the BERI and *The Economist* models, but it shares drawbacks with these and other analytical models.[51] Specifically, none of the models effectively addresses cultural differences, ethnic or race considerations, or religious dimensions that would affect investment decisions. Consequently, an Israeli company attempting to use one of these models may face entirely different risk criteria than a U.S. company when considering foreign expansion in the Middle East or Southeast Asia. Likewise, a Japanese company may find that it faces a different set of risk criteria than an American or European firm when investing in a western country. Quantitative analyses also imply "objective" rigor when, in fact, the studies reflect only panel opinions. They may be very good, but they are still subjective evaluations. Statistical analysis of the results of such surveys does not automatically provide better results than intuitive judgments. An additional drawback is that analytical methods generally orient their risk assessments toward specific countries, yet global companies often pay more attention to comprehensive pictures of their interrelated foreign activities. Particular investments or location decisions in any one country may exert little influence within a worldwide scope of operations. Still, a combination of the intuitive and analytical approaches coupled with access to outside advisory services constitutes the best available technique for political risk analysis.

MANAGING POLITICAL RISK

Few companies make a simple yes/no decision about foreign investments. Of course, if a multinational has the luxury of choosing to invest in a risky country or walking away, the decision may be to avoid the risk and invest elsewhere. In most instances, international managers face more complicated situations. For example, if the nature of risk suggests that a foreign government could expropriate assets, the situation is much different than risk associated with currency fluctuations. Therefore, two countries with a similar high-risk rating may be quite different in terms of the nature of risk-related losses.

Risk management is concerned with choosing an appropriate mode of entry to a foreign market, or determining the appropriate level of investment in foreign operations. Alternative modes of entry and investment strategies are addressed thoroughly in Chapter 6 as strategic decisions, but in general, an enterprise has a wide variety of choices for its foreign activities. For example, expanding into new foreign markets by contracting sales through a foreign agent (an export management contract) may be preferable to establishing a joint venture or taking ownership of a wholly owned foreign subsidiary. The question of risk management is more acute for an established foreign operation. A company may suddenly face host-country difficulties that increase risks and prompt new decisions about staying there, downsizing, or withdrawing. Unlike the choice between making an initial entry or avoiding a country (a no-cost decision), decisions regarding existing foreign assets will always have significant costs.

In addition, a global company must decide how a particular foreign activity will affect its worldwide network of activities. A specific foreign operation may represent a crucial link in the organizational chain of activities, so even extremely high risk may not deter the company from investing there. This dilemma is faced by oil exploration companies that often have significant assets in the Middle East, Southeast Asia, South America, and risky offshore locations. Companies such as Exxon, Texaco, Shell Oil, and British Petroleum must maintain their presence in many different environments, regardless of the risk involved in any one location. The issue is not simply whether to do business in a particular country, but how to reduce the overall risks facing a company. Risk management, therefore, focuses less on whether to do business in a particular country than on how to reduce unavoidable risks of doing business overseas. International companies manage risk through two general approaches, known as *defensive strategies* and *integrative strategies*.[52] Figure 3.3 contrasts these strategies.

Defensive Strategies for Risk Management

A **defensive risk-management strategy** is an intentional effort to minimize a company's dependence on a host country. If a foreign operation can be easily relocated, the firm faces the minimum threat of losing control in a specific location. If it can purchase materials elsewhere or rely on a wide range of markets, the multinational avoids becoming hostage to one channel of supply for needed resources or one high-profile customer base. If the company can spread its financial resources, it can insulate itself against currency problems or direct intervention by a single foreign government.

FIGURE 3.3
Defensive and Integrative
Strategies of Managing Political
Risk

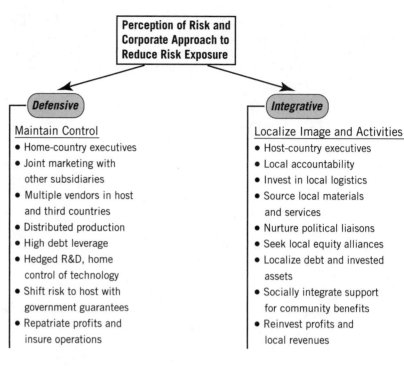

Perception of Risk and
Corporate Approach to
Reduce Risk Exposure

Defensive

Maintain Control
- Home-country executives
- Joint marketing with
  other subsidiaries
- Multiple vendors in host
  and third countries
- Distributed production
- High debt leverage
- Hedged R&D, home
  control of technology
- Shift risk to host with
  government guarantees
- Repatriate profits and
  insure operations

Integrative

Localize Image and Activities
- Host-country executives
- Local accountability
- Invest in local logistics
- Source local materials
  and services
- Nurture political liaisons
- Seek local equity alliances
- Localize debt and invested
  assets
- Socially integrate support
  for community benefits
- Reinvest profits and
  local revenues

Also, limiting financial or market exposure prevents undue risk of loss from unexpected problems such as war or terrorism. The important factor is the *degree of control* that a multinational can maintain to avoid being victimized by circumstances. The following paragraphs summarize several specific defensive considerations, each with its own relative benefits for different types of risk.[53]

Management Concerns

To ensure effective management, a firm might maintain home-country control over strategic management positions in the foreign subsidiary and minimize local management involvement in executive decisions. This precaution ensures decision-making control by the parent company. As the same time, the company would train its lower-level managers in its operational systems to improve continuity of activities in the host country and among interrelated foreign activities.

Marketing Considerations

The parent company could maintain control over local marketing activities, perhaps through joint marketing with other subsidiaries. As a corollary for manufacturing, it might establish joint production systems for parts or components. These measures reduce the risk associated with local intervention such as imposed price controls, import-export quotas, procurement restrictions, regulatory constraints, or, in extreme situations, expropriation. If the company can also control its distribution and transport systems, it can insulate itself somewhat against disruptions such as strikes or civil strife. Perhaps the best protection is to establish strong global trademarks and an organizational image that cannot be arbitrarily replicated. IBM's worldwide recognition prevents others from selling knockoff products under similar names. For similar reasons, companies with branded software products, such as Microsoft and Lotus, aggressively protect copyrights, logos, and trademarks to maintain marketing control.[54]

Operational Controls

Control over host-country operations can be held tightly by managing foreign activities with expatriates through the parent company's home offices, or by taking complete control through a wholly owned subsidiary. For years, IBM refused to enter a country without first establishing operational control through a wholly owned subsidiary. In less risky environments, a company may exert less direct control by staffing subsidiary operations with local host-country managers, or by forming joint ventures with shared management responsibilities. Foreign alliances are more common today, and most companies, including IBM, prefer some measure of shared management in foreign operations.[55] Coca-Cola did not have operations in India until 1993, and then only when it was able to acquire India's largest soft-drink company, Parle Exports. This capped nearly two decades of negotiations with Indian government authorities, yet Coke would not enter India without effective operational controls in a country that was perceived to have unacceptable political risks.[56]

Many multinationals hedge the risk of disruptions to production by replicating operations in several countries. For example, Sony manufactures identical parts for its modular telephones in Malaysia, Indonesia, Mexico, Japan, and the United States.[57] By spreading the risks, Sony accepts the cost of making some components in high-cost environments such as Japan and the United States, but it moderates those costs by sourcing a high percentage of those components from low-cost countries. The components themselves may be shipped to Japan, the United States, Britain, or Germany for assembly. Consequently, Sony reduces its overall average production costs by accepting an increased risk of distributed manufacturing. It also reduces the risk that events in any one country will cripple its total production system. The same strategy can be applied to external logistics; by sourcing materials from multiple suppliers, a company can reduce the threat of disruptions to particular input streams. Also, by maintaining R&D in its home country (or concentrating it in another low-risk environment), a company can maintain control over foreign process technology. Thus, a distributed system of activities often ensures that each foreign activity plays only a limited role in the total production process, reducing the risk of host-country intervention.

Financial Factors

By reducing a company's equity investment, management can reduce the risk of financial loss due to foreign intervention or unexpected changes in host- and home-country relations. This can be accomplished by maximizing the debt component of capital expansion, so that any detrimental effects of intervention will by felt by creditors more than by investors. As a further precaution, the company can secure debt financing in the host country (directly or through loan guarantees), placing the host country government in the position of protecting the multinational's interests as a way of protecting its own assets or those of local creditors. Regardless of whether a company is structured primarily through debt or equity, it can reduce the risk of financial loss through a portfolio of financial resources. Management should pursue multiple channels of finance from local banks, government, local customers, suppliers, and perhaps international development agencies.

In their operational arrangements, managers can reduce financial risk by creating multilateral ventures or consortia with companies from other nations. For example, the AsiaSat communications satellite system involves companies from the United States, Canada, Britain, Hong Kong, Japan, and Sweden, and the consortium has subscriber investments from China and six Southeast Asian nations. The relative risk exposure of each party is small, and the risk of political or regulatory intervention by any of the constituent interests is minimal.[58] Most multinationals also try to minimize local retained earnings; put another way, they try to quickly repatriate profits or set up transfer costing systems to extract excess cash holdings. Finally, they secure loan guarantees, government securities, or purchase risk insurance from organizations such as OPIC to reduce financial losses that occur through currency fluctuations, defaults, and foreign-exchange constraints.

Integrative Strategies for Risk Management

The ultimate objective of an **integrative risk-management strategy** is to transform the foreign activity into a local enterprise. It may still be recognized as part of a foreign company, or perhaps have very close ties with a global organization, but the nature of its operations, staffing, investment, and image is that of a local firm. This is accomplished through a variety of methods, as summarized in the following paragraphs.[59]

Management Concerns

Transforming foreign activities into local enterprises requires a multinational to employ and train host-country managers. When at all possible, the central office delegates local operational control entirely to host-country executives. In many instances, local managers are trained at the parent-company headquarters, and their career opportunities extend to higher-level regional posts or home-office appointments. To complement this profile, the parent company takes extra care to train expatriates in the host-country cultures where they will work. For example, Coca-Cola Company's China operations are co-directed by an expatriate and a Chinese manager, and the company hires more than 100 employees every week. All operational managers and key staff members are Chinese, and Coke spends more than $2 million annually on management training, including a special training facility in Shanghai that offers resident instructional programs to subsidiary managers and newly hired employees.[60]

Operational Considerations

Integrative risk management leads a company to pursue marketing, production, and logistics initiatives that often contradict those appropriate for a defensive strategy. Such moves emphasize local sourcing of materials and procurement of supplies, parts, components, and services rather than outsourcing through other foreign activities. In many instances, multinationals contract to buy resources through government procurement systems, enhancing their political connections as well as providing inflows of revenues to their host countries. These decisions increase a firm's dependency on local suppliers and labor sources, but they also decrease the risk of government intervention or restrictive regulations that would endanger the foreign enterprise. Indeed, the multinational may gain substantially from reciprocal benefits such as tax incentives and government subsidies or perhaps even from *supportive* intervention by the host government.

Many companies pursue host-country alliances for local and export distribution systems, thus blending parent-company and host-country financial interests. These arrangements can be rather simple, such as contractual agreements for export marketing. They can also be more substantial, such as joint ventures and locally registered, publicly listed subsidiaries. In many instances, governments also invest in these activities, giving every party to the enterprises a compatible stake in their success. Whether a company is wholly owned by the parent or involves significant local participation, managers can solidify its image as a local enterprise by actively working with local suppliers or downstream wholesalers and retailers.

Financial Considerations

An integrative risk-management strategy implies a conscious effort to raise equity capital locally and to share profits fairly with local investors. This effort also implies that the company reinvests a substantial portion of the subsidiary's profits in local development rather than repatriating them. These decisions provide investment opportunities to local constituents, either privately or through public stock listings, and multinationals commonly try to secure local debt capital. Unlike the blatant defensive strategy of shifting risk to creditors, the integrative company builds an identity as a source of profitable business opportunities to local creditors. Nevertheless, local debt and equity financing also offer a defensive benefit regardless of the motive, and these measures reduce the risk of adverse government intervention.

Because the integrative company favors reinvesting and expanding with local profits, it is less likely than a defensive company to create systems that extract cash and profits. In other words, transfer-pricing policies among its foreign subsidiaries seek to ensure equitable levels of profits in all foreign subsidiaries. This arrangement helps to cement relations with the host government, which benefits from added taxable revenues, enhancing the credibility of the foreign enterprise.

Government Relations

While a defensive strategy would encourage a company to maintain a distance from the host government, an integrative strategy suggests a proactive effort to develop strong government relationships. The company's managers actively cultivate ties with the political elite, but they must carefully avoid an image of political manipulation. This can be accomplished through nonpolitical activities, such as corporate support for social development programs in health, education, transportation, or housing.

The multinational's activities must be acceptable without subversive undertones, and sometimes this is difficult to achieve. For example, Honeywell helped to establish housing for Mexican workers at its twin-border plant in northern Mexico, and the company also provided food benefit programs for families of workers. Unfortunately, local politicians felt embarrassed by this "big brother" spending, because neither local industries nor the government itself could provide similar benefits. They pressured Honeywell to make broader contributions by providing the government with funding support that would be redistributed through political channels. Honeywell objected to payments made to any government agency, and in retribution, found itself entangled with both labor unions and politicians.[61]

Implementing a Risk-Management Strategy

A multinational seldom chooses between purely defensive and strictly integrative strategies to manage political risk. Each foreign environment requires independent consideration that takes into account many factors beyond political risk. As noted at the outset of the chapter, some country risks stand apart from political risk, and political risk scenarios fail to fully account for cultural and social distinctions. Consequently, even if a country has a low-risk rating, a multinational may not choose to pursue an integrative strategy where cultural integration would be difficult to achieve. Indeed, the host country may not welcome such an approach.

A defensive risk-management posture suggests a degree of isolationism, and a globally integrated company may not be able to implement this strategy in light of its worldwide network of operations. It may accept risks only as part of its industry structure, pursuing selective risk management that combines certain aspects of integration and certain actions that could be deemed defensive to make the best of the situations it finds. Whether a firm chooses one strategy or the other for a specific country, it may follow a different course of action in another location. These choices must also account for risk preferences of parent-company managers, and corporate executives often have very different philosophies about managing foreign activities.

CONCLUDING COMMENTS

In conclusion, multinational managers can seldom make distinct choices between pure risk-management strategy models. This is particularly true if the companies have already established foreign activities and become involved in local initiatives from which they cannot easily retreat if circumstances change. These facts make political risk forecasting even more important, because it helps a company to be forewarned of as many contingencies as possible. As a general rule, multinationals try to configure foreign activities to preserve as many options as possible without sacrificing the benefits of foreign business activities. As this chapter closes, it is important to note that these decisions cannot be made in isolation from the social responsibilities faced by multinational corporations. Managers must weigh their decisions within an ethical framework for business behavior, which involves important topics that are addressed in the next chapter.

REVIEW QUESTIONS

1. Identify the macro and micro issues concerned with country risk and political risk. How do the concepts of country risk and political risk differ?
2. How does culture influence a country's political and legal systems? Contrast two familiar governmental systems, and discuss how culture may have influenced their development.
3. How do major societies perceive business roles, and what effect do these perceptions have on a multinational operating abroad?
4. Describe several of the primary considerations in a company's relations with a host-country government.
5. How does a firm's home-country government influence multinational activities?
6. Describe the concept of a global platform and how it influences international management decisions about the relative risk of doing business abroad.
7. Identify the principal risks associated with direct intervention in business by foreign governments.

8. What are the major risks associated with government regulatory intervention?
9. Briefly describe the major ways in which companies assess political risk. What major issues do most assessment techniques address?
10. Describe the two general approaches by which multinationals manage political risk, and explain three principal methods by which each approach reduces risk.

GLOSSARY OF KEY TERMS

Advisory risk assessment   The use of published risk ratings, consulting reports, government advisory services, or contracted consulting services to assess risks of foreign operations or investments.

Analytical risk assessment   Formal methods of evaluating political risks, often using statistical methods to track changes in foreign nations based on objective information such as economic indicators supplemented by expert opinions on political and social factors that could affect a company.

Chance factors   Unpredictable economic or natural disasters, unforeseen technological developments, disruptive social events, wars, revolutions, and terrorism that could affect a company's ability to compete.

Country risk   The uncertainty associated with government continuity; national or regional politics; legal, regulatory, and monetary systems; and chance circumstances in a foreign country.

Defensive risk-management strategy   An intentional effort by a multinational to avoid undue dependence on a host country, to minimize risks of consolidated markets or production facilities, and to insulate the firm against financial losses.

Exchange control   A government-imposed tax, rule, quota, or penalty that restricts foreign activities in a host country.

Expropriation   One form of intervention in which a government takes over a foreign company's assets and operations in exchange for appropriate compensation and with a legal transition in ownership.

Global platform   The concept of a firm's operations in a country as part of a base for regional or international activities within a global network of multinational interests.

Integrative risk-management strategy   A proactive effort to transform a multinational's foreign subsidiary into a local enterprise with close ties and interdependent operations within the host country.

Intuitive risk assessment   The process through which executives evaluate threats to foreign business activities based on in-house judgment or management opinions.

Local-content rule   A government requirement that defines domestic products as those that include a certain minimum percentage of value (costs, materials, labor, or other measurable resources) from local sources, exempting them from restrictions on nonqualified foreign-made products.

Ministry of Finance (MOF)   In the Japanese context, the senior government ministry responsible for financial management, banking, currency reserves, foreign exchange, and economic policy.

Ministry of International Trade and Industry (MITI)   A major government bureau in Japan with extensive influence in domestic and international trade, industrial policy, and industrial development.

Political risk   Uncertainty associated with commercial interests, currency transactions, political instability, government intervention, and unforeseen events that could lead to losses for a company doing business in a foreign country.

Rule of law   Government based on accountability of a nation's leaders to constitutional and statutory laws that prevail over individual prerogatives or succession privileges.

Rule of man   Government at the sufferance of individual rulers whose successional prerogatives prevail over constitutional legislative bodies, if any exist.

EXERCISES

1. Research the rapid growth of China and the continuing concern about politics and international relations between its government and those of western nations. How would you

assess the political risk of doing business in China? Describe the major issues confronting a foreign multinational doing business there, and briefly contrast arguments and information recently published about doing business in China.

2. Terrorism has become a major concern for international managers and their families. Explain how this risk affects efforts to do business in a relatively stable, industrialized environment and in a relatively unstable environment within a developing foreign nation. Defend your suggestions from your home-country perspective.

3. Briefly list home-country initiatives that influence the business activities of foreign enterprises in your own country. Interview a foreign manager in your home-country environment about government policies and activities that affect the company's business decisions. Does the foreign manager consider this country a high risk? Is this government viewed as one that intervenes in business decisions?

BEN & JERRY'S MELTDOWN IN MOSCOW

Ben & Jerry's, the upscale American ice-cream maker, built a plant in Russia in 1992—only to pull out in early 1997, citing the "impossibility of managing" its assets under current conditions. The venture was not the first foreign expansion for the Vermont ice-cream maker. Ben & Jerry's has formed profitable alliances with franchised names and licensing in a dozen European locations and several Latin countries. It also has made investments in rain-forest countries such as Brazil, where the company has been active in conservation activities through purchasing contracts for harvested nuts and other natural ingredients used in special-flavored frozen desserts. The company encountered an entirely new experience, however, with the Russian plant in Karelia, a developing area near the Finnish border northwest of Moscow. By some accounts it was highly successful; by others it was a disaster.

Ben & Jerry's rode the wave of free-market expansion into Russia. Working for a company noted for its social awareness, its managers openly preached market economics and democracy; but the plant was motivated not only by missionary zeal. To the contrary, Ben & Jerry's fully expected to make a substantial profit by serving an area where demand for ice cream is among the highest in the world. People there annually consume nearly 350,000 tons of ice cream, produced through antiquated technology and sold by limited vendors. The company also received a major development grant from the U.S. Agency for International Development (USAID) in 1994 to effect a significant transfer of American technology and to develop a distribution system for northwestern Russia. Planners envisioned a prototype of American ingenuity. Ben & Jerry's facility was underwritten by company assets in partnership with a Russian firm. The new venture, called Iceverk, created an exceptionally well appointed factory, introduced American management techniques, and established accounting and control systems. Ben & Jerry's spent slightly more than $700,000 of the $850,000 USAID grant before pulling up roots, but U.S. officials said the company had successfully implemented the systems and project services called for in the grant.

What went wrong is still not entirely known. The Russians perceive Ben & Jerry's management as running out on them after failing to cope with the reality of local customs and market problems. From Ben & Jerry's viewpoint, the company made a rational business decision to get out of an unprofitable venture and cut cash-flow losses. Unofficial reports from USAID describe Ben & Jerry's managers in part as victims of the environment itself and in part as unprepared for the risks of a Russian investment. They point out that Ben & Jerry's was one of 11 American-Russian partnerships that received a total of $20 million in grants under an agribusiness partnership program including several other successful ice-cream and frozen-dessert ventures. In 1996, for example, Baskin-Robbins completed a $30 million factory outside Moscow, and Mars and Nestlé have bought into existing local ice-cream factories. However, these multinationals have built up experience under fire, selling many other products in many challenging locations throughout the world. Indeed, they may not do any better than Ben & Jerry's in Russia, but the demise of Iceverk illustrates the demands of working in an unfamiliar society.

At the project's inception, Ben & Jerry's invested more than $500,000 to renovate an existing facility and bring in equipment. The company carried 70 percent of the total financial package and transferred managers to run the new operation. Demand started off briskly, and the Iceverk venture opened American-style "scoop shops" in Moscow and regional cities. By 1995, sales were approximately $750,000, and the company expected substantial growth in 1996. Ben & Jerry's seemed like an overwhelming marketing success, with Muscovites lining up under the familiar cow logo to buy whimsical flavors such as "Chunky Monkey" and "Cherry Garcia." The catchy American-sounding terms for brands with cult-like followings rapidly spread to other outlet stores. However, Iceverk's managers—Americans and local Russians—knew that success depended on the intricacies of the Russian distribution system. They were also up against currency problems, troubles with government controls, and bureaucratic glitches. They had their hands full.

Russia still lacks a developed wholesale-distribution system capable of delivering products to stores on time, consistently, and in good condition. To ensure quality, Ben & Jerry's and other companies had to create a soup-to-nuts distribution system, buying trucks and training staff at stores that sell their products. Managers worked through USAID contacts and networked with other American entrepreneurs to sort through the difficulties. They found themselves wrestling with an underground system of payoffs in which only graft would get materials delivered. More often, they had to resolve official problems such as high rents on shipments of equipment coming in through customs offices. Factory equipment could be delayed for months, and Russian customs officials would charge unusually high storage fees while taking their time in releasing shipments to the importing companies. Without payoffs, materials often disappeared into the Russian black market. To hire employees, the firms had to find friends with "connections," who put forward their own candidates for the best positions. Shipments required special licenses from minor government clerks, who felt obliged to charge special fees for the privileges. The local and regional host-government agencies controlled access to facilities, telephone lines, licenses and permits, and cargo invoicing systems. The central government's multitiered regulations governed standards for inspecting goods as well as shipping, packaging, and storing products, and tax schemes provided neither clarity nor controlled, predictable demands. Repatriation of income and currency transactions passed through several different banks, and Ben & Jerry's, for example, had to deal with both commercial foreign-exchange banks and domestic agricultural banks, often without knowing who had authority for payments, currency clearances, or foreign-exchange accounting.

Simple problems began to plague Iceverk, and Ben & Jerry's managers felt as if they were floundering when the USAID grant arrived to help underwrite transition costs. The venture was never completely able to resolve problems with ice-cream shipments melting and then refreezing before reaching their final destinations. The Ben & Jerry's formulas are very sensitive to freeze-thaw cycles, and the desserts break down under careless handling. Often the shipments had to be thrown out on their arrival. Regulations and common cost efficiencies required local production of Ben & Jerry's products, but the quality of milk, flavorings, and other ingredients were seldom consistent or equal to the blends familiar from Vermont. Ben & Jerry's managers also discovered that few of the 10 stores they had opened in Moscow or the more far-flung franchises on the Black Sea resort coastline had adequate freezers, and power outages sometimes disrupted services. The operation also needed a good freezer truck, but equally important was an adequate highway over which to transport the company's products.

Ben & Jerry's venture was certainly not the victim of unusual problems, but small issues apparently compounded to the point that management decided to opt out of the Russian market. In early 1997, Ben & Jerry's literally gave away all of the 70 percent investment it had made in Russia to the minority host partner, simply abandoning the factory and technology and returning home to Vermont. However, an interesting observation in Moscow described Russian consumers as intensely concerned with "buying things Russian," and the early fascination with American brands such as Ben & Jerry's socially conscious ice-cream products, supported by claims of environmental sensitivity, were no longer appreciated. Nestlé, for example, purposely created a Russian chocolate brand with traditional flavoring, and even McDonald's revised its menus to serve burgers, chicken entrees, and side dishes with traditional Russian flavors and ingredients.

After Ben & Jerry's withdrew from Russia, Iceverks reconstituted most of the ice-cream flavors, changed packaging, and closed down the scoop shops. The Russian firm continues to sell ice cream in familiar ways, but it produces the products with efficient American technology. Meanwhile, Ben & Jerry's learned important lessons about their limitations as an international organization capable of managing foreign markets. The company began searching for an alliance with a seasoned multinational company that could provide international management experience and the ability to integrate Ben & Jerry's wide-ranging foreign interests. In April 2000, the Anglo-Dutch company Unilever acquired Ben & Jerry's, adding the $240 million ice-cream company to its global portfolio of brands such as Breyers All Natural, Good Humor, Popsicle, and Klondike ice cream products. Unilever, a $45 billion company with 225,000 employees and markets in 88 countries, will keep Ben & Jerry's company intact as a self-managed U.S. division. However, Ben & Jerry's loosely organized foreign markets and distribution outlets will become part of Unilever's international marketing networks.

QUESTIONS

1. Describe the types of risks that Ben & Jerry's faced in the Russian market. In your opinion, was the venture a good idea?
2. What role did culture play in the difficulties encountered by Ben & Jerry's Russian venture?
3. How might Ben & Jerry's managers have responded differently to the commercial, social, and regulatory problems that they encountered? Could they have succeeded eventually, or did they make the right decision in leaving?
4. What risks might be reduced or eliminated when Ben & Jerry's products become part of Unilever's globally integrated market system?

BIBLIOGRAPHY

Ben & Jerry's Homemade, Inc., corporate website <www.benjerry.com>, News Release and Financial Information Summary sites [cited 12 April 2000].

Banerjee, Neela. "Ben & Jerry's Is Trying to Smooth Out Distribution in Russia as It Expands." *Wall Street Journal*, 19 September 1995, p. A18.

McKay, Betsy. "In Russia, West No Longer Means Best: Consumers Shift to Home-Grown Goods." *Wall Street Journal*, 9 December 1996, p. A12.

Rao, Sujata, and Jeremy Weinberg. "Ben & Jerry's Bids a Bittersweet Farewell." *Moscow Times*, 13 February 1997, p. 1.

Vitullo-Martin, Julia. "Manager's Journal: Moscow Entrepreneurs Seize Golden Opportunity." *Wall Street Journal*, 20 January 1997, p. A14.

CASE 3.2

"CLICKS AND MORTAR"—B2B REDEFINES GLOBAL COMMERCE

In 1994 Glen Meakem, then a young technician employed at General Electric, met with the company's senior planners to propose a new project. He suggested that GE create a "business-to-business" (B2B) procurement system based on Internet auctions among suppliers hoping to land contracts with the company. At the time, the Internet was in its formative years; e-mail was just beginning to be used by a few novices, and the concept of "e-commerce" was unknown. General Electric seldom gets things wrong, but in this instance the company entirely missed the boat. The GE brass chuckled when Meakem boldly announced that business-to-business would "transform the global economy." No one is laughing now.

Meakem left GE soon after his proposal was rejected, set up his own B2B home office, and became one of the pioneers of e-commerce. Barely five years after he incorporated *FreeMarkets Inc.*, Meakem's company reached a market cap of more than $7 billion, and Meakem became one of the first megamillionaires of the Internet world. The company's first-quarter 2000 portfolio included nearly 4,000 registered suppliers from 67 countries, 37 client-buyers from the *Fortune 500*, and at least 2,000 buyers from medium and smaller companies. Major accounts included General Motors, United Technologies, Raytheon, Quaker Oats, Navistar, and Owens Corning, together with public buyers such as the State of Pennsylvania. Each of these reported savings between 15 percent and 43 percent on conventional purchasing through FreeMarkets' auctions, with products ranging from cardboard packaging to sophisticated semiconductor circuitry.

Meakem's FreeMarkets was among the first (perhaps *the* first) successful enterprises in the B2B Internet market, but the company is no longer alone. No one counts how many such companies exist, because their numbers change almost as rapidly as stock prices on the Dow ticker. But several front-running entrepreneurial ventures like FreeMarkets are poised to quickly become billion-dollar businesses, and several very large "old economy" companies are setting up their own B2B network systems. For example, in early 2000 GM announced that it would soon leave FreeMarkets as a client and establish its own 30,000-supplier internal network for procurement. Soon after, Ford and DaimlerChrysler announced they would partner with GM for a global automotive supply system. Corning Glass—long associated with glass pots and dishes as a rust-belt company—now has more than half its corporate assets in new IT supply systems as a client-based B2B provider. Many of the large B2B networks are focused within specific industries. Steel has *e-steel* and *MetalSite*, and the plastics industry has *PlasticsNet.com*. In Europe, the Virgin Group (Virgin Air, Virgin Records, Virgin Travel, and 17 other similar divisions) now has the largest e-commerce site in the EU, appropriately called *VirginOnline*. International alliances for auction purchasing have now attracted some surprising players. For example, Sears and the giant French retailer Carrefour have launched a retailer's network, emulating the automotive industry's model.

The world market for B2B commerce is being called the "auction economy," and it is projected to top $5 trillion for industrial parts and supplies before the year 2010. By early 2000, sales by B2B auction were just over $3 billion—a pittance in the near-term scheme of things—yet five years earlier, barely $10 million in parts and supplies were sold through Web resources.

Everyone is fascinated by the "dot.com" revolution, and virtually every securities exchange and business publication follows the companies involved in this phenomenon. The headline heroes and heroines of this segment of the new economy are those young entrepreneurs in the fields of on-line entertainment, games, home retailing, and services such as travel and sports commentary. However, the combined market for these activities is unlikely to be one-tenth that of industrial purchasing. More important for investors, fields such as on-line retailing and entertainment are not yet predictable; most have serious problems, such as the Internet's inability to offer video entertainment or realistic sports coverage. In contrast, there is a known market and extremely high demand for industry goods. Consider that by the end of 2000, Emerson Electric had nearly one-fifth of its $1 billion procurement budget for MRO products sourced through on-

line auctions, and United Technologies sought to place its entire $14 billion procurement orders on the Web. MRO (maintenance, repair, and operations) requirements are among the least glamorous aspects of the business. They include everything from office pencils to toilet paper and factory needs such as sandpaper and lubricating oil.

MRO and the vast range of business equipment required for daily operations accounts for $1 trillion in annual sales between U.S. supply companies and client organizations, which explains the current success of B2B auction sites. However, production equipment (such as machinery and tools), and process materials (such as steel, plastics, circuit boards, chips, and construction materials) exceed $3 trillion annually. On a global scale, these figures are tenfold and growing. This is where the B2B market is headed, and it is where major companies are investing their capital assets. It is also where venture capitalists are underwriting the largest proportion of new start-up companies. The entrepreneurs involved are not in the glamorous limelight of Internet growth, yet they are attracting not only the bulk of new venture capital but also the so-called old-economy corporate partners, who are anxious to invest in small companies with platforms capable of global supply sourcing and worldwide client procurement contracts. For example, consider *EqualFooting.com*, a Virginia-based B2B industrial supplier launched in November 1999 with four individual partners and four employees in rented warehouse facilities. The company had no sales until early 2000; yet by August the company had 146 employees, $50 million underwriting, pending deals of more than $200 million, and a projected market cap by early 2001 of $1 billion. EqualFooting attracted more than 300 suppliers with 7,000 different product items, supplied from nine countries in its first three months of operation. This generated sales of $10 million before employees had desks to work from. The company quickly found itself in a bidding contest among corporations such as Germany's Deutsch Bank and U.S. Textronics, which were offering huge investment packages to EqualFooting for a minority interest in a B2B platform. At latest count, Wall Street and a London investment house are now in the contest.

The implications for global development by companies like FreeMarket, EqualFooting, and their industrial counterparts have been called seismic. Indeed, the industry is so new to global commerce that no one knows quite what to expect. One who criticized the French government's proposal to "regulate control of the Internet in Europe," quipped that such a notion defies reality in a world where "bricks and mortar" are being replaced by "clicks and mortar—with the mortar quickly turning to dust." Clearly, the ability to conduct instantaneous business electronically with no time or space limitations will change the fundamental nature of all commerce. The B2B industry promises to be the catalyst of this change that will require commensurate financial transaction networks, integrated logistics networks, and a new generation of international managers and technicians capable of creating and controlling these systems.

The B2B epic will also require an entirely new international legal system for addressing the complexities of these borderless networks. In that regard, the French government certainly was on the mark when it raised the issue of regulation. At the moment, there is tremendous apprehension about how governments might intervene in B2B electronic commerce—and consequently, what risks might arise from government efforts to tax transactions, impose quotas or duties on cross-border transactions, control content of on-line transmissions or databases, and protect their own industries from devastating competition. Meanwhile, governments have few ideas how to pursue any of these initiatives, or how multilateral government alliances could be established to form an effective regulatory body.

These points are illustrated by two questions, both yet unanswered, commonly asked of companies like FreeMarkets and EqualFooting. Client buyers ask, "If we buy, how do we know what we bought will be delivered, and if it's not delivered, what legal recourse do we have?" Client suppliers ask, "If we sell, how do we know we will be paid, and if we are not paid, how do we collect?" In the bricks-and-mortar world, buyers have physical delivery systems, pay on (or after) delivery, and have clear legal recourse under their own court systems or through regulatory agencies empowered to enforce commercial contracts. Suppliers have a national home base with well-articulated commercial laws governing sales transactions, logistics, trade, and collection procedures. However, an e-commerce company may be located almost anywhere that a communications center can be established, and registered in almost any country. Yet it can do business throughout the world, often with buyers or suppliers in countries where commercial codes are nonexistent. To complicate matters further, in many countries there is no certain way to document hard facts of a transaction, to trace electronic currency exchanges, or to hold companies accountable for contractual performance. Finally, the Web itself has not yet proved to be secure, because files and data can be readily accessed, accounts can be pirated or convoluted (a new brand of commercial terrorism), and proprietary company information can be copied or converted—a form of commercial espionage.

QUESTIONS

1. Identify the risks envisioned for client companies in an international B2B network, and describe how these risks might be categorized under one of the political risk assessment scenarios.

2. Studies are beginning to emerge on the questions governments face about regulating, taxing, and controlling e-commerce. Research these issues, perhaps through government websites, World Bank, EU, and similar sources, to formulate a summary of related issues and recommendations.

3. What risks would you perceive as most likely to threaten the entrepreneurial B2B companies, particularly those with international suppliers and clientele?

BIBLIOGRAPHY

Banham, Russ. "Servicing Global E-Commerce." *World Trade*, July 2000, 35–42.

Brown, Eryn. "Big Business Meets the E-World." *Fortune*, 8 November 1999, 88–98.

"Business: The Failure of New Media." *The Economist*, 19 August 2000, 53–55.

Green, Heather, Mike France, Marvin Stepanek, and Amy Borrus. "Online Privacy: It's Time for Rules in Wonderland." *Business Week*, 20 March 2000, 83–94.

Mandel, Michael J. "The New Economy—It Works in America. Will It Go Global?" *Business Week*, 31 January 2000, 73–77.

Swartz, John, and Nadine Joseph. "E-Commerce: 2B or Not 2B." *Newsweek*, Special Issue, July 2000, 40–44.

Tully, Shawn. "The B2B Tool That Really Is Changing the World." *Fortune*, 20 March 2000, 132–145.

ETHICS AND SOCIAL RESPONSIBILITY

CHAPTER OBJECTIVES

Explain the concepts of social responsibility and corporate responsiveness.

Describe business ethics in terms of ethical relativism.

Discuss the dilemma of balancing respect for global ethical concepts against expectations to accommodate local practices.

List ways in which governments influence international ethical standards.

Detail the controversy concerning ethical standards for bribes.

Demonstrate how social priorities are influenced in host countries and why companies must honor implicit social contracts in foreign environments.

CHAPTER 4

George Eastman, founder of Eastman Kodak Company, coined a phrase that seems almost trite today: "Doing the right thing is the Eastman way." This phrase has been the guiding principle of the Eastman empire since 1880, when the company opened for business as a small photography shop in Rochester, New York. George Eastman was an innovator who began manufacturing photographic plates and providing supplies to professional photographers and camera buffs. However, he soon had to face a stomach-churning ethical dilemma. His customers had returned a huge quantity of his dry plates because they failed to produce an image when developed. Facing the crisis, Eastman had few options. He could close his business and leave town, or he could replace the defective plates and risk bankruptcy. The right thing to do was to make good on his products, and he mortgaged everything that he owned to replace the plates or repay his customers.

Thirty years later, George Eastman opened Eastman Chemicals in Kingsport, Tennessee, and hung a sign on the front door on the first day of business. It was the Eastman pledge: "Do the right thing, always." A framed copy of this is on the wall of every workshop and office in every Eastman facility throughout the world, and George Eastman's successors have been chosen on the basis of their commitment to that simple code of ethics. The Tennessee plant, now an employee-owned company with more than $5 billion in sales, is one of four major U.S. facilities and 10 foreign subsidiaries. The company has been a champion of employee rights and community affairs for decades. Harvard scholar Jay Lorsch recently said, "There are still a few large companies that say employees and their communities are just as important as shareholders....Eastman Chemical is one." Lorsch explained that Eastman's record has been extraordinary, spanning a century of turmoil in which the company's founding ethical principles have remained constant.[1]

Eastman Chemical is the largest chemical facility in the United States, with more than 500 buildings on its home site of 1,200 acres. Like other Eastman sites, the company provides extensive recreation facilities, health clubs, family centers, full access to facilities for its retired employees, and company-sponsored activities that include hiking, computer networking, league basketball, theater arts, and continuing education. Employees and their families have been able to attend movies free at the plant's theater for a half-century, and Kingsport citizens use the company theater and recreation facilities for community events. During the 1930s in the midst of depression, Eastman spent liberally to keep employees. He also established career training programs, and paid for employees to participate in public works projects. A legacy of George Eastman is the practice of encouraging company scientists and technicians to be substitute teachers in local schools, and they do so on company time. Employees do not punch time clocks, and since the company's inception, they have had a voice in decisions.

Eastman Chemical's corporate code of ethics is a replica of the company's worldwide commitment to five constituent interests: customers, employees, shareowners, plant-site communities, and the environment. "Doing the right thing—the Eastman Way" is achieved by honoring three fundamental principles. First, integrity is a foundation of all business policy; second, good business policy must include good environmental policy; and third, trust that the company and its managers will always seek to do the right thing. Eastman Chemical's CEO, Earnest A. Deavenport, recently explained this commitment in these words: "People don't do business with a company. They do business with the people of that company. . . . If your customers can trust the people within your company, you will be in business a long time." Deavenport added an important message to his international managers: "I sense that the world is entering an era of unparalleled growth. The global environment can be the ultimate benefactor if this new growth leads to world prosperity."[2]

MANAGING BY WHAT RULES?

International managers often develop chameleon-like behavior in adapting to foreign environments where employees, customers, and competitors represent a broad range of social values. Unfortunately, their behavior is not always appropriate. If they attempt to conform to local customs, they often breach their own code of ethics; and if they do business strictly in accord with their ethical standards, they can violate host-country expectations for ethical conduct. How *should* managers behave overseas? Should they "pay off" government officials in Zambia to obtain export permits, as many companies do? While in Mexico, should they treat women with less dignity than they would at home because women there are commonly placed in socially inferior roles? Should international managers ignore environmental protection standards because host countries lack protective laws? What rules should they follow in hiring or disciplining employees? How should they handle graft, intellectual piracy, corrupt politicians, or exploitation of child labor? What do they do when political ideologies present ethical dilemmas? These questions perplex international managers, who struggle to find some sense of consistency in foreign relationships that do not contradict their personal values or their company's code of conduct.

From a corporate perspective, global companies are concerned with "responsible citizenship" that upholds human rights and safeguards the environment. Managers also must protect their company's business interests, and differences between social and business responsibilities are often irreconcilable. In a world where laws, customs, and cultural values vary tremendously from one society to another, managers cannot always determine what constitutes "appropriate behavior." This chapter addresses business ethics and corporate social responsibilities in the context of doing business in often-sensitive foreign environments.

Clarifying Terms

Defined broadly, the term *ethics* is concerned with what is right or wrong, and this implies judgments about what is moral or immoral. **Business ethics** are concerned with personal conduct perceived to be right and moral by individuals within an enterprise, thereby taking into account the human welfare of those affected by decisions and behavior.[3] **Ethical standards** describe expectations for companies and individuals to conform to widely accepted codes of conduct. These principles emanate from cultural customs and values, and consequently they vary among all societies. What is perceived to be right or wrong in one culture is seldom the same elsewhere. There are no ethical absolutes. One person or one society may hold dearly to one set of beliefs considered sacred and absolute, yet those same beliefs can be rejected by others. Also, because societies are constantly evolving, their systems of values and beliefs change. Therefore, ethical standards are not static ideals, but dynamic patterns of human conduct.[4]

These statements suggest that ethics are relative, not universal, which is a hotly debated topic. Although some ethical concepts are generally accepted as universal, most still are subject to interpretation within each of the world's societies. For example, most human beings believe that it is wrong to kill another human being, yet even this horrific act can be justified by self-defense or war. Nevertheless, many people argue that killing any human being is *absolutely* immoral, while others argue that circumstances determine the morality of killing—such as assisted death for individuals who are terminally ill, and justifiable abortion. Thus even the human act of killing can be condemned as the ultimate crime, but can also be regarded as commendable. Many other moral concepts can be equally controversial, such as perceptions of love, hate, respect for human dignity, and ecological protection. International managers face difficult choices on these and many other concepts, because cultural values are shaped differently in each of the world's societies.

While ethics are concerned with personal conduct, *social responsibility* is concerned with an organization's role in society. **Corporate social responsibility** is defined as an organization's obligation to conduct business in such a way as to safeguard the welfare of society while pursuing its own interests.[5] Although an organization is an inanimate legal entity, it is responsible for its actions through the collective decisions, policies, and conduct of managers who are held accountable for activities within the context of their organization's social and ecological environments. In this viewpoint, organizations have been given a sense of organic life, so it is common to speak of "corporate" or "business" ethics as if a company could be right and moral, or wrong and immoral. Ultimately, managers are responsible for organizational ethics, and although corporations can be held legally liable for violating laws pertaining to business conduct, managers are liable specifically for decisions that constitute organizational endeavors. A corporation is judged by the *responsiveness* of its managers to meet society's expectations for organizational performance; individuals are judged by their behavior *in response to* those expectations.[6]

These relationships have been dramatically emphasized by several incidents. For example, the Exxon *Valdez* Alaskan oil spill in 1989 resulted in a legal fiasco in which the company, Exxon's CEO, and several key managers were indicted on violations ranging from safety issues to duplicity in corporate decisions that should have prevented the tanker accident. Exxon was held liable for damages, and the tanker's captain was held accountable for criminal neglect. However, the critical issue was whether Exxon's executives had acted in a responsible manner to reasonably prevent such an incident.[7] The Exxon *Valdez* problems have yet to be fully resolved, but another incident illustrates the issues more dramatically. In 1984 a deadly gas leak at Union Carbide's plant in Bhopal, India, killed more than 2,000 people and injured nearly 200,000 more. The Bhopal incident has been called the worst industrial accident in history. The company, Union Carbide, was indicted in India on charges ranging from minor supervisory infractions to major crimes of negligence. Union Carbide's CEO was formally charged with murder by the Indian government. Most of the charges were never pressed, but Union Carbide, its Indian partners (including local government authorities), and several local managers were held accountable for malfeasance. The company settled resulting lawsuits and took full responsibility for the disaster. There was no effort to thwart investigations or cover up facts of the incident.[8]

Antecedents of Corporate Ethics and Social Responsibility

Although each society draws on its history and cultural values to determine how business should be conducted, the concepts of corporate ethics—and specifically the idea of social responsibility—are associated with American business development and the obligations of managers in a free-enterprise system. Research and much of the debate in recent years concerning ethics and social responsibility have been concerned with regulation of business. Underpinning the research and debates is an implicit assumption that business leaders must be forced to accept social responsibilities. However, long before government became involved in regulatory efforts, business leaders took it upon themselves to pursue social initiatives.

For example, Stephen Girard, a French immigrant who arrived in America in 1776, has been called the father of philanthropy. Girard was a seafarer who created a sprawling commercial empire of trade, mercantile stores, warehousing, shipping, and banking. On his death in 1831, he left an estate estimated to be the largest in America, exceeding even that of John Jacob Astor. Girard bequeathed his estate to establish Girard College, which was initially founded to provide comprehensive support for indigent boys (food, shelter, clothing, education, and special schooling). Today the school is part of a permanent trust fund that provides education, shelter, and scholarships to boys and girls with special programs for the gifted and the needy. Girard pursued philanthropic interests throughout his life, including a joint effort with John Jacob Astor to underwrite the War of 1812. He promoted employee health, provided homes for fatherless children and abandoned wives, and built hospitals. In 1793 Girard paid almost entirely from his own wealth for the medical care of yellow-fever victims in the city of Philadelphia. Girard's efforts to help the destitute in society were among the first initiatives to bring business resources to bear on social issues.[9]

Another immigrant, Andrew Carnegie (1835–1919), came to America from Scotland, founded the U.S. steel industry, and subsequently coined the phrase "corporate responsibility." In his view, industrialists had an obligation of *stewardship* in which the rich had an ethical obligation to use their corporate resources to improve social welfare. Carnegie endowed colleges and universities, promoted public education, created museums, established hospitals and medical treatment centers, promoted housing and community projects, and pursued programs to support early environmental initiatives, human rights, and a wide variety of fine arts. The Carnegie name is associated with many of America's foremost institutions and fine-arts trusts, and Carnegie interests extend to Europe and Asia through endowed educational programs and research.[10]

There is no doubt that many managers must be prodded to respond to social issues, but business leaders more often than politicians have laid the foundations for much of the social legislation people now take for granted. Social legislation, and specifically the regulation of business, differs widely among nations; and these differences create additional dilemmas for managers working abroad. As noted later in the chapter, there are efforts to solidify global initiatives into social legislation concerning human rights and environmental protection, but pervasive social legislation, whether business related or not, may be impossible to formulate.[11] In a practical sense, managers are more concerned with how to respond to social and ethical questions that arise daily and are specific to the environments in which they find themselves.

Corporate Responsiveness

During the 1960s and 1970s, social legislation became prominent in North America and Europe, and models of corporate behavior began to appear in management literature. Business round-table consortia also began to emerge to specifically address "codes of conduct." Business leaders began in earnest to ask how they should respond to society's expectations, and many debates surfaced about the appropriate role for government in regulating business conduct. This was the era of new regulatory initiatives concerning equal opportunities, affirmative action, occupational safety, consumer rights, and environmental protection. Regulatory agencies also proliferated with enforcement power, and regulatory noncompliance could result in fines, restitution, or even imprisonment for managers found guilty through government-initiated indictments. Consequently, companies began to interpret their social responsibility through meeting regulatory mandates as a gauge of social conduct. Compliance became the standard of performance.

Merely *complying* with laws, however, proved to be shortsighted. Instead, the concept of **corporate responsiveness** emerged as a broader criterion that called for judging a company by how well it was *perceived* to respond to an issue rather than by what it actually did. For example, when the first models of the Ford Pinto were found to have design flaws that caused their gas tanks to leak, often exploding in rear-end collisions, it was not the flawed cars that became an issue, but the reluctance of Ford to admit that the cars were unsafe and to recall Pintos for correction. The public was outraged that Ford executives tried to skirt the issue. More recently, Ford faced a new and even greater challenge. In July 2000, the company was implicated in accidents and mishaps connected with faulty Firestone tires on thousands of its vehicles worldwide. Although Firestone had become a Japanese-owned company, and Ford was simply a corporate purchaser of the faulty tires, there was an outrage at deaths and accidents that prompted Congress to act on a broad range of regulatory and criminal charges. Ford's new CEO, Jacques Nasser, took the unprecedented step of closing three major Ford assembly plants so that the company could redirect its stockpile of 70,000 new (and safe) tires as replacements for suspected Firestone tires on consumer vehicles. In August 2000, there were an estimated 6.5 million faulty Firestone tires in circulation by all automakers worldwide, and Ford's high visibility simply drew the spotlight. The record will show, in time, that Ford responded to the problem almost immediately upon hearing of the tire defects—and well ahead of congressional hearings or public pressure to address the problem. There was no hesitation by Ford executives to constructively respond, even at an enormous cost; yet the company's exhaustive effort was still met with an onslaught of negative media. Meanwhile, congressional reporters compared Ford's behavior during the Firestone problem with its handling of the Pinto debacle and concluded that "Ford's response to the tire crisis [was] light-years ahead of its actions in the 1970s."[12]

Corporations often go to great lengths to avoid these problems. By creating a *code of ethics*, a company can send strong signals to its managers and to the public about how it intends to respond to social issues. Of course, a company must then act accordingly; but also, public opinion must agree that the company's intentions and its actions are sufficient to be considered socially responsible. Consider, for example, Nelson Mandela's viewpoint on American behavior toward South Africa during the struggle to bring social justice to his country. While touring the United States in 1990, Mandela urged the continuation of sanctions against his country to press for democratic changes, but he was critical of American and European firms for doing too little. He commented that although many companies were taking the correct ethical posture by complying with the boycott against South Africa, they were doing little to actively improve the situation. In Mandela's view, "compliance" may have protected companies from accusations of unethical behavior, but merely having a record of no unethical behavior was not a sufficient response to a serious social problem.[13] On the eve of the 2000 Olympics, Mandela addressed the European Investment Bank's development conference in Brussels and applauded initiatives by European and American business leaders who, in his words, "were wise enough to reach beyond the platitudes of political agenda to bridge the gaps that exist among peoples of the world through social enhancements of ethical commerce."[14]

Responsiveness implies a *proactive response* to prevent potential social problems. It is a self-initiated action by a company to resolve a problem or to protect against unethical behavior without being provoked by events. Responsiveness can also mean a *reactive response* in which a company is forced by crisis, by legal intervention, or by external pressure groups to deal with a perceived breech of ethical behavior. To say that a company is "responsive" suggests that management has attempted to be proactive in its ethical policies. A reactive response is perceived to be a reluctant answer, and even if a company handles the situation well, its credibility suffers. Nevertheless, managers are faced with both situations, and even the best company cannot proactively plan for every contingency. With that said, there are guidelines to help managers make decisions when faced with social responsibility issues. Figure 4.1 illustrates a *continuum of social responsiveness* that reveals public *perceptions* of corporate behavior.

At the low end, *obstruction* is a response that categorically rejects wrongdoing, perhaps even to the point of fighting compliance laws in court. This is the public perception of how American tobacco companies are responding to antismoking legislation and to an anti-tobacco lobby that is spreading worldwide. Tobacco companies are also perceived as following the second response of *defense*. In this situation, the companies are rationalizing their behavior as "in compliance with" legal requirements (such as meeting restrictions on smoking advertisements). They defend their positions as being socially responsible within the law while protecting corporate interests. From an international perspective, this is interesting because in many countries, such as China, Japan, Indonesia, and most of South America, smoking is not only socially acceptable but widely encouraged through relatively unrestricted advertising.[15] Tobacco companies are not perceived as being obstructive or defensive in these societies, and even in Europe, there are few confrontational problems about smoking.[16] The third type of response is *accommodation*, which implies that a company takes positive actions to rectify questionable activities. Accommodation assumes that a company candidly takes responsibility for problems, and then seeks ways to prevent them from recurring. It suggests that managers can be caught off-guard by events, yet by taking expedient corrective actions, they can behave in an ethical manner. The highest point on

FIGURE 4.1
Continuum of Social
Responsiveness

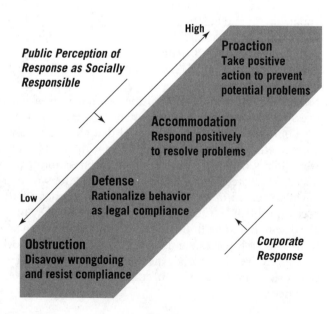

the continuum is *proaction*, which presumes that managers make a planned effort to identify potential problems and take effective steps to prevent them from arising.[17]

The logical conclusion is that companies should always strive toward high-end, proactive behavior; but even so, the best intentions can fall short. Companies and their managers are subsequently judged by how they respond to the inevitable crises that occur without warning, and that are often beyond their control. The annual list of *Fortune*'s *Most Admired Companies* consistently includes companies ranked as "stellar performers" on *social responsiveness* measures. Yet among the top 10 on *Fortune*'s 2000 list, every company has recently faced serious ethical dilemmas. Merck & Company has had to pull several controversial pharmaceutical products from the market after unexpected problems occurred from dosages and side effects. Merck not only responded candidly to the issues but also introduced new testing procedures more rigorous than those of the National Institutes of Health to prevent future problems. Johnson & Johnson swept Tylenol from store shelves after a tampering scare revealed poisonous substances in Tylenol bottles, but the company also invented tamperproof bottles and new packaging procedures that have since become industry standards. Target Stores, a company many were surprised to see on the top-10 list, was ranked #1 in the United States for environmental policies, yet the company had faced a number of waste-dumping incidents by local subsidiaries over the years. Target responded with sweeping policies and incentive programs to challenge its employees and competitors to set the highest standards for pollution prevention. *Fortune*'s *Global Most Admired Companies* has an equally star-studded list. These companies also are consistently among the top performers for responding to social issues with well-articulated codes of conduct, and in every instance candidly faced crises quickly and effectively. They include General Electric, Nokia, BP Amoco, Royal/Dutch Shell, Nestlé, and 15 other companies that also rank among the top companies in their respective home countries.[18]

A Social Contract

In every culture, an implied **social contract** exists between business and society that permits companies to pursue commercial interests within certain parameters of conduct.[19] The implied contract constitutes a set of expectations for the role of a corporation and its managers in a particular society. These expectations are shaped by cultural values, religious codes, ideologies, regulations, and economic conditions of both home and host countries. These relationships are illustrated in Figure 4.2.

In a free-enterprise system with a capitalist ideology, companies have a wide berth in pursing private business interests. Corporations are expected to operate on behalf of their stockholders and commercial constituents. In a socialist system, that mandate is less clear. In marketing economies with socialist leanings, such as France or Sweden, businesses may seem to operate unfettered, but governments impose rather extensive regulations on their enterprises and often become directly involved in business activities, labor issues, and capital management. In highly centralized socialist societies, business enterprises may exist only to the extent that they create jobs or provide society with prescribed goods and services. And of course, in autocratic or communist regimes, business may not exist apart from government itself.

In many less-developed countries, businesses are expected to support political priorities for economic development—and in so doing, individual rights and constituent interests are of little importance. Under these conditions, business practices may be lax, patent laws may not exist, and concepts of equal employment or environmental protection may be ignored in the quest for rapid economic growth. International

FIGURE 4.2
The Social Contract

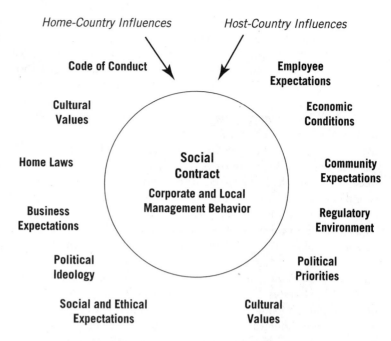

managers must understand expectations under various ideological systems, and the nature of the social contract subsequently rests with interpretations of ethical conduct and the role of business in each society.

BUSINESS ETHICS

Business ethics are framed in several different ways. In a global sense of universal human relations, ethics are concerned with how a company conducts business to support widely held human rights and to protect nature. This does not mean that every culture will endorse the same ethical standards. It does mean that in a general way everyone recognizes, for example, that humans have the right to life, and thus every society has penalties for those who take another person's life. All societies also have a sense of ecological protection. Corporate conduct that results in violations of these rights is subsequently condemned, and if individuals within the company can be held responsible, they are punished. However, these so-called *universal rights* are subject to so many interpretations that few laws exist on an international scale to guide corporate conduct.

More specific corporate conduct concerns ethical relationships between the company and people beyond the organization who are directly affected by a company's decisions. This category would include, for example, competitive conduct (predatory pricing, fraud, bribery, corporate espionage, or patent infringements), environmental protection measures, financial accountability, and community relations. Regulatory activities of international watchdog organizations focus on these relationships to monitor business conduct. Ethics also are concerned with close-constituency relationships. These include, for example, internal hiring practices, ethical treatment of employees, consumer rights, product safety, and protection of shareholder interests. Companies also are concerned on a daily basis with behavior among employees, such as sexual harassment. Many other examples could be cited, but they would all support the point that ethics are concerned with the perception of moral behavior by individuals within the context of their work relationships.[20]

Relativism and Business Ethics

At any level of consideration, ethics reflect *relative* standards in the sense that they require interpretation. **Ethical relativism** incorporates four perspectives that help to explain business ethics: naive relativism, role relativism, group relativism, and cultural relativism. They are summarized in Table 4.1.[21]

Naive Relativism
The most prevalent explanation of ethics is from an *individual* interpretation of what is right or wrong. **Naive relativism** is the belief that every human being is solely responsible for deciding what is right and moral, or wrong and immoral. In this extreme viewpoint, the individual must make a personal moral judgment on every ethical issue. Consequently, everyone can freely judge the appropriateness of murder, cannibalism, lying, cheating, and every other human activity. Of course, few people would approve of murder or cannibalism, but an avid naive relativist would argue that individuals still have the right to judge what is right and moral according to their personal values. Indeed, in some societies both murder and cannibalism are acceptable practices. Such dramatic human events seldom lead to ethical dilemmas, but interpretations become much more complex for behavior such as cheating, lying, or discriminatory hiring of particular ethnic groups or races. Everyone makes moral judgments that reflect a sense of naive relativism, but these decisions are often trivial, or at least not always apparent. For example, driving in excess of a posted speed limit is not just a matter of violating the law. It is a choice people make in their own self-interests; implicitly, those who speed are rejecting a standard imposed by society in favor of their own judgment of a safe speed to drive.

Naive relativism rejects universalism in favor of a personal moral code of conduct, and in some ways this is a strong argument for individual rights. The absolute right of an individual to guide his or her own spiritual life, for example, is supported by a personal moral code that says each person can believe in a chosen supreme deity (or none at all), and everyone has the right to worship in a personal manner. However,

---

TABLE 4.1

FOUR EXPLANATIONS OF ETHICAL RELATIVISM

Belief in Relativism	Interpretation of Belief
Naive relativism	Individual is solely responsible for deciding what is right or wrong
Role relativism	Moral obligations are inherent in professional or work roles
Group relativism	Individual morals are determined in context of a reference group
Cultural relativism	Morality is relative to each culture and defines society in context of a nation or people

extending this principle to other activities such as speeding, cheating, taking drugs, exploiting minorities, or simply making decisions that affect other people destroys the argument: Religious worship can occur in isolation, while other behavior can become an imposition on the environment or on other human beings. Religious worship also can become an imposition if it results in denying another person the same choice of worship. Naive relativism therefore becomes a self-defeating argument unless an individual lives in a complete vacuum.

Nevertheless, naive relativism does influence behavior, and everyone makes individual moral judgments about basic activities such as speeding and cheating on exams, usually with justification to their advantage. Managers may avoid hiring African Americans through a personal belief in racial inequality. Employees may "take a few things home" from the office, justifying this theft because they feel that the company doesn't pay them adequately. People make similar rationalizations about intellectual property rights, like copying software, and about more sensitive issues, such as what constitutes sexual harassment. Ultimately, if everyone acted this way, people would live without rules for human coexistence or protection for private property; society would be chaotic. These issues are even more complicated for international managers. In their foreign assignments, they must make decisions in unfamiliar environments where questions such as product safety, environmental protection, and child labor may have substantially different meanings from their own interpretations of what is right and moral.

Role Relativism

Ethical dilemmas occur when individual beliefs clash with role expectations. This is called **role relativism,** and it is based on the premise that certain moral obligations are inherent in everyone's professional role, yet these are often distinct from personal moral beliefs. A duality of ethical systems can result in which managers are expected to behave in a particular way even when that behavior contradicts their sense of what is ethical. This is a common problem that is known in management literature as *role conflict*. Role conflict, or the clash of personal and professional ethics, is particularly difficult in highly specialized societies where doctors, lawyers, teachers, psychiatric counselors, engineers, and sales professionals must conform to social expectations beyond their control. In many instances, they are members of professional associations or referent groups with codes of conduct that override personal convictions.[22]

For example, medical doctors are expected to treat all patients the same. They cannot choose to ignore a patient because the individual is Hispanic or a woman, and they are not expected to make moral judgments about the right to medical care of one patient or another. Medical questions such as whether a woman should have a legal abortion can be difficult. If the law permits abortion (and even if circumstances suggest this is best course of action), a hospital team that must perform the procedure may still have grave doubts about it. For moral reasons or religious beliefs, the doctors and nurses involved may be adamantly against abortion, yet find themselves faced with doing the procedure. Lawyers and professional counselors must observe client confidentiality; consequently, even if they know that their clients are criminals, they cannot reveal their clients' crimes to authorities. In foreign societies, these rules may not apply. In China, abortion is required by law to limit population growth under the country's one-child-family rule, and in Moslem countries, criminals are not protected by client confidentiality laws.

All managers are expected to act in a moral way to protect the interests of their companies' owners. It is called a *fiduciary duty*, and within the limits of law, managers therefore *should* put stockholders and investors first in their decisions. Obvious conflicts arise when other constituent interests are considered. Consumers should not be exploited with high prices or cheaply made products merely to maximize profits. Employees should not be exploited through unfair wages to compensate for other costs. The environment should not be exploited to save money. Yet in the international arena, these prescriptive rules may not be so obvious. Managers often find that it is easy to ignore what they "should" do by their own society's standards, and instead behave in concert with local expectations. More often, managers try to behave within their home-country frame of ethics, and subsequently have difficulties abroad or suffer anxieties about their responsibilities.

The *role relativist* argues that, in the extreme, a person does whatever is required by his or her role. When individuals are caught in a dilemma between personal beliefs and role expectations, they are subsequently expected to either set aside their personal viewpoints or resign their positions. Many managers do resign or transfer out of uncomfortable positions; but for the international manager, the situation is more complicated because the role itself may be substantially different in every foreign assignment. Multinational companies recognize the potential for role conflict or ethical dilemmas, and valuable employees are placed where they can be productive with a minimum of role stress. This subject is treated in later chapters on human resource development where recruitment, selection, and expatriate training are addressed.

Group Relativism

As members of social groups, ethnic groups, religious organizations, communities, and families, everyone is influenced by group affiliations. **Group relativism** refers to moral judgments in context with group expectations. As noted earlier, professional associations for doctors, lawyers, and other specialists often have codes of conduct that dictate expected behavior. From a business standpoint, these expectations do not necessarily suggest legal or regulatory constraints, but are more often "group norms" about individual conduct. For example, in the United States, *generally accepted accounting procedures* determine how books should be kept, assets valued, and profits recorded; yet these procedures are not widely accepted overseas. An American multinational following these standards overseas may be charged with inappropriate behavior. Several leading U.S. companies, including Coca-Cola, Goodyear Tire & Rubber, and Procter & Gamble, were charged with unethical accounting procedures by Japan's National Tax Administration. The Japanese claimed that the companies engaged in artificial transfer pricing to avoid paying taxes. From an American viewpoint, company accountants were doing nothing more than following standard procedures to legally minimize tax liabilities.[23]

Many ethical conflicts occur as an extension of the pluralistic nature of society. Individuals develop a sense of personal conduct by adopting standards of their referent groups. These include, for example, close friends, professional associations, religious affiliates, and ethnic groups. Church members define moral conduct according to their specific religious group, ethnic minorities reflect behavior in their subcultural groups, and people from New York, London, Dallas, or Tokyo learn to conform to expectations of their urban societies. Expectations for conduct can be imposed by specific group membership, such as those in the pro-life movement or the National Organization of Women. At the other extreme, implicit and informal expectations can shape behavior according to role identities, such as management attitudes versus those of blue-collar workers. Regardless of the group affiliation, the point is that individuals often adopt group standards as if their particular interpretation of ethical behavior is right while others are wrong.

International managers face a more perplexing problem of group expectations that often bear little resemblance to values held by comparative groups at home. Managers in France, for example, do not necessarily rise from the ranks or earn promotions; instead they are products of a socially stratified culture, where they often gain positions according to birthright or family connections. French managers are channeled into ranks, called *cadres*, which offer very little vertical mobility. Thus foreign managers stationed in France find that authority is structured to maintain social distance between themselves and their subordinates. This can result in rather uncomfortable patterns of human relations and awkward decision-making situations for managers from other countries.

Cultural Relativism

Closely associated with group relativism, but in distinct contrast to naive relativism, **cultural relativism** claims that morality is relative to a particular culture or society. In a sense, it is a "nationally bounded" viewpoint. This approach is more appealing than others because it avoids the chaos of individualist naive relativism, yet it recognizes that substantial ethical differences exist among the world's cultures. Cultural relativism does not imply that one system of ethics—or one sense of national morality—is better than another. To the contrary, it encourages the acceptance of cultural differences without assuming universal prescriptions of right and wrong. Therefore, managers are in the position of having to understand foreign cultural values, but not judge them. Companies are in the position of having to adapt their practices to accommodate local expectations, yet neither impose their home-culture standards on foreign operations nor relinquish their own corporate codes of conduct.

Advocates of cultural relativism would agree with the age-old saying, "When in Rome, do as the Romans do." Critics of cultural relativism say this is nonsense, that if something is ethical it should be a moral standard for all human beings—it should be *universal*. No one has resolved this argument, but it is important to recognize how both sides see it. For example, many people would say that taking a human life in any form is absolutely wrong, yet as noted earlier, different cultures certainly have their own justifications for various forms of killing. Aside from war and self-defense, specific practices such as abortion and euthanasia (mercy killing, or physician-assisted suicide) are dramatically different among the world's societies. The "Global Viewpoint" feature presents an example of the controversy over euthanasia.

If there is little agreement among people on major ethical issues such as killing, consider the extraordinary number of less dramatic issues that can lead to heated debates. In Japan, for example, men and women have developed a social differential that relegates women to subservient roles. Indeed, this male superiority is common to Confucian and Islamic societies, and it is not uncommon in Mexico and many Latin societies. Consider, then, how an American man should treat women if he was assigned to Japan, China, Mexico, or Saudi Arabia. Should he treat women with a sense of equality, or follow local customs and treat women as subservient? To better appreciate the argument, turn the situation around. Should a man from Japan, China, Mexico, or Saudi Arabia working in the United States treat American women the same way he would at home? The cultural relativist would say that in every instance, the man should learn appropriate behavior toward women in the host country and adapt his behavior to conform to those values. An advocate of the universal view would say that there is only one ethical way to behave between men and women. Ironically, if the universalist is speaking as an American, the ethical standard may be a sense of equality;

EUTHANASIA: MURDER OR MERCY?

Euthanasia has many names, but the kinder ones are *mercy killing* or *physician-assisted suicide*. Some simply call it murder. By whatever name, terminally ill patients, soldiers beyond help on battlefields, and hopelessly insane people have been helped to die throughout human history. Those who have helped have achieved near-sainthood in some quarters, and have been prosecuted for the acts elsewhere. Perhaps many have simply lived without self-guilt or notoriety—or perhaps they have suffered in silence, unable to reconcile their acts.

Whether euthanasia is morally right or wrong is a controversy with no end in sight. The chief justification for euthanasia is to provide relief for patients who are suffering excruciating pain, and of course, who are likely to die soon in any event. However, international research has shown that in North America and Europe, relief of pain was the sole motivating factor in only 5 percent of all cases, and it may have played a role in 30 percent of the cases studied. The remaining 70 percent suggests a more complicated picture. Depression, hopelessness, anxiety, extreme psychological tendency toward suicide, and other less personal factors such as money or family security all influenced patient requests for a merciful death. Many patients simply take their own lives. Often family members help. But in most instances, a physician or medical professional is involved.

Some cases in the United States have been dramatically reported in press articles and court cases. Studies by the Sloan-Kettering Hospital in New York of cancer patients and AIDS victims, together with state-supported investigations in Washington and New York, conclude that as many as 25,000 Americans succumb to euthanasia each year. Officially, there are no clear records beyond the courts, but it occurs all the same.

In other nations, euthanasia may be more prevalent than in the United States, and it is less controversial. The Netherlands, for example, has recognized justifiable euthanasia for years. It began with a quiet acceptance of assisted suicide for the terminally ill that has prevailed for generations, and then it moved to a broader acceptance of euthanasia for the chronically ill. The presumption was that euthanasia was voluntary—instigated at the patient's request—but a study by the Dutch government has documented more than a thousand cases of involuntary euthanasia each year for the past several decades. The official term is "termination of the patient without specific request." Case reports show that the problem has increased with HIV-positive patients who, although not immediately in danger, have been hastened to death by family members or friends. But in many instances, it has been a matter of accommodating those who have lost control of their lives, fear becoming a burden on loved ones, or suffer from severe depression.

The Netherlands is grappling with the problem because every effort to regulate euthanasia has been modified or violated with impunity. Since 1993, when a Dutch court acquitted a psychiatrist who had assisted in the suicide of his patient—a 50-year-old woman who was distraught after losing her two sons—there has been legal precedent for justifiable assistance in death. In the Dutch sense of value-related criterion, doctors should put the welfare of their patient above the law. Thus, when circumstances can be judged as best for the patient (whether physical or psychological), law can be set aside. In December 2000, the Dutch Parliament made euthanasia legal in the Netherlands as "assisted suicide" under medical supervision. This contrasts sharply with other European and North American countries, where no such legal measure exists. Legal realities, however, are often subservient to social customs. In many of the world's nations euthanasia, as we know it, is honorable. Death in many cultures is regarded as a transition in time, and those who assist the hopeless, the infirm, and the elderly are instruments of divine providence. Foreigners to these societies may be shocked at the ethics of death and practices such as euthanasia. Laws do not prevail over human values, and human values are not universal.

Sources: Ezekiel J. Emanuel, "The Painful Truth about Euthanasia," *Wall Street Journal*, 7 January 1997, p. A16; "The Dutch Way of Death," *Wall Street Journal*, 7 January 1997, p. A16; and "The Permissive Dutch, in Life and Death," *The Economist*, 2 December 2000, 51.

but if the person is from a Confucian or Islamic society, the universal standard would imply a system of gender inequalities.[24]

When international business behavior is in question, the challenge of ethics is even more bewildering. Should you bribe officials in Mexico, if that is common practice there? Can you take another company's innovation if there are no patent laws in a particular country? Can you "knock off" or pirate software because that is how businesses compete in China or Indonesia? Can you deny someone a promotion in France because he or she did not graduate from an approved school? Can you hire, fire, or discipline employees on the basis of race, ethnic group, or tribal caste, as they do in many societies? International managers may find themselves in situations where they have little control over these matters. They may personally avoid unethical behavior, yet work in environments where their foreign peers openly engage in such practices with no sense of wrongdoing.

A further complication is that global companies now have so many international alliances and subsidiaries that one set of standards is difficult to implement throughout an organization. For example, Bristol-Myers Squibb (BMS), a highly respected global pharmaceutical company, recently acquired Argentia SA, which is one of Argentina's largest and most reputable pharmaceutical companies. The acquisition was a logical move for both companies and gave BMS a strong market share and major operating base in South America. Unfortunately, after the purchase, BMS found that Argentia SA was a major producer of pirated drugs, selling versions of at least five major anticancer agents and antibiotics patented by U.S. and European companies. Ironically, Argentia SA even made pirated versions of Bristol-Myers Squibb's leading drugs. BMS continues to produce and market the knock-off drugs in Argentina even though by U.S. and European patent laws this would be illegal. In Argentina, where there are no patent laws to prevent this (and where many companies pirate products), BMS's behavior is not viewed as illegal or controversial. BMS has stated that it intends to honor international patent rights as quickly as possible; however, in the Argentine market, its subsidiary there will continue to operate as usual until changes can be introduced.[25]

The problem with cultural relativism is that a company cannot "do as the Romans do" and merely switch ethical gears in each country. Managers cannot ignore their own ethical standards, nor can they set aside home-country moral and legal codes. They are caught between conflicting moral and legal demands, and none of the relativist approaches provides a sufficient answer to the dilemma. Universal values, although philosophically sound, offer few guidelines. Nevertheless, all societies have developed cultural values systems with *internal consistency*. Understanding these value systems helps managers to make informed decisions that are ethical under the circumstances.

Global Concepts and Local Practices

Global concepts of ethical behavior are emerging through efforts by international organizations to consolidate the best corporate policies into guidelines for multinational enterprises. The Organization for Economic Cooperation and Development (OECD), the International Chamber of Commerce (ICC), and the International Labor Organization (ILO) have all created corporate codes of conduct to assist international managers. The UN Commission on Transnational Corporations has also sought to establish a code of ethics. A summary of recommendations by these organizations is presented in Table 4.2.

Many of the recommendations from the international codes of conduct sound sensible, but they can be controversial. For example, under the heading "Laws and Regulations" in Table 4.2, all multinationals are advised that they are subject to the laws, regulations, and jurisdictions of the countries in which they operate. While it is true that local laws prevail over all others, each home country also has laws governing multinational companies that must be observed. The U.S. Foreign Corrupt Practices Act (FCPA) affects all American companies, and it specifically outlines the nature of gift giving or payments that could be considered bribes by U.S. managers working abroad. American multinational managers may therefore behave according to local customs and protocols, yet find themselves in violation of home-country FCPA regulations. U.S. multinationals face a similar dilemma in employee relations. Under the 1991 Civil Rights Act, American citizens employed in a foreign country or by a subsidiary or alliance that has a controlling U.S. interest are covered by all U.S. civil rights legislation. However, there is an exception when compliance with the U.S. laws would violate local laws.[26] In other words, local laws prevail, and Americans working abroad may find that they have none of the civil rights that they would have at home.

The international codes also suggest that multinationals should cooperate with host governments to create employment opportunities. MNCs often find in less-developed countries that governments want them to create as many jobs as possible, and this presumes that the companies will lean toward labor-intensive technology. As a result, multinationals can be put in the position of constraining their foreign operations to relatively low-skilled processes or refraining from introducing new methods that could improve productivity, if such measures would reduce local employment. The MNC therefore risks being criticized as a company that exploits local employees. In contrast, the same country may shift its political priorities and expect companies to pursue new technological development. Under the international code, this too is encouraged; but it can contradict the commitment to employment. Multinational managers can subsequently find themselves facing a dilemma where either choice of strategies risks some form of criticism.

Multinational companies walk a thin line between what is viewed as appropriate and inappropriate behavior in a host country. For instance, American multinationals in Mexico are expected to pay somewhat better wages and benefits than local companies; but to do so draws criticism from Mexican competitors, who claim that Americans are "buying" their best workers and inflating wages.[27] Meanwhile, if American firms pay comparable wages and benefits, they are accused of exploitation. A further complication is that American firms in Mexico have tried to introduce U.S. standards for equal employment opportunities, but Mexicans view this as contentious intervention or "cultural imperialism" by the Americans.[28]

International Convergence of Ethical Perceptions

Business leaders in North America and Western Europe have similar views of business ethics, and there are relatively few controversies involving corporate behavior, patent rights, or workers' rights. Cultural differences exist, of course, but European and American companies have converged toward common standards of ethical behavior. There may not have been a conscious effort by Europeans or Americans to accommodate, and eventually integrate, a common platform of business behavior; indeed, the evolution of transatlantic business simply made it a necessity. Mergers and acquisitions amounting to more than $1 trillion during the past decade have brought hundreds of major corporations together. Many are American in origin, yet equally as many are Europeans that have bought (or bought into) U.S. industries. Chrysler is

TABLE 4.2

INTERNATIONAL CODES OF CONDUCT—COMPOSITE GUIDELINES*

MNEs† and Host Governments

Economic and Development Policies
- MNEs should consult with governmental authorities and national employers' and workers' organizations to assure that their investments conform to the economic and social development policies of the host country.
- MNEs should not adversely disturb the balance of payments or currency exchange rates of the countries in which they operate. They should try, in consultation with the government, to resolve balance-of-payments and exchange rate difficulties when possible.
- MNEs should cooperate with governmental policies regarding local equity participation.
- MNEs should not dominate capital markets of the countries in which they operate.
- MNEs should provide to host government authorities the information necessary for correctly assessing taxes to be paid.
- MNEs should not engage in transfer pricing policies that modify the tax base on which their entities are assessed.
- MNEs should give preference to local sources for components and raw materials if prices and quality are competitive.
- MNEs should reinvest some profits in the countries in which they operate.

Laws and Regulations
- MNEs are subject to the laws, regulations, and jurisdiction of the countries in which they operate.
- MNEs should respect the right of every country to exercise control over its natural resources, and to regulate the activities of entities operating within its territory.
- MNEs should use appropriate international dispute settlement mechanisms, including arbitration, to resolve conflicts with the governments of the countries in which they operate.
- MNEs should not request the intervention of their home governments in disputes with host governments.
- MNEs should resolve disputes arising from expropriation by host governments under the domestic law of the host country.

Political Involvement
- MNEs should refrain from improper or illegal involvement in local political affairs.
- MNEs should not pay bribes or render improper benefits to any public servant.
- MNEs should not interfere in intergovernmental relations.

MNEs and the Public

Technology Transfer
- MNEs should cooperate with governmental authorities in assessing the impact of transfers of technology to developing countries, and should enhance the technological capacities of developing countries.
- MNEs should develop and adapt technologies to the needs and characteristics of the countries in which they operate.
- MNEs should conduct research and development activities in developing countries, using local resources and personnel to the greatest extent possible.
- When granting licenses for the use of industrial property rights, MNEs should do so on reasonable terms and conditions.
- MNEs should not require payment for the use of technologies of no real value to the enterprise.

Environmental Protection
- MNEs should respect the laws and regulations concerning environmental protection of the countries in which they operate.
- MNEs should cooperate with host governments and with international organizations in the development of national and international environmental protection standards.
- MNEs should supply to appropriate host governmental authorities, information concerning the environmental impact of the products and processes of their entities.

TABLE 4.2 *Continued*

MNEs and Persons

Consumer Protection
- MNEs should respect the laws and regulations of the countries in which they operate with regard to consumer protection.
- MNEs should preserve the safety and health of consumers by disclosure of appropriate information, proper labeling, and accurate advertising.

Employment Practices
- MNEs should cooperate with host governments' efforts to create employment opportunities in particular localities.
- MNEs should support representative employers' organizations.
- MNEs should try to increase employment opportunities and standards in the countries in which they operate.
- MNEs should provide stable employment for their employees.
- MNEs should establish nondiscriminatory employment policies, and promote equal employment opportunities.
- MNEs should give priority to the employment and promotion of nationals in the countries in which they operate.
- MNEs should assure that adequate training is provided to all employees.
- MNEs should contribute to the managerial and technical training of nationals of the countries in which they operate, and should employ qualified nationals in managerial and professional capacities.
- MNEs should respect the right of employees to organize for the purpose of collective bargaining.
- MNEs should provide workers representatives with information necessary to assist in the development of collective agreements.
- MNEs should consult with workers' representatives in all matters directly affecting the interests of labor.
- MNEs, in the context of negotiations with workers' representatives, should not threaten to transfer the operating unit to another country.
- MNEs should give notice of plant closures and mitigate the resultant adverse effects.
- MNEs should cooperate with governments in providing income protection for workers whose employment has been terminated.
- MNEs should provide standards of employment equal to or better than those of comparable employers in the countries in which they operate.
- MNEs should pay, at minimum, basic living wages.
- MNEs should maintain the highest standards of safety and health, and should provide adequate information about work-related health hazards.

Human Rights
- MNEs should respect human rights and fundamental freedoms in the countries in which they operate.
- MNEs should not discriminate on the basis of race, color, sex, religion, language, social, national and ethnic origin, or political or other opinion.
- MNEs should respect the social and cultural objectives, values, and traditions of the countries in which they operate.

---

*Consolidated from guidelines independently developed under the United Nations Commission on Transnational Corporations, the International Labor Organization, the International Chamber of Commerce, and the Organization for Economic Cooperation and Development. Not all organizations subscribe to all items in the summary of codes.

†MNE, rather than MNC, is the more common European and world organization usage.

Source: Adapted from Kathleen A. Getz, "International Codes of Conduct: An Analysis of Ethical Reasoning," *Journal of Business Ethics* 9 (1990): 567–577.

now part of DaimlerBenz, GM owns a substantial portion of Italian Fiat, U.S Best Foods is now part of Anglo-Dutch Unilever, Ford owns Sweden's Volvo, Lockheed Martin's Aerospace is amalgamated with Britain's BAE Systems, and even Burger King is British owned. It is a long list that expands virtually every day. The crucial point, however, is that management represents a broad cross section of nationalities, and many employees are readily transferred or promoted into positions beyond their native countries. Consequently, there is a genuine melting pot of corporate expectations, policies, work cultures, and behavior.[29]

Widely accepted ethical standards also govern international financial behavior and securities trading. For example, when Japan's Daiwa Bank was indicted for fraudulent bond trading and illegal financial reporting in the United States, Japanese and American authorities quickly agreed on the improprieties and pursued a joint investigation. A Japanese executive, Toshihide Iguchi, was convicted of fraud under U.S. law and went to prison. Daiwa Bank subsequently lost more than $1.1 billion in making restitution payments, and Iguchi was ordered to personally pay $2.6 million. In Japan, Daiwa executives moved quickly to establish a new internal code of conduct for international employees, and several managers implicated in the resulting cover-up were prosecuted.[30] Another example of convergence is the platform of international resolutions on international banking that grew out of the Bank of Credit and Commerce International (BCCI) debacle (described in the following "Global Viewpoint" feature).

Ethical Dilemmas in Developing Countries

Business leaders of industrialized countries often have difficulty reconciling ethical behavior in less-developed countries, where political ideologies are in sharp contrast to western concepts of governance. As a result, some multinationals try to avoid political controversies by conducting business according to their own standards. They make no attempt to intervene with host-country politics or to influence how business is done locally, yet a growing number of multinational executives feel obliged to press for reforms. This is particularly apparent with regard to human rights.

Although this may seem altruistic, some business leaders believe there are universal ethics, and they use their corporate resources to pursue change. For example, Bruce J. Klatsky, president and CEO of Phillips-Van Heusen, a billion-dollar New York apparel manufacturer, adamantly insists that all employees of his company throughout the world should enjoy the same constitutional rights as his U.S. employees. Klatsky also requires that vendors, suppliers, and foreign licensees within the Phillips-Van Heusen empire comply with his company's code of conduct. He goes beyond legal standards to limit work hours each week, avoid child labor, provide employee housing and benefits, and develop local employees in his Asian and Latin American factories. The company does not make payoffs—not even for incidental "tips"—and the company clearly demands that managers avoid becoming involved in local politics. By working "on a high moral plane," Klatsky says, "Phillips-Van Heusen demonstrates to foreign countries its determination to make a human and economic contribution within a framework of its corporate code of ethics."[31]

Levi Strauss & Co. has "Guidelines for Country Selection" that prohibit the firm from using or selling products made by prisoners or residents of forced-labor camps. The company brought world attention to human rights issues when it withdrew from China, citing its abhorrence of unsafe working conditions and politically motivated human rights infringements. Levi has also withdrawn from Burma and Peru due to human rights concerns, and other major international companies have joined Levi in protests. As a corporate sponsor of Amnesty International's "Human Rights Now" program, Reebok presses hard for reforms throughout the world; and through the

GLOBAL SCANDALS BUT NO ANSWERS FOR QUESTIONS OF ETHICS

When news of fraud at the Bank of Credit and Commerce International (BCCI) became public in 1991, headlines described it as the world's most complicated and expensive example of bamboozlement. Indeed, the BCCI disaster involved principals from London (BCCI's international headquarters) to Saudi Arabia and Pakistan—domiciles of the company's behind-the-scenes investors—and the United States, where most of the commercial banks under BCCI became victims or tools of illegal money laundering, fraud, and stock manipulation. As the BCCI case unfolded, it tainted independent Saudi businessmen, Pakistani investment clans, and American political figures. But most important, it revealed blatant activities to siphon off between $4 billion and $10 billion in earnings, stockholders' equity, and depositors' interest through uncontrolled money laundering, foreign exchange maneuvering, and asset manipulation.

During congressional hearings, stories of BCCI's illegal acts revealed that they were rooted in unethical behavior by the principals. Such behavior included actual money laundering; influence peddling by BCCI attorneys and lobbyists; questionable methods of tax avoidance by the principals; and widespread bribes, payoffs, and unusually large "consulting fees" or retainers paid to individuals for unidentifiable services. The British deplored this unethical behavior, and London authorities opened investigations that uncovered far-reaching illegal activities in that country. In America, in addition to the violations of federal banking laws, the unethical behavior could lead to criminal indictments against the bank's principals,

consultants, attorneys, and lobbyists. Most lawsuits related to the scandal will be settled in the United States, where most of the bank and investment fraud occurred and where taxpayers will ultimately cover fraud losses.

Unfortunately, BCCI's behind-the-scenes investors and foreign principals from the Middle East may not only escape unscathed but also enjoy some notoriety in their homelands. Some issues revolve around fundamental differences in business ethics of the individuals involved. In Saudi Arabia, business is often conducted through "connections," which resembles influence peddling, payoffs for lobbying, and outright bribes when viewed from outside. In Pakistan, laundering money and manipulating assets simply represent smart business practices rather than illicit foreign-exchange deals or fraud. Also, beating Uncle Sam through tax loopholes may seem more like gamesmanship than illegal business to Middle Eastern investors; some sense that the fiasco merely amuses many of those involved. However, the British and Americans see nothing amusing about another banking disaster, quick on the heels of the savings and loan debacle of the mid-1980s.

Sources: Stephen J. Hedges, "Inside the BCCI Megascandal," *U.S. News & World Report*, 12 August 1991, 27, 30–32; Susan Dentzer and Leslie Mandel-Viney, "How to Avoid Another BCCI," *U.S. News & World Report*, 12 August 1991, 33; and Marcus W. Brauchli and Peter Truell, "Family Shipping Firm Is One Reason BCCI Lost So Much Money," *Wall Street Journal*, 15 August 1991, pp. A1, A8.

Reebok Foundation, the company sponsors annual "human rights awards" for peaceful activism by employees who volunteer to help local communities and workers to improve their standards of living.[32]

Government Influence on Global Ethics

Although individual efforts by companies such as Reebok, Levi Strauss, and Phillips-Van Heusen influence behavior in host countries, international political alliances are instrumental in fostering widespread changes in business ethics. The treaty that established the North American Free Trade Association (NAFTA), for example, includes a number of provisions for trade transactions, financing, payment methods, contracts, labor negotiations, and employment practices that require conformance to human rights standards, working hours, child labor restrictions, workplace safety, and international patent protection. Disputes among NAFTA participants can be arbitrated or adjudicated through an international tribunal, and although the agreement includes only the United States, Canada, and Mexico, future participants from Latin America will have to measure up to these conditions. Potential NAFTA candidates are not entirely comfortable with the mandates, since they clearly reflect U.S. prerogatives. Existing laws and social behavior in Brazil, Argentina, Uruguay, and Paraguay would not be acceptable under NAFTA. In these countries, for example, child labor is still prominent, currency regulations are lax, and corruption is common. Leaders in these countries are not insensitive to their nation's problems, but they cannot easily induce fundamental changes in cultural and economic values.[33]

Powerful countries also bring pressure to bear on developing countries through bilateral trade agreements. For instance, in the face of severe pharmaceutical pirating, the United States threatened Argentina with trade sanctions to sway recalcitrant lawmakers to pass effective laws for protection of intellectual property.[34] The United States has for years tied its trade agreements to human rights or social issues, although critics argue that trade commerce and social justice should be pursued independently. The most notable U.S. trade initiative has been the annual awarding of MFN (most-favored nation) status to the People's Republic of China. Following China's major change toward global economic development in 1979, the United States granted China MFN status to encourage rapid trade development. MFN status is a poor term. On a scale of 1 to 5, MFN would rate a score of about 3—1 being completely closed trade, which has been the case with Cuba and Burma, and 5 being unrestrained trade, which is similar to the relationship between the United States and Canada. MFN status means that a country can export to the granting country any nonrestricted goods under normal quotas and import duties for a period of time determined by the granting government. During the Bush administration (1989–1993), MFN was described as a "constructive engagement" with China. The argument for MFN was that more foreign trade and international investment would improve transparency in China's activities, subsequently fostering better human rights policies. President Clinton began his administration by threatening to end MFN and to impose economic sanctions if China did not eliminate prison labor and crack down on violations of intellectual property rights. China did make significant changes, but observers say that China's actions were motivated by its efforts to become a member of the World Trade Organization, not to placate U.S. trade missions. In November 1999, the United States and China signed a sweeping bilateral trade agreement that is coupled with social and government regulatory changes by China in its bid to be sanctioned for WTO membership before 2002. However, analysts are pessimistic about China's ability to implement human rights and commercial reforms.[35]

No nation is without ethical problems. When outsiders look at the United States, they see high-profile crime, congressional scandals of unethical conduct, courtroom dramas, and presidents under investigation. Japan has ousted several prime ministers following scandals, and both Germany and France have senior leaders removed or expelled after political malfeasance and cover-ups that date to Nazi connections of World War II.[36] Nevertheless, stronger nations such as the United States, Japan, Germany, France, and Britain attempt to use their economic power to influence values systems elsewhere. For example, Japan is a leading advocate for world environmental protection. The Japanese bring pressure to bear on other countries through trade alliances and financial leverage of their multinationals. Ironically, Japan is also under pressure by other western nations to change its foreign employment policies, which are viewed as discriminatory, particularly with regard to hiring women and African Americans.[37] The European Union has sought to establish a universal code of ethics under the Maastricht Treaty, which addresses commercial transactions, intellectual property rights, and industrial employment policies. The treaty's Social Charter includes 173 guidelines on business conduct, yet within Europe, there is little agreement on these initiatives. Sweden, for instance, says that its national social legislation is far more comprehensive than anything the EU has introduced, and Britain has refused to endorse the Social Charter as an imposition on its national industrial policies. France does not agree with Germany on social or ethical issues, citing preservation of its cultural heritage in criticism of the Social Charter, and Germany believes that its environmental laws and employee relations systems are superior to those of its neighbors.[38]

The important point of these international initiatives is that ethical standards are being openly discussed, and differences in national practices and corporate behavior are being aired. Governments are becoming more sensitive to human rights, environmental issues, trade practices, global transactions, and the *interdependence* of societies. Whether this has occurred for altruistic reasons or through pressure from special interest groups is beside the point. There is convergence toward common agreement on a broad range of ethical issues. International managers, however, are still perplexed by the uncertainty of what rules they and their companies must follow. Even though individual prerogatives and nation-bound moral codes of conduct will become progressively less acceptable, most of the world still presents international managers with ethical dilemmas. One model of conduct has had remarkable influence on international conduct through its guidelines for American businesses operating abroad, and for foreign companies or alliances that cooperate with U.S. interests. This is the U.S. Foreign Corrupt Practices Act, which is addressed in the following section.

The Foreign Corrupt Practices Act

During the 1970s Americans became acutely aware of questionable payments and contributions by U.S. and foreign businesses to both domestic and foreign officials, in order to gain contracts or secure political favors. Following the Watergate Hearings and alleged offshore laundering of contributions to Nixon's 1972 presidential campaign, Congress was pressed to control illegal payments. The triggering event, however, was when the U.S. multinational, Lockheed Corporation, was found to have paid an estimated $25 million to Japanese officials to win an aircraft contract for its Tristar L-1011. The investigations in Japan not only became an embarrassment for the United States but also led to the criminal conviction of Prime Minister Kanjuie Tanaka under Japan's anticorruption laws. In the United States, the Justice Department, Securities Exchange Commission, and Internal Revenue Service studied major international companies and determined that at least 100 of the *Fortune 500* companies had made questionable foreign payments totaling more than $300 million. In reality, estimates far understated the extent of these payments, since researchers studied only a sample of major companies.[39]

As a result of these investigations, the U.S. Congress passed the **Foreign Corrupt Practices Act (FCPA)** in 1977. The FCPA was an attempt to curtail unethical and illegal payments, fees, gifts, and other forms of exchange that could be considered as bribes.[40] The act distinguished bribes to government officials, which it prohibited, from minor "gratuities," which it allowed as legal payments to relatively low-level officials in order to facilitate business. This controversial distinction separated illegal bribery from acceptable gratuities primarily by the amount of the payment. It set a pragmatic standard because few countries had established their own laws against bribery, while gratuities had been common in most cultures for centuries. In many developing countries, for example, it is common to tip a customs official to gain release of a package. Foreign customs officials often earn so little that everyone assumes they will supplement their incomes by providing better service to those who pay a bit of pocket change for their help.

In China, a traveler can gain a good seat on a train by adding a bit of change to the ticket price. In Mexico, as in many countries, motorists avoid traffic tickets by paying the arresting officers, who probably never report the tickets or the payments. Customs clerks and other minor officials in developing countries often welcome small gifts, such as a carton of cigarettes or a bottle of imported wine. These minor payments and other similar gratuities do not constitute illegal acts under the FCPA, mainly because they create no commercial advantage to the person offering the gift or making the payment. The act also allows payments made "under duress," such as threatened arrest or denial of an entry visa, although the offending recipient may have engaged in an illegal act under the host country's laws.

Specific Criteria for Illegal Bribes

The FCPA makes three distinctions about payments. First, bribery occurs and is illegal when a payment is made voluntarily to encourage an unlawful act; the size of payment is not relevant. However, if the payment is made under duress, it is extortion, and the individual who is forced to pay is a victim, not an offender. Second, bribery occurs and is illegal when the payment is "significant" and meant to secure an advantage in trade or commercial activities. These payments are illegal. "Insignificant" payments intended only to expedite services considered to be normal are legal "grease" or "lubricant" gratuities. Third, the FCPA prohibits any payments to an agent or third party that could be used to illegally bribe an official or to secure an unlawful act if the individual making the payment knows, or should have known, that secondary illegal payments would be made on their behalf. This provision guards against a company or individual "laundering" money by passing it through someone else's hands.

These rules can be confusing for several reasons. For example, a payment that appears to be made under duress may be ruled an illegal bribe if there was no clear intention of extortion. Foreign officials may "not exactly" spell out the consequences of not paying for a service, so that if an American tenders some form of payment, it is the American (or the company) that is held liable, not the foreign official. Also, the relative size of a payment could be judged as a gratuity or a bribe, but this is not delineated in the FCPA. Consequently, many companies—such as IBM, GE, and Tenneco—avoid the risk by prohibiting all possible payments as a matter of policy. However, international managers can still get tripped up, even in the best companies. For example, Tenneco managers in India were charged with illegal payments made by the company for mobile telephone calls placed by an Indian official during contract negotiations. Subsequently, Tenneco spelled out a "no excuses" policy for all employees in more than 180 foreign locations and 25 countries, forbidding all payments and gifts of any kind. Unfortunately, overseas employees working under such strict restrictions often find that they cannot obtain permits, process transactions, or even arrange telephone service in many countries without gratuities to workmen or government clerks.[41]

One way to understand this dilemma is to compare small payments with tips, which are commonly paid to restaurant waiters and taxi drivers in the United States. The western system of paying a waitress or waiter low base wages and then expecting them to supplement their income through tips is not considered unethical. Tipping in the United States and most of Europe extends to a wide range of services. In many foreign countries, the same tipping gestures are expected for services ranging from telephone installation to approving export permits. Local people see nothing wrong with these practices.

Third-party payments under the FCPA are more difficult to assess. As the law reads, a company is liable for secondary payments or bribes if it knew or *should have known* that an illegal payment would be made on the company's behalf. This is meant to prevent "slush funds" and "blind packages" from making their way through networks of relationships. Companies are required to practice due diligence in investigating their agents and in making a reasonable effort to determine that gifts do not solicit illegal acts. In China, where *quanxi* (pronounced "gwan-she") is a common form of exchanging favors (gifts, actions, or actual bribes), almost all payments go through third parties. Trade agents often build a premium into their pricing systems to cover quanxi costs, and these can range from small tips to sizable payments. Ironically, China is considered one of the most corrupt nations by U.S. standards; yet internally, the Chinese harshly condemn bribery. Quanxi is not considered to be a bribe, but there are formal rules for illegal bribes that, in effect, are acts of extortion. Anyone caught taking an illegal bribe or benefiting from extortion can be executed.[42]

Requirements for Compliance

The FCPA guidelines require U.S. companies to keep reasonable records and specific accounts of all foreign transactions. This prevents the use of cash slush funds for sizable payments of any kind, and it limits kickback payments or the ability to pad transactions. Unusual accounting controls are not required, but the Securities and Exchange Commission monitors publicly held firms, and all multinationals are under the watchful eye of the Justice Department. Information technology has made it easier for regulators to gain access to data, and foreign countries also supply data for FCPA monitoring. For example, the People's Assembly in Cairo instigated an investigation several years ago of its state-owned airline, *Egyptian*, and sparked U.S. investigations into Boeing Aircraft Company's sales of aircraft to Egypt and Jordan. Comparing data, they found that Egypt paid a significant premium for the same aircraft sold elsewhere at a lower price. As it turned out, Boeing had been placed in the position of charging a higher price, then rebating the excess to Egyptian government officials who had controlled the aircraft purchase.[43]

International transactions can be difficult to administer when companies transship parts and components throughout the world. Companies themselves are often duped by agents. For example, Cargill Corporation, one of the world's largest commodities companies, ships billions of dollars of fertilizer, feed, flour, sugar, and hundreds of similar bulk products to nearly 80 foreign countries. Bulk tonnage is invoiced to buyers or foreign agents, who often break down shiploads into commercially packaged products such as household cereals. Cargill has to be extremely diligent to catch the "baker's dozen" scam. Specifically, Cargill will bill an importer for, say, 12 tons of product, but the importer will create a local invoice for 13 tons that its customer (often a government agency) will purchase. The buyer pays for 13 tons, and the agent pays for 12 tons. The hidden profit is typically passed on to customs people or corrupt officials. Cargill has not benefited from the transaction (and probably is not aware of the infraction), but FCPA regulators could charge that Cargill should have known about the transaction and kept a better audit trail. A twist on this is when an importer creates a local invoice for 11 tons, but receives and actually pays for 12 tons. Customs duties are levied on only 11 tons, and if those duties would have exceeded the purchase price for the unregistered ton, the importer benefits from a lower total cost of the transaction. This is not uncommon in trade where customs duties can be extremely high. Somewhat poor countries like Sri Lanka have 20 to 50 percent import duties on commodities, thus inviting such behavior.[44]

Compliance regulations improved following the Omnibus Trade Act of 1988, which clarified ambiguous provisions of the original FCPA. Specifically, gratuities were defined according to a long list of actual transactions that would be considered legal and necessary to do business. Included in the list are payments for water services, telephones, mail, cargo loading, unloading, special handling of perishable products, transit of goods, obtaining visas, work orders, security permits, and transactions to ensure police and fire protection. The Omnibus Act labels these as *transaction bribes*, conceding that in practical terms, they are similar to tips for services with no connotation of illegality.

Companies can be fined as much as $1 million for each infraction of the FCPA, and individual managers can be fined up to $10,000 and jailed for up to five years. The fines are also regulated so that companies cannot pay fines imposed on their employees, nor can they assist individuals in obtaining funds for fines. This particular rule is designed to hold individuals fully accountable for their offenses, thus risking their personal assets if they are found in violation of the FCPA. Their companies cannot offer immunity or cushion their financial risk. The U.S. Government can also seek an injunction against the company, revoke export or import licenses, and ban the firm from government contracts. Those involved are also subject to civil lawsuits by competitors, who may sue for damages using the criminal evidence in support of a civil claim.

Effects of FCPA on Business

The impact of FPCA regulations on U.S. business has not been extensively researched. Some evidence exists that American companies have suffered losses in Latin American countries by refusing to make questionable payments, subsequently losing contracts or operating licenses. However, studies during the early 1980s of bribery-prone and bribery-adverse nations showed that U.S. exports and investments were not significantly different between the two groups.[45] Recent research focuses on problems in specific countries. In Russia, for example, researchers found that it is impossible to do business there without payoffs, kickbacks, and deals with black-market suppliers. For the Russians, this isn't a matter of international trade or exploiting foreign companies; local Russian businesses face the same corrupt practices, and government agencies are deeply involved in bribery schemes.[46] In another report ranking 54 countries on corruption, Nigeria, Pakistan, Kenya, Bangladesh, China, Russia, India, and Indonesia were rated the most corrupt. Multinationals could choose not to operate in these countries, but they would cut themselves off from markets representing more than half of the world's population. Table 4.3 illustrates the rankings in which Japan and the United States were 38th and 40th respectively; both were rated as relatively more corrupt than Scandinavian and European countries.[47]

The FPCA and the Omnibus Act have provided U.S. multinational companies with some reliable guidelines on ethical practices. Only Sweden has comparable antibribery legislation, yet social legislation enacted by the European Union includes new regulations for business conduct. Foreign countries recognize that U.S. companies are expected to honor U.S. laws; in this sense the regulations have helped Americans, who are less susceptible than others to overtures for illegal payments. Foreign governments are also beginning to emulate ethical codes in their antibribery acts in order to attract investors from North America and Europe. Public outcries in Japan against securities violations and corrupt payoffs by lobbyists have resulted in convictions of bribery among leading politicians and industrialists.[48] New legislation in Japan—together with changes in China's laws and those of Singapore, Malaysia, and

TABLE 4.3

CORRUPTION: A NATIONAL RANKING

(1 = most corrupt, 54 = least corrupt; in 1996 survey by employees of multinational firms and institutions through Transparency International, Berlin)

1. Nigeria	15. Brazil	29. Malaysia	43. Britain
2. Pakistan	16. Ecuador	30. Czech Republic	44. Ireland
3. Kenya	17. Mexico	31. Poland	45. Australia
4. Bangladesh	18. Thailand	32. South Africa	46. Netherlands
5. China	19. Bolivia	33. Portugal	47. Switzerland
6. Cameroon	20. Argentina	34. Chile	48. Singapore
7. Venezuela	21. Italy	35. Belgium	49. Norway
8. Russia	22. Turkey	36. France	50. Canada
9. India	23. Spain	37. Hong Kong	51. Finland
10. Indonesia	24. Hungary	38. Japan	52. Sweden
11. Philippines	25. Jordan	39. Austria	53. Denmark
12. Uganda	26. Taiwan	40. United States	54. New Zealand
13. Colombia	27. Greece	41. Israel	
14. Egypt	28. South Korea	42. Germany	

Source: "Commercial Corruption," *Wall Street Journal*, 2 January 1997, p. 6.

the Philippines—have brought about major transformations in Asia to curb commercial corruption.[49]

ETHICS IN PERSPECTIVE

Headlines about scandals, laundering, payoffs, illegal contributions, and other questionable behavior reinforce public skepticism that business leaders are ethical. Unfortunately, the skepticism extends to public officials both at home and abroad, and debates frequently surface over claims of one society being relatively more ethical than another. Without a doubt, some individual managers are unethical, and this often becomes generalized to all business endeavors. Some countries have patterns of unethical conduct more troublesome than others, especially for managers working in those environments. However, any generalizations are dangerous. It may be more useful for international managers to understand the differences between perceptions of ethical and unethical conduct, as well as the contrasts among prominent world cultures, for countries in which they might work.

Misconceptions about Unethical Conduct

In a recent study of young professional managers, Harvard researchers found that most respondents had been asked to do what they called "sleazy tasks" by their companies. Respondents also reported that their companies have sensible codes of ethics, but few managers consciously considered the implications of behavior that violated these codes. Behavior, the respondents suggested, is based on four commandments of business, and ethical conduct within the framework of these priorities. First, performance is what really counts, not always how results are achieved. Second, loyalty to the organization as a team player influences behavior more than policies or codes of conduct. Third, no one should break the law; to do so is unacceptable regardless of the organization's performance requirements or expectations. And fourth, individuals should not "overinvest" in ethical behavior.[50]

Responses to the Harvard study suggest managers are expected to behave lawfully, yet the definition of what is ethical might be subject to broad interpretation. Managers explained their responses in terms of questionable tasks they had been asked to do by their superiors. These included such things as "massaging numbers" and "hyping reports" to enhance a company's performance profile, and "shading issues" or "hiding information" to protect the company's image. Only a very small number reported more serious infractions, and none that were unlawful. To the contrary, even though they characterized some of their behavior as sleazy, the respondents all felt that their companies were generally ethical. They also said that a large majority of staff and managers did not act inappropriately. The results that emerged from the study indicated that no more than 3 percent of all managers behaved "questionably," and of those, only a few would be characterized as "unethical." Those individuals represented idiosyncratic shortcomings, while the rest were "solid citizens" just doing their jobs.

Unfortunately, misbehavior by a few individuals is too often generalized to entire companies, although the companies will suffer the burden of public criticism. For example, General Electric is an acknowledged leader in pursuing corporate ethics programs, and it has a worldwide reputation for its commitment to socially responsible behavior. Indeed, the company's executives have won public acclaim for leadership and business acumen. But since 1990, GE has been cited for environmental violations and held responsible for 72 Superfund environmental clean-up infractions that have cost the company more than $500 million. GE has also paid more than $163 million in fines for 16 major cases of abuse, fraud, and malfeasance in government contracting. Further, the Justice Department is investigating GE on alleged contract violations at its aircraft engine plants, and the company faces international charges for price fixing and other violations in its industrial diamond markets. GE is still involved with reconciling more than $350 million in false trading profits that occurred in 1994 at the company's Wall Street financial subsidiary, Kidder, Peabody.[51] The evidence would suggest that GE has a great many ethical problems, yet these difficulties do not account for the scope and complexity of the corporation. GE has approximately 225,000 employees worldwide, $60 billion in revenues generated through more than 600 businesses, and operations in 140 countries or territories. The company's infractions were traced to a few individuals or incidents that, combined, involved or affected no more than 0.01 percent of GE's employees or operations. CEO Jack Welch still had to answer charges on behalf of the entire company in congressional hearings, but the company's executives and board of directors have a reputation for rapid and candid response to environmental issues. Their ability to minimize social responsibility difficulties and maintain corporate transparency for such issues has consistently earned GE a top rating for socially responsible companies, and for the company with the best American board of directors.[52]

Researchers involved in the Harvard and GE studies reached similar conclusions: Infractions will prevail through idiosyncratic behavior of individuals, no matter how rigorously a company pursues ethical policies. In comparing ethical conduct over time, the researchers concluded that companies behave much more ethically today than they did in the past, often as a result of voluntary efforts to create socially responsive organizations. Managers also are cognizant that today, more than in the past, any company delinquency is transparent to an educated public that is well informed through penetrating media technology.[53]

Ethics across Cultures

Cross-cultural research on ethical practices yields sparse information. National comparisons are difficult because the criteria on which to judge ethical behavior remain open to question. For example, the studies cited earlier emphasized measures of illegal bribery and payments involving foreign politicians, but these issues were based loosely on U.S. and European rules without considering ethical standards in other countries. Whose priorities determine what standards govern the highest ethics? For example, in Ecuador, illegal bribery and contract manipulation are considered to be widespread problems for multinational firms; but from the Ecuadorian viewpoint, they are not problems *within* the country's culture. Instead, they are problems brought to Ecuador by foreign companies. In fact, in an effort to reduce importation of unethical practices, an association of Ecuadorian businesses called *Transparency Ecuador* joined with its government to press foreign companies into signing pledges not to offer bribes.

In another example, UN representatives from several developing nations in Africa with reputations for corruption have pleaded for changes in European regulations to protect their countries from unethical behavior by outsiders. The representatives specifically cite countries such as France, Belgium, Greece, Germany, and Luxembourg that allow firms to deduct foreign bribes as business expenses from their taxable income. Multinationals from these and several other countries can actually itemize costs on their tax forms as "bribes" or "extortion payments." In Germany, tax deductions are called *nuetzliche Ausgaben*, or "useful expenditures." These laws give a degree of legitimacy to bribery and extortion. Many foreign leaders therefore suggest that corruption does not always originate in their societies but can be introduced to their cultures by foreign interests.[54]

Comparative studies also attempt to distinguish how ethical behavior is defined and enforced among the world's societies, but these differences are difficult to document. Researchers have been able to conclude that European ethics are predominately concerned with employee relations, whereas U.S. codes are heavily weighted toward relationships with foreign governments and customers. Although perceptions of ethical behavior are similar in North America and Europe, European firms focus more intensely on internal conduct while U.S. and Canadian firms focus more intensely on external relations. Also, Europeans are less apt to codify business ethics in written regulations, while U.S. and Canadian companies are sensitive to compliance behavior and therefore favor well-articulated regulations.[55] North Americans, in Canada as well as the United States, are much more likely to create policies and document employment rules than Europeans, Japanese, or Arabs. Another distinction is that Europe welcomes broad-based social legislation that creates national codes of conduct, such as that in Sweden and Germany.[56] In contrast to North American and European societies, Japan relies on social homogeneity and a deeply ingrained national code of ethics to inspire self-directed conduct rather than enacting conformance regulations.[57] Consequently, observers find little real evidence on which to judge the relative ethical performance of one nation against that of another, and such comparisons become extremely difficult when studying developing nations and transition societies.

Guidelines for Avoiding Ethical Dilemmas

As long as there are differences in individual and cultural values, there will be differences in expectations for ethical behavior. Thus international managers will almost always face ethical dilemmas in their foreign assignments. Multinational corporations try to minimize ethical problems by establishing codes of conduct, but these will have little effect without education and reinforcement. Therefore, companies also establish ethics training programs to sensitize their people to cultural norms in host countries and to instruct managers in company expectations for ethical conduct. Specific topics of ethics programs for U.S. companies include, for example, elements of the FCPA and Title VII of the U.S. Civil Rights Act. Programs also include development training in topics such as managing diversity and negotiating contracts to help managers adapt to foreign assignments. Many multinationals, such as GE, Texas Instruments, Motorola, and AT&T, spend a great deal of money on *predeparture training* to acculturate employees scheduled for overseas positions.

Ultimately, a multinational must stand behind its commitment to ethics by reinforcing appropriate behavior and maintaining a disciplined approach to ethical business decisions. This implies a comprehensive consideration for human resource management, as discussed at length in Chapters 12 and 13. In providing ethics programs, specifically, companies have several options. Modules on various components can be provided through in-house training, consultants may contract to provide acculturation training with specific interests in ethics, or managers can attend university or professional programs on business ethics. Universities and consultants usually offer pre-planned seminars or courses, but the following guidelines offer useful principles for developing the internal ethics component of such a program:[58]

- Determine the major ethical issues of a foreign assignment. In some instances, a foreign assignment may present sensitive problems for bribery. In another, the religion of the host country may require an understanding of critical moral values. In others, inequality of sexes or hierarchical power differences may lead to ethical conflicts.

- Institutionalize appropriate behavior through a corporate code of ethics, developed by the participants in conjunction with company leaders. This document should establish a value-based framework of guidelines for self-directed behavior in foreign posts.

- Provide realistic opportunities to experience ethical dilemmas and methods to resolve them. A program at the parent company can utilize case studies, guest speakers, role playing, or simulation. Programs in the host country can be realistically presented through local mentors and nonthreatening ethical confrontations that simulate potential situations.

- Whether at home or abroad, managers should be encouraged to attend seminars on cross-cultural management, including ethics components. When possible, they should network with others in the industry to attend seminars or conferences organized by professional organizations. By attending these sessions, managers learn the best practices and bring benchmark criteria back to their companies.

- Create an ethics review process that generates regular feedback from field managers and program participants. In this process, participants should reexamine the company's core values and its code of ethics to determine their relevance and practicality.

Personal ethical decisions are far more difficult to categorize than company policies. If any message is apparent in this chapter, it is that ethical standards are difficult to define apart from cultural values. Therefore, researchers have suggested several points to bear in mind:[59]

- Explore the facts of an ethical dilemma and clearly understand the alternatives before taking any action.

- Understand what parties will be affected by a decision, how they will be affected, and what rights they have to influence the outcome of a decision.
- When considering an alternative action or decision, consciously evaluate its fairness to everyone involved.
- Ensure that the action or decision conforms to legal standards and, if so, if it is the most ethical alternative under the circumstances.
- Determine that an activity or decision can be successfully and ethically implemented.

At the outset, the chapter defined *business ethics* with reference to conduct perceived to be right and moral by individuals within an enterprise. As these guidelines suggest, ethical decisions are personal actions that must take into account human dignity and a sense of community. No one lives in isolation, and a society needs foundations of values for individuals to live and work together in relative security. Ethical behavior, however, can be attributed to a company, and in this sense the inanimate corporate entity bears responsibility for collective behavior by its members. As the next section explains, a business firm's social responsibility is part of the more pervasive concept of business ethics.

SOCIAL RESPONSIBILITY

Corporate social responsibility is an organization's obligation to conduct business in a way that safeguards the welfare of society while pursuing its own interests. This was the definition provided early in the chapter, but *responsiveness* was emphasized as the perception of how an organization deals with social issues, not necessarily what it actually does. Therefore, corporations are not concerned with always doing the right thing (which may be impossible), but with making a reasonable effort to prevent problems—and when problems occur, with addressing them in an ethical manner.

International Priorities for Corporate Citizenship

The composite behavior of corporations, defined by policies, practices, and decisions of senior managers, determines the public's perception of a company's citizenship. Social responsiveness is thus reflected in the behavior of managers, and researchers have found that managerial values vary widely throughout the world. A study by Harvard University compared the social values of 12,000 senior managers from major multinationals in Europe, Asia, and North America. The results revealed a general consensus among the respondents that environmental protection, human rights, poverty, and education were the most important social issues; but the study also found little agreement about the priorities of these problems. The top five priorities that a large majority of executives identified were environmental protection, human rights, poverty, drug and alcohol abuse, and education. However, differences in social values resulted in substantially different rankings by respondents in each country. The Japanese ranked environmental protection as the single most pressing issue to be addressed by business and government leaders, but American executives ranked environmental concerns fifth. One explanation given for this dichotomy was that Japan has experienced escalating industrial and urban pollution in a country where population density accentuates environmental concerns, while Americans enjoy a very low population density and isolated areas of industrial or urban pollution. Several other contrasts were equally puzzling. Americans ranked drug and alcohol abuse as the top priority, while European and Japanese respondents placed this problem at the bottom of the list. Americans ranked education second highest, but Japanese and Europeans were reluctant to consider education as among the top priorities. Instead, they put greater weight on human rights issues and poverty.[60]

Explanations for these differences in social priorities were based on twentieth-century events that changed each society, and on fundamental differences in cultural values. The United States has been the primary target market for illegal drugs, Europe has experienced two world wars in which human rights were pervasively violated, and both Japan and Europe suffered massive human indignities and poverty from wars or political upheavals. Ethnic and religious differences among Asian cultures have stratified societies for centuries, and in Europe, social ideologies have created different patterns of expectations for education and human rights than in America. Consequently, while most managers from the world's leading economies have a sense of problems common to all countries, managers from each country have very different priorities about the problems their particular societies face.[61]

Managers are expected to respond to social problems in their particular societies, but those expectations differ in every culture. Japanese managers are not expected to take active roles in solving social problems. Instead, the Japanese rely on social awareness and culturally embedded sanctions to influence individuals and corporations toward compliant behavior that is congruent within their society. In contrast, German managers are expected to participate in public initiatives such as waste management, pollution control, corporate sponsorship for education, and employee development. They are also expected to commit corporate assets to these public programs.[62] A *patron system* in Mexico shifts the burden of social problems such as unemployment and poverty onto government. Mexican companies tend to become involved in social issues such as human rights or environmental protection to support government programs, but they seldom initiate activities beyond the scope of their own enterprises.[63] In social welfare countries such as Sweden, and to a lesser extent Britain, corporations are not expected to take an active role in solving social problems. Corporations in the United States are expected to respond to social issues such as employee welfare and waste management, but they are not expected to respond to broader issues such as education and human rights. These are generalizations that have many exceptions; but clearly, managers from one society working in another will face substantially different perceptions of how corporations are expected to respond to social problems.[64]

Corporate involvement in social issues can be expected and warranted, yet it can also be criticized as inappropriate intervention. This was emphasized recently at an international conference of corporate executives who met specifically to discuss social responsibilities of multinational companies. The conference included managers from Lotus Development, Levi Strauss, The Body Shop, Au Bon Pain, Ben & Jerry's Homemade, MBW, The Gap, Honeywell, British Petroleum, and many others.[65] The executives concluded that local norms for corporate activities had to be institutionalized in the context of the host-country cultures. For example, Honeywell supports community health and social services programs in the United States through charitable funding, but also through corporate sponsorship of programs such as Honeywell's "New Vistas High School." This program offers pregnant teenagers and teenage mothers a way to continue their education at corporate expense. However, Honeywell has been unable to pursue similar programs in Eastern Europe or Latin America because religious beliefs and social sanctions keep social problems such as teen pregnancy out of public view. They are guarded as family affairs, and efforts by companies to help are considered intrusions. The Gap, like many distributors of clothing made in less-developed countries, is sensitive to products made by child labor or fabricated in "sweat shops." The Gap tries to closely monitor its foreign sourcing, but in many

A 12-year-old child works at a rug loom near Casablanca, Morocco, where two of every five children are homeless. Children are hired off the streets or from impoverished families, but if these children did not work, they and their families would face a worse fate. Most would not have an opportunity to attend school or to learn a skill, so child labor is often viewed as a benefit to developing societies. It is often the only means of survival for destitute families and homeless children.

countries, youth aged 12 and 13 typically work in factories to help support their families. If the company refuses jobs to youngsters, many would be put on the street, adding to their poverty problems. The Gap addresses this dilemma by limiting employment ages and restricting the type of work youth can do, but not by withdrawing from these markets and ignoring the problem.[66]

Responding to Local Expectations

Laws and social norms in each country dictate how corporations are expected to participate as local enterprises. When a subsidiary fails to achieve these expectations, the company may be tolerated only to the extent that it generates jobs or adds to the nation's economic well-being. To be accepted as a socially responsible organization, the company must at least comply with local expectations—and often go beyond those expectations—to demonstrate its commitment to good corporate citizenship.[67] World cultures differ in too many ways to try to explain specifically how international managers should respond to local expectations, but research has identified several mainstream issues. These are presented in Table 4.4; several examples that follow may help to illustrate these concerns.

International companies often bring new standards of conduct to their foreign operations that influence changes in the host countries. For example, BMW pushed for new environmental protection measures in its home country of Germany long before the "Green Party" emerged as a political force in the 1980s. BMW executives also encouraged their subsidiaries to pursue environmental protection measures in other European locations and among their Asian affiliates. BMW believed that the company could not only reduce waste and create a cleaner industrial environment, but it could do so without eroding profits. A unique effort by BMW was a prototype "disassembly

TABLE 4.4

CORPORATE CITIZENSHIP—RESPONDING TO LOCAL EXPECTATIONS

Multinational corporations and their managers should be responsive to local laws and expectations with respect to:

- Environmental and pollution controls
- Employment of women and minorities
- Employment of local citizens and expatriates
- Personnel issues, including remuneration, pension plans, recruitment and dismissal procedures, and training
- Management-union relationships
- Taxation and financial controls
- Securities and investments
- Purchase of local and foreign materials
- Purchase, lease, and location of land, building, and plant
- Market competition
- All other business activities constrained by law

Source: Adapted from Richard Mead, *International Management: Cross Cultural Dimensions* (Cambridge, Mass.: Blackwell Publishers, 1994), 295–296.

line" to recycle entire cars. The idea was to retrieve good parts and accessories, recondition them for the secondary market, and recycle the remaining metal from old automobiles. The project was so successful that BMW set up a subsidiary dedicated to dismantling cars, where nearly 80 percent of a vehicle's parts are reconditioned at a profit. European observers studied BMW's effort, and in 1992, German politicians sponsored a law requiring all heavy industries to collect and recycle packaging, cans, cardboard, paper, and plastics. Legislation, all aimed at industrial recycling, subsequently emerged in Austria, France, and Britain; today the European Union has pervasive guidelines for its member nations.[68]

As noted earlier, many societies do not always appreciate efforts by multinationals to address local social problems, because the foreign company usually approaches the problems from its home-country perspective. This unwanted intervention is called **cultural** or **ethical imperialism,** which is the perceived imposition of social standards by one country on another society. Conflicting viewpoints about social standards thus represent serious dilemmas for many managers who try to maintain standards of conduct according to their values in overseas assignments. For example, sexual harassment and sexual discrimination are sensitive issues in North America and Western Europe, but treatment of women (and behavior toward female co-workers) is judged differently elsewhere. When measured by U.S. standards, treatment of women in Saudi Arabia, for example, would be exploitative. Women cannot negotiate with men, they cannot travel alone, and, indeed, many cannot get a driver's license.[69] The gender situation is worse in Oman and Kuwait, where women cannot get passports and in most instances cannot collect their own wages or handle bank accounts.[70] In many Latin and African cultures, behavior by men can be exceptionally condescending.[71]

American firms such as Goodyear Tire & Rubber Company, E. I. du Pont de Nemours (DuPont), and SmithKline Beecham—all known for their proactive policies to eliminate gender discrimination and sexual harassment—find that they cannot impose the same expectations on foreign workers. They report few actual complaints of sexual harassment or discrimination among their foreign subsidiaries, not because problems do not exist, but because men and women in their foreign operations do not recognize that the problems exist according to their customs. Consequently, Goodyear relies on local managers to determine appropriate behavior while trying to maintain equitable policies. DuPont conducts extensive sexual harassment training in the United States, but does not transport those programs overseas. Instead, the company works with diversity consultants in trying to minimize foreign practices that clash with corporate policies, and when possible, to enforce hiring and disciplinary rules that do not conflict with local norms.[72]

CONCLUDING COMMENTS

The examples of social responsiveness cited here barely scratch the surface of international relationships that would constitute good corporate citizenship, but they do illustrate the difficulty of generalizing standards of behavior or encoding universal policies on conduct. They also reinforce the point that social responsiveness is a matter of perception. A company's actions viewed as commendable in one country may be ridiculed in another. International managers constantly navigate through cultural clashes and ethical dilemmas, and in order to achieve recognition as socially responsive businesspeople, they must engage the controversies one at a time.

Business ethics and social responsibilities are difficult to reconcile. Perplexing differences in cultural and individual values preclude any universal sense of appropriate behavior, although individual firms and international consortia are attempting to establish guidelines. Discussions of these crucial dimensions of international management appear early in the book because they deserve consideration among the foundations of international business and as building blocks for understanding managerial careers. Chapters in Part Two are concerned with decisions about global strategies and competition. These topics are often best understood in the context of the ethical environment of business and the nature of foreign relations.

REVIEW QUESTIONS

1. Define the terms *social responsibility* and *business ethics*. In the process, explain the concept of corporate responsiveness.
2. International managers can influence their companies to adopt either *reactive* or *proactive* responses to achieve social responsiveness, leading to public perceptions of more or less ethical approaches to social problems. Describe and contrast four patterns of behavior that illustrate these approaches.
3. Explain the logic of *ethical relativism* from four different viewpoints, and discuss the arguments for and against universal values.
4. Cultural relativism is particularly important to international managers. Explain how cultural values influence multinational activities in host countries and how this process generates ethical dilemmas.
5. Major governments frequently use their economic power to influence ethical conduct in foreign countries through trade and alliances. Explore the merits of this form of government intervention.
6. The U.S. Foreign Corrupt Practices Act differentiates between illegal bribes and legal gratuities. Explain how firms can justify controversial payments to foreign parties as legal expenditures. Do you agree with these provisions of the FCPA? Defend your position.

7. Contrast the methods by which different countries develop and instill in citizens social codes of ethics. Discuss the similarities and differences in cultural priorities that would affect convergence toward a common international code of business conduct.

8. How can multinationals encourage perceptions of their organizations as socially responsible citizens? Argue for or against this statement: The business community and its leaders participate in society in a socially responsible way at home and abroad.

9. Multinationals face sensitive situations in developing countries, sometimes facing charges of *ethical imperialism*. Explain the foundations of these charges, and describe how managers can avoid conflicts.

10. Being a socially responsive organization is often a matter of perception. Describe the dilemma of a firm trying to be a good corporate citizen in a host country yet also trying to protect its own business interests.

GLOSSARY OF KEY TERMS

Business ethics   Standards for conduct perceived as right and moral by individuals within an enterprise, taking into account the human welfare of those affected by decisions and behavior.

Corporate responsiveness   The public perception of an organization's reaction when it learns of social issues or problems, or of its proactive efforts to prevent problems.

Corporate social responsibility   An organization's obligation to conduct business in a way that safeguards the welfare of society as it pursues its own interests.

Cultural relativism   The influence on standards of morality of priorities within a particular society or culture, often bounded by nationality.

Ethical imperialism   Efforts to impose one society's ethical norms on another through political or commercial influence by governments or multinationals. Also called *cultural imperialism.*

Ethical relativism   A belief that standards for behavior require interpretation.

Ethical standards   Expectations to which companies and individuals must conform to remain consistent with widely accepted modes of conduct.

Foreign Corrupt Practices Act (FCPA)   A U.S. law that attempts to define ethical and legal behavior of U.S. companies with respect to payments, fees, gifts, and other forms of exchange.

Group relativism   The influence on moral judgments and individual behavior of expectations defined by membership in a referent group.

Naive relativism   The belief that every individual retains sole responsibility for deciding standards for right or wrong in a world without absolute criteria.

Role relativism   The concept that certain moral obligations are inherent in work roles, and they often create expectations distinct from personal moral beliefs.

Social contract   A set of expectations for the role of a company and its managers in a particular society or community consistent with its values, customs, ideologies, and economic realities.

EXERCISES

1. Obtain a recent copy of a corporate code of conduct from library resources, the Internet, or by contacting a multinational company. In class, list key concepts from each company's code on a board, and keep count of how many codes refer to the same concepts. The result should be a list with some items ticked often and others ticked seldom, perhaps only once. Prioritize these lists and discuss reasons for similarities or differences in priorities.

2. Choose a law not mentioned in the chapter, such as an environmental protection act or affirmative action regulation (perhaps one enacted by a foreign nation), and ask someone from another culture (student, faculty member, or manager) how that law would be perceived in his or her country. Would it be ridiculed? accepted? modified? Be prepared to discuss your findings.

3. Select teams of four or five students. Each team will prepare a list of three situations or decisions that international managers might face overseas that could present sensitive ethical dilemmas. Each team will describe these situations to another team and ask for a brief response in class. All remaining teams will assign scores for their perceptions of each answer, from 1 (low) to 10 (high). Questions and answers should be limited to about 10 minutes each. In the end, tally the scores and discuss the results. Which problems were most difficult to resolve? Why?

ENRON CORPORATION HOLDS THE LINE ON ETHICS IN INDIA

Seven years after plunging into India, Houston-based Enron Corporation secured the largest international strategic power development project yet for a U.S. multinational. The $3.1 billion natural gas facility in the western Indian state of Maharashtra is the first phase of a $10 billion international joint venture, entirely owned by non-Indian investors. Enron—arguably the largest U.S. company in natural gas and pipeline delivery systems—has 80 percent of the venture, and the remainder is shared by American partners General Electric and Bechtel Corporation.

However, the entire project has been highly controversial, not because of its foreign ownership but because of the extraordinary infighting required by Enron just to remain in India and to stand fast against three different governments riddled with corruption. Between 1992 and 1999, the company fought and won 27 international lawsuits, all brought by Indian officials, charging unethical bribery and graft involvement. This period also brought intense negotiations. Some saw the project as an organizational battleground as the Indian government and private Indian interests in the state of Maharashtra tried in vain to gain control of up to 30 percent of the project through political maneuvering, backroom pressure, and outright intimidation.

Early attempts by India's various interest groups failed to influence the Americans to ante up part of the equity ownership, particularly when no one seemed able or willing to pay for the assets, so retaliation brought charges against the Americans for everything from petty bribery of national politicians and local officials to land graft and ethnocentrism. This ploy had little effect, so the Indian government at the time simply canceled Enron's business contracts and operating permits. This move enraged the Texas executive staff, and they responded with lawsuits of their own to enforce contract terms. During international hearings, that Indian government was voted out of power. Subsequently, several senior politicians, including the ousted prime minister, were indicted on corruption charges and various allegations of extor-

tion. Many of the charges apparently involved foreign investors from Asia and Europe who fell victim to India's well-known proclivity to fleece anyone with deep pockets.

The new government, however, had little power and relatively little control over regional politics or India's state bureaucracies, and it did not last a full term before itself being overwhelmed in a forced election by a 13-party coalition government. In its wake, the Congress Party, which had ruled India for half a century, left a quagmire of useless regulations and confusing commercial policies that have seriously thwarted foreign investment. By 1997, for example, foreign investment had risen only slightly, falling short of projections by nearly 70 percent, and the Bombay Stock Market had lost nearly 20 percent of its value in less than a year.

The critical problem was government credibility. The 13-party government had not demonstrated that it could control the provinces or politicians. Corruption, extortion, fraud, and petty hand-greasing substantially increased, and foreign multinational corporations simply looked elsewhere for investments or markets. Enron, however, stayed and faced charges brought by the old Congress Party when it was in power. These suits ran for more than five years, and Enron was successful in having them litigated under British law in London, where the company won every point. Then a new coalition government came to power, largely on the strength of anti-Enron sentiment that resulted in the company's office being bombed and its employees harassed by local pro-Socialist activists. The new coalition government promised to oust foreign multinationals, and for those in India, the government buried them in red tape.

When this government dissolved under the weight of democratic elections, all prior decisions about Enron's contracts were reversed. Indeed, the new government gave official sanction to the energy project, but also demanded an equity interest as a "cooperative" partner. Fortunately, the coalition ministers involved seemed to be clean. Enron saw no hands held out for favors, and officials seemed determined to encourage industrial development without blatant corruption that had existed under prior regimes. Unfortunately, the government agency involved in the negotiations lacked funds to actually become an invested partner with Enron. The state-owned electricity board was not only in the red at the time but also has continued to suffer from entanglements in the Finance Ministry's problems with petroleum subsidies, which drain more than $1 billion a year from the country's cash reserves. Somewhat reluctantly, Enron and its American partners were given a clean slate and full license to launch the multibillion-dollar power project that was inaugurated by Rebecca P. Mark. As CEO of Enron International, Mark launched a system of liquefied natural gas plants in India and elsewhere in Asia.

Mark explained that doing business in India almost always involves decisions in grey areas, and although her company has always remained well clear of any suspect behavior, it has also had to acknowledge some realities for "doing business the Indian way." For example, because Enron brings into the country billions of dollars in materials and equipment, it faces an official import duty of 20 percent. "But when it comes right down to it," Mark said, "very common in a project is that it doesn't end up being 20 percent but whatever the customs inspector wants it to be on the day you get there." Encountering the Indian way of business—based on cutting deals, trading favors, and opening doors with so-called palm-oil money—Enron has stayed focused and sought changes in the system. "People thought we were pushy and aggressive," Mark reported. "But think of the massive bureaucracy we had to move that has done things one way its entire collective life." In effect, companies such as Enron face delicate decisions about what constitutes proper behavior; it is not always clear which demands simply reflect "customary practices" and which are violations of business ethics.

Although government actions have become more transparent today, based on established democratic, legal, and judicial systems, politicians and bureaucrats still wield enormous and arbitrary powers to change and interpret complicated rules and regulations in a rapidly changing business environment. Enron faced an unusual situation; being highly visible during the years of legal proceedings, the company had to avoid any ethical infraction, such as bribes. In the end, Enron won because it followed international legal guidelines on corporate conduct. Success by a major

business enterprise without bribery or suspect deals shocked most Indian observers. Indeed, when earlier governments brought charges against Enron and wild rumors circulated in regional newspapers, reporters from the *Wall Street Journal* investigating the incident found a quick assumption among Indians: "Of course they did these things. How else does a company do business? How else would a billion-dollar project get approval unless appropriate government officials got rich in the process?" Current investigations of government dealings during the 1980s and early 1990s have revealed that substantial payments were made by both domestic and international companies—including foreign government agencies—on key Indian defense contracts, power plants, franchise licenses, telecommunication ventures, and virtually all infrastructure construction, such as road contracts. Sadly, kickbacks and other forms of side payments were generally accepted because the money went mainly to finance political parties, especially the ruling Congress Party. In many instances, intermediaries and ministers skimmed off money; Indian business has always contended with relatively minor corruption, such as widespread payments for telephone installations and customs clearances.

An opinion poll reported in the *Times of India* during the sensitive 1995 elections found that 98 percent of respondents believed politicians and ministers were corrupt, followed by 97 percent for police, 88 percent for bureaucrats, and 80 percent for lawyers. One high-ranking Indian business executive quoted in the poll said of his competitors, "They don't bribe ministers. They just have every politician in the country on their payroll." Apparently this witticism drew very little attention, other than a countercharge that the executive's family had a reputation for cutting in government agencies on nearly every business they controlled. According to an unspoken rule of thumb, politicians and provincial officials can expect about 10 percent of a project's investment value simply to win their cooperation. Foreign journalists know that they must pay license fees for publishing rights. Dealers and foreign brokers collect so-called expediting premiums beyond their official fees. Customs officials have for years set their own duty rates and conditions for storing or releasing imported goods and materials. In many instances, bribery is openly conducted. Recent investigative reports, for example, describe how an unnamed U.S. firm lost an Indian contract for a development project when the Americans refused to pay an official request for $30 million to a minister in the Congress Party. A European firm apparently paid the fee and got the bid. Meanwhile, executives from Germany and France spend officially sanctioned funds of up to $4 million annually to "take care of necessary payments" in India. These payments are officially recorded and listed on German and French tax returns as business expenses.

Amid this dirty business, Enron apparently stayed clean, and the company persisted in its contracts. Critics suggest that the company and its partners should have looked elsewhere and avoided the problems in India. Enron officials respond that while corruption in India is serious, it is worse in China, nearly as bad in the Persian Gulf, and complicated by terrorism or regional warfare in the Middle East and many parts of Latin America. At least in India, they say, they now know the game and the players, and their adversaries know that Enron will play by the rules.

An interesting twist to the Enron saga is that through the long legal debates and political turmoil, India's sadly inadequate commercial laws and mysterious business regulations became focal points in the European courts and arbitration tribunals. Consequently, business laws were substantially reformed, new legal codes were written—such as those to allow arbitration in India—and laws governing insurance, finance, and currency controls were legislated. Enron is credited with fostering fundamental changes in India's business methods, including adoption of new anticorruption laws and environmental protection regulations. These changes improve the business environment for all companies, including domestic Indian interests as well as multinational corporations.

QUESTIONS

1. India obviously has major problems with business ethics, but many little conditions contribute to the "Indian way of doing business." How does a company deal with issues such as bribery, and by what rules does an international manager play in a foreign country such as India?

2. Could a cultural relativist make a case that India's business practices are ethical by local standards? How are ethical business practices defined in such instances as bribery by American and European authorities? Indeed, do any universal rules of ethical conduct apply in India?

3. If foreign companies accommodate corruption in India and foreign laws take into account practices such as bribery, can India be blamed for its corruption, or can a case be made that corruption is imported? Take a position and defend your points.

BIBLIOGRAPHY

Elliott, John. "India's Slide into Sleeze." *Asian Wall Street Journal*, 13 November 1995, p. 6.

"Enron and On and On." *The Economist*, 14 June 1997, 74.

Jordan, Miriam. "Indian Leader Rao Quits Post to Face Charges." *Wall Street Journal*, 23 September 1996, p. A17.

Karp, Jonathan. "India's Gowda Belatedly Advances Economic Reform." *Wall Street Journal*, 19 February 1997, p. A12.

Kripalani, Marjeet. "You Have to Be Pushy and Aggressive: How Rebecca Mark Helped Enron Bounce Back in India." *Business Week*, 24 February 1997, 56.

O'Reilly, Brian. "The Power Merchant—Enron, No. 18 on the Fortune 500." *Fortune*, 17 April 2000, 148–160.

CASE 4.2

CHILD LABOR AND HUMAN RIGHTS: STARBUCKS TAKES NEW MEASURES

Starbucks Coffee Company, concerned about human rights violations among its foreign suppliers, has adopted broad guidelines aimed at improving working conditions at plantations and foreign supplier operations. The guidelines are specifically aimed at Starbucks coffee suppliers, but they are gaining attention in many other agricultural sectors and among multinationals engaged in textile contracting. The company's guidelines were the first ever to be adopted by a big U.S. importer involved in an agricultural commodity. Starbucks executive managers initiated their code of ethical conduct for foreign suppliers in late 1995, and field observers for the International Labor Organization and several human rights groups from the United States and Europe reported that by 1997, the initiatives had had a major effect on child labor practices. Observers also found that the code of conduct had influenced wage structures for agricultural workers, and subcontracting practices for many continental and North American companies operating in Latin America and Southeast Asia.

The Starbucks guidelines call for the Seattle company's suppliers abroad to pay wages and benefits that at least "address the basic needs of workers and their families." For example, the company wants suppliers to allow child labor only when it does not "interfere with mandated education." In addition, Starbucks has strongly advocated broader public education for agricultural workers in countries such as Brazil, Colombia, Tanzania, and Kenya. It also wants suppliers to help workers gain "access to safe housing, clean water and health facilities and services." Although the company does not actively manage overseas facilities or have the level of direct foreign investment abroad comparable to those of major multinationals, its extensive supply contracts allow management to bring considerable economic pressure on export-dependent nations. In addition, the guidelines endorse the right of workers to free association and to "work because they want or need to, but not because they are forced to do so." This provision strikes deeply at practices such as forced labor and economic enslavement, which seldom come to people's attention despite protests by worldwide human rights groups.

Global human rights activists applauded the guidelines, saying they substantially widen the possibilities for corporate codes of conduct. "This is going to be a benchmark for a lot of importers of agricultural commodities," said Robert Dunn, president of Business for Social Responsibility, a trade group. "Starbucks has drawn a roadmap that will make it easier for other companies to assess whether what they currently do is adequate." Dunn noted that a small but growing number of western consumers object to buying imported goods made by children, bonded labor, or workers paid below the legal minimum wage in their home countries. Still, multinationals encounter extremely difficult obstacles when they try to influence foreign practices. Consider, for example, that more than half the world's population relies on agriculture for both minimum subsistence and for a large majority of national income derived through exports. In most developing countries, any able-bodied individual, no matter how young or old, expects to work in fields, processing plants, textile facilities, or some aspect of agricultural and fiber-based industries. A fine line separates a company providing valued work and one exploiting human beings.

Of course, child labor and worker exploitation are not confined to poor, low-wage, developing countries; and they certainly are not limited to only the agriculture and textile trades. Companies everywhere are willing to hire children, not only because they are cheaper but also because they are docile workers. According to the Geneva-based International Labor Organization (ILO), an estimated 61 percent of child workers live in Asia, 32 percent in Africa, and 7 percent in Latin America. The ILO census did not include developed countries and Eastern Europe. Children in developing countries work in agriculture or as domestic servants, but they also toil in mines, construction, fishing fleets, glass factories, apparel industries, and mills. Some of these jobs pose serious health hazards. Children also are victims of unacceptable forced labor, such as prostitution. In one report, the ILO found evidence of international networks trafficking in children, including one in Eastern Europe that transported girls from Belarus, Russia, and the Ukraine to Hungary, Poland, and the Baltic states—and perhaps onward to developed neighboring states.

The particularly small slice of human rights concern is, by itself, vast enough to overwhelm most responsible companies with foreign operations. Prior to the accelerated pace of globalization, European and U.S. consumer companies relied on their own employees to make most products, and standards were easier to enforce. They were part of a social consensus of what constituted appropriate work and compensation. Today, many name-brand products are made by foreign contractors, severing the direct link between workers and western companies. Foreign subsidiaries managed locally have little understanding of U.S. or European work rules, and neither the managers nor their employees are aware of social values or human rights expectations beyond their own (often very localized) communities. From a child-labor-rights perspective, there is little consensus of what is right or wrong apart from obvious problems such as forced prostitution.

In this uncertain environment, socially conscious multinationals have attempted to implant some criteria for improving human rights among their foreign contractors and suppliers. Like Starbucks, Levi Strauss Associates Inc., Reebok International Ltd., Nike Inc., The Gap, and numerous other importers and retailers have endorsed codes that threaten to cut off any contract suppliers that allow substandard working conditions. Starbucks does not plan to punish suppliers that violate its code. Indeed, agricultural and textile-related commodity markets are too vast to be influenced by one or even a few major companies. Cutting off a contract would only mean that the supplier would sell to a competitor, probably without changing its work practices. However, despite the grim realities of labor on plantations and small farms in many parts of the world, human rights advocates are hopeful about the guidelines. The fact that Starbucks does not threaten punishments may make it easier for the company to sell its concepts of child labor practices and ethical work conditions to foreign suppliers.

"The last thing I want is for people to start shaking in their boots when they see me coming," says David Olsen, Starbucks vice president. Olsen added, "It's going to take a long time to improve conditions for agricultural workers in many foreign countries, where child labor, poor sanitary conditions, and near-subsistence wages are common."

Experts disagree about the best ways to reduce reliance on child labor. Proposed responses range from punitive restrictions on international trade in products made by children to the adoption of voluntary programs by government, business, and social service agencies to steer children into schools and out of workplaces. Unfortunately, no one has yet found a cost-effective way to address these issues. U.S. Senator Tom Harkin backed a measure to ban imports made by children, and the World Trade Organization has pressured its constituent members to adopt a social clause that forbids the worst labor abuses. These efforts have gained praise, but even sympathetic advocates say they may do little good. According to a Columbia University Policy Study Group, "Such measures may make your conscience look good, but won't get desired results because displaced child workers won't necessarily end up in school, where

they belong, but may be forced into even more degrading labor, such as pornography and prostitution."

Companies that do try to take individual measures find themselves in awkward situations, and they are seldom appreciated. Some human rights advocates, for example, say that Starbucks should have done more. "Without some mechanism to force the selection of better suppliers, this falls far short of being a serious lever for change," said Pharis Harvey, director of the International Labor Rights and Education Fund, an advocacy group in Washington. Indeed, only recently, human rights advocates picketed Starbucks stores around the United States and briefly boycotted the company's products. They cited concerns that Guatemalan workers supplying beans to Starbucks toiled under dreadful conditions. Starbucks Vice President Olsen said that protestors "prodded" the company into forging a rights policy tightening guidelines on suppliers in Guatemala, yet the company could not have a substantial effect on its own accord. Nevertheless, Starbucks invested heavily in a planned study of working conditions and introduced stricter monitoring systems. These initiatives will take concerted efforts by foreign and domestic interests, and continued support by organizations such as the Business for Social Responsibility group. Olsen is sympathetic with protesters and notes that their pressure—even when directly aimed at his own company—has value in alerting everyone to issues such as child labor exploitation. Responding hurts the company's bottom line, but that cost may represent a necessary price of greater social awareness.

Although Starbucks has taken a leadership role in this particular aspect of social responsiveness, many companies in North America, Germany, the Netherlands, and Britain, have, in particular, focused their efforts on commodity imports. Nestlé has brought its considerable economic strength to bear on child labor rules among coffee and cocoa growers in South America and Africa, and a small but growing percentage of coffee already carries a label purporting to guarantee that beans were picked by workers earning a fair share of coffee profits. In September 2000, Starbucks joined forces with the Ford Foundation and other donor groups in *TransFair International*, a nonprofit organization that circumvents agents and middlemen traders to work directly with growers, farmers, and agricultural cooperatives in poor countries. TransFair guarantees to purchase or arrange buyers for these people, passing on profits of between 30 and 50 percent while helping them plan their crops and market products without being exploited. Starbucks will market a special line of coffee products under the TransFair label, thereby certifying to customers that quality coffee beans were purchased at a fair price from independent growers, and that the company had assured each grower of a substantial profit. More important, TransFair and its supporters, like Starbucks, are active in assuring that growers and farmers do not exploit child labor guidelines; through the revenue guarantees, improvements are made in local education and housing facilities. TransFair, together with organizations such as CARE and Conservation International, is beginning to exert tremendous leverage on foreign governments to address human rights, and in particular child labor issues. Starbucks is a sponsoring company and active member in these and several other organizations. With patience and continued effort, Starbucks may make a difference.

QUESTIONS

1. Would you describe Starbucks as a leader among socially responsive companies, or merely a pragmatic business making limited efforts to resolve human rights problems among its foreign suppliers? In your opinion, what constitutes social responsiveness?

2. Could business develop universal standards for child labor and workers' rights? If so, what are a few of the guidelines you would envision within such a code?

3. If international organizations like the ILO or World Trade Organization could introduce measures to protect against child labor abuses, how could multinationals implement the standards? What pressure could companies, foreign suppliers, or governments apply to enforce these rules?

BIBLIOGRAPHY

"Human Rights: The Bloodhounds of History." *The Economist*, 12 April 1997, 19–21.

David Olsen, quoted in 25 September 2000 news release by Starbucks, "Starbucks Joins TransFair," at <www.starbucks.com>, "News" website.

Sweet, Charles. "Cosmology and Centrality: Personal Decision Making in Today's Changing World." *World Trade Organization, Human Rights in Developing Countries, Proceedings* (1997): 344–376.

"TransFair Certifies Quality and Products for Independent Growers and Farmers," at <www.transfairusa.org>, "Organization" website [cited 26 September 2000].

Zachary, G. Pascal. "International News: Starbucks Adopts Guidelines to Aid Foreign Workers." *Asian Wall Street Journal*, 23 October 1995, p. 2.

Zachary, G. Pascal. "Developing Countries Have 250 Million Kids at Work." *Asian Wall Street Journal*, 12 November 1996, p. 2.

MANAGING A PLANETARY BRAND— MICROSOFT VS. THE WORLD

Thanks to the world's most extensive marketing campaign, by 1995 most people on the planet had heard of Microsoft and its microcomputer operating system, Windows. That was a banner year for the company, when *Financial World* identified Microsoft as the best-managed brand in the world and the sixth most valuable one, rivaling other global brands such as Coca-Cola and Kodak. At the time, three-quarters of the world's 130 million PCs ran on Microsoft software, and the company's name recognition transcended language and cultural barriers in 170-plus countries.[1] By the end of 1999, when Microsoft's antitrust battle with the U.S. Justice Department was nearing a verdict in the U.S. District Court, the company's Windows platform had an even greater market share. It also had extended its penetration to 199 countries, and Microsoft's profits eclipsed those of the next 40 software companies, combined.[2]

U.S. District Court Judge Thomas Penfield Jackson rendered a final ruling on June 7, 2000, finding Microsoft guilty of antitrust violations under the Sherman Act, and directed that the company be divided into two separate entities. In his ruling, Judge Jackson condemned Microsoft as a "predatory monopolist" that had used its "prodigious market power and immense profits to harm any firm that insists on pursuing initiatives that could intensify competition against one of Microsoft's core products."[3] Soon after the ruling, Microsoft appealed, and the U.S. Justice Department sought a rapid conclusion by the U.S. Supreme Court under a little-known legal procedure called "fast tracking." That could have resulted in a summary ruling by the Supreme Court with little legal debate, a situation that greatly favored the Government's case. However, on September 26, 2000, the Supreme Court sent the case to the lower U.S. Court of Appeals in an 8-to-1 decision, a situation that would allow comprehensive appeal arguments by both the Justice Department and Microsoft. The case

itself is not expected to be resolved for several years, and the appeal postponed—at least temporarily—the breakup of Microsoft.[4]

Although it is premature to include in this text anything on Microsoft while appeals are in process, and sensitive because circumstances change almost daily for Microsoft and the U.S. software industry, the company provides an extraordinary example of management challenges. Microsoft only recently was considered an exceptional study in entrepreneurial verve and exceptional marketing; but with the legal entanglements, it has emerged with a tarnished image. Time will determine which perception is more accurate, and further speculation is beyond the intent of this case. The focus here, however, is on the opportunity to question how a company with globally branded products and markets in virtually every corner of the world can effectively manage its planetary assets.

Ironically, despite making global products, Microsoft itself is not viewed as a global enterprise. Indeed, it is more often characterized as an entrepreneurial venture of its founder, William H. Gates III, as a distinctly U.S. firm selling a U.S. product through U.S. methods to the rest of the world. This perception may not be entirely accurate, but it is a continuing legacy created by Gates in the firm's early years. His greatest challenge may be to transform Microsoft into a transnational corporation in the coming millennium, even if it is broken up in a fashion similar to the fate of AT&T, Standard Oil, and early twentieth-century trusts. In hindsight, Microsoft has already gone through several transformations in its brief history.[5] That story began in 1975, when Paul Allen and Bill Gates developed the BASIC language program for the little-known Altair minicomputer. This youthful hip-pocket fantasy was inspired by an article in *Popular Electronics* magazine that forecasted "one day, people will be able to have personal computers like home television." Allen and Gates realized that the prediction could never come true without a language program that did not require a Ph.D. from MIT. Within a few months, the two men walked into Altair's offices with their BASIC translator program.

The product did not achieve immediate success, however, because Altair and many other entrepreneurial computer companies toyed with BASIC and other languages. Some sold their ideas to larger companies, and many failed, leaving Microsoft little more than a two-man partnership centered in a small shop. In 1979, however, Allen and Gates redefined the BASIC translator to run on the Intel 8086 microprocessor, which soon became a component of machines from IBM and other mainstream players. The partners waited two more years before IBM announced the release of its PC in 1981, which was packaged with their disk operating system. Suddenly, Microsoft was an industry contender. At that point, Microsoft could have remained a small think tank of technically savvy software designers, or it could have actively pursued software and systems development as a corporate enterprise. Gates led the company toward full industry development, creating the first 16-bit MS-DOS operating system software. During this first major transformation, the founders struggled through nearly eight years of start-up turmoil, managing only a few young associates supported by a marginal capital base.

IBM's extraordinary success, followed quickly by industry demand for MS-DOS systems by literally hundreds of hardware companies anxiously trying to get a foothold in the PC market, led to the second transformation. IBM needed design support by Microsoft in Europe. Several leading British firms needed MS-DOS technical design systems, and both North America and Europe were gearing up to compete against a rising onslaught of Japanese innovations. IBM's pressure almost forced Microsoft to enter international markets, and Gates somewhat reluctantly agreed. He set up a British subsidiary unit in 1982 for design and marketing support in Europe.

Despite this tentative move, however, Microsoft remained firmly entrenched at its Seattle home base, where Gates and company began to design the first Windows operating system. In late 1983, he announced the first version of Windows as an extension of MS-DOS, but it was not until 1985 that the company was able to bring the product to market. The delay revealed a serious flaw in the company's structure: It could not deliver its products on time or support them with an adequate marketing system. Nevertheless, the solid position of MS-DOS, which was running most of the world's microcomputer systems, allowed Microsoft to survive its shortcomings.

Windows was not well received, and Microsoft was labeled by its critics on Wall Street as a company of youthful "geeks" who, with proper leadership and solid management, could dominate the software industry. Enter the big guns of corporate finance and American management. Microsoft was completely restructured, and in March 1986—11 years after Allen and Gates began tinkering with the Altair system—the company went public, generating $61 million in a stock underwriting. Within a year, MS-DOS and the early versions of Windows were running on more than 20 million systems in 80 countries. A year later, the company had 40 million systems on-line, and Microsoft was no longer an industry vendor but an industry leader. All that said, Gates and his relatively small corporate staff were still clustered in Seattle. They were distinctly young Americans and stereotyped as West Coast "techies" with little sense of the rest of the world and little desire to consider anything or anyplace beyond the cult-like computing enclave.

Gates's own persona reinforced this image, as did the 1989 decision to build his company headquarters near Seattle, at One Microsoft Way in Redmond, Washington. Known as *the campus*, it established an environment where techies and young geniuses could cluster in cubicles, working feverishly on technical projects and communicating almost exclusively by e-mail. Then, as today, employees were extremely well paid. Indeed, many became wealthy through profit sharing and company stock. Nearly all Microsoft employees were very young. Even today the company's 16,000 employees average barely 26 years old, and a constant, rapid turnover of new talent keeps that number from rising.

That corporate profile was similar in early 1990, when Microsoft announced worldwide availability of Windows 3.0. Unfortunately, the company had not yet developed the marketing maturity to deliver on its promises. It suffered prolonged embarrassment before placing the first feasible Windows program on dealers' shelves in May 1991. The so-called *worldwide* distribution of the package actually reached only 24 countries that could accommodate an English-language program. These drawbacks were especially galling in the wake of the company's two-year marketing program that had encompassed more than 100 languages and portrayed Microsoft as the global company of the future. Critics were genuinely annoyed by its heavy-handed marketing techniques, compounded by fears of a U.S. attempt to monopolize information technology.

Antitrust and fair-trade charges plagued Microsoft for several years. Indeed, government officials in several European countries and in major Asian markets sought injunctions against Microsoft and its marketing alliances. Mainland Chinese officials literally blocked market entry of Windows because Microsoft was marketing the product through a Taiwanese company. This was a major error in judgment considering the discordant relations between the PRC and Taiwan.[6] Nevertheless, the popularity of MS-DOS and Windows proliferated through gray-market channels and, unfortunately for Microsoft, through software piracy.

None of these problems could stop Microsoft's ascent, but the company clearly had not positioned itself as a global enterprise capable of managing worldwide interests. To solve the problem, Microsoft tried to counter opposition with mass advertising and aggressive promotions. The company's announcement in 1994 of Windows 95 once again proved a premature step, and it finally delivered the product in August 1995. The move to Windows 95 was also controversial and fraught with errors. Indeed, early versions on CD-ROM included viruses from the factory that caused panic and significant difficulties to many worldwide systems and users.

During 1997, over 2,000 IT executives met for a technology symposium in Cannes, on the French Riviera. Many voices in the gathering condemned Microsoft for lack of technical support and insensitivity to international markets.[7] With Gates in attendance, critics assailed his company for launching products at exorbitant prices with little or no systems support. European firms reported spending more than 10 percent of their IT budgets on software maintenance, and in 1996 alone, they paid nearly $5 billion for technical help and systems support, which they described as unnecessary costs that should have been covered by Microsoft as their primary vendor.

Executives also complained of "American colonialism," charging that Windows 95 and its thousands of enhancements were idiomatic of American culture and language structure. Although foreign versions of the company's software were widely distributed, they seldom provided the same capabilities as the English-language versions. European and Asian IT specialists condemned Microsoft as a culturally bound recluse, and they joined foreign government leaders at Cannes to challenge Gates to create a world organization capable of implementing human values comparable to the company's technological genius.

This conference was not the first time that Gates had heard these messages. In 1994, Chinese Communist Party chief Jiang Zemin effectively boycotted Microsoft's entry into China, and he later blocked introduction of Windows 95 there.[8] When Gates visited Jiang in Beijing, he received a frosty reception marred by charges that Microsoft was totally insensitive to China. Jiang advised Gates to "learn something about the 5,000 years of Chinese culture."[9] Outside the United States, Microsoft was viewed as little more than a collection of traveling glad-handers hawking quick-fix miracle medicines, an image far from the desired one of a leading multinational corporation.

Jiang's reaction may have been a wake-up call; Gates returned home determined to take his company to a new level of international business. He immediately began development of a Chinese version of Windows, sacked the entire staff in China, and reorganized a series of Asian alliances with local management and regional accountability for a full range of services and support. He called on his executives to reposition Microsoft as a global player with appropriate management systems and capabilities for intercultural cooperation. Gates then returned to China on an extensive personal tour of the country, engaging in months of study to prepare for an East Asian launch of Windows. He arranged a second visit with Jiang, who at the time was also president of the People's Republic of China, and set into motion a coordinated program of long-term technical development in China.

The company's transformation apparently had not progressed far enough for the Cannes delegates in 1997, although Microsoft had made major changes in Europe. It had reorganized its U.K. offices, for example, to begin developing a comprehensive European support system for marketing, distribution, and after-market technical services.[10] This office, established as Microsoft's first foreign operation in 1982, had remained no more than a sales office reporting directly to the Seattle headquarters until the company ran into criticism for its Windows 95 program. Microsoft had long emphasized direct marketing rather than technical support, design services, or systems implementation. Most of Microsoft's other foreign operations had followed similar patterns. Driven by confrontation in China and substantial criticism for poor support of both domestic and foreign customers, Gates targeted the company's U.K. headquarters and East Asian operations for the first wave of many moves toward global transformation.

Meanwhile, Gates had to face the stark reality that Microsoft lacked two essential assets for any global transformation—a service organization capable of supporting multinational clients and a corps of experienced managers capable of working in a multicultural world environment.[11] Gates personally worked hard to overcome these barriers, completing a 25-nation world tour in an effort to understand the markets and cultures that Microsoft served. In India, for example, he was stunned to discover 14 distinct written and spoken languages, enough diversity to prevent a single version of Windows software—even one written specifically for India—from effectively supporting users unless it could be rapidly adapted to varying dialects with different structures. In Gates's words, "Now that I understand that, we are going to invest a whole lot more in localizing our products."[12]

These laudable personal efforts fell short of the transformation required to make Microsoft the worldwide computing empire that Gates envisioned. Marketing and technical snafus plagued Windows 98 and the Millennium Edition (Windows 2000)—both with delayed launches, both prone to viruses, and both suffering compatibility problems with other Microsoft products. Microsoft has always had the skills required for technological development, but critics believe that the company has not yet established the human resource capabilities to manage its systems. For example, Microsoft has never provided technical support beyond staffing telephone help lines, and access to customer services is complicated. Indeed, Microsoft has trouble answering calls from domestic companies, let alone international clients, and surveys of its U.S. business clients show that nearly 80 percent are disappointed in its customer service systems.[13]

Microsoft has pursued alliances with more than 30 hardware and software service corporations, including Digital and Compaq, in an effort to tap their international management expertise. Several of these alliances have proved beneficial—such as Compaq's strength in China, where the company can service Microsoft products running on its hardware. Clients receive the full range of Microsoft systems software with every Compaq computer they buy, and they also gain the hardware maker's full-service warranty, backed up by a worldwide network of host-country

technicians and well-traveled home office representatives. This alliance also helps Microsoft to resolve pirating problems, particularly in China, because Compaq sells a system already loaded with software. Resellers, known as *alley vendors*, find no market among these customers for their knock-off versions of Windows.

Since the early meetings with President Jiang in 1994, Gates has extended the company's Chinese alliances, and he has begun to strengthen other international markets with powerful local alliances. Compaq is Microsoft's primary partner in China, yet Gates recently signed a joint agreement with the powerful China Great Wall Group and the Shanghai Computer Applications and Industry Development Association to provide ethical marketing of Microsoft products in cooperation with Compaq and other companies. Consequently, Gates has been able to repair the damage that Microsoft had suffered in Asia, creating more than 300 major distribution centers in China alone.[14]

This level of international activity is characteristic of dozens, perhaps hundreds, of Microsoft's foreign alliances and marketing agreements. Microsoft is indeed in the middle of a major transformation, but it is one that differs substantially from the technological revolution that Gates helped to engineer. It must also manage such dramatic change in the heat of substantial competition. Microsoft may be a vast organization with a dominant current position in microcomputer systems software, but it cannot expect to operate without opposition, despite the most unusual "campus" full of design and development brainpower on the planet. Oracle Corporation, Netscape, Sun Microsystems, HP, Intel, and others—not to mention IBM and the entire Japanese industry—pursue their own agendas, and many of them have strong international teams with exceptionally well entrenched corporate systems capable of dealing in a globally diverse information industry. The question is whether Microsoft can reconstitute itself as a global contender with human resource capabilities comparable to its technological acumen. The pending breakup may actually help the company reorganize its management systems, concentrating Windows software and its associated applications under one entity while placing all other activities under a separate entity. Meanwhile, how the company approaches its "dot.net" dilemma and resolves its antitrust difficulties is an enigma. Clearly, Microsoft has several of the world's most prominent globally branded products in existence, but there is no clear evidence of how the company intends to manage these assets.

QUESTIONS

1. Identify and discuss the problems of global expansion facing Microsoft. How do these issues compare with similar expansion problems and foreign competitors of other multinational corporations?

2. Can Microsoft establish an international enterprise with the same transnational and transcultural identity that it wants for its products? In your estimation, what must Microsoft do as an organization to achieve this goal? If the company does not make these changes, what threats does it face from domestic and foreign competitors?

3. Vocal critics deride Microsoft as a firm so focused on its marketing goals that it has failed to consider customers' needs for service and technical support. Setting aside the antitrust violations now being contended in the Court of Appeals, many observers believe that Microsoft has not behaved ethically as a business entity. Indeed, the company has made a significant number of cultural blunders, such as marketing to the PRC through Taiwan, selling poorly translated software in India and Southeast Asia, and ignoring client support services in Europe. Limit your opinion to these incidents and Microsoft's marketing strategies to conclude whether the company has behaved unethically, or simply failed to manage its international interests.

4. Microsoft has battled software piracy throughout the world. Explain the risks associated with marketing intellectual property and the ethical dilemmas of marketing expensive products in less affluent or developing economies. What measures can Microsoft or similar companies take to protect themselves?

5. Identify the major "political risks" that Microsoft faces in foreign markets and with foreign governments. What could Microsoft do in the coming years to minimize those risks while maintaining a credible reputation and market presence in its foreign operations?

STRATEGY AND GLOBAL ORGANIZATION

GLOBAL STRATEGIC PLANNING

CHAPTER OBJECTIVES

Explain the concepts of international competitive strategy and global trends that affect international management.

Detail industry-level strategic planning and strategic options for globally integrated and multidomestic companies.

Relate company-level strategies, and show how companies position themselves in foreign markets.

Describe the cornerstone competitive strategies for multinational corporations.

Discuss the strategic planning process and how firms formulate strategies from the perspective of an international manager.

CHAPTER 5

Michael Dell, founder of Dell Computer Corporation and its chairman and CEO, has come of age along with his highly successful company. Dell launched his venture from a University of Texas dorm room in 1984 when he was not yet old enough to vote. During the next few years, Dell found himself managing a growing company with demand that outpaced anything that he could deliver. His strategy was simple: Deliver factory-direct PCs with a 100 percent guarantee and the lowest price in the industry. In 1987, he was proclaimed Entrepreneur of the Year by the Association of Collegiate Entrepreneurs. In his acceptance speech, Dell predicted that his company would sell $300 million in computers before he turned 30 years of age.[1] This claim drew skeptical reactions—Michael Dell looked much like a schoolboy, and his business was still an upstart venture. Although Dell's sales had topped $100 million, the company was up against Compaq, IBM, and Apple, among others in the PC industry.

Today, Dell Computers is the world's leading direct computer systems company and premier supplier of technology for the Internet infrastructure.[2] The company, a global corporation with worldwide sourcing and a fully integrated production and marketing system, can deliver a computer on order as rapidly as 36 hours after receiving an order from a customer in any of more than 65 countries on three continents.

Dell competes through a focused strategy of cost effectiveness and customer service. Speed, which the company refers to as "Dell-ocity," is the key. All Dell computers are made with a just-in-time philosophy that calls for assembly precisely to customers' orders. Each system is made, packed, and shipped within two days. By regionalizing the firm's global operations, Michael Dell has configured a rapidly responsive organization, built on integrated factories in Austin, Texas; Limerick, Ireland; and Penang, Malaysia. The company has established a network of vendors and contractors that deliver parts and assemblies overnight (or sooner) from numerous worldwide locations. Minimal stocks of components and parts are stored in warehouses close to each factory. Ideally, Dell would like to operate 100 percent just-in-time systems worldwide, and the firm comes close, with inventory levels that rarely exceed a few days' supply.

The result has been a global system that can change on a dime. The company assumes very little risk of loss due to obsolete inventory and has very little capital tied up in stock or overhead. Any Dell plant stocks less than one day's materials on hand for production, relying on suppliers to deliver components within hours of requests. Dell's globally integrated "rapid response" system translates to cost and profit advantages over slower rivals.

Dell runs its sales operation with equal efficiency. Dell collects and studies lots of data regarding customer service, measuring customer satisfaction in a multitude of ways. For example, Dell knows how long it took to ship a computer from the time it was ordered, whether a problem was encountered, and how it was resolved—including whether a service call was needed and when the service person arrived. Through its website, Dell also studies its customers' buying patterns.[3] Understanding its customers' buying behavior, coupled with industry and competitor trends, Dell can anticipate customer needs more effectively.

A globally integrated strategy, coupled with cost leadership and the fastest factory-direct service in the industry, helps Dell to lead competitors in profitability (measured by rate of return on invested capital). It achieves the industry's fastest conversion of orders to cash (one day from invoice to cash in hand), and it offers the most complete customer warranty (a 100 percent guarantee, with immediate replacement and no questions asked). The company's ultimate strategy is to become a global enterprise operating in cyberspace with instantaneous response to customers and worldwide distribution.[4]

A GLOBAL FRAMEWORK FOR STRATEGY

Multinationals undertake global strategic planning at three levels in different sets of circumstances. At the *international level*, multinational companies are drawn into the politics of international trade and negotiations. Leaders of every country are concerned about making their industries more competitive, and governments devote tremendous amounts of their resources to foreign relations and forging trade agreements that affect multinational companies. Consequently, international managers often find themselves significantly involved in national political agendas. At the *industry level*, international managers are concerned with trends in global industries, and they must position their companies to compete effectively within their industries. At the *company level*, strategic planning reflects the traditional concepts of how a company develops its markets, products, technologies, and organizational systems in ways that help it to achieve its objectives. Strategic planning occurs at all three levels, and most multinational companies cannot detach planning at one level from the others. A small export firm, however, may focus keenly on company issues rather than on national priorities. In contrast, a major corporation such as General Motors may find itself embroiled in international trade issues while managing complicated industry competition.

Strategic planning is too complex a subject to be adequately addressed in one chapter; separate courses study this process in depth. This chapter seeks to foster an understanding of the international manager's role in strategic decision-making and to describe strategic priorities for multinational companies. It begins by exploring each of the three levels of strategy summarized in Figure 5.1.

International Competitive Strategy

Although a tremendous amount of press coverage focuses on national trade policies, negotiations, and political initiatives aimed at fair trade, no particular body of knowledge constitutes a field of international competitive strategy. No single theory explains international competition, and no global model lays out a process for competitive strategy. Perhaps the closest anyone has come to an encompassing concept of international competition is Michael Porter in his classic work, *The Competitive Advantage of Nations.*[5] Porter argues that success depends on a specific strategy, but even the most effective one will not succeed for long in a dynamic world environment. This does not mean that chaos governs all strategic initiatives—only that adaptation is essential as important changes occur to undermine prior assumptions about international competition.

For example, Porter and other scholars have explained how the Japanese have succeeded by building a managed economy in which major industries act in concert with government support. Japanese strategists have concentrated on targeting foreign markets and selecting specific industries in which to compete. They have achieved major growth through orchestrated government policies to position the nation as one

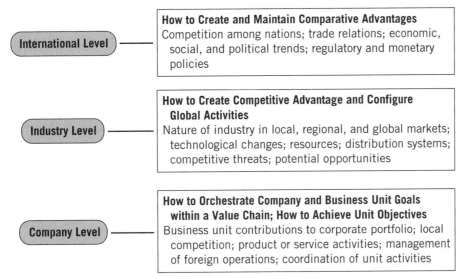

FIGURE 5.1
Focal Issues and Objectives at Three Strategic Levels

of the world leaders in consumer electronics, automobiles, robotics, and microelectronics innovations. Japan has accomplished this ambitious goal by solidifying a national psyche for high quality and productivity, and by centralizing home-based industries within giant consolidated consortia. This combination of factors has resulted in major cost advantages and quality standards that differentiate products made in Japan from those made elsewhere.[6]

Japan's strategic success is well documented in both academic and popular literature. But prior to the 1960s, when the concept of managed demand emerged there, the country consisted of large conglomerate trading companies with feudal atmospheres managing haphazard product portfolios and merely seeking markets of opportunity. These firms enjoyed huge advantages in low-cost production, due mainly to very low wages, and their leaders formed an autocracy that significantly influenced Japan's national commercial psyche. The country built on these advantages to spearhead a generation of global growth, but these conditions no longer exist. Today, Japan's managed-demand strategies have little meaning in industries that are diffused throughout the world. Although Japanese companies maintain their national reputation for high-quality products, they no longer enjoy wage advantages or closely orchestrated interindustry leadership. Consequently, many Japanese companies are contemplating and executing major changes in their global strategies. They are locating manufacturing facilities overseas, including the United States, and they have begun to pursue new strategies in North America and Europe through international joint ventures.[7]

Alarmed by Japan's success over the past several decades, political leaders in North America and Europe became concerned about competing with Japanese companies. This priority led them to establish restrictive trade barriers to protect home-country markets. In hindsight, these stopgap measures have failed to solve those countries' problems. Lester Thurow, a former dean at MIT and a critic of government economic policies, argues that defensive protectionism has never worked well for long in any society. In his view, trade barriers have served as only temporary measures to protect inefficient industries, thus further weakening a nation's long-term capabilities for global competition.[8] Ironically, politicians of almost every nation continue to favor protectionism in trade negotiations, as many individual companies, trade unions, and consumer groups clamor for protective government policies.

The polar opposite of protectionism is unbridled free-market trade. Under ideal economic conditions, such an environment encourages countries to consolidate strategies based on *distinct comparative advantages*. Chapter 2 described this classic model of economic competition, and it noted that **comparative advantage** is a strength one nation has relative to another in a factor of production or trade. A comparative advantage can thus be achieved when a country has relative strength in natural resources, such as Saudi Arabia's oil reserves; in technology, such as the U.S. dominance in aerospace; or in human resources, such as low-cost labor in China. A country can also create an advantage, such as low tax rates that draw international firms to Hong Kong and Singapore. However, comparative advantages also are short lived; resources run out, labor rates rise along with growth, technological advances soon become commonplace, and tax systems can change with governments. Consequently, a nation can vigorously pursue and seek to benefit from some comparative advantage, but each program offers only a springboard for more lasting economic development initiatives. In this regard, a nation's comparative advantage becomes a temporary platform for supporting domestic enterprise and foreign investment.[9]

Comparative advantages, protectionist initiatives, or other strategies—such as Japan's managed demand—change rapidly as international competition changes. Because even small changes can significantly affect international business, managers of major international companies become intensely involved in national economic policies. For example, the ongoing U.S.–Japanese confrontation over import-export agreements on automobiles has brought U.S. accusations of Japanese protectionism, leading to countercharges that U.S. automakers cannot make automobiles that prove acceptable to Japanese consumers. Neither side seems to gain more than a temporary advantage in negotiations that usually fail to reach conclusive resolutions. Both sides include input from leading business executives, legal counselors, and consultants from auto companies, international banks, and trade union associations in their negotiating teams. Government trade legations have drawn business interests into the political fray, so that business leaders find themselves as deeply involved in trade negotiations and diplomacy as the politicians.[10]

Several implications for international managers are apparent. Managers cannot isolate themselves; they must accept involvement in international relationships with foreign governments and multilateral political or trade organizations. They must also consider national priorities of foreign host countries and the postures that these countries adopt relative to others for trade agreements, alliances, and economic cooperation. Because managers often participate in international negotiations, they find themselves representing home-country interests beyond those of their own companies, so they must also consciously consider home-country political agendas. Further, because multinational companies may be targeted by foreign governments as threats to domestic industries, managers can find themselves aligned against the combined forces of a foreign industry and its government. Most important, international managers must comprehend foreign nations' strategies and likely changes in them. Due to changing conditions, a firm operating overseas may experience a sudden transformation from a friendly and economically beneficial host environment to a contentious one that places it on the verge of ejection, expropriation, or intense trade restrictions. International managers must choose between remaining alert to these situations and actively participating in global initiatives—or remaining isolated and becoming passive victims of circumstances.

Raymond Vernon, known respectfully as the "oracle of globalization," wrote hundreds of articles and many of the leading books on international business and economics prior to his death in 1999. As the son of a Russian Jewish immigrant, Vernon worked his way through college and entered government service during the 1930s, then served in diplomatic missions for nearly two decades. During his early career, he was involved with the Bretton Woods agreement to establish the IMF and the charter for the UN. He also helped establish the Marshall Plan following World War II, helped to author the first General Agreement on Tariffs and Trade (GATT), and was instrumental in post-war Japan to establish international trade agreements. In 1956 Vernon joined Harvard and launched an academic career that spanned more than 40 years. He advised four presidents and was awarded Japan's highest civilian honor, the Order of the Rising Sun, for international economics and theories of globalization. Four of his books have become standards in international literature: *Sovereignty at Bay* (1971), *Storm over the Multinationals* (1977), *Beyond Globalism* (1989), and *In the Hurricane's Eye* (1998).

Industry-Level Strategy

Although multinationals often find themselves entangled with national priorities and trade policies, their strategies are keenly focused on their own industries. They formulate strategy at the industry level, some for intensely localized industry conditions and others for globally integrated competition.

Recall that Chapter 1 defined two broad categories of international companies' *multidomestic enterprises* and *global enterprises*. Each defines the scope of its industry and the nature of its competition in a different way. The multidomestic firm competes in an industry where products and company business systems are localized for each market. Examples include retail merchandising of home, health care, and hygiene products; insurance services; and commercial banking. The multidomestic enterprise formulates a *multilocal strategy* in which it tailors products to meet local consumer needs and expectations. Therefore, the multidomestic enterprise competes simultaneously in many differentiated markets, directing strategies at specific countries or more immediate market segments. The industry consists of predominately multidomestic competitors, each with a similar mandate to intensify its activities in local markets. In contrast, the global enterprise faces worldwide, integrated competitors selling universal goods and services. Examples include automobiles, semiconductors, audiovisual equipment, and most petrochemical products. Some observers suggest that financial services have become universal products, since money and investments have global channels with fluid transactions.[11]

A multidomestic enterprise must, by definition, unbundle its goods and services, thus creating a decentralized portfolio of strategies. Its managers cannot presume that they can replicate operations merely because their strategies have succeeded in domestic markets. Something as simple as Campbell's canned soups, commonly sold in the United States in condensed form, meets with rejection in the U.K. British consumers know Campbell's reputation well, but they are accustomed to buying canned soups fully prepared and ready to cook without dilution. The British also prefer a blander taste in soups than American consumers. After years of struggling to export products packaged under U.S. guidelines, Campbell now manufactures and distributes its products from a British subsidiary. Campbell faced similar problems in trying to market canned soups to Germans, who traditionally mix soups from powders or pastes. The company repositioned operations in Germany to distribute dehydrated soups in environmentally friendly recycled packaging.[12]

A global enterprise must formulate a more complicated strategy. Porter's model of global competition at the industry level is perhaps the easiest to understand. He begins by explaining a *value chain* of activities that a firm must address, and he then identifies how a firm pursues these activities in its worldwide markets. This arrangement constitutes what Porter calls *configuration*. After defining a configuration, the company must orchestrate the various activities in the value chain in a process called *coordination*. Thus a company will define globally which activities it must pursue, from initial steps of purchasing through to final sales. It then configures the enterprise by defining where these activities will take place and how they will be coordinated. The ultimate strategic objective is to establish a *sustainable competitive advantage within the global industry.*[13] The concept of a value chain and the two processes of configuration and coordination are explained further in the following paragraphs.

The Value Chain

The industry in which a firm competes is defined by a typical value chain of productive activities, and the manner in which a company competes is defined by how it carries out the activities within its particular value chain. Formally defined, a **value chain** is an accumulated set of discrete activities that are interdependently related through a progression of coordinated processes.[14] This definition is translated from Carl Menger's nineteenth-century Austrian work, in which he established a body of econometric theory that subsequently became known as the *general theory of production*. Menger explained how a chain of events progressively transforms resources with little useful value of their own into goods and services with far greater value. The chain creates new value with each progressive activity, and consumers willingly pay premiums for the *added-value* benefits they receive as a result.

Conceptually, this activity completes the simple sequence in the model shown in Figure 5.2. Common resources, such as potatoes growing in a field, are harvested, sorted, cleaned, packaged, transported to market, and finally offered to consumers in convenient local stores. Each activity in the chain is a discrete step in the process of growing, picking, sorting, cleaning, packaging, transporting, and selling potatoes.

In Paris and Vienna during the nineteenth century, this apparently simplistic process offered a revolutionary new benefit for city dwellers, who before that time could not purchase a small bag of fresh potatoes at a neighborhood grocery. Companies and entrepreneurs profited by adding value at each link in the chain. The same process works today for products as diverse as potatoes, gasoline, commercial jetliners, mutual funds, and international telephone services.

To understand an industry, study the value chain that defines how the industry works. Realize also that an industry's composite sequence of activities may incorporate dozens of embedded value chains. This is important, because very few companies are fully integrated to the extent that they can control their entire value chains. Even the most sophisticated organizations rely on inputs from agents, subcontractors, transport

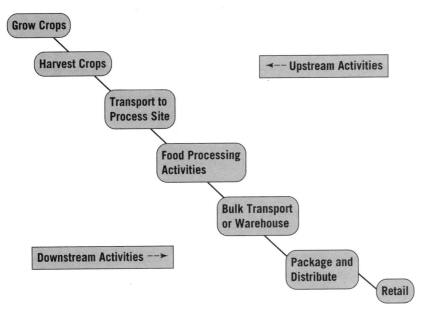

FIGURE 5.2
Conceptual Example
of a Value Chain

companies, telecommunications systems, equipment manufacturers, wholesalers, retailers, and many other companies to commercialize their goods and services.

Porter built on Menger's model to develop a contemporary theory of global competition based on *systems of value chains*.[15] A simplified view of Porter's model is shown in Figure 5.3. This matrix creates a vertical array of *support activities* and a horizontal array of *primary activities*. Support activities contribute in various ways throughout the chain, from the earliest involvement in a primary activity until the final primary activity is completed. Primary activities perform discretely identifiable functions in the chain, and they are linked through an interdependent, progressive system. Observers distinguish primary activities as **upstream activities**—relatively close to original resources or part of early stages of conversion—or as **downstream activities**. Upstream goods and services have accumulated less added value (e.g., growing potatoes versus harvesting them) than downstream activities, which occur relatively close to final

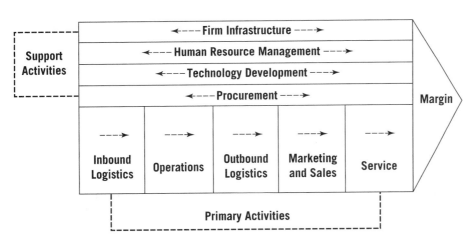

FIGURE 5.3
Interdependent
Activities of the Value
Chain

Source: Copyright (c) 1986, by
The Regents of the University
of California. Reprinted from
the *California Management
Review* 28, no. 2. By permission
of The Regents.

completion of the chain of events. Goods and services accumulate progressively greater added value throughout the process.

Configuration of Activities

Every organization, from a large global conglomerate to a small domestic enterprise, operates within and is part of a value chain. In Porter's model, **configuration** explains what activities to pursue in a company's value chain and therefore how to organize these activities to achieve optimal integration. The local retailer operates at the extreme downstream point, where the ultimate sale occurs, yet its business is substantially influenced by upstream activities of wholesalers, suppliers, and manufacturers. The retailer may choose to expand into the value chain by buying delivery trucks or warehouses, thus eliminating intermediaries and taking over their functions. The retailer also might become an intermediate supplier or become involved in product design and manufacturing. However, because it competes in an intensely localized industry, the retailer concentrates its efforts in downstream activities. Even when such companies enter the international arena as multidomestic organizations, they remain focused on point-of-sale considerations and closely related downstream activities. That focus constitutes their strategic configuration.

A global organization is not anchored to any specific point in the chain. To the contrary, in order to compete globally, a company often must be strategically involved in all stages of the value chain. Therefore, a global configuration should *optimize* each discrete activity with the ultimate aim of optimizing the total organization through integration. For example, Motorola's Project Bandit appears to be a domestic U.S. operation based in Boynton Beach, Florida, producing the Bandit Pager, a state-of-the-art, high-growth mobile pager—one of many innovative products in the firm's global product portfolio.[16] The Bandit group has earned an exceptional reputation for delivering a custom-ordered product of leading-edge quality at a good price to clients anywhere in the world within 48 hours. Despite its domestic appearance, the company is globally configured to orchestrate more than 50 activities in 24 countries to bring the tiny pager to market. Simple electronic parts and components are made in China, Malaysia, and Indonesia. Downstream microcircuit assembly is accomplished in Singapore and Hong Kong. Partial component systems are transported to points in Europe, Japan, and the United States for pagers, telephones, and other products. Meanwhile, research and development that precedes product design for many of Motorola's products occurs in the United States and Japan. The firm largely contracts for plastic molding and fabrication to make pagers, mobile telephones, and other components through subcontracting partners or foreign joint ventures located in India and Southeast Asian countries. Finally, marketing activities, customer service, and retail distribution are located as near to end customers as possible. Motorola's Bandit group focuses on a concentrated product line, and its system "pulls" the various components and parts through different operations to the final assembly point and then to distribution.

Motorola Hong Kong is a high-skill facility that manufactures and assembles major circuitry and integrated components. It is not a low-cost operation; Hong Kong's per-capita income exceeds that of the United Kingdom. But Motorola's Hong Kong location facilitates bringing together materials and subassemblies from China and Southeast Asia, where the firm can find huge cost advantages, after which it exports a range of value-added components to other company subsidiaries. Motorola buys quality goods from Hong Kong, where it pays low duties and benefits from excellent worldwide shipping facilities. At the same time, it locates low-skill tasks such as plastic molding and component fabrication in low-wage countries—but only when it can also find other benefits in procurement or distribution; low wages alone do not drive location decisions. Location decisions and most other activities in the company's value chain reflect the net result of optimizing materials, labor costs, market accessibility, distribution capabilities, regulatory considerations, and the entire carefully orchestrated process, including logistics and finance.

This type of configuration appears throughout many global operations, and configurations can change rapidly as conditions in a foreign country change. For example, GM has shifted several U.S. operations to Mexico, where it can carry out metal stamping, engine work, and assembly more inexpensively than at its U.S. facilities. Ford has similar operations in Ireland, Malaysia, and Spain. Chrysler has formed strategic alliances for manufacturing in South Korea, Mexico, and Indonesia. All three have distributed their upstream activities to offshore locations as part of an accelerated effort to reconfigure their global enterprises.[17]

It may be helpful to think of the global configuration decision in terms of a confederation of interests within a flexible system of alliances. Figure 5.4, sketched from a model of a cellular phone manufacturer's organization, illustrates the point. The company reaches beyond the limits of its own resources and skills to combine ownership and control of activities with negotiated alliances, contracts, and licensing deals. It takes an equity interest when it sees advantages in such an action, but it works above all to establish a synergistic competitive advantage on a global scale.

Coordination of Activities

In Michael Porter's model, **coordination** constitutes how a company achieves an optimal integration of activities and manages its system of operations within the global

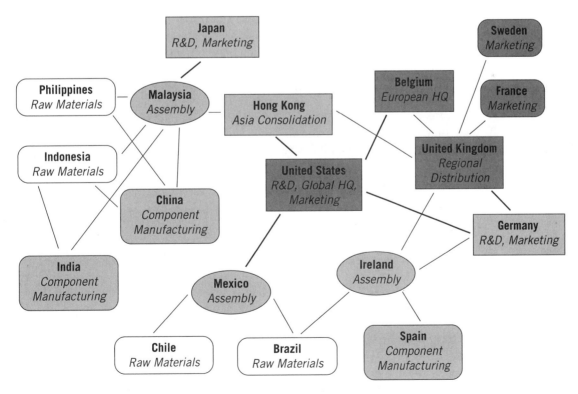

FIGURE 5.4
Alliance Network of a U.S. Manufacturer of Cellular Phones

configuration.[18] Specifically, the company defines its system of global operations, together with those provided by any alliances and contractors, and determines how activities within the system as a whole will be managed. Strategists have struggled to understand how to treat coordination as a consideration apart from configuration. Perhaps coordination can be viewed as the operational authority required in each location to achieve effective functioning in a particular configuration.

The least complex configuration is a fully integrated facility where most, if not all, activities are performed under one roof. In this situation, coordination occurs through a centralized management system. In reality, few organizations implement this model; most that do are small firms with simple products and local markets. A global enterprise operates at some point within the spectrum of complexity, often near the polar extreme where systems must coordinate hundreds of activities by many different participants. Between the extremes, firms find many options for practical configurations. As a result, they define a broad range of coordination roles.

One company may employ several different configurations. For example, a chemical plant manufacturing agricultural pesticides might configure most of its activities in each major plant location. A plant in India could include R&D, materials procurement, manufacturing, and all the downstream activities required to market and distribute chemicals in a fairly broad geographic area. In contrast, the firm may choose to configure the Indian plant to combine procurement and manufacturing in one location, and then send bulk shipments of pesticides to worldwide centers for redistribution. The same company may have widespread interests in mining, processing, and logistics. Most major petrochemical companies rely on this model to achieve economies of scale in separate processes for making bulk products such as oil and plastic resins, yet they rely on regional distribution systems and local marketing.

As observed at the outset of this section on industry-level strategy, a multinational is concerned with trends in global industries in which it competes. Porter's model suggests that an enterprise must create a sustainable competitive advantage and then configure global operations to suit conditions in its industry. Coordination explains how the company chooses to sequence its activities and delegate authority for operations within the value chain. If it is a company that competes in several industries with a variety of goods or services, it may balance several different strategic scenarios at the same time. Ultimately, the company's major objective will be to optimize its composite global activities through industry-specific strategies.

Company-Level Strategy

Prevailing patterns of competition and global configurations determine strategic boundaries for individual companies. Within these boundaries, companies formulate strategies specific to their missions. Some traditional business policy courses focus on company-level management decisions as a foundation for instruction in strategy formulation, followed by an evaluation of industry-level competition as part of the decision-making process. In contrast, this chapter has started at the global level and then discussed industry-level competition as a prerequisite to understanding company-level strategic management.

It is important to envision a company as something more than the traditional hierarchical enterprise serving a homogeneous market. In the global arena, the concept of a company in this respect has little meaning. But the term can productively indicate the focal organization—such as IBM, GM, Sony, or Phillips—that plays a primary role in a value chain. All establish their own organizational identities, but they also develop complicated networks of subsidiaries, foreign alliances, and widely dispersed foreign operating units. These operating units often are sufficiently large to constitute companies in their own right within the larger enterprises. Each formulates its own competitive strategies. This chapter distinguishes such companies by the term *strategic business units (SBUs)*. Strategies associated with SBUs are distinct from those at the company-wide level (also called the *portfolio level* of management). To clarify, then, the SBU competes within a narrowly defined range of its industry or within a geographic region. Consequently, the SBU tends to pursue a country-specific strategy. In the grand scheme of portfolio management, the focal organization competes on a global basis.[19]

Strategic Orientations

Companies develop patterns of decision-making, sometimes called *predispositions*, that reflect managers' characteristic orientations toward decisions within the organization's structure. These patterns powerfully influence company strategies, because the entire organization becomes oriented to a certain way of getting things done. In the context of global management, the concept of *ethnocentricity* makes an important contribution to such predispositions.

Ethnocentricity is a predisposition to believe that one's native culture is superior to others. This also implies a strong tendency to impose one's own values on others. Some have associated this trait with early colonists and religious missionaries, and many people level similar charges at politicians, trade negotiators, and activists involved in human rights issues.[20] In business, extreme ethnocentricity implies an effort to impose home-country values and management methods on foreign operations. It is considered one of four orientations that influence strategic decisions. These four orientations are ethnocentrism, polycentrism, regiocentrism, and geocentrism, which are explained below.[21]

- *Ethnocentrism.* A company that displays this orientation tends to centralize decision-making in the home-country headquarters, controlling foreign operations through home-country people groomed for overseas positions. The hierarchical model of a domestic company tends to prevail where home-country values, methods, and priorities underpin foreign affairs. Profits are repatriated to the parent company, and expansion projects often implement vertical integration strategies that place control in the hands of home-country managers.
- *Polycentrism.* In contrast to the single-centered ethnocentric organization, a polycentric organization distributes control through many centers. Widely dispersed governance allows autonomous local decision-making by managers hired and groomed for executive roles in their native countries. The firm's hierarchical structure includes divisions and subsidiaries, often as part of a vertical integration strategy—but one with a focus on national responsiveness. The company seeks to take into account local customs, values, and culture, and it often repatriates only a portion of profits while reinvesting in its host-country subsidiaries.
- *Regiocentrism.* The regiocentric organization works toward cross-cultural integration *within a region* where similarities among a group of nations allow consolidation of marketing or production. Decision-making authority is delegated to national and regional group managers. The company's strategy emphasizes regional integration of activities. It seeks to create a system for responding nimbly to local markets, yet one that remains competitive within its regional industry. These firms often develop local managers within their native countries while grooming executives for regional responsibilities. This arrangement keeps management attuned to both local and regional cultural characteristics and customs, and it

fosters rapid response capabilities. Most profits and resources tend to remain with regional subsidiaries to underwrite their growth.

- *Geocentrism.* The phrase "think globally and act locally" epitomizes a geocentric orientation, with a priority of optimizing the global network of company activities. The network organization reflects regional and national activities, vesting operational authority in local managers. The strategic mandate within such a firm, even its small foreign operations, calls for contributing value-added activities as required for worldwide integration. Because the organization spans diversified activities, its success depends critically on being responsive to local cultures and markets. Consequently, the firm grooms local managers for their respective activities while drawing executives from anywhere in the world. An emphasis on global configuration optimizes the company's total competitive advantage.

These four orientations do *not* constitute a continuum of characteristics, nor do many companies fit nicely into one category or another. The orientations are models for understanding companies' *tendencies for conducting business.* Most multinational companies tend to reflect ethnocentric characteristics. Studies of cultural values have revealed that home-country managers often bring strong ethnocentric biases to their foreign assignments; this probably reflects human nature for businesspeople of all nationalities.[22] When an ethnocentric company expands vertically, it tends to maintain substantial control within its foreign operations through homegrown expatriates. This arrangement institutionalizes the parent company's core characteristics while maintaining decision-making continuity for its financial and strategic considerations. In high-risk businesses, the system also helps to protect proprietary technology and capital resources. However, the perceived advantages must be weighed against handicaps of limited responsiveness to local or regional interests.

In contrast, polycentric and regiocentric organizations can achieve rapid *national responsiveness.* Locally managed foreign operations can make quick decisions from positions close to their customers. They can accommodate local customs, cultural differences, and both political and economic interests. Unlike a polycentric enterprise, which is composed of local operations with well-defined national boundaries, the regiocentric enterprise transcends and blurs national boundaries. It often develops goods and services within a region. Products made in one country can be shipped throughout the region, and marketing can leverage common characteristics of regional customers. Therefore, a regiocentric firm operating in Europe, the Middle East, or Southeast Asia often can achieve economies of scale in both downstream and upstream activities.

The geocentric organization is not a progressive form of either polycentric or regiocentric orientations, and many organizations combine all four orientations. A company's management orientation can influence its configuration and competitive strategies. Few companies align themselves entirely with one orientation or another, and the nature of competition in an industry often dictates how a company must be organized to achieve effective competition. The combination of characteristics of industry competition with a company's predisposition results in its *strategic posture.* This characteristic places the firm at a point along the continuum shown in Figure 5.5.

Strategic Posture

A firm's strategic posture can characterize the entire global organization, or a single business unit within it. At one extreme, the company or business unit may adopt a multidomestic posture and conduct itself as a polycentric organization. Such an enterprise competes intensely in local markets with differentiated goods or services, and it

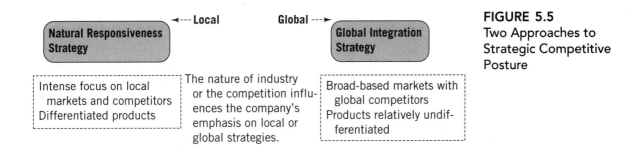

FIGURE 5.5
Two Approaches to Strategic Competitive Posture

keeps downstream activities specifically focused on local customer requirements. In management parlance, the enterprise is pursuing a **national responsiveness strategy.** At the other extreme, the company may adopt a global posture and conduct itself as a geocentric organization. Such an enterprise competes in global markets with relatively undifferentiated goods and services. It standardizes activities throughout the value chain as part of a **global integration strategy.**

Between these extremes, a company can position itself to compete more or less intensely in local markets by offering more- or less-differentiated goods and services. Few global companies position themselves at either extreme. Recall that some multidomestic companies, such as retail merchandisers, must compete in well-defined local markets. In contrast, some global organizations, such as major oil companies, must compete in worldwide markets. The retail merchandiser, even an outlet of a large company with international holdings, must address local customer needs and compete with neighboring retailers, often mom-and-pop shops.

However, an international company such as Toys 'R' Us or Marks & Spencer can generate economies of scale in global procurement, bulk warehousing, and standardization of products. Even firms that compete intensely and maintain *responsiveness* to local markets can seek competitive advantages through integration. Global companies such as Exxon and Royal Dutch/Shell must develop huge-scale economies to successfully market their mainstream petroleum products. They implement highly standardized methods for extraction, refining, and shipping of nearly identical products. In addition, they pursue very similar downstream marketing and service activities. Nevertheless, neither Exxon nor Shell can ignore local market characteristics, currency and exchange rate differences, cultural idiosyncrasies that require different approaches to marketing, and social realities of managing facilities in unstable foreign economies.

Factors That Influence Posture

Almost every aspect of a firm's business influences its strategic posture, and strategic decisions are made in complicated environments. Home-office executives with their own ideas about how to manage might impose an ethnocentric philosophy of leadership and constrain foreign managers from making decisions. The result could be a less responsive company that cannot compete as it should in local markets. Some companies, such as large steel producers and shipbuilders, require massive facilities with consolidated activities, so they would encounter extreme problems in trying to coordinate widely dispersed activities. National laws, such as commercial banking regulations, prohibit foreign firms from participating in specific industries in many countries. Therefore, most banks must organize under local laws as subsidiaries. Customs duties and tariffs in nearly every nation dictate substantial differences in costs for importing and exporting. Tax structures on imports and exports, on foreign income, on value-added activities, and on profits are important considerations. International treaties (or their absence) and other political risks affect posturing decisions. Of course, operating cost factors concerned with labor, materials, manufacturing, distribution, and services must be considered. These factors fall into one of three categories: economic, political, or cultural influences.

Economic Influences

By generating significant economies of scale in the upstream activities of its value chain, a company can configure worldwide operations to compete as a globally integrated enterprise. Even if it must address local market requirements, the company can compete effectively through regional or global organizations. Nevertheless, it must generate those scale economies or adopt a more focused approach to local markets.[23] Oil companies such as Exxon and Royal Dutch/Shell enjoy these global economies, yet many smaller oil companies effectively serve proprietary home markets and compete effectively with larger rivals through small-scale, low-cost distribution systems. A firm must generate relative cost advantages in some way to enter a market or to locate facilities overseas. It judges the effects of these requirements on a national responsive strategy according to local industry conditions, much as any domestic company would evaluate its immediate competitors. When the global enterprise evaluates relative costs, it must also consider how a foreign operation will contribute to the optimization of the company's worldwide network. Thus, a relatively high-cost facility may be necessary to provide essential materials or components to downstream operations, resulting in overall lower costs or better products. Posturing decisions, therefore, depend crucially on economic factors, yet the criteria for these decisions are not always clear-cut.

Political Influences

Every nation recognizes several common priorities, such as growth, economic development, and security. Each nation arrives at its own political arrangements to fulfill these priorities. Some simply enact regulatory barriers to protect domestic industries, while others open their borders to international development. Many nations have stern restrictions on imports and exports, yet others encourage unbridled competition and trade. Also, as Chapter 3 explained in its discussion of political risk, ideologies dictate potential trading partners or restrain trade with other countries. Consequently, host-country politics can dictate a foreign company's emphasis on national responsiveness. For example, a globally integrated oil company may be required to set up domestically owned subsidiaries, to procure materials locally, or to guarantee domestic employment in order to locate activities in a foreign country.[24] These conditions often apply to companies doing business in China or India, yet similar restrictions exist in Mexico, Ireland, France, and most Middle Eastern countries. Many companies are simply barred from entering specific countries, perhaps by foreign laws or by home-country diplomatic positions. Therefore, any company may decide to posture its foreign operations based on criteria that management cannot control.

Cultural Influences

The values, beliefs, customs, and collective behavior of a people or a nation constitute its culture. These cultural factors influence a company's decisions not only about positioning operations overseas but also about managing its foreign facilities. Much of this book is concerned with these issues, but two cultural considerations exert especially powerful forces on strategic postures: the *work ethic* and *consumption preferences*.

The local work ethic must be carefully evaluated to determine whether a planned foreign facility can function as required. Economic conditions may reveal low wages or ample materials (or both), promising relatively inexpensive operations. Unfortunately, a people unaccustomed to the type of work expected—or those who lack the required skills—may offer little help to a foreign subsidiary.[25] The term *work ethic* may not capture the complete meaning of this influence. It does, however, remind international managers that planned projects can look lucrative on paper yet have unsatisfactory results because local workers cannot meet performance requirements. In an age when quality is crucial, a country that produces large quantities—but without the required quality—is a poor choice for expansion. Nevertheless, significant economic advantages and acceptable political risks may induce a company to go forward with facilities, concurrently posturing itself with appropriate local involvement to train employees or transfer in needed technology.

Consumption preferences refer to the way products are used in a foreign culture. A company's strategy must ensure that it has a viable market for its products or services. For example, an oil company that sells motor oil in one-quart cans will find significant problems distributing its product in most developing countries. In India, Bangladesh, Pakistan, Peru, Brazil, Chile, and most of the African continent, most people travel by scooters, motorbikes, or commercial three-wheelers powered by tiny engines. They purchase gasoline in used soft-drink bottles and buy oil in small jars. A one-quart can of oil would possibly cost a day's wages, and gas station owners cannot afford to stock large inventories. An oil company serving these markets cannot realize cost economies when it must repackage its products and distribute them in small quantities to many small outlets.

Reconciling International, Industry, and Company Priorities

A multinational company clearly faces a complex situation when considering its strategy, and there is no easy model of decision-making to guide management actions. However, firms follow a general order of priorities. First, company executives must consider how their enterprise fits into the overall world picture and how its plans can be affected by economic, political, and sociocultural phenomena. Within this broad interpretation, strategists then must consider the nature of the industry in which their company competes, the configuration of global competitors, and how they will coordinate activities. This requires strategists to define the value chain for each product group within their global enterprise, and then they must identify discrete activities that the firm must optimize to achieve effective competition. Finally, the company must choose a strategic posture. This decision often requires decision makers to unbundle the firm's portfolio of global businesses. Each group of goods or services can compete independently as a separate business unit, or it can compete as part of an integrated system of activities. This determination rests partially on the company's orientation and industry characteristics, but also on economic criteria, political realities both at home and abroad, and cultural factors in foreign markets.

Company strategists must weigh many perplexing considerations as they try to pull all these issues together. International affairs are difficult to unravel, political risks and economic changes are nearly impossible to forecast with much accuracy, and global cultural differences often cannot be explained or understood. Also, no matter what scenario company strategists derive from their investigations, changes occur so rapidly that management cannot assume that "one best strategy" will endure for long. Consequently, international managers acknowledge a premium on speed of responsiveness in strategies and flexibility in repositioning a company. A further complication is that no matter what strategy seems optimal, management prerogatives can take precedence, and the enterprise also must accommodate shareholder expectations and investor biases.[26] With these points in mind, the next section examines various strategies that international companies often pursue.

INTERNATIONAL AND GLOBAL STRATEGIES

International managers define how they will pursue company objectives by consolidating company efforts in a focal strategic direction. This unified **strategic intent** implies that the firm implements a single master strategy, yet a complex company may well combine a variety of strategies for diversified foreign operations. The following sections will demonstrate how a company establishes its strategic intent, formulates its cornerstone strategies, and determines how it will effectively compete within its industry.

Cornerstones of Competitive Strategies

The cornerstones of competition are **generic strategies** that establish basic models for strategic management. They are based on two general conditions of *value-added* goods or services provided to consumers, and *cost-effective* performance within the organization's value chain. There are three generic strategies: cost leadership, differentiation, and a focus or niche strategy.[27] Every company establishes a framework based on one (or a combination) of these strategies as its major strategic intent. The resulting model determines the primary criteria on which the multinational will try to outperform other firms in its industry. Each generic strategy (or combination), therefore, constitutes an alternative way in which a company can build a *core competency*. These generic strategies are described in Figure 5.6.

FIGURE 5.6
Generic Strategy
Choices for Building
Core Competencies

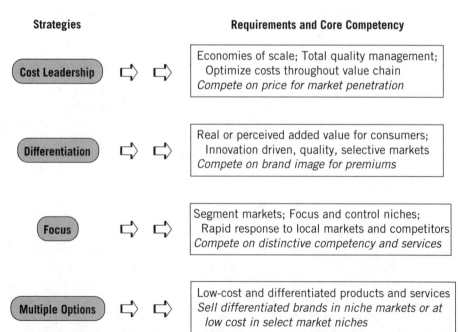

Strategies	Requirements and Core Competency
Cost Leadership	Economies of scale; Total quality management; Optimize costs throughout value chain *Compete on price for market penetration*
Differentiation	Real or perceived added value for consumers; Innovation driven, quality, selective markets *Compete on brand image for premiums*
Focus	Segment markets; Focus and control niches; Rapid response to local markets and competitors *Compete on distinctive competency and services*
Multiple Options	Low-cost and differentiated products and services *Sell differentiated brands in niche markets or at low cost in select market niches*

Cost Leadership

A company can succeed by achieving the lowest overall cost of operations among its competitors, allowing it to sustain the lowest prices. It can subsequently choose to undercut competitors and gain market share or to match industry price levels and achieve high profits. This strategy option seems obvious, yet its implementation requires a total commitment throughout the value chain to minimizing costs. A cost-leadership strategy depends to a large degree on a company's ability to achieve economies of scale. Consequently, it must configure operations for the most efficient use of material and financial resources, seek the most productive methods for total quality performance, and ensure the most efficient use of facilities. Activities such as research and development, procurement, manufacturing, distribution, marketing, customer service, and personnel management must contribute to the goal of *optimizing costs.*

A driving force behind cost leadership is *quality.* For nearly 20 years, Japanese automakers have succeeded in the U.S. market by designing, manufacturing, and delivering cars that are better made, more reliable, and less costly than competing models. Toyota, Nissan, and Honda all developed more efficient production processes, achieved scale economies by minimizing defects and waste, and beat the prices on domestic models, despite the expense of delivering cars halfway around the world and paying import duties. Today, all three Japanese firms manufacture cars in the United States for domestic sales, and they export from U.S. facilities to Europe and back to Japan. The success of Japanese automakers, therefore, has come from effective implementation of a cost-leadership strategy. U.S. automakers have adapted to this competition by retrenching and redefining their companies around quality-driven philosophies. This effort has become known as **Total Quality Management (TQM).** Many companies, such as Ford, consider TQM the ultimate generic strategy, with cost leadership as a major result.[28]

Differentiation

Companies can also succeed by creating goods or services with features unique within their industries. These distinct products can attract substantial customer traffic at competitive prices, or the firms can charge premium prices and enjoy unusual profits. The key to differentiation is *perceived superior value* as compared to industry competitors.[29] Managers who consciously choose to compete by differentiating their products are often customer-driven people, acutely aware of the expectations and needs of the consumers they serve. Companies often try to create these expectations by introducing new products and exciting innovations. They can differentiate products in many ways, but almost all rely on an underpinning assumption of superior quality and added value.

Rolex watches, Rolls Royce automobiles, Cartier jewelry, and Herman Miller furniture stand out in their industries for exceptional products and unusual designs. Apple Computer established an early reputation for a unique, user-friendly computer operating system. Liz Claiborne crafted an unusual line of women's fashions. Nintendo outran competitors and set new industry standards in video game technology. Levi Strauss built a brand reputation through consistently reliable products. In each instance, at least one driving force propelled the differentiation strategy. Actual priorities varied—ranging from design quality, reliability, and generating consumer trust through exceptional service to emphasizing the intrinsic value of the products, materials, or work. Many psychological considerations influence differentiation, such as brand satisfaction, pride of ownership, image, or simple pleasure in owning something unique.

Differentiation and quality (real or perceived) go hand in hand. A company may achieve cost efficiencies by differentiating its products, but costs are secondary to characteristics that set its efforts apart from those of competitors. Most well-differentiated companies spend more than their competitors on research and development, materials, technology, custom fabrication, and selective distribution. Further, they often hire more skilled people than competitors do, pay higher compensation, and allocate more to marketing and customer services. Because high expenditures on differentiation usually require premium prices, savings can often be achieved through quality improvements that exceed associated costs. Therefore, some companies can combine differentiated products and lower costs. By passing on cost savings through lower prices, the firm can build market share, or it can charge premium prices and reap unusual profits. Liz Claiborne has earned a fine reputation in women's clothing, but the company keeps prices moderate—less than comparable designer clothing, but above the prices of off-the-rack clothes.[30] The chapter's opening profile on Michael Dell illustrates how he has succeeded by differentiating Dell Computer Corporation through extremely efficient factory-direct services, full-service warranties, and lower prices relative to industry competitors.

Focus

A company may also succeed by focusing on one segment of a market or concentrating on one good or service. In this way, many firms try to achieve competitive advantages *within particular segments or niches* over more diversified competitors. Entrepreneurs and small-business owners prove the value of this strategy every day by positioning their ventures in well-defined market niches and fulfilling customer needs that larger companies do not meet. Large global companies can find similar opportunities, however, to position specific product lines in highly focused local markets. As discussed earlier, a global enterprise can unbundle its operations to establish multiple locally responsive operations rather than pursuing global integration, and the nature of its industry often dictates this configuration. Global franchising has generated a wide range of globally branded goods and services, each positioned as a local enterprise. These include McDonald's and 7-Eleven stores, yet companies such as Coca-Cola and Kodak have followed their own focus strategies for years.[31] Today, unusual upscale companies such as Tiffany's, Saks, and Marks & Spencer leverage their global brands in very narrow niches worldwide.[32]

The focus strategy offers an advantage relative to broad-based competitors, because the locally responsive firm can usually create a *distinctive competency*. It reacts more quickly than rivals to customer needs, behaves more flexibly than integrated companies, and sometimes achieves lower operating costs. The strategy helps a company to attract and retain customers through exceptional services, even if prices exceed competitive levels. If the company can leverage its distinct advantages, it can often charge premium prices and achieve above-average returns. If it cannot distinguish its goods or services from other competitors, however, then it can compete effectively only by establishing a cost advantage.

Competitive Strategies

To avoid confusion, consider generic strategies as core determinants of how management intends to position a multinational corporation in its industry. These broadly defined strategies describe the pivotal direction for a company. However, they require translation into *competitive strategies*, which are pragmatic alternatives for attaining a sustainable advantage against the competition. Porter refers to competitive strategies as "strategic alternatives" under the umbrella of a focal generic strategy, but corporate executives tend to speak of a *grand strategy* (generic strategy) as a framework for pursuing a competitive strategy within the company's industry. From a multinational perspective, there are four alternative competitive strategies: broad-line global competition, global focus, national focus, and protected niche, as summarized in Figure 5.7.[33]

Broad-Line Global Competition

A company pursuing this strategy competes worldwide with a full range of products in its industry. It maintains a competitive presence in all market segments, and success depends on achieving low-cost leadership through scale economies and global integration or establishing differentiated product lines. These priorities require a tremendous commitment of resources and few impediments to entering foreign markets on a major scale. Perhaps this strategy is more an ideal than a reality, yet many organizations aspire to broad-line postures. IBM may be the only company in its industry to take this approach, competing in every foreign market that it has entered with a full range of products. Bayer AG, the German pharmaceuticals company, is one of several in its field with globally branded goods and a broad-line strategy. Sony Corporation comes close to a broad-line strategy with market entries in nearly all of its audio and entertainment-based product lines.

Global Focus

Most companies must concentrate on more selective product lines, choosing particular offerings for global markets. This option constitutes a global focus strategy. For example, Merck & Company is comparable to Bayer AG in both size and product range, but Merck tends to focus on serving institutional markets while avoiding the foreign retail ethical drug segment. Merck goes head-to-head with Bayer, Ciba-Geigy, and Glaxo-Wellcome in domestic markets with a full range of products in all

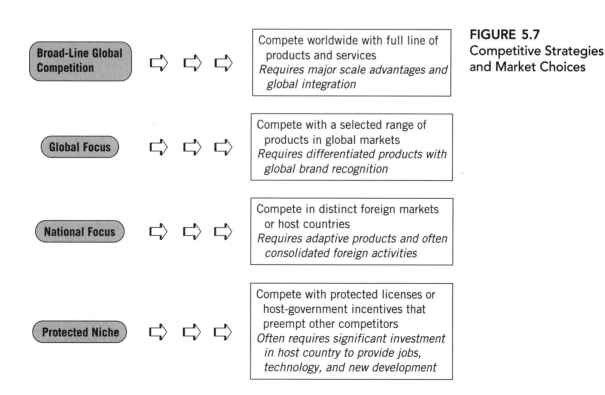

FIGURE 5.7
Competitive Strategies and Market Choices

| Broad-Line Global Competition | ⇨ ⇨ ⇨ | Compete worldwide with full line of products and services
Requires major scale advantages and global integration |

| Global Focus | ⇨ ⇨ ⇨ | Compete with a selected range of products in global markets
Requires differentiated products with global brand recognition |

| National Focus | ⇨ ⇨ ⇨ | Compete in distinct foreign markets or host countries
Requires adaptive products and often consolidated foreign activities |

| Protected Niche | ⇨ ⇨ ⇨ | Compete with protected licenses or host-government incentives that preempt other competitors
Often requires significant investment in host country to provide jobs, technology, and new development |

market segments, but it targets product markets in Europe and Asia. Many companies lack extensive product lines, so they compete globally but only in select segments. For example, Compaq has built a global distribution system nearly as extensive as IBM's, yet the company is positioned in the microcomputer segment. Meanwhile, Hewlett-Packard is strong in larger information systems for institutional and industrial segments, and has entrenched its printer technology worldwide. In most instances, a global focus strategy implies concentration on differentiated products specific to each market segment. Companies such as Procter & Gamble and Kimberly-Clark, however, compete with globally branded personal care products that are close substitutes, so they pursue scale economies to achieve competitive advantages.[34]

National Focus

Many companies find that they can concentrate their efforts in specific national markets and defend these markets against much larger competitors. Success requires effective differentiation or cost advantages relative to global competitors, thus raising entry barriers for other firms and protecting particular foreign markets. A company pursuing a national focus strategy must maintain extreme sensitivity to host-country political priorities; success often requires a company to overcome substantial entry barriers in order to entrench itself ahead of competitors. Such a firm seldom builds a globally integrated operation, opting instead for a locally responsive configuration, for two reasons. First, host nations welcome companies that bring extensive upstream activities, which create jobs and introduce new technologies. Second, in order to protect its position and reinforce relationships within the host country, a foreign enterprise must be highly responsive to local conditions. Consequently, such firms tend to make substantial foreign investments with long-term commitments.

Black & Decker Corporation has become a global competitor in hand tools and power appliances by locating consolidated facilities in more than 50 countries. It often positions upstream factories as well as downstream marketing offices in places such as Newcastle, United Kingdom, where low wages and local inducements give the company significant cost advantages.[35] Fujitsu, Nissan, and Samsung have followed similar strategies in Ireland, Portugal, Spain, and Greece. Royal Dutch/Shell, known for its globally integrated activities, also has consolidated activities in Japan, Brazil, and India to anchor itself as the market leader in those countries. Procter & Gamble has established consolidated and proprietary positions in Mexico and China to preempt competitors.[36]

Protected Niche

Unlike a simple niche strategy, in which a company seeks to establish a narrowly defined market segment, a firm creates a protected niche by forming a special relationship with the host nation. This relationship helps to insulate the company against competition through proprietary licensing, favorable import or export quotas, special tax concessions, low-cost facilities, or advantageous contracts. The contracts might include, for example, government guarantees for either supplies of domestically procured materials or government purchases of the firm's products. Foreign governments often hold equity stakes in these enterprises through joint venture agreements, cementing the relationship.

Developing nations are particularly keen to offer incentives, thus attracting companies that can bring with them advanced technologies, jobs that expand domestic employment, or opportunities to enhance exports and foreign exchange. A protected niche establishes a defensible position in which an enterprise can stand off threats by strong competitors. For example, U.S. Sprint, France Telecom, and Deutsche Telekom created a strategic alliance to provide a telecommunications network specifically to link the United States and European systems to potential markets in Eastern Europe. The European utilities are government-supported monopolies with protected licenses, conditions that preempt moves by competitors such as AT&T and MCI WorldCom.[37] India is notorious for selective licensing. For years, the government preferentially awarded licenses to PepsiCo and European bottlers and excluded Coca-Cola.

Companies in protected niches often face substantial political risk. They may suffer from weakening government ties, especially when new politicians come to power and pit foreign competitors against one another. AT&T, for instance, has enjoyed preemptive licensing protection in India for decades; but it found its Indian telecommunications markets up for auction by a newly elected government.[38]

GLOBAL STRATEGIC PLANNING

For global companies, strategic planning is an extremely complicated process that spans multiple organizational levels. As demonstrated in the previous section, executives of multinational companies can decide to compete in a wide variety of ways, and combinations of strategies can emerge for different business units. Planning thus requires a consistent approach to strategic decision-making. Most companies follow a strategic planning process such as that shown in Figure 5.8. Strategic planning begins with a clear idea of a strategic intent, as defined by a firm's mission and company-wide objectives. Then managers evaluate their industry and competitors through a process known as *environmental analysis.* These first two steps involve managers in extensive planning activities to provide a foundation of information for formulating strategies. At this point, managers consciously choose a strategic action plan and then move into

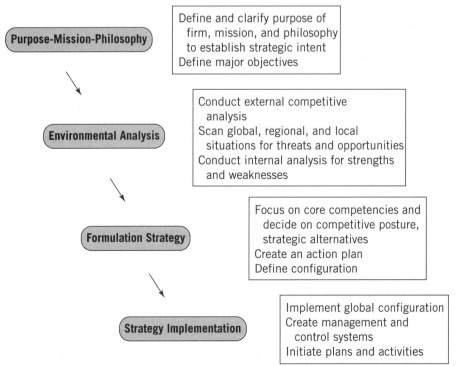

FIGURE 5.8
The Strategic Planning
Process—A Global View

the final stage of strategic implementation, where the difficult work of configuring the organization occurs.

Formal Statements of Strategic Intent—Mission and Objectives

Every company has a strategic framework of ideas that explains why it exists and what it should accomplish. A formal statement of these ideas is commonly called the company's mission, but perhaps a broader definition is needed to include an organization's **purpose, mission, and philosophy (PMP).** An organization's purpose defines why it exists. For example, a university exists to provide postsecondary education, and IBM exists to provide computer systems and services to its clients. An organization may refine the statement of its purpose to enhance its meaning, perhaps explaining that a particular university is a state-owned institution that focuses on undergraduate studies in liberal arts or a private institution with extensive graduate programs in science and technology. IBM elaborates in its purpose statement by explaining that it is a publicly listed corporation with a broad line of computer systems, components, and software directed primarily toward business applications. The purpose in each example is differentiated to give everyone a reasonable understanding of how a particular organization fits into society.

A mission statement captures the essence of what an organization does and, in broad terms, the activities it intends to accomplish. For example, IBM has settled on a mission to be the premier computer-services company with full-line integrated systems serving a global business clientele. This statement differs substantially from Apple Computer's mission to focus intensely on innovative microcomputers and small network systems for office and educational markets. Both differ from the missions of Sun Microsystems and Hewlett-Packard, which emphasize those firms' divergent core competencies in scientific computing systems, computer-integrated design and manufacturing, and computer imaging equipment.[39] A company's mission thus explains what it does and for whom, as well as how it intends to be positioned in its industry.

Finally, the company's philosophy helps to define appropriate organizational conduct. A company's philosophy is implied by its predisposition toward competition and by its organizational culture. It is not something easily reduced to writing, yet many companies try to differentiate their images through philosophy statements. Ford Motor Company launched a major advertising campaign in the early 1980s to drive home a message of "customer commitment" and a "focus on total quality." These two messages have permeated Ford's efforts to design new cars with unusual styles and enhanced operating characteristics, to improve employee training in quality performance, and to retool its factories for greater quality and reliability.[40] A global firm's philosophy pays special attention to international priorities such as managing from an ethnocentric viewpoint, establishing a decentralized geocentric system, or laying out a form of polycentric configuration that positions the company in national or regional markets with related managerial responsibilities. A company develops systems and methods that conform to the principles of its philosophy, and two companies with virtually identical purposes and similar missions competing in the same industry can have divergent philosophies, perhaps dictating entirely different patterns of competitive activities. Consequently, the combined effect of PMP underscores a company's strategic intent.

Company-wide objectives identify a firm's intended accomplishments. They offer verbal evidence of a company's commitment to achieve specific results. Both global and domestic companies must address the same categories of objectives: *profitability, market growth, financial stability, product/service performance,* and *stakeholders' interests.*

Companies define these objectives differently within their specific operating environments, but the principles behind their objectives remain quite similar throughout the world. For example, profits are universally defined in terms of returns on sales, assets, or investments, and, for publicly held corporations, in terms of stockholder equity and earnings per share. Market growth is described as sales volume, revenue, and relative market share. Financial stability is reflected in share prices, debt-equity leverage, capital structure, and various operating ratios. Product performance objectives for a firm's goods or services are more difficult to describe, but criteria relate to product characteristics, quality measures, or the portfolio of products that the firm intends to offer. They can also include statements about the services and measures of costs associated with operations. Finally, objectives for stakeholder interests can amount to relatively simple statements, such as ensuring a stable return to equity stockholders, or they can become very complicated promises about customer safety, environmental protection, and employee health and welfare, among other criteria.

A global company specifies objectives at the highest level, as composite results of worldwide operations, and at lower regional and national levels, as results of business-unit operations. Because most business units do not operate completely independently, and because they seldom perform consolidated activities within the firm's value chain, they set relatively few strategic objectives of their own. Instead, they usually concentrate on accountability for specific operational results. Each foreign operation also faces unique circumstances, however, that lead to specific and often unusual objectives.

Environmental Analysis

Environmental analysis, also called **environmental scanning,** is a system of forecasting that provides managers with strategic information on activities across their company's range of global interests. Forecasts are not limited to existing operations or geographic areas in which the firm already has a presence. To the contrary, forecasts must encompass all potential areas of interest, potential markets, and any area in which competition could arise. An international company is concerned with *potential* threats and opportunities, as well as those that it already recognizes.

A multinational organization typically conducts several types of environmental analyses, beginning with a macro scan covering a global sweep. As shown in Figure 5.9, this general inquiry includes forecasts of global political trends, global and regional economic and social trends, changes in technology, and demographic profiles of both regional and national markets. Analyses at this level are considered prerequisites for more specific evaluations of potential markets or foreign operations. They comprise a first scan of major trends and global changes to support development of broad-based criteria for weeding out unstable or overly risky countries or regions. This macro scan also profiles countries or regions that seem to offer promising opportunities.

A second scan narrows the company's attention to create detailed forecasts for high-potential areas. These analyses encompass market potential, competition, economic factors, social characteristics, and political risks for each region and nation under consideration. Market potential is evaluated in terms of total demand for the company's goods or services within the industry for a specific geographic area. Traditional demand models commonly supply forecasts of consumer income figures, market sizes, growth rates, and consumption patterns. If the company contemplates foreign production or operations such as procurement and distribution systems, then it analyzes labor markets, materials costs, capital requirements, and various

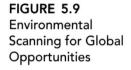

FIGURE 5.9
Environmental
Scanning for Global
Opportunities

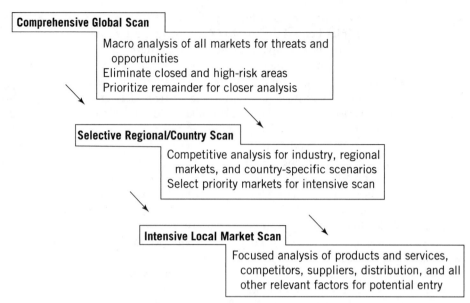

infrastructure issues (e.g., transportation, communication, and technology availability). Studies of social characteristics can run the gamut from broad reviews of consumer habits to minute forecasts of changes in complicated cultural beliefs. Political risk is assessed in terms of government stability, nationalism, advantageous government policies, disadvantageous government regulations, trade constraints, and potential conflicts of interest between home and host countries.

In a third pass, scanning focuses on the remaining short list of foreign opportunities. This in-depth environmental analysis closely resembles traditional models presented in business courses. It involves a *competitive analysis* to evaluate the nature of an industry in specific markets under consideration, and it also evaluates the company's own capabilities to compete in these markets. Michael Porter provides one of the best-known methods for conducting a competitive analysis, called the *five forces model*, as illustrated in Figure 5.10.[41]

The five forces model makes more complicated demands of the international firm than of a domestic company. Analysis of the first of the five forces, *threat of new entrants*, must encompass possible new competitors at any weak point of the global value chain. Consequently, international strategists always watch for subtle changes that threaten foreign operations. These might include, for example, revaluation of a foreign currency or a change in host-country tax policies, either of which might entice new foreign investment to that market. A multidomestic company or one pursuing a protected niche strategy must also monitor many factors that could change to dramatically increase competition.

The second force, *threat of substitute products or services*, may threaten the market positions of goods or services as new entrants to the market offer potential substitutes for the firm's own products. These substitutes often emerge as a host country develops the technological ability to support its own industries. A globally integrated company may encounter new substitutes through strategic alliances (discussed in Chapter 6) or simply due to continuous expansion of international trade. Foreign enterprises pursuing new markets may see its customers as opportunities to exploit their own competitive advantages.

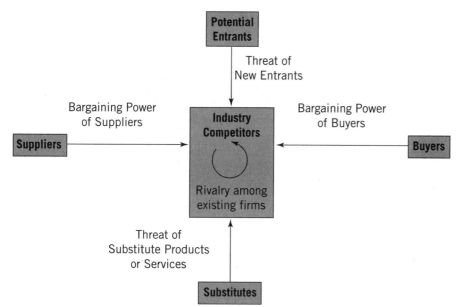

FIGURE 5.10
Forces Driving Industry Competition

Source: Reprinted with the permission of The Free Press, a Division of Simon & Schuster, from *Competitive Strategy: Techniques for Analyzing Industries and Competitors* by Michael E. Porter. Copyright (c) 1980 by The Free Press.

The third competitive force, *bargaining power of suppliers*, and the fourth, *bargaining power of buyers*, depend on the company's configuration. For example, a global company with foreign interests such as mineral extraction may well face threats from host-country controls on exploration and mining. Similarly, if a company relies on inputs from foreign procurement of materials or offshore manufacturing facilities, it must consider its relative strength as an investor in or customer of the host country. If the company is simply one of many foreign organizations that buy overseas, the host country or local suppliers can dictate prices and terms, thus dominating negotiations. On the other hand, major firms such as Boeing and IBM, although not unchallenged in their industries, buy enough inputs to be courted by foreign interests. Their large purchasing budgets give them extensive bargaining power.

To analyze Porter's fifth force, *rivalry among existing firms*, a company must evaluate the intensity of competition with its nearest rivals. Among other things, management wants to know how a competitor is likely to react to market changes, and if an aggressive move by one will prompt retaliation by others. Unlike domestic companies serving well-defined markets, global companies must consider worldwide markets with continuously changing legions of competitors. PepsiCo and Coca-Cola compete with one another domestically and globally, and strategists in each company keep themselves well informed about the other's activities. However, both companies face threats from local rivals in foreign domestic soft-drink markets. They also face often-unpredictable behavior by foreign distributors, political intervention, and cultural constraints that can drastically affect their competitive advantages.[42]

Analysis often fails to predict how a foreign competitor will react. For example, the major Japanese automobile companies—Toyota, Nissan, and Honda—dramatically reduced exports to the U.S. market in 1995 because changes in the dollar-yen exchange rate threatened huge losses in repatriated income. However, all three firms also made a major policy shift toward manufacturing cars in countries where they had markets. American competitors watching only import statistics might have perceived a sudden gain of a significant marketing advantage; in reality, however, Japanese automakers had become even more competitive through enhanced U.S. manufacturing capabilities.[43]

A crucial criterion for competitive analysis demands that it focus on the future. Recall the statement at the beginning of this section that the environmental scanning process seeks to understand *potential threats and opportunities*. Therefore, scanning at all levels must look toward the company's strategic planning horizon. This period may span a few seasons for dynamic industries such as fashion clothes and toys, or several decades for infrastructure-related industries such as electric power generation and containerized commercial shipping. Power plants take years to develop, and many more years to become profitable, and containerized shipping requires enormous capital investments in port facilities, equipment, ships, and support services. Chapter 6 explores how companies evaluate future threats and opportunities and considers how they can seek to insulate themselves against uncertainties through global alliances.

Formulating Strategy

International managers formulate strategies based not only on the results of environmental scanning but also by keeping a close eye on their company's capabilities. For example, few companies can become globally integrated enterprises, simply because they lack the resources to do so. Many firms do not have the managerial skills they would need to expand into foreign markets, and others may not have the technology, finances, or organizational systems to consider overseas expansion. Therefore, although environmental scanning may uncover exciting new opportunities, managers must determine their own firm's strengths and weaknesses before pursuing any strategic initiatives. This internal analysis often occurs in concert with, or subsequent to, the external environmental analysis. Together, the external and internal analyses are called a **SWOT analysis,** and they include the elements shown in Figure 5.11.

SWOT Analysis

The term SWOT comes from *strengths, weaknesses, opportunities*, and *threats*, and SWOT analysis is among the most common approaches to strategic planning for companies of every type and size. Many strategy texts present the model as a sequential process of evaluating each dimension, but in reality managers complete a two-part

FIGURE 5.11
SWOT Analysis—
Factors for
Consideration

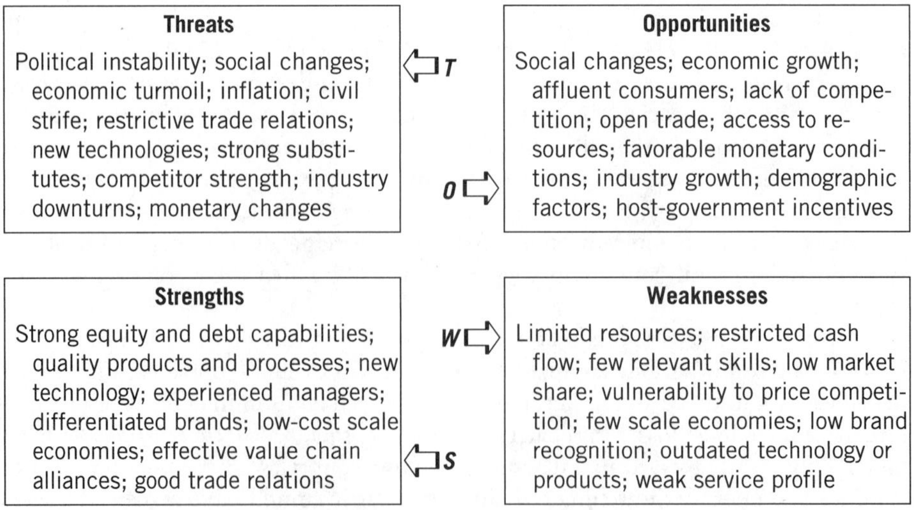

Threats	**Opportunities**
Political instability; social changes; economic turmoil; inflation; civil strife; restrictive trade relations; new technologies; strong substitutes; competitor strength; industry downturns; monetary changes	Social changes; economic growth; affluent consumers; lack of competition; open trade; access to resources; favorable monetary conditions; industry growth; demographic factors; host-government incentives
Strengths	**Weaknesses**
Strong equity and debt capabilities; quality products and processes; new technology; experienced managers; differentiated brands; low-cost scale economies; effective value chain alliances; good trade relations	Limited resources; restricted cash flow; few relevant skills; low market share; vulnerability to price competition; few scale economies; low brand recognition; outdated technology or products; weak service profile

process that probably flows in the reverse order: TOWS. Companies tend to emphasize monitoring activities that reveal threats first as a sort of early warning system to reveal competitive changes that would affect business decisions. This part of the environmental scanning activities, mentioned earlier, also tends to point out opportunities. If the process repeats any particular sequence, it tends to favor study of potential opportunities.

After concisely summarizing potential threats and opportunities, management can then ask whether the company has the capabilities to defend against threats or to take advantage of potential opportunities. This determination involves an evaluation of the firm's weaknesses and resulting vulnerability to competition. Through global evaluations, management must develop strategic scenarios based on opportunities it would like to pursue, followed by a review of any critical constraints that would prevent the company from implementing the plan.

The final consideration in strategy formulation looks at a company's *strengths*. Recall that successful companies develop distinctive competencies on which they rely to gain competitive advantage. They evaluate these strengths in terms of strategic scenarios, often using sophisticated simulation exercises and forecasting methods to determine whether the firm can apply a particular competency in the projected scenario. Owens Corning is the market leader in fiberglass insulation for both North America and Europe due to substantial cost and technological advantages that give the company vast economies of scale. This strength has, in turn, given Owens Corning an entrenched brand position that the company uses effectively to expand in almost any foreign market it chooses. Similarly, 3M Corporation has long held a lead position in abrasives and adhesives through constant innovation programs that differentiate the company's portfolio from those of its competitors for nearly 2,000 products, such as Scotch tape and Post-it Notes. Canon has leveraged its expertise in optical reproduction technology to succeed in cameras, photocopiers, and a wide array of lithography equipment.[44]

Most of these companies also enjoy competitive advantages due to their past performance records and reputations. These strengths contribute to enviable financial capabilities, the ability to commit significant resources to R&D, management depth with skilled international staff, procurement networks, and well-developed distribution systems. In addition, established global alliances allow these firms to enhance foreign capabilities and gain access to markets, production, and technology not available to other competitors.

Strategic Alternatives

After completing a comprehensive environmental analysis, developing a profile of company strengths and weaknesses, and evaluating potential competitors, international managers are prepared to consider feasible alternatives. The term *alternative* implies a discrete choice among strategies, but reality seldom presents such simple situations. Consider the complexity of considerations discussed earlier for *configuration* and *coordination*. Also, consider that an enterprise can set up different configurations at different levels of its organization. In addition, it faces a continuum of choices between the polar extremes of global integration and multidomestic localization. Managers often feel caught in a quagmire of alternatives, with many subtle nuances affecting separate choices. In fact, this is precisely the situation faced by strategists, and increasing global diversification brings greater complexity of decision-making.

The process begins at the apex of the organization with identification of a specific strategic intent, defined earlier as the primary determinant for pursuing a particular strategy. The company must decide whether it will compete as a globally integrated or multidomestic enterprise. After settling on one of those predispositions, it can then consider one of the dominant generic strategies—cost leadership, differentiation, or focus (niche). It can also form some combination, such as developing differentiated products that are also cost leaders in their fields or pursuing specific market niches with well-differentiated products. Perhaps the company can bring together elements of all three.

The extent to which the firm can follow any of these strategies (or any combination) depends on the company's relative strengths and weaknesses with respect to its competition. By bringing together the results of their competitive analyses, managers can anticipate potential portfolios for expansion and subsequently create local scenarios for specific foreign operations. As discussed earlier, each of these portfolio choices can emphasize one of three approaches—globalization, regionalization, or localization. Therefore, most international companies compare strategic alternatives by answering questions such as where to compete, which goods or services to compete with, how to compete, and how to organize the company to coordinate these activities.

Companies determine where to compete based on the competitive analysis that identifies opportunities. This decision also depends on the firm's capabilities. Managers decide which products to deploy by considering the company's distinctive competencies as compared to the strengths and positioning of competitors within chosen target markets. They determine how to compete based on the company's ability to employ one or more of the generic strategies.

Finally, decisions about how to organize the company may reflect not choices but mandates. For example, if Honda chooses to compete in dozens of countries with hundreds of distribution points for its motorcycles, it may be able to build globally branded products (i.e., implement a globally integrated manufacturing strategy), but it must ensure locally responsive marketing. Consequently, Honda's central organization takes the form of a holding company that coordinates 22 divisions concerned with upstream procurement, R&D, technology, finance, and manufacturing. In addition, a business-unit level of organization links foreign alliances, regional distributors, and autonomous dealerships and agencies.[45] Organizational choices also are influenced by company alliances with foreign partners and by location requirements. Specifically, many countries require local equity interests in foreign companies, often through joint ventures. Some also mandate licensing through local government interests or purely domestically owned subsidiaries. In each instance, the company may find that it cannot repatriate revenues, must hire locally or set up joint senior management groups, and perhaps must purchase local materials.

Entry Decisions

For domestic companies that have not yet entered the international arena, strategy formulation is concerned with how to "go global." Of course, all the planning criteria mentioned in preceding sections apply equally to domestic and international companies without regard to the extent of their holdings, but the domestic company often faces additional uncertainty as it steps into unknown waters. Chapter 6 is devoted to strategic alternatives for entry decisions that relate to both domestic companies and expansion options for international firms. It is sufficient to point out here that entry decisions bring together the two concerns of how to compete and how to organize the international company. For example, a company that seeks only to export products is taking a minimum risk with little or no foreign investment and simply placing products with foreign distributors. Exporting can be far more complicated, of course, but most companies begin global business by testing the water with minimum involvement. At this stage, the organization is not substantially altered; the enterprise remains configured as it was before entering export markets. However, as a company becomes more involved with foreign markets, it can graduate to licensing, franchise agreements, foreign distribution, manufacturing, joint ventures, or more complicated strategic alliances. With each incremental change in its international business, the company alters product decisions, location options, and methods of competing.

Strategy Implementation

Implementation has two general connotations. The first is concerned with positioning the company according to its strategic intent, so that it can pursue a well-defined mission and achieve its stated objectives. When a company decides where to compete and with what portfolio of goods or services, then it brings together the necessary resources and capabilities to realize these plans. Implementation in this sense may require reorganization or strategic alliances to gain access to new markets or resources. Strategic alliances also influence how the company competes, thus solving one of the implementation questions. As discussed in the next chapter, alliances often help a company to overcome its competitive weaknesses by combining complementary resources or skills of each partner. Alliances also can solidify relationships within the value chain by linking activities through contracts or reciprocal agreements. Consequently, the first connotation of *implementation* implies global configuration decisions to pursue the organization's mission and strategic objectives.

The second connotation of the term concerns management within the firm's chosen configuration. This process involves coordination, and much of the remainder of this text reviews how managers deal with their international responsibilities. Implementation in this regard centers on how to develop foreign operations, how to organize and lead in a multicultural environment, and how to address the functional requirements of both integrated and locally autonomous foreign activities.

DEVELOPING EFFECTIVE STRATEGIES

Managers in global enterprises face extremely complicated circumstances for planning, and their companies often formulate multiple levels of strategies in uncertain and volatile environments. Therefore, the task of developing effective strategies eclipses the ability of one executive, and it often goes well beyond the capabilities of experienced management teams. The intuition and experience of key managers are crucial, but the decisions involve such complex competitive issues that strategic planning requires a continuous effort to collect information, analyze worldwide trends, and track circumstances along many different vectors.

As this chapter concludes, it is important to emphasize that its portrayal of a general planning process offers only a starting point for strategic management. Further, Chapter 6 may appear to oversimplify the various methods described for competing in the international arena. Bear in mind that global companies must orchestrate strategies at several organizational levels, each with very different priorities and criteria. Consequently, no single approach to planning or preferred planning model can apply to all international management teams. It is equally dangerous to suggest that a specific strategy will be best for a particular company. If one model stands out, it is unlikely to endure for a significant period of time because competitive circumstances change. These facts support one essential conclusion: Adaptability is an international manager's greatest asset.

REVIEW QUESTIONS

1. What is *strategy* in the international context? How do comparative and competitive factors influence strategic decisions?
2. Distinguish between the different levels of strategy and how international, industry, and company priorities contrast.
3. Explain the *value chain* and its role in a globally integrated enterprise. How do relationships differ within a value chain for an integrated company versus a multidomestic enterprise?
4. Define *configuration* and *coordination* in Porter's model of competition. How do these priorities contrast for a global strategy versus a multidomestic strategy?
5. At the company level, a firm's *strategic orientation* or predisposition often determines how it will structure and manage international activities. Describe these predispositions and their relative merits.
6. A multinational adopts a *posture* of a globally integrated or locally responsive organization. What do these terms mean, and what factors influence management's choice of one posture or another?
7. Identify and describe the three *generic strategies*. How do they differ, and what are the relative advantages and disadvantages of each strategy?
8. Within the broad context of a generic strategy, a multinational further refines its approach to competition through so-called *strategic alternatives*. What are they, and how does each alternative influence management decisions?
9. Explain the terms *strategic intent* and *purpose, mission, and philosophy*. After defining these important strategic criteria, how does a company go about strategic planning?
10. How does a multinational complete an *environmental analysis?* What levels of environmental scanning do managers carry out, and what factors are important at each level?
11. Briefly describe Porter's *five forces model* of competitive analysis.
12. What is a SWOT analysis, and how does it influence strategic decisions?

GLOSSARY OF KEY TERMS

Comparative advantage   A strength that one nation has relative to another in a factor of production or trade.

Competitive analysis   The process of evaluating an industry within a specific market under consideration for a strategic initiative, as well as the company's own capabilities to compete in this market.

Competitive strategy   One of the specific alternatives for attaining a sustainable advantage against competition, including *broad-line global competition*, *global focus*, *national focus*, and *protected niche*.

Configuration   Porter's concept that explains how a company organizes the activities in its value chain, and thus how it selects activities to pursue and integrates those operations.

Coordination   Porter's concept of methods by which a company interconnects value-chain activities and manages for optimal integration of global interests.

Downstream activity   A component of a value chain that occurs relatively late and close to final completion of the chain of events, such as market distribution and retailing.

Environmental scanning   A system of forecasting that provides managers with strategic information on activities across their company's range of global interests.

Ethnocentricity   A predisposition to believe that one's native culture is superior to others, often implying an effort to impose these beliefs on others.

Generic strategies   The cornerstones of global competition that establish basic models for strategic management: *differentiation*, *cost leadership*, and *focus* or *niche* strategies.

Global integration strategy   The model for a company with a global strategic posture that competes in global markets with undifferentiated products and relatively standardized activities throughout the value chain.

National responsiveness strategy The model for a company with a global strategic posture that focuses intensely on local markets and niches, tailoring its products specifically for well-defined customer bases.

Purpose, mission, and philosophy (PMP) A broad definition of a firm's strategic framework that explains why it exists, what it should accomplish, and guidelines for its overall conduct.

Strategic intent The sum of a company's unifying principles, including its mission; its company-wide objectives; its philosophy, which determines how it will pursue its mission; and its long-term expectations for global development.

SWOT analysis A competitive analysis to strategically assess a company's strengths, weaknesses, opportunities, and threats.

Total Quality Management (TQM) An initiative to retrench and redefine a company around a quality-driven philosophy as part of a cost-leadership strategy.

Upstream activity A component of a value chain that occurs relatively close to original resources or materials or in an early stage of the overall conversion process.

Value chain An accumulated set of discrete activities that are interdependently related through a progression of coordinated processes.

EXERCISES

1. Select a company within a well-defined industry that interests you, such as Compaq or Toys 'R' Us, and trace its value chain. Identify key elements of the value-chain activities from as far upstream and downstream as you can. How is the company configured within this value chain? Has it sought to integrate (linking activities)? If so, how does it coordinate these activities (by ownership, alliance, licensing, or contracts)? What opportunities do you envision for the company to expand by pursuing greater linkage within the value chain?

2. News and magazine articles offer many examples of companies' foreign operations, manufacturing, and market tactics. Find an example of a company that demonstrates each of the three *generic strategies*—cost leadership, differentiation, and focus or niche. In your opinion, why does each one succeed or fail? What are the critical issues for each, and how would you suggest the companies could improve?

3. Form small teams to present arguments for and against the competitive strategies *broad-line global competition*, *global focus*, *national focus*, and *protected niche*. Companies can choose among these, but often they are constrained by the nature of their industries. Therefore, select a company to support your arguments and be prepared to briefly present the case in class.

DISNEY ENTERS A NEW GLOBAL ERA

Mickey Mouse and Donald Duck, global brands well known around the world, are a small part of the worldwide Walt Disney Company, yet they are the heart and soul of the Disney image. The friendly mouse radiates the wholesome character of childhood innocence that once gave the Disney empire its singular competitive advantage in a rugged entertainment industry. Unfortunately, the company's rapid growth and activities outside its traditional areas of business led many stockholders and analysts to question whether the company had lost its way. Three major issues seemed to confront Disney CEO Michael Eisner. First, he and his staff had to decide how to manage the rapidly diversifying global enterprise. Second, they had to study how to position the Disney company to retain the "magic" that led it to greatness. Third, they had to discover how to compete in worldwide markets as an American company with a distinctly American character to its goods, services, and management systems.

The magnitude of these strategic problems was reflected in how the company had expanded in recent years. As a result of Walt Disney Company's $19 billion acquisition of Capital Cities/ABC Inc. in 1995, financial analysts and company officials expected international growth to drive the new entertainment behemoth into the next century. The acquisition brought a major new international dimension to Disney. Soon after the deal was done, the Disney Channel brought U.S. family-style programming to China and India, where Capital Cities' ESPN cable network already had a presence.

Meanwhile, Disney solidified its foreign theme parks in Japan and France. The Japanese experience was highly successful as a fully replicated American export of values, characters, behavior, songs, shows, and company icons. In France, the Americana that Disney offered was less well received, and the company had to respond to sensitive charges of ethnocentrism and misplaced emphasis on selling the American culture. Nevertheless, Disney Chairman Michael Eisner mentioned a strong possibility of new Disney theme parks in South America, perhaps Brazil, and of another park in Asia. Despite the initial financial debacle in Paris, Eisner said that the company was searching the globe looking for potential sites and partners in countries from Spain to China.

Theme parks aside, the core of Disney's expansion has been in media, and the announcement of the Capital Cities/ABC deal emphasized the combined company's new international role. "More and more, as I've traveled around and watched our company grow and expand, I have noticed that its expansion is outside the U.S.," Eisner said when announcing the deal. "We think the combination of ABC and its assets, particularly outside the U.S., like ESPN, coupled with the Disney Channel . . . gives us the ability to grow." Indeed, the strategic combination of the companies created synergies and cross-promotion opportunities, particularly in television programming and distribution between outlets such as ESPN and the Disney Channel.

However, this activity was just the tip of the iceberg. The Walt Disney Company had equity stakes in two major European program production companies and interests in broadcast and cable distribution. In addition, Disney completed a satellite uplink broadcast facility in Singapore, launched a wholly owned Taiwan-based outlet for the Disney Channel, and formed programming alliances with satellite and cable TV interests in Hong Kong and Korea. ESPN took advantage of the Asian uplink facility to expand to the East Asian market, and ESPN International Networks now reach 70 million homes in at least 150 countries. The Disney network of interests includes many local TV and radio affiliates, domestic and foreign media agreements for program support, and a huge international productions division.

Global growth was expected to be particularly strong in Disney retail theme stores and a new concept of a Disney mall with integrated stores and entertainment. The company has nearly 500 stores worldwide, and it opened a high-profile location on the Champs Elysees in Paris. Currently, Disney has some of its strongest retail stores in Asia, and numerous others serve Europe. The company says that the bulk of new stores will be opened outside the U.S. market.

Disney has yet another dynasty of interests somewhat less famous than its broadcasting and core entertainment businesses of Disney Studios and theme parks. The company owns or holds major interests in Miramax Films, Touchstone Pictures, Buena Vista Home Video, Hollywood Records, and Wonderland Music. Indeed, these holdings have been responsible for much of the company's entertainment revenue. But, they have also stirred some controversy due to the nature of some of the films and records released.

The company's image suffered from other criticism concerning objections to ABC's yearlong story line on its sitcom, *Ellen*, that related a lesbian coming-out experience. Also, an ill-fated attempt to create a "historical" theme park next to the Bull Run Civil War battlefield in Virginia angered some observers. Disney also had to substantially modify production of a movie featuring the nearsighted cartoon character Mr. Magoo in the wake of charges by the National Federation of the Blind that it would prove degrading to blind people and repugnant to most viewers.

Wall Street securities analysts were left wondering, though, whether Disney, and Eisner in particular, had lost their sense of direction. In the minds of America, Disney is "American" and the "wholesome" company that provides entertainment reflecting "core values" of ethical behavior. Consequently, the company was expected to run its business on the same ethical grounds. With nearly a third of its total revenues and an even greater percentage of profits generated outside the United States, foreign fans of the Disney culture were beginning to question the ethics of CEO Eisner and his executive staff. Headlines about Eisner's extraordinary multimillion-dollar annual bonuses and multimillion-dollar executive buyouts and benefits for other top executives brought charges of compromised ethics and misplaced strategies.

Indeed, some characterized the global enterprise as having a strategically split personality. On one hand, it dominated the niche of American-style family entertainment, but on the other hand, it had some controversial, if profitable, bedfellows. Ultimately, the question was whether Disney could keep its reputation intact—and continue to leverage the "magic" that differentiated the company from all other competitors, or would it expand, diversify further, and eventually disintegrate?

Today, Disney continues to diversify its interests. In 1998, Disney took a 42% stake in Infoseek Corporation, an Internet company, to form the Go Network and later increased its stake to 72%. In addition, Disney formed a joint venture with Hearst Magazines in 1998 and established ESPN the Magazine. Plans are currently underway to launch an extreme-sports magazine, EXPN, for extreme-sports enthusiasts. In early 1999, Disney restructured its overseas operations in an attempt to better market its brand internationally and take advantage of growth opportunities overseas. By the end of 2000, Europe was one of Disney's primary targets for international expansion. The expansion includes the 2002 addition of another theme park to Euro-Disney in Paris, Disney retail stores and consumer products associated with Disney movies.

While Disney will close 100 of its 508 stores nationwide, the company recently announced that it will redesign the existing stores to be more interactive and carry more contemporary clothing. In addition, the stores will feature merchandise for the entire family including a housewares line. The redesign will begin in July 2001 and is expected to take approximately three years.

Disney also found a partner in Hong Kong for its third theme park outside of the U.S. Hong Kong International Theme Parks Ltd., a joint venture between the Hong Kong government and Walt Disney Company, was formed to build Hong Kong Disneyland, which is a 311-acre theme park to be located on Hong Kong's Lantau Island. Under the terms of the agreement announced in 1999, the government owns 57% of the company and Disney's stake in the company is 43%. The theme park is scheduled to open in 2005.

QUESTIONS

1. Disney created a global image, and perhaps even a company-wide identity, through a distinct niche strategy in entertainment. How would you describe its strategy? From what you know about the Walt Disney Company, how would you describe its distinctive competencies and competitive advantages within the entertainment and media industries?

2. Critics charged that Disney and its CEO had "lost their way." Do you agree? Did the company seem to have a clear strategic direction for its growth and global expansion? Critique the company's collection of interests from the viewpoint of a global company in search of a sound long-term strategy.

3. What strategic management problems would you envision for Disney as it manages cultural mismatches and other conflicts in its worldwide interests? Can it retain the all-American image while selling globally branded products and "exporting" the cultural values of its founder's image, or should the company localize?

BIBLIOGRAPHY

Bannon, Lisa. "Expanded Disney to Look Overseas for Fastest Growth; a Disney Channel for China and India, New Foreign Theme Parks Are Possible." *Wall Street Journal*, 2 August 1995, p. A3.

"Chase Bank Arranging Hong Kong Disney Financing." *Amusement Business*, 11 September 2000, 55. [Retrieved 5 March 2001 from Dow Jones Interactive database.]

Goldblatt, Harry. "How Can Disney Do So Badly with Family Programs? ABC's Lame Sitcom Lineup." *Fortune*, 17 March 1997, 32.

Grover, Ronald, and Eric Schine. "At Disney, Grumpy Isn't Just a Dwarf." *Business Week*, 24 February 1997, 38.

Guy, Sandra. "Disney Revamps." *Chicago Sun-Times*, 20 February 2001, p. 48. [Retrieved 9 March 2001 from Dow Jones Interactive database.]

"Hong Kong Puts Financial Secretary in Charge of Disney Joint Venture." *Dow Jones Business News*, 16 March 2000. [Retrieved 5 March 2001 from Dow Jones Interactive database.]

Keegan, Jeffrey. "Deals of the Year: Guarding the Keys to the Magic Kingdom." *Investment Dealers Digest*, 13 December 1999. [Retrieved 6 March 2001 from Dow Jones Interactive database.]

McIntosh, Bill. "Disney's Eisner Targets Europe for Acquisitions." *The Independent*–London, 7 December 2000, 22. Retrieved 6 March 2001 from Dow Jones Interactive database.]

Orwall, Bruce. "Disney Names Iger to Major Overseas Post." *Wall Street Journal*, 26 February 1999, p. A3. See also "Disney Restructures Overseas Operations." *Wall Street Journal Europe*, 26 February 1999, p. UK5A.

Streisand, Betsy, and William Holstein. "It's a Divisive World After All." *U.S. News & World Report*, 14 July 1997, pp. 45-46.

CASE 5.2

PEPSICO STUMBLES AND REVAMPS ITS GLOBAL STRATEGIES

Not long ago, visitors to India could get a Pepsi but not a Coke, travelers on Aeroflot to Moscow would be served Pepsi, Hungarian workers quenched their thirst with Pepsi from a factory cooler, and East German kids thrived on Pepsi. Coca-Cola Company was quietly in the background and, in many instances, not in the market. Similar signs of success for PepsiCo Inc. showed up in Latin markets. News articles and industry analysts around the world applauded Pepsi and questioned Coke's strategies in the so-called cola wars. However, the fall of the Berlin Wall abruptly ended Pepsi's Eastern European influence. A subsequent change in India's government opened the doors to international competition, scrapping a proprietary contract with PepsiCo, and the economics of competition in Latin America changed. Today PepsiCo is in better financial standing than it was in 1996, but getting there required new domestic and global strategies.

PepsiCo derived 70 percent of its sales from domestic markets, in contrast to Coca-Cola with nearly 80 percent of its revenues generated outside the United States. To change this disparity, PepsiCo launched a multibillion-dollar international expansion plan in 1994 to capture new world market share. The goal was to begin the campaign to capture 20 percent of the national market share in Brazil, which is the world's third largest soft-drink market after the United States and Mexico. By 1996, Pepsi's plans were in shambles. Its Brazilian "superbottler," Buenos Aires Embotelladora SA, or Baesa, was facing insolvency; three top executives stepped down in wake of Baesa's problems; the company defaulted on international loans; and Pepsi's Venezuelan bottling partner defected to Coca-Cola. At the same time, Coca-Cola took the market-share lead away from Pepsi in the heart of Russia and much of Eastern Europe.

Pepsi's problems in Latin America and Europe suggested that its biggest enemy overseas was not Coke, but itself. In Brazil, say industry analysts, the company made an ambitious charge into the country, focused on pumping up sales and outgunning the competition rather than on building brand loyalty and long-term profitability. In its rush, it made costly mistakes. The firm implemented a go-for-broke beverage strategy not just in Latin America, but worldwide, and Brazil was to be the company's first major engagement.

But Brazil is Coke country. Coca-Cola has weathered the ups and downs of the Brazilian economy for more than 50 years, building a brand name, slowly winning more than 50 percent of the market, and leaving Pepsi with about 10 percent or less. The main reason is that Atlanta-based Coca-Cola has spent some 10 years lashing together its hundreds of overseas bottlers and independent franchisees to make and sell soft drinks. Coke's regional bottlers, called *anchor bottlers*, have developed deep local ties, huge capital budgets, and finely honed distribution systems. In contrast, Pepsi struggled in Brazil, shifting among three bottlers in 25 years without having those bottlers build a brand name or customer loyalty for the products. In addition, PepsiCo switched to a regional Latin strategy, centered its operations in Puerto Rico, and established an elaborate distribution hub to serve Chile, Brazil, Argentina, and Uruguay. When this failed, the company "relaunched" national market systems, such as the one in Brazil with Baesa. Pepsi's plans called for opening four state-of-the-art plants in Brazil, each capable of producing 250 million cases of soft drinks a year. The company also bought new trucks and rolled out several new products and packages. The new plants were rushed into service, and people were hired and rapidly trained. Pepsi brought in local managers from other locations, as well as executives from the United States and other Latin subsidiaries. The result was an environment where chief executive officers not meeting expectations were replaced, and plant workers were fundamentally unskilled. Pepsi suffered costly quality problems with bent cans, broken bottles, leaky caps, and shoddy distribution and wholesaling services.

Learning from its past mistakes, Pepsi has spent the past four years restructuring. The restructuring has involved cutting back on its international operations and selling restaurants and bottling operations in order to revitalize the company. In particular, PepsiCo has revamped its strategy and focused on what it does best and where it has the potential to be a dominant player in the industry—packaged foods and drinks. By utilizing the strengths of Frito-Lay Snacks, Pepsi Cola Beverages, and Tropicana Juices, the company has developed a strategy that centers on supermarkets. Pepsi's new strategy has proven effective in a number of non-soft drink areas. The concept, "Power of One," places Frito-Lay and Pepsi products side by side on grocery store shelves to encourage shoppers to purchase Pepsi when buying snacks. This strategy has increased the odds that consumers will select Pepsi when purchasing snack foods. In addition, Tropicana has 44 percent of the market share, which is more than double that of Coca-Cola's Minute Maid, and Pepsi's Aquafina holds the bottled water market share.

Overseas, PepsiCo still faces challenges in the soft drink arena. But it has learned that going head to head with Coca-Cola in overseas markets where Coke is the dominant brand may not be the best strategy. PepsiCo has decided instead to focus on emerging markets such as India and China, where there is the potential to gain a greater share of the market. Coca-Cola continues to hold over 50 percent of the market share in China; however, Pepsi-Cola has the greater market share in India.

Pepsi's product line is solid, and its executives are not afraid to take risks. Pepsi-Cola may never edge out Coca-Cola, but its current strategy has made Pepsi more competitive. It has created synergies resulting in increased operating margins, higher return on invested capital, and a stronger position in the marketplace. And with a new CEO stepping up to the plate, Pepsi may grow even more and increase its global position.

QUESTIONS

1. How would you describe PepsiCo's primary strategy? What strategy would you suggest, and why would it succeed?

2. Using Porter's competitive model, analyze the environment in Brazil for PepsiCo. As an alternative, use the model to suggest difficulties for

competing and gaining soft-drink market share in China.

3. How might PepsiCo gain greater market share in emerging markets?

BIBLIOGRAPHY

Byrne, John A. "PepsiCo's New Formula: How Roger Enrico Is Remaking the Company." *Business Week*, 10 April 2000, 172+. [Retrieved 21 November 2000 from Dow Jones Interactive database.]

Frank, Robert. "Adding Some Fizz, Once-Stodgy Coca-Cola Races to Sate Global Thirst." *Asian Wall Street Journal*, 23 August 1995, p. 1.

Frank, Robert, and Jonathan Friedland. "Coca-War Casualty: How Pepsi's Charge into Brazil Fell Short of Its Ambitious Goals." *Wall Street Journal*, 3 September 1996, p. A1.

"Hong Kong: Pepsi, Coke Duke It Out in India, China." *Advertising Age International*, October 2000, 1. [Retrieved 6 March 2001 from Dow Jones Interactive database.]

Lavelle, Louis (Aleta Davies, ed.). "Thirsty for Growth at Pepsi." *Business Week*, 16 October 2000, 64. [Retrieved 21 November 2000 from Dow Jones Interactive database.]

McKay, Betsy. "Juiced Up: Pepsi Edges Past Coke, and It Has Nothing to Do with Cola." *Wall Street Journal*, 6 November 2000, p. A1. [Retrieved 21 November 2000 from Dow Jones Interactive database.]

Schwartz, Nelson D. "Time to Cash in Your Blue Chips?" *Fortune*, 21 July 1997, 120–123, 126–128, 130.

Sellers, Patricia. "How Coke Is Kicking Pepsi's Can." *Fortune*, 28 October 1996, 70–75, 78–80, 84.

GOING GLOBAL AND IMPLEMENTING STRATEGIES

CHAPTER OBJECTIVES

Distinguish between proactive and reactive approaches to international strategy.

Describe the factors that influence location decisions within various generic strategies and approaches to international competition.

Identify and explain ways in which companies enter foreign markets or establish foreign operations.

Detail the advantages and disadvantages of various forms of international expansion.

Highlight the primary management considerations for implementing international strategic plans.

Alexander J. Trotman began to dismantle the monolithic bureaucracy of the Ford Motor Company only three weeks after becoming its chairman in 1993. He announced a new global strategy based on world-class auto designs, consolidated U.S. and European engineering activities, and created international management teams to coordinate worldwide interests. The U.S.–Europe consolidation brought together engineering by German, British, and American divisions to establish a common automotive chassis and new aerodynamic designs. Trotman looked to the year 2000 to mark a new era for globalization of the Ford line, bringing together a streamlined organization with distributed worldwide manufacturing and marketing for the new century. Ford already had laid the foundations for this change, but Trotman also had begun to internationalize its management. Staff members could no longer think in parochial terms as American, British, or German managers; they had to function as world managers. Corporate headquarters remained in Detroit, but the executive core was no longer exclusively an American stronghold.[1]

When Trotman was named chairman, the company's profits were failing, and Ford's world market share was rapidly eroding. Consequently, people anxious for change welcomed Trotman's announcement of a sweeping new strategy called "Ford 2000," a vision to create a unified global company. Within two years, an established global mandate called for replacement of a rigid bureaucracy with an internationally focused team management program. Car design became a cooperative global effort, and 20 percent of the executives who did not share the global vision departed. Ford reconciled its worldwide purchasing systems and redefined upstream activities, generating reductions in global costs by $3 billion a year. New ventures were opened in China, Vietnam, India, and Poland, and South American operations were consolidated into a major division.

While Ford is far from reaching its objectives, it is the world's second largest automaker behind General Motors. The company has shored up the erosion in European market share, but it faces an uphill battle against foreign competitors. Over the years, Ford has added Volvo, Mazda, Lincoln, Mercury, Jaguar, Aston Martin, and Land Rover to its fold, making the company stronger and more competitive. But, unlike its global competitors, Ford still does not have a strong presence in Asia.

Alexander Trotman retired as chairman of Ford at the end of 1998, but he laid the groundwork for Ford to entertain opportunities in Asia long before he left. Recently, Ford, under the leadership of current CEO Jacques Nasser, considered buying bankrupt Daewoo Motors in South Korea. After months of negotiations, Ford pulled away from the deal, leaving it with a weak presence in Asia. In contrast, General Motors is building Buicks in Shanghai and has the opportunity to grow its Asian market share. But Nasser is not giving up. He is still searching for opportunities in Asia and the world over that will contribute to Ford's growth.[2]

Nasser, Lebanese-born and raised in Australia, developed a new strategy for Ford after his appointment as CEO on January 1, 1999. Nasser has begun restructuring Ford around its global brands, treating the company as a group of consolidated smaller companies. In time, this will create the culture of a consumer company. One example of Nasser's consolidated groups is the Premier Automotive Group, a division of Ford that manages Ford's luxury-car brands such as Volvo and Land Rover. In this type of organization, the luxury-car brands have the opportunity to effectively compete with other brands such as Mercedes-Benz and BMW while maintaining the benefits of the Ford group.[3]

IMPLEMENTING STRATEGIC PLANS

Strategic implementation is the process of setting into motion organizational activities required to meet the company objectives for strategic competition. In one sense, implementation is part of the planning stage of strategy development, because management must decide at that time where to compete, how to organize foreign operations, and how to manage them. These questions raise planning issues, but when these activities begin to take place, the full range of management responsibilities unfold. This chapter focuses on *decisions* related to implementing strategies. Those decisions, illustrated in Figure 6.1, are where to compete, or the *locations* of foreign operations; how to *enter foreign markets;* and how to *manage foreign operations.*

Before beginning to explore these three points, it is important to distinguish between firms that can choose among many options in location and entry strategies and those that have few choices. Chapter 5 described a planning process based on a *proactive model* of competition that assumes available time and resources to evaluate international competition. Managers in these organizations have the luxury of choosing where to compete and how to structure their foreign operations. They can deliberately formulate plans and make appropriate decisions to implement those plans.

In contrast, many companies must *react* to competition or respond to unexpected circumstances that preempt more leisurely systematic planning. This reactive stance often forces managers to accept decisions thrust upon them.[4] Consider, for example, Robertson Marketing Group (RMG), a small company in Salem, Virginia, founded by three brothers soon after they graduated from college.[5] The company began in a rented shop making premiums, small gift items imprinted with company logos, names, or advertising slogans. The range of products reaches from inexpensive ballpoint pens to expensive limited edition gold jewelry; imprinted T-shirts, gold-embossed Bibles, and "concept" fashions with embroidered designs are mid-range items. The Robertson brothers began by printing college sweatshirts, and then expanded to serve business accounts, developing a client list that includes, for example, *USA Today,* Disney, and Texaco.

RMG expanded into computerized methods for mass production and quickly began searching for low-cost, foreign-made bulk materials. The firm felt compelled to buy caps, shirts, toys, jackets, backpacks, leather goods, and dozens of other items through Taiwanese brokers to retain competitive prices. This was especially true as competition intensified for orders from chain stores marketing entire lines of promotional premiums and massive orders for promotional items from clients such as McDonald's. The Robertson brothers decided to contract for manufacturing overseas,

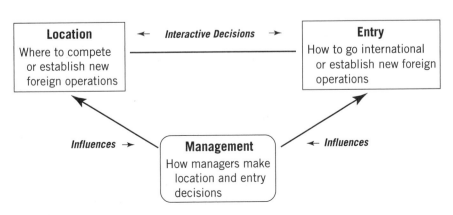

FIGURE 6.1
Implementing International Strategies

but none of the family had even been outside the United States except on brief vacations. Nevertheless, two brothers flew to a trade conference in Hong Kong. Within a year, RMG was contracting with firms from the Far East to manufacture its products. The brothers also began importing from Mexico, and their exports soon reached Canada and Scandinavia. RMG had not planned to become involved in international sourcing or foreign contracts. These decisions were mandated by an explosive growth in their industry, and the company was pulled into international business while under fire by competitors.

Competitive pressure often forces companies such as RMG to take action, but changes in international trade relations can prompt similar reactions. For example, companies such as UPS and FedEx have pulled or pushed one another into Asian and European markets. Also, changes in trade laws, such as restrictive European Union rules, mandate that many North American and Asian companies establish new foreign joint ventures or European subsidiaries rather than export products to gain access to EU markets. Reversing the model, Japanese automakers have recognized a need to open domestic plants in the United States to counter protectionist trade quotas, and the European firm Rover Group allied with Honda to establish a gateway organization in Japan.[6]

Limited resources have forced companies into foreign investments for many years. Major oil producers had to establish drilling and refining operations in the Middle East, West Africa, and the North Sea to gain access to the oil fields' enormous reserves as compared to limited domestic supplies. Extractive industries, such as metal mining and chemical production, have had to join with foreign interests to gain access to international supplies of minerals. Service companies face similar challenges. Citigroup (formerly Citicorp) and other major international banks must follow their customers, so they set up subsidiaries wherever substantial international finance and trade occur. Insurance companies, freight companies, public relations firms, advertising agencies, public accounting companies, and travel organizations are quickly drawn into foreign operations. The point is that the rapid growth of global companies has forced internationalization of the service sector, as these firms follow their customers abroad.

Managers of a company in a *reactive* stance may have decisions thrust upon them, but they usually retain some discretion about location. They can also choose how they will enter foreign markets, and they must always decide how to manage activities. Proactive companies obviously benefit from greater discretion when they decide in advance what to do, and they make decisions with better preparation. With that caution in mind, the next section examines the choice of a location as the first consideration in a strategic move toward international competition.

LOCATING ACTIVITIES—GLOBAL ALTERNATIVES

Managers of domestic companies face the least complicated location decisions of any firms when they simply export or import products. They need only identify the most lucrative foreign markets for their products, or the best foreign suppliers of needed inputs. At the other end of the spectrum, managers of globally integrated companies face the most complicated location decisions. They look for the optimal overall pattern of foreign activities throughout the company's value chain.

Between these extremes, researchers have identified two benchmarks to differentiate broad categories of foreign location decisions. First, a country-centered strategy leads a multidomestic company to choose specific foreign countries for its operations. This situation represents a progressive step beyond exporting or importing, in which the firm may establish a foreign sales office or an overseas manufacturing operation. The second benchmark is associated with extensive foreign investments requiring major coordination of international interests. This situation defines the stereotype of a multinational corporation (MNC), but even this setup involves location issues much less complicated than those for a globally integrated enterprise. These four explanations serve as reference points on a continuum, as shown in Table 6.1. They are not discrete choices; yet in each category, managers encounter distinct circumstances that affect their location decisions.

Location Criteria for Export-Import Operations

Foreign market potential is the primary consideration for a company seeking to expand through exports. In formulating its strategy, the company will pursue some version of one of the alternatives introduced in the previous chapter: broad-line competition, global focus, national focus, or protected niche. A small domestic company making its first effort at exporting will not command the product line or resources it would need to pursue either a broad-line or global focus strategy. Instead, comparatively small and inexperienced companies act as "target shooters," seeking specific opportunities in well-defined markets—and this usually means a national focus strategy. Those with very unusual products or proprietary services find opportunities to secure protected niches through special licenses or foreign government contracts. However, even large companies such as IBM, Ford, and Shell have relied on national or niche strategies for many years before evolving global strategies. Therefore, exporters, regardless of size, encounter similar location criteria.

All companies must base decisions about international business on potential **competitive advantages** that they can achieve within the limits of their generic strategies. Recall that generic strategy choices include low-cost leadership, differentiation, and

TABLE 6.1

CONTINUUM OF LOCATION ALTERNATIVES

	Focus of Strategies			
	Export/ Import	Country	Diversified Centered	Globally Multinational
Integrated				
Investment strategy and risk exposure	Minimum exposure	National focus with risks and responsibilities depending on country conditions	Multilocal focus with risks diversified on major foreign investments	Maximum exposure and interrelated responsibilities
Management structure	No foreign management or host-country control	Expatriate or host-country management with significant local involvement	Parent-company strategic control, possibly with significant expatriate and local management	Parent-company control of strategic core activities, typically supplemented by local management with regional or global responsibilities

focus (possibly in combination). A small company such as Robertson Marketing Group, described earlier, can compete successfully in a price-sensitive industry by maintaining a low-cost edge over competitors. This was the company's primary strength as a domestic competitor, and when management decided to compete for Canadian and European business, RMG sought to win markets on cost-price relationships. Its management spent a great deal of money on market research to discover where the firm could successfully export its products, and they found potentially lucrative opportunities in eastern Canada and the Scandinavian countries. At the same time, they ruled out nearly all other European nations on cost criteria. This analysis considered actual product costs, as well as shipping, customs duties, foreign distribution costs, transaction fees, and incidentals such as insurance and brokerage fees.

Until the late 1980s, IBM competed primarily on a national basis with a limited product line in order to restrict the complexity of its product distribution system and also to maintain control over its foreign assets. The company traditionally positioned its line of mainframe computers in specific countries under subsidiaries owned and managed by IBM, but it has reorganized as a broad-line competitor under a complex regional distribution structure. Throughout its expansion efforts, IBM has relied on a generic strategy of differentiation, initially entering Europe through the United Kingdom, where it enjoyed strong brand recognition and weak competition. IBM has never been a low-cost competitor, but it has traded on brand-name recognition, turning rules about country of origin into a distinct advantage.[7] Today, competition throughout the world requires IBM to follow a regionally integrated responsive strategy with a broad-line profile, yet it still must consider nation-specific market criteria. For example, IBM competes in China with a select product line; and the company limits its investment exposure and product line in developing countries where it finds high political and economic risks.

Import decisions are based on criteria similar to those for export decisions, and they are predicated on similar generic strategies. Domestic companies that import supplies do not, however, pursue strategic alternatives related to global expansion or foreign markets. If they rely on specific countries as supply sources, then they must be sensitive to trade restrictions, export-import regulations, customs practices, and risks associated with economic or political instability. Changes in any of these factors can threaten supply channels or costs. A company that imports a scarce commodity, such as petroleum derivatives or minerals, must watch for competitors who might outbid it or negotiate more skillfully for favorable contracts. In the language of trade, an importer will *source* from selected foreign locations that offer the optimum combination of low risks and cost characteristics.

Most importers also hedge their options by sourcing from multiple locations. Hedging implies contracting with suppliers in several locations, often raising overall costs but reducing the risk of disrupted supplies from any single provider by ensuring immediate access to alternatives. Those who do not, or cannot, hedge this risk are hostage to events beyond their control in the source countries. For example, during the 1980s, Whirlpool competed as an American appliance manufacturer with limited foreign markets in South America. Once considered among the top three appliance makers in the world, Whirlpool was rapidly losing market share to top Japanese and European companies. It could neither sustain foreign markets nor successfully bid for foreign materials.

During the early 1990s, however, Whirlpool repositioned itself to contend for world leadership, and now its sales place it second only to Matsushita. This turn-around resulted from a calculated strategy of globalization—first through acquisition of the appliance business of Dutch electronics giant Philips, giving Whirlpool access to Europe, and then by systematically opening five regional Asian divisions with facilities in 22 countries. South American activities expanded from a core Brazilian market to 18 Latin markets. This rapid diversification and global expansion strategy proved essential to Whirlpool's survival. Prior to implementing the new strategy, the company found itself easily victimized by competitors in all but its closest home markets, and its profits were seriously affected by performance in a few concentrated markets. Inflation and exchange rate instability in South America often turned profits into losses. Also, because the company relied on a few foreign facilities to supply appliance components, changes in production costs or vendors seriously affected operating costs. By 1995, Whirlpool had reversed these situations by distributing manufacturing among more than 50 worldwide locations, thus hedging production costs and reducing its reliance on each facility to between 10 and 13 percent of total output. Its diversified marketing and regional development initiatives reduced risks associated with foreign exchange and changing market conditions. Equally important, Whirlpool created a number of international joint alliances, thus diversifying its product line and subsequently penetrating a network of more than 3,000 Asian and European dealerships.[8]

In the simplest configuration, an importer seeks low-cost foreign resources, often as a way to reduce domestic prices. Some importers seek unique foreign products, so they genuinely need to ensure supply lines to safeguard their competitive advantages. Nevertheless, when competitors begin to penetrate foreign resource channels, such an importer must step up to more active international involvement. Exporters face similar circumstances when other firms penetrate their foreign markets, or when domestic companies emerge to compete in those host countries. If the importer or exporter hedges these risks by links to other sources or markets, then competition poses a less serious threat.

Location in Country-Centered Strategies

The next step along the continuum of foreign activities leads a firm to adopt a country-centered strategy. This choice actually represents an arbitrary benchmark. It is a conceptual zone between operating as a domestic export-import enterprise and actually committing resources to foreign operations. The country-centered strategy encompasses a broad range of possible foreign activities rather than an absolute point on the continuum. The least active country-centered company tries to minimize its investments in either foreign distribution or manufacturing; for example, a service company might cautiously open a few foreign branch operations. Similarly, a small exporter may break into this level of international business by assigning one marketing manager to serve a host country with little more than an expense account and a fax machine. A bolder exporter might establish a local office staffed by foreign nationals. An importer may take the plunge by investing in a comanufacturing facility to secure its supplies, or perhaps the company might set up a small wholly owned *foreign subsidiary*.

Some companies accumulate rather large foreign investments as they pursue country-centered strategies, and they also clearly assume some management responsibility for their foreign operations. These firms fit the definition of multinationals, yet they fall short of true MNC operations in the broader sense of managing diversified international interests. Many companies cross a second imaginary demarcation line and become "true" multinationals when they collect diversified foreign subsidiaries or autonomous business units. Under a country-centered strategy, however, a firm positions each foreign activity to help it compete in specific countries. Therefore, location decisions depend heavily on host-country conditions and local competition.

A company in this situation engages in a multitiered environmental scanning analysis to develop a short list of potential host countries. Management then evaluates each country for its unique advantages. Multidomestic companies (i.e., those not concerned with integrating regional or global activities) independently evaluate separate countries as potential hosts for consolidated business activities or as hedges against risk in other operations. Competition may also require simultaneous entry into more than one foreign location, but the strategy precludes establishing integrated activities. The scanning process gathers sufficient accurate information to support management decisions on these choices. It often begins with a thorough political risk analysis, as explained in Chapter 3, and then proceeds with a systematic industry analysis, as explained in Chapter 4. These investigations generate only broad-based planning scenarios, but they usefully eliminate inappropriate foreign locations as well as identify the risks associated with doing business in particular countries and within specific industries. Managers then focus their scan on a competitive analysis of their own organization and its potential match with the conditions in each foreign location. Finally, they conduct a careful analysis of the company itself and its potential for success in each of the foreign locations under consideration.

Country-centered decision criteria must also account for social and cultural factors, since companies that favor such strategies often face initial choices to commit resources to new cultures, new customers, and new employees. The company's managers must accept the challenge of working in foreign environments. In particular, a **multilocal** business requires that management must establish a locally responsive configuration. Therefore, the company is concerned with cultural values, work ethics, consumer behavior patterns, labor skills, social trends, educational variables, and ideologies, among many other factors. In the end, a nation that seems to be a logical candidate for expansion based on competitive factors may be entirely wrong for a company that cannot accommodate likely social and cultural issues within the constraints of its own organizational culture and management capabilities.

When a country-centered company identifies more promising alternatives than it can afford to underwrite, each nation must compete for selection. This rivalry adds an important twist to the location decision, because every nation actively courts foreign investments. Indeed, states and regions within countries compete for foreign investments, and that statement applies to the United States as well as small, underdeveloped countries. For example, Nissan was enticed to locate its U.S. truck manufacturing plant in Tennessee by favorable state tax rates, concessions from local authorities to upgrade transportation infrastructure serving the Nissan site, and a cooperative program to establish a U.S.–Japanese trade legation in the state. These perks did not constitute direct subsidies by American interests, nor were they the primary reasons for Nissan's decision, but they helped to tip the scales in favor of Tennessee over other locations. Often, new businesses enjoy substantial direct subsidies such as "tax holidays," exemptions from export taxes or duties on imports, rent-free facilities, land allocations, government-backed loans, guaranteed government purchase agreements, and favorable domestic supply allotments. These benefits were discussed in Chapter 3 on political risk, and governments and trade development agencies commonly promise such important incentives to attract multinational companies.[9] The Republic of Ireland has pursued this strategy, emphasizing that a foreign company locating there also benefits from the country's privileged access to other EU markets.[10] Similar regional development efforts promote development projects in Scotland, northern England, and the south of France. China packages incentives for western multinational joint ventures, Mexico has boosted its economic success through its attractive cross-border programs, and the practice is beginning to emerge in former Soviet

JORDAN ATTRACTS OFFSHORE FOREIGN INVESTMENT

The Haashemite Kingdom of Jordan is seeking to regain its historic position as a regional center for international trade. As part of this effort, the government has sought to attract offshore investments in Jordan by foreign multinational companies. In 1989, the newly enacted Companies Law allowed organization forms familiar in the West such as general partnerships, limited partnerships, limited liability corporations, public-share holding companies, and joint investment firms (mutual funds). In addition, the law created a new category of so-called exempt companies.

An exempt company can take any legal form allowed under Jordanian law (e.g., private or limited partnership, public-share company, etc.). It must register with the government as a Jordanian entity, but it cannot conduct business within Jordan. It must operate as a complete offshore facility of a foreign enterprise, but it derives all income from export, trade, or regional service transactions beyond Jordan's borders.

No Jordanian citizen can invest in an exempt company, nor can the company offer public shares for subscription by Jordanians. Firms accept these rather unusual restrictions to gain substantial tax benefits. An exempt company incurs no tax liability on its foreign income, by definition all of its revenues. It is also exempt from capital gains assessments, property taxes, the country's schools tax, and various registration duties. Dividends paid to shareholders are also fully tax exempt, and the government actually subsidizes the company's export-oriented development.

Together with the Companies Law, Jordan has passed legislation to reduce taxes on private partnerships and joint ventures. The kingdom has also set up "free zones," in which a foreign-owned firm or joint venture that meets certain qualifications can engage in export or transit trade with a 12-year tax holiday, exemptions from import and export fees, subsidized rent for facilities, and special privileges such as freedom to import equipment and private cars. These provisions seek to stimulate employment, collecting no income or social taxes from Jordanian citizens who work for free-zone or exempt companies. These assessments can run as high as 55 percent of a worker's income, so people actively pursue jobs with such foreign firms.

Because Jordan has enacted incentive legislation, foreign investment there has outpaced that in any other Middle Eastern state since 1990. Companies and foreign contractors find attractive environments for their headquarters as well as lucrative opportunities in development projects for Jordan. In the process, they can realize extraordinary cost advantages. Through arrangements such as these, in a few short years Jordan has transformed a domestically sealed economy with close ties only to its regional Arab neighbors into a transnational economy.

Sources: Saif Ali Zu'bi, "Jordan: Inviting Investment," *International Corporate Law*, February 1995, 34–38. Also see *Private Enterprise Development in Jordan* (Amman: U.S. Agency for International Development, July 1994), 1–3, 15; and "Private Enterprises Development in Jordan," *USAID Advisory* (Amman: U.S. Agency for International Development, August 2000), 1–2.

states and Eastern Europe.[11] The "Global Viewpoint" feature profiling Jordan illustrates how a country uses incentives to attract foreign investors.

Government incentives exert relatively minor force in a total location decision, yet they can influence choices between close alternatives. The most important general categories of location decisions within a country-centered strategy are infrastructure factors, environmental risks, and government policy variables.[12]

Infrastructure Factors

Location decisions often hinge on air and ground transportation capabilities, port facilities, freight handling and export-import forwarding functions, communications systems, effective access to utilities, and human resources with appropriate skills. A company that intends to locate significant upstream activities in a host country will focus especially closely on availability of a skilled workforce, local management talent, training or educational systems that support private-enterprise growth, supply systems, access to domestic materials, and appropriate transport and communications systems. If research and development activities are important, as they are for companies such as Ford Aerospace and Textronics, decision makers evaluate postgraduate technical education and scientific capabilities in the host country.[13] In contrast, companies concerned with downstream activities focus on marketing and distribution factors such as mass media and advertising capabilities, warehousing functions, port facilities, and support services.

Environmental Risks

Political risk and unique business risks also strongly influence location decisions in country-centered strategies. Specifically, companies look for political stability, and for welcoming attitudes of host-country leaders toward private-enterprise development and free-market competition. They also are sensitive to a country's ability to make peaceful transitions when governments change. Relevant macroeconomic variables are taken into account, including inflation, wage rates, monetary stability, disposable income, and employment statistics. A company operating in one country and selling to neighboring nations also considers how the host nation relates to its neighbors and the likelihood of hostilities between them.

Most companies regard exchange rate volatility as the single most important business risk variable. For example, Brazil has been listed by the U.S. Commerce Department as one of the top 10 prospects in the world for foreign investment, yet private investors are deterred by that country's unpredictable exchange rates.

Government Policy Variables

Official policies might influence location decisions by restricting profit repatriation, imposing bureaucratic constraints such as licensing procedures, requiring undue paperwork, or unpredictably enforcing rules. Managers are also concerned whether a country has effective commercial laws to protect patent rights, security of trademarks, and ownership of copyrights. In addition, while some policies provide incentives for development, as discussed earlier, some can impede it and deter foreign investment. For example, Australia has reduced taxes on profits to entice foreign companies to relocate regional or international headquarters to the country, yet the Australian tax office has independently clamped down on transfer pricing rules, making local investments less attractive to foreign companies. Consequently, an international company such as Mitsubishi must price its exports higher than anticipated, thus paying higher taxes in Australia relative to those in other export destinations.[14]

The most important policy-related consideration involves the combined tax effects of doing business in a particular country. For example, residents and businesses within the commonwealth of Puerto Rico pay no income tax, and even U.S. companies with operations receive substantial tax credits against offshore earnings for U.S. corporate income taxes.[15] In addition, Puerto Rico passed laws that reduced or eliminated property and municipal taxes on foreign-owned local operations. Similar offshore tax havens entice companies elsewhere in the Caribbean, among island republics off the coasts of Britain and France, and in Southeast Asia.

Oddly, the United States is considered a tax haven by many foreign corporations and nonresident aliens. Both are taxed under the 1966 Foreign Investors Tax Act, which was enacted by Congress to entice Japanese investments and offshore mutual funds to the United States. The rules are too complex to address thoroughly at this point, but in general, they exempt foreign corporations and nonresident alien investors from capital gains and earned income taxes on transactions for stocks and other securities. Foreign securities and commodities traders are exempt from all U.S. federal taxes, and other businesses can avoid taxes on passive income such as rents, royalties, interest, and dividends. They can further enhance their tax profiles if they generate jobs or engage in activities that qualify for environmental protection incentives. As a result, companies such as Nissan, Toyota, and Honda—located in Tennessee, Kentucky, and Ohio, respectively—enjoy some tax incentives not available to domestic competitors.[16]

Location Decisions for Multinational Corporations

Multinationals choose international locations based on their individual requirements. The traditional concept of a multinational identifies an international company with *substantial* foreign investment and management responsibilities, but one that has not configured its organization as a globally integrated enterprise. Consequently, location criteria for a multinational with diversified interests are roughly similar to those for a company with a country-centered strategy. Some differences do set apart diversified companies from narrowly focused firms, however.

In many decisions, a multinational corporation's location criteria differ from those of a country-centered firm in intensity more than in content. The country-centered enterprise often hunts for a specific foreign location rather than scanning for multiple entry points, and its management intensely evaluates candidates to narrow the range of choices. In contrast, a multinational considering multiple entry points maintains a wider range of opportunities with greater diversification of foreign investments. Consequently, a particular location decision represents a small part of its total risk as compared to the same investment decision by its country-centered counterpart. Unlike the country-centered enterprise, which consolidates activities in each subsidiary, a diversified multinational can adapt its configuration to match upstream or downstream activities in a particular location to the constraints of those host countries.

For example, Canon Inc. runs research and development facilities outside Japan, all near centers of scientific research in North America and Europe. The company also has manufacturing divisions in low-cost countries such as Malaysia and Indonesia. Further, it customizes downstream activities in Europe to support regionally managed marketing, but in North America it relies on distinct sales teams and distribution hubs. Canon attempts to integrate worldwide operations, but it configures location-specific operations according to market needs and relative advantages of each location.[17]

Similarly, Cathay Pacific, Hong Kong's flagship airline, has repositioned several critical functions in foreign locations.[18] The airline created a $100 million training center in Australia to take advantage of that country's highly skilled, technically capable workforce and a state-of-the-art maintenance center for commercial aircraft established by the Australian government. However, Cathay moved its entire world communications network for reservations, accounting, and scheduling to Guangzhou, China. These communications functions involve tedious and repetitive operations that could be efficiently performed by low-skilled personnel in a cost-efficient centralized facility. Meanwhile, Cathay has established marketing systems in Los Angeles and

London, but it maintains a low investment profile in Japan through subcontracted services. Each decision took into account different criteria, suiting some operations to emphasize local responsiveness and others to provide global support services.

Location Choices for Globally Integrated Companies

All-encompassing evaluation criteria guide location decisions for firms operating on a global scale. Management must consider simple relationships between export products and foreign markets as well as complex relationships that arise in managing integrated foreign subsidiaries. A globally integrated company must balance interrelationships among all of its operations, foreign and domestic. The firm treats every location as a business with its own independent operations, yet each plays a role in the larger value chain and contributes its share to the ultimate results envisioned for the combined company. The traditional location criteria of comparative advantages for specific countries lose importance as a firm pursues synergistic benefits from interconnected business units.

For example, Ford Motor Company acquired an interest in Mazda to gain access to the Japanese market and also to shift certain component engineering functions to Asia. Meanwhile, Mazda benefited from access to Ford's European design team, which spearheaded its introduction of new aerodynamic models. Ford built its plant in Hermosillo, Mexico, in cooperation with Japanese process engineers, and it coproduced cars with Mazda in Mexico, Japan, and Taiwan for U.S., Asian, and Canadian markets. In each instance, the company distributed engineering, design, component technology, manufacturing, and marketing in various foreign facilities and its overseas business units to optimize location-specific advantages.[19]

Location choice seeks to *optimize* production by assigning specific activities to particular foreign units. Individual costs or competitive criteria are less important than total synergy within the value chain. Efficiency does influence decisions about which activities to allocate to specific foreign enterprises, and this priority calls attention to traditional criteria of comparative advantage, both in manufacturing parts or components and in completing final production. Typically, final product assembly is located close to end markets, allowing minor modifications in product makeup to accommodate differences in consumer preferences. A company selling globally branded products may lay out final assembly points for convenient access to regional distribution centers. In such an instance, the configuration of activities such as packaging and warehousing is more important than cost factors. Location decisions for upstream manufacturing activities often focus more keenly on business-unit costs.

Country of origin restrictions may play a major role in a location decision, because a global company typically generates its products by accumulating the efforts of many different business units, and these products become inputs for different foreign downstream activities. A small shift in activities from one country to another may affect the definition of a product's country of origin, thus triggering changes in export classifications for customs duties and import quotas.

A globally integrated company combines three sets of factors in the process of configuring its international locations. First, it considers its value-chain activities and allocates responsibilities among business units according to traditional measures of *comparative advantage*. These priorities include costs, political risks, social factors, and environmental conditions such as availability of resources and infrastructure. Second, the company considers market and industry characteristics that constitute competitive advantages in its foreign locations. These concerns include market size, growth, industry structure, and strategies employed by competitors. They also include opportunities for successful competition on the basis of low-cost product differentiation or a favorable market niche. Third, the company must consider where it must establish a presence to maintain its global identity, either reacting to industry competition or proactively opening new markets.

No single category of criteria prevails over the others. Instead, each global company emphasizes one set of criteria over others depending on the nature of its business. For example, oil companies such as Exxon and Shell compete in an industry where success requires economies of scale throughout an integrated value chain. Their undifferentiated petrochemical products earn them no particular advantage, so they succeed by controlling comparable cost advantages. Therefore, location decisions for sourcing, production, and marketing are influenced primarily by low-cost strategies.

In contrast, consumer-goods companies such as Procter & Gamble, Colgate-Palmolive, and Unilever compete by selling differentiated brands. These companies value cost efficiencies, but their crucial competitive advantages come from their market identities, so location decisions depend on market factors and industry competitiveness. Companies that serve niches—such as Hewlett-Packard, Fujitsu, and Okidata, each with distinct lines of computer printers—must alertly monitor competitive positioning. Consequently, they configure foreign operations to establish location-specific activities that maintain niche advantages. Comparative and competitive factors are vital to their success, but these companies emphasize arrangements that keep them extremely responsive to potential threats from rival firms.

Location Decisions in Perspective

The early part of this chapter mentions three general dimensions of strategy implementation: location, entry strategies, and management capabilities. Although all three are interrelated, location is a prerequisite planning consideration that defines basic arrangements in a company's foreign interests. Firms more complex than small exporting companies seldom resolve location decisions by making simple choices among discrete alternatives. For example, a company's entry strategies determine *how* it will establish global operations, further complicating location decisions. Also, as explained in a later section of the chapter, the third factor—management capabilities—can affect the feasibility of particular locations. Still, that discussion requires prior consideration of the strategies that determine how a firm will establish foreign activities, that is, its foreign entry alternatives.

FOREIGN ENTRY ALTERNATIVES

A company can "go international" in many ways, and certain common choices are called *entry alternatives* or *entry strategies*. The word *strategy* may seem overused in this application, and the connotation of *entry* implies opening new markets. These terms are holdovers from the traditional approach to international business as an exporting activity. Clearly, exporting is one major strategy alternative, and initiatives to enter foreign markets demand significant attention. Today, however, international business encompasses far more activities. Figure 6.2 compares these alternatives as part of the

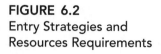

FIGURE 6.2
Entry Strategies and
Resources Requirements

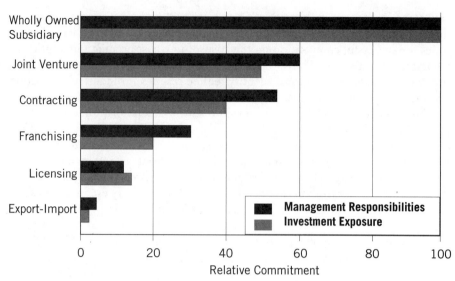

strategic implementation process. In each instance, there are differences in resource demands for ownership and in management responsibility for foreign assets.[20]

Exporting

The most fundamental international entry alternative, **exporting,** involves selling domestically produced products in foreign markets through brokers or overseas distribution centers. By maintaining its manufacturing facilities at home, an exporting company escapes the need to make substantial organizational or technological changes other than to establish distribution channels to reach foreign markets. This is the least risky method of expanding into international business. Initially, it may cost little to become an exporter, and it is relatively easy to withdraw from a foreign market. By marketing its products through foreign agents, an exporter avoids extensive investment and management responsibilities, but the company also has little influence on how its products are marketed overseas.

Companies that market through their own personnel rather than agents and brokers are called *direct exporters.* Those that choose to rely on intermediaries are *indirect exporters.* Direct exporters bypass intermediaries to sell directly to overseas buyers. They take responsibility for selecting overseas markets, making contacts with foreign customers, arranging shipments, and handling documentation required by the transactions. Intimidated by these demanding tasks, most small companies choose to export indirectly through the services of intermediaries.[21] Large companies may also favor this alternative and agree to brokerage contracts for exports to small markets that do not justify investments in overseas facilities.

Still, large firms often develop their own export networks to exert some measure of control over marketing operations. For example, prior to its reorganization in 1986, DuPont generated nearly half of its $1.3 billion in foreign income by selling polymer products through agency contracts in more than 100 different countries. By 1990, DuPont had consolidated most foreign marketing activities for polymer products under an international division, but the company maintains agency contracts in many developing countries throughout Central America and Africa. Brokerage and agency relationships continue to offer the best alternatives for selling in small, relatively un-stable markets.[22] Decisions about direct and indirect exporting, however, involve more complex analysis than simply choosing to avoid intermediaries, and firms can approach each method of entry in several ways.

Direct Exporting

Direct exporting has the advantage of keeping control in the hands of company man-agers, but they can exploit this advantage only if they understand foreign markets and have experience negotiating with foreign customers. For products that need no special modifications, a direct exporter's major task is to select a *distribution channel* to reach target markets. This choice requires that managers negotiate sales to foreign cus-tomers within that channel. Direct exporters market through three standard channels:

- *Foreign agents.* A foreign agent is any person or company legally entitled to import goods to an overseas location. An exporter can sell directly to the agent as a dis-tributor or wholesaler, which then resells the goods in its local market. Most for-eign agents are citizens or legally registered companies of the nations into which they import goods. This statement sounds obvious, yet the class of foreign agents also includes international companies with worldwide interests. For example, Gilman Office Supplies contracts directly with Apple Computer Corporation and Hewlett-Packard through its offices in California to import Apple microcomput-ers and HP laser printers to Hong Kong. Gilman is a division of Inchcape, a British corporation that distributes several hundred products constituting $11 bil-lion in annual sales.[23] Gilman sells Apple and HP equipment in Hong Kong, but in California it is a registered foreign agent of Inchcape.

- *Foreign retailers.* An exporter can also sell directly to foreign retailers, which resell in their local markets through stores, catalogs, direct-marketing promotions, trade shows, or telemarketing. This possibility offers an attractive alternative for entrepreneurs with unusual products. Some Rolex watches, for example, are re-tailed by licensed dealers; but the firm sells nearly half of all products directly to jewelry stores in 47 countries under contracts that ensure its tight control. Ralph Lauren sells its sports accessories through airline catalogs, duty-free airport shops, major department stores, and specialty retailers. In selling directly to for-eign retailers, exporters must assume the burden of negotiating contracts, trans-porting products, and arranging financial transactions.

- *Direct sales to end users.* Transactions between domestic companies and overseas end users constitute a sizeable export business. For example, major companies such as Boeing sell aircraft directly to foreign-owned airlines. Nearly 200 U.S. and Canadian companies sell medical instruments and pharmaceuticals directly to independent foreign clinics, physicians, hospitals, and government agencies. Nearly half of these medical equipment suppliers are privately held companies with less than $10 million in annual sales. Although small firms often market through agents, the nature of the medical equipment industry dictates direct con-tact between manufacturers and end-user clients.[24]

Indirect Exporting

Companies can simplify the export process by marketing indirectly through an expert intermediary. When someone else handles foreign negotiations and legal transactions, this assistance minimizes management responsibility. More important, intermediaries usually have excellent market connections. Several types of intermediaries support in-direct exporting:[25]

- *Commission agents.* These traders act simply as intermediaries to find outlets for exporters' products or to find products to meet purchasers' import demands. They may receive "finder's fees" or commissions from one or both parties to the transactions they arrange, but they do not become involved beyond this brokerage role. In most western countries, commission agents must be registered traders holding government licenses to transact business. Once licensed, they act as wholesale brokers, finding buyers and sellers, negotiating terms, handling transaction details, and clearing products through customs. In some countries, only government branches can act as agents. For example, in Russia, agents appointed through the Ministry of Foreign Trade monitor trade activity, handle transactions through the State Bank of Foreign Trade, and negotiate with foreign companies as representatives of Russian enterprises.[26]

- *Export management companies (EMCs).* An export management company is a private business that acts under contract as a manufacturer's representative for exporting firms. Most EMCs develop reputations in specific industries, such as chemicals or electronics, and handle export trade transactions in many different markets. Unlike a commission agent, which focuses on one country, an EMC will market wherever it finds profitable sales. Such a firm seldom handles more than a few product lines in an industry, but it often represents many companies at once. This division of loyalty represents a potential danger to the exporter, because the EMC could represent its competitors' products alongside its own. Consequently, an indirect exporter must carefully select an EMC that adequately handles similar products without playing competitors against each another. An EMC usually represents exporters directly, selling their brand-name goods without modifications, but it may also be licensed for other functions such as buying in bulk for resale under local brand names, providing support services, and expediting physical distribution.

- *Export trading companies (ETCs).* Prior to 1982, export trading companies were private companies similar to EMCs but representing special product lines. After the U.S. Congress passed the Export Trading Company Act of 1982, however, the breadth of ETC activities expanded with support from government-funded programs and loan guarantees intended to enhance trade through foreign buyers.[27] ETCs now can trade in exports for direct sales, whereas EMCs manage exports only on commission. ETCs customarily take title to the goods they handle, either through direct purchase or a guarantee that, in effect, ensures that the exporter will receive proceeds from a specific sale. In addition, exporters can create their own ETCs. This step is common in Japan, where ETCs are the primary marketing channels for nearly 60 percent of all exported goods. In Europe, virtually every major international company maintains its own ETC, often with substantial government backing.

- *Export merchants or remarketers.* Although they are called *brokers*, export merchants are really remarketers of exportable products. They buy directly from manufacturers, take full title to goods, and then resell them in foreign markets. The success of this business depends critically on expert negotiations. A manufacturer negotiates for sales to broaden its global markets against merchants seeking the best possible purchasing terms. Still, export merchants offer a convenient export channel to manufacturers that relieves them of overseas marketing responsibilities. Merchants typically cluster in port cities and industrial zones because many of their activities include physical warehousing, packaging, loading, and shipping products.

The choice between direct exporting and indirect exporting, as well as details of implementing the decision, depends largely on the company's management capabilities. An enterprise with little international experience may prefer the obvious choice of a low-risk brokerage arrangement. As a substantial market develops for its products, an exporting company may decide to establish a foreign distribution center to take control of its marketing strategies and distribution systems. This move results in organizational change and added management responsibilities for strategic control of overseas activities. The seller also must invest in facilities and staff the foreign office. Most host countries also require companies to obtain licenses to engage in trade, and the exporters' home countries often require their own licensing and registration to export goods. Therefore, while a decision to export goods is a major change for most domestic companies, a decision to become a direct exporter with foreign responsibilities is a giant leap into international business.

Importing

Importing is a common strategy for many companies in both developed and less-developed economies. Affluent countries import resources and commodities when they find comparative advantages in sourcing from foreign locations. Developing countries often must import resources, food, and services (i.e., contracting for people with certain skills or knowledge of advanced technologies). As described in Chapter 5, a nation can gain a comparative advantage from relatively low resource costs, low wage levels, or economies of scale generated by foreign networks of manufacturing. When countries must import, they usually suffer disadvantages in trade, so government programs often must subsidize the importing companies or assist in re-exporting products made from imported resources.

In the least complicated importing scenario, a company seeks foreign products for sale in its home markets. Such transactions establish a flow of products in a single direction from foreign sources to domestic markets. In the most complicated scenario, a company with a global network of manufacturing and services manages an equally complex network of domestic and foreign sources and markets. In effect, the company is constantly engaged in physically importing and exporting products through a variety of market channels.

Conceptually, importing reverses exporting, with similar choices for going directly to foreign sources or working through intermediaries. However, importing differs because a company often must look abroad in its search for very specific resources rather than looking for potential markets. Consequently, exporting is primarily marketing while importing is primarily procurement or *sourcing*. Firms accomplish this activity in several ways.

Direct Sourcing

International managers can send buying delegations overseas, attend foreign trade shows, or negotiate with foreign representatives who maintain offices in their own home country. Direct sourcing is a purchasing process in which companies contract directly with foreign manufacturers. No intermediaries participate in these exchanges, and foreign manufacturers often transport goods directly from their facilities to the domestic points of sale. For example, executives of the American toy retailer Toys "R" Us take buying trips to Hong Kong and Taiwan twice yearly to conclude toy contracts. Toys are typically manufactured seven to nine months before the scheduled beginning of merchandising, so Toys "R" Us completes its purchasing for Christmas during the annual New York trade show held in late February or early March. Large companies such as Toys "R" Us often establish long-term relationships with foreign manufacturers and negotiate directly for specific products.[28] This approach requires little foreign investment, and the importer need not manage foreign assets, but it does require negotiating expertise and knowledge of foreign suppliers who, from their perspective, compete as exporters for foreign markets.

Subcontracting

Many domestic importers contract for overseas production, specifying the products that suppliers make. The Franklin Mint, for example, is one of many telemarketing companies in the United States that design collector chess sets, coins, and model cars for sale through TV merchandising. The company subcontracts manufacturing to foreign companies, which produce, package, and deliver the final goods directly to U.S. distribution points. The Franklin Mint contracts for production of its collector car series with Perfekta Toys, Ltd., of Macau, which in turn runs manufacturing facilities in the People's Republic of China.[29] Franklin Mint is strictly an importer without investments of its own overseas; it pays for products when suppliers ship them. However, the company becomes obligated under its purchase contracts, so it assumes the risks of adverse foreign-exchange moves and changes in domestic demand.

Indirect Sourcing

Many importers deal with intermediaries in sourcing or arranging for production of needed inputs. They work through the same channels as indirect exporters; however, agents or brokers act on behalf of their import clients. They earn commissions based on percentages of the contracts' value by locating products, arranging contracts, and handling details necessary for importation. In some instances, they receive retainer fees in ongoing import representative relationships in which they relieve importers of transaction services.

Other Methods of Sourcing

Direct importing offers the most reliable way to source products, but the easiest method is to contract indirectly through a broker. However, some importers use other methods. In one option, buyers advertise in trade journals and foreign newspapers to let potential sellers know what products they seek and how to contact them to submit bids. Another common method is to register with domestic or foreign government trade agencies. The United States and Foreign Commercial Services (US&FCS), for example, maintains trade lists, publications on particular classes of goods and services, and a vast array of commercial intelligence. US&FCS, an agency of the Department of Commerce, maintains posts in 63 nations that represent the most active U.S. trading partners.[30]

More than 50 registered trade organizations represent the European Union, and each European country fields government-supported trade legations, sometimes organizing them as quasipublic organizations. China maintains a New York office for its Trade Council, and the United States and China have formed a joint alliance, the U.S.–China Business Council, that maintains a global database of business opportunities for the two countries. Even small developing countries maintain official or quasigovernmental trade offices called *export* or *development boards*. All of these organizations work to stimulate international trade. They help foreign companies connect with domestic interests, and in some cases, they facilitate actual transactions required for export or import activities.[31]

Licensing

A common type of international business in this high-tech age involves licensing. In **licensing** deals, firms contract with other companies, granting to the licensees proprietary rights to use technology, patents, copyrights, trademarks, or specific goods and services.[32] Licensing is a simple way to expand foreign business, because the licensee assumes the risk and funds the investment necessary to do business. The domestic licensor may do little more than grant the right to use a trade name in exchange for royalties. Disney Corporation, for example, licenses the right to manufacture Mickey Mouse electric toothbrushes to Hasbro Toys, which makes the units in its manufacturing facilities in Europe and the Far East. In turn, Hasbro pays Disney a royalty on its sales of the product. Licensing arrangements have typically focused on marketing successful products overseas through licensed agents. With sufficient sales, firms may also license overseas manufacturing. Today, licensing extends to thousands of products, including both goods and services. Some licensors contract with retailers to distribute product lines such as Estée Lauder perfume or Liz Claiborne clothes. The practice is also common among companies with globally branded products, such as pharmaceutical firms. Licensing helped Biogen to expand globally, as summarized in Figure 6.3.

Licensing is a particularly effective option for small companies that lack managerial resources they would need to expand effectively into global markets. Large companies also find that licensing offers an expedient way to position proprietary products or brands or unique technologies in host countries. The major advantage of licensing is that it avoids direct investment in foreign facilities, but it also allows firms to avoid the pitfalls of customs duties, trade quotas, and export-import restrictions.[33]

The major disadvantage of licensing is the lack of control; the licensor can control foreign operations only to the extent that management can enforce contract terms. In reality, the foreign licensee controls quality, marketing, and services. If it delivers marginal performance in these areas, the licensor can suffer damage to its reputation. Licensing may also compromise patents, technologies, or copyrights in countries where intellectual property rights are not adequately enforced. This is a major concern for U.S. companies operating in Eastern Europe, Russia, and China.[34]

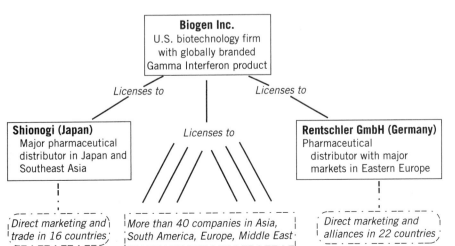

FIGURE 6.3
Biogen's Licensing Network

Sources: Saul Klein and Jehiel Zif, "Global versus Local Strategic Alliances," *Journal of Global Marketing* 8, no. 1 (1995): 51–71. Also see *Annual Report 1995*, Biogen Corp., Cambridge, Mass., January 1996.

Franchising

Franchising is a special form of licensing in which a franchisor contracts to provide assets that comprise a complete business to a franchisee in return for certain fees and royalties. International franchises resemble American franchises in which a franchisee gains the right to offer, sell, or distribute goods or services under a *business system* created by the franchisor.[35] Franchise agreements vary widely, but the franchisor usually provides facilities, equipment, materials, services, patent or trademark rights, management systems, and standardized operating procedures. Taken together, these elements constitute the business system for an outlet of the parent firm, such as McDonald's, Precision Tune, or 7-Eleven.

International franchising allows a firm to enter foreign markets rapidly with a complete business concept that has proved successful in the home country, giving the franchisor a competitive advantage over independent domestic competitors. At the same time, it takes relatively little investment risk. The foreign franchisee often gains a successful business in the host country, but this person or company assumes the major investment risk.

Foreign franchises are highly visible examples of global expansion by western interests. McDonald's opened a giant restaurant in Gorky Street, Moscow, and headlines celebrated the Soviet free-enterprise venture before its grand opening in 1990. It was by no means the first western investment in the former Soviet Union, and it was a Canadian organization that took McDonald's into Moscow, yet the venture seemed to represent a turning point in East-West relations. Visitors to Beijing are often stunned to see a Kentucky Fried Chicken franchise in the heart of an enclave of government buildings. Tourists in Tokyo, Hong Kong, and Singapore can shop at 7-Eleven markets, rent Hertz cars, and, of course, eat at McDonald's.[36] International franchises present management challenges because they have become the fastest-growing economic sector in nearly every major nation. Although franchisors can keep things simple, they can also become actively involved in global negotiations, facilities planning, training of foreign workers and franchisees, marketing strategies, and development of goods and services with cross-cultural appeal. Therefore, franchising offers a wide range of options for international participation, often with franchisors becoming major investors in foreign alliances.[37]

Contracting

International contracting constitutes a special form of foreign entry strategy, covering a range of activities from single agreements for specific services to substantial long-term alliances. At one extreme in this wide spectrum of opportunities, a domestic company behaves much like a small exporter, but rather than marketing products to buyers in a host country, the company enters into an agreement for specialized services. The firm acts as a consultant "exporting" knowledge, technical expertise, or management skills, perhaps through an individual effort or as an organizational endeavor. At the other end of the spectrum, companies contract for build-operate-and-transfer operations that produce full turnkey projects such as power-generating stations, transportation systems, and port facilities. Between the extremes, companies contract with foreign enterprises or governments to extract minerals, jointly manufacture exportable products, or complete private industrial development projects such as establishing food-processing plants. The following paragraphs look more closely at each contract type.

Service Contracts

Individual consultants or organizational groups often contract with foreign private companies, governments, or international development agencies to provide expertise, management, or knowledge of technical systems in exchange for fees or periodic retainers. For example, Bill Gorman, an information technology (IT) specialist who originally designed the software for Citigroup's (then Citicorp's) global electronic transaction systems, contracts to provide similar services to foreign governments that want to develop banking and securities-trading systems. In 1994 and 1995, Gorman contracted with the Commonwealth of Independent States (CIS) to establish a computer-based commodities exchange system, with Sri Lanka to implement a securities exchange and transactions system, with Jordan to evaluate computer vendors bidding on an electronic foreign exchange system, and with India to link regional stock-exchange database systems. Each contract covered a specific term ranging between several weeks and a year and laid out specific objectives, called *terms of reference*, for the project. The terms of reference set out contract expectations for so-called *deliverables* to emerge from the exchange and other obligations of the parties.

Large companies such as Accenture, Ernst & Young, Saatchi & Saatchi, and J. P. Morgan contract to provide accounting, finance, advertising, promotion, and investment banking services to foreign governments, private foreign corporations, and international development agencies. Consultants also frequently contract to perform these and other functions through economic development agencies such as the U.S. Agency for International Development, World Bank, Asian Development Bank, or European Reconstruction Bank. Service consultants seldom incur significant investment risk, and their foreign exposure remains slim throughout their contracts. Consequently, they can penetrate foreign markets rapidly with minimum investments, and they can withdraw upon expiration of their contracts with little difficulty.

Diversified Contracts

Manufacturers often contract with foreign firms to comanufacture products that can be made inexpensively overseas. The finished products are exported to regional markets or imported to the home country. Often, the partners comanufacture for host-country domestic markets, develop extractive technology to mine minerals, or fabricate components for transshipment as part of an integrated global manufacturing strategy. These contracts can form part of joint ventures and other long-term alliances, but simple agreements more commonly bind a prime contractor and a foreign host. Diversified contracts go beyond mere comanufacturing agreements to include management services, technology development, process design, equipment supply, training, foreign-exchange transactions, and distribution. In many ways, these contractual alliances create relationships that resemble those of foreign subsidiaries to parent companies, but they fall short of this qualification due to the temporary nature of their agreements and limitations on investments. For example, Anne Klein fashion clothes for women are made in several Asian countries under specific contracts that place the major burden of manufacturing on foreign companies. The American contractor designs the clothes, sends quality control managers and technicians to the foreign locations, and handles import logistics.

Build-Operate-and-Transfer (BOT) Contracts

A contract may call for creation and operation of a facility commonly called a *turnkey operation*, because the prime contractor accepts responsibility for an entire project from its early planning stage through construction to full-scale operations. Once the

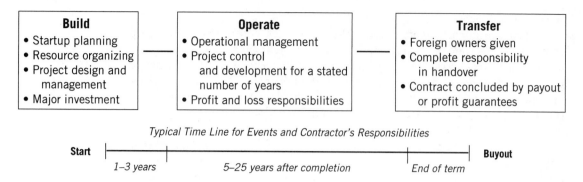

FIGURE 6.4
Build-Operate-and-Transfer Model

project is on line and a capable host-country organization has been established, the contractor "turns over the keys" or *transfers* complete responsibility to the foreign owners. The process is illustrated in Figure 6.4.

The **build-operate-transfer contract** model emerged during the late 1970s as a method of rapid economic development for major infrastructure projects. Only very large companies or international alliances attempt to undertake BOT contracts, and the model is still evolving as a form of international business. Early contracts were short-term agreements, but most now specify that contractors assume complete development responsibility to bring projects on line over periods of perhaps 3 to 5 years. The contractors agree to gradually staff the facilities with local labor and management, providing training as necessary, then to transfer ownership and authority to foreign organizations (usually government agencies) in return for buyout fees. A foreign contract authority provides equity or financial support and usually a profit guarantee from government-supported funds. The BOT contractor, therefore, can rely on a future revenue flow and a huge transfer fee without creating a permanent foreign organization. Unfortunately, any cost overruns or snags in project management can quickly erode profits, and inflationary effects or fluctuating foreign exchange rates can threaten the company. Today, BOT contracts tend to span longer periods of 10 to 20 years. They also include built-in safeguards against inflation and currency fluctuations, and many contain revenue-sharing clauses that divide income between the contractors and host governments. Most BOT contracts are financed through alliances of investors, who thus hedge their individual risks.

A good example of a BOT contractor is Hopewell Holdings, a multibillion-dollar heavy construction firm that has undertaken approximately 20 BOT projects in Asia, including six complete power-generating plants in southern China, two major power plants in the Philippines, a 600-kilometer tollway linking southern China and Beijing, the entire municipal ringway road system in Bangkok, and a water-treatment system for the city of Jakarta, Indonesia.[38]

The end of the American embargo on Vietnam has elevated BOT contracts to become the favored investment vehicle for U.S. and European companies entering the Vietnamese market. Major companies such as ABB, Elf Aquitane of France, Shell Oil of the Netherlands, and AT&T South Asia of Singapore have contracted for billions of dollars in Vietnamese alliances to complete infrastructure projects under BOT agreements. Vietnam also has attracted less well known companies such as Emerging

TABLE 6.2

U.S. INTERNATIONAL STRATEGIC ALLIANCES FORMED 1990–1999

Alliance Partner	Number	Percentage
Japan	198	14.3%
Commonwealth of Independent States	163	11.7
People's Republic of China	162	11.6
Germany	79	5.7
France	74	5.3
United Kingdom	87	6.3
Malaysia	44	3.2
South Korea	41	2.9
Mexico	111	8.0
Switzerland	37	2.7
Vietnam	35	2.6
Canada	28	2.0
Hungary	27	2.0
Taiwan	14	1.0
Italy	13	0.9
Rest of the World (non-U.S.)	276	20.1
Total	1,389	

Source: *International Strategic Alliances and Commercial Agreements*, OECD Data Series on CD-ROM (Paris: Organization for Economic Cooperation and Development, 2000), Tables 4 and 5.

Markets Partnership of Washington, D.C., the Nexen Group of Canada, and Braxton Ltd. of London that have huge BOT investments in Vietnamese BOT projects.[39]

Joint Ventures

Firms can also realize foreign expansion goals through **joint ventures** that bring together companies from different nations to form commercial alliances. As Table 6.2 shows, this is a common method of entry for companies everywhere. Each partner assumes a partial ownership position in the new enterprise, and such a deal can involve two or more private firms, private and state-owned companies, foreign government interests, or a broad network of organizations from many different nations. A typical joint venture emerges from a contractual arrangement between a multinational company and a foreign host company, each contributing equity capital to a new, jointly managed enterprise. More than 70 percent of all joint ventures fit this description, and their primary purpose is to expand the businesses for both partners with limited risk while achieving a synergistic benefit in the alliance.

A joint venture often represents the only legal way a company can do business in a foreign country, since many governments mandate that foreign investors can operate within their borders only in combination with local equity interests that share commensurate management authority. This model has prevailed in China, the CIS, Mexico, Brazil, India, Indonesia, and Saudi Arabia, to name a few. Although contracts have constrained foreign companies to less than a majority equity interest (50 percent or less) in the past, this practice has softened in most countries in order to attract foreign investment.[40]

Companies invest in joint ventures to coalesce their unique strengths, and most of these ventures have achieved success. Another term, **international strategic alliance (ISA),** has come into use to expand the meaning of *joint venture* to include consortia and other membership structures beyond the two-entity model. The participants in these ventures do not necessarily hold equity positions in the new ISAs. Indeed, many joint ventures are not based on equity investments but on cooperative links between individual capabilities, such as marketing channels, technologies, or proprietary goods and services. ISAs often resemble contractual consortia rather than new joint-stock companies.

Still, the most common ISA, the two-company *equity joint venture*, is formed when two firms join to establish a new comanufacturing facility to make a specific product. The equity joint venture is an investment-based partnership with carefully negotiated investments and responsibilities for the participating parties. For example, GM joined with Toyota in 1983 in a venture to expand its small-car line in the United States. Toyota brought the technology and expertise in small-car production needed to make a high-quality product, and GM contributed the marketing and distribution strength to rapidly penetrate the American automotive market. The new enterprise, located in California, is New United Motor Manufacturing Inc. (NUMMI).[41] Along with its unique capabilities, each partner contributed $100 million in cash and assets to start NUMMI, and the original management team included an equal number of Japanese and American executives. Responsibilities for R&D, product design, automotive manufacturing, distribution, and administration were carefully delineated, and profit allocations to Toyota and GM were defined according to complex but precise formulas based on investments and asset contributions. Today, NUMMI's line managers are all U.S. nationals, while Toyota personnel act as coordinators; 4 senior Japanese executives serve as vice presidents among the 11 top positions. NUMMI produces the Geo Prizm for GM dealers and the Corolla sedan for Toyota dealers, manufacturing both models using Toyota production technology, imported Japanese engines and transmissions, and other parts from U.S. suppliers.

The prevailing pattern of joint ventures (about 57 percent of new formations) has shifted toward securing new markets, either in the host country or in other countries to which the combined efforts of the new enterprise allow access. Consequently, many new joint ventures have linked major North American or Japanese companies with European companies offering similar strengths, providing a popular means of gaining access to the EU regional trade bloc. MCI Communications and British Telecom, for example, desired to penetrate continental telecommunications markets, so they formed Concert Communications, which eventually became part of the MCI World-Com merger. In response, AT&T created an alliance with Denshin Denwa Company of Tokyo to form World Partners as a direct competitor of Concert Communications. Not to be outdone, Sprint Corporation, France Telecom, and Deutsche Bundespost Telekom formed Atlas/Sprint to counter the other global telecommunications ventures competing in Europe.[42]

No single reason explains why companies enter into joint ventures. As the examples related so far show, market entry often motivates the deals, but access to scarce resources and low-cost manufacturing are also sound reasons. In addition, companies join forces to combine their research technologies. This was the primary incentive behind the alliance between DuPont and the Dutch electronics firm, Philips, to develop compact discs.[43] Companies also come together to spread the financial burden of product development. This was the reason behind a consortium that included Boeing, three Japanese heavy-industry companies, and a Japanese government agency that subsidized development of the Boeing 767.[44] Partners often combine complementary skills that launch both companies into entirely new industries. Kubota, Japan's largest producer of farm equipment, had exceptional mechanical design and manufacturing capabilities, but its marketing was narrowly focused on agricultural equipment. Meanwhile, six small Silicon Valley companies involved in computer systems development had access to exceptional technological innovations but no experience in manufacturing. Kubota and the Silicon Valley entrepreneurs teamed up to create mini-supercomputers, which currently dominate that industry sector.[45]

As a general rule, partners establish ISAs in less-developed countries to carry out upstream value-chain activities in locations with low wage and resource costs. Multinationals form these ventures in order to optimize costs or patterns of resource utilization. Thus, they locate activities overseas as a way to achieve economies of scale or establish competitive advantages. In contrast, globally integrated companies tend to form ISAs in developed countries to complete their downstream value-chain activities. These multinationals join forces to seek market access or competitive advantages, either within regional market sectors such as North America or the EU or in specific countries such as Japan, China, or the CIS. Additional alliances have included financial services ventures in Hong Kong, logistics systems in Eastern Europe, and projects for government-supported military assistance in places such as Israel.[46]

Managers involved in joint ventures work at the cutting edge of global business. Because partners to every venture contribute not only equity investments but also expertise and ownership responsibility, managers find themselves deeply involved in foreign societies. Joint ventures are the preferred organizational vehicle for doing business in countries with unstable politics or unconvertible currencies. The higher risk profile in these environments also raises the risk of failure for the venture itself, because it typically involves managers with diverse interests and cultural backgrounds who face more complicated coordination problems than found elsewhere. Research has shown that successful alliances satisfy four criteria, as illustrated in Figure 6.5:

- They join together complementary skills or organizational capabilities.
- They unify cooperative cultures or effectively reconcile cultural differences in management.
- The partners have compatible strategic goals for the new ventures that do not conflict with individual company objectives.
- They create levels of risk commensurate with the equity and exposure of each partner.

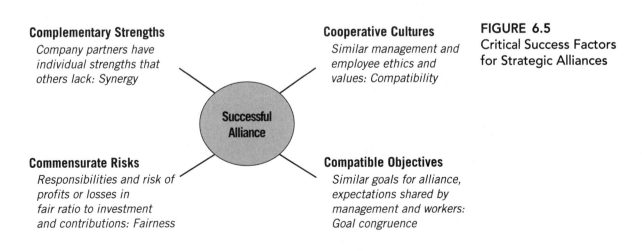

Complementary Strengths

Company partners have individual strengths that others lack: Synergy

Cooperative Cultures

Similar management and employee ethics and values: Compatibility

Commensurate Risks

Responsibilities and risk of profits or losses in fair ratio to investment and contributions: Fairness

Compatible Objectives

Similar goals for alliance, expectations shared by management and workers: Goal congruence

Successful Alliance

FIGURE 6.5
Critical Success Factors for Strategic Alliances

When participating companies cannot reasonably meet all four criteria, they often have rocky relationships that cripple the joint venture. A venture can be doomed early by poor choice of partners or by entering into agreements too quickly without establishing well-developed ground rules. Even when ISAs are well structured, approximately one-third dissolve as relationships among the participating companies sour or they change their priorities. Changes in foreign operating environments, political instability, or conflicts between governments of the participants often threaten these ventures. Consequently, international strategic alliances are not low-risk entry alternatives; they require participants skilled in cross-cultural management.[47]

Wholly Owned Foreign Operations

Unlike joint ventures, which limit each partner's ownership and control, a **wholly owned foreign operation** is entirely owned and controlled by the parent company. This is the ultimate form of international involvement in countries that allow foreign ownership. It also represents the highest risk profile of available options, but it assures the most extensive management control.

Foreign ownership has been the preferred mode of entry for western multinationals, a bias that often has reflected a sense of ethnocentricity. Even now, many western managers prefer to hold tight to operational controls rather than relinquish authority to host-country managers. A foreign enterprise 100 percent owned by a parent firm provides that control, whereas a joint venture, franchise, or other form of ownership requires shared governance. Firms in multidomestic industries often prefer full ownership of foreign subsidiaries, and local laws sometimes require it, as they often do for bank service. The insurance industry, for example, differs substantially in every country, and few practices common in one legal system work the same way elsewhere. Therefore, it makes sense for an international insurance carrier to localize its global interests. Further, in some countries, the process of business registration requires domestic ownership.

Many companies decide to establish wholly owned foreign operations to meet their needs for strategic coordination of activities throughout an integrated value chain. Citicorp (now Citigroup) has worldwide international banking systems that require local registration control of bank acivities. Consequently, Citicorp's strategy required a centralized strategic nerve center for global monetary transactions yet locally registered and managed branches. Although the company was among the earliest financial institutions to expand internationally, its assets in one country were indistinguishable from those elsewhere. Consequently, while the banking industry constituted a collage of country-specific financial enterprises, the parent company represented a highly coordinated organization with integrated assets. Therefore, the firm settled on wholly owned bank subsidiaries, each registered within a specific country, as a logical choice.

Global alliances are becoming more common than fully owned foreign operations, yet many companies argue that they can expand more rapidly and reduce risks more effectively through autonomous foreign business units. Those that favor strategic alliances point out that local equity partners assume some financial risk, and they help to avoid difficulties with currency repatriation. Supporters also emphasize that a joint venture is less likely than a wholly owned foreign enterprise to generate hostility from host-country citizens and politicians. Those who favor wholly owned enterprises do not dispute the validity of many of these risks, but they contend that a parent company can isolate each foreign subsidiary through independent registration and insulate central assets from anything that might happen to the foreign subsidiaries. Thus a devastating problem in one business unit would have little effect on global operations. The strength of either position seems to rest with the size of the foreign investment relative to total company-wide holdings.

A wholly owned foreign company can be created from scratch as an overseas branch, or the parent company can acquire an existing company as a foreign subsidiary. An **overseas branch** is part of the parent company and simply an extension of domestic operations.

Unless the parent has established a global reputation (e.g., Citigroup or IBM), a branch will have to fight for a competitive position alongside local companies. In contrast, a **foreign subsidiary** is a separate company organized under a foreign nation's legal code with accountability distinct from the parent company.

An acquisition provides rapid access to established foreign markets. By acquiring an existing overseas company, the parent immediately penetrates trade barriers and avoids start-up complications by having a functioning organization in place. A constant flurry of activity joins acquisitions to large international companies of every nationality, but entrepreneurs are also attracted to the acquisition strategy because it allows them to avoid the problems of creating an international management team. Compared to larger companies, entrepreneurial ventures have fewer resources to pursue in acquisitions, but a relatively small purchase can yield huge dividends.

MANAGEMENT CAPABILITIES

The third consideration for implementing strategy is management, or, more specifically, whether a company's managers are capable of implementing the firm's strategic plans. The best-laid plans, detailed neatly on boardroom letterhead, require managers to actually do something, and it may sometimes mandate impossible tasks. The remainder of this book, hundreds of other books, and thousands of articles spanning centuries of colonial trade and international history reflect the human quest for answers about how to survive in a global community of diverse cultures and societies. Clearly, a few short paragraphs will not unravel these mysteries. They can, however, point out several pivotal factors that relate specifically to implementing international strategies.

Management Prerogatives

Each kind of global business strategy, from exporting to acquiring foreign subsidiaries, must account for top management intentions (including the CEO's personal preferences). Strategy does not become reality until senior management buys into it. Objective analyses, computer simulations of optimal situations, and solid competitive scenarios can only map out a preferred and rational strategy, but a strong executive with other ideas can veto the most logical plan. Just as important, the executive's intuition may lead to better decisions than those based on the results from objective planning analyses. Choosing a location, for example, has been explained primarily on assumptions of comparative or competitive advantages, but these dry concepts do not account for unexplainable differences between a company's internal culture and the antecedents of culture in a host location. An experienced executive may have a "feel" for what the organization can tolerate. These decision makers may understand or fear the effects of social, cultural, religious, or ethnic differences on their organization or how their people will react to conditions in a foreign land. Therefore, they may exercise

Ben & Jerry's cofounders Ben Cohen (left) and Jerry Greenfield (right) offer a sample of their ice cream to Unilever's U.S. chief executive Richard Goldstein. Unilever bought Ben & Jerry's in May 2000, creating a new division for gourmet ice cream and frozen desserts and launching the popular American ice cream products in European and Asian markets.

their prerogatives to deviate from planned courses of action, or they may choose to avoid international involvement altogether.

Personal biases of executives may block certain foreign options. Many senior executives and company board members fought in World War II against the Japanese or Germans, and some may still resist doing business with people from these countries. More recently, the fateful changes in Eastern Europe and the former Soviet Union may have left lingering distrust in Europeans and North Americans brought up during the intense cold war era. Indeed, there are acute sensitivities among Eastern Europeans and both western interests and former allies. The reconciliation of relations between the United States and Vietnam does not sit well with everyone either. Consequently, even the most glowing reports of opportunities in Russia, Eastern Europe, Japan, or Vietnam can fall on deaf ears. Trade with China is violently opposed by human rights groups, and the intricacies of trading with Arab states while also supporting Israeli interests can confuse capable analysts.

American and other western managers—as well as company stockholders—may recognize these limitations, but other countries view the same situations from their own equally important perspectives. Some Japanese citizens, for example, simply don't want Americans doing business in their country. Many Israeli citizens avoid doing business with foreign firms that also do business with Arab states; some Arab leaders are equally anxious to avoid those who do business with Israel. American or British observers see tremendous benefits for China from cooperative trade relations, but many Chinese believe that the Americans and British would benefit most, and they are not necessarily eager to open their borders.

Executives on both sides of an international alliance, therefore, have their reasons to exercise management prerogatives and block international agreements or discourage trade. Political leaders exert their influence for many of the same reasons, but some also want to protect ideologies or their own domestic interests. Of course, all these priorities can also accelerate international trade, and executives of any nationality can be enticed to consider foreign expansion in places that they would not have considered without foreign intervention. Still, few decisions are isolated from the intricacies of human interactions and psychological implications of cross-border relations. *Management prerogative* is merely a collective phrase to try to capture the spirit of those decisions.

Obviously, executive decisions can redirect a company's strategic configuration and explain why it suddenly becomes a global competitor. Executives are paid to lead their companies in effective strategic initiatives, but their personalities also play crucial roles. Earlier examples implicitly reinforce this conclusion.

Management Cooperation

Whether executive prerogatives coincide with objectively determined strategic goals or the executives make preemptive decisions to go global, successful implementation of those strategies requires the cooperation of company managers, who must make things happen in field activities. The chief executive is the catalyst, the team coach who calls the plays; the remaining executives and division managers execute the game plan. No one should assume that managers automatically implement company plans; therefore analysts should question any strategy, location decision, or choice of entry vehicle. Cooperation breaks down for many reasons, but researchers have found several patterns of behavior peculiar to international companies, as described in the following paragraphs.[48]

Implementation problems tend to occur far more frequently among multidomestic enterprises than among globally integrated organizations. Within a multidomestic configuration, foreign managers and company expatriates in foreign subsidiaries compete through country-centered strategies, and they become accustomed to locally responsive business methods. In contrast, subsidiary managers of a globally integrated company compete as part of a network of organizational interests, often pursuing broad-based strategies of globally branded goods or services. Consequently, managers in multidomestic companies tend to expect autonomy within focused national strategies and local decision-making systems, while their globally oriented counterparts enjoy autonomy and decision-making authority only within networks of interrelated activities. Company-wide strategies therefore seem less important to multidomestic managers of foreign subsidiaries than to managers in globally integrated firms. In fact, corporate-level strategies may directly conflict with local priorities, worrying subsidiary managers that their operations are jeopardized by distant priorities. These polar opposite configurations reinforce two distinct patterns of behavior; one can result in open conflict between subsidiary managers and home-office executives, and the other tends to reinforce support for mandates from the top.

The question of managerial compliance, however, is far too complex for a simple explanation based on differences in priorities. Actions result from an entire range of psychological and social considerations related to individual career aspirations, personalities, managerial values, and ethics. These subjects go well beyond the purpose of this book, yet they must be considered by company executives who announce a new strategy that will affect the lives and careers of thousands of people. The change may not be very dramatic for a small company making a modest effort to export products; managers may simply have to make a few trips abroad or learn about their new foreign customers.

CONCLUDING COMMENTS

The past several chapters have emphasized the new complexity of international business and the difficulty of formulating and implementing international strategies. Strategies in and of themselves represent not discrete choices from set menus of options, but multitiered sets of company-wide and business-unit priorities that combine alternatives drawn from several spectra. A company brings together generic strategies discussed here to define a strategic intent; then it formulates competitive strategies under that generic umbrella. Further refinements determine the manner in which a company will compete within local foreign interests or globally integrated interests. Altogether, these factors comprise a strategic scenario on which the firm builds specific action plans, and successful implementation of the action plans determines the effectiveness of the grand organizational strategy. Implementation, in turn, is complicated by location decisions, modes of entry to foreign markets (how the company positions itself internationally), and how company managers take the actions required to succeed with a new strategy.

Implementation is also concerned with organizing the company's resources and reorganizing it in order to meet international management challenges. It is difficult to isolate any of these considerations from one another; but looking forward, the next chapter addresses organizational structures as part of this puzzle. As discussed in Chapter 7, companies cannot implement strategies or compete globally through traditional hierarchical organizations. This principle has been implicit throughout earlier examples. Closer examination of organizational issues will reveal combinations of strategic planning and organizational configurations that dramatically redefine the foundations of international management. In turn, those foundations influence multicultural leadership, human resource management, and many other issues discussed throughout the remainder of this book.

REVIEW QUESTIONS

1. Ideally, managers *proactively* plan their firms' strategies, but in reality their strategic decisions often result from *reactive* gestures in the face of unanticipated conditions. What circumstances result in a reactive mode of strategic decision-making?
2. How do companies hedge foreign investments and protect their foreign interests against host-country risks?
3. What determines a country-centered strategy, and what primary considerations affect decisions related to foreign locations under this strategy?
4. Contrast differences in location decisions for multinational and globally integrated companies.
5. Describe the differences between direct and indirect exporting, and those between direct and indirect importing. What are the advantages and disadvantages of each approach to business?
6. Contrast the entry modes of licensing and franchising. What benefits and limitations influence each entry strategy?

7. Joint ventures are the most common form of international strategic alliances, but their ownership structures do not necessarily imply equity holdings, nor are their activities limited to the stereotypical joint manufacturing. What are some other common forms of joint ventures?
8. Describe the advantages and disadvantages of wholly owned foreign subsidiaries.
9. How do management prerogatives influence location decisions and competitive strategies?
10. Explain how expectations for host-country management cooperation differ for multidomestic and globally integrated companies. What management problems can you envision for a company under each mode of operation?

GLOSSARY OF KEY TERMS

Build-operate-transfer contract   A development initiative in which a foreign company plans, develops, builds, and fully manages a project such as a toll-road system or power-generating plant, until it eventually transfers ownership and control to the host-country government or private owners.

Competitive advantage   The relative competitive strength of a company within its industry or specific markets.

Country of origin   A determination that a product comes from a particular country based on predetermined standards for the percentage of content contributed by that country. This classification affects customs duties and quotas established by treaties.

Exporting   An international entry alternative marked by selling domestically made products in foreign markets through brokers, agents, or company representatives, as well as a variety of other channels and intermediaries.

Foreign subsidiary   A separate company organized under a foreign nation's legal code with accountability distinct from that of the parent company.

Franchising   A special form of licensing that confers the right to implement a complete business system.

Importing   Sourcing materials or products, often through contract manufacturing, for use or sale in the importer's home country.

International contracting   Individual or corporate agreements for many different forms of professional services, technical projects, or activities generating foreign income.

International strategic alliance (ISA)   Another term for joint ventures; it encompasses consortia investments and other multiparty deals that combine equity interests by several companies.

Joint venture   A cooperative equity investment by two or more companies that creates a new third venture by contract. Often it expires after a limited life.

Licensing   A contractual agreement in which a firm permits specific usage of products, processes, or technologies, often with restrictions on the licensee or time-based conditions, in exchange for royalties or other payments.

Multilocal   A description of a company that competes through a *locally responsive configuration* in which foreign operations remain independent of one another.

Overseas branch   An official type of subsidiary.

Wholly owned foreign operation   A company branch or division located overseas and entirely owned and controlled by the parent organization.

EXERCISES

1. Identify a foreign company located in your home country. Perhaps an apparently local enterprise is actually a subsidiary owned by foreign interests. A local company may also hold foreign license rights to produce or market the parent's goods, or it may be a joint venture involving a foreign partner. Visit the company or use on-line services and publications to discover what you can about the enterprise and its reason for being located where it is. Does this location give the firm a comparative advantage relative to locations in its home country? How do conditions such as taxes, labor costs, market access, and resources compare between the two location options?

2. For the firm you contacted in Exercise 1 or a new company, explore the competitive advantages for marketing in its current location. What is its core competency, and does it enjoy a particular advantage through a distinct difference or an entrenched position in a market niche? How does it compete, and how does it maintain a competitive advantage? Is it a consolidated multilocal enterprise competing with domestic firms on their own terms, or is it a globally integrated company competing through optimal support relationships among foreign networks and activities? How is it configured to compete?

3. Scan issues of a publication such as the *Wall Street Journal, Business Week,* or *The Economist,* and create a list of five or six companies with international interests. Select articles that describe why the companies are in particular foreign markets and perhaps also why they seem to enjoy success (or have difficulties) due to their "entry" decisions. Be prepared to discuss these in class.

GENERAL MOTORS' DECISION TO BUILD CARS IN SHANGHAI

Anticipating a lucrative market and future in China, General Motors (GM) decided to build luxury Buick sedans in China. China showed great promise because of its large population, development of new roads, and rise in individual wealth. The port city of Shanghai attracted GM because of its population of about 14 million people and a newly developed industrial area designed to attract foreign investors.

In an effort to move quickly into China, GM began building a $1.5 billion plant in Shanghai while still negotiating its joint venture with Shanghai Automotive Industry Corp. (SAIC). In addition, GM invested $100 million in the deal without a signed contract. Convinced that the variables were appropriate for this venture, GM's Chairman, John F. Smith Jr., moved forward with the deal by bringing in over 100 U.S. auto executives and transferring its technology to its local partner. Hundreds of design changes were made to accommodate the Chinese tastes, and workers were trained around the world at various GM plants. In 1997, with a site selected and negotiations continuing, site preparation work began for the Shanghai plant.

In May 1998 the first car built by the GM plant in Shanghai rolled out, with a price tag of about $40,000, and sales seemed to be on target. By all accounts, it appeared that GM had accomplished its goal of successfully entering the Chinese market with a product that met consumer demand. Unanticipated, however, was China's bid to be considered as a member of the World Trade Organization, which may prompt its leaders to cut import tariffs and lower prices. In anticipation of this, Chinese consumers postponed their car buying decisions. As a result, sales at the Shanghai plant slowed down, inventories increased, and GM scaled back its output target for the year by 20,000 cars.

In response to the Chinese market, GM decided to produce a new mid-sized 1.6-litre Buick with its joint venture partner, SAIC, that is more affordable for China's middle class. The Buick Sail is based on GM's Opel Corsa, which is built in Brazil and sold in about 80 countries. The Sail will be priced at around $12,000, and full production is expected to begin in April 2001.

GM's commitment to the Chinese market remains strong, despite the disappointments since entering the market two years ago. While the production and sales of a smaller car will help offset the unmet demand for GM's luxury Buick sedans in China, GM still faces challenges if it wants to remain the world's largest auto company. Once China joins the World Trade Organization, European, American and Japanese automakers are all expected to compete, because China will have to open its doors to car imports. Volkswagen, who also has a joint venture with SAIC, and Toyota are both expected to offer smaller cars in the same price range as the Buick Sail. Ford also is expected to enter the small-car market in China.

QUESTIONS

1. Explain the mode of entry in the General Motors strategy. What other options might be open to an automaker?
2. Explain GM's comparative advantage in the auto industry.
3. Describe GM's commitment to the Chinese market. How might management prerogatives have played a role in this decision?

BIBLIOGRAPHY

Graham, Mark. "Paddy Fields to Full Production." *Industry Week*, 6 November 2000. Retrieved from *Industry Week* website <www.industryweek.com> [cited 21 November 2000].

Leggett, Karby. "GM Confirms Plans to Produce Less Costly Buick for the Chinese." *Wall Street Journal*, 24 October 2000, p. A21. [Retrieved 22 November 2000 from Dow Jones Interactive database.]

Leggett, Karby. "Asia Focus: General Motors Plans to Introduce New Compact Car for China Market." *Wall Street Journal Europe*, 24 October 2000, p. 36. [Retrieved 22 November 2000 from Dow Jones Interactive database.]

Smith, Craig S. "The Race Begins to Build a Small Car for China." *New York Times*, 24 October 2000, p. 1, col. 3. [Retrieved 22 November 2000 from Dow Jones Interactive database.]

CASE 6.2

ACER GROUP: "REVERSE THINKING" IN A WORLD-CLASS COMPANY

While the world watches IBM, Apple, Compaq, Packard Bell, Dell Computers, and several other famous-name technology companies, Acer Group of Taiwan is quietly taking over major markets. The company is currently ranked as the world's third largest PC manufacturer. Acer's founder, Stan Shih (pronounced "she"), pursues a worldwide vision and global strategy that goes against all other practices in the microelectronics industry. Rather than developing tightly controlled central management and promoting a high-end brand name, Shih's Acer Group is a loose confederation of global subsidiaries with tremendous autonomy for local operations. Instead of protecting its technology and software applications, Acer openly shares everything it does with every distributor and any group subsidiary. Its organizational knowledge is an open book.

Compaq and Dell centrally control proprietary manufacturing to produce distinctly American-made products, primarily with U.S. components and parts. In contrast, Acer operates a globally integrated manufacturing system that includes manufacturing sites and assembly plants in 10 countries. Any manufacturing manager can source materials and components anywhere, as long as they meet quality specifications and cost guidelines.

Shih provides the vision and moral leadership for Acer Group and its world network of subsidiaries. "Our philosophy is to make it possible for everyone everywhere to enjoy these technologies by driving down costs and making PCs easy to use," Shih explains. "And this will be our calling card when we challenge Sony, Toshiba, Hewlett-Packard, and other companies in many other product lines."

Acer's unique strategy encourages cooperation within a loose confederation, extending as far as public ownership of separate organizations when possible. Shih believes that allowing subsidiaries to control their own destinies helps the parent company to retain its razor-sharp edge in innovations and cost efficiencies; otherwise, local stockholders will pressure their enterprises to turn to competitors for components and technical support. Shih describes this interesting strategy as "having a global name and a local touch," yet it presupposes a broad-based, generic product line. His approach to management works toward a self-managed global network of affiliates, an approach he calls "reverse thinking," and it moves away from the autocratic models of most global competitors.

Today, the Acer Group offers a broader range of products than its previous line of PCs and related components and competes head-on with Sony, Toshiba, and Hewlett-Packard, to name a few. Acer's products span a broad range of PC products—from PC servers to computer peripherals to Internet technologies.

The Acer Group also participates in several joint ventures and comanufacturing partnerships that account for several billion dollars in annual sales. For example, Acer recently named Mustek Zimbabwe, a distributor of IT products with a wide range of dealers in the country, to distribute its products exclusively in Africa. This combination of a known name brand and an established distributor was a move by Acer to increase its share of the Zimbabwean market.

Repositioned as an Internet-enabling company, Acer has developed several innovative sales strategies to bring thousands of people in other countries online. For example, by teaming up with companies such as Telmex, Bital, and BBV banks in Mexico, Acer Latin America has boosted sales in that country by providing services such as direct shipment to buyers in 48 hours and in-home installations. In Argentina, Acer Latin America worked with Central Bank as one of the key suppliers for the "Argentina Digital Project" that offered customers low-cost loans to purchase computers. The success of these programs has encouraged Acer Latin America to develop similar opportunities for other countries such as Chile, Peru, Brazil, and Colombia.

Acer remains the top-selling computer brand in Central American and Southeast Asian markets, despite the currently slow global demand for personal computers. While Acer's major competitors are keenly aware of Stan Shih, his philosophy, and his vision, few industry analysts give Acer more than a nod; few consumers even know the name. Nevertheless, Acer ranks as one of the world's largest manufacturers of personal computers.

QUESTIONS

1. Has Acer pursued a proactive strategy or a reactive one? In your answer, describe the primary generic strategy of the founder, Stan Shih, and explain why his approach has succeeded.
2. Acer has entered foreign markets through various alliances and entry strategies. Describe these, and explain their relative merits with respect to well-established U.S. and European markets and the less-developed countries of Mexico and Chile.
3. Briefly explore the management implications of Shih's philosophy of expansion and control over foreign subsidiaries. What potential difficulties might arise from his management style, and what

benefits might the Acer Group realize from this system?

BIBLIOGRAPHY

"Acer Appoints Zimbabwe Distributor to Grow Market Share." *African News Service*, 18 October 2000. [Retrieved 18 November 2000 from Dow Jones Interactive database.] (Distributed via Africa News Online by Africa News Service.)

The Acer Group, "About the Acer Group." Retrieved from Acer website <www.acer.com> [cited 19 November 2000].

Chen, Kao. "Acer Believes in Playing an Open Hand." *Straits Times*, 10 November 1996, p. 6.

Clark, Robert. "Acer Plans New Generation Internet, Consumer Products." *Newsbytes*, 25 March 1997, p. 16.

DiCarlo, Lisa. "Acer to Expand beyond PCs: Company Moving into U.S. Networking, Consumer Markets." *PC Week*, 22 April 1996, 125.

Engardio, Pete, and Peter Burrows. "Acer: A Global Powerhouse." *Business Week*, 1 July 1996, 22.

Richards, Kathleen. "Portable Window for Acer: Deal for TI Division Lets It Vie with Bigs." *HFN Weekly*, 3 February 1997, 67.

"Technology Tools Help Latin Managers Flourish in Today's New Economy." *Latin Trade*, October 2000, 88. [Retrieved 18 November 2000 from Gale Database/The Gale Group (Article A65949467).]

"Taiwanese PC Maker Acer Cuts Fiscal-Year Forecasts Amid Weak PC Demand." *Dow Jones Business News*. [Retrieved 22 November 2000 from Dow Jones Interactive database.]

Zbar, Jeffery D. "Latin America: Computers Tap a New Market in Latin Region." *Advertising Age*, 11 March 1996, 134.

CHAPTER SEVEN

Designing Effective International Organizations

CHAPTER OBJECTIVES

Discuss the concepts of global expansion and the contrasting forces of disintegration and integration.

Describe how company structures change to support exporting activities and foreign subsidiaries under international divisions during early growth stages.

Detail organizational alternatives for large, diversified multinational corporations.

Explain the transformation in which a diversified MNC becomes a fully integrated global enterprise.

Show how a transnational corporation can become a "seamless" organization.

Summarize the implications for international managers as restructuring redefines power and hierarchy, altering roles in a global organization.

Last year Procter & Gamble, the largest U.S. household products maker and one of the most well-known companies worldwide, experienced turmoil while trying to re-structure into a global operation and improve sales. In the process more than half of P&G's executives were forced to change jobs, and thousands of jobs were cut world-wide. Employee morale suffered. Some employees complained about the changes, while others decided to pursue new opportunities. P&G's chairman, Durk Jager, re-signed. Under a new CEO, A. G. Lafley, the company is now trying to restore its management structure, increase sales and profit earnings, and improve employee morale.[1]

Procter & Gamble's restructuring plan, Organization 2005, appeared to be a good one, but it did not take into account the effects the plan would have on employees. For example, instead of having its organizations in each country function separately as in the past, P&G's new plan called for employees to be grouped by product in "global business units." As a result, managers of product areas were reporting to bosses over-seas and communicating via conference calls thousands of miles away. Organization 2005 also called for a focus on new product innovation, leaving behind P&G's core business. Further, costs were getting out of hand while managers were trying to pur-sue sales growth.

During that time, P&G was experiencing lower earnings than in the previous year, and operating profits were declining. After 17 months on the job, Durk Jager stepped down as CEO and was replaced by Lafley in June 2000. Lafley, previously president of P&G's global beauty care division, was faced with several challenges as the new CEO. In particular, he needed to restore employee morale while staying fo-cused on improving sales and earnings growth.

To get the company back on track, Lafley made changes in several areas. He reeval-uated the global locations of product area executives, simplified the company's struc-ture, encouraged young managers to remain with the company, and persuaded some who had left to return to P&G. On the marketing side, Lafley restored core brand mar-keting efforts and boosted advertising efforts for new products. He also enticed former P&G chairman, John Pepper, to come out of retirement and rejoin the team.

Lafley knows that employee morale, sales growth, and earnings growth cannot be restored overnight, but he is encouraged that P&G is back on the road to recovery. His objective is to get the company back in balance while keeping it on a growth track.

STRUCTURES FOR INTERNATIONAL ORGANIZATIONS

International businesses display many different organizational forms, and few are sim-ilar to their domestic parent companies. Only rarely can a firm extend its domestic structure into a global environment, and no ideal model defines the optimal multina-tional organization. The configuration of an international company changes so often with circumstances that a "snapshot" definition, commonly shown as a two-dimen-sional organizational chart, is outdated almost as soon as it is made. Nevertheless, companies try to establish stable systems for management. These can be studied in the context of *patterns* of decision-making authority and the *processes* of managing global resources. This chapter focuses on these patterns and processes.

International companies seldom make drastic changes in their organizational structures unless they face grave crises. Instead, structural elements evolve as the nature of a firm's international operations changes. During this evolution, the authority structures and management systems change to fit new competitive strategies. These changes can be categorized to reflect strategies, thus leading to an important observation: Structure follows strategy. More accurately, a company must forge an organizational structure consistent with its strategy to successfully implement plans through effective management systems. However, managers can often develop an effective strategy more easily than they can alter an organizational structure. This difference will become apparent as the chapter relates how organizational systems evolve and, at times, how the inertia of prevailing management systems impedes change.

The Organization as a Global Network

The term *organization* takes on new meaning for a company that goes international. A small domestic company, for example, can often trace a clear hierarchy of management authority downward from owners to operating employees. In contrast, a large, globally integrated company may coordinate hundreds of diversified international operations through multidimensional networks of management systems. These functions imply complicated structural relationships. Between the extremes, a particular company may assign regional headquarters staff to coordinate activities in particular market segments, product groups to address globally branded products, or various combinations of market and product configurations orchestrated through a wide variety of systems.

For example, Stanley Works, the world's leading manufacturer of hand tools, operated primarily as an American exporter for more than half a century.[2] It served worldwide markets through a home-based export office, but intensifying competition from companies such as Black & Decker forced Stanley to establish overseas offices and eventually to group them under national and regional distribution centers. With greater expansion, Stanley found itself in a so-called *matrix structure* that allowed for cross-management of products and markets. In July 1997 Stanley implemented its restructuring efforts, consolidating U.S. operations and vertically integrating many of its value-chain activities. The plan also involved unifying Stanley's global operations.

The Stanley Works example illustrates how conditions may force a company to rapidly create new structural systems in order to implement effective strategies. For Stanley, a simple model of exporting worked well in an earlier era, but competition and growth dictated new systems of management for its expanded international operations. When the organization expanded beyond a linear model of integration to pursue many interrelated activities, uncertainty clouded the management picture at Stanley. In the course of gaining more than 20 percent of a $12 billion global market in hand tools, Stanley spread throughout many different locations with a diversified product line and many interdependent activities. Stanley—like many large, diversified multinationals—has evolved toward a global *network* of overlapping systems in which foreign and domestic operations interact and depend on one another in many ways.[3]

Despite the difficulty of envisioning these different structures, the example illustrates how changes in a company's international interests complicate its management structure, and that the emergence of structure follows a logical evolution in strategy. Thus, a company periodically must reposition or "stage" itself. These stages represent patterns of organizational systems, each congruent with a company's development. At any stage of development, one structure may perform better than another, but no structure permanently qualifies as the best one. Each is *contingent* on existing circumstances and expectations for management processes required to implement strategies. Therefore, as strategies change, new structures evolve. Businesspeople create charts to illustrate structural relationships, but these superficial abstractions seldom reveal how processes occur within the system.

Contrasting Concepts of Organizational Structure

The fundamental concept of structuring a company's organization changes as the company becomes a progressively active global player. For nearly a century, organizational theory has focused on *specialization* and *vertical coordination* as the primary determinants of structure. This historic focus has led to mechanistic models based on a legacy of hierarchical authority. Most management books still focus on these models and on the importance of specialization and associated functional or operational unity of command. They address the task of coordination as relationships between either management strata or functionally specialized departments. This oversimplified account acknowledges the essential contributions of specialization and vertical coordination, but it also reveals their inappropriate criteria for organizing international management systems. In fact, tendencies toward specialization and vertical coordination act in direct opposition to the international mandate for a *globally integrated* organization capable of coordinating a complicated network of interrelated activities.

Consequently, a company may specialize tasks as it evolves until it creates a structure of extremely well delineated activities. Although this pattern may serve its purposes well while it remains a domestic enterprise, the resulting departmentalization may cripple efforts to integrate global operations. Specialization and hierarchical coordination are important stages in development, but at some point structural relationships must accommodate the complexity of dozens (or hundreds) of international operations providing goods and services to one another and selling to outside customers in many different markets. Managers of these global activities engage in multiple networks of cross-cultural communications, and they can do so only within a system of coordinated *interdependent* activities. More specifically, specialization and vertical coordination imply *dis-integration*, while global coordination implies a move toward greater *integration*. Figure 7.1 illustrates the two viewpoints, in which vertical and horizontal relationships suggest different fundamental organizational structures.

The design of an organization, therefore, is contingent on several factors. All organizations must divide tasks and activities into well-defined operations and delineate authority to coordinate those activities. Strategy determines the interrelationships among these activities within the constraints of industry competition, technology, and the company's markets. The complexity of international operations redefines information needs throughout a company, and patterns of information show the influence of cross-cultural issues such as diverse languages, work values, and leadership styles. Altogether, these factors influence management choices in organizing a complicated process to both facilitate the firm's strategy and ensure responsibility throughout the company.

STRUCTURAL PATTERNS IN DEVELOPMENT STAGES

During two centuries of industrialization, companies have evolved through a form of **creeping incrementalism.** Structures have evolved from solitary entrepreneurs

FIGURE 7.1
Disintegration and
Integration—Contrasting
Organizational
Relationships

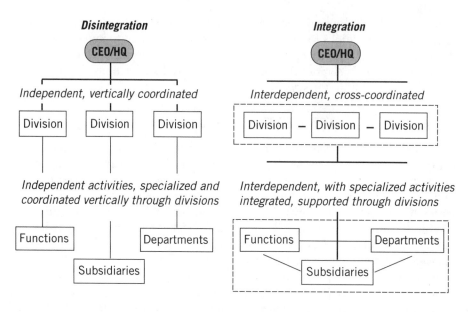

through expanding staffing and ever-greater reliance on specialization and subsequent delegation of authority. Therefore, managers have become comfortable with hierarchical power relationships that define patterns of communication and decision-making. They expect hierarchical "pecking orders" consistent with well-entrenched principles of management with names such as *unity of command* and *chain of command*. Indeed, scholars of international management at Europe's INSEAD recently concluded that managers, leaders, and politicians have for centuries treated hierarchy as a "sacred science" to protect their power through "universal subordination" of other people.[4] Unfortunately, hierarchies imply assumptions of coinciding knowledge and human ability, so they foster unidirectional communication and influence. Hierarchical authority does, however, stabilize control and accountability, even though it may impede cooperation and stifle relationships that could benefit the organization.[5]

Incremental changes in organizational structure imply a progression of adjustments within the boundaries of a particular hierarchical system; the system may not change, yet behavior within the system does change. This requires new assumptions about power, hierarchy, and status. International activities require changes in fundamental systems. Procter & Gamble is undergoing a shift in its pattern of organization; and as noted earlier, Stanley Works has had to adopt an entirely new approach to international management. In both companies, incremental developments have required managers to adapt to new ways of thinking, and infrequent structural shifts have required dramatic changes in organizational relationships. The fundamental forces affecting organizational structures in the international arena are different from those in purely domestic enterprises, and international managers face challenges never encountered by managers in domestic roles.

Fundamental Structural Forces

The principal force affecting organizational structure is specialization. As noted earlier, specialization generally results in **disintegration**. A more familiar term is *departmentalization*, and both describe a process that occurs in all organizations, even families. No one can be everything to everyone in a family, any more than a marketing manager can concurrently handle production, engineering, and finances in a growing company. Departmentalization evolves through delegation, which enhances efficiency by separating responsibilities. By definition, this tendency creates a form of disintegration, with definite costs due to potential conflict and isolation. Just as family members often struggle to define their role responsibilities without allowing separate identities to erode family relationships, companies struggle to achieve departmental efficiencies without creating machinelike bureaucracies.

Of course, firms gain important benefits from specialization and departmentalization. Individuals and departments become highly skilled at specific roles, generate economies of scale, and leverage knowledge through focused systems of functional expertise. Paul Lawrence and Jay Lorsch have studied organizational processes through benchmark research over a period of several decades. They have concluded that role *differentiation* provides an essential foundation for understanding how people work together in a complex work environment.[6] By first differentiating roles, these analysts came to understand the dynamics of decision-making, differences in structured and unstructured work environments, and the idiosyncratic demands on individual managers. Armed with this information, the analysts could then *integrate* each role into the fabric of organizational coordination systems, thus defining the structure of a company according to how decisions were made and who participated in the process.

The Lawrence and Lorsch differentiation model resembles the organizing concept of departmentalization, and both attempt to address the problems of organizational accountability and control. In a well-defined, differentiated organization, decision-making authority is unambiguous. Clear communication channels carry orderly streams of information, while less-obvious integrating activities bind elements in a departmentalized hierarchy. For example, Citigroup manages a broad array of financial products and services in over 100 countries. Until a few years ago, nearly 900 Citigroup (then Citicorp) executives managed all of that work, each retaining a carefully differentiated role with well-defined communication channels. Unfortunately, the company found its activities strangled by demarcation disputes, untimely decisions, and a global collage of uncoordinated bank services.

Recently, Citigroup simplified its management structure and created a single management structure that aligns the company's operations to meet customer needs and respond to growth opportunities.[7] Citigroup, like other global organizations, is attempting to achieve global integration by redefining its organizational system based on a logical consolidation of activities and extensive coordination among interdependent worldwide operations.

The essence of integration is coordination of interdependent activities that transcends departmental boundaries and minimizes unproductive demarcations of authority. As an immediate benefit of integration, interdepartmental communication improves, often resulting in higher quality, greater innovation, and organizations that are more responsive to competitive and environmental changes. Integration also creates difficult challenges for management, however, and the firm must bear certain costs. Managers and employees accustomed to power-based hierarchies cannot easily adapt to integrated activities with somewhat ambiguous authority channels. Blurring of demarcations between departments leaves intermingled responsibilities and shared governance. While this ambiguity may strain relationships, group or composite company objectives become paramount, overshadowing individual or departmental objectives. Independence is less valued than interdependence, and ironically, individual initiative gains substantial importance—but it is defined within systems of people working toward synergistic results, not narrowly defined specializations.

During the early stages of a company's evolution, disintegration dominates its structure. As the company expands into multiple foreign markets, perhaps with multi-faceted operations and diversified product lines, integration becomes the dominant force. Early growth requires delegation and incrementally greater specialization. During early periods of international expansion, a company disperses operations to pursue comparative advantage through specific foreign activities. Downstream activities are intensely managed within multilocal operations in order to achieve competitive advantages.[8] Comparative and competitive advantages are optimized through closely managed and highly specialized subsidiaries. As the company becomes more global, it develops upstream activities as well as consolidated foreign interests, many of them supplying other operations within the same organization. Networks begin to develop among regional enclaves, and further expansion forces the company to manage many different systems of activities. Specialization and local intensity may retain importance, but hierarchical relationships become cumbersome and inhibit effectiveness. Individual responsibilities are no longer defined by vertical management systems, but by cross-cultural relationships. Comparative advantage no longer depends on aggregated performance efficiencies in individual foreign activities but, rather, on the synergistic effects of interrelated systems. These contrasting forces relate less to the size of a company than to the nature of the global industry in which it competes; even a small enterprise may find itself managing complex relationships. Figure 7.2 emphasizes how priorities change for a company as it becomes more involved in global business.

Structural Change and Incremental Growth

During the early growth stages, an organization is characterized by the traditional pyramid of stratified authority. At inception, a firm is too small to delegate responsibilities; but as it grows, a hierarchy emerges. This structure usually distributes authority along *functional* lines, and those boundaries can remain intact as the organization achieves a rather large size. However, organizations can establish several other structural options, such as a *product pattern* that bases its primary divisions on product-line groups. Each product division oversees its own functional activities, such as marketing, research and development, and human resources. Another alternative is to create divisions based on a *geographic pattern* that groups mainstream functional activities (production, marketing, human resources) and replicates them for distinct market areas. An organizational model may also display a *consumer orientation*, concentrating product-centered and functional activities on a market niche defined by a distinct consumer group.

As an enterprise ventures into foreign sales by exporting domestically manufactured goods, it adds an *export department* to its organizational structure. Rather than an autonomous function, this department is identified as an extension of the marketing function. As the company continues to grow, exporting becomes specialized, and the department expands its range of responsibilities to include sales and distribution activities through locally responsive foreign subsidiaries. Perhaps the term *subsidiary* is too strong here, because foreign interests at this stage may be limited to agency, brokerage, and licensing relationships. Nevertheless, the company can expand within this model to include extensive foreign offices, wholly owned subsidiaries, and various types of cooperative ventures.

To emphasize the difference between merely creating an export department and the more involved task of managing foreign investments to facilitate exports, the latter model is referred to as an *export department with subsidiaries*. Although the subsidiaries may not be autonomous, they imply an increasing role for the export department and

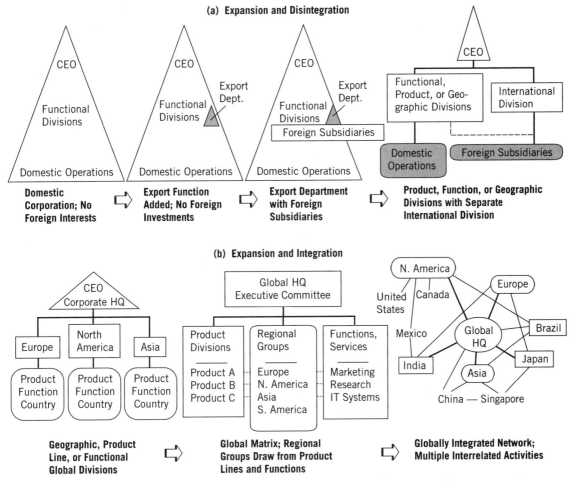

FIGURE 7.2
Structures for Expanding Business

an important change in the management process. Export marketing staff no longer simply sell homegrown goods overseas; associated local operations give them responsibility for foreign interests. As a later section discusses in more detail, a growing number of subsidiaries can eventually overwhelm the capabilities of an export department and create a need for a different approach to international management.

Incremental growth causes tensions that eventually reach crisis proportions if management does not continuously adapt the organization to retain its competitive edge. In one common crisis, an export department often plays a limited role in marketing decisions, yet it manages huge foreign interests. For example, Rubbermaid (now Newell Rubbermaid, Inc.) has successfully marketed its household and consumer rubber goods worldwide, yet its image suggests a Midwestern small-town company. Rubbermaid sold into export markets through a home-based export department until conflicts erupted between export personnel and the company's manufacturing division. Tension occurred because export sales were growing faster than the company's ability to provide products. In addition, the export staff wanted modifications in products and packaging to take advantage of foreign demand. Although it remained a small department with little influence, by the early 1980s it was generating more than 30 percent of the company's gross income and nearly 50 percent of its profits. To reconcile the problem, management decided to shift support toward worldwide distribution, elevating the export department to a senior function reporting directly to the CEO. This resulted in a decade of sustained global growth and record profits though a core international division.[9]

Integration becomes apparent as an export-driven company reorganizes to form **global groups** with geographic, product-oriented, or functional focuses. These three options, shown earlier in Figure 7.2, appear more or less attractive in individual situations based on industry characteristics and company strategy. Most multinational enterprises currently fall into one of these three categories, but they also face difficulties of coordinating functional activities, divisions organized around specific goods or services, and overall international operations.

This group structure represents a fundamental departure from hierarchical departmentalization. The organization moves toward horizontal cooperation along all three dimensions, forming a **global matrix.** This matrix approach falls short of full integration, but it does move beyond the principle of unity of command to establish dual authority channels within geographic groups. A matrix organization requires managers throughout a company to engage in joint (or multilateral) decision-making and to share authority to resolve common problems or to achieve shared objectives. This process can be extremely difficult, and many companies avoid the matrix structure with its potential for conflict. Texas Instruments, for example, found that its matrix system created too much ambiguity and too little cooperation; the company subsequently scrapped the structure. Dow Corning also found a matrix structure troublesome. Instead, both Texas Instruments and Dow Corning reorganized around global product divisions with integrated functional support systems.[10]

Global companies do not necessarily adopt matrix structures, although they have been popular among enterprises selling multiple groups of goods or services in many different markets. Ultimately, a company outgrows national limits on functional authority, and it pursues **global integration** to achieve a fully networked world enterprise. This step may bypass a matrix structure and comprehensively redefine divisions as interdependent systems. For example, AT&T created a globally integrated company while abandoning its product-based, divisional structure.[11] The old structure divided AT&T's activities among three primary divisions. Lucent, a telephone equipment manufacturer, was AT&T's primary hardware company. The acquisition of NCR led to the formation of a separate division for computer systems and software. The core AT&T division was the consolidated telecommunications unit that remained after deregulation. By 2005, AT&T expects to have spun off manufacturing and computer systems. It will then nearly triple its global activities by organizing four "interrelated systems" of services: local/domestic telephone services, on-line systems (e.g., Internet, videoconferencing, and teleconferencing), long-distance calling services, and support systems (e.g., credit cards, wireless transmissions, R&D). If the company's plans are successful, an independently managed long-distance unit will fully integrate its activities with the firm's global Internet services, videoconferencing and teleconferencing capabilities, and comprehensive network of links to local telephone systems. The new systems seem to stand alone on an organizational chart, but they will act as fully integrated partners. Without global integration, the services envisioned by AT&T would be impossible to achieve.

These categories of structures represent a progression of organizational change. As the examples show, however, companies do not necessarily pass through every stage. Nevertheless, the progression provides a general framework for understanding multinational enterprises. The following sections describe individual structural alternatives in greater detail, in the process illustrating how management roles change through globalization.

Domestic Organization with an Export Department

Exporting and importing represent the lowest risk profile of alternative methods of international involvement, and they require relatively simple changes in a domestic firm's organizational structure. Foreign sourcing, or importing, often requires no specific change; the procurement function merely expands to include overseas opportunities. This statement may oversimplify the purchasing process for companies that strongly rely on foreign materials. Companies such as Pier 1 Imports, Anne Klein clothes, and Toys "R" Us manage substantial foreign interests concerned almost entirely with worldwide procurement activities. As small companies initially reaching beyond their home borders, these organizations defined purchasing responsibilities according to the expertise needed to deal with foreign brokers, import agents, or companies selling into their home markets.

In contrast, the export function is a responsibility distinct from domestic marketing. As a company establishes foreign markets, it must develop the ability to facilitate the necessary transactions. This process often requires new abilities to respond to unfamiliar customers, negotiate with foreign buyers, and expedite sales and services. These activities extend beyond adjunct marketing responsibilities, and firms usually acknowledge the separate needs by staffing *export offices* with people skilled in international business. Figure 7.3 illustrates the basic export-department structure under a functionally organized enterprise. Many companies—even those with rather extensive foreign sales—retain this structure for long periods of time, merely expanding export office staff as required. Occasionally, companies with product structures position their export offices directly under the CEOs to ensure coordination of sales for several different product lines. This option is shown in Figure 7.4.

Subsidiaries under an Export Department

When a company's export activities become sufficiently complicated to require overseas facilities, its structure evolves further to include foreign subsidiaries. This move constitutes a major change for most companies, yet a block diagram representing the management hierarchy changes only by arraying a lower level of subsidiaries under

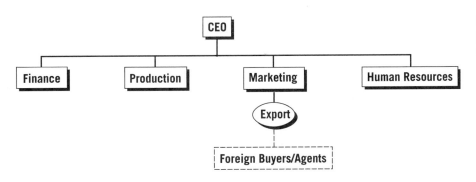

FIGURE 7.3
Functional Structure
with Export Department

FIGURE 7.4
Product-Oriented Division
Structure with Export
Department

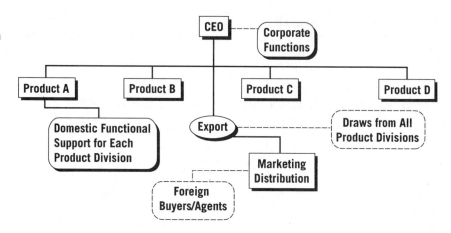

the export department. Figure 7.5 shows an abbreviated model of a company with several subsidiaries, but a real MNC may encompass several hundred of these foreign offices. Although the addition of foreign subsidiaries makes the company a multinational, it may retain its fundamental pyramid of authority. The established *organizational script* need not move beyond the embedded concepts of cascading authority and unity of command. Nevertheless, the *organizational process* changes substantially as two critical forces imprint themselves on the enterprise. First, home-country managers gain responsibility for important foreign resources and for direct interactions with people of other cultures. Second, foreign managers and employees become part of the parent company. Their diverse interests and values can substantially influence organizational processes.

Block diagrams do not reveal the mysteries of the processes through which tasks get done; they show only the formal relationships that officially link various subsidiaries to the company. At one extreme, subsidiaries may be no more than branch sales offices with little authority of their own other than to transact foreign business

FIGURE 7.5
Functional or Product-
Oriented Structure with
Separate Export Division
and Foreign Subsidiaries

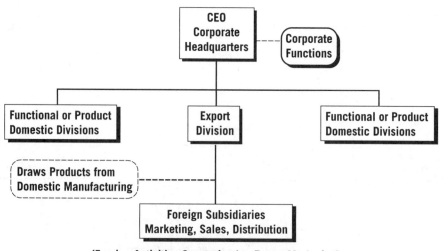

(Foreign Activities Constrained to Export Marketing)

on behalf of the parent company. At the other extreme, subsidiaries may have significant autonomy and their own identities that bear little resemblance to the parent company's operations. They may be independently constituted entities or part of extensive, multifaceted strategic alliances. Their size and influence can rival those of their parent organizations, with paradoxical effects for a hierarchical authority system. Block diagrams also fail to explain the activities of subsidiaries, which can range from simple processing of sales transactions to pervasive decision-making for marketing, distribution, and foreign exchange. However, as long as the subsidiaries retain identities as marketing or service operations, the company can retain its structure, with foreign activities stratified under an export function.

International Division Structure

An **international division** structure represents a significant change in an enterprise's strategy and organizational authority. In particular, the *process* of coordinating foreign operations implies a major reconfiguration. Subsidiaries are no longer extensions of parent-company marketing efforts. Further, an international division's comparative advantage in production capabilities (not merely market opportunities) drives performance expectations. A company's capabilities for rapid redeployment of foreign activities depend on its strategy and management's commitment to international expansion. Specifically, the international division could evolve as a stepchild alongside traditional functional or product divisions. This arrangement often reflects a reluctance by managers to separate foreign and mainstream interests, yet the separation into divisions can help resolve conflicts while improving controls.

At the other end of the spectrum, a new international division may represent a fundamental change in the way a company competes. By creating a new division, management may begin to write a new organizational script for relationships between divisions and between elements of the company and its foreign interests. Such an international division does not report through a hierarchy; rather, it remains responsible directly to headquarters. Meanwhile, the rest of the company usually remains steadfastly anchored to its old hierarchical script. This situation may signal the transformation away from a structured chain of command for company responsibilities and toward interdependent coordination among division managers.

This fundamental shift can result in an international division that appears to operate parallel to and separate from the parent company, as shown in Figure 7.6. Yet the diagram does not reveal the firm's processes of decision-making and strategic operations. Depending on management's philosophy for directing operations, the structure shown could easily be steeped in traditional status-based systems, or it could emphasize horizontal coordination between semiautonomous divisions.

An international division allows the company to pursue any one of the generic strategies described in earlier chapters. Most important, the firm can also configure foreign activities to pursue both competitive and comparative advantages. Foreign locations for downstream sales and marketing activities should optimize competitive advantages; the configuration of upstream activities should favor locations that optimize national comparative advantages. Recall that competitive criteria focus on marketing and distribution; comparative criteria are concerned primarily with scale economies and resource management. Therefore, foreign subsidiaries redefine their business-unit strategies and their internal processes to match expectations for these enhanced roles. This development marks the beginning of *integration* and movement toward global networking.

FIGURE 7.6
Nonintegrated Product-
Oriented International
Division Structure

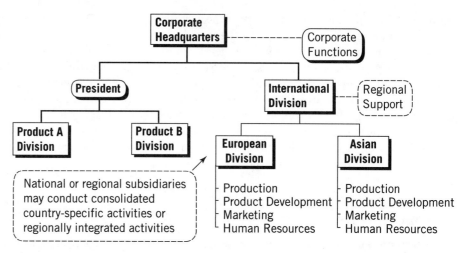

An enterprise may not necessarily move rapidly toward integration, and by creating international division structures it does not presume activities are interdependent. In fact, integration often emerges in a slow process of change that transforms one subsidiary previously constrained to export marketing into a more complete system with local production and materials sourcing. In this way it improves its local responsiveness, creating the appearance of a multilocal organization. If the company-wide strategy dictates this direction, then the subsidiary's actions may not reflect a drive toward **vertical integration** to establish control over value-chain activities nor a shift from marketing to manufacturing. The approach may simply be an incremental step toward improving local competitive advantage.

This important distinction has emerged in the development of companies such as IBM and Procter & Gamble, both of which have followed the multilocal approach very successfully for several decades. Many of their foreign subsidiaries resemble miniature versions of the parent structure. These firms did not consciously pursue integration and coordination of global activities, and many successful companies continue to implement similar practices, including PepsiCo, Levi Strauss, and Kellogg's. Each of these companies enjoys wide recognition for its globally branded products, but those goods must compete intensely in local markets.[12]

The international division structure enhances geographic identity for all foreign activities. The international division head typically reports to the CEO and oversees a network of foreign subsidiaries with country-specific business-unit strategies. Performance is judged in relation to the nation in which a unit competes, and the thrust of local responsiveness dictates whether each foreign unit remains focused on downstream sales or expands into upstream functions such as manufacturing, procurement, and R&D.

Because the structure maintains a clear locus of control over well-defined operations, the central office can make effective decisions about where and how to compete. As the foreign unit expands, the home office also acquires a great deal of knowledge about comparative advantages. Further, each element in a diversified network of operating units represents a low-risk investment relative to the organizational portfolio. The result is diversification of foreign interests and reallocation of activities in support of worldwide affiliates. As the company grows and the momentum of integration increases, an international division is likely to create a second tier of coordination under regional headquarters. This change strengthens interdependent roles for regional and national managers.

Global Group Structure

As mentioned earlier, increasing complexity in an international division's activities forces a company to reorganize. A new structure is typically based on logical groups of activities, and these become global divisions. Unlike the slow and incremental evolution of an international division, reorganization based on global groups requires a company-wide realignment. This upheaval results in an amalgamation of organizational interests to establish geographic, functional, or product-oriented groups, thus replacing the international division structure with a new worldwide organization.

Geographic Groups

The most common form of the group structure defines activities by geographic regions, as shown in Figure 7.7. This change continues the consolidation of regional clusters of activities that began under the authority of an international division. In the process, it also redefines the entire organization. The parent company's core domestic business may become a North American group with an expanded role encompassing Canadian, Caribbean, and Mexican operations formerly under the international division. A European group might include the entire EU as well as Scandinavia and Eastern Europe. Similar geographic group boundaries may be established for the Middle East, Asia, Africa, and South America, if the company's activities extend that far.

Restructuring is concerned with the logical fit among national and regional activities to improve the efficiency of asset management, reduce duplication, improve distribution of regionally or globally branded products, and respond effectively to regional and local competition. Automotive companies such as DaimlerChrysler prefer a geographic group focus, to consolidate distribution channels that serve similar consumers within each region. Consumer-goods companies such as Nestlé, Unilever, and Procter & Gamble achieve regional economies of scale by making globally branded products, but they also benefit by consolidating their marketing efforts to compete in distinct regions through regional marketing alliances and locally responsive distribution systems.[13]

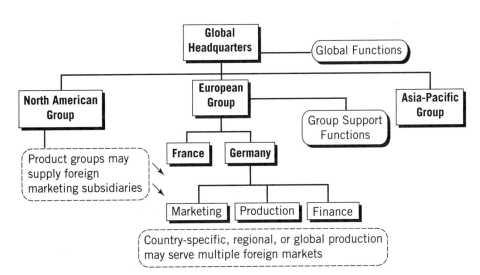

FIGURE 7.7
Global Geographic Structure

Redefining the organization and setting boundaries for its geographic groups may seem like a simple principle, but it is seldom easy to implement. For example, managers might easily diagram a European group by calling for an arrangement of foreign national operations under a regional group headquarters. Perhaps this plan would simply designate all EU countries as part of the new group. Unfortunately, this assumed arrangement ignores cultural, social, political, and economic differences among those nations. Existing subsidiaries in each country may have deeply embedded nationalistic biases that prevent them from cooperating under one organizational roof.

Merrill Lynch & Co., which carefully monitors European competition, advises that a company making any effort at consolidation must recognize the potential for mismatches among at least 15 primary national systems, each with political and language characteristics, major dichotomies in foreign exchange and buying power, and unique management cultures. Structures created on paper may differ substantially from reality. Fila and Hugo Boss, for example, are two fashion empires in direct competition. One is Italian and one is German, yet both operate under a single closely held industrial holding company, Germina SpA, which is also a European publishing powerhouse. Germina carefully avoids revealing how these companies are linked to headquarters; instead, management prefers to keep them separated and identified with their national origins. Fila and Hugo Boss both define their own global group systems with divisions in the United States, Asia, Europe, and South America.[14]

A configuration of global groups differs from one based on an international division, mainly because its managers have made a major commitment to restructure the entire company. The motives behind this move are based solidly in the range of global strategies addressed earlier in the chapter. Specifically, the company has *proactively* decided on a globalization strategy that requires a structure capable of simultaneously responding to global markets and providing more effective coordination through *selective integration*. Integration proceeds selectively because grouping partially combines activities rather than mandating a total unification of a network of worldwide operations. Also, the selection process often retains many independent national subsidiaries that do not fit logically into one of the group clusters. Consequently, during the early stages of defining global groups, managers may establish a master plan that designates regional groups, but full realization of this idea represents the final objective of a long implementation process.

Functional Groups

The functional group structure illustrated in Figure 7.8 results from an effort to integrate functional specialization and gain economies of scale. The international division is replaced by global groups, which are defined by specialized capabilities. Group directors report directly to the CEO, usually from offices located in a central headquarters. This form of organization extends the traditional domestic functional hierarchy, and its development often bypasses the international division stage. When it does evolve from an international division structure, functional grouping represents a rationalization of foreign activities according to *specific product lines*. This system may seem to duplicate a product-oriented configuration, but it does not. Foreign subsidiaries focus on specific lines of goods or services, but management control is defined by functional authority. This structure works well in small companies, or in those with narrowly defined technologies where integrated manufacturing or service activities can achieve economies of scale. The subsidiaries tend to feed products back into mainstream company marketing and distribution systems, or they serve narrow segments of consumer markets. Thus subsidiary activities are coordinated through a

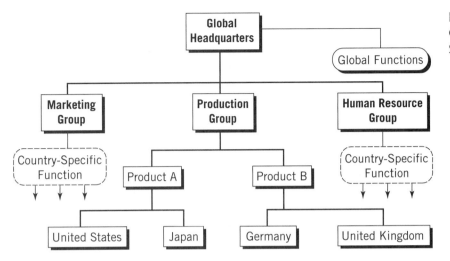

FIGURE 7.8
Global Functional Structure

central executive cadre representing production, marketing, finance, and home-office activities.

The global functional group structure is difficult to implement for most companies, yet an organizational inertia born of traditional functional specialization draws managers to this model. Often, the functional configuration seems like a natural result of growth. As a multinational expands, each foreign subsidiary develops its own functional systems for essential activities. As noted earlier, a multilocal organization that competes through locally responsive operations may need to establish local capabilities for functional activities, yet most companies find that such foreign activities represent tremendous duplication. Business units in a dozen European locations may each support extensive departments for marketing, research, finance, and purchasing, many of them replicating manufacturing and distribution functions of other subsidiaries. Similar duplication of functional activities worldwide often represents an enormous collective cost by sacrificing scale economies and losing strategic control over resources.

Functional duplication and the resulting bureaucratic compartmentalization eventually force management to reorganize a company to achieve better efficiencies and improved management control over operations. This can be accomplished without abandoning the functional structures. The company simply centralizes and consolidates functional expertise, thus repositioning subsidiaries to focus on select product lines in well-defined market niches. This system can work extremely well when units offer narrow product lines to similar customers, or when the company can leverage its technology through centralized manufacturing. Until recently Volvo, the Swedish carmaker, followed this model almost exclusively—with centralized manufacturing and product development, executive coordination of worldwide marketing, and executive service teams. Volvo is now part of Ford's global auto group, and the company has evolved to include more distributed manufacturing and marketing alliances. Nevertheless, a functional philosophy still prevails at Volvo.[15]

Product Groups

A company that sells a diversified selection of goods or services will likely organize based on a product group structure. The term *product* is a convenient description of a logical cluster of activities based on a company's primary business endeavors. Along with familiar tangible goods, it applies equally to services, such as those offered by hospitality, air transport, logistics, and telecommunications firms. It also applies to technological processes such as petrochemicals, mineral extraction, and pharmaceuticals. Industry characteristics often dictate a product orientation. Petrochemical companies, for example, serve global customers with product lines in oil, resins, plastics, and refined fuels; all competitors in the industry implement essentially the same technological processes. The core business demands that companies strive to achieve economies of scale, often through vertically integrated technology and distribution systems. Because the petrochemical industry giants compete with similar products in many different markets, their structures must focus intensely on product lines (services or processes). Research and development, procurement, distribution, and other activities are positioned under each division. Downstream marketing activities are established for each line of goods or services, and these are further differentiated for regional and local markets. Figure 7.9 illustrates this configuration.

The net effect of a product-oriented company's organization is to establish broad-based scale economies while achieving local responsiveness through intensive marketing. On the surface, the structure seems to duplicate functional activities unnecessarily, but this is not the case. Divisions usually handle product categories so distinct that they require specialized skills that seldom interchange effectively with other divisions.

An organization with global product divisions constantly wrestles to reconcile two opposing forces. It must try to optimize scale economies in global upstream activities as it competes through responsive downstream marketing activities, which become less cost effective with greater specialization. A logical solution to the dilemma is to reorganize along the lines of global groups, thus subordinating product and market activities to control by a regional headquarters group. If this solution maintains scale economies, it remains a feasible option; but many companies cannot make it

FIGURE 7.9
Global Product
Division
Structure

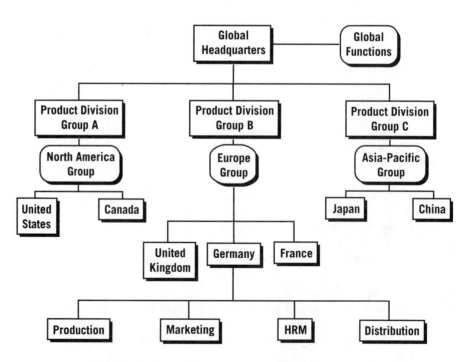

work. They face a three-dimensional problem of reconciling product (service or process) requirements, functional specialization, and geographic (regional or national) coordination. A new configuration that emerges from this dilemma is called the *matrix structure*.

Global Matrix Structure

Product diversification usually leads a firm to sell a variety of products in many different markets. Unlike the product group orientation, which dedicates marketing and support services to each distinct product line, the diversified company maintains multifaceted marketing and support services for several product lines. The common denominator is a regional (or country-specific) market. Consequently, a global matrix structure attempts to coordinate the three dimensions without losing the scale economies of manufacturing or the competitive advantage of locally responsive marketing. Further, the company seeks to maintain the effectiveness of regional coordination. Figure 7.10 is an attempt to show, in two-dimensional form, this three-dimensional relationship.

The matrix structure has not proved itself as an acceptable configuration for more than a few major companies, and many have abandoned attempts to implement a matrix system.[16] Nevertheless, the matrix form offers several strong advantages to a company that can coordinate the necessarily complex management relationships. The chief advantage is the ability to achieve close coordination of locally responsive marketing activities while pursuing global product development. Functional specialization that would be weakened under a global product structure is thus enhanced in the matrix approach. This arrangement brings the company much closer to the customer by speeding and enhancing market feedback. In turn, this information supports effective product development, responsive distribution, and opportunities to leverage broad-based product lines. Effective managerial control created through the matrix's third dimension, geographic coordination, is the critical success factor. In theory, an area manager is equivalent to a project manager. This position requires a general manager who ultimately coordinates product or business divisions with functional support systems.

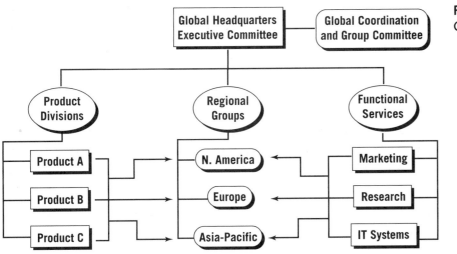

FIGURE 7.10
Global Matrix Structure

The obvious disadvantage of this system is that a foreign subsidiary (or project) must coordinate three channels of communication and authority. The general manager forms part of a geographic hierarchy through which local or country managers report to regional managers, who in turn report to headquarters. Managers within each field unit report through their links in the functional support hierarchy, or their dominant product groups, yet they must satisfy parallel responsibilities to the general manager and coordinate cross-functional activities.

This scenario represents an entirely different psychological script for managers culturally conditioned to linear power structures. Most cannot adapt to the uncertainty of multiple channels of authority or expectations for cross-functional coordination.[17] They also find themselves working in complex multicultural environments, since foreign operations tend to draw varied staff members from across the organization as well as local employees. Communications become complicated because of the diversity, and because messages move through multiple reporting channels. As a result, the efficiency expected of a locally responsive matrix system is often difficult to achieve.

Despite those limitations, several excellent organizations have formed highly effective matrix structures. Companies such as Bectel Corporation and ABB Group (formerly Asea Brown Boveri), both known for major infrastructure engineering projects, have implemented global matrix systems, and both are renowned for achieving worldwide success in their fields.[18] Bectel and ABB also have long histories of effective project management in which foreign activities are directed by country managers (or project managers) with extensive use of expatriate staff. Bayer AG, the giant German pharmaceutical company, is actually a consortium of companies, each with matrix characteristics, that operate in specific countries to market globally branded products drawn from product-based group divisions. In all three examples, country managers (or regional general managers) enjoy extensive autonomy to attract staff from throughout their companies. They also recruit locally, form alliances, and pursue independent strategies. Central executives assume global coordination roles rather than the directive roles typical in linear systems, and executive committees formed by managers with cross-functional and geographic responsibilities provide team-based support systems.

The matrix structure may never become widely implemented, particularly by companies committed to traditional management systems or by people whose cultures reinforce patterns of hierarchical authority. Researchers who have studied highly successful matrix companies note a rapid movement beyond this model and toward a networked form of global integration.[19] Although some firms appear to be making this transition, their cases do not imply that every organization must pass through a matrix stage to pursue an integrated structure. Transition from a divisional structure to global integration may often be easier than superimposing a product-market matrix on a globally diversified organization.

Globally Integrated Enterprise

The ultimate form of an earth-spanning organization is a globally integrated enterprise that removes the meaning of two or three matrix dimensions; perhaps space development will stimulate evolution of yet-to-be-defined models. At this moment in history, the concept of a global company evokes images of a fully networked, multidimensional organization. In this model, the company is defined not by its formal structure but by how its processes are linked together. Perhaps more accurately, the company is characterized as a *system of interrelated subsystems*. Figure 7.11 is a modest effort to illustrate such a hypothetical company with several satellite subsystems.

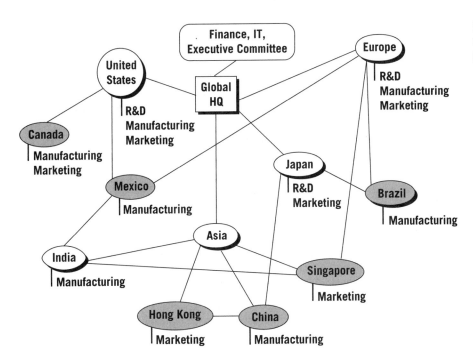

FIGURE 7.11
Globally Integrated Structure

The closest available model of this structure is a client-server computer network, in which a central unit serves as an information resource base and distributed subsystems operate under their own power and through close connections to the main server unit. Like the business structure, these systems are in their infancy. But as computer networks expand and interact with other networks, all sharing systems data worldwide, they establish a globally integrated process of information technology. The resulting interlinked network begins to explain the structure of a globally integrated company. Extending the analogy to include Internet relationships and global multimedia resources adds even more interest. This potential has prompted several researchers to explain international organizations in terms of *information processing systems.*[20]

Organization as Information Processing

In an effort to explain how a globally integrated company coordinates activities, theorists have proposed an **information processing theory** that defines a multinational organization as a communications system.[21] These researchers explain the global company as a fluid system of communications exchange processes. The organization is thus defined by information requirements and resulting communication channels among strategic offices, and throughout its regional, functional, and divisional operating units. The network also expands to external alliance partners or affiliates. Like the ideal model of a globally integrated company, information networks reach beyond political boundaries or territorial rules; they are virtually borderless systems. Indeed, communications acknowledge no hierarchical patterns; information networks transcend time and space by carrying messages and facilitating business transactions without regard to time of day or proximity of the parties.

Of course, information technology provides more than a model for a global organizational structure. It is one of the influential tools that link and coordinate hundreds of worldwide operations. Through advances in telecommunications, electronic networking of financial systems, database-oriented paperless purchasing systems, marketing through facsimile transmissions, and many more applications, companies can now realistically develop seamless organizations.[22]

This approach has great appeal, and companies such as Logitech have quickly adapted IT concepts to configure management systems. Logitech, the world leader in computer-control devices (the computer mouse, various joysticks, and interactive instrumentation), is headed by an "office of the president" that provides direction not from a single person or CEO but from a global team. The members of this group define their individual roles not as controlling employees, but as serving their "in-company clientele" with information and support in a knowledge-based system. Logitech operates on three continents with manufacturing in Ireland, Taiwan, and several Southeast Asian locations. It has product development in the United States, Europe, and Japan, and distributed marketing through network alliances in 80 countries. Founded in Switzerland, Logitech appears to be headquartered in the United States, yet members of the executive team represent both of these countries in addition to Italy and Japan. Shared decision-making occurs through "distributed teams" that control its global network operations.[23]

Although the analogy to information processing helps to explain the company's global organization, it seems to create a somewhat mechanical image. In fact, a global organization is a vibrant collage of human interactions. Management theorists are still groping for an adequate definition of the globally integrated organization. Most of the world still lacks an understanding of information processing or the types of systems that global companies require, and most organizations must still rely on face-to-face management with both formal and informal relationships that do not neatly fit into any structured model of behavior. This fact has prompted organizational theorists to refer to global companies as *relational networks*, a term that emphasizes the trend away from hierarchical structures and toward systems of human relationships.[24]

Relational Networks

The concept of a **relational network** emphasizes that organizations are reservoirs of human capabilities in dynamic circumstances. Within the network environment, decisions are made and activities occur through an interactive association of the people involved.[25] The organization has a structure, much like a human body has a skeleton, that defines the entity. Like a human body, the organization functions as an interrelated system of discrete elements and processes. It is defined according to the dynamic relational networks among many subsystems. The concept of structure implies no assumption of symmetry, hierarchy, or linear channels of communication. In fact, a relational network is probably not created consciously as much as it evolves from the interdependent activities that occur during the transformation from a divisional structure toward an integrated organization.

Relational networks are more likely to develop in a company with globally branded products than in one with highly differentiated products or markets. For example, Coca-Cola, arguably the world's most recognized brand, has established highly standardized systems throughout the world. The cola-based drink formula, bottling methods, packaging, and distribution are quite similar everywhere. However, even Coca-Cola must compete fiercely with other major producers, such as PepsiCo, and both companies produce many other soft drinks, juices, and snack items. In addition, growing lines of independent business units compete through differentiation or niche strategies. These conditions do not suit creation of interdependent and standardized networks.

In contrast, Canon sells a globally branded line of cameras, image-reproduction equipment, and optical electronics gear. It achieves economies of scale in production through global standardization, yet Canon must compete intensely in local markets by differentiating its products.[26] Standardization and efficiency through scale economies are important goals for any global enterprise, but they push a company toward offering commodity-type products. (Commodities are standard goods with notoriously low profit margins and relatively low growth potential.) Therefore Canon pursues global integration, not only to achieve efficiencies but also to gain competitive advantages in distinct markets through various means of differentiation. A company may forge these advantages through cost benefits if it can achieve superior margins through flexible pricing. Similar advantages may result from preemptive market penetration, foreign alliances that create protected niches, unusually effective distribution systems, control over resources, or rapid response capabilities to cope with environmental changes in local markets. Standardization becomes secondary to the efficiency of the relational network, in which pervasive information can be shared among many interrelated global activities.

An optimal network includes dynamic relationships throughout a company's value chain. These relationships may be effected not only through the company's own systems or subsidiaries but also through strategic alliances that bring together coordinated subsystems of suppliers, agents, contractors, manufacturing units, distributors, and downstream marketing activities. With many different goods or services positioned in many international markets, the optimal network defies a singular line of vertical coordination. To suggest that such a firm works through one value chain ignores the reality of hundreds of different potential sources for upstream activities to serve any one downstream market—or conversely, hundreds of potential downstream customers for any individual upstream system.

Reconciling the Approaches

Neither the information processing analogy nor the relational network explanation provides an unambiguous model for the structure of a globally integrated company, but that is just the point: International managers can draw on no specific model for this form. Characteristics that define other formal organizations help to describe contrasts between traditional models of multinationals and the integrated global company, but none of these identify the principal features of an integrated enterprise. Specifically, references to hierarchical authority structures, power relationships, linear integration within a value chain, and decision-making guidelines (i.e., functional, product, or geographic alternatives) fail to adequately explain the human dynamics of organizational integration.

Every other form of organization *institutionalizes* one or more of these characteristics, but the globally integrated firm avoids institutionalizing any of them. It cannot enforce hierarchical authority and at the same time seek multidimensional cooperation among its worldwide activities. It cannot encourage power relationships among managers of diversified activities and still expect them to work responsively and interdependently within a larger network. The globally integrated company cannot expand into diversified markets with multiple product lines established through well-defined value chains, because it has abandoned linear chains of activities.

To illustrate this point, consider an example from a manufacturing plant. Sony's Malaysian facility assembles digital telephones, drawing components from 26 other Sony subsidiaries or joint alliances. Five of these suppliers provide exactly the same microchip component, and six others provide exactly the same telephonic circuitry. The percentage of component orders drawn from each upstream supplier depends on capacity allocations and scale economies that can change significantly for each supplier in response to fluctuations in foreign exchange rates, transport schedules, and import-export quotas. In addition, the company hedges the risk of supply disruptions due to political instability or regulatory changes by always maintaining access to several comparable supply sources. Sony's organizational structure cannot be rationalized along functional, product, or geographic lines, because these forces promote *distintegration*—the precise opposite of the interorganizational cooperation that the enterprise is trying to achieve throughout its network.[27]

At the risk of oversimplifying, a globally integrated company is a *noninstitutionalized* form of organization that flexibly distributes responsibilities among all the activities within the primary (company-wide) system, as well as *relational* networks among the secondary subsystems of subsidiaries and alliances. Boundaries are fuzzy, and operational relationships are fluid. The crucial role of executive management is to ensure autonomous self-organization by worldwide operations according to priorities that optimize the company's overall objectives.[28] In that sense, central management directs strategies, controls major resource allocations, and defines company-wide objectives. Regional and local managers retain responsibility for their differentiated networks. In effect, the network structure is defined by reciprocal relationships and shared responsibilities for contributing to the company's major strategic goals. The ultimate challenge is to form an organization of elements with sufficient operating independence to justify accountability for specific activities and responsiveness to competition. At the same time, the firm must retain an organizational identity with sufficient interdependence to coherently leverage human, financial, and technical capabilities through global reciprocity of management systems.[29]

These complicated relationships have far-reaching implications for managing across cultures and for developing new paradigms of organizational relationships. These topics are addressed in relevant chapters later in the book, but it is important to look more deeply into the meaning of the global organization. The terms *global* and *integration* tend to be confusing, and they are used in many different contexts. To remedy this ambiguity, some researchers offer the concept of a *transnational corporation* as an important way to distinguish between the globally integrated company and traditional multinational models.

A TRANSNATIONAL PERSPECTIVE

Recall from earlier chapters that a transnational corporation (TNC) is not a distinct form of organization; rather, the term describes a globally integrated company with extensive international alliances. It is a convenient label for a company with *global systems of interrelated networks*. The focal or parent organization is only one part of a global web linking it to other organizations through many different forms of alliances.[30] As more and more companies generate foreign alliances, industries are undergoing redefinition as still larger systems of transnational companies. Competition within an industry is no longer strictly confined to national markets, because companies can quickly respond to conditions almost anywhere in the world through their allied interests.

The concept of a TNC represents a conscious shift away from traditional assumptions about a formal organization. Specifically, a TNC may retain its national identity (e.g., an American, Swiss, or Japanese firm), which is legally required for registration and tax purposes, but the actual headquarters may be no more than a small suite of offices at some location with a communication infrastructure adequate to support a global information system. Meanwhile, several major foreign offices act as nodes or centers of international activities, and these often host larger facilities with more complicated operations than the worldwide headquarters. The nodes may be located in Brussels, Tokyo, or Buenos Aires to coordinate upstream activities in their respective regions. More important, they consolidate manufacturing, R&D, and related services such as financing. Consequently, the nodes provide the worldwide system with certain product-line services such as product development or funding. A company may maintain several dozen of these centers, each with responsibility for consolidated activities (such as manufacturing a globally branded product). The key point, however, is that the centers seldom actually engage in the activities that they control. Instead, they *take responsibility for* specific activities within the entire global network system.

Strategic Alliances and the TNC

The concept of an alliance is a mutual exchange agreement in which two or more parties join forces to leverage their individual strengths and create a synergistic competitive advantage. Joint ventures and other forms of equity-driven alliances generate entirely new companies owned by the participating companies. The concept of a transnational corporation extends this principle of strategic alliances to entirely new dimensions. In the conventional sense, alliances allow a company to rapidly enter foreign markets or to gain access to technology and resources, but the transnational corporation seeks alliances in order to contribute elements to its total global network of operations.

Many of a TNC's foreign subsidiaries may be partnerships or joint ventures with other independent companies that are equally strong and perhaps larger than the so-called *parent*. Consider the alliance by Amdahl, Fujitsu, and Peritas to create KnowledgePool, a joint venture designed to become the world's largest technology education group.[31] Amdahl, known for its computer hardware and scientific workstations in North America and Europe, competes directly in many product lines and markets with Fujitsu, known worldwide for computer systems, printers, and telecommunications equipment. Peritas is among the world leaders in IT training and multimedia educational software, itself operating as a subsidiary division of ICL, the giant British petrochemical company. KnowledgePool is expected to rival parent Amdahl in size and client base, and it will be far larger than Peritas. Neither of these alliance partners, nor the new enterprise, can approach the size or influence of Fujitsu, one of Japan's major global corporations. Nevertheless, each alliance partner gives the new venture a link to other important divisions within its own organization, and new links will connect KnowledgePool to external alliances. The new company is estimated to form beneficial **exchange relationships** with nearly 2,000 other organizations in 25 countries beyond those brought to the agreement by individual alliance partners. The identity of the "parent" is not a relevant issue, because no single organization creates the new unit and each company is substantially changed by the new relationships and integrated network of accountability created with the new enterprise. The new configuration does not necessarily displace activities within the existing companies, but it is clearly a powerful federation that influences activities of each alliance member.

Transnational organizations cannot operate only under their own inertia; they need management coordination of often widely diversified activities. Consequently, authority structures do evolve, but they form part of the organization's communications system. Decisions are coordinated, often through teams, at strategic points and at the regional nodes. The complexity of the structure overwhelms the idea of a "boss" or a single control point (office, partner, controlling company, or director). Nevertheless, a global organization must develop a centralized strategic control system. One TNC may acknowledge a single global headquarters with one executive committee and CEO, but this office represents only one of several spheres of influence. On paper, it may appear to form a hierarchy, and certainly demarcation lines define authority relationships, but in practice elements function more in liaison than in directive control, one managing another. These elements include the TNC strategic center (perhaps coordinating its own activities with those of several equally influential world centers), regional network groups that coordinate alliances and their subsidiaries, and widely distributed, semiautonomous operations with locally responsive subsidiaries. Their spheres of influence obviously do recognize differentiated hierarchical authority, but the relational network eliminates management by fiat. Instead, management communication and decision-making become *information exchange* processes.

Although the TNC may seem to centralize authority and intensely control information, this appearance holds true only within the metaphoric model of a client-server network. Rapid decentralization occurs simultaneously with this recentralizing process. Production, marketing, sales, and support functions such as supply, logistics, and distribution often require intense localization, and the TNC depends critically on these activities because they form part of its interdependent network. Downstream activities still compete through local subsidiaries, and local responsiveness still remains a crucial goal. Thus the transnational organization must delegate more actively to its operational subsidiaries than a less decentralized organization would. Again, as in the client-server metaphor, the TNC relies on a central core of information and systems control; but the distributed network scatters significant autonomy to manage operations and flexibility for local managers to self-organize within their area subsystems.

Power Dynamics within a TNC

Managing a transnational corporation is a delicate balancing act. Strategic authority cannot be easily delegated, but all participants expect significant interaction. This priority is particularly strong among executive centers and major participating companies in global alliances. Executives are fully responsible for total system results, yet effective management requires that they hold firmly to their commitments to delegate authority, thus empowering their subsidiary and alliance managers. Two important factors influence the dynamics of power and authority in the TNC: *density of relationships* and *resource configurations*.

Density of Relationships

An organizational chart cannot describe the trust between alliance partners, nor can it explain the full range of relationships between companies and their subsidiaries. These relationships also include government agencies, customers, special interest groups, and other social organizations. Nevertheless, the power dynamics of a transnational organization—and therefore the patterns of management behavior—are influenced by the *density* of relationships. **Density** refers to relationships developed through trust and mutual obligations. It also refers to the significance of social ties, cultural antecedents, ethnic proclivities, and any other factor that cements relationships to the benefit of both parties.[32]

Within a transnational system, relationships can be tenuous, and organizational cooperation may occur only in a formal manner through alliance contracts or prescriptive role requirements. This form of linkage would suggest a somewhat fragile network. At the other extreme, relationships can represent tight bonds of almost feudal devotion. These can be built entirely on trust, ethnic links, or cultural sanctions, creating a very dense association.

Loose associations require comparatively intense management control and active assertion of power. A TNC with extensive loose associations presents an extremely difficult management challenge. It may grow slowly and delegate authority through cumbersome procedures. A company with few dense relationships consequently may struggle to achieve integration. In contrast, a company with significantly dense relationships can rely on willing cooperation among its constituents. Highly dense relationships allow extensive delegation, with little management intervention, through coordinated action by empowered subsidiaries and managers. Density is concerned with power and power-dependency relationships, both internal to company activities and external among a broader range of constituents.[33] Figure 7.12 contrasts these relationships.

Companies with extremely dense relationships tend to stifle subsidiary managers. They also can dominate relationships with other constituents. This assertiveness clearly brings a potential for detrimental effects, and it can limit a company's opportunities to expand. The density of a company's relationships affects where it can do business and how it must manage its worldwide interests. On balance, relatively high density benefits an organization, while weaker ties present more difficult problems of coordinating worldwide activities.

Resource Configurations

The locus of control for most decisions in an organization tends to correspond to accumulations of resources. A small domestic company has all of its resources under one roof—and, of course, the prevailing hierarchy defines the locus of control. In a typical company, the core competency determines how internal power relationships evolve. For example, in a manufacturing firm, production decisions often take precedence; in a strong marketing organization, sales activities take center stage. These relationships

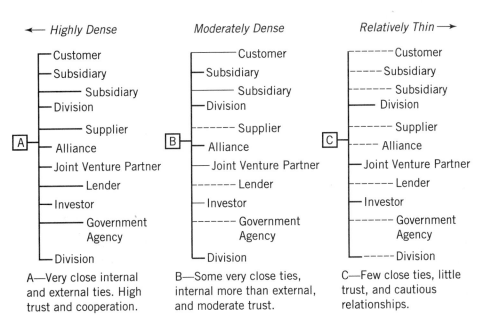

FIGURE 7.12
Density of Constituent Relationships

← Highly Dense

A

- Customer
- Subsidiary
- Subsidiary
- Division
- Supplier
- Alliance
- Joint Venture Partner
- Lender
- Investor
- Government Agency
- Division

A—Very close internal and external ties. High trust and cooperation.

Moderately Dense

B

- Customer
- Subsidiary
- Subsidiary
- Division
- Supplier
- Alliance
- Joint Venture Partner
- Lender
- Investor
- Government Agency
- Division

B—Some very close ties, internal more than external, and moderate trust.

Relatively Thin →

C

- Customer
- Subsidiary
- Subsidiary
- Division
- Supplier
- Alliance
- Joint Venture Partner
- Lender
- Investor
- Government Agency
- Division

C—Few close ties, little trust, and cautious relationships.

do not imply that one orientation or the other is the ideal option, only that relative influence for company decisions tends to flow to the areas where resource strength is concentrated. In this context, resources include production capacity, capital assets, finances, technology, marketing skills, services, and management capabilities. Possession of physical materials and natural resources, or access to them, strongly influences authority relationships in companies that compete in the fishing, lumber, and mineral extraction industries. In contrast, insurance companies, banks, marketing organizations, and hospitality services rely heavily on the market strength conferred by their customer bases.

As a company begins to disperse its activities, particularly as it develops extensive international interests, resources are reconfigured. An exporter may retain all of its manufacturing at the home location and therefore preserve its home-based power center, but other resource activities become more diffused with expansion. This change subsequently requires decentralization of decision-making as well, so power relationships change. A transnational corporation's resource configurations become extremely important, because they represent significant redeployment of managerial authority over a broad range of decisions.

Organizations with highly dense relationships, as noted earlier, tend to retain control over critical resources; consequently, they consolidate power as well as resources. For example, Matsushita, the giant Japanese keiretsu known worldwide for consumer electronics products, tightly controls 100 percent of its research facilities and product development in Japan. The company also maintains nearly 90 percent of its manufacturing at home, with relatively few alliances in Europe. Although Matsushita is one of the world's largest multinationals, it has remained firmly anchored to its centralized power base. Despite operating literally thousands of worldwide distribution channels and sales offices, power is vested in a home-based cadre of Japanese executives.[34]

In contrast, Philips, another of the world's largest electronics companies, widely distributes authority. Headquartered in the Netherlands, Philips has located nearly 80 percent of its total assets outside the home country, and no single subsidiary controls more than 15 percent of the company's resources. Philips configures its foreign manufacturing to replicate most characteristics of world-branded products in dozens of European, Asian, and North American facilities. Marketing, research, product design, procurement, and many support services are widely dispersed; yet they are interlaced through local production subsidiaries. Decisions relating to strategic portfolios and organizational finance remain with home-office executives, but power relationships elsewhere in the Philips network clearly reflect transnational priorities based on interdependent exchanges.[35]

Power Deployment

Power configurations become most sensitive when a company's interests become threatened by the sheer weight of foreign influence. In the Philips network, the parent company maintains strategic control through financial leverage, not by consolidating the firm's remaining assets. It exerts only marginally greater control over product development and manufacturing at home; controlling only about 20 percent of the company's total assets, the home-country facilities are only slightly larger than other subsidiaries. Nevertheless, regional groups of subsidiaries in North America and Asia outweigh the home-country asset base, and the foreign groups contribute nearly 92 percent of the company's profits.[36] Philips managers must thus recognize the need to nurture cooperative relationships among all worldwide operations to minimize power struggles.

Difficulties in achieving integration often result from problems with redeploying power. For example, GE has been held out as a model of global integration for more than a decade, yet organizational change has been a difficult and time-consuming ordeal for the company.[37] GE has been very successful, largely through the efforts of its legendary CEO, Jack Welch, who has become something of a guru for proponents of drastic restructuring. GE's metamorphosis took the giant firm from a widely diversified company with marginal growth and questionable control in many of its product lines to a globally focused electronics and aerospace enterprise. Welch sold off entire divisions in household appliances and consumer goods, combined worldwide R&D for product development, and entered into major new strategic alliances for robotic development, aircraft engines, and telecommunications. He also trimmed corporate activities and established what has been called a "virtual company" through outsourcing for technology, supplies, component manufacturing, and distributed marketing.

Today, GE has all the makings of a truly global corporation. It has made numerous acquisitions worldwide and developed internal processes to assist in the transitions. GE's success, in part, comes from its ability to transplant its global corporate culture into different international locations as evidenced in Europe and Japan.[38] Recently, Welch began incorporating GE's corporate culture values into its Asian businesses. The plan appears to be working—the Asian market is growing.[39] Welch is scheduled to retire in April 2001.

MANAGEMENT IN PERSPECTIVE

International managers face many challenges as their organizations change. Most new organizational systems require entirely new assumptions about how to manage activities in an international enterprise. As a company expands and changes from a

Legendary CEO of General Electric Jack Welch planned to retire in 2000 but has remained with the company that he transformed into one of the world's leading global corporations through innovative leadership. Welch set new standards for corporate leadership and inspired a new breed of international managers during an often-controversial executive career.

domestic enterprise to a diversified international competitor, managers must cope with increasingly intense specialization. They also face growing complications in challenging multicultural relationships. Each stage of change expands requirements for cross-border management that force staff members to learn new human resource skills, languages, and technical requirements of trade, finance, and international logistics. Up to a point, however, managers can stay safely within traditional scripts based on hierarchical authority and linear relationships.

But when organizations begin to consolidate global activities and reconfigure worldwide resources, international managers must embrace a new paradigm. The fundamental assumptions that have served them well during earlier expansion stages come to inhibit their effectiveness as the international enterprise evolves toward becoming a *global system*. Instead, managers must begin to think and act as participants in a *relational network* with the ultimate goal of *optimizing total system benefits*. Strategic mandates may remain the same, such as pursuing global cost leadership or becoming globally differentiated for locally responsive marketing of goods and services, but drastic changes transform the ways the company works to implement these strategies. Managers must also understand that growth is not limited to redeployment of company assets but often occurs through expansion of global alliances and by mergers and acquisitions. Indeed, although the details of mergers and acquisitions are beyond the scope of this discussion, they represent tremendous changes that are reshaping international competition and redefining many of the world's leading companies.

Organizational change and international transformation redefine the management process. The fundamental requirements of planning, organizing, leading, and controlling remain intact, but they challenge international managers in ways that domestic managers do not experience. Planning assumes a worldwide scope, spanning diversified interests and activities. Organizing—the focus of this chapter—can involve remarkably complex new international alliances and entirely new models of relationships. Leading requires new multicultural perspectives and new human resource skills. Leadership requires exceptional capabilities to manage in foreign societies, with foreign associates, and among people with substantially different values. Controlling an international organization requires entirely new relationships and behavior within systems of alliances and multifaceted operations.

The management process in the international arena reflects these pervasive relationships, which often display little resemblance to traditional patterns of organizational governance. Managers must strive to achieve an optimal configuration of interrelated activities, accepting responsibilities for integrative roles that span borders, cross cultures, and defy definitions based on time and space. *Management* is redefined in terms of spheres of influence, not bounded by rationalizations of political, social, or economic criteria. Simple forms of international business, such as exporting, may not require such a complicated perspective; but managers working in a transnational environment must prepare for entirely new roles.

Roles and Relationships

Earlier in the chapter, it was noted that organizations often have difficulty making transitions to new competitive postures because managers bring with them a shared imprint, or *script*, that determines how they expect an organization to function. All organizations have historical roots in their particular societies that reflect national ideologies. These ideologies partially explain how organizations will be structured. All managers reflect cultural values and patterns of behavior rooted in their own personal histories. Managerial culture, more than any other factor, may explain the structures and processes explored in this chapter.

Christopher Bartlett and Sumantra Ghoshal—two highly respected scholars in the field of international business—explain this phenomenon as a company's **administrative heritage.**[40] Specifically, it is the collective history of organizational processes and the management culture that has evolved that determine how a company is structured as well as how it defines management roles. As Bartlett and Ghoshal explain, companies are captives of their experience, and managers are shaped by their values, norms, and expectations. Consequently, managers in a European multinational become accustomed to loose confederations of authority. They may thus adapt to relational networks within a globally integrated company more easily than managers from the United States, who are more accustomed to independent control within focused hierarchies. Americans are generally more comfortable with vertically structured organizations and well-defined systems of power and status. In contrast, Japanese managers are uncomfortable with independent decision-making authority. Although they share a proclivity for group processes, their historical imprint does not encourage relationships with others outside their particular referent groups, often causing them difficulty in coping with alliances that span other cultures.

These cultural considerations affect both organizations and management roles, and they raise important questions about international management. The remainder of this book is devoted entirely to the behavioral issues of managing multinational corporations. Nevertheless, it is important to emphasize here that organizational structure and the processes that determine roles for international managers are crucially linked to the heritage of business systems in each society. Therefore, as a multinational expands and establishes new alliances, each new business formation brings together distinctly different historical imprints of managerial systems and role behavior. In the transnational environment, with many diverse systems operating together, international managers participate in federations involving often-dichotomous patterns of behavior. Indeed, as a transnational corporation evolves, these diverse systems may blend, each contributing to the new organization until the management process itself no longer reflects any particular cultural perspective but, instead, develops an identity of its own.

Management in Transition

As global competition changes and organizations complete the transition from uncomplicated domestic enterprises into international systems, management itself is being transformed. Managerial skills for dealing with a focused organization may no longer adequately prepare a member of an international enterprise. Instead, effective management may require multidimensional skills for working within a multicultural organization defined by fluid relationships and unbounded patterns of global relationships. An understanding of international management begins with an understanding of the antecedents of international strategies and the foundations of organizations as they evolve toward a transnational world.

The term *transnational* may not become a permanent part of the business lexicon, but it captures the essence of current tendencies in world competition. Although today's businesspeople lack a good metaphor for this organizational phenomenon, *systems concepts* provide a useful model. Indeed, information systems, coupled with the human dimension of behavior and value systems, may well describe relational networks. The organizations are systems of people and repositories of human capabilities in which managers forge relationships, determine through behavior the density of those relationships, and adapt in a continuous learning process. Management itself is in transition, away from prescriptive roles of a bureaucratic-control model to roles appropriate for and characterized by flexible and responsive structures. In this new environment, managers face new challenges of rapid and continuous response in systems driven by flexible decision-making processes. Management is being redefined in the context of international teams and alliances, thus escaping the limits of linear, hierarchical governance.[41]

Reflecting on earlier chapters, the discussion so far has introduced the concepts of company strategies and explored how managers posture multinational corporations to compete successfully in global industries. This chapter has addressed the different models for organizing companies to compete in international markets. Throughout these presentations, cultural values and the dimensions of human behavior have been recurrent themes, yet these themes have not been cultivated beyond introductory remarks. The chapters that follow concentrate on the human side of international management on themes of culture, values, communications, negotiations, human resources, and leadership in the new millennium.

REVIEW QUESTIONS

1. The concepts of *specialization* and *unity of command* are important aspects of management, but how can they create complications for international managers?
2. Explain the meaning of the term *disintegration*, and show how *integration* redefines the roles of international managers.
3. Describe and contrast the primary patterns of organizational relationships, and explain the advantages and disadvantages of each model for a multinational corporation.
4. How does a company structured to compete internationally through an *export department* differ from one structured with an *international division*, and why would a company choose one or the other?
5. Outline relationships between elements of a company organized around the concept of *global groups*. How do managerial relationships differ for product-oriented and functional structures?
6. Describe the configuration of a *global matrix*. What chief advantages and disadvantages does it offer? In what situations would it be an effective model for managing foreign activities?
7. Information processing theory attempts to explain the concept of a globally integrated company. Explain the system of relationships that evolves in an MNC as a network for information processing.
8. How are management roles defined in a *relational network*, and how is authority structured in contrast with traditional concepts of management?
9. Describe the power dynamics within a transnational corporation. How does the *density* of relationships influence activities between TNC alliances and their affiliated interests?
10. The role of an international manager differs substantially from that of a domestic manager, particularly for globally integrated companies and those characterized as transnationals. How will management roles change in response to the global changes taking place in organizational structures, particularly with the proliferation of international alliances?

GLOSSARY OF KEY TERMS

Administrative heritage   The collective history of an organization's processes and managerial culture that determines how a company is structured and the pattern of roles for its managers.

Creeping incrementalism   The evolution from solitary entrepreneurs to expanding staffing and ever-greater reliance on specialization, with subsequent delegation of authority to broadly differentiated structures.

Density   An indication of closeness (or distance) of ties within an international network of relationships among an organization's activities, alliances, and external constituents.

Disintegration   The process by which an organization's structure develops through expansion, incrementally greater delegation, diffusion of interests, and diversification, ultimately becoming too complicated to manage through traditional power hierarchies and leading toward reintegration and consolidation of global interests.

Exchange relationship   The concept of horizontal cooperation and exchange of information in a mutually beneficial manner rather than through a hierarchical system of authority.

Export department   A subordinate activity within the marketing function that handles foreign sales of domestically manufactured goods.

Global group   A structural element with responsibility for foreign operations, often organized as a geographic division with broad regional authority, a product-oriented division, or a functionally specialized division.

Global integration   An optimal configuration of worldwide activities through system networking and interdependent relationships throughout the organization; contrast with *vertical integration*, which assumes linear links within a distinct value chain.

Global matrix   A structure that attempts to manage regional interests, product considerations, and functional activities within cooperative dual or triple reporting systems.

Information processing theory   Means by which a multinational corporation is defined in terms of a fluid system of communications exchange processes rather than a hierarchy of authority.

International division   A separate division apart from other functional or product divisions with full responsibility for foreign activities, investments, and configurations.

Relational network   An interdependent system of linked, multidimensional channels of communication and coordination with limited regard for hierarchical power structures.

Vertical integration   A linear linkage within a value chain to control or own activities in upstream or downstream operations, or to fully integrate all activities for maximum ownership and control.

EXERCISES

1. Outline an organizational structure, either from a published case or one that you can devise, for a firm with a simple global product line. Structure your outline to reflect *global groups*, a *global matrix*, and a *globally integrated enterprise*. Keep it simple, but provide sufficient detail to identify at least one line of goods or services, several functional specializations, and at least one foreign regional market area. Argue for the advantages and disadvantages of each structural design.

2. Use your outline or one from a published case to create a job description for the senior manager in charge of marketing under an international division structure. Formulate a job description for a similar manager under a regional group structure with markets in the United States, Europe, and Japan. How do the marketing executives' jobs differ? What responsibilities emerge from their relationships with other division managers and with the parent-company headquarters? How would you describe the organizational systems in which they manage?

3. Interview a domestic manager who has worked for a foreign company, and interview a foreign manager who has worked for an MNC in his or her home country. In their perception, how did their foreign enterprises structure authority? What communications, reporting, and "exchange" relationships did the companies expect? Did the companies encourage trust and cooperation (dense ties) or rely on separation of power in stratified organizations?

CATERPILLAR RESTRUCTURES ITS WORLD ORGANIZATION

Before 1990, Caterpillar Corporation was known as one of the most highly centralized companies in the world. It was run from Peoria, Illinois, and any decision, say, in a road-stop company facility in Nigeria, had to come through headquarters. No one moved without blessings from home. Unfortunately, this ultrafocused organization bogged down in the mud of international competition. By the 1970s, Caterpillar found itself losing out to Japanese and European rivals, which could respond rapidly to local markets and service dealerships with hands-on decisions. More importantly, all technology and innovation came directly through the functional vice president in Illinois, and the company's global operations merely fell in line. The organizational chart showed a simple traditional hierarchy, organized by function with divisions for engineering, manufacturing, finance, marketing, and accounting. For years, each functional area was evaluated on its specialized performance objectives, and continuing sales of globally branded products fostered a secure feeling within the company.

Following a decade of domestic labor unrest, major turnover among top executives, and huge losses in international market share, the giant awoke to reality. It could survive only by winning in head-on competition with Komatsu, Kato, and large French and German industry consortia. The changes began in the mid-1980s when the International Division, then a unit within the marketing function, gained a separate identity. Within a few brief years, the International Division had stopped a downward spiral in market share. At its peak in the 1970s, Caterpillar controlled nearly a third of world market share in off-road heavy equipment and generated more than half of its overall revenues from foreign sales. By 1988, it had barely 20 percent of the world market share, excluding Japan, and revenues from foreign sales had dropped to nearly 45 percent. The International Division plugged the gap and achieved a slight increase in market growth by 1990.

A second stage of change occurred in mid-1990. Caterpillar had begun to engineer this change several years earlier by repositioning several major functional activities. The firm created Caterpillar Financial Services as a separate subsidiary, moved the unit to Tennessee, and gave its managers near autonomy for complete capital asset underwriting of the global business. The division subsequently relocated its world capital development center to Dublin, Ireland, where it could achieve tax advantages and leverage international debt to improve service to the entire corporation. The company had massively redefined its world organization, eliminating all functional divisions and departments other than essential administrative centers for accounting, legal and regulatory affairs, and various executive support systems.

In place of the functional divisions, Caterpillar created 13 profit-center divisions and four service centers. By 1997, the company had expanded to 16 integrated profit centers and five global service centers. Product groups within these divisions focused on customers associated with related product lines and full control over engineering, manufacturing, and marketing. Accounting and finance, two of the service centers, remained logically specialized on their unique functional responsibilities, serving all divisions as well as Caterpillar's worldwide network of dealerships.

In the process of adopting this structure, Caterpillar strengthened its foreign subsidiaries and dealerships, placed all customer contacts under local control, and retired the International Division. Today a customer receives full sales and service support through an alliance office or dealership, including swift handling of financing or foreign-exchange transactions through worldwide regional offices of the company's subsidiary. Under the old system, a customer who wanted to purchase a hydraulic excavator had to work through the massive Caterpillar organization to place an order, get it shipped from the factory, and, if necessary, finance the purchase through the U.S.-based corporate accounts system.

Each division is now organized internally as a group of cross-functional teams, and team-based standards govern division performance evaluations, bonuses, funding, and accountability. Each division also acts as part of a global network of companies within the parent, so that parts made in one Caterpillar activity and shipped to another are actually sold through the procuring division. The divisions often must use proprietary Caterpillar parts and components, yet they are free to outsource on the competitive market if they can find materials of acceptable quality. Many common items—nuts, bolts, core metals, plastics, cables, and other items—now come from outside the company, purchased directly by divisions responsible for their own profit-and-loss performance.

This competitive posture has created new opportunities for many divisions that previously worked only within the limits of the central procurement system and limited geographic markets. For example, Caterpillar de Mexico, the company's heavy-manufacturing unit in Santa Catarina, near Monterrey, has weathered a five-year economic storm in Mexico by leveraging its newfound flexibility to court customers within Caterpillar as well as to export to lucrative Latin American markets. The subsidiary manufactures heavy-equipment accessories, including backhoe loaders, frames for wheel loaders, truck bodies, rippers, buckets, and bulldozer blades. It also produces a substantial line of components for sale back to the U.S. divisions or other company assembly plants in Europe and Asia. Under the old system, the Mexican plant would not have been able to pursue markets or to alter its product lines. Major financial problems in Mexico—the devalued peso, labor unrest, debt defaults, and substantial losses in sales as the country's economy stalled—probably would have forced Caterpillar de Mexico to lay off a major portion of its workforce. Many dealerships may have been closed, and perhaps many of its product lines would have transferred to other countries. Instead, it remained profitable, kept the entire labor force intact (and even increased the hire rate), and met its debt obligations. Caterpillar de Mexico also benefits from complete authority and local management. It is free to design, manufacture, and market an expanding range of products.

For several years, Caterpillar has been decentralizing foreign operations in an effort to network international activities, but it has also aggressively pursued foreign alliances to break into new markets. Recently, Caterpillar and DaimlerChrysler's commercial division agreed to form a global alliance to "develop, manufacture, market and distribute medium-duty engine, fuel systems and other powertrain components to serve the needs of third-party customers and for use in their own products." This 50/50 global alliance will give both companies the ability to meet the demands of the worldwide engine market and the potential for future growth.

Caterpillar executives cite a goal of becoming a transnational corporation, but critics say they are a long way from reaching this goal. Indeed, some recommend managing the firm under a project-based matrix system. Company executives reject this notion, holding to their belief that Caterpillar can create a borderless organization through its divisional structure. Clearly, whatever happens, Caterpillar has taken off its organizational blinders and empowered its organization with new energy.

QUESTIONS

1. Briefly trace the evolution of the organizational structure at Caterpillar, and compare the result with a more general history of multinational developments. How would you describe the existing structure at Caterpillar?

2. What advantages and disadvantages must Caterpillar consider under its new strategic organizational plans? Do you agree that Caterpillar should pursue a transnational structure, or would you agree with critics who suggest a matrix organization? Explain your conclusions.

3. Although Caterpillar has said little about management difficulties, clearly it has created a much flatter organization that emphasizes decentralization and localization. Explain how management roles may have changed in this reorganization, and note the relationships that parent-company executives must consider with alliances and subsidiaries.

BIBLIOGRAPHY

"Caterpillar and DaimlerChrysler to Form Global Alliance." PR Newswire, 22 November 2000. [Retrieved 30 November 2000 from Dow Jones Interactive database.] See also "Caterpillar Deal." *Birmingham Post*, 23 November 2000. [Retrieved 30 November 2000 from Dow Jones Interactive database.]

Hendricks, James A., David G. DeFreitas, and Delores K. Walker. "Changing Performance Measures at Caterpillar." *Management Accounting* 78, no. 6 (December 1996): 18–24.

Lewis, Steven F. "Bulldozing Economic Obstacles: Exports Help Caterpillar de Mexico Plough Through." *Business Mexico*, January 1996, 14.

Stober, Richard. "Caterpillar Profit, Sales Set All-Time Record." *Financial News*, 21 January 1997, 1.

CASE 7.2

CLUB MED REVITALIZED

Club Mediterranee, the global vacation and travel organization founded more than a half-century ago in France, recognized a need for major restructuring. The company's dilemma was with an entrenched centralized management system that could be understood only in the historical context of its formation years. It was undoubtedly a "French" company in spirit and tradition, founded by a well-educated entrepreneur who emerged from World War II with a dream of creating "rough-and-back-to-nature" holiday experiences. Club Med's early vacations took travelers to remote "villages" of tents and huts, where the company provided village managers and hosts (or hostesses) who looked after the vacationers' every need. In the early days, the campers cooked and washed for themselves and brought their own equipment for trekking, fishing, diving, or whatever sport the village area offered. The Club Med team provisioned the group, arranged activities and entertainment, and took care of travel.

The concept rapidly caught on throughout the world. The founder's son, Serge Trigano, effectively took control in 1950; within 10 years, he had grown Club Med into the premiere adventure travel company in the world. The company subsequently became one of France's best-known enterprises, with more than 400 village clusters on four continents. As the firm grew, Trigano established a U.S. subsidiary for North American sales, a Latin American regional hub office, an Asian center for travel in Tokyo, and service branches in nine African countries, as well as in the Middle East, India, Australia, Scandinavia, and the Caribbean.

The number of village clusters grew tenfold by the mid-1970s, and the nature of Club Med vacations changed dramatically, supported by computer-based travel and reservation systems. As the company expanded, it began to cater to a jet set that wanted luxury ski-village vacations, educational adventures such as anthropological excursions, and even polar treks. It also offered company retreats, family villages, and even nudist or adult-restricted holiday packages. Club Med pursued all of these opportunities, and by 1980 its customers could choose among more than 8,000 different holiday configurations, including extended cruises offered by a new division. The company custom-built a high-speed luxury liner equipped with sails. This unique vessel featured landing pads for helicopters, water bays for ski boats, diving craft, and even a set of recreational submarines.

However, expansion created many unexpected challenges for the Trigano family. Serge and his father had made every attempt to retain full family ownership and control, even to the point of personally interviewing village staff. These young recruits often visited Paris for screening, whether they were recruited from Kansas City or Lima, Peru. Everyone on the payroll knew without question that he or she reported to Paris, and thus to the family. Growth took money, and expansion into other cultures such as America and Japan required looser reins on power. The Triganos issued stock and created several stand-alone subsidiaries for worldwide provisions and capital asset development.

The company also had evolved into a multinational system of geographic divisions, with no intention of creating such a structure. This change was promoted during the 1970s by the unusual nature of business in Japan and by the structure of travel bookings in North America. Japanese vacationers almost always bought packaged fares, including many company-sponsored travel arrangements. Indeed, many Japanese travel and vacation in tours and company-related social groups. Few individuals or families buy one-off tickets to anywhere. These customers also expect firm agendas for travel, excursions, entertainment, meals, and even "free time." In contrast, American consumers have rarely traveled in tours until recently; even now, most tours are booked through travel agents for older clients who favor cruises, or for families with young children. Most Americans avoid group endeavors, although a growing set of company clients book promotional tours and annual social events.

The traditional Club Med "village" (the heart of the business) is marketed differently in most parts of the world. In Japan, agents and company travel offices are essentially the key marketing contacts for group sales of bookings in resort villages in Bali, golf enclaves in Thailand, and upscale beach areas on the Riviera. Few Japanese groups or their sponsoring companies consider options such as nature villages or adult programs. Language barriers also present a problem for Club Med staff in most locations, and Japanese in particular avoid mixed ethnic-group vacations.

The company books sales almost exclusively through independent affiliates of travel networks. North America is a competitive market of integrated travel-related services that competitors promote, sell, and service through networks of agencies, travel counselors, airline travel subsidiaries, and entrepreneurial travel offices. Club Med found that success in the North American market requires franchising or licensing its programs, while in Japan, it has a group/tour development system that serves company buyers. Meanwhile, European and Mediterranean operations are in control of the Paris headquarters, and a large majority of European Club Med sales came through company offices and direct-marketing strategies.

As these systems evolved and the company added the "Global Oceanic" cruise division, at least four distinct types of markets defined how the company operated. These variations presented significant problems for Club Med's centralized French management, which favored mandates of central authority for decisions, staffing, and expenditures. Club Med demonstrated insight in creating an international division for accounting and finances to handle the more than 120 different currencies and foreign transaction systems. It also created regional procurement centers for provisions and rapidly delegated authority to village managers for the local purchasing of foods and supplies. Local staff are also responsible for medical care, insurance, ground transportation, and security.

Unfortunately, the Trigano family never quite stepped aside from direct management of Club Med as a whole. With so many different types of customers and markets demanding such diverse vacation plans, villages, and sport/cruise/adventure options, management was drowning in its own creation. This difficulty was becoming apparent during the mid-1980s, when market growth in the United States staggered somewhat in the face of increased competition and price pressure, coupled with a slow response from Club Med. The company lost market share in Europe as new operators launched similar packaged systems and travel affiliates spread. Club Med also failed to recognize that changes in Eastern Europe would open vast markets, and the firm hesitated to cooperate with national tourist boards (government-sponsored agencies) in promoting foreign travel. In the early 1990s, Club Med barely broke even, managing only a narrow operating profit in its village system, bolstered through new and exotic luxury vacation programs and co-op destinations in high-demand areas such as the French and Swiss Alps. The Japanese affiliates had never been entirely comfortable with the French approach to proprietary marketing, which was widely criticized for insensitivity to Japanese culture and to their preferences in foods and activities.

Problems peaked in 1994, when Club Med recorded its first annual losses. Profits were not only flat, but the company also took huge write-offs and closed numerous villages and services to meet cash-flow requirements. The earnings performance scorched share prices, and the sell-off prompted a financial realignment in 1995. In 1996, after more than two years of free-falling profits and massive downsizing, Serge Trigano announced that he and the family could no longer manage Club Med, nor could they reconfigure the company to turn around performance. In early 1997, however, Trigano made another announcement that he had lured the chairman of Euro Disney, Philippe Bourguignon, to become Club Med's new CEO. This stunning move brought an end to 50 years of family control of the French firm. The Trigano family remains active through board seats, but they have further diluted their ownership and relinquished all operational responsibilities. Bourguignon immediately set about a massive restructuring of Club Med's global interests, repositioning its debt-equity underwriting and rationalizing its management structure.

Today, Club Med is realizing the benefits of its restructuring strategies. It has renovated properties, developed new resorts, and revamped its marketing and advertising campaign in an effort to restore Club Med to its roots. North America-based executives also have gained more control over daily operations due to the decentralization of operations in the United States.

Although Club Med started its financial recovery in 1998, reestablishing its image with travel agents remains a challenge. To address this issue, Club Med gave its image an overhaul by changing the orientation of its resorts. Today, the more than 90 vacation villages around the world are marketed as family, adults only, or everyone resorts. In addition, "Baby Club Med," "Petit Club Med," and "Mini Club Med"—organized activities for children of all ages— are in place at 18 Club Med Villages. New brochures project the new image as well as a revamped website. Club Med's emphasis is once again on sports, activities, food, and vacations for everyone.

QUESTIONS

1. How would you describe the Club Med organizational structure as it existed in the 1950s, later during the 1980s, and perhaps at the crisis point of restructuring in 1997? What advantages and disadvantages might have occurred during each period?

2. How would you evaluate Club Med's new restructuring strategy? What additional changes would you recommend? Explain the logic of your recommendation.

3. How would you describe the power dynamics of management under the old system?

BIBLIOGRAPHY

"Club Med Still Expanding After 50 Years." *Toronto Star*, 14 October 2000. [Retrieved 30 November 2000 from Dow Jones Interactive database.]

Covey, Claudette. "Club Med Emphasizes Distinction Between Its Vessel and Villages." *Travel Weekly*, 6 June 1991, 52.

Jack, Andrew. "Club Med Hopes Disney Magic Will Offset Loss." *Financial Times*, 22 February 1997, p. 1.

Kiesnoski, Kenneth. "Club Med Rebounds." *Leisure Travel News*, 11 September 2000. [Retrieved 30 November 2000 from Dow Jones Interactive database.]

Shillinglaw, James. "Club Med's Half Century." *Travel Agent*, 21 August 2000. [Retrieved 30 November 2000 from Dow Jones Interactive database.]

Spitzer, Dinah A. "Club Med Seeks to Broaden Image: Not Just a Singles' Paradise." *Travel Weekly*, 22 April 1991, 54.

YANTANG KNITTING FACTORY

Organized in 1979 under the State Enterprise Mandate for Economic Development of the People's Republic of China, Yantang Knitting Factory (YKF) was among the first competitive companies in the country. The first factory site was equipped to produce multicolored woolen yarns for use in export-quality sweaters. This opportunity arose when a Hong Kong textile wholesaler offered to provide the equipment under a loan agreement in which YKF would repay the cost of technology in products shipped to the wholesaler. At the time, this arrangement suited both parties well because China had not established a system of foreign exchange, complicating currency-based transactions with the outside world. By setting up the countertrade deal (a form of barter), YKF obtained western equipment as well as some cash flow from the Hong Kong dealer, who also benefited by acquiring exportable products at very low costs with a commensurate low tax burden. YKF also gained tremendous knowledge in applying this advanced technology and basic skills training for its factory workers and managers.

Unfortunately, the Hong Kong agreement prevented YKF from selling its products to anyone other than the Hong Kong wholesaler until shipments had covered the cost of the equipment. One of the YKF managers later characterized this limitation as "fishing in a bountiful sea with only a shallow bait net." Indeed, by the mid-1980s China's open markets, coupled with an influx of foreign investors, had created a huge demand for Chinese-made goods. Labor and material costs were so low at the time that U.S. and European companies rushed into the China market to gain cost advantages over western rivals. In 1985, Levi Strauss tried to open negotiations to buy products from YKF working as its subcontractor, but the agreement with the Hong Kong wholesaler prevented an alliance. Support from the Bank of China eventually allowed YKF to convert its equipment from a liability to an asset and terminate the Hong Kong contract. By then, however, Levi executives had turned to other prospects, leaving YKF to seek re-gional export markets for woolens in Australia, Taiwan, and Japan on its own.

This strategy worked well as YKF converted its yarn business to production of actual knitwear, such as low-priced sweaters, children's garments, and winter work clothes. Business literally doubled every nine months for several years, and YKF opened a second factory, expanding employment from about 50 spinners to nearly 250 production workers. With continued growth, the company opened a third factory near the border of Hong Kong in the Shenzhen Special Economic Zone in 1990, and three years later it had doubled its total capacity in all plants.

By year-end 1993, YKF employed a workforce of 820 employees in four different production systems. One focused on yarn goods and wholesale wool weaves. Another produced a wide range of knitwear for contract buyers in Europe and North America, including a small specialty line for Anne Klein fashion clothes in New York. A third system made mixed cotton and synthetic undergarments for domestic markets and a limited export line to Japan. The fourth and newest line was established through a comanufacturing agreement with an Australian textile firm to produce bulk woven fabrics on Jacquard looms, a process developed in France to weave intricate designs resembling tapestries for use in commercial upholstery.

To underwrite its growth, purchase equipment, and find skilled technicians, YKF sought state support. As a state-owned enterprise, it obtained financing with relative ease, but the company had to be reorganized under the State Enterprise Authority for Agricultural Management as a textile subsidiary. Although its status as a tightly controlled state subsidiary brought financial benefits to YKF (including preferred tax status and access to domestic supplies), it also entailed several major drawbacks. The most serious problem resulted when executive management gave way to a shared "directorship" control system with a company manager and a state-appointed bureaucrat at the helm. In addition, a representative of the Chinese labor union, clearly an appointee of the Chinese Communist Party, sat on the board. Consequently, company decisions often emphasized political priorities rather than realistic commercial considerations. For example, the company had to buy certain supplies from other state-owned enterprises even when better materials could be purchased on the open market from overseas vendors.

A second constraint resulted from the limited interest of foreign investors in direct comanufacturing agreements or equity alliances such as joint ventures with YKF. The company also discovered that international relations could disrupt its operations. When the U.S. Congress brought political pressure on China and threatened withdrawal of MFN status over human rights issues, companies such as YKF were "urged" by the Beijing authorities to retaliate by charging premium prices to U.S. buyers or withholding export sales entirely by cutting shipment quotas. This demand seriously interfered with several lucrative contracts with New York importers, including the Anne Klein line of fashions, which apparently were contracted to several other Asian locations.

Nevertheless, YKF's turnover in sales increased steadily between 1993 and 1995, and in 1996 President Clinton's approval of MFN status for China eased tension on the company to pursue restrictive marketing policies. By year-end, orders from western textile and clothing buyers increased by 41 percent, and YKF began yet another major round of expansion. These rapid increases in sales allowed the firm to pay off nearly all equipment loans, including those for new technology brought in from Japan. This financial independence allowed YKF to consider other financial markets apart from government-controlled sources and the Bank of China. New laws had also come into effect during this transition period. China's Private Company Act of 1988 had allowed companies to incorporate as wholly owned for-profit ventures, and new provisions in 1992 allowed public sales of stock and broader hard-currency investments from foreigners. Amendments to China's Company Laws also permitted, for the first time, majority interest in a joint venture by a foreign partner. These changes attracted many U.S., European, and Japanese investors, who actively sought Chinese companies as equity partners in new international export ventures.

On the down side, U.S. government negotiators and special interest groups further increased pressure on China to institute a number of legal protections against abuses of human rights, child labor, theft of intellectual property, enforcement of corrupt practices guidelines, and protection for several critical domestic industries. Among these U.S. laws, the Lautenberg Amendment changed the U.S. Foreign Assistance Act in ways designed to affect trade in textiles and agricultural products. In effect, the law created broad-based restrictions for U.S. foreign aid (and related investments) to ensure that it would not benefit foreign production of textiles and certain imports that would compete with U.S.-made goods. Similar types of regulations, including import restrictions imposed by individual states such as Massachusetts and New York, curtailed investment in China and discouraged new contractual business. YKF managers struggled to sort out international treaties, problems with cross-border transactions, and the dynamics of uncertain markets that were seriously influenced by political initiatives.

The external problems were only part of the grand picture. In many ways, foreign relations remained generally good with strong exports, but YKF management still contended with complicated issues, beginning with serious domestic problems. Waves of inflation in China brought price increases ranging between 10 percent (annualized) in early 1987 to as much as 28 percent in 1992. Government austerity measures dampened inflation in 1993, limiting increases to about 18 percent, but factory workers' wages consistently rose at an annual average rate of 18 percent between 1987 and 1996. The cheap-labor advantage that had attracted comanufacturers in the 1980s had evaporated by the early 1990s. Indeed, many foreign contract buyers had begun to source products in remote regions of India, Indonesia, and Bangladesh, where they found wage levels half those in the industrial coastal areas of China. Put another way, Chinese factory wages in the high-growth areas of Shanghai, Guangzhou (Canton), and the special economic zones along the coast had more than quadrupled in less than 10 years, while average wage levels had remained extremely low in rural parts of China and in competing Asian economies. For YKF, this change powerfully influenced its costs in three of four production systems high in labor intensity. At the same time, inflation fueled increases in materials prices, storage costs, transport expenses, and energy overhead. The net effect expanded YKF's total costs by approximately 14 percent annually through 1996, while it could raise prices only in concert with world markets, which allowed less than 9 percent annual increases.

The company was fortunate to experience continued rapid growth, although it remained somewhat unpredictable due to international political disputes over trade. Rapid expansion kept the factory working near capacity, generating huge-scale economies during peak seasons. Through astute management and dedicated retirement of its major debts, YKF was able to keep a positive cash flow. It also improved its technology and its quality levels, thus attracting new clients in an otherwise confused market environment. For example, the company was awarded the Certificate for Quality Assurance by the International Wool Secretariat in 1986, and it won the award again in 1991. These awards brought important recognition in Australia and New Zealand, where woolen products and export markets headed for Europe are top commercial priorities. Consequently, YKF was thrust into the limelight for bids on worldwide purchases of woolen products, and its contract work gained wide acceptance by fabric mills and "converters" in the industry. Each year, YKF actively participated in the Guangdong Annual Textile Trade Fair, which attracts thousands of foreign buyers; the company also displayed products in Frankfurt, Germany, and New York during major trade shows. Orders generated from these networking activities permitted YKF to gain liberal export trade quotas from the Beijing authorities that further boosted output.

YKF also changed its method of distribution. Prior to 1994, all orders were shipped directly from the factory in containerized consignments. These bulk shipments were cost effective for most orders, but increasing order sizes and new systems of designing and producing standard products such as undergarments and upholstery fabric also raised costs. The firm spent more and more to lease and store containers and to hire transport. The cumbersome containerized shipping system also delayed shipments, required payment of intermediate storage fees, and boosted losses from handling errors. To combat these problems, YKF leased several wharf-front warehouses in 1995 and then built a facility with automated materials handling in 1996. These investments reduced operating costs and inventory losses, but they stretched the company's financial resources to the limit.

At the end of 1996, YKF managers felt that they were in a strong position to expand nearly all of the firm's international markets, thus generating foreign exchange and a secure level of profitability. They could not, however, finance growth or actively market products in North America and Europe. As a state-owned enterprise, they enjoyed a slightly better tax rate on inventory turnover than private companies and foreign joint ventures paid, but they operated under offsetting restrictions in purchasing and market strategies. For example, YKF could not negotiate licensing agreements for overseas markets, and it could not procure from or sell into certain markets restricted by legislation in the United States. The company managers could easily gain travel visas to participate in foreign trade shows, but they could not negotiate agency agreements with foreign organizations to market finished goods. The YKF enterprise on its own could not issue stock or seek bond funds, and it could not invest in foreign ventures, such as European or Australian distribution centers.

These limitations interfered with the company's efforts to compete on an equal footing with foreign competitors. Internally, the state-owned company was locked into state (and party) control of its labor force, leaving management little control over wages, recruitment, or employment levels. In fact, YKF had to provide a rather extensive employee benefit package, including housing assistance, food allowances, educational support, and family supplements. It could not directly hire or fire employees without completing a complicated process involving party and labor union committees, and it could not alter its workforce or technology without similar bureaucratic headaches.

Management concluded that YKF had to privatize, restructure its financial base, and eventually seek foreign investors. Beijing authorities supported the idea, because a private plant would probably grow more rapidly than a state-owned enterprise, generate higher tax income, and attract foreign exchange. It would also fit well with the government's political objectives to attract new technology and, in a small way, improve China's record of commerce in support of its bid to become a member in the World Trade Organization.

Several problems confronted YKF's managers as they planned for the new initiative. First, they could not go private without help from major private-equity stakeholders. Second, the textiles and fashion fabrics industry lacked the high margins that readily attract foreign investors. Third, the cost profile in YKF's region of China was no longer an advantage compared to many other areas of Southeast Asia and Latin America. Costs were still low relative to developed countries, and YKF retained several advantages that management felt it could sell. The company had established a quality record and was certain that it could meet ISO 9000 requirements for access to preferential markets in Europe. The company's skilled workforce and reasonably sophisticated technology would allow it to manufacture a diversified line of products. Compared to most regional competitors, YKF also had excellent distribution and expediting systems.

Management was concerned about going forward with privatization plans quickly in 1997 or 1998, due to several international situations. The European Union had discussed imposing quota restrictions, and several nontariff restrictions were already being introduced. For example, the British Wool Council had raised standards for imported garments, thus forcing overseas companies to both conform to ISO guidelines and link up with a British (or EU) company that already had market access. No Chinese companies in the industry could meet these requirements. Germany also introduced protectionist measures requiring inspections of imports and charging premium duties to stem an alarmingly high unemployment rate. Although the German policy measures were aimed primarily at plugging Eastern European market channels, they would effectively block trade with China, as well. France reduced import control points, where merchandise could pass through customs, from four to two—thus strangling distribution by jamming imports into expensive intermediate storage facilities. Further, although U.S. President Clinton had supported MFN, congressional approval was still a question mark in coming years. YKF's executive management council concluded that their best option involved partnering with a "fat cat company with New York and London offices."

By an odd twist of fate, this ideal situation almost developed. A New York agent whose father owned a Shanghai fabric printing company came across sample headers of YKF's jacquard weaves while visiting the offices of Burlington Industries. Headers are small swatches of finished fabric, each about two feet square, attached to a cardboard hanger similar to a standard coat hanger. The cardboard lists design information, company source, and promotional information. A company such as Burlington—perhaps the largest fabric and textile mill in the United States—samples hundreds of these headers from independent companies every month. It selects designs that would fit into its own seasonal collections for clothing or upholstery clients. Burlington creates many of its own fabrics and designs, but it also subcontracts a significant part of its low-end production from overseas suppliers who can create bulk materials at competitive prices.

The New York agent who noticed the headers was a Chinese national who represented his father's Shanghai factory in the United States, calling on clients such as Burlington to solicit orders. When he saw the YKF imprint, he jotted down the information as intelligence about a possible competitor that he would have to investigate when back in China. Indeed, he visited YKF's headquarters pretending to be a New York buyer and was given a complete tour of the facilities. He was so impressed that he recommended that his father try to buy out YKF. The family lacked sufficient resources to complete the deal on its own, and the agent returned to the United States, where he was able to interest Burlington in a possible minority equity stake. Burlington subsequently pulled out when negotiators discovered that they would have to deal directly with the Beijing government rather than a private enterprise, yet the seed was planted. The New York agent subsequently approached several other mills and converters in the United States and the Netherlands, eventually involving YKF in two initial fact-finding meetings with serious negotiators interested in a China investment.

The Dutch offer sought a 52 percent interest in a two-party international equity joint venture with YKF, with no government interest or third-party position. This deal threatened to cut out the Shanghai family, but they suggested to YKF that they could underwrite a buyout from the government together with short-term loans; the new entity partnership between YKF and the Shanghai interests could then deal with the Dutch bidder. YKF management liked the proposal because it would immediately give the venture market access to the EU without restrictive tariffs or prohibitive import duties. However, it would damage relations in the U.S. market. The equity would give the new venture nearly $20 million to fund expansion, an ample amount to completely reposition the company in high-yield quality fabrics and textiles manufacturing. On the down side, the Dutch wanted no part of cotton goods or mass-produced domestic undergarments, which represented about 30 percent of YKF's productive capacity and contributed nearly 36 percent of its profits. To pursue this deal, YKF would have to close down its entire cotton plant or spin it off at a huge loss.

A competing U.S. proposal called for a three-party equity joint venture. YKF and the U.S. bidder would each own a 40 percent interest, and the Chinese government would retain 20 percent through an official investment agency. This arrangement would help the new venture retain its domestic contacts, while unshackling its constraints as a state-owned enterprise. The Beijing authorities did not actively oppose the idea, but they expressed political reservations. Meanwhile, the Shanghai family would be excluded, unless YKF wanted to create a private-equity arrangement with them. The U.S. bidder admitted some interest in working with the Shanghai plant for contract work, but it did not want to invest direct equity funds. YKF would benefit from the deal by gaining immediate entry into the heart of the U.S. market through agreements between the new venture and the U.S. mill, and by licensing a large number of popular designs. Several of the designs are used in very profitable bedding ensembles and household fabrics sold through K-mart and other mass merchandisers. The prospects of very attractive scale economies seemed enticing to YKF managers. The U.S. bidder would provide $12 million in hard currency and assume the full cost of one plant conversion with its own equipment and technical staff. Compared to the Dutch offer, YKF would gain slightly less capital for expansion but better conversion technology.

The crucial issues that surfaced during the early talks concerned management structure. The Dutch intended to co-manage and share profits and losses according to the equity positions. The new venture would officially be headquartered in Maastricht, the Netherlands, and all marketing and transactions would be centered there. YKF would effectively become a manufacturing subsidiary registered under the China Company Act as a foreign joint venture in Guangzhou. The Dutch envisioned intermediate shipments from China to sewing facilities and garment fabricators in Southeast Asia to further reduce costs and upgrade the volume at YKF, which would become a primary supplier of components as well as a producer of finished high-end knitwear. YKF could become part of a system of overseas activities under a family of Dutch-owned facilities. This arrangement left YKF managers uncertain of their future roles in the global enterprise. In contrast, the

U.S. alliance would be primarily registered in China, and it would stand alone, headquartered in Guangzhou. YKF management would become the core executive staff of the local subsidiary with a joint director appointed by the U.S. partner. The new venture would become part of a global network of alliances with potential contract and licensing agreements, much like the Dutch proposal, while retaining its domestic markets and cotton business. Uncertainty clouded its management systems and the roles of local staff, but government would retain a strong influence.

QUESTIONS

1. Outline the advantages and disadvantages you perceive in both negotiations and the market-entry strategies, and explain what they imply for YKF.

2. Explain the benefits and risks of each arrangement for local management control and decision-making. Is one situation better for YKF than the other? Explain your position.

3. YKF may not actually need to privatize or secure a deal with a major foreign partner. It has achieved impressive success on its own. If it remained intact, what options would the company have for penetrating lucrative western markets or for attracting other buyers?

4. What major issues would management have to address in conducting an environmental scan of the conditions facing YKF? What industry and competitive factors would you identify as opportunities and threats? What competitive profile should YKF management consider within Porter's analytical model?

Source: This case was written by co-author David H. Holt in conjunction with Qiu Hai-Xiong and Zhao Wei, graduate students at Zhongshan University, Guangzhou, PRC. It is intended to provide material for classroom discussion concerning the effects of regulatory change on private enterprises in China.

PART THREE

SPANNING BORDERS FOR CROSS-CULTURAL MANAGEMENT

CHAPTER EIGHT

CULTURAL DIMENSIONS OF INTERNATIONAL MANAGEMENT

CHAPTER OBJECTIVES

Define culture in the context of global management.

Describe the effects of values, beliefs, and attitudes on behavior among different peoples.

Contrast four dimensions of cultural differences, and show how human values influence international management behavior.

Explain the concept of Confucian dynamism, and contrast values in a Confucian society with those common in Western Europe and North America.

Illustrate methods for making cultural comparisons and clustering societies in cultural profiles.

Demonstrate how culture influences managerial behavior in multicultural environments.

The fashionable German clothing manufacturer Hugo Boss penetrated global markets on the strength of its "culture-sensitive" men's products, gaining nearly 10 percent growth annually since 1994, and topping $1 billion by the end of 1999. Repositioning Hugo Boss as a global company was a vision of Peter Littmann, who came to the company in 1993 as CEO. Littman was given the challenge of transforming the rather stodgy and provincial company into a major international clothier. He inherited a long-standing company reputation for high-quality traditional men's clothing, based on a single product line known primarily in Germany as *Boss*. For many years, the company's image emphasized clothes that appealed to the mature, strong, dominant male personality; but Littmann began designing clothes for European Yuppies. As the company's new designs caught on, Littmann decided that he had to establish a global reputation for Hugo Boss product lines.

Although the Boss line dominated the company's core business, Littman set out to create what he called "culture brand images" for worldwide distribution. He created three distinct new lines of high-quality clothing, designed especially for men with different value orientations. The old *Boss* line was changed to *Hugo Boss*, and new designs were created specifically for conservative businessmen. The name change softened the company's image, and the combined effort of its designers and marketers became focused on an expanded range of refined products and accessories. A second line called *Hugo* was carefully positioned to appeal to younger men, with styles and materials having a distinctly casual Italian flair. A third product line, called *Baldessarini*, became the company's select line of handmade items; some were designed to order using only the best fabrics, others marketed in limited editions through exclusive men's stores.

"We do not have cheap clothes," Littmann declared in 1997. "All three lines are very high quality." This priority sets Hugo Boss apart from most competitors, who create less-expensive, low-end brands to supplement their primary high-quality products. Clothing manufacturers also tend to mass market to broadly defined groups of customers. Each season, styles may change, but each retailer stocks a company's entire range. In Littmann's view, this practice did not address distinctions among men of different social values and fashion tastes. Consequently, he has positioned each line among retailers who seldom offer more than one of the company's product lines. In Hong Kong, the Hugo Boss line is popular, and stores that feature the name also sell shirts, outerwear, higher-priced lotions, and complementary accessories. The strong male image of the Hugo Boss line appeals to Asian buyers, and today Hugo Boss has flagship retailers in Tokyo, Hong Kong, and Singapore. With more than 160 franchise shops under the Hugo Boss group, this particular clothing line also has penetrated major American and European cities. In Latin countries and areas of major cities that attract younger affluent shoppers, the Hugo brand has excelled. With a more faddish image and riskier continental styles, Hugo is marketed through selected retailers that compete against other clothiers such as Armani. Meanwhile, Baldessarini is almost hidden within the industry as a deliberate effort to provide exquisite clothing to a discerning customer.

For each product line, Littmann developed independent design and marketing organizations to create a distinct approach to clothing. Manufacturing methods, personnel selection, and marketing activities reflect the values of their target customers. For example, new employees are screened for their sensitivity to cultural trends in each country, and Littmann himself was recruited for his multicultural experience. Littmann was born in Prague, educated as an engineer, and worked in the carpet industry, where he headed a company with international sales. His experience also included being vice president for Rosenthal AG, a porcelain company known worldwide for its excellent glass products and designs. Drawing on a lifetime of working with multicultural customers, Littmann was well suited to the Hugo Boss challenge. During the four years following his appointment, company profits increased by more than 73 percent, fed by a dramatic expansion into more than 20 new global markets. An important success factor, according to Littmann, was not trying to create special clothing for everyone, but to create clothing with special meaning for those who the company serves.[1]

Littmann retired from Hugo Boss and was replaced by the current CEO, Werner Baldessarini, in November 1998. However, Littmann's vision of global expansion and exquisite clothing with culturally sensitive brands has continued. The company has since grown by more than 10 percent annually, added complementary accessories, and recently introduced a women's designer-wear division. The supervisory board (equivalent to a board of directors) and the management board of operational executives represent a rich mixture of several nationalities with young men and women as well as older members who can bring a culturally diverse dimension to design and marketing strategies. Baldessarini himself is German-Italian and the head of the fashionable Baldessarini clothing design family, with a vision that Hugo Boss will one day be "the fashion statement for customers of every cultural persuasion."[2]

THE NATURE OF CULTURE

The term *culture* appeared throughout earlier chapters in references to different ethnic groups, nations, and peoples. It also has become part of management terminology for organizational value systems as a symbolic suggestion for cohesiveness within a reference group. These partial explanations fail to convey the importance of the concept to an understanding of human behavior, yet no consensus has emerged to give a clear definition of culture. Indeed, comprehensive anthropological studies reaching back more than a century have only narrowed the field to slightly more than 160 definitions.[3] This chapter does not address the comprehensive issues of culture; it tries to provide a sensible explanation that can be used in the context of international management. The definition used here is offered by Gary P. Ferraro in his book, *The Cultural Dimension of International Business*: "**Culture** is everything that people have, think, and do as members of their society."[4]

The definition is rather broad, yet the operative words provide a robust framework for understanding differences among cultural groups in organizations and world societies. People *have* things—physical objects, tools, weapons, languages, laws, music, art, material resources, technologies, and systems—that are both real and symbolic. Collectively, what a society has helps to explain its historic development and to define what it is today. People *think*, and therefore a society develops systems of ideas, values, attitudes, beliefs, and ideologies. Collectively, these represent *shared interests* that help to explain religious preferences, political mandates, customs, and a wide variety of social relationships. People *do* things, and within a particular group or society, what is done represents a collective prescription of accepted behavior. These three elements—*have*, *think*, and *do*—represent culture when they collectively represent behavior of members in a society. Culture is an anthropological concept that relates to a *shared system* of beliefs, attitudes, possessions, attributes, customs, and values that define group behavior. In this context, culture can relate to a family, an ethnic group, a commercial organization, or a society.

An important aspect of culture is that it is *learned*.[5] Everyone is born into a culture, and must subsequently learn how to behave within that society. Culture is transmitted through interaction with others in a reference group or a community, and by living within and experiencing that environment. Everyone therefore adapts to a system of values that have evolved as a cumulative effect of past generations. Each member of a society learns its values in terms of patterns of possessions, symbols, languages, relationships, religious beliefs, eating habits, and other dimensions of life. They also learn what *not* to do, to have, or to think. Consequently, children will learn "taboos," or become ingrained with ethnic, religious, or ideological prohibitions. They will share both biases and beliefs. This does not mean that everyone will always behave the same; but most of the time, most people will behave in predictable patterns and within boundaries defined by their cultures. Therefore, culture is a constructive abstract of expectations that determine limitations to individual behavior as accepted members of a society.

Culture evolves through a learning process that begins in early childhood with parental guidance and continues throughout life with systems of laws, regulations, social sanctions, and ethical standards of conduct. Formal education systems implement society's expectations by reinforcing these values while preparing youth in necessary knowledge and skills; as a result, methods of education differ widely among the world's societies. In Scandinavian countries, for example, students are evaluated more on their classroom behavior than on actual grades, and students work hard to control emotions, develop friendships, and be courteous. In Norway, grades do not exist in primary and middle schools. In contrast, Japanese children are pressed hard to excel, and they compete fiercely for grades to gain entrance to higher education. Nevertheless, once Japanese students reach tertiary levels, their grades are relatively unimportant compared to demonstrating their acceptance of cultural norms. Consequently, Japanese college students will maintain acceptable grades, but also join college clubs, volunteer for civic duties, and strive to become officers of student associations.[6]

From a management perspective, these shared systems of learned patterns of behavior influence our perceptions about authority, leadership, work attitudes, and ethical practices. On a practical level, cultural antecedents influence how workers perceive quality performance, job responsibilities, their roles in decision-making, and whether they will readily accept directions from superiors. Cultural norms also influence daily conduct, such as punctuality, conformance to safety standards, and personal hygiene.[7] In more important situations, culture affects attitudes toward male and female roles, and toward social perceptions of human rights. Therefore, subtle differences between value systems of any two cultural groups (even within a given society) can generate tremendous friction. Managing in an international environment populated by many potentially different competitors and alliances requires sensitivity to these cultural differences and to appropriate ways of doing business. The "Global Viewpoint" feature illustrates several difficulties of doing business in a Muslim culture as an example of these challenges.

Understanding Why Cultures Differ

All human beings face similar problems. Some problems are universal, such as meeting basic physiological requirements for food, water, clothing, housing, and security. These resources are limited, and each society must develop systematic ways of acquiring food and water, providing clothes and housing, and protecting its members. Even among small tribal communities, solutions to these problems evolve into systems of social and economic behavior. For example, certain tribal members hunt or gather

GLOBAL VIEWPOINT

You Can't Compare a Refrigerator with Nature

An appliance company in Iran manufactures refrigerators named after the nation's most prominent mountain, but it faced censorship of advertisements that included images of the mountain. Mount Damavand, an 18,000-foot snow-clad peak near Teheran, was photographed as background for the company's Damavand refrigerators. It seemed like the perfect pitch to promote the appliance. Then the government's Ministry of Islamic Guidance stepped in to pull the plug. "You can't compare a refrigerator to nature," the censor said. "That's God's territory."

Not long ago, Iran's ruling clerics forbade all advertising, but a form of Islamic capitalism now allows advertising within certain guidelines. To guard against moral decay, Iranian ads may include no images of women, no English, no celebrities, no jokes, no product claims, and no evidence whatsoever of sex, aristocracy, or anything American. A billboard to advertise lingerie, for example, showed only a plain green box with the words "soft and delicate" written alongside. Unfortunately no one understood the ad.

In another incident, Aladdin Vinegar, a common product marketed throughout the Middle East, created a mascot of an Aladdin character holding a bottle of vinegar. An ad showed the mascot saying, "It's not magic. It's 25 years of experience." The mascot and the advertisement were banned because Iran, being a Persian nation, holds centuries-old grudges against Arabs—and Aladdin was an Arab.

American companies are not immediately affected by Islamic law as practiced in Iran, because only a few American products reach that country. Nevertheless, GE found itself the victim of zealots who disfigured its signs, and Parker Pen was censored for using "suggestive" words on its packaging. The French telephone firm Alcatel had to redesign advertising that showed a picture of a man wearing a tie—very unorthodox dress in Iran. Billboards for TV sets sold by Japan's Sharp Ltd. were painted out because they implied some "entertainment value" for television.

Islamic law is equally important in countries other than Iran, but practices vary. Malaysia combines a significant Muslim population with a mix of nationalities and religions including Hinduism, Buddhism, and Christianity, so people make accommodations for one another. For example, Christians avoid displaying crosses or other religious symbols, and Buddhists mute their temple bells and cymbals except on religious occasions. Islamic followers in Malaysia accede to the presence of mixed western fashions and Malaysian clothing, but they maintain strict rules within their own communities. Islamic women cannot hold passports or travel without their husband's permission. They dress fully covered from head to foot in traditional attire, seldom speaking to men unless addressed first. Therefore, Motorola, which employs many women in its Malaysian operations, often must hire women through interviews with their husbands, and female employees remain restricted to certain types of jobs by Islamic law. In its Malaysian facilities, South Korea's Lucky Goldstar—one of the country's largest producers of television sets—provides separate rest areas for women and men as well as prayer facilities for Muslim and non-Muslim employees. To accommodate Hindu employees, the firm allows idols and altars in protected places on factory grounds.

Source: Peter Waldman, "Please Don't Show Your Lingerie in Iran, Even if It's for Sale," *Wall Street Journal*, 21 June 1995, p. 1. Also see P. S. Ching, "Doing Business in East Asia," *Straits Times*, 20 March 1996, p. 6.

food, others cook, make clothes, construct shelters, or attend to children. In more economically developed societies, roles evolve not only for work and domestic affairs but also for maintaining the systems of production and distribution required to support large communities.

As early tribal societies evolved, they reflected the conditions of their natural environments. Those in continental Europe found ample game to hunt for food and clothing, forests for wood fuel and building materials, and seasonal changes that replenished water. Their environment also required sturdy homes and methods of storing food for winter months. Adapting to these conditions, Europeans settled in agricultural enclaves that were often self-sufficient and isolated from one another. In contrast, Scandinavian societies evolved along rocky shorelines with little game to hunt, short growing seasons, and severe weather conditions. They came to rely on seafood and trade with coastal cities—often, as Viking history illustrates, traveling tremendous distances to raid or to acquire resources. Desert societies of Asia and North Africa, unable to grow sufficient crops or to store food, had to travel great distances in search of water and food for themselves and their flocks. Consequently, people in each of these regions developed substantially different systems for acquiring basic resources. In each tribe or community, people worked out solutions to their physiological problems, and patterns of behavior became established through generations of development.

Eating habits among desert peoples, for example, emphasized foods that would not spoil or that could be hydrated with goat milk or small amounts of water. Dry grains, figs, and lean dehydrated meats became common, and dangerous foods such as pork were carefully avoided. Subsequently, many food products and methods of food preparation were either institutionalized or banned through religious tenets to protect societies from disease. Islamic law, for example, prohibits followers from eating pork; and in many instances, people cannot touch the skin of a pig. Northern Europeans favor ham and pork products. The kosher rules followed in the Jewish faith help ensure safe food preparation. Over the centuries, similar religious teachings have evolved in many societies to institutionalize how foods are acquired, prepared, and eaten.

Each society also has developed patterns for mating and child rearing to perpetuate itself. Agrarian cultures traditionally require labor-intensive fieldwork and herding, and large families working together can achieve greater economies in farming than small families working independently. Thus farming societies have typically encouraged large families, and in many cultures there are polygamist marriages that nurture new generations in a cooperative community. Social systems for marriages have evolved to protect dependent children, and therefore to secure each society's future through new generations. Marriage often has less to do with romance than with perpetuating the species, and it is not uncommon today to find arranged marriages, taboos against marrying outside one's religion or social class, or prohibitions against mixed ethnic relationships. Marriage is therefore part of a broader system of social control that assures population growth and perpetuation of a society's cultural infrastructure.

Future generations of a particular culture are ensured by social and marital customs, but also by systems of education that perpetuate a society's values, beliefs, and knowledge. Education systems in Japan, for example, emphasize group harmony and loyalty. They also stress rigorous conformance to group and social norms, and to diligence for work. These are values that mirror the broader profile of Japan as a collectivist society. In contrast, education in the United States encourages self-achievement and independence. These reinforce concepts of self-determination, debate, and innovation that characterize the United States as an individualistic society.[8] Each nation also explains history in its own cultural context, thereby ingraining beliefs and values in future generations, even though they often conflict with teachings of other societies.

Communities also evolve social control systems or mechanisms to ensure that cultural values and practices are observed in most instances by most people. Ultimately, controls are needed to avoid anarchy. These are the laws and regulations put in place to provide a formal system of protecting individual and group rights within society.

Federal, state, and local laws ranging from traffic rules to penal codes constitute an elaborate system of institutionalized behavioral norms. Few people in any society will obey all its laws all the time, and idiosyncratic behavior is accepted more in some societies than in others; but these control systems establish limitations within which behavior can vary without penalty. When the majority of people follow the laws, society can solidify its systems of values and beliefs, thus enhancing its internal security.

Societies also nurture deeply ingrained supernatural beliefs, and despite the ridicule of other societies, these beliefs are important to understand.[9] Many beliefs form part of religions, or they have been adapted to religious practices; but many others are simply cultural elements in the sense that they have emerged through generations of social conditioning. In China, for example, the concept of *feng shui* prevails even though no scientific evidence exists to support the concept. Feng shui is the art, or belief, of spatial continuity. It teaches that what people construct (houses, buildings, offices) and configurations in which people arrange their physical possessions (placement of office desks near windows or leaving a doorway open to face a stairway) can be good or bad in the sense of welcoming good spirits or discouraging bad spirits. In the Chinese way of thinking, ignoring feng shui invites problems from bad spirits—even perhaps calling forth dragons from within the earth. To avoid disasters, contractors and architects often consult feng shui masters before work begins on a building, and once a building is completed, a feng shui master will ceremoniously inspect the premises and either approve its opening or recommend alterations.

The headquarters of the Hong Kong and Shanghai Bank, one of the 10 largest bank holding companies in the world, was found to have "bad feng shui" when it was completed because the front entrance faced directly to the harbor. The expansive entranceway was viewed as too inviting for devils that might lurk in the harbor waters. To rectify the problem, two giant bronze lions were crafted and carefully positioned at the street entrance to ward off malevolent spirits. Although this accommodation may seem puzzling to westerners, had the bank not acted on the recommendations of the feng shui masters, many Chinese customers probably would have taken their banking business elsewhere. In a related incident, a police district in Hong Kong had experienced several unsolved rape cases targeting schoolgirls, and a feng shui mystic laid the blame on a poorly positioned district police office. The problem was resolved by attaching a huge iron weather vane shaped like a fighting cock atop the police building and placing several mirrored windows in the offices to ward off evil spirits. Inexplicably—at least to western observers—assaults on schoolgirls ceased, and in the year that followed, several major cases were solved.[10]

Cultural variations can be enormous with respect to supernatural beliefs, religions, social values, marital patterns, education, and social controls. These are only a few of the dimensions that comprise small parts of the total interrelated system of a culture, yet they are shaped by a society's efforts to respond to its sphere of universal problems. Therefore, people solve their community problems and explain their behavior within the context of the environment in which they live. They maintain steadfast beliefs in their own ways, as long as conditions in their environments support their beliefs. In fact, when values are deeply embedded—perhaps through religion, laws, or supernatural beliefs—environmental changes may have little effect. Refrigeration, for example, is common enough in the Arab world to permit safe processing and storage of pork, but Islamic law is far more important than technological change, and pork remains a forbidden food.

The world has an extraordinary number of distinct cultures. In Africa alone, there are more than 800 separate cultures with distinct languages, customs, and values. Only a few of these cultures are defined by national boundaries.[11] China may have as many

GLOBAL VIEWPOINT

SOLAR ECLIPSE DARKENS MANY OFFICES

The solar eclipse of October 1995 was seen most prominently in Thailand, where superstitions gained as many headlines as the eclipse itself. Four native-language newspapers, including Thailand's largest mass-circulated newspaper, *Thai Rhath*, ran front-page stories and features full of astrological predictions for nearly a month before the occasion. Most warnings spelled doom and gloom for the country. Supported by astrological calculations, soothsayers predicted famine, inflation, flooding, and other national calamities, including a military coup by the end of the year.

The eclipse was the third this century, and crop failures and civil unrest had indeed followed previous events. Researchers described the dire threats as nonsense, explaining that seasonal weather may have been difficult and political demonstrations self-serving, but neither resulted from eclipses. That assurance aside, Thailand's prime minister, Banharn Silpaarcha, known for his superstitious beliefs, made a point of leaving the country on a visit to New York during the eclipse. He was one of many Thais who chose to go abroad, fueling more than a 100 percent increase in travel bookings by wealthy Thais during the eclipse period.

Events of the year also prompted many people to take precautions. Thailand's queen mother and the former prime minister both died unexpectedly during the year, Bangkok experienced unusual floods, and meteorologists predicted more than eight major monsoon storms for the season. Nakhon Sawan, an area that lies directly in the path of the eclipse, was devastated by floods, and political infighting had led to military intervention to prevent a coup. Also, the royal princess changed her plans for the week and substituted a secret itinerary, and many merchants announced that they would close their doors. Nearly one-third of the population was expected to shut themselves indoors and cover their windows.

Hindu mythology explains eclipses as the result of an act of a misfit god, Rahu, who drank Vishnu's sacred water to achieve immortality. He was discovered by Vishnu, the most powerful god in Hindu beliefs, who hurled a disc at Rahu, cutting him in half. Unfortunately, Rahu had already absorbed the water in half of his body, so he lost only the mortal lower half. In revenge, he ate his brothers the sun and the moon, thus causing the first eclipse and centuries of periodic reoccurrences accompanied by disasters.

In an effort to placate Rahu, anything connected to the number 8 formed part of religious devotions. No one knows exactly why the number 8 is so mysterious; in many Asian cultures "8" is ominous, often associated with death—yet in others, it is a lucky number. In any event, during the recent eclipse, people with the number 8 on identity cards, driver's licenses, addresses, license plates, and telephone numbers felt compelled to follow certain rituals to ward off trouble. For eight weeks prior to the eclipse, devotees made offerings to Rahu of eight black objects every Wednesday night. (Black also has significance to thwart the effects of an eclipse.) These objects included black whiskey, black sticky rice, black candles, and so-called black "thousand-year-old" eggs (eggs that are fermented in salt with spices, often for several months, but commonly called black or thousand-year-old eggs due to the discoloration and fermented taste). Some worshippers burnt incense, created blackened images, and scattered eight joss sticks in auspicious places. In centuries past, it was not uncommon to make animal and human sacrifices; but today the rituals are limited to preparing blackened chicken meals as sacrifices to the mythical misfit.

Some businesspeople welcomed the eclipse. Hotels with prime viewing sites were fully booked nearly a year in advance. Everyone in the tourist trade enjoyed windfalls, and those who supplied the offerings had record sales. However, foreign business representatives who did not fully appreciate the significance of the event found themselves in trouble. Many employees did not show up for work, and those who did often avoided work on any product with a hint of a connection to the number 8. At one telephone assembly plant, every eighth item on the assembly line was mysteriously rejected (some say purposely broken), units with 8 in their serial numbers were packed off or avoided, and one executive's car with the number 88 in its license plate was hauled away to ward off bad luck at the company's offices.

Little significant damage accompanied the eclipse, and many welcomed it as a once-in-a-lifetime event worth celebrating. But for many others, it was a rude awakening to the power of cultural beliefs and the importance of preparing for even the most unusual superstitions.

Sources: Charlotte Bevan, "Superstition over Today's Solar Eclipse Has Fired Forecasts of Death and Destruction in Thailand," *South China Morning Post*, 24 October 1995, p. 17. Also see Atthaviroj Sritula, "Ignore Rahu at Your Peril," *Thai Rhath*, 18 October 1995, p. 12; and A. Roth, "Thais Edgy, but Eclipse Business Is Booming," *Asia Today*, October 1995, 24.

as 200 distinct cultural groups. Canadians can be identified by their French, English, or native heritage, which is further distinguished by geographic locale, religions, or tribal antecedents. So culture is not a "national phenomena," although we tend to describe cultures based on national identities. The point is that a vast number of cultures and subcultures exist with an equally vast number of differences, yet they all have distinct community solutions to universal human problems.[12]

Cultures within Cultures

Clusters of cultural values within a particular society are identified as subcultures. Every society has subcultures, yet people often ignore the fact that societies other than their own have similar disparate groups. In the United States, for example, there is an obvious difference between Caucasian Americans and African Americans, between northerners and southerners, between New Yorkers and Los Angelenos. Buffalo has a reputation for a large Polish population and a significant number of Catholics, and Santa Fe has a rich mixture of several Southwest Native American cultures and Hispanics. But are these distinctions sufficient to describe any particular aspect of American culture or, indeed, American society as a whole? Has anyone met a typical New Yorker? Most Americans sense cultural differences in people from other areas, and they stereotype certain groups by their ethnic roots, religions, creeds, or skin colors; but subsidiary cultural systems do exist, and they have distinctly different patterns of behavior.

Group differences within subcultures can be as sensitive as differences between broadly defined cultures. For example, at a recent academic conference, an African American colleague was presenting a paper on discriminatory wage practices, citing research that showed how African American business professors were underrepresented, paid less, and promoted less often than members of other groups in a number of universities. He also emphasized the lack of similar discriminatory practices in Nigeria, where he had recently spent a sabbatical. He noted that he traced his roots to Nigeria and felt that Nigerians represented a cohesive society with more equitable rules and less discriminatory practices than those in the United States. At the end of his presentation, another African American colleague stood up to question the remarks, sternly denouncing Nigeria as an elitist tribal society that had come close to committing genocide in the 1960s against the Ebo tribe, from which the questioner had descended. A second colleague raised her hand and asked if the presenter would classify her as African American. The obviously light-skinned woman revealed that she was of Arab descent from Morocco, and she resented the restriction of the label *African American* to Blacks in America, when she too was from Africa and American. Clearly, she identified with a different subcultural group. Similarly, the individual with the Ebo heritage resented being identified together with the African American colleague with a Nigerian tribal heritage.

Nearly all societies have their subcultures and distinct groups, often with their own languages, religions, beliefs, and unique customs. Nevertheless, it is common to identify them collectively within their national political boundaries. There are societies with relatively more homogeneous populations than others, such as Japan, so generalizations about national cultures are not entirely unreasonable. However, generalizations are usually not credible. For example, when someone says, "that is typical American behavior," it probably has very little meaning. When a Scotsman is asked about his country (meaning the United Kingdom) and the person asking the question refers to "England," the Scotsman is likely to be rather annoyed. When Chinese are asked where they are from, they tend to reply in terms of a specific city or province, such as Shanghai or Guangdong, even if they are second- or third-generation American citizens. Chinese often identify with their ancestral roots, such as being Cantonese, Manchu, or Hui, and many Chinese attach great importance to these regional differences.[13] In Malaysia, the Cultural Ministry created a slogan to celebrate Malaysia's National Day that meant, in English, "Culture Determines Achievement." This was an attempt to emphasize national unity for economic development, but two translations led to open demonstrations and street riots. One of those translations in Malay (an unofficial but common language) meant "culture makes you tired." The other translation in Behasa Melayu (the majority dialect) implied that having a sense of national culture is unattainable. Rioters accused government of subverting their national language, and demonstrators were angry that government would try to impose a single cultural perspective on their country.[14]

Tourists often stub their toes on cultural issues, but they are usually forgiven for their ignorance. International managers are not as easily forgiven. If they are newcomers to a foreign post, they may be permitted minor infractions, but major errors are seldom tolerated. Unlike tourists, expatriate managers are expected to adjust quickly to their host environments, and therefore cultural blunders can incite severe ridicule. One way to gain insight to cultural protocol is to first understand one's own cultural perspective. If managers can come to grips with the evolution patterns of their own cultures, then they can more easily recognize how practices have evolved in other societies. With that recognition, they can adapt more easily to foreign cultures and accept differences among people with whom they work.

Cultural Sensitivity

Trying to reconcile cultural differences on a global scale is like opening a Pandora's box of potential misunderstandings. Successful international managers take great care to avoid misunderstandings by trying to understand cultural differences, which is a conscious effort to be *culturally sensitive*. **Cultural sensitivity** means to have the empathy to accept cultural differences without allowing one's own values to surface in unproductive or confrontational ways.[15] It implies that an individual has become sufficiently aware of differences to function effectively without becoming openly judgmental. Expatriate managers do not have to abandon their values to be empathetic, but they must avoid imposing their personal cultural beliefs on others. Even when "their way" seems to be right, and other ways seem to be wrong, managers must accommodate cultural differences to be effective. It is not a matter of right or wrong, or win or lose, but of avoiding *ethnocentric* or *parochial* behavior.[16]

The concept of ethnocentrism was introduced earlier, in the context of business ethics, and as a perplexing dimension of international strategy. Ethnocentrism is a way of saying that people tend to believe their way of doing something is always best (or right), and subsequently, they impose those beliefs on others. Parochialism is similar,

Pepperoni may be the number one pizza topping in the United States, but tastes are more eclectic around the world. In Japan, Domino's Pizza responds to local tastes and customs by offering specialities such as Chiki-Teri, All-Star Seafood, and All-Star Vegi.

and it implies an expectation by people that others will readily adapt to their standards of behavior. Ethnocentrism carries the connotation of conscious imposition of one's viewpoint, while parochialism implies a lack of sensitivity born of ignorance. In a study of Japanese managers working in Germany, the Japanese viewed their German counterparts as abusive, argumentative, blunt, and uncooperative. In contrast, the German managers felt that Japanese managers were arrogant, reclusive, and indecisive. Both tried to avoid imposing their viewpoints on the other group, but both believed that their foreign colleagues were trying to influence them to behave according to the other group's values. Consultants studying the situation found that neither the Germans nor the Japanese understood how the other group made decisions. No conscious imposition was intended by either group, yet neither the Japanese nor the Germans could reconcile the other group's behavior. The study involved nearly 30 Japanese-German alliances, and in nearly all instances, relationships were strained.[17]

Managers can learn to be less parochial by expanding their knowledge of other cultures; they can also learn how to become sensitive to potential misunderstandings. The ultimate goal is to be able to honor differences in cultural values, and if irreconcilable differences occur, to recognize these hazards before misunderstandings can escalate into serious conflicts. This is difficult enough for individuals working entirely within their own cultural environments, but for managers working in cross-cultural situations, it can be a tremendous challenge.

CULTURAL VALUES AND BEHAVIOR

The single most important question asked by anyone involved in international affairs is, "How do other people behave?" Diplomats wonder how foreign officials will behave in talks, what protocols will be appropriate, and what perceptions foreigners will have concerning the business at hand. Export managers wonder how foreign consumers will behave, how they will respond to products or packaging, and what marketing techniques will be appropriate. International managers in foreign assignments pose the question in an effort to understand how their foreign colleagues will make decisions, how employees will respond to leadership styles, and what values foreign workers place on wages, quality workmanship, and personal relationships. Domestic managers of foreign enterprises wonder how they should behave to be consistent with expectations of their foreign owners, and in multicultural work environments, managers question how employees of different backgrounds will get along together. Obviously there is no simple answer to the question, but it is extremely important to ask.

People behave according to their *values*, *beliefs*, and *attitudes*, which collectively constitute culture in a given society. **Values** are basic assumptions about how things should be in society. They are convictions regarding what is right or wrong, good or bad, and important or trivial.[18] Values are subconsciously ingrained and may be impossible to measure or to consciously articulate. They are the accumulated effect of culture and social conditioning reflected in a social psyche. Consequently, values are extremely difficult to change.[19] For example, the United Arab Emirates (UAE) is an Islamic country with laws that require women to cover themselves from head to toe. Women are not supposed to reveal their ankles, and indeed, men also are expected to keep their feet and ankles covered. In early 1997 Haworth Inc.—a Holland, Michigan, furniture maker— sent $3.5 million in desks to the UAE under a government contract, and subsequently had them all rejected. Haworth had to modify the desks by extending the front panels to the floor to avoid exposing workers' ankles. This was a very costly error.[20]

Beliefs are conscious assertions about what is right or wrong, what is good or bad, or whether something exists or not. Unlike values, beliefs are not necessarily ingrained. They are malleable and somewhat more fragile than values, and therefore changeable. For example, a society may put great *value* on a particular religion, yet there may be hundreds of different *beliefs* by people of the same religion about how to worship. Beliefs can also be subtle. For example, IBM's direct marketing division operates from U.S. headquarters for worldwide sales, and key staff are drilled rigorously in foreign customs that would affect the company's business. Consequently, IBM is adept at avoiding mistakes that conflict with local beliefs. In China, IBM found that its direct marketing business could not rely on mass-produced offers or mail-order promotions. Each letter or offer had to be handwritten, simply because postal promotions are considered an "affront." Although the Chinese readily accept mass advertising and some use of catalogs, they believe that dignified offers require personal communications.[21]

Attitudes are preconceived ideas held by individuals about appropriate behavior, and although attitudes are formed within the context of social values and group beliefs, they are usually idiosyncratic. Individual attitudes do not necessarily reflect social values or beliefs, yet those of influential people can create serious difficulties in foreign relations. For example, Ecuador was, for decades, among the top oil-exporting countries in the world. At one time, it ranked third in the world outside the Middle East and North Sea fields. Since 1993, however, Ecuador has tumbled far down the list of oil producers, and the country has gained a reputation for unfriendliness to foreign oil interests. Observers blame ousted president Addala Bucaram for this change, since he made a political point of attacking foreign investors through unpredictable policy changes and turned Ecuador into what an American oil executive called a "maddening place to do business." Bucaram was known as "El Loco" for his policies, and a new government is trying to repair international relations.[22]

Cross-cultural research, and in particular research on international management, is concerned with identifying patterns of values on which to predict behavior within foreign societies.[23] Understanding these patterns of collective values helps managers to adapt easier and to avoid many cultural blunders. Understanding systems of beliefs is also important, yet because beliefs are less intransigent than values and in many instances individualistic, they are less valuable as foundations on which to base assumptions of behavior. Attitudes are important to the psychology of individual relationships, and while they cannot be ignored, understanding individual attitudes does not provide insights about cultural behavior required for effective foreign relations. Management's task is to reach deeply into cultural values to try to understand the fundamental forces that shape behavior within a society.

HOFSTEDE'S MODEL OF CULTURAL DIMENSIONS

Dutch researcher Geert Hofstede is noted for the largest cross-cultural study of organizational behavior ever conducted. During the 1970s, Hofstede queried more than 116,000 IBM managers from 72 countries to create a comparative profile of cultural differences related to management.[24] Hofstede and his colleagues have continued to pursue cross-cultural studies and to refine a global model commonly called the *four dimensions of culture*.[25] This work is somewhat controversial because it attempts to classify patterns of behavior for individual countries without taking into account subcultural differences or ideological orientations. Nevertheless, the model has significantly changed the prevailing view of behavior in various cultures and, in particular, how to understand work-related values among many of the world's nations.

The Four-Dimension Model

Hofstede defined *culture* as the aggregate of values, beliefs, and customs that define common characteristics of a human group. Therefore culture defines the human group, much like personality explains an individual's identity. Hofstede then explained culturally based value systems as comprising four dimensions: *power distance, uncertainty avoidance, individualism,* and *masculinity*. These dimensions are identified from collective attributes, or value orientations—such as achievement, creativity, autonomy, and self-determination, among others—that provide a relative measure of group characteristics. Taken together, they represent a society's predispositions to react to human problems with relatively strong or weak emphasis on each value orientation. These predispositions are used in cross-cultural research as well as practical management situations to contrast values and patterns of behavior among nations and organizations.

Power Distance

Power distance is the degree to which human inequalities are emphasized. A culture high in power distance would place great value on hierarchical status and authority. In this sense, it implies that less powerful members of a society or an organization accept their subordinate status, and they are expected to conform to authority enjoyed by members in superior positions. Figure 8.1 illustrates a continuum of high and low power orientations. Hofstede found that Mexico, Indonesia, Pakistan, India, and Japan are particular nations that scored high in power distance. In these societies, for-

FIGURE 8.1
Power Distance Scale

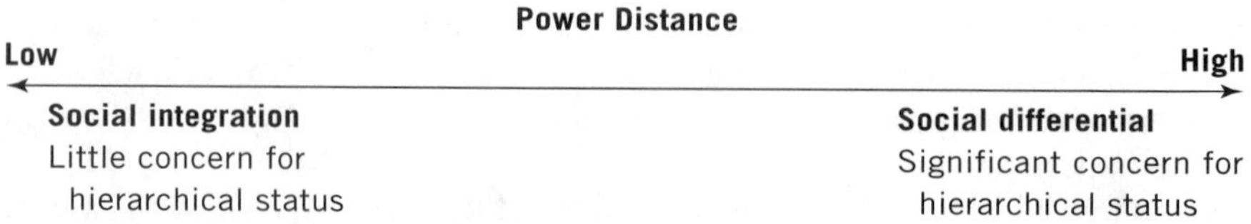

Power Distance

Low   High

Social integration   Social differential
Little concern for   Significant concern for
  hierarchical status   hierarchical status

mal hierarchical authority is respected, and employees seldom violate a chain of command or openly question decisions by their superiors. In contrast, countries that scored low on power distance included Australia, New Zealand, the United States, Denmark, and Finland. In these cultures, superiors and subordinates were found to be more at ease with shared decision-making, and employees were not expected to rigidly conform to authority.

Hofstede discovered an interesting twist to these results in later research; some societies high on power distance were found to embrace systems that reward social differentiation. This implies that upward mobility within a centralized or hierarchical environment is valued. Examples of countries that fit this description included Spain, Belgium, and Italy. A further refinement from the research showed that a society low in power distance could be expected to reduce human inequalities. These cultures also tend to reject differences in social strata, yet respect the right of individual self-achievement. The United States, Canada, Great Britain, Israel, and the Netherlands were among those in this category.[26]

Individualism

The dimension of **individualism** is the degree to which independent initiative is valued relative to collective effort. A culture high in individualism would emphasize personal achievement, innovation, autonomy, and adventure. A stronger interpretation of this dimension is that individuals are likely to put themselves and their families ahead of others, often neglecting the broader needs of society. This is an extreme interpretation, yet many societies reveal patterns of behavior that rank relatively high on the individualism scale shown in Figure 8.2. They include the United States, Australia, and Great Britain, where individual achievement is clearly a mark of success. In contrast, a society low in individualism would likely endorse group harmony, social order, conformity in group relationships, deference to reference group norms, family relationships, and loyalty to consensus viewpoints. These societies exhibit collectivist behavior, and they include many Asian, Latin American, and West African nations.

Uncertainty Avoidance

This dimension reflects the degree to which ambiguity prompts anxiety in a society. A culture high in **uncertainty avoidance** seeks to reduce ambiguity, and members of the society feel relatively uncomfortable in unstructured situations. Figure 8.3 illustrates this continuum. This measure also relates to a society's philosophical or religious beliefs in absolute truth. Cultural traditions based on Judaism, Christianity, and Islamic fundamentalism reflect clear beliefs in absolute truth that exclude similar claims in other societies. Consequently, societies that value their images of ultimate truth seek definition and clarity in both past and future events. Japan, Greece, Portugal, and Korea are examples of societies that seek to avoid uncertainty, leading to relatively well-articulated laws and expectations for scrupulous conformance to social standards.

Individualism

Low   High

Collectivity   **Self-determination**
Concern for group   High concern for
   harmony versus   achievement and
personal achievement   personal growth

FIGURE 8.2
Individualism Scale

FIGURE 8.3
Uncertainty Avoidance
Scale

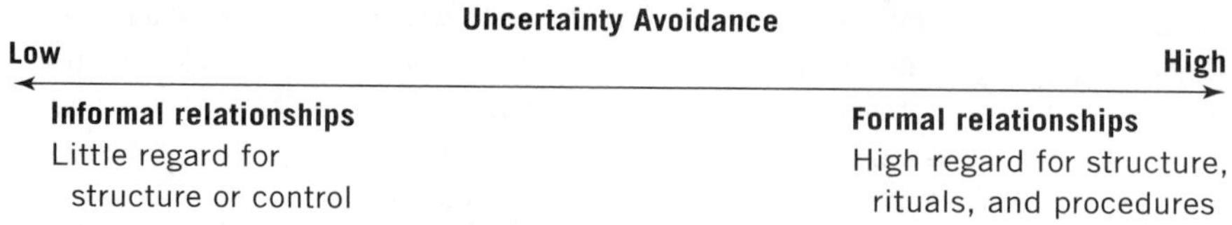

Uncertainty Avoidance

Low ← ——————————————————————————— → High

Informal relationships
Little regard for
   structure or control

Formal relationships
High regard for structure,
   rituals, and procedures

Many South American countries fall along less certain points of the continuum, and France scored relatively higher in uncertainty avoidance than its European neighbors, suggesting that France is less tolerant of ambiguous social standards.

In contrast, societies with dualistic social philosophies or multidimensional religions place little value on any absolute truth. Instead, these "uncertainty-accepting" cultures practice religious and social relativism, and they tolerate ambiguity relatively easily within their organizations. The list includes, for example, the United States, Canada, Great Britain, and several African nations. Company practices in these societies are likely to be more informal and relaxed than those companies in societies with highly structured environments. Also, they often are less concerned with ceremonies and company rituals, such as those associated with Japanese or Korean companies, and within these societies, job mobility is more readily tolerated.

Masculinity

The fourth cultural dimension, **masculinity,** is the degree to which motivational behavior is associated with value systems as described in masculine versus feminine terms. This dimension is not concerned with biological contrasts, but with behavior conveniently described in gender terms. A society scoring high on masculinity tends to value decisiveness, assertiveness, and competitiveness. These reflect men's values that emphasize control over events, perhaps wealth accumulation, and concern with material possessions. In contrast, women's value orientations tend to be associated with nurturing relationships and human interaction, compared to more competitive behavior among men. These polar views are shown in Figure 8.4.

Gender labels and assumptions of differences in values are controversial, but the descriptions are helpful in explaining behavioral orientations toward work, decision-making, and relationships. In masculine-oriented societies such as Japan, Austria, Mexico, and Argentina, men are generally expected to hold the primary jobs. Women are expected to remain at home and raise families. Organizations are male dominated and assume characteristics such as assertiveness that create competitive and often highly stressful work environments. Male offspring are groomed for work roles and higher-level education, while female children are relegated to supporting roles. So-called feminine societies include the Scandinavian countries, Portugal, Spain, and several Pan American nations. In these cultures, women are prominent in

FIGURE 8.4
Masculinity Scale

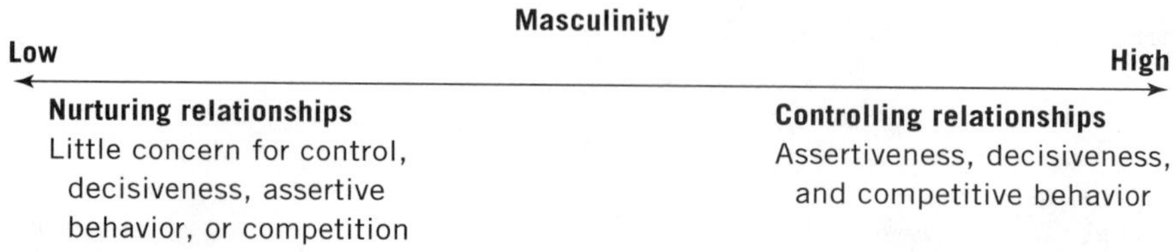

Masculinity

Low ← ——————————————————————————— → High

Nurturing relationships
Little concern for control,
   decisiveness, assertive
   behavior, or competition

Controlling relationships
Assertiveness, decisiveness,
   and competitive behavior

management and professional fields, and the work environment is less assertive. Hofstede found that organizational competition is less apparent in these societies compared to male-oriented cultures, which also suggests less value placed on individual achievement.

Dimensional Relationships and Externalities

Hofstede's four dimensions are individually useful for categorizing cultural values, but combined, they also reveal patterns of social behavior. A significant tendency toward power distance, for example, is generally associated with collectivist behavior; so most societies that score high on power distance also score relatively low on individualism. Consequently, cultures that emphasize individualism, such as the United States, score relatively low on power distance. A practical interpretation suggests that Americans are relatively independent minded and value self-directed behavior. It seems consistent, therefore, that they also put relatively little emphasis on social status or group conformity.

The combination of power distance with uncertainty avoidance yields interesting results. Several countries combine high power distance and strong uncertainty avoidance. A practical interpretation of this combination is that a society such as France maintains clear differences in social status through hierarchical authority coupled with intricate labor laws and social legislation that preserve these status differentials. Thus, people expect little ambiguity in formal roles or job descriptions. Strong uncertainty avoidance also is associated with a low rank on masculinity, but Hofstede's research is inconclusive on this point.[27]

These interrelated dimensions present several dozen patterns of behavior. They also illustrate how difficult it is to identify well-defined sets of cultural values. The relationships suggested by Hofstede are oversimplifications, and each has exceptions and paradoxical explanations. Hofstede has been able to resolve some of these inconsistencies by mapping "clusters" of societies with general cultural similarities.[28] These clusters provide some consistency in explanations so that, for example, a cluster of Anglo countries and a cluster of Scandinavian societies both seem to have little regard for maintaining power distances or creating intricate regulatory systems to avoid uncertainty. Put another way, countries in these two clusters put little value on hierarchical power, and they are comfortable with informal relationships. Figures 8.5 through 8.7 illustrate Hofstede's mapped clusters, and the abbreviations he uses for countries are listed in Table 8.1.

A thorough explanation of all possible combinations and clusters would be exhausting, but a detailed study of Hofstede's cultural maps can be interesting for those concerned with specific comparisons of national patterns of behavior. Bear in mind that clusters represent generalizations. Also notice that each of the four dimensions represents a continuum, so that when societies are categorized as being high or low on a particular variable, few actually rank near the polar extremes. To the contrary, most countries have moderately high or low rankings, with some so close to the midpoint that there is room for conjecture. Studies in Japan, for instance, support the contention that the Japanese maintain relatively greater power distance than Anglo societies, thus placing greater value on organizational status; but the Japanese propensity toward group harmony moderates the severity of differences found in other societies that have extremely rigid power hierarchies.[29] Consequently, there is evidence beyond Hofstede's cultural dimensions that factors peculiar to each society can either moderate or intensify patterns of behavior.[30] Many of these factors reflect ideological priori-

FIGURE 8.5
A Plot of Power
Distance against
Individualism

Source: Adapted from Geert
Hofstede, *Cultures and
Organizations: Software of the
Mind* (London: McGraw-Hill
U.K., Ltd., 1991), p. 54. Used
with permission.

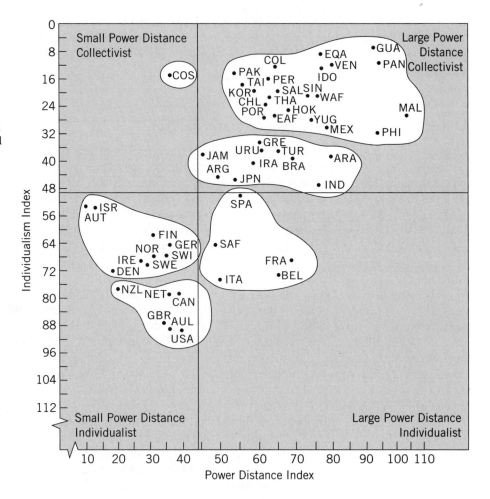

ties, such as socialist influence or extreme communist mandates that accentuate power-based systems with centralized authority.[31]

Economic development also influences the results. Less-developed countries are likely to have relatively fragile legal and commercial infrastructures, which result in economic instability. These difficulties often lead to polarized power structures and governing systems in an effort to control societies where both economic and political ambiguities persist. In contrast, developing nations with strong growth rates are likely to introduce greater regulatory controls while, paradoxically, softening power differentials in hierarchies as market economies emerge.[32]

Researchers also found that technological advances such as those in telecommunications systems alter patterns of commerce, education, and human relations. Technological development reduces status barriers and social ambiguities while empowering people with information and encouraging personal growth.[33] Globalization also has important effects. As borders soften between nations, more international commerce occurs, foreign investment accelerates, and multicultural environments increase.[34] These influence value systems in the sense of accommodating values of other societies or adopting foreign practices. Research on globalization is sparse, and little is known about actual changes in cultural values, but there is some evidence that developing economies are acclimating to values common to free-market societies.[35]

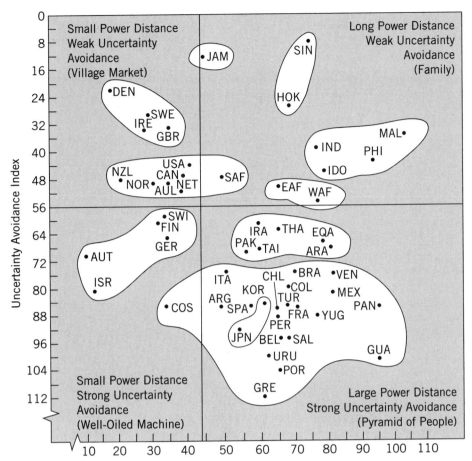

FIGURE 8.6
A Plot of Power Distance against Uncertainty Avoidance

Source: Adapted from Geert Hofstede, *Cultures and Organizations: Software of the Mind* (London: McGraw-Hill U.K., Ltd., 1991), p. 141. Used with permission.

The interdependence between Hofstede's four cultural dimensions coupled with external factors suggests that cultural maps may offer useful approximations of behavioral tendencies, but they do not account for evolution of cultures. Societies change, ideologies change, and governments are usurped. New technologies introduced to developing countries require new organizational systems and, with them, new patterns of work and human relationships. International trade and foreign investments break down barriers between nations and open opportunities for new relationships. A further consideration, addressed in later chapters, is that interactions between people from different cultures result in reciprocal influences. For example, international managers bring their particular value orientations to overseas assignments, thus influencing their foreign associates; yet in turn, they are influenced by the experiences of foreign cultures in which they work. When societies have significant international interests, reciprocal influence can be considerable.

Limitations to Hofstede's Model

Hofstede has been criticized on a number of issues, and although the criticisms are valid, they do not outweigh the importance of his work.[36] His initial study, though global in scope, was limited to IBM; critics point out that IBM employees are not

FIGURE 8.7
A Plot of Masculinity against Uncertainty Avoidance

Source: Adapted from Geert Hofstede, *Cultures and Organizations: Software of the Mind* (London: McGraw-Hill U.K., Ltd., 1991), p. 123. Used with permission.

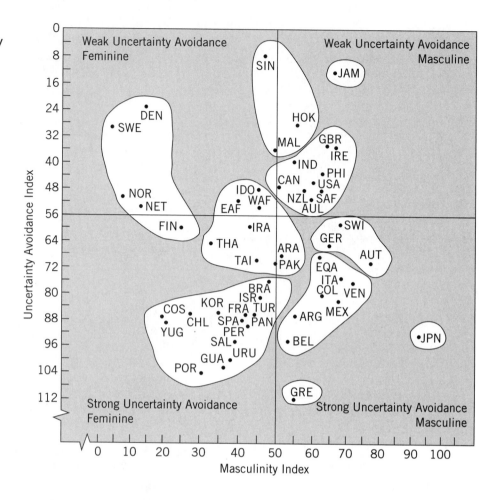

necessarily representative of society at large. In addition, Hofstede worked mainly with managers, not a full complement of employees. He recognized these limitations and subsequently broadened his scope of inquiry to a wider range of employees and organizations. He also accumulated results from other researchers using his methods. Generally, the patterns of cultural behavior found in the initial study have been upheld.[37]

Two serious limitations have plagued Hofstede, and these have been the focus of much of his research during the past decade. First, his study is western in context, as are most of those that subsequently used his methods. Specifically, words, terms, meanings, and interpretations in the research instruments have reflected European or American values. Because his surveys involved value judgments, many terms were bound to have different meanings to respondents from different cultures. For example, questions about "spirituality" were answered in European terms in the context of organized religious practices or values based on Judaism, Christian, or Moslem beliefs; but many Africans and Asians responded in terms of nonreligious customs. "Being spiritual" did not mean simply attending religious services; it was often interpreted as being superstitious. The second issue was that most of Hofstede's work on value systems was abstracted to national identities without regard for subcultural differences within a given country. A nation-bound perspective also ignores the tran-

TABLE 8.1

COUNTRIES AND REGION ABBREVIATIONS IN HOFSTEDE'S RESEARCH

ARA	Arab countries (Egypt, Lebanon, Libya, Kuwait, Iraq, Saudi Arabia, UAE)	JAM	Jamaica
		JPN	Japan
		KOR	South Korea
ARG	Argentina	MAL	Malaysia
AUL	Australia	MEX	Mexico
AUT	Austria	NET	Netherlands
BEL	Belgium	NOR	Norway
BRA	Brazil	NZL	New Zealand
CAN	Canada	PAK	Pakistan
CHL	Chile	PAN	Panama
COL	Colombia	PER	Peru
COS	Costa Rica	PHI	Philippines
DEN	Denmark	POR	Portugal
EAF	East Africa (Kenya, Ethiopia, Zambia)	SAF	South Africa
		SAL	El Salvador
EQA	Equador	SIN	Singapore
FIN	Finland	SPA	Spain
FRA	France	SWE	Sweden
GBR	Great Britian	SWI	Switzerland
GER	Germany	TAI	Taiwan
GRE	Greece	THA	Thailand
GUA	Guatemala	TUR	Turkey
HOK	Hong Kong	URU	Uruguay
IDO	Indonesia	USA	United States
IND	India	VEN	Venezuela
IRA	Iran	WAF	West Africa (Nigeria, Ghana, Sierra Leone)
IRE	Ireland		
ISR	Israel	YUG	Former Yugoslavia
ITA	Italy		

Source: Adapted from Geert Hofstede, *Cultures and Organizations: Software of the Mind* (London: McGraw-Hill U.K., Ltd., 1991), p. 55. Used with permission.

scendent nature of ethnic cultures that are borderless. These two problems have had important implications for studying Asian cultures. Hofstede and others who study cultural values discovered conflicting results in China and India, where multiple cultures exist. Studies of ethnic groups have also been difficult because of migration. For example, Chinese and Indians are among several major ethnic groups found in many other countries.[38] The western semantic bias also presents major difficulties for explaining Asian, African, and several Latin American societies. In many instances, a social philosophy characterized as eastern (or Confucian) has influenced value systems since long before western doctrine emerged.[39]

Hofstede chose to view these issues as opportunities for further research, and his early endeavors have subsequently become the building blocks for a significant number of studies in eastern culture. Some limitations remain, such as the common practice to think in terms of national cultures and thereby generalize about people according to whether they are French, Chinese, or American. These shortcomings become obvious in places like the former Yugoslavia, now splintered through ethnic strife, or the former Soviet Union, which was an amalgamation of more than 160 ethnic societies. The realigned Central and Eastern European countries have not only severe ideological and economic differences but also significant ethnic differences that preclude consistent interpretations of cultural norms.[40]

Extending the Four-Dimension Model to Confucian Societies

To address the problems of western interpretations, and to learn more about Asian cultures, Hofstede teamed with Michael Bond to develop a fifth, eastern dimension called **Confucian dynamism.**[41] This dimension is comprised of eight distinct values that have special significance in cultures that reflect a Confucian social philosophy. Societies demonstrating a high degree of Confucian dynamism would rank all eight values as being characteristics of their cultures; but they would rate four values of high importance, and concurrently rate four values as unimportant *relative to one another.* Those considered important are (1) persistence or perseverance; (2) ordering relationships by status and observing this order; (3) thrift; and (4) having a sense of shame. Those considered relatively unimportant are (1) personal steadiness or stability; (2) protecting one's "face"; (3) respect for tradition; and (4) reciprocation of greetings, favors, or gifts. These eight values are summarized in Table 8.2.

Hofstede and Bond explained these values specifically in terms of East Asian entrepreneurship and the unusual success of private-enterprise development in non-communist Asian economies. "Persistence and thrift," for example, were associated with aspiring entrepreneurs. "Ordering relationships by status and observing this order" implied a sense of predetermined social structure; yet in Confucian social philosophy, it was associated with "filial piety" and complementarity of social relationships. Therefore, entrepreneurship as practiced among Asian families was found to be enhanced by formal business connections, but also by informal associations. "Having a sense of shame" was explained as a form of self-efficacy in the Asian context. This does not have a direct western translation; but in Confucian societies, being self-effacing is a pattern of behavior that enhances group cohesiveness. In contrast, low ratings of unimportant values such as "personal steadiness" and "respect for tradition" suggested resistance to Confucian doctrine, and consequently a greater propensity to embrace change or to take calculated risks. A low rating on "saving face," or less concern with protecting one's image, would allow greater freedom to take risks or to pur-

TABLE 8.2

ELEMENTS OF CONFUCIAN DYNAMISM

Relatively Important
Persistence or perseverance
Ordering relationships by status and observing that order
Thrift
Having a sense of shame or a self-effacing attitude

Relatively Unimportant
Personal steadiness or stability
Protecting one's "face"
Respect for tradition
Reciprocation of greetings, favors, or gifts

sue individual achievements. "Reciprocity" is a social expectation entrenched in Confucian ethics, and it implies a system of dependence or social debt. In the Confucian dynamism model, it is explained as a social function; however, there is a closely associated concept in China called *quanxi*, which is a system of reciprocal favors usually associated with commerce.[42]

It may sound confusing that a society rated high in Confucian dynamism would score low on any of the eight values. Indeed, the values are all Confucian, but Bond's research revealed a consistent pattern of high scores for the four important values and low scores for the four unimportant values among the world's fastest-growing economies, including Japan and the four Asian dragons of Hong Kong, Singapore, Taiwan, and South Korea. This pattern indicated a strong *future orientation* that embraced change and growth. In contrast, those Confucian societies that scored high on the unimportant variables also scored consistently low on the important variables. These societies were static and entrenched in traditions that impeded economic development, thus indicating a *current or past orientation*. Confucian dynamism is not proprietary to Asian cultures. Parallel values were found among a number of South American and African populations, as well as people from Indian Ocean nations. However, the composite concepts were conspicuously missing in western value systems. Specific considerations, such as saving face, merely puzzled individuals in western societies; yet the notion of an absolute truth was equally puzzling to those from eastern cultures. Other Confucian behavior, such as self-efficacy and reciprocity, do not have comparable meanings in western societies.[43]

CULTURAL COMPARISONS

Cultural comparisons are equally important for corporations and for individual managers. From a strategic viewpoint, companies need to be able to understand foreign markets, customer behavior, factors that influence investment decisions, and relative advantages of locating facilities overseas. From a personal viewpoint, individual managers need to be able to differentiate patterns of behavior, work values, standards of conduct, and the cultural antecedents of people with whom they will interact in management, working, selling, and community activities. Grouping countries with similar characteristics into clusters and creating country-specific profiles are two methods of categorizing patterns of behavior. These help companies and managers to develop the adaptive skills necessary for international business.

Country Clusters

While Hofstede was developing his four-dimension model, Simcha Ronen and Allen I. Kraut were studying similarities among countries with respect to employee work habits and leadership methods.[44] They clustered their findings into five groups, based on approximately 4,000 respondents surveyed in 15 countries:

- *Anglo-American*, including Australia, the United Kingdom, and the United States
- *Nordic*, including Denmark, Finland, and Norway
- *South American*, including Chile, Mexico, and Venezuela
- *Central European*, including Austria, Germany, and Switzerland
- *Latin European*, including Belgium and France

Ronen and Kraut demonstrated that individual societies often have similarities enabling companies to establish regional operations compatible with countries within a particular cluster. This helped companies like Procter & Gamble to enter the European market with branded commodities developed specifically for Central European customers, while modifying those products for Latin Europeans. Companies conduct cluster analyses, based on compatible profiles of employment and leadership methods within regional groups of nations, in order to locate their foreign production and distribution facilities. Companies also employ studies based on Ronen and Kraut's model to evaluate personnel assignments and overseas appointments.

Following these early studies, Ronen teamed with Oded Shenkar to identify eight global groups consisting of 46 countries.[45] These clusters, shown in Figure 8.8, were based on several separate studies conducted during the 1970s and early 1980s. Ronen and Shenkar analyzed four categories of organizational variables from the studies, briefly described as: (1) work goals; (2) job satisfaction; (3) leadership and organization; and (4) interpersonal roles. The eight clusters were based on what Ronen and Shenkar called "attitudinal dimensions" which defined general patterns of attitudes about work habits, leadership, organizational procedures, work roles, job satisfaction, personal needs, compensation, rewards, and interpersonal relations. In addition, countries were positioned within their clusters according to *per-capita gross national*

FIGURE 8.8
A Synthesis of Country Clusters

Source: Simcha Ronen and Oded Shenkar, "Clustering Countries on Attitudinal Dimensions: A Review and Synthesis," *Academy of Management Journal* (September 1985): 449. Used with permission.

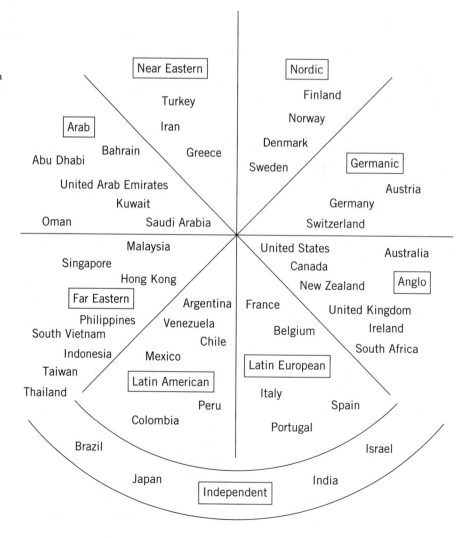

product. The logic of using this measurement was that economic development evidenced by a high or rising per-capita GNP significantly influences cultural values related to work customs and organizational behavior.[46]

The Ronen and Shenkar model has been controversial, due in part to the underpinning assumption of a strong connection between GNP and convergent cultural values. Further, it defined an "independent" category, beyond the eight clusters, that included Brazil, Japan, India, and Israel. These nations were excluded from the eight clusters, but they were not grouped into a separate cluster. Each was considered unique in the Ronen and Shenkar research. Brazil, for example, did not reveal a value system similar to those of other Latin American countries; instead, it demonstrated patterns of attitudes reflecting colonial ties with Portugal. Nevertheless, Brazilians did not fit along with Portugal in the group of Latin Europeans. Israel clearly stood apart from Arab or Near Eastern clusters as a composite nation of global immigrants sharing a similar ethnic culture, yet one with regional foundations. Japan has always practiced a distinct Asian culture, and its society developed in isolation from its neighboring countries. Finally, India could not be easily identified with Asian or Near Eastern cultures. Nevertheless, the clusters provide a useful framework for more detailed studies of cross-cultural management.

Country Profiles

A country profile is a focused analysis of characteristics that can help describe a foreign society. The extent to which a company goes to gather information about a particular society depends on why it needs the profile. For example, if a company is only interested in exporting to a foreign market, a profile may be little more than a brief marketing report with a reasonable description of economic buying power and customer preferences. On the other hand, if a company intends to make a significant investment in a foreign society or manage foreign operations, it will require a comprehensive environmental analysis, as described earlier in Chapter 5. Researchers have identified six categories of cultural information that may be included in a country profile: material culture, social institutions, man and the universe, aesthetics, language, and religion.[47]

Material Culture
This category describes the economic and technological capabilities of a society that determine its material standard of living. An economically underdeveloped country, for example, may not have the per-capita income to afford products or services common in more affluent societies. When Procter & Gamble entered the China market in 1989, the company initially introduced a range of soaps and personal care products that included disposable diapers and sanitary napkins. P&G soon realized that a vast majority of Chinese families with an average annual income of little more than $400 could not afford such luxuries. The company wisely withdrew its disposable diapers and sanitary napkins. Instead, the company focused on hand soaps and shampoos, which were very successful. Procter & Gamble learned that while the Chinese quickly accepted new soaps and hygienic products, their material cultural had not yet adapted to disposable personal care products.[48]

Technology determines the ability of a society to use machine tools, processes, and production techniques. It also relates to the ability to utilize services, such as checking accounts or telecommunications. Many developing countries lack the basic infrastructure to generate sufficient electric power to support computer systems or production equipment. Many also lack telecommunications, transportation, water supplies, or waste systems to support industrial development. These conditions also affect behavior, because societies that lack experience with sophisticated tooling or industrial maintenance cannot supply the skilled workers needed for economic development. In many instances, local employees simply have no sense of how to use or maintain technology required for quality performance and profitability by a foreign company. Consequently, a host country that seems to offer a comparative advantage based on low wages or inexpensive resources may still be unattractive to a multinational enterprise.

Social Institutions

All societies have formal institutions of government, education, and commerce that significantly influence the risk profile associated with foreign investment decisions. But they also have informal or social institutions that influence cultural characteristics. Patterns of family life, for example, will determine whether a husband, wife, or both will work, and what values will prevail concerning family loyalties. In India it is common for companies to hire relatives, and with an entrenched caste system, the country practices exclusionary hiring practices that would be unacceptable in most western societies. Japan has a dominantly masculine society in which women are expected to remain at home, or if employed, to accept subordinate positions with few promotion opportunities. An American woman living in Japan may be very uncomfortable with the level of masculinity; but most Japanese women fully support the gender differentials as part of their culture.

Islamic cultures institutionalize powerful social and legal systems associated with their religion. Saudi Arabia, for example, has "cultural police" on patrol, watching for offenders who violate Islamic codes of dress or personal conduct. Some societies are paternalistic, such as China and Korea, and behavior within social hierarchies reflects long-standing Confucian values of conformity to a prescribed system of authority. Leadership methods, decision-making, and work standards differ substantially in these societies from those in North America and Europe.

Man and the Universe

This category was labeled before the age of inclusive language. Perhaps a better term might be *inherited beliefs and rituals*. Many cultures—and subcultural groups within a society—believe in varying supernatural phenomena, ghosts, fortune-tellers, the psychic power of healing, and unique ceremonies, all of which have tremendous effect on cultural values. These are distinct from religious beliefs, yet they often influence how business is conducted in a foreign society.

For example, it is common in many Near Eastern societies to seek astrological advice before concluding a contract or meeting with a business associate. The Chinese avoid doing business on days identified on ancient Chinese calendars as risky or fateful. They also associate certain numbers with good or bad luck. The number 8 means "prosperity" or "good fortune" to the Chinese, and a good day to sign a contract would be the eighth day of the eighth month. (Many Chinese also identify dates using lunar calendars.) In Hong Kong the number 8 is restricted, because it actually has commercial value. A license plate with the number "A8" sold at auction recently for nearly $50,000.[49] Meanwhile, the number 4 signifies death; there are no telephone exchanges in Chinese societies beginning with multiple fours or with 14, which means "sure death." Some restaurants will not serve meals with four items on a plate. From a management perspective, pricing and labeling products must be number sensitive, and there are preferential days and times to schedule meetings or to entertain guests.

Aesthetics

Art, music, drama, and folklore are more than artistic expressions. They are often symbolic of values held in a society, or reflections of traditions and beliefs. Foreigners often do not appreciate the significance of what might be perceived as off-key music or odd dramas, yet these performances may be quite important to the host society. Certain ceremonies and gestures also have special significance in foreign societies. For example, the Japanese are known to bow as a form of greeting; but they use many different bows, from slight nods to very deep bows. The former may be an informal greeting or acknowledgment, while the latter is meant to show deference to a superior of some importance. The act of bowing is a refinement of feudal rituals to reaffirm unspoken acknowledgments of rank and status.[50]

Language

Learning a foreign language is often important, but when developing a country profile, it is equally important to understand language usage and patterns of oral and written communication. Singapore, for example, has four official languages: English, Chinese, Malay, and Tamil. Business and government activities are conducted officially in English, yet most practical business affairs are pursued in several dialects. As part of the Malay Peninsula, Singapore has a significant Malay population. Since Malays are predominately Islamic, communicating with them involves certain language requirements and sensitive situations calling for a bilingual capability. Tamil is an Indian dialect common to a minority caste in India that found its way to Singapore, Sri Lanka, and other British colonies in the nineteenth century. Consequently, doing business in Singapore often requires multilingual capabilities ranging from product labeling to managing a multicultural workforce. Subtle language meaning also influences choices for product names, company logos, advertisements, and most company communications.

Religion

Without a doubt, religion clearly influences cultural values, and it often has a significant effect on business activities. For example, Islamic societies recognize Friday as a day of worship. Saturday is the Jewish Sabbath. In Christian cultures, Sunday is the day of worship. In non-Christian societies, most people work Sundays, and in most of the world's societies, a normal workweek is 5½ days. (The half-day off varies from Wednesday afternoons in Britain, when stores and banks often close, to Saturday afternoons in Southeast Asian nations.) In many instances, half-days reflect religious practices; but even during normal working hours, Muslims stop to pray several times each day. Religious holidays present problems for scheduling work, and seasonal patterns of vacation time often coincide with traditional pilgrimages or religious ceremonies. Religious tenets also restrict financial transactions, such as limitations on debt in Islamic societies and extreme restrictions that forbid interest or restrict profits.[51]

Food preparation is also regulated by religious beliefs throughout the subcontinent of India, the islands of the Indian Ocean, the Middle East, and much of North Africa. For example, slaughter is permitted only for certain animals, and then only as essential foods. Also, the means of killing animals must conform to religious codes, including prayers chanted for each animal as it is processed. Religion dictates eating habits, which often means excluding particular types of food such as pork for Muslims and Jews, prescribing foods on certain occasions, or prohibiting certain combinations of foods.[52]

Religious practices are also interpreted differently within subcultural groups. For example, two French businessmen in Afghanistan recently held a small party for several Afghan colleagues and office workers. The women dressed in western clothes; and although the Frenchmen were careful to observe Islamic laws and avoided music and alcoholic beverages, a neighbor reported the party to authorities, who promptly arrested everyone there. The Frenchmen were convicted of "evil and corrupt sessions with half-bare women," (i.e., the women were unveiled), and the Afghan businessmen were convicted of "insulting the Afghan nation and violating Islam" for looking at corrupt western magazines and having trimmed beards (forbidden by strict Taliban Islamic codes). The offenders were sentenced to severe lashings and imprisoned; the women were to be "re-educated," but reports neglected to explain the meaning of this sentence.[53] Often, even local hosts do not entirely understand social expectations that reflect religious values, and in many societies correct standards of behavior are unpredictable.

IMPLICATIONS FOR MANAGERS ON FOREIGN ASSIGNMENTS

The most successful international managers are those who are capable of adapting their behavior to be effective members of multicultural organizations. That includes not only job-related factors but also the ability to live in a foreign society and to accommodate cultural differences among their employees and among members of the host-country society. There is no formula for acquiring these skills, but through various methods of education and training, managers can achieve a level of cultural appreciation that will allow them to approach their foreign assignments mindful of potential cultural blunders.[54] Unfortunately, too many expatriate managers cannot adapt, and many multinational companies are hesitant to send managers overseas where they risk failure in their assignments.

Cross-cultural research consistently reports that managers who fail in their assignments do so because of intercultural problems, not because they are technically incompetent.[55] Unfortunately, failure rates cannot be accurately measured, but the number of expatriates who face career disruptions due to difficulties with their assignments is probably double that for domestic managers. These difficulties result in reassignment, recall, demotion, or disenfranchisement (having their careers sidetracked by dead-end assignments or isolation). Perhaps as many as 40 percent suffer career setbacks in foreign assignments.[56] (Expatriate management and career problems are addressed in depth in Chapter 11.)

On the positive side, the increased pace of globalization has emphasized international education, and the combined efforts of company-sponsored training, improved methods of orientation for expatriates, and fundamental changes in international curricula have significantly reduced problems associated with foreign assignments. Also, because more multinational companies have better career opportunities for international managers, the traditional concepts of competitive advancement through mainstream functional departments are becoming less important. This heightened demand for capable managers has prompted many multinational corporations to create innovative programs, such as cross-cultural management exchanges and cultural mentoring, to fill international positions. (Human resource training and development are topics addressed in Chapter 13.) Consequently, notable companies now have many senior executives—including some chief executives—who were foreign born and promoted through international assignments. Examples of American companies include Ford, IBM, P&G, Colgate-Palmolive, GE, Digital, Hewlett-Packard, Compaq, and

Heinz.[57] Nevertheless, cultural problems are persistent, and managers rarely appreciate the challenges that they face in overseas assignments.[58]

An important part of resolving cultural adaptation dilemmas is to achieve a conscious understanding about cultural diversity. This insight develops through a journey of education and experience that can start by building a better understanding of one's own home culture.[59] Hofstede's research on dimensions of cultural values provides a useful model for this line of inquiry. For example, understanding that Americans will demonstrate a greater sense of individualism, relatively less concern with power distance, and greater tolerance for ambiguity often helps American managers recognize how their values correspond to those from different societies. A practical interpretation of this example is how difficult it will be for an American manager to adapt to an assignment in Japan or Mexico, where both countries strongly avoid uncertainty, maintain relatively large power distance relationships, and place little value on individualism. However, the very fact that a manager consciously understands these contrasting value orientations can reduce cultural shock.

American managers working in Japan expect a certain degree of culture shock. Indeed, much is written about Japanese behavior in U.S. management literature, so those Americans who have taken time to study Japanese systems will be alert to potential cultural dilemmas. However, they may not be as alert to potential problems if assigned to Mexico, which now has so many foreign companies operating there that few people perceive the serious cultural gaps that exist. Organizations in Mexico demonstrate even greater power distance than in Japan. They maintain strict differences in status and rank, and decision-making reflects paternalistic characteristics of Confucian social ethics. These differences are reinforced by social expectations for group conformity to authority, and individualism is discouraged to a far greater extent in Mexico than in Japan. Consequently, many American companies are caught off guard by perplexing behavior in their Mexican subsidiaries. In contrast, Japanese managers working in Mexico have little difficulty adjusting to that society; yet like managers from all societies working in foreign countries, they will face cultural shocks. Some contrasts will be more difficult to accommodate, and others will be relatively easy to reconcile; but in each situation, managers must understand their own value systems before they can determine how to adapt to their host-country environments.[60]

Managers can prepare themselves for foreign assignments by developing contrasting cultural scenarios and country profiles, but nothing replaces actual experience. No document or report can explain the sights, sounds, odors, foods, living standards, or recreational behaviors that characterize another culture. Vacation travel seldom provides the insights required, because tourists rarely get past superficial activities to participate in local cultures. Travel is a valuable experience, but while local people tolerate tourists—even those who make gross cultural blunders—expatriates are given little time to accommodate themselves to their surroundings. Blunders are not easily forgiven, and minor improprieties often have major consequences.

For example, when a British executive went to Oman to close a deal, he packed a miniature bottle of gin purchased at an airport. After the formal negotiations, he celebrated with a quiet drink in the privacy of his hotel. He was unaware that even a drink in private was unacceptable practice under the country's strict Islamic law, and when his indiscretion was discovered, the executive was asked to leave the country. Later, his company was expelled from Oman because the hosts felt that neither the executive nor his company respected its laws. In another incident, an American insurance executive arrived in Germany to take part in a claim negotiation. Dressed nicely, but wearing cowboy boots, the American portrayed a sense of informality that offended European executives. Negotiations failed; the American went home and was later told that his behavior had led to contract cancellations. As a final consequence, his company was exempted from further business with the German clients.[61]

Entire books chronicle the cultural blunders of businesspeople, and although many examples seem odd or humorous, most incidents have had disastrous results for the transgressors.[62] Studying these books can be enlightening, but the main point is that managers in the international environment must develop a cultural sensitivity and an open mind to adapt to unfamiliar societies. The next several chapters address specific problems related to cultural differences with communications, negotiations, and labor relations. These subjects constitute several major considerations for becoming a successful international manager.

REVIEW QUESTIONS

1. Define *culture* in the context of global management. How do cultural values evolve?
2. How do *values*, *beliefs*, and *attitudes* differ? How do they influence international managers in their decisions?
3. Describe Hofstede's power distance dimension of culture. How does this principle affect management authority and decision-making?
4. Describe the cultural dimension of individualism, and contrast it with the concept of collectivism. What problems would you envision for a manager from a culture with one orientation working in the other?
5. What does the cultural dimension of uncertainty avoidance measure, and what does it imply for organizing work and exercising leadership activities?
6. Describe the cultural dimension of masculinity. Ignoring physical and gender characteristics, what traits do high and low positions on a masculinity scale imply?
7. Explain the concept of Confucian dynamism. How are Confucian values different from those in western societies?
8. Explain how managers can use information from cultural clusters and country profiles to adapt themselves to host-country customs and norms.
9. Researchers have identified several categories of culture. What are they, and how could they influence a company's foreign activities?
10. What steps would you recommend to someone preparing for an overseas assignment that would help that person adapt to an unfamiliar cultural environment?

GLOSSARY OF KEY TERMS

Attitude   A preconceived idea about appropriate behavior or about what is proper, improper, important, or unimportant to an individual.

Belief   A conscious assertion about what is right or wrong, or good or bad or about an existing condition.

Confucian dynamism   A behavior dimension composed of eight attributes that describe relatively important and unimportant values in eastern cultures.

Cultural sensitivity   The capacity to accommodate differences in cultural values by understanding the antecedents of a society rather than judging foreign behavior according to one's own cultural assumptions.

Culture   Everything that people have, think, and do as members of their society.

Individualism   The degree to which a society values independent initiative and self-achievement.

Masculinity   A society's association of motivational behavior with values such as its emphasis on control over events, decisiveness, assertiveness, and competitiveness, traditionally characterized as manly values.

Power distance   A society's emphasis on perceived human inequalities that foster rank and status differentials.

Uncertainty avoidance   A society's intolerance of ambiguities, leading to high value on rules, order, and conformity to social systems and controls.

Value   A basic assumption about how things should be in society—what is right or wrong, good or bad, important or unimportant—constituting ingrained characteristics of a majority group psyche.

EXERCISES

1. Make a list of the common problems faced by most societies, and then identify how your home culture has developed solutions to these problems. What environmental factors in your society led to these solutions? How were they translated through the generations to become ingrained as cultural values? Distinguish between values and beliefs in your answer, and give an example of each.

2. Select another culture to study, and identify the universal problems and solutions prominent in that society. What environmental factors might have influenced that society's development, and what values can you identify that persist today? Compare your home culture with that society's values regarding these universal problems, and summarize the differences.

3. Using Hofstede's four dimensions, and the Hofstede and Bond fifth dimension of Confucian dynamism, select a country in which you would like to work. Develop a profile of that country, and make a prioritized list of differences that you would have to address as an expatriate manager there.

PHARMACIA: MERGERS WITH UPJOHN AND MONSANTO ARE CULTURAL CHALLENGES

Pharmacia is not a well-known name among American multinational pharmaceutical companies, but most people will recognize the names Searle, Upjohn, and Monsanto. These three major corporations, together with the former Swedish company Pharmacia S.A., are now under one corporate banner following Pharmacia's acquisition of Monsanto on March 31, 2000. Monsanto had purchased Searle & Co. in 1985, forming a separate ethical drug division while repositioning its core business under agricultural products and biotechnology research for food and crop development. The Swedish arm complemented both drug and horticulture with European sales and research facilities in Britain, France, and the United States.

American executives, once part of Michigan's Upjohn Corporation, became part of Pharmacia's international executive group after Upjohn merged with the Swedish firm in 1995. In the years between the Upjohn merger and Monsanto's acquisition in 2000, management groups from five rather different countries found themselves pulled together in one multicultural organization. The Americans and Swedes became intensely familiar with London, where executives from the two main headquarter groups jointly formed a new "world headquarters" for Pharmacia & Upjohn Inc. The headquarters was located in London because an unobtrusive building near Windsor Castle was the only site the executives could agree upon.

Selecting a corporate headquarters took months of negotiations, foreshadowing subsequent problems of merging two very different corporate cultures. Initially, the Americans wanted their Swedish counterparts to move to Kalamazoo, Michigan—a proposal that was unilaterally rejected. An alternative suggestion was to relocate in Mississippi, where Upjohn had extensive R&D facilities. Managers from both Michigan and Stockholm rejected this option. Italy was considered, since Pharmacia had substantial subsidiaries in southern Europe, but the site was rejected because few managers in either group felt comfortable with language and cultural requirements of an Italian location. France also was quickly rejected due to the country's complex legal requirements, language barriers, and just gut-level resistance. London presented a relatively bland compromise. Neither partner had facilities in London, no one had particular connections or biases in the United Kingdom, and all executives could at least communicate in English.

Having decided on London, the managers had to agree on a style of building. Americans rejected an upscale building with modern facilities. They also objected to Swedish proposals for open-style rooms and conference areas without walls. Instead, the Americans wanted well-insulated offices appointed in such a way as to reflect rank and status of executives. They also wanted lockable rooms and secure conference areas. The solution was to remodel an aging red-brick Victorian building with closed office spaces for Americans and open space for the Swedes. When Italian managers arrived as part of the executive group, they felt suffocated by the American areas and too exposed in the Swedish areas. The Italians also wanted access to flower gardens and large new windows. The French, mainly Parisians, simply felt affronted by everything as being "forced into a stifling Anglo environment."

The company has been buffeted by hundreds of relatively minor business-culture problems since its inception, but major conflicts have also surfaced. Soon after the headquarters problem was resolved, the new American chief executive, John Zabriskie, moved in and brought with him a style of management described as "brisk, fast-lane, driven, and a full charge to take no prisoners." Within three months of relocation, Zabriskie left in what was called "a mutual agreement over unreconcilable management differences." Jan Ekberg, the CEO who replaced Zabriskie, said that difficulties had little to do with Zabriskie himself, other than his obvious entrenched American approach to business. Still, cultural problems created friction among the ethnically diverse employees throughout the company.

"We have half a merger," Ekberg said in an interview. "The companies were ideally suited, each with compatible product lines and extensive research and manufacturing in their respective regions. Neither had markets in one another's areas. Upjohn needed Europe and a world presence after being anchored in the U.S., and Pharmacia could not compete in North America without the strength of Upjohn. What we missed was that a merger has less to do with accounting than with human beings."

At the outset, American executives tried to graft their U.S. management style onto an established European business. In Ekberg's view, the hard-driving, mission-oriented American approach that Upjohn executives brought with them shocked the more gradualist, consensus-oriented Swedish managers. American managers wanted plans, actions, results—immediately—and a reporting system or committee process that followed inflexible lines of power relationships. It was not unusual for an American to make a proposal, and encountering no obvious contention, assume that the proposal was acceptable to everyone without further debate. The American would move directly toward implementing the proposal as if a decision had been made to do so. Meanwhile, Swedish colleagues assumed that the Americans had merely put forward ideas that required contemplation. Consequently, where Americans were often charging ahead, the Swedes were talking matters over, expecting to move more carefully toward a consensus.

Although the Swedes and Americans made decisions differently, often creating unnecessary anxiety, they always arrived promptly at meetings and attended carefully to business. In contrast, Italian managers were often late, sometimes not even showing up for meetings, and they seldom followed prescribed business procedures. Instead, they complained that Americans and Swedes were far too preoccupied with time and procedures to appreciate the finer points of life. French managers stayed at home when they had the choice, and sometimes insisted on bilingual interpretations or translated documents. One American executive, who decided to take early retirement rather than trying to adapt to the situation, said "these people just rubbed each other the wrong way...[W]e couldn't even agree on a new name for the company, and Pharmacia Upjohn was the default....[I]n fact, many of us are too

set in our ways to even try to understand a new culture."

Organizational differences present a set of problems that compound human relations. Americans were accustomed to bonuses in stock options, deferred income, and supplemental retirement benefits. Throughout the Upjohn company prior to merging, management compensation had a strong component of non-cash (or tax-advantaged) benefits. A Swedish company has no use for these methods, coming as it does from a social system that provides universal medical care, a social-welfare approach to taxation, and pervasive benefits for all employees with limited differentials between lower-level employees, managers, and higher-level executives. European accounting systems simply do not accommodate stock-option bonuses or selective, nonmonetary rewards.

At the same time, Americans came to work early, stayed late, took few vacations, and coupled holidays with business trips. Not so for Europeans. Ekberg explained that the American managers from Kalamazoo could not begin to comprehend how their European counterparts could take off the entire month of August for vacation. "They were astonished at European vacation habits," said Ekberg. "I must admit there are different traditions, and I think Europeans are much more international. We are used to working across borders, in different languages. We are used to treating people in a different way. The Americans are really not very international because they have this huge home base. American companies sell their products abroad, but that does not necessarily make them international." Ekberg said that his most pressing task during the next few years would be to meld together an organization that could be tolerant of different expectations.

Goran Ando, the executive vice president for research at Pharmacia & Upjohn, offered some insight into the culture clash. "I am a Swede who has lived in both Britain and the United States for a number of years, and I see in Americans a more can-do approach to things," Ando said. "They try to overcome problems as they arise. A Swede may be slower on the start-up. He sits down and thinks over all the problems, and once he is reasonably convinced he can tackle them, only then will he start running. But I don't know which style is the best." Ando said he had found that one solution was to move American and European managers back and forth across the Atlantic, even for brief visits. This, he said, "may help to speed up the development of contacts, and it will enhance understanding because you develop respect for each other."

The Pharmacia & Upjohn situation was not easily rectified. The organization was flattened, more in line with Swedish methods of team management and fewer hierarchical ranks. Global communications systems were developed in London, and international accounting and information systems were benchmarked worldwide to American practices. However, the French maintained a dual accounting process that has yet to be reconciled. Major cross-border training was introduced to raise levels of understanding among several continental European groups and regional U.S. interests. Unfortunately, the company also launched a major downsizing program to cut excess facilities and staff. Close on the heels of these changes, negotiations began with Monsanto, and the company began rebuilding with new talent.

The pending acquisition of Monsanto prompted Pharmacia & Upjohn to reorganize around three global divisions. Pharmacia itself—including Upjohn, with 60,000 employees and $7 billion in sales in 60 nations—established global-brand production and marketing (Upjohn no longer exists apart from Pharmacia). Searle was to remain a distinct biotech research and ethical drug division under Monsanto; and Monsanto, although entirely under the corporate umbrella of Pharmacia, was to reposition its agricultural and horticultural products, continue with its biotech research in food products, and provide the major international distribution centers for all corporate business. After five years of mergers and acquisitions that included several other European and regional U.S. companies, the new company—under the name of Pharmacia—is headquartered in Michigan with global marketing and communications centers in London and Stockholm, and managed by a six-nation executive board. Team management and consensus decision-making methods have become more common for the new 100,000-employee, $20 billion-plus multinational; but several French and Italian subsidiaries have been sold or amalgamated into other European groups.

QUESTIONS

1. Using Hofstede's dimensions of cultural values, contrast the differences in American and Swedish managers. What other problems might arise among European and American managers in the London corporate center, even though headquarters are now in the United States?

2. With the primary merger of Pharmacia and Upjohn, two equally strong companies, could the new corporation have made the transition easier if located in Michigan or Stockholm rather than in London? What problems might have emerged had the central offices been located in Milan?

3. In your opinion, why did the two organizational systems clash? What issues might seem to be extremely difficult to reconcile? The newly expanded Pharmacia with Monsanto does not necessarily shift corporate culture more toward American systems, because Monsanto already had widely diversified international management teams and foreign offices; but with a distinctly U.S. corporate headquarters location, new cross-cultural problems may emerge. What problems would you envision for French, Italian, and Swedish managers in this new corporate scenario? How would you reconcile such problems?

BIBLIOGRAPHY

"Ekberg's Prescription for P&U." *Financial Times*, 17 April 1997, p. 42.

Friedman, Alan. "A Case of Corporate Culture Shock in the Global Arena." *International Herald Tribune*, 23 April 1997, p. 1.

Pharmacia Corporation, Monsanto, and Searle company websites at <www.pharmacia.com>. Retrieved from each under the Corporate home page, "News" [cited 31 March 2000] for Monsanto acquisition, and "Company Profile" [cited 28 September 2000].

"Pharmacia and Upjohn to Close 24 of 57 Plants." *Reuters European Business Report*, 7 May 1997, p. 1.

"SESAME STREET"—CULTURAL VALUES REFLECTED IN CHILDREN'S POPULAR TV PROGRAM

Can you tell me how to get to Sesame Street? In the Middle East, the directions are downright confusing. If you want the Israeli Sesame Street, look for a boardwalk with an ice-cream parlor and a view of the Mediterranean. For the Palestinian versions in the same episode, head for a street with a water well, a shop selling Arab sweets, and a backdrop of West Bank-style hills and olive trees.

Americans have participated in this aspect of the peace process since the New York producers at Children's Television Workshop, creators of the original "Sesame Street," came up with the idea of a joint Israeli–Palestinian version. According to their logic, if former enemies like Yitzhak Rabin and Yasser Arafat could shake hands, why couldn't Israeli and Palestinian "Muppets"? Both sides loved the idea, but with changes. After so many years of conflict, the Israelis and Palestinians didn't want to live together, even on Sesame Street. "They each insisted on having their own street," said Lewis J. Bernstein, the show's executive producer.

This isn't the first time the program has been tailored for a foreign audience. Children around the globe watch 17 foreign versions of "Sesame Street," each with its own idiosyncrasies. The Russians came up with plotlines resembling those of a Tolstoy novel, arguing that their children aren't used to lighthearted fare. The French, Bernstein said, insisted on giving "Big Bird" a face-lift so he has a profile akin to Charles de Gaulle's. But the Israeli–Palestinian show is unique; it's the only one made by former enemies. In uncanny ways, the production mirrors the difficulties of the peace process itself.

"At one point I thought to myself, if it's like this between puppets, just imagine resolving all the difficulties between people," said Dolly Wolbrum, the Israeli producer.

From the start, conflicts large and small have disrupted production. The Israeli and Palestinian television studios signed separate contracts with the New York–based production company, rather than with each other. Each side has its own production crew, writes its own scripts, and looks at (but can't veto) the other's story lines. The two sides' skits appear together on each episode, and both make concessions on dialogue and characters—often after seemingly endless discussions.

The Palestinians, for example, wanted one of their characters to say he learned Hebrew while serving time in an Israeli jail. The Israelis said that wasn't the right message. In the end, the Palestinians agreed the character could say that he learned Hebrew while working in Israel.

The Palestinians insisted that the Muppets could come to the Palestinian side only if they were invited, in contrast to real-life conditions under Israeli military occupation, when soldiers could enter homes at any time. The Israelis wanted more informal relationships, but they acceded to the Palestinian request. As a compromise, two of the characters were made cousins in order to facilitate visits. Even so, the Palestinians insisted that the Muppets not be portrayed as overly friendly to each other. "The Israelis wanted full 'normalization,'" said Daoud Kuttab, the Palestinian producer, echoing the terms Israelis use in peace talks with their Arab neighbors. "They wanted the Muppets to start dancing right away. We said no kissing, no hugging. There is still a tension between our two peoples. If the characters are too happy, the show won't succeed."

In many ways, the resulting "Sesame Street" program (which is titled on the same screen as "Rehov Sumsum" in Hebrew and "Shara'a Simsim" in Arabic) is similar to the American original. The 60 half-hour shows include classic skits involving characters such as "Bert," "Ernie," and "Cookie Monster." The program promotes awareness of the environment, health, safety, and tolerance; but a big issue has been language. In some scenes, Ernie asks a question in Hebrew and Bert answers in Arabic. Producers try to use a core of 3,000 words that are similar in both Semitic languages. Subtitles are out, for reasons both practical (most viewers can't read yet) and cultural: "We insisted that there should be no Hebrew subtitles when our characters speak Arabic," Kuttab said. "We wanted Israeli children to accept us as we are. And Arabic is part of who we are."

The program has a Middle Eastern flavor. The Israelis created their own "Oscar the Grouch," named "Moses"; he lives in a broken-down car and often says "oof," a favorite expression of disdain among Israeli children. The Palestinians decided to pass on Oscar. "One Israeli grouch is enough," Kuttab said with a smile.

Each side was eager to create its own version of a Big Bird-type character—a lovable creature who would play a central role in the show. The Palestinians came up with "Karim," a rooster typical of their villages and a symbol of national pride. The Israelis initially considered using the American Big Bird character but with an eye patch to make him look like Moshe Dayan, the famous one-eyed war hero. Ultimately, the Israelis decided to revive "Kippy," a giant purple porcupine who had starred on a Hebrew version of "Sesame Street" produced in the 1980s. The porcupine was chosen as a symbol of the Israeli persona—tough on the outside, but sweet and generous on the inside.

On the set at Israeli Educational Television's Tel Aviv studio, actors say that politics do not intrude. During a break in filming, for example, one Israeli crew member discovered that Husam Abu Eshee, a Palestinian actor who plays a music teacher on the show, learned to speak Hebrew in an Israeli jail while serving a four-year sentence on security charges. They shrug it off. Guy Friedman, who plays Kippy, served as an Israeli medic in the Gaza Strip during the Palestinian intifada, or uprising. That isn't a problem. Nevertheless, politics are in the backdrop. Security guards check Palestinian belongings for bombs.

After the Israelis and Palestinians nixed the idea of living together on one Sesame Street, the Americans suggested building a third set, a park where residents of both streets would meet and play. The Israelis say they were willing to consider the proposal, but the Palestinians wanted to know who owned the park. "There is no neutral ground . . . and we felt strongly that there should at least be a sign in the park marking the border between Israel and Palestine," said Kuttab. From Wolbrum's perspective as the Is-

raeli producer, ownership of a park is an adult concern. "I kept arguing that no child would ask who the park belongs to," she said. "The Palestinians kept saying that isn't how things are in real life. That's true, but is there an Israeli street with a purple porcupine walking around it in real life?" The park never came to fruition.

Another American compromise was to create a joint water fountain located between the two streets, but that was nixed by the Israelis because the word for a spring, while similar in both Hebrew and Arabic, has a connotation in Hebrew similar to the word *none*. But some problems have resulted in successful resolutions. In one skit, for example, a Palestinian Muppet called "Haneen" comes to buy a book on the Israeli Sesame Street. In another scene, an Israeli boy takes a wrong turn on his bicycle and ends up on the Palestinian side, where he has a flat tire. The Palestinian Muppets help him fix the flat and quietly go on his way. Kippy also learns that the Arabic and Hebrew words for body parts sound the same, and that Palestinians and Israelis both like to eat falafel and hummus.

For Israelis and Palestinians, who have spent years viewing each other as terrorists or occupiers, these images of normal daily life represent a dramatic change. Some see cautious stirrings of hope amid a peace process that has all but broken down. The Israelis and Palestinians have completed work on separate theme songs, and in New York Bernstein is already worrying about weaving the two tunes together. "I know we'll get there in the end," he says, "but there are times when I want to stand up and shout, 'Hey you guys, enough already, we're talking about Sesame Street.'"

QUESTIONS

1. Describe examples of cultural values, beliefs, and attitudes in the Muppet world. How would you distinguish these elements from one another?

2. The production company taking "Sesame Street" worldwide is involved in international management as surely as any other multinational enterprise. Examine the issues the producers from the United States, Palestine, and Israel face in bringing together an organization that can accommodate disparate value systems.

3. Many American shows, such as TV series and movies, are marketed globally with modifications only to avoid sensitive scenes or language. In ef-

fect, they are American exports with dubbed languages and subtitles. In contrast, "Sesame Street" is actually trying to create local versions of an American media institution. What problems do you see with this project? Do you agree with the strategic choices it implies? Should the producers just dub voices and export the American show? Should they not try spreading it outside the United States at all? Should they produce entirely local programs with unique characters and situations?

BIBLIOGRAPHY

Marcus, Amy Dockser. "Ernie Uses Hebrew, Bert Speaks Arabic; Moses, He's a Grouch." *Wall Street Journal*, 5 June 1997, pp. A1, A13.

CHAPTER NINE

INTERCULTURAL COMMUNICATIONS

CHAPTER OBJECTIVES

Define and contrast *intracultural* and *intercultural communications.*

Describe how cultural characteristics influence patterns of communication in foreign societies.

Detail the communication process and important considerations it implies for international managers.

Identify problems with oral communications and their implications for cross-cultural management.

Explain the characteristics and implications of nonverbal communications.

Outline ways in which managers can improve their intercultural communication skills.

Georginia Wyman is managing director of Bata Limited in the Czech Republic, the world's largest shoemaker. Registered as *Bat'a, a.s.*, the company was originally established as Bata Shoes in Zlin, Czechoslovakia, by a ninth-generation shoemaker, Tomas Bata, in 1894.[1] After the communist government seized their firm in 1945, the Bata family fled to Canada, but continued to make shoes worldwide. Today the company is headquartered in Toronto, with an organization of 51,000 people in 70 countries and regional divisions managed through Paris, Mexico City, Singapore, Calcutta, and Harare. The company sells more than 150 million pairs of shoes each year through 4,700 company-owned stores and over 20,000 other retailers.[2]

The rebirth of the company's Czech division, however, was the fulfillment of Thomas Bata's dreams. As the last descendant of the founder to head the company, Thomas Bata had narrowly escaped the communist takeover at the end of World War II. When the velvet revolution ousted the Czechoslovakian communists in 1989, he actively encouraged expatriates and Czech exiles from around the world to return home and help rebuild the country. Thomas Bata was among the first to petition the new Czech government to privatize his family's historic factories and the remnants of 30 major department stores. Nearly 80 years of age and in no position to actively manage a facility in the Czech Republic, Bata searched for a younger person who could meet the challenge of rebuilding the company's Eastern European business. He was fortunate in hiring Georginia Wyman, another native Czech living in Canada who was anxious to pursue the project.

Wyman was expected to negotiate the privatization, create a new organization, and position the new enterprise eventually to become the flagship of the Bata global family. She had no manufacturing experience, but her multilingual abilities complemented a proven track record in tough negotiations. She was also enthusiastic about returning to the Czech Republic. Wyman had left her native land in 1948 at the age of two when her father, a notable industrialist, fled persecution by the communists. The family lost everything in confiscation raids and barely escaped with their lives. Georginia was brought up in Canada, but taught to value her native language and to appreciate the cultural heritage of her homeland. After college, she worked for several years as a historian, and then entered government with the Canadian Public Sector Administration. During her public service tenure, she worked in the Department of Indian and Northern Affairs, where she handled sensitive native claims, and then as a negotiator for the Department of Energy, Mines, and Resources. This post led to her appointment as Deputy Minister of Supply and Services for Canada.

In 1990, Georginia Wyman met and was hired by Thomas Bata, a direct descendant of the founder, Tomas Bata. It was a time of enthusiasm for the independence of the new Czech Republic. Her first task as head of the company, supported by few established guidelines for private-sector development, was to negotiate terms with the Czech authorities. Indeed, the new republic had created only a fledgling legal code and no commercial infrastructure. The firm contended with other bidders, including U.S. buyout teams headed by eager lawyers and German industrialists backed by their country's powerful banking industry.

Wyman never wavered, however, making effective use of a communication style that everyone applauded. Rather than negotiating to "narrow" margins of differences, she sought always to "widen" the scope of opportunities. Rather than approaching conversations as confrontations, she always found win-win positions for everyone involved. While U.S. bidders promised rapid profits for the host economy, noting how they could leverage the country's low-cost labor structure, Wyman envisioned a highly skilled and well-paid workforce making quality shoes. Profits would come, she promised, but only when the company and its employees had rebuilt their country's industrial base on a foundation of sound technical skills. She understood the cultural strength and pride of the Czech people, while Germans and Americans talked numbers and rolled out financial statements. After three years of exhausting negotiations, the Czech government granted Bata the privatization license, taking a 30 percent interest in the enterprise for itself.

Once the company began operating, Wyman faced new problems. Employees worked in dusty relics of buildings, and they were accustomed to meeting volume objectives with little regard for quality or efficiency. For a long time, they had made cheap shoes that were mass shipped to Russia or other parts of the former Soviet Union, so they had developed no concern for customer preferences or conditions in the markets. Worker skills were not particularly relevant to modern processes, and people did not talk to one another or to their bosses. Wyman inherited a workforce that feared anyone in authority and suppressed any thought or comment that could be considered a criticism. Workers had learned to keep their heads down, their thoughts private, and any associations with management remote from themselves.

Wyman tackled this problem by starting informal group meetings. She also sent managers and line supervisors to foreign conferences, brought in expatriate Czech nationals who had been living elsewhere, and initiated training programs. Eventually, employees began to accept her ideas. They began to speak out, to try new ideas, and to trust management. During a two-year period, a sense of teamwork and open communications emerged in the company. Staff members began to "share meanings" about quality and the "pride of the Bata shoe." Wyman avoided bringing in outside consultants because she did not want her people to feel hammered by messages about the advantages of western methods. Instead, she sought to help them learn these lessons through their own efforts.

Marketing problems proved to be more difficult to solve. Wyman began a program to create a system of consumer-oriented service in the company's stores. On her first tour of the main store, she noticed a distant and uninterested attitude among her employees. She asked a clerk why she didn't smile at customers, and received the candid answer, "Why should I smile at customers? They don't smile at me." Wyman picked up on body language and obvious behavior that conveyed an uncaring attitude to customers. Shoes were stacked in cluttered aisles, not displayed. Window displays followed no themes. Everything seemed to communicate a single message to customers: "Just pay and get out." Using the same tactics of patient conversation, training, and setting a good example herself, Wyman transformed the retail stores into fun places to work and shop.

Today, the Czech division of Bata is known for its customer service, outgoing employees, and exquisite store displays. The company sells only well-made shoes, ranging from sports shoes that compete with Nike and Puma to dress shoes with fashionable Italian styles. The Czech facilities export more than half of all shoe production to Scandinavia and Western Europe, and manage stores or licensed franchises in seven East European countries. The company has grown from several hundred employees working in run-down buildings to a domestic industry with more than 2,000 employees in renovated facilities. Wyman annually travels to more than 100 countries to visit Bata customers and to coordinate international sales. Everything that she does and says communicates one message: Bata is a global family that respects people's needs.

BRIDGING BARRIERS—INTERCULTURAL COMMUNICATION

People maintain their cultural heritages, and therefore protect their value systems, by passing on to new generations deeply embedded patterns of language and communication behavior. Indeed, anthropologists often distinguish societies and their value systems by patterns of communication behavior *within* a culture. This is called **intracultural communication**, and encompasses the combined behavior, language, nonverbal gestures, and patterns of interaction through which members of a society bond together. In contrast, **intercultural communication** occurs between individuals, groups, organizations, or societies with different cultural antecedents. This chapter emphasizes differences among societies in their communication behavior, focusing mainly on the implications of intercultural—or *cross-cultural*—communication for international managers.

The communications field is vast, including written and electronic media, interactive systems, mass media, organizational media, the conversational dimension of oral communication, and the behavior and gestures that constitute nonverbal communication. These are all important, but this chapter is concerned primarily with **interpersonal communications**—specifically oral and nonverbal communication behavior—that underscore international management roles in a multicultural environment. This coverage begins with an introduction of intercultural communication concepts necessary to provide a fundamental perspective of cross-cultural management. The chapter then addresses how cultural differences influence communications, contrasts patterns of verbal and nonverbal communications behavior for selected societies, and concludes with a model of intercultural communications. These broad-based presentations culminate with practical recommendations that can help international managers better understand and communicate with people of other cultures.

A Fundamental Perspective

Intercultural communication becomes important to international managers in three different situations. The most obvious situation is when managers of a home-country multinational are assigned to positions in foreign countries. Alternatively, managers may find themselves employed by a foreign enterprise located in their own home country. Another situation, becoming more common as more multinationals form complex international alliances, is that managers can find themselves working for a foreign company and be assigned to yet another foreign location. This can occur, for example, when an American employed by a company like Unilever (Anglo-Dutch) is deployed to Brazil, or an Australian manager working for Ford is assigned to the company's German subsidiary.

Most Americans give little thought to working for a foreign company at home, although more than two million Americans work for more than 3,000 registered foreign companies, including giants such as Honda, Volvo, Sony, Nissan, Seimens, and Bayer AG. Many companies do not appear to be foreign, yet they are foreign owned, including, for example, Intercontinental Hotels, Tiffany's, Ramada Inns, Benetton, and Columbia Pictures. In most instances, there is no sense of working for foreigners, yet patterns of behavior will be different from those of a domestic firm, and communications can become complicated by cultural differences. From an American viewpoint, foreign owners bring with them some unusual characteristics that often become stereotyped as typical Japanese, German, or British. From the foreign owners' perspective, they are managing a diversified workforce in a host country, which can be difficult in America because the country is a melting pot of global cultures with an indistinct mixture of language protocols. This can also be said of work populations in Canada, Australia, and Great Britain, which are relatively heterogeneous cultures. By comparison, countries such as Japan, Saudi Arabia, China, and Sweden are relatively homogeneous, with distinct language protocols.[3] Communication theorists have identified patterns of behavioral characteristics in heterogeneous cultures and have defined these cultures as *low-context societies*. They have also identified different patterns for behavioral characteristics for homogeneous cultures and refer to these cultures as *high-context societies*. These patterns subsequently influence relationships and interpersonal communications.[4]

America has become the model of a low-context society, and Japan is the prominent model of a high-context society. Figure 9.1 illustrates differences between the two societies. In a low-context, heterogeneous culture, there is greater social and job mobility, relationships are shorter in duration, and insiders and outsiders are less closely distinguished; with this diversity comes a wider variety of behavior. Consequently, foreigners find it relatively easy to assimilate into low-context countries like the United States, yet ironically that also means that communication is often ambiguous or has many different meanings and interpretations. Therefore, in low-context countries, there is more reliance on explicit written contracts, messages often must be clarified, and nonverbal communications can be easily misinterpreted. In contrast, high-context societies with a history of homogeneity have a closely shared system of communication encoding. Oral and nonverbal communications have rather explicit meanings because there is little cultural diversity. Insiders and outsiders are clearly distinguished, there is little social or job mobility, and relationships are relatively long lasting. In these societies, there is little ambiguity in behavior or communications. For example, managers from the United States or Canada discover that it is extremely difficult to learn the precise intricacies of Japanese language and communication behavior in order to be understood correctly. In contrast, a Japanese manager can get along rather well in North America with only a marginal knowledge of English because variations in language usage and communication behavior are more readily accommodated than elsewhere.

FIGURE 9.1
Characteristics of Low-
and High-Context
Societies

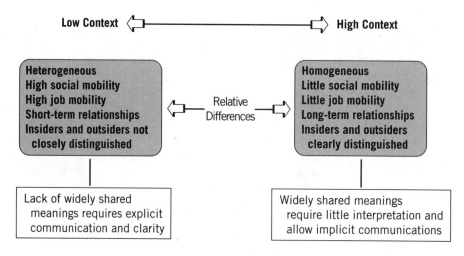

Multicultural diversity does not preclude stereotyping, as demonstrated in the "Global Viewpoint" feature. Stereotyping, of course, has its advantages as a shorthand way of grasping differences between cultures. Its implications for effective communications become obvious when stereotyped characteristics are compared among societies with significantly different cultures. For example, Italians are demonstrative in their expressions; Greeks use hand and face movements similar to Italians but often gesture more elaborately; and both seem emotional when compared to the British or Germans. Americans are considered loud, impatient, and arrogant by people in many other countries, yet they are also considered friendly to the point of excessive informality. Americans are also considered to be hard-working and time-driven individuals who are prompt, observe deadlines, and are particular about keeping appointments. On the other hand, Italians, Greeks, and French are less sensitive to meeting time requirements or working to schedules. Italians and Greeks, and to some extent the French, also are bold in their tone of voice, and they often accentuate conversations with metaphors or emotional adjectives to make a point. Americans are generous and seldom overly concerned with social status, yet the British are viewed as conservative and reserved, often to the point of seeming impersonal in their polite use of language. Consequently, patterns of communication and language protocols can be substantially different among these societies. The contrasts become even more dramatic when comparing societies in Africa, Asia, and Latin America.[5]

The greatest contrasts are probably seen when comparing Japanese or Chinese cultures to European or North American societies. Westerners view these two Asian cultures as inscrutable and apprehensive about foreigners. They are considered soft-spoken but extremely formal, status sensitive, and group oriented. Consequently, Americans and Europeans find the Japanese and Chinese difficult to understand—at times polite and considerate, at other times contemptuous and withdrawn.[6] To outsiders, the Japanese and Chinese may appear similar; but they have distinctly different ethnic cultures with significantly different value systems that influence communication patterns and relationships.[7] Americans and Europeans have difficulty communicating in Asia due to extreme contrasts in social philosophies and histories of human relationships. As noted in the previous chapter, the Confucian, Islamic, and Hindu cultures existing in Asia have entrenched value systems that emphasize different human needs and priorities compared with Judeo-Christian societies. But this is a dangerous generality because countries such as China, Indonesia, Malaysia, Thailand, and Vietnam have diverse subcultural groups and mixtures of religions that represent a broad range of multicultural differences in that region of the world.

From an *intra*cultural viewpoint, managing in America can require multicultural sensitivity to assimilate differences even within a wholly domestic company. Indeed, efforts to manage diversity in the domestic workplace have become major considerations, not only to resolve gender and age differences but also to bridge ethnic, racial, and religious differences in a heterogeneous society. (The topic of managing diversity is addressed in Chapter 14.) When domestic managers interact with foreign owners, communication issues become still more complicated; but as noted earlier, heterogeneity permits a certain sense of accommodation.

From an *inter*cultural viewpoint, managers in foreign assignments are exposed to potentially major cultural clashes. An expatriate manager in a foreign land encounters well-entrenched, sometimes inflexible patterns of communication behavior that can be impossible to understand. Host-country employees are less inclined to accept diverse behavior or to understand perceived ineptitudes in communication by foreign managers. In the past, the somewhat brash and arrogant image of Americans has led to

WHAT OTHERS THINK ABOUT AMERICANS AT HOME AND ABROAD

Americans prefer to be casual and informal in their relationships. They sometimes offend others by being too informal, such as when they use first names to address others despite their being only recent acquaintances. This is one view, expressed by a British manager; but American informality can also cause awkward situations in relations with Latin Americans, Asians, and Arabs, many of whom observe titles and carefully address others according to rank and protocol.

Americans have created an image of well-dressed, self-confident people. Yet their behavior can seem paradoxical when they use jargon in conversations or joke to make points. Latin Americans are sometimes confused by how quickly Americans make decisions. Indeed, Latin managers often resent American impatience, and many Europeans feel that Americans can jump to premature conclusions by their hasty approach to decisions. Managers from Latin America in particular, but also those from several Scandinavian countries and southern Europe, are accustomed to having long, social discussions devoted to establishing tranquil relationships before business is discussed. Managers from these countries also are more likely than Americans to avoid talking about business at social events or during lunches and dinners.

Most people outside North America—perhaps with the exception of the French—put little emphasis on lengthy contracts and legal documents. Therefore, the American fascination with contracts steeped in legal terms and iron-clad clauses can be perplexing. In Japan, China, and other parts of Asia, the perception of American commercial legal procedure is that American contracts leave no room for trust in a relationship. Then again, American managers are very mobile, and their contracts transcend personal priorities, so agreements can endure despite changes in personnel. Americans also are perceived to display a sense of superiority, sometimes without justification. Of course, most American firms can negotiate from positions of economic strength, and many of their executives are excellent managers. Still, foreigners perceive a tendency in Americans to flaunt their capabilities.

Some American characteristics are confusing, some are not appreciated, and others simply surprise foreigners. Americans working abroad often embarrass their foreign friends with their commitments to work and their "can-do" energy. Americans tend to mow their own lawns, do home repairs, clean, and cook. These jobs are often beneath a person of stature in other cultures, where even relatively junior managers rely on housekeepers or hire tradespeople to attend to such duties.

Perhaps more bothersome is the American willingness to strike up a conversation with almost anyone of any status. American wives living abroad seldom hesitate to talk freely to visiting tradespeople or to carry on personal conversations with maids, sales clerks, or people they meet in passing. Managers talk with shop-floor employees with little regard for their lower social status, and American tourists may treat anyone as fair game for a friendly chat. Foreign hosts are more likely to maintain social distance and avoid unnecessary conversations with fellow citizens of different social status.

American friendliness can also create a heart-warming feeling. Japanese managers comment that Americans are more than generous with those around them. Although they may not always observe differences in rank, Americans are sensitive to feelings and quickly make friends. Well-traveled Asians and Latin Americans appreciate this sense of egalitarianism, but foreign subordinates who do not understand Americans often cannot accept such familiarity. They sense their places in their organizations and acknowledge the subtle differences of others in both superior and subordinate positions. By ignoring those differences or speaking as equals, Americans can embarrass these people. Fortunately, Americans earn respect by their jovial behavior, and their ability to laugh at their own mistakes can be pleasantly disarming. Americans send a message of friendship by their demeanor, and even when they seem impatient, time bound, and workaholic, they are often warmly received abroad.

Sources: Gary Althen, *American Ways: A Guide for Foreigners* (Yarmouth, Me.: Intercultural Press, 1988), Chapter 1; R. E. Axtell, *Dos and Taboos of International Trade* (New York: John Wiley & Sons, 1991), 83–84; Farid Elashmawi and Philip R. Harris, *Multicultural Management: New Skills for Global Success* (Houston: Gulf Publishing, 1993), 52–56; and Clarke Clifford and Mitchell R. Hammer, "Predictors of Japanese and American Managers' Job Success, Personal Adjustment, and Intercultural Interaction Effectiveness," *Management International Review* 35, no. 2 (1995): 153–170.

an unpleasant stereotype of the insensitive "ugly American." Globalization has diffused this image somewhat, yet the global forays of Japanese companies have begun to prompt a similar stereotype of an "ugly Japanese," who acts in inflexible and arrogant ways. Consequently, Japanese expatriates are now more often schooled in how to behave in foreign assignments, and in how to respond to communication difficulties.[8]

Although communication is culture sensitive, this does not necessarily mean that communication patterns are defined by national boundaries. French, British, Japanese, or Chinese cultures, for example, are broad abstractions of social identities. Meanwhile, religious and ethnic characteristics of one society may be found in many other societies. For example, while Islamic and Confucian beliefs are identified with prominent societies in the Middle East and Asia, they also prevail among subcultures throughout much of the world. Therefore, stereotypes and generalizations can be substantially misleading—paradoxes are common—yet by identifying these abstract characteristics, managers can prepare themselves better with a foundation on which to sharpen their communicative skills.

CULTURE AND COMMUNICATION

Recall from Chapter 8 that culture evolves in response to each society's approach to solving problems for its people. In individual environments, the universal problems of food, water, shelter, economic survival, and security have historically required different responses. Consequently, societies can be compared by studying the systems they have evolved. The earlier discussion classified these systems in broad terms as economic, political, and social systems. It also identified the importance of family and marital customs and demonstrated how educational systems serve as conduits for these standards, ensuring the succession of social values in future generations. Each of these systems influences, and reacts to influence by, patterns of *intracultural* communication. Thus the search for an understanding of intracultural communications must evaluate how these systems function.

Communications in Economic Systems

Market economies such as the United States and Canada are characterized by open, free-flowing patterns of communication. Available communication media support a wide range of advertising and relatively unrestrained journalism. High mobility and relatively open trade relations foster wide-ranging information exchanges. In contrast to many other economies, substantial informality encourages accessibility in both public and private communications. Communist economies have notoriously restricted media and information exchanges, and these restrictions influence private communications in which organizations, groups, or even families are reluctant to share information with others. Just as products and services are controlled in extreme socialist environments, information is controlled as a vital resource.

Ironically, mainland China is the ultimate model of a closed system, while the Chinese society of Hong Kong is arguably the ultimate model of an open free-enterprise system; yet the Chinese members of both societies share an entrenched common ethnic culture. The former British colony of Hong Kong was returned to China in 1997 as a Special Administrative Region under a separate political structure, and communication differences have become sensitive problems. Beijing favors severe limits on journalism, outright bans on public debates about any topic that relates to political or commercial interests, strict codes for advertising and entertainment media, and the official Chinese language in place of English. (The official language is *Putonghua*, a dialect of what westerners call *Mandarin*, spoken in Beijing. Two versions of written Chinese include a "classic" script common in the south, Hong Kong, and Taiwan, and a "simplified" version that prevails in most mainland areas.) Following the handover, Hong Kong and Chinese officials identified more than 280 issues relating to language, customs, regulations, commercial codes, private rights (including limits on free speech and public assembly), media licensing, contract procedures, and private company registrations.[9] Most of these issues are not yet resolved; when they are, the way business is conducted in Hong Kong may be very different than it is today. Although Hong Kong's difficulties may seem unimportant to outsiders, they are very important to multinationals with interests there. Hong Kong has approximately 27,000 registered foreign businesses—including more than 50,000 American expatriates in residence, nearly 30,000 British, and 180,000 people of other nationalities from 89 countries—and the territory's financial infrastructure in banking and securities is closely tied to United States markets.[10]

Contrasts in communication behavior are most noticeable among countries with significantly different economic profiles. Many tribal societies in South America, Africa, and the South Pacific still barter or survive through village systems, and the concept of commercial enterprise often does not exist. Instead, village cooperatives or tribal customs prevail. These high-context cultures have little need of written formalities or legal codes, and communications are patterned on village relationships. Recall from Chapter 8 that researchers identified clusters of societies in which economic development was a significant factor in classifying cultural differences. Less-developed economies were found to place little importance on individual enterprise, and extremely underdeveloped societies were characterized as isolated and communal.[11] Therefore, communication patterns are substantially different among these societies, and international managers working in less-developed countries must be extremely sensitive to unusual languages and customs.

Communications in Political Systems

Each society will have its own unique approach to politics that sets it apart from others, even when they have similar ideologies. The United States is a federation of states with representative government, states rights, and both national and state laws. Canada is a parliamentary system with provincial controls, but relatively more widespread national systems such as health care, insurance, and commercial law compared to the United States. Meanwhile, the United Kingdom is a constitutional monarchy with an entirely different parliamentary system. In each nation, political leaders exert different influence. Political power rests on differences in oratory skills, cooperation among different branches of government, and public acceptance of leadership behavior.

Greater differences exist between democratic systems and autocratic countries. China demonstrates something close to a cult environment, where not only is the Communist Party in control, but national leaders such as Mao Zedong and Deng Xiaoping were elevated to almost supernatural personages. France is a democratic society with socialist characteristics, yet it is also a country where elected heads of state have extraordinary power. Some observers say France has elected emperors who seem to remain in power for life, even though contentious politicians may win relatively minor positions in government.[12]

The way countries elect leaders and appoint legislators permits power to accrue to those leaders in different ways. The process also dictates how the state will influence public and private relationships, such as business negotiations, contracts, dispute resolutions, and daily commerce. The influence of political leaders may be substantial or minimal, and communications may be stifled or encouraged according to prevailing ideologies. Decisions may follow hierarchical patterns of authority or broad participation, and these behavior patterns will follow through to personal relationships and organizational behavior. These and many other factors affect patterns of individual development and communicative behavior.

From an intercultural viewpoint, these differences can require sensitive adaptations to language, semantics, use of written documents, contracting, and conversational context. Singapore, for example, is a democratic nation with an elected government, but it has been governed exclusively by one party since its independence. When Singapore held its first open election in 1965, the People's Action Party established a constitutional democracy, but one that became an acknowledged socialist system. For nearly three decades, Prime Minister Lee Kuan Yew ruled Singapore without opposition. Mr. Lee voluntarily stepped down in 1989 to become a senior minister. By all accounts, he is still the most powerful person in Singapore, and his son is the deputy prime minister and heir apparent.

Ironically, Singapore is also one of the world's most open economies, with vibrant trade and a showcase of entrepreneurial zeal. Yet government, and more specifically Mr. Lee, controls much of what is written or said. For example, the *Asian Wall Street Journal* was banned for a mild back-page criticism of the senior minister, and Singaporean officials sued the *International Herald Tribune* for questioning whether they had received favors to sway political decisions. More recently, Singapore censored U.S. papers that carried President Clinton's criticism of Singapore's practice of caning lawbreakers.[13] Although these sound like repressive measures, Mr. Lee is very popular among Singaporeans. He has openly advocated a "visible hand" society in which government penetrates almost all aspects of socioeconomic life, "exhorting, guiding, motivating, innovating, and in exceptional circumstances coercing, through public speeches and campaigns, advisory bodies, statutory bodies, government companies and legislation."[14]

Communications in Social Systems

Social institutions include governmental, educational, religious, regulatory, and family organizations, but a *social system* is the culmination of these institutions within a society's physical and economic environment. Perhaps even more important, the system itself is grounded in the culture's social philosophy. Recall that these characteristics represent important distinctions among Confucian, Judeo-Christian, and Islamic cultures.

Social systems can be dramatically different, but they have common priorities to define how people coexist in their communities. Each society will establish individual rights, responsibilities of individuals to the society as a whole, customs pertaining to property ownership, inheritance, protection of private assets, and prescriptive roles for their leaders. The social philosophy of Confucianism that evolved more than 2,500 years ago in China anchored property rights to the ruling elite. This disenfranchised the lower echelons of society. Communist land reforms following World War II sought to remedy this by restructuring property rights and instituting pervasive land reforms, but commoners still have few claims to real property.[15] Similar feudal systems evolved in Europe, disenfranchising serfs and concentrating ownership among nobles. Revolutions of the eighteenth and early nineteenth centuries coupled with industrialization led to major land reforms and common-law rights of asset ownership.

In contrast, India and neighboring cultures that share a rich Hindu tradition display a social dualism. The so-called *Raj* mentality awards absolute control over assets and property to certain castes, which hold them in trust for all people. In practice, perpetual ownership rights vested in individuals pass to their heirs through generational bloodlines. On the other side of the dual social system, Hinduism and Buddhism as practiced in the Indian Subcontinent seek to minimize the importance of material property and earthly ownership; these doctrines stress the identity of the Earth itself as part of the cosmos that no human can own or claim.[16] Material and property rights substantially influence how people in a society relate to one another and to their environment. Language is a reflection of these beliefs, and patterns of communication are usually dictated by social hierarchies that evolve through systems of ownership rights.

Social systems also reflect class structures. The Confucian philosophy developed a very severe differentiation between four major social components. Rulers occupied the highest social class; members of the military supported them from the second stratum; the agrarian masses were third; and the least-esteemed members of society were those engaged in commerce. Thus, uneven power distributions became deeply ingrained. Therefore, hierarchical power systems have permeated Confucian societies over the centuries, reaching downward through organizations and families.[17] This fundamental social hierarchy is still very much in evidence today in many parts of the world, and it brings with it a strong sense of allegiance to authority and conformity.[18] Figure 9.2 illustrates this hierarchy, nowhere written explicitly into law but reinforced by patterns of social behavior in many nations.

Throughout Europe and the Middle East, social hierarchies similar to those in China and India prevailed until the rise of colonial mercantilism and the acceleration of industrialization. Christian and Islamic cultures included a very strong clerical element, often one that was not distinguished from the ruling aristocracy. Meanwhile, socialist ideologies stifled the aristocracy and created centralized systems of control under the guise of "stewardship" by rulers to protect society's collective interests.

In contrast, most Middle Eastern nations remain autocratic, ruled by monarchs or their equivalents, but governance is often based on an institutionalized religion. In Saudi Arabia, for example, laws do not exist apart from the Koran; law is the Islamic code, not a civil code. Language, behavior, and social relationships in Saudi Arabia and many of its neighboring countries are reflections of Islamic law. Therefore, business communications such as negotiating and contracting must conform to expectations within these social theocracies. Each nation's religious doctrine, however, can be substantially different. Iran, Iraq, Kuwait, Jordan, and Saudi Arabia, for example, have

FIGURE 9.2
Confucian Structural
Priorities: A System of
Inequalities

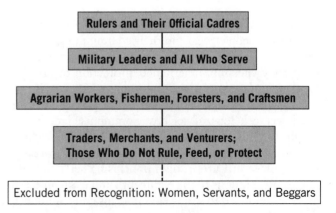

distinct social theocracies, and although all are based on Islamic code, the societies often clash.[19] Language protocols, patterns of communication, and—in particular—methods of conducting business are distinct in each of these nations.

Communications in Educational Systems

Education, by definition, is an information system. Language, traditions, customs, behavioral norms, beliefs, and all forms of artistic and creative expression are perpetuated through a nation's educational system. Combined, these are the building blocks of cultural development. Education systems also provide the scientific and technological knowledge base, which can be a country's most important asset. Societies with high literacy rates typically have well-developed general education systems, and high-context societies such as Japan rely on primary and secondary education systems to solidify social behavior among successive generations. Indeed, research by the World Bank concludes that superior education systems in Japan, South Korea, Hong Kong, Taiwan, and Singapore were primary determinants in rapid economic growth; and in each instance, education was the key determinant of social progress.[20]

Patterns of communication that form information-exchange relationships through education are shaped by several factors. Socialist political systems, for example, tend to dictate what can be taught, read, spoken, and shared in classrooms by teachers and students. Consequently, educational development is influenced by political ideologies, but also by political priorities. For example, during the Cold War era, the Soviet Union focused on rapid technological advancement and specifically channeled educational programs toward applied sciences. Unfortunately, fine arts and social sciences were generally sacrificed to put resources into scientific and military endeavors.[21] In developing countries, individuals in government positions often enjoy elevated social status, and consequently, higher education has been focused on public administration. This ensures that the political elite can pursue government careers, often at the expense of education systems that fail to provide technical and commercial skills for a sufficient student population. Countries such as Sri Lanka, Malaysia, the Philippines, Chile, Colombia, and Kenya are now anxiously trying to establish commercial and technology programs to enhance skill levels for coming generations.[22]

Differences in educational systems, priorities of each society that influence curriculum content, and methods of instruction result in wide variations in relationships and information processes. The consensual society of Japan, for example, puts great emphasis on a university student's club memberships and extracurricular team activities. These reinforce social values of harmony and loyalty. Meanwhile, individual achievements such as class rankings or high grade-point averages may be important, but they are not emphasized.[23] The Japanese have one of the lowest illiteracy rates in the world (about 1 percent, compared to 8 percent in the United States), but it is achieved by compulsory education, strict methods of memorization, and rigorous discipline in primary and secondary schools. In contrast, individuality in the United States permits greater educational choices with significant variations in compulsory education among the individual states. Compared to Japanese, Americans rely little on memorization, instead emphasizing interactive teaching methods that reinforce individual creativity. At the same time, American schools have less-rigorous disciplinary systems than those in Japan.

Although both Japan and the United States have well-educated populations, their social learning processes are very different. These societies, as well as most of the other affluent nations, have similar education priorities, but their methods, communication protocols, and expectations for interpersonal behavior often contrast sharply. Unfortunately, many societies have relatively weak education systems, and they suffer with high illiteracy rates, few skilled workers, and few opportunities for growth. Therefore, multinational managers working in these countries find it difficult to communicate with their employees or to train them in new technologies necessary for economic progress.[24]

Communications in Family Systems

The definition of a family unit varies widely among cultures. Marital laws and customs determine biological family ties and responsibilities, but in many societies, *family* means several generations of blood relatives, with close associations among aunts, uncles, cousins, and other families connected through marriage. Several generations may live together, share work, build extensive businesses, or develop clans of associations. North American and most European families splinter into independent family units as young adults marry and move away from home. Indeed, part of the transition to adulthood is to become independent of family ties even though kinship bonds remain intact. At the other extreme, some African and Southeast Asian cultures have communal responsibilities, which means children are raised by the group rather than solely by their biological parents. In effect, non-blood relatives become surrogate parents, and children are not distinguished as belonging to a particular family but as young members of the community. In these societies, cultural traditions are taught through community involvement and rituals. Patterns of communication and role development occur through group activities and ceremonial rites. Similar characteristics can occur among nuclear families in the Middle East, South America, and the Indian Subcontinent. Figure 9.3 suggests three models in which the core parental influence is relatively different among these societies.

Family systems therefore encourage specific communication patterns within a culture. At the same time, these patterns limit communication with outsiders. For example, a woman from one of the Arab cultures rarely converses with a non-family member, and she avoids foreigners. Business associates of Arabs are seldom invited to an individual's home unless there is a social occasion, and foreigners are seldom introduced to family members except in formal circumstances. In any event, conversations rarely include family matters. Men and women maintain separate lives in most Arab countries, and families seldom socialize together in public.[25]

In Japan, men spend most of their time with other men. They work together, attend social events together, and recreate in segregated activities. Japanese women tend to remain close to home and congregate with neighborhood friends. This may be changing as more Japanese women are beginning to pursue independent careers, but their work relationships often remain distinctly separate from those of their male colleagues. Women generally handle family affairs, and men concentrate on relationships outside the family unit. Nevertheless, the Japanese family is very closely affiliated, with close generational allegiances. The traditional Chinese family reflects deeply rooted Confucian ideals. Relationships between husband and wife are very clearly based on a dominant male role, and the wife is handmaid to the husband's dictates. "A husband sings, the wife hums along," as one Chinese saying explains.[26] There are family rules about what can be said and to whom, and when a woman or child can speak. This social philosophy of hierarchical rights also dictates that women should speak in a subservient manner around men, and male children are taught to be assertive, even with their mothers.[27]

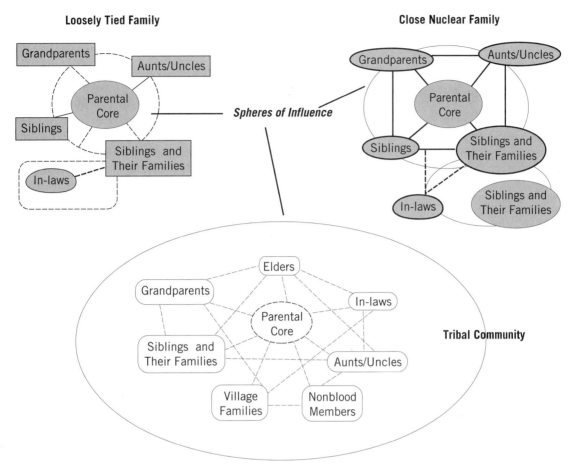

FIGURE 9.3
Patterns in Family Relations

International managers often have difficulties with customs that involve family relationships in host countries. In Muslim countries such as Jordan or the United Arab Emirates, for example, a foreigner can easily violate the sanctity of a family simply by greeting a woman without being properly introduced. Westerners often bring up personal issues in social gatherings, which is a breach of protocol, but even an innocent compliment can lead to unpleasant misunderstandings. For example, an American executive working in Jordan attended a reception for a local businessman, and when he was introduced to the businessman's wife, he complimented her on having an exquisite silver sash as part of her evening gown. The sash was stunning and expensive. Later, he noticed her again, but without the sash. It seems that after the compliment, her husband became annoyed and made her take the sash off because he felt that it drew "sensual attention" to her midriff.[28]

These examples barely begin to illustrate the fascinating differences that exist in families of other cultures. In developing countries, managers must avoid conversations or nonverbal behavior that could be construed as inappropriate, and this can be difficult. In host countries where women are prominent in lower-skilled positions, employee relations can be sensitive, and disciplinary actions may be impossible without involving the male head of the household. In most societies, men and women do not communicate as equals. Although a western manager may try to speak respectfully to a local woman employee, kind gestures or friendly conversations can be viewed as improprieties by her co-workers or by her husband.[29]

Implications for Effective Communication

Patterns of communication are affected by the cultural underpinnings of a society. But it is seldom a clear cause-and-effect relationship, because patterns of communication also help shape and perpetuate a society's culture. Therefore, cultural values may run deep; but as a nation's communication capabilities change—and as the economic, political, educational, and social systems evolve—cultural values, beliefs, and attitudes are affected. For example, people in a less-developed country may not have access to news media or to television, but as the country prospers, news and entertainment media will reach them. In time, they will become better informed about national and world events, consumer products, and circumstances of other communities and social groups within their own cultures. Society itself changes with the development of information media as people become aware of other societies and their value systems. A better-informed population also becomes aware of different value systems and new opportunities, and people can become intrigued with new technologies or frustrated by comparisons between themselves and others.

Foreign managers working in developing societies must therefore be alert to how their presence—and their knowledge and technologies—influences social change. With that said, researchers have several suggestions to help international managers become more effective in their interpersonal communication roles.

Respect Differences

Becoming *culturally sensitive* is necessary to appreciate and respect differences in a foreign environment. It means being open-minded, and therefore a better listener who is alert to nuances in language, customs, and behavior in a host country. Managers can begin by having more patience with local customs. They can also learn the communicative rules of a foreign society—when to speak and to whom, and under what circumstances it is proper to address another person.

Managers can also learn when not to speak to someone, how to avoid improper body posture, and what gestures may be inappropriate.[30] Earlier examples have emphasized these points, such as not speaking to Arab women unless introduced, using proper surnames and customary titles, and avoiding business topics during meals or social meetings. Even subtle gestures can be troublesome. For example, in Muslim societies, it is a demeaning gesture to point the sole of one's foot or shoe at someone. It implies that the person toward whom the foot is pointed is considered loathsome, and therefore the common western practice of crossing the legs to reveal a protruding foot should be avoided.[31] Demonstrating efforts to use appropriate gestures and conversational protocols gains respect in a host country, even if a person makes minor blunders.

Avoid Quick Judgments

A second precaution is to become more *tolerant* of unfamiliar customs. International managers must try to be *nonjudgmental* about how other people speak and act. Tolerance develops as people learn how to accept the ambiguities of another culture. For example, attentive outsiders learn to recognize vague patterns of communication in a high-context society such as Japan, despite initial difficulties of interpreting the nonverbal language of bows, smiles, and unexplained silence.

Nonjudgmental behavior also means being able to hold your own emotions in check. In China, for example, there are many words for *please* and *thank you*, each with several tonal variations reserved for specific circumstances. However, Chinese clerks, storekeepers, waiters, and other service staff seldom "thank" a customer. When customers say "thank you," clerks seldom say "you're welcome." Expressions of gratitude in public situations or commercial transactions simply are not part of Chinese communication behavior.[32] Consequently, foreign tourists visiting China or other Chinese societies often feel affronted by what they consider rude behavior. Perceptions that Chinese lack etiquette or purposely behave indifferently toward others are common in business. For example, the Chinese custom of sitting side by side rather than face to face in meetings seems remote, and it is sometimes or often uncomfortable for foreigners. It is also rare for a Chinese negotiator to make direct eye contact during a meeting. Western visitors often must be patient and nonjudgmental when encountering unfamiliar circumstances such as these, even though they may feel somewhat humiliated by the experience.[33]

Effective communication behavior is enhanced by *withholding judgment* of events or customs until a better understanding can be achieved. Everyone has a strong tendency to judge another person's actions from a personal frame of reference, and although this is normal, it often leads to inappropriate responses. Effective managers will learn to withhold judgment, instead trying to empathize with the other party. This suggests an *adaptive role* to accommodate perceptions and behavior that may seem different. Assuming an adaptive role is important for a manager from an individualistic culture—such as the United States or Canada—who is working in a collectivist society like Japan or South Korea. As a manager, the individualist may have to develop consensual decision-making behavior, or become a group facilitator who listens well and prompts participation.[34]

Listen for Implicit Meanings

Perhaps cultural influence is most apparent in the way it shapes patterns of *explicit* and *implicit* communications. North Americans, British, and several other heterogeneous peoples in Europe tend to have very explicit patterns of communication. These are low-context cultures in which people learn to say exactly what they mean, to be precise in written communiqués, and to take great care in preparing contracts. Such patterns of communication minimize implicit meanings, thus reducing ambiguities that can occur in a multicultural environment. In contrast, the high-context societies of Japan, Saudi Arabia, Pakistan, and Greece have less need for explicit messages and formal, written documents because language, nonverbal gestures, and the context in which communication occurs have well-understood implicit meanings within these homogeneous societies. Often, meanings in these societies cannot be explained in objective terms; there are no exact translations that suffice. A word conveyed with a slightly different tone of voice or a subtle nod can have many different interpretations.

All cultures rely to some degree on subtle gestures to convey implicit meanings. For example, in France, Britain, and Italy, language rules are well developed; but local people have learned how to embellish meanings with physical gestures that foreigners seldom understand. Italians are noted for emotional facial expressions and expressive hand gestures to punctuate meanings. The British are seldom demonstrative, yet they make liberal use of adjectives and adverbs to modify language. The French are better known for voice inflections and altered tone levels that add subtle meanings to messages.[35] Indeed, speakers in most cultures often convey stronger messages "between the lines" than in their explicit statements, and foreign managers may never fully understand language subtleties. Nevertheless, they must remain alert for clues that

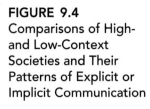

FIGURE 9.4
Comparisons of High- and Low-Context Societies and Their Patterns of Explicit or Implicit Communication

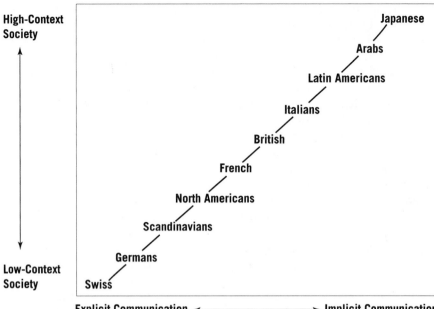

would help to avert misinterpretations. Contrasts in explicit and implicit language patterns are shown in Figure 9.4.

CONTRASTS IN ORAL AND NONVERBAL COMMUNICATION

Communication is the process of sharing meanings. It involves our total behavior, from uttering words to making subtle physical gestures. The term **communication** is derived from the Latin root *communicare*, which means "to make common." In that sense, communication fails to occur if the participants do not arrive at a common meaning.[36] Exactly how meanings are shared is difficult to analyze, and cultural differences described earlier emphasize the potential for miscommunication. All messages are packed with a sender's personal perceptions, and it is easy to assume that what is being said is also what is being heard. In fact, much can go wrong with a message.

The miscommunication problems that can occur in foreign relations are explored in this section, with specific emphasis on oral and nonverbal communications. *Oral communication* is the process of speaking with others and expressing ideas or thoughts that can be understood within the context of how others speak, listen, and interpret messages. *Nonverbal communication* refers to the meanings exchanged between individuals through physical gestures; behavior; sensory implications of touch, smell, and eye contact; and silence. Oral and nonverbal communications are explained by considering a model of the communication process.

The Communication Process

The basic communication model in Figure 9.5 represents a familiar process commonly presented in business and communication courses. The **sender** originates a

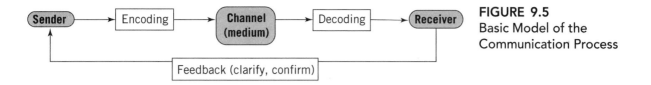

FIGURE 9.5
Basic Model of the Communication Process

message and is responsible for **encoding** it using symbols, words, pictures, or gestures. The method of encoding partially depends on the **channel** of communication. Obviously, e-mail messages cannot include gestures or other nonverbal symbols, and are therefore limited by the lack of behavior to embellish meanings. Nevertheless, language becomes important for encoding and subsequent translation, and personal style of using words, such as slang or modifiers, embellishes a message. Encoding is important because it is the process of formulating *meanings* in a way that is not likely to be easily misconstrued by a receiver. For that reason, choosing the correct channel should be a conscious decision with the receiver in mind.

The choice of a communication channel (or medium) can be a problem in foreign environments. For example, although the Japanese are world leaders in computer technology, Japanese managers seldom use e-mail or computer-generated messages in daily business affairs. Instead, they prefer face-to-face meetings, and they rely on handwritten memoranda. The Japanese are accustomed to proximity in personal communication; they avoid impersonal media, which cannot convey the implicit meanings common to interpersonal communication in Japan. Even telephone conversations are not always considered appropriate, because they do not provide physical proximity. In contrast, Chinese in Hong Kong and Singapore have no hesitation in using fax, e-mail, and mobile telephones almost anywhere for any business.[37] Hong Kong has the highest per-capita use of electronic media and mobile telephones in the world, and this has created some problems. Movie theaters, for example, warn people before performances that phones, beepers, and other devices must be turned off, and many restaurants forbid using mobile phones during dining hours.

Having consciously selected an appropriate channel or medium for communication, the sender begins a transmission; but this act alone does not constitute communication. An effective message requires a **receiver** who is capable of decoding the transmission. This is the person or audience to whom a message is addressed. **Decoding** is a perceptual assessment of information by the receiver, who *gives meaning to the message* by interpreting it. Communication begins as the receiver responds in a way that indicates how a sender's message is being received. During this exchange process the sender and receiver switch roles; the receiver becomes the sender, and the sender is now the receiver. Once a message has been sent, acknowledged, and verified (i.e., a response that indicates the intended meaning was received), then communication has taken place. Peter Drucker summarizes this sequence in the following passage:

> It is the recipient who communicates. The so-called communicator, the person who emits the communication, does not communicate. He utters. Unless there is someone who hears, there is no communication. There is only noise. The communicator speaks, or writes or sings—but he does not communicate. Indeed, he cannot communicate. He can only make it possible, or impossible, for a recipient—or rather "percipient"—to perceive.[38]

From an international management perspective, encoding and decoding activities are pivotal. They are the points at which communications often fail; yet they both depend on an effective medium that is suitable not only for encoding by the sender but also for decoding by the receiver. Some channels allow only a limited exchange of information, while others are capable of extensive communication that includes non-verbal and subtle meanings. Communication theorists refer to differences in these channels as *measures of media richness.*

Media richness is the capability of a given form of communication to convey in-formation.[39] At the lowest level, media are considered *lean* because they convey only limited and impersonal information. They lack information on attitudes, perceptions, or emotions of senders that give meanings to messages. Indeed, these impersonal media may have no specific senders or well-defined recipients. Consider how com-puter-generated reports can be massively replicated and automatically distributed through extensive databases. Advertising flyers, e-mail, and Internet home pages can be electronically flung into global markets. Telephone systems with auto-answering, auto-pay, and auto-order features cannot convey human feelings, and they provide no opportunity for an interactive response. Ironically, before "auto" features became common, the telephone was considered a *rich* media because of the human voice con-nection. Today, the telephone can often be a nuisance as people find themselves speak-ing into plastic mouthpieces to emotionless recordings. Indeed, they can feel betrayed or silly when they try to call humans and encounter recordings.

The highest level of media richness is face-to-face, one-on-one communication. This is enhanced when the surroundings are conducive to conversation, such as a pleasant office or a quiet place away from the clutter of work. Consequently, those who advocate effective communications emphasize that managers should consciously select a place where there is little physical or psychological noise. Interactive media are relatively rich, and they permit human exchange. Personal telephone conversa-tions or teleconferences with response-and-feedback capabilities are examples. Static media, such as memoranda and letters, have a delayed response capability. Facsimile and electronic mail messages have more rapid connection times than printed matter, yet until receivers acknowledge messages and respond, fax and e-mail messages are unilateral transmissions. Impersonal mass-generated messages and unidirectional di-rectives are very low on the media richness scale. These relationships are summarized in Figure 9.6.

FIGURE 9.6
Relative Richness of
Channel Media

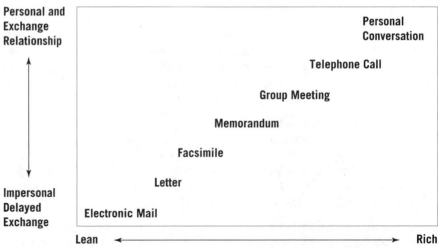

Oral Communications

Among the most common problems for managers on foreign assignments are misunderstandings that occur through translation or interpretation errors. Lack of foreign language skills strains oral communications, yet just learning a foreign language is seldom sufficient to avoid misunderstandings. Certainly learning the technical language skills of a foreign society is important, but understanding communication behavior requires an appreciation for cultural nuances in that language. For example, having knowledge of the Russian language will permit only a superficial ability to communicate in a country where approximately 150 million people represent 128 different cultural groups spread across 11 time zones. Nearly 60 different cultural languages exist in Russia (exempting other CIS republics) in addition to the official Russian tongue, and there are many variations in dialects.[40] Nevertheless, language skills are important, even if they are rudimentary, because managers will earn a host country's respect by sincerely attempting to communicate in the native tongue. The complexity of oral communication is emphasized by the unusual pattern of languages that exists in Luxembourg, profiled in the "Global Viewpoints" feature.

Paralanguage

More difficult to master than formal rules of a language is *paralanguage*, which is the pattern of conversational dialogue. **Paralanguage** is the rate of speech, the volume and intonation used in conversations, and the intention conveyed in the context of words and their meanings. Arabs, for example, tend to speak loudly compared to Europeans, and southern Chinese (Cantonese) speak extremely loudly compared to almost any other society. The Cantonese use at least seven different primary tones to embellish words; in northern China, the official Putonghua language (the Beijing dialect of Mandarin) has four tonal combinations. Mandarin speakers criticize Cantonese as a rough, loud, and complicated language, and Cantonese speakers complain that Mandarin is a "lazy" dialect. Cantonese and Mandarin speakers rarely understand one another.[41] Men tend to speak louder than women in most societies, yet women tend to speak more rapidly. However, most Asians, Arabs, and people from the Indian Subcontinent speak extremely fast compared to European and North American societies. In contrast, native Latin American cultures often have a soft and slower-paced style of conversation.

Voice inflection in China, Japan, and Korea can completely alter word meanings; but then again, most languages have some inflection characteristics that convey different meanings. The word *no* said loudly can reflect its absolute meaning of "No, and that's final!" It can be said softly as "maybe," or "I'm not sure." It can take on many more meanings, which English speakers convey subconsciously through voice inflection. The Japanese are famous for being able to avoid saying no, or seeming to say yes but meaning no. Because many Asian cultures have bisyllabic languages in which one word seldom has meaning by itself, clauses or "two-symbol" words are linked to convey a meaning. Even then, conversational meanings vary by context. Most words, even common ones like *water, wind, no, yes, good,* or *bad,* take on meanings only when they are linked with other words.

The example using *no* is extremely basic and does not reveal the complexity that occurs through variations in word usage. For example, there are 413 inflection sounds in Chinese that can modify any bisyllabic character set. Yet by comparison, Chinese is not that complicated; there are 420 inflections in Japanese, 468 in French, 437 in German, and 493 in Russian. Western languages, including English with about 462 inflections, are simpler than Chinese or Japanese because they are based on an alphabet of 26 characters. In contrast, the Japanese have 51 and the Chinese have 167 root

GLOBAL VIEWPOINT

LANGUAGE LUXURY IN LUXEMBOURG

Luxembourg may be small, with a population of barely 400,000, but it is the strategic center of the European Union and rich in language and culture. Unfortunately, the Grand Duchy has been invaded, conquered, settled, or controlled by nearly all of its neighbors at one time or another during the past several hundred years. Since the end of World War II (during which it remained neutral while armies from several continents marched around its territories), Luxembourg has been occupied by world diplomats and foreign executives. It is the provisional seat of European Union institutions and the center for the powerful European Coal and Steel Community. It was a founding member of the European Economic Community (EEC) and the European Atomic Energy Committee. The European Court of Justice, Bank for European Investment, and European Court of Auditors are based there. Luxembourg is also the home to the Secretariat General of the European Parliament. The World Economic Forum has ranked Luxembourg as the most competitive economy in Europe and fifth in the world behind Singapore, Hong Kong, New Zealand, and the United States.

With these credentials, the Grand Duchy attracts an unusual assortment of global interests, and language has become a sensitive issue among Luxembourg residents. The courts dispense justice almost exclusively in French, but nearly half of all legal documents are in German, many are in French, and a few are in English. Although Luxembourg is primarily a Catholic country, its church influence comes from Germany. Consequently, written religious communications tend to favor German; yet scriptures in Latin, French, and several other languages are common. Priests tend to speak French in their daily lives, but they deliver sermons in Luxembourgish, the country's native tongue. Children learn German as a mandatory language until the age of seven, after which they study almost exclusively in French. However, most daily conversation, shopping transactions, and local entertainment media are in Luxembourgish, the native tongue. Speaking at least four major languages, Luxembourgers may have the most colorful communication characteristics in Europe—perhaps in the world. Certainly, languages have taken on styles not common beyond the Grand Duchy, and locals often speak in a manner called Letzebuergesh that few foreign linguists can sort out.

Foreign diplomats and business travelers may encounter even greater challenges while the country solidifies its native tongue as the official language. The citizens of Luxembourg are determined to shed French, German, and English usage for every public function. Some years ago, the population voted overwhelmingly to adopt Luxembourgish as the official language, but officials could not implement the new law. Only one dictionary, created during the 1950s, recorded the vocabulary and grammar of the language. It was not until 1975 that the government published a substantial manual on "How to Speak Luxembourgish." Consequently, hundreds of words in daily use have no equivalent in the official language. Nevertheless, in 1984 Luxembourgish became the national language; government documents, court records, negotiations, contracts, and even many church scriptures are now written in that language.

Although many people in the world have never heard of Luxembourg, it is perhaps the single most important strategic center of European activity, which now extends into Central and Eastern European states. A tourist may be mildly amused by the extraordinary mix of language and communication behavior, but those who must do business there are scrambling to learn how to communicate in the Grand Duchy.

Sources: Adapted from Luxembourg government special reports on National Day, 21 June 1996, including "Mother Tongue Triumphs," "Neutral Position Aids Compromise," and "Open, Flexible Economy Tops European League."

characters. To complicate things further, Chinese grammar has no genders, plurals, tenses, cases, or conjunctions. The Japanese have many of these conventions, and other Asian languages often have very distinct language protocols for use with and by each gender.[42]

Metacommunication

Language nuances are difficult to interpret even when someone is fluent in a foreign language, but metacommunication is more troublesome. **Metacommunication** is the implied meaning of a message, whether conveyed intentionally or subconsciously during a conversation. Voice inflection, tone, and the speed of conversation can impart different emotional meanings. For instance, an increase in speed often suggests anger or impatience. A slightly higher pitch might imply apprehension or uncertainty, and subtle differences in the context in which words or phrases are used can send unexpected messages.

For example, an American woman visiting Indonesia for her consulting firm arrived at a business meeting in a fashionable pants suit. She was greeted by the local director, who said, "My dear, *that's* a lovely outfit." He emphasized the word *that's*, sending a subtle message that her attire was inappropriate. The woman did not get the message but felt some sense of discomfort by the director's tone. As she left the meeting and walked to her hotel, she began to notice that all women were in dresses or skirts. She discovered later that pants suits are not uncommon, but they are rarely worn in business meetings with Muslim clients.[43]

Conversational Behavior

Cultures have different patterns of conversational behavior that result from their orientations to time, physical proximity of speakers, and thinking processes. These factors directly affect oral communications through relationships between participants, but they are also dimensions of nonverbal communications.

Chronemics

Attitudes toward time are called **chronemics**, and researchers broadly classify most societies as either *monochronic* or *polychronic*.[44] Figure 9.7 illustrates the concept. In a monochronic culture, people think in linear terms; activities and events occur in sequence. People tend to take time commitments seriously, concentrate on one thing at a time, and treat time as an asset. In a polychronic culture, people think in relational terms, which are often called "circular" patterns, and they often are rather casual about time commitments. They often do several things at once rather than in sequence, and they often "talk around points" rather than "getting to the point." Germans and Swiss are monochronic and very time conscious, whereas Americans,

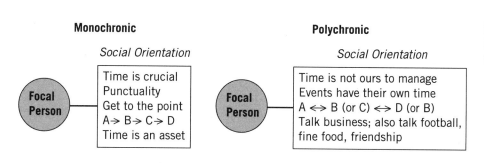

Monochronic

Social Orientation

Focal Person

Time is crucial
Punctuality
Get to the point
A → B → C → D
Time is an asset

Polychronic

Social Orientation

Focal Person

Time is not ours to manage
Events have their own time
A ↔ B (or C) ↔ D (or B)
Talk business; also talk football,
fine food, friendship

FIGURE 9.7
Monochronic versus Polychronic Behavior

British, and Scandinavians, although also monochronic, are relatively less time-driven. At the other extreme, time seems to have little meaning in the Latin countries of Chile, Peru, and Mexico. Punctuality is not a virtue in most Latin cultures, so business meetings can be very casual and last for hours with no apparent agenda. Polychronic societies also include North African and Middle Eastern Arab states, where time is considered a dimension of religion—God decides man's priorities and when things are accomplished.[45]

Proxemics

The physical proximity of people engaged in conversation is known as **proxemics**.[46] Arabs, Greeks, and Turks tend to stand very close during a conversion. This seems almost oppressive to Americans, who prefer to talk at a comfortable distance from one another. An American typically considers a distance of about 18 inches too intimate for conversations among business colleagues. Instead, most Americans prefer a distance of about four feet for informal relationships, and perhaps a bit more during social or business engagements. Latin Americans often seem to press closely together, creating situations too personal for comfort among Europeans or North Americans.[47]

In contrast, Japanese and Chinese societies are considered low-touch, private societies. Chinese people often carry on conversations standing several feet apart and at angles to one another. The Japanese prefer a formal amount of separation; after being introduced and exchanging business cards, a Japanese business colleague usually steps back a pace or two to maintain distance. Outsiders can misinterpret such actions as withdrawal, arrogance, or rudeness; but conversely, the closeness of a conversation with an Arab or Greek can create an overbearing atmosphere. Indeed, Arabs are accused of creating an "intimidating closeness" when they converse.[48]

Proxemics also affect meetings. Arabs and Latin Americans are likely to arrange meetings in rather close quarters, which can seem stifling to foreigners. On the other hand, Japanese are likely to arrange spacious meetings with formal seating for participants, who are carefully positioned according to ceremonious conventions.[49]

Thought Processes

Conversation patterns are substantially different among societies with fundamentally different ways of thinking. For example, in most Asian cultures, people resist making fast decisions. They ponder issues, negotiate at length, talk around issues (or so it seems to more time-conscious outsiders), and in general work deliberately to find solutions to problems. This casual pace can be frustrating to Americans and Europeans, partly because they bring different time orientations to the relationships, as noted earlier, but also because people in Asian cultures tend to make *inductive* decisions. Specifically, they solve problems by starting with details and factual observations, gradually building toward generalizations or conclusions. As a model for inductive reasoning, consider a medical diagnosis that begins with a careful examination of specific symptoms, then proceeds toward diagnoses, and culminates in a decision about treatment.

In contrast, managers in western societies tend to favor *deductive* reasoning. They solve problems by starting with broad categories and then evaluate details and more specific information to reveal the nature of a problem and potential solutions. This tends to be a rapid process, one that people from inductive cultures perceive as jumping to conclusions. Although people in all cultures engage in both inductive and deductive reasoning, each society is likely to have one prominent pattern of thinking. People brought up to think and act in one frame of reference experience difficulty in adjusting to the other without misunderstandings.[50] Figure 9.8 contrasts the two processes.

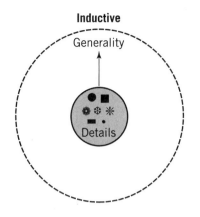
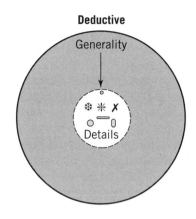

FIGURE 9.8
Inductive versus Deductive Reasoning

Nonverbal Communications

Cultural orientations toward concepts of time, space, thought processes, proximity to one another, language intonations, and voice inflections are all part of the oral and nonverbal communication process. Each of these factors influences nonverbal behavior in personal relationships, but there are several characteristics to emphasize in addition to those already mentioned.

Kinesics

The term **kinesics** refers to any body movement that embellishes or amplifies communication. It includes gestures, facial expressions, and mannerisms such as posture.[51] The Italians and Greeks are known for arm and hand gestures to give extra expression to words, but Chinese and Japanese tend to keep their arms still and their hands clasped in their laps. Americans are known for scratching their heads or tweaking an ear lobe when talking, but most gestures are subtle. Americans have telltale habits of crossing their arms or legs when bored, and when coupled with a backward shift in their chairs, this posture often suggests a sense of defensiveness. In Japan, crossing the arms or leaning back stiffly in a chair does not carry the same meaning. Infamous misunderstandings have resulted from the "thumbs up" gesture, which to Americans commonly means "okay." The same gesture has an angry and obscene meaning in Latin American societies. The two-finger "V for victory" sign in America is a crude obscenity in Britain when flashed with the palm inward. In Sri Lanka and several groups in India, a quick sideward nod of the head, which would be taken as a "no response" elsewhere, actually means "yes, I agree." If the nod is slight, it is like saying "well, maybe."

Facial expressions create special meanings, and all cultures have developed subconsciously ingrained habits to convey meanings for anger, happiness, contempt, sadness, and many other emotions. People also learn how to hide feelings such as crying, or to intimidate others by purposely scowling. The Japanese tend to smile as a way of masking other emotions, not necessarily to imply a sense of pleasure. The Chinese seem to stare almost without expression, and such a fixed gaze can be quite disconcerting to a westerner; in fact, it can mean anything from disinterest to intense concentration, or from disgust to deep respect.

Eye contact, or **oculesics**, is a special form of facial expression. Most Asians with cultures rooted in Confucian social philosophy can purposely use a fixed gaze to show disrespect; but it would be risky to assume this meaning as a foreigner. In their own cultures, Japanese, Koreans, and Chinese will lower their eyes, focusing on the other person's chin or neck during a conversation. This is a common sign of deferential respect. Many subordinates try diligently to avoid direct eye contact with their superiors, but superiors are expected to glare as a way of reinforcing their authority. Male Arabs and men from southern India stare intensely into another person's eyes as they speak at very close quarters. Women from these regions, on the other hand, are careful to maintain distance and only indirect eye contact.[52]

Mannerisms can be very sensitive. Germans consider a slouched stance as rude, but in North America it merely suggests a sense of informality. The left hand is considered unclean in Muslim societies, so not only do people from these societies avoid touching others with their left hands, but they use their right hands for many gestures—for eating, opening doors, or greeting friends. Americans often put their hands in their pockets, even in formal meetings, but in Britain this gesture is too casual for comfort and implies a sense of arrogance or disdain. Latin Americans prefer a casual stance, which they interpret as a signal of personal warmth in conversations, but a hand in a pocket in Japan or South Korea can be a sign of disgust. Greeks and Italians—true to their expressive characters—often toss their heads vigorously or jerk their shoulders upward, coupled with various facial expressions, to reinforce a point. People in every culture display many mannerisms, and although most are related to common courtesies, many purposely convey hidden meanings.

Physical Contact

A tremendous number of emotions can be conveyed through body contact. It's the stuff that romance is made of—kisses, hugs, and gentle touches. It is also the stuff that can fuel conflict—a strong-arm grapple, an unpleasant nudge, or a push. In practical business situations, a variety of emotions can be conveyed by the way people shake hands, or when someone pats another on the shoulder. Many societies avoid physical contact, while others reinforce communication through touch. Japan, Finland, and Sweden are known as "don't touch" cultures, and the French and Chinese are characterized as being "physically remote." In contrast, Italy and Greece are high-touch societies, where body contact can become intrusive to those from low-touch cultures. Americans and Canadians fall between the extremes, but are slightly more likely to touch others than to remain at a physical distance.[53]

To most foreigners, the Chinese seem to avoid personal contact. They reluctantly shake hands, and when they do their grips are limp with no hand pumping. The Chinese try hard to avoid brushing other people, and they do not engage in back patting or hugging among colleagues. Paradoxically, Chinese men and women walk hand in hand publicly (men with men or women with women). Foreigners often construe this custom as homosexual behavior, yet it is a common practice among close friends.[54] The Japanese have become comfortable with shaking hands with foreigners, but among themselves, distance is more common; body language, facial expressions, or various methods of bowing replace human contact.[55] In contrast. Arabs, Turks, people from the Balkan states, and most Russians will kiss colleagues repeatedly on the cheeks with no regard for gender. These are forms of greeting or gestures of friendship. Latin Americans are also high-touch societies in which back patting, lingering handshakes, and hugging are common. In Brazil, for example, two men may begin a conversation with a hearty handshake that quickly becomes an *abraco*, a term that distinctly means "a male embrace." Such tight embraces may last several minutes among close friends.[56]

Differences in nonverbal gestures and habits of human contact can be entertaining to study, but they all have serious communication properties. People use expressions purposely to send messages or to convey implied meanings in place of direct statements. There are advantages to being able to demonstrate disgust with another person by turning away, fixing a glare, or making a cross-armed withdrawal gesture rather than directly confronting them. In the high-context societies of North America, a person may be more direct and simply vocalize disgust. But in Asian and Middle Eastern societies, where "saving face" and harmony are important, the nonverbal clues are essential.

Not least among these nonverbal clues is *silence*. Many societies use silence as a response that implies disapproval or dissent, but in others it is a sign of respect. The Japanese are a quiet people who value silence in meetings. They carefully choose words and use long pauses between points in negotiations. Silence is a mark of self-control, a highly desirable trait in Japan that dates back centuries to the *bushido code* (way of the warrior, or samurai). This code emphasized the qualities of calmness and inner strength for men.[57] In contrast, Italy, Greece, Turkey, and the Arab states are characterized as noisy cultures in which conversations are rapid, people often interrupt or overlap other speakers, and moments of silence are quickly interpreted as disinterest or disapproval.

The combined effect of intracultural patterns of behavior, oral communications, and nonverbal practices reinforces the point that *intercultural communication* can be extremely complicated. Some suggestions for improving communications have been woven into earlier discussions, but researchers have a few well-developed recommendations for international managers; these are explored in the next section.

GUIDELINES FOR EFFECTIVE INTERCULTURAL COMMUNICATION

Effective communication begins by being able to **acclimate** to foreign values and customs. This does not mean that a person should compromise his or her own values, but it is necessary to accommodate those of a host country. This requires learning about, and when possible living within, a foreign society to achieve an appreciation of cultural differences. Expatriates who have resided abroad for much of their careers tend to develop the flexibility required to quickly adapt to unusual conditions. Even if expatriates find themselves in new situations where values and customs starkly contrast with their own, they can usually acclimate far more easily than individuals with limited foreign experience.[58] International managers may not always learn a foreign language, but their experiences abroad condition them to sensitive language differences. With that in mind, several suggestions for improving communication effectiveness follow.

Going beyond Language Training

Trotting the globe is the ultimate prerequisite to becoming culturally sensitive, but that does not help younger managers about to embark on their first international assignments. Learning a second or third language can help individuals prepare for international careers, but often more can be gained by studying foreign literature for its metaphors, philosophies, and customs. This may not require knowledge of a foreign language, since many of the world's great works of literature have been translated. Also, many guides to foreign cultures have been written, aimed at both tourists and professional travelers, and foreign embassies have information about their countries. This includes not only hard data such as economic performance but also soft information such as historical vignettes and portfolios on fine arts and cultural events.

International e-mail and networks provide exceptionally rich sources of contacts throughout the world, and today it is quite easy to connect with other people through Internet websites. Each new contact or bit of knowledge about a foreign country enhances the ability to understand how cultural values differ.

Many companies have formal training programs to acclimate employees slated to work abroad. In addition to language skills, the programs can include negotiating skills, training in dispute resolution, decision-making, and nonverbal communications. General Electric conducts training for expatriates and their families based on anthropological concepts that address diverse issues such as living abroad, diet, shopping, social customs, and religious practices. AT&T brings foreign-born managers to the United States, often for as long as two years, and they participate with American managers in cross-cultural sensitivity training to build communicative skills. At McDonald's Hamburger University in Illinois, nearly half of the 250 students in each program are from outside the United States, and translation is available in 22 languages.[59]

Communication effectiveness is enhanced by immersion in a culture, but when that is not possible, formal college courses and company training programs help to develop an appreciation of multicultural differences. Government agencies also provide special training in multicultural diversity, for people going overseas as well as for those who work with foreign organizations at home. Motorola runs proprietary training programs, and it contracts with universities in the United States, Singapore, Europe, and Latin America to provide development programs for employees and their families specifically to enhance communication effectiveness. Typical modules in Motorola's training programs include, for example, transcultural competencies, systems philoso-

Employees learn to use team-based network communication systems at Motorola University, the company's training headquarters in Illinois. Motorola provides interactive coursework in 24 languages for its international staff in more than 80 countries to create a corporate fabric of cross-cultural communications and fully integrated data resource systems.

phies of communication, measurement systems, managerial practices, coaching be-havior, and strategic planning.[60] Unfortunately, most companies offer little in the way of cultural training beyond the technical requirements of an overseas assignment. Re-searchers have found that nearly 90 percent of all North American and European multinationals provide little more than orientation sessions for their expatriates, and fewer still include family members in the process.[61]

Language and Expression

Learning a language goes beyond a simple ability to recall usable phrases and expres-sions. It also requires an awareness of embedded sociocultural nuances. An American on the way to Germany, for example, would need to know that people there expect formal business greetings, and they address one another by last name preceded by title. In Germany, *specific titles* are extremely important to remember. Not all univer-sity lecturers are called professors; only those with full professor ranks are addressed in that manner. An executive with a Ph.D., although not an academic, will be properly addressed as *doctor.* In Spain, individuals in the same positions may be introduced by their first names and, as a matter of conversation, identified as a professor, managing director, vice president, or some other title.[62] In the Philippines, a foreign manager may be greeted with a precursory sound that often seems like a rude grunt; Filipinos often use honorifics of *po* and *ho* to convey respect for others of superior rank or social status. In many societies, very subtle variations define gender-specific language usage. For example, in Thailand, male speakers use the expression "sawasdeekrab" to say "hello" or "welcome," but female speakers say "sawasdeeka" to mean the same thing. Neither a man nor a woman in Thailand would dare to use the other gender's propri-etary words or language markers.[63]

The wording of a statement is not always what it seems to be. *Euphemisms* are common in most Asian conversations because unlike western societies, Asian societies prefer to avoid direct confrontations. Consequently, their linguistic behavior often seems to be loaded with ambiguities. For example, a Japanese manager reviewing a letter in English typed by his secretary said: "This is very good—very few mistakes—keep up your studies of English." The message intended was: "This is not very good—there are too many mistakes, and you need to study English." The secretary, inciden-tally, was not pursuing any formal training in English, but she got the message and quickly enrolled in an evening course.[64] Each language also has its slang, proverbs, and conventions that seldom show up in foreign language courses. A few examples of

---

GLOBAL VIEWPOINT

AMERICAN SLANG AND FOREIGN INTERPRETATIONS

"Let's do a deal"	To an Arab means: "Let's do something unethical."
"What's the bottom line?"	To a Japanese means: "What is your starting bid?"
"Okay" or "That's okay"	To a Chinese means: "Not really good, could be better."
"That's a shame"	To an Indian means: "You have insulted me."
"I get a kick from that"	To a Japanese means: "It hurts."
"Can we close on this?"	To a Chinese means: "We should stop, cancel this."
"This is too good to be true"	To a Malaysian means: "You must be cheating me."

American slang and foreign interpretations are shown in the Global Viewpoint feature. Several publishers have dictionaries of slang, and in some foreign universities, students are required to study American slang because it has surfaced in so many international business situations.[65]

Perceptual Differences

People from different societies may be schooled in common business practices, but hold very different perceptions about how to do business. Consider the transition taking place in Russia, and how people differ in their thinking. Many Russian managers have been formally trained in western marketing techniques during the past few years, and many more Russians have studied in the United States or Western Europe, with internships lasting from several months to several years. Nevertheless, few of these managers are able to adapt to western business values. When asked about how they segment their markets or identify customers, for example, most can recite definitions, but few can explain differences in customer preferences. For generations, Russian factories produced standard goods for the masses without customer preferences in mind; people trained in these assumptions cannot yet accept the concept of demand-driven marketing, so terms such as *segmentation* mean little to them. Consequently, communications between Russian managers and their western associates often fail due to fundamental differences in perception about business practices.[66]

There is not much a person can do about perceptual differences, yet becoming more aware of the social, ideological, and cultural underpinnings of a foreign society often reveals important clues about potential perceptual problems. Companies such as AT&T, Kodak, British Petroleum, Sony, and Banque Nationale de Paris have created extensive management development programs, which concentrate on fundamental perceptual differences that their managers are likely to encounter in foreign assignments. Some companies such as Xerox and CitiGroup have developed language manuals for training employees in perceptual differences and potential problems that occur through misinterpretations.[67] Often, however, students can gain valuable insights from discussing concepts such as marketing or consumer behavior with foreign students or visiting professors.

Rules and Customs

It is important to understand the dangers of violating religious, moral, and social codes in foreign societies. It is also important to avoid generalizations that gloss over specific differences of host countries. Most cross-cultural research and educational programs generalize about clusters of countries or regions, such as Europe, Asia, or the Middle East, but each society in these regions can be remarkably different. In the sub-Saharan region of Africa, for instance, there are more than 40 independent nations with at least 800 linguistic communities and cultural identities. The Middle East has at least 20 national cultures and 60 languages, including 200 or more independent dialects. This part of the world has several diametrically opposed societies with equally diverse values, such as those found in Lebanon, Israel, Turkey, Egypt, Cypress, and Saudi Arabia.[68]

Encoding and Decoding

Effective communication in any language, and between any parties anywhere, requires clear encoding by senders and accurate decoding by receivers. By definition, any person involved in communication must be responsible for both roles. The process begins with the selection of an appropriate medium for a message. The richness of the medium should be consistent with the nature of the intended communication. Personal contact arranged through a formal office meeting, an informal chat at work, or a social coffee are some options, but keep in mind that the selection of a venue sends an implied message before actual conversation begins. For example, scheduling an office staff meeting or just calling a subordinate into your office suggests formal roles and a clearly work-related agenda. A formal statement scheduling a meeting, such as an official memo, may strike a chord of seriousness or create trepidation among those invited. If this implication is part of the intended communication, then the memo is an appropriate medium; but the same message delivered through the same medium for a relatively unimportant matter could do more harm than good.

Foreign managers can breach protocol by meeting with an employee several levels down, thus circumventing a supervisor. Although the purpose of the meeting may be nothing more than having a casual chat, the fact that the meeting occurred could seriously disrupt relationships. Using the wrong channel can aggravate receivers. As noted earlier, the Japanese do not appreciate computer-generated memoranda; they expect more personalized handwritten memos or face-to-face contact in most instances.[69]

Managers can choose several different media with mutually reinforced messages. For example, announcing an important new safety procedure might first be set down carefully in a written directive, summarized in a notice, and reinforced at staff meetings. If this communication takes place in a foreign location where several languages are spoken, the actual encoding may require translation and "back translation" to ensure that the meaning is clear. For example, at Motorola's Hong Kong facility, important notices, letters, and fax messages that are intended for local Chinese employees are first written in English and then translated into Chinese. The Chinese version is then back-translated into English by a third party. The original and back-translated documents are compared to ensure that an accurate message has been written and translated. It is not unusual, however, to discover that messages can change substantially in translation. An example is shown in Figure 9.9.

Unfortunately, this translation process is often ignored, which results in unpleasant blunders. General Motors struggled to market its Nova car model in Puerto Rico and several other Latin countries before it discovered that the name sounded like the Spanish words *no va*, which mean "it does not go." Ford discovered several years ago that the name of its *Caliente* model meant something like "streetwalker" in Brazil.

Question asked in English on a survey questionnaire of Chinese managers concerning their cultural values. The question was translated into simplified Chinese characters and then back-translated by a third party into English.

FIGURE 9.9
Back-Translation to Clarify Meanings

Question in English: **Do you value spirituality?**
     Intended meaning: Do you value religious practices?

Translated into Chinese: **Do you believe in ghosts or demons?**

Back-translation into English: **Do you know ghosts or demons?**

Sunbeam Corporation promoted its hair-curling irons in Germany as *mist-producing* appliances, only to find out that in German the word *mist* suggested excrement. These and many other international blunders are compiled in tongue-in-cheek books, but they often have serious consequences.[70]

Decoding is a form of psychological translation, and being an effective receiver requires a person to *listen with empathy*. Put yourself in the shoes of the sender and try to grasp the meaning of a message with as little psychological distortion as possible. Reinforce your understanding of the message with a reply or question, and then refine or verify what you hear. For example, a popular American manager at the Marriott Hotel in Hong Kong was nearing the end of an overseas assignment and preparing to return home. His secretary, a Chinese woman with whom he had worked closely for several years, remarked: "Mr. Brice, you look very happy to be going home." The remark caught Brice a bit off guard, and he sensed a hidden message of some kind. He replied: "Yes, I look forward to seeing family and friends again, but, Alicia, do I 'look different' somehow?" She said: "Well, Mr. Brice, you *do seem* very bright and cheerful." Brice thought for a moment, and it dawned on him that she was really saying: *Mr. Brice, you seem TOO happy about leaving.* Brice tested this by commenting: "Alicia, my assignment here has been wonderful, and in many ways I'm actually sad to leave such good friends like yourself. I'm not as 'bright and cheerful' inside as you think, but everyone also needs their families, so going home will be pleasant. Perhaps I can come back one day." His secretary seemed delighted, and Brice realized that what Alicia was communicating was the need to recognize their friendship. He jotted a note to himself to give her a nice parting gift as a gesture of that friendship.[71]

Develop Feedback Systems

Individuals as well as organizations need effective information feedback systems. A company announcing a new safety procedure could broadcast a new policy, disseminate well-translated notices, and even emphasize the procedures with key staff members, yet fail to adequately communicate the necessary information. To make sure the message is received and understood, a manager should *solicit feedback* and evaluate it to ensure that the message has been understood. For example, the manager concerned with a new safety procedure could set in motion a follow-up program to monitor employee safety habits or hold small group meetings with employees and their supervisors to gain insight about their perceptions of the new procedures. The process of translation and back-translation at Motorola is a quality control device for ensuring effective communication, but the company also utilizes focus-group meetings to solicit feedback and recommendations.

On a broader scale, international companies face system-wide problems in gathering feedback, such as appropriate links between headquarters units and diversified field units. Large multinationals must implement extraordinary measures to accumulate information from hundreds of foreign managers and operations in foreign cultures, often with major variations in language. Even if all communications conform to a single language, such as English, differences in language skills throughout the company can lead to misunderstandings. Consequently, firms use multiple media as feedback systems. Through telephone calls, fax messages, reports, memoranda, letters, and meetings, they purposely duplicate or reinforce important messages. For example, S. C. Hayward Associates, an American exporter with offices in 16 Latin American countries, follows a standing policy that any invoice or customer inquiry must have a confirmation follow-up through a second medium in both English and the native language. This requirement complicates office procedures, yet staff members encounter at least one significant communication incident every day that requires clarification. Effective feedback has helped the company avoid many costly problems.[72]

Enhance Boundary-Spanning Activities

In conclusion, both individual managers and global organizations can improve communications by *enhancing boundary-spanning activities*. Boundaries divide peer groups, functional departments, and geographically dispersed operations. These distinctions can be loosely referred to as *horizontal* boundaries, because they emerge when people and groups at similar levels in a company maintain compartmentalized barriers that thwart communications. *Vertical* boundaries also divide people and groups, since formal hierarchies differentiate authority. This tendency is often especially apparent in organizations where cultural dimensions emphasize power distance, as described in the previous chapter. One answer to both horizontal and vertical boundary problems is to engage in activities that soften the barriers. Researchers have found that the best vehicle for accomplishing this goal is **interpersonal dialogue**.[73]

The process of an interpersonal dialogue ideally begins with senior executives. These executives meet in small groups with managers at one or two subordinate levels, with the purpose of building a better team understanding of how they can improve communications. Consultants often facilitate these meetings, but if the participants are willing to try to learn from one another, self-directed meetings can achieve important gains. The meetings can involve two or more individuals, but they should be limited to no more than 12 to 15 to allow active participation. Any real issue or problem can serve as the topic for these meetings, but the main purpose is to reconcile differences in communication techniques. By openly discussing their problems and misunderstandings, the participants can collectively improve patterns of both oral and nonverbal communication. By replicating this process at successively lower organizational levels, a company can systematically encourage cooperation and reduce communication problems.

The concept of a dialogue is common to those in organizational development training, and it is one of the fundamental intervention methods for team building. Effective communication *is* effective team behavior, and in the global organization, this is a critical requirement for developing effective *relational networks*. Recall that relational networks are characteristic of global organizations where pervasive cooperation is achieved among worldwide operations. This is not achieved unless effective communication systems exist, and within those systems, individuals have the ability to understand one another through shared meanings. The next chapter addresses *intercultural negotiations* as an extension of this concept.

REVIEW QUESTIONS

1. What are the major differences between high-context societies and low-context societies?
2. How do economic and social systems influence patterns of communication?
3. Explain how political ideologies affect business communications and personal relationships.
4. How does the educational system in Japan differ from that in the United States? What role does an educational system play in molding communication patterns?
5. Describe the basic communication process and its component activities.
6. What is paralanguage? How can foreign managers guard against misunderstandings that arise from imputed meanings due to the nuances of language?

7. Explain the concepts of chronemics and proxemics. What problems would these conditions cause for western managers?
8. Describe nonverbal communications. What can a manager do when working abroad to prevent difficulties that arise from subtle meanings of nonverbal messages?
9. Contrast differences in the way people think. How do these variations in thought patterns affect communication behavior?
10. Explain four things that managers can do to become more effective at communications in a foreign assignment.

GLOSSARY OF KEY TERMS

Acclimation   The process of developing a sufficient understanding of a culture to accommodate differences and tolerate contrasts in patterns of behavior, attitudes, beliefs, and customs.

Channel   The method of communication selected to encode a message; also called the *medium*.

Chronemics   Attitudes toward time; monochronic societies tend to think of time sequentially and work on one task at a time, while polychronic societies think relationally and handle disruptions or interruptions without worrying about lost time.

Communication   From a Latin word meaning "make common," the exchange of information or meanings in such a way that both parties share a common understanding.

Decoding   The perceptual assessment of information by a receiver that eventually gives meaning to a message.

Encoding   The process of arranging symbols, words, gestures, pictures, and other elements to formulate a message with an intended meaning and a particular receiver in mind.

Intercultural communication   Patterns of exchanging meanings between individuals, groups, organizations, or societies with different cultural antecedents.

Interpersonal communication   Exchanges between individuals using the oral and nonverbal indicators of meaning.

Interpersonal dialogue   Exchanges that bring people together to reconcile differences in communication habits, thus building teamwork and improving understanding through participative training.

Intracultural communication   Patterns of exchanging meanings within a society that create shared understandings among a people, community, or ethnic group.

Kinesics   Commonly called *body language*, or any expressive use of the body—hands, arms, head, and facial movements or expressions.

Media richness   The capability of a given form of communication to convey information. Lean media support impersonal exchanges and convey limited information; rich media support personal exchanges and offer many ways to embellish meanings through gestures and behavior.

Metacommunication   The implied meaning of a message, which can be conveyed intentionally or unintentionally through voice inflection, choice of words, tonal qualities, or nonverbal embellishment.

Oculesics   A special form of kinesics that concerns eye movements, including glaring, staring, or the direction and focus of the eyes.

Paralanguage   The rate of speech, volume, tone, and context of oral communications that combine to enhance the explicit wording of messages.

Proxemics   The behavior patterns common in societies that govern the proximity of people engaged in conversation, ranging from relatively close and intense to relatively distant and disengaged.

Receiver   The intended audience for a message.

Sender   The person who originates a message.

EXERCISES

1. As a group or individual exercise, list 10 slang terms common in your home language and how people in several foreign countries might interpret them. You should research slang

dictionaries or popular books on business blunders, which cite many examples for English and other selected languages.

2. Form teams and select one member of each to communicate a simple message (perhaps several paragraphs long, or a brief conversational presentation). Challenge the listening team members to jot down the message received and its meaning, and then to note all possible gestures, facial expressions, and other nonverbal clues used by the speaker. This activity can take place in a classroom setting where team members alternatively act as speakers and prepare messages in advance, planning intentional use of nonverbal communications and both explicit and implicit meanings. Compare the results and discuss conclusions of individual team members and groups.

3. Develop three distinct ways to say exactly the same thing, but assume three different cultural orientations. Use the following statement for this exercise, or formulate your own basic statement: "No, I will not pay that much for a product of such low quality." Choose any three variations that you like (e.g., Japanese, British, French, Indian, Chinese, Arab, etc.), but be prepared to explain why you reformulated the message and the meaning it conveys.

TRANSPRINT USA: AN OPEN DOOR IN CHINA

Transprint USA is a rapidly growing manufacturer of heat-transfer printing paper with sales in more than 15 countries. Transfer paper has rapidly become the preferred method of coloring synthetic fabrics used in clothing, fashion designs and accessories, upholstery materials, household products such as drapes and bedding ensembles, and promotional imprint products. Most people are unaware of the many different applications of heat-transfer technology, but they will recognize promotional items such as NFL-branded jackets, Disney collectibles, and T-shirts promoting the Hard Rock Café. Many of these products are printed by a dry-heat transfer process that applies a design to fabric.

This technology has gone far beyond decals and T-shirts to become a mass-production method of creating colorful designs on fabrics, plastics, and even certain types of metal or composite surfaces. Indeed, it is a billion-dollar industry with tremendous growth opportunities because the dry transfer process requires only inexpensive equipment to press together the master-design paper and untreated fabric. A fabric mill no longer requires complicated presses with ink stations for each color and feature. The advantage of the transfer process over wet-ink printing is tremendous for mass-produced fabrics or synthetic vinyls. Domestic markets in Europe and North America are very profitable, with goods contracted for retailers including K-Mart and Wal-Mart; commercial buyers such as Burlington Mills also fabricate millions of meters of each design for clients such as Holiday Inn Resorts. The process also allows unusual and intricate designs seldom achieved through ink-printed processes, so upscale clients such as Victoria's Secret can create their own patterns, produced with transfer paper, for products such as women's lingerie.

This technology is particularly attractive to mills in developing countries, where there are huge markets for inexpensive home products and clothing. Transprint USA has reached many of these emerging markets, but set its sights especially on China, where

the technology is almost unknown. The president of Transprint USA, Bill Boyd, recently contacted consultants in Hong Kong to assist in opening the China market for his company. The consultants provided marketing information and industry data on Chinese printing techniques, factories, and distribution systems. They advised Boyd to enter the China market cautiously through a contract agent—an established mainland company that would ethically market Transprint products without pirating and had proper connections to printing mills. The consultants recommended a company called IBD International, Ltd., located near the border of Hong Kong in Zhuhai, PRC. This state-owned enterprise had trade interests in computer components, software, wines, plastic components for office equipment, and home furnishings. Under a new government mandate, the managers were expected to compete for profits and conduct business very much like a private-sector enterprise. Consequently, IBD was anxious to consider a product like transfer paper that would introduce the technology in China.

Boyd was advised to come to China personally to open negotiations. As CEO, he would be expected to create the relationships required for IBD and Transprint USA to pursue an agency agreement. Boyd had come to the United States from his homeland in Scotland, and he had traveled throughout Asia, so he was reasonably comfortable with the idea of going to China. He joined his consultants in Hong Kong, and together, they went to Zhuhai for two days of scheduled meetings.

When they arrived at IBD's offices, the managing director, Mr. Nei, met Boyd and his team with a translator, who introduced herself as Jenny. She also introduced three senior IBD executives. Boyd's team consisted of an American consultant, a bilingual Hong Kong consultant who was included for his understanding of cross-border relationships, and a Chinese interpreter. Mr. Nei's translator, Jenny, escorted both teams into a pleasant but austere conference room with a long oval table and identical straight-backed chairs. Tea glasses were set out at each attendee's place at the table, and bottled water was carefully centered on the table. Boyd was seated at one end of the oval table, a position that seemed to be opposite the head of the table. Jenny seated Boyd's two consultants on either side of him, and the Hong Kong interpreter at a center side position. She took up a position opposite the other interpreter, and then IBD's team members seated themselves. Mr. Nei took a seat just to the right of the head of the table, more like a corner position, and two other managers sat in side positions. The head seat was oddly left vacant.

Tea was served, and the meeting began shortly after 9:00 AM. The American consultant whispered to Boyd that he should scoot his chair around to a "corner" position, and make a light comment about "this being a bit more comfortable for conversation." He did so, graciously, which brought smiles to the IBD people. Boyd didn't realize until later that the Chinese often purposely position one another in side positions during meetings, sometimes actually sitting next to one another rather than facing other parties. This is a deferential gesture of humility or respect for the parties to a conversation. As the conversation began, little was mentioned about business. Instead, Mr. Nei seemed anxious to hear how the Americans liked their jet foil ride from Hong Kong to Zhuhai, and then commented about American TV and the NBA games being shown there on Chinese broadcasts. Boyd responded well to the social talk, but having traveled halfway around the world for this meeting, he was anxious to get on with business. Whenever the occasion presented itself, Boyd spoke about Transprint or his products, laying samples on the table several times during the morning. The Chinese were polite, but seemed disinterested. All conversation went through the interpreters, so the morning meeting was rather long and seemed to the Americans almost subdued.

During the meeting, Mr. Nei spoke in a low voice, and glanced into his tea or fixed his gaze at the window when talking. Only rarely did anyone other than Nei and Boyd, and their interpreters, speak. It was a strangely quiet meeting with little business mentioned. At 12:15 Mr. Nei announced lunch, and the two teams walked a short distance to a Chinese restaurant where several more IBD employees were already waiting. In fact, Nei and his staff had arranged a special two-hour lunch banquet. Everyone was seated at a huge, round table, Mr. Nei with Bill

Boyd to his right, and Jenny to Boyd's right. Then other team members were seated in alternate places next to Chinese hosts. A Chinese wine was served, along with a toast by Mr. Nei to "new friends in America." Boyd reciprocated with a toast to "future friends in China." Lunch conversation was the polar opposite of the morning meetings. Everyone on the Chinese team seemed anxious to engage one of the Americans in conversation, and the room was extremely noisy and busy.

Lunch conversation, however, did not include business. Instead, the Chinese asked questions and made comments that were often very personal and, at times, embarrassing. Some were humorous. For example, one Chinese manager commented on Boyd's bright suspenders, and apparently noticing that Boyd also had a belt, asked: "Will your trousers not stay up without one or the other?" A Chinese woman asked the American consultant if his wife was slim or fat, because she had visited Chicago at a trade fair and noticed how heavy most Americans were. Another Chinese manager, having slurped his tea loudly while Boyd sipped his tea quietly, said: "We will bring you better tea . . . you do not like this tea." (In China, a slurping sound is expected to show enjoyment.)

Boyd tried chopsticks and was instructed by Mr. Nei, who seemed to enjoy Boyd's naiveté. However, Boyd was somewhat puzzled by the food. A variety of plates had been served, most with unfamiliar tidbits of food or vegetables that seemed strange, perhaps unpalatable to a westerner. Boyd asked about several of the items served, and the Hong Kong interpreter advised him to just try it. "Even if it seems odd, try a nip to be sociable," he said. In fact, it was important to try everything, and Boyd followed Mr. Nei, matching him by at least taking a few bites of every dish. This was an important gesture, because Mr. Nei had purposely ordered food several weeks earlier. It included Chinese delicacies such as pickled jellyfish, marinated chicken feet, steamed pigs' ears, sharkfin soup, an appetizer made of bird's nest, and unborn octopus in oyster and garlic sauce. Fortunately, most food items were not recognizable for what they were.

After lunch the teams reconvened in the conference room, where social talk and quiet behavior replaced the noisy atmosphere of lunch. By the end of the day, Boyd had managed to show most of his sample products and to explain how the heat-transfer process worked, yet Mr. Nei and his managers responded only with polite comments or questions.

Once again they seemed remote and disinterested, often looking into their teacups or at someone other than Boyd when speaking. Indeed, there were pronounced periods of silence. The meeting ended at 5:00 PM. Everyone shook hands, nodding and smiling politely, and departed.

At dinner later that evening, Mr. Nei introduced a visitor from Beijing, who was seated next to Boyd and at the head of the table. This was a clue to the consultants that the visitor was someone of importance, and indeed, it was later discovered that he was a "political observer" assigned to evaluate the American proposals. However, he avoided any mention of Boyd's business and was careful to provide no opportunity for Boyd to talk about business. The evening was entirely social; yet except for Jenny, the interpreter, no other women were at the dinner. Boyd remained patient and never violated social protocol, but later, as he and the American consultants took an evening stroll in their hotel gardens, Boyd exploded. "Bloody [expletive deleted]!" He exclaimed. "Can't these people talk a simple business deal? At least they could *act* interested or look you in the eye once in awhile. The fat fellow with gold teeth that asked me why I wear both suspenders and a belt was the only person today that uttered an intelligent sound."

The next day's meetings were much the same as the first, but coupled with a tour of the city and a visit to a plant site that made naugahyde for furniture upholstery. By day's end, no serious business issues had been discussed, and the American team prepared to leave for the jet foil ferry back to Hong Kong. Typical of these occasions, the Chinese presented several wrapped gifts to Boyd. In return, Boyd gave Nei and his team gifts of Cross pens that he and his American consultant had selected and wrapped before leaving Hong Kong. Boyd began to unwrap his gifts, but was stopped with a nudge by his interpreter. In China people do not open gifts in the presence of those who give them, for fear that gifts of unequal value will embarrass one party or the other. Boyd did not understand, but he put the gift in his briefcase and turned to thank Nei with a handshake. He also laid a hand on Nei's shoulder, a gesture of friendship common in the United States. Nei momentarily recoiled at the touch, then smiled and bowed farewell.

Nei and his interpreter then escorted Boyd and his team to the ferry landing and expressed his gratitude for the visit. Then quite unexpectedly, Nei said that he would welcome a discussion about a joint venture between the companies, quickly adding that Transprint USA would prosper if Boyd invested in China. He then asked Boyd to send to him extensive samples, price lists, and financial performance data on Transprint USA, noting that the visitor from Beijing had approved of the venture and would help the parties set up local manufacturing, gain proper permits, and develop marketing channels. This entire conversation lasted no more than two minutes, and it represented more about business than had been discussed in the previous two days. Boyd was somewhat stunned as he boarded the ferry for Hong Kong.

In the end, Boyd decided not to enter the China market because he had no intention of risking a substantial investment there in manufacturing or a joint venture. However, the experience of trying to conduct himself in a business meeting with Chinese had been interesting. Boyd had also especially enjoyed one of the lunch entrees; he later asked his Hong Kong consultant what it had been. The consultant replied, "I'm afraid, sir, that you ate sautéed dog brains." Boyd has not returned to China.

QUESTIONS

1. From a communications viewpoint, both the Chinese and the Americans displayed behavior and made comments that could have been discomforting to one another. Identify these issues, and describe how both parties could have improved their meetings.

2. Both teams attempted to accommodate the other, but minor infractions of protocol occurred. Several important gestures probably benefited the talks as well. Identify these and describe why they were important.

3. Relationship building is crucial to the Chinese. Describe the cultural implications of relationships between the companies, and between Boyd and Nei. What should an American expect in a country such as China, in terms of cultural exchanges and conversational protocol? How would the meetings have been conducted had the parties met in the United States to discuss business?

Source: This case was written jointly by the author, David H. Holt, and Huen Sui-yip for classroom use at Zhongshan University, Guangdong, the PRC. Copyright 1997 by David H. Holt.

CASE 9.2

COMPAQ'S NEW CEO EXPECTED TO TRANSFORM COMPANY CULTURE—AGAIN

Michael D. Capellas officially became chairman, president, and CEO of Compaq Computer on September 28, 2000. He had been acting president and chief executive officer since July, while the company's board of directors completed an exhausting evaluation of candidates to head Compaq in the new millennium. In fact, the company had been without an official chairman or CEO since April 18, 1999, when Eckhard Pfeiffer resigned the executive posts. In the interim, Compaq established an Executive Office—a team comprised of two board members and the chief operating officer. The interim period was marked by uneasy shareholder behavior and unstable stock prices while the Executive Office redefined how the company would be managed.

Examining the differences between the outgoing CEO, Pfeiffer, and the new CEO, Capellas, reveals what has happened at Compaq during this transition. Michael Capellas is characterized as a conservative, soft-spoken American businessman with a strong technical background in software engineering, a history of success at several major hardware and software engineering companies in senior positions, and a person with "traditional" American values. He ascended to the top job at Compaq through promotions and job mobility, and as a graduate accountant with years in the information technology field, he is the model of an American executive who has carefully worked his way into the executive suite. His executive colleagues are all U.S. natives, and few have had international appointments or foreign affiliations.

In contrast, Eckhard Pfeiffer, the outgoing CEO was characterized as a "driven man" and a perfectionist. When he came to office in 1991, Pfeiffer convinced employees, stockholders, and many industry analysts that he could make Compaq the leading computer company in the world. Pfeiffer nearly reached that goal before resigning—he left Compaq with annual growth rates at 20 percent or more, major global expansion, and hundreds of international alliances that placed Compaq computers in more than 100 countries. By April 1999, Compaq was No. 1 in the world in sales of commercial PCs, and it was the market leader in web servers. At one of Pfeiffer's first press conferences in 1991, he had calmly announced that annual revenues would quadruple within four years. Instead, they quintupled from $3.3 billion to $14.8 billion by 1996, and then nearly tripled again by 1999 to $38 billion. Indeed, Pfeiffer regularly set outsized goals and met them against competition such as IBM, Fujitsu, and Hewlett-Packard. Today, Compaq is the second-largest computer company in the world, and during Pfeiffer's reign as CEO, many analysts came to believe that his style of leadership may be the clarion call for management in the future.

Pfeiffer was audacious, quick tempered, and demanding with an emphasis in both his business and personal affairs on efficiency and precision. Pfeiffer was also German, physically imposing, and far different from most American executives. He was once characterized as the personification of German management, running Compaq like a finely tuned Grand Prix racecar. Indeed, the gray-haired Pfeiffer—in his late 50s—drove a black Porsche convertible to work each morning in a ritual that epitomized his approach to life. Wearing expensive sunglasses and a European designer suit, he literally hurtled through traffic, racing from his exclusive high-rise home in Houston's ritzy Tanglewood section 25 miles northward to Compaq's steel-and-glass enclave. Predictably, he received more than a few traffic citations; and other executives who followed a similar route to work knew that they could maneuver their cars closely behind Pfeiffer's and, if they could keep pace, let him run interference with police.

Speed was not everything, though; change, redirection, innovation, and adaptation were key words during his time at Compaq. Pfeiffer pushed for innovative marketing, stressed the importance of foreign sales and alliances, and was absolutely demanding of quality-driven performance by everyone. On the other hand, he created a fluid organization without sacrosanct principles, thus inspiring change and innovative thinking.

Pfeiffer was self-groomed as an international executive before his Compaq years. After an early career in accounting for German companies, he grew into international roles, learned several foreign languages including English, and became financial controller for Texas Instruments in Munich during the early 1960s. Pfeiffer's communication skills were put to use by colleagues who asked him to assist as a translator and negotiator in sales, leading to a career switch from accounting into sales. Eventually, Pfeiffer headed European marketing for TI. Compaq recruited Pfeiffer in the 1980s to launch the company's European operation, and he made it a stunning success. His subsequent record made him an attractive candidate for a senior executive role.

Pfeiffer brought with him a German mentality that shook the company's foundations, but he also remained somewhat of a mystery. Tenacious, driven, highly competitive, and an unabashed workaholic, Pfeiffer spent 60 to 70 hours each week on the job. His workday began at 7:30 AM, and evenings often stretched into the next day. He set an unflagging pace, yet was described by colleagues as a "supremely confident and calm" leader. For all his speed and mastery at innovative changes, Pfeiffer rarely showed emotion. When answering a question or making a point during meetings, his response seemed like a well-rehearsed script; it was precise, crisp, and directly to the heart of an issue. He was patient in team situations and fully controlled under stress, yet absolutely insistent that everyone who worked for him strictly conform to schedules, commitments, and project objectives. He displayed an image of autocratic "German-style" demeanor but without imposing decisions.

He was also capable of unpredictable—even outlandish—behavior. For example, Pfeiffer was known for his reckless abandon on the dance floor; he loved to dance at company gatherings. At a company celebration in the Summit sports arena, home of the Houston Rockets, Pfeiffer came out in lederhosen and had himself hoisted 70 feet up to the ceiling on a cable. He arrived at another company meeting wearing a four-foot-wide cowboy hat. Pfeiffer had been known to hang out with the Rockets' Hakeem Olajuwon and occasionally with George Bush. As a Rockets season-ticket holder, Pfeiffer often sat near bearded ZZ Top guitarist Billy Gibbons, and he was always an avid fan of unorthodox jazz, fast-paced sports, and international athletic competition.

In business, Pfeiffer presented a controversial profile—the staid German manager in total control of every situation whose public gestures, unorthodox antics, and passion for action ran counter to expectations. With a single secretary as his entire office staff, he personally handled all communications. E-mail, fax messages, memos, and directives were just "too impersonal" for his taste. Pfeiffer believed that any message that needed to be communicated should be conveyed in a personal exchange; words that needed to be said should be spoken face to face.

Most of his American colleagues expected Pfeiffer to display the stereotypical German autocratic behavior, but their expectations were not met. Pfeiffer did indeed behave much as he would have in Germany—but the German tradition is one of making decisions in scheduled committee meetings, encouraging team projects, engaging in conversations with subordinates, and socializing with other company executives and staff. He encouraged those around him to share information and to air differences openly. However, Pfeiffer's conversations and behavior with people outside the company were described by business journalists as "pressed and pleated" with a sense of Germanic formality.

Pfeiffer did not engage in American informalities such as back-slapping, nor was he likely to praise employees for work well done. In the German scheme of things, employees are not apt to get feedback on their accomplishments. Still, Pfeiffer was adept at public ceremonies that chimed the virtues of his people and Compaq. One executive remarked that Pfeiffer drove everyone crazy, but admitted that just following in his slipstream could be an exhilarating experience. Pfeiffer's accomplishments—and his idiosyncrasies—will be long remembered at Compaq. So also will the clashes that Pfeiffer and other Europeans on his staff created between themselves and their American colleagues. The company paid a price, with heavy turnover among American executives who could not adapt to Pfeiffer's leadership methods.

In contrast, Michael Capellas has demonstrated behavior totally in line with American values. He has a strong support staff and delegates authority readily through an organizational hierarchy that reflects a high degree of specialization. The board that elected him has high expectations of a "return to normalcy" at the company, yet in an environment that can mobilize Compaq's resources to continue to climb up the ranks of the *Fortune 500*. Compaq ranked 28th in 1999, and improved to 20th in the 2000 annual *Fortune 500* list. Although Capellas has only begun his career as CEO at Compaq, he is gaining a reputation as a polished executive who systematically organizes people and resources. At the same time, he is becoming known as a shirtsleeves kind of CEO who prefers first names and informality in meetings, often complimenting people on their work and joking over coffee. Pfeiffer's era is over, along with the mysteries of his approach to management; in his place is Cappellas, a stable homegrown American who is expected to bring with him an era of predictability.

QUESTIONS

1. In America, Pfeiffer faced a new experience as a foreign expatriate. How might cultural differences have shaped his expectations? What specific challenges might he have faced in working with American colleagues?
2. What aspects of German behavior did Pfeiffer introduce at Compaq? In your opinion, did his approach to management create difficulties or

did it result in beneficial changes? How did his behavior and organizational changes affect patterns of communication in the company?
3. If you had been a manager at Compaq working with Pfeiffer, what problems might you have had in adapting to expectations for behavior and interpersonal communications? Contrast these expectations to those you might have in working for Capellas as the company enters a new era.

BIBLIOGRAPHY

Chakravarthy, Bala. "A New Strategy Framework for Coping with Turbulence." *Sloan Management Review* 38, no. 2 (1997): 69–82.

Compaq Computer, Inc. "Company Management," "News," and "History." Retrieved from website <www.compaq.com> [cited 2 October 2000].

Francis, Bob. "Branching Out." *Informationweek*, 3 February 1997, 36–42.

Kirkpatrick, David. "Fast Times at Compaq." *Fortune*, 1 April 1996, 120–128.

Stamps, David. "Welcome to America: Watch Out for Culture Shock." *Training*, November 1996, 22–30.

CHAPTER TEN

INTERCULTURAL NEGOTIATIONS

CHAPTER OBJECTIVES

Define and contrast distributive and integrative negotiations with respect to international business.

Explain the negotiation process and the responsibilities of negotiating teams.

Describe how cultural differences affect relationships during international negotiations.

Identify four alternative forms of agreement that constitute successful conclusions of negotiations.

Detail how conflict occurs and how participants can manage it during international negotiations.

Highlight the essential characteristics of effective negotiations.

Sten Elgstrom was born to Swedish parents in Belgium, where his father was a lumber import agent. Groomed for a future in international business beginning early in his life, Sten learned English, French, Swedish, and local dialects of Flemish.[1] His father had pointed Sten toward university studies in the United States, but he chose to study engineering in the Netherlands. After graduating, Sten began his career with Philips N.V., at the Einhoven, Netherlands, plant. Very quickly, he found himself on Philips field teams negotiating manufacturing rights in South Korea and Japan.

"I have no idea why they had me on the team," he explains. "Maybe because I spoke several languages or never seemed to get upset." Sten had a knack of self-control and a forthright attitude instilled in him by his Swedish parents. Tall, blondish, and athletic, he seemed to glide through perplexing situations unruffled, yet he could stand his ground on matters of importance. These traits served him well when, after nearly 10 years with Philips, he was recruited by ASEA Brown Boveri in Sweden (now ABB Global, a major European engineering company). As an engineering consultant, Sten was assigned to projects in Asia, where he worked on a joint power-plant development with the South Korean government. He then worked in Indonesia on a major water treatment system for the capital of Jakarta. Six years and four projects later, Sten was promoted to senior project consultant and lead negotiator for joint engineering projects. The company reorganized in 1990 following a merger, and Sten was assigned to a project in Poland, but he was uncomfortable with this post and resigned. He returned to Asia and recalls those early days:

> I was in a bit of a panic at the time, but with my knowledge of Asia, I tried to sell my services to a South Korean engineering firm. I also had pretty good contacts in the region and in Europe, and some money, so my father suggested that I do something on my own. My Korean friends then said why not do a business together. So we started to talk seriously, and we have the new company called PacRim Engineering that does a lot of work outside Korea for bridge and seaport developments. We are all good friends now, but we had some trouble working together at first.

Sten explained that although he and his Korean partners had known one another since his first visit with Philips, when they sat down to negotiate the new business, they seemed like strangers.

> It was almost crazy. As soon as we started talking, my two Korean friends acted like enraged. They would shove their fists in the air and talk very loudly, just absolutely rejecting my ideas. Even on small points, they would get angry. We met four times, and on each visit it was the same. No concessions. No pleasant talks. Just anger. But then we would go out to dinner and agree not to talk business, and everybody was friendly. One day Kim Jong, the senior guy and now my partner said to me: 'Sten, you really expected us to agree on the terms you gave us at the beginning, but why don't you Swedes offer something else so we can fight a little bit?' I said that I didn't want to fight. I just wanted a good business, and I wouldn't change my mind about this.

Two weeks after that meeting, the Koreans called Sten and formed the new joint-equity company on terms close to Sten's original proposal. Kim, being an older man with trade experience, told Sten that he would have to learn to be tougher and more emotional when he worked with Koreans, or he would not be respected. Since they launched PacRim Engineering, Kim and Sten have had five years of rapid growth, more than doubling their initial projections to exceed US $20 million in annual contracts. With operations in Taiwan, the Philippines, Malaysia, and Singapore, PacRim expects business to accelerate even faster in the early years of the new century.

Meanwhile, they have created a winning approach to negotiating business. Kim and Sten always meet clients together. Kim handles opening bids and tends to respond to early offers on terms. He does so in his Korean style of flamboyant gestures and stage manners. Sten is the calming force who develops close relationships and disarms the combatants with Swedish efficiency and factual positions. He always works hard to find hidden clues to the opponent's motives and makes creative proposals that no one expects. He explained:

> When we were negotiating in Malaysia to design an expanded container port, we were deadlocked on the types of cranes and their capacity. The Malaysians wanted a big off-loading crane on a pier that would not hold the weight for more than one unit. But the pier was long enough to have four major cranes if it could be redesigned. The expense seemed too much. My thought was that they would build on the cheap and just have to rebuild it all again later, but they were anxious to get a crane operation going as soon as possible. I discovered that two things motivated them. First, the Malaysians are super sensitive to being beaten by the Singapore container port, which is their main competitor. They really don't like being treated as second-rate by the Singapore people. Second, their own government was breathing down their necks on cost containment, and the bureaucrats didn't seem to appreciate long term prospects for economies of scale—they just wanted results now.
>
> So I went to work to work on these two things, and I showed how they could capture a big chunk of Singapore bulk shipping with multiple cranes and a stronger pier system. This was exciting, but the costs were too much. Then I found out who the government guy was who was pushing for efficiencies, and I talked with him several times. Finally, I gave him a free report on all Malaysian ports, and compared it with Singapore's record. I let that ride for a couple of weeks and made a new proposal to our clients based on the same data that I gave to the government. By just talking, I let them decide that maybe they should pass this proposal along to the government for advice, and I suggested the fellow that I had met. Our clients did that, and they looked like heroes to the government. The government guy also looked like a hero because he took credit for the information that I gave him. This was okay with me. They came back with a proposal and acted like it was all their idea. Kim stopped playing the bad guy and gave some concessions, and we signed the deal.

Kim and Sten had a final debate about the negotiation. Kim was perplexed that Sten let the clients and government take all the credit. He said to Sten: "Why you have no sense of pride! This was your work and our ideas all the way, and you just sat there when they made it seem how smart they were and us not so smart?" Sten replied: "We have the contract because we helped them be proud. That's the whole point."

NEGOTIATIONS IN THE GLOBAL CONTEXT

International negotiations are far more complicated than the typical model of one-on-one bargaining or group resolutions such as those found in domestic labor-management relations. Cross-border negotiations are complex because they involve people from societies with different cultural values and ideological perspectives, but also because of socioeconomic differences. Parties to negotiations often have different motives and priorities for doing business.

At the international level, diplomats negotiate to free hostages, strike trade agreements, or initiate peace agreements. International managers are engaged in negotiating a wide variety of multilateral agreements ranging from export contracts to complicated strategic alliances. In global commerce, managers may be involved in team-based negotiations with other companies, other governments, foreign trade unions, financial intermediaries, and even shop-floor employee groups. With the rapid increase in global business, negotiation skills are important to all international managers.

The Concept of Intercultural Negotiation

Negotiation is an art form and a communication process that occurs in every aspect of management. **Intercultural negotiation** is distinguished from personal and domestic bargaining to emphasize the cross-border, culturally complex nature of global management.[2] This chapter is focused on intercultural negotiations, specifically on those issues related to managing in a foreign environment. It does not address labor-management issues, personal disputes, sales tactics, or diplomatic bargaining, but how international managers negotiate business situations in a multicultural environment. With that said, the *process* of negotiation is the same for diplomats at a peace table as it is for a young couple deciding on who will mow the lawn and who will do the dishes. The stakes are different, but the fundamental elements of negotiation are the same.

Before examining the negotiation process, it is important to distinguish between *bargaining* and *negotiation*, and also to explain how *conflict* relates to the process. **Bargaining** is a limited concept that suggests a competitive exchange process. It does not necessarily suggest a win-lose situation, but often that is the case. **Negotiation** is a comprehensive concept that suggests a joint effort by two or more parties to find a mutually acceptable solution to a problem, opportunity, or conflict. In this sense, negotiation often includes bargaining, but requires a greater breath of activities, perhaps without trade-offs or compromises. Indeed, negotiations often result in win-win situations, such as corporate mergers or profitable contracts that benefit all parties. Figure 10.1 suggests how the two concepts differ.

Bargaining

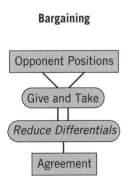

Negotiation

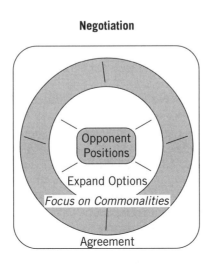

FIGURE 10.1
Conceptual Differences between Bargaining and Negotiation

Conflict in its simplest form can imply disagreement or opposition, but more precisely, it means *interference* by individuals engaged in pursuing individual goals that cannot be achieved simultaneously.[3] This is addressed thoroughly later in the chapter, but it is important to bear in mind that conflict plays a crucial role in negotiations. People define conflict differently and therefore approach negotiations with different expectations for behavior.

The Intercultural Negotiation Environment

Situations that involve international negotiations can become complicated by many factors, such as economic conditions, political priorities, differences in social or legal environments, and, of course, cultural differences of those involved. Negotiations become extremely complex in foreign business affairs, particularly when they are concerned with foreign investment, trade, currency exchange rates, terms of trade, payment methods, repatriation of profits, and contingencies for changes in financial or economic conditions. Locking in a contract for materials procurement, for example, might seem to be a simple situation. But if the contract specifies a fixed payment in a particular currency, and then the exchange rate changes, one of the parties is likely to suffer while the other makes an unexpected gain. Also, sudden changes in host-country regulations can alter custom duties, tax rates, or trade quotas affecting business transactions. Political leaders can mandate trade sanctions. Religious difficulties or ethnic confrontations can disrupt trade agreements, and so on. Many unexpected things can occur that negotiators must try to take into consideration when doing business abroad.

Negotiations typically involve bilateral contracts between two parties, yet in many countries, governments interject themselves into business talks. Until recently, for example, international joint ventures in India or China were exclusively tripartite—involving a foreign company, a domestic company, and a government agency. Still today, most international joint ventures in these and other less-developed countries must go through government channels for approval. Consequently, negotiators find themselves bargaining with a foreign company, perhaps a local municipal or provincial agency, and in extreme situations, the national government itself. Closely tied to this is the influence governments and politicians can exert through incentives (e.g., tax holidays for preferred foreign investments) or disincentives (e.g., restrictions on resources, imports-exports, or profit repatriation). It is not unusual for a foreign government to pressure foreign negotiators to transfer in technology, make concessions on hiring and training, guarantee employee housing, or develop infrastructure as conditions for doing business there.[4]

Ideological differences also come into play. Negotiators from developed European or North American countries where market economies exist often find it extremely difficult to come to terms on business negotiations in socialist countries where commerce is heavily regulated or centrally controlled. Foreign companies simply do not always have the luxury of making independent decisions. In addition, business negotiators may find that effects of home politics of ideological differences work against them. Ethnic and religious differences have similar effects. In some Muslim countries, it is unlawful to have joint business interests with members of certain other ethnic or religious faiths, but even when these restrictions are not absolute, foreign companies often face severe limitations on ownership and management.[5]

Culture will be the most pervasive issue, because people differ in their priorities about why they are negotiating and what they want to achieve in the process. Consequently, the actual negotiation process assumes different characteristics in each society. In cultures where time has little meaning, a simple contract may take months to conclude. In societies where personal relationships outweigh the importance of contractual terms, negotiations may seem more like long-term social developments than business affairs. Indeed, the "final agreement" that emerges from this process may be little more than a general conclusion that the parties will work together in good faith while details evolve later within the context of that general agreement. Cultural values dictate the cadence of negotiations and the type of agreement sought by both parties. With these points in mind, the next section explores the fundamental nature of the negotiation process.

THE NATURE OF NEGOTIATION

Many different models of negotiation have been put forward by theorists to explain subtle distinctions among bargaining parties, but they generally follow one of two mainstream concepts called *distributive* or *integrative* approaches.[6] **Distributive negotiation** is a zero-sum model in which parties are in competition to maximize their share of outcomes, and because the total outcome pool is fixed, whatever one party wins, the other must lose. **Integrative negotiation** is a collaborative model in which parties seek to expand the range of possible outcomes and thereby maximize their individual benefits by sharing in the collective results. Distributive bargaining creates win-lose situations, while integrative bargaining presumes that the parties seek win-win results. This contrast is shown in Figure 10.2.

Characteristics of Distributive Negotiations[7]

In a distributive situation, the goals of one party are in direct opposition to those of the other party. For example, a customer shopping for a new car clearly wants to pay as little as possible and get the best package for the money, and the car salesman on commission wants to get the highest possible price. Most customers are uncomfortable in this situation, because they know the game before they set foot on the car lot. Both parties also know that the total pie to be divided up is finite; it is the margin the dealer has between zero profit (actual cost) and the car's listed sticker price. These are arbitrary limits, and like most bargaining situations, many other factors influence the outcome. For example, the customer may be willing to take a low trade-in value for his

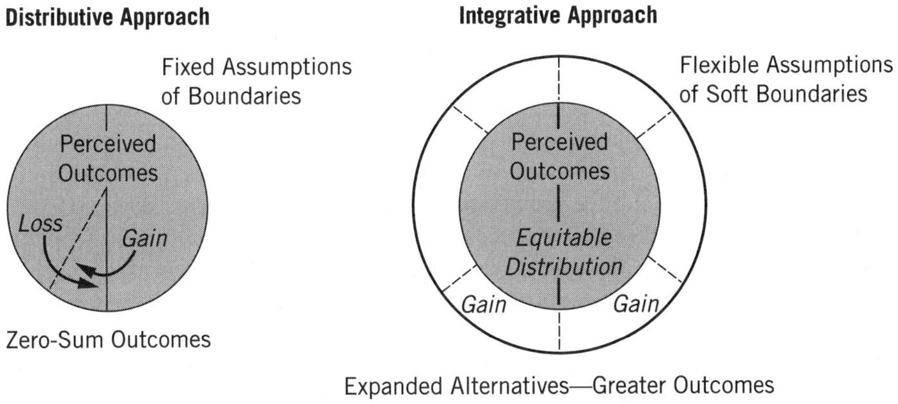

Distributive Approach

Fixed Assumptions of Boundaries

Perceived Outcomes

Loss / Gain

Zero-Sum Outcomes

Integrative Approach

Flexible Assumptions of Soft Boundaries

Perceived Outcomes

Equitable Distribution

Gain   Gain

Expanded Alternatives—Greater Outcomes

FIGURE 10.2
Distributive versus Integrative Negotiation

or her old car, thus giving the dealer an additional profit opportunity by reselling the trade-in car. Perhaps the dealer has attractive financing that would support a higher price within the bargaining range, or, conversely, the customer could accept unfavorable dealer financing if the price were lowered. Give-and-take details surface, such as equipping the car with deluxe tires or a stereo system, or dickering over incentive discounts or rebates. Nevertheless, there is still a fixed value in the total transaction with floor and ceiling conditions that restrict both the salesman and the customer. Between these extremes, each party has a comfort zone based on their personal perception of the value that they will receive from an agreement. This constitutes a perception of a fair price that each party hopes to obtain.

Labor negotiations have characteristics similar to those of many selling situations, including automobile bargaining. Employees bargain for a share of profits paid through wages and benefits, and managers who represent owners bargain for a share of profits achieved through retained earnings. If wages rise, earnings decrease relative to a fixed amount of profits. In this situation, profits will always be finite even though they may not be precisely determined. Like buying a car, labor negotiations can have many mitigating circumstances. These distributive negotiations are competitive and win-lose situations, but they are not necessarily bad. In fact, they constitute the most common form of negotiation behavior. Purchasing a house is a distributive bargain process with price and cost limitations, but also with room for concessions or sweeteners by both parties.

Some negotiation experts claim that "everything is negotiable," and they base their popular seminars on examples of distributive bargaining. One unusual example of this bargaining behavior occurred in Los Angeles, where a real estate agent built a small fortune by paying *more* than listed prices for houses or agreed to *higher interest rates* than lenders requested. He would analyze a property for its potential rental income, and if he could envision a positive cash flow, he would offer the seller a premium price *if* the seller would finance the down payment. Therefore, for a small premium in price, the buyer bought with no money down and every dollar of net cash flow represented a large-percentage profit at relatively low risk. The alternative was to bargain with a lender for a low down payment and accept an interest rate several percentage points higher than required. This gave the bank additional leverage, reduced the buyer's risk, and increased the profit ratio. The same salesman made a game of paying less than full price for groceries. Once at the cash register, he would debate the value of dented cans of food, or complain that his lettuce looked a bit yellow. By making a fuss in a busy checkout line, he often succeeded in getting the store manager to discount items.[8]

These examples illustrate how parties in a distributive negotiation seek to win something, and in the end, each party may believe that he or she has won or lost less than the other person. However, there is much more to negotiation. The grocery-line situation is not unlike international trade negotiations, in which price and cost factors are only a part of the overall package of outcomes that might include psychological satisfaction, winning an ideological point, or just feeding one's ego. In most distributive situations, the objects of negotiation are resources (money, wages, income, profits, or investments) and although the psychological benefits of winning are extremely important, the conflicts focus on these outcomes.

International negotiations to create equity joint ventures, for example, involve percentage ownership or equity contribution, values placed on assets, or share distribution of profits. In each instance, whatever one person achieves in the bargain will necessarily affect the other's outcomes. For this reason, negotiators guard information closely and often go to great lengths to disguise their own objectives. Ambiguity and confusion are allies of both parties. A seller does not want to reveal his or her cost basis, because the buyer will automatically seek to drive a bargain toward that point; and a buyer does not want to reveal his or her notion of a fair price, because the seller will push to those limits. On the other hand, both parties negotiate in an effort to discover as much as possible about the other person's limitations. Gaining tidbits of information is part of the distributive negotiation process. It is the classic model of trying to discover cracks in the other party's armor, to prompt reactions that would reveal hints about an opponent's comfort zone, and then seek ways to take advantage of that information.

Distributive negotiation is the stereotype of smoke-filled, back-room machismo, and good distributive negotiators are described as "tough nuts to crack," or revered for their "poker faces" and "thick skins." In many instances their ethics are questioned, calling to mind images of used-car salesmen, or characters like "Fast Eddy" who know all the angles. Unfortunately, there is a great deal of truth to many of these stereotypes, yet when people hire real estate brokers to sell their homes, or when governments send diplomats overseas to negotiate trade issues, those brokers or diplomats are expected to "talk tough" and get "no-nonsense results." Consequently, it is difficult to categorically dismiss distributive bargaining as deplorable, and there is no reason that it cannot be conducted ethically.[9]

A more appropriate way to characterize distributive negotiation is that it is a necessary way of resolving differences between parties with mutually exclusive goals. This does not mitigate the point that it is a win-lose situation. Parties to the negotiation will withhold as much information as possible to gain an advantage, and at the same time they will seek as much information as needed to disarm their opponents. Effective negotiators will have a good mental picture of their *target outcomes* (their own concepts of fair results) and a clear idea of their *resistance points* (the floors or ceilings beyond which they will walk away from negotiations). They should also have a *zone of potential agreement* that defines the variance from ideal target outcomes that they are willing to accept, and define for themselves the *bargaining mix* (price, terms, or concessions) that could influence their comfort zone. Table 10.1 summarizes these considerations.

Negotiators will also have a clear idea of what they are trying to accomplish and keep this idea firmly in their minds. This is perhaps the most critical point of skillful negotiation because too often people lose sight of the real reason for negotiating. Instead, they find themselves arguing to protect their egos or to win minor concessions; in the end, they win small skirmishes but fail to achieve a satisfactory agreement. This unfortunate analogy accounts for many remorseful buyers who, having emotionally purchased a car or house, wake up to realize that they have not made a very good deal. Keeping focused also allows negotiators to consciously keep in mind *alternatives*. All negotiations have alternatives. Ultimately, anyone can walk away from a negotiation, even international managers involved in large acquisitions or mergers.

Characteristics of Integrative Negotiations[10]

Integrative negotiation is a process in which the parties jointly work toward goals that are not mutually exclusive; one party does not necessarily gain at the other's expense. In addition, the resources for which the negotiators are bargaining are not necessarily fixed, but they can be expanded. For example, consider the situation in which a young couple living on the U.S. East Coast is trying to decide on a vacation. Both work and can spend a week together on vacation, but they have a tight budget and different ideas about what to do on their vacation. The husband wants to go to the beach,

TABLE 10.1

ESSENTIAL ISSUES TO CLARIFY PRIOR TO NEGOTIATIONS

Example of a negotiation by an America company with a Peruvian exporter to purchase leather handicrafts for importing to the United States.

Primary objective	Create a reliable source in Peru for purchasing leather handcrafts.
Target outcomes	Secure an initial purchasing contract, create broker-age agreement, and ensure profitable procurement terms.
Resistance points	Define points on price, quantity, quality, delivery terms, commissions, payments.
Zone of potential agreement	One-time agreement with least attractive terms to long-term agency contract for scale economies at attractive profits.
Bargaining mix	Partial shipments, split terms, advances, custom designs, bonuses, guarantees.

where he can relax, swim, and also enjoy nearby golf. His wife wants to go to New York City, where she can shop, see a Broadway play, and visit her parents on the way. As they begin discussing their options the conversation turns ugly, because whichever vacation option is taken, one or the other person will be forced to make a major concession. The husband creates a major error by personalizing the issues when he remarks, "Visiting the in-laws is the last thing on my mind for a vacation." His wife responds, "Being a golfing widow for even a few hours of my vacation has about as much appeal as going to the dentist." Both argue that "their" hard-earned money is not going to be spent doing something they don't enjoy. This type of conversation can lead to open warfare, degenerating into the type of behavior that makes distributive bargaining so unpleasant at times. Soon, the young couple loses track of the original point of the discussion—the *substantive* issue of a vacation—and find themselves arguing merely to "win" or to extract some price from the other for hurtful words. However, both could have found a win-win solution without painful concessions by approaching the problem in an integrative manner.[11]

At the outset, the couple should have defined the problem, expressed their individual preferences, and agreed to attempt to find a solution that would meet both party's goals. They both wanted a vacation, had limited funds and time, and had individual special interests. Integrative negotiators seek to identify *alternative solutions* that benefit both parties. In order to do this, each party needs to fully appreciate what the other hopes to achieve in the negotiation. Unlike distributive bargaining, during which information is purposely withheld and ambiguity is an advantage, integrative bargaining requires a willingness to share information. The parties must conceal as little as possible in an effort to understand exactly what is at stake. In our example, the couple had several critical interests in their vacation. The husband wanted some form of relaxation and the opportunity to play golf. However, during a vacation week, he is unlikely to play golf every day; and although he likes the beach, he clearly does not intend to spend the entire week there. Meanwhile, the wife wants to visit her parents, but there is no need to spend more than a day or two with them. She also wants to do some big-city shopping and enjoy an evening out. When the couple begins to analyze the situation, they also find a deeper interest in having some time together. This is an **intrinsic interest** of the bargain—an outcome of the actual vacation well beyond the **substantive issues** of the vacation itself; the vacation is a means to an end, not an end in itself. By sharing this information and talking through each party's interests, the integrative negotiation becomes a positive force of collaboration. At that point, the couple can begin to search for mutually beneficial solutions.

Integrative negotiation encourages those involved to focus on substantive issues for their real values. This often reveals the intrinsic issues, thus reducing the risk of conflict that occurs when parties *personalize* bargaining points. If the husband recognizes that a day or two visiting his in-laws will not preempt other activities, then it is less of a threat. Perhaps it may be a very nice visit, and if his father-in-law plays golf, the men can go to the course while his wife and mother-in-law go shopping. This may be a relief to the wife as well, since she can spend time with her mother without feeling like a golf widow. The husband probably would also enjoy a night out, a romantic dinner with his wife, or attending a show in New York. In the end, both may not get all that they want. The wife may have to settle for a night out at a disco or a jazz club because her husband really doesn't enjoy ballet or a heavy Broadway show. And maybe that's okay, because the more important *intrinsic interest* of enriching their relationship rather than seeing a particular play has been fulfilled. Perhaps the husband will go to a Broadway musical for the same reason and feel okay about that decision. The husband may have conceded his beach time—and if so, the honesty of the negotiations will reveal this, so that his wife may suggest an alternative trip to the beach on an upcoming weekend holiday. Perhaps they will settle on the city vacation now, and at the same time agree to go to the beach the next time. Everyone wins.

This example illustrates several critical elements of integrative negotiations. First, there is an earnest effort to openly share information, and therefore to identify both the substantive and intrinsic motives of both parties. Second, the parties communicate effectively to arrive at an understanding of the priorities, and also to understand the actual limits of each person's needs. In the language of negotiation, both parties have determined *target outcomes* and *zones of potential agreement*. Third, by focusing on issues and not hidden motives, they are collaborating to seek positive solutions. In negotiation language, they are searching for the right *bargaining mix* or the *alternatives* that benefit both parties. Fourth, they are interested in helping one another find winning solutions, and by doing so they also win. Conflict is defused. What seemed to be irreconcilable differences at the outset dissolved in the negotiations. Fifth, both parties began with the intention of finding similarities in their interests, not differences. Perhaps that is the most critical point, because both can achieve more from the solution than either could realize with their own agenda.

Integrative bargaining also has the important dimension of building relationships. If there are concessions, such as the husband forgoing the beach or the wife relenting on a Broadway play, these can be *relationship-building equities*. Whoever made the sacrifice has built up a small emotional savings account that can be used later to buy back an equal favor. Perhaps it just sits there gathering interest in terms of bonding the parties closely together. However, the concession must be voluntary, and the person granting the concession must feel that it was fair to both parties. If the concession is then misused as leverage to win a point, the value of that equity is lost—or worse, it may seriously damage the relationship.[12] Suppose the husband in our example wants to go fishing on a long weekend several months later, and says to his wife: "Hey, I gave up my beach vacation time so you could shop with your mother, so it seems fair to take a couple of days to go fishing." This is counterproductive. What originally appeared to be a grateful concession now becomes an ugly game in which the couple is "keeping score."

International managers face precisely the same circumstances in their negotiations. Consider the situation in which an American company opens negotiations with a Mexican company to form a joint venture. The American company ostensibly wants to establish a manufacturing facility in Mexico to take advantage of substantially lower labor costs. Management also recognizes the market potential for its products in Mexico, and the proximity of Mexico to the United States for importing finished goods. The Mexican company envisions substantial benefits from the joint venture in terms of capital investment, improved technology, and new jobs. Both see profit potential and a win-win possibility. Under these circumstances, negotiations can lead to a joint venture agreement that mutually benefits both parties. However, the two companies will have many sticky points to resolve. For example, who will control policy? How will the new venture be managed? At what premium will the actual wage levels be settled to realistically benefit Mexican employees? What will each bring to the table in terms of equity investment, technology, facilities, and other resources? Who will be responsible for actual operations, marketing, training, and other functions? How will profits be allocated? Searching for answers to these types of questions can quickly become confrontational. Both parties can get bogged down in the fine points of relative trade-off positions and eventually begin "keeping score" on who is winning and who is losing. The initial purpose of the joint venture, the substantive issue, is lost in the bickering, and the intrinsic value of the collaboration is lost as the parties become adversaries. Even if they reach an agreement, relationships between the two partners may always be strained, degenerating further as the parties fall back into the trap of win-lose distributive bargaining behavior.

However, if the American and Mexican negotiators begin on the premise of sharing information, they have a very good opportunity to discover *beneficial similarities* in the details of their agreement. If, for example, the Americans understand Mexican wage rates, skill levels, and employee expectations for wage premiums, then actual wage negotiations will not be a battle over money but a positive motive to arrive at a consensus compensation package. Taking this a step further, Mexican workers, like most workers anywhere, would want high wages, and the American negotiators would want low wages to obtain a competitive advantage in labor costs. However, workers really want what good wages can buy, not merely premium wages for their own sake. Consequently, the Americans might be able to create a medical and dental benefits package, an employee retirement plan, and perhaps subsidized housing in lieu of monetary income. Also, given that wages are taxed while most benefits are not, the total package may far exceed the workers' expectations, yet cost the company less than a premium wage level. Both win, and even more important, they have created a special relational bond—an important intrinsic benefit—well beyond negotiated outcomes. Table 10.2 provides examples of contrasts in substantive issues and intrinsic interests.

An integrative approach can be taken with almost any specific bargaining point, but cultural differences often force negotiators into adversarial situations. For example, during trade talks between the United States and China over intellectual property rights, both sides seemed poised for a major trade war. The United States wanted an end to pirated CDs, software, and U.S.-branded products. Many of these were being made and sold in China as well as exported. The United States had threatened trade sanctions against China if an agreement could not be reached, and the U.S.

TABLE 10.2

SUBSTANTIVE ISSUES VERSUS INTRINSIC INTERESTS

Substantive Issues	Intrinsic Interests
Couple has different ideas for vacation plans	Both parties seek time together for relationship, but husband also has recreational needs and wife has need to visit her family
Japanese firm negotiates joint venture with Irish manufacturer	Japanese want to access EU market; Ireland is an entry choice. The Irish want employment opportunities and future development options.
U.S. company negotiates to invest in Malaysian electronics company	U.S. company will enjoy cost advantages but really wants access to SE Asia markets. The Malays want U.S. investment but are more concerned with new skills and technologies for future development and growth.

government also could withhold its support for China as a candidate for membership in the World Trade Organization (WTO). Meanwhile, American businesses had invested more than $100 billion in China, which Chinese authorities threatened with restrictive regulations and reciprocal trade sanctions.[13] Negotiations were conducted at very high government levels, and presidents of both countries made very bold public statements that were clearly confrontational. The language and cadence of negotiations were emotion-packed with repeated charges and countercharges by both sides that the other was not bargaining in good faith. The U.S. team accused China of failing to comply with international laws, and the Chinese team accused the United States of trying to incite political changes in China through economic trade leverage. Negotiations seemed to stall; then, only moments before the deadline that was set for the negotiations to close, the two sides reached an agreement.[14] The extraordinary thing about this event was that both China and the United States had mutual interests in enforcing restrictions against intellectual piracy and establishing a more pervasive trade agreement for many other goods and services. The illegal trade in China of intellectual property such as software, for example, cost U.S. manufacturers hundreds of millions of dollars in lost revenues, and the United States also lost revenue from import duties. Meanwhile, the Chinese government had been losing huge sums in unofficial foreign exchange and tax revenues from illegal software trade. World publicity also seriously threatened China's credibility for seeking membership in the WTO. By all accounts, both sides had every reason to collaborate not only on the core issues of intellectual rights, but on a broad range of trade issues between the two countries. What was missing, according to some accounts, was the *intrinsic value* of the negotiations. Beijing Communist Party officials were less interested in the trade issues than in winning an ideological battle against the United States. At the same time, the Clinton administration, having already backed down from trade sanctions several years earlier, wanted to enhance its record in foreign affairs as the 2000 election year approached. Negotiations had stretched over several years, and although a new China–American trade pact was signed in November 1999, the talks were characterized as having been "tough-talking brinksmanship for the benefit of hardliners in Washington and Beijing."[15]

A FRAMEWORK FOR SUCCESSFUL NEGOTIATIONS

There are two distinct characteristics of all negotiations. The first is the *substance*, such as pursuing a joint venture, reaching a marketing agreement, or resolving a dispute. The second is the *process* itself, and this includes how the negotiation will occur, procedures that must be observed, behavior, and relationships that evolve during negotiations. When people negotiate within their own cultures, process is not a sensitive consideration because they typically share common expectations within a familiar business environment. These negotiators also have a common understanding of how their society resolves conflicts.

In negotiations between parties from different societies, however, process can become the most important consideration. This is because expectations for how negotiators conduct themselves, communicate, and resolve conflicts are based on entirely different sets of cultural values. Americans and most Western Europeans with similar histories of business and economic development, for example, can negotiate contracts on the *substantive* issues with only minor variations in negotiation protocols. In contrast, Japanese, Chinese, and many Latin Americans place great importance on relationships among the participating parties, both within their own societies and with those of other societies. In these cultures, negotiators must be cautious about relationships and differences in protocols. Consequently, the negotiation *process* becomes a predominant consideration through which trusting relationships must be established before substantive issues are addressed.[16]

Successful negotiations require several stages of activities, each with different responsibilities and patterns of behavior. Researchers differ slightly in their definitions of these stages—some identify four stages, others five—and each uses different labels for these activities. However, there is a general consensus on what must be done within the negotiation framework regardless of the substantive issues being addressed. The negotiation process is defined by how negotiators from different societies pursue these activities. This section presents a model of the process with five distinct categories of activities: planning, relationship building, exchanging task-related information, persuasion, and reaching agreement.[17]

Planning

The initial planning stage is concerned with **prenegotiation activities** that prepare negotiators with relevant information about *circumstances*, *negotiation issues*, *participants*, and *applicable processes*. Effective negotiators begin well in advance of actual meetings to gather information about political, economic, financial, and other considerations that could affect negotiations. They also start well in advance to study the other party's motives and characteristics. In addition, each side tries to clearly determine their own objectives and expected outcomes. These activities are common to all forms of negotiation, but when managers are involved in international negotiations, planning activities must include a competent study of the other party's culture, methods of negotiation, priorities, customs, and negotiation behavior. Categories of planning activities shown in Figure 10.3 are described in the following paragraphs.

Circumstances

Preparation for intercultural negotiation requires a thorough profile of relevant information about the foreign country, its economy, currency, infrastructure, government,

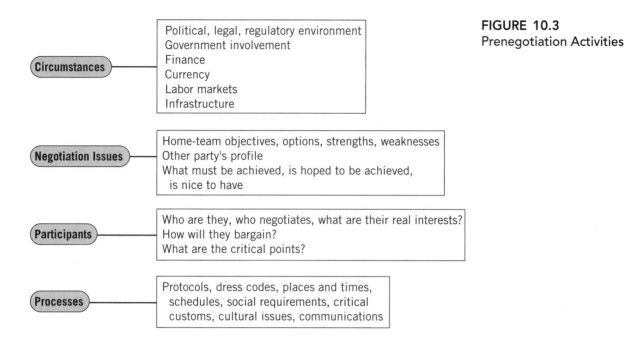

FIGURE 10.3
Prenegotiation Activities

and legal system that could affect negotiations. There may be a considerable list of issues if an enterprise intends to operate in a foreign country, but if the negotiations concern a sales contract or an export agency agreement, less extensive preparation may suffice. Several relevant issues merit specific consideration, including[18]

- *Political and legal systems*—Identify regulatory requirements, operating constraints, foreign ownership requirements, foreign tax policies, and intellectual property rights.
- *Foreign government intervention*—Evaluate potential demands for control or representation in the enterprise by foreign governments, role of officials in negotiations or operations, and the effects of political ideology on negotiation procedures or outcomes of agreements.
- *International finance*—Consider the stability and convertibility of foreign currency, debt and equity markets, restrictions against repatriation of profits, and monetary policies that could influence capital markets or economic stability.
- *Social stability*—Analyze the political and economic climate for potential changes, power shifts, risk factors, and future scenarios of growth, change, or social evolution.
- *Infrastructural considerations*—Identify characteristics of foreign labor markets, technological capabilities, physical development (roads, harbors, utilities, air transport, telecommunications), and commercial support systems (banking, transshipment expediting, insurance) that could influence decisions important to the negotiating parties.

If negotiations are concerned with establishing a major foreign enterprise, such as a manufacturing subsidiary or a regional marketing center, many of these considerations can be critical. Prenegotiation planning may therefore take months and involve exceptionally detailed reports by consultants or international agencies. For example, a manufacturing enterprise will need to know a great deal about its potential labor force—worker skills, wage rates, benefit requirements, labor laws on hiring and re-dundancies, labor union structure, labor relations, availability of local training, performance expectations, quality workmanship profiles, and so on. If the negotiating company intends to import raw materials to be subsequently processed, there will be very sensitive regulations on such things as import quotas, customs duties, export-import licensing, and constraints on types and sources of material imports. If the facility will then re-export products or components, destinations for exports and trade constraints must be considered. Each category of considerations has many potential questions that a company's negotiating team must answer through diligent investigations.

Negotiation Issues

The primary purpose of a negotiation may be obvious, yet parties may also have hidden agendas that would not be reflected in the final agreement. By planning ahead, negotiators will be able to clearly define all relevant issues, prioritize their objectives, and then develop alternatives that would meet those objectives. This stage of planning can be summarized by the phrase *know yourself first*. The negotiators want to have a clear idea of *why* they are negotiating and *what* ultimate objective they want to achieve. For example, a company may enter negotiations with a foreign company to establish a joint venture, but in reality the joint venture is only a means to an end; the company's real interest is to gain access to a new foreign market. With a little homework, the company would discover many other ways to gain market access, ranging from a brokerage agreement to establishing a foreign subsidiary. Viable options might include foreign licensing, entering a co-marketing agreement, or setting up regional sales distribution offices. However, if the negotiators begin with the presumption that they must successfully secure an agreement for a joint venture, they may miss more beneficial opportunities to achieve the company's real objectives. Negotiators need to be clear about what they intend to accomplish as well as the resources they bring to the table.

An American company from Wisconsin recently found itself in the situation of changing its approach to doing business overseas. The company imports foreign handicrafts for mass retailing and catalog sales, and managers travel worldwide on purchasing excursions several times each year. Recently, they went to Sri Lanka and scheduled negotiations with several small manufacturers to buy wooden figurines and toys. However, one of their primary Sri Lankan sources with very attractive items refused to consider any further export orders. The Sri Lankan claimed that periodic purchase agreements were too uncertain, and the company wanted a joint venture or long-term contract that would allow them to buy new technology and expand their operational capacity. The Americans were not prepared to consider foreign investment or to make a long-term agreement that involved anything other than trading. Instead, they negotiated on terms by trying to sweeten the offer. They offered to pay for a larger share of shipping costs, and they raised the purchase offer slightly. As a marketing organization, the Americans had always negotiated direct short-term purchases, and they had no experience with other options. The negotiations failed. A year later the Wisconsin people were back, but they had investigated several other possibilities. They were prepared to work with a Sri Lankan company to comanufacture products and to provide seed capital for new machinery, in return for a supply of proprietary items not sold to competitors. They also suggested the possibility of a licensing agreement or a small joint venture for special product lines. Any of the options would give the Americans products they wanted at attractive costs, and each could provide attractive benefits to a Sri Lankan company for expansion. The Wisconsin managers met with several Sri Lankan companies, quickly concluded a contract for licensing with the company where negotiations had previously failed, and signed a separate agreement for comanufacturing with a second enterprise. This gave the Americans a cost-effective supply of reliable products with low-risk investments, and helped two Sri Lankan companies more than quadruple their capacity.[19]

Negotiation issues are rarely cut and dried; research has shown that companies that spend more time preparing options and understanding their negotiating boundaries are far more successful than those that spend less time in preparation and have fixed objectives.[20] Research specifically found that successful negotiators are likely to have more than five options prepared in advance, while less-successful negotiating teams tend to focus on one primary objective, perhaps with only one backup alternative. Skilled negotiators were also found to pursue nearly twice as many long-term agreements than less-effective negotiators, and the best negotiating teams spent more effort on finding common ground between the parties than most negotiators who often became bogged down in confrontational differences.[21] From a planning perspective, *finding common ground* is particularly important. It involves not only a study of the negotiators and their organizations but also a self-study in order to determine three different sets of objectives for each party:[22]

- What *must* be achieved by both parties;
- What both parties *hope* to achieve; and
- What both parties *would like* to achieve.

By understanding what each participant *must achieve*, negotiators define the core objectives and each party's reason for entering the negotiation. Sometimes, the principals state these objectives clearly at the outset, but often they remain masked by other positions. Negotiators who begin by talking about an "interest in" a joint venture either do not understand why they are pursuing the agreement or they are being somewhat deceptive about their *real* reasons. As noted earlier, a joint venture is a vehicle for accomplishing some goal, such as opening a foreign market. The real reason—what the negotiations must achieve—may be to gain market access or to move production into a low-cost country. When that fact is understood, then the negotiators can develop a range of viable options, perhaps including a joint venture, without being blinded by the constraints of bargaining for a joint venture agreement.

Understanding what the parties *hope to achieve* involves research. Neither party is likely to reveal what it hopes to achieve, and perhaps both parties have only vague ideas about the possibilities. In any event, negotiators will be better prepared for making offers (or considering concessions) when they understand the possible outcomes. For example, a company that wants a joint venture for foreign manufacturing may envision lower wage costs, access to raw materials, or proximity to new markets. In the process, they hope to achieve certain negotiated wage concessions, perhaps preferential access to raw materials, and incentives from the host government such as tax holidays and favorable export quotas. These and many other issues become important points for both negotiating teams, and research is essential. Research seldom provides all the answers, but it helps negotiators to understand important issues before they engage in talks.

What the parties *would like to achieve* often reflects entirely subjective priorities, yet these priorities are critical to reaching an agreement. In talks about a proposed joint venture, for example, a foreign company may have a long-term vision of acquiring state-of-the-art technology or achieving major diversification. Although these goals may not represent realistic outcomes of the immediate negotiations, a new alliance might open the door to technology transfer and future diversification. Consequently, the host-country negotiators may consider short-term concessions in order to create an opportunity to move toward their long-term interests. At the same time, a multinational company may envision a foreign base as part of its global network; the company's negotiators may look favorably on a proposal that is not highly profitable on its own if it contributes products or services to other company operations. This is common where one subsidiary may provide partial components that are shipped elsewhere for assembly, or where labor-intensive unskilled work is accomplished in one operation with products shipped to affluent countries for further processing and marketing. In each situation, information about the foreign environment serves as a foundation for understanding the objectives and motives of both parties.

Participants

The most successful international negotiators are those who have prepared well in advance to understand the people with whom they will negotiate. They will try to form clear ideas of the importance of protocols that build appropriate relationships (or do not damage them) and to learn the negotiating styles of their foreign counterparts. Recall that in high-context cultures, people place greater importance on individual relationships than people from low-context cultures. Consequently, individuals from Latin America, the Arab world, Japan, China, and Mediterranean societies will focus their negotiations on building trust.[23] They seldom get to the specific details of negotiation until they feel a solid relationship exists between the parties, and until that has been established, details of the negotiation are somewhat incidental.

Few people in the world negotiate the same way or with the same expectations. Americans come straight to the point more quickly than people from other countries do, and they tend to emphasize the substance and details of negotiation. Americans also rely on company teams or experts to bargain. In contrast, Muslims typically emphasize relationships, avoiding discussions on details until the parties develop acceptable trust. Once this precondition is established, they are willing to cooperate on the finer points of an agreement. Arab executives often rely on third-party negotiators or intermediaries not necessarily connected with their enterprises, whereas northern European and American executives are more likely to participate directly in negotiations.

Japanese principals are always involved in negotiations, but they seldom address details. Instead, they rely on *Shokai-Sha*, or third-party "introducers" who bring the parties together, arrange negotiating sessions, conduct meetings, and sort through proposals and the negotiation points as semiofficial intermediaries. They often act as mediators to resolve contentious issues. The Japanese principals focus on relationship-building activities, usually relying on associates or outsiders to pursue substantive details as their agents.[24] Because negotiators view their roles differently in each culture, the process itself is significantly influenced by their role expectations. The "Global Viewpoint" feature illustrates contrasts in cultural differences.

Negotiators from different cultures have unique patterns of behavior, as described in the previous chapter on intercultural communications. Therefore, planning for negotiations should include an effort to anticipate communication methods and effective responses. For example, Mexican negotiators are often purposely selected to represent their companies based on their oratory styles and stage presence. In Mexico, negotiation is a performance that places high value on grand gestures and exquisite protocol, yet with a certain confrontational manner. Negotiators from Europe or the United States may find this behavior very distracting if they are not prepared for it.[25] In contrast to Mexicans, Swedish negotiators adopt quiet, cautious, and nonconfrontational postures, and they value clear and honest positions requiring little compromise. They put their terms on the table and earnestly expect to settle near those terms or abandon negotiations.

GLOBAL VIEWPOINT

VALUE DIFFERENCES ACROSS THE RIO GRANDE

Ron Kingstone headed for Mexico with great expectations for establishing a profitable maquiladora plant near Monterrey. Since devaluation of the Mexican peso, wage costs had fallen in real terms, materials costs were far lower than in the United States, and the Mexican government offered a lucrative system of tax incentives and favorable sites to lure American investment. Kingstone had been contracting a small amount of production from Mexico for his KanTite container company, but after several years of sustained growth, he hoped to relocate most of his plant capacity south of the Rio Grande.

Having already spent a year in preliminary talks with several Mexican companies, Kingstone was near a decision point. He had developed options of establishing a joint venture or a subsidary with the Monterrey company that had been contracting to supply part of his production. He anticipated greater benefits for a wholly owned subsidiary, but Mexico's regulations would require the plant to export substantially all production. Kingstone's marketing people felt that a significant domestic market could be developed for container packaging, and this action would require a U.S.–Mexican joint venture. KanTite's employees also had sent not-too-subtle messages that they favored a joint venture expansion, because the proposed subsidiary meant a major shift in production that threatened their jobs.

Kingstone reviewed these priorities as he prepared for a meeting scheduled with a Mexican labor union official and a government representative. He would not proceed far toward either option without government approval on a long list of requirements, and the union boss exerted influence, as well. Actually, Kingstone failed to understand why he was meeting with the union official except perhaps to satisfy protocol. He was more concerned with the government people. In that frame of mind, he landed in Monterrey and changed into a light suit to head for the first of several meetings.

During the first hour of discussions at the hotel's veranda cafe, no business was discussed. Two government people had arrived early and briefly mentioned that they had received all the papers and proposals that Kingstone had sent. They introduced him to two more men, one a local union representative and the other an investment banker. Before long, several more people arrived. One of them was a senior union official, who made a point of saying that he had just flown in from Mexico City where he had met with another major American company on a serious grievance matter.

After four hours of social talk and drinks, little business had been discussed. During the evening, Kingstone had stayed closely involved in conversations with the government official, who seemed to him the likely kingpin of the deal. He had made a few minor errors in names and titles but committed no serious breach of protocol. The government official that he had been cornering all evening was groomed like a diplomat and seemed to orchestrate things. The second official had spoken only a few social words and excused himself early. The union boss was dressed casually but flashed large gold rings and a Rolex watch. He was almost flamboyant at times, and Kingstone was uncomfortable with his sense of arrogance. He reacted pleasantly to the fellow while focusing his attention on the groomed diplomat and banker.

The meeting ended late that evening with no obvious references to the business at hand. The next day, formal meetings resumed with the Mexican company director and union representatives. After four hours, Kingstone felt a bit irritated with the proceedings. The parties had talked about almost nothing critical to his decision. They had not mentioned investments, products, technology, market potential. No one made any remark about government involvement or requirements for licensing or permits. The union representatives spoke at length about minor details, such as giving employees meal vouchers or setting up food services and creating a cash bonus scheme to bolster an unstable peso. They wanted Kingstone to hire local managers, bringing in Americans only to train and to develop the technology. They questioned Kingstone about his plant structure and employees in the United States, and someone even described a hypothetical disciplinary problem and asked how he would resolve it. Kingstone tried to answer these questions, but when he posed questions about the proposed new venture, someone changed the topic.

During lunch, the government man in diplomatic style showed up, and a second bank representative joined the table. Kingstone eased into what he believed was a fruitful conversation about investments and market potential for his company. Then he asked if the parties could meet on those issues that afternoon. The Mexican parties discussed this suggestion among themselves in Spanish, and the well-groomed diplomat said that they should meet briefly at around 4:00 PM. Lunch ended, and the company director escorted Kingstone on a tour of Monterrey, stopping to sample beer at a local brewery.

At 4:00 PM, Kingstone sat in the lobby lounge waiting for the appointed meeting. By 5:00 PM, no one else had arrived. He called the government office. No one was there. He called the company director's office and left a message. At 5:45 PM the well-groomed diplomat arrived, expressing sincere apologies. He sat down, ordered a drink, and then said: "Well, Mr. Kingstone, we enjoyed your insights, and we hope you enjoyed our wonderful city. My superior, whom you met yesterday, feels that we need more time to consider your proposals, and I'm afraid that our union leaders may want a great deal more information before they can endorse your ideas."

Kingstone was nearly ready to explode, and he showed it. In the course of the next 10 minutes, he learned that the well-groomed diplomat was a relatively low-level official in a position something like a public relations representative. The truly influential person was the modestly dressed fellow to whom Kingstone had given little more than nodding attention during the previous evening. The bankers attended as de facto observers for the government. The senior union leader that Kingstone had written off as someone trying to impress beyond his status was, in fact, in a position to veto the proposal.

Kingstone returned home with only a diplomatic promise of further meetings "in due course." They never occurred. Kingstone discovered later to his regret that everything he did and proposed probably irritated the Mexican hosts. He had not done his homework, and when he shrugged off the union's questions and pushed business issues during lunch, he showed a serious lack of respect. While the plant manager toured Kingstone around Monterrey, the union boss was meeting with government officials and booking a flight to Mexico City. He would not do business with Kingstone, and if the government approved the venture, union employees would not work for the new company.

Source: Ronald J. Kingstone, "How to Trump Your Own Hand in a Friendly Game," workshop presentation to the Association of Venture Capitalists, La Costa, California, May 1995.

Negotiators need to do their homework on the other team's negotiators and the executives who ultimately make decisions. This can be difficult if the other negotiating party is an intermediary. In fact, one reason that mediators are employed in Islamic nations is to insulate the owners, thus protecting them from the possibility of indignant confrontations or situations in which they could be shown to weaken or be bettered by the competition. When Arab principals are directly involved, they will be concerned with the relationship issues and avoid points of contention. When disagreement seems eminent, they will break off talks and appoint mediators to resolve details.[26] Consequently, prenegotiation planning can be challenging when trying to accurately assess the interests and behavior of those in critical decision-making roles.

Processes

By understanding the negotiators and their styles, each party gains a great deal of useful information about the actual negotiation process, yet cultural subtleties influence behavior and relationships between negotiating teams. In some societies, for example, a formal dress code is expected for business meetings, and negotiators involved in foreign assignments must understand expectations by host-country participants. In many Latin American cultures, it might be assumed that hot weather would permit more casual attire, but business executives dress in suits with cuff-linked shirts and fashionable ties. In Japan and China, an unwritten code seems to demand conservative dark blue, black, or dark gray suits with equally demure ties and plain shirts.[27] Exactly what is expected of women is unclear, because in many instances women are not expected to take part in negotiations. In orthodox Islamic cultures, women seldom have any role in business.[28] This sense of culture is captured in a recent anecdote about an American businesswoman on a visit to the Sudan. She was invited to a male colleague's home, served fine food, and treated to a ritual of washing with rose water after their meal. Later, the woman asked a local colleague why her host had treated her with dignity usually only afforded to men. "Oh, it's no problem," she was told. "Women do not do business, therefore you are not a woman."[29]

There are many peculiar formalities and restrictions to observe in foreign countries. For example, in Japan, prenegotiation "negotiations" often occur to settle issues that seem trivial to westerners. The Japanese will take great care to determine things such as the shape of a negotiation table or the seating of delegates. The Chinese dwell on minor scheduling issues, rest breaks, meal menus, agreements about photo sessions (or explicit prohibitions of them), detailing how to address participants, and how minutes will be taken. Such considerations seem rather unimportant to an American or European negotiator, but preliminary arrangements are very much a part of the actual negotiation process in Japan and China. Delegates from these countries often judge other negotiators according to concessions made on these details. An American who gives in easily on a procedural detail will lose some respect from host negotiators, possibly weakening negotiations or eroding trust between the negotiating teams.

Negotiators must be prepared to make sensitive decisions about where, when, and how to negotiate. It would seem logical that holding negotiations on one's home turf would be an advantage; the team will have support, rapid access to assistance, and the comfort of familiar surroundings. There is no evidence that negotiating at home or abroad yields better results for one party or the other, but cultural traditions often dictate the negotiating venue. The Chinese, Japanese, and most Middle East Arab cultures believe that it is important to host both diplomatic and business negotiations. If they cannot host talks, then they wish to meet in neutral surroundings. Therefore, the party serving as host has a sense of control over procedures, or if not acting as host, control is not yielded to the other party in neutral surroundings. American and European business negotiators, and most western diplomats, typically will go to the foreign venue. Many business negotiators themselves prefer to hold talks at, or near, the foreign parties' facilities. The visiting team can then gain an advantage of firsthand evidence of the other parties' capabilities and weaknesses, while at the same time revealing little about their own organizations. This separation can be an important advantage for small enterprises with few assets to flaunt, a point demonstrated in the "Global Viewpoint" feature. Such visits also can be crucial for organizations expanding into developing countries about which they lack reliable operating information. Personal experience may be the only way to validate the veracity of information about the other party and the foreign environment.[30]

Negotiators must plan dates and times of meetings to avoid conflicts with foreign holidays and religious restrictions. According to a religious calendar, the Muslims set aside a month each year for fasting and pilgrimages. During this month of Ramadan, many Muslim businesspeople focus on religious affairs, and many people reserve the time for religious pilgrimages. Indeed, entire businesses often close, and travel in Muslim countries can be very difficult.[31] In Japan, religious holidays follow a lunar calendar that marks out special periods, typically in early April and late November. Ethnic Chinese cultures almost everywhere in the world shut down completely during the Lunar New Year period in late January or early February; this time of celebration

GLOBAL VIEWPOINT

TAKE IT ON THE ROAD—DON'T NEGOTIATE AT HOME

Bill Boyd, president and founder of Transprint USA, keeps a suitcase handy and believes in negotiating anywhere but at the home office. "Take it on the road," Boyd says. "At home, you open your life to inspection. Although I take great pride in our company, it's a factory environment with no frills, and that doesn't always impress people." Boyd enjoys leading guests on tours of his factory, because he has a good operation, but it is still a relatively small business that some would not associate with global interests.

Transprint USA, however, earns revenues of $30 million a year printing special transfer papers for dry-heat transfer dying processes used in creating high-quality fabrics. Boyd's customers are typically large manufacturers of synthetic textiles created for the upholstery and fashion industries. His factory turns out millions of yards of transfer paper each month, which it ships worldwide. Transprint USA holds rights to nearly 4,000 registered designs, and through variations in dyes and inks, the company can create more than 2 million design combinations. This highly specialized industry is dominated by a few global companies, and although Transprint USA generates a modest sales volume, it is the leading U.S. company and third in the world behind German and French competitors.

Boyd developed an early preference for negotiating in the other company's backyard. He has explained how a mistake put him on the road:

> I signed an agency contract with a Taiwanese company several years ago after we negotiated an agreement in our New York sales office. We had good initial sales, then nothing. The guy just seemed unable to close sales, and then time lapsed, and I soon discovered that my European competitors were making a ton of money in Taiwan. When I visited there, I was shocked to find my agent selling everything from computer parts to wigs, but none of our products. The guy barely remembered that we had a contract, but he quickly held me to it. Unfortunately, I was locked in for another 6 months as long as he said that he was trying to get business. He never did another dollar's worth.

Transprint USA has since renegotiated with a new agent, but its business in Taiwan runs well behind that of other competitors. Meanwhile, Boyd has expanded into Malaysia, Thailand, and Japan, and his European offices have more than tripled their volume, including sales to new customers in the Middle East. With fewer than 400 employees, Transprint USA relies on contract agents, regional distributors, and, in a few instances, company-supported design centers in major domestic and foreign cities. Consequently, the company must maintain a network of well-coordinated business associates, and that activity keeps Boyd on the road most of the time.

"The Taiwan situation taught me a hard lesson," Boyd explained. "Had I known ahead of time how that guy operated and the crazy collection of products he tried to sell out of one back-alley office, I would never have signed with him. I don't sign anything anymore without visiting sales offices, potential customers, and learning everything that I can about the places where we intend to ship products." Boyd described how he avoided several other mistakes by traveling to China, India, and Malaysia, in each instance negotiating with several potential trade companies without signing agreements. "Each group I talked with had weaknesses that were discomforting," he said. "They looked good on paper, but either lacked quality or had questionable practices. These are things you have to see for yourself."

Boyd always does business firsthand, supported by a team that negotiates the details; they too go to the source. The team includes his New York chief designer and vice president of marketing, a senior manager in process technology, and an independent export executive from Italy. The team members make site visits after Boyd has made initial contacts, meeting and developing preliminary plans before returning several more times to pursue contractual agreements. The company also frequently brings in outside consultants or local intermediaries to bolster the team's effectiveness. In Boyd's view, the cost of these activities is a drop in the ocean compared to the cost of contracting with the wrong person and losing millions of dollars in sales.

Source: Co-author David H. Holt's experience as a consultant and negotiator in China with Transprint USA.

might make sense to an American only as Christmas, New Year's Day, and the Fourth of July rolled into one very long holiday. Each society observes its own regular Sabbath, prayer time, or day for religious services, and violating these schedules would be disastrous for a negotiating team.[31]

These examples of cultural issues are among many important, and often subtle, dimensions that constitute the art of negotiation. Consequently, *forming the appropriate negotiation team* can be a vital planning decision, especially when experience of a foreign culture is required, but also because foreign parties to a negotiation have very explicit expectations of who should be involved in the talks. Diplomatic missions take great care to match ranks, ages, status characteristics, and personal traits of negotiators with those of their foreign counterparts, and business delegations should take the same precautions. In most Asian societies, company presidents or senior directors head negotiating teams, and they expect similar status in western teams. Senior executives may do little more than observe social decorum, while junior executives or specialists handle details, but an Asian delegation would perceive a serious breach of etiquette if an American group were to meet them headed only by a junior executive.[32] Unlike Americans, Asians are not accustomed to having lawyers involved in negotiations, and a team that brings along a corporate attorney may be unwelcome. In almost all high-context societies, negotiations involve small, close-knit teams of key corporate staff who anticipate an equally well-balanced visiting team with whom they can establish relationships with a reasonable degree of parity.[33]

Relationship Building

Most international negotiations outside North America and Western Europe focus on personal relationships, not on technical deliberations. As emphasized earlier, the strength of foreign relations in Japan, China, Latin America, and much of the Middle East depends on building long-term commitments. The Japanese negotiate to develop a high degree of long-term confidence between the individual parties; they negotiate between people, not organizations. In their view, if a proper relationship exists, an agreement will have the stability it needs to change with conditions without threatening either party. However, if the relationship is weak, problems will always become magnified and difficult to resolve.[34]

Similar viewpoints are common to other high-context cultures where negotiators seek to establish relationships that remain constant over time. This *trust* in the relationship, rather than complicated legal clauses, allows enforcement of contract terms or a congenial modification of the agreement should circumstances change. In a recent contract between a major consortium of western contractors with the People's Republic of China, a two-page agreement was the end result of 14 months of negotiations. The document simply identified the parties and their commitment to jointly build a $25 billion highway. In the agreement, the Chinese representatives and the consortium principals exchanged mutual pledges of trust to support one another in the pursuit of their joint project, with proportionate sharing of development costs and profits. The 14 months preceding that agreement were consumed by weekly meetings, luncheons, dinners, and social events. Often, the principal executives participating in the consortium simply visited one another without discussing business.[35]

Mutual trust within the framework of a long-term relationship does not mean that either side will make unnecessary concessions or be any less determined to protect their interests. Russian negotiators place high value on relationships, yet they are extremely hard-nosed about terms and conditions. In Brazil, negotiators seem to follow a paradoxical pattern of behavior in which warm and friendly relationships can exist, yet negotiators are likely to be vague (often purposely misleading) about details of an agreement.[36] One reason for this behavior may be that in high-power-distance societies, negotiators are highly protective of information and their personal control over decisions. (Recall from the discussion of Hofstede's value dimensions that status differentials are very important to high-power-distance cultures.) Consequently, even though a sound relationship exists, there may be unavoidable rigidities in professional negotiating roles.[37] The Chinese typically bargain fiercely for long periods of time, yet despite the great value they place on protocol and personal etiquette during official meetings, they can easily resort to blatant "shaming" techniques and ambiguous charge-and-countercharge tactics. This can be a perplexing paradox to western negotiators.[38]

Prenegotiation meetings, as discussed earlier, help to develop the format of bargaining; they also contribute crucial time for relationship building. Behavior by the parties during these preliminary activities influences expectations and personal bonding between the parties. Relationship building begins with the earliest correspondence between the parties, and it continues long after an agreement is reached—as long as the parties share joint interests. Although Americans are considered impatient and too focused on immediate results, research has shown that they value strong long-term relationships as highly as anyone else. Foreigners regard Americans as among the most trustworthy people in the world with whom to do business.[39] The difficulties surface in how these relationships evolve. Specifically, many Americans simply do not make relationship building a priority, and they often lack the patience to let business arrangements develop on their own accord. In domestic negotiations, American contracts are likely to be in force and operative before negotiators find time to get to know one another.[40]

Relationship building is partially a matter of common sense and partially a matter of good research. Common sense suggests that negotiators should consciously make time to socialize and allow the "hard" issues to surface without undue pressure. Meanwhile, they should take precautions to avoid errors in communication or behavior that could be misconstrued. Common sense also suggests a need for research to understand the cultural perspective of the other party. Negotiators must be aware of religious, social, and ideological conventions, and this knowledge often comes from careful research and preparation. Being prepared with cultural knowledge does not mean that negotiators must change their stripes. They should be true to their own values, but appreciate the other party's priorities and values.[41]

Exchanging Task-Related Information

During this stage of negotiations, both parties are expected to make formal presentations, perhaps in several rounds of talks beginning with the most general remarks. Senior managers typically open the proceedings with philosophical statements about the purpose of the parties, and then make general pledges of "good faith." In many instances, the exchange process is a summary of months of prenegotiation planning, and it is often a crucial stage when the parties initially come face to face to present their agenda. From a *distributive* bargaining position, this stage represents the opportunity for opponents to show their teeth, to put demands on the table. It is the stereotypical combative stance that permeates so much of the literature. From an *integrative* position, this is the opportunity to gain a deep understanding of the other party's needs and expectations.[42] It is the time when negotiators can learn about one another and the contributions that both parties bring to the table.

Most parties begin to negotiate at positions not entirely acceptable to one another. The exchange process brings out the necessary information to clarify both positions and to create opportunities for new solutions. As emphasized earlier, negotiators must *learn about the other party's interests*, and interests are not the same as stated *positions*.[43] Through effective information exchanges, interests surface and usually change the bargaining positions of both parties. As discussed earlier, the types of interests that may arise include relationship issues or ideological concerns. The exchange process allows both parties not only to articulate their differences, but to thoroughly explore their mutual interests. When these objectives are pursued in a constructive manner, negotiators can jointly formulate a *problem statement*—a focal point of negotiation.

The term *problem statement* is emphasized because negotiators often are cast in the roles of problem solvers. In international negotiations, participants may find the most success if they treat the core issues as opportunities to reach agreements that mutually benefit both parties. In this win-win approach, discovering more about one another reveals how the parties can achieve greater results working together.

Negotiators exchange several categories of information. The obvious categories include background data on the companies, market opportunities, economic changes, and any other factual or statistical information relevant to the negotiations. A second set of information covers background for relationships, including personal and professional profiles of the principals, the negotiators, and anyone who may become involved in future business activities. Third, negotiators may exchange technical information specific to the negotiation issues, such as product characteristics, process methods, logistics, costs, pricing data, marketing support, and so on.

A fourth category, appropriately called *stakeholder interests*, includes both formal and informal positions, objectives, interests, and motivations of anyone affected by the results of a negotiation. As shown in Figure 10.4, primary **stakeholders** include principals, stockholders, employees, customers, and creditors. This group may also include members of a community in which the principal parties have an interest (such as a population area where, for example, a proposed factory might be located). Stakeholders also include politicians who may have an ideological interest in the negotiations and foreign suppliers who could be affected by the bargaining results.

Each category of information adds an important element to negotiations, and methods for handling this information differ substantially among the world's cultures.

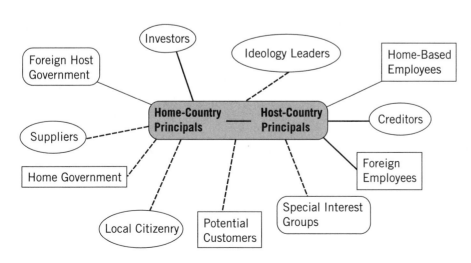

FIGURE 10.4
Stakeholders in
Intercultural Negotiations

Prenegotiation planning pays large dividends in dealing with these variations, and negotiators are better prepared for adapting to unfamiliar circumstances in foreign environments.

Persuasion

Closely associated with the stage of information exchange is the stage of *persuasion*.[44] Often, negotiators engage in extensive give-and-take during the information-sharing process, but persuasion raises the difficult issues that may prompt aggressive behavior or lead to concessions. At this stage, one party can offer promises, make threats, or ask for concessions while trying to persuade the other to accept conditions or give way on points. Unfortunately, sensitive differences can also lead to serious confrontations or misunderstandings. Negotiators may work very hard up to this point and feel as if they have established a mutual understanding on many issues, only to be surprised when the other party makes an absurd offer or takes a tough stance against any concessions. These developments are confusing because they send *metamessages* that, despite good relations between the parties, they remain far apart on the issues. Perhaps by making an absurd offer, a negotiator is sending a signal that the parties have not yet developed sufficient trust to realistically pursue the issues. In either event, bargaining can regress into a confrontational mode.

In contrast, parties may open with a great deal of differences in their positions, but their relationship may be sufficiently sound to *intone* messages in a way that suggests a desire to cooperate. This practice can soften disagreements, even over seemingly irreconcilable issues. A metamessage is a signal that negotiators should begin to search for constructive alternatives on which both sides can concur.

Negotiation style plays a crucial role in persuasion. Chinese and Japanese negotiators are likely to ask many questions about relatively small details, avoid giving direct answers on substantive issues, and use periods of silence either to build tension or to defuse pressure on themselves. Conversely, Americans are likely to push hard for direct answers and fill potential periods of silence with rhetorical embellishments.[45] Latin Americans may simply change the topic when it becomes too pointed or uncomfortable. Brazilians take this a step further by becoming purposely vague in their conversations, thus avoiding threats or clouding promises by disarming their counterparts with relatively minor and ambiguous issues.[46] In contrast, Americans are not reluctant to make promises or to use threats. Japanese negotiators, though slower to react than Americans, will not hesitate to use threats when they have been backed into a corner. They will also yield to well-conceived promises after members of their decision-making team have properly discussed them. Chinese negotiators try to avoid conceding any points until the talks near their culmination point. They may also interject threats without hesitation at any time on almost any point under consideration.[47] The Japanese seem unemotional in their persuasive techniques, but Koreans, Italians, and Middle Eastern negotiators often rely on bravado and intimidation tactics.[48]

Though understanding the psychological dimension of negotiating is difficult for international managers, the core objectives must be kept firmly in mind. Negotiators must be considered within the relationship, yet the agreement must substantially meet the objectives of both principal parties. Consequently, persuasion is concerned with presenting the relative advantages of the agreement to each party according to what they can realistically contribute and subsequently realize in outcomes. Skillful negotiators who understand these points are therefore better armed to make reasonable offers or concede to reasonable counter-offers. Skillful negotiators will look beyond the distractions caused by unfamiliar negotiating behavior, thus preventing tactics and idiosyncrasies of negotiators from jeopardizing an agreement. They will be able to remain constructively focused on the essential issues, thus helping both parties reach their objectives in an equitable manner.

Reaching Agreement

What constitutes an agreement is not always clear. Though actual terms in formal contracts or legal agreements may be obvious, *understandings* and *intentions* are seldom written down—yet they form the backbone of most international alliances. These are the implied conditions of an agreement and the expectations that define relationships between the parties. Unfortunately, these undocumented ambient factors result in contentious alliances or failed contracts more often than specific violations of negotiated agreements. For example, researchers estimate that between 30 percent and 60 percent of international joint ventures fail after their formation, and although many failures are blamed on poor contractual terms or unexpected changes in circumstances, more often alliances degenerate through misunderstandings and mistaken expectations that destroy relationships between the alliance partners.[49]

A significant number of international joint ventures do not survive in the long run simply due to unsatisfactory performance. In turn, disappointing performance may be the result of circumstances beyond the control of either party to an agreement, such as war, political instability, economic difficulties, and so on. However, negotiators too often fail to reach a complete *meeting of the minds* about their association, and despite the actual terms and conditions of the formal agreement, the parties soon realize that they did not really solidify a satisfactory agreement. Perhaps one party compromised too much, yielded to pressure, or surrendered to intimidation, thus resulting in a fragile relationship. The parties may have come to an agreement in good faith, only to discover in hindsight that they failed to reach a proper understanding of one another's performance expectations, and the agreement subsequently unravels.

These points become important for negotiators in several ways. First, preparation and planning significantly reduce the risk of failure. Recent research indicates that negotiators who spend more than double the average time in planning not only double their likelihood for success, but they also reduce negotiation time by more than two-thirds.[50] Second, well-planned negotiations with an integrative focus result in agreements with half as many compromises as agreements concluded through confrontational bargaining.[51] A third implication is that agreements based on sound relationships can be relatively easy to modify by the parties when circumstances change. In effect, *the agreement reflects the relationship and its personal understanding*, not merely the terms and conditions within a legal agreement. Japanese negotiators consider any agreement *invalid* (among themselves or with foreigners) that is so detailed that it requires litigation. Even the threat of legal action destroys the agreement, and although the Japanese partners will honor judgments and settle grievances, they will not consider themselves morally obligated to the other party.[52]

The implications of negotiated agreements go well beyond this presentation. However, some insight can be gained about agreements by recognizing how contractual relationships have changed in recent years. Formal international arbitration systems have evolved, such as those built into the European Union and the North American Free Trade Agreement. Dispute-resolution rules on more than 400 trade issues have been introduced through GATT and the World Trade Organization. In addition, the World Court and regional legal systems have vastly expanded their roles to interpret both provisions of agreements and the behavior of parties in global alliances.

All international agreements and alliances also must function in the context of country-specific commercial codes and legal systems.[53]

All things considered, no single set of standards determines what constitutes an agreement. Consequently, international managers find it more productive to recognize four general postures commonly associated with *culminating negotiations*:[54]

- *Formal agreement.* The parties may indeed reach a contractual agreement, put their terms and conditions into writing, and subsequently expect all parties to perform to the specific content of the agreement. Acquisitions of foreign subsidiaries, joint ventures and other alliances, comanufacturing agreements, sales or distribution contracts, purchasing agreements, trade pacts, agency contracts, and many other international transactions require formal agreements.

- *Informal agreement.* Parties often "reach an understanding" that is stronger and more resilient than anything written into an agreement. Indeed, Japan has become famous for implicit expectations developed between parties through historic family or organizational ties. Reliance on personal pledges and a deep-rooted understanding of allegiances carries far more weight than formal agreements among Japanese companies. Chinese business agreements are similar to those in Japan; both cultures are based on ancient traditions of group loyalty and filial piety. Unwritten loyalties bind many ethnic and religious groups in other foreign societies, and these cultural characteristics influence all agreements within their societies and outside their societies. Parties to an informal agreement share a mutual commitment to one another's long-term objectives; within this broad relational umbrella, they may pursue any activities that they jointly favor. A psychological contract is created, and negotiations in the traditional meaning take place throughout the life of the alliance.

- *Agreement not to agree.* A successful closure can also result when the parties end formal talks with no agreement. This outcome can be as important as a signed contract because negotiators must acknowledge when they find no common ground on which to base an agreement. To push harder, to concede more, or to refuse to "admit defeat" almost ensures failure of the agreement. Too often, negotiators disregard their own criteria and decline to walk away when they should. Successful negotiators, however, do not consider an agreement not to agree as a failure. Few partners ideally suit any particular situation, and a congenial parting often leaves the door open for future opportunities should conditions change or the parties find new grounds for collaboration.

- *Agreement to continue.* Few negotiations are singular in purpose or focused on one set of issues at one point in time. Whether the parties achieve a formal or informal agreement, they may also agree to conduct future negotiations. If they do not reach an agreement, but both agree that some potential benefit might come of remaining in touch with one another, then a successful agreement may do no more than begin to build bridges between the parties. They can agree to the possibilities, express their future interests, and perhaps even make pledges to one another for further cooperation. These understandings can be extremely important in many cultures, even though neither party incurs a distinct legal obligation.

Obviously, *reaching an agreement* means much more than achieving the objectives initially set out in formal negotiations. Negotiators should conceive a full range of possible agreements before they actually come to the table, and they should then recognize these possibilities as viable objectives of a successful negotiation. A successful agreement also depends critically on being able to manage conflict. All negotiations have contentious points and conflicts to resolve, and successful agreements are the result of how well negotiators manage conflict to achieve constructive results. The next section explores conflict within the context of intercultural negotiations.

MANAGING CONFLICT IN NEGOTIATIONS

Conflict was described earlier as interference by one individual or group in another party's efforts to achieve goals. This definition avoids many different dimensions of conflict, ranging from armed combat to the personal psychological problems of *intrapsychic* conflict. These are beyond the scope of this chapter, although some negotiators may be involved in every type of conflict situation. The most common form of conflict in negotiations occurs at the *group level.*

There are two classifications of group conflict. First, **intragroup conflict** concerns disputes and confrontations that arise within a particular group or organization. Negotiating teams often face internal differences about their negotiation strategies, objectives, and roles, thus creating disharmony within the group. Second, **intergroup conflict** is outward disagreement between two or more groups or organizations. This type of conflict includes, for example, disputes or confrontations between unions and management representatives, between buyers and sellers in a commercial contract, between organizations such as partners in a strategic alliance, between parties to a commercial litigation, and between ideologically opposed nations, trade legations, and diplomatic missions.[55]

Intergroup conflict is the most pervasive type of situation experienced by negotiating teams. When negotiations open, both parties begin with a degree of apprehension, and negotiators are usually far apart on most initial issues. Everyone would like to believe that negotiations will lead to a mutually beneficial and harmonious outcome, but until relationships are well developed, negotiations remain minefields of potential conflicts. Close proximity of the negotiators and the intensity of meetings increase the probability that one group will try to interfere with the other, thus creating potentially serious confrontations. The negotiation process itself may be disrupted, or one party's objectives and expectations may be frustrated, by the other party's mannerisms, threats, intimidation behavior, or verbal assaults.

Tactical Attributes of Conflict

Several patterns of negotiations described earlier demonstrate that conflict may be a normal consequence of bargaining, especially when aggressive negotiators purposely elevate talks to flash points. In these situations, conflict may be considered a proper tactic to gain a bargaining advantage. For example, Chinese negotiators were described earlier as individuals who often try to shame or frustrate their opponents through misdirected questions and trivial charges, or by stonewalling talks. Arab mediators are respected for their ability to draw the other side into emotional debates, thus putting their opponents on edge. Russians reinforce their bear-like image through stiff opposition to everything, subsequently consolidating their position for a dramatic closure on comprehensive bargaining points.[56] These types of behavior can be extremely stressful to negotiators who are unaccustomed to confrontational tactics, and minor differences often escalate into major distractions.

Differences in styles of negotiation clearly demonstrate that some parties may create conflict without remorse. Those negotiators regard conflict as a good technique. To others, conflict is a dysfunctional practice that serves no constructive purpose. Therefore, it is a bad technique. Whether conflict is inherently good or bad is an unresolved debate.[57] Proponents of conflict argue that individuals or groups without a certain degree of disagreement grow stale in their ideas; too much harmony prevents constructive questions or effective criticism, eventually robbing an organization of its competitiveness. Participants in international business who support conflict as a positive force point out that multicultural differences can be effectively resolved only by allowing conflicts to surface and then addressing them in constructive ways.[58]

For example, an American firm in Singapore struggled for several years while making only marginal profits and operating below home-office expectations. When consultants studied the company, they initially found no outward difficulties with the workforce. Employees were cooperative, expressed confidence in their managers, and were competent. Nevertheless, productivity was low, and no one seemed particularly motivated to improve. A more thorough investigation revealed resentment by many host-country staff toward their American managers. They perceived the Americans as making unilateral decisions and dictating work situations while giving lip service to new ideas or employee initiatives. The workers, accustomed to conformist behavior, simply kept quiet and never challenged decisions. Meanwhile, the Americans perceived their subordinates as docile people with little initiative. Consequently, the managers seldom challenged members of their staff to take significant initiatives or make recommendations. Through intervention workshops, the consultants created conflict situations that led, in due course, to a turnaround in the company. Americans learned how to challenge their subordinates and to manage controversial initiatives, and local managers and employees discovered that they could speak up constructively without repercussions.[59]

The classic debate about conflict raises issues of creativity and entrepreneurship. Large organizations that run smoothly are generally considered complacent and lacking innovation. Small companies anxious to compete often embrace challenges and treat conflict as just one dimension of successful entrepreneurship. Most people on both sides of the issue would agree with these points, but an ethical question remains whether deliberate use of conflict tactics to generate stress is exploitative. Though no one has a clear answer to this question, there is general agreement that companies should manage conflict within the ethical boundaries of human rights, yet sustain tension within the organization that can result in constructive change.[60]

Critics of conflict assert that interference is dysfunctional in any situation. They draw attention to a fundamental difference between conflict and competition, where competition can occur without purposely antagonizing the other party. They cite American football as an example of conflict in which individuals act with the sole purpose of disrupting their opponents, often to the point of physical harm. In contrast, swimming, sailing, sculling, and all field and track events are noninterference games. Competitors win or lose on their own abilities or teamwork. In these sports athletes pursue objectives, such as winning, that all participants cannot simultaneously achieve; but they cannot purposely interfere with their opponent's efforts. Runners cannot block other runners, swimmers must remain in their lanes, and rowers cannot tangle with other boats. Violations of these rules can result in disqualification.[61]

Commercial regulations in every country place similar constraints on business activities. Indeed, the U.S. Justice Department's antitrust case against Microsoft was based entirely on conduct by the company's executives that interfered with the performance of other competitors.[62] Further, cultural values exert tremendous influence on behavioral norms, but conflicts that arise across cultures are due in large measure to differences in people's distinctions between competition and conflict. The Japanese and Chinese cultures are often stereotyped collectively as Asian societies that share analogous characteristics. In fact, major cultural differences distinguish practices of negotiation and conflict in these societies. The Chinese are confrontational while the Japanese go to extremes to avoid confrontations. The Chinese also view "winning" as pressuring the other side to capitulate or to make concessions, while the Japanese consider winning much like an athletic event where a victor emerges on merit.[63] As a result, Japanese managers do not like to negotiate with Chinese managers, yet they feel comfortable dealing with Americans or Canadians. The Japanese like rules. They set up elaborate systems of negotiation, and although they expect to compete vigorously, they also expect all parties to stay within these rules and avoid hostile behavior.[64] The Japanese do not want the other party to feel defeated, but to achieve honorable results within the negotiating rules.

Alternative Approaches to Managing Conflict

In a conflict situation, opponents recognize two considerations: their personal needs and their opponents' needs. This duality can lead to four possible resolutions:

- Trade-offs, in which one wins at the other's expense
- Compromise, in which both win or lose in roughly equal proportions
- Contention, in which both agree to let the best competitor win through competition
- Collaboration, in which both seek to maximize their outcomes

The duality can also result in no resolution when both parties walk away to avoid the situation. These trade-offs underscore the **dual concern model** shown in Figure 10.5.[65]

In the lower left corner of the model, individuals show little concern about outcomes, either for themselves or for their opponents. Perhaps they view the point of

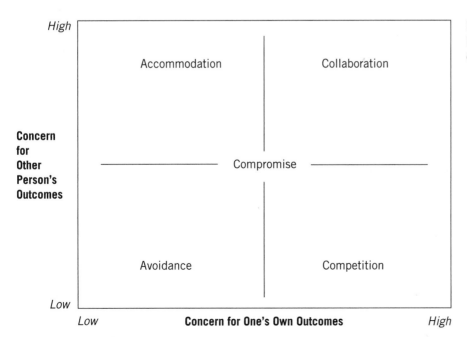

FIGURE 10.5
Dual Concerns for
Conflict Resolution

conflict as too trivial to pursue. This combination may also result from cultural values that encourage passivity, leading people to withdraw or avoid confrontation. This behavior characterizes a conflict management strategy called **avoidance** (or *inactivity*). In negotiations, it appears as a quiet nonresponse, yet it does not imply capitulation because nothing was gained or conceded.

In the top left quadrant, labeled **accommodation** (or *yielding*), a negotiator displays a high concern for the other party. Capitulation is a viable option. In high-context relationships, such as sensitive marriages where couples sincerely care about one another, conflicts are often dispelled when one party gracefully gives in to the other's demands. In business negotiations, this situation may arise when people value maintaining a relationship more than winning a particular point, leading one party to yield.

The lower right extreme describes negotiators strongly concerned about their own interests. They engage in *competition* (or *contention*), since each party assumes an aggressive stance in resolving differences. Both parties are out to win, and if the rules in place support a competitive environment, then both firms behave within those parameters without resorting to interference. On the other hand, this approach is clearly a win-lose situation, and it can incorporate dysfunctional aspects of conflict. Minor issues can be escalated, communication can become personally antagonistic, both parties may try to create confusion and misunderstandings, and differences may become focal points of contention.

The quadrant at the top right is called *collaboration* (or *integrative problem solving*). It can accommodate aggressive actions by the negotiators comparable to those in competitive situations, but activities focus on finding mutually beneficial solutions. The parties are concerned for their own outcomes as well as those of the other party. This situation is the ultimate form of constructive behavior in international negotiations, but it requires cooperation by both parties. One negotiating team cannot pursue this pattern of bargaining while the other team is determined to be confrontational.

Finally, the center of the diagram defines a zone for *trade-off* or *compromise*. Neither party can claim a win or loss, nor does either yield or walk away. Although a compromise agreement is the stereotypical expectation of any negotiation, it seldom yields ideal results. Neither party fully achieves its objectives, and the final compromise agreement may leave both in relatively weak condition. A joint venture born of compromise agreements may result in less than optimal investment funding, mediocre performance expectations, and reservations by both parties about the other's commitments.

The optimal approach is to seek collaboration with a commitment by both parties to resolve conflicts before they escalate. They do not avoid conflict or yield without contending the issues. Indeed, they may compete fiercely to defend their interests, but they do not regress to dysfunctional behavior. Finally, negotiators resist compromises and make concessions only when they contribute to more important collaborative objectives. Concessions are not made merely to balance accounts. Unfortunately, this ideal scenario rarely occurs, and most negotiations depend on conciliation and compromise. When compromises cannot be engineered or when competitive parties become deadlocked, negotiations may simply fail. However, conflicting interests can be addressed through a dispute resolution process or through arbitration.

Dispute Resolutions

The ultimate forum for resolving serious disputes is a civil court, but this is not a popular option. To sue another party for perceived damages or to force performance on a contract usually requires a hearing under a foreign legal system, and many nations lack effective commercial codes or the means for enforcing judgments. Nevertheless,

Youthful demonstrators left World Trade Organization talks in shambles when, in November 1999, thousands of marchers jammed buildings and facilities during the WTO's Seattle summit meetings. They gained worldwide attention for their protests against the concept of the WTO and its mandate to liberalize trade for member nations. Indeed, since its founding in 1996, the WTO has sought to negotiate "trade-off" concessions among countries in Western Europe and North America, often intervening in sensitive disputes over trade commodities and interpretations of trade terms under GATT. However, protesters see such interventions as lopsided political maneuvering and "corporate protectionism" through an organization that has not yet become an effective agency to fairly resolve international trade disputes.

companies often must resort to legal remedies. In some countries, special tribunals hear civil disputes and hand down binding rulings. In others, formal mediators or systems of arbitration exist for resolving disputed claims. Domestic and international grievance agencies also address specific problems such as labor contract violations, employee complaints, insurance losses, and payment defaults.

Some disagreements may involve international legal proceedings on trade or cross-border business, but these procedures do not redress past wrongs as much as search for acceptable solutions to disputed issues. Consequently, negotiators occasionally must call upon international agencies such as the World Trade Organization to clarify the parties' positions. The WTO and similar agencies seldom become involved in the affairs of individual companies, but instead address industry-level problems or conflicts in national trade activities. For example, the WTO was involved in a series of rulings that upheld U.S. State Department claims against European Union trade practices that created unfair duties and price advantages by European businesses for American-processed fruits, foods, and beef products. The State Department joined American food industry legations in claims, and later in legal proceedings at the World Court in Brussels.[66]

Litigation that cannot be handled through domestic court systems may require intervention by the International Court of Justice (ICJ). However, the ICJ deals more often with international political issues and treaties than with commercial interests. The Overseas Private Investment Corporation (OPIC) intervenes to expedite transactions between parties to international contracts, but OPIC works mainly through transaction insurance rather than litigation. It is not a legal tribunal but an intermediary with substantial influence to affect contract performance. Activities of these and many other international organizations, regional trade councils, and the United Nations substantially influence the legal parameters of negotiations and agreements.[67]

Another option for dispute resolution is **arbitration,** in which both parties agree to intervention by a neutral third party.[68] When the parties choose an arbitrator, they agree to honor the third-party ruling without recourse, but this limits future options and deters many companies from accepting arbitration. A somewhat friendlier approach is to appoint a neutral mediator. In effect, a mediator acts as a negotiator for the negotiators; rather than making final rulings, the mediator intervenes to help both parties work out acceptable solutions. Arbitration and mediation are two of the most powerful and efficient methods for resolving commercial disputes. The Paris-based International Chamber of Commerce (ICC) is perhaps the best-known international arbitration institution; the ICC handled 529 industrial cases in 1999. Nearly 1,300 arbitration tribunals are registered by the United Nations or the American Arbitration Association, which together resolve more than 5,000 international commercial cases each year. Indeed, they are so effective that many international companies require a clause in negotiated agreements that contractual parties will submit to arbitration should they encounter problems with their agreements.[69]

Many disputes occur from conflicts over enforcement of terms or performance rather than deadlocked negotiations. Parties who bargained in good faith may have promised more than they could deliver, or perhaps conditions have changed to block shipments, upset investment plans, or otherwise violate contract terms. In emerging nations in Eastern Europe and the former Soviet Union, contracts are often vague and difficult to enforce. Changes in Russia, Bulgaria, and Poland, for example, have blurred the lines between public and private interests, further compounding the problems of cross-border trade and responsibilities for contract enforcement.[70] In these situations, the parties are no better off than when they were initially negotiating agreements. Without some method of ensuring performance, contracts have little meaning.

One method of dispute resolution gaining in popularity is the use of hostages. The term *hostage* is misleading because in this sense, it has nothing to do with forcefully holding someone for ransom. A better term would be an *exchange of observers* or *liaison officers*. A hostage may be an individual who represents one company while working closely with the other as a condition of the agreement. This person receives significant access to the host company's operations and carries authority to resolve problems as they arise.

In a different sense, contract terms can be *made hostage to* conditional performance. For example, when two parties cannot agree to terms on purchasing, the buyer may agree to accept stock-in-trade or a percentage of output. Some resolve disputes by accepting shipments of a different product than originally specified, requiring the selling party to obtain those products from a party outside the agreement. This method amounts to *countertrade*, and it helps to avoid or resolve disputes over price, cost, or impediments to trade such as customs quotas or high tariffs. A buying company itself can become hostage by providing the foreign seller technology that is amortized through future trade shipments. The buyer owns the equipment and loans it to the seller, so that the company can make the products the buyer will purchase. As the seller completes future shipments, the loan is paid down in proportion to the value placed on goods shipped. This approach can avoid deadlocks in which the parties cannot fully agree to terms for a joint investment.[71]

A full understanding of dispute resolution procedures would require in-depth study of commercial law, supplemented by country-specific investigations. Informal dispute-resolution techniques comprise the formal and informal terms of contracts, side agreements, countertrade arrangements, and various forms of third-party intervention. Negotiators often find new strategy alternatives for their companies when searching for help to resolve disputes. In these instances, a grounding in relevant commercial law can be an important advantage, and mediators are often hired precisely for their skills at uncovering alternative ways around difficult issues. Consequently, effective negotiators are often those who can achieve satisfactory agreements by identifying innovative ways to resolve potential conflicts.

CONCLUDING COMMENTS

Effective negotiations result from participation by well-informed, sincere, and experienced negotiators who understand the benefits of collaborative behavior as well as the dangers of confrontational tactics. These culturally sensitive people display genuine interest in learning about the values and concerns of others. They also bring to the negotiations the communication skills necessary to build relationships, and they are alert to the nuances of the negotiating process. Perhaps most important, effective negotiators expand everyone's opportunities with innovative efforts to seek new opportunities through joint endeavors that neither party could pursue independently. These synergistic opportunities often provide the rationale behind growth in global enterprises and improved international relations.

Looking forward, the chapters in Part Four expand the theme of cross-cultural management to the practice of human resource management. Intercultural negotiation and communication are important cornerstones for these chapters, which look closely at international labor relations, the difficulties associated with life as an expatriate manager, and the challenges of managing in a multicultural environment. These chapters examine human resources from a labor-management perspective and explore how different cultures organize work. They also describe problems associated with recruitment, selection, and discipline in foreign subsidiaries. Finally, they introduce methods of international management development and training in both home and host countries.

REVIEW QUESTIONS

1. How do the *distributive* and *integrative* approaches to negotiations differ?
2. Identify activities associated with *prenegotiation*. What should a negotiator take into consideration during the planning period?
3. Contrast differences between parties to a negotiation. How would American, Japanese, Egyptian, and Brazilian negotiators differ in their behavior?
4. All parties pursue three types of objectives in a negotiation. What are they, and how do they influence the behavior of the negotiating principals?
5. People try to persuade others to accept their viewpoints in many ways. How does this activity affect negotiations? Give four examples of persuasion methods common to other cultures.
6. Negotiators can reach four kinds of agreements. Identify and explain each one.
7. How do *substantive issues* contrast with *process issues?* Explain how negotiators from Latin America, Asia, and North America generally emphasize each of these considerations.
8. Explain the arguments for and against conflict as a bad or good aspect of negotiations.
9. How do the four quadrants of the *dual concern model* explain how people attempt to resolve conflict?
10. Explain the concept of hostages within a negotiated contract. Why would two parties need such conditions?

GLOSSARY OF KEY TERMS

Accommodation   A nonaggressive resolution to conflict in which one party yields or capitulates its own interests to satisfy the other party's needs.

Arbitration   A process by which parties to a contract agree to a binding decision by a neutral third party when there is a dispute concerning contractual performance.

Avoidance   Turning away from issues and walking away from a conflict or an entire negotiation, thus resolving nothing for either party.

Bargaining   A limited concept that suggests competitive bartering or exchange processes to narrow choices of competing parties to an outcome agreeable to all.

Conflict   Interference by one party with another in the pursuit of individual goals that they cannot simultaneously achieve.

Distributive negotiation   A zero-sum model in which parties compete to maximize their individual shares of a fixed pool of outcomes, thus creating a win-lose situation.

Dual concern model   A matrix of conflict resolutions based on competing concerns for two parties' positions.

Integrative negotiation   A collaborative model in which parties seek to expand the range of possible outcomes, in the process maximizing their individual outcomes by sharing in collective results.

Intercultural negotiation   Distinguished from domestic negotiation; cross-border, culturally complex exchanges of positions common in international business affairs.

Intergroup conflict   Outward disagreements between separate groups.

Intragroup conflict   Disputes and stressful problems that arise within a particular group or organization.

Intrinsic interests   The underlying needs and motives, often unrealized or unspoken, of negotiators or their principals, which, if satisfied, usually prove far more important than substantive issues.

Negotiation   A comprehensive concept that suggests a joint effort to find mutually acceptable responses to problems, opportunities, or conflicts.

Prenegotiation activities   Planning responsibilities during the initial process of negotiations to identify circumstances, issues, participants, and protocols involved in pursuing formal initiatives.

Stakeholders   Those who have an interest in, will be affected by, or can influence negotiations or outcomes proposed by the parties.

Substantive issues   The objective initiatives and bargaining positions of negotiating parties.

EXERCISES

1.   In almost every negotiation situation, *substantive issues* arise from openly stated objectives, and unspoken *intrinsic issues* motivate each participant. Recall three different negotiation situations in which you have participated. Identify the substantive issues and briefly jot down the conditions, terms, and results. Then project your thoughts to answer the following questions: Why were you involved? What really motivated your behavior? What were your real needs? Now examine the outcomes of those negotiations and determine whether you resolved your substantive issues and whether you addressed your intrinsic needs. How could you have improved your negotiations?

2.   Within the framework of Exercise 1, consider the intrinsic interests of the parties with whom you negotiated. How did the outcome of your negotiations meet their interests or motivate them? If you had realized those interests before you actually began bargaining, how could you have changed the terms or improved the outcomes? Set up one example that you can discuss in class, and identify at least one viable alternative that would have created a satisfactory win-win situation for all parties.

3.   Based on what you have learned from this and previous chapters on cultural differences, select a foreign society as an example for a hypothetical negotiation to set up a joint venture

for an export office. Choose any product or commodity you like, and then identify the main negotiation issues you would expect to face. Also identify the interests that you believe would be most important to the foreign parties. In your answer, describe possible stakeholders who might influence this agreement.

A Gaijin Takes Charge at Mazda

Japan's fifth largest automaker, Mazda, is managed in Japan by a foreigner, Henry D. G. Wallace, who also represents the first *gaijin*, or western foreigner, to head a major Japanese company. Wallace was the first non-Japanese executive in Mazda's history, during which generations of tightly knit relations under the watchful eye of Sumitomo Bank have ensured that a few families wielded power in one of Japan's strongest industrial groups. Mazda Corporation is the largest organization in Hiroshima, representing nearly 28 percent of the city's economic activity. Since the end of World War II, Hiroshima has been etched in history as the first devastating target of atomic warfare. This ordeal, and the rebuilding of Hiroshima through industrial development by companies such as Mazda, has created a very tight bond among Japanese.

Indeed, Hiroshima is a distinctly homogeneous Japanese city, more so than Tokyo, Yokohama, and other cities with somewhat more cosmopolitan populations. It also is a "company town," and many of its citizens were stunned when Mr. Wallace was appointed as Mazda's president in 1996. Only weeks before Wallace's appointment the outgoing president, Yoshihiro Wada, had insisted that he didn't intend to step down, and that he alone would name a new president when the time came for him to retire. His response came during a press interview following Ford's announcement that it had acquired a significant position in Mazda. When speculation mounted about Ford bringing in outsiders, Wada had publicly assured his employees that neither he nor his colleagues could possibly imagine a foreigner running Mazda. Wada was subsequently eased into a ceremonial position on the company's board, and replaced by Wallace.

Wallace is a tall, fair-skinned Scotsman who was raised in England. During his 17-year career with Ford, he held management posts in six countries on three continents—including stints as Ford's finance director in both Europe and Mexico, and as president of Ford's subsidiary in Venezuela. He speaks English, Spanish and German, but cannot read or write Japanese. However, Wallace is a quintessential global executive, and he is well versed in Asian culture. His position at Mazda was part of the groundwork laid two years earlier when Ford influenced the appointment of Wallace and a trio of British, American, and Australian executives to sensitive positions at the Hiroshima headquarters. Together, they cemented Ford's behind-the-scenes power at Mazda, taking charge of most of Mazda's major functions. When Wallace's appointment became official, it was a shock. Indeed, Wada and nearly all of his loyal executives strongly opposed foreign management, but Sumitomo Bank executives actually engineered the change. The bank owns about 3 percent of Mazda and holds a significant creditor position, but it is also the powerhouse behind the *keiretsu* (industry group) in which Mazda is an entrenched member.

Wallace has solidified his position with the backing of the keiretsu elite and his Ford connections, but he has faced extraordinary challenges in his leadership role. Language barriers presented difficulties for communicating with his executive staff. Wallace could not write memos, hold team meetings, or maintain social relationships easily when everything had to be translated. Language difficulties are critical, Wallace concedes, "not because a person cannot speak fluently, but because, even if he did, a non-native speaker will never fully think in the foreign language." In Japan, communications—particularly negotiations—between people who work closely together is based on a concept called *shinyo* (gut feeling). This literally means having an intuitive understanding of the other's needs, and these perceptions are important for building cooperative relationships and reaching understandable agreements.

The Japanese give even greater meaning to the concept of *shinyo*, where their cultural homogeneity has created a pattern of behavior called *ishin-denshin* (communication without words). This is far more important in Japan than in heterogeneous western societies. Among Mazda's Japanese managers, subtle nonverbal communication conveys more meaning than explicit messages. Unfortunately, Wallace and his western staff cannot grasp the meanings associated with Japanese nonverbal behavior. For example, one of Wallace's senior Japanese managers was asked to make a change in production procedures, and he responded "we will make efforts to do so," but Wallace sternly replied that making an effort was not sufficient. "Will you do it?" he pointedly asked. A Japanese witness to this exchange explained that Wallace was seeking a firm personal answer from his manager, and the Japanese executive was making a very strong commitment on behalf of his team. Wallace was unable to recognize the deferential manner of his manager, which conveyed obedience and a commitment on behalf of himself and his staff.

"We speak from different cultures as well as languages," Wallace says. Consequently, he finds himself constantly in negotiations because to accomplish work that must be done, he must first elicit agreement on decisions—much like a psychological contract or a joint understanding of expectations that transcend the cultural barriers. "I can't tell you how many times I've been told, 'You don't understand Japanese business practices'," Wallace says. He believes, therefore, that honing his negotiating skills will eventually create a pattern of relationships within the company to bind together his executive team. Japanese who know him say that he has mastered several traits essential for managing in their country: a calm demeanor inside the office, an ability to schmooze on the golf course, and a knack for karaoke. These may not all seem to be serious relationship-building activities, but they are important as well as symbolic of Wallace's efforts to adapt to the Japanese society.

Wallace has gained respect for listening to employees while building close associations both in the plant and in social settings. Indeed, Mazda employees and suppliers say that he appreciates the art of *nemawashi*—a Japanese phrase meaning to "prepare the roots," or to build sound relationships before conducting business. A Sumitomo adviser who was involved in the decisions that changed management at Mazda characterized Wallace as a person capable of "growing tall trees by nourishing strong roots rather than fertilizing a weak plant." An Australian standing nearby heard this comment and questioned its meaning. "What's the point?" he asked. The adviser answered, "In the vernacular that you are accustomed to, sir, Wallace doesn't [expletive deleted]."

Wallace is gaining a reputation of being firm and direct, but also fair and gentle in his selling approach to getting things done. "We think he's a Buddhist," says Mazda executive Hiro Akutagawa. "If he were shoving things through all the time, nobody would follow him." In contrast to most westerners who seem too abrupt for Japanese sensitivities, Wallace spends a great deal of time negotiating before he ever takes a seat at a negotiating table. Decisions are made, or at least the issues are well understood, before the parties convene. This is the Japanese way. Traditionally, managers who needed to discuss important issues gathered in bathhouses or restaurants, walked in gardens, or shared tea. Negotiation occurred through informal meetings and conversations, and also through a relationship called *hara-gei* (literally, "stomach art"). This technique for solving problems relies on negotiations among individuals without using direct words or confrontational persuasion tactics. What is in one's *hara* is akin to saying what is in one's "heart." Therefore, individuals find ways to effectively communicate what is in their hearts—leaving unmistakable clues about their desires, needs, demands, or intentions—without blatantly exposing their positions to attack.

Wallace practices *hara-gei* on the golf course, in private meetings, and during casual office conversations. Consequently, when he convenes a meeting with managers or sits down with suppliers over contracts, the occasion seems more like a ritual approval than bargaining. When an impasse does occur, or a point is contended, the Japanese tend to become silent, or they change the subject. An Australian expatriate on Wallace's team is likely to argue or to strongly press his points. Two Americans on the team tend to offer persuasive arguments or appeal differences on factual evidence. Wallace can stand firm when necessary, but he also recognizes when it is time to end the meetings, short of confrontations, and go back to laying better groundwork to ensure an understanding among those involved.

Wallace has established a successful performance record with new models of the Mazda line, but coming into the new century, he also has established *nagai tsukiai* (long-term trust in relationships). This is the crucial point on which success turns as anxieties between East and West melt. Mazda employees, their union leaders, and citizens of Hiroshima recognize that Wallace has brought a strong dose of western decisiveness to the organization—and they welcome the change—but he also has gained respect for observing the traditions of how Japanese get things done. Contracts will not suddenly replace relationships or become legal documents written for their enforcement value. They remain as formal expressions of trust—*nagai tsukiai*—that underscore long-term understanding among parties. Clearly, negotiation does not end with a contract in Japan; instead, negotiation begins when a contract provides the foundation for trust.

QUESTIONS

1. The Japanese concept of negotiation differs dramatically from the western approach. Using the model of negotiation presented in the chapter, contrast these differences for each stage in the negotiation process.

2. Several important Japanese concepts were described in the case. Describe how unique thought processes and perceptions are influenced by culture, and how an international manager's role would change when dealing with Japanese negotiators.

3. How does the Japanese approach to communication influence negotiations? In particular, how can managers at Mazda avoid distributive bargaining behavior and nurture integrative relationships?

BIBLIOGRAPHY

Graham, John, and Yoshihiro Sano. "The Japanese Negotiation Style." In Roy J. Lewicki, Joseph A. Litterer, David M. Saunders, and John W. Minton, *Negotiation: Readings, Exercises, and Cases*, 2nd ed. (Boston: Irwin, 1993), 541–552.

Menger, Richard. "Japanese and American Negotiators: Overcoming Cultural Barriers to Understanding." *Academy of Management Executive* 13, no. 4 (1999): 100–101.

Reitman, Valerie. "Foreigner Takes Driver's Seat at Mazda: Japan Gasps as a Gaijin Takes Charge at Mazda." *Asian Wall Street Journal*, April 16, 1996, p. 1.

Tezuka, Hiroyuki. "Success as the Source of Failure? Competition and Cooperation in the Japanese Economy." *Sloan Management Review* 38, no. 2 (1997): 83–93.

CASE 10.2

CHILE: A LATIN EXPERIENCE IN PATIENCE

Hector Raos McLachlin is a Canadian citizen from Vancouver. He also is part Chilean, a heritage that he traces through his grandmother, who married a mining engineer shortly after World War II. Hector's mother was born in Chile before the family moved to Canada, and as a young man Hector came to be known by the name Raos, after his maternal family name. He grew up hearing intriguing stories about the mountains and streams of his grandmother's home in the wine country some distance from Santiago. Raos majored in commerce while at college. As a young adult he worked in a trade office, where he learned about international transactions, including much about Latin American trade. He had also been brought up to understand Spanish, although he was not well schooled in the finer points of Latin culture. Nevertheless, lifelong preparations set the stage for Raos to take the entrepreneurial plunge in 1996 when Canadian customs regulations changed to favor importation of foreign wines.

Financed by a legacy from his grandfather's will, Raos went to Santiago to establish a cooperative venture with a winery that offered wholesale capabilities and government backing to expand export trade. To Raos's surprise, the Chilean wineries made excellent products, and he hoped that government subsidies and tax breaks on export quotas would help him to build a thriving trade through Vancouver connections.

On his first visit to Chile, Raos met with two members of the Allende family, who owned the winery in which he was interested. During a four-day visit, he examined the fields, toured several of the family's facilities, and studied their warehousing system and retail outlet in Santiago.

The Allendes were very cordial hosts, but they adopted unexpectedly formal attitudes. Dressed exquisitely in European suits, an elder family member and his twenty-something son seemed to follow an agenda of meetings and site visits coupled with long lunches and dinners that began near midnight and lasted well into the early morning hours. After their initial meeting, Raos quickly shopped for an up-market suit and several expensive shirts, clothing that he had not brought with him. He matched the Allende protocol in appearance and demeanor—a smart move in retrospect, since these occasions included introductions to bankers, government officials, merchant friends of the family, and several cousins, uncles, and in-laws.

In each instance, casual conversations stretched over long periods, almost always covering the same ground. His acquaintances wanted to hear about his grandparents, where his mother had been born, what relatives they had in Chile now, and what his family did in Vancouver. The questions were so patterned that Raos became weary of answering them. Throughout the visit, little was said about why Raos had come to Chile. The Allendes knew of his proposal for a cooperative venture through correspondence prior to the trip, but whenever Raos tried to speak of business, the elder Allende would change the topic with a somewhat boisterous anecdote or story. In one conversation with a banker, for example, he broke into a long explanation of how the family had fought through a drought that had almost devastated their vineyards. In another instance, he explained an ordeal of finding a supplier of wine bottles. During dinner with a government trade counselor, Raos was left to chat with the official's wife while the Chileans debated changes in politics. Raos was tempted to interrupt these stories, and he felt irritated by what he perceived as self-centered boasting by the elder Allende. Even as Raos was escorted to his flight home, the elder Allende made an odd remark that Raos, being "paled by the lack of sun in Canada," should "return to the warmth of Chile."

Several months later, Raos visited again. During the interim, he had corresponded in detail with the younger Allende about an agreement either to import wine to Canada as a broker or to make an equity investment in a separate export company that would wholesale the Chilean wine in Vancouver. Raos wanted to create an equity joint venture, and his correspondence was weighted toward persuading the Allende family to agree with his plan. However, on arriving in Santiago to pursue the negotiations, Raos was met by the younger Allende and an uncle who seemed to convey very guarded messages about any business venture. Talks dealt more specifically with business prospects than those during the first visit, but Raos was left with the feeling that the family was quite happy with its current business without the complications of exporting wine to Canada.

General details about price points and margins were discussed, questions about shipping wine and whether it would "travel well" were brought up, and various issues such as bottling, case-quantity storage,

and currency differentials were raised. But legal issues and contract terms were not discussed. The Allende uncle often told boastful anecdotes, much as the elder Allende patron had done, but he was a gracious host and agreed to visit Vancouver in the spring of 1997. The younger Allende promised to discuss Raos's questions more carefully with his father and then get back to Raos on the finer points of doing business.

Several months passed, and Raos finally sent a detailed proposal to the Allendes with an offer of a direct equity stake in an export company. He outlined price points and projected sales and summarized a very thorough market report on potential customers. He put the offer in terms that he felt deserved a clear response—either acceptance or a counter-offer—that would move the negotiations toward a conclusion. Instead, he was met with silence. The Allende family made absolutely no reply other than a brief fax to acknowledge receipt of his proposal. The uncle never came to Vancouver, and Raos's telephone calls seemed to be ignored.

Angered by the silence, Raos made an unannounced trip to Santiago in June 1997. He showed up in casual dress wearing no tie—and although tidy, he looked ready for a backyard barbecue rather than an important business meeting. The elder Allende, dressed as though he were going to the theater at 10:00 AM, greeted Raos with some reserve. He said that they would meet for lunch at the hotel about 1:00 PM. Raos went to the hotel at the appointed time, took a seat on the patio with a cool beer, and waited. An hour passed, and no one showed up. At 2:40, the barman brought a message that his party would be coming soon. By 3:30, Raos was ready to leave. In fact, he was almost anxious to leave, to return to Vancouver and just forget the whole thing. He went back to his room and mentally wrote off the whole deal.

Shortly before 7:00 PM, the younger Allende arrived with a driver. He apologized for a difficult day and the missed appointments, and then invited Raos to pack his clothes and come out to his house to stay. He explained that his father would talk with him soon at home. Raos reluctantly allowed the driver to help pack him out of the hotel. On the way to the Allende home, Raos was told that the family had a surprise for him—someone to meet. When they arrived, Raos was escorted by the driver to a very nice upstairs room in a large villa and invited to refresh himself and come downstairs. The Allendes would be on the veranda, and he could come as he was or in even more casual attire.

Raos rinsed his face and hands, ran his fingers through his hair, and wished that he had gotten a haircut before leaving Vancouver. When he reached the veranda, he was surprised to discover the entire family gathered amidst an impressive spread of catered foods, chilled wines and beer, and two musicians who played a lively tune on their guitars when Raos arrived. The elder Allende immediately extended a hand in greeting and clasped his other hand over Raos' hand in a strong and unexpected gesture. He was dressed in perfectly creased casual slacks, his graying hair carefully combed, yet he sported a colorful shirt that was purposely opened to reveal, in macho style, a golden chain and cross.

"We celebrate a new member of our family today, Raos," Allende said. "You will be our adopted son and you will sell our wines, and make everyone very proud. Our grape will be the toast of Vancouver, and you and my other sons will make their mothers very happy."

This grandiose announcement left Raos unable to speak. Before he could gather himself even to think straight, the elder Allende continued. "And this, Raos, is my personal surprise for you." He made a sweeping gesture with his arm and introduced a lovely lady, probably in her 70s, who stood up from a small straight chair. She nodded her head with a slight smile of greeting. "This is your grandmother's youngest sister who we fortunately found living peacefully in a beautiful valley near your home."

Raos was still unable to respond with composure; but he greeted the lady somewhat awkwardly, and they exchanged a sincere but reserved hug. After refreshments, several more songs, and somewhat difficult chats with his newfound relative, Raos spoke with the younger Allende. "I don't understand," he said. "I was ready to go home, and no one even bothered to meet with me or to discuss our proposals . . . what's going on?"

"My father was waiting to see the *real* Hector Raos," Allende said. "He liked you from the first day. We all did. But he could not see what was inside you. You were behind new clothes and too quick with your answers. We are not like that, and it was my father's decision to see what you were about."

"And what of my, uh, let's see . . . my great aunt?" Raos asked.

"My father wanted to know your bloodline," Allende said. "So much can be said through one's relatives, but father also wondered why your people had not stayed close to one another."

"That's a good question," Raos said. "I knew, vaguely, that grandma had two sisters and perhaps a brother, but we never spoke much about them."

"Oh, we understand," Allende said. "Your grandmother's sister is very proud of her Canadian relatives, but they are simple people. You have other relatives who are on the boats. They are fishing from a village, but the lady here, she lives in a valley, and she even has old letters from your grandmother. But she does not read or write very well. Father brought her here with a friend's help who owns a plane. That's why we were not at the hotel. My father, he is very impressed that you dare to come to his offices and speak your thoughts. He said 'We will work with this man' and that was it."

QUESTIONS

1. Describe the negotiation process by comparing a model of behavior that would be expected in Canada and the negotiations that actually occurred in Chile. What contrasts can you identify, and how can you explain these differences?

2. Behavior like that of the elder Allende—the head of the family, or patron—would be expected in most Latin cultures. What elements of Latin American culture do you perceive in his behavior, and how do they influence behavior by other parties to a negotiation?

3. Relatively few details were agreed upon before these negotiations reached agreement. In fact, no formal contractual agreement was settled. How would negotiations proceed from the situation at the end of the case? What would you expect if you were Raos?

Source: This case was prepared by co-author David H. Holt and Edward Raos McLachlin, an MBA exchange student. It is intended only for classroom use, and, although real, the Chilean names are disguised. Copyright ©1997 by David H. Holt.

ABB—Global Integration in a Borderless World

Zurich-based ABB Group has an unusual reputation for developing a global cadre of managers capable of comfortably working in many different cultures. Formerly known as Asea Brown Boveri, ABB was created through a merger in 1988 of two international engineering companies—one Swedish and one Swiss. Today it is a $40 billion company with 160,000 people working in nearly 5,000 profit centers and 140 countries. ABB's core business coming into the 1990s was its engineering. It was a worldwide builder of power plants, transportation systems, industrial factory complexes, port facilities, and telecommunications systems. By the end of the century, the core segment of engineering represented 30 percent of ABB's business, and through acquisitions and expansion, the group now has about one-third of its business in process automation and one-third in software engineering. By 2001, ABB will have 25,000 software engineers, compared to 1990 when the company employed fewer than 1,000.

An example of ABB business is its contract, signed September 20, 2000, to design and operate South Australia's entire power-transmission system through 2020. Another example is Pittsburgh's international airport rapid-transit and logistics systems, which ABB designed, built, and operated in conjunction with the airport authorities. It also has a $260 million contract with the UAE to network the country's offshore gas-drilling rigs through remote-entry process controls. These are three examples from among 280 international contracts and 5,000 foreign activities that require an extraordinary organization of multicultural, multilingual personnel. ABB's managers invariably have cross-function skills ranging from engineering to procurement, and from marketing to strategic contract negotiation. Consequently, ABB has created a corporate culture of "global missionaries" who can move swiftly from a plant in India to one in Mexico, Hungary, Norway, or the United

States, and management capabilities to operate in Madagascar as well as Tokyo.

One example is Swedish-born, blond-haired, blue-eyed Benny Karl-Erik Olsson, who until recently was ABB's country manager in Mexico. When asked where he was from by a Wall Street journalist, Olsson reportedly looked the journalist straight in the eye and replied, "I'm Mexican." Then he explained that nine months earlier "he was Venezuelan," and before that, "he was from Madrid," and for a time, "a Barcelona man." Olsson began his 20-year career with ABB on assignment to South Africa, and while he has not lost track of his Swedish roots, he characterizes himself as a "global citizen with ABB bloodlines." He recently joined the ABB alliance group near Paris, where the company is involved in a $1.5 billion restructuring of France's electric power-generation systems.

Few companies have been so successful as quickly as ABB at creating a corporate culture that embraces a deeply rooted commitment to what the company calls *internationalism*—a borderless organization of highly adaptable people working toward a common purpose. Many other companies have spent decades creating a corporate culture. GE, PepsiCo Inc., Coca-Cola Co., and International Business Machines Corp. are renowned for their efforts to establish corporate profiles of international management, yet only ABB has been rated consistently among the best-managed companies in the world. Indeed, it was ranked No. 1 three times during the 1990s, and was voted "Europe's Most Respected Company" in 1997 and again in 1999 by the *Financial Times* and the annual global survey of best businesses by PriceWaterhouseCooper.

Much of the company's success is attributed to Percy Barnevik, ABB's former CEO, who masterminded the company's global growth strategy between 1988 and 1997. Unlike its giant American competitors, ABB did not try to create a "home-based" corporate culture, but instead built a unique culture on its global diversity. Consequently, the company is not distinguished as being Swiss, Swedish, or anything else. ABB elected to conduct all business in English, even though it maintains headquarters in Switzerland. Accounting systems are a composite of American and European practices that accommodate international standards, yet financial data are reported in U.S. dollars. All local operations among the 140 countries in which ABB does business utilize fully translated documents and local language protocols. Compensation, contracts, and transactions are localized.

ABB has no master plan with a carved-in-granite mandate for how to do business; yet there is a carefully prepared philosophy for management, encased in a 55-page "bible" that is translated into more than 40 languages. The essential messages are to respect local customs, meld into local cultures, to "be at one" with host-country operations, and to encourage an "internationalist" approach to every business endeavor. "Our strength comes from pulling together," Barnevik said when he introduced this approach to management. "We will have to cooperate, we will have to buy from each other, we will have to help each other. If we can make this work real well, then we will get a competitive edge out of the organization which is very, very difficult to copy."

ABB is, in effect, a global matrix of cooperative organizations working in hundreds of local markets. In contrast, most American companies still view their home market as the center of the universe. The ABB approach to integrative management is even more imaginative when you consider that the parent company has acquired more than 230 other enterprises in 50 countries in less than a decade. Each of these has been woven into the ABB fabric, and at the same time, they have changed ABB to become a more universal corporation. Although Barnevik recently stepped up and out of executive management to be its emeritus chairman, he left a legacy of an organization unbound by traditional constraints where, in his words, "people are in a perpetual learning situation in a global classroom."

Barnevik began honing his idea of a company with no geographic base during the 1988 merger. The concept was simple: Draw on expertise from around the globe, but glue the company together through managers who could understand and adapt to local cultures while also executing ABB's global strategies. This global view, he explained, comes more naturally to managers from small countries who

have never had the luxury of big home markets such as the United States or Germany. "From day one, they are part of a global team," Barnevik said, "and ABB will become what they make it—from a rich fabric of diverse linguistics to a rich diversity of talent and international values."

ABB's new CEO, Goran Lindahl, also is chairman of ABB's powerful executive committee. The committee, acting as a core team, consists of three Swedes, two Swiss, an American, and a German; only the American and one Swiss live in their native countries. Some 171 staff employees from 19 countries populate Zurich headquarters. Similar corporate diversity is reflected throughout the company, which does not account for hundreds of major international alliances.

ABB's global-local perspective is illustrated by its expansion in India, where the government is liberalizing its power industry and actively courting foreign investments. ABB landed a $200 million contract for the country's first private power plant as one element of a billion-dollar infrastructure program. The plant's steam turbine was made in Sweden, gas turbines were made in Germany and Switzerland, and boiler systems were designed and manufactured in the United States. ABB's Indian operations dealt with the customer, GVK Industries in Hyderabad, and supplied engineering, construction, and associated electrical work, which accounted for 40 percent of the total contract value. The country manager, Arun Thiadarajan, is an Indian educated in Sweden, and one of ABB's "internationalists." He coordinates more than 10,000 people working in 10 production plants and 23 offices that cover four regions of India, each with different dialects and cultural roots.

The Indian experience is repeated time and again. In Malaysia, ABB heads a consortium to build a $5.4 billion dam and hydroelectric system. It will be the world's second largest power-generating project next to China's massive Three Gorges Dam project. Partners with ABB for the Malaysian project include a Brazilian contractor, Thai cement company, Swedish turbine-engineering firm, German electrical contractor, several Asian developers, underwriters from Malaysia and regional development banks, and subsidiary power-generation divisions from the United States. At the head of it all, back at headquarters, is Alexis Fries, a Beirut-born Swiss citizen who speaks seven languages, has worked in five countries, and runs ABB's businesses in the Asia-Pacific region. Fries has demonstrated an unusual ability to quickly adapt his behavior local circumstances, to negotiate through language and gestures congruent with local customs, and to manage diverse ethnic constituents.

Fries also is one of the company's most astute negotiators, known for his ability to find win-win situations in any contract meeting. This is a critical skill for ABB because the company's entire pattern of business relies on a constant number of new contracts. Some of the projects last for years, such as building and operating major power plants, but the majority of ABB's contracts are for shorter durations, such as the Pittsburgh airport transit system. This contract took several months to negotiate, several more months to plan, and less than a year to complete. In contrast, the Malaysian dam project was in negotiations for nearly three years, and the planning and design stages will culminate soon, after an additional five years. The project may then take only several years to complete. Fries was involved in several aspects of the Malaysian negotiation when the company perceived that the Malaysian constituents and government officials would expect ABB to spend time and money to build relationships before actual contract negotiators would sit down to write the agreement. Fries's Middle East upbringing permits him the patience to socialize or engage in friendly chat, often for hours, without turning conversations to business topics. In contrast, ABB has mistakenly sent well-qualified Swedish employees into foreign contracts and failed to win contracts because Swedes, unlike many people of other nationalities, do not "bargain." They often begin with terms and conditions of an offer very near to their expected point of agreement, expecting and offering little compromise.

Barnevik learned early that his local managers and host-country team members could do a far better job during preliminary contract talks and for many of the planning activities than his expert European executives. Barnevik was himself a student of negotiation styles and became very good at adapting to local situations. It was Barnevik who, some years ago, coined the phrase, "Go global, but behave local." After leaving active management of ABB, he was recruited as a board member at General Motors—precisely because he was adept at handling multicultural situations and had a more diversified view of world cultures than other GM board members or, indeed, most of the company's executives.

At ABB, Barnevik's legacy has carried through to Lindahl and the ABB executive committee members, all of whom place very high premiums on "being global, but acting local." This principle permeates many decisions, such as forming teams for contract negotiations, selecting staff to represent ABB in foreign relations, and customizing projects and company products for foreign clientele. Today, ABB spends $2.5 billion annually on research and development, and nearly $1 billion on cross-cultural research, training, and management development. As ABB enters the new century, however, even these efforts may be dwarfed by new challenges of information technology and entirely new approaches to how the company does business.

In a keynote speech before the World Economic Development Congress in September 1999, ABB's CEO Goran Lindahl challenged international executives to change the fundamental way in which companies and their people think about global commerce. He explained this vision as how ABB expected to recruit its people and manage its assets in the new century. An excerpt from that speech illustrates his point:

> Globalizing leadership for a world without boundaries is not a dream but a reality. We are creating shared values within the company, expanding our values beyond the Northern European ethics and values, and beyond U.S. business school thinking, to adopt values that motivate the people we want to attract from the global talent pool.

Lindahl went on to explain that ABB is now faced with a new challenge of borderless communications and process technology that is neither constrained by time nor limited by engineering infrastructure. ABB's history has been one built on success in constructing massive facilities, providing machinery and technology for control systems, and staffing the activities with hands-on operating personnel. "Today," he said," the Internet and its penetrating systems of electronic commerce have redefined human processes." Lindahl declared boldly in his closing remarks:

> We have seen the death of distance...the death of planning as we knew it.

Lindahl emphasized that the Internet would not replace people or reduce the need for local managers, but create an even greater need for globally minded managers sensitive to local cultures and customs. International managers will be expected to communicate, negotiate, and operate within a vast network of disparate interests and activities, he explained. Process controls will no longer be the responsibility of engineers and technicians, climbing around plants and turning valves or reading gauges; instead they will be the responsibility of process systems teams, monitoring and controlling operations through time and space from wireless communications centers. In turn, those centers may be in the plant complex itself or thousands of miles away. Information technology will provide instantaneous access to such activities as energy technology diagnostics with equally instantaneous response time to process control decisions, virtually in a world society.

The future of ABB—and in Lindahl's view, the future of the world's global companies—rests with having software engineering and development capabilities to create the systems required in a global communications environment. Even more important, companies must have personnel capable of not only using such systems but also communicating with hundreds of different people in hundreds of societies with vastly different values and cultures.

QUESTIONS

1. In Fries's role, and specifically for the Malaysian project, what considerations would you envision for intercultural communication among the high-context and low-context associates in the consortium?
2. The Malaysian project, like many other ABB contracts, involves partnerships and alliances that span several cultures. What are some of the primary problems you would identify for negotiating such contracts?
3. Olsson, the Swedish-born country manager who worked in Mexico and then moved on to France, has a strong record of success managing in several cultures where hierarchical relationships would be quite different than in Sweden. What contrasts in communicative behavior might Olsson have encountered in his career postings?
4. Much of ABB's strategy is predicated on effective communications linkage and well-coordinated information systems in a multicultural environment. What problems might the Swiss-Swedish headquarters group encounter for its executive core, and in particular, how might cultural differences influence behavior among the senior executives?
5. Lindahl envisions extraordinary challenges for future managers of ABB, who must consider an entirely new world of borderless communications systems, new ways to manage foreign projects, and new responsibilities for the company's project managers. Briefly explain what changes you believe will occur in ABB's organization, its approach to negotiations, and its communications systems.

BIBLIOGRAPHY

ABB Group websites including "News," "Company History," and "Company Strategies," specifically on Project Alpha and ABB's Internet Commerce and Software Engineering. Retrieved from <www.abb.com> [cited 4 October 2000].

"ABB-led Consortium Gets $5.4 Billion Dam Contract." *Wall Street Journal Europe*, 14 June 1996, p. 3.

Guyon, Janet. "World Citizens: At ABB, Globalization Isn't Just a Buzzword; It's a Corporate Culture." *Wall Street Journal Europe*, 1 October 1996, p. 1.

Guyon, Janet, and Margaret Studer. "Lindahl to Succeed Barnevik as Chief Executive of ABB." *Wall Street Journal Europe*, 11 October 1996, p. 4.

Lindahl, Goran. "Globalizing Leadership for a World without Boundaries." Reprint of the *World Economic Development Congress, CEO/CFO Summit Meetings*, Washington, D.C., 22–24 September 1999.

Lopez, Leslie. "New Worries Surface as ABB Signs Bakun Pact." *Asian Wall Street Journal*, 3 October 1996, p. 3.

HUMAN RESOURCES IN THE GLOBAL CONTEXT

PART FOUR

CHAPTER ELEVEN

International Labor Relations

CHAPTER OBJECTIVES

Explain the process of labor relations within an international environment.

Describe collective bargaining practices and various roles for management, unions, and government.

Define and compare methods of conflict resolution pertaining to workplace issues.

Highlight prominent cultural and social themes that influence labor relations in global companies.

Discuss the controversy over international convergence in labor relations practices.

Detail specific ways in which labor relations practices are becoming internationalized.

Review recent initiatives for employee participation in management and industrial democracy.

Eurotunnel, the company that operates the tunnel beneath the English Channel between Kent in the United Kingdom and Pas de Calais in France, is among the first organizations in Europe to qualify as a genuinely transnational corporation. The company was created through a joint British and French alliance specifically to be "neither French nor British, yet to fully accommodate requirements of both societies."[1] The most challenging problem for Eurotunnel founders was not the extraordinary engineering problems of boring the giant tunnel but reconciling differences in human relations. Long before the tunnel began carrying traffic, organizers recognized that the contrasting structures of industrial relations in France and Britain would create tension. Along with French-British differences, relations would have to encompass other companies that contracted to provide engineering services, freight handling, passenger service, and financing.

The company began with a set of underpinning principles for human resource management that grew to become an extensive employee handbook. This document states policies on issues such as a general commitment to customer service, safety performance, and security rules. More important, it lays down guidelines for rather sensitive points such as the right of all employees to express ideas and to communicate in their mother tongues. Company organizers negotiated common terms and conditions to establish parity among employees from both societies, and this initiative had rather interesting results. All employees put in a standard work year of 1,700 hours based on a 37.5-hour workweek. They have 25 days annual leave with a bonus of 2 days for those unable to take leave during the summer. Employees may choose optional private medical insurance paid through the company, and sick pay begins on the first day of absence. No one can be summarily fired without review by an employee tribunal, and all terminated employees must receive at least one month's notice. Employees with longer seniority enjoy longer periods of notification, up to 12 weeks at full pay and benefits. Life insurance is provided for up to eight times an employee's annual salary. An appraisal-linked system controls promotion and bonuses, and workers may retire at age 65. Social benefits include child care and canteen services. The company has also worked out a complicated system of overtime pay, holiday bonuses, and shift premiums, yet base compensation is substantially different for British and French workers.

Independent French and British works councils elect employee representatives to fulfill responsibilities for decisions relating to staffing, safety, employee rights, benefits, and intervention in grievances. Works councils, now mandated by the European Union for most international companies, are also required under French law. Britain has not endorsed a similar legal process, but the British contingent in Eurotunnel voluntarily established a works council system. Both British and French councils are chaired by the Eurotunnel CEO, and although they make autonomous decisions relating to their national employees, the two councils convene as a strategic co-governing body.

Many of Eurotunnel's employment guidelines reflect the influence of national rules from either France or Britain, and all practices are required to conform to laws or customs of both countries. For example, workers receive 12 official holidays in Britain and 14 in France, but the lists differ; therefore, all employees enjoy 18 holidays to accommodate events peculiar to each society. In Britain, union membership is voluntary, and collective bargaining contracts lack support from legal enforcement mechanisms; in France, however, union representation legally obligates a company to contract with the union, and agreements are enforced through French courts. Consequently, Eurotunnel operates simultaneously in a trade union environment on the French side of the channel but in a primarily nonunion atmosphere in Britain.

Although the company has established one management system for unified authority, and it recognizes comparable employment or skill grades for all workers, human resource managers find that they often must coordinate three different sets of responsibilities. They behave according to British expectations for less-formal labor relations without prospects for government intervention. At the same time, they must accommodate French customs, which emphasize formal labor laws and government-mandated intervention for contracting practices and dispute resolution. As managers in a cross-border EU enterprise, they find themselves coordinating yet another set of employment practices that differ under British and French regulations. Company executives must also coordinate contracts for engineering and other services with international companies from the United States, Sweden, Belgium, and Germany. No one reacted with surprise, then, when a recent commentary by Eurotunnel executives noted that although their firm represented perhaps the first genuine transnational company in Europe, they were "still in search of a meaning for transcultural human resource management."[2]

OVERVIEW OF HUMAN RELATIONS IN THE WORKPLACE

A study of human relations in the workplace deals with the fundamental question of *how work gets done.* As previous chapters have shown, a unique profile of behavior in every organization and each society influences how work is accomplished there. These sociocultural profiles emanate from complex systems of human development. With this premise in mind, the chapter concentrates on *labor relations within the sociocultural context of how work gets done.*

In the minds of many people, the term *labor relations* conjures up images of trade union members walking picket lines or irate workers battling with recalcitrant company managers over contract issues. The term often implies grievances and win-lose collective bargaining in factories torn by conflicts between blue-collar employees and managers over wages, benefits, work rules, and fair (or unfair) labor practices. As a professional field, many treat labor relations as a specialized function of human resources and thus not something that everyone needs to know about. Unfortunately, these images *do not* adequately represent the field of labor relations; managers and employees in all organizations (whether unionized or not) are involved with or affected by labor relations in the workplace.

This chapter explains labor relations within the broader context of employment relationships, and it distinguishes relationships and their differences among the world's societies. The presentation focuses on exploring how international managers deal with significant variations in systems of labor and with employees in various societies who have substantially different expectations about work relationships. In addition, the chapter addresses government involvement in workplace regulation and how new trends such as industrial democracy are affecting workplace relationships. The chapter is primarily concerned with labor-management issues, but it addresses this topic within a cross-cultural framework relevant to international management.

The Importance of Labor Relations in Global Management

As Michael Porter pointed out in his classic work *The Competitive Advantage of Nations*, technology has become freely accessible to almost anyone, and investment capital moves effortlessly across borders. Consequently, the most critical element of competitive advantage is the social organization of production. Put another way, competitive abilities depend on how capital and technology are harnessed by workers through their skills and collective capabilities. More specifically, Porter states that a firm gains a durable competitive advantage through the combined effect of processes, capabilities, and competencies, woven together by the prevailing systems of the work environment.[3]

As globalization increases, and as new international relationships emerge through developments such as the North American Free Trade Agreement and the Single European Market, few organizations can ignore the resulting competitive pressures and their effects on human endeavors. In the past, societies could barricade themselves against others so that, for example, events that shaped the national system of labor in Great Britain had little effect in France or the United States. Even within a specific society, strikes, labor contracts, and working conditions had little effect on other national systems. Today, however, complex cross-border ties and global networks in both manufacturing and service industries create sensitive interactions between differing national labor systems. Wage effects or industrial unrest in one country no longer remain isolated from those elsewhere.

For a global company with highly integrated activities, labor conditions in one location can have significant implications for other operations. For example, a strike against General Motors in Ontario by the Canadian Auto Workers union forced the firm to shut down an engine plant in Ohio for lack of parts made in Canada. Also, a component supplier to GM-Canada located in Tennessee, unable to ship products, had to put half of its workforce on leave.[4]

Recall from earlier chapters that Porter's model describes how global functions often incorporate well-diversified activities both upstream and downstream, and the way a firm accomplishes work often determines its configuration within its value chain. With that in mind, the field of labor relations evaluates how employees are persuaded to work and to generate a surplus of productivity over the cost of labor to create a competitive advantage. Related questions concern the nature of work and whether the work environment emphasizes cooperation, compliance, discontent, or open hostility. In any of these situations, how is a sense of order established? How does an organization sustain productive effort and a well-managed workforce? How are the often diverse and conflicting interests of management and workers mediated? Finally, in a global organization, how are *systems of human resources and labor relations* managed?

Contrasts of differences in workplace relationships begin to clarify the nature of the questions and to answer some of them. For example, in some cultural settings marked by collective behavior and compliance, labor issues seldom result in hostility. In other societies where individuality is highly valued, personal disputes and grievances can rapidly surface. These generalities obscure many subtle differences in work behavior. Social development, ideologies, and cultural expectations affect how labor is organized and managed. Political systems and the history of labor movements in each nation also affect how work is regulated there. Taken together, these forces affect management responsibilities for collective bargaining and labor contracts.

Ironically, while globalization has increased integration of activities, it has also promoted *disintegration* of human resource management practices. Labor relations, in particular, are distinctly *multilocal systems*. Myriad national regulations and work customs require companies to reconcile their procedures with location-specific realities.[5]

This fact prompted management theorist Peter Drucker to comment in an editorial printed in the *Wall Street Journal* that the notion of a "global human resource function" should be rejected in favor of a system of coordinated, multiple, and localized human resource management (HRM) activities. Drucker emphasized the local nature of labor-related decisions and the danger of oversimplifying comparisons such as wage rates or productivity measures among diverse locations.[6] This approach to global human resource management is shown in Figure 11.1.

The Framework of Labor Relations

Researchers began in earnest to examine human behavior in organizations during the 1960s. But for a century before that time, labor relations was a poorly defined concept associated with the ebb and flow of militancy among workers (often with Marxist overtones). With the rise of a behavioral school of management thought during the 1960s, management theorists began to explain labor relations as a *process*. Clark Kerr and his colleagues at Harvard described this process according to the ways in which management established "systems of control" (e.g., job descriptions, compensation packages, work rules, procedures, and disciplinary codes). In Kerr's view, effective labor relations systems should avoid exploiting workers while motivating employees to work productively, even though they subordinate themselves to a company's terms of employment.[7] In the parlance of this theory, *organized labor relations* implied a process of forging a collective agreement, jointly determined by management and workers, to delineate the terms of employment and specific methods for enforcing terms or redressing grievances. As labor relations became more distinctly associated with collective bargaining (specifically in the western Anglo-centered world), it evolved as a regulatory discipline more closely associated with legal issues than with management initiatives.[8]

Today, the term **labor relations** carries a more encompassing meaning that suggests a process through which management and workers determine job relationships.[9] This definition is not restricted to union representation, nor does it carry an industrial connotation that excludes other forms of organization. Labor relations no longer necessarily implies legally mandated conditions, nor is it limited to nations with formal labor laws. More precisely, the concept of labor relations is concerned with the question posed earlier: *How does work get done?*

FIGURE 11.1
Global Human Resource Function

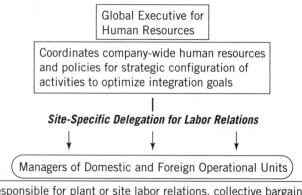

Labor relations can be better understood by defining the scope of human activities that concern managers, yet the field itself clearly suggests a preoccupation with labor laws and negotiations under collective bargaining agreements. In the United States, labor law is embodied in federal and state legislation, and similar national and provincial legislative measures exist in Canada. In Europe, however, labor laws vary from nearly nonexistent (as in Britain) to deeply embedded in social legislation (as in Germany). Later sections of the chapter will address these variations in greater detail. This overview of labor relations must note a general concern with substantive rules or work norms, some of them determined by company-specific contracts (as in the United States and Canada) or decided through industry-wide agreements (as in many European nations).

Labor relations also encompasses mediation and arbitration systems, some with the force of law (as in North America) and many based on civil processes for dispute resolution (as in Europe). Asian societies such as Japan, Taiwan, and South Korea put little emphasis on formal labor laws or what western managers would consider due process. In many developing countries of the Indian Subcontinent and Africa, labor regulations do not exist apart from religious codes that constitute law. In Islamic countries, for example, due process and other facets of labor relations are determined according to interpretations of underlying religious doctrines.[10]

Traditional work systems, defined broadly by industrial relations systems of the early twentieth century, have changed dramatically during the past several decades. Quality circles, teamwork, participative decision-making, shop-floor management, and self-directed work groups have emerged as important themes. Some of these developments have seemed to come and go like fads, yet they have produced very real effects, including a clear shift toward employee involvement that transcends contract language or legal mandates. The form and content of work has also changed. So-called *lean production systems* underscore trends in downsizing, and although the term seems specific to manufacturing, reorganization of work systems is a pervasive trend throughout business organizations.

Not least of all, management must be concerned with *industrial democracy*. This broad term refers in part to movements toward formal employee (or union) representation on company boards, works councils, and work-unit committees. As a later section will explain, industrial democracy can spread through political intervention, through contractual agreements, or as a culturally influenced accommodation that alters the control aspect of a labor relations process to create a more collaborative approach to employee involvement.

National borders have not impeded the flow of new *work processes and methods*, however. Many of these are associated with Japanese management techniques, including the *kanban* system, *just-in-time* manufacturing, and *flexible* manufacturing. Work relationships are being redefined, driven by a shift away from traditional manager-employee hierarchies and toward cooperative work environments. Work-to-rule contracts and management-controlled decisions are giving way to self-managed systems and integrated work activities.

Principal Themes for Comparative Labor Relations

Work systems differ in many ways throughout the world, but three prominent themes recur in comparisons of domestic and foreign labor relations: the nature of collective bargaining, the tactics of labor-management confrontation, and the methods for conflict resolution. The following paragraphs briefly consider each of these subjects, supplying selective comparisons of mainstream issues in North America, Europe, and

Asia. More specific comparisons of national labor relations systems follow in a later section.

Nature of Collective Bargaining

In North America and most European countries, **collective bargaining** refers to formal trade union representation on behalf of workers. Union representatives negotiate contractual agreements with employers to specify wages, benefits, working hours, fair labor practices, and conditions of employment, including issues such as grievance procedures, profit sharing, and safety rules. In many countries, collective bargaining and trade union representation are rights created by law. In other countries, no legal enforcement mechanisms support collective agreements, nor are trade unions sanctioned by legislation. In some countries, trade unions operate as literal extensions of political parties; this arrangement is especially common where the government exerts substantial influence in the collective bargaining process.

Regardless of their political affiliations or legal status, unions in Europe and North America are organized in several different ways. They can be craft associations with local, national, or international membership; industry-wide affiliations that blanket many different crafts and jobs on a national scale; or amalgamated confederations of smaller independent unions. In Japan, a unique form of company unions represents workers, as discussed in a later section on the Japanese system of labor relations. The primary forms of western trade unionism are listed in Table 11.1. The ability of a country's trade unions to bargain and to enter contracts varies widely according to their legal status and scope of representation. Laws in each country define formal union authority to represent employees, and substantial differences in such laws prevent generalizations about collective bargaining.

Tactics of Labor-Management Confrontation

The topic of labor relations involves a fundamental contradiction in interests between workers and managers. Workers seek equitable compensation in exchange for their efforts to transform labor into economic surplus. In doing so, they yield to management a certain amount of control for work-related decisions. In contrast, managers represent a firm's owners, who expect them to seek maximum surplus returns to investors through high productivity; this expectation affects labor relations, because it implies high labor efficiency. Consequently, nearly all organizations (other than egalitarian

TABLE 11.1

TYPES OF UNIONS AND REPRESENTATION

Craft union	Represents workers in a specific craft or skilled occupation	Most common in the United Kingdom
Enterprise union	Represents all employees and managers of a specific enterprise	Unique to Japan
Industry union	Represents all employees working in a specific industry group or sector	Most common in Germany
National union	Represents all employees in a specific company through local unions that are amalgamated nationwide	Dominant in the United States and Canada
International confederation	Represents member unions from national and industry groups	Primarily known in Europe and North America

consensus groups, if any exist) build certain disparities into their structures. Extreme differences can lead to conflict, but the potential for conflict always remains within what one group of authors has called *systems of structured antagonism*.[11] Each side of this confrontation has developed informal tactics for advancing its viewpoints or pressuring the other side for concessions. For example, employees might organize work slowdowns, sit-ins, or walkouts, or they might sabotage production to make a point. Also, where law permits, they have the right to strike or to demonstrate. Employers might resort to **lockouts,** in which they prevent employees from working, or they can hire nonunion "scab" workers to replace strikers. All of these practices are legally constrained in most countries.

Methods of Conflict Resolution

Given the nature of structured antagonism in organizations, managers are responsible for reducing conflict and resolving differences. Ideally, they maintain workplace harmony while ensuring optimal profitability for the enterprise. Formal labor laws help workers and managers in this regard by providing legal recourse in case of disputes. These options take the form of grievance procedures, mediation, and arbitration. All differ substantially among countries, and they offer ways of addressing procedural justice without resorting to formal legal prerogatives. Most disputes arise from disciplinary decisions, dismissals, and issues related to claims of misconduct or incompetence.[12]

A **grievance** is a complaint against an employer, usually brought by individuals or through union representatives on behalf of employees who believe that they have been treated improperly under the terms of a labor agreement. In the United States, labor contracts usually spell out grievance procedures. These can require nothing more complicated than a reconciliatory meeting between a supervisor and a shop steward acting on behalf of an employee, but more serious issues as unresolved grievances may require intervention by higher-level union representatives and company managers. In extreme situations, the parties may resort to legal action or seek mediation.

Mediation is a method of third-party intervention in which labor and management agree to ask a neutral outside party to propose a mutually acceptable solution. Mediation does not bind the parties to a ruling, but most formal labor contracts associate it with **arbitration,** which is an enforceable judgment affecting both parties.[13] When the parties agree to arbitration, they explicitly agree to accept a ruling by an appointed arbitrator. An arbitrator could rule in favor of either party or devise a compromise. After this person issues a judgment, neither party can easily challenge it without resorting to complicated judicial procedures.[14] This option is viewed as a last resort by both union officials and company managers, who prefer to settle disputes between themselves. Mediation and arbitration are compared in Table 11.2.

Cultural and Social Influences on Labor Relations

International managers must concern themselves with the legal and contractual dimensions of labor relations, but legal knowledge and ability to interpret contracts are far less important than understanding the cultural and social foundations of a foreign work environment. Understanding results from experience, not classroom exercises, yet managers clearly need to study foreign labor relations to discover potential patterns of behavior and differences in work systems. For example, Japanese companies rarely encounter confrontational tactics such as strikes and walkouts; few labor-management disputes result in mediation or arbitration there, and both labor and

TABLE 11.2

MEDIATION AND ARBITRATION

Mediation	Arbitration
Employees or union agrees with management to submit grievance to a third party for help resolving contested issues.	Union and management deadlocked on a grievance or contract issue may agree to accept an arbitrator's judgment.
A neutral person or tribunal suggests settlement conditions.	A neutral person or tribunal, often working under authority of a government agency, determines a solution.
Parties can accept the mediator's ruling or pursue arbitration or civil action.	Parties agree in advance to accept the arbitrator's ruling.
Mediation seldom applies the force of law and parties can rarely enforce resulting provisions.	Arbitration has the force of law to arrive at a final adjudication of a dispute; an appeal is possible but rare under most legal codes.

management view labor difficulties as problems to be jointly resolved without conflict. In the United States and Canada, confrontational behavior commonly characterizes labor-management relations; indeed, conflict itself is viewed as beneficial when it motivates constructive debates that lead to improved decisions. These results make sense, since a collectivist society such as Japan places a greater premium on harmonious relationships between labor and management than does an individualistic society such as the United States. Even the definition of conflict and the criteria for a dispute differ dramatically among the world's cultures. As noted in previous chapters, patterns of group behavior and methods of resolving differences in the Arab world can involve emotionally charged and almost combative exchanges; similar behavior is characteristic of Italy, Greece, and some Latin societies. In contrast, Scandinavians go out of their way to avoid emotional confrontations.

Social systems that have evolved in individual countries also significantly influence how labor-management issues are resolved. In Germany, nationwide industrial unions tend to represent labor, and organizational interests are represented through large-scale industry associations. Unions and employer groups in France and Italy are organized substantially around political affiliations under socialist ideologies. In Britain, the Labour Party is politically and monetarily supported through the Trades Union Council and its affiliated union locals. In Canada, the New Democratic Party relies on support from the labor movement, even though unions and the political party are not as closely associated as comparable institutions in Britain. In contrast, the Democratic Party in the United States benefits from union voting support, but political parties and union organizations are not formally associated with one another, nor do union members vote consistently with a particular party. In each instance, labor relations reflect national customs and embedded social philosophies.[15] A closer look at systems of labor relations in selected countries requires close attention to cultural and social forces, which pervasively influence the nature of collective bargaining, the tactics of labor-management confrontation, and methods for conflict resolution.

CONTRASTING SYSTEMS OF LABOR RELATIONS

International managers must adapt to different systems of labor relations in order to define systems for organizing and accomplishing work. In a multinational environment, where managers often cope with several disparate social systems, work is coordinated with substantially different priorities and expectations. A company may find itself negotiating with strong national trade unions in one country, forging separate agreements with dozens of small craft associations in another country, and dealing with state-regulated affiliations elsewhere. It must achieve dispute resolution and contract enforcement in societies with rigid government regulations as well as countries without due process of law. The following sections profile selected regions to describe some of these contrasting systems.

Labor Relations in North America

The United States and Canada follow a similar pattern of organized labor relations known as the *North American model.* This general statement oversimplifies many cultural differences that influence labor relations, yet the two countries have many similarities in how work is organized and regulated through collective agreements. Perhaps in time, Mexico and Caribbean nations will adopt labor relations practices common in North America. The influence of NAFTA may speed this process, but for the moment, Mexico and other neighbors differ substantially from either the United States or Canada. The following paragraphs examine labor relations in the United States and Canada, and later discussions address Mexico separately as the third principal country in NAFTA.

The United States and Canada

Under the New Deal administration of the 1930s, the U.S. government interceded in labor-management conflicts to establish a regulatory system based on legislation intended to protect both employee and employer rights. Laws were passed that aimed at ensuring individual worker rights, such as child-labor restrictions, mandates for employer-supported social security, and national standards for workweeks. At the heart of labor regulation, however, legislation empowered trade unions as collective bargaining representatives. Canada pursued similar regulatory controls during the early 1940s, and both the United States and Canada have developed complex and detailed systems of labor law.[16] Most unionized workers in North America belong to a **national union** that represents specific groups of workers, such as truck drivers, air traffic controllers, auto workers, or steel workers. *Union locals* undertake collective bargaining after becoming certified to represent employees of a particular plant or company. Labor contracts apply specifically to certified locals and individual companies, not to a union's national membership or to other companies within an industry.

National laws govern certification criteria. In the United States, for example, the National Labor Relations Board (NLRB) oversees an election process that culminates a union's drive to "organize" a company; by a majority vote, employees can vote to accept representation by a new union or to decertify an existing one. This broad description oversimplifies actual conditions in both the United States and Canada, because complicated procedures govern actions by all parties to permit voting and certification. In addition, substantial variations distinguish the individual states and provinces of each nation regarding union eligibility and rights for collective bargaining. Nevertheless, in general, national unions with specific company bargaining rights are fundamental to both systems.

Collective bargaining contracts in both countries commonly cover periods of two or three years, and then they are renegotiated. While these contracts are in force, legislation prohibits strikes, thus reducing potential disruptions to work. Nevertheless, unauthorized *wildcat strikes* can occur. These and other means of labor protest, such as sit-ins and sick-outs, are not part of organized union activity. Companies respond with similar unofficial actions, such as lockouts to counter employee-initiated work disruptions. In North America, when a contract expires and the union and company management have failed to agree to a new one, employees can legally strike to bring pressure on the negotiators. Because companies often deal with several unions representing different groups of employees, each with contracts ending at different times, a company could face a strike by one group while others remain at work under their contract terms. For example, Chrysler, GM, and Ford negotiate independent contracts with the United Auto Workers, Teamsters, and Machinists unions, each with different terms and contract dates. This situation has prevailed since the early years of the auto industry, and when the different unions have become involved in one another's protests, chaos has dominated collective bargaining.

In a further complication associated with multiple bargaining situations, contract terms won by one union typically affect later negotiations by others. This is known as *patterned bargaining*, and it encourages one union group to build on the successes of another group to win similar concessions within one company. Alternatively, a union may succeed in negotiations with one company and then use that contract as leverage to win concessions from another company in the same industry. The UAW pressured GM by this method in 1996 after it gained guarantees of job security, enhanced benefits, and wage increases in excess of a cost-of-living index from Ford.[17] These rather complicated relationships have often created crippling industrial disputes, inspiring extremely detailed legislation in North America intended to prevent conflict while protecting the rights of all parties.[18]

Part of that legislation establishes a legal framework for redressing grievances. Once a contract is signed, it carries the force of law. Terms of employment, wages, benefits, individual and collective employee rights, working hours, and anything else specified by the collective agreement can be enforced through the courts. At the same time, both union representatives and management must follow very detailed grievance procedures. Labor contracts in Canada and the United States tend to be comprehensive, with precise language covering most issues that might conceivably arise in the worker-employer relationship, including grievance procedures. This is an unusual characteristic of the North American model of labor relations, because although a contract specifies methods for dispute resolution and holds the parties legally liable for fulfilling its terms, the actual grievance, mediation, or arbitration process operates outside jurisprudence systems. Union and management representatives must resolve differences between themselves without guidance from the law, and they may make private arrangements for mediators, arbitrators, or third-party tribunals. The government has intervened in labor disputes that threaten public safety, however, such as when U.S. President Ronald Reagan mandated an end to the strike by the Professional Air Traffic Controllers union during the 1980s. As a rule, however, the governments of Canada and the United States remain apart from business-labor relations.[19]

Despite these similarities, labor relations in Canada and the United States show many subtle differences, and a company involved in cross-border operations may find that it must adjust to different patterns of labor relations. The U.S. labor market has experienced a downturn in union membership; only about 12 percent of the national labor force is unionized (excluding public-sector associations that lack official certification). For comparison, at one time shortly after World War II, nearly one-third of the U.S. workforce was unionized. In contrast, unions remain robust in Canada with approximately 28 percent of the labor force working under collective bargaining contracts.[20]

Canada also inherited from Britain a history of **craft unions,** which organize workers within specific trades such as carpentry (joinery), tool and die making, and weaving. Craft unions operate in the United States also, but not as actively as they do elsewhere. Canada's formal apparatus for arbitration is much stronger than that in the United States, and it forms a separate body of jurisprudence to regulate and enforce grievance and arbitration decisions. Consequently, Canada's governmental involvement through social legislation is more comprehensive than in the United States, and through government regulations there are greater controls on wages, disciplinary procedures, terms of employment, and individual rights of nonunion employees. In effect, U.S. employees work under two distinct systems. One is union based, with well-defined contractual and legislative guidelines for organized labor relations; the other is nonunion, with few guidelines or social legislation related to individual employee rights. Canadian social legislation sets more specific standards for business interests that concern the rights of all employees and employers.[21]

Mexico

Labor relations in Mexico are important to neighboring American and Latin countries, due in part to the influence of the North American Free Trade Agreement (NAFTA). Also, increasing cross-border joint initiatives with U.S. partners highlight contrasts, as do expanding European and Asian ventures in Mexico. Recent economic and political changes there have pushed the country into a regional limelight, and Mexican labor relations are being rapidly transformed.

NAFTA includes a provision for joint review of sensitive labor issues by the U.S., Canadian, and Mexican governments, including minimum-wage regulations, child-labor practices, and industrial safety. Disparities between Mexico and its northern neighbors often make these issues very sensitive, but as the borders soften and more manufacturing and trade activities originate there, the nation's enterprises feel increasing pressure to bolster wages and implement new labor practices. At the same time, North American unions have used the NAFTA provisions to push for broader roles in Mexican union activities. Several U.S. unions, for example, have become involved in cross-border disputes resulting in legal complaints filed with government agencies. The Teamsters Union—along with several others—filed grievances specifically aimed at General Electric's plant in Mexico, accusing GE of violating Mexican labor laws when dismissing employees. Another complaint accused Honeywell of interference with union-organization rights.[22] Companies that pursue operations in Mexico therefore face new complications of cross-border scrutiny by unions. They also face new laws emerging in Mexico under a social system in transition, and foreign companies must manage disparities, such as substantially different wage rates between Mexico and the United States.

U.S. interests in Mexico increased rapidly when the **maquiladora** program was established in 1965 to attract foreign investors. The program was specifically designed to entice U.S. plants to move operations into northern Mexico, where unemployment levels often exceeded 30 percent. The U.S. Department of Commerce strongly supported the program, expecting it to drastically reduce illegal immigrant traffic into the southern United States. By 1992, when NAFTA came into effect, more than 2,000 U.S. firms operated maquiladora plants in Mexico alongside more than 400 plants of firms from Japan, Germany, Sweden, and Britain.[23] Under the program, a foreign company can import machinery, parts, and raw materials to Mexico for use in fabrication or assembly of products specifically designed for export. Products made at a maquiladora plant cannot be sold in Mexico, but manufacturers pay customs duties and other taxes only on the value added at the Mexican facilities. Consequently, the imported materials and equipment represent temporary duty-free transfers of assets. The company not only benefits from the tax provisions and an open export-import conduit, but it can also generate substantial savings in low-cost Mexican operations. Mexico gains through economic development, employment, and improved technology. These points are summarized in Figure 11.2.

Although the maquiladoras have been successful, they have also stirred controversy. American unions claim that companies flee to Mexico, taking many U.S. jobs to relatively low-wage, nonunion Mexican factories. Supporters of offshore manufacturing acknowledge this effect, but they point out that Mexican facilities employ people primarily in low-skilled jobs, and the companies might well have closed domestic plants or downsized to remain competitive if they had not found more economical options in Mexico. Also, U.S. and Canadian social watchdog groups have criticized the safety of products made in Mexico. Some of these claims may be true, but many Mexican plants have also won quality achievement awards. Further, recent research has shown that, although Mexico trails far behind its industrial neighbors in many ways, Mexican workers can quickly learn new processes and work to the highest standards. Nevertheless, unions in the NAFTA countries have exerted tremendous pressure to force unionization in maquiladora plants, and tensions are rising between labor and management there.[24]

Labor itself cannot be separated from government or politics in Mexico. The *Congreso del Trabajo* (or Congress of Labor, known as CT) is an official branch of the *Partido Revolucionario Institucional* (or Industrial Revolutionary Party, known as the PRI). The PRI has effectively ruled the country since taking power during the Mexican Revolution in 1918. At that time, unions represented no more than 10,000 workers; but by the end of the revolution in 1924, more than 500,000 Mexican workers were union members, and the core union movement was a major force in politics. In fact, the CT has the legal right to nominate candidates for election to congressional and regional offices. Approximately 26 percent of the entire labor force belongs to unions under the umbrella of the CT, and a count that includes federal and "unoffi-

FIGURE 11.2
The Maquiladora Process and Its Benefits

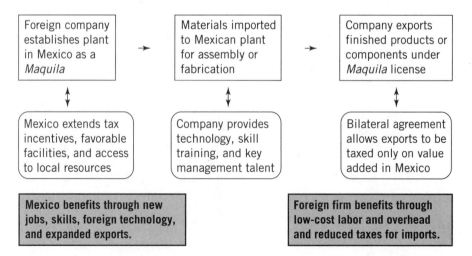

cial" unions would encompass nearly 40 percent of the country's workers. Unofficial unions are grassroots organizations that have evolved independently in opposition to government control of labor organizations and the PRI. They have campaigned as the only true unions in Mexico, and they have subsequently gained significant power in many local areas.

Together, the CT and the independent unions include craft unions, company unions, industry unions, and confederations defined by geographic locality. All unions have constitutional rights to bargain collectively and to strike. In addition, they can enforce grievances and force arbitration of disputes through government-supported systems. The Mexican legislature has enacted strong labor laws, modified to reflect the tenets of NAFTA. Through social security funding and a mandatory "employee fund," underwritten by enterprise contributions, Mexican workers have free national health care, retirement, and other social benefits. Legislation also mandates wage floors, holidays, vacations, compensation for occupational risks, and maternity leave. Additional regulations periodically enacted and enhanced by the government require companies to pay Christmas bonuses and contribute through profit sharing to a federal housing-assistance program. Federal laws also dictate rules for dismissal and severance pay, with provisions strongly weighted in favor of employees. Consequently, an employer often finds it extremely difficult to trim employment, and any layoffs can expose the firm to expensive severance payments.

Collective bargaining contracts in Mexico seldom specify time periods; rather, they are indefinite in length. Each long-term contract is reviewed annually for wage rates, and every two years for benefit adjustments, but the parties can renegotiate it at any time. Unlike contract terms elsewhere, these indefinite agreements result in numerous "reopenings" and potential strikes. Unions have the legislated right to strike over any substantive contract issue, unfair labor practice, or contest between competing unions to represent a company's employees. They also frequently strike over demarcation disputes, such as union control over particular work functions or skill categories. Because unions are viewed as extensions of government—and therefore conduits to political benefits—nearly a third of all strike activity is politically motivated and aimed at national economic or social policies. In these circumstances, an enterprise may not be the target or even remotely involved with the substantive issues in a dispute, yet it can be shut down by the strike. Unions also strike in sympathy to support other unions, thus creating a domino effect that amounts to a boycott of an entire industry.[25]

The Mexican political system, commercial practices, and union affiliations have all evolved within an environment dominated by patronage. Networks of relationships conform to clear patron-client hierarchies and allegiances. The Mexican culture emphasizes clear distinctions between the haves and the have-nots, and individuals as well as companies prosper only according to the support they elicit from a patron who is in a position to protect their interests.[26] Unions maintain extremely active operations, but often in direct support of government initiatives and in line with political priorities of those in power. Unions remain strong only within the context of patronage by the ruling party, and when they exceed the limits of patron-client loyalties, government leaders intercede without hesitation. Several years ago, for example, the transport workers staged a national protest against government wage and benefit cuts. Within a few days, the government summarily fired all 23,000 union workers, blacklisted organizers, and in some cases employed squads to "reinforce" standards for acceptable behavior through physical attacks.[27] Independent unions and nonunion employees find themselves outside the protection of a patron relationship, and the government regularly backs company managers or CT constituent groups against independent and nonunion groups.

As Mexico becomes a more active trading economy with greater foreign investment and exposure to international market forces, traditional networks of patron-client allegiances may lose importance. In the near term, however, doing business in Mexico requires appropriate connections. Like other practices, labor relations are contingent on relational networks and subsequently on political priorities. Collective bargaining agreements, wages, benefits, and dispute-resolution processes reflect political agendas more than market realities. Nevertheless, labor conditions in Mexico are becoming more transparent due not only to cross-border interests of U.S. and Canadian unions but also to exposure of Mexican workers to global union federations. The International Labor Organization (ILO), discussed in a later section, has taken an active interest in promoting humane and equitable working conditions in Mexico. ILO studies conclude that Mexican workers are capable of "first-world quality" and "productivity comparable to both the United States and Canada," but they work "in a system questionable for its political veracity."[28] These studies coupled with headlines about corruption and political abuses in Mexico are bringing pressure on authorities to address disparities and human rights in the workplace.

Labor Relations in Europe

Some international managers make the dangerous assumption that labor relations are similar throughout Europe, or at least among the EU members. In reality, each European society has a unique approach to labor relations. A comprehensive comparison is beyond the scope of this book, but the following paragraphs contrast the main themes of labor relations among the selected nations of the United Kingdom, Germany, Sweden, and Italy.

United Kingdom

The British have a history of strong unions dating to the early craft guilds of the industrial revolution. One of the two leading political parties, the Labour Party, has been closely tied to workers' interests, and during the 1930s it was identified with the Marxist movement. The association of political liberals with industrial employees fostered a distinct class conflict between workers and the owners of industry. Trade unions in the United Kingdom, and British workers in general, have enjoyed government regulatory support that encourages collective bargaining, provides substantial unemployment benefits, and ensures social welfare benefits for workers nationwide. British unions operate under fewer restrictions than their U.S. and Canadian counterparts, such as the ability to strike while a contract remains in force and to boycott in sympathy with another striking union. Grievance procedures, however, are not regulated, and arbitration works through informal and voluntary programs.

The U.K. economy experiences more strikes than any other major nation, and they can occur at any time.[29] However, strikes tend to be short-lived and may affect only small segments of targeted companies; often strikes are not actions against companies as much as protests against unfair labor practices or demarcation disputes between unions. The nation has known its share of devastating nationwide strikes in the coal and steel industries, and by transportation workers, but most strikes involve relatively few employees and are limited to specific locations.

Several causes contribute to this unusual pattern of industrial conflict.[30] Most British trade unions are craft unions, rather than conglomerate affiliations or national unions as in North America. Each local craft union reaches a separate collective bargaining agreement with a company. Therefore, one firm may be party to dozens of labor contracts, each one specific to a particular group of employees in one craft or skill classification. This plethora of craft-based contracts prevents a company from shifting labor around freely; members of one union cannot work in a skill area controlled by another. For example, if a metal worker were to receive an assignment to complete work normally done by a machinist, the shop steward representing the machinists union would protest the "encroachment" and argue that the company should hire from the proper union to carry out the machining work. In a team environment, this obstacle presents difficulties in cross-training or reassigning workers, since unions aggressively protect their turf and their members' jobs.

Collective bargaining in Britain is shaped by the multiplicity of craft and trade unions, compelling many companies to constantly negotiate contracts with one union or another. When disputes arise, any union could walk out or call a formal strike, and if those workers perform tasks crucial to the company's overall operations, then the entire organization could come to a halt through action by only a handful of employees. On the other hand, unions face serious coordination problems to bring together all the employee groups in one organization to threaten a company-wide strike such as those common in the United States or Canada. Figure 11.3 contrasts these approaches to collective bargaining.

British unions also negotiate collective bargaining agreements unlike those found elsewhere. A British contract can range from an informal "understanding" between the parties to a fully articulated agreement; however, labor contracts are *not* legally enforceable commitments in the United Kingdom. They are considered personal bilateral agreements between private parties, and while the terms can be questioned in a civil action, labor contracts do not come under statutory law.[31]

Unregulated and informal methods of dispute resolution give employees a great deal of latitude to bring grievances, seek mediation, or voluntarily enter into arbitration with company managers. Employees can also resort to common-law procedures or challenge rulings made by mediators and arbitration tribunals. Along with these benefits, the informality of the system and problems with enforcement inflate grievances into cumbersome and costly ordeals for everyone. The fragmented and localized British approach to dispute resolution works inefficiently and unpredictably from one location to another. This condition does not, however, allow employers to exploit workers or force them to operate in a chaotic labor environment. Most labor contracts incorporate broad provisions rather than the detailed mandates common in the United States and Canada; many considerations resolved by negotiations in North America are settled in the United Kingdom through social legislation. British law regulates terms of employment, working hours, rules for overtime pay, definitions of se-

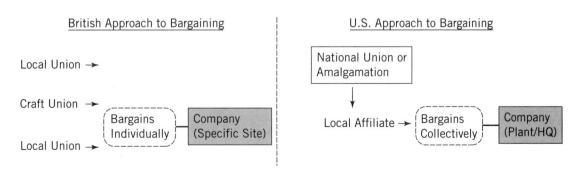

FIGURE 11.3
Union-Employer Relationships in the United States and Britain

niority, hiring and termination practices, unemployment benefits, medical programs, and many other issues. These provisions reflect the close alignment between British politics and organized labor's priorities as compared to North America.

Germany

Collective bargaining in Germany pits strong **industry unions** against affiliated organizations of employers to determine working conditions at the national level. Few contracts are negotiated by independent entities. For example, IG Metall, Germany's largest industry union, represents employees from all crafts and skill levels within most metal-related industries, including steel production, smelting, fabrication, aluminum production, alloys, metalcrafting, and so on. Employers belong to a similarly broad-based association for the entire metal industry. When a German union such as IG Metall negotiates a contract with the corresponding employer association, all members of the union and all employers that belong to the association are bound by the same terms and conditions. Wage rates, working hours, holidays, benefits, seniority systems, workers' rights, and other major negotiation points are set in place on a national scale. In practice, these broadly stated guidelines often act as wage and benefit floors.

Local unions negotiate for finer points, such as bonuses and cost-of-living adjustments, benefits in excess of national standards, terms of employment specific to a company, and variations on grievance procedures. Although IG Metall represents only about 20 percent of the nation's metal workers, its members comprise the core workforce of Germany's major companies. At the same time, only about 25 percent of all employers in the industry are members of the national association, but they are the major employers. Negotiations between the two giant institutions result in a patterned bargaining system of labor relations. Specifically, the national contract broadly influences relations between nonunion employees and employers outside the national association. It is estimated that IG Metall substantially determines employment characteristics for more than 80 percent of the German metal industries.[32]

German unions number fewer than those in North America, and they seem like only a handful relative to the number in the United Kingdom. These industry-wide labor organizations wield tremendous power, however. As in North America, German unions can rely on legal enforcement of their contracts, and the law prohibits them from striking while a contract is in force. A German company may also require contracts with several different unions, forcing it to belong to several employer associations. Still, the system of industry-wide bargaining avoids the problems caused by the multiplicity of local craft unions in the United Kingdom. Because labor contracts are legally enforceable in Germany, the country also has established well-defined grievance procedures, mediation services, and formal arbitration tribunals. Disputes related to contract terms are handled in highly structured ways. In addition, Germany constitutes a unique model within Europe in that it relies on federal laws to govern a broad range of labor issues.[33]

Unlike the comprehensive and detailed contracts negotiated by U.S. and Canadian unions, German labor contracts are written in broad terms, leaving many details for interpretation by specific companies. However, this imprecision does not create unnecessary ambiguities, because German social legislation mandates many employment conditions that would be subject to private negotiation in North America. These include employment and unemployment benefits, standardized working hours and conditions, and safety issues, as well as social welfare, insurance, and retirement systems. In this sense, German law plays a social role somewhat comparable to that of British law, and neither workers nor employers can debate the issues in labor negotiations. Nevertheless, the labor contract leaves much to be monitored, and individual grievances and disputes must be handled by individual companies.

In contrast with the United Kingdom, Canada, and the United States, Germany's national system of *industrial democracy* establishes a broadly defined participative approach to labor relations. This system involves workers or union representatives in company decision-making by giving them seats on company boards and membership in works councils. This approach to labor relations is known in Germany as **codetermination.** Based on provisions enacted in the Works Constitution Act of 1972, this system seeks to ensure democratic representation for both labor and management in organizational matters.[34]

At the heart of the codetermination system, **works councils** encourage interactions between members elected by employees from various work units and managers appointed to allotted positions. In unionized organizations, trade union representatives also are appointed to strategic councils and boards. Works council members typically serve three-year terms, and the councils act as intermediaries for decisions related to working conditions, administration of labor contracts, and resolution of grievances. To some degree, works councils become involved in external relations such as vendor liaisons, community affairs, and advocacy for legislative proposals relevant to the company or its employees. An implicit advise-and-consent philosophy underpins the concept of industrial democracy, ensuring that many potential points of conflict are resolved through the representative committee rather than through labor-management confrontations.[35]

Sweden

Labor relations in Scandinavian countries reflect a socialist ideology, which encourages active participation by government in all aspects of industrial regulation. Despite ideologies, important distinctions separate Scandinavian nations. For example, Denmark emulates the German approach to industrial democracy, but other countries in the region show less pronounced tendencies in this direction. A state-centered labor relations system plays a prominent role in Sweden, but the state is less obvious in Norway, Denmark, or Finland. Sweden, however, provides a representative model to explore.[36]

During the 1920s, severe industrial unrest in Sweden frustrated both employees and employers due to their inability to resolve industrial conflicts. Similar social unrest disrupted all of Europe during that time, closely following successes by Marxist movements and the communist revolution in Russia. While Sweden sought to avoid the dangers of revolution, its people also favored an equitable system of social legislation that emerged under the existing monarchy. In 1928, Sweden enacted substantial legislation that predated by several years the New Deal legislation in the United States. The country also established a state-regulated system of labor organizations and confederations of employers.

In the highly socialized Swedish form of government, the state mandates working hours, employment rights, benefits, and welfare systems. Through a system of heavy taxes and monetary redistribution, Sweden pays for and administers what has become known as a "cradle-to-grave" social welfare economy. These provisions eliminate discussions of labor-management negotiating issues that commonly lead to confrontations in North America. Neither employees nor employers are concerned with health care, family support, insurance, or retirement benefits. Employees in Sweden, whether members of unions or not, enjoy state-mandated holidays, sick leave, maternity leave (for both fathers and mothers), unemployment protection, and state-funded training or redundancy education.

Collective bargaining in Sweden has been controlled through government agencies since the labor movement emerged in the 1920s. In effect, one nationwide labor organization, the Swedish Trade Union Confederation (the Swedish term is commonly abbreviated as LO), represents all workers. The LO encompasses constituent membership groups based partially on craft skills and partially on industry classifications. Therefore, local representatives deal with companies for administering contracts, resolving disputes, and enforcing terms of employment; but contract negotiations occur under the state auspices as a national system of collective bargaining. A counterpart to the LO, the Swedish Employers' Confederation (abbreviated as SAF), represents private enterprises as well as nationalized industries. Membership of the SAF also includes public-sector organizations and joint government cooperatives such as telecommunications, postal, and energy enterprises. The LO and SAF bargain collectively for national contracts, and they often form coalitions to influence social legislation. Both negotiate under constraints established by extensive social regulations, however.[37] These relationships are illustrated in Figure 11.4.

Although Sweden appears to be one of the most regulated countries in the industrialized world, employers and workers have tremendous freedom in decisions relating to workplace behavior, work rules, enterprise management, and company-specific discipline and grievance procedures.[38] This freedom within a protective umbrella of social legislation has led to many innovative changes in labor-management relations. For example, the Swedish automaker Volvo gained worldwide attention in the 1970s for its team-based production system. The program became associated with leading theories of motivation and job enrichment. Similarly, the forerunner of the current Swiss-Swedish giant ABB (Asea Brown Boveri) developed a global model of project engineering management based on distributed participatory teams.

Swedes enjoy the benefits of social legislation and an environment where government administration eliminates most potential conflicts over work issues. On the other hand, the country struggles with its invasive regulation and national control over employee and employer rights. The system results in a heavy burden of involuntary taxation and industrial management through state systems, national wage scales

FIGURE 11.4
Swedish System of
Workplace Regulation

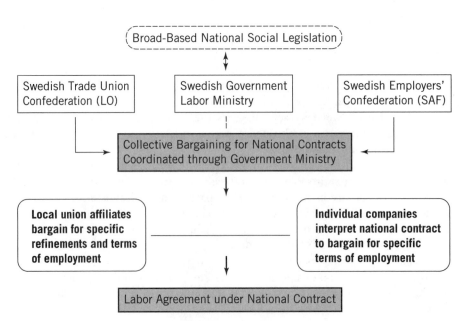

and benefits, and blanket collective bargaining agreements that affect both union and nonunion organizations. This central control also results in fewer strikes than most countries experience, and most disputes are handled peaceably through company intervention groups. Sweden does have grievance systems and legal tribunals to resolve especially serious complaints.

Italy

The structure of union activity in Italy resembles that in Germany, with national federations of local unions whose membership is defined by the industry. Major federations of unions combine labor relations in the metals, chemicals, banking and finance, automotive engineering, postal and telecommunications, and transportation industries, among others. Collective bargaining is channeled through these federations, resulting in national contracts that set terms within entire industries. However, individual unions within the federations often negotiate with companies on issues outside the national contracts. For example, when a company wants to introduce new technology that would alter employment configurations, the local union almost always negotiates actively to protect job security for potentially redundant employees or to pressure for employee retraining programs. Work rules, disciplinary codes, bonus systems, family benefits, and terms of employment that affect hiring and termination can be negotiated locally or by one of the industry unions. Larger issues such as wage rates, holidays, employee leave rights, unemployment protection, safety measures, and major benefits are typically determined by agreements between the national federation of unions and industry employer associations.[39]

Italy's unions are much more politically active than those in Germany. This reflects the country's socialist underpinnings and significant links between unions and left-wing political parties. Social legislation in Italy establishes somewhat more intricate rights than comparable German laws create, but legislation is not as comprehensive as that in Sweden. Consequently, since Italians lack the social protection that Swedes enjoy, workers rely on their employers for many benefits. Dental care, for example, is taken for granted in Sweden; but it remains a voluntary benefit subject to negotiation in Italian employment contracts. Nonunion employees, as well as most small-company managers and employees, do not enjoy benefits structured under national contracts unless those benefits are specified by social legislation.

With greater latitude in bargaining and less extensive support from social legislation than some other Europeans enjoy, Italian labor-management relations can become strained. However, Italy experiences no more strike activity than Germany does, and workers strike less frequently than those in Britain—for two reasons.[40] First, collective bargaining contracts are legally enforceable and cover broad categories of companies and employees. This arrangement complicates efforts to organize a coordinated strike, and wildcat walkouts seldom garner support from the unions' national representatives. Second, like Germany, Italy established a system of industrial democracy after World War II with works councils at each plant location. Although German codetermination laws are much more comprehensive than Italian counterparts, works councils are common in Italy, and employees have a strong voice in company decisions. Council members are elected from company operating units, and managers can be elected or appointed according to the council charters.

A works council plays a crucial role in resolving labor conflict. Its members help to mediate grievances and intervene in potential labor-management differences, and a council almost always participates in decisions that affect any aspect of employment. For example, changes in technology such as introducing computer-assisted manufacturing receive substantial attention from a works council; if the new technology will alter work patterns or employment levels, the council may advise the union to open negotiations to protect employee rights. On the other hand, the council may see the change as an opportunity for increased business and subsequent growth in employment. Under this scenario, the council and company management may act in concert to develop the technology. Cooperation between works councils and their companies is far more common than confrontation, because council representatives defuse many potential problems informally. Grievances can emerge, and serious ones may reach arbitration through third-party adjudicators or state tribunals.

Italy displays many similarities with other European countries. Its labor-management systems compare closely with those in Germany, and several important similarities link provisions of social legislation in Italy and Sweden. Historically, Italy and Britain have shared similar political antecedents and alliances between unions and political parties. Nevertheless, Italian culture contrasts sharply with other European nations. While unsanctioned work stoppages and public demonstrations are rare elsewhere, they can occur frequently in Italy. Therefore, managers of multinational companies in Europe often find that they must take careful account of differences in employee expectations and behavior among their continental operating divisions. This interaction becomes even more complicated for companies with North American operations, where labor relations differ substantially from those in Europe. Managing in Asia presents an entirely different cultural perspective on labor relations.

Labor Relations in Asia

With more than one-third of the world's population and prominent societies with high international growth profiles, Asia is the world's most rapidly expanding region. Global companies have a significant presence in Asia, and their managers face unusual challenges in cross-border relationships. As emphasized in earlier chapters, however, no one should generalize about a universal Asian perspective. Each Asian culture features distinct characteristics, and labor relations in the region cover a widely diversified spectrum. Japan and China represent the major Asian nations for international business, and although similar in many ways, they have divergent systems of labor relations.

Japan

Prior to World War II, all attempts to organize labor were severely repressed by a society built on the strength of a monarchy and constituent interests of a feudal aristocracy. After the war, the American-led Allied occupation forces under General Douglas MacArthur established a constitutional government and helped to rebuild Japan. One of MacArthur's earliest changes was to encourage Japan to enact labor legislation. Consequently, the country's first Labor Union Law, modeled on U.S. legislation, was signed in 1945. This preceded Japan's constitution by nearly four years, and it inspired the spontaneous foundation of an astounding number of unions. By the time the Japanese constitution was enacted in 1949, approximately 55 percent of Japan's labor force was unionized. Unions were formed at each plant site or company, and workers actively battled management through strikes and walkouts. They also pressured politicians for economic reforms, measures to improve employee rights, and social legislation to provide broad-based human benefits. As a result, Japan's constitution was drafted with a strong pro-labor mandate ensuring three fundamental rights for all organized labor (unions, associations, and most public-sector affiliations): the right to organize, to engage in collective bargaining, and to engage in legal strikes without retribution.[41]

Spontaneous and rapid union organizing focused on individual plants or service organizations, and the Japanese labor movement became rooted in specific enterprises. The resulting **enterprise union** contrasts sharply with industry-wide unions found in continental Europe. It also differs from craft unions in Britain and amalgamated unions in the United States and Canada. No explicit restrictions bar membership by managers, limit a union to blue-collar or white-collar employees, or exempt individuals due to skill differentials or personal characteristics. Consequently, a trade union in Japan is a *company union*, and union leaders are elected without regard to status, longevity, or skill; many union representatives are managers. Indeed, many union shop stewards elected from nonmanagement ranks earn promotions into management after their stewardship terms.[42]

Although unions in Japan are company-specific organizations, the constitutional protections for the labor movement created national controls on work rules and employment procedures. Specific clauses of the Japanese constitution obligate the state to ensure employment opportunities to all who are capable of working and desire to do so. At the same time, the constitution imposes a duty on adult citizens to pursue constructive employment. This approach to a balanced labor environment has worked extremely well in a society that values harmony and group welfare over individual priorities. Therefore, the government has sought to provide employment, to protect those who cannot be employed, and to promote training to assist them in finding meaningful work. If citizens hold up their end of the bargain by actively seeking stable work, they gain from a system that provides so-called *lifetime employment* and benefits such as housing subsidies, family benefits, medical care, training and education, and well-founded retirement income. On the other hand, severe penalties await those who opt out of the system or otherwise fail to meet social expectations to pursue productive employment (if they are capable). These consequences range from loss of benefits and social compensation to vagrancy charges and actual penal judgments.[43]

Collective bargaining in Japan rests with the enterprise owners and company union, but these parties find relatively few points to negotiate compared with systems in other countries. Wage rate structures, insurance, working hours, provisions for overtime, industrial safety, job security, and health benefits are legislated. Labor contracts tend to focus on local employment issues, working conditions, and wages or benefits that exceed national mandates. Dispute resolution procedures also are the responsibility of local unions and companies. Grievances, however, are not a significant concern because the collectivist Japanese ethic leads individuals to carefully avoid confrontations.

Japanese workers do resort to strikes, and although these work stoppages last only a few hours or days, they can be highly visible. A strike typically represents a last resort after the parties involved in negotiations have failed to reach a reasonable consensus on the bargaining points. A strike is viewed as a show of force to rally workers through a membership vote and to demonstrate that they are genuinely adamant about a particular issue. Many strikes involve company-wide walkouts rather than labor actions against management; in fact, an enterprise may strike to bring pressure on the government to influence legislation by making a public showing of unity. Confrontational strikes do place employees in opposition to company *owners* (distinguished from managers), and these events have increased as Japan's economy has suffered setbacks leading to company reorganizations and rising unemployment.

Regional and national federations of unions have also raised their profiles. Although they do not participate in collective bargaining, the large federations hold major annual conferences with government officials, and together the delegates create advisory guidelines for pervasive issues such as wage levels and benefit systems. Local unions notice these guidelines and bargain accordingly, and nonunion organizations pattern their employment policies on these national proceedings as well as on union contracts. Business owners and managers join national industrial associations that hold council with government officials in a similar fashion. Thus, Japan's tripartite system of labor relations involves the government as a key player that interfaces with unions and industry leaders through their national associations. These groups also provide financial support and voting power to political parties. Consequently, Japanese industrial relations represent an intricate web of formal and informal networks, industry relationships, political connections, and integrated enterprise organizations. No other society has such a complex system, and foreign companies operating in Japan must adapt to the Japanese model or risk competing without significant connections in a nation where success depends crucially on these network relationships.[44]

The People's Republic of China

Under the communist system in the PRC, four major participants influence how an organization operates: the factory director, an Enterprise Party Committee, a Workers' Congress, and a trade union.[45] The factory director is a member of senior management (or a cadre), perhaps a government official in a state-owned enterprise or cooperative. The director is appointed by the central government, which is also called *state bureaucracy* to distinguish it from the Chinese Communist Party (CCP). The CCP is the second group with authority to appoint its own representative to an organization through a formal Enterprise Party Committee (EPC). No institution outside China compares to this committee, which is effectively a CCP-controlled board of directors. A party secretary in the EPC wields substantial authority, reporting directly to the CCP and sharing *de facto* joint management authority with the factory director. The EPC has hierarchical precedence over the factory director, and it can veto manager decisions when necessary. The state interests are ostensibly separate from those of the CCP, and these officials concern themselves with operating responsibilities such as production, services, financing, and human resource management. The party secretary tends to avoid operational decisions but is the guardian of communist dogma.

A Workers' Congress (WC) operates under the EPC with representatives drawn from employee ranks, party interests, and trade union members. On the surface, a WC is created for each organization as an egalitarian committee that serves to link internal organizational interest groups as well as external interests such as banks, trade organizations, and *citizen communities* (i.e., public and community groups, municipal agencies, and interrelated suppliers and vendors). These congresses often represent consortia of companies within a specific industry group or geographic enclave. Enclaves are equivalent to industrial parks controlled through national or provincial directorates and CCP officials. An enterprise WC has significant power to adopt or challenge resolutions concerning production, procurement, budgets, employment, allocation of rewards (bonuses or benefits), disciplinary measures, wage adjustments, and training. The WC also makes recommendations to the EPC secretary on management appointments. The Chinese regard the Workers' Congresses as the ultimate form of industrial representation. (The term industrial *democracy* is carefully avoided.)[46]

The fourth group within this system is the trade union itself. Over 300,000 trade unions represent workers in China. Most are rather small and enterprise specific, yet their membership includes more than 100 million workers. All unions are subordinated to the All-China Federation of Trade Unions (ACFTU). On paper, the ACFTU enjoys a social status nearly equal to the state bureaucracy and the CCP. Officially, the ACFTU is the third leg of a tripartite national socialist ruling system working jointly with the government and the Chinese Communist Party. In reality, it is an arm of the party and an extension of the political system fulfilling a mandate to communicate party interests between the CCP and the masses. The ACFTU is also responsible for implementing government decrees related to enterprise development, and it is ultimately responsible for protecting workers' rights and their material well-being. Figure 11.5 summarizes relationships.

This extraordinary system of interlocking responsibilities joins labor relations together with political ideology. No labor laws protect Chinese workers apart from ACFTU and CCP mandates. Collective bargaining does not occur, yet the Workers' Congress and local trade unions do set terms of employment, with approval by the EPC. The WC has unilateral authority for resolving disputes and handling disciplinary cases. Consequently, although workers have grievance rights, the WC is the ultimate judge and jury, subject to CCP intervention.

Workers in China do not have the right to strike, but strikes are neither officially forbidden nor sanctioned. A gray area of circumstance determines judgments about any collective action to stop work, but strikes have occurred with increasing frequency. In China's heavily industrialized northeastern region, dozens of state-owned enterprises ran short of cash and were unable to pay their employees, sometimes for as long as three months. More than 100,000 workers took to the streets in four provinces, refusing to work until they were paid. They also pressured the government to intervene with financial restructuring and to remove incompetent managers. The action drew praise for the workers' courageous effort to help national leaders understand the plight of troubled companies. Beijing did intervene to privatize, shut down, or reposition finances for many companies.[47] In contrast, similar strikes in Beijing and the northern provinces in 1994 drew different reactions. Despite claims of almost identical motivations by nearly as many workers, the uprising ended with mass firings, imprisonments, and "employee repositioning" (i.e., reassignment or reeducation).[48]

The capricious reactions to strike activity are revealed in more than 100 independent strikes that have occurred in China's special enterprise zones (SEZs) of Shenzhen and Zhuhai. These SEZs in the southern Guangdong province were created to attract foreign investment; and most foreign joint ventures work from facilities in China's coastal SEZs, where they find lucrative access to foreign trade and soft-border financing. Strikes have occurred with greater frequency in the SEZs since 1986, when trade was liberalized and the Private Company Act allowed China's entrepreneurs to establish independent enterprises.[49] The strikes have focused mainly on wage rates,

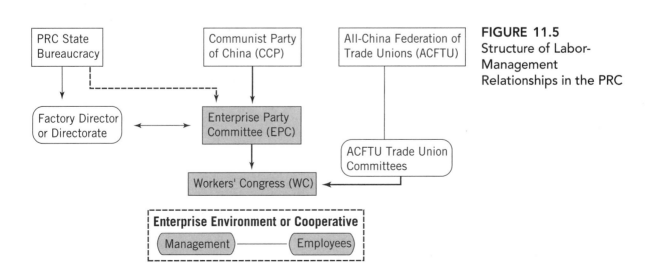

FIGURE 11.5
Structure of Labor-Management Relationships in the PRC

working hours, and benefits. But in 1995 massive work stoppages and demonstrations protested unsafe working conditions following collapses in several factories, mine cave-ins, and dozens of factory fires that killed thousands of people. Because these incidents often involved foreign joint ventures, Beijing not only endorsed the strikes but also brought pressure on foreign companies to compensate bereaved families and to adjust wages and benefits of all workers. Observers say that the official response might just as easily have gone the other way; Beijing could have smothered the demonstrations and criminally indicted the strike leaders, but perhaps the officials perceived political benefits in supporting strikes targeted at international companies.[50] In the end, Beijing mandated unionization by the ACFTU of all enterprises with foreign equity interests. This move extended a program that was under consideration in 1994, but after purging managers from a number of state-owned enterprises following the accidents, the Workers' Congresses pushed for greater control in foreign joint ventures.[51]

Complicating the system of labor relations in China, each community has a social system called a *danwei* (pronounced "don-way"). The **danwei** is a powerful quasiofficial social group run by bureaucratically appointed community leaders who wield exceptional influence over housing assignments, rights to medical care, access to rationed supplies, jobs, and even births, abortions, and funerals.[52] A danwei leader may be a mature housewife, a factory manager, a blue-collar worker, or a bank teller; the only criterion for selection is recognition by the local community for loyalty to China's ideological values. Every Chinese citizen identifies with a local danwei. It is that person's umbrella of social infrastructure. When someone violates the expectations of the danwei, such as seeking material wealth through entrepreneurial activity, the danwei members (i.e., the community) often oust the individual. An entrepreneur is said to be "swimming naked in the ocean," and similar social isolation can occur for any number of infractions, including improper behavior at work or disturbing harmony (such as strike activity). Deviation draws a decisive response in a society that expects conformity.[53] The ousted individual may therefore find it difficult to buy necessities, to arrange for proper housing, to obtain approval for a job transfer, to qualify for training programs, or even to arrange a simple travel permit for a vacation outside the district.

For an international manager working in China, labor relations present a number of challenges. Even the best-honed human resource skills will not ensure a full understanding of the intricate relationships among the state bureaucracy, the CCP, and the ACFTU. Perhaps the most important accommodation by international managers is to recognize that the current policies and procedures were instituted only a few years ago by a government capable of dictatorial reversals. Reforms are indeed taking place; China's workers have gained a louder voice in industrial governance than they once had. Private enterprise has rapidly grown, and China is sensitive to its prospects for success in global commerce. Many of the changes taking place today may lead to an even more dramatic transformation in the future, but China will remain an enigma well into the twenty-first century.[54]

Labor Relations Elsewhere in the World

The national systems discussed in previous sections hardly represent the full diversity of labor relations in the world, and several additional examples merit attention. For example, France differs in important ways from its EU counterparts.[55] French labor relations evolved under the influence of strong socialist movements in the 1930s, creating an entrenched system of national unions closely aligned to political ideologies. The dominant unions in France openly support either communist or socialist priorities, and they have backed political candidates in those parties. Several smaller, independent unions have defined themselves as far right or conservative institutions, but nearly all unions in France are national confederations based on industrial classifications. Industry-wide collective bargaining involves exchanges between the confederations and national employer associations within industry groups such as steel, shipping, transportation, and telecommunications. French contracts incorporate indefinite provisions considered as extensions of political mandates. Social legislation stipulates wage brackets, benefits, holidays, insurance, employee benefits, retirement, working hours, and job security issues. Although national agreements and laws leave few topics for bargaining at the company level, employees and managers debate continuously over local differentials, such as contract-specific wage premiums, or disputes between supervisors and employees over work ratings. Most debates and confrontations are handled through company committees mandated by law.

Workers in France strike less frequently than those elsewhere in Europe, and most strikes concern national ideological issues. Unions and employer associations known as *cadres* have relatively little to say about labor issues or terms of employment, yet these politically powerful organizations can substantially affect industry-wide decisions. France recognizes its unique status within Europe and goes to great lengths to protect its institutionalized system of labor relations.

Israel is similarly unique in the Middle East. With its complicated history and tenuous position in the region, the country has developed an unusual system of centralized controls. Labor relations in Israel extend to all sectors of society, including government, and although the nation's politics emphasize democratic free enterprise and a market-driven economy, its people adhere closely to the collectivist principals of a social welfare state. With an unusual pattern of industrial development coupled with political sensitivities, labor relations have evolved through both national and community movements. The unique characteristics of Israeli labor relations are profiled in more detail in the "Global Viewpoint" feature.

South America lacks a regional identity comparable to that of the EU. Although several Latin economies are vibrant and important to both European and North American interests, relatively few researchers have studied their labor relations. This situation may change as countries such as Chile, Brazil, and Argentina become serious candidates for membership in NAFTA. Chile has set its own course for stabilization and rapid growth through relatively cooperative relationships among unions, company managers, and the government. Unlike its Latin neighbors, Chile has pursued the goals of building a market economy influenced by legislation on workers' rights. These conditions opened its borders to foreign investment and at the same time created a competitive labor market.

In contrast, labor relations in Brazil trace their roots to Portuguese colonialism tempered by years of military rule, and the system steadfastly resists change.[56] Oddly, labor organizations in Brazil were modeled on Mussolini's Italian system of authoritarian control prior to World War II, but they have subsequently come under state control as government-sponsored organizations. They are supported through public funds and mandatory contributions from companies. Since unions depend on the state for their existence, they participate in a collaborative environment in which the government ensures workers of broad-based social protections, state-defined benefits, and legislated wage rates. Unions bargain directly with companies for terms of employment, incentive pay in excess of legislated minimum rates, and company benefits beyond those provided by social regulations. Unions gained the right to strike only in

Israeli Labor Relations—The Quest for a Dead-Level Playing Field

The foundations of Israeli labor relations were laid several decades before the country gained its independence in 1948. During those earlier years, the nation's forefathers were part of a mixed society of Arab and Hebrew heritage living in agricultural communities. They established their own unofficial institutions with a view toward creating a Zionist state, subsequently forming collective settlements known today as kibbutz and moshav. During that time, an Israeli federation of labor was created to protect workers from inhumane working conditions and exploitation. When Israel became a nation, this informal labor group became the formal arm of the Israeli labor movement. Today, this is the General Federation of Labor, more commonly known by its historic name, the Histadruth. The organization has become the most influential nongovernmental organization in the country. It represents every individual and industry union for nearly every profession and craft, counting more than half of all Israelis among its members.

The Histadruth is one of three recognized economic sectors in Israel with widespread business interests. The other two are private-sector industry and public-sector services. However, the Histadruth's influence extends throughout all three sectors through a pervasive representation of unions and government workers. Consequently, nearly every organization finds itself bargaining with the Histadruth either directly or indirectly—with the single exception of Histadruth enterprises, which are themselves employers. This odd situation has grown out of its role as the grassroots spearhead of Zionist interests, during which time the organization created holding companies and cooperative enterprises within the kibbutz network. It also established medical services, personal insurance, financial services, and industrial plants. Consequently, the Histadruth is not a labor union confederation comparable to those in Europe or North America, but a social institution born during an ideological struggle to become both employer and employee representative on a major scale.

Collective bargaining in Israel occurs on two levels within all three sectors. So-called collective agreements negotiated at the national level cover entire industries or, in the case of civil service workers, the entire union membership of government workers.

Specific agreements are negotiated with individual enterprises. The extensive holdings and commensurate union strength of the Histadruth establish it as the largest of the three sectors, but contracts are not negotiated at this level; they are determined by edict. However, these agreements reflect the terms of national contracts negotiated in the private and public sectors, and they include Histadruth unions as the key negotiators.

Public-sector agreements are negotiated by the respective unions with the government, through the Ministry of Finance or high-ranking politicians. The government is totally unionized apart from its elected officials, and civil-service employees negotiate contracts in the same way that union employees negotiate in a private industry. Private-sector bargaining between the unions in the federation and national employers' associations results in collective nationwide contracts. Specific contracts for individual enterprises and public agencies must conform to the national agreements; wages, benefits, and terms of employment cannot exceed those specified in the national agreements except for cost-of-living adjustments and exempt conditions such as professional differentials.

This unusual structure of labor relations is further influenced by substantial social legislation. Israel shares the priorities of a social welfare state well known in Sweden, and an exceptional range of laws governs child labor, women's rights, maternity leave, holidays, standard workweeks, retirement benefits, medical privileges, rights to strike, and so on. Collective bargaining contracts cover indefinite periods of time, and workers have no right to strike while the contracts remain in force. Theoretically, this provision legally prohibits any strike because national contracts are essentially always in force. Nevertheless, under social legislation, strikers are immune from prosecution when they are contesting contractual terms. Consequently, Israel experiences many strikes, and civil-service workers account for nearly 40 percent of all lost days from work stoppages, placing them among the most active groups in labor disputes.

Also, although contracts are established for indefinite periods of time, literally hundreds of new ones are written every year. Labor laws require reviews of national agreements every two years, yet the law provides no guidelines for negotiations. Consequently, contract reviews prompt strikes or re-openers intended to gain changes in agreements. In contrast to most European and North American countries, no Israeli laws establish procedures for collective bargaining. Therefore, everyone knows that each of the three sectors will negotiate national contracts and review them at least every two years, yet no regulations specifically empower unions to participate in this process by organizing, striking, or bargaining. As a result, enterprise-level contracts (specific agreements) are debated, reopened, and rewritten whenever the national contracts undergo changes or when union groups feel that they have due cause to confront management. Individual parties determine how these negotiations take place and how contracts are created. The process generally reflects social patterns that evolved during preindependence underground activities and are ingrained in the national concept of social consensus through collective action.

Despite variations in specific situations, national contracts and extensive social legislation represent a highly centralized form of social governance devoted to creating nationwide patterns of equitable wages, benefits, and terms of employment. In effect, any development in the private or public sector, or within the Histadruth, is closely emulated by the other sectors of the economy. Even slight variations in working conditions or compensation spread quickly from one sector to all others. This tendency derives substantially from the early Zionist days, when the Israelis drew tightly together in their cooperatives and supported the Histadruth as an independent force to protect community welfare.

The Israeli people have always sought a dead-level playing field for all, and although unions, companies, and nonunion groups compete fiercely among themselves, few economic differentials are permitted to surface. When they do, workers quickly protest. This activity has prompted the government to initiate yet another tool to level the playing field—called an extension order. An extension order can mandate any contract or labor condition to apply to an entire industry, to one or more economic sectors, or to the nation as a whole. A sectoral change in wages, therefore, can quickly become a national wage norm by fiat.

Sources: Amira Galin, "Israel," in Mariam Rothman, Dennis R. Briscoe, and Raoul C. D. Nacamulli (eds.), *Industrial Relations around the World* (New York: Walter de Gruyter, 1993), 187–204. Also see R. Dubin and Y. Aharoni, "Ideology and Reality: Work and Pay in Israel," *Industrial Relations* 20, no. 1 (1981): 18–35.

1988, when Brazil liberalized its labor laws to shift more responsibility to negotiations between unions and companies. Before that time, however, strikes often occurred in the guise of political demonstrations for across-the-board wage and benefit changes.

Argentina's labor relations evolved from Spanish colonial influence. Although conditions there are similar to the strong union-government alliance in Brazil, Argentine unions are independently constituted. This trait reflects British influence, which encourages formation of craft and industry unions under a loose confederation. Unions can strike individual companies, and they have responsibility for labor relations similar to those in Brazil, but they operate with no comparable central government patronage. Therefore, Argentina experiences more independent strike activity than its neighbor, and unions pursue more grievances against employers. Brazil handles disputes through state court systems, while Argentina prefers reconciliation tribunals. In both countries, unions exert significant political influence under collaborative systems, and they have relatively little bargaining power with individual companies. These examples do not reflect conditions in other Latin countries. With the exception of Chile, organized labor relations in the region range from chaotic systems devoid of formal labor laws to dictates of autocratic government agencies.

On the other side of the Pacific, Asian labor relations reflect equal diversity. An earlier section presented Japan and China as the two most prominent nations in Asia. That focus ignores countries such as Australia, New Zealand, South Korea, Singapore, Hong Kong, Malaysia, and Indonesia, among others, each with a unique culture and its own system of labor relations. The Australian system, for example, is not simply an extension of European antecedents; instead, the country is an Asian nation with elements of a European profile. Australian leaders developed a federal system of politics and commercial law in the nineteenth century that has evolved into a welfare democracy based on strong priorities for individual rights. This characteristic separates it from socialist environments, but the strongest political party, the Australian Labour Party (ALP), was formed by unions in 1891. Today, the ALP is still firmly entrenched as a union-backed party.[57] Australians do not have a legal right to strike, and when they do their unions can be deregistered and their members fired. Nevertheless, Australia experiences a notoriously high number of lost days from unofficial work disruptions. During a dispute with management, employees simply create a "stop-work" demonstration in which a company's entire workforce might walk out en masse or suddenly all report sick and stay home. The effect is the same as a strike, and such actions often give a brutal character to Australian labor relations. The government intervenes regularly to mandate arbitration or to enforce regulatory mandates.[58]

In contrast, the predominately Islamic nations of Indonesia and Malaysia do not ensure universal access to unions in the western sense. Both countries permit collective bargaining within provinces where local governments agree, but some provinces (literally individual states within each country) strictly follow Islamic law. Like nearly all Islamic cultures, workers' rights in Indonesia and Malaysia are protected through government ministries, and the custodial patronage model of government is rigidly followed in orthodox states. Consequently, employers must conform to government mandates for nearly all terms of employment, wages, benefits, and workplace practices. Employees expect government leaders to prevail on their behalf. Collective bargaining sets some conditions in the cosmopolitan areas of each country, but employers bargain with government ministries acting on behalf of employees. Strikes occur, but they almost always take the form of public demonstrations on ideological issues. Workers align themselves with political parties or social causes, but the government remains responsible as the guardian of human activities and individual rights. By western standards, labor relations are relatively calm in these countries, but employees and employers are substantially constrained by social sanctions deeply embedded in cultural and religious values. Formal labor laws have only recently begun to evolve, and disputes are often resolved under the jurisdiction of ministries or judges appointed according to religious tenets.[59]

These contrasts in national labor relations serve to illustrate the difficulty of generalizing about labor concepts. International managers cannot presume that they will encounter similar workplace behavior even in two adjacent countries such as France and Germany, or in those that share similar ethnic and social profiles such as the United Kingdom, Canada, and Australia. Employment practices do not easily cross borders, and substantial differences distinguish not only laws but also employee behavior and expectations. Rules that generally prevail in one society may not apply readily elsewhere. Nevertheless, as the spread of global companies leads to development of integrated networks, and as labor becomes more mobile through regional initiatives such as political alignment in the EU or improved trade through NAFTA, observers see signs of convergence toward common labor practices.[60] As discussed in the next section, certain trends in international labor relations are encouraging convergence, but, in the process, managers are facing increasingly complicated work environments.

TRENDS IN INTERNATIONAL LABOR RELATIONS

Union membership throughout the world has changed in several important ways. Prior to World War II and until the 1950s, unions concentrated their strength in the industrial sector, representing primarily blue-collar workers. During that era, union membership ranged between 30 and 50 percent of a nation's workforce. Growing numbers of white-collar unions later emerged to represent service workers and public-sector employees. But union membership as a percentage of the total national workforce did not significantly increase, because industrial union membership began to decline. This common transition appeared in most industrialized nations as manufacturing grew at a progressively slower rate (or declined), while services increased dramatically and public-sector employment expanded. Meanwhile, union activity increased significantly in less-developed countries as their economies began to establish strong manufacturing profiles, although these tendencies have reached plateaus or declined slightly with new social legislation. In some nations, such as Sweden, very high union membership has not declined because organized labor has become closely associated with the social welfare system itself, rather than acting as a countervailing force to industrial power. In other nations, such as Brazil, unions operate as extensions of government or under government jurisdiction; consequently, union activity often targets political issues rather than commercial interests.

In most nations with traditionally confrontational relations between unions and employers, union membership has shown sharp declines. However, no evidence suggests that unions are disappearing. In many instances, lower membership figures can be misleading, because the strength of national and industry unions may be even greater today than it was in the past. This transformation is due in part to legislation that mandates industry conformance to contract terms or regulations that support employee participation in business-related decisions. This situation has emerged unmistakably in Western Europe, and the trend forces a vast number of nonunion companies to accommodate the terms in union contracts or to adapt to legislated labor-management processes.

In general, union activities worldwide have become less pronounced, and both union and nonunion employees participate in fewer confrontations with employers. Governments have enacted growing bodies of legislation to address grievances once championed by unions, such as unsafe workplace conditions, unfair labor practices, and child labor. Social legislation also has taken the sting out of labor-management problems by providing all citizens with a wide range of benefits and by advocating humane working conditions.

The growth of international companies and cross-border strategic alliances also has significantly contributed to changes in labor relations in two primary ways. First, international companies act as conduits for exchanges of information on employment practices, and the resulting flow of ideas influences foreign and domestic operations. Second, foreign workers and their employers are at least aware of, if not integrated into, foreign labor-management systems. As growing numbers of companies establish global operations, people from diverse cultures often find themselves accommodating similar technologies and work methods.

Global labor relations also are affected by information technology, which provides pervasive access to world news about economic changes. The combination of these factors empowers most societies with knowledge of international labor initiatives and comparable workplace standards. Employees in Mexico can easily compare their own wages and benefits with those of workers doing similar jobs in the United States or Canada. Workers in Spain can follow labor debates in France or Germany as easily as switching on their television sets. Indeed, employees in Denver, Yokohama, or Hong Kong can go online through the Internet and share information on everything from an employer's attitude toward sexual harassment issues to rumors of impending strikes. Consequently, the field of organized labor relations has passed through a major transition, and significant external forces have brought about change for employees and employers in all organizations. These changes raise the awareness of three emerging themes: convergence in labor relations, internationalization of labor relations, and labor participation in management.

Convergence in Labor Relations

Continuing trends toward globalization and integration of international operations create a natural urge to standardize work processes and converge management systems. **Convergence** is defined as a process of assimilation of different management concepts and subsequent reduction of workplace disparities among the world's societies.[61] The desirability and even the reality of convergence have stirred debate for nearly a century. In a convergent world, technology and human skills would adapt in every society, and managerial systems would be similar everywhere. Organizations would rely on similar systems of accounting, financing, procurement, production, and service support activities, and leadership processes would ensure and expand compatibility. In such an ideal system, similar labor relations would prevail throughout the global network, and a multinational corporation could confidently predict how work would be accomplished anywhere.

No one has yet observed these ideal conditions, and if they are evolving, then many ask what major system is providing the common model for others to emulate? Although globalization seems to invite standardization, cloning of industrial systems is an abstract and highly doubtful concept. It is not even necessarily a desirable concept, since every society would lose cultural identity, and worldwide the richness of social diversity would evaporate. The French will not soon buy into an American industrial culture any more than Americans will emulate a Japanese model, so why should the Chinese, Mexicans, or Russians give any thought to French, American, or Japanese concepts?

Arguments such as these have not, however, prevented a significant migration of concepts. American and European companies have indeed adapted a number of Japanese practices, and the Japanese have selectively adopted many American and European management concepts. Mexicans have aggressively sought to incorporate North American work methods into their society. Russian companies are in a rapid transition toward suitable adaptations of western systems. Along with their products and jobs, global companies are bringing changes in labor practices to the developing countries of Africa, Southeast Asia, and Latin America.[62]

Recall Michael Porter's assertion that technology and work processes are being infused in company operations on a global scale. He emphasized that capital flows freely across borders, information is instantaneously accessible to most countries, and technology itself is easily transferred or duplicated in all but the most underdeveloped societies. These transfers of concepts and technologies generally flow from developed countries toward less-developed countries, but this pattern does not imply a pervasive or unilateral exchange. Global companies and most societies borrow from one an-

Starbucks Coffee is one of many global brands that transcend cultural barriers. Global branding and borderless commerce are rapidly creating a convergence of products, services, and concepts. Nationalism and cultural isolationism are mellowing, particularly as a younger generation begins to integrate foreign ideas and adapt behavior introduced through international companies in a seamless world.

other. This interaction has not been studied extensively, and researchers who undertake the task must navigate an emotion-laden field of inquiry, because most people strive to protect their cultural roots. In fact, many explicitly advocate divergent models of development to purposely insulate domestic activities from foreign influences.[63] The primary forces for and against convergence are illustrated in Figure 11.6.

Internationalization of Labor Relations

Trade agreements and regional political affiliations create new regulations that affect labor relations between member nations. NAFTA, for example, lays out explicit guidelines for monitoring U.S., Canadian, and Mexican employment practices, and labor legislation in Mexico is beginning to reflect NAFTA principles. More generally, all Mexican labor practices also are beginning to emulate U.S. and Canadian guidelines, in part due to intervention by American unions in Mexican labor disputes, as noted earlier, but also as a result of actions by international labor organizations. The

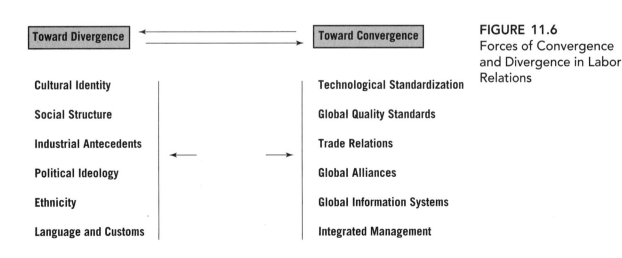

FIGURE 11.6
Forces of Convergence and Divergence in Labor Relations

World Confederation of Labor (WCL) and the International Confederation of Free Trade Unions (ICFTU) have become involved in many national labor issues, circulating publications throughout the world to spread information about wages, work hours, industry conditions, terms of employment, and benefit systems. These organizations also advocate improvements in humane working environments and workplace safety. Mexican unions, employer associations, maquiladora associations, politicians, and government agencies have equal access to information from these organizations.

In addition to international union associations, the **International Labor Organization (ILO)** was created under the United Nations following World War II to promote fair labor standards and employee health and welfare throughout the world. The ILO has actively supported social legislation, and it focuses particularly on efforts to track employment practices of multinational organizations. As global communications improve, information from the ILO, international associations, and national labor movements is readily available to anyone in the literate world. Employees and employers everywhere are thus becoming well informed about foreign labor practices, and conditions in many emerging nations are approaching world standards.

Multinationals, in particular, faced major changes following a European Council mandate that all of them must institute consultative works councils by September 1996. Many multinationals were unable to comply with this ruling, and they were forced to accept interim works councils appointed by government. Some companies, such as General Motors, adapted with fewer difficulties. GM welcomed the concept of works councils as an extension of its own effort to improve employee participation, but the automaker rejected the EU's process for establishing the councils. Specifically, European unions pressured the EU's regulatory commission to require multinationals to appoint full-time union representatives to company works councils, and GM rejected this provision as a move by unions to strengthen their own control over both companies and their employees. GM was not alone in its opposition; Volkswagen, Daimler-Benz, and other major companies also fought the initiative. Ultimately, however, union supporters won the contest.[64]

On other fronts, European unions are losing ground. The large industry unions in France and Germany have had to agree to major employment reductions, across-the-board wage concessions, and new rules for standard job classifications throughout Europe. These initiatives have reduced union membership and circumvented collective bargaining agreements, but they also have reduced wage and benefit disparities. Additional changes have emerged since the launching of the European Monetary Union (EMU), mandated by the Maastricht Treaty, which required member nations to establish economic parity in currency values by 2000. In response, those nations actively tried to reduce budget deficits and stabilize wage and price differentials. The unions claim, with rather strong justification, that they speak for a majority of European citizens when they warn that legislated interchangeability of money, jobs, and benefits will threaten individuality in any European state.[65]

Serious obstacles impede implementation of regulations stipulated by the **Social Charter** of the Maastricht Treaty. In Austria, for example, unions are closely identified with major political parties. Unlike Germany, where industry unions have traditionally controlled collective bargaining and industry-wide employment issues, in Austria the government has imposed state guidelines for job classifications, wage systems, and employee benefits. Therefore, while Germany and Austria both ratified the treaty, German unions oppose only particular aspects of EU policy, and the Austrian government (and by definition its associated unions) sees the entire Maastricht Treaty as an imposition on sovereign rights.[66]

Labor Participation in Management

The trend toward worker participation in management affects labor relations, because it implies formal programs of employee involvement in company decisions. German codetermination and similar works council systems throughout the European Union, described earlier as *industrial democracy* initiatives, reflect formal employee involvement efforts. Many of these are mandated by law, and the Social Charter now requires pervasive efforts in this direction by every EU member country. The EU emphasizes that the common purpose of these initiatives is to ensure a fundamental system throughout Europe that addresses employee rights and benefits.[67]

Shortly after World War II, social practices regarding commerce as business interests began to emerge throughout Europe. In particular, regulators and union leaders sought to enhance employee rights and union representation in relevant management decisions through formal legislation. This effort took different forms in each European country. As explained earlier, Sweden developed a highly centralized system of social welfare through direct government intervention. Germany initially developed informal employee works councils, but later social legislation established participation throughout the nation. The resulting codetermination system has become the prevalent model for comparison and is shown in Figure 11.7. Meanwhile, Italy instituted several forms of employee councils at various levels in the country's business organizations, all with union membership. The close alignment of unions with politics in Italy ensured that the country would take a short step to legitimize these practices through amendments to labor laws. Despite the United Kingdom's resistance to the EU Social Charter, the British have a long history of employee involvement in shop-floor committees and politically supported company works councils.[68]

In each instance, and among the remaining countries in Western Europe as well, *labor participation* has come to mean a formal approach to employee representation in decision-making bodies, despite variations in actual practices from one country to the next. For example, the German system encourages *industrial* democracy, and this term emphasizes the concentration among works council activities on workplace decisions. In contrast, the Austrian system of *social* democracy focuses works councils on efforts

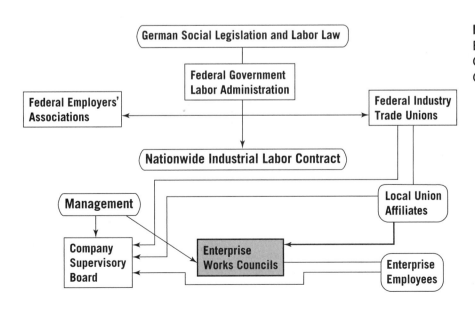

FIGURE 11.7
Employee Participation in Germany under Codetermination

to improve social legislation through national labor regulations. On the surface, works councils seem identical in Germany and Austria; but in practice, Germany's system deals with industrial activities while Austria's system extends throughout the society and interweaves its activities with national politics.[69]

Laws in North American countries have established no formal system of industrial democracy. U.S. and Canadian social and political systems strongly resist any legislation that would impede management prerogatives or "socialize" commercial interests.[70] Consequently, companies can independently pursue employee-involvement programs as individual choices. Nevertheless, employees in the United States and Canada are actively involved in workplace decisions, and a growing trend toward more active participation is quite noticeable. In both countries, participation is associated with specific organizational initiatives to create team-oriented work environments. Company programs include, for example, efforts to develop autonomous work teams, quality circles, group incentive programs, performance-based empowerment systems, and various forms of job enrichment. Specific provisions range from consultative decision-making processes to formal membership by employees or union representatives on company boards. However, participation is linked not to labor relations or union activities but to empowerment initiatives intended to improve labor productivity.

Japanese management techniques have become largely synonymous with participation and integrated group activities, yet industrial democracy has evolved in Japan through the country's cultural values, not as a result of political ideology. Similar situations have emerged in other Confucian societies, such as China, Taiwan, and South Korea. The importance of group harmony and consensus often leads to involvement by employees or union groups in organizational decisions. None of these societies approach the level of worker participation common in Japan, however. In fact, ethnic Chinese societies, South Korea, and most other Asian nations are steeped in paternalism, which encourages very hierarchical decision-making structures. These contrasting societies were described at length in earlier chapters on culture, and their different value systems were emphasized through research by Geert Hofstede.[71] Nevertheless, Chinese employees have gained a significant voice in company matters through their union and party affiliations. In Taiwan employers are extremely sensitive to employee rights; but in the Chinese manner, they avoid confrontation by maintaining elaborate committee systems to encourage employee consultations. In Korea, unions, nonunion employee groups, and students sometimes act with extreme militancy, thus bringing pressure on management decisions through public demonstrations; employers therefore tend to consult with employees in order to maintain harmony and avoid unpleasant public disputes.[72]

As more companies go global or become involved with European trade, the concepts of social or industrial democracy are likely to spread across borders and diffuse into integrated operations. Managers from U.S. and Canadian organizations must accept legal mandates for participation to continue their interests in the European Union, and any western manager involved in Japan must accommodate pervasive cultural values that require group decision-making. At the same time, Japanese managers working in Europe face rigorous legal requirements for implementing formal works councils and acquiescing to union representation unknown in the enterprise unions of their homeland. Indeed, Japanese managers in Europe have encountered significant difficulties in adjusting to industrial trade unions and to the aggressive tactics of union leaders.[73] No one should doubt, however, that international managers are assimilating practices of their foreign operations, nor that employee participation, both formal and informal, is becoming a common feature of business activity.

MANAGING INTERNATIONAL LABOR RELATIONS

A multinational corporation must manage its labor relations at two distinct levels. At the strategic level, it must manage globally to coordinate work activities throughout an integrated company. At the local level, subsidiary managers interact with employees, local unions, and political interests much as they would if their operating units were autonomous organizations. This bipolar approach to international labor relations is necessary because national labor laws, customs, and practices differ substantially, yet a global company must try to optimize productivity by allocating work efficiently among its subsidiary units. Local managers often know little about labor conditions in other operations, so they seldom understand how their subsidiaries compare with others in the organization. Meanwhile, strategists seldom understand local conditions well enough to make realistic long-distance decisions about labor issues such as wages, benefits, scheduling, staffing, and resolving disputes. As a result, decisions about resource allocations and the configuration of company-wide activities come from headquarters executives, who evaluate their subsidiaries largely on cost effectiveness and productivity criteria. Significant responsibility for human resource management and labor relations is delegated to subsidiary managers.

This scenario implies that relatively high labor costs in one country could persuade headquarters to shift operations to a lower-cost location. On the other hand, priorities for quality performance and workforce stability often prompt companies to locate in premium-wage areas despite high costs. Trade issues, such as customs duties and export-import quotas, also affect international labor decisions, as managers attempt to ensure an uninterrupted flow of components or supplies from local operations in a global configuration. Thus a subsidiary with few work stoppages and a record of good labor relations may play a more highly valued role in a global value chain than one with substantially lower wage levels that cannot achieve reliable performance due to labor problems. Nevertheless, choices between comparable environments, such as between European subsidiaries, may hinge on small variations in wages or labor costs. Although relocation based on such criteria can generate strong controversy, a country with substantial comparative advantages in labor costs can often attract significant investment, thus draining jobs from its neighbors.

Managing labor relations in the international environment requires substantial knowledge of worldwide labor market conditions and workplace practices. Local managers may focus primarily on domestic labor issues, but effective decisions require a keen appreciation of competitive forces in their industries. In order to bargain effectively, structure human resource programs, or respond to union demands, managers must understand their own limitations and the likely effects of concessions on their viability within integrated structures of activities. They cannot assume that local labor relations will compare favorably with those of foreign subsidiaries, and they often must compete for resources within their own organizations. On the other hand, they cannot ignore the local labor market or cultural characteristics of their subsidiary societies.

Expatriate managers working in foreign environments face an even greater challenge of maintaining effective labor relations in unfamiliar territory. These managers generally bring with them knowledge of practices in their home countries, but industrial relations vary so widely that they often must give up hopes of managing from home-country perspectives. Expatriate managers must therefore attempt to understand foreign labor relations systems while looking for ways to adapt to local expectations for workplace behavior.

REVIEW QUESTIONS

1. What factors prompt companies to focus human resource management at the subsidiary level?
2. Create a conceptual framework that contrasts how work gets done in North America, Europe, and Asia.
3. Identify the four principal themes for comparing labor relations. How does each theme influence the management of labor relations?
4. Define *grievance*, and differentiate between *mediation* and *arbitration* as methods for resolving grievances or disputes.
5. According to the four principal themes of labor relations, how does the United States compare with Canada? With the United Kingdom? With Germany? With Japan?
6. Describe the cultural environment for labor relations in Mexico. How do labor practices differ in Mexico compared to those in the United States or Canada?
7. What is the concept of codetermination, and how does it affect work relationships and management decisions in Germany? What roles do employees and unions play in Italian companies under similar regulations? How does worker participation differ in Europe, North America, and Japan?
8. Describe labor relations and social legislation in Sweden. How do these conditions differ from systems in the United States?
9. How does Japan's enterprise union structure compare with American or European systems? Explain how strike activity differs in Japan, as compared to strike activity in the United Kingdom, Germany, the United States, or Canada.
10. What three groups participate in Chinese industrial relations systems? What are their roles, and how do they influence foreign managers in Chinese joint ventures?
11. France presents an unusual model of labor relations. How are labor unions formed there, and what role does the government play in labor regulation?
12. What does *convergence* mean, and how is this trend affecting countries such as Mexico? Are U.S. and Canadian management practices converging toward those in other systems? Explain your viewpoint.

GLOSSARY OF KEY TERMS

Arbitration   A formal process of third-party intervention to adjudicate a dispute in which both parties agree to accept an arbitrator's ruling, which usually carries the force of law.

Codetermination   A right protected by formal legislation in Germany that establishes works councils and employee representation in company decision-making bodies that deal with workplace issues, creating a form of industrial democracy.

Collective bargaining   Formal negotiations and trade union representation on behalf of workers to establish a contractual agreement with an employer specifying the terms of employment.

Convergence   In labor relations, the trend toward standardization of work processes and employment practices that transcends national borders and cultural differences.

Craft union   A trade union that organizes workers within skilled trades or crafts, rather than representing company employees or industry interests.

Danwei A powerful, quasiofficial social group in Chinese communities with authority to administer social benefits such as housing, jobs, family births, and funerals within a local environment.

Enterprise union A company-wide union in Japan with members spanning all employee and management groups regardless of status or position.

Grievance A complaint against an employer brought by an individual or a union representative for redress of an alleged wrong, violation of terms of employment, or unfair labor practice.

Industry union A trade union, often national in scope, that represents all employees in a particular industry, such as Germany's IG Metall.

International Labor Organization (ILO) An international association, independent of trade unions or governments, that serves as a worldwide information and research agency on labor-related issues.

Labor relations A process through which management and workers determine job relationships.

Lockout A company tactic to prevent union employees from coming to work, often accompanied by hiring of nonunion "scab" labor and usually in retaliation to an employee protest or work stoppage.

Maquiladora A Mexican processing or assembly facility encouraged by a government program to promote international investment by allowing foreign companies to import materials for manufacture or assembly in Mexico without taxes or restrictions, with the stipulation that finished goods will be exported.

Mediation A method of third-party intervention to resolve disputes in which both parties agree to work with a neutral outsider.

National union A trade union that represents a broad range of skills and workers through the amalgamation of local unions, such as the United Auto Workers.

Social Charter A major section of the EU's Maastricht Treaty that seeks to establish unified standards of conduct for employment relations, a foundation for social benefits common to all EU member states, and a legal mandate for industrial democracy through works councils and regulation of employment practices by multinational companies engaged in European business.

Works council A worker-management decision-making group in a European company composed of elected employee representatives, management appointees, and often trade union officials or government officials.

EXERCISES

1. Find a recent article on a foreign company or labor dispute from a publication that carries international news, such as *Business Week*, *Fortune*, or the *Wall Street Journal*. Bring the article to class and be prepared to discuss how it reflects concepts presented in this chapter.

2. Many reports appear in the press and on the Internet of companies that periodically move production, close plants, or reconfigure their foreign operations. Research the labor-management tactics of one or more companies featured in these stories, and suggest priorities that might have influenced the organizational changes. How did social or cultural considerations affect the actions? Compensation or cost advantages? Quality issues? Be prepared to discuss these issues in light of this and previous chapters.

NEW ZEALAND: LABOR RELATIONS TURNED UPSIDE DOWN

New Zealand is one of the world's most interesting countries. Remote and somewhat isolated in the South Pacific, this diverse nation is populated with a rich mixture of early Scottish, Dutch, and English adventurers along with native islanders and a growing population of Chinese. Travelers know New Zealand for its expansive beauty—towering, snowcapped mountains and glaciers, a countryside dotted by grazing sheep, and cities that might have been transported intact from Europe. New Zealand also is a politically charged environment currently undergoing a transformation that is shaking the foundations of its industry.

For years, New Zealand has favored socialist ideology, even though its government is modeled on the British parliamentary system modified by adaptations of the German electoral system. Until recent years, the government owned or controlled virtually all key industries, utilities, transportation, airlines, and major services. Also, protectionist legislation literally banned foreign investment and severely restricted imports. New Zealanders had barricaded themselves for more than eight decades against global trade, yet they brought troops and logistics to allied forces in major wars, UN actions (such as the Korean war), and Vietnam. The government has played a major role in regional trade associations (ASEAN and SEATO) and in trade organizations with global membership (GATT and WTO). Far from a backward country, New Zealand has excellent universities, skilled workers, world-class manufacturing capabilities, an extremely active financial system and securities market, and sufficient infrastructure to be a force in world affairs. Indeed, New Zealand has displayed a dual personality, socialist at the core yet very closely aligned with the world's major free-market economies. Today, the duality is rapidly dissolving in favor of a competitive economy that welcomes trade and open foreign investment.

Telecom Corp. of New Zealand, the country's biggest telecommunications company, is now controlled by U.S. firms Verizon Communications, Inc.

(formerly Bell Atlantic) and Ameritech. The huge timber tracts that blanketed the rugged archipelago were purchased by the U.S. giant International Paper Company, which has listed shares on the New Zealand stock exchange. The national railroad is steered by a Wisconsin company that developed private freight systems and port-based shipping lines. Australians dominate international banking, and a steady stream of Japanese and Hong Kong companies have registered operations in Auckland. Agricultural production and marketing, telecommunications and postal services, oil and gas production, banking, air and rail transport, insurance, and steel and shipping—all of these industries once owned outright by the government are now almost entirely private, with international financing through global alliances.

The transformation from an entrenched socialist society to a competitive market system that approaches its polar opposite began in 1984 when the Labour Party won national elections while facing a national financial crisis. The crisis had been brewing for years as New Zealand struggled to remain apart from world commerce, but when Labour took the helm again, some feared deeper social reforms and even more intense isolation. People were already suffering from inflation, poor wages (at survival levels in many sectors, maintained through government subsidies), paltry consumer goods, and a declining standard of living. The country was at a standstill. For example, people waited months to have telephones installed, nearly as long to get car loans approved, and perhaps years to arrange home mortgages if they could afford to buy. New Zealanders wanted to work and to enjoy the fruits of their labors. Consequently, when the Labour government came to power, fears led to sell-offs in securities, the New Zealand dollar crumbled, and foreign exchange virtually evaporated. The obvious answer was to unleash the economy and privatize.

In 1985, the government decided to let the value of the New Zealand dollar float in relation to other world currencies. Once it was detached from its peg to the U.S. dollar, the New Zealand dollar rose in value and attracted new foreign investment. In 1986 the Commerce Act was passed, allowing unrestricted private enterprise and open foreign trade. In 1987 a new Labour Relations Act uncoupled the labor unions from government controls. Wages, terms of employment, benefits, incentives, and collective bargaining provisions were almost entirely deregulated. Also in 1987, the first major block of government-owned enterprises was put up for bid. The telecommunications and forestry industries were the first to go private, followed by Air New Zealand, port facilities, and other transportation resources. The postal service remained government owned, but it gained a new mandate as a competitive, profit-oriented organization. In 1988, the State Sector Act further relaxed regulations over labor relations, giving more autonomy to private enterprise and unions for workplace development, grievance procedures, and benefits such as retirement pensions that had previously been tax-funded government services. Perhaps the two most important legislative changes came in 1991 with the Employment Contracts Act, and in 1994, when the government eliminated all restrictions on foreign investments. The Employment Contracts Act ended 107 years of union domination, during which labor groups together with political interests controlled nearly all wage and benefit systems. After the act was passed, employers could bargain directly with employees rather than through unions. They also could pursue independent wage rates, bonus systems, and incentive and benefits plans.

A favorable environment for capital growth coupled with a highly attractive labor market enticed Bell Atlantic and Ameritech to bid successfully to buy Telecom of New Zealand. Japanese companies such as Sony, Toshiba, and NEC had been reluctant to consider New Zealand prior to the Employment Contracts Act, but they became heavily involved there through more than $5 billion of joint contracts and licensing operations. Indeed, within two years, more than 3,000 multinationals from the United States, Britain, and Japan alone accounted for half of the new economic growth in New Zealand. To be sure, New Zealanders bought the lion's share of privatized companies, but more than half of the country's stock market capitalization is foreign money.

For labor relations, change and global growth have brought mixed blessings. The postal service dropped from 12,000 rural workers to 6,800 as new efficiencies replaced a welfare state devoted to job security. The Communication and Energy Workers Union, once the central force in influencing wage and benefit practices, shrank from more than 46,000 members to less than 20,000, and the union has lost its bargaining authority to speak for a nonunion workforce in nearly a third of the country's enterprises. The Public Service Association, a civil-service union whose membership dropped to 69,000 from 80,000 several years back, no longer has the political status to mandate national wage scales or to protect redundant jobs. Overall, union membership has dropped since 1991.

Good things come at a price, though. Unemployment is disproportionately high among workers long accustomed to protected jobs and government-subsidized benefits. Few multinational companies have been pressured to provide extensive social services, such as comprehensive health benefits or retirement options that would match benefits under the old system. These companies have created largely nonunion environments, and workers are not organized well enough to speak with authority about work processes or terms of employment. Monetary rewards are higher than New Zealanders were accustomed to before the change, but they remain substantially below regional benchmarks for comparable skills. In addition, workers now find that they must deal with expatriate managers from the United States, Japan, and Europe, who bring with them foreign systems. In fact, some see the possibility of a backlash by workers, perhaps headed by labor leaders who may well gain support from the population at large.

Issues continue to surface reflecting the somewhat sensitive interface between New Zealanders and the managers of their foreign employers. European companies have introduced workplace democracy through employee works councils, and although it is a voluntary program, it is palatable to workers brought up in a socialist society. Still, the works council system disturbs those who only recently embraced a pervasive movement toward an unfettered free-market economy. New union models have begun to emerge in the fashion of craft shops and skilled-trade locals. These developments reflect British antecedents, but they prove discomforting to Canadian and U.S. interests. The Japanese actively support company-based employee/management unions, but they display fierce antagonism toward national unions and politically connected employee groups common in New Zealand. Individual wage and benefit structures are preferred by U.S. companies such as Sprint and Bell South. Both of these companies compete there against the privatized Telecom of New Zealand, which recently announced its integration with Australia's third largest telco, AAPT, Ltd. The combination of these two companies will include the creation of six business units in an effort to build market share in Australia.

President Clinton's recent signing of the American Competitiveness in the 21st Century Act stands to affect New Zealand's shortage of high-tech workers as well. The law increases U.S. opportunities to attract highly skilled workers to fill its IT vacancies by loosening immigration restrictions on these workers. According to industry watchers, this move by the United States may have direct and indirect effects on New Zealand. While New Zealanders may be attracted to the U.S. jobs that offer higher earnings, the U.S. law may also affect New Zealand's ability to attract workers to fill an increasing demand for high-tech jobs. But it is not just the United States that can affect New Zealand. Germany also has eased its immigration restrictions in order to attract similar types of workers. To compete for foreign workers and retain its high-tech workers, New Zealand may have to rethink its competitive strategies.

QUESTIONS

1. What cultural conditions will most likely concern U.S. or European employers who must manage labor relations in New Zealand?
2. What roles and contrasts would you envision for New Zealand's labor leaders, government offi-cials, and private employers as the country emerges from a centralized socialist system?
3. If you were an expatriate manager for a foreign firm in New Zealand, what labor relations and employment issues would you expect to face in your effort to maintain an effective work environment?

BIBLIOGRAPHY

Brauchli, Marcus W. "The Foreign Invasion: New Zealand Discovered the Benefits of Letting Global Companies Be a Part of Reform." *Asian Wall Street Journal*, 23 October 1995, p. S3.

Chan, An. "Kiwis Have Strange Bed-Fellows with Foreign Firms: Japanese Introduce the 'Company Song.'" *Straits Times*, 12 February 1997, p. 3.

James, Andrew. "Bill's Double Whammy on NZ Skills." *Independent Business Weekly*, 29 November 2000. [Retrieved 2 December 2000 from Dow Jones Interactive database.]

"New Zealand: Two-Faced." *The Economist*, 14 June 1997, 70-71.

"New Zealand: Telecom Combines Units to Integrate AAPT." Reuters English News Service, 26 November 2000. [Retrieved 2 December 2000 from Dow Jones Interactive database.]

"Privatization and Foreign Investment: Growth and Development Outlook." *AZN Annual Report*, AZN Bank, Ltd., December 1996, 1-4, 8.

Wood, Alan. "New Zealand Telecom Separates into Six Units." *Dow Jones Business News*, 27 November 2000. [Retrieved 2 December 2000 from Dow Jones Interactive database.]

CASE 11.2

EUROPE AND THE NEW ECONOMY

During its inception, Europe's monetary union created labor unrest, high unemployment strikes, and a politically charged environment in which unions played a major role. The euro, launched on 1 January 1999 and adopted by 11 of the 15 participating countries, created an opportunity to integrate capital markets across the continent and lower exchange risk. But the more recent focus seems to be on the New Economy, high-growth sectors, and labor relations in a rapidly changing European labor market.

The Neuer Markt, a Frankfurt-based exchange for growth stocks, has played a vital role in bringing the New Economy to Germany. Neuer Markt companies are typically young, high-growth companies in sectors such as telecommunications and technology. Unlike German codetermination, which uses work councils to make decisions and resolve issues between employees and management, Neuer Markt companies use open-door policies, employee share-ownership programs, staff meetings and training programs to involve employees in decision-making processes.

Given that the labor market in the high-growth sectors is tight, employees of the Neuer Markt companies do not seem to be concerned about work councils or formal structures. According to Ingo Kipker, author of a recent Deutsche Boerse study on Neuer Markt companies, only 16 percent of the companies in the Neuer Markt's NEMAX 50 Index have work councils. Instead, most of these companies use a different work culture to resolve issues such as regular staff meetings and the Internet to communicate, consult, and inform employees. Companies such as Micrologica AG, a maker of call-center software with 270 employees, and GFT Technologies AG, a 600-employee enterprise that provides an information-technology service, both use the Internet as a communication tool to provide information and consult with employees.

Unions, however, argue that this new working culture may not last. They suggest that the Neuer Markt companies are still in their infancy and growing, so the need for codetermination has not been realized. In addition, unions point out that while share-ownership programs do offer employees stock options or shares, they do not protect the employees from unfavorable working conditions or layoffs. But unions also are trying to find their way in this rapidly changing European labor market. As membership in European unions has decreased over the years and technology-related companies continue to emerge, unions have decided to pool their resources. In November 1999, five German unions set forth a plan to establish the world's largest union, Verdi, with 3.2 million members. The merger was planned for February 2001. Nevertheless, some advocates of codetermination wonder if the New Economy will bring about new variations of the Old Economy working culture model.

Recognizing that people are important to the vitality of an organization, the New Economy also has suggested management changes in the human resources field. In the New Economy, stock options are being used at some start-up companies to recruit, retain, and develop employees. In addition, human resource departments in these companies are becoming a focal point, moving away from the traditional function of administrative-type tasks toward measuring human capital and maximizing human potential. This move is creating opportunities for human resource managers who seek to participate on the strategic level in organizations. For example, some consulting firms that were losing employees to Internet start-up companies established in-house incubators to allow employees to explore their own business ideas.

While the Old Economy with its traditional structures and hierarchies may still exist for some European companies, it does not seem to be the direction of young companies in the high-growth sectors. What remains to be seen is whether some of these start-up companies will revert to codetermination or a variation of it.

QUESTIONS

1. Because work councils enjoy widespread acceptance in Europe, what major adjustments in labor relations will U.S. managers of high-growth companies located in Europe face as part of the New Economy?

2. If you were a strategic manager in a multinational corporation currently operating in Europe, how would the changes in labor relations brought on by the New Economy influence your decisions about human resource management?

BIBLIOGRAPHY

Richter, Konstantin. "Germany Rethinks Labor Relations in New Economy—Confident Employees Give Up Protection of Work Councils." *Wall Street Journal Europe*, 6 June 2000. [Retrieved 9 December 2000 from Dow Jones Interactive database.]

Richter, Konstantin. "Managing Change (A Special Report on Management in the New Economy): Renaissance for Human Resources." *Wall Street Journal Europe*, 30 May 2000. [Retrieved 10 December 2000 from Dow Jones Interactive database.]

Richter, Konstantin. "Managers and Managing: European Unions Quietly Combine in Unifying Trend—Merged Organizations Face Challenge of Changing Labor Market." *Wall Street Journal Europe*, 11 January 2000. [Retrieved 9 December 2000 from Dow Jones Interactive database.]

"What Holds the Euro Down Recently in Brussels." *Business Line (The Hindu)*, 9 December 2000. [Retrieved 10 December 2000 from Dow Jones Interactive database.]

CHAPTER 12

HUMAN RESOURCES: MANAGING EXPATRIATES

CHAPTER OBJECTIVES

Describe the expatriate system as a process or cycle of activities.

Define the term *adaptation* with reference to the emotional cycle an expatriate experiences overseas.

Show how career development programs are particularly important to expatriates.

Explain the major issues expatriates confront on repatriation.

Identify the major elements of compensation and benefits in an expatriate contract.

Detail the difficulties experienced by expatriate spouses during a foreign assignment.

Elizabeth McDougall never remotely imagined herself as owner of a recreation consulting firm in Hong Kong, but today she manages a fascinating company halfway around the world from the home of her birth. Her status as an entrepreneur in Hong Kong is not unusual, but she followed an interesting path to get there. Born in Canada, she attended a U.S. university under a tennis scholarship and graduated with a degree in management in 1984. Although she had dreams of a professional tennis career, she found herself working in a Toronto sporting goods store. Motivated to achieve greater things, however, McDougall set about interviewing for a business-related job while taking evening courses in an MBA program. Her efforts resulted in a modest entry-level job with the Toronto office of Namura Securities, one of Japan's largest investment houses, where, she explains, she "served coffee and clipped newspapers for a year." But she was a charming young woman who worked hard and took the opportunity to study Namura's portfolio of investments in Asia.

Recognizing her abilities, McDougall's boss, a Japanese expatriate, encouraged her to consider working toward an international assignment. Several months later, he was transferred to Korea, and he recruited McDougall to fill a research position in Namura's Seoul office. Although she did not understand at the time why the company would go to the expense of sending her to Korea, she soon discovered that Japanese companies often hire Canadians to work in offices where relationships between the Japanese and host-country nationals are strained. It seems that Koreans readily accept Canadians, which helps the Japanese companies avoid problems with Koreans' lingering resentments that can be traced to a bitter period of Japanese occupation earlier this century. McDougall's contract imposed several conditions, but these worked to her advantage. She had to learn both the Korean and Japanese languages and to continue her MBA studies.

After three years, McDougall had fulfilled all three requirements and earned her MBA from a Korean university. During that time, she was promoted from research to a fast-track sales position, where she became somewhat of a novelty. McDougall was the only western woman in sales, literate in three languages, and an expert on the emerging markets of Southeast Asia. Her academic achievements and an excellent sales record prompted Namura management to send her to Hong Kong, where the firm was expanding operations. In Hong Kong, McDougall became an institutional broker specializing in Indonesian and Malaysian mutual funds. Her income nearly tripled, enabling her to move into an expatriate apartment complex with membership in an exclusive tennis club. After living away from tennis for nearly six years, she found the club a welcome perquisite, and she renewed her interest in the game. By 1991, she had become almost as well known for her tennis abilities as for her professional activities, and she found herself teaching tennis to the spouses of other expatriates.

Unfortunately, McDougall was becoming disenchanted with Namura. She felt that the company promoted men more rapidly than women and preferred Japanese brokers for its important clients. So when a relatively young Japanese manager arrived from headquarters as her new boss, she felt "topped out." She soon quit Namura and returned to Toronto, where she was hired by a major insurance company to handle international investment services. However, after only four months at home, McDougall felt like a fish out of water. She explained:

> I was just one more person in a huge office complex, and no one cared if I had been down the street or on the moon. My language skills were of no use, and I could not relate my experiences to anyone. I was telling my boss, one day, about meeting the Sultan of Brunei, and he had no idea where Brunei was or that the sultan was one of the wealthiest men on earth. Maybe that was excusable, but

when he asked me how I had survived among "those little yellow people," I cringed. That was it. I was on a plane for Hong Kong.

Back in Hong Kong, McDougall opened a business as a tennis instructor and soon found herself with more clients than she could handle. By 1994, she had hired two locals as instructors and opened an upscale boutique selling tennis clothing. Since then, she has added a second location, and her staff includes 14 employees from six different nationalities. Her clients include many of Namura's expatriate wives, British and Chinese executives, and a large Korean contingent ranging from children to senior diplomats. McDougall reflected on her success and concluded that she had finally become acclimatized to the role of an international citizen. "How else can you describe it?" she asks. "I came to Asia as a Canadian with a U.S. degree, working for a Japanese firm, making deals with Koreans. Then I began trading in Hong Kong with Chinese clients—plus a few Brits, Aussies, and Yanks—selling Indonesian and Malaysian securities. Now I'm into tennis and fitness training with everyone under the sun. Canada is still home, and someday I'll go home, when the time is right."[1]

THE EXPATRIATE EXPERIENCE

The opening profile illustrates the events through which many individuals become involved in international management. A young securities broker can become an entrepreneur and a foreign resident managing local staff. Similarly, many expatriates either work for multinational companies or become world citizens in the course of their adventures. Also like Elizabeth McDougall, many expatriates find both rewards and disappointments in their international assignments due to the relationships they form and their own adaptations to foreign environments. This chapter is about these relationships and techniques for managing people who take the opportunity to venture overseas into unfamiliar societies and cultures.

A substantial part of international management activity concerns human resources, specifically managing expatriates in foreign assignments. In the broadest sense, an **expatriate** is anyone working in a foreign environment, from a common laborer to a senior diplomat. In business, expatriates are employees assigned by their companies to work in foreign operations. If these international employees are native to a home-country organization, they are called **parent-country nationals (PCNs)**. If they are foreign employees assigned to posts outside their native societies, they are referred to as **third-country nationals (TCNs)**. These terms serve more academic than practical needs, and people working abroad are unlikely to recognize the labels *PCN* or *TCN*. They simply describe themselves and any accompanying family members as *expats*.

Regardless of the labels that describe them or their nationalities, expatriates share a common bond, and they face similar challenges as foreigners. They may be Japanese citizens working in the United States, U.S. citizens working in China, or Swedes working in Saudi Arabia. They may also be Canadians working for a British company in India or Portuguese people working for a German enterprise in Brazil. All live as minorities in their foreign assignments. They work with people from unfamiliar cultures, often communicating in nonnative languages and living in societies with rules and laws that seem curious to them. Expatriates usually remain "outsiders" even after working in foreign environments for many years, and most remain citizens of their native lands with good intentions of going home in due course. They straddle two worlds at the same time, leading to both exhilarating and devastating experiences.

The parent company views an expatriate as a vital link between a foreign operation and headquarters. Consequently, if the expatriate finds excitement in his or her assignment, the company will likely enjoy success in its deployment of personnel abroad. On the other hand, if the expatriate finds the experience too much to endure, the assignment may fail, and both the expatriate and the company may suffer. Therefore, companies benefit from energetic efforts to prepare their expatriates for overseas assignments, yet few companies have established effective expatriate training programs. Ironically, even though globalization has increased the demand for capable international managers, companies have only begun to respond with well-planned human resource development initiatives.

This situation underscores the main theme of this chapter, which is to study the *expatriate experience* in the context of *international human resource management.* This opening section introduces the concepts of expatriation and international human resource management. These principles serve as foundations for later explorations of methods by which companies select employees, prepare them for overseas assignments, and eventually bring them back home.

The Expatriate System—A Process Model

Expatriates are important members of an international system of management. They are the field operatives who link global activities to parent-company interests, and they are often the vanguard, the adventurers, who break new ground for their organizations. A company hopes that expatriates provide an element of home-country control over foreign operations; they act as insiders in distant facilities, dealing with the externalities of international markets and foreign workforces. Expatriates view themselves as set apart from the normal system of management. They step out of their parent-company hierarchies, risking alienation from domestic activities. The expatriate system is distinct from a company's domestic system, creating a particular career cycle based on international assignments. Figure 12.1 illustrates this cycle as a *process* during which an employee experiences various stages of career changes; success for both the company and the employee depend on careful management of these developments.

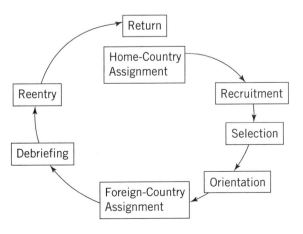

FIGURE 12.1
Expatriate International
Career Cycle

Source: Nancy J. Adler, *International Dimensions of Organizational Behavior,* 2nd ed. (Boston: PWS-Kent, 1991), reprinted by permission.

The career cycle is a useful model for international human resource management, because it emphasizes a sequence of activities that all companies must address when staffing foreign posts with expatriates.[2] The cycle begins with recruitment and selection, a sensitive responsibility because few employees bring foreign work experience to their assignments or understand what they may entail. Consequently, recruiters have difficulties evaluating how candidates will perform in the field. Further, candidates who may be interested in a foreign assignment may have family responsibilities that would present problems. For example, spouses' careers may be disrupted, and children may be uprooted from their schools and friends.

The second part of the cycle is concerned with preparing employees for assignments. This activity involves predeparture training and preparation for new cultural experiences. Once expatriates arrive at their foreign posts, they face new challenges of working and living abroad. During this phase, they experience significant changes in their lives and a different period of adaptation.

Assuming that they succeed in their assignments and return home, they must then readapt to their home environments. This final stage of repatriation can bring difficulties of its own, because expatriates cannot simply arrive home and resume old jobs. Their old jobs are probably filled, but few want their old jobs back. They prefer new challenges, because they return with stronger career profiles and international experience that they want to apply. Some do resume their old jobs, and others are promoted into positions that make good use of their international experience, but many expatriates find themselves isolated in demeaning jobs. Those who feel disenfranchised often move on to different companies looking for opportunities to leverage their international acumen. As discussed later, companies need effective repatriation programs to help homebound expatriates reestablish themselves. The expatriates' family members also must readjust to home environments, and those who have been away for several years may encounter difficulties. This cycle of activities represents a system of exciting but perplexing changes. Success or failure depends on how well a company supports its expatriates and on how well expatriates adapt to the circumstances they experience.

When Expatriates Fail

The expatriate experience brings a significant risk of failure. Perhaps the term *failure* overstates the potential problem, and in any case it is judged by relative criteria. It could mean returning home after achieving less than the company expected, which may limit future advancement opportunities. It could mean returning with a record of successfully fulfilled job expectations, but only after sidetracking the expatriate's own career or compromising that of a spouse.

Failure could also mean recall to the home office or premature termination of an assignment, with predictable consequences such as banishment to a career-ending position or even dismissal. This is the most common criterion by which researchers define expatriate failure.[3] Recalls are not uncommon, and they can happen for many reasons. Perhaps the expatriate simply could not handle the technical dimensions of the foreign assignment. Perhaps the individual's style of management did not match the expectations of foreign employees. Many recalls result when expatriates cannot adapt to living in their host countries, or when family members cannot make the necessary transitions. The reasons for premature recall can range from innocent breaches of protocol to irreconcilable family problems, but the true reasons for failure are often traced to inept company practices and poor preparation for expatriates themselves or for their accompanying family members.

Failure rates for American and Canadian expatriates have been estimated at between 25 and 40 percent over the past several decades. Although the rate of failure may be declining as more companies develop programs to prepare their expatriates, some estimates for managers working in developing countries run as high as 70 percent.[4] Studies of European companies show much lower failure rates, ranging between 3 percent for Swedish firms and 14 percent for French firms; on average, approximately 10 percent of European managers terminate assignments early, or they are recalled.[5] In recent studies of Japanese multinationals, failure rates were estimated to be as low as 5 percent.[6]

Although these research findings clearly illustrate that international companies must resolve significant problems in staffing their foreign operations, the studies have been inconclusive and often based on small samples. Such research is difficult because few companies are willing (or able) to document their failures, and expatriates who experienced difficulties are seldom available to explain their circumstances.[7] Nevertheless, the problem is real; Table 12.1 sheds some light on the nature of problems faced by expatriates.

The Role of Human Resource Management

Human resource management in a global company differs significantly from that in a domestic enterprise. It involves many of the fundamental activities for staffing, but an international company must undertake them with a strategic consciousness of its diverse human resource responsibilities. **International human resource management (IHRM)** may even emerge as a distinct profession because it requires a unique concern with a multinational configuration of subsidiary operations and integration of foreign and domestic human resources.[8] The IHRM professional fulfills interesting responsibilities, such as management planning for foreign operations, tracking the composition of workforces in different cultural settings, recruiting and selecting foreign nationals, setting compensation and benefits for employees in varied economic environments, cross-cultural training, and ensuring regulatory compliance under foreign labor laws.

IHRM is explicitly concerned with recruitment, selection, predeparture training, compensation, and repatriation of employees. This responsibility extends to every dimension of the expatriate experience, including assistance for the expatriate family prior to departure, logistics of foreign relocation, overseas support for the expatriate and his or her family (such as housing, schooling for dependents, access to medical facilities, and transportation), reentry processing to the home-based job and society, and career guidance. It also involves liaison duties with headquarters during the foreign assignment, an activity crucial to an expatriate's success.

These IHRM responsibilities suggest that managing the expatriate process is, by itself, a distinct concept. Unfortunately, no concise body of theory suggests effective methods for managing expatriates. A growing consensus among leading executives and management theorists indicates, however, that organizations must create comprehensive programs for sending personnel abroad, supporting their efforts while away, and repatriating them.[9] The expatriate career cycle provides a framework for developing these organizational programs. It implies three major elements of an IHRM program: (1) preassignment, or home-country, activities, (2) foreign assignment activities related to the work and social environment of the foreign post, and (3) reentry assignment activities related to the company position after returning home.[10] The American Society of Personnel Administration International (ASPAI) has suggested that international companies should implement comprehensive programs composed of three

TABLE 12.1

INCIDENCE OF INTERNATIONAL PERSONNEL PROBLEMS

Type of Problem	% Japanese Firms Reporting Problem* (n = 34)	% European Firms Reporting Problem (n = 23)	% U.S. Firms Reporting Problem (n = 24)
Expatriate Related			
Lack of home-country personnel who have sufficient international management skills	68 (60)	39	29
Lack of home-country personnel who want to work abroad	26 (27)	26	13
Expatriates experience reentry difficulties (e.g., career disruption) when returning to the home country	24 (20)	39	42
Average of expatriate-related problems	39 (36)	35	28
Local National Staff Related			
Difficulty in attracting high-caliber local nationals to work for the firm	44 (53)	26	21
High turnover of local employees	32 (20)	9	4
Friction and poor communication between home-country expatriates and local employees	32 (47)	9	13
Complaints by local employees that they are not able to advance in the company	21 (20)	4	8
Local legal challenges to the company's personnel policies	0 (0)	0	8
Average of local national staff-related problems	26 (28)	10	11

*Researchers draw a subsample of Japanese respondents to validate results of the primary sample with compared results in parentheses.

Source: Rochelle Kopp, "International Human Resource Policies and Practices in Japanese, European, and United States Multinationals," *Human Resource Management* 33, no. 4 (1994): 590. Copyright John Wiley & Sons, Inc., reprinted with permission.

components: preparation, adaptation, and repatriation.[11] These components, diagrammed in Figure 12.2, reflect the activities described earlier in the expatriate career cycle.[12]

Preparation

In broad terms, the preparation stage includes recruitment, selection, orientation, and training activities. Recruitment resembles internal searches to evaluate potential candidates, determine their qualifications, and develop a short list of those who seem best suited for a foreign assignment.

Selection activities start with interviewing candidates, and in the best programs selection also includes interviewing family members who would accompany the em-

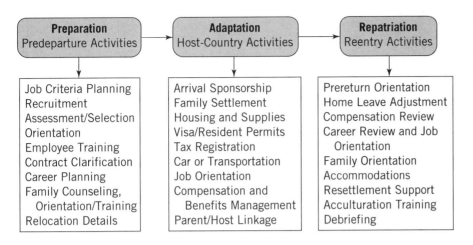

FIGURE 12.2
Components and Activities for a Comprehensive Expatriate Program

ployee overseas. Selection also includes skills testing (such as verifying language capabilities), psychological evaluations (such as assessing the candidate's motivation and adaptability), and professional evaluations (such as assessing individual characteristics or leadership skills).

Orientation activities prepare the expatriate for entering a foreign society. Relatively simple activities include obtaining entry visas and inoculations. This step also involves complicated activities such as preparing for the culture shock of living in a foreign country. *Orientation* implies a form of briefing, while *training* implies a systematic effort to prepare the expatriate for both technical and social requirements of the foreign assignment. Therefore, **predeparture training** can range from rather simple activities to thorough and extensive instruction; the choice depends on the nature of the assignment and the candidate's capabilities. For example, a company may send managers bound for Russia to intensive language courses, programs of study about the country's daily life and social customs, and instruction sessions in practical problems such as negotiation tactics. In contrast, a U.S. manager assigned to the United Kingdom will need no formal language instruction, but the societies are sufficiently different to warrant some cultural sensitivity training.

Adaptation

Activities associated with **adaptation** begin prior to leaving home, often as part of a formal training process. These preliminary training sessions are designed to ease the impact of moving to a new society by addressing topics such as acculturation, foreign currencies, housing, social customs, education, medical services, and foreign laws. Some organizations invite family members to participate in training programs, but the practice is not yet commonly known.[13] During the adaptation stage, IHRM focuses on efforts to successfully position the expatriate in the foreign post and then to provide ongoing support during the often difficult time of adjustment to the new environment. This long-term effort begins with predeparture planning, and it extends throughout the assignment period until the expatriate prepares to return home.

Specific IHRM activities include job-related responsibilities, such as administering compensation and benefits. In addition, home-office staff must assure the expatriate of access to technical support through channels such as e-mail accounts or other correspondence links. Expatriates need assistance in handling transition requirements, such as required registration with the foreign government for residence, travel, and tax purposes. More important, the home office must help the expatriate to enter an unfamiliar society without undue culture shock, perhaps including provisions for dependent schooling, housing, assistance with local transportation (e.g., providing a company car or assisting with car rental or purchase), and attending to other personal and family needs. As described in a later section, the adaptation stage can include complicated services such as providing security protections.

Repatriation

Near the end of a foreign assignment, an expatriate begins to focus attention on returning home. Some accept transfers to other foreign assignments, and they focus on those transitions. In either case, **repatriation** begins before the expatriate actually leaves the existing assignment. Initial IHRM activities are concerned with preparing the expatriate for reentry, including arrangements for the physical logistics of relocation, travel, paying local income taxes, and "clearing the country." Expatriates often express interest in their next assignments or home jobs, and IHRM staff must provide a conduit of information related to job responsibilities and new role expectations. Expatriates returning home with families encounter additional considerations with transportation, housing, and dependent schooling. IHRM activities are therefore concerned with minimizing the pain associated with readjustment. Many of the same adaptive activities associated with leaving on a foreign assignment are duplicated for the homecoming. In addition, employees who return from long or difficult foreign assignments may face substantial psychological adjustment problems.

Organizational Initiatives in Expatriate Management

Although many companies express concern with the difficulties of managing their expatriates, relatively few have implemented programs to address these problems. Studies of leading U.S. and Canadian multinational corporations have found that barely half offered any form of preassignment orientation for expatriate managers, and orientation often excluded in-depth predeparture training. Also, only 31 percent had established human resource management policies to assist in repatriation. Of those multinationals that reported operating formal assistance programs, less than one-third included expatriate family members or addressed domestic issues.[14] Research on the few firms that offered formal predeparture training (beyond mere orientation processes) revealed that fewer than 25 percent included cross-cultural considerations; instead, most focused primarily on technical job-related issues.[15] Subsequent studies have investigated the content of training programs, finding that fewer than 40 percent of the companies addressed problems of adaptation to foreign societies.[16]

In contrast to these findings, notable companies such as General Electric, Motorola, and Procter & Gamble have for years pursued complete programs of selection, training, acculturation, foreign entry, and location assistance. These leaders provide continuous support for expatriates during foreign assignments, preparation and training for reentry, and systematic procedures for repatriation.[17] Japanese companies such as NEC, Mitsui, and Sony operate similar comprehensive systems, including intensive acculturation training for staff, spouses, and children prior to departure. However, Japanese companies are generally known for their homogeneity, and they go to great lengths to maintain ethnocentric control over their foreign interests.[18] Consequently, Japanese expatriates face greater problems of foreign acculturation than expatriates from other cultures, and they experience more difficulty assimilating into host-country societies. In contrast, American and European expatriates often feel more at ease in unfamiliar cultures.[19]

European companies have longer and richer histories of expatriate development than North American or Asian enterprises, many dating from early colonial expansion. However, unlike American or Japanese expatriates, managers of European firms have traditionally undergone conditioning to prepare them for overseas careers rather than short-term assignments. Companies such as Unilever, British Petroleum, Philips NV, and Bayer AG select and train managers specifically for assignments to foreign posts with indeterminate contracts. These expatriates often become "global citizens" with permanent international careers.[20] A somewhat faddish term has emerged to describe these individuals—**transpatriates,** which refers to global managers whose careers transcend national borders and are no longer anchored to home-country positions.[21]

The concept of a global career has not yet reached the mainstream of international management research. It is just as elusive as an example of a *truly* global company, yet career development issues are becoming critical elements of the globalization process. With that in mind, the next section of the chapter returns to the career cycle to look more closely at the expatriation process.

RECRUITMENT AND SELECTION

Companies cannot rely on traditional models of recruitment and selection to fill foreign posts. Foreign management positions are not structured in organizational hierarchies where candidates wait in the wings for opportunities to open. Unlike a domestic model of organization, a global company lacks any predictable channels of career promotion. In the traditional organizational structure, most employees—managers and others—form mental outlines of their potential career paths. Each one develops a feeling of a sequence of steps through which to ascend within the company, and all consciously groom themselves for these opportunities. Foreign assignments are seldom part of this mind-set, and relatively few employees prepare themselves for these opportunities. Therefore, companies seldom can choose among pools of eager candidates ready for assignments overseas. The selection process must begin with the basics of searching for those with the potential and the motivation to work abroad.

Recruitment at Home and Abroad

The model shown in Figure 12.3 presents recruitment as the primary activity of the selection process.[22] Recruiters must always answer a fundamental question about whether a position can be filled by a **host-country national (HCN)** rather than an expatriate. Experienced managers always ask: "Can we go local on this?" If they can, the firm can gain obvious benefits from the local experience of a host-country manager who does not have to adapt to a foreign environment. A North American company recruiting for a European office (or vice versa) can find good people with only marginally greater difficulty than it experiences in filling domestic positions. There may be additional language requirements and organizational idiosyncrasies to adjust to, but locally hired managers will not face severe social hardships or major cultural dilemmas. Unless the host country's culture differs considerably from that of the parent company, few major obstacles will prevent local hiring. However, when cultural differences are pronounced, a firm may experience serious difficulties trying to hire locally. In less-developed countries, it may not find any local managers with requisite skills and experience.

FIGURE 12.3
Expatriate Selection Process

Source: Adapted from Rosalie L. Tung, "Selection and Training of Personnel for Overseas Assignments," *Columbia Journal of World Business* 16, no. 1 (1981): 68–78.

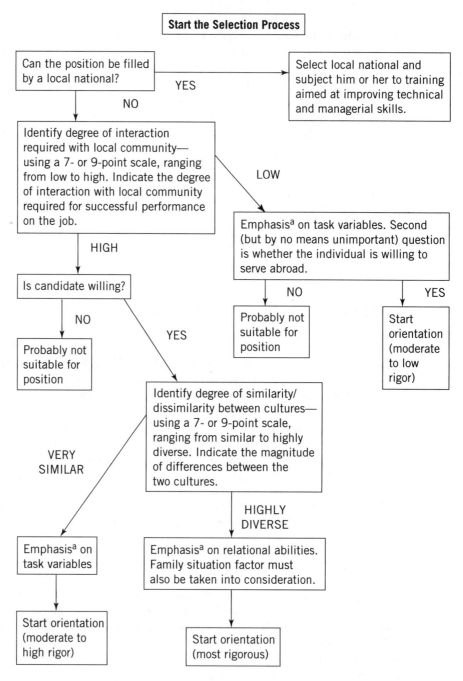

^a*Emphasis* does not mean ignoring the other factors. It only means that it should be the dominant factor.

The most important limitation on recruiting locally is the company's perceived need to maintain central control over foreign operations. Hiring a foreign national prompts questions of loyalty, and such a decision sometimes risks compromising proprietary technology or company information. Placing a homegrown expatriate in the foreign post often seems like the better choice to ensure accountability and control.

This attitude reflects a clear ethnocentric bias, yet it is common for many European companies that emerged from a colonial era when nearly all foreign activities operated under close parent-company management.[23]

U.S. multinationals exhibit a less pronounced preference for parent-company control, but Japanese companies very seldom consider recruiting foreign managers. They retain extremely tight control of culturally dependent management systems through predominantly home-country staffing assignments.[24] Nevertheless, efforts to fill foreign operations with expatriates, regardless of nationality, encounter obvious limitations. The parent company may retain control, but it also faces considerable expense to maintain expatriates working in unfamiliar cultures. More important, the expatriates will always be aliens within their foreign environments; to the local employees, an expatriate is a visitor sent on behalf of the parent organization. Host-country nationals experience similar problems of not being fully accepted within the parent organizations. Both groups come up against cultural boundaries, however slim, and one party or the other often feels reservations about a manager's loyalties.[25]

The choice between recruiting locally or dispatching an expatriate is determined by a combination of factors specific to each situation. The primary concern is a company's perceived need to control information, technology, or foreign activities. Also, the stage of development of the foreign country and its political and social stability affect the decision. Less-developed countries with high political risk profiles or significant social unrest often call for parent-company managers in key positions to ensure accountability. In societies sensitive to religious or ethnic considerations, the potential for relational problems with local employees encourages local recruitment. Where language barriers are extreme, such as in Russia, the parent company often finds few qualified candidates and must therefore recruit locally or at least provide an expatriate executive with capable host-country support.

Many countries require by law that foreign-owned or joint-venture enterprises must establish locals as senior directors or codirectors. Some insist that foreign companies operating within their borders must maintain prescribed percentages of host-country personnel in all technical and managerial positions.[26] For example, until 1992 when China relaxed provisions of its Private Company Act, any foreign-invested enterprise had to assign a Chinese national at the executive rank of managing director, even if an expatriate wielded equal authority. Today, a foreign manager can hold the position, but only in a majority-owned joint venture and only with the approval of a convening government board.[27]

Foreign management often evolves through the globalization process rather than through a deliberate choice between parent- or host-country candidates. For example, joint ventures or comanufacturing contracts usually specify block reassignments of staff and employees from the host-country partner. Often the agreement itself establishes systems for management control as a local directorate or another shared system of governance. Also, when a multinational acquires a foreign interest, it usually considers the purchase as an ongoing operation, maintaining current management and staff in place. Most newly acquired organizations gain expatriates in key positions, but local management groups typically remain intact. In contrast, a *build-operate-transfer (BOT)* organization (described in Chapter 6) begins under an expatriate system fulfilling a contract to launch a project and operate it for a period of time. At a predetermined date, the project is transferred to local management control. In the interim, host-country managers join the organization accompanied by a commensurate reduction in expatriates, leading to a smooth transition.

Expatriates can also be drawn from other foreign operations. These *third-country nationals (TCNs)*, as mentioned earlier, are parent-company employees of nationalities other than the home or host country. Globally integrated organizations often favor this option, because foreign managers typically bring substantial regional experience to their posts. They also tend to adapt more easily than a manager sent from the home office to the new environment. For example, when Procter & Gamble (P&G) established a manufacturing joint venture in southern China in 1988, an Australian was named as senior managing director. This individual had worked for P&G in his home country, Japan, and Hong Kong, so he knew the region and was well suited to manage in China. Other key executives included a director of marketing who was originally from Britain but had worked in Asia for 16 years, a Canadian finance manager, and an American accounting executive transferred from a South American position. In addition, P&G brought in Americans on short-term assignments to initiate product development and to oversee plant engineering. The management configuration that evolved at P&G in China included managers from five countries, with a senior Chinese executive as codirector.[28]

Caterpillar Corporation has followed a slightly different approach. Its ethnocentric policy of expatriate control in most key positions prevailed until the early 1980s. As the company went through a decade of difficult reorganization, however, Caterpillar began to move toward a global approach with integrative staffing patterns. By the 1990s, most foreign subsidiaries were locally managed, and executives had become very mobile.[29] For a specific example, Caterpillar's senior executive for quality assurance, Sam Black, works at the firm's home base in Illinois. He is a native-born Scotsman who worked in several European divisions early in his career, followed by a post as a senior manager for the company's French manufacturing subsidiary. He has traveled extensively for the company, working in Japan and Southeast Asia, and helped Asian teams restructure foreign offices in Hong Kong and Singapore. When Caterpillar began to adopt a global reconfiguration, Black was promoted into the American headquarters group.[30]

Staffing a major foreign subsidiary often involves formation of a cadre of managers from host-country, parent-company, and third-country operations. For each specific position, however, the choice of personnel rests on a selection assessment. As the model in Figure 12.3 illustrates, companies often attempt to use rating scales to quantify these assessments, but many of the criteria reflect subjective judgments and measurements. Point systems can be developed to rate technical attributes and candidate qualifications, but relational skills, ethnicity considerations, and cultural adaptability depend on human judgment. Most companies do not rely on predictive assessment models. More often, they determine job attributes and evaluate candidates according to insights by experienced executives.[31]

Qualifications for Selection

Formal job descriptions seldom adequately explain the full range of requirements for candidates, but they do provide the primary criteria for technical competence and preferred experience. As in most professional positions, *technical competence* is the cornerstone qualification, and it can usually be measured objectively through familiar methods of performance reviews and certifications. However, domestic performance may have no bearing on how a person will perform overseas. Unfortunately, too many companies rely on this element of evaluation while paying too little attention to broader *relational* issues. Studies of expatriates in Europe, Asia, and the United States have shown that technical competence is a poor predictor for success in an international assignment. It remains important, but the critical consideration is an individual's ability to *adapt*.[32] This point is emphasized in Table 12.2, which summarizes the 10 most prominent criteria for selection.

TABLE 12.2

RANK ORDER OF EXPATRIATE SELECTION CRITERIA

1. Ability of an expatriate candidate to adapt to a foreign culture
2. Ability of a candidate's spouse and family members to adapt to a foreign culture
3. Technical capabilities and competence for a foreign assignment
4. Human relations skills (relational characteristics and abilities)
5. Motivation and desire to work in a foreign environment
6. Understanding of host-country culture and society
7. Extent of relevant overseas experience
8. Academic qualifications and job-related credentials
9. Language skills and literacy applicable in the host country
10. Understanding of the home-country culture and society

Sources: Adapted from Raymond J. Stone, "Expatriate Selection and Failure," *Human Resource Planning* 14 no. 1 (1991): 10. Also see Meg G. Birdseye and John S. Hill, "Individual, Organization/Work and Environmental Influences on Expatriate Turnover Tendencies: An Empirical Study," *Journal of International Business Studies* 26, no. 4 (1995).

Adaptability and Personal Characteristics

Descriptions of adaptability often stress terms such as *sensitivity to different cultures* and *ability to work in an international environment*. These expressions are difficult to evaluate, and their definitions vary by company for specific positions independent of other considerations.[33] Although an individual's potential for adaptability can be assessed through personality and psychological tests, few companies use these types of evaluations, because they are culture-bound techniques. Specifically, most assessment instruments have been developed in the United States or Western Europe, and they reflect American or European values. These do not provide the insight required to judge a candidate's ability to adjust to a position in Russia, Japan, Argentina, or some more exotic place. Also, none of the existing psychological or personality assessment models have been found to provide consistent results for employees in a multinational organization with diversified international interests.[34] Therefore, companies rely heavily on a consensus of opinions by a candidate's superiors and members of a selection committee that subjectively rates the individual on adaptability. The company wants to know whether a candidate will be responsive to laws, work behavior, social protocols, ethnic factors, ideological differences, and perhaps conflicting religious doctrines in a specific foreign assignment.

Adaptability also includes a candidate's potential resilience to culture shock. Will the individual recoil from a wave of unfamiliar circumstances and become overly stressed by daily anxieties, or will the person adjust and work in an effective way? Will the shock of entering a new culture be a positive learning experience or a negative one? Obviously, the answers to both questions should indicate that the potential expatriate would be flexible enough to adjust to culture shock, exhibit sufficient self-control to roll with the daily punches, and find positive rewards in the assignment. Research has shown, however, that individuals who are immune to culture shock—those who seem totally resilient to cultural differences—are unlikely to be good candidates for expatriate posts. In practice, they often lack capabilities of responding to local problems and host-country expectations, so they fail to understand local cultures.[35] In contrast, highly adaptable people—those who can rapidly assimilate into new environments—can be equally poor candidates. These individuals may too easily "go native," thus becoming overly responsive to local needs and subsequently disengaging themselves from their parent organizations. Selecting a candidate with the appropriate balance of adaptability is an important first step toward staffing the overseas position. Managers must be selected who are least likely to flounder from culture shock, as well as least likely to "go native" and lose their perspective.

Relational Skills

An individual's ability to appreciate a foreign culture and to communicate and behave appropriately results from **relational skills.** As shown in Table 12.2, adaptability and skill at human relations are distinct criteria. The human relations skills of expatriate managers determine their *relational attributes* for effective leadership in a culturally diverse work environment. (The topic of leadership is addressed more thoroughly in Chapter 14.) These skills also include the abilities to interact with constituents outside the organization such as host-country government officials, to work with local customers, and to cooperate with managers of other foreign activities within a company's globally integrated network.

Relational skills also depend on an individual's understanding of both a host-country culture and the firm's home-country culture. Some firms try to measure these characteristics through value-rating tests or anthropologically based evaluations, but most base their judgments on subjective interviews. Understanding both home-country and host-country cultures is important because an expatriate manager must distinguish how his or her values differ from those of foreign constituent groups. This capability not only reduces the risk of making naive mistakes in human relations but also eases the anxiety associated with culture shock.

Spouse and Family Adaptability

Academic literature uses the gender-inclusive term *spouse*, but in reality companies are concerned with the adaptability of wives. In fact, an overwhelming majority of married expatriate employees are men, and the few women in overseas assignments are relatively young and unmarried.[36] Wives accompany husbands who go abroad, but there are few husbands who follow their wives overseas. This tendency is particularly important, because wives seldom contribute to company decisions regarding their husbands' appointments, and it is equally rare for a company to provide predeparture training for wives. Husbands at least benefit through company orientation initiatives, however slim, but wives are often ignored.

This oversight is not a trivial issue. Many wives have careers of their own, and they often fulfill pressing family and social responsibilities in raising children. When a husband announces that he is being assigned to a foreign country, his wife may suddenly face the prospect of uprooting her career, leaving friends, breaking off social obligations, and if she has children, taking responsibility for transferring school records and planning the family move. Husbands may share in these responsibilities, but wives do not benefit from the same preparation and support that their husbands receive. Unfortunately, few companies provide wives with support or resources for these relocation responsibilities.[37]

Effective selection and training programs do indeed include family members in decisions about foreign assignments and relocation, although research shows that barely 5 percent of multinationals provide support and orientation training for wives. Companies such as Monsanto, GE, AT&T, Eli Lilly & Co., ABB, and Intel, for example, offer comprehensive family programs.[38] They include wives and children in meetings that govern foreign assignments, and selection programs evaluate them together with their husbands, include them in committee interviews, and provide orientation and training specifically designed to address family issues. These companies honor judgments about whether a candidate's assignment would serve the best interests of the family as a way to reduce the risk of failure. The inability of wives to adapt to host-country culture is the primary reason cited for early return and assignment failure.[39] Therefore, selecting the appropriate candidate requires that a firm select the appropriate family. A responsible approach to selection benefits not only the company; it is important to both husbands and wives in their career aspirations, and to the development of their children.

Matching Candidates to Host-Country Needs

Job descriptions and assessment instruments do not necessarily reflect practical host-country requirements. The potential for mismatch is particularly important in filling a new post or one that involves expansion of foreign activities in a host country where only firsthand experience can support sensible staffing decisions. Candidates seldom know much about these positions when they apply, and they respond to offers in the context of their limited domestic experience. Often they base expatriate career aspirations on romantic suppositions about exotic places or misguided apprehensions about others. Firms may try to resolve these dilemmas by involving experienced foreign managers in the selection process.

Some firms implement these programs by convening foreign advisory boards responsible for developing job criteria and requisite characteristics for successful candidates. A candidate may visit the host country and meet with an advisory committee there. He or she might also work on a brief project in that location to give the employee and the company a feeling for the potential fit of the larger assignment. Site visits and collaborative interactions between company executives and host-country representatives for job design and assessment are common practices at leading companies.

For example, as a matter of policy, Xerox and Philip Morris both require site visits and joint evaluations by foreign advisory committees for all senior managers and employees on long-term assignments. AlliedSignal Corporation works through a system of regional human resource coordinators to write job descriptions and coordinate selection criteria at the host-country level. Ford relies on international human resource teams that include local and regional managers to conduct personnel assessments for management and technical staff vacancies.[40] European companies such as British Petroleum, ABB, Unilever, Volkswagen, and Bayer AG operate regional assessment centers staffed by selection committees with plant-level representatives who evaluate all international appointments.[41] These companies invest substantial resources in the selection process—a far better use of the funds than wasting them in cleaning up after failed assignments.

TRAINING AND ORIENTATION FOR FOREIGN ASSIGNMENTS

Despite the high rate of expatriate failures and evidence of persistent problems in foreign assignments, few companies provide adequate training to prepare their employees for international positions. Statistics on predeparture training described earlier for North American and European firms might be summarized as a "story of halves." Less than half of the multinationals studied offer any form of training; only about half offer more than one week of general orientation; of that small proportion, less than half include family members. The numbers fall even lower for companies that offer cross-cultural development programs. As a result, perhaps no more than 14 percent of western multinationals maintain acculturation training programs, and only 5 percent provide predeparture support for family members.[42]

Most training focuses on technical job dimensions for the selected employee, along with introductory language skills when required. The short-course approach (one or two weeks in duration) typically includes an environmental briefing weighted toward job-related issues. This pattern evolved during the 1970s and has persisted with only marginal improvements. The primary reasons why companies do not invest more in expatriate training programs (summarized in Table 12.3) reveal several themes that may be difficult to overcome. First, top management is not convinced that training works, or that it is cost effective. Second, employees who should be motivated by the training are dissatisfied with the programs. Third, training sessions are often squeezed into predeparture schedules at a time when expatriates and their families are already extremely busy preparing to move. Fourth, companies expect to employ rising numbers of host-country managers, thus reducing their needs for programs to train expatriates.[43]

These arguments are difficult to support. Although top management may not be convinced of the cost-effectiveness of training, estimated costs associated with failures range between $50,000 and $150,000 per incident, not including losses directly related to the performance problems created by the expatriate's early return.[44] Researchers have not studied the subject sufficiently to conclusively determine that training would reduce failure rates, yet if results achieved by Japanese companies represent valid comparisons, then training (particularly in-depth, cross-cultural training) is an extremely effective expenditure. Several major studies of Japanese companies show that approximately 80 percent operate formal predeparture development programs that involve substantial acculturation training lasting for several months. Japanese expatriates experience extremely low failure rates, perhaps no more than 5 percent.[45]

Employee dissatisfaction may indeed be a valid criticism if poorly planned training programs squeeze instruction into last-minute schedules. A seemingly obvious

TABLE 12.3

PRIMARY REASONS COMPANIES DO NOT INVEST IN EXPATRIATE TRAINING PROGRAMS

- Top management perceives no need for expatriate training.
- Cross-cultural training programs have not demonstrated effectiveness, and no evidence indicates substantial benefits to trainees or companies.
- Training is not a cost-effective investment; temporary short-term assignments (those lasting one to three years) do not warrant training expenditures.
- Selection leaves too little time before relocation to new assignments to allow in-depth, cross-cultural training to expatriates.
- Companies prefer to hire locally, creating a trend toward assigning fewer expatriates overseas and weakening the need for expensive training programs.
- Employees feel dissatisfied with training programs and see little value in lengthy or intensive sessions beyond orientation programs.

Source: Adapted from Mark E. Mendenhall, Edward Dunbar, and Gary R. Oddou, "Expatriate Selection, Training, and Career-Pathing: A Review and Critique," *Human Resource Management* 26, no. 3 (1987): 331–345. Copyright John Wiley & Sons, Inc.

answer suggests that trainers plan more effective and timely programs that can be both meaningful to employees and sensible for companies.[46]

If companies could rely on local managers rather than expatriates, then training would be a moot point. Indeed, increasing numbers of companies are hiring host-country managers, and they are also expanding their reliance on third-country transfers, but demand for qualified expatriates has increased at an even greater pace with accelerated globalization.[47] International staffing patterns actually place a growing burden on human resource programs to train personnel. Further, host-country nationals need training themselves to integrate company interests; although such a program is separate from expatriate training, expenditures of this kind are gaining importance as companies strive to integrate skills, allowing them to transfer workers among their international divisions. Training third-country managers is, by definition, a form of expatriate development, and expanding numbers of foreign managers are joining domestic organizations, substantially increasing the need for effective cross-cultural training.[48]

Effective Predeparture Training

Evidence for a less-than-optimistic training outlook clearly implies a great deal of room for improvement. First, top management must support training and orchestrate human resource programs with strategic planning activities, so that appropriate cross-cultural content is addressed in a timely fashion. Every company encounters unique training requirements, so no single comprehensive model can meet every set of needs. Nevertheless a general approach can be followed, with varying emphasis on topical coverage. Figure 12.4 illustrates a three-tiered model of organizational training that is gaining credibility.[49]

A comparison of the approaches to training in Figure 12.4 with the earlier model of selection in Figure 12.3 reveals a pattern. At one extreme, training can be abbreviated to little more than short-term orientation for someone entering a foreign culture similar to the home-country society. At the other extreme, training may require several months of cultural immersion when a candidate is slated for a long-term assignment in a location where life sharply contrasts with the home culture. Between the extremes, companies can adapt to their particular needs, varying rigor between a cursory orientation and a comprehensive immersion program.

One determining factor will be language differences. A U.S. native scheduled for an assignment to London, for example, would need little language training; but an assignment in China would present major communication obstacles. Often English is the preferred language of commerce, but European languages are common in many parts of South America, Africa, and Southeast Asia. Assignments to these regions may require intermediate language training. Business negotiations also require acculturation to host-country social customs, legal systems, and cultural patterns of behavior. In these instances, an *affective training approach* may be most promising, with elements such as simulation exercises, role playing, case work, and assimilation exercises including brief site visits or work-related experiences under foreign mentors.

A brief assignment probably does not warrant rigorous training; language capabilities and cultural assimilation will not be expected, and the expatriate is unlikely to reside in the country long enough to suffer extreme stress. However, a person on a longer assignment, perhaps one lasting several years, may benefit substantially from an extensive program of cultural immersion. This is particularly true if family members will accompany the expatriate. One technique used by Japanese companies is to place candidates and their families with foreign host families for several weeks. The

FIGURE 12.4
Training Approaches
Related to Length of
Assignment and Degree
of Integration

Source: Adapted from Mark E.
Mendenhall, Edward Dunbar, and
Gary R. Oddou, "Expatriate
Selection, Training, and Career-
Pathing: A Review and Critique,"
Human Resource Management 26,
no. 3 (1987): 331–345. Copyright
John Wiley & Sons, Inc., used
with permission.

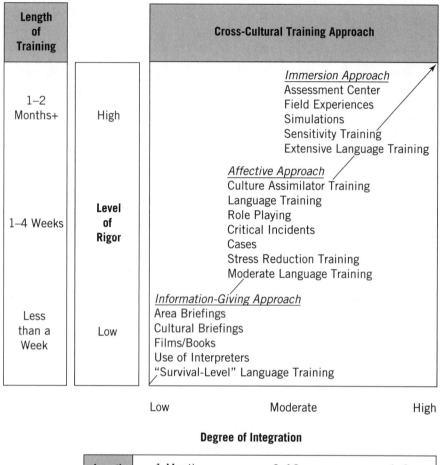

host families provide living experiences or "social internships" that force the expatriate families to test their limits before committing to the new assignments.

Many other considerations govern specific features of training programs, including technical and legal aspects of working overseas, labor relations, management protocols, and relations with foreign governments. Cross-cultural training might address perceptual differences in sex roles, health and nutrition, standards for ethical conduct, dependent education, and security. The most important consideration is the *degree of integration* required in the host-country culture. A long-term assignment often requires substantial integration, since a family must live on local terms and become resident in the community. In contrast, a short-term assignment may allow an individual to live in an expatriate enclave and remain culturally insulated. Training is therefore tempered to expectations for cultural integration as well as to specific assignments.

Career Development

Individual career development in the United States has focused on fast-track domestic careers; some have always recognized international aspirations, but this calling has influenced fewer people in fewer organizations in the United States than elsewhere. Over time, however, international career development in U.S. firms has moved to the forefront of successful management development programs. IBM, GM, Procter & Gamble, General Electric, and Westinghouse, among others, have implemented internal career-tracking programs as part of their overall management development systems. Many of these programs have existed since the 1940s. American oil companies and mineral extraction conglomerates such as Exxon and Alcoa established many early international subsidiaries, and assignments to them required international career training before World War II.[50] U.S. banking interests were among the country's first companies to establish Asian subsidiaries. Citibank (now part of Citigroup), for example, was the first foreign financial institution to establish a subsidiary in China when it opened a currency trading house in Shanghai in 1922.[51] IBM is among the leading advocates of international career development, perhaps due to its historic policy of maintaining financial and managerial control of foreign interests through wholly owned subsidiaries.[52]

Effective career-development programs will groom managers for international positions over periods of years, starting with their initial, entry-level positions. Before sending an employee overseas, a thoughtful company establishes a **succession plan** with the candidate in order to map out company and employee expectations for a foreign assignment and eventual repatriation to the parent organization.[53] If an employee aspires to hold multiple foreign posts or international transfers, the succession plan identifies these options. This kind of succession planning is a method of providing career continuity within the organization. In the process, it helps to bridge the difficult gaps of leaving home, working at a distance from the parent company, and returning to a domestic position.

Succession planning is a convenient term for the larger process of career development planning, but with a particular emphasis on the expatriate career cycle. Most companies apply their own program titles to this planning activity. For example, IBM creates a *career profile* for each new employee at hiring, and GE's process called *global brains* seeks to establish a register of high-potential recruits.[54] Both companies, and most other leading companies, require annual reviews of managerial career-planning documents, and many devote periods of one week or more each year to management development training that incorporates career-tracking elements. IBM and GE infuse training for international assessments into the annual review processes for those involved in (or candidates for) foreign assignments.

An organization that lacks this depth should still establish a succession plan prior to an expatriate's departure. The plan should consist of the terms and conditions of the assignment, the employee's position before leaving and during the assignment, job skills and expectations, growth potential in the foreign assignment, and progress checkpoints toward repatriation or further assignment. The plan should also identify the most likely position to which the expatriate will return. This designation does not promise a promotion—companies can seldom issue such guarantees—but it constitutes a *psychological contract* of mutual commitments by the company and the expatriate to pursue sustainable performance and jointly determined objectives.[55]

A succession plan helps to smooth expatriate transitions, and it provides a benchmark for periodic reviews during the foreign assignment. The plan is not merely written and filed away; it continues to function as a liaison tool between the expatriate and the parent company. It can become a focal point for ongoing discussions and reinforcement between headquarters and the field manager. For the company, a succession plan provides an important channel for communication, and it helps to solidify the control that parent-company executives often crave.

Career planning is a major concern for expatriates because many foreign assignments often remove them from mainstream promotional channels. Over the years, expatriates have consistently returned home to find their jobs eliminated and themselves sidelined. Often, they have lost touch with their parent companies and no longer feel part of the home environments. A sort of "out-of-sight-out-of-mind" phenomenon threatens every foreign assignment and every expatriate's career. Fewer than half of all repatriated employees gain promotions on their return, despite successful and tremendously enriching experiences.[56] As mentioned earlier, a significant number of repatriated employees leave their companies or change careers. Of those who remain, about one-quarter experience serious career problems. A process of periodic career review and communication during the assignment helps to minimize these problems and provides a sense of cohesion between the company and employee. Further, such a plan greatly reduces family anxiety. Although little research offers support for this conclusion, studies among Japanese firms attribute success in long-term expatriate assignments in large part to career planning that includes family members.[57]

Although a succession plan offers important benefits, it is not a panacea for all career problems. A company must also maintain an effective IHRM program to integrate employees into its global network, thus utilizing their unique talents and leveraging their experience to benefit both the employee and the company. Employees share commensurate responsibilities for career management. The plan is likely to identify expectations, performance factors, and gaps in qualifications that the expatriate must address. If a language skill is needed, then, in addition to predeparture training, the employee may be expected to learn a third language that will influence future career posts. The employee should also expect to demonstrate cultural literacy in his or her assignment and to maintain company cohesiveness. These are elements of acculturation and relational skills needed to balance the difficulties of being a member of the parent organization and, at the same time, part of a host-country team.

ASSIGNMENT AND ADAPTATION

An expatriate leaving on foreign assignment often feels intense anticipation as the airplane leaves the tarmac; the adventure is launched. Culture shock can begin shortly after the airplane lands and a rush of people, most of them foreign, scramble for bags and struggle through customs. An expatriate flying from New York to Tokyo will arrive 12 to 14 hours after leaving, and in a rest-deprived condition, immediately face a sea of confusion. Smells, sights, mannerisms, and often just the press of people there can be unnerving. Assuming that all goes well with customs, the next challenge is to obtain some local currency and then get out of the terminal, into a taxi, and safely to a hotel. The entire ground transportation process may take several hours—and if the expatriate's destination is less developed than Tokyo, such as Sri Lanka or the Sudan, the flight will have included several transfers, perhaps 24 hours of travel time, and additional hours clearing customs. Then the expatriate is confronted by a confusing mob of taxi drivers eager to charge double the normal rate to foreigners. Landing in a less-developed country often brings an immediate sensory shock outside the terminal as beggars and mobs of children relentlessly press for handouts. A foreigner who makes a handout, however noble the gesture, may be approached by even more beggars and bands of small children who cannot be dissuaded until the traveler escapes behind locked taxi doors.

This scenario is not uncommon, and it illustrates an opportunity to reduce stress through predeparture orientation by someone who has been through the experience and can prepare the uninitiated person for the shock. More important, a company can plan to avoid such a painful scenario by dispatching a local employee to meet the arriving expatriate and arrange transportation. Many companies and government agencies provide these services, particularly when assignments involve expatriate families and locations in developing countries. A more active company might appoint a local host coordinator who not only meets and escorts the expatriate but also remains close at hand throughout the early period of the assignment.[58] A coordinator can be extremely helpful with domestic resettlement, housing, negotiations with utility companies, providing transportation or assisting with a car purchase, providing advice on health hazards and local customs, and orienting the expatriate to services such as laundry facilities, banking, and shopping.

A comprehensive program will include a coordinator, in-country orientation, and a transition process that helps to settle the new expatriate. This can include help with cutting through legal red tape for visas, resident permits, family amenities, and complications such as school registration for children. The social dimension is mirrored by job-related orientation and an "associate" or mentor who is assigned to the expatriate much like a professional aide.[59] Japanese companies link married expatriates to host families in destination countries; Mitsui, for example, assigns mentors at home and abroad for all international employees.[60] Minimizing initial culture shock is important, and a friendly reception is essential.

Research has shown that expatriates cycle through an adjustment process that begins on arrival and is accompanied by high anticipation—but equally high potential for culture shock.[61] After several months, the mood changes. Anticipation is quickly replaced by a sense of confusion as the "newness" of the adventure gives way to frustration. The decline in attitude continues for several more months, dropping into an emotional trough as the expatriate feels engulfed by cultural differences. At that point, the expatriate either begins to adapt successfully, thus finding some sense of normality, or fails to adapt, becoming cynical and unable to function effectively. This cycle is illustrated in Figure 12.5.

A smooth initial entry process cannot completely eliminate culture shock. Instead, companies try to help expatriates reduce unnecessary stress while maintaining enthusiasm for the new assignments. For example, a firm gains nothing by trying to insulate newcomers from the poverty common in developing countries, but preparation and support help to keep them from being immediately overwhelmed by the jolt

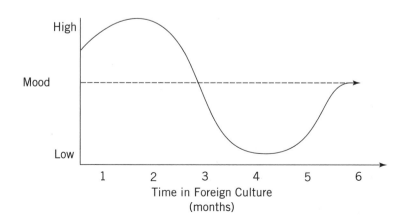

FIGURE 12.5
Culture Shock and Adaptation Cycle
Source: Adapted from Nancy J. Adler, *International Dimensions of Organizational Behavior*, 2nd ed. (Boston: PWS-Kent, 1991), 227. Copyright PWS-Kent Publishing Company, reprinted by permission.

of unexpected circumstances. During the first few weeks, a firm can minimize other stressful situations without isolating the expatriate from cultural reality. An effective local support program seeks to reduce the potential for *maladaptive* responses during the transition. Change creates stress, and stress is accompanied by psychological and physiological responses such as headaches, anxiety, insomnia, misapprehension, frustration, poor digestion, and perhaps more serious medical ailments. Consequently, the company benefits by cushioning the impact of stark cultural contrasts.

During the few months an expatriate experiences an emotional downturn, he or she needs reassurance and some relief from the local culture. One solution is to establish a **stability zone**—a comfort zone that separates the expatriate from daily responsibilities in an unfamiliar society. An activity that provides a touch of home may also encourage adjustment.[62] Expatriates have felt comforted by many examples of stability zones. For example, U.S. expatriates working in Hong Kong often join the American Club, a facility that offers lunch and dinner, special events, guest speakers, and competitive events such as golf tournaments and sailing contests. Many British expatriates in Singapore hold memberships in colonial country clubs, yacht clubs, and art societies. Swiss residents in Sri Lanka congregate in a restaurant near Colombo's embassy section that has become known affectionately as "the Swiss house." For their guests, the local owners have developed a familiar cuisine, prepared by a Swiss chef and complete with imported Swiss wines. U.S. members of the U.S. Foreign Service in Indonesia have established weekend picnics with American-brand hotdogs and snacks, a touch-football schedule, and Little League baseball. German expatriates working in the Middle East congregate regularly in coastal resorts of Greece or Italy to enjoy "beer fests" or to celebrate European Christian holidays.

By far, the most popular stability zone involves company-sponsored club memberships. Japanese companies have become notorious for sponsoring expensive golf memberships for their employees, and European companies endorse golf club memberships throughout the world. British and German expatriates also participate actively in social clubs, performing arts, and sports associations. U.S., Australian, and Canadian workers are drawn to health clubs in their foreign locations. Travel agencies also do a brisk business in expatriate getaway vacations. Asian travelers tend to take long weekends or brief breaks with their families, often through organized tours and educational development programs. Whatever the choice, a stability zone allows a regular brief respite from foreign experiences and a chance to reconnect with one's own culture through friends, events, or social activities.[63]

The protection of a stability zone limits the downside effects of the inevitable slump that occurs after an initial period of acclimatization to a new society. Outsiders often envy expatriates who seem to have good compensation packages with social benefits and perks seldom provided to domestic employees. Besides club memberships and expense accounts, many expatriate contracts provide for periodic home leaves that amount to full-fare paid vacations for expatriates and their families. A company may require that the employee return home rather than traveling elsewhere, and the trip may include a working visit to the parent organization for meetings or brief progress conferences. Still, many companies provide travel allowances equivalent to the cost of returning home and then permit employees to go wherever they wish within those budgets.[64] Educational allowances for children to attend international schools or home-country boarding schools assure expatriates that their children will have appropriate educational opportunities. These and many other benefits are common, but they are also expensive. Consequently, although international companies recognize the importance of providing these benefits, the high cost of support systems adds to the firm's incentives to hire locally when it can do so.[65]

As the adjustment cycle progresses, and assuming that an expatriate successfully adapts to the local culture, an upward emotional lift improves attitudes. This change can occur subtly over a period of several months or emerge rather suddenly as the expatriate "gets into" the new surroundings. The positive readjustment is attributed partially to a broader understanding of the foreign environment (and therefore acceptance of differences), and partially to individual adaptability. As noted earlier, adaptation requires a sense of balance in which an individual is not so malleable as to go native, yet is sufficiently broad-minded to accept cultural differences without inappropriately compromising his or her own cultural values. The result is an ability to live peacefully in a foreign society, work effectively there, and appreciate the benefits of an international assignment.

REPATRIATION: THE RETURN HOME

Returning home is often more traumatic than going overseas. Returning expatriates encounter problems because they have changed in many ways during their assignments, and because few repatriation programs effectively help employees to reenter their own societies. Most return to jobs that no longer suit them, so they must wait until the company can determine what to do with them. Many returning expatriates are alienated from their own home societies. On the other hand, good companies with effective repatriation programs can preserve the rewards of the expatriate experience. This section looks at the personal and organizational effects of repatriation.

The Personal Challenge of Returning Home

All who experience living and working in foreign cultures are changed by those environments.[66] They return with a broader appreciation for the world, global events, and people of different cultures. They also return with a better awareness of their own cultures and the relative benefits and shortcomings of their native societies. Very few people can articulate these changes or explain the transformations they have experienced. Equally important, they can rarely share their emotions or explain what has happened to them with others who have not had similar foreign experiences. They are looking at the world, and at themselves, with entirely new eyes. How does this change occur? What events shape personal changes?

In their professional lives, most expatriates experience more autonomy and independence in their foreign assignments than they knew in previous jobs at home. During their foreign assignments, they often feel empowered to make unexpected contributions to their own growth and to their organizations through the intensity of their involvement. In addition, they often feel more important and more valued in the foreign assignments than they felt at home; in fact, they often do accept far greater responsibilities for much more challenging activities. Many foreign assignments amount to promotions; if not, the overseas posts still may bring prestige among local employees. A large majority of expatriates return home with global insights into their company's global business and, consequently, deep appreciation of their firm's strategies, strengths, weaknesses, and opportunities. Indeed, they return better equipped as managers than when they departed, having grown professionally in ways that are beyond the scope of their home-rooted peers. These expatriates return with diversified interests, enriched appreciation for communication, and empathy for cultural differences. In short, they bring back a different conceptual framework of how the world works.[67]

People's values may change, for better or for worse, during foreign assignments; but their visions of themselves and their companies certainly differ from those they took with them to begin their assignments. Their experiences enrich their appreciation of their home-society advantages in important ways; phenomena that they took for granted several years earlier often become very important when they return home. For example, a U.S. employee of Marriott who had worked in Hong Kong for several years returned to a suburban home near Washington, D.C., and was enthralled by the "fun" of mowing grass and doing yard work. After two years in a concrete jungle, he was starved for space, trees, and the pleasure of mowing a yard. A young Bostonian woman who had just returned from a stint in Bangkok reported laughing at Boston traffic and its notoriously nerve-wracking reputation; in Bangkok she had spent two hours each way, driving in daily rush-hour traffic, just to go a few miles. A man who had just returned from Ethiopia watched a colleague throw away his half-eaten lunch and reported that he had cried silently; he had just spent a year watching starving children try to eat weeds and suck water from handfuls of mud. Similar discontinuities surface at work, particularly when employees and other managers complain about conditions such as the sanitation in rest rooms, the length of breaks, or the amounts of work they must do. Many expatriates become comfortable in situations with scant access to rest rooms, few work breaks in 10- or 12-hour workdays, and expectations to work six days a week.[68]

A returning expatriate therefore has a new psychological orientation. Most return with high aspirations for comparable work or equally challenging circumstances. They return armed with more behavioral tools for coping with change and diversity, and as a general rule, their expectations for meaningful work and recognition of their accomplishments exceed reality. Their old jobs simply may not satisfy them anymore; even a new position that lacks the breadth of responsibility experienced overseas may seem shallow to them. If they find themselves sidelined or circling in career holding patterns, their disappointment grows. Consequently, they must complete a reacculturation process in adjusting to their own societies. They must ease back into their organizations and communities—a task that often requires extra sensitivity and patience with their new surroundings. They must be prepared to feel ignored, undervalued, and misunderstood by others. Also, they often must constrain themselves from imposing their newly formed opinions and worldly visions on others who may feel resentful or confused by the expatriate's perspectives. This adjustment is a personal struggle, often involving deeply rooted values (and new value perspectives), and some expatriates simply cannot reconcile the difficulties of returning home.[69]

Organizational Dimensions of Repatriation

An organization benefits when it helps employees to repatriate smoothly into productive and motivating jobs. As noted earlier, however, few companies have repatriation programs. Why does this contradiction continue? Part of the answer rests with false assumptions, persisting among expatriates and their home-country colleagues, that returning home requires no adjustment. People commonly expect that values and behaviors learned since early childhood will prevail, and returning employees will adapt without difficulties. In some instances, both parties also assume that the foreign assignment is a mere interlude, a "time-out period," after which an individual will fall back into step in a previous job or line of work. Often, people also assume that few changes occur during the assignment period.

These assumptions are erroneous on several counts.[70] An expatriate often must recognize pervasive changes in personal values and behavior, although some expatriates return home relatively unaffected by their experiences. Individuals who have been abroad several times or in several different societies can adapt quickly without much reentry shock. Even the most experienced veteran can return home to unexpected changes, though. Home-company executives, even if they are well traveled, may not recognize the contrast in conditions over periods of several years for either themselves or their companies. The employee has lived out of touch with events at home, so whatever changes have occurred to change the individual are often hidden well below the surface. Meanwhile, the company has probably experienced changes of its own, hired new people, introduced new products and technologies, expanded (or contracted), and perhaps redefined its strategic objectives.

Home-based managers who have participated in those changes may not recognize that a returning expatriate is uninformed about them. Most organizational changes accumulate gradually in the minds of domestic managers, but returning expatriates experience the accumulated effect of change over several years as a single overwhelming wave.

Society has also changed; nothing stands still. Prices for housing, food, and automobiles probably have gone up, perhaps by a large margin. New legislation imposes unfamiliar demands, and new expectations now govern activities such as managing companies, hiring employees, or communicating in inclusive language. Friends and family members may have changed, aged, or moved. Things just are not the same. However, the expatriate probably retains an image of home, friends, community, prices, and everything else formed at departure—only to return to a strange world. Assumptions frozen in time have lost their validity.[71]

Expatriates return to vast ranges of new circumstances, and they need assistance to cope with the changes. The methods of assistance resemble those for preparing employees for foreign assignments, with certain modifications. Figure 12.6 shows the primary forms of assistance. Before the final exit, predeparture orientation can help to reacquaint the employee with the parent company. This instruction can be accomplished at the foreign site, but it often works better if the firm brings the employee home for a brief visit to attend meetings, meet new personnel, and discuss future job responsibilities. This

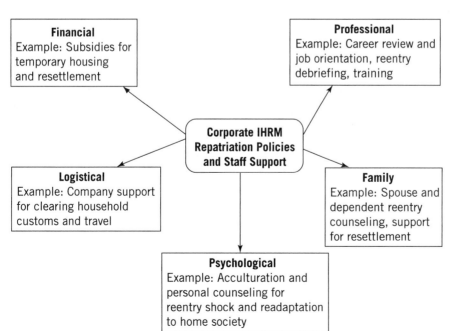

FIGURE 12.6
Categories of Repatriation Assistance and Examples

step provides a channel of communication between expatriates and their coworkers, thus reducing the potential for misunderstandings. A predeparture home-orientation process also provides an opportunity to explain compensation and benefits plans, which can be substantially different (and usually lower) at home than abroad. Royal Dutch Shell, with offices throughout the world, implements a standard practice of "pre-return" visits that allow managers to both solidify job-related details and investigate housing, schools, and family-related interests. Expatriates being rotated home often want to purchase new houses and have them ready for arrival. If a family has rented their home while overseas, they must probably recondition the premises before moving back in. If this can be accomplished before the move, then reentry transition is less traumatic.[72]

Training and career-development activities may accompany the pre-return orientation, or they may begin soon after the expatriate arrives home. Firms appear to follow no standard practice, but expatriates who will assume new posts may coordinate training with their transfers. This instruction focuses primarily on technical and administrative considerations, although it should include acculturation training. Career-development efforts often include assignments to brief projects at home and other foreign locations. European multinationals favor joint project responsibilities for senior managers as a way of both smoothing repatriation and creating a sense of esprit de corps within the organization. Japanese companies often include their foreign-based managers in home-country job responsibilities, assign them to parent-company committees, and expect them to remain involved in home-country activities throughout their foreign assignments. These practices reinforce the Japanese proclivity to maintain a cohesive cultural identity.[73]

Companies that maintain succession-planning systems seldom need to arrange special briefing sessions or unusual training programs. Each employee's succession plan preserves an ongoing dialogue between the parent company and its expatriates. Recall that a succession plan is established well in advance of the initial assignment, and the company periodically reviews expatriates' performance and objectives. Consequently, few surprises await returning employees, because their new positions, compensation, and future responsibilities are at least broadly determined. Succession planning also keeps expatriates abreast of company changes, thus reducing the risk of reentry shock.[74]

Mentoring programs, such as those in Japanese companies, are not popular in the United States and Canada. Instead, a similar form of support is provided through *company sponsors*. These are short-lived arrangements to help in the transition. Effective sponsorship programs are usually concerned entirely with job-related duties or reorientation to organizational systems, yet because the contacts are initiated several months before expatriates return, they benefit the company and employee by facilitating job reentry. Unfortunately, research has shown that U.S. expatriates generally view sponsorship efforts, mentoring, reentry development programs, and career-counseling services as superficial efforts. Thus, they do not always perceive a need for company intervention programs. Good programs, however, are appreciated. U.S. companies like GE, Alcoa, and Exxon, along with European companies such as ABB, Fiat, and Shell, receive high marks from their international managers for providing effective reentry programs.[75]

Companies can also provide assistance in specific forms to lighten the burdens of moving back home. Most expatriates return to compensation packages less generous than they received in their foreign assignments, even though at home they may face higher prices for housing, tax complications, and expenses required for resettling their families. Few U.S. companies provide financial assistance to defray these expenses, but almost all U.S. and European firms provide per-diem moving and relocation allowances. For U.S. employees, these allowances are seldom sufficient to offset relocation costs.

Japanese companies typically cover all explicit expenses and oversee the relocation process, yet Japanese employees often return home to lower standards of living than they enjoyed in other countries. For example, those who work in the United States for Sony, Nissan, Honda, or Toyota live in spacious American-style homes. They also pay what they perceive as bargain prices for staples, meat, gasoline, and clothing, and send their children to relatively inexpensive schools. Upon returning home, Japanese expatriates pay relatively high prices for small apartments in busy cities, pay three or four times as much for gasoline and automobiles as they paid in the United States, and revert to simple meals that can fit their budgets. Their children are assigned to public schools, where parents pay premiums for most college preparatory courses and few students qualify for limited university positions. Toyota has provided some relief for its expatriates through home loans and education allowances, and Sony often arranges both housing and transportation. Overall, however, the returning Japanese managers must financially retrench and adjust to the parsimonious conditions of life in their homeland.[76]

Making the Transition Succeed

Companies have already made substantial investments to support international managers by the time those employees arrive home. By comparison, additional costs of repatriation amount to relatively small sums. Therefore, at a small cost, organizations can do much to help ensure smooth transitions. As part of this process, many organizations *debrief* employees. This information exchange reconnects expatriates with their parent-company managers after they return. Debriefing benefits both the company and the employee by systematically reviewing the foreign assignment, results achieved, and problems envisioned by the expatriate. Companies often discover new opportunities or insights about their foreign operations through debriefings, and equally important, superiors enhance their understanding of the expatriate's abilities and aspirations. This information proves valuable for planning future assignments and for improving the company's human resource activities. Debriefing is a significant activity at Monsanto, for example, where the company "showcases" the experiences and careers of returning expatriates, includes families in company presentations, and couples these efforts to an "enthusiastic," comprehensive repatriation process. This activity reassures expatriates that the company values their experiences and wants to promote smooth transitions back into American life.[77] Table 12.4 summarizes a set of recommendations to help expatriates make successful reentry transitions.

Ultimately, the repatriation process is concerned with creating a win-win situation for the company and its employees. As they notice a growing need for qualified international managers, global companies throughout the world are making concerted efforts to attract new globally minded employees, to develop their current staff members into competent international managers, and to retain those with experience and skills in cross-cultural responsibilities. They fund significant investments in each foreign assignment, and as the field of international human resource management begins to mature, comprehensive IHRM planning will further enhance repatriation programs. Nevertheless, some controversies persist, and even astute planning cannot fully resolve problems such as how to structure equitable compensation packages.

TABLE 12.4

COMPANY INITIATIVES FOR REENTRY TRANSITION

- Succession planning before and after assignment to promote career development and transition management
- Reentry sponsorship to ensure that someone meets and greets the expatriate and family on return and aids in their transition
- Relocation assistance to facilitate concerns regarding housing, transportation, customs and duties, children's schooling, and necessary temporary accommodations
- Pre-return orientation to clarify company and home-society changes, as well as job-related information about duties and expectations
- Pre-return home visit for brief transition review concerning housing arrangements, reentry job expectations, and compensation issues
- Financial support, perhaps through bridge loans, for housing, temporary accommodations, transition expenses per diem, family requirements, and resettlement costs
- Tax advice or return preparation for both in-country and home obligations
- Spouse assistance, including redirecting career interests or new reentry positions
- Family counseling to minimize reentry culture shock and resocialization in home culture
- Follow-up acculturation counseling and necessary training during early post-return period

Source: Adapted from Richard Mead, *International Management: Cross Cultural Dimensions* (Cambridge, Mass.: Blackwell Publishers, 1994), 400–401. Also see Charlene Marmer Solomon, "Repatriation: Up, Down, or Out?" *Personnel Journal* 74, no. 1 (1995): 28–30.

COMPENSATION AND TERMS OF EMPLOYMENT

Foreign assignments often seem like financially lucrative opportunities because they entail extensive compensation and benefits that, on face value, exceed the terms of domestic employment. As a general rule, expatriates enjoy higher gross incomes and more substantial benefits than they would receive in comparable home-country positions, but their *net* income and benefits may not differ so much.[78] A company spends substantially more to maintain an expatriate in his or her position than the same job would warrant at home, and an expatriate earns much more than a locally hired manager would make for the same job.

Contract administration is concerned with providing equitable compensation and benefits sufficient to reward good employees in challenging positions while also guarding against financial losses to expatriates or their families due to unusual overseas expenses. Direct comparisons with home-based positions cannot be made. Instead, a firm judges equitable compensation according to perceptions of the requirements to attract competent applicants for specific overseas situations and to maintain acceptable living standards once those employees begin their assignments. Consequently, companies must spend more to motivate employees to risk overseas assignments or to work in unsafe locations, such as those experiencing civil strife. Likewise, an assignment to Germany or Switzerland, where living costs can be quite high compared to those in North America, will require income premiums.

Compensation is the centerpiece of expatriate contracts, commonly called *expat packages*. These packages incorporate benefits as part of the terms of employment, and although contracts vary according to company policies, they typically include base salaries, bonuses, medical coverage, contributions to retirement plans, provisions for dependent education, passage allowances for expatriates and family members, baggage allowances, home leave and vacation benefits, and hardship differentials. In addition, they can include car allowances (or arrangements for company cars), home furnishings, club membership privileges, daily transportation allowances, security provisions, expense accounts for travel and entertainment, food allowances, and reserve accounts designed to equalize the effects of exchange rate fluctuations on expatriates' income. Most companies also defray excess income taxes incurred by employees. Each of these provisions varies for different foreign assignments and customary practices of doing business there.[79]

Policies on direct compensation reflect company and industry income scales. As for domestic employees, multinationals in manufacturing industries pay higher base salaries than those in consumer goods industries or banking, but they probably pay somewhat less than firms in professional services such as accountancy. Base pay standards are then adjusted for conditions in specific host countries; a U.S. employee assigned to a post in Europe may earn a base salary 30, 50, or even 100 percent higher than the same job would pay at home. No hard-and-fast rules govern these differentials, but large companies usually rate individual jobs according to indexed cost-of-living reports from the World Bank or government foreign service studies. For example, if the U.S. salary base is set to 100 and the index rating for Germany is 145, then base salaries for U.S. employees assigned to Germany would have to be 45 percent higher than for homebound employees to provide comparable buying power.

Adjustments also are made based on occupational hazards. For example, a U.S. national IT engineer working in Sweden might earn the equivalent of U.S. $80,000, while a comparable employee at the parent company is paid U.S. $40,000. Both earn approximately equal effective incomes after taxes and costs of living are considered. On the other hand, if that same American engineer is sent to India where IT engineers are paid the equivalent of $10,000, the higher U.S. pay scale will be retained. This would ensure the American of maintaining home-based benefits, such as retirement funds, and provide the American with a style of living abroad comparable to that at home.

Salaries can also be adjusted to neutralize tax differentials. Most expatriates owe taxes to their host countries and to home authorities on the same income. Special tax provisions set rates in each country (a full discussion exceeds the scope of this section). For example, however, a U.S. citizen who meets IRS qualifications can exempt $70,000 of foreign-earned income. (The exemption is being raised by a formula by the IRS through 2005.) This person would then pay U.S. taxes on all income over $70,000, but would be liable to the host-country government for taxes on all income earned there. Someone who happens to work in Hong Kong or Singapore enjoys very low tax rates—approximately 15 percent—but the same person working in Sweden, Belgium, France, or Germany might incur a tax liability exceeding 50 percent. Consequently, a high base salary could result in a net after-tax loss compared to a comparable home salary.

A company can equalize tax effects by raising an employee's gross salary or by directly paying the excess tax. In addition, many countries tax the value of certain benefits as income; the list includes housing allowances, educational benefits, provisions for cars, and reimbursements for travel and entertainment. Few countries allow tax-deferred retirement benefits, as the United States does, further increasing a covered employee's foreign tax burden. Therefore, a compensation package may seem to be more attractive than it really is; tax effects, reduced retirement allowances, and higher costs for education and local transportation all affect employees' earnings. Companies can resolve these problems by increasing gross pay packages and by providing company-owned overseas housing, impounding retirement funds at home, creating company-sponsored education funds or scholarships, and maintaining fleets of cars or transportation pool services. Some provide interest-free loans or subsidies for purchasing cars, foreign housing, furniture, food, and clothing.[80]

Additional complications plague the compensation issue. Exchange rates can change, often very quickly and in dramatic swings, as they did in Mexico several years ago when the peso was drastically revalued. Foreign employees paid in Mexican pesos may have lost half of their buying power without some form of protection by their companies. Similar problems occur in countries where inflation erodes buying power or in places such as China, where foreigners are charged premiums for everything they buy as a matter of public policy. Simple exploitation also occurs, but firms cannot document this problem in their accounting ledgers. Nevertheless, companies must recognize that their employees will face these unusual costs.

They must also ensure appropriate education for employees' children through international schools with instruction in their native languages. In many countries, expatriates find few (if any) international schools, and children must attend boarding schools at home or in other foreign countries. Paying for education, arranging transportation, and coordinating school holidays can be a difficult and expensive undertaking.

Hardship payments present yet another challenge. For example, Sri Lanka's continuing civil war requires almost every foreigner to install special security alarms on their quarters and hire security guards; those in high-visibility positions may need personal bodyguards.[81] In addition, expatriates in East Africa are subject to risks through border wars. These circumstances require extra security, and they also create psychological hardships and daily problems such as food shortages and disruptions in supplies. Calm places may involve their own hardships due to lack of economic development, unsafe sanitary conditions, poor roads, sparse shopping, and few recreation facilities. Hardships may characterize even the most advanced nations. Americans living in Japan, for example, must rent very small apartments at very high rates, rely on extremely busy public transportation, and pay very high prices for western-style meals. They also live without television, movies, or performing arts because few forms of entertainment offer programs in English.[82]

These situations add to culture shock, and they persist (and change) throughout contract periods. Companies design their compensation programs to minimize unpleasant effects and to ensure that compensation makes foreign assignments attractive in spite of unusual difficulties. Administration of these programs is complicated, and they must comply with specific and variable host-country regulations. A global company may deal with hundreds of employees on foreign assignments in dozens or hundreds of countries, creating a monumental task of managing compensation and benefits.

WOMEN'S ROLES AND FAMILY CONSIDERATIONS

Women encounter the elements of expatriate life in two distinct roles: as accompanying spouses and as overseas employees themselves. These roles include family considerations; and as mentioned earlier, the gender-free term *spouse* does not adequately explain the special problems encountered by wives, who comprise the overwhelming majority of expatriate spouses. Considerations for children and their adjustment problems returning home merit comparable attention, yet very little research has been published on the problems children have as expatriates. It is also important to consider the roles of women who work as expatriates. These topics are addressed separately in the following sections.

Wives and Families Abroad

Although foreign travel and the romance of living in exotic places can invoke alluring images, expatriate wives often encounter rough conditions. Unlike their husbands, who are involved in the decision to go abroad and do so for definite professional purposes, many wives simply follow their husbands into overseas assignments. Their expatriate experiences typically begin when husbands bring home news that they may be transferred overseas. The couple may have serious discussions about the assignment, but, because it often represents an important step in the husband's career, the wife seldom voices strong objections.

Of course, this is not always the case. In dual-career families, the implications of uprooting a wife from her career often influence a husband's decision to avoid foreign assignments or to make considerable efforts to accommodate his wife's interests. Many companies with enlightened managers also go to great lengths to assist wives with their own careers, perhaps by providing comparable positions in the company's foreign offices. They also contract with foreign job-search professionals to help wives find meaningful work during the foreign assignment. Some dual-career couples decide temporarily to go their own ways, and companies may raise total compensation packages to allow frequent trips home or extended holidays that permit the family to periodically reconnect. These initiatives are not uncommon for short-term assignments, but for those spanning several years, wives are more likely to quit their jobs and accompany their husbands overseas.

A strong case could be made that wives value predeparture orientation, and in particular acculturation training, more than their husbands do. They often bear responsibility for deeply integrating into local cultures through daily activities of shopping, dealing with school administrators, paying household bills, adjusting to unusual food products, and living in unfamiliar social systems. While husbands may be able to communicate in their home languages at work (or rely on professional translators and company-appointed assistants), wives often must meet these challenges on their own. Consequently, although they face the most stringent requirements for cross-cultural adaptation, they and their children generally have fewer support systems to aid in their daily activities. Often wives of other expatriates establish welcome committees or social clubs that soften the culture shock. To their credit, some companies and foreign service agencies budget funds to support newly arrived wives, and through these company-sponsored programs, wives and their dependents are able to establish new friendships and find family assistance.

These initiatives have become important dimensions of international human resource management programs, but they do not fully relieve the sacrifices that wives make in their careers or when they are not principal participants in assignment decisions. Many wives experience isolation, stress, and a sense of personal loss if they put their careers on hold to support their husbands' aspirations. These problems may be more or less pronounced depending on individual situations and host-country environments. A U.S. executive's wife may have little remorse about interrupting her career for a tour of duty in Paris, but an assignment in Bangladesh may accentuate her sense of isolation and sacrifice.

In contrast, Japanese wives coming to the United States express serious apprehension about the nation's drug problems and violence, and many Japanese families purposely isolate themselves from American society. Japanese wives tend to keep to themselves or remain socially clustered with other Japanese nationals, seldom allowing their children to venture too far beyond the family enclaves. This separation can lead to acute adjustment problems, but to some extent everyone living in a foreign country tends to seek their own kind. Social clustering certainly helps to provide a family stability zone, but it also can barricade the family and create a self-imposed social cage for wives.

On balance, foreign assignments provide substantial benefits that usually far outweigh the difficulties. Wives can actively participate in the global experience, and they often return home with deeper insight into world cultures that can serve them well in later careers or personal activities. Many seize opportunities to learn new languages, apply their career skills in local jobs, pursue cultural interests, become involved in host-country arts communities, and join voluntary organizations. Most research is anecdotal, but it suggests that many wives feel enriched by their foreign experiences. Although they report loneliness and frustration in their efforts to find meaning in daily activities, they also indicate that they have experienced personal growth and come to appreciate foreign lifestyles. In many ways, their responsibilities evoke an assertiveness and independence, but often under compulsion, rather than through company-sponsored programs that prepare them for living abroad.

Children experience many of the same benefits and frustrations as their parents. They may not have to be concerned with shopping or paying bills, but they must adjust to new friends, new schools with different philosophies of teaching, and new expectations for social behavior. If they are not sufficiently challenged to maintain academic levels consistent with home-country schools, they risk falling behind others their age. If they find local educational standards too rigorous, they may experience distress. Young teens may find themselves in societies with more permissive standards than they know at home. On the other hand, some societies impose more rigid rules that result in teenagers getting into serious trouble for behavior that would go unnoticed at home. By far, the most important consideration is to provide opportunities for young people to develop friendships and peer-group activities to prevent them from becoming reclusive and socially isolated.

Repatriation of wives and children can be a difficult problem. A wife seldom can expect to return to a specific position. Instead, she simply arrives home with a new set of responsibilities for getting the family settled and children registered in school. She must reestablish social ties and adjust to a new community, leaving her somewhat adrift in her own society for a time. Meanwhile, children will be equally adrift as they return to school. They will have changed, and their friends will have changed. Peer expectations change in the course of normal growth, and children who live abroad for several years may assimilate foreign behaviors and values that alienate them at home.

These problems can occur in any culture when families face significant changes. For example, a Japanese youth of 16 and his younger sister, returning to Japan after four years in New York, found themselves shunned for their "Americanized" behavior. Their former friends ridiculed them for speaking Japanese with a foreign accent and for their lack of discipline. Neither could accept expectations for compliant behavior common in Japan, and they were severely disciplined by their teachers. They received failing marks in school for being "too independent minded," and they lost access to school activities. Their parents felt compelled to get the children back to the United

States, and six months after they had arrived in Japan, they returned to New York, where both finished school as class valedictorians and subsequently attended major U.S. universities.[83]

Women in Expatriate Roles

Women may be more suited to expatriate roles than men. Although fewer women are sent abroad by their companies, they perform more successfully than their male counterparts. These conclusions seem to defy logic, because traditional roles for women in most societies relegate them to domestic duties and lower-profile management responsibilities. Also, the stereotypes of managers in foreign cultures suggest a sense of machismo that would impede a woman's effectiveness. Without a doubt, parochial views of women and gender biases create many problems for women, but women expatriates also enjoy distinct advantages.

Research has shown that women bring social and interpersonal skills to their assignments that allow them to work especially effectively in multicultural environments. Women accommodate others more easily than men do, and they also establish social networks more effectively, feel less confined by trappings of power relationships, and form more conciliatory personal relationships. These strengths help them to integrate into foreign social environments more easily than men, and they are viewed as more cooperative in their behavior. In male-centered foreign cultures, women certainly face many disadvantages, but foreign women in responsible positions often receive unusually respectful treatment. Expatriate women are not treated the same way as domestic women. Instead, they evoke a sense of admiration from foreign male colleagues. Perhaps this occurs because men encounter few women in these positions, and perhaps it is also because the women are well-qualified professionals with excellent relational skills. Women are generally more trusted than their male colleagues, and in societies where trust building is important, these relational characteristics are major advantages.

Nevertheless, women must contend with "glass ceilings," misgivings about their capabilities, and social biases that reflect prevailing attitudes in both the host country and their parent organizations. Their foreign experiences often result in mixed blessings, a point emphasized in the opening profile of Elizabeth McDougall, who was treated extremely well by some foreign colleagues and rather poorly by others. The situation is further illustrated in the "Global Viewpoint" that profiles Carol Raffray, a well-qualified woman who was often underutilized and had to overcome obstacles that men seldom face.

The experience of Carol Raffray is not unusual. Female expatriates almost always hold graduate degrees, many from top American and European business schools. More than 75 percent have traveled internationally, and most speak at least two languages; some are adept at three or more languages. Upon joining their companies, female candidates for expatriate posts often bring international interests or exposure to multicultural work environments, and most are young (under 30) and single.[84] Nevertheless, research on North American companies shows that more than half are reluctant to send women overseas, and more than three-quarters believe that foreign prejudices against female managers would present insurmountable difficulties for these expatriates.[85]

Subsequent research has demonstrated that such beliefs are myths. Indeed, parent-company biases are far more pronounced than foreign cultural constraints. Surveys of American women interested in foreign assignments have shown that more than 70 percent believed the primary reason they were not selected for international positions was reluctance by their parent organizations to consider women as

Heather Killen, senior vice president for international operations at Yahoo!, may be one of the most traveled women in the world. Born in Australia and educated in Europe and the United States, she is based at Yahoo's headquarters in California but spends the majority of her time airborne. She travels a quarter of a million miles each year, speaks several languages fluently, and can converse about Yahoo business in 23 languages and dialects. Having held the managing director position for Yahoo Europe while still in her mid-thirties, she is among the company's executive elite in her early forties. She also is among the company's prestigious multicultural, multilingual staff that is equally at ease working in Germany as in Japan, or negotiating in Hindi or in Chinese.

acceptable candidates.[86] Statistics confirm this bias. In studies of Canadian and U.S. firms, barely 3 percent of all international managers sent abroad were women, yet among the companies surveyed, more women reported that they were interested in foreign assignments than men. Company beliefs seem to confirm the biases; executives responding to the surveys gave three primary reasons for not selecting women:

1. Women do not want to be international managers.
2. Women in dual-career marriages are poor candidates.
3. Foreigners are unwilling to accept women in managerial positions.[87]

Mounting evidence suggests that in the future significantly more women will fulfill foreign assignments. Unfounded biases are beginning to disappear in favor of selection processes that seek the best-qualified candidates. In many assignments women will be preferred candidates, since they will likely flourish where foreign cultures emphasize the importance of relational skills, trust, and cooperation. Obstacles will remain, certainly in societies with deeply embedded religious codes that suppress women's rights; many Middle Eastern nations and Islamic cultures simply do not recognize roles for women outside their homes and families.

On the other hand, western women are likely to discover greater equality and fewer biases in many countries outside their own. Female executives in Hong Kong are not uncommon, and women hold many senior government appointments throughout the world. Women have held, or currently occupy, powerful positions as prime ministers, presidents, and party leaders in Pakistan, Sri Lanka, India, and Bangladesh. European nations have also elected women to similar high political positions, demonstrated by examples in the United Kingdom, France, Denmark, Finland, and Sweden. In each of these nations, international companies employ far more expatriate women managers than comparable North American companies, and although women are still in a minority and face a prevailing glass ceiling that shields many top jobs, cultural barriers are receding.[88]

GLOBAL VIEWPOINT

OVERQUALIFIED AND UNDERUTILIZED: ONE WOMAN'S SUCCESS AS AN EXPATRIATE

Carol Raffray was intent on an international career when she enrolled as a freshman at Cornell University to major in Asian studies. Ten years later, and armed with impeccable credentials, she had her chance. She became an investment analyst in Tokyo for a major American securities firm. Raffray recalls her experience in Japan as "frustrating and deprecating, but also the two most exhilarating years of my life." She was assigned as a junior analyst in Tokyo after spending six years on Wall Street, where she had been a rising star in international mergers and acquisitions. Though the position in Japan was a slight demotion, to Raffray it seemed an intriguing opportunity. With an undergraduate degree in Asian studies and an MBA from Cornell University, she spoke three languages and had traveled extensively in Europe, South America, and Asia. Once in Japan, however, her role was reduced to "desk jockey and gofer." She praises the Japanese but spares few words of kindness for her U.S. colleagues:

My buddies from home "expected me to do their leg work, to get coffee, and play receptionist to their clients." They would introduce me by my first name with a throwaway title like "she's in research." Then they would sit me near the door in meetings—which, in Japan, is a mark of lower status. The Japanese men in the company "invited me to tea" and always introduced me to clients as "Ms. Raffray," with a flattering explanation of my position, such as "our M&A expert on Asia." When they arranged luncheons or meetings, I was always seated according to my position, and when I was promoted, my seating position and respect improved. However, there were lines drawn, and I had to respect the differences in our cultures. I was never invited to the "boys' nights," to karaoke bars, or to "power lunches."

These were "guy things." On the other hand, I was always included in sensitive social engagements, often to the exclusion of my American male colleagues because I spoke Japanese fluently and understood how to behave. I hesitate to say that few of the company men could do as well. Japanese clients often insisted that I handle account negotiations, and many became trusted friends. I never felt like I was being patronized by the Japanese men, but their wives ... well that's another story. You ought to be home having kids in their view.

After her two years in Tokyo, the company planned to transfer Raffray back to her old job, which would have been another demotion. Instead, she quit the company and joined a Japanese executive search firm. She describes the experience:

Hey, talk about challenges! I was the only female in the office and held a senior associate management post with several Japanese men reporting to me. I might as well have been from Mars, but they respected me for my professional abilities and my position. Still, I had to earn my spurs and go the extra mile to cement relationships. Had I not gone to Hong Kong with my husband shortly after we were married, I would be a senior partner with the firm in Tokyo. But I am still visited in Hong Kong by Japanese friends, and I am confident that I could resume my career here, in Tokyo, or Tim-buk-tu. I went further, faster, and had more fun doing it in Tokyo than I could ever imagine in New York.

Source: Interview with Carol Raffray, Cornell Club Executives-in-Asia meeting, February 1995, Hong Kong.

REVIEW QUESTIONS

1. Describe the expatriate system as a process or cycle of activities. What are the primary characteristics in each stage of the cycle?
2. What are the three components of expatriate staffing, and how does IHRM address each one?
3. What are the main criteria for recruitment and selection of candidates for foreign positions?
4. How would you describe the adaptation problem for an expatriate living abroad? What emotional cycle affects an expatriate during a foreign assignment?
5. Explain what companies can do to provide effective predeparture training. How does acculturation training assist an expatriate?
6. What elements would a succession plan include to provide an effective career-development instrument for an international manager?
7. What are the major issues facing an international manager during repatriation to a home position?
8. How can repatriation problems be minimized?
9. How can a company ensure that the reentry transition represents a positive and successful process that benefits both the company and the expatriate?
10. Describe the elements of an expatriate compensation plan. Why are the costs high for expatriate support systems? Are they justified? Defend your answers.
11. Why do expatriate wives struggle more to adjust to foreign assignments than most male expatriate employees? What particular problems do wives face, and how can these be minimized?
12. Describe the profile of a typical expatriate woman. What characteristics give her advantages in an international assignment, and what problems must she overcome in the foreign assignment and after returning home?

GLOSSARY OF KEY TERMS

Adaptation   Emotional and cultural adjustment to a foreign society and work environment.

Expatriate   Anyone working for a parent organization in an environment outside his or her native society.

Host-country national (HCN)   An employee of a foreign-owned company working for its local subsidiary in his or her native society.

International human resource management (IHRM)   A field distinct from domestic human resources due to its unique responsibility for expatriate personnel, foreign staffing, labor relations, host-country employee and management relations, and management of related compensation and benefits.

Parent-country national (PCN)   A native of the parent company's society assigned to one of its foreign operations.

Predeparture training   Expatriate's training before leaving on an overseas assignment to develop technical, social, and cultural skills required to successfully adapt.

Relational skills   Personal attributes and interpersonal communication or behavioral abilities that help international managers to accommodate or adjust to people and situations in a foreign culture.

Repatriation   The process of reintegrating expatriates into parent organizations and their home societies after they complete foreign assignments.

Stability zone   An activity, event, or social interest that allows expatriates to periodically decompress or break away from living and working in a foreign culture, often in ways that reconnect them with their own culture and other people who share common cultural interests.

Succession plan   A formal career plan that integrates the expatriate cycle into a wider sequence of prospective foreign and domestic assignments to ensure continuity of company and personal interests prior to, during, and following the cross-border assignment.

Third-country national (TCN)   An expatriate employee working for a parent company in one of its foreign operations outside the individual's native society.

Transpatriate   A global manager whose career transcends national borders, with no anchor to a home-country position.

EXERCISES

1. Interview someone who has worked as an expatriate to identify his or her viewpoints about the benefits and difficulties of working abroad. The interview can be more meaningful if you create a brief list, from the chapter, of questions and issues to cover. If possible, interview two or more subjects to provide a contrast, including a woman who has been in an expatriate role. Often, faculty members have worked in foreign assignments; if you can find one, determine what university programs support the expatriate experience.

2. Contact a company with international interests to arrange an interview with a human resource manager involved with expatriate assignments. Assemble a profile of the firm's IHRM activities and programs related to selection, training, sponsorship, and repatriation. Determine how the company measures success or failure of expatriates and whether it relies on a career-tracking process to help expatriates reenter, and perhaps advance themselves, within their home environments.

3. Interview a family that has been overseas on assignment and subsequently returned. Develop a profile of the wife's problems (assuming she accompanied an expatriate husband) and children's difficulties and a scenario of company programs or other means available for family assistance. As a team effort, interview a family, school officials concerning expatriate children, and a company concerning family support programs. Develop a profile of your findings for class discussion.

MOTOROLA: HOMEGROWN TALENT THROUGH SIMULATION

Motorola's experience shutting down Iridium, which cost the company 3.5 billion, taught this multinational company a valuable lesson in global business. The Iridium telephone system, a global satellite-based wireless system designed to "go anywhere," appeared to be a technological solution for consumers who depended on telephones for communication when traveling anywhere in the world. By all accounts, it appeared that Motorola had done its homework and prepared for the launching and positions of the 66 satellites. So what went wrong?

A number of marketing-related factors contributed to the failure of the Iridium project—product, price, place, and promotion. Not only did the phone set weigh about one pound, which was much heavier than the newer PCS phones that weighed ounces, but its shape made it awkward and difficult to access. In addition, the worldwide travelers needed several attachments in order to take advantage of the Iridium system's benefits. The initial cost of an Iridium phone and the airtime charges far exceeded the costs of cellular phones and the more contemporary PCS phones. The opportunities to use the Iridium systems also turned out to be limited. Although the Iridium system was marketed as a go-anywhere system, it turned out there were common places in the world that could not be accessed by the orbiting satellite system. Finally, while the advertising and public relations campaigns designed to promote Iridium in more than 20 countries were effective in getting about 1.5 million people to inquire about the system, many of the calls went unanswered.

The North American sales efforts did not prove to be fruitful. The promotional campaigns, however, were well orchestrated and included television campaigns and advertisements in journals such as *Fortune* and *The Wall Street Journal*. But such was not the case with the efforts of Motorola's international partners, who did not have strong backgrounds in marketing high-technology telephone equipment. The advertising and public relations campaigns were able to pique interest in Iridium and avoid the issues addressed earlier (price, product, place, etc.). Salespersons, on the other hand, could not; so only about 20,000 of the 1.5 million inquiries resulted in actual subscriptions. In effect, Motorola was unable to generate the cash flow needed to keep the project afloat.

A lesson was learned—Motorola now relies primarily on homegrown talent to run its global businesses. Global business is becoming increasingly complex and multinationals are finding it harder to locate the talent needed to run global businesses. According to Kelly Brookhouse, who directs Motorola's executive-development program, "We realized we need to develop our next-generation managers." Building upon evaluation tools that have been around since World War II, Motorola uses workplace simulation exercises to identify and evaluate potential candidates for international management positions. According to Brookhouse,

> We put people into a simulated environment and throw business challenges at them to see how they respond. . . . We get a fairly comprehensive picture of people's leadership profile.

Here's how the program works. Foreign work candidates are flown to central locations for evaluation. Lasting from one day to three weeks, the evaluations are administered through the use of role-playing exercises, trained assessors, and Motorola's Internet-based test (developed with Aon Consulting Worldwide). Due to a shortage of management talent in China, Motorola established a pilot program there that evaluated over 150 subjects by the end of 2000, according to Brookhouse. In addition, Motorola plans to assess the management talent of nearly 500 executives in 2001 through the use of its life-like program. After participating in the program, Mandy Chooi, a human resource executive at Motorola who is based in Beijing, said, "It was hard. A lot harder than I had expected. It's surprising how realistic and demanding it is."

QUESTIONS

1. Why would major companies such as a Motorola make such fundamental mistakes in managing a global business? What measures could Motorola have taken to improve the potential success of the Iridium project?
2. Explore the benefits of Motorola's "homegrown talent" program. What more could the company do to evaluate candidates for foreign work?
3. How would you respond to participating in Motorola's executive-development program?

BIBLIOGRAPHY

Olson, Eric M., Stanley F. Slater, and Andrew J. Czaplewski. "The Iridium Story: A Marketing Disconnect?" *Marketing Management*, 1 July 2000, 54–57. [Retrieved 11 December 2000 from Dow Jones Interactive database.]

Woodruff, David. "Your Career Matters: Distractions Make Global Manager a Difficult Role." *Wall Street Journal*, 21 November 2000, p. B1. [Retrieved 11 December 2000 from Dow Jones Interactive database.] See also "Conjuring Up a Crisis— Firms Put Candidates through a Battery of Tests." *Asian Wall Street Journal*, 17 November 2000, p. P3. [Retrieved 11 December 2000 from Dow Jones Interactive database.]

CASE 12.2

GLOBAL MOBILITY: WOMEN AND THE GLOBAL MANAGER SHORTAGE

Many multinationals operating overseas are experiencing a shortage of management talent and looking for innovative ways to attract and retain global managers. In the past, generous allowances and expatriate benefits packages have been used to attract people into the global management arena. But current studies have revealed that other issues come into play when considering global mobility.

TMP Worldwide, an executive search consultancy, surveyed Britain's largest 500 companies. The survey found that while nearly 90 percent of senior managers place importance on the global mobility of executives, over 50 percent of top managers said they were now less likely to make the personal sacrifices necessary to accept an overseas assignment. TMP's UK managing director, Andrew Simpson, believes "the causes include the rise in dual-career families and the fact that people who have divorced and remarried are reluctant to consider a lifestyle that could put their second marriage at risk. Other factors include an unwillingness to interrupt children's education and the need to care for elderly parents."

Women represent 49 percent of all American managers and professionals; however, only 13 percent are given global assignments. A new study by Catalyst, a nonprofit research organization, called "Passport to Opportunity: U.S. Women in Global Business," was designed to explore reasons why women are not sent abroad. It revealed several misconceptions about women. According to the study, in which Catalyst interviewed and surveyed over 1,000 current and former women and men expatriates,

> Survey respondents believe that women are not as "internationally mobile" as men, yet 80 percent of women expatriates (working abroad) have never turned down a relocation, compared to 71 percent of men. A second powerful assumption is that women encounter more work/life conflict managing a global schedule. However, nearly half of both women and men report they find work/life balance difficult. Lastly, the survey respondents believe clients outside the US are not as comfortable doing business with women as they are with men. In fact, 77 percent of women expatriates report being very effective at building business relationships with men of other cultures.

The majority of human resource executives who participated in the survey indicted that their companies, like many companies that have overseas operations, are dealing with a shortage of global managers. In addition, developing global talent is a high priority for nearly 50 percent of these respondents. An overwhelming majority (90 percent) of women expatriates responded that they would accept their current assignment again, yet U.S. companies barely utilize this pool of global management resources. Sheila Wellington, president of Catalyst, said:

> The bottom line is that these stereotypes—one on top of the other—makes it less likely that decision makers are going to think of women managers when they build executive global teams. . . . This is destructive because as it turns out, women want these assignments, they do well abroad, and they told Catalyst they would seize the opportunity again.

Some companies have altered their strategies for attracting and retaining global management talent in order to address people's concerns about working abroad and to reduce the costs associated with expatriates. PriceWaterhouseCooper, a consultancy, surveyed over 270 top European businesses and found that options such as short-term assignments and travel home every weekend from workplaces were being used to make the global experience more attractive to employees. In addition, increases in the use of technology such as videoconferencing and e-mail are reducing the frequency of travel for global managers.

Such changes will require changes in how global managers are trained for overseas experiences. According to Chris Crosby, managing director of human resources at TMA for Europe (a human resources consultancy):

> The traditional route for expatriate training focused on briefing people about the country they were gong to live in and how to survive "culture shock." Now we're training people to work collaboratively with people from a range of other cultures. This type of cross-cultural training is more about attitudes and behavior and requires a deeper understanding of other cultures and your own.

It is not known whether changes such as short-term assignments and the use of technology will attract company employees into the international arena, but the picture remains clear—developing global managers is a high priority for many companies. Even airlines such as British Airways are responding to the needs of international business travelers on short-term assignments by offering services such as showers, massages, and aromatherapy while these passengers wait for the next flight.

QUESTIONS

1. How do you think U.S. companies should address the shortage of globally mobile executives? Given the concerns addressed by top managers, what strategies would you consider to make the international experience more palatable for employees?
2. What program would you recommend for a company to improve preparation of promising recruits for foreign positions?
3. How would you go about encouraging U.S. companies to utilize their qualified pool of women managers for international assignments? Support your views.

BIBLIOGRAPHY

Baker, Peter. "Work: Just How Far Will You Go for Your Job? Paris? Tokyo?" *The Guardian*, 17 May 2000. [Retrieved 11 December 2000 from Dow Jones Interactive database.]

"Misconceptions about Women in the Global Arena Keep Their Numbers Low: Shortage of Global Managers Hindering Companies' Ability to Expand Globally." *PR Newswire*, 18 October 2000. [Retrieved 11 December 2000 from Dow Jones Interactive database.]

HUMAN RESOURCES: STAFFING, TRAINING, AND DEVELOPMENT

CHAPTER OBJECTIVES

Highlight the roles and responsibilities of international managers for human resource development.

Explain the primary means through which a company can develop capable international executives.

Describe the major considerations for staffing foreign subsidiaries with host-country managers.

Contrast the advantages and disadvantages of hiring locally for subsidiary management.

Detail important problems associated with recruiting local employees in host countries.

List the training techniques best suited for foreign employees.

Discuss methods that international companies employ for human resource development.

CHAPTER 13

Gillette sells more products to more people in more countries than any other consumer goods company ever. According to the company's chairman, Alfred M. Zeien, the Gillette name is arguably the most recognized brand in the world (with due credit to contender Coca-Cola).[1] Zeien (pronounced "zane") attributes Gillette's success to two principles. First, it does the best job of any firm worldwide in its core businesses and in responding to customer needs. Second, it maintains a fast-moving organization staffed by globally minded people. With 34,000 employees spread over 200 countries and territories, the company is, Zeien says, a "cosmopolitan" firm. Internationally trained line managers are to Gillette "what the telegraph was to the early railroads." If anything keeps the chairman awake at night, it is his concern about developing competent managers capable of global effectiveness.

Zeien believes that growth at Gillette is constrained only by "the rate at which we can build management." The company has been growing at a 20 percent annual clip since 1991, when Zeien became CEO, but it had experienced stiff competition and financial difficulties during the previous decade. The French giant Bic ripped into Gillette's market share with the first disposable razors in the 1980s, and then Revlon targeted the company's men's care products. Parker Pen eclipsed Gillette's fledgling interests in writing instruments, and Germany's Braun became a global player threatening its foreign markets. Gillette dug in its heels and began creating new shaving systems, men's care products, personal appliances, and toothbrushes. It became the leading innovator and strongest global distributor in the industry. Along with beating rivals, the company bought out several of its competitors, including Parker Pen, Waterman of France, and Braun of Germany.

When Zeien took over, Gillette was a centralized, hierarchical, and U.S.-centered enterprise driven entirely by decisions made at its Boston headquarters. Since 1991, Gillette has become a globally integrated company with research and development in the United States, Germany, China, and India; manufacturing on three continents; and intensely localized marketing and distribution functions that can respond to any customer order within hours. Today Gillette is the world market leader, with more than half of total global sales in razor blades and shaving systems. It is also the market leader in writing instruments and men's toiletries, and it holds its own in nip-and-tuck rivalries for global leadership in electric shavers and personal appliances. More than 70 percent of the company's total sales and operating profits are generated outside the U.S. market, but Zeien cannot find the managers he needs to fulfill the company's growth potential.

"It takes 10 to 14 years to develop a capable international manager," Zeien explains, "and we are only in the middle of that cycle." Gillette had placed more than 350 U.S. expatriates in foreign positions between 1991 and 1996 and had placed an additional 700 U.S. expatriates overseas through 1998. U.S.-born foreign managers currently number about 15 percent of the company's total complement, but that will more than double by 2002. Currently, nearly 3,000 host-country managers run foreign operations, and 1,000 more are in early development stages of their careers. Gillette is a less attractive employer to young U.S. talent than to foreign-born managers, making recruitment by Gillette often difficult. U.S. natives require language training, global orientations within responsible foreign assignments, and motivation to go abroad, according to Zeien.

"Say you're born in Pakistan," he explains, "and you study at an American university . . . [Y]ou speak English well. You say, 'Gee, if I work for Gillette, I can work in four or five countries, it's a nice career.' So Gillette is a magnet that attracts many non-Americans." The problem with U.S. recruits, Zeien explains, is that too few are prepared to accept the reality that the world does not end at their native borders. He feels that young managers are just not prepared culturally or socially to compete in a global market. He also believes that Gillette and most other major companies in the *Fortune 500*—whether they are in manufacturing or services—must accept that competition is global, and survival depends on competing with the same intensity. He concludes that most goods and services relate to global markets, and managers must do the same thing in a hurry.

PERSPECTIVE ON INTERNATIONAL HUMAN RESOURCE MANAGEMENT

International human resource management is primarily associated with meeting a company's needs for expatriate talent and staffing its subsidiaries, but the field encompasses much broader considerations. Once expatriates are sent abroad, for example, they assume new roles in foreign operations, but their careers remain rooted in their home countries. IHRM staff must help those expatriates succeed in one world while maintaining viable careers in another. In a global company, expatriates are involved in *interdependent* systems of activities that create complicated issues of coordinating work in *multicultural* environments.

IHRM is concerned with developing human resource capabilities to meet the needs of multinational configurations with little resemblance to traditional organizations. As the previous chapter emphasized, an expatriate steps into a somewhat uncertain world where his or her career path is vague, and where there are higher risks of working abroad. Helping these expatriates manage their careers is a challenge, yet almost everyone involved in a multinational enterprise is affected to some extent by the international nature of the company's business. Executives at home and abroad must meet more extensive responsibilities than a purely domestic business would impose, and they must help young managers to develop the skills they need to compete in global markets. Home-based staff must learn new skills of international business in order to work with foreign customers and alliance partners. Human resource managers, in particular, must staff and train both domestic and foreign employees so the firm can meet these challenges.

A company's human resource profile changes dramatically as it evolves through stages of internationalization. During this evolution, IHRM is concerned with three broad levels of development. First, as the strategic configuration of an enterprise expands, the company requires executives capable of managing a diversified international system of activities. Second, as foreign activities gain prominence, managers of overseas subsidiaries must develop the capabilities of working within an interdependent global system, and they must provide capable leadership within their local enterprises. Third, as a company expands its network of foreign subsidiaries and alliances, needs for local workforces create requirements for staffing, training, and harmonizing employee groups to reflect the priorities, processes, and technologies of the emerging multinational enterprise. This combination of activities suggests substantial new responsibilities for line managers and professional HRM staff, who must develop unique systems to support international human resource capabilities.

As this chapter will explain, an international organization's human resource requirements differ in important ways from those for a domestic enterprise. Management must therefore take a different approach to recruiting, staffing, training, and employee development. The configuration of a company's human resources also depends on power dynamics and the parent company's philosophy of how to manage its foreign operations.

The Human Dynamics of Power

A company's management philosophy determines its structure and staffing needs, and this relationship extends from the executive suite to the most remote foreign outpost. A human resource manager views a firm's philosophical orientation as a system of *human dynamics*, that is, as a configuration of *power relationships* defined within the global structure.[2] Figure 13.1 identifies four philosophical orientations introduced earlier in the book, together with the influences on human resource decisions in each one.

In some instances, these four orientations could be viewed along a continuum with *ethnocentric* staffing defining one extreme and *geocentric* staffing defining the other. A continuum offers a useful model for describing management prerogatives, because those decisions may vary in centralization or decentralization, reflecting distinct mind-sets about sharing power and authority. Almost every other aspect of human resource management—staffing, development, training, communications, and labor relations—depends on the company's predisposition toward power and authority relationships. An ethnocentric orientation implies a tendency to impose values or viewpoints on others. A centralized organization does not necessarily imply ethnocentrism, however; some care must be taken in using the term. Nevertheless, a centralized decision-making environment characteristically relies on decisions from parent-company executives, who control worldwide operations directly or through carefully selected managers. *Control* is the central goal, and it is best achieved by parent-company expatriates, through whom headquarters can call the shots in foreign operations.

A polycentric management approach, in contrast, would distribute authority for operating decisions among foreign subsidiaries but under limits defined by an executive umbrella. Foreign managers or expatriates may work relatively independently in such a system, but they must fulfill direct reporting requirements to the parent company. The polycentric model implies no presumption of control for interdependent

FIGURE 13.1
Influence of
Philosophical
Orientations on
Staffing Decisions

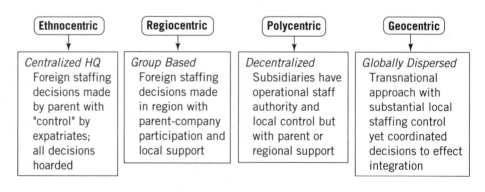

activities or network relationships. Therefore, human resource activities may reflect traditional systems of staffing, and HRM responsibilities may be guided by home-office policy.

In contrast, *regiocentric staffing* reflects the priorities of groups of foreign business units. A regional group usually encompasses a geographic area, such as Europe or South America, in which units function autonomously as a system of subsidiaries. Their managers assume responsibilities for investments, regional development, and within-group staffing patterns. A group might also be defined by a product-market profile. Aerospace companies tend to follow this pattern; they distinguish units according to product lines and associated client bases, creating separate groups to sell fighter aircraft globally to military buyers and commercial aircraft globally to national airlines. The concept of a region can therefore become ambiguous as it takes on structural characteristics of a matrix organization. Human resource managers apply the term *geographic staffing* to describe employment requirements in this system. The concept suggests a borderless approach to management decisions, where international alliances and affiliations operate with substantial autonomy within boundaries defined by interdependent responsibilities for related operations. In this situation, parent-company executives do not control decisions; instead, they coordinate and orchestrate decisions by others.

These distinctions in management philosophies determine different patterns of relationships, as well as different responsibilities for human resource staffing, training, and development. More important, as a company grows and alters its configuration, managers must rapidly respond to new priorities for meeting its human resources needs. As an organization's operations become progressively more globally dispersed, human resources are deployed differently, and both parent and subsidiary operations experience a power shift. This change requires managers to improve coordination skills so they can work effectively in multicultural environments. Consequently, management systems change, and IHRM professionals must recruit differently or help current employees to develop the skills required in new multinational roles.

Unfortunately, this task is easier said than done. In a recent survey, *Fortune 500* companies identified shifting priorities as among the most perplexing problems that managers encounter, and few of the respondents felt that they had adequate systems in place for properly staffing their organizations. Executives who responded to the survey from Texas Instruments, Honeywell, IBM, and Texaco adamantly agreed that the field of human resource management is being transformed to meet the growing challenges of multicultural management in a competitive global economy.[3]

Focus of the Chapter

The scope of international human resource management represents a comprehensive field of activities. Although this chapter cannot address all the issues, it does explore the primary concepts. The chapter builds on the framework of four organizational perspectives to address executive staffing and development responsibilities within the *general management system* of a multinational enterprise. The focus then shifts to issues of staff development and training for *subsidiary managers*, which differ substantially between companies configured according to each of the four models. Each configuration determines priorities for *staffing local enterprises*, and later sections will examine the various means of recruiting and training employees in foreign subsidiaries. Finally, the chapter introduces some aspects of *management development* programs, and it concludes with recommendations to help companies prepare managers for international careers.

GENERAL MANAGEMENT AND EXECUTIVE DEVELOPMENT

In an attempt to describe changes in roles for senior international managers, a round-table of executives met at the Cranfield School of Management in Britain. A summary of the group's conclusions reveals a significant challenge for the new millennium, including a worldwide technological revolution that has created many new occupations and functional specializations that did not exist a few years ago.[4] In addition, clear career tracks, particularly for international managers, have disappeared; in many countries, such as Sweden, Denmark, Germany, and Italy, part-time workers, job sharing, short-term contracts, and a growing "gray-collar" workforce of aging professionals have redefined organizational priorities. With rationalization (often described by euphemisms such as *downsizing* and *rightsizing*), core organizations have shrunk and flattened. At the same time, organizational alliances, outsourcing, subcontracting, and networks of mutually dependent enterprises have dramatically widened systems of associated tasks that ignore borders, cross cultures, and blur boundaries among companies, suppliers, and customers. Cheap labor in the Pacific Rim, South America, and Eastern Europe has exerted a downward pressure on prices and factor costs, yet accelerated trade activities within and between regions have boosted demand. These forces have often created spiraling systems of prices and wages in high-growth economies.

An international executive is now expected to act as a competent leader who can manage in this dynamic environment and be an insightful architect of organizational change. A global executive in Europe, North America, or Asia faces potentially conflicting challenges of redefining the parent company as a center of global coordination between small, relatively independent teams of experienced people. Meanwhile, globalization also affects organizational values. Rapid expansion through global alliances and multifaceted workforces brings many different people together, in the process eliminating personal characteristics of race, creed, color, and gender as variables in a transnational world governed only by performance. Within this framework, general managers with company-wide responsibilities must define their organization and how its work is accomplished.

Roles of General Managers

The international roles of general managers are changing in two fundamental ways. First, technical capabilities have become far less important than relational skills required in global alliances and integrated organizations. Second, executives can no longer manage from a particular national perspective; instead, they must participate in a transparent network of multicultural interests. Who, then, are general managers— and what do they do?

International general managers hold positions with pervasive multifunctional responsibilities that span multiple business units unrestricted by national borders or home-country cultures.[5] The category of general managers includes chief executive officers, managing directors, and senior operating officers. In regiocentric organizations, these executives act as group heads with titles such as *regional president* or *director* and similar responsibilities. Often, their regional responsibilities include overseeing miniature multinationals within the broader frameworks of global enterprises. At the national level, country managers may also hold titles such as *president* or *managing director* within individual subsidiaries; they too assume broad-based responsibilities that often require cross-border coordination and multifunctional networking.

Titles of general managers can lead to confusion about their specific roles, and such a label does not always accurately describe the range of an executive's authority. For example, the managing director of Canon Europe is responsible for the company's activities in Western Europe, but not in Central and Eastern European countries previously associated with the Soviet bloc. In addition, the boundaries of Canon Europe's territory also include parts of North Africa and western Asia.[6] Canon's overall management structure is shown in Figure 13.2. Similarly, Ernst & Young, the U.S.-based multinational accounting and consulting firm, has headquartered its European operations in Brussels, from which the regional director manages operations in 35 countries ranging from Estonia to Nigeria. In contrast, AT&T assigns the title of general manager Europe to an executive who spends more time in the United States than in the European office in Zurich—which carries out regional responsibilities almost seamlessly with those of New York, Berlin, London, and even less developed places such as Sophia, Bulgaria, or Riga, Latvia. Consequently, management responsibilities and the

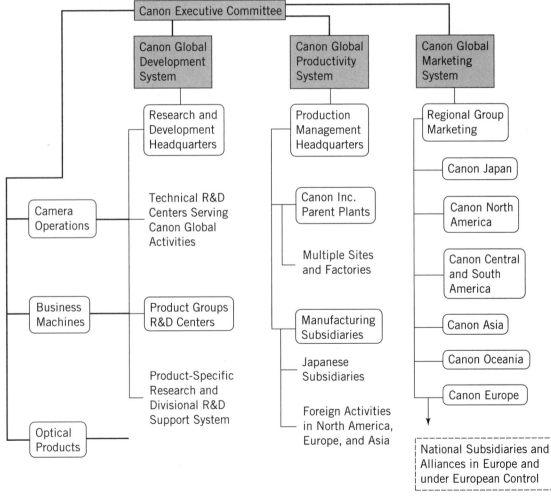

FIGURE 13.2
Canon Global and Group Organization
Source: Adapted from *The Canon Story* (Tokyo: Canon Inc., 1989).

scope of a business unit's activities cannot be explained simply by geographic boundaries, nationalities, specific markets, services, or product lines.[7]

Until recently, many American and European multinationals have favored patterns of management responsibilities similar to the chain-of-command *executive-head* system that prevailed prior to World War II. An executive-head system positioned the CEO as an overlord commanding subsidiary executives, who subsequently maintained control of regional groups through intermediate officials. Today, only a few of the largest firms retain this model of management control. Instead, a typical CEO now assumes the role of a **coordinative head** of a confederated organization. A progressive change in organizational configurations (described in Chapter 7) often alters managerial decision-making responsibilities. As a company breaks away from a centralized system of dominant executive control to establish a matrix or integrated system, the power dynamics and interpersonal relationships of senior executives undergo dramatic changes. In many instances, the concept of an executive no longer implies a single person, referring instead to a company-wide team. At Eastman Kodak, a CEO, a vice chairperson, and two joint assistant operating officers comprise a governance committee.[8] One individual officially heads the team, but its collaborative and coordinative responsibilities require a team effort of diverse skills and executive talents. For example, Sony Corporation maintains a distinctly Japanese organizational culture with a traditional strong CEO, yet operating management rests with an *executive committee*. Sony's regional management centers, such as Sony Europe, respond to instructions from similar executive committees composed of general managers drawn from subsidiary divisions.[9]

A third approach to general management creates a system particularly well suited to organizing regional executive systems. The firm establishes **representative heads** adept at integrating subsidiary activities.[10] Country and subsidiary managers who appear to report to a regional representative head do not necessarily interact with that executive in superior-subordinate relationships. Instead, these managers exercise nearly autonomous operational authority, while the representative head performs an integrative role as a coordinator and team facilitator. Subsidiaries and divisions report to product or marketing groups or through functional channels, not to the representative head. Although he or she may exert extremely powerful influence due to rank and home-office connections, the position seldom confers direct decision-making authority over foreign operations. The representative head suggests and recommends, and the firm holds this official accountable for activities in relational networks, but it does not assign accountability for profits and losses. Companies such as GE, AT&T, and ABB have spearheaded this ambassadorial approach.

The Japanese proclivity toward homogeneous parent-country control keeps most foreign interests under the authority of a Japanese executive corps. Hitachi has diverged from this model by creating relational networks among nearly 700 global operating units. These units are grouped by geographic regions and coordinated through consensus-oriented committees of executives drawn from subsidiaries within each group.[11] Management roles are therefore changing to emphasize horizontal coordination over vertical authority. Executives exert less direct control over decisions than they once did; instead, they rely on persuasion and power sharing. A conceptual view of the representative-head organization is shown in Figure 13.3.

Developing Executive Talent

The innovative, boundary-spanning roles of today's executives require new interpersonal management skills and multifunctional insight into organizational systems.

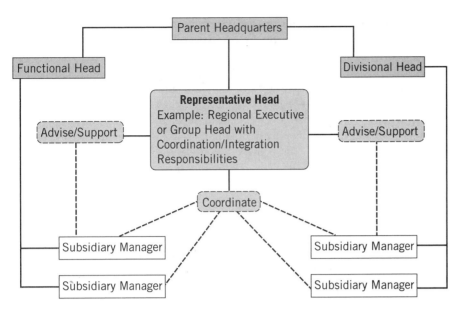

FIGURE 13.3
Managerial Relationships
of a Representative-Head
Organization

Consequently, executives are developed into these roles, but practices differ significantly in North America, Europe, and Asia. North American multinationals (and more specifically those from the United States) favor division-specific **career development** by which managers rise to senior posts through their respective affiliates or operating divisions. They tend to remain in their functional areas of specialization and earn promotions into senior positions over periods of years. Many U.S. companies expect their executives to acquire international experience, and they promote this development by posting managers to foreign assignments. In the past, these positions have seldom taken employees outside their divisional hierarchies or functional specialties, but that tendency may have begun to change. Six of the ten senior group executives at 3M Corporation, for example, have developed at least eight years experience in three different interdivisional positions, and Kodak's president and vice chairman was appointed over domestic contenders based on spending more than half a career overseas in multidimensional posts.[12]

Few foreign executives ascend to executive positions in U.S. companies, and their careers are often territorially bounded (or specific to particular divisions). Obviously, this practice limits their access to regional and parent-company executive positions, yet U.S. multinationals are more likely than Europeans or Asians to rapidly promote host-country managers to senior foreign posts within their respective divisions. Foreign managers bump against an imaginary ceiling in U.S. companies, despite notable exceptions. For example, Ford's former CEO, Alex Trotman, is British, and Ford's new CEO, Jacques Nasser, is a native of Australia. Also, the recently retired chairman of H. J. Heinz, Tony O'Reilly, came from Ireland. Many other U.S. companies have appointed foreign directors, senior line managers, and group executives, but indeed, they are exceptions.[13]

To counter this limitation, and to develop stronger cadres of experienced executives, several U.S. companies have established international development programs. Ford initiated a series of management exchanges that began in 1992 by assigning nearly 500 midlevel and junior executives from the United States to British and German positions, while British and German managers were reassigned to Detroit. This program has grown to include interdivisional reassignments among European offices and between the United States, Europe, Asia, and South America.[14] Similarly, GE created an International Division specifically to initiate executive training for cross-cultural assignments. This division identifies high-potential junior managers and then provides in-house development training based on job rotation through several foreign positions. The junior managers' careers are tracked toward international executive posts, not toward traditional channels in department or functional specialities. As an essential part of this development, the company creates joint activities that bring international managers together in team environments, thus breaking down hierarchical barriers and compartmentalized behavior fostered by functional specialization.

Exxon has established a similar program that seeks to diversify the company's workforce to broaden representation of minorities and women in the international career development processes. Exxon's program, called *compensation and executive development* or *COED*, brings together selected managers with international potential at several distinct organizational levels; it then monitors their development and rates participants both qualitatively and quantitatively during their assignments. Managers are subsequently selected for international positions based on progressive performance and evaluations. The Ford, GE, and Exxon programs are long-term efforts designed to help develop executives for postings 10 to 20 years into the future. Consequently, individual job assignments span several years in each position, leading toward progressively greater management responsibilities coupled with periodic formal training.[15]

In contrast to the U.S. approach, European firms rely extensively on country-specific staffing patterns and give their subsidiaries extensive autonomy to develop young managers. However, European parent companies draw executives from their subsidiaries much more readily than U.S. multinationals do, so their management teams tend to display more diversified backgrounds. European headquarters participate less actively than U.S. companies in training executives. Although home-office personnel seldom become involved in actual recruitment, senior European executives are more directly involved than U.S. executives in orchestrating management assignments.

Eugene Matthews is among a growing number of African Americans thriving in foreign management positions for multinational corporations. He has worked in Vietnam as a business consultant since 1990 and represented U.S. publishers in Southeast Asia. Matthews will soon be in Japan as an investment specialist providing venture capital to smaller international companies. An African American colleague of Matthews explained that they can succeed comfortably abroad because, ironically, foreigners have had so little experience with Black expatriates that there are few racial boundaries or preconceived stereotypes.

In this regard, they powerfully influence executive development. Fiat, the leading Italian carmaker with operations in more than 100 foreign countries, has initiated an unusual approach to executive development. The company created a subsidiary called *ISVOR* (an acronym for the Italian term that translates as *internal corporate executive development*) with authority for training, development, job rotation, performance reviews, and interdivisional transfers. ISVOR acts somewhat like an executive consultant firm with unusual authority for worldwide management development. Along with technical training for general leadership roles, it supports language studies, cross-cultural sensitivity training, and internships for foreign nationals in parent-company posts, where they become acquainted with Fiat's home culture and organizational systems.[16]

Executive development in Japan contrasts vividly with the U.S. and European approaches. The importance placed on homogeneity and company allegiance in Japan has created a system of organizational development that bonds employers and employees to one another. Employees and prospective managers typically go through an extensive culling process at the job-entry stage, survivors of which develop into their individual careers as "company people." Consequently, an individual's functional specialization has always been less important in Japan than seniority and performance within the total organization. Managers are not territorially locked into one division or one occupational field, and they commonly transfer between divisions. Therefore, a manager ostensibly educated as an engineer may have amassed several years of experience in marketing, production, research and development, and administrative posts at the company's headquarters.

Companies look for promising executive talent as employees progress in seniority, purposely assigning the best candidates for advancement as "assistants" to important executives, who mentor them for still higher posts. International managers are groomed in similar ways, but before they go into the field, they are extensively trained by the parent company in Japan and work as liaisons at headquarters. Often, the career prospects of these employees are associated with the executives to whom they are assigned; the best candidates work under the most senior executives, and those with the greatest international potential are routed toward the most important foreign subsidiaries. The rigorous culling process common in Japan continues throughout these development efforts, and managers earn advancement opportunities based on performance. Those who do not measure up may be reassigned to more suitable positions or perhaps parachuted to divisions where their careers take undemanding routes. In all instances, seniority is a major factor in rank and compensation; a Japanese manager rarely moves on a fast track past other managers or circumvents the chain of promotions.[17]

In Japanese companies, the combination of mentoring, formal development training, and broad-based interfunctional and interdivisional experience results in well-seasoned managers in executive roles. As a result, few people who are not native Japanese have opportunities to pursue executive positions in Japanese enterprises. The country's multinationals have, however, begun to purposely hire externally in host countries, recognizing that foreign subsidiaries must achieve some cultural assimilation. Honda's U.S. operations in Ohio, Nissan's truck facility in Tennessee, and Mitsui's regional European group headquartered in Brussels are among the Japanese firms with senior host-country directors. In each instance, the companies filled these posts with externally recruited executives who had significant international experience. Also, all were assigned to the parent company in Japan to work closely with Japanese executives as they made the transition into their new appointments.[18] Relatively few Japanese companies pursue host-country executives, despite good reasons for doing so. Often, firms need to project local company images, and local employees may be very sensitive about working for foreign executives. Many foreign subsidiaries must coordinate complicated alliances, and a host-country national often can identify with local customs and leadership expectations in ways that an expatriate cannot match. Table 13.1 emphasizes the main reasons why companies hire local executives.

Multinational companies actively try to create cadres of international managers drawn from host-country and third-country sources. They also are improving their external recruiting to draw candidates from other multinationals, although most generally rely on internal development and progressive promotions along recognized international career tracks. Procter & Gamble and Royal Dutch Shell, among other multinationals, work aggressively to "denationalize" their general management ranks.[19] They do so by requiring managers to work in multiple foreign assignments, to exhibit diverse language skills, and to demonstrate adaptation skills through

TABLE 13.1

WHEN COMPANIES FAVOR HOST-COUNTRY EXECUTIVES OVER EXPATRIATES

Situation or Consideration	Advantage to the Company of a Host-Country Executive
Need for local image	A foreign or host-country executive reduces the contrasts that an expatriate creates; customers and local employees often feel more comfortable working with others like themselves.
Severe cultural differences	A host-country executive understands the nuances of a society, eliminating potential problems with culture shock.
Political sensitivity/ instability	Host and home countries may exhibit delicate ideological differences; a host-country executive reduces political risk and the potential for misunderstandings.
Contrasting business methods	Subtle ways of doing business may be deeply ingrained in local traditions, requiring a local manager capable of networking and dealing in familiar ways with government officials, vendors, customers, and investors.
Difficult methods of negotiation	A host-country executive understands a country's subtle protocols, behavior, emotions, methods of negotiations, and communications.
Complicated foreign alliances	Expectations, behavior, and priorities of foreign partners and investors may require involvement of a host-country executive with strong integrative skills.
Economics of foreign assignment	In a less-developed country, a host-country manager may work at a lower cost than an expatriate with comparable skills relevant to the assignment.
Major social/economic differences	Stark socioeconomic differences between host and home countries may create insurmountable obstacles for an expatriate; host-country executive needs no acclimatization to such conditions.
Differences in leadership expectations	Local biases, expectations, and roles of leaders may force a difficult adaptation challenge for an expatriate; a host-country executive may bring a more complementary style to the assignment.

experience in cross-cultural negotiations and by participating in foreign team projects. These managers are not *selected* in the traditional sense of the word; rather, their employers encourage them to pursue international management careers through supportive training and opportunities for foreign postings.

SUBSIDIARY MANAGEMENT AND STAFF DEVELOPMENT

Companies recruit people to manage foreign subsidiaries internally from home-office staff, among incumbents in existing host-country positions, and from qualified candidates in third-country subsidiaries. Recruiters might also canvas external sources. Home-office or third-country recruiting focuses on placing expatriates in management positions. Although local recruitment for host-country managers differs in many ways from the process for assigning an expatriate, firms fill their foreign management posts in fundamentally the same ways under all the options. Two questions affect these staffing decisions: What qualities and characteristics are required in the foreign position? Where can recruiters find an appropriate candidate? Answers to both questions may sound simple, but many factors complicate staffing decisions. This section begins with an examination of these factors, leading up to an explanation of the recruitment process.

Factors Affecting Subsidiary Staffing Decisions

Competition among global companies, specifically in foreign countries operating domestic enterprises, influences the staffing decisions of foreign subsidiaries. A company may be strongly motivated to fill key management posts with expatriates if competition in its industry chiefly pits major global companies against one another, and particularly if competitive advantage in the industry depends on integrated activities that involve many diverse foreign operations. An expatriate can apply a broad range of experience to such a management task, along with an understanding of the dynamics of an integrated multinational enterprise. On the other hand, in an industry with distinctly multilocal competition (i.e., each subsidiary competes within its own national market independently of others), a company may have good reason to seek out local management talent. However, neither of these polar scenarios is typical of global business conditions; most foreign subsidiaries undertake mixed selections of activities, some on their own and some interdependent with other operations. Therefore, the optimal answer implies seeking the best management talent regardless of the candidates' national origins or personal characteristics.

This conclusion may be an idealistic solution, because a company cannot realistically ignore the personal characteristics of management candidates. Individuals may experience difficulties in particular assignments due to irreconcilable religious conflicts or clashes between deeply rooted personal values and local beliefs. Although gender discrimination causes controversy in many societies, in others, gender is an important criterion for selection. Similarly, a manager's ethnic background may create tension with host-country employees, customers, or officials.

Staffing decisions also depend on the host country's stage of economic development. A country that lacks sophistication in transportation, basic necessities, and

GLOBAL VIEWPOINT

FINDING EXECUTIVE TALENT IN "OLD EUROPE"

Many observers regard Central and Eastern Europe as the "old Europe," with cultures and national societies predating many modern European states. Hungary, the Czech Republic, Bulgaria, Latvia, Lithuania, Poland, Estonia, and several former Soviet states have come to be known as "new" or "emerging" capitalist economies. Indeed, they are emerging from a half-century of industrial retardation, and they are new in the sense that they have reestablished (or created for the first time) democratic political and economic systems. These changes cannot overshadow the rich heritage of the region, however, and each country nurtures a tremendous sense of pride in its society. Each one also offers tremendous human resource capabilities among extremely well educated citizens. Many speak multiple languages, and most are skilled in science and technology. Unfortunately, very few have any idea about how to manage in a competitive environment, or to succeed in a market-driven industry. In short, few able managers populate old Europe, and fewer still show any vision of international management.

Foreign companies eager to do business in the old Europe have discovered new challenges in recruiting local managers. Recruiters cannot rely on hiring criteria such as applicant credentials, experience, education, or skills. Instead, they must look for fundamental characteristics that indicate management and leadership potential. Because judgments of these crucial characteristics are almost entirely subjective, staffing decisions often produce interesting results. Today's managers may have been medical doctors, professors, engineers, or even cooks under former regimes. One example illustrates the point.

Darinka Despotova is general manager of Kraft General Foods International, located in Svoge, Bulgaria. Kraft GFI took over a former state-owned chocolate factory in 1993, inheriting a workforce of several hundred employees. Surveying the acquisition, the company found itself without managers capable of western-style production or marketing activities. A search for raw talent turned up Despotova in the Bulgarian Ministry of Light Industry, where she held a research post as a Doctor of Science. Her enthusiasm prompted Kraft to hire her to bring the old factory to life. She did. The Kraft facility now has more than 400 full-time employees, a multicultural and multilingual management group, and rapidly expanding domestic and international sales. It has built a reputation as Bulgaria's leading chocolate manufacturer, surpassing the Swiss giant Nestlé SA in domestic sales.

Hiring Despotova to manage a foreign multinational's name-brand subsidiary may seem an unusual choice. She began the job with no experience in the field, having trained as a theoretical physicist. She came to the senior position a relatively young 40 years of age, with no knowledge of western management techniques or leadership systems. Nevertheless, she created a vision of success by working 65 hours a week to learn competitive business practices, subsequently translating that knowledge into training courses for her employees. Today, Despotova is involved in negotiating purchases of new plants and privatized facilities for Kraft while running one of her country's most successful privatized companies. Is she an unusual case? In many respects, she is—few women in old Europe (or much of new Europe) are considered for management posts. But in the emerging nations of Central and Eastern Europe, multinationals are looking past stereotypes and social biases to find management talent in any quarter. Despotova is not unusual in that regard. She is one of many from unexpected professions and organizations being hired and developed by global companies that emphasize performance first.

Old Europe hides much latent talent in survival jobs or beyond the recruiting reach of foreign companies, yet its citizens are often far better educated and experienced in sciences, engineering, math, and linguistics than their western counterparts. Some observers predict explosive growth and sustained development in old Europe, fueled in part by the emergence of this latent talent. Multinationals are fully aware of that potential and have placed heavy educational and development resources into the region.

Sources: Lori Ioannou, "A Worldwide Shortage of Quality Managers Forces U.S. Companies to Become Gender Blind When Staffing Foreign Operations," *International Business*, December 1994, 57–60. Also see Greg Steinmetz, "Hi, You're Hired: Workers of the World Who Need a Job Fast Might Look in Prague," *Wall Street Journal*, 2 December 1996, pp. A1, A16.

information technology presents a significant hardship for expatriates who generally are not accustomed to such rigors. Consequently, a host-country manager may be a better choice. On the other hand, less-developed economies sometimes demand the skills of expatriate managers who can function autonomously and effectively protect their companies' interests under difficult circumstances.

The stage of a country's development influences staffing decisions in other ways as well. Specifically, a start-up operation in an underdeveloped environment often requires close control by an experienced expatriate who, together with other qualified expatriate managers and technicians, can effectively launch the new enterprise. As the subsidiary grows and develops local talent, expatriates can be replaced by local personnel. In effect, a foreign operation passes through a life cycle marked by dynamic activities in new ventures and those in rapidly changing environments where expatriate talent is important. As the economy stabilizes (or the company becomes more stable), experienced expatriates are less needed; local managers may then be preferred.[20]

Development of regional markets and political alliances may also affect subsidiary staffing patterns, since managers within the region may have to maintain intercultural relationships. The unification of Europe, for example, has resulted in consolidation of manufacturing and marketing systems to serve a combined European Community. Therefore, a plant in France may draw employees from several other nations, deal with clients in a dozen different languages, and source parts and materials on a global basis. Consequently, a North American expatriate who lacks substantial continental experience may be at a severe disadvantage in this environment. Regionalization also forces large global companies to recruit managers according to their expertise and cultural adaptability *within particular regions.* A Japanese manager's extensive experience in North America may offer little help to a company regionally headquartered in the Netherlands. Regionalization is also important in Asia, where economic agreements such as ASEAN require intricate relationships among member nations in a politically sensitive environment.

A concern of all multinationals is a pervasive sense of nationalism that may lead to conflicts between countries. Nationalism has caused growing problems in developing economies, but strong feelings of national superiority also affect activities in the United States, France, and Germany. Of course, Japan has been criticized for its controversial protectionist measures; but all countries seek to protect their domestic industries, to maintain or enhance employment among their people, and to counter trade imbalances. Protectionism, with all its ramifications, constitutes a major deterrent to foreign expansion, and specifically to tolerance of foreign nationals in management positions. Most countries establish laws to regulate the number of expatriates and other foreigners who can work in particular companies. Also, as noted in Chapter 12, many countries require outside firms to place host-country managers in senior posts. Even when a company may technically choose between expatriate and local management, political sensitivities may compel it to staff a foreign operation with local personnel.

Finally, the prevailing management philosophy of parent-company executives may supersede all other considerations (within the constraints of foreign laws). Some organizations mirror Dow Chemical's resolve to recruit the best available talent, and Dow attempts to hire both internally and externally, without regard to nationality. Honeywell leans toward managers with regional experience, so it sponsors regional development programs specifically intended to generate a pool of diverse local talent. Its European division, for example, includes 12 non-American executives among its 20 most senior positions. Recall that Mitsui and a few other Japanese firms place non-Japanese managers in host-country positions. At the other end of the spectrum, the

Anglo-Dutch firm Unilever believes in hiring only local managers for all foreign subsidiaries.[21]

Recruitment Problems

Recruiting capable junior or midlevel managers is not a problem for those few companies with international human resource programs capable of sustained development efforts. Recall that GE, Procter & Gamble, Exxon, IBM, ABB, Philips NV, Bayer AG, and Fiat are world leaders in building core competencies among parent-company managers. They identify junior managers with strong potential and interest in international careers, establish career development plans for these staff members, and ease them into appropriate career tracks through periodic training and foreign assignments. However, these companies are in the minority; Chrysler Corporation's initiative to bolster its expatriate ranks reflects a more likely scenario.

In a 1996 press release, Chrysler announced that it was going to "beef up" its foreign offices with knowledgeable employees from headquarters who could take their expertise overseas as well as acquire the skills they would need to manage in a global environment. Specifically, the company intended to send several hundred "high-potential and upwardly mobile employees" to posts in Europe, the Far East, Latin America, the Middle East, and Africa. Citing the success experienced by Ford and GM in strengthening their international competitive profiles, Chrysler said that it was determined to rapidly expand overseas activities. Therefore, the company sent personnel staff from headquarters to meet with foreign subsidiary general managers in each region to determine the types and number of people required. The company then began selecting home-country employees for three-year stints abroad. According to a Chrysler spokesperson, each employee selected would undergo extensive preparation, including "significant cross-cultural training, language instruction, and an overview of the country" in which he or she would be living.[22] This announcement sounded like an enterprising effort by Chrysler, but the actual selection process was questionable. The company rushed its internal job searches to quickly recruit candidates, then squeezed the entire training and development program into two weeks at one of the company's facilities in Colorado or Illinois. The initiative included no apparent consideration for family orientation or career planning. Indeed, the entire program was disappointing, and Chrysler abandoned it shortly before the company was acquired by Daimler-Benz, thus bringing global access to Chrysler through the newly amalgamated DaimlerChrysler organization.[23]

Comprehensive development programs at GE, P&G, and other leading companies provide both depth and scope for international managers, but they also suffer from several drawbacks. The programs require expensive, time-consuming efforts that do not always benefit individual managers' careers. Firms can incur enormous costs to train managers over periods of several years, ensure progressive job rotation and foreign experiences, and support their career initiatives. Many companies simply cannot justify the expense unless they can realize a particular return on their investment. More to the point, a company can accumulate a pool of management talent only by filling its system with more candidates than it needs for current assignments. As a result, some of the time and money it invests in developing candidates' skills may sit idle in the form of latent potential, and only a few individuals will be drawn for foreign assignments at any one time.

Recruitment is further complicated by competition between home-based employees and expatriates already on overseas assignments. A company may prefer to reassign an employee currently working abroad to a new foreign post rather than send a fresh recruit overseas. The overseas expatriate has the advantage of foreign experience and a performance record that the firm can evaluate more objectively than that of a domestic manager. Reassignment also costs less than repatriation and subsequent replacement from the parent-company ranks. The existing expatriate often requires less training than a domestic manager would, and he or she commonly experiences fewer adjustment problems and represents a lower risk to the company. Nevertheless, recruiting these individuals also has its problems. Current expatriates may not always want to extend their contracts to move on to new foreign locations, especially if they have families that have been away from their home cultures for prolonged periods of foreign duty. A company with a centralized development system may also lack the ability to prepare overseas managers for reassignment without complicated arrangements to bring them home for reorientation. In many cases, the apparent benefits in transferring managers among overseas assignments are not justified. Expatriates with excellent track records may have been so intensely preoccupied with their foreign activities that they have disengaged themselves from broader parent-company objectives. Also, they may have honed their skills and become so acculturated to their particular posts that they lose the flexibility to adjust to new positions, while a fresh recruit from headquarters who has not yet gone abroad may do so with less difficulty. Although this situation is probably rare, it does suggest a compelling reason for companies to bring their people home regularly for rejuvenation and reassimilation into the organizational culture.

Another alternative is to recruit externally, perhaps from foreign competitors or other multinationals with effective development programs. Firms accomplish this type of recruiting in traditional ways, such as placing advertisements and job placement notices. For relatively senior positions, they may deal with executive search firms that specialize in international recruitment. Smaller companies may find external recruitment a cost-effective alternative compared to the difficulty of maintaining in-house development programs. Also, by recruiting externally, these firms may attract managers with significant experience.

International recruitment continues to grow more challenging over time as companies evolve and their patterns of organization change. Groups of executives meet annually in roundtable discussions, and their recommendations emphasize a global company's need for a strategic human resource focus that includes executive HRM managers in company-wide planning systems.[24] This participation provides a coordinated method of effectively matching international strategies with competent talent. In addition, companies should endeavor not only to develop adequate management pools but also to ensure that each person selected articulates an **individual development plan (IDP)** that systematically supports realistic career goals while protecting the employee against underutilization. An IDP is a broader instrument than the succession plan described for expatriates in Chapter 12. It is a permanent record of an employee's development rather than a transitional planning tool. Although IDPs follow no standardized formats, Figure 13.4 outlines key components that should be considered for such a career plan.

Going Local with Host-Country Managers

The decision to hire locally reflects management's philosophy about how to staff foreign activities, but it also involves other factors such as economic development in the host country, perceived need for control by the parent organization, and the relative costs associated with local versus expatriate managers. Of course, it also depends on

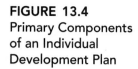

FIGURE 13.4
Primary Components
of an Individual
Development Plan

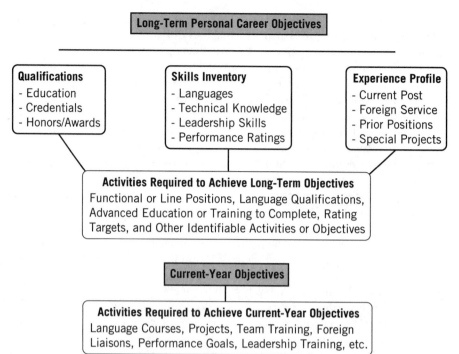

the availability of qualified local candidates. Staffing patterns reveal sharp contrasts between multinationals from various nations. U.S. multinationals generally employ fewer expatriates and more local managers at all levels than companies from other major nations. In their Western European operations, U.S. companies employ approximately one-third parent-country nationals (PCNs) in higher-level executive positions; slightly less than two-thirds of the executives are host-country nationals (HCNs); and a small number of executives are third-country nationals (TCNs). In contrast, Japanese companies employ nearly 80 percent parent-country nationals and barely 20 percent local managers for higher-level positions; Japanese companies seldom hire third-country executives. Between these extremes, but closer to the U.S. staffing pattern, European companies employ nearly 40 percent parent-country staff and slightly more than 60 percent host-country nationals in senior positions. These data reflect patterns in the European region, and the percentages change dramatically for business units in Latin America and Asia, where U.S. multinationals typically favor direct parent-company control. In Latin America, more than 40 percent of U.S. senior managers are PCNs; there are only slightly more HCNs and a few TCNs. In Asia, U.S. companies staff more than 50 percent of posts with PCNs and less than 40 percent with HCNs. European and Japanese companies tend to rely heavily on parent-country expatriates in both Latin America and Asia.

These statistics suggest a stronger tendency for U.S. companies than for European firms to "go local." Both U.S. and European companies tend to hire locally for senior posts, while Japanese organizations ensure that they retain home-country control.[25] The magnitude of the ratios makes a convincing argument for effective recruiting and development of host-country managers. Unfortunately, recruiters find no model to follow, and practices vary widely among multinationals, establishing no discernible pattern.[26]

Recruiting Local Managers

The most reliable method of recruiting local managers is by promoting them from within the foreign subsidiaries they will manage, but many companies also employ local executive search firms to recruit and screen external applicants. For senior posts, regional human resource offices often establish collaborative search committees composed of subsidiary managers who understand the vacant posts and their demands. For example, Motorola's Malaysian electronic parts subsidiary supplies components to the company's assembly facilities in the United States and Japan, making it a vital link in the overall value chain. Motorola fills any top management vacancy in the Malaysian plant through a search committee with U.S., Japanese, and Malaysian representatives convened by regional HRM personnel located in Singapore. The committee reviews job requirements, screens applicants, and makes recommendations to Motorola's regional director, who makes the final placement decision. Texas Instruments sometimes relies on headquarters staff to act as coordinators in overseas search and selection processes; or more commonly, regional search teams or group managers make hiring decisions. The president of EDS (Asia/Pacific) located in Hong Kong, for example, has authority for all management positions in Taiwan, South Korea, Singapore, Australia, New Zealand, Thailand, the Philippines, and, most recently, Vietnam. He does not, however, have a voice in staffing decisions for EDS Japanese subsidiaries, which are purposely structured under the parent headquarters in Texas and staffed through a U.S.–Japanese liaison committee.[27]

Large global companies have begun to establish regional human resource assessment centers to consolidate foreign recruiting activities. For example, Ford recently opened a European center in Brussels to help coordinate management deployment in the region. The center also collaborates with other regional centers in Southeast Asia and South America to ensure continuity of recruitment standards. This program is a small part of Ford's comprehensive human resource development system, called the *Employee Development and Assistance Program.* Launched in 1990, the program encompasses training and development activities for employees at all levels on a global basis. During the first five years of the program, more than 100,000 Ford employees participated in an assortment of personal and occupational training efforts. By early 2000, more than 400,000 employees had been involved through global on-line training systems established by Ford's new CEO, Jacques Nasser. Through its regional human resource centers, Ford established extensive host-country and cross-cultural management development projects to complement hiring and deployment of managers and technical staff. These have now become core programs for computer-based international training and assessment throughout Ford's corporate network.[28]

Many companies contract for the services of international consulting firms or divisions of larger consulting operations that specialize in helping multinationals to manage their human resource activities. Ernst & Young, a U.S. multinational known primarily for accounting and auditing services, also operates a global division called *Ernst & Young Resources,* with regional centers in London, Atlanta, and Dallas. Through 94 foreign offices under the direction of these regional centers, the company contracts with other multinationals for expatriate administration, outsourcing, compensation management, foreign taxation, and development programs. An Ernst & Young program called *Global Expatriate Support Systems (GESS)* has also created a network of professional alliances with companies such as Berlitz, Selection Research International, and PaineWebber to help companies assess candidates for management positions, advise them on foreign pay issues, and provide language training.[29]

Advantages of Recruiting Local Managers

Firms can minimize many of the problems associated with expatriate staffing by hiring local talent. A host-country manager, by definition, does not require acculturation training, and the firm incurs none of the expenses that it would pay to relocate a parent-company employee overseas. Companies do not have to match domestic compensation rates or provide the extensive foreign assignment benefits that expatriates would expect. They immediately gain recognition as "locally managed" companies, often resembling local entities more than subsidiaries of foreign multinationals.

Further, local managers often have the political, social, and business connections necessary to work effectively in their countries, while expatriates may run into insurmountable barriers in such foreign relationships. Local managers mesh culturally and socially with their employees, customers, public officials, and local vendors. They may not necessarily be politically aligned with their countries' leaders, but they understand their native social systems and the nuances of government regulations. In addition, qualified local managers are often among the most motivated and well-educated members of their respective societies. This is particularly true in less-developed countries, where positions in foreign multinationals represent choice opportunities that attract cream-of-the-crop applicants.

Disadvantages of Hiring Local Managers

Many of the disadvantages of relying on host-country managers reflect associated arguments, presented earlier, for staffing with expatriates. Multinational executives are always concerned about home-office control over foreign operations, and they believe they can maximize accountability by staffing with expatriates. Host-country managers, once they have achieved recognition in reputable foreign companies, are often pirated by competitors; or they leverage their experience to land high-profile domestic positions. Consequently, turnover among host-country managers can be a problem. Also, communications by parent-country headquarters with regional offices and subsidiary managers are often complicated by language differences and lack of personal contact. Communication problems also can result from failure to assimilate host-country managers into the parent company's organizational culture, leading to potential difficulties in understanding home-office priorities. For example, local managers seldom have the breadth of experience to understand the overall strategies associated with a globally integrated company. Of course, managers in Europe and developed Asian societies will be technically competent and well-educated people—perhaps comparing favorably with parent-country candidates—but educational standards and technological development in most foreign countries are inadequate to prepare local managers with the professional skills they can gain in developed countries. Further, local managers seldom qualify for reassignment to other foreign posts as third-country expatriates, so they have difficulty relating to organizational expectations such as meeting quality standards or understanding standards for ethical behavior.[30]

Recruitment in Host Countries

The discussions of the advantages and disadvantages of recruiting local managers have illustrated some of the more perplexing human resource management problems facing multinational corporations. The most sensitive problems concern the integration capabilities of host-country managers and thus the ability of a company to orchestrate international activities through a system of somewhat autonomous foreign managers. Contrasting management styles and fundamental differences in work-related values also create apprehension about disparities in productivity, work standards, and management succession. Indeed, research has shown that comparable work in different company locations can produce significantly different costs and performance results, and these differences are generally traced to contrasting styles of leadership by host-country managers.[31] Therefore, one of the most pressing problems of IHRM is to attract competent host-country managers, particularly in labor markets distinguished by intense competition for relatively few well-qualified individuals.

A primary reason for hiring locally is to limit labor costs, but this benefit does not always extend to management positions. Mexico, for example, is famous for low labor costs, yet management compensation can be quite high. In its annual survey of executive compensation, however, Korn/Ferry International discovered that more than two-thirds of the multinational companies operating in Mexico pay Mexican executives at least as much as, or more than, comparable expatriates would cost. The study, which was conducted among notable international companies with Mexican subsidiaries managed by locally recruited executives, included DuPont, Ford, Chrysler, GM, Volkswagen, Colgate-Palmolive, IBM, Black & Decker, Kimberly-Clark, Warner-Lambert, Campbell Soup, and AT&T. Many more of the nearly 3,000 North American, European, and Japanese companies sampled reported strong local management contingents in second-tier positions, and total compensation was only marginally different between senior Mexican managers and those from the United States, Europe, and Japan.[32] Expatriate packages still cost employers more due to relocation costs and home-based benefits, yet firms often face high relocation costs to move the relatively few qualified local managers they recruit to Mexican sites of the foreign multinationals' operations. The problem is compounded in Mexico because multinational facilities often are located in ports or near the U.S. border, far from urban centers or universities where managers are recruited. Moving an employee in Mexico also can involve resettling a sizable extended family. Consequently, the demand for Mexican managers has raised the cost of recruiting and escalated local employment costs.[33]

Management Development in Host Countries

Although management development is addressed more extensively later in the chapter, this section requires a discussion of several distinct issues related to host-country managers. Unlike expatriate managers, who are usually trained at parent-company facilities, local managers seldom have opportunities to participate in similar development programs. Instead, they learn primarily through experience while on the job, perhaps reinforced by occasional consulting workshops and seminars held in major cities near their locations.[34] Foreign subsidiaries cannot always send managers to formal development programs, and they often lack sufficient resources to sponsor extensive in-house training. Small subsidiaries with few managers are subsequently overlooked in the development process.

In addition, because host-country managers are seldom reassigned to other company activities as third-country expatriates, they gain limited cross-cultural exposure. Often their experience and backgrounds are confined to the foreign enterprises that initially recruit them. Local managers in less-developed countries also suffer disadvantages because they lack access to training through local education systems. Equally scarce technology and managerial materials may exacerbate this problem. Unlike North American and European environments rich in opportunities, such as executive MBA programs, most developing countries lack fundamental business programs for career development.[35]

The picture may seem bleak. Yet many foreign managers study in North American and European schools; and though they represent a small, elite group, their numbers are growing. Also, a recent rapid expansion of educational alliances between indigenous schools and western universities has created new learning opportunities in strategic cities such as Manila, Singapore, Lahore, Bangkok, Beijing, Lima, and Mexico City. Participants study through distance learning, often reading and listening to presentations in English (although some offer bilingual instruction and materials). The rapid infusion of information technology and electronic networking is bringing training and development opportunities to expanding audiences throughout the world. Of course, many world-class Asian universities teach students in Japan, Australia, Hong Kong, and Singapore, but demand for education far exceeds supply.

Western multinationals are particularly challenged in Russia, where domestic companies and foreign enterprises are sending promising managers back to school. In the words of a Columbia University instructor working there in an executive education program, "U.S. companies operating in the former Soviet Union immediately discover that key local managers may be well-educated in the classical sense, especially when it comes to math and science, but don't know beans about even the most basic business concepts."[36] The demand for capable managers has attracted at least nine leading American universities to St. Petersburg, the emerging center of Russian capitalism, including schools such as Columbia, Duke, U.C. Berkeley, and the Universities of Massachusetts and Maryland. British, French, German, and Japanese undergraduate institutions are there as well, offering programs ranging from four-year bachelor's degrees to compact four-week executive immersion courses. Practically all universities promote resident and exchange programs as well as modular development courses offered on their home campuses.

Employers themselves have also made substantial investments in global development, such as Ford's global Employee Development and Assistance Program mentioned earlier. In response to the demand in Russia, R. J. Reynolds, Delta Telecom, U.S. West, and at least 64 other U.S.–Russian joint ventures sponsor work internships for local managers at U.S. facilities. These mentoring or "twinning" programs match candidates to work alongside American managers on joint projects. Asea Brown Boveri, currently one of the highest-profile global companies, established its own university in China. The ABB China Business School was launched in 1994 with carefully selected international faculty members and 100 young Chinese managers from ABB's joint ventures in Beijing and Shanghai. Courses range from "mini-labs" teaching specific language and marketing skills to an organizational version of an MBA degree. Gillette is also in China—and Boston, London, and Singapore—with 18-month management "exposure courses" that involve foreign students in formal training and joint business projects. Gillette draws students to its regional centers from several hundred foreign locations, returning them to their home countries for assignments in Gillette's subsidiaries upon completion of their courses. Motorola, another high-profile global company, took the initiative to create the Motorola University in China with a mission to provide long-term education to aspiring young managers there. The company also set up an institute called the *China Accelerated Management Program (CAMP)* that runs short-term seminars for all employees as well as intensive executive development programs for senior managers.[37]

Management development and management recruitment in host countries are becoming linked as complementary activities. Unlike managers from developed countries, who bring sometimes extensive qualifications to new job opportunities, many managers from less-developed countries depend on company-sponsored development initiatives to develop qualifications after they are hired. Put another way, multinational companies often hire people with management potential, and then help them mold their careers. Therefore, foreign recruitment often brings with it an implicit responsibility for management development.

Management development is therefore an expensive investment for multinational corporations. It also has difficult complications of delivering effective instruction to company facilities throughout the world. Each foreign facility has distinctive host-country characteristics and individual challenges.

LOCAL ENTERPRISE STAFFING AND TRAINING

Recruiting line workers, office staff, and field employees can succeed through relatively uncomplicated programs in cultures with similar characteristics to those in the home country. Throughout Europe and in the developed Asian economies, most occupations share similar job descriptions and qualifications. Even among less-developed economies, most skilled and semiskilled jobs exhibit commonalities. Therefore, recruiting local operating employees is not as difficult as recruiting managers or professionals—yet multinationals do face some complications that need to be addressed.

Employee Recruitment

In developing countries with high unemployment, traditional methods of recruitment, such as advertising vacancies, can attract only limited numbers of qualified candidates. This problem occurs for several reasons.[38] First, in countries such as Bangladesh, Chad, Senegal, Bolivia, and Venezuela, high illiteracy rates mean that few people read newspapers or encounter other media messages. Second, in a typical developing country, only a limited number of urban general-circulation newspapers, a few radio or television stations, and widely separated employment centers provide information on job openings. Third, most people in these societies live in village environments where their employment opportunities must lie within walking distance or in the range of humble transportation options; they cannot aspire to jobs even short distances from their homes. In Mexico, for example, sufficient numbers of people look for work along the U.S. border, but they are limited to jobs near their homes.

In contrast to U.S. practices, even literate members of other societies often do not hunt for jobs in newspapers. Instead, they rely on government agencies or village offices that fill vacancies. Many jobs are filled through trade unions, and in some countries a foreign company cannot hire directly but must rely on official agencies to assign workers. For example, China only recently began to permit foreign companies to hire employees without going through a state bureaucracy for allocating jobs. In Central and Eastern Europe, governments still substantially control jobs and regulate qualifications. Direct hiring may not be any easier in developed countries. Germany and France exert pressure on hiring through social legislation, and strong trade unions promote their own systems. A multinational cannot expect to hire only through advertisements or direct applications.[39]

Companies run into legal recruitment barriers and constraints on employment that grow out of religious or social customs. In India, Pakistan, and other west Asian countries, women seldom can be hired without the approval of their husbands or fathers. Islamic nations in the Middle East and Southeast Asia often prevent women from working in jobs specifically defined as men's positions, and employers frequently must negotiate terms of a wife's or daughter's employment through the family patriarch. Rather than hiring for specific job vacancies, a firm commonly must hire family members or relatives who work as a group, or at least within the same organization.

Foreign employers often adjust to this cottage-industry environment, or they find ways of dealing with nepotism as a constraint on recruitment.[40]

Recruitment is further complicated by national laws that restrict hiring choices by a foreign company and the ratio of local-to-foreign employees that it must maintain. In Mexico, for example, no more than 10 percent of a company's total employees can be non-Mexican nationals. Consequently, a new foreign venture that assigns five expatriates to help start the enterprise must hire at least 45 Mexican employees before it can open for business. McDonald's faced a challenging problem due to this requirement. Initially, it planned to staff each new outlet with at least one senior expatriate and several temporary U.S. employees to help establish the franchise and train local employees. As soon as the first McDonald's franchise was opened in Mexico City, government officials threatened to shut it down after counting 4 expatriates and 12 local employees, a clear violation of the 10 percent rule. Through back-room negotiations, McDonald's convinced the authorities to count the expatriates as part-time workers, but it still had to hire extra counter clerks and night cleaners to balance the ratio.[41] Table 13.2 describes employment regulations in Mexico that complicate staffing decisions.

Of course, cultural differences always present difficulties. For example, Dragon Air, a regional airline based in Hong Kong, had hired airline maintenance and reservations staff in Kuala Lumpur, the capital of Malaysia. The company was surprised when half of the employees quit two weeks after the company first landed there. In this predominantly Muslim state, Dragon Air had allowed its Hindu employees to place religious shrines in communal employee work spaces (a common practice in Malaysia), but it had provided no facilities for its Muslim employees to attend to daily prayers. Upon solving that problem by renovating offices and maintenance areas, Dragon Air faced a work stoppage by Hindu employees protesting work schedules that accommodated Muslim religious days but failed to acknowledge Hindu religious holidays.[42]

Along with religious and cultural issues, companies also must deal with antiwestern attitudes or intense nationalistic feelings in some foreign countries. These issues cause particularly sensitive problems in the emerging market economies of Central and Eastern Europe, where countries such as Hungary, Romania, Slovakia, and the Czech Republic take great pride in centuries-old traditions and cherished national heritages. For example, Volkswagen gained a majority interest in the Czech Skoda automobile company, planning to expand employment and institute German-based engineering systems. After several months of operations, an enraged Czech workforce staged a mass protest, complaining that they received lower wages and fewer benefits than German counterparts. In addition, the workers seriously resented being treated as less competent than Germans. As a result, Volkswagen had to replace many of its German workers with Czech nationals and retrain its expatriate technicians to be culturally sensitive to their Czech coworkers. The company subsequently agreed to a comprehensive domestic employee development program.[43]

Recruitment problems differ throughout a company's global activities, but an understanding of typical employment systems in a particular country can substantially reduce the anxiety of staffing that foreign operation. Recognizing the enduring probability of networking and personal allegiances in Mexico's paternalistic culture, for example, allows human resource managers to turn these links to their own advantage by establishing recruitment networks. With an effective screening system and appropriate policies to ensure that hiring decisions reflect valid qualifications, a company can benefit from the cultural practice by forming a cohesive workforce. Although loyalties may depend on personal relationships, they result in a stable and harmonious work environment.

TABLE 13.2

LEGAL AND COMPENSATION PRACTICES IN MEXICO

Labor Law Overview
- Labor law is part of the national constitution, and individual employment contracts or collective agreements are subject to regulation by the government. Failure to meet legal requirements by any party amounts to a violation of constitutional law. In the event of a dispute, the burden of proof is on the employer.

Compensation
- Employees' workweeks and minimum wages are established by law, as are several additional requirements:
  - Overtime is limited to three hours per day, three days per week.
  - All overtime is a worker's voluntary choice, and the employer pays a 100 percent premium (double time).
  - Firms must offer tax-free savings funds to employees at negotiable rates.
  - Firms must pay punctuality bonuses in cash for 15 out of 20 days of perfect attendance; the government encourages extra prorated payments, as well.
  - Firms must pay annual incentive bonuses for executives in negotiated amounts.
  - Firms must pay short-term incentive bonuses to plant or site employees.

Benefits
- Mandatory social security benefits include old-age and survivor's benefits, disability pensions, medical coverage, and maternity leave.
- Employers must contribute 2 percent or more of each employee's base pay to a mandatory retirement fund.
- Mandatory severance pay equals 12 days' pay for each year's service at rates at least double the minimum wage.
- Employers retain full liability for severance without just cause; poor performance is not adequate reason for dismissal.
- Employers must make cash payments to fund programs such as housing assistance, food plans, child care, maternity care, education, family care, and hardship support, subject to government review.
- Holidays are established by law, with time off paid at overtime rates; employees who work on those days earn double the time-off rates.
- Vacations are mandated by law and paid and funded by employers.

Training Host-Country Employees

Training employees in a foreign country emphasizes technical skills and job-related duties. Training in less-developed countries requires unusual emphasis on safety, quality control, and work standards. Otherwise, training programs are similar in most of a company's subsidiaries. A few large multinationals provide extensive programs for employees with subject matter ranging from fundamental self-improvement skills to complicated cross-cultural insights. For example, GE's Hungarian joint venture, Tungsram Ltd., has trained more than 1,000 local employees in a variety of elective courses including finance, marketing, project leadership, customer relations, and environmental protection. GE also offers courses to foreign affiliates at U.S. facilities. Selected Hungarian employees of Tungsram are trained at GE's Lighting Division in Cleveland, Ohio. The employees reside there for several weeks, working on projects ranging from international account management to product line engineering, and they are trained to pass their skills on to other employees in Hungary.[44]

Texas Instruments has been developing a comprehensive global training system for more than 15 years, and today the company claims that it can offer an overseas employee "virtually everything available to a U.S. employee."[45] The TI program began as a global delivery system for its total quality management program. It grew until it eventually encompassed all forms of training and development in the company. The primary goal of this activity has been to harmonize training with worldwide standards that ensure consistency in employee qualifications and a global workforce with interchangeable skills.

Other international companies, such as Procter & Gamble, Coca-Cola Company, American President Company, and AT&T, have built equally comprehensive programs. P&G is particularly keen on providing opportunities for employees of foreign subsidiaries to work toward self-advancement through on-site seminars and sponsorship of off-job education at schools and universities. AT&T has a similar program, but it adds remedial education in fundamental math skills, reading, and language for educationally disadvantaged employees. Coca-Cola has anchored its training to a theme of performance quality, and instruction emphasizes global consistency. Therefore, the company runs continuous on-site education programs to prepare employees in the same methods and work processes wherever it does business.[46]

Without a doubt, some employers exploit cheap labor and do little to train or develop employees, but competing through immediate wage advantages is a false economy. Wage advantages quickly disappear with economic expansion. For example, wage rates in growing Asian economies have increased on average 20 percent annually during the past decade. In Hong Kong and Singapore, where workers earned meager wages only a few years ago, per-capita incomes now exceed those of nearly all European economies. Consequently, labor-intensive industries in these countries—and in South Korea, Taiwan, and to some extent Malaysia—are moving further offshore to China, Indonesia, and Bangladesh. Observers have attributed much of this economic growth to improvements in training, much of it provided by multinational companies. These companies have benefited from increased productivity, while the exploitative companies capture only temporary advantages in labor costs.

An American Management Association study conducted among domestic U.S. managers and foreign executives concluded that too many companies have been shortsighted in pursuing labor economies. Eventually these firms face severe downsizing problems—not because they accumulate too much organizational fat, but because their cost-driven priorities push them toward typical responses to rising costs. That is, they ask fewer people to do more work with fewer resources. In contrast, a company that builds a skilled workforce creates a stable platform for long-term improvement that yields dividends in productivity and sustained growth.[47] Common methods of training recommended for foreign employees are identified in Figure 13.5 and described in the following paragraphs.

On-the-Job Training

The most common form of training emphasizes on-the-job learning under direct supervision. This kind of instruction is supplemented by intervention programs that periodically focus on job-related skills such as using new computer software or implementing new inventory-control procedures. Supervisors and in-house training specialists can arrange brief classes or work with employees at the job site through a tell-show-do process. They tell employees about a new process, demonstrate the process, and then have employees practice by actually doing hands-on tasks. Less formal methods of learning while doing include cross-training in complementary skills (such as machine operation and setup functions) and self-monitoring for quality. The

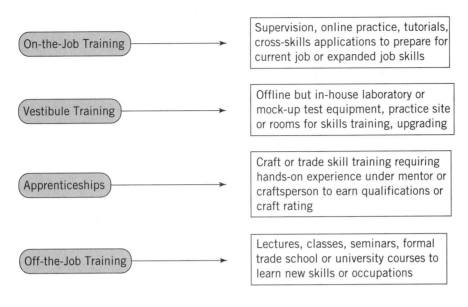

FIGURE 13.5
Training for Foreign Employees

point of on-the-job training is to upgrade employee skills during normal work routines with actual production equipment. Sales representatives, bank tellers, data-entry staff, clerks, and other service personnel can be trained in the same manner. They actually engage in work as they learn it, albeit at a slow pace and with considerable latitude for errors.

Vestibule Training

This off-job method keeps training in the facility, often using simulation techniques or laboratory equipment and training aids. For example, employees learn to use quality-control instruments and methods of measuring work against standards in mock-ups or simulated environments. Small groups improve their computing skills in on-site computer labs. New work methods are developed through programmed instrument manuals and test modules. This method is particularly effective for teaching skills that require repetitious practice, such as language proficiency. Vestibule techniques can also provide self-paced learning in specially equipped laboratories.

Apprenticeship

Trade skills such as carpentry, tool-and-die making, and printing are usually learned through apprenticeships. Technical skills such as marine surveying and draftsmanship can also be taught through apprenticeship programs. Employees begin their careers as apprentices by working alongside qualified specialists, where they progressively learn the trade and earn credentials through performance assessments. Most programs require apprentices to work for specific periods of time, perhaps several years, during which they rotate through predetermined sequences of jobs. Once they have completed these requirements and passed any formal tests or other evaluations specified for the occupation, they are recommended to trade boards by their supervisors for licensing.

An apprenticeship is a preferred form of training for many trades, in which only experience allows workers to hone individual skills. European companies, particularly those in Germany, favor apprenticeship methods. Many German students are tracked into vocational apprenticeships during their early teens. European multinationals introduce these systems to their foreign subsidiaries, and employees in Southeast Asia and Latin America have enthusiastically adopted apprenticeship methods. Those who complete the training earn widely recognized qualifications for crafts and trades, and these credentials qualify employees for improved job mobility.[48]

Off-the-Job Training

While managers often attend public seminars or other formal programs offered through universities and training institutions, operating employees have few similar opportunities. Nevertheless, many companies encourage self-development through tuition-assistance plans, release time to attend courses, and sponsored scholarships. Certain skills are best taught away from the work environment. For example, language instruction can be provided through a vestibule-training program, but it may be more cost effective to send groups of employees to private language schools or adult education programs. Institutions that offer these programs gather capable instructors and create effective support systems, such as practice laboratories and libraries. Trade school programs are also popular in countries with sufficient educational infrastructure to support them. In some fields, such as information technology, vendors provide public seminars and packaged off-the-job training programs. Skills such as data entry, software utilization, office systems, and computer-assisted bookkeeping can be taught similarly in most countries because IT skills do not vary greatly from one country to another.[49]

GLOBAL HUMAN RESOURCE DEVELOPMENT

Human resource development is the responsibility of line managers to create an integrated organization of competent people capable of pursuing organizational goals while also aspiring to fulfill their individual potential in rewarding careers. It is important to emphasize development as a line-management responsibility for working with all employees regardless of rank or status, but this statement is too broad to be useful in practice. Instead, the field is compartmentalized into *management development* and *training*, with a vocational connotation for the second term. This distinction can be confusing, because people often talk about *executive* or *staff* development. The chapter would gain little by debating semantics, but it is important to realize that human resource development is only partially concerned with training, and it is a pervasive organizational responsibility.

Development is even more pervasive in international management than in domestic management, because it implies global integration of cross-cultural interests and the infusion of a shared vision of the organization.[50] This process begins with executive development devoted mainly to creating an organizational vision; all else cascades downward. Therefore, this section explores development programs by referring to what they are intended to accomplish and whom they are intended to benefit. Figure 13.6 illustrates the cascading relationship of development objectives and programs.

Executive Development—Creating a Shared Vision

Although executive development is a continuous process, it becomes highly visible when strong leaders make major strategic changes in the core characteristics of their

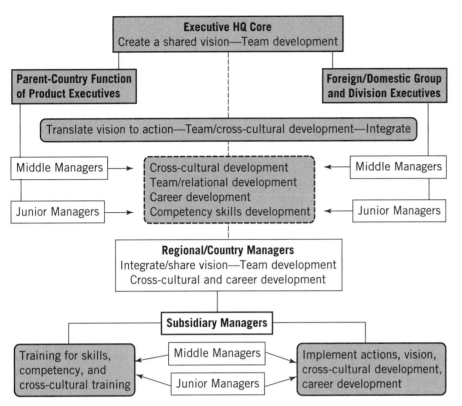

FIGURE 13.6
Cascading Effect of
Human Resource
Development

organizations. These are headline events, and visionary leaders become part of the society's folklore. Jack Welch, CEO of General Electric, is famous for re-creating GE as a global electronics and aerospace company. Prior to his appointment, GE was better known as a somewhat dull blue-chip manufacturer of lightbulbs and appliances. Few people knew that the company made jet engines, pioneered propulsion and power-generating technology, and pursued interests in robotics and telecommunications. Welch created a new core vision and a strategy that repositioned GE as a world leader in advanced systems technology. Percy Barnevik, former chairman of ABB, rose to prominence by masterminding creation of the company's global network that includes nearly 1,000 companies in 140 countries, all coordinated through the Swiss-Swedish headquarters in Zurich. Barnevik may have coined the phrase *seamless corporation*, but his vision of ABB as a *relational network* of global engineering businesses made the company an extremely successful enterprise. Alex Trotman, former CEO of Ford Motor Company, launched "Ford 2000" in 1990 as a 10-year program aimed at redefining the company's identity as a leading global automaker based on fully integrated European and American design functions. Trotman also created an international network of multiskilled and multicultural managers. This transformation resulted in prize-winning new automotive designs that have rejuvenated Ford along with international systems of managers that took more than 1,000 senior managers into foreign positions.[51]

Many other companies have become prominent through strong core visions and shared values. In each instance, organizational success began with a new sense of purpose that, by itself, provided important guidance for creating distinctive competencies for the companies. The visions and values became embedded—institutionalized—through years of persistent executive development, recruitment, and career development. Each company made a sustained effort to instill in the minds of every employee, supplier, and customer the organization's new vision of its enterprise. Executive development was one small slice of a very large pie, but it was a crucial one. These companies began by announcing programs of organizational development that combined the efforts of perhaps 20, 30, or 50 key executives in strategic planning and restructuring initiatives. Executives who spearheaded these programs from GE, ABB, Alcoa, Ford, and IBM all applied substantial foreign experience to these activities, gaining even more international exposure in the process of creating their programs. The new insights began to cascade through their organizations when the key executives involved second-tier managers in the process. Consequently, growing numbers of managers ventured overseas, many exchanging positions with foreign counterparts and some assuming new executive roles in regional groups instituted under the sweeping changes. Literally all executives participated in formal development programs, and the collaboration and teamwork that emerged through this process powerfully influenced efforts to reshape the organizations and their leadership cadres.[52]

Executive development does not always create dramatic situations. Sometimes it inspires sustained incremental change in organizational values. For example, when total quality management (TQM) was introduced in the face of intense Japanese competition, some western companies reacted with quick-fix solutions, perhaps mandating quality circles and adaptation of Japanese work methods. However, most successful companies began long-term processes of reeducating senior managers to develop ingrained commitments to quality improvement. Incremental changes in work processes and technology increased the emphasis on team development techniques and promoted pervasive acceptance of TQM concepts. These principles cascaded through the organizations as senior managers set strong examples and inspired changes at successively lower management levels. Development programs repackaged TQM and team-empowerment concepts for application by division line managers and functional staff executives. In turn, these were translated into specific quality improvement training programs at lower levels in the organizations. Throughout international organizations, TQM improved integration among diverse subsidiaries and guided reconfiguration of work methods. Foreign managers subsequently have had to learn new leadership skills and methods for improving coordination among multinational activities.

Cross-Cultural Development—Pursuing Integration

Cross-cultural *training* is normally associated with preparation for expatriate assignments, but **cross-cultural development** is concerned with creating an organization of international managers capable of working in many different societies.[53] The distinction is an important one, because cross-cultural training prepares employees by communicating knowledge about the principal values, beliefs, behaviors, and cultural norms of specific countries to which they will be assigned. Cross-cultural development prepares managers for ongoing responsibilities of working within an interrelated framework of multicultural interests. The objective is to create a broad-based appreciation of contrasting societies, beliefs, work-related behaviors, and fundamental values among a corps of international managers.

An expatriate post may be the first step in a comprehensive development effort, but third-country assignments and development programs for host-country managers also add important contributions. IBM, Shell, P&G, and Unilever prefer to place local managers in charge of host-country activities, but almost no one gains a senior management position without compiling a successful record working in other foreign environments. Progressive sequences of foreign job assignments represent one major approach to developing cross-cultural competencies. A variety of formal cross-cultural training programs also are offered by private companies, government agencies, consultants, and universities as elements of this development process. Management development implements several different training methods, some emphasizing cross-cultural considerations more than others. Table 13.3 summarizes these approaches, and the following paragraphs describe them.[54]

Information Training

The most common element of management development programs is fact-based training. This instruction relies on traditional education processes such as lectures, seminars, reading assignments, and orientation programs to improve learners' knowledge about a particular foreign culture. Managers may be trained in this information through in-house programs, public seminars, predeparture briefings, or formal university courses. Companies may hire specialists to present technical information, such as how to use market research statistics or how to comply with specific sets of labor regulations. Government agencies also often present programs for overseas managers.

Attribution Training

This kind of training attempts to condition managers to understand *why* people of another culture behave as they do. It works to instill a sense of appreciation for values and beliefs of a foreign culture, thus preparing managers to adapt to conditions they encounter while working overseas. Formal courses and exercises help in this regard, but, as mentioned earlier, many companies also implement mentoring systems to help sensitize managers to foreign behavior. Also, some use short-term cross-cultural assignments to provide real-life experiences. Brief internships support effective development by providing hands-on experience without full accountability in a permanent position.

Cultural Awareness Training

An alternative name for this training might be *home cultural awareness*, since it tries to sensitize managers to their own cultures and value antecedents. Cultural awareness

---

TABLE 13.3

TRAINING METHODS FOR CROSS-CULTURAL DEVELOPMENT

Information training	Fact-based instruction to communicate information or data related to the foreign environment or assignment
Attribution training	Study and experience of foreign culture and values to improve sensitivity
Cultural awareness training	Conscious evaluation of home-country culture and values as basis for understanding international differences
Cognitive behavior modification	Participation and repetition of behavior to condition "reflexes" to foreign incidents through rewarding and painful consequences
Experiential training	Role playing, case analysis, and simulation to emulate real-work situations

may seem an odd topic to address, but most people grow up without giving serious thought to why they behave the way they do or how they have formed their values. They may know how they differ from other people, but they can seldom explain why. Conscious awareness of their own cultures substantially helps people to accommodate differences elsewhere. Formal classroom training can contribute to awareness programs, but interactive learning techniques, role playing, and simulations are also useful to illustrate behavioral responses to critical incidents. These techniques contrast how managers are conditioned to behave at home and how they must adapt in foreign societies under similar circumstances.

Cognitive Behavior Modification

This kind of training works to instill response behavior related to rewards and punishments. It is a form of operant conditioning that helps managers to become accustomed to behaving in ways that will help them avoid painful consequences or that will result in pleasant results. International managers use this method to instill behavior that will not violate expectations in a foreign society in situations of leadership, communications, social protocols, and other host-country relations. Case analysis, simulation exercises, and role playing are very useful techniques for behavior modification programs; lectures, seminars, and reading assignments are less effective because learners must participate to gain the true value of this training—evoking responses.

Experiential Training

As the title implies, this kind of training exposes managers to actual experiences, or representations of experiences, that they might encounter in a foreign society. Role playing, simulations, mentoring programs, internships, and team-based case research methods add a real-world dimension to cross-cultural training. The most useful of techniques may be on-site project work that brings together foreign and domestic employees to pursue a joint project. Participants benefit not only from the work itself but also from the personal associations and social activities they encounter during a short assignment.

One additional development technique should be mentioned. Although it is a relatively old and somewhat expensive technique, companies such as Procter & Gamble and AT&T have used **culture assimilator** training successfully for years.[55] An assimilator program begins with a questionnaire listing hypothetical foreign situations. Respondents select from several multiple-choice answers to indicate how they would respond to the problem presented in each question. Questions are grouped in modules, and as employees finish successive sets of questions, they can turn to answer booklets that explain the logic behind the correct answer. Most important, the booklet explains the likely consequences of any of the other choices in each situation. Each module poses a more complicated set of questions than the preceding one, building upon the previous modules. Assimilators can include as few as several dozen questions in two or three modules or as many as several hundred questions in more than a dozen modules.

The extent of the assimilator and its rigor depend on the relative similarity of the foreign environment for which the learner is preparing compared to the home-country culture, as well as on the extent of interaction with the new culture that the assignment will require. P&G combines culture assimilators with information and attribution training. In addition, when possible, it provides hands-on experiential exercises such as field trips and intercultural projects.[56] Development techniques are not mutually exclusive choices, and all work toward the same ultimate objective: to create a corps of managers capable of working in a variety of foreign situations.

Team Development—Building Relational Networks

Team development has become a very important element of multinational corporations' efforts to expand through alliances and broader networks of international subsidiaries. Managers at home and abroad must work together effectively, although separated at sites distant from one another in the global company, creating an essential need for cooperation to achieve successful integration of company-wide activities. Thus a manager's career advancement often depends on their ability to work in a team environment.[57] (Chapter 16 addresses team concepts and methods for forming international teams.) Cross-cultural development techniques are designed to create strong international teams and, through *organizational development (OD)* techniques, to build relational networks. Managers and technicians at all levels can join together in teams to work on international projects. They can also be drawn from both parent and foreign locations to generate groups that cut across formal organizational lines. The resulting collaboration is a valuable acculturation experience, whether the team is composed of foreign managers working at headquarters or managers from the parent company and foreign subsidiaries working together in third-country locations.

Career Development—Optimizing Human Potential

Career development efforts do not necessarily amount to career *pathing*, which implies defining narrow tracks with well-defined upward routes. Specialization sometimes requires close pathing, and, as discussed earlier, U.S. firms specify tracks for both domestic and international managers more often than European companies do. Therefore, a U.S. electronics specialist may complete several foreign assignments without ever venturing beyond electronics-related positions or subsidiaries within his or her product division. American firms are gaining flexibility, however, through broader exposure by managers involved in foreign alliances. In Europe, an electronics specialist may have served in posts related to customer relations, marketing, logistics management, or other functional areas. At the same time, the European specialist may have worked in several subsidiaries that dealt with a variety of products, such as microcircuits, power systems, and aerospace equipment. Consequently, a European's range of experiences can differ substantially from the experiences accumulated by a U.S. employee. Career development in Japan is based on a widespread exposure to different functional tasks and divisional operations, giving Japanese employees greater interdisciplinary mobility than Americans or Europeans.

These comparisons emphasize that international career development is being systematically redefined in terms of *mobility*.[58] An organization needs more than technically competent managers; success often depends on promotable and mobile individuals in management roles. Multinationals are thus interested in development programs that enhance opportunities for horizontal mobility (team management, cross-cultural assignments, etc.) and that lead to progressive advancement in managers' careers. Mobility implies a sense of cross-functional sensitivity. An accountant may not suddenly have to fill a foreign sales job, and a marketing manager may function effectively without understanding accounting, but development should reduce functional barriers and enhance coordination among activities that do not always share common interfaces.

Skills Development—Enhancing Competence

The least complicated element of a management development program, and probably the most common one, is job-related **skills development** training to upgrade the technical competencies of staff members (e.g., computer utilization, new accounting systems, sales training, and so on). As managers rise to positions with expanded responsibilities, they must acquire new skills in leadership, strategic planning, negotiation, general management responsibilities, and particularly sensitive areas such as dealing with sexual harassment and ethical conduct. These capabilities are more pronounced for international managers than for domestic ones, because cultural practices and social customs dictate different sets of rules in separate locations. The challenge of skills development training is to establish a fundamental company-wide approach to leadership, ethics, and management processes; and then to prepare managers for specific foreign environments, where they will be expected to adapt to unfamiliar circumstances.[59] The methods used in the culture assimilator process described earlier are often adapted to these specific categories of training, but training institutes and consulting organizations also provide in-house and off-site programs to address these needs.

CONCLUDING COMMENTS

At the beginning of the chapter, the "Profile" included a comment from former Gillette CEO Al Zeien that his most pressing problem was a lack of qualified international managers—in particular, a lack of U.S. managers capable of working in a global environment. Throughout the chapter, subsequent discussions have tried to illustrate how leading multinational corporations are meeting this challenge through well-conceived human resource training and development programs. Nevertheless, firms face a clear shortage of well-qualified people willing to accept foreign assignments. Many of the problems in recruiting good candidates result from a lack of global vision by the generation of executives now heading major companies. Yet many of the success stories—such as those of GE, P&G, Shell, IBM, Motorola, ABB, Sony, Canon, and Gillette—have resulted from the actions of enlightened executives who provided new visions for their companies.

A manager creates such a vision by promoting shared values and committing a company to develop human resource capabilities among domestic and foreign operations. The field of international human resources is only beginning to emerge as a strategic force in global business; but already new and exciting initiatives are beginning to be accepted, together with the concept of a career in international management. The next chapter addresses motivation, which is an important element of this concept.

REVIEW QUESTIONS
1. How are roles changing for general managers in multinational corporations?
2. Define the management roles of *executive heads*, *coordinative heads*, and *representative heads*. In what types of organizations are you likely to find each?
3. How would you describe executive development in the United States and Japan? Contrast the two approaches to management training and development.
4. What are the most important influences on staffing decisions in foreign subsidiaries?
5. What arguments do parent companies cite to support decisions to staff subsidiaries with their own expatriate managers rather than with local managers from the host country?
6. What benefits and potential problems are associated with decisions to staff subsidiaries with host-country managers?

7. What methods do multinational corporations implement to develop foreign managers?
8. Describe the main issues for staffing local organizations. What problems do companies face in recruiting employees abroad?
9. Assuming that a foreign employee requires training in computer utilization, what training methods could a company consider? What are the advantages and disadvantages of these methods?
10. What forms of training support cross-cultural development programs? How do these activities relate to team-building efforts and to managerial career development?

GLOSSARY OF KEY TERMS

Career development   A process of developing a pool of qualified and motivated managers capable of working in multicultural and integrated global activities while also enhancing the upward mobility of individuals who aspire to international management careers.

Coordinative head   The emerging executive role that emphasizes responsibilities of coordinating worldwide activities rather than directing operations.

Cross-cultural development   The process of preparing employees for foreign assignments and international cooperation, often involving intercultural team projects, foreign assignments, formal acculturation training, assimilator exercises, mentoring, and cultural sensitivity training.

Culture assimilator   A training technique using programmed questionnaires based on critical incidents that elicit responses and provide feedback for specific foreign cultural experiences or problems in which managers might find themselves.

Human resource development   A pervasive concept of creating a viable organization with capable employees and managers at all levels; *development* is commonly associated with management instruction, in contrast with *training*, which implies a vocational focus.

Individual development plan (IDP)   A career development plan developed jointly by a high-potential employee and IHRM staff to track and monitor progress in skills, thus assuring advancement, proper job assignments, cross-cultural opportunities, and appropriate training.

International general manager   An executive whose broad-based knowledge of multifunctional international environments spans multiple business units with associated responsibility for coordinating integrated activities.

Representative head   A regional or group manager who operates outside direct chain-of-command authority to integrate activities in the region or group; the position implies an advisory and supportive role, often with tremendous influence despite the lack of direct involvement in and authority over operating decisions.

Skills development   A targeted program for honing specific management skills, leadership behavior, language capabilities, and technical knowledge essential to international assignments.

Team development   In the international context, an effort to bring together people from widely dispersed operations to jointly work on organization-wide projects or simulations to improve self-direction and interdependent coordination in global operations through personal development of team members.

EXERCISES

1. If you are majoring in international management or have career interests in the field, draft an outline for your own individual development plan. Specify a planning horizon of five years after you graduate for long-term career objectives. (Looking too long into the future risks ineffective stargazing, but if you have longer-term objectives, please address them.) List your probable qualifications on graduation and your skills and experience; then identify the activities you might consider essential to fulfill your needs between now and graduation. What position would give you an ideal start?

2. Select a country that interests you as a possible foreign assignment. Assume that you would go there in a management capacity with responsibility for local employees. Research the labor and employment laws of that country, and develop a summary for class discussion.

3.   Arrange to interview a staff specialist in human resource management (or a line manager) who has had experience with recruiting managers in a foreign subsidiary. Determine the advantages and disadvantages of local recruiting for the company, and identify unique difficulties associated with recruiting and management development. What programs does the company operate to address these issues?

Volkswagen: Managing for the Future

German managers are notorious for tough, single-minded rule from positions of power. But in a world of global competition, the most successful German firms are those that have built strong international teams of executives and well-developed host-country managers. German businesses are among the most competitive in the world. With global competition more intense than ever, German companies are making themselves progressively more international competitors—and in many cases, more American ones. Nevertheless, old stereotypes persist, and ample evidence casts doubt on the enlightened view of international management in German multinationals. Volkswagen, one of Germany's leading multinational companies, provides a perspective on managing a global business.

Volkswagen's record has been characterized by Wall Street critics as "one of the worst examples of a distant-headquarters stewardship" in recent history. VW employs more than 300,000 employees worldwide, and about 38 percent of them are Germans. Many of those are expatriates working outside Germany, yet VW has established a reputation for hiring host-country managers. An organization chart for VW would suggest a widely decentralized host-country management. In reality, VW keeps tight control over host-country operations and does not hesitate to press decisions from headquarters.

A case in point is Volkswagen's approach to managing its Audi of America division. During the mid-1980s, consumer advocates and the U.S. media assailed the Audi 5000 for problems with unintended acceleration. Consumers condemned the car's safety record, prompting several years of investigation by the National Highway Traffic Safety Administration. Consumer lawsuits cropped up across the country.

At the time, VW Chairman Ferdinand Piech looked upon the fiasco as an engineering problem. He concluded that the cars performed as expected and blamed problems on unsophisticated U.S. drivers. However, product failure was less a problem than the public perception of VW's poor response to consumer complaints. VW was so distant from the group's U.S. market that it had no understanding of how American consumers hold companies responsible for their products. Industry analysts in New York said that Piech destroyed his position in the U.S. market by a "lack of local sensitivity and foreign arrogance." Audi of America appears to have been managed entirely by U.S. executives, but the official picture hides the activities of German executives in accompanying offices, who second-guessed every decision made. In effect, all decisions were made in Wolfsburg, Germany, not Detroit or Troy, Michigan.

This became apparent to auto industry analysts when Volkswagen fired John B. Damoose, the American executive in charge of Audi's U.S. operations. He was succeeded by another American, Richard C. Marcy; but matters did not improve to Wolfsburg expectations, and Marcy was also fired. Successors included Joseph Tate, Audi's general sales manager, and finally in 1989 Richard M. Mugg, who became Audi's chief executive as the company hit its low point. Since then, the National Highway Traffic Safety Administration has attributed the vehicle's misfortunes to "pedal misapplication," vindicating VW's engineering record but solving nothing. VW had ostensibly designated more Americans to take executive control while pushing the German presence into the background, but in the aftermath of Audi's disaster, the company seems to have changed little. Critics point out that Volkswagen still puts little trust in its U.S. managers; as in many other foreign operations, management development does not deal sufficiently with company-wide affairs or the VW culture to afford host-country employees the confidence they need to make executive decisions. In effect, they are not connected to the company's central activities.

In a special report, analysts from the *Wall Street Journal* suggested that the U.S. market is too large and potentially too profitable to be managed from a distance or, as in Audi's case, by a distant mentality. They conclude that Audi of America could have avoided the damage "had it installed a powerful, knowledgeable, well-connected, highly respected American automobile executive as its chief executive officer in America and then backed his judgment. They did not, and they have suffered."

In a recent interview with *Wall Street Journal Europe's* Scott Miller, Ferdinand Piech was asked what he had learned about the differences between running Audi and Volkswagen. Piech responded:

I have learned to lead federally like the Swiss do with their cantons. This is a big difference between how VW and other competitors are led. Others lead out of their headquarters and it is wholly what comes out of there. We lead in a more decentralized way, and we let our brands do whatever they like as long as they bring in 6.5% (return on sales). But in the principles of finance, we are like other companies. Only a direct line works. If someone from Germany fails abroad in these areas, he never comes back to Germany.

In describing his management style, Piech said:

I would say that during my five years at Audi I was not well liked. I can't say what it is like here. I'm older now, and perhaps I've mellowed. During the time when VW had a 1.9-billion-mark [971.5 million euros] annual loss (at one point in the early 1990s), I must have been difficult, and I couldn't let anyone make two mistakes because I needed to be convinced that they had learned something after one mistake. After the second mistake we would have been dead. Today, if someone doesn't learn, we give him six months, and a good report to look for something new. We leave mistakes out of the evaluation.

Today, Volkswagen AG Chairman Piech is taking on a new challenge that may require yet a different management style. Slated for retirement in 2002, Piech is focusing on the financial performance of the company, whereas in the past, Volkswagen was more concerned about engineering and worker job security. Unlike its competitors in the auto industry, such as Ford Motor Company and General Motors Corporation, Volkswagen has been willing to accept low profit margins and avoid cutting the workforce. This has been due in part to Volkswagen's 19 percent market share in Western Europe—up from 16.7 percent in 1995.

To achieve his profitability goal and show analysts that VW has changed, Piech hired a new head of investor relations, agreed to adopt international accounting rules, and established regular meetings with analysts. Previously, VW kept its financial information closely guarded and company forecasts were confusing to analysts.

While these changes have shown some positive effects, the question remains, can Volkswagen, the world's fifth-largest auto maker, put profits in front of its workers and convince analysts that its views on profitability have changed? German unions are strong, the state's priority is to keep jobs local, and VW invests heavily in Germany, where labor costs are high.

QUESTIONS

1. Who should manage a foreign operation? Identify the issues and the circumstances that might influence how a company chooses to staff its foreign executive positions.
2. Putting personalities aside, VW has compiled an excellent record worldwide for engineering and marketing quality automobiles coupled with a somewhat dismal reputation for managing people. What lessons could it learn about developing executive talent from other companies such as Shell Oil and GE, profiled in the chapter?
3. If you were a U.S. manager for VW in Troy, Michigan, what career prospects would you envision for your future development with the company?

BIBLIOGRAPHY

Lehner, Uban C. "Who's the Boss? A Group of Experts Debate a Crucial Question: Who Should Run the Overseas Operation?" *Wall Street Journal*, 26 September 1996, p. R15.

Miller, Scott. "The Mellowing of a Pit Bull?— VW Chairman Piech Says His Management Style Has Changed—The First Thing He Did: Give Audi Back Its Sales." *Wall Street Journal Europe*, 13 December 2000, p. 1. [Retrieved 16 December 2000 from Dow Jones Interactive database.]

Miller, Scott. "Shareholder Value Still Hard to Prove at Volkswagen—German Workers' Interests Come Before Stock Price—Old Wine in a New Bottle." *Wall Street Journal Europe*, 13 December 2000, p. 1. [Retrieved 16 December 2000 from Dow Jones Interactive database.]

Miller, Scott. "VW Starts on a New Model: Profits—Feisty Chairman Faces New Challenge." *Wall Street Journal*, 13 December 2000, pp. A1, A8. [Retrieved 16 December 2000 from Dow Jones Interactive database.]

Steinmetz, Greg, and Matt Marshall. "Foreign Policy: How a Chemicals Giant Goes about Becoming a Lot Less German." *Wall Street Journal*, 18 February 1997, pp. A1, A8.

TRAINING MANAGERS TO BE TRAINERS AT SHANGRI-LA HOTELS

"The most important role for an expatriate manager is being an effective trainer," according to John Petersen, director of human resources for Shangri-La Hotels and Resorts in Hong Kong:

> Service industry training in particular has become an entire industry. My associates at ITT Sheraton, Holiday Inns, New World, and Regent International Hotels recently met at a world conference on hospitality in Singapore, and there were two emergent themes. First, our people—the maids, housekeepers, waiters, waitresses, and clerks—are grossly unprepared for what we expect them to do. Second, our managers—those who do know what to do—haven't the foggiest notion of how to impart that knowledge. Training is the key, but it's not a popular word. We not only must train staff, but train managers to be trainers.

For a growing number of international companies, training managers to train others effectively is a major headache. An expatriate manager typically earns an overseas assignment based on a performance record and qualifications, but that selection process rarely addresses the ability to build a human resource base of capable people in a foreign culture. "How could it?" asks Petersen. "Most of our younger managers are out here for the first time, or perhaps promoted from their own country to another Asian location where they have no cross-cultural experience."

The Shangri-La organization operates 37 of the world's leading hotels in locales such as London, Paris, Shanghai, Beijing, Manila, Bangkok, Singapore, Hong Kong, Indonesia, Malaysia, Philippines, Fiji, Thailand, and Taiwan. It recently announced plans to launch its first hotel in the Middle East, which is scheduled for completion by late 2001. It also manages about 300 hotels and resorts elsewhere in Asia and in major U.S. cities. Senior managers are drawn from more than 40 different countries, and all of them bring extensive cross-cultural management experience to their posts. Former CEO, Pho Ba Quan, an ethnic Vietnamese, is a U.S. citizen who worked in Washington, D.C., for 20 years. Quan explains the dilemma of training partially as a cultural issue and partially as a cost factor. "From a cost standpoint, the staff turnover means that we have a revolving door," Quan says. "All hotels face a similar problem, and the money you put into training is quickly lost as your people leave. In China alone, we run a huge 'hotel college' program with 400 new recruits every few weeks."

Shangri-La can build these costs into its overall budget, but more perplexing cultural issues continue to cause problems. Quan observes:

> We have people in China that don't understand the fundamental concept of a modern bed. The managers on site may only be vaguely in touch with service concepts and hygiene standards, and most of them have no experience outside China. It is different in Singapore, where a whole society is squeaky clean and you have some of the world's best hotels competing for business. Staff there have been part of a higher class of service. But when we bring in someone from Singapore or Hong Kong for Chinese training, it is traumatic. These managers try to hammer down rules and policies, but local people don't understand what they are trying to achieve. Too many expatriates are insensitive to the locals, who are clueless about foreign standards.

Managers brought in from Europe or North America often experience more severe difficulties, according to Quan and Petersen. "They face a culture shock for which few are prepared," says Petersen. "We literally hand-hold most newcomers, and the senior people here recognize that they too are trainers. But, still, who trains the trainers? And what do they need to know? How do they approach their training roles?"

Shangri-La apparently found some of these answers. In early 1995, Shangri-La Hotels announced its intention to open two new training facilities—a management training center in Beijing and an Institute of Management in Shenzhen—in order to provide training and development for local people. The Beijing facility is a partnership between Shangri-La and Beijing Second Foreign Languages Institute, which houses the management training center. According to Phil Stephenson, Shangri-La's group director of human resources at that time, "Experienced managers and supervisors are simply not readily available in China. . . . We are therefore taking a proactive stance by developing our own hotel educational institutes." A Shangri-La spokesperson further stated:

> In Beijing, we are not grooming an elite executive corps. We are training to meet our area of greatest need, which is at the middle-management and supervisory levels. There are no accredited hotel management schools either in China or in the region, and there is a real need to teach basic concepts of management and delegation of responsibility, something that is not part of current Chinese society.

The training programs are between two days and eight weeks in length. Training for managers begins with home-country orientation, when possible including at least two days of cultural sensitivity seminars. For employees facing dramatic changes in environments—such as someone from Dallas, Texas, going to Thailand—seminars may run as long as two weeks and include preassignment trips to local facilities, where the candidates work under experienced mentors for month-long stays. Programs pursue four objectives: They introduce local cultural expectations and customs; they address technical aspects of the candidate's job in the host country; they address human resource issues, which include disciplinary guidelines, compensation requirements, contrasts in work rules, and leadership behavior; and they communicate candidate responsibilities for job training. Quan explains the program:

> We didn't arrive at this approach overnight. We had to learn the hard way, and we are far from where we want to be. Training methods are currently the biggest question. If a person is coming to Hong Kong, there is little difficulty. We can train staff through on-job techniques and by example. We put new people with experienced

staff, and the manager simply must provide a systematic way of coordinating the learning process. The same person going into China has to be able to explain the importance of having clean sheets every day—or providing toilet paper, clean towels, and soap. These things never occur to most Chinese, who lack the amenities in their normal lifestyle. They can't learn by example, because they would often just learn poor habits. Instead, we provide "model training." We have fully prepared guest rooms and actors—other managers who portray hard-nosed guests—and then drill the recruits in a tell-and-do process. We burn them when they are wrong, and praise them publicly when they do things correctly. We rely on many little rewards, real and psychological, to motivate new staff to want to understand what good service is all about. Getting good managers to be able to do this is not easy.

Indeed, Shangri-La runs courses for training managers at key facilities in the United States, Europe, and the Hong Kong headquarters. During an intensive two-week series, participants learn how to develop a training plan, how to write instructions and objectives, how to demonstrate techniques, and how to evaluate performance. Although the company has not yet established a pervasive mentoring program, pilot projects in Thailand and Manila have shown great success. As part of the mentoring process, candidates scheduled for reassignment fulfill adjunct duties presenting training programs to local staff. This contact provides a hands-on experience with local workers, and managers quickly learn standards for acceptable and unacceptable practices. In China, for example, employees expect explicit instructions. They are accustomed to a superior-subordinate relationship based on conformance, so established policies will be followed—if the workers understand them. In Thailand, workers do not appreciate such a directive approach; instead, they expect managers to behave in tutorial roles. Policies will be ignored as often as obeyed, but workers will respond favorably if the manager can instill a sense of obligation—a sense of pride in doing something without being told.

In an interesting twist to the hotel training program, Shangri-La assigns Asian staff members for training duties in the United States and London. They train host-country minorities who in many instances are immigrants. Quan describes the program as a cultural bridging process:

Immigrant Asian workers in Texas or New York typically do not have an appreciation of American quality standards, but more important, they don't particularly like working for non-Asian Americans. They'll do what they are told to do, but that doesn't get it. We find that bringing in a good employee from a home-Asian society provides a role model. This creates a bond that works on the individual psyche. We're trying to do the same thing in reverse—send our western-resident Asians to the Far East. The bottleneck is that among all our managers and staff, there just are not enough people who can do training well.

QUESTIONS

1. Discuss the role of trainer and its requirements for international managers. Career profiles often omit this activity. How can a manager acquire training skills, and what might be the most important things to learn for a manager headed for a foreign assignment with training responsibilities?

2. Shangri-La seems to have created an entire operational training element of management responsibilities, and the firm's executives suggest that cross-cultural training is becoming an industry by itself. How would a private training organization approach the problem of preparing hotel staff members for their duties? What methods would best promote this goal?

3. How would you improve the training process at Shangri-La or a similar organization with worldwide facilities in many different cultural settings?

BIBLIOGRAPHY

Brady, Diane. "Asian Economic Survey 1995: Training Trauma." *Asian Wall Street Journal*, 9 October 1995, p. S46.

Brady, Diane. "Beijing Hotels Struggle in Bid to Boost Service." *Asian Wall Street Journal*, 29 May 1997, p. 4. [Retrieved 14 December 2000 from Dow Jones Interactive database.]

"Hospitality Dilemma: Training and Retaining Qualified Staff." International Conference on Human Resource Management, Singapore, 10 June 1996.

Personal interview with Pho Ba Quan and staff, Shangri-La Hotels & Resorts, Hong Kong, 10 December 1995.

Seiwitz, Robert. "Shangri-La Plans Two Hotel Schools." *Hotel & Motel Management*, 9 January 1995. [Retrieved 12 December 2000 from Dow Jones Interactive database.]

"Shangri-La Begins Management Restructuring." *The Star (Malaysia)*, 15 June 2000. [Retrieved 12 December 2000 from Dow Jones Interactive database.]

"Shangri-La Spreads Its Wings in the Mideast." *Travel & Tourism News,*15 February 2000. [Retrieved 12 December 2000 from Dow Jones Interactive database.]

DEVELOPING PRIVATE ENTERPRISES IN LATVIA

Ask someone where Riga is, and you probably will get a blank stare. Someone may correctly answer, however, that it is the capital of Latvia, a small state with a population of 2.8 million on the Baltic Sea. It shares a border with Russia and sea links with Sweden. To the south lies Lithuania, and slightly southeast is Belarus. Poland is somewhat farther south. To the north of Latvia, tiny Estonia also borders on Russia. Latvia is one of the so-called newly emerging Baltic economies. The country regained its independence in 1991 after the dissolution of the Soviet Union, but it is far from a new nation. Indeed, Latvia has a rich cultural heritage that residents proudly trace to the Viking age. Riga was a major seaport for the Baltic region before Columbus sailed for the Americas. Even today, the heart of Riga preserves buildings and houses first erected in the early 1700s. Several are still in use as renovated offices and facilities for Latvia's new stock market and central bank.

Until 1991, more than 200,000 Soviet troops controlled Latvia, and Russian tanks were more common sights there than city buses. Latvia came under Soviet domination as Stalin's lightning-fast tank brigades advanced toward Berlin during World War II. After the war, the country became a Soviet industrial satellite, the most heavily industrialized sector under Soviet control. As a port, Riga gave the Soviet economy a relatively ice-free channel to the sea—access that was crucial for dispatching submarines and electronically equipped trawlers into the North Atlantic. Latvians and Estonians maintained huge fishing fleets that provided a vital lifeline of seafood, much of which was transported directly to Moscow along two highways. The Soviet Union's oil and natural gas supplies came through Latvian ports, and the people themselves provided some of the best-skilled technicians in the Soviet engineering system. Latvians were required to learn Russian, which for nearly two full generations was the official state language. All young men were subscribed into military service, and most were educated in science and engineering

professions. Latvian women were commonly pressed into factory work, often completing technical studies themselves. So when Latvia regained self-rule in 1991, the nation began its new life with a reasonable infrastructure—the inefficient, Soviet-style equipment notwithstanding—and an extremely well educated workforce.

However, the country was not in a position to support itself. The old Soviet system had created a dependent industrial state that sacrificed farming and agriculture for production in defense, petrochemicals, and heavy-engineering plants. Food grains, beef, and most staples were allocated through the old state system from other Eastern European enclaves or the Balkans. Latvia had no independent banking system, transactions were handled entirely through Soviet monetary processes, and no lending process could supply capital in a country where private ownership of any asset other than household needs and clothing was outlawed. Job assignments were decided by fiat, and Russian managers generally controlled all key government and industry posts. Wages were paid through the state system in Russian currency, and Latvia began independence without a national currency. Indeed, this ancient culture with a sense of history and pride in its people had to redefine much of its economy and create entirely new social systems.

With the help of international agencies and foreign aid from Sweden, Germany, the European Development Bank, the IMF, and the U.S. Agency for International Development, Latvians established the foundations for a market economy. Within two years, they formed a central bank, launched a securities exchange, and established a national currency while also holding inflation in check. In the process, they attracted more than 400 multinational companies to do business there. Nevertheless, Latvia inherited defunct fiscal and monetary systems that continue to create enormous problems for economic development. With no recent history of private enterprise and a huge demand for development funds, the country is swamped with taxes. A private company will pay turnover taxes (taxes on gross income), employee taxes, business and profit surcharge taxes, and an odd assortment of specific levies on property, transportation, exports, and imports. The government distributes these funds among crucial public-service projects, so it needs a strong tax income. Still, the combined tax burden for a company often exceeds its total costs of production and operations. Net profits are therefore rare, and private citizens accumulate almost no capital. Consequently, the economy can supply little money to fund investments in private enterprise, precisely the engine that the country hopes will drive its growth for the future.

Still, Latvia is making progress in business development. The old city center of Riga houses thriving small businesses, retail stores, and entertainment. The opera house has been renovated, and a few nice dining areas have appeared alongside busy open-air markets, fish mongers, a farm market, and a remarkable supply of homegrown foods and vegetables provided by a rural population that has suddenly recovered ancestral lands. The country is surviving, however, only through massive foreign investments and international aid, much of it in forms other than money. Indeed, most foreign aid is channeled through volunteer organizations and hundreds of experienced international managers funded by U.S., Swedish, German, and other governments. This international entourage represents some of the best minds in the world with extensive private-sector business experience. At any one time, the country may host several dozen retired executives from U.S. multinationals, an equal number of German financial advisers, trade specialists from London, New York, and Tokyo, 50 or more active executives from major companies, and MBA students on volunteer assignments from U.S. graduate schools. These outsiders work with Latvian companies to help them establish successful businesses, with further support from a Peace Corps cadre and foreign government advisers, foreign teams that look for current trade or investment opportunities, and Latvians returning home from overseas to take part in their country's reconstruction. By and large, these people all act as international managers in every way, even though they may not have direct management stakes in business ventures.

Latvia's biggest economic challenge is human resource development. Building infrastructure, creating financial systems, and generating capital are all cru-

cial activities, but converting Latvians from a subjugated population into a self-determined free-market nation is a monumental task. International contractors such as PriceWaterhouseCooper and Andersen Consulting focus primarily on capital markets and private-sector financing, but they seldom become involved in human resource development. Management is relegated to specialists brought in and funded by nongovernment organizations (NGOs) that work independently of government foreign service offices, usually entirely through volunteers. One of the most extensive NGOs is the International Executive Service Corps (IESC), a Connecticut-based organization with more than 12,000 seasoned businesspeople volunteering to advise firms in nearly 150 countries worldwide. The Latvian program is a microview of how IESC works to assist private enterprise development; similar and much larger programs operate, for example, in Russia, Poland, Chile, Brazil, India, Sri Lanka, Jordan, and Kenya, to name a few.

U.S. foreign-assistance programs contract with IESC to place expert managers and senior executives in host-country enterprises as advisers for periods that vary between several months and several years. The IESC matches a local client's needs with U.S. volunteers drawn from lists of retired managers, supplemented by university staff members and active executives who can take time from their schedules to work with host-country enterprises. Similar NGOs are backed by government development agencies in Japan, Sweden, and Britain, all with worldwide interests in private enterprise. Such agencies often generate multilateral assistance projects or joint interventions. After 1991, when foreign-assistance providers began to direct substantial allocations into Eastern Europe and Russia, the U.S. Agency for International Development (USAID) contracted with IESC for approximately 200 company intervention projects over a five-year period in Latvia. Two examples of this program illustrate the successes and failures of human resource development under USAID assistance. These activities mirror results of other NGO efforts from other developing countries.

Dailrade Production Association

Dailrade was approved as a joint-stock company after privatization distributed equity shares to its managers and 520 employees in 1992. The company was spun off from a light-manufacturing division of one of the large Soviet-run defense installations. The old state-owned defense works typified industrial management under the communist regime. At one time, it employed nearly 20,000 people in five divisions to manufacture weapons components, military hardware, and various metal products ranging from field utensils to aircraft fuselage parts. The Dailrade division, located near Riga, specialized in metal fabrication, plastic molding, extrusion processes, and an odd range of associated products and technologies working with ceramics, glass, and leather. The Soviet collapse decimated the Riga division. Approximately 1,200 Russian technicians and indigenous Russian workers either returned to their homeland or abandoned the factory to pursue subsistence farming and jobs that could pay survival wages. At the same time, nearly 3,000 Latvian workers faced the choice of trying to convert the remaining shell of Dailrade into a profitable business or going their own way. Because they saw no obvious product lines or markets for anything that Dailrade could make, most employees simply left.

The remaining 520 employees committed themselves to begin manufacturing a wide range of small products that they hoped to sell in local markets, to tourists, and especially to overseas customers. They were supported by small government development grants and a trickle of funds generated through the privatization stock offer. Most stock was issued through vouchers to employees who made no cash investments, so little capital flowed into the company from equity holders. Nevertheless, the new owner-employees dug in their heels and created 2,040 different products that could be sold for profit. This extraordinary selection of products demonstrated their skills and production capabilities. The company established domestic sales for new kitchenware and agricultural hand tools (plows, animal feeding troughs, shovels, forks, and so on). Sales were encouraging, but no one in the nation could purchase more than minimal tools and supplies. The company also made handcrafted dolls, key chains, and Latvian tourist mementos that sold well to foreigners working in Riga. Employees adapted their machinery to produce ceramic insulators required by state electric power projects and telecommunications exchanges. They quickly expanded into leather goods, such as gloves, hats, belts, women's purses, and winter jackets. Many of the company's families leveraged their resources under a cottage-industry arrangement by handcrafting woolen clothing, colorful shawls, sweaters, and socks that could be sold through company channels. The glass workers established a line of housewares

and, with the help of metalcrafters, fashioned jewelry for sale to tourists.

After nearly a year of difficult struggles encouraged by promising prospects, Dailrade faced a quandary similar to those of many other struggling companies privatized after the Soviets departed. It had the skills and equipment to manufacture a wide range of interesting products, supported by engineering capabilities and a physical infrastructure in the form of a huge Soviet-style factory. Employees were disorganized and barely surviving, however, and they had no concept of how to operate a private enterprise. No one, not even the senior managers, knew anything about marketing, cost accounting, purchasing, personnel management, compensation systems, or how to control cash flow and transactions. Not one employee understood the meaning of a checking account, because none had ever existed in Latvia until the newly liberated banks began to introduce commercial accounting for private businesses. No one understood concepts of advertising, pricing, sales marketing, or distribution; the company simply made products and trucked them to wholesale customers, who in turn sold them in handshake agreements for whatever price they could bring. In the plant, employees still worked 10-hour days under a works supervisor. But the plant's organization scheme lacked job classifications and training programs, and it had no more than a skeleton system of rules fashioned after Soviet-style management. Basically, this autocratic supervision system dictated work routines and quotas, controlling activities through a severe disciplinary code. Under the new ownership this system lay in ruins, because supervisors had lost the command authority of a state-owned council. Employees viewed themselves as free owners, often neglecting to show up for work for casual reasons such as working on handicrafts or tending gardens.

When IESC volunteers first arrived to help Dailrade, employees had not been paid in three months. Sales also had slowed to a trickle, and a haphazard assortment of inventory was piled everywhere. Most of the inventory was useless, except for clothing and household items that most employees whisked away for themselves or hawked in open-air markets. The company maintained no sales office—indeed, no one was even designated as responsible for sales. No one pursued marketing activities or personnel, employee welfare, compensation, safety, or benefits management. Individual managers juggled all of these tasks.

Nevertheless, Dailrade had a development plan generated through a U.S. business advisory service, and its technical capabilities suggested a huge untapped potential for manufacturing exportable products. Indeed, the company could offer a very low cost profile. Wages at the time amounted to approximately $80 a month for factory workers, and the abandoned Soviet plant and equipment came free of charge. The company could buy raw materials and supplies cheaply from other Latvian enterprises also struggling to survive, and most workers and their families accepted very basic accommodations in cost-free, barracks-style quarters erected under the old system.

IESC advisers faced the task of instituting organizational changes required to bring the company into an export market with appropriate products that would generate foreign exchange—and, perhaps, attract foreign investors. One volunteer, a retired vice president from General Electric's Aerospace division, took on the task of overhauling manufacturing systems. Another volunteer, a New York advertising executive who had sold his business and was independently wealthy, began to build a marketing program. A third IESC executive, a successful CPA with a thriving Connecticut business, volunteered his time to restructure Dailrade's administrative systems. IESC headquarters also began a worldwide market research effort to identify potential markets for Dailrade's products or foreign investors that might contract for the Latvian company's output.

Within three months, a marketing office was established, a cost-accounting system and production control system put in place, new administrative processes introduced, and a product development department formed. The volunteers stayed on to mentor Dailrade's managers, and U.S. trainers visited for short stints to assist plant workers. Several experienced MBA students arrived from North Carolina under a separate NGO contract to train all employees in fundamental business practices. Two experts in foreign trade arrived from Washington, D.C., to formulate strategies for export development and to train managers in negotiating skills. English and German language skills were developed through Peace Corps programs and a Deutsche Bank grant for language instructors. In addition, 12 Latvian workers in leadership roles visited U.S. and Swedish factories, where they interned with production technicians.

After many months, volunteer assistance declined. All NGO programs are structured to jump-start new projects or to intervene temporarily with platforms of support. Eventually, however, they leave foreign enterprises to go it alone. Such companies can draw on a broad range of continuing support, such as subsidized market planning, financial advice, export development assistance, and education. Dailrade continued to benefit from several in-house training programs and IESC connections for export trade. The company recovered to a point where it began to break even, and the Latvian government suspended taxes on products that generated foreign exchange through international markets. The euphoria lasted only a short while, however; unfortunately, the company closed down operations in 1996.

A postmortem evaluation revealed that neither managers nor employees could sustain a private-enterprise psyche. Once volunteers left, old patterns of behavior reemerged. The product line, which had been trimmed from 2,000 to 60 exportable items, had quickly ballooned again to 800 products, most designed and manufactured opportunistically rather than through decisions reflecting solid marketing research. The purchasing officers could not bring themselves to procure materials in economic quantities; for nearly a half-century, they had known Soviet-style systems in which they amassed any allocated supplies, even if they did not use the goods. Slow change in habits prevented the company from achieving good health, and the deathblow came when Dailrade failed to service international accounts that IESC had established. For example, it failed to deliver on an order from a New England importer for more than $40,000 in leather jackets and accessories, supplying only 20 percent of the contracted goods on time with the remainder shipped piecemeal up to three months late. Meanwhile, the company leveraged its contract with a bank for cash operating loans and spent the money long before it received payments. This behavior was repeated several times, creating a cash-flow crisis that the company could escape only by rapid export growth. In another example, Dailrade contracted with a German electronics firm to make ceramic insulating components for computer circuit boards. The company delivered on time, but the shipment was rejected for poor quality. In that instance, Dailrade had leveraged its contract and spent the cash, but it never received payment; it had to swallow the production losses and default on loans.

To counter its cash-flow losses, Dailrade trimmed employment, down from 520 at inception to barely 80 employees after the German fiasco. One salesclerk and one accountant remained, skilled technicians capable of working elsewhere quit, and all but a few managers disappeared. The facility was gutted, and those employees who remained reminisced about the "good old days" of communism when people had food to eat and no worries about paychecks or paying bills.

Grindex Pharmaceutical

A former state-owned chemical plant was privatized at about the same time as Dailrade, and the transformation was similar. When the Soviets departed, the plant site stayed intact, but employment dropped suddenly from nearly 6,000 to less than 800 workers. The remaining personnel were all well-educated, experienced Latvians eager to establish a profitable enterprise. IESC sent in several teams of volunteers, including engineers retired or on leave from U.S. giants such as Merck and AlliedSignal Corporation. The Germans supported a product research team with volunteers from Bayer AG and two independent agricultural products laboratories. The U.S. government assigned FDA consultants to assist in compliance with international standards in exportable pharmaceuticals. IESC marketing and accounting volunteers intervened to rebuild a market-driven company, train managers in private enterprise, and coordinate in-house training programs similar to those provided to Dailrade.

Unlike Dailrade, Grindex hired two U.S. executives who had retired from multinationals. One worked jointly with the company's new marketing director, and one worked in liaison with the chief operating officer. Both executives were experienced in Europe and in pharmaceuticals. But more important, they had worked in several foreign countries under rugged development conditions, and they understood that Grindex had to transform its entire philosophy of management. They set in place a four-year plan for development, including travel to the United States for Latvian managers, joint involvement in international negotiations for contracts and procurement, and a broad range of plant visits in Europe and America for managers and key employees. They instituted quality-control procedures learned through site visits to U.S. firms and developed CPA-audited records to meet international accounting standards.

During the first two years, Grindex operated constantly on the verge of collapse. The company failed to meet payroll on several occasions. It endured a strike by workers, who had organized themselves and sought heavy guarantees for wages and benefits that reflected the old Soviet profile of protected entitlements. Grindex managers initially met this challenge with force, threatening workers and rejecting all offers. The U.S. managers and German volunteers, however, convinced Grindex to negotiate a profit-sharing contract, introduce works councils similar to those in Europe, and support an employee-directed benefit program of self-help and personal development. Not having cash flow to meet union demands, the company sought win-win solutions through joint responsibility projects with employees.

The result was a company that focused on just nine products, all with export potential. They included processed ingredients or additives that major companies, such as Merck in the United States and Hoechst in Germany, required for making retail pharmaceuticals. In its third year of adhering to a marketing plan for producing economical-scale quantities of intermediate goods, Grindex landed a $1 million contract with a New England company.

By industry standards, this total amounted to petty cash; for Grindex, it was the beginning of a success story. In the following two years, the company landed 21 similar contracts, drawing repeat business from Munich, Stockholm, New York, and Toronto. During the early going, the employment level had dropped to 600 employees, but after four years Grindex had reemployed nearly 1,500 idled workers. Management also introduced a Director's Club, an association of pharmaceutical employees devoted to providing self-help, training, and family assistance to displaced workers. This program spread beyond Grindex to other Latvian companies, through which IESC volunteers supported a system of cross-cultural training and skills development.

By late 1996, IESC had introduced 48 foreign companies to Grindex, each with teams that visited the plant site and worked with the Latvians to develop marketable products. The crucial determinant of success was a pervasive change in behavior. Early difficulties were overcome by small but important successes that fostered a sense of belief that market systems could work. Management became knowledgeable about trade and foreign management techniques, and many employees witnessed firsthand overseas production and marketing systems. Those who did not travel were introduced to foreign methods by their well-traveled peers or through international managers from the volunteer corps and client companies.

The two key expatriate managers were instrumental in perpetuating foreign work systems adapted for Latvian cultural characteristics. For example, works councils were created, but the firm made no effort to establish team-based work processes. The Latvians simply were not accustomed to self-directed decision-making after two generations of autocratic leadership. Nevertheless, the American expatriates counseled Latvian supervisors on communications skills, making decisions as expected, but phrasing orders as recommendations or seeking advisory meetings with employees before implementing directives. Employees participated in social programs and employee support services, but they remained distant from work-related decisions, much as the advisers expected them to do. Labor relations improved through a system of open communications. Employees were keenly aware of product developments, marketing plans, compensation programs, and distribution of company income. Fully 25 percent of operating profits were channeled into training and education for both employees and managers.

Dailrade and Grindex represent companies at two ends of a spectrum of private enterprise in Latvia and most neighboring countries in Eastern Europe. They hope for international assistance but not handouts. They seek self-determined enterprise and knowledge about global markets. They aspire to participate in world markets, almost naively expecting the world to beat a path to their doors. They have the capabilities to compete and to grow, and most accept foreign management ideas. But they are also part of an entrenched ethnic culture whose roots require careful protection. In one way this is a tremendous benefit, because Soviet domination did not eradicate values ingrained over centuries. Soviet influence subverted the economy and subsequently fashioned industry on communist ideology, and the remnants of that system still present difficult problems. On reflection, Dailrade was not a business failure as much as an uphill battle against ideologically conditioned behavior. Grindex was successful because it met those challenges.

QUESTIONS

1. What are some of the major cultural and perceptual barriers to developing private enterprise in Latvia?

2. Should American, European, or other foreign management concepts be adopted in Latvia? What international concepts of human resource development would be most beneficial there without imposing on local culture or customs?

3. Training is a critical dimension of economic development, but under the circumstances in Latvia, some methods offer far more important benefits than others. What approaches to training employees and developing managers would you suggest for companies such as Dailrade and Grindex?

4. Thousands of foreign service employees, volunteers, consultants, and business advisers from nearly all major developed countries work throughout the world in private enterprise. They are deeply involved in trade, finance, exports, investments, and management of enterprises in virtually every field of commerce. Are they international managers, or do they fulfill ambassadorial roles defined by political priorities? Describe how you envision roles (or careers) for representatives of NGOs who work in private-enterprise development.

BIBLIOGRAPHY

The Grindex Director's Club: Achievements and Lessons Learned. Grindex Corporation, Riga, Latvia, July 1996.

Holt, David H., and Armands Jurves. "Intervention Success and Development of International Markets for Latvian Privatized Companies." *IESC Report to Central Bank of Latvia*, Riga, December 1996.

Sweet, Charles, David Holt, Andrea Love, Paul Prentice, and David Harbin. *A Program Evaluation of A.I.D.'s Investments in Voluntary Assistance to Private Enterprise Development in Central and Eastern Europe* (Washington, D.C.: U.S. Agency for International Development, 1993), 16–22, Appendices E6 and E13.

MANAGING PEOPLE: THE LEADERSHIP DIMENSION

PART FIVE

MOTIVATING PEOPLE: THE CHALLENGE OF DIVERSITY

CHAPTER OBJECTIVES

Explain how people's concepts of work influence behavior in different cultural environments.

Contrast job content and job context factors for motivating foreign employees.

Demonstrate how achievement motives can differ substantially among countries.

Describe how expectancy theory can help to account for situational contingencies.

Show how social values influence the types of incentives that effectively influence foreign activities.

Identify the three main viewpoints of diversity and their implications for resolving conflicts.

Dan Westford, president of PolyChem Inc., closed down the company's Italian plant located near Milan, frustrated by his inability to maintain competitive levels of production there.[1] He had opened the plant in 1990 to serve growing European and Middle Eastern markets in highly absorbent polyacrylamide crystals used in agriculture and environmental applications. The PolyChem products are small, salt-like crystals that absorb hundreds of times their weight. Farmers in desert or semiarid regions use them to hold and retain water; mixed in with a plant's roots, the crystals provide a long-lasting source of moisture. Variations of the crystals fill "socks" that absorb oil, not only in the form of small tubular units for cleaning up oil leaks on boats but also as huge booms for collecting oil from major spills. The business was profitable and growing, but PolyChem's Italian subsidiary was plagued with work stoppages, labor-management disputes, and low productivity. When Westford tried to introduce performance-bonus incentives, the situation deteriorated. After he brought in American consultants to help build production teams, production slid to even lower levels. To counteract high absenteeism, Westford tried to create attendance premiums, but absenteeism only increased.

The Milan plant was managed by a British engineer who had worked extensively in the United States for several major chemical companies. He too was frustrated by events, but he explained the situation in part by what he called "an Italian mentality"—some individuals seemed to come to work only when it suited them, but many more simply "punched the time clock" to be there. In either case, they also seemed to expect a premium wage paid by an American multinational. Most employees also seemed very cynical about the bonus system, which evidently did little to motivate anyone. Bonuses were awarded quarterly to departments and to task groups based on performance that exceeded target output levels. After the plant shut down in 1994, Westford discovered that his group-based incentives probably were not welcome in Milan, where a strong socialist movement among factory workers molded attitudes.

In 1995, a German chemical company leased the Milan plant site and established a very successful operation. What was the difference? Westford discovered that the firm had implemented a company-wide profit-sharing plan that never singled out any group for differential bonuses. The competitor enforced attendance and work rules vigorously, even requiring a strict dress code, yet workers apparently respected management. Westford recalls that his British manager had been much more considerate by comparison, yet apparently never gained the respect of the Italian employees. A colleague in Rome told Westford that he just didn't understand Italians. "They respect strong and decisive people," he said, "and that's not the way you guys managed. But Italians also want to feel in control, like having a brotherhood. Your group incentives probably pitted these guys against each other. Attendance incentives? Forget it! That's like waving a red flag to a bull. They are going to throw the money back at you and take even more days off just to show you who's the real boss."

Several months after that meeting, Westford and his site manager in Monterrey, Mexico, decided to change a few local practices to improve motivation. First, the local Mexican manager was given greater authority to make decisions, and he was presented with an expensive Rolex watch to mark a recent promotion. Westford was told that the watch would become an important status symbol—and, indeed, it became the talk of the office. The manager also began to dress in more expensive suits, flaunting his watch and attire so much that Westford felt somewhat uncomfortable, since he often visited the plant in jeans and an open-collared shirt. Westford was urged to dress even more exquisitely than his manager did, and when he responded to the advice, strange changes occurred in workers' attitudes. "It's crazy," Westford said. "I noticed that each time I visited, the staff seemed more and more pleasant. How can a suit of clothes or a flashy watch make a difference? It's as if they expected me to prance around like a movie star. That kind of behavior back home or in England would get me ripped. I can see where I might have acted that way in Italy—maybe it would have helped—but Mexico confuses me. Now I have to get a gold watch that's better than the one I gave the guy in Monterrey because he says that I don't look important enough. These things turn on the employees. They like to see status differences, so we'll work on that theme right down the line."

THE CHALLENGE OF MOTIVATING PEOPLE

One theme has recurred throughout earlier chapters: Because people and societies differ, international managers must adapt to unusual circumstances and become culturally sensitive to differences in foreign work environments. In no instance is this requirement more important than when managers are challenged to motivate foreign employees. They can rely on *no universal rules* to accomplish this goal. That statement does not mean that well-founded concepts of motivation contribute nothing, only that the principles of motivation theories cannot be generalized to all cultures. Managers must find the methods that work best within their own environments and with their particular employees. As this chapter will show, research about motivation in the international context has revealed interesting contrasts.

This chapter tries to reduce the confusion about motivating people in other cultures and subsequently to suggest broad guidelines that may help international managers to understand their own situations. This chapter does not attempt to assess the viability of motivation theories in themselves. Instead, the chapter briefly reviews the foremost theories, assuming that most students need only a refresher discussion about fundamental concepts. The theories are then discussed in relation to human values and how people from different parts of the world seek fulfillment at work. Many points introduced in earlier chapters will reemerge. For example, an understanding of differences in human values among the world's societies is crucial to a further understanding of why people from one nation may eagerly pursue monetary gains, yet people elsewhere have little regard for wage incentives. In other instances, employees put high value on group harmony and criticize co-workers who want to achieve individual recognition. As the chapter will show, the concepts of *work* and a *job* evoke different meanings among people from other cultures; therefore, incentives to work must also differ.

Differences in values, lifestyles, ideologies, and social systems create patterns of behavior that can be perplexing to managers working in foreign locations. These considerations become still more complicated for managers responsible for cross-cultural activities and global networks; they must develop exceptional skills at managing *diversity*. Consequently, the essential theme of this chapter is to explore differences in motivational characteristics of culturally diverse workforces. Examples highlight countries with especially pronounced contrasts, because they often create the greatest human resource management challenges for international companies.

MOTIVATION IN THE CROSS-CULTURAL CONTEXT

In broad terms, **motivation** is the stimulus that drives behavior. It consists of all the forces that cause people to behave in certain ways, including forces from within the individual, from other people who can influence behavior, and from the surroundings.[2] Figure 14.1 illustrates a process in which these three sources of motivation combine in the first stage to activate behavior, then are coupled to performance, and eventually become linked to perceived rewards. Motivational factors at the heart of this model can be examined individually; but as discussed later, they are not mutually exclusive influences.

The first characteristic emphasizes the origination of motivation within a person, creating a capability for generating one's own momentum for working or taking initiative. The second characteristic implies that motivation is influenced by other people; in occupational situations, it is influenced by external stimuli such as pay, promotion opportunities, supervisory praise, threats, potential ridicule, and disciplinary action. If a manager could identify cause-and-effect relationships between each of these variables and how well individuals work, then motivating people would be a relatively easy task, but causal effects cannot be reliably determined. This is particularly evident in an evaluation of the third characteristic, called *situational factors*. Individual behavior is influenced by the work environment, which includes influences from society, close associates, technology that defines what people do and how they work, leadership behavior, and circumstances that arise in the process of working.

These three forces can easily be seen at work every day, although many people never become consciously aware of them. For example, a teenager with decent moral values may not be tempted to shoplift, yet the same teen roaming through a store with a group of friends may be challenged to pick something up. Within the group context, that person may become a shoplifter. On the other hand, a teenager who might shoplift on his or her own accord may be prevented from doing so merely through a belief that group members would not approve of such behavior. Work behavior is subject to the same type of influence, exerted through social or cultural expectations, peer pressure, or personal values. Individuals subconsciously evaluate their circumstances and then act, speak, dress, work, and play in ways that they perceive to be congruent with their environments.

The three characteristics of motivation become much more complicated in an international context. International managers may have very little understanding of foreign cultures or social systems, and they are often uninformed about deeply embedded individual values. The international manager's job would be much easier if values were universal, but these values differ substantially among the world's societies. People are

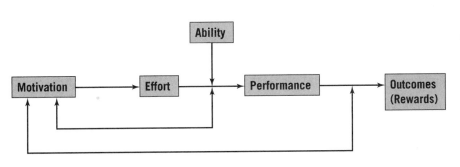

FIGURE 14.1
The Basic Motivation Process

not motivated by the same rewards in different societies. They do not have similar expectations for pay, promotion, or personal recognition. Workers in one society may respond well to certain types of incentives that are unacceptable elsewhere. People have different expectations about their jobs and careers. Their work-related behavior differs from one society to the next, and, in each society, employees expect different rewards for their efforts. Work-related values are not universal but instead reflect patterns of behavior ingrained in each culture.

Nevertheless, researchers looking for common bonds across cultures have found some evidence to suggest that motivation can be modeled along international lines. Before exploring these principles, it is important to make several preliminary observations. First, because motivation theories have evolved primarily in the United States, they represent a western or U.S.-based perspective. Contrasts among Asian, Middle Eastern, African, Latin American, and even many European societies reveal anomalies in the fundamental assumptions on which the leading theories are based.[3] Second, research has failed to show that motivation theories can be consistently generalized; even within specific societies, attempts to validate them have not escaped controversy.[4] Third, none of the theories have resulted in clear recommendations that managers can reliably employ on a broad scale. With those caveats in mind, this section reviews the contributions of each theory to the current understanding of what people expect from their labors and what motivates them to do effective work.

Universality of Needs

All people pursue goals that have value for them. But, since few societies display similar values, employees in different societies set varying goals. For example, Americans characteristically show a high regard for individual achievement, so they pursue promotions, individual recognition, and differentiated monetary rewards at work. Similar values motivate most Western Europeans, but in Japan people put a higher value on group harmony and collective achievement. Because these motives prevail over individual goals, Japanese workers who transparently aspire to individual promotion or monetary rewards can be severely ridiculed. In China, group affiliation and harmony are also important, yet this tendency is tempered by more than 2,000 years of Confucian social philosophy that puts an even higher premium on acquiescence to authority. The brand of communism practiced in mainland China has reinforced a social order that values conformity. Therefore, contrasts of social values between the United States and Japan, or between the United States and China, reveal obvious differences in *priorities of values;* equally severe differences separate the Japanese and Chinese societies.

Values in Israel present another interesting contrast. Some observers have characterized Israelis as a strongly communal people with collectivist values similar to those held by Japanese. However, studies of their kibbutz organizations reveal an important qualification of this judgment. While Israelis are indeed collective *as a culture* with respect to outsiders, *within their culture* they display highly individualistic values.[5] Consequently, a study of Israeli value systems might draw different conclusions about behavior and motives depending on whether the research focused on behavior among Israelis or between Israelis and members of other societies.

The now-famous studies by Geert Hofstede continue a process that already has spanned two decades. Hundreds of parallel studies delving into human values and motives have extended this work to nearly all national cultures. About one-third of those studies have found evidence to support some common values across cultures, but the researchers have carefully avoided any implication that motivation techniques can be universally applied.[6] (See Chapter 8 for a detailed discussion of Hofstede's cultural values.) Nearly half of those studies have found no support for common values, however, and the researchers argue that cultural values remain strongly ingrained and *divergent* in each society. The remaining studies have yielded no conclusive arguments either for or against universality. Hofstede has added his voice to those who strongly refute a universal model of motivation. His extensive data suggest that there are extreme variations in values among the world's cultures, and that prevalent cultural values determine priorities of needs within a society.

Hofstede has criticized **content theories,** which explain motivation largely in terms of *human needs,* pointing out that variations among cultures in needs such as achievement, monetary rewards, and individual recognition prevent the possibility of arousing people in the same way by the same phenomena.[7] **Process theories,** which explain motivation largely in terms of expectations about perceived outcomes of behavior, have drawn less severe criticism because they allow for contingencies in specific environments. The most common model of a process theory, expectancy theory (discussed later in the chapter), asserts that individuals subjectively judge whether they can accomplish assigned tasks and whether they will be properly rewarded for their efforts. This expectation of a work-reward outcome is tempered by the importance an individual attaches to the potential reward. If it doesn't seem to bring important benefits, then the person feels little motivation to work for that reward. Of course, an individual may be confronted with some form of punishment (or loss of potential rewards) for failing to perform as expected, and this sense of apprehension certainly influences behavior. However, rewards and punishments are perceived much differently throughout the world. Recent research has shown that even within a culture, these perceptions vary substantially among different social strata and occupational groups.[8]

As mentioned earlier, this chapter is not concerned with debating the research about motivation, but with the dangers of extrapolating views held in one culture to others. Recent studies in Russia, for example, have shown distaste for initiatives based on teamwork and participative processes associated with worker empowerment in western societies. In fact, the Russians tend to strongly prefer structured hierarchies and directive styles of leadership. Attempts to motivate workers through team involvement and group recognition actually result in cynicism rather than improved performance.[9] Comparative studies of U.S., Japanese, and Taiwanese managers have found that people in all three societies value achievement, but each one interprets achievement in a different way. In the United States, achievement is reflected in measures of individual success. In Japan, it is associated with organizational success or social objectives. In Taiwan, achievement is indicated by family well-being.[10]

Comparative studies among Middle Eastern societies have found striking contrasts in work-related values between Arab and non-Arab cultures.[11] For example, the Saudis rank family esteem as far more important than individual achievement or public recognition. Muslims from non-Arab states, such as Turkey, rate a commitment to the Islamic state as a paramount consideration, placing less value on family or individual needs. The Muslim cultures in both Arab and non-Arab societies value conformity and social power relationships. This result may explain greater comfort with authority and autocratic behavior among these peoples than among Israelis, who strongly value ethnic group harmony. Consequently, Israelis place less value on authority while endorsing more egalitarian principles of democratic socialism than their Middle Eastern neighbors. Each society reveals a different pattern of motives for working together and different expectations for leadership behavior.[12]

These examples illustrate the extreme sensitivity of cultural values. Accordingly, international managers cannot presume that behavior, rewards, external incentives, or personal inducements that prove effective in one country (or perhaps in one ethnic group within a country) will have similar behavioral effects in other countries or groups. International managers also must recognize that people from different societies often exhibit substantially different viewpoints about the meaning of work itself. Figure 14.2 suggests different viewpoints about work, as described in the next section.

The Meaning of Work

Work is an economic necessity for nearly everyone, and income from a job is tied to basic physiological needs. Work also contributes to self-perceptions, however, and it helps to define purpose within individual societies. Through work, people pursue many of their achievements and social activities—yet, odd as it may seem, they spend very little time actually working. Of the 168 hours in a week, a standard full-time job in North America or Western Europe fills no more than 40 hours. Work occupies less than 25 percent of a person's time. The remainder of the week is spent eating, sleeping, and pursuing personal interests such as hobbies, leisure activities, and family activities. After subtracting vacations and holidays from total work hours, most people actually work very little of their time. Of course, many people spend more time working, including entrepreneurs, self-employed professionals, and most managers. In each instance, these people may work long hours and full weeks. Work can dominate a person's life or hold a relatively unimportant place among other priorities.

The importance of work relative to other interests is called **work centrality.**[13] One person may hold two jobs and do little more than eat, sleep, and work; work centrality is a commanding force in that person's life. Work centrality is more evident in some societies than others. For example, the Japanese society gives the appearance of a nation of workaholics. Several years ago, a *Meaning of Work (MOW)* research team rigorously studied work habits among eight nations. Not surprisingly, they found that Japanese people value work far more than any other nationality studied.[14] The United States also ranked high in the sample, but work centrality is not nearly as strong among Americans as among Japanese. Israel ranked slightly higher than the United States, as did respondents from the former Yugoslavia. Respondents from Belgium,

FIGURE 14.2
Variations in the Meaning of Work

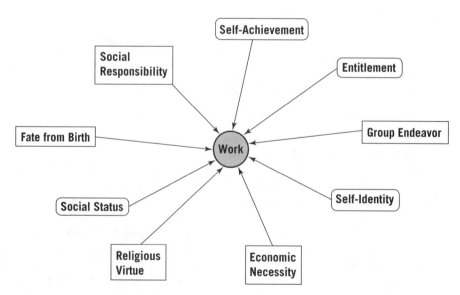

the Netherlands, Germany, and the United Kingdom ranked work as a somewhat less central consideration than respondents from the United States, Japan, Yugoslavia, and Israel.

The MOW research also provided insights about the reasons why people perceive such importance in work. Monetary necessity was the most important reason for work in every instance, but countries share little agreement about other reasons for working. After providing income, respondents from the Netherlands, Israel, and Belgium valued work as an interesting activity that provided a sense of personal satisfaction. Ironically, the Japanese saw little interest or personal satisfaction in work, though they emphasized its importance. In another interesting result, all nations in the study except Israel ranked work as an important way to make meaningful social contacts; Israeli respondents saw little social value in working. The researchers also questioned the value of work as a means of providing status or personal prestige, both points on which the U.S. respondents ranked highest of all countries. Respondents from the other countries did not associate status or prestige with their work, and Japanese respondents rated status or prestige among the least important reasons for working.

Studies have not extensively cataloged work behavior and the importance of work in people's lives, yet the results revealed so far emphasize an important point. Beyond the obvious benefit of providing income, people have substantially different viewpoints about work itself. Therefore, they are likely to have significantly different motives for pursuing work. For example, the relatively low value of status as a benefit of work in Japan suggests that few Japanese workers would react to motivation based on prestigious job titles, individual recognition, or promotions. Indeed, research has shown that Japanese workers appreciate recognition when it is *shared* among their work groups or colleagues, and they take pride in promotions viewed as equitable rewards within their firms' seniority systems. However, they shun individual recognition or promotions based largely on individual performance. Indeed, individual attention can be a source of embarrassment and invite ridicule by co-workers.[15] Japanese employees work very long hours. Office workers and managers often work well into the evening each day and then dine together before going home. This tendency may be changing as Japanese work habits show some slight moderation. Still, unrelenting work schedules coupled with the lack of personal satisfaction from work results in very high stress levels among Japanese workers. Their single highest motive for working is the social cohesion that they realize through group activities. In this sense, long hours at work and time spent with colleagues outside the workplace may bring hidden dividends.[16] Thus, effective incentives in Japan are oriented toward influencing group behavior, not individual productivity, and satisfaction is closely associated with social benefits, not personal rewards.

Extensive studies of work values among Arab nations reveal several interesting patterns.[17] First, although work is associated with economic necessity there as elsewhere, wealth is not associated with work. Instead, wealth or success are either inherited or attributed to adherence to Islamic religious principles. Work is viewed as a virtue in the Arab cultures, and hard work within one's capabilities has a religious significance. This attitude flows from a logical chain of reasoning: If people are faithful to the Islamic code, they will work hard; by working hard, they prove their faithfulness and thus earn appropriate rewards according to their capabilities.

Research has also shown, however, that these general patterns of beliefs do not hold consistently among the Middle Eastern Arab nations, nor do they necessarily remain consistent within any one nation. Egyptians and Palestinians appear to favor conformity, and they view work as a benefit. In contrast, Saudis and natives of Bahrain, Kuwait, and the United Arab Emirates often adopt more opportunistic views of work.

They tend to seek personal rewards more aggressively than residents of other Arab countries, but this tendency is still constrained by Islamic religious beliefs. Also, Arabs working as expatriates in other Arab states are often viewed as more materialistic than domestic employees, and working abroad is a way to alter one's wealth and social status. These apparent contradictions do not seem to create problems within Arab societies, where religious tenets can reflect a variety of interpretations. Consequently, it is not only difficult to generalize about Arab cultures but also hard to suggest uniform values that motivate behavior in all Arab states, or even among members of different social strata within a single Arab state.[18]

The Value of Rewards

Motivation is inextricably concerned with real or perceived rewards that result from work efforts, and the value of rewards reflects the meaning of work itself. Recall from Chapter 8 that culture is the construct by which people differentiate meanings of work, values, and work-related behavior; it is the collective mental programming that distinguishes one group of people from another. Therefore, culture can define boundaries at many different social levels among different groups, but the common convention is to identify culture with a nation bounded by one political ideology or its geography. Culture can also be ascribed to ethnic groups, but this definition may not correspond to national boundaries. Ethnic Chinese can be found in enclaves throughout the world, and the high-growth "dragons" of Taiwan, Hong Kong, and Singapore are predominately Chinese cultures that today rank among the world's most affluent societies. The Hebrew culture (more commonly identified with the Jewish religion) spans significant ethnic subcultures in many western and Asian nations.

The term *culture* also applies loosely to regions within countries, such as the southern culture of the United States, the Chechyen culture within Russia, and the distinct culture of the Punjab area of India. Additional group cultures are defined by organization membership or occupational status within society. Thus, businesspeople speak of organizational cultures as well as blue-collar, white-collar, and gray-collar cultures; similar distinctions create recognizable groups such as the computer generation, Yuppies, and Wall Street "suits." Members of each group share cultural norms, or collective mental programming, along with patterns of behavior that reflect common fundamental values. Hofstede used the metaphor of a forest to explain his definition of culture:

> Culture can be compared to a forest, while individuals are trees. A forest is not just a bunch of trees: it is a symbiosis of different trees, bushes, plants, insects, animals and micro-organisms, and we miss the essence of the forest if we only describe its most typical trees. In the same way, a culture cannot be satisfactorily described in terms of the characteristics of a typical individual.[19]

Managers risk serious error when they attempt to generalize human motives or to assume that pervasive values cross cultural boundaries. A value esteemed in one group may have little meaning to others. Perceptions of rewards vary according to such values, and behavior reflects the importance of those rewards to the group.

Management itself is not even a common concept in every culture. In the United States, people view a manager as someone who controls, leads, motivates workers, makes decisions, and accepts responsibility for organizational assets and resources. The U.S. managerial class is distinct from other groups of employees. In Germany, a manager is a *meister*, meaning a technical expert in an authority role who helps employees to resolve organizational problems; the concept includes no presumption of responsibility to motivate or control that a U.S. manager would expect.[20] Japanese businesspeople are controlled by their peer groups, and managers essentially provide social stability within their organizations. In fact, management may not exist in Japan in the same sense that it does in the United States or parts of Europe. French employees do not even think in management-nonmanagement terms. People born into a social class very much like a caste system accept only the limited possibility of aspiring to higher status, perhaps by attending prestigious schools and forming the right connections that make them members of *social cadres*. Such mobility is rare, however, because each cadre protects its privileges based on social class, and outsiders seldom gain access to a higher-level echelon. French managers do not rise to their positions in the sense recognized in the United States of earning qualifications to gain promotions through the ranks.[21] Each managerial culture is specific to an individual society, but the U.S. idea of management is an elusive concept to many people in other countries.

Because so many differences separate cultures, the task of motivating employees leans heavily on *situational factors*—the environment of work and the employees involved. International managers determine what incites employees to perform and the values they place on potential rewards by considering combinations of contingencies. In this judgment, they benefit in important ways from the research of Hofstede and many others who have conducted similar cross-cultural studies in human values. A review of Hofstede's four cultural dimensions, supplemented by Hofstede and Bond's concept of Confucian dynamism, lays a foundation for understanding varying perceptions of rewards.[22]

Recall that the first dimension, power distance, is the degree of inequality among people considered normal in a culture. In a culture with little concern for power distance, people expect relative equality and rather consensual work environments. Strong power distance supports a tendency toward hierarchical differentiation and a relatively autocratic environment with expectations for conformity. The second cultural dimension, individualism, reflects people's preferences to act independently rather than as members of cohesive groups. Consequently, a society ranked high on individualism will reflect a propensity of people to pursue individual achievements or personal recognition. The opposite of individualism, collectivism, implies a proclivity toward group identity and a corresponding identification with group-based rewards.

The third cultural dimension, masculinity, suggests a profile strong in attributes commonly associated with male behavior, such as assertiveness, competition, and performance-based results; Hofstede identifies feminine characteristics as congeniality, sensitivity to the feelings of others, caring, and service. Although these distinctions have sparked controversy, they imply that motivation in a highly masculine culture should honor toughness, winning through competition, and outward symbols of success. Those in feminine cultures should emphasize appreciation for caring roles and personal relationships. The fourth cultural dimension, uncertainty avoidance, measures people's preference for structured over unstructured situations rather than more dynamic and unstructured environments. Societies high in uncertainty avoidance base rewards on adherence to detailed rules, conformity within well-defined career paths, and objectively determined performance; any behavior that suggests deviation from the norm draws sanctions as a dangerous activity. In contrast, societies low in uncertainty avoidance are comfortable with ambiguous regulations, flexible career interests, and individual mobility; new or unusual activities may be rewarded rather than viewed as deviant behavior.

Confucian dynamism, also called a *long-term orientation*, emphasizes an orientation toward future objectives. Societies high on this dimension value patience,

TABLE 14.1

HOFSTEDE'S TEN-COUNTRY COMPARISON ON CULTURAL DIMENSIONS

	Power Distance	Individualism	Masculinity	Uncertainty Avoidance	Long-Term Orientation
United States	40 L	91 H	62 H	46 L	29 L
Germany	35 L	67 H	66 H	65 M	31 M
Japan	54 M	46 M	95 H	92 H	80 H
France	68 H	71 H	43 M	86 H	30 L[a]
Netherlands	38 L	80 H	14 L	53 M	44 M
Hong Kong	68 H	25 L	57 H	29 L	96 H
Indonesia	78 H	14 L	46 M	48 L	25 L[a]
West Africa	77 H	20 L	46 M	54 M	16 L
Russia	95 H[a]	50 M[a]	40 L[a]	90 H[a]	10 L[a]
China	80 H[a]	20 L[a]	50 M[a]	60 M[a]	118 H

[a]Estimated

H = top third, M = medium third, L = bottom third among 53 total countries studied for the first four dimensions and among 23 countries studied for the fifth.
Source: Geert Hofstede, "Cultural Constraints in Management Theories," *Academy of Management Executive* 7, no. 1 (1993): 91.

persistence, thrift, family security, and cultural harmony. Table 14.1 summarizes the collective results of past studies and more recent cross-cultural comparisons with Chinese and Russian societies.

The categorical differences identified in Hofstede's research provide hundreds of paired or grouped comparisons that could be evaluated for their effects on the motivating power of rewards. Many of these traits are relevant to motivation theories and they are addressed later in the chapter, but a few current examples will illustrate the variability that international managers must accommodate.[23] Note that U.S. respondents scored relatively low in power distance compared to those from Russia, who scored highest of all nations studied. Thus one would suspect there is a more favorable reception to group participation, team-building efforts, and employee recognition programs in the United States than in Russia. Recent studies have supported this conclusion; Russians seem very reluctant to work in participative environments, instead preferring differentiated status and trappings of power that are generally uncomfortable for American managers.[24]

In another comparison, U.S. subjects displayed extremely high individualism, whereas Chinese, Indonesian, and West African subjects favored collectivism. Correspondingly, achievement motives—and the rewards associated with risk, entrepreneurship, and personal performance—are very strong in U.S. businesses, while these characteristics earn little recognition in the other societies. The collectivist societies value group recognition and appreciation of harmonious relationships.

The table indicates very high masculinity for Japan, compared to a more feminine profile for the Netherlands. Therefore, rewards in Japan should reinforce a sense of assertiveness and a certain attitude of fealty to the organization. The Dutch reputedly emphasize rewards for accommodating behavior, which shows relatively more sensitivity for human differences than in Japan. Japan and Russia both display high uncertainty avoidance, and organizations in both countries impose extremely rule-bound, rigid performance expectations. Both societies reward conformity and link promotions to seniority and hierarchical loyalty. In contrast, the Hong Kong Chinese tolerate ambiguity with ease, caring little for formalities, thriving in an opportunistic environment, and therefore prospering in a somewhat ambiguous society. In Hong Kong, the victor seizes the spoils, and businesses reward entrepreneurship more generously than seniority or conformist behavior.

A final comparison on long-term orientation (Confucian dynamism) also yields interesting results. Mainland Chinese people emphasize long-term values, and they expect rewards that complement these values. Thrift, patience, and persistence are recognized, while the U.S. emphasis on immediate priorities such as short-term profits and rapid decision-making has little appeal. Japan and Hong Kong also favor long-term concerns, and research confirms expectations for related patterns of behavior—such as saving a high proportion of one's income, displaying a concern for harmony and consensus decisions, and earnestly fulfilling job responsibilities with few complaints.[25] Rewards in these Confucian societies reflect group incentives. Variations in compensation between hierarchical levels are compressed to avoid emphasizing individual differences, and benefits accrue to entire groups or organizations with little regard for individual performance.

Another interesting study compared values among U.S. workers in three eras, based on responses from similar samples of blue-collar and white-collar workers in 1946, 1981, and 1986. The adult respondents were grouped by age into four categories: 30 and under, 31 to 40, 41 to 50, and 51 to 60 years of age. Researchers factored responses from a questionnaire designed to assess values and perceived job rewards to identify the top 10 considerations in each survey. These are summarized in Table 14.2. The nonsupervisory employees perceived quite different rewards in their jobs than supervisors saw. The researchers also found that the 30-and-under group responded more like their supervisors than older groups did, rating the top three rewards as good wages, job security, and promotion and growth. The older workers showed less concern with wages and promotions.[26] Other research using the same methodology supported these results for U.S. workers overall, but not for workers from other societies. For example, in Germany, good pay and job security still merited important attention; but workers showed comparable concern with interesting work and good interpersonal relationships. The Japanese rated "a good match between the person and the job" as their primary concern. Interesting work and job autonomy were rated next in order, but the Japanese placed money and security well down the list. Opportunities for promotion were the least important rewards of work in both Germany and Japan.[27]

Recent studies of work-related values among Russian, Japanese, Chinese, and U.S. managers reinforce Hofstede and Bond's observations, but the new results also draw attention to changes in these societies.[28] Several hundred respondents in each country answered an extensive 56-item questionnaire in their native languages, and the results revealed interesting differences. Specifically, Chinese managers seemed more likely to adhere to authority than Japanese, Russian, or U.S. managers. However, unlike the Japanese respondents, who expressed feelings of allegiance to their organizations, the Chinese subjects expressed loyalty to families or other referent groups. The Chinese subjects also were more likely than Japanese or U.S. respondents to avoid uncertainty, limiting the tendency of Chinese organizations to initiate innovations.

In this sense, the Chinese results resembled those for Russians, both revealing expectations for structured environments with predetermined job activities, compensation, and benefits. The Chinese and Russian subjects also both scored significantly lower than others on measures of individualism, suggesting a psychological resistance to personal responsibilities for achievement. Both groups viewed promotions and authority as results of social status, not performance. Ironically, Russian managers cared

TABLE 14.2

PERCEPTIONS OF JOB REWARDS: U.S. INDUSTRIAL EMPLOYEES AND SUPERVISORS

U.S. Nonmanagement Employees		U.S. Supervisors
1946 Survey	1981 Survey	1986 Survey
1. Full appreciation of work done	1. Interesting work	1. Good wages
2. Feeling of being in on things	2. Full appreciation of work done	2. Job security
3. Sympathetic help with personal problems	3. Feeling of being in on things	3. Promotion and growth in organization
4. Job security	4. Job security	4. Good working conditions
5. Good wages	5. Good wages	5. Ineresting work
6. Interesting work	6. Promotion and growth in organization	6. Personal loyalty to employees
7. Promotion and growth in organization	7. Good working conditions	7. Tactful discipline
8. Personal loyalty to employees	8. Personal loyalty to employees	8. Full appreciation of work done
9. Good working conditions	9. Tactful discipline	9. Sympathetic help with personal problems
10. Tactful discipline	10. Sympathetic help with personal problems	10. Feeling of being in on things

Source: Kenneth A. Kovach, "What Motivates Employees? Workers and Supervisors Give Different Answers," *Business Horizons*, September–October 1987, 58–65.

little about individual achievement, yet they strongly emphasized *self-determination*. This sense of self-determination, however, was expressed in terms of assertiveness, self-control, and ability to endure hardships. Chinese, Russian, and Japanese managers shared high masculinity, but while the Russians associated this trait with dominance and directive decision-making, the Chinese associated it with paternalistic behavior. Both Chinese and Japanese emphasized a Confucian perception that men are more important than women.

Chinese and Japanese respondents were also similar in expressing strong feelings of collectivism, but again the Chinese defined their priorities according to their specific referent groups or families. The Chinese revealed a sense of pragmatism and willingness to accept the uncertainty of managing private enterprises, yet they also showed reluctance to endorse concepts of individual profit-seeking behavior. These workers tended to view bonuses and other incentives as entitlements for all employees, not rewards for individual achievement. Young Chinese managers who have recently entered the workforce apparently respond more favorably to personal rewards than do older managers who matured under a state-controlled economic system, yet young managers still embrace traditional values with respect to cultural power differences and risk sharing.

Despite detailed results such as these, international managers cannot look to research on cross-cultural values for predictive models of motivation. Indeed, most of the studies reveal contradictions that are insufficiently explained, and managers must take great care in trying to use the same motivational techniques in several different societies. Programs that work in one place can fail disasterously in another. Consequently, an experienced manager working in one country cannot automatically transfer to another country and expect to find the same reaction to motivational techniques among different groups of employees. With that caution in mind, the next section takes a closer look at mainstream concepts of motivation and how they can help international managers to interact effectively with their workers.

CROSS-CULTURAL COMPARISONS OF MAINSTREAM CONCEPTS

Domestic and international studies on motivation have emphasized three recurrent themes: human needs, culture-bound motives, and achievement. These studies have focused primarily on content theories. Specifically, mainstream research has been concerned with Maslow's hierarchy of needs, Herzberg's two-factor theory, and McClelland's acquired-needs theory. This section need not provide detailed explanations of these theories; instead, it attempts to provide insights gained through cross-cultural studies about their applicability to international management.

Hierarchy of Needs

Abraham Maslow's **need hierarchy** model emphasized a *progressive* hierarchy of five categories of human needs in which fulfillment of lower-order needs leads to the emergence of successively higher-order needs, which a person then works to satisfy. When employees perceive an unmet need, according to Maslow, they behave in a way intended to satisfy that need—to remove the deficit; they then proceed in sequence to attend to the next-higher-level unmet need. The model has always been controversial, but it also has profoundly affected managerial thinking. It not only identifies human needs but also provides a framework for understanding why some people are preoccupied with basic needs such as food and shelter, while others seek self-esteem or satisfaction derived from personal achievements. From an international management perspective, the model is controversial because people from different cultures define their needs in different ways. The importance they attach to their needs influences work behavior; therefore, motives to work or to achieve various needs will vary across cultures. The obvious questions are whether the *priority* of needs remains the same across cultures and whether individuals across cultures can be motivated by similar stimuli.

An international team of researchers sought to answer these questions by surveying 3,641 managers in 14 countries during the early 1960s.[29] They found a generally consistent priority for the needs in Maslow's hierarchy in all 14 societies. The importance attached to lower-order needs remained reasonably similar in all cultures studied, and all felt compelled to meet those needs before higher-order needs became prominent motivators. But the results did not yield conclusive answers. Respondents in several European and Latin American countries were uncomfortable with the single higher-need category of esteem, and they responded by interpreting this concept in two different ways. Some associated esteem with pride or personal prestige, while others associated it with autonomy for independent activities. The study also revealed a slight difference from Maslow's model in the importance respondents attached to categories of needs. Latin American and Nordic clusters of respondents emphasized high-order needs of self-actualization and personal autonomy, while U.S. and British respondents saw no reason to include autonomy as a priority. Social needs were also more highly valued in the Latin and Nordic clusters than in the U.S.–Anglo cluster. However, these observations did not refute the need hierarchy in its fundamental pattern of motives.

Several later studies included wider samples of management and nonmanagement respondents from the United States, Canada, Europe, the Middle East, South America, Japan, and Southeast Asia.[30] The results supported Maslow's hierarchy only in a very general manner, and researchers found more exceptions than domestic U.S. studies had revealed. Specifically, physiological needs associated with money (or products that money could provide) were less important in many places than social needs associated with group identity and personal relationships. In many instances, strong priorities for the higher-order needs associated with esteem and self-actualization were correlated with high levels of education in developed societies. The results of these studies have accumulated over a period of several decades, leading to the conclusion that in general, people share common hierarchical *clusters* of high-order and low-order needs; but *within* these clusters, people show tremendous variation in the priorities of needs and the importance they attach to specific motives.[31]

Most cross-cultural studies on Maslow's need hierarchy have sought to establish the priorities of various needs through a questionnaire that would allow researchers to arrange responses on scales. These studies have also attempted to determine the degree to which respondents felt that their needs were being satisfied. Respondents expressed considerable dissatisfaction with organizational initiatives to address their higher-order needs. This frustration may have resulted from lack of organizational attention to employees' desires, from ideological constraints, or from a fundamental difference in cultural values; no studies have successfully evaluated these issues.

An interesting example of the discrepancy between perceived satisfaction and importance of needs was reported in a study of managers in Thailand's top 500 firms.[32] Table 14.3 reveals major disparities between satisfaction and importance scores. Thai managers also expressed physiological needs as elements of security, and they ranked esteem as a lower-order need. Their definition of autonomy as a higher-order need coincided with results from earlier studies that treated it as a sense of control over work-related activities as opposed to acquiescence to autocratic decisions. Although results

TABLE 14.3

PERCEPTIONS OF NEED IMPORTANCE AND SATISFACTION AMONG THAI MANAGERS

Need Importance Ranking	Need Satisfaction Ranking	Maslow's Hierarchy
1. Self-actualization needs	1. Autonomy needs	1. Self-actualization needs
2. Autonomy needs	2. Social needs	2. Esteem needs
3. Social needs	3. Security (physiological) needs	3. Social needs
4. Esteem needs	4. Esteem needs	4. Safety (security) needs
5. Security (physiological needs)	5. Self-actualization needs	5. Physiological needs

Source: S. Runglerkrengkrai and S. Engkaninan, "The Motivation and Need Satisfaction of the Thai Managerial Elite," *Asia Pacific Journal of Management* 3, no. 3 (1986): 194–197.

on specific work-related values raised questions about Maslow's model, the study did not refute the concept of general clusters of high-order and low-order needs.

Several studies in the People's Republic of China, Hong Kong, Taiwan, and Singapore—and among several other Southeast Asian societies—have revealed a need hierarchy that is dramatically different from Maslow's model. In line with Hofstede and Bond's value dimension called *Confucian dynamism*, research results have revealed more importance for social factors such as loyalty to one's referent group and conformist behavior within a hierarchical social system. These are not clearly articulated in Maslow's model.

Bond's research extended well beyond China to include national samples drawn throughout South America, Southeast Asia, India, and selected African societies. He discovered characteristics of Confucian social philosophy in many cultures, not only in China and East Asia. Those characteristics reflected culturally ingrained systems of structured social relationships, strong emphasis on group loyalty, obedience to a social order, and a sense of pride in work, even within predetermined work roles. In this framework, self-esteem is not a highly valued characteristic except as a reflection of filial piety. The prevalence of self-effacement often allows individuals to deny basic physiological needs if their sacrifices serve the larger needs of their families or referent groups. In these cultures, self-actualization does not imply achievement in the western sense, but it can suggest meanings such as effective self-control or the ability to be humble; humility is often seen as a sign of virtue in Asia.[33] Validation studies comparing East Asian and Chinese managers with U.S. managers support Bond's results.[34] The resulting need hierarchy in Table 14.4 reflects East Asian values, specifying four (not five) categories and citing brief explanations from a Chinese perspective.[35] In this model, the lowest-order need is belonging (a sense of social acceptance), followed by physiological needs, then a higher-order need of safety (security for self and family), and finally self-actualization (defined in collectivist terms of contribution to society).

This Chinese need hierarchy is no less controversial than Maslow's model, and no one can say for sure whether either can be generally accepted as representative of other societies. Despite extensive research in motivation theory, no study has yet adequately unraveled the mystery of why people behave the way they do. However, the research has yielded extremely helpful results in several ways. Indeed, it does show that human needs, real or perceived, are crucial elements of any understanding of human behavior. Studies also confirm that behavior is strongly influenced by cultural values, and that motives cannot be explained apart from specific work environments. Other studies have revealed that most western concepts of motivation (those common in the United States, in particular) are based on psychological concepts concerned with individual behavior, while many other cultures treat motivation as a sociological

---

TABLE 14.4

EAST ASIAN HIERARCHY OF NEEDS: A CHINESE PERSPECTIVE ON MASLOW

1. (Highest)	Self-actualization needs (achievement) in service to society
2.	Safety needs (security) of self and family
3.	Physiological needs (endurance)
4. (Lowest)	Belongingness needs (social) within group, society

Source: Edward C. Nevis, "Cultural Assumptions and Productivity: The United States and China," *Sloan Management Review* 24, no. 3 (1983): 17–29.

phenomenon concerned with referent group, community, or social behavior. One practical conclusion from cross-cultural research is that most people do not feel that their work or organizational affiliations satisfy their needs, and therefore tension results from a gap between the needs that firms should address and those that they actually do address.

The Two-Factor Theory

Frederick Herzberg introduced his **two-factor theory** of motivation to describe distinct sets of variables that affect work-related behavior.[36] According to Herzberg, job satisfaction is one dimension of motivation that depends on the nature of work itself (made up of intrinsic satisfaction with the job, recognition, achievement, advancement and personal growth, and responsibility). Management can try to improve employee morale by addressing these so-called *satisfier factors* through predominantly psychological rewards. Herzberg's second factor in motivation reflects dissatisfaction caused by perceived deficiencies in working conditions, relationships with supervisors and co-workers, compensation, supervision (disparities in expectations for leadership behavior), company policies, and personal dimensions of an individual's life, status, and security. Herzberg called these variables *hygiene factors* that management must address to minimize their negative effects on behavior. Hygiene factors relate to the work environment, or the *job context*, while satisfier factors relate to *job content*.

In Herzberg's view, hygiene factors generally cannot inspire employees to strive for improved productivity, and they do not lead to satisfaction. Instead, they must be controlled as potential sources of dissatisfaction that can stifle productivity. In contrast, satisfier factors can inspire performance and provide satisfaction. They are often influenced by managerial actions, such as by improving career opportunities, recognizing employees for quality performance, and involving employees in decisions, which enhances their sense of responsibility for work-related issues.[37] The two-factor theory is illustrated in Figure 14.3.

Herzberg's hygiene factors generally coincide with Maslow's lower-order needs, and they are considered *extrinsic* variables—those outside the job itself. The satisfier factors generally coincide with Maslow's higher-order needs and are considered *intrinsic* to the job. Like the need hierarchy, the two-factor theory is criticized both domestically and internationally—and like Maslow's work, Herzberg's concepts still generate controversy. Critics point out that the distinction between a satisfier and a hygiene factor is a matter of degree, not an absolute difference in kind, and international operations can further obscure that distinction. For example, researchers have found an association between dissatisfaction and job context factors such as wages, material benefits, working hours, working conditions, and job security in most (but not all) developed countries. However, the same extrinsic factors are motivators in many (but not all) less-affluent countries.

In general, poor wages or unpleasant working conditions can lead to employee dissatisfaction almost everywhere, but such problems are more apparent in well-developed economies. Meanwhile, wage increases, incentive pay, and enhanced working conditions with little motivational value in these societies can produce marked improvements in morale in less-developed economies. Perhaps the difference simply separates "have" and "have not" societies, but researchers note substantially different patterns of behavior related to extrinsic rewards. They could not, however, explain dichotomies among societies with comparable economic profiles. For example, a study of European employees found that while the behavior of British workers was not significantly affected by job context factors such as wages and benefits, French workers

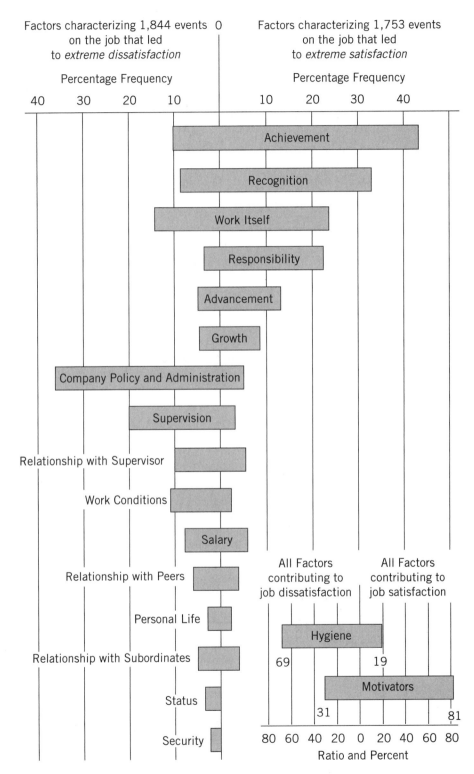

FIGURE 14.3
Herzberg's Research
Findings on Hygiene
and Satisfier Factors

Source: Reprinted by permission
of the *Harvard Business Review*.
An exhibit from "One More
Time: How Do You Motivate
Employees?" by Frederick
Herzberg, issue
September/October 1987.
Copyright 1987 by the President
and Fellows of Harvard College.
All rights reserved.

put a high value on compensation and security benefits, leading to a close association between extrinsic rewards and productivity.[38]

Another criticism of the two-factor theory notes that job context and content factors may not be independent or mutually exclusive elements. Herzberg's model regards advancement and achievement as separate aspects of job content, yet they are often interdependent in practice. Responsibility (part of job content) is often associated with salary (part of job context). Recognition (content) can be associated with supervision (context) or relationships with peers, superiors, or subordinates (all context factors). Personal status may depend on recognition, and many other practical links provide similar interconnections between job content and context. Therefore, critics assert that it is not possible to definitely determine what factor actually motivates, nor whether a causal relationship connects specific factors.

A third criticism claims that Herzberg's classifications are not uniformly predictable in the nature or intensity of their effects. Several variations alter this basic premise. First, young workers and those in particular jobs for only a few years are likely to value job context factors such as salaries and status more than longer-established workers do, although job content factors such as advancement and growth retain their importance. In contrast, older workers particularly value security, relationships, and the intrinsic rewards associated with their jobs. Therefore, a factor that may be a source of dissatisfaction to one person may motivate another. Another variation points out that workers in less-developed countries, or during economically distressed periods in affluent societies, may attach more importance to salaries, benefits, and security factors than to advancement or recognition rewards. Also, cultural values influence the relative importance that a society attributes to any intrinsic or extrinsic factors.[39]

Cross-cultural research specifically concerned with the two-factor theory has been limited, but the criticisms raised here do not invalidate Herzberg's concept of two categories of factors, each with particular motivational effects. To the contrary, research generally supports the concept. Nonetheless, these studies question the consistency of the variables and their intensity for particular groups of employees in different cultural environments. Several international examples may be helpful to clarify the issues.

In Mexico, where a rigid hierarchy of power prevails, subordinates are rewarded according to their submissive behavior and personal service (allegiance) to authority figures. Managers are expected to make paternalistic gestures, to protect their employees, and to ensure equitable compensation without singling out individual employees. These characteristics, described in detail in the previous chapter, affect motivation by establishing expectations between Mexican managers and employees that reduce the importance attached to job context factors such as wages, incentive pay systems (which seldom are accepted in Mexico), and job security (which is considered a social right, not a performance-based reward). Individual status is important in Mexico, however, and materialistic trappings of position and power give obvious signals. Ostentatious status symbols such as jewelry, fine clothes, and well-appointed offices are highly prized rewards of high achievement. Advancement, however, is not associated with performance but with personal relationships and ability to work harmoniously with others. These job context factors powerfully influence motivation, and international managers working in Mexico find that employees seldom react positively to rewards that emphasize individual achievement or performance-based incentives.[40] Similar systems of authority and paternalistic relationships appear in other Latin American states and in Asian cultures. These differences require firms to reorder priorities among job content and job context factors in each society.[41]

In an important initiative commonly associated with the two-factor theory, companies often try to alter both job content and context factors through *job redesign* programs. Such an effort may encompass three separate elements: job rotation, job enlargement, and job enrichment. Each creates structural changes in work relationships with the ultimate purpose of enhancing productivity by improving workforce motivation.[42]

Job Rotation

By rotating an employee's assignments among several jobs, a company introduces the individual to a variety of work and job responsibilities, thereby reducing the boredom associated with repetitive tasks. More important, an effective job rotation program helps to create a multiskilled workforce capable of internal flexibility, enhancing both productivity and career mobility. This is a particularly helpful benefit for international managers who want to improve their relational skills within systems of multinational subsidiaries. An individual may welcome job rotation as a way to enhance job security, status, and self-esteem through growth and recognition of achievements.

However, job rotation is mainly concerned with individual roles; employees in collectivist societies have reservations about reassignments that take them outside their work groups. To them, job rotation can produce a destabilizing effect that weakens the group. Ironically, job rotation is common in Japan as an institutionalized human resource development practice, and Japanese employers expect cross-training in varied skills. In deterministic societies such as Mexico and China, however, well-differentiated occupations and job categories inhibit job rotation. To some extent, job rotation is not favored in France, yet it is a common practice in Germany and Sweden.

Job Enlargement

This aspect of job redesign involves a permanent change in specifications to incorporate multiple tasks within an individual job. It is an amalgamation of tasks that reduces job specialization and breaks down barriers between compartmentalized activities. For example, a machine operator may be trained in routine maintenance and machine setup procedures (two tasks often assigned to separate individuals). As one person gains responsibility for a broad new range of tasks, according to Herzberg's theory, the added responsibility should enhance motivators such as status, job security, and self-esteem.

Unfortunately, this result does not always emerge. Employees may view an enlargement program as an effort to get them to do more work without corresponding increases in benefits. Further, some societies highly value job specialization, and people there may view enlargement as a loss in identity. This effect is compounded in collectivist societies where tasks within a work group are often highly orchestrated, each with a prescriptive responsibility in an interdependent system. In some instances, job enlargement may be seen as manipulation by management to break down group identity or devalue individual roles within the group.[43]

Job Enrichment

The concept of job enrichment calls for expanding a person's responsibilities to give more meaning to work. Enriched jobs feature expanded depth through extension of decision-making responsibilities, leading to comparatively autonomous individual or team efforts. Job enrichment is often associated with initiatives to improve the *quality of working life (QWL)*, based on the premise that individuals will then feel satisfied with their work environment and gain self-esteem. In a group environment, these motives translate to improved compatibility among co-workers and collective rewards that are commensurate with the group's combined productivity.[44] Job enrichment involves employees in downstream or upstream activities, and it creates team-based environments for joint initiatives to make important decisions.

This element of job redesign presumes that employees want to participate in management or in self-directed activities, so they will enjoy enhanced job satisfaction. Many of these programs work extremely well in societies low in power distance, such as Sweden with its widespread egalitarian values. They do not work well in societies with high power distance (such as Mexico, China, Brazil, and France). Japan is unique with its relatively high power distance and respect for authority, coupled with a cultural homogeneity that emphasizes both vertical and horizontal collaboration. In fact, many QWL practices have evolved from Japanese group-work processes.[45]

Job enrichment programs cannot be haphazardly applied across multinational subsidiaries without careful consideration of cultural values and underlying expectations for work-related behavior of employees. Evidence from European studies suggests that enrichment programs (or their recent counterparts, *employee empowerment* initiatives) have emerged in a wide variety of applications with equally varied results among individual European nations. Researchers point out that no single characteristic constitutes a sufficient clue about how employees will react to motivation techniques. Instead, the applicability of motivational techniques depends on a composite of job-related factors, social legislation, labor relations (including formal activities such as those under Germany's codetermination laws), perceptions of status and power (as in France's cadre system), and values associated with collaborative work systems (such as Sweden's affinity for self-managed teams).[46]

Achievement Theory and Expectations

Another theory of motivation, the **acquired-needs theory** proposed by Harvard psychologist David C. McClelland during the 1960s, suggests that people develop a profile of needs that determine their behavior.[47] The concept maintains that needs are *learned* through life experiences, and if they can be learned, then instruction can develop desired *need sets*. In McClelland's view, people acquire needs as they learn to adapt to particular orientations. McClelland based his theory on research conducted by John W. Atkinson, who hypothesized that everyone carries an energy reserve that can be tapped to fulfill personal goals. Through research on personalities and behavior, Atkinson suggested three distinct personality profiles called *achievers, power-centered persons,* and *affiliators.*[48]

McClelland built on this foundation to suggest tendencies toward one of these three profiles based on acquired needs, including a *need for achievement,* a *need for power,* and a *need for affiliation.* He proposed that everyone experiences all three sets of needs, but one orientation generally emerges as dominant through the culmination of experience and life learning. Each person is therefore a product of a particular environment; by altering the environment, one can condition an individual to accept a desired set of needs. These needs and their related values are illustrated in Figure 14.4 and discussed in the following paragraphs.

Need for Achievement (nAch)

Defined as a desire to take on tasks and to accomplish them in a satisfactory manner, *nAch* characterizes individuals who enjoy challenges and thrive on stimulating environments. They prefer independent responsibility and autonomy to pursue self-determined goals, and they garner strength from constructive feedback. Achievement theory highlights the profiles of entrepreneurs and a spirit of calculated risk taking. Indeed, high achievement profiles often distinguish creative and venturesome individ-

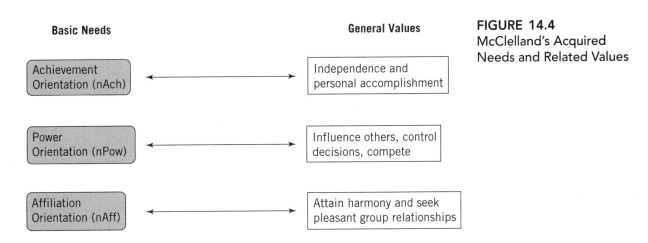

FIGURE 14.4
McClelland's Acquired
Needs and Related Values

uals. McClelland devised ways to measure the three dimensions through value-based personality scoring systems, and research indicates that employees with high nAch profiles earn more raises and faster promotions than those high in power or affiliation. Ironically, the research also reveals that achievers are not always the best managers, because organizations expect people to work within hierarchies, take only limited risks, and respect the parameters of accepted organizational behavior. Achievers often have difficulty living up to these expectations.[49]

Need for Power (nPow)

The word *power* here refers to a sense of desiring influence and control over events and, in particular, responsibility over other people. Individuals who score high on *nPow* are comfortable with executive positions where they can make decisions in highly competitive situations. They place high value on status and advancement opportunities. Such behavior often suggests an autocratic mind-set, but a high power orientation also suggests strong leadership behavior and willingness to accept unilateral responsibility (attributes that reflect Hofstede's cultural dimension of masculinity). No evidence suggests that individuals high in nPow manage more effectively than achievers do, nor are they less likely to achieve important results. Some of the world's greatest leaders as well as its worst demigods might have scored high on this dimension had they been evaluated in their time. Unlike achievement, the need for power is not associated with creativity or entrepreneurship, yet many successful new ventures have resulted when power-focused people pursued risky enterprises.[50]

Need for Affiliation (nAff)

Defined in social terms, *nAff* is the desire for a sense of belonging and thus to participate with other people, create friendships, and seek social interactions. An individual high in nAff seeks to attain a sense of social esteem, prefers conciliatory and low-conflict environments, and values group harmony above individual achievements. In this regard, affiliators display aversion to risk and discomfort with managerial responsibilities. They seldom become involved in difficult decisions such as enforcing policies or disciplining subordinates, but they work extremely well in egalitarian situations and team environments. Perhaps they reach their peak performance as coordinators who can help integrate activities in interdependent work processes. Few affiliators occupy executive or line management positions, and there is little evidence to indicate that they seek promotions or place high value on status.[51]

The acquired-needs theory, and in particular the concept of achievement, has raised many interesting questions. The presumption that anyone can learn one set of values is central to McClelland's model. Although the presumption that people are products of their environments seems intuitively sound, some may question whether people set in their ways can learn and retain new traits. However, if the theory abandons this learning assumption, then it degenerates into a deterministic model of personality that implies inability for most people to change their behavior. Because achievement orientation cannot be directly observed, McClelland and his colleagues conducted training experiments in India and among groups of less-educated people and foreign workers in Africa to observe their learning behavior. By following the careers of these subjects for several years, McClelland and his team determined that achievement training made a significant difference in performance and personal success.[52]

However, critics point out that attributes associated with achievement are distinctly individualistic traits bound up in western social values. The emphasis on individual achievement can thus have unpleasant—even antisocial—connotations in places such as China, Indonesia, and Malaysia and perhaps in African and Latin American countries where people value collective behavior.[53] In paternalistic societies, achievement may not be conceived apart from the family or close referent group. In hierarchical cultures such as Mexico's or countries with strong Confucian values, McClelland's achievement need may be devalued as a destructive element in societies where conformity and duty prevail. In these societies, power may be more highly valued as a leadership attribute, while affiliation may be more highly valued among subordinates. This duality has been observed in Mexico, in several Latin American societies, and among the Islamic cultures in Southeast Asia.[54] Finally, in societies with low power distance (or, alternatively, in societies with feminine characteristics), affiliation behavior may be valued above all others. In Scandinavian and certain Latin nations, motivation for both managers and employees reflects social esteem, human interaction, and friendship bonds far more vividly than it does in other societies.[55]

Criticisms of the acquired-needs theory do not invalidate the model. It makes important contributions to management practices, especially for international managers who need tools for understanding differences in motives among different groups of foreign employees. The research cited strongly supports McClelland's claims that many motivating characteristics can be taught or learned through experience. This implies that people can benefit from human resource development programs aimed at improving team-building and decision-making skills. Another important implication suggests that as global companies expand into new countries, they face variations in familiar orientations. For example, where culture suppresses achievement motives, the experience of working for a multinational subsidiary creates new expectations and subsequently influences people to strive for self-achievement goals.[56]

Expectancy Theory

Introduced by Victor Vroom during the 1960s, expectancy theory suggests that people are driven by needs, but they also make choices about what they will or will not do. **Expectancy theory** proposes that individuals make work-related decisions according to their perceived abilities to perform tasks and the rewards they will likely receive for that performance.[57] The model shown in Figure 14.5 indicates three variables influencing these work-related decisions:

- *Expectancy*—A person's confidence in his or her ability to successfully perform a task

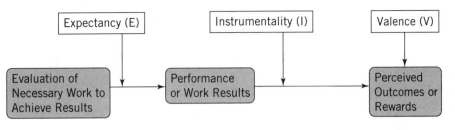

FIGURE 14.5
Expectancy Model of Motivation

Source: Adapted from Victor H. Vroom and Arthur G. Jago, *The New Leadership: Managing Participation in Organizations* (Englewood Cliffs, N.J.: Prentice Hall, 1988), 121–127.

- *Instrumentality*—A person's confidence that successful performance will bring appropriate rewards
- *Valence*—The value that a person places on expected rewards

The strength of each variable changes according to individual perceptions in Vroom's model. Therefore, in order to use the model, an individual is required to assign subjective probabilities between 0.0 and 1.0 to each of the three variables. Because the model multiplies these probabilities, strong motivation results only when all three variables exhibit high positive values. If any variable falls toward zero, the probability of motivated performance declines with it.

For example, if you believe that you can do a particular task—that it is within your capabilities and you have the necessary support and resources—your self-confidence will lead you to assign a high value to expectancy. When you also believe that you will gain rewards commensurate with the effort required to complete the task, you will assign a high value to instrumentality. Finally, if you perceive value in the potential reward (if it offers attractive prospects for fulfilling an important need), then you will assign a high value to valence.

Cross-cultural evaluation of expectancy theory is appealing because it eliminates the presumption of cultural influence on behavior and also because it requires no judgment about the relative merits of individual needs.[58] Specifically, because an individual assigns personal subjective probabilities to three variables for any task, these reflect individual perceptions unique to a task and the environment; culture is not a consideration. Also, rewards are judged in terms of individual perceptions of value, and they too vary in different situations. Managers must understand how workers value rewards in order to offer the right inducements, and they must also follow through by equitably distributing those valued rewards to meet individuals' perceived needs.

Expectancy theory is not without difficulties, though. Detractors worry that it is a normative theory. (It explains how a person should behave, not how he or she will actually behave.) Also, it supposes rational, conscious calculations of individual probabilities; in reality, few people rigorously complete such calculations to determine their choices. Expectancy theory also articulates a model of individual behavior, not collective expectations that can be generalized. Nevertheless, expectancy theory describes a process—a way of thinking—that helps managers to understand employee behavior. For example, if employees are assigned tasks and promised rewards but they fail to perform, then managers can ask where the problem arose. Did the assignment misjudge the difficulty of tasks relative to employees' capabilities? Did the employees feel manipulated by promises of rewards that would not be realized? Did the rewards fail

As more multinational corporations enter foreign markets, they bring with them new opportunities and new expectations for independence. Avon Products entered China in 1993, for example, and has since established a legion of fashionable Avon Ladies. Selling western-made products and earning self-determined commissions has fueled expectations for individual achievement among Avon representatives. Here, a female doctor earns more part time with Avon than as a senior resident in a Chinese medical center, and she enjoys the freedom achieved with her new earning power.

to impress employees? Even if managers cannot quantify these expectations, the theory gives them a framework for diagnosing what works and what does not work.[59]

Neither expectancy theory nor other motivation theories consistently predict how people behave in particular situations. Human nature simply varies in too many ways to be reduced to a formula. This variation is amplified for international management, since widely diverse cultures and human values prevent any one universal method from fitting all situations. Unfortunately, managers cannot just ignore these theories regardless of their limitations. Instead, they must try to understand the advantages and disadvantages of each concept and then develop techniques that work well in a given situation.

MOTIVATION IN A CULTURALLY DIVERSE ORGANIZATION

Global companies, by definition, are culturally diverse organizations that require executive coordination of practices that accommodate a variety of perspectives from many different people. Addressing diversity is, therefore, an important dimension of international management. Within a business unit, diversity compels attention for the human dimensions of managing small teams and personal relationships. The conceptual framework for managing a globally diverse workforce is not significantly different from that for addressing domestic diversity issues, but the range of issues spans more complicated variations in a globally integrated firm.

Diversity encompasses differences in human characteristics that arise from national origin, gender, race, ethnicity, religion, language, age, socioeconomic status, and cultural values. Sensitive distinctions also arise due to differences in marital status, sexual orientation, physical abilities, and political ideologies. Perhaps the list does not end there. Clearly, any definitive prescription for managing a workforce with substantial variations in these characteristics would pose a difficult challenge. International managers can approach the topic in three ways. First, from a domestic perspective, they must allow for changing demographics, immigration, and employment practices that influence diversity in their home-country organizations. Second, managers must evaluate their responsibilities in foreign subsidiaries, where patterns of expatriation introduce new and diverse individuals and where local workforces exhibit diversity judged by internal standards, despite the appearance of homogeneity to outsiders. Third, diversity affects management of home-country employees by domestic managers reporting to foreign owners.

Domestic Workforce Diversity

Cultural diversity has always been a prevalent feature of U.S. society, with a population composed almost entirely of immigrants; although a distinct U.S. culture has evolved, immigration continues to influence it. Today, first-generation immigrants make up approximately one-quarter of the U.S. workforce, and within a few years nearly one-third of workers will be immigrants or their offspring.

Along with immigration, several other factors also affect diversity. The U.S. population is growing more slowly now than at any time since the 1930s, and the average age of the workforce continues to rise as baby boomers mature and fewer young workers enter the labor market. Participation by women in the workforce, and particularly in managerial positions, has continued to increase. African Americans comprise slightly more than 10 percent of the U.S. workforce, Hispanics nearly 8 percent, and Asians 4 percent, but the early twenty-first century will bring significant increases in those numbers. The proportion of African American and Hispanic employees is expected to increase by more than 20 percent, and the component of Asian workers may nearly double in the next few years. At the end of the twentieth century, white male workers constituted only a slight majority, and white female workers represented almost as large a group, yet all workers displayed a wide definition of skills, education, and personal interests—much more so than past generations.

Just as the American workforce has become more diverse, so have consumer interests. In coming years, companies will have to serve more culturally diverse customers with ethnic tastes and language characteristics that demand substantial adaptations in goods and services. Schools have already begun to implement multilingual programs, and both students and teachers will function within an increasingly multicultural environment. In fact, the number of foreign nationals living, studying, and working in the United States will more than double in the coming decade, as growing numbers of foreign companies enter the U.S. market and universities expand their horizons to include international programs.[60]

Consider the example of Ralph Lauren, a merchandising empire that spans 26 major product divisions ranging from wholly owned subsidiaries in paints and furniture to men's and women's fashions, eyewear, and fragrances. The $5 billion company sells worldwide to customers in more than 130 nations; it also imports, exports, comanufactures, and licenses products on four continents. Design and marketing staff at the company's New York offices represent 12 different ethnic groups and speak 20 different languages. The company's foreign subsidiaries are actually less diverse, because they serve more focused client groups with locally recruited staff; yet Ralph Lauren's international marketing operation works through a culturally and linguistically complicated network. Ultimately, the company tries to market in a high-end niche to fashion-conscious consumers, but the diversity of its interests and clientele requires sensitive attention to differences in customer tastes as well as managing an organization characterized as "undescribable" in one report. Yet Lauren explains that the company thrives on diversity and nurtures it. Creativity, he adds, is the result of thinking differently, and the company's managers work hard to encourage diversity without allowing one viewpoint or another to become an imposition.[61]

Modeling a Diversity Program

Many new diversity management programs are modeled on human resource development systems that were established by global companies such as GE, AT&T, and Texas Instruments. Still, specific efforts to manage diversity are appearing in domestic companies that have no international interests. For example, Wisconsin Power and Light (WP&L)—a company in the heartland of the country and seemingly distant from diversity problems—found that nearly one-third of its employees were ethnic or racial minorities, and nearly half were women. The company developed a program called Diversity of Workforce Awareness to head off clashes among workers with different backgrounds, establish equitable guidelines for minority recruitment, and create team-based projects that improved employee retention. The WP&L model program is simply an effort to encourage mutual respect and sensitivity for all employees and to accommodate "differences in race, gender, age, physical and mental abilities, lifestyles, culture, education, ideas, and backgrounds."[62] An executive policy statement developed jointly by managers and employees emphasizes the following objectives:

- Appreciation for diversity at all levels of the organization
- Respect for and recognition of one another's differences
- Company commitment to provide a work environment that supports diversity
- Encouragement to seek and nurture different perspectives
- A mandate for workplace behaviors consistent with the objectives of equal opportunity and building a diverse workforce

The company communicates these objectives through workshops and a steering committee with specific responsibility for motivating employees to accept and behave within the diversity guidelines. WP&L also maintains support teams, counseling programs, and tutorials created jointly with consultants to address diversity issues.

Team Performance and Diversity

Studies of group behavior that have compared mixed-culture teams with homogeneous teams have found that mixed groups consistently outperform groups of similar individuals.[63] The researchers evaluated mixed teams composed of both men and women employees with Caucasian, African American, and Asian backgrounds and, in some instances, with wide differences in ages and educational qualifications. For comparison, they evaluated homogeneous groups made up of individuals with similar ethnic or racial characteristics, some confined to one gender. The subjects were existing work groups in major companies such as Hewlett-Packard, Alcoa, GM, and Kimberly-Clark. Other groups were purposely created to study the formation of patterns of behavior, and their team performance was subsequently measured against that of existing mixed and homogeneous teams. Some existing teams experienced relational problems and disagreements that reflected cultural, racial, and gender differences, yet

MANAGING DIVERSITY AT THE MARRIOTT MARQUIS

Prickly racial, ethnic, and gender differences underscore virtually all work relations at New York's Marriott Marquis. The hotel's 1,700 employees represent racial and ethnic groups from 70 countries and speak 47 different languages. Nearly half are immigrants from Asia or Latin America, many are African Americans, and the mix includes recent arrivals from Eastern Europe, the Middle East, and former Soviet states. Most employees are women in housekeeping and hotel service jobs, and many women hold management positions supervising minority men. Even among native-born Caucasians, the Italian, Polish, and Hungarian elements stand out for their differences. The hotel also employs Muslims, Jews, and Buddhists among representatives of other religions, many of them quite sensitive about their beliefs. Managing people with such diverse interests is a daunting challenge.

Functioning with such a multiracial and multiethnic staff requires unusual tolerance. For example, when a guest with an overflowing bathtub needed immediate attention, manager Victor Aragona chose to fix it himself rather than call the maintenance worker on duty. The call would have interrupted the man's daily Islamic prayers, and in Aragona's words, "My priority was a flood, his was God . . . it wasn't fair or efficient to have him fix the problem." The hotel respects employee religious practices, and while daily prayers could disrupt guest services, managers have learned to be flexible and to schedule around dozens of different religious practices and cultural holidays.

Work assignments can also become sensitive issues. Susan Gonzalez, the rooms director, finds that she must delicately rotate room-cleaning assignments so that everyone performs a comparable assortment of preferred and less attractive tasks. Slight differences in assignments, such as assigning an African American worker to a busier floor than a Hispanic worker, will bring discrimination charges that Gonzalez had favored "her own kind." On the other hand, a favorable assignment for a non-Hispanic risks ridicule from her Hispanic employees that she is placating other staff members.

Jessica Brown, a second-generation American of Jamaican and Honduran parentage, finds herself oddly stereotyped by her housekeeping staff. When she is in the employees' good graces, she is known as

either African American or Hispanic, respectively, to African American or Hispanic employees. When she must reprimand a worker or correct shoddy work, however, she is known as "that black [expletive]" to Hispanics and "that [expletive] from the Caribbean" to the African Americans. Racial epithets constantly flow, and Brown cannot commend one person or another without being chided about playing favorites.

Helena Blat, a Jewish immigrant from Latvia, had never met a person of Hispanic, Asian, or African lineage before coming to the United States. As a supervisor in hotel services, she walks a thin line on religious differences; being Caucasian, she is extremely cautious about how she asks people to do things. Blat has studied cultural differences and communications, and she effectively applies that knowledge. "You address a Haitian or African American in a sober tone and 'ask' them for help," she says. "With a Hispanic, you have to make it sound like a party." Blat says that minority European or Middle Eastern workers would scoff at her if her tone wasn't almost authoritarian; what works with one never works with another. "There are cold people and hot people," she says, "and Spanish people are party people. They're willing to help out, but you approach in a fun way when you need something. Others need to know that it's serious when you need something done."

Gonzalez notes that Latin women prefer to work for Latin men. They willingly accept the authority of men, even those without direct authority over them, but the reverse is not true. She finds that Hispanic and Asian men even in relatively minor positions also expect submissive behavior from women—even their superiors. Other men in management positions often must run interference for their female colleagues, but women managers such as Gonzalez and Brown have learned how to deal with gender issues. They focus on results and hold their ground.

"I don't lower my standards for anybody," Brown explains, "and when people realize that, gender and race are not problems." Gonzalez advises focusing on work and never overcompensating for individual differences. The resentment of gender or racial differences usually goes away when people know that you are capable, she explains.

Marriott benefits from cultural clustering, but it also suffers from ethnic segregation. Members of similar racial or ethnic groups commonly band together. They find their own and develop strong ingroup perspectives. Consequently, various groups constantly conflict with one another. Every order, word of praise, personal gesture, or disciplinary action carries a cultural message. Relatively minor squabbles have sometimes reached all the way to the Marriott headquarters for resolution. Yet, at the same time, cohesive group behavior can be beneficial when informal group leaders rise to the surface and help to reconcile multicultural interests.

Ethnic clustering is also helpful in recruitment. Each group tends to bring prospective employees to Marriott, and although this practice often verges on an uncomfortable form of patronage, the newcomers learn quickly with help from their peers, and they carefully avoid embarrassing their sponsors. Nevertheless, in-group hiring makes Marriott managers wince. Richard Morse, the resident manager at the Marquis, says that it is crucial to be color-blind when filling any position. Diversity is essential, Morse believes, because the hotel serves an equally diverse clientele; group membership cannot be allowed to degenerate into biased behavior, though.

Marriott requires diversity training for employees, and classes bring to the table every possible aspect of conflict that could result from multicultural diversity. The program has been a feature of Marriott's management development program for years, and it emphasizes communication and perceptual differences. People touch one another, learn to appreciate body language, and sort through problems with language use and interpretations of individual and cultural meanings. They become aware of differences in religious practices and beliefs, learn to understand differences in work-related norms, and complete trial-and-error exercises to refine their behavior. Gonzalez observes that the training made her face her own prejudices, many of which she was not even aware of before the sessions. Veteran managers at Marriott say that diversity training causes them discomfort, and it is among the most difficult parts of their jobs, yet they describe it as beneficial to their personal growth and to their careers.

Source: Adapted from Alex Markels, "How One Hotel Manages Staff's Diversity," *Wall Street Journal*, 20 November 1996, pp. B1–B2.

their problem-solving abilities exceeded those of homogeneous groups, which experienced less friction and no cultural or gender issues.

The newly formed groups struggled early to establish cooperative team environments, but they evolved into cohesive teams that collectively demonstrated stronger motivation to pursue organizational objectives than researchers observed from comparable homogeneous control groups. Similar studies have shown that creative problem solving increases when job context difficulties are minimized and group rewards such as recognition and performance ratings are attached to group results. The researchers concluded that if diversity is encouraged and if team members respect one another's differences, they boost organizational synergy and strengthen team-based commitments to objectives. Teamwork also effectively breaks down barriers and stereotypes, thus improving overall job performance by enhancing social relationships among coworkers.[64]

Foreign Workforce Diversity

Motivation and leadership issues in foreign subsidiaries can be just as sensitive as those in domestic companies when employees come from different backgrounds. When ownership and management involve interests from outside the host country, however, differences can be further magnified. A global company must coordinate activities among people from multitudes of different cultural perspectives, and this diversity can bring about many puzzling relationships. However, managing diversity in both local and global operations involves similar intervention skills to encourage integration.

Host-Country Diversity

When expatriates manage a subsidiary, they play highly visible roles, and people are alert to contrasts in behavior. Obvious differences in characteristics of the foreign managers can lead to temperamental situations that create barriers between managers and their employees. Most of these expatriates are men, and a significant number of foreign employees are women, a distinction that can further complicate relationships. This problem becomes particularly troublesome in less-developed countries for specific industries such as textiles, garment manufacturing, and electronics assembly, which are dominated by low-skilled handwork.

Subsidiaries managed by locals rather than expatriates may experience diversity problems of their own, and these seldom become apparent to their parent companies. For example, residents of some countries are sensitive to class distinctions among employees or between workers and managers. This is common in less-developed countries, where managers often come from elite social classes with economic and educational advantages over their workers. However, even in well-developed societies such as France, social stratification can accentuate class differences. Managers and employees often come from distinctly different ethnic groups, creating a prevailing atmosphere of tension that cannot be easily reconciled. This situation emerges in African and Indian Ocean societies, where sentiments of tribal or ethnic superiority support divisions between ruling and ruled classes. Of course, developed nations, including the United States, have not escaped underlying currents of ethnic or racial supremacy.

International managers must understand a critical fact: Few workforces—foreign or domestic—reflect homogeneous backgrounds. Outsiders may feel tempted to believe that everyone in an overseas subsidiary displays similar characteristics, or that all employees share very similar values, but these are dangerous abstractions. Consequently, companies rely on team-building efforts to reduce diversity problems; in some societies, however, subcultural tensions interfere with teamwork. Four general guidelines, outlined in Table 14.5, can help international managers to understand subcultural motives:[65]

- *Group-based incentives.* Effective rewards include bonuses, formal recognition, competitive awards, social recognition, holiday awards, and similar efforts equally distributed throughout the membership of a group, task force, team, department, or operating unit. These measures work best when utilized in highly team-oriented cultures (or subcultures), especially those with histories of successful group efforts and internal cohesiveness. Group incentives also effectively motivate workers in nations that have not yet fully stabilized or completed the transition toward rapid economic development. Subcultural cohesiveness is a common feature of behavior during prolonged periods of economic or social unrest, when individuals become focused on family security, cohort interests, and referent group associations.[66]
- *Egalitarian incentives.* Some firms provide rewards such as bonuses, public recognition, extra holidays, social events, recreation facilities, and other similar incentives in equal measure to all employees without competition or association with specific performance. This motivation technique is best employed in cultures that

TABLE 14.5

MATCH BETWEEN INCENTIVE SYSTEMS AND CULTURAL ENVIRONMENTS

National Characteristics	Cultural Characteristics	Effective Incentive Systems
Frequent disruptions of political stability	High team spirit	Group-based incentives
Long-established socialist system	Strong preference for egalitarianism	Equal distribution of awards
Isolated geographic location	Emphasis on social needs	Rewards that enhance social interaction
Highly equivocal language	High tolerance for ambiguity	Nonspecific rewards tied to overall performance

Source: Y. Paul Huo and Richard M. Steers, "Cultural Influences on the Design of Incentive Systems: The Case of East Asia," *Asia Pacific Journal of Management* 10, no. 1 (1993): 81.

value equality in social and human welfare. Such conditions often accompany social legislation and other outward signs of democratic socialism as well as histories of relative political stability.

- *Social incentives.* Many of the rewards associated with group or egalitarian incentives also allow special emphasis on social affiliations of people through company, community, or ethnic and religious identity. Such incentives can also extend to public ceremonies that recognize cohesive associations, reward individual or group efforts on behalf of the referent group, and accommodate equitably differentiated individual or group incentives for those who advance the referent group's interests. This motivational technique works best in homogeneous societies and in those with well-guarded ethnic, religious, or cultural identities. Social incentives also work well in societies that are geographically, culturally, or politically isolated from their neighbors. An example is the kibbutz system in Israel.[67]

- *Nonspecific performance-based incentives.* In some cultures, rewards may take the form of bonuses, individual or group payments based on performance-based compensation systems, public or private recognition, noninstitutionalized gestures such as occasional symbolic acts by supervisors that show gratitude for excellence, periodic competitions, and company-sponsored social events. These techniques work well in cultures that easily tolerate ambiguity. In Germany, for example, such awards would be considered haphazard gestures signifying organizational ineptitude; they might well do more harm than good. In China, however, ambiguity is almost an art form that pervades negotiations, personal communications, and exchanges in which superiors compliment or reprimand workers. The Chinese language itself encourages equivocation in its capacity for variable meanings depending on the context of communications and subtle gestures. Words and gestures by themselves seldom convey exact meanings, so behavior that "gives face" through praise can mystify non-Chinese observers.[68]

These guidelines may not provide concrete recommendations for motivating employees, but they can help international managers to avoid serious mistakes. As a rule, ad hoc incentive programs may result in ridicule rather than exuberance in structured social environments where employees feel little tolerance for uncertainty. In contrast, highly structured team incentives may have similar ill effects in individualistic societies where employees are accustomed to personal achievement. By matching incentives to expectations, however, and avoiding those that may cause problems, an organization can reduce the differences created in diverse environments and often inspire new employee affiliations.

Global Diversity

A global organization must resolve large-scale issues created by diversity to achieve international coordination. As part of this effort, it must motivate employees throughout a widely diversified system of subsidiaries. In particular, a multinational with an integrated system of management must rely on cooperation among a rather broad-based network of executives and foreign managers. Consequently, the key to success is *team building*. As explained in Chapter 13 on management development, many of the foremost global companies credit their success to teamwork and a commitment to building effective boundary-spanning relationships. Nestlé has carefully integrated teams throughout its long history, establishing a reputation for cooperation among a highly diverse group of international executives. Its senior management ranks include as many as 100 different nationalities, and its practices encourage multilingual and cross-functional decision-making.

In contrast, few U.S. firms can count more than a handful of different nationalities among their executives.[69] The leadership style of a company's top managers often may dictate a closely controlled autocratic organization with little teamwork. Management practices may also reflect the ethnocentricity of those in command. Fortunately, a powerful trend is moving businesses toward greater team development and integration of managers with diverse backgrounds. Earlier chapters have cited examples illustrating recent developments in global teamwork: GE's coordination system in Hungary, AT&T's international executive training system, ABB's fully integrated network of team activities among more than 2,000 world projects, and Shell Oil's unique approach to self-learning teams. The "Global Viewpoint" feature in this section describes another example demonstrating how GM's European affiliate, Opel, has overcome difficult cultural constraints to reposition itself as an international competitor.

Effective global team development is a crucial activity, but its goals do not represent a universally palatable prescription. Cultural values can make teamwork difficult to achieve. Managers from paternalistic societies, for example, are unlikely to share decision-making authority; indeed, their employees are unlikely to expect them to behave that way. Managers from societies accustomed to autocratic behavior find teamwork even more difficult to accept. Further, managers from individualistic societies cannot always appreciate the benefits of the collaborative environment required in teamwork.[70] Still, diversity management can succeed in these societies through constructive efforts by executives to minimize human resource problems. Research has produced several recommendations that do not specifically require team-based management, yet they can provide equally effective support for companies developing global teams:[71]

- Headquarters should consciously recognize that the company is managed from a home-culture perspective with explicitly local values and assumptions.
- Parent-company executives should recognize that foreign subsidiaries manage people in unexpected ways, and these methods may prove more effective than familiar domestic practices.

- Senior managers and staff members responsible for international relationships should openly acknowledge cultural differences and encourage discussion and accommodation of these variations.
- The firm as a whole should make a proactive effort to encourage an organizational attitude accepting creative and effective new ways of managing people through cross-cultural learning.

Managing diversity thus implies an ability to accept a multidimensional organization with talented people who can contribute in their own ways from their unique cultural perspectives. Success depends not on compromising one's own cultural values to accommodate others, but on constructively orchestrating the strengths of individual differences. Teamwork may be the ultimate goal for a globally integrated company—indeed, it may be essential for long-term success—but a company can achieve synergistic effects from diversity when executives make a conscious effort to accept differences and look for positive contributions from all managers and employees. When parent-company executives set an example for this behavior, others follow. Although diversity problems may not disappear or teamwork instantly materialize, proactive steps to manage diversity provide essential support.[72]

Foreign-Owned Enterprises and Home-Country Diversity

When U.S. multinationals expanded into Europe and Asia following World War II, the dominance of the country's foreign investment became known as the "American challenge." Today the situation has changed—foreign investment in the United States is at record levels, and the world faces a new American challenge that is far more daunting than managing abroad. It is the challenge of managing foreign affiliates in the United States.[73] Aside from the economic problems of opening subsidiaries on U.S. soil, foreign companies have identified three obstacles as the most difficult to overcome: management, culture, and workforce organization.

Managerial Challenge

Foreign companies tend to mix expatriates and local managers for their U.S. subsidiaries. In particular, European firms prefer to fill key positions with their own people. Although American executives sometimes work in European subsidiaries, it is a relatively uncommon phenomenon. Few American managers actually want to work for European companies, because they can seldom envision more than limited careers. The same argument can be made for natives of almost any European host country considering employment with U.S. or other foreign firms, but Japanese companies carry this preference for home-country talent to extremes.

Only rarely do Japanese firms recruit host-country executives for their U.S. or European operations, and those who have been hired have only recently taken their positions. Japanese companies strongly prefer to staff their entire senior management cadres with Japanese nationals. For example, Matsushita assigns more than 700 senior managers to foreign posts at any one time, many of them in the United States. This known tendency creates serious problems for domestic recruitment of both managers and employees. U.S. workers experience serious difficulties working under Japanese managers, beginning with language and cultural constraints. Given their choice, most would rather work for U.S. companies where they understand the reward systems and career opportunities.

Cultural Challenge

Descriptions of U.S. culture, from hundreds of research efforts ranging from contrasts between Mexican and U.S. workers in maquiladoras to Hofstede's decade of

GLOBAL VIEWPOINT

TEAM BUILDING AT GM OPEL: PROFITING FROM DIVERSITY

General Motors operates worldwide with regional subsidiaries and model names. Made in Germany, GM Opel has been the leading American brand throughout Europe for nearly a half-century. However, a few years ago, Japanese competition nearly drove the company out of business. In fact, the entire German car industry has been fighting rugged competition from Japan, and Opel has been one of several European companies extremely vulnerable to foreign competition. The Japanese have manufactured between 55 and 60 cars per year per employee (the industry measure of competitive production). U.S. manufacturers have averaged roughly 45 to 50 cars per year per employee; only a few U.S. plants can match Japanese output ratios.

Meanwhile, German competitors have averaged approximately 24 cars per employee per year. Considering that German workers earn extremely generous compensation, enjoy 10 weeks each year of paid holidays, and receive exceptional benefits, the German automobiles are extremely expensive products. Of course, they are also exceptionally well engineered. Despite this perceived quality differential, however, in the early 1990s Opel was in trouble, and 1995 brought still larger problems due to the assimilation of East Germans and the influx of other Eastern European workers. This change in the workforce led to strained relationships among employee groups, which divided along ethnic and cultural lines. The company also experienced problems due to differences in work-related values and concepts of work quality.

By introducing new team-building processes, GM Opel has turned its situation around and become one of Europe's most efficient companies. The plant produces 58 cars per year per employee, equal to or better than all but the most efficient Japanese plants. It has accomplished this transformation through a total commitment to team-based enterprise with incentives that emphasize group and organizational achievements rather than competition for individual awards. For example, all employees and managers share common lunchrooms, recreation facilities, and rest areas. Everyone earns a salary, and the lack of hourly workers eliminates debates about overtime pay, inequitable job ratings, or individual differentials. Bonuses are structured as profit-sharing payments distributed to everyone according to seniority and skill level. Salaries are based on group qualifications and established ratings, not on measures of productivity or efficiency. The company sponsors family days, children's parties, and sporting events to bring employees and their families together. All employees have access to educational funds and support for after-hours development activities. The factory design follows the Japanese kanban system, complete with just-in-time production methods and self-managed quality assurance operations. This layout complements other conditions to foster an extraordinary atmosphere of open communication in which team members have access to all company information. In addition, Opel has allocated nearly one-half day each week to employee development, including career training and diversity training.

This process was launched by GM Opel as a way of resolving sensitive conflicts among workers, but the program has been so successful that it is spreading to other European activities. GM has begun to transform its continental operations into regional teams and to purposely build bridges between diverse cultural interests through integrated development efforts. The program is still in its early stages, and it may take several years to implement, yet the GM Opel plant has won high praise for its initiatives.

The real kicker is that this program and its manufacturing facilities are in the old East German area of Eisenach. Many of the company's highly productive employees were part of a smoke-belching, Soviet-style industrial system just a few years ago.

Source: Adapted from Adolf Haasen, "Opel Eisenach GMBH-Creating a High-Productivity Workplace," *Organizational Dynamics* 24, no. 4 (1996): 80–85.

investigations, emphasize attitudes of *independence*. This country's people easily tolerate ambiguity, job mobility, informality, and self-determined careers. They prefer independence in work behavior and decision-making. Europeans and Asians wonder at these characteristics. Instead, they prefer structure to relationships, predictability in careers, and broad acceptance of authority. U.S. society is also considered to be overly litigious and intolerant of infringements on individual rights. Japanese managers frequently experience problems in the United States in their relations with female employees; Japan's generally accepted masculine prerogatives do not travel well. U.S. society also favors confrontation more than foreigners expect, as illustrated in a quote from a London-born manager of British Air in New York: "Going to America is like stepping into a page of an American Western novel. Even in New York, you have to strap on your 'shooting irons' and be ready for the proverbial showdown at High Noon, and this happens with regularity, whether it is negotiating with a cab driver or negotiating an international business alliance."[74]

Japanese visitors perceive the United States as a dangerous environment, with its obvious conflicts among ethnic minority groups as well as prominent racial tension and high crime rates. In commenting on his early return to Japan, a Nissan executive said: "America is a wonderful place with so many opportunities and so much to offer that it is sad that we must lock our doors against one another and worry for our children even as they wait for a school bus."[75] All societies have their social ills, but the striking contrasts in the United States often create unusual challenges for managing diversity within the foreign-owned enterprise. Most of the difficulties arise from disparities in the cultural values of independence and personal freedom. U.S. nationals going abroad encounter just as many difficulties, as earlier chapters have documented, so they should not feel like their isolated nation stands against the world; indeed, problems prevalent in the United States are comparable to those in many other countries.

A foreign company operating in the United States must resolve the same issues of managing diversity as it would when managing a domestic enterprise, but it confronts more sensitive situations that result from obvious differences in foreign management practices. Team building remains the key to unlocking pent-up disparities, and developing a sense of integration is an essential activity for foreign multinationals. Japanese or European managers must accept the heterogeneity in North American companies and pursue shared interests that transcend language, cultural, and organizational differences. These are not idle recommendations, nor are they exclusive to the United States. Japanese companies, for example, have had similar difficulties in their Latin American subsidiaries, and Europeans have struggled with similar problems in Japan.[76]

Organizational Challenge

The cultural and managerial difficulties of foreign companies operating in the United States result in a chronic source of friction within multinational firms. U.S. multinationals succeed abroad by integrating foreign subsidiaries into the U.S. model, but individual U.S. nationals often fail to integrate into foreign organizations. This difference suggests an uncomfortable hint of ethnocentricity, but it is also the result of the geographic dispersion of U.S. markets, where affiliates of foreign-owned parent organizations rely extensively on locally managed operations. Consequently, tension results from disparities in expectations between U.S. managers and their foreign superiors. Swedish companies such as Volvo, and Japanese companies such as Honda, bring concepts of self-managed groups and worker autonomy that far exceed the expectations of U.S. workers. Ironically, the independent U.S. character tends to stifle hierarchical power as it sets up barriers against group-based activities. Workers may not, therefore, accept participative systems that exist in many foreign organizations.

MOTIVATION IN PERSPECTIVE

No standard set of principles for motivation can provide a prescription for managers either at home or abroad, and almost any recommendation seems to vary between trivial and too complex to allow practical implementation. Nevertheless, several general guidelines can help managers to cultivate sensitivity to cross-cultural differences in motives. At the same time, certain measures may help to reduce conflicts that arise in diverse multicultural environments.

The first point to bear in mind is that motivation can emerge from individual values or self-directed initiatives. Therefore, success requires an understanding of how and why each person behaves as they do, but this need imposes a perplexing responsibility on international managers. Motivation also can result from external influences, organizational incentives, and leader-member relationships. Because these motives vary with cultural values, locations, ethnic profiles, and many other factors, they are called *situational* variables. International managers should therefore avoid making assumptions about motivation within their home cultures. Instead, they should reach for a deeper understanding of the expectations and customs that influence local behavior. For this reason, motivation theories that favor a contingency approach often prove more effective than rigid theories. Variations in situational variables within a foreign subsidiary with a culturally diverse workforce require a continuous balancing process, challenging managers to consider individual motivational characteristics, patterns of cultural values, and situational variables that underscore multicultural differences.

Understanding differences in the concepts of work and jobs throughout the world provides an equally important foundation for effective motivation. The notion of work takes on many different meanings in Mexico, Germany, Russia, China, and the United States or Canada. Organizations in different countries must accommodate underpinning beliefs in the value of work. They must adapt to relationships with co-workers, superiors, and subordinates; and in the end, seek to understand the priorities assigned to rewards received for work-related behavior in each environment.

International managers find their greatest personal rewards in success through new relationships with people from other cultures. They also experience their greatest frustrations in efforts to understand and adapt to expectations of their foreign colleagues and employees. This diversity creates psychological and sociological challenges that simply do not arise in a home culture, ranging from perplexing problems to exciting opportunities. The next chapter builds on the theme of challenges by exploring international dimensions of leadership.

REVIEW QUESTIONS
1. How do content theories and process theories differ in their characterizations of motivation?
2. Why does the concept of achievement differ in Russia, Japan, and the United States? What conditions influence these differences in value perspectives?

3. People often inappropriately generalize values to a region or a nation. Explain the problems with a description of values for the Middle East. Do all Arabs share similar values? Do all Muslims acknowledge similar motives to work?

4. What is the meaning of the term *work centrality*, and how does it influence attitudes toward the rewards of work? Explain using two or more contrasting cultures as examples.

5. Explain how people differ in their motivations according to Hofstede's four cultural dimensions.

6. How accurately does Maslow's need hierarchy apply in regional clusters such as Latin American, Anglo, and Nordic cultures?

7. Do Chinese, U.S., and Latin American people perceive the same priorities for human needs? Explain differences or similarities.

8. Contrast Herzberg's two-factor theory of motivation as perceived by U.S. and Mexican nationals. What differences separate hygiene factors and satisfiers in the two cultures?

9. Why is expectancy theory attractive as a concept for motivation in the international arena?

10. Describe how team management can help to minimize problems associated with human diversity. What are the primary goals of organizational diversity management programs?

11. What problems are associated with diversity in host-country management?

12. How does a company address the problems of managing diversity on a global basis? Ultimately, what does managing diversity mean?

GLOSSARY OF KEY TERMS

Acquired-needs theory   McClelland's model of motivation is based on orientations toward power, affiliation, and achievement and a presumption that behavior is learned, allowing constructive development of desired orientations.

Content theories   Principles of motivation based on human needs and behavior.

Diversity   Encompasses differences in human characteristics that arise from national origin, gender, race, ethnicity, religion, language, age, socioeconomic status, and cultural values.

Expectancy theory   A rational model of motivation that combines individual evaluations of the efforts, the potential rewards, and the importance of those rewards to explain work-related behavior.

Job redesign   A program with elements of job rotation, job enlargement, and/or job enrichment to improve individual capabilities, individual and team performance, and job satisfaction.

Motivation   The stimulus that drives behavior, consisting of all the forces that cause people to behave in certain ways.

Need hierarchy   Maslow's theory that behavior is motivated according to unmet needs that occur in a progressive hierarchy of importance, in which satisfaction of the lower-order needs leads to the emergence of higher-order needs as important motivators.

Process theories   Principles of motivation based on expectations about perceived outcomes of behavior.

Two-factor theory   Herzberg's theory of motivation based on two distinct sets of factors: satisfiers that motivate behavior and hygiene factors that may cause dissatisfaction.

Work centrality   The importance of occupational tasks relative to other human activities.

EXERCISES

1. Choose a country not specifically described in the chapter but researched in studies available to you. (See the citations on the work of Hofstede and others.) Develop a cultural profile of values related to that country, and then list potential incentives that would be most relevant for a subsidiary located there. Be prepared to show why the incentives you have selected would motivate workers in that society.

2. List specific values that would influence work-related behavior (e.g., personal achievement, group harmony, etc.), and then interview foreign students or managers to develop a small sample of opinions. You could structure this as a survey questionnaire, asking respondents

to rank the importance of each item according to a scale of one to five (least to most important). You should be able to identify at least 20 values in your list; many published research surveys cite 50 or more possibilities. Try to get enough responses so that you can contrast at least two cultures.

3. As a class assignment or group effort, student teams can administer one survey instrument as suggested in Exercise 2. Each team would select a nationality to study (e.g., U.S., Canadian, British, German, Chinese, Japanese). In universities with substantial foreign enrollments, each team should be able to gather sufficient responses for a reasonable cross-cultural comparison of values, perceived needs, and potential incentives. Run simple statistical tests on these responses, and perhaps collectively evaluate the team results by analyzing variance. Each team should present its findings and make recommendations for motivational incentives.

Move toward Performance-Related Philosophy in Thailand

Thai workers may be among the happiest in the world, but growth and a rapidly expanding international community of multinationals are changing Thai expectations for work and rewards. "When I first visited Thailand some 16 years ago, I was struck by a sense of peace and self-satisfaction among the people," says Jon Terpstra, a management consultant. "When I visit now, I'm more aware of a restlessness—a sense of rushing toward 'getting more and more' and doing less for it. The Thais are still among the happiest people on earth. They are born smiling—a gentle folk."

Terpstra was part of an important focus group of international consultants and government officials assembled in early 1997 to try to resolve the problems of a wave of violence and labor strife that has swept through Thailand's workforce. Most affected are multinational companies that have been hard hit by unexpected worker demands, strikes, walkouts, and physical violence. Workers rioted at a Sanyo Universal Electric PCL, a division of the giant Japanese Sanyo Electronics Corporation, and burned down the company headquarters in December 1996. Within hours, other Sanyo workers burned down the company's warehouse. They publicly denounced management as exploitative and insensitive to Thai workers. Several days later, four factories of Delta Electronics, a Taiwanese joint venture listed on the Bangkok exchange, were shut down over bonus disputes. In January 1997, Crosby Associates, an international brokerage investment firm, lost nearly 20 percent of its most experienced analysts over compensation debates. And in February, managers at a U.S. facility under the Motorola flag came to work only to find that employees had locked them out and barricaded themselves behind banners decrying "performance inequities."

Thailand is known as a land of harmony, and prior to 1990 the country averaged no more than about 200 labor disputes per year. Most of these were localized and concerned typical problems of wage levels or working conditions. By 1995, the number had risen to about 300 disputes—still very low by international standards, yet somewhat alarming to Thais. Foreign-invested companies reported 28 work stoppages in 1995, but none with violent overtones. In 1996 the disputes escalated to more than 350, with 35 work stoppages including the year-end violence at Sanyo and Delta Electronics. The number of labor dispute cases in 1997 reached a record number, according to the Thai Control Labor Court.

The Thai government subsequently called together experts in human relations management, company representatives from leading multinationals and domestic firms, and trade representatives from other nations. They were to identify potential causes for worker unrest and suggest ways to reduce future difficulties. At the outset, a Sanyo spokesman made it very clear that his company's problems involved a disputed bonus system that, from the company's viewpoint, was unrealistically high. "We have paid workers the equivalent of more than five months' wages in year-end bonuses," he explained. "That is four times what we pay elsewhere, and as everyone here knows, it is extraordinary. Asian workers outside Japan are accustomed to their '13th-month' bonus, but our Thai workers have become very aggressive for very big bonuses."

The Thai manager representing Taiwan interests for Delta Electronics explained the problem of "bonus expectations." He noted, "Thai workers rejoiced at quarterly bonuses of 10 percent just five years ago, but now scream for double that amount. It has become commonplace and seen as part of their standard pay to take home excess bonus dividends every three months—yet no bonus reflects productivity. In Taiwan, this is not even legal, but in any case, bonuses are meant to reflect workers' productivity. They are motivators, incentives, not obligations of the company without regard for results."

Terpstra, who was asked to represent four U.S. companies through the American Chamber of Commerce, explained bonuses as "incentive seeds gone sour by making them too common to have purpose." If a monetary reward is to succeed, he explained, it must have emotional value to Thai workers. "Chinese workers in Hong Kong, Singapore, and Malaysia are indeed used to a 13th month payment, and it is seldom linked to performance," he said. "We all know this, yet we have lost track of the payment as an incentive. Today, it is an expectation. The Thais, however, have never thought about bonuses in this manner until recently. They used to take exceptional pride in a bonus, almost like a badge of courage. When we first introduced bonuses at Motorola, they were issued in person by the country manager. He would present each bonus payment personally, often in fresh new currency. After awhile, that became a payment sent out by the payroll people, and in time, an added sum to periodic pay envelopes."

In response to this, a trade adviser from the Japan External Trade Organization (JETO) in Bangkok said that incentive bonuses are very common in Japan, but employees understand the spirit and intent. They have a reciprocal obligation to perform well, and bonuses change as the company's fortunes change. But he also noted that Thais, Chinese, Malays, and other Asians with whom JETO works have entirely different expectations. "We find that we must help our home-based employers understand the nuances of each culture, and for this situation, when Sanyo or Delta try to restrain bonuses, it is like clipping the lion's mane—you snip at their pride. But the statistics suggest much deeper issues. Thai workers simply are not the happy, carefree people they once were. I wonder if we have not helped instill expectations in them far beyond the symptoms we see in errant bonus disputes."

Now, through governmental efforts, a more performance-driven philosophy and culture are on the rise in Thailand. The Thai government recently announced plans to implement performance-based bonuses in state enterprises as well as remuneration systems, according to Lawrence Watson, the Bangkok representative of the U.S.-based Hay Management Group. The Hay Management Group is an internationally recognized organization with expertise in "leadership, human motivation, performance, and compensation." For approximately the past 10 years, Thailand has experienced positive economic growth; but in recent years, the country has not enjoyed the same level of growth. Speaking to Hay Management Group directors in Bangkok, Watson, a 22-year veteran of the company, said, "This is not only radical in a regional context, it is also extremely rare for a government to select implementation of performance-driven remuneration programmes." Watson stated that Thai companies should follow the government's lead and implement similar programs in order to get companies focused on results.

Corporate clarity, according to Watson, is the key to improved performance. Watson attributes some of the bonus problems in Thai companies to this issue. In addition, employees should know how a company determines or defines criteria for bonuses. Watson said:

> Research shows conclusively that high performance can be directly correlated with clarity in the minds of employees. Clarity means they see clearly the overall vision and mission of the organisation as well as their own specific role. Once companies can ensure their message is clear, they can effectively institute a "Pay-for-Performance" plan. To do so, however, they will need to liberate themselves from old ways of doing business and reengineer both base salary increments and the traditional concept of guaranteed bonuses.

Watson views "Pay-for-Performance" from two angles—base salary increments and bonuses. Base salary increments, he says, are a reward, not a right. Bonuses, on the other hand, should be directly linked to performance with formulas for different positions and responsibilities and not thought of as a deferred salary. According to Watson, "Performance-related pay is all about cause and effect. If you achieve a certain result, you will be rewarded in a certain way."

QUESTIONS

1. Why would Thai needs be different from those of Japanese or American workers? Why would managers from more affluent countries such as the United States, Japan, and Taiwan have difficulty understanding workers' motives in this regard?

2. Examine the controversy over bonuses. In Thailand, they seem not to be performance based; according to the conference participants, bonuses are tied to corporate results in Japan. Yet among Chinese societies, bonuses are almost standard—the 13th-month payday. Why do bonuses differ as incentives?

3. Based on differences in cultural values explained in the chapter (and elsewhere in the text), what do you believe would be most important to Thai

workers? How might a multinational company address problems in motivation for its local Thai workers?

BIBLIOGRAPHY

Au, Tanya. "Bonuses in Bangkok Fuel More Violence." *Straits Times* (Singapore), 22 February 1997, p. 1.

"Experts Hail Thai Drive for Performance-Driven Culture, Nation." *Nation*, 8 February 1999.

[Retrieved 19 December 2000 from Dow Jones Interactive database.]

Sherer, Paul M. "Labor Unrest Still Smolders in Thailand; Foreigners Wait for Government Reaction to String of Bonus Disputes." *Asian Wall Street Journal*, 26 December 1996, p. 1.

Strategic Forum on Labor & Worker Rights. Chulalongkorn University, Bangkok, Thailand, 7–9 March 1997.

"Thailand Sees Rising Labor Disputes." *Xinhua English Newswire*, 9 September 1997. [Retrieved 19 December 2000 from Dow Jones Interactive database.]

CASE 14.2

SHELL BECOMES MORE ENTREPRENEURIAL DURING RESTRUCTURING

In 1995, Royal Dutch/Shell announced the largest corporate shake-up the company would experience in more than 30 years. Shell intended to shed its matrix-style organization in favor of a global team approach, with strategic divisions headed by small groups of senior managers. The team concept would then trickle down to virtually every operating unit. At the time, analysts predicted the move would devastate Shell's ranks and endanger performance over the next few years. About 1,200 of the 3,900 staff at service companies in The Hague and London were expected to lose their jobs in the proposed restructuring, and shock waves were expected throughout the global organization. Cornelius Herkstroter, chairman of Shell's top-level committee of managing directors (CMD), said the company's flagging performance against its international competitors had triggered the changes. In the long run, he added, the company would rid itself of several layers of bureaucracy, streamline decision-making, and become the leading oil company in the world.

By 1997 the restructuring had begun to take effect, but predictions of upheaval had not occurred. Indeed, the company had exceeded Herkstroter's future vision of Shell, becoming the most profitable corporation in the world and overtaking Exxon in both assets and sales performance. Shell had redefined itself with six major strategic divisions around

the company's main businesses of exploration and production, refining and marketing oil products, chemicals, gas, coal, and ancillary polymers. This in turn generated more than 100 worldwide operating divisions for the $121 billion company. Many of these divisions are in themselves major corporations or subsidiaries in the United States, Britain, Asia, and Latin America.

Shell used a systematic approach to teamwork that put the actual restructuring decisions in the hands of managers and employees who would be affected. At the top, the CMD makes joint strategic decisions and coordinates worldwide divisional interests. Each operating division or incorporated subsidiary under the new group structure has its own agenda for change, its own strategies to orchestrate, and its own lower strata of managers to reorganize.

Speaking at the Howard Weil Energy Conference in New Orleans, Maarten van den Bergh—vice chairman of Royal Dutch/Shell Group and president of Royal Dutch Petroleum—said, "Shell has undergone a dramatic transformation, since the beginning of a company-wide restructuring in 1998." In particular, he was talking about the company's move from a bureaucratic organization to one that is more entrepreneurial. Van den Bergh further commented:

In the mid-1990s, we realized that our ROCE [return on capital employed] was not good enough and something had to be done. The events of 1998 galvanized the restructuring process. Today, there are more direct reporting lines and every project has to complete for capital.

In a 1999 article, "Redrawing Boundaries," that appeared in *Executive Excellence* and was written by van den Bergh, he said the Royal Dutch/Shell Group of Companies was redefining its own boundaries in order to respond innovatively to global forces such as communications technology. In particular, he said the company was

taking bold steps to transform its structure, management style and ways of doing business. Success in such a complex environment demands an equally complex mix of imagination and pragmatism, caution and courage. We are using today's expertise to chart a successful course into tomorrow's world.

For businesses seeking new prospects, van den Bergh said they will face three challenges: "1) Pressures from the need for global competitiveness in a troubled global economy; 2) Pressures from new expectations of business from society; 3) Pressures to find structures that can respond fast and effectively to both commercial and societal demands." For Royal Dutch/Shell, this means flexible organizations, flexible structures, and a cohesive culture.

When asked if recent mega-mergers in the oil industry would affect Shell's leadership position, Steve Miller, group managing director of the Royal Dutch/Shell Group of Companies (who was recognized in the April–May 1998 issue of *Fast Company* as a role model for his grassroots approach to leadership), responded:

If anything . . . all of this merger activity has made grassroots leadership an even greater imperative. We want to create hundreds of small, entrepreneurial businesses that come together to make one big business. Grassroots leadership lets you break down a massive company into a series of bite-size, manageable, highly effective pieces.

At Shell, "retailing boot camps" were used to encourage frontline employees to work together to "develop products, to share ideas, and to foster continued innovation." The effects of the boot camps? Since 1996, they have added over $300 million to the company's bottom line. Miller credits the value of the boot camps to employees' abilities to "create learning opportunities on their own." He said:

We're scrambling to keep up with the phenomenal rate of learning around here. It's as if, in the first year, people weren't sure how to add and subtract—and now, a year later, they've already licked calculus. So we're trying to figure out how to create a grassroots-leadership graduate school. In other words, how do you get your doctorate in this stuff?

While some in the industry have looked to mergers and acquisitions for growth, Royal Dutch/Shell says it will engage in "highly selective joint ventures aimed at exploiting individual opportunities." For now, it appears that Royal Dutch/Shell's restructuring strategies are paying off; the company started showing signs of record profits.

QUESTIONS

1. Shell faces questions of global diversity and managing people in a variety of cultures. What diversity issues are most important for understanding how structural changes might affect host-country operations?
2. What are the benefits of moving from a bureaucratic structure to one that is more entrepreneurial?
3. How can companies address the three challenges identified by Maarten van den Bergh as they seek effective ways of going "beyond the edge"?

BIBLIOGRAPHY

Fan, Aliza, and Christina Katsouris. "Changes at Royal Dutch/Shell Represent Historic Upheaval." *Oil Daily*, 11 April 1995, p. 2.

Guyon, Janet. "Why is the World's Most Profitable Company Turning Itself Inside Out?" *Fortune*, 4 August 1997, 120–125.

Haines, Leslie. "Execs Looking Beyond Traditional Business for More Returns." *Petroleum Finance Week*, 10 April 2000, 21. [Retrieved 19 December 2000 from Dow Jones Interactive database.]

Muoio, Anna. "Updating the Agenda: A Second Look at the 1998 Agenda Role Models." *Fast Company*, 1 April 1999, 184. [Retrieved 19 December 2000 from Dow Jones Interactive database.]

"Shell, Ocean Report on Growth Strategies." *Gas Daily*, 4 April 2000. [Retrieved 19 December 2000 from Dow Jones Interactive database.]

"Shell Plans Shake-up in Effort to Compete More Effectively Worldwide." *Financial Times*, 5 April 1995, p. 1.

Van den Bergh, Maarten. "Redrawing Boundaries." *Executive Excellence*, 1 February 1999, 3. [Retrieved 19 December 2000 from Dow Jones Interactive database.]

CHAPTER FIFTEEN

LEADERSHIP IN THE GLOBAL CONTEXT

CHAPTER OBJECTIVES

Define and contrast the trait, style, and contingency approaches to leadership.

Describe the process of transformational leadership and its importance to international managers.

Explain how subordinate expectations can make crucial contributions to leadership effectiveness.

Compare trends and differences in European leadership behavior.

Detail the major challenges managers in Central and Eastern Europe face as their societies adapt to new patterns of organizational behavior.

Indicate the effects of Confucian social philosophy on leadership behavior in Asia.

Show how cultural values influence patterns of authority in contrasting societies in Asia, Latin America, and the Middle East.

Jerry Florence is the first African American to become an executive in a Japanese enterprise with operations in the United States.[1] His success has little to do with personal characteristics and a lot to do with leadership skills that he learned as a professional baseball player. From 1966 through 1971, he played for the Chicago White Sox organization, achieving some notoriety for his team spirit and on-the-field leadership. Today, Jerry Florence is Nissan's U.S. vice president for marketing. His position is extraordinary given the company's reputation for placing Japanese executives in charge of key foreign operations. Indeed, Nissan seems to have broken ranks with other Japanese firms in the United States which, in many instances, place U.S. natives in middle management posts but prefer Japanese natives in executive positions.[2] However, Florence is an unusual person with leadership qualities that transcend ethnic and racial barriers.

After leaving baseball, Florence began a business career in marketing that eventually led to General Motors in 1983, where he worked in sales and product planning. During the ensuing 10 years, he developed and negotiated contracts with buyers in the Soviet Union and Japan, traveled widely, and was instrumental in bridging cultural gaps. His success soon led to his appointment as general director of marketing and product planning for GM's Cadillac division. Responsible for worldwide sales of luxury vehicles, Florence dramatically improved GM's market share, and in 1993 Nissan Motor Corporation brought him on board to spearhead marketing for the new Maxima and 240SX models. He immediately set about to lead a strategic team effort, and within two years established both models as front-runners in the U.S. market. Part of that success resulted from his vision of an integrated network of partnerships, but the real reason was his ability to inspire a multicultural team to look past individual differences and strive toward a unified goal. Florence was also able to bridge the cultural gap between Japanese and U.S. management methods by leading from a group empowerment perspective.

"In America, we place a big premium on individual superstars," Florence explained. "In your career, you try to do something big and impactful that will make you stand out from the crowd. In the Japanese culture, that's not the case. The idea is for the organization—the team—to win." Florence was a team player from the moment he set foot on a baseball field. He never let individual priorities or personal differences interfere with the objective of contributing to a winning team.

Florence brought with him an attitude compatible with Nissan's belief in group effort rather than a traditional American expectation of relying on individual merit. He recognized that the Japanese had always discouraged individual gain and instead had rewarded group excellence. In his view, that was one key to success for Japanese automotive firms. But he also brought with him a goal-directed vision of leadership—a vision of creating team contributions for total organizational success. "I had to understand that you can't always do things in a vacuum," he said. "I had to make sure that the goal fit with the overall vision and direction of the company."

Florence was immediately comfortable with this team-oriented style of leadership, but he also emphasized that U.S. staff members could learn from Japanese practices such as *nimiwashi*, the name for the grueling process of encouraging proposals through participative methods and then questioning those proposals thoroughly to dig down to the root of the idea. In Florence's view, the Japanese could also learn a thing or two about innovation and leadership from the United States, and Nissan seemed more than willing to accommodate management practices that represent the best of both worlds. Florence and his colleagues at Nissan have subsequently begun to look beyond stereotypes and individual traits to encourage a multidimensional organization in which the capability to lead effectively is a common value.

LEADERSHIP: INFLUENCING BEHAVIOR

Leadership is the process of influencing other people to behave in preferred ways to accomplish organizational objectives. In the business world, it is the management activity intended to optimize progress toward organizational objectives while also inspiring individual employees to fulfill their potential.[3] Although many researchers and philosophers have tried to explain how great men and women have persuaded people to follow them, scholars still search for an unambiguous explanation of leadership. The definition offered here emphasizes a *process of influencing behavior,* a *stimulating effect* on group and individual performance. This concept is broad enough to be generally accepted almost anywhere in the world, but every culture puts a different imprint on the meaning of *leadership.*

No universal prescription describes how managers can best influence behavior or stimulate performance. Indeed, while observers may agree on a definition of the term, this conclusion does not resolve controversy over the nature of leadership and what it means to be a leader. Research has supported many insights about the meaning of leadership, but studies also have deepened the mystery surrounding it. This contradiction is captured in a statement by Manfred F. R. Kets de Vries, an international scholar at the European Institute of Business Administration (INSEAD), who recently wrote:

> When we plunge into the organizational literature on leadership we quickly become lost in a labyrinth: there are endless definitions, countless articles and never-ending polemics. As far as leadership studies go, it seems that more and more has been studied about less and less, to end up ironically with a group of researchers studying everything about nothing. It prompted one wit to say recently that reading the current world literature on leadership is rather like going through a Parisian telephone directory while trying to read it in Chinese![4]

With that caution in mind, this chapter will summarize the prevailing theoretical approaches to leadership and examine managerial roles in what is called today the **new leadership.** The *new leadership* concept accentuates the process of influencing others through *charismatic* and *transformational* roles that managers must consciously develop.[5] International exchanges give many meanings to these terms, and the chapter will illustrate how managers practice the art of leadership in different societies. With a literature encompassing tens of thousands of articles on leadership, a simple overview in this chapter covers the topic superficially at best; but everyone should be aware of the richness of the available literature. International managers can benefit from studying the work of great thinkers such as Confucius and Sun Tzu, two Chinese leaders whose ideas underscore modern managerial behavior for nearly one-third of the world's population. The religious tenets of Islam and historical development of Middle Eastern cultures emphasize an entirely different approach to leadership that affects nations from the heart of Africa to the borders of Russia. Judeo-Christian societies are steeped in a leadership philosophy of their own, with insights dating to Pericles and the Golden Age of Greece.

The Dionysian concept of charisma, for example, was a focus of study by German sociologist Max Weber (1864–1920). Weber attempted to define leadership apart from a divine right; instead, he suggested that effective organizations are built on "rational relationships." He is best known for his impersonal view of bureaucratic organizations, yet the heart of his work was concerned with *influence relationships*, a subject that has resurfaced in contemporary western literature.[6]

Available literature offers many opportunities to read about the histories and philosophies of other societies, resources that can be very beneficial to an international manager. Limitations prevent this chapter from probing deeply into these issues, yet it is important to understand that leadership behavior is a reflection of values well entrenched in a society's cultural heritage and of the evolution of its social philosophy. It is also important to note that any single sociocultural summary of leadership principles will certainly contrast sharply with other viewpoints, and these differences are unlikely to dissolve, reinforced as they are by hundreds of years of social conditioning. International managers can learn much from other cultures, and although each person may believe that his or her approach to management is better than others, in reality no one can claim to practice the best way to manage people. Consequently, a drive to become an effective leader may be the most profound challenge facing an international manager in a rapidly expanding global economy.[7] With these caveats in mind, the next section looks more closely at leadership theories.

CORNERSTONES OF LEADERSHIP THEORY

Western theories of leadership are separated into *trait*, *style*, and *contingency* approaches. Each set of principles constitutes a field of knowledge incorporating several distinct models of leadership attributes. These models have evolved sequentially during the past half-century, one building on another. However, the emergence of each new approach has not meant the demise of others. Instead, each treatment offers an alternative way of explaining leadership.

The Trait Approach

The longest-surviving leadership concept, the **trait approach,** probably dates to ancient times, when tribes, clans, city-states, and nations clung to the belief that leaders gained power over others through divine intervention. Effective leaders were viewed as endowed with superhuman qualities. Beginning in the era of rapid industrialization and lasting until after World War II, advocates of the trait approach progressively abandoned the idea of divinity, yet they firmly believed that leaders were born, not made. In many societies, leaders held mysterious sway over populations. History offers examples such as Alexander the Great, Mohandas Ghandi, religious prophets and saints throughout the ages, and, on the darker side, Adolph Hitler. None of these individuals duplicated the traits of others, yet the stories of their development convey a sense that they were born to their destinies.

Even today, people search for individuals born with leadership characteristics. They revere TV heros for their physical prowess and heroines for their beauty. These judgments bend under the strength of biases about sex, race, and ethnic roles for leaders. Some value individual characteristics such as intelligence, self-confidence, and a sense of morality. Although some of these attitudes reflect insupportable biases, reality justifies people's reverence for many attributes.

In business organizations, three categories of characteristics seem to distinguish effective leaders: physical attributes, abilities, and personalities. A person's physique and appearance can influence others' behavior, and those who have demonstrated scholarship, fluency of speech, intelligence, or performance attributes (such as star basketball players) become celebrities often emulated by others. Whether their performance abilities or physical attributes relate in any important way to people's real interests is beside the point. Some years ago, management theorists sought to identify a set of universal characteristics of successful business leaders, arriving at a short list of personality traits: *persistence*, *self-confidence*, an *achievement drive*, *capability to influence others*, and *originality*.[8]

During the first half of the twentieth century, and particularly among independent-minded Americans, these traits seemed credible. Yet notable research published by Ralph Stogdill in 1948 cast grave doubts on the evidence.[9] Ensuing years have brought a substantial stream of criticism of the trait approach, yet certain personal characteristics have clearly been associated with effective leadership. The need for achievement, for example, when expressed in performance terms as a desire to succeed, is high on the list. Self-assurance, or a feeling of competency in problem-solving situations, is another example. Intelligence, revealed in judgment, reasoning skills, and creativity, is yet another. Decisiveness may also be an important attribute of leadership. However, these are behavioral traits, and researchers cautiously point out that they find too many exceptions to suggest universal effectiveness by leaders with any or all of these traits.[10]

Observers periodically advance new traits as evidence of leadership potential—honesty, assertiveness, extroversion, ambition, tenacity, energy, and so on—but their justifications tend to cite situational variables. George Patton was an outstanding wartime general, but he may not have been equally successful in business. H. Ross Perot, an extraordinary leader in his field who founded data-processing giant Electronic Data Systems (EDS), may not achieve equal effectiveness in government or in a different business field.[11] Jack Welch, the tough-minded CEO of General Electric, attributes his success to his "characteristics for good chemistry at GE." Welch also quickly points out that he would feel like someone with two left feet trying to manage some of GE's businesses, so he relies on managers who can "lead their own parades."[12]

No one doubts an *association* of many traits with effective leaders, and certain characteristics, such as intelligence or self-assurance, may be important for success. Still, little evidence identifies individual traits as *causal factors* in successful leadership. A person rich in preferred traits may not necessarily become an effective leader. Some research suggests the opposite possibility—successful leaders who may have learned how to become decisive or competent decision makers, rather than succeeding because they started out with those characteristics.[13] The main problem with the trait approach is its exclusionary tendency. It attempts to identify individuals with specific personal characteristics and exclude others who lack those characteristics. Efforts to avoid excluding potentially effective leaders result in an ever-widening range of characteristics to consider (or situations to help explain a connection). This interpretation stretches the concept of a trait so far that little meaning remains.

Despite such theoretical drawbacks, the trait approach surfaces in almost every culture, yet attributions of desirable characteristics differ widely among cultures. In societies high in masculinity, for example, people associate leadership roles with male behavior such as decisiveness and assertiveness. In contrast, less masculine societies value conciliatory behavior in leaders, which allows them to create harmonious work environments. Hofstede's work on cross-cultural values, described in Chapter 8, illustrated these contrasts. His research also revealed that societies with high tolerance for power distance (a proclivity for maintaining systems of inequalities and status differences) tend to value power linked to social positions, often supporting paternalistic leadership traits. Although little research has specifically targeted cross-cultural comparisons of leadership traits, some studies have suggested that while all societies have developed a sense of what traits are important to them, these conclusions vary significantly across cultures.[14]

The Style Approach

Following Stogdill's criticism of the trait approach in 1948, management scholars began to define leadership according to *patterns of behavior*. These patterns were labeled **styles** as a shorthand code for describing actions through which effective leaders influence the behavior of their subordinates. The foundation research behind this movement was the Ohio State studies published during the 1950s.[15] In evaluating successful leadership behavior, researchers recognized a clustering of results along two dimensions. The first dimension was *consideration*, or the extent to which leaders influenced behavior through camaraderie, mutual trust, and respectful relationships with their subordinates. The second dimension was *initiating structure*, or the degree to which leaders influenced behavior by structuring work content, scheduling, controlling activities, and defining role responsibilities.

The Ohio State researchers identified consideration and initiating structure as separate sets of variables, not two dimensions along a single continuum. Consequently, a leader's behavior could be defined in four ways: high on both factors, low on both, low on consideration and high on initiating structure, or high on consideration and low on initiating structure. Obvious profiles emerged from these descriptions. In one, a leader might abdicate the responsibility to structure work and display neither consideration nor effective control. Another theoretical profile identifies a leader capable of tremendous control and extreme consideration. Two more would include leaders who relied either on considerate relationships or control systems to guide their followers. These relationships are shown in Figure 15.1 as a general model for understanding the style approach.

FIGURE 15.1
A Basic Model of
Leadership Styles

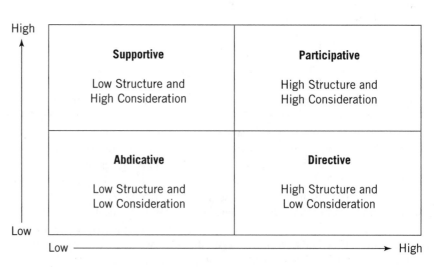

The Ohio State studies set in motion a great deal of research on leadership behavior by rejecting the born-to-lead presumption of the trait approach. New possibilities emerged when theorists defined leadership behavior as an attribute that could be learned. Leaders could develop styles in concert with organizational expectations. Rensis Likert introduced his **System 4** model to explain styles in terms of procedures by which managers make decisions.[16] At one extreme (System 1), managers make autocratic decisions and employ exploitative techniques in top-down directive relationships with their subordinates. At the other extreme (System 4), managers seek full participation with employees to forge consensus decisions. Between the extremes, managers could display decision-making behavior labeled in somewhat controlling (System 2) or rather consultative (System 3) categories. These four points were quite similar in concept to the Ohio State model.

Robert Blake and Jane Mouton established their *managerial grid* model as a more complex extension of the Ohio State model, plotting leadership styles along a one-to-nine scale for each of two dimensions—*relations-oriented* and *task-oriented* behavior.[17] The model implied an obvious ideal of a nine-nine style, maximizing attention to both relations and tasks. Likert's System 4 and the Ohio State model drew similar conclusions. All three approaches and subsequent refinements have been attractive to western managers (U.S. managers in particular), because they are grounded in democratic values. Specifically, the concepts of participation, employee involvement, team building, and consensus decisions "feel right" to members of western cultures. They accommodate human tendencies and consideration. In contrast, the concepts of control, structured tasks, unilateral decision-making, and directive behavior cause a certain degree of discomfort.

The viability of the style approach to leadership, however, is based on results. Theorists suggested that participative or democratic styles would generate systematically better performance and greater job satisfaction than other alternatives. In fact, most research has found reasonably high correlations between the favored leadership styles and performance results; however, the studies have not supplied data strong enough to conclusively endorse any of the models.

One problem has been causality. A high correlation between variables does not establish a cause-and-effect relationship. If research could establish cause-and-effect links between management behavior and results, then one ideal approach to leadership could be prescribed in a universally euphoric environment. However, equally plausible arguments support the opposite of the assumed causal relationship. Specifically, researchers have found that performance often dictates leadership style rather than the reverse. For example, when a company experiences difficulties in productivity or with underperforming employees, management often initiates a more rigid structure; more controls are emphasized with closer supervision. When operations are going well—productivity is up and employees feel challenged—managers can relax controls and adopt more conciliatory patterns of behavior. Another problem is that the style approach assumes that managers consciously choose how they will behave. Research has not confirmed that managers have this capability and, if they did, whether they could assess a situation accurately enough to purposely select fitting leadership styles.[18]

Perhaps the strongest criticism of both the trait and style approaches is that neither considers *situational* variables.[19] In international management, this is a significant problem because neither approach can accommodate cultural differences such as work-related values, subordinate and superior expectations, assumptions of ethical conduct, and organizational culture. Cross-cultural research that has addressed leadership styles, such as work by Hofstede, strongly emphasizes the influence of culture on leadership. For example, Mexican employees appreciate considerate treatment, yet they are uncomfortable with participative methods that involve working in partnership with their superiors. In this authority-structured society, managers are expected to look, act, and behave as superiors. They are expected to make firm decisions and to establish unambiguous control systems ranging from specific job descriptions to rigid disciplinary rules. High in power distance, Mexican society contradicts the selectivity assumptions of a style approach.

Paradoxically, even in Japan where participative management is prevalent, an authoritative pattern to leadership is pronounced. Japanese leaders are expected to observe rank and status, to manage through well-articulated control systems, and to expect uncompromising loyalty by subordinates. Yet they also value group involvement and consensus decisions. This duality of behavior is consistent with Confucian values of social structure and conformity, but it perplexes outsiders.[20] Similarly, many societies disdain the fundamental concept of an effective leader who is strong, considerate, and able to motivate subordinates. Malaysian workers, for example, respect leaders who show religious devotion and humble or self-effacing characteristics yet who are confident in their superior social status roles; no one presumes that they must actively motivate employees or share decision-making authority.[21] In France, India, Saudi Arabia, Brazil, and many other countries, leadership status is associated to some degree with social class, not necessarily with behavior or performance. In Germany, leadership qualities lean toward the trait approach, with high respect for intellectual ability and decisiveness.[22]

The Contingency Approach

In an effort to account for situational variables, researchers adapted earlier models of leadership to establish **contingency theory.** Introduced by Fred Fiedler in 1967, this approach is based on the concept that no single leadership style works well in all situations. Further, because each manager develops a predominant style of behavior that is unlikely to change significantly, firms should match individuals with situations that suit their capabilities.[23] This statement does not mean that managers cannot adapt to circumstances, but that they are relatively predisposed to their own styles of leadership behavior. These predisposed styles may be highly successful in certain work environments yet disastrous in other situations.

Fiedler identified two familiar dimensions of leadership style—*leader-member relations* and *task structure*—to differentiate work environments; but he also included a third dimension called *position power.* This variable describes organizational culture, such as formal management hierarchies and patterns of expectations for decision-making behavior. Contingency theory represented an important advancement in leadership studies because it implicitly took into account differences in expectations for management behavior. Fiedler's work was controversial, however, and it suffered from inconsistencies. Critics also questioned the notion of matching managers with specific work environments and employee expectations.

Robert J. House and his associates expanded the contingency approach into a plausible model called the **path-goal theory,** based on the assumption that leaders can adapt their behavior to different situations.[24] A conceptual view of the path-goal theory is provided in Figure 15.2. Inextricably related to the expectancy theory of motivation, this model emphasizes people's desire to benefit from their efforts, leading them to assign probabilities (expectancies) that particular behavior will result in certain outcomes. If employees value these outcomes (rewards or avoidance of unpleasant

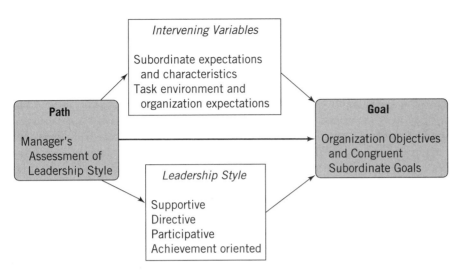

FIGURE 15.2
Conceptual View of Path-Goal Leadership

consequences) and if they confidently believe that they can achieve the desired results, then they will be strongly motivated to perform.

Recall from earlier presentations on motivation that expectancy theory also emphasizes the need that employees must have faith in the company's ability to fulfill their expectations. Path-goal theory is directly associated with this dimension of expectancy theory. It assumes that leaders can adapt their behavior in concert with employee expectations and then build on an understanding of the goals that are important to employees to facilitate progress toward those goals and compatible company objectives. Leaders therefore constructively intervene to remove roadblocks, offer support, provide resources, and personally supervise work in a way that smoothes the path toward goals.

House and his colleagues proposed four general patterns of leadership behavior.[25] *Supportive leadership* works well, they asserted, for tedious or boring jobs. In these situations, workers expect managers to enhance the work environments through personal, friendly associations. *Directive leadership* would work best in unstructured work environments where employees expect close supervision and are willing to accept direct oversight. *Participative leadership* emphasizes team building. This would work well in an unstructured and ambiguous work environment and for tedious or unpleasant tasks. Finally, *achievement-oriented leadership* would be advantageous in an uncertain environment with nonrepetitive tasks. Achievement criteria also assume that employees expect to be challenged and can accept responsibilities. The path-goal model has attracted substantial support, but researchers have not yet clearly distinguished among the four categories of behavior or verified that adherence to the model improves performance.

Another model associated with contingency concepts is a rational expectations theory of Victor Vroom and Phillip Yetton. These theorists brought together the expectations formula and Likert's System 4 approach to decision-making.[26] Vroom and Yetton also reversed the cause-and-effect relationship proposed by the style theorists to suggest that leadership style does not determine decision-making patterns; instead, the nature of decisions influences choices of decision-making behavior. Consequently, subordinate expectations coupled with situational variables (such as task structures or stress levels of work) dictate the extent of autocratic, controlling, consultative, or participative management. Vroom and Yetton rely on quantification of their variables, and little subsequent research has attempted to validate or refute their contentions.

A final model to consider is the **life cycle theory** put forward by Paul Hersey and Kenneth Blanchard.[27] Like other contingency models and mainstream style approaches, it proposes four patterns of leadership behavior—*telling, selling, participating,* and *delegating.* These are arranged along a continuum, and each of these approaches depends on the maturity of subordinates. By *maturity,* Hersey and Blanchard mean the composite profile of a work group that takes into account their job abilities, skills, experience, and confidence to perform tasks. It also includes their collective willingness to assume task responsibilities. At one extreme, an immature work group may be composed of young or inexperienced employees (perhaps unskilled workers) with little desire to participate in decisions or to assume responsibility for directing their own work. They expect managers to tell them what to do and how to do it. At the mature extreme, skilled and experienced workers know their jobs well and are likely to feel comfortable with little supervision. Indeed, they may resent detailed instructions and instead may expect to be responsible for their work. Unfortunately, the life cycle model does not take into account other important situational variables, such as the task environment, authority structures, or problems such as mixed work groups made up of employees with diverse interests or a wide range of capabilities.

Contingency theories have serious shortcomings, but they are important to international managers as a way of thinking adaptively about their assignments. Instead of stereotyping leaders (or followers) according to personal traits, contingency theories encourage managers to study employee expectations in the context of their work environments and organizational cultures. International managers may not be able to quantify expectations or to clearly assess work-group maturity, but they can conscientiously judge how employees perceive their leadership behavior.

The models all reflect distinctly U.S. foundations, yet that identity does not detract from their usefulness for understanding the psyches that drive employee expectations and performance in other societies. Unfortunately, none of the contingency models directly accommodates cross-cultural variables such as work-related values, social philosophies, or religious beliefs. They also fail to account for cultural dimensions. Therefore, as western concepts, they have limited appeal in pluralistic and Confucian societies. The most important criticism is that global companies cannot adopt these models for universal application or as guidelines for management development. Multinationals must manage in widely diversified societies with complicated multicultural environments. Any prescriptive model that advocates a particular set of traits, a specific style, or a single contingency framework will have limited value.

TRANSFORMATIONAL LEADERSHIP

More than four decades of intense research on leadership have produced a series of theories and models that entirely satisfy no one. **Transformational leadership** is not meant to be another theory, but instead, a different way of thinking about leadership. This concept asserts that effective leaders need the ability to make *profound changes* in their organizations, to introduce new *visions,* and to *inspire people to become part of the leadership process itself.*[28] This focus incorporates the fundamental idea that an entire group or an organization can be responsible for its own leadership. Within this environment, managers act as catalysts of change who not only create the vision but also ensure a common commitment to pursue that vision.

Vision and Commitment

Transformational leadership is a process of forming a vision, evoking commitment to that vision, and then ensuring that everyone becomes part of the process to achieve the vision. The term *transforming leadership* was coined by James McGregor Burns in 1978 as part of an effort to refute existing leadership theories, which he criticized as "transaction-bound" failures.[29] Indeed, nearly every statement about motivation and leadership mentioned in this chapter has emphasized transactional responsibilities narrowly concerned with daily management of resources or incremental changes in performance. Advocates of a transformational viewpoint argue that management and leadership have been misdirected.[30] They point out that throughout history, the world's most revered leaders have made exceptional changes in human endeavor; in an organizational sense, they have often reinvented meanings for people and for work itself. Thomas Watson Jr. (IBM), Jack Welch (GE), Sam Walton (Wal-Mart), Jan Carlzon (Scandinavian Airlines), and Akio Morita (Sony) are conspicuous for their international reputations as transformational leaders.

On a grander scale, people regard leaders such as Nelson Mandela, Winston Churchill, and Martin Luther King Jr. with awe, and the list could also include other visionaries, such as Mother Teresa and Mohandas Gandhi. These are people whose deeds and philosophies of leadership transcend time and borders, yet many individuals go unnoticed by the world while displaying similar attributes and earning similar respect from their colleagues or employees. They are not CEOs, Nobel laureates, or political leaders, but supervisors, team leaders, and informal group leaders whose inspiration binds organizations together. These bonds often develop as a result of the leader's charisma.

Charismatic Leadership

The term *charismatic leadership* has become synonymous with *transformational leadership;* together they are considered as founding concepts of the new leadership premise.

John T. Chambers, CEO of Cisco Systems, has become one of the few executives to gain global recognition as a transformational leader. He has a reputation for strict rules and no-nonsense behavior, yet he is charismatic and ethical to a fault. He built Cisco Systems through a vision of innovative alliances and world markets and has demonstrated an unswerving commitment to ensure that Cisco is a model organization of inspired leadership. Indeed, Cisco was second only to GE on *Fortune*'s annual list of "America's Most Admired Companies" at the beginning of 2001. Chambers was cited for his "tireless innovation" and for creating a company that "continues to reinvent itself."

As mentioned earlier, however, the concepts are hardly new ones. Max Weber wrote extensively about charisma during the first few decades of the century, advocating leadership that could inspire "consequential" changes rather than maintenance of the status quo.[31] Robert House, known for the path-goal theory, also wrote energetically during the 1970s about the need for charismatic leaders who could communicate visions of high achievements and weld organizations together in unified pursuit of "transcendent" goals.[32] Bernard Bass, who is usually associated with research on trait theories and Stogdill's behavioral models, spoke of transformational team endeavors guided by leaders capable of "getting us to transcend our own self-interests" to collectively accomplish things beyond individual imagination.[33] He emphasized that transformational leaders raise people's aspirations to higher-order needs.

Based on their studies of the sociology of organizations, British scholars in Manchester, England, have concluded that transformational leadership and charismatic leadership are universal concepts that people have forgotten in an effort to create menu-driven leadership styles. These styles, they say, suggest contingent results and a how-to approach to management that implies an ability to select behavior that yields administrative efficiencies rather than dynamic changes.[34] Hofstede from the Netherlands, Kets de Vries from INSEAD, and Laurant from France also ascribe a universal and timeless character to transformational concepts, but they worry that organizations and their members have become mired in "prodding and detached" models of leadership.[35] A British observer concluded recently that successful endeavors launched by farsighted leaders are inevitably taken over by managers whose vested interests in preserving the past ensure that they hasten the demise of their organizations.[36]

Historically, the giants of industry have been transformational leaders capable of mobilizing their organizations to pursue new dreams. Some have been entrepreneurs, but more of them have acted as charismatic organizational leaders inducing performance through group loyalties and individual allegiances; such an individual steps forward to set a new cadence. In many instances a person may be thrust into a leadership role by employees who sense leadership capabilities and willingly subordinate themselves. To succeed, the transformational leader must satisfy three requirements. First, he or she must establish a vision of the future that defines a shared purpose within the organization. Then, the leader must clearly understand the organization's current vision, if it has one, to become the catalyst for empowering the organization to transcend the present and achieve future goals. And finally, the transformational leader must sustain the inspiration and energy necessary to achieve those goals.[37] Figure 15.3 identifies the patterns of thinking associated with these three elements of transformational leadership.

FIGURE 15.3
Elements of
Transformational
Leadership

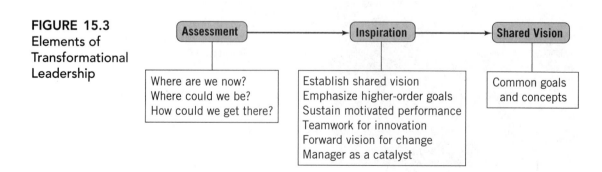

No one should be surprised that the so-called *new leadership* premise is firmly rooted in team management concepts. It is implemented through continuous involvement of everyone in many little activities that, combined, transform an organization. The concept of total quality management, for example, sometimes faddishly implemented as a quick fix for specific problems, is nonetheless a fundamentally sound vision of organizational purpose. Efforts to differentiate companies by aspiring to goals of continuous quality improvement have substantially redefined the concepts of competition and business ethics. Reengineering, another idea sometimes used to mask cost-driven downsizing, has also legitimately urged managers to rethink the fundamental purposes, processes, and behaviors behind their endeavors.[38] Jack Welch has gone through the GE organization in this way. He has sold divisions, downsized operations, divested entire lines of business, bought into new alliances worldwide, created team-based group processes, and ripped down hierarchical organization charts, replacing them with "relational maps." His transformational leadership has repositioned the company in potentially high-growth industries for the twenty-first century. Indeed, GE has orchestrated all of its management activities in earnest pursuit of visionary changes.[39]

Transformational leadership is unable to provide specific guidelines for effective leadership activities. It is a unified concept that defines leadership within the social context of organizational activities. No one can say specifically that one situation calls for telling employees what to do rather than letting them make their own decisions. Charismatic and transformational leadership are not based on deductive "if this, then that" reasoning. Consequently, research cannot be easily structured to evaluate transformational leadership or to measure its efforts or performance. Some studies offer evidence from personal profiles or executive interviews to reveal some patterns of common success factors.[40] These studies give enlightening guidance, but they also tend to supply only ambiguous suggestions. Perhaps the studies are more notable for what they have not found. Apparently, no cultural, ethnic, racial, gender, or physical similarities characterize transformational leaders. Mother Teresa, Akio Morita, Jack Welch, Jan Carlzon, Mohandas Gandhi, and Martin Luther King Jr. share few common traits. It is not something fixed in western values or unique to western cultures.

Subordinate Expectations

Expectations of subordinates are important because they influence leadership behavior. Hofstede emphasized throughout his research that he was studying employee attitudes toward leadership, not managerial behavior. His research on work-related values implicitly questioned perceptions of how managers and employees believed leaders should behave within their particular cultures. He suggested, however, that leadership was really about *subordinateship*, or the relationship of employees to their superiors.[41] Transformational leadership complements this bottom-up flow of influence, and the central theme of charismatic leadership builds solidly on perceptions and expectations of subordinates. This relationship is illustrated by a somewhat tongue-in-cheek explanation of a charismatic leader: "If a man runs down the street proclaiming that he alone can save others from impending doom, and if he immediately wins a following, then he is a charismatic leader. If he does not win a following, he is simply a lunatic."[42]

The cultural dimensions of work-related values described by Hofstede clearly reflect subordinate expectations.[43] One of his four dimensions described in Chapter 8 was individualism, or more accurately a continuum between individualism and collectivism. Highly individualistic cultures, notably the United States, Canada, and the United Kingdom, were shown to share a strong preference for independent decision-making.

These Anglo countries also scored low on power distance, suggesting less importance attached to status and rank. This contrast in values results in an interesting dilemma because low power distance is associated with cultures well suited for participative leadership methods, yet individualism emphasizes independent leadership roles. In practice, the strength of individualism often simply outweighs other considerations. Therefore, when compared to other societies low in power distance, such as Scandinavian countries, people from Anglo countries are less likely to prefer participative leadership techniques.

In contrast to the Anglo cultures, Malaysia, Mexico, and Indonesia show very high power distance. Even though they also display low individualism, their cultures emphasize status differentials and tightly structured authority systems. Consequently, subordinates are not accustomed to group decision-making or participative leadership, despite their tendency toward collectivity. Employees in Mexico, Malaysia, and Indonesia all work well together *within their social strata*, but expectations for leadership behavior favor more autocratic methods and maintenance of large power distances. Similar clusters of expectations and values have emerged in almost all studies to validate differences in subordinate expectations and therefore in perceptions of appropriate behavior for those in leadership roles.[44]

This conclusion is reinforced by values associated with Hofstede's dimension of uncertainty avoidance. Mexico scored relatively high on uncertainty avoidance, meaning that people there feel uncomfortable with ambiguity; they prefer explicit statements and policies. Employees expect to work under clear job descriptions, and they are comfortable carrying out specific directions from management. This tendency coincides with their high score on power distance, reinforcing a strong signal to international managers in Mexico: Expect to maintain status differentials, give clear directions, and avoid relying on employees to pursue goals on their own. This summary may oversimplify the situation, but such a general guideline is useful if managers accept power differentials in a patronage environment. They must take command positions but carefully avoid abusing their responsibilities as superiors.

In contrast, Malaysian and Indonesian societies scored high on power distance (as Mexico did), but the Asian societies also scored rather low on uncertainty avoidance. These results suggest that employees in these Asian cultures feel comfortable with a certain degree of ambiguity. People do not expect managers to devote as much effort to spelling out responsibilities. Indeed, job descriptions in these Asian societies seldom lay out clear duties, and employees do not always follow directions or observe rules. Ironically, these cultures value authority and status, yet managers often hesitate to specifically tell employees what they should or should not do. By comparison, in the United States, Canada, and the United Kingdom, all with relatively low uncertainty avoidance, people can deal with a certain degree of ambiguity. Ironically, job descriptions, work rules, and procedures often are articulated clearly in all these countries. Directive styles of leadership are not easily accepted in Anglo cultures, yet when compared with cultures with similar high tolerances for ambiguity, such as Sweden, Denmark, Singapore, and Hong Kong, the Anglo cultures seem rather rigid in their preferences for rules and directives.

Hofstede's fourth dimension of masculinity, which measures behavior associated with male characteristics such as decisiveness and dominance, remains somewhat controversial in this situation. Mexico scores high on masculinity, reinforcing the concept of a strong system of structured authority, but its culture emphasizes the value of a subordinate's personal allegiances. This tendency amplifies the role of charismatic leaders. Indonesia and Malaysia, however, do not score high on masculinity, suggesting that employees in these cultures would feel comfortable with conciliatory group processes. Theory suggests that they should expect leaders to help them nourish relationships and build social ties. In fact, research has supported these conclusions, but because both cultures also exhibit high power distance, relationships and social ties remain limited within social strata; managers and employees observe proprieties between rank and status levels, but they attempt to do so in a congenial manner.[45] U.S., Canadian, and British cultures fall near the middle of the scale on masculinity (although slightly skewed toward the high end). Clearly, leaders in each of these countries favor masculine characteristics, especially in relation to examples from the Nordic countries, yet it would be misleading to suggest that they are prone to machismo such as that observed in Mexico or Japan.

Comparisons such as these reveal that *cultural contingencies* mold subordinate perceptions of values related to leadership behavior. In turn, differences in subordinate expectations influence leaders to behave in certain ways in order to inspire employees to pursue performance goals. Therefore, participation—or even subtle concessions toward consultative management—will produce little effect in many countries. In some instances, any leadership gesture with less than explicit direction will meet with ridicule or cynicism.[46] The "Global Viewpoint" feature describes several additional contrasts in subordinate expectations.

LEADERSHIP IN A CROSS-CULTURAL CONTEXT

Leadership has meaning only in an organizational context, and only in the sense of managing within a system of inequalities. Superior-subordinate relationships help to define leadership behavior, and the culture in any particular society influences the nature of these relationships. Two leadership roles are common to all societies, however. The first is the **charismatic role,** or the capability to provide vision and inspiration. This is emphasized by transformational leadership concepts. The second is the **instrumental role,** or the capability to design effective organizational processes, control activities, and meet organizational objectives. This describes the functional expectations of someone in a leadership role. However, each society determines the relative importance of each role and therefore what makes a good leader.[47]

Cross-cultural research has identified a pattern of characteristics common to effective leaders in these two roles, but these commonalities do not constitute shared traits. They include

- *Conscientiousness* Dependability, achievement orientation, and perseverance within the scope of one's responsibilities
- *Extroversion* Open, accessible attitude, as opposed to remaining insulated from group activities
- *Dominance* Appropriate use of authority in a system of inequalities
- *Self-confidence* Comfort in one's own skills and abilities for managing

Recent research has also suggested that regardless of cultural contingencies, effective leaders tend to display *intelligence, energy, emotional stability*, and *openness to experience*. In the international context, this last characteristic encourages cultural sensitivity without ethnocentric imposition.[48] Because each society assigns unique meanings for most of these characteristics, their importance varies in all societies. For example, mainland Chinese people agree with those in the United States that perseverance is an essential attribute of a conscientious manager, but the two societies do

GLOBAL VIEWPOINT

COLGATE-PALMOLIVE—INCENTIVE LEADERSHIP WORLDWIDE

For several years now, Colgate-Palmolive has focused on recognizing employees who demonstrate unusual leadership through hands-on results. The program, called You Can Make a Difference, brings winners from around the world to New York for ceremonies to honor their achievements. Management doesn't quibble over expenses, and participants arrive in style, stay at the Waldorf-Astoria, dine like royalty, and rub elbows frequently with CP's chairperson, senior executives, guest dignitaries, and other program celebrities from dozens of countries. This treatment can be an extraordinary experience for someone from a rural Brazilian plant or a quiet Thai village who has never ventured more than a few miles from home. Honorees return from the ceremonies carrying customized gold medallions, blazers, award letters, and memories for life of trips to the famed Rainbow Room, Ellis Island, and the Bronx Zoo. They tell colleagues about lunches at Planet Hollywood or the Hard Rock Cafe, evenings out at Broadway plays, or attending Mets or Yankees baseball games. In addition, they take home CP stock worth $1,000.

The company's program manager, Michele Macchia, was named "Motivator of the Year" in 1996 by *Incentive Magazine* for her unusual work with foreign managers. As she explains it, the program is not just a new twist on handing out company kudos to motivate employees; it is a method of empowering all staff members at every level to provide the inspirational leadership appropriate for their people and their particular work environments. A Kenyan employee was honored because he inspired others through his community volunteer efforts. Leading by example and charisma, a moral dimension, was recognized for its cohesive effect on the workforce in Kenya. A seven-

time winner from Italy was given a "global award" for leadership qualities; he was nominated and supported by subordinates in a groundswell of enthusiasm. An Indonesian participant was noted for his strength and command responsibilities—not an expected profile in many countries, but an important one to the Indonesians. A Thai team award recognized simple acts of kindness that were uncommon and had uncommon effects. A local operation provided workers with their own rice pots and quality rice at company expense. This paternal gesture in a hierarchical society coupled with other small gestures created a team spirit that transformed the entire subsidiary.

Leadership activities that resulted in the awards showed no more similarity than the dozens of languages spoken by the participants. Ceremonies held three times a year have produced a winners list as diverse as the United Nations. The company hires almost as many interpreters as it has guests, and each award is described in the context of the contribution made by the person or team honored. Often, people from other cultures listening to an award presentation cannot understand the unusual character of the acts it honors. Some individuals are recognized for their team-building efforts, some as patrons to their employees, many for their independent initiative, others for their benevolence, and still others for compassion, humility, strength, command abilities, or ethics. Colgate-Palmolive does not keep score, and it intentionally disregards theories, believing that effective leadership begins in the hearts of those involved.

Source: Judy Quinn, "Motivators of the Year," *Incentive Magazine*, January 1996, 26–30.

not interpret achievement in the same way; unlike Americans, the Chinese ascribe little value to individual success. Other terms, such as *dominance*, carry value-loaded and controversial meanings, but the root meaning of accepting the mantle of leadership is worldwide.[49]

In confronting such shared attitudes, researchers have focused on how leadership roles vary across cultures and how these characteristics of leadership behavior are interpreted abroad. As this section reviews examples, bear in mind that cross-cultural research is seldom meant to epitomize one cultural pattern of leadership as superior to others (although biases prevail); instead, researchers try to illustrate differences that can help international managers to function effectively in foreign societies.

Variations in European Leadership Behavior

Countries in Europe have made significant progress toward consolidating the European Union (EU), but many unresolved issues remain. Not least among EU problems is the difficulty of managing multicultural organizations within the region. Although EU unification of commercial regulations and labor laws has dominated government and company agendas, the activities of leading companies in this complicated environment have received little attention. The obvious question is whether a common European leadership approach will emerge from the economic union, or whether leadership practices will remain culturally bound to each nation. One group of observers expects that as Europe's nations converge economically, a hybrid form of leadership will replace individual cultural practices. An opposed group asserts that cultural values are so ingrained that any effort to consolidate management practices will meet strong resistance. They firmly believe that leadership behavior will remain differentiated in each nation. From a U.S. perspective, it is easy to speak of "European methods" as some common stream of consciousness, but research in Europe leaves no doubt that leadership behavior varies substantially among the individual countries. A recent study at Ashridge Management College in the United Kingdom surveyed senior managers in 14 European countries to compare leadership behavior and concluded:

> Such is the cultural diversity of Europe, that at this moment there is no single model or theory of leadership which is capable of taking into account the complete range of national values. . . . Leadership as a concept is either not as salient as it is in the United States, or, it occurs but within different paradigmatic boundaries. Clearly, it is not as "romanticized" in Europe as in American cultural life.[50]

The Ashridge study found vast differences in perspectives among European countries. At one end of the spectrum, managers from France nearly unanimously defined leadership and management as the same thing. Those from Belgium concurred, but with a somewhat less unified voice. Respondents from these countries viewed managers as leaders by the rights and responsibilities inherent in their positions. Managers, they suggested, hold their positions because they are capable of leading; although some fail and some outperform others, leadership qualities generally emerge in individuals as they assume management responsibilities.

At the other end of the spectrum, managers from Denmark and Finland described leadership as a reflection of trust and confidence afforded by subordinates to those in *stewardship* roles. A manager earns the right to lead as subordinates recognize his or her capabilities to energize an organization. German respondents emphasized the foundations of leadership roles in technical expertise, not positional power or relational skills. To them, leadership is the intelligent use of knowledge and experience to guide organizational activities. Spanish and Portuguese managers, however, described leaders as their organizations' reservoirs of strength; benevolent in their behavior, effective leaders adopt protective attitudes toward their charges, yet remain steadfast in their authority. Leaders, they say, must be moral people involved emotionally with their followers to build relationships. They must also be trustworthy, so that they can direct their people toward effective completion of the right tasks.

The Ashridge study suggested a rough structure of four types of behavior within Europe. In northern Europe, a sense of group endeavor emerges from leadership associated with subordinate acceptance; leaders act as stewards and facilitators, but not as paternalistic overlords. In the Latin nations of southern Europe and to some extent in Greece, managers favor a hierarchical approach to leadership based on charisma and, more important, on "benevolent authority" and **paternalism.** In Germanic and Anglo countries, leadership emphasizes formal skills and intellectual capabilities, but also the ability to form consultative relationships with employees without resorting to directive or paternalistic behavior. France seemed to stand alone, entrenched in the concept that leadership flows as a natural extension of a pyramid of authority; leadership is a responsibility carried out at a distance from subordinates and in ways commensurate with management rights.[51] Comparisons of attitudes such as these across cultures leave little evidence of something like European management.

Another important study conducted during the 1960s, now rather dated, surveyed 3,641 managers across 14 countries on a variety of leadership criteria.[52] The researchers found that nearly all respondents endorsed concepts of participation and shared governance, but in practice their behavior spanned a wide range: highly authoritarian attitudes in France, less authoritarian but work-centered preferences in Germany, benevolent but dictatorial tendencies in Italy and Spain, consultative postures (but not significantly participative ones) in the United Kingdom and the Netherlands, and highly participative practices in Scandinavian countries. The study compared the United States to the United Kingdom in its proclivity for consideration of others, but U.S. managers still were seen to rely heavily on individual initiative. The researchers found that autocratic systems prevailed in Argentina, Chile, and India, but subordinates expected "inspirational" guidance, creating a paternalistic profile similar to that of Latin Europe.

Results of these early studies are not significantly different from those of more recent Ashridge research, although contemporary explanations of leadership behavior are better understood after three decades of investigation. These and other studies support a similar conclusion: Even after major changes brought about by the EU's Single Market Initiative, leadership behavior within each of the European cultures has not changed significantly in a very long time. Nevertheless, unification in Europe will force managers to find a way of managing that is compatible in many countries. Because labor can now cross borders with little constraint and because European companies are becoming more involved in regional alliances, managers who lead these organizations must adapt to a single, composite multicultural environment.[53]

A further explanation of differences in leadership practices throughout Europe was recently offered by Fons Trompenaars, who identified four distinct approaches to management.[54] He characterized the first as a *Family* model, organized around a power orientation in which the leader is regarded as a "caring father" or *patron*. Research consistently identifies this model with Latin countries in Europe and the Americas. The second model, which Trompenaars called *Eiffel Tower*, was explained as a formal, depersonalized organizational culture with pervasive rules and procedures. Leaders must therefore enforce rules and command through hierarchical channels. These patterns of behavior were ascribed to German and Austrian managers. A third model, called a *Guided Missile* approach, was typical of behavior in the United States and the United Kingdom. It was characterized by a task-oriented culture in which leaders emphasize performance and objectives, but not necessarily in autocratic commands—an important condition. Within such a system, a leader could achieve results through project teams or more conventional superior-subordinate relationships by showing measured concern for the individuals involved. Trompenaars labeled his fourth model as an *Incubator* approach to signify a sense of nurturing, innovation, and intellectual response to new ideas through participative, democratic styles of leadership. He suggested that leadership behavior in Sweden closely reflected many of these characteristics.

Trompenaars's descriptions seem to favor stereotypes, and some have criticized his research methods. Still, the four-category approach provided a useful tool for a major British research study by the Cranfield School of Management. Cranfield researchers developed profiles of more than 2,500 European executives over a period of six years.[55] This study was rigorously controlled through interviews, internal company investigations, and validation procedures to evaluate differences in management styles. The results correlated rather well with Trompenaars's and Hofstede's research, leading to the four categories shown in Table 15.1.

The Cranfield leadership categories provide descriptive labels for managerial behavior commonly associated with countries in Europe. In the *Leadership by Consensus* style typical of Sweden (and to a lesser degree in Finland), employees and managers valued teamwork and open dialogue. The study's Nordic participants emphasized a high regard for efficiency and organizational stability, expecting organization members to adhere to procedures without sacrificing participation to achieve efficiency.

TABLE 15.1

MANAGEMENT STYLES: A EUROPEAN VIEW

Model of Leadership Behavior	Location of Emphasis
Leadership by Consensus Emphasis on participation and team effort Open dialogue Self-discipline in activities Consensual decision making	Nordic cultures
Leadership toward a Common Goal Emphasis on authority in disciplined systems Reliance on functional expertise Clear roles and responsibilities Identity with controls	Germanic cultures
Leading from the Front Emphasis on charisma in leaders Reliance on manager's abilities Avoidance of rules and procedures Benevolent dominance	Latin cultures
Managing from a Distance Emphasis on authority, rank, and status differentials Pursuit of personal agendas Little vertical communication Ambiguity in relationships and roles	French culture

Source: Adapted from Andrew Myers, Andrew Kakbadse, Tim McMahon, and Gilles Spony, "Top Management Styles in Europe: Implications for Business and Cross-National Teams," *European Business Journal* 7, no. 1 (1995): 21.

The study also revealed that although this profile fit approximately 50 percent of the companies studied in Sweden and Finland, the stereotype tends to obscure the lack of universal consensus on team processes. Some firms featured quite hierarchical leadership styles (more often in Finland than in Sweden), and some managers favored directive or consultative approaches with relatively little participation. This variation was explained in part by industry characteristics as well as the influence of multinational alliances with Anglo or Germanic interests.

The style called *Leadership toward a Common Goal* typified German and Austrian behavior. In these countries, respectively, 84 percent and 79 percent of the respondents agreed that decisions should remain in the hands of managers within hierarchical systems of controls. However, these respondents identified leaders as those who had earned their positions and rights to leadership through functional and technical expertise, not longevity, birthright, or social status. Consequently, the profile of a leader in these cultures emphasizes authority to command from a position of demonstrated capability, bringing the organization together to achieve well-defined goals.

The category *Leading from the Front* described cultural values of individual initiative, charisma, and self-motivated behavior. The researchers had some difficulty explaining respondents' tendencies to favor dominance in their positions, noting that the concept of dominance itself had different meanings in Anglo and Latin countries. Nearly 74 percent of the Spanish respondents, for example, fit the criteria for this category, including dominance defined as hierarchical rigor legitimized by benevolent paternalism. In contrast, 73 percent of the British managers also reflected these characteristics, but for them dominance carried a connotation of accountability for decisions within a range of acceptance by subordinates based on instrumental role responsibilities.

The final category of *Managing from a Distance* was unique to France. Approximately 83 percent of the French managers endorsed concepts of high power distance (separation by rank and status), command environments with little regard for subordinate participation. They also preferred ambiguity that would allow managers to pursue their own agendas with minimal constraints imposed by organizational rules, procedures, and control systems.

The results of these European studies forewarn of potential collisions between managers from different cultures who might find themselves working together in a consolidated European organization. The Cranfield researchers identified several dramatic cases in which managers could not reconcile their differences. For example, in one British-German alliance, the British staff members felt frustrated by German expectations for rigorous job descriptions and narrowly defined authority for decisions. Meanwhile, the Germans were equally frustrated by the British willingness to delegate authority freely and to make decisions through informal methods. Germans and Swedes in another merged company ran into difficulties over employee participation. Although German social legislation requires companies to invite employees to participate in works councils and board meetings, few German managers enthusiastically included subordinates in meetings, and they were not always open to dialogue with subordinates.

The Cranfield researchers concluded that European firms do not practice representative styles of leadership. In spite of European unification, no evidence suggests a likely convergence of leadership behavior. Instead, the continent features at least four clusters of behavior, each with similarities among several countries. Further, each country in the cluster carefully guards its managerial prerogatives. Nevertheless, the researchers also concluded that although the process will be a slow one, the proliferation of cross-national teams will eventually require European managers to accommodate one another's differences.

Central and Eastern Europe

Many conflicts seen in Western Europe are magnified by including Central and Eastern European enterprises. Although not formally defined as a region, Central Europe includes the Czech Republic, Poland, Slovakia, Hungary, Slovenia, and the Baltic states of Estonia, Latvia, and Lithuania. Eastern Europe includes the Commonwealth of Independent States (CIS), Romania, Bulgaria, Albania, and five nations independently established from the former Yugoslavia. Obviously, the region spans several disputed territories, and some definitions incorporate border states such as Belarus and Ukraine. The CIS alone encompasses 14 internal states that do not entirely agree on the terms of their participation in the CIS. Although many observers refer to these entities collectively as *Russia*, that label is inaccurate, even if a convenience.

Virtually all of these countries must manage rapidly expanding trade relations with partners in Western Europe, Asia, and North America. They represent at least 28 distinct cultures and a combined population that rivals those of North America or Western Europe. The countries of Central and Eastern Europe share the common experience of emerging from communism, but few share comparable histories. Each country has its distinct ethnic roots, languages, and cultures, and often regions within its borders vary among themselves. Some evolved from feudal systems or autocratic kingdoms, others were early satellites of the Austrian-Hungarian Empire, and still others sprang from Latin cultures dating to the Roman era. Only a few developed from democratic societies. Before their subjugation under communism, several countries had built thriving industrial and trade economies, and prior to World War I most enjoyed infrastructural resources, educational systems, and social systems not unlike those of Western Europe.[56]

These are not countries that have suddenly emerged from the Dark Ages. Their peoples recall rich heritages of cultural and linguistic diversity, but several generations of communist domination ensured that all but the youngest employees and managers worked within tightly structured systems commanded through political and military interests. Individuals in nearly all walks of life became subservient to inflexible bureaucracies that stifled individual initiative. The collectivist mandate of the ideal communist state was intended to serve the welfare of workers. However, it was expressed in an extremely autocratic environment where people worked in collectives and bent to a conformist mentality. No one ever pursued individual initiatives or varied from the dictates of those in control.[57]

As a result, western multinationals involved in Eastern bloc countries have encountered severe difficulties with human resource management. Recent studies of companies from the United Kingdom, Germany, and the United States conclude that firms have "substantially underestimated cultural differences and their impact on the establishment of operations and the nature of the local workforce."[58] People who have been accustomed to taking orders, doing no more and no less than what they are told to do, find it difficult to accept responsibility for their own endeavors. For several generations, industrial managers have gained their positions through political appointments, maintaining allegiance to the party or state apparatus, not to their organizations or employees.

Although western executives find the people of these emergent countries enthusiastic to adopt new methods, these workers cannot merely discard old patterns of behavior. Most managers and nonmanagement employees still expect dominant leadership, directive decision-making, and central control of operating procedures. They are highly skeptical of participative processes or paternalistic gestures. In addition, host-country managers are extremely sensitive to expatriate intervention, which communicates a sense of colonialism. Ideological differences aside, local workers often resent outsiders who seem determined to impose their own brands of management.[59] These generalities, however, do not account for individual national cultures or their historic precedents. Leadership behavior that eventually works well in Hungary or the Czech Republic may be disastrous in Bulgaria or Poland.

The economies of Central and Eastern Europe promise to grow rapidly through substantial foreign investment and international alliances. Leadership is expected to evolve within unique management systems that coincide with distinct cultures, and although it is too early to suggest how these systems will develop, researchers agree that two general patterns of behavior are important to international managers. Generally, a sense of collectivism prevails throughout the region, but it is constrained by an autocratic psyche that undercuts individual initiative. Indeed, individual initiative retains a connotation of exploitation in many people's minds. As the same time, socialism has provided a legacy of collective effort that could become a cornerstone for rapid growth in new management systems.[60]

A Russian Profile

Leaders in the Russian federation face the difficult task of introducing sweeping economic, political, and social changes without provoking mass movements calling for restoration of the previous Soviet ideology. At the core of the change process is nearly 75 years of deeply rooted socialist doctrine and a rigid sociopolitical hierarchy exerting monopoly control over resources and the means of production. Until recently, only a select body of the Supreme Soviet or its appointees had authority to make substantive decisions. Today, however, Russia is attempting to denationalize its economy. The transformation is accompanied by a mandate to reposition companies as market-driven enterprises. Consequently, managers are gaining expanded responsibility for organizational performance. Managers are, in fact, expected to provide the impetus for transformation, an undertaking that requires a pervasive change in managerial values.[61]

The Russian people have experienced neither the freedom of individual endeavor nor responsibility for independent decision-making. Instead, they have become accustomed to suppressing their personal interests in favor of commitments to the collective welfare of the state. Unlike many Eastern European countries where some can recall precommunist practices, the Russian federation is making a unilateral effort to introduce an entirely new socioeconomic system based on private enterprise development. Unfortunately, this transformation must begin from an extraordinary network of monopolized industries under state control. Until recently, Russian managers had no experience in the priorities of competitive enterprises and no need to concern themselves with employee motivation or welfare. The state provided the decision-making framework, dictated reward structures and punishments, and allocated resources. The system provided employees with protected entitlements, and management practices reflected political priorities.[62]

On the positive side, Russian managers are generally well educated in scientific or engineering fields, and most have compiled intense organizational experience in their respective industries. A system of technical education in Russia has created a broad base of skills among most workers and craftspeople, and the country's military technocracy has generated highly capable specialists. Russian industry thus can rely on a sound human resource base and on an extensive educational system that will support future development. However, the process of managing private enterprises and the psyche of responsible leadership remain mysteries to most Russian managers.

By western standards, Russian managers have not yet grasped the concept of leadership apart from rigid, autocratic roles.[63] Specifically, a legacy remains of one-person leadership with unquestioned authority in an absolute chain of command. From an employee viewpoint, this system demands nothing but absolute compliance from subordinates. Managers under the communist regime felt ambivalent about accepting responsibility because superiors in the previous system allowed them no voice in larger matters. Indeed, subordinates often expected them to demand no more than passing on directives and quickly delegating responsibilities. Consequently, if something went wrong, a manager could easily point to a subordinate as the culprit. If their organizations lacked resources or support, they could look to superiors who controlled allocations. Achievement was expected, but available energy and support were channeled toward government or bureau priorities, not individual development. Ambition and initiative risked punishment or ridicule. Managers were expected to show self-confidence in making decisions, direct work toward efficiency goals, and demonstrate above-average intelligence. Over four generations, employees came to expect of leaders the same behavior that leaders expected of themselves, and the tsarist traditions that gave way to communism featured even more hierarchical and autocratic systems. Beyond obvious ideological differences from the West, Russia has been a military-oriented, centralized, command environment based on rigid rank and status differentials for centuries.[64]

The Russian people carry a great deal of social and psychological background into the twenty-first century. Managers are still expected to take firm stands and lead from positions of authority, yet citizens now expect to voice opinions about decisions related to work and politics. They do not, however, look kindly at participative behavior or even consultative approaches.[65] The few studies conducted on collectivism and participative management methods showed a difference between having a voice in decisions and taking responsibility for those decisions. U.S. companies in Russia, including McDonald's, U.S. West, Pizza Hut, Apple, Ford, and Digital Equipment, have found that they must initiate change slowly and accept archaic management behavior.[66] Meanwhile, European and Asian companies such as Fiat, Imperial Chemical Industries, Lucky-Goldstar, and Hitachi have had less difficulty; they have brought to their Russian alliances histories of relatively structured management and noticeable power distance.[67]

The Japanese Approach

U.S. scholars have paid attention to Japanese management systems and contrasts in leadership styles for several decades. This interest has increased along with the exceptional success of Japanese industry and highly visible advantages gained by those companies in quality production. The Japanese system is widely known for its lifetime employment guarantee, a seniority system that rewards loyalty and commitment to organizational harmony. In fact, Japanese management success has rested on three pillars: developing employee loyalty, improving productivity, and pursuing continuous quality improvement. Within this broad outline, several characteristics of Japanese companies emerge. First, employees, once hired, rarely leave for jobs at other companies even though they always have that choice. Second, because of Japan's insular character, it has retained a homogeneous population that maintains cultural and linguistic integrity; in effect, it is a closed social system of relationships among companies, groups, and political interests. Third, Japan developed a so-called bottom-up decision-making environment that relies on active participation by all employees. The name of this management approach, *ringi-sei* (or *ringi*), literally means "reverential inquiry."[68]

Japan's approach to leadership is difficult to understand apart from its industrial history. At the time of the Restoration in 1868, growth depended heavily on the strength and private fortunes of feudal families. These social institutions amounted to military clans with strong internal networks of political and merchant relationships. As they began to establish Japan's industrial base, they created family-dominated holding companies that competed with one another in commerce much as they had in war. Known as *zaibatsu*, these conglomerates established huge trading companies to reach beyond Japan for technology and industry resources on which to build their domestic business empires. By World War I, nearly 80 zaibatsu controlled enterprises that represented more than 75 percent of Japan's total GNP. The top five included Mitsui, Mitsubishi, Fusanosuke, Sumitomo, and Suzuki. The largest was the Suzuki zaibatsu, whose trading volume equaled nearly 10 percent of the country's total GNP.

Within this heavily centralized private enterprise—literally, a nation composed of a handful of extremely powerful conglomerates—management methods mirrored autocratic feudal systems. Family members could not directly manage all companies or activities under their umbrella organizations, and although they maintained extraordinary power, the zaibatsu were only as strong as the loyalty of their subordinates. Consequently, Japan developed a business philosophy of hierarchical control maintained through detailed protocols. Top managers cemented internal relationships through a form of benevolent dictatorship, creating a society where subordinates enjoyed the benefits and security of their organizations as long as they remained loyal and worked hard to ensure organizational success.[69]

The zaibatsu were disbanded by the U.S. occupation forces after World War II, but hundreds of rebuilt independent companies carried on both the traditions and the names of Japan's leading industrial and financial empires. In the 1960s a new system emerged, made up of very strong industrial conglomerates. Many of these were family controlled, as they were during the era of the zaibatsu. However, the new conglomerate systems were heavily capitalized through interconnected company, banking, and government interests. Management systems did not evolve in the same manner. Through the upheaval of military defeat and occupation, the core attributes of the old zaibatsu management system showed few signs of significant change. Centuries of embedded patterns of behavior that defined leadership relationships, and, indeed, broader social and business relationships, were not obliterated by legal prohibitions. Instead, new organizational giants were formed through relational networks. These are now called *keiretsu*—a concept described at length in Chapter 2.

Roughly translated, that term means an association of mutual interest for trade and industry. The management values of paternalism remained intact in the keiretsu, and the value of company loyalty pervaded the nation's economy. Japan's industrial strength has been based on tightly controlled mass-manufacturing systems, supplemented in today's technocracy by a high regard for authority and conformity within the system.[70] Such priorities often seem dichotomous to outsiders, because Japan has built its system of loyalty and commitment through one of the world's most participative management systems. How can conformity to a hierarchical system coexist with widespread participation? The answer rests largely on the concept of consensus and methods for achieving it in Japan.[71] Every member of an organization is encouraged to recommend improvements and to participate in cohesive team-oriented activities. Teams, such as the well-known quality control circles, establish consensus-oriented decision-making environments that cast managers as facilitating leaders. These groups are self-managed in their problem-solving and decision-making activities about workplace issues *within the frameworks of their specific environments.*

For example, a work group might meet to discuss ways to improve the efficiency of work schedules. Every participant is encouraged to offer suggestions or to debate alternatives. Initially, the group works to expand the range of available alternatives (not to quickly settle on one best choice). Consequently, group members may spend a great deal of time just brainstorming new ideas. In due course, the members begin to focus on several of the best ideas, and they devote increasing effort to "urging one to the surface." This process continues until the group identifies an obvious choice (or at least a strong preference for one alternative). Most groups arrive only at majority interpretations of their problems and preferred solutions; they seldom reach unanimous agreement. Indeed, several members in a group may strongly object to the majority's preference. In this instance, the group will patiently try to win over the dissenting members; but in the end, even if persuasion fails, the majority decision will be adopted. The dissenting members are then expected to fully accept the group's decision and give their uncompromising support. All members pursue the decision as if they were in total agreement. Most decisions are communicated upward as "recommendations" to be reviewed at appropriate management levels. After review and approval, they carry the weight of authority, yet the group seldom receives explicit instructions. The system legitimizes their recommendation, and even if management objects to the group's decision, it is not vetoed except in extreme cases. Instead, it is "referred" back to the group for reconsideration.[72]

Some see irony in the expectation that Japanese managers will act decisively within their firms' hierarchies. They maintain this balance by guiding subordinate groups toward making good recommendations and fulfilling organizational objectives. Decisiveness does not suggest that managers impose unilateral decisions. As long as managers fulfill subordinates' expectations, they conform to authority and rigorously observe rules and procedures that, by definition, they have been instrumental in creating. When individual employees violate procedures or threaten group harmony, their superiors are expected to exert authority to correct the problems. In such cases, managers wield exceptional authority and can impose ruthless decisions expecting the full support of their subordinate groups because the errant individuals have proven themselves unworthy of group allegiance.[73]

The Japanese approach to leadership also involves expectations that managers bring expertise to their organizations that assist subordinates in solving problems. Managers are expected to apply their experience and intellectual capabilities to help work groups fulfill their potential. In addition, they must act as inspirational leaders and role models who can instill vision and moral purpose in work groups. These expectations are not substantially different from characteristics described for transformational leaders in western cultures, and through effective development and selection of managers, organizations communicate these role expectations to everyone. A foreign expatriate, however, would have tremendous difficulty fulfilling these composite role expectations in Japan. At the same time, a Japanese manager has a great deal of difficulty managing local workers in a foreign country. This is a problem because Japanese systems rely on reciprocal relationships between managers and employees that are uncommon elsewhere. The Japanese system of leadership cannot be transported to another culture unless their foreign employees willingly accept participative methods and group responsibilities. Expatriate managers in Japan must also accept subordinate group processes and understand workers' expectations for leadership.[74]

These tendencies may change as globalization expands the involvement of Japanese managers in foreign operations and also because a growing number of foreign enterprises do business in Japan. Observers thus believe that Japan is on the brink of major changes in its management systems.[75] They emphasize that traditions of insular relationships and company solidarity worked extremely well in a rapidly expanding economy, but today's slower growth requires the country's businesses to adjust to international management practices to retain their competitive strength. Consequently, industry leaders are beginning to realize the need to abandon practices that depend on homogeneous companies and culture-bound commitments to the organization. A growing group of observers expects that Japanese companies will relinquish centralized control of overseas posts, and that firms will scale down large headquarters staff. Some companies have begun to adapt U.S. management techniques that reward individuals on merit; some also accept the idea of employee mobility and hire outside talent. In effect, some evidence indicates reconciliation of western management practices, but change is likely to be slow, and it is unlikely to affect enterprises in Japan as much as Japanese activities in foreign countries.[76]

Chinese Leadership and Confucian Values

Leadership in China is deeply embedded in the Confucian social philosophy, which prescribes a rigid social structure. Superiors are neither managers nor leaders, but they are *heads*. And leadership qualities are explained within the paternalistic concept of *headship*, similar to the role of the head of a family, the head of a clan, or the head of state. Heads are born to their positions or thrust into them by fate or natural circumstance. In this context, effective leaders are those that can fulfill two roles. The first is to maintain order through a system of inequalities in which the head has a distinct obligation to enforce the social structure. The second is to maintain harmony through adherence to social rules in an ordered hierarchy.[77]

The Confucian ethic requires people to accept their positions and to conform to roles within their social strata.[78] As described in Chapter 8, the values and traditions of Chinese society reinforce a hierarchical structure of organizations that aligns interpersonal relationships with rank and status. This concept of social order is apparent not only in mainland China but also in many Southeast Asian societies. The leader in a headship role can expect deference, respect, and obedience from subordinates without coercion. Compliance is expected, much like a child conforms to the natural order of a family. However, the system relies on the benevolence of the head of an organization. As in a parent-child relationship, the underling expects care and protection and in return offers filial piety. Individual members of this social family owe allegiance to the family first, and they band together against all outsiders. Leadership in the Chinese context is distinguished from autocratic leadership because the head position is legitimized by the responsibility for subordinates. Research on this relationship has detailed eight characteristics of Chinese leadership.[79] These characteristics are summarized in Table 15.2 and described in the following paragraphs.

Subordinate Dependency

Everyone depends on others within various group structures, and members of every group expect heads to act as responsible leaders who guide and protect them. Dependency on others is the natural order of life, according to this concept; thus, subordinates gain the right to be nurtured and protected by obediently accepting their positions.

Personalism

The quality of personal relationships, not formal rules or criteria, governs behavior. Organizational decisions may take into account objective information, regulations,

TABLE 15.2

PATERNALISTIC PRIORITIES IN CHINESE LEADERSHIP

Subordinate dependency	Maintain the natural order of life, in which each person has an appropriate station in a family or group.
Personalism	Personal relationships govern behavior; informal ties prevail over rules or procedures.
Moral leadership	Authority demands worthiness of respect, humility, self-effacement, and trust.
Harmony	Leaders ensure harmony to maintain social order.
Conflict avoidance	Leaders are expected to diffuse conflict and prevent confrontational behavior.
Social distance	Proprieties of rank and status must be maintained; inequalities are natural expressions of individual roles.
Didactic role	Information is a guarded resource to be sparingly shared; ambiguity is a benefit to be preserved.
Proper dialogue	Leaders should nurture and support subordinates but at a proper distance; they always protect "face."

Source: Adapted from R. I. Westwood, *Organizational Behaviour: Southeast Asian Perspectives* (Hong Kong: Longman Group, 1992), 134–135. Also see S. Gordon Redding, *The Spirit of Chinese Capitalism* (Berlin: Walter de Gruyter, 1990), 153–158.

laws, and rules that imply an impersonal bureaucracy, but behavior toward other people depends on personal knowledge of those involved. More to the point, people cannot judge how to behave properly unless they know whom they are dealing with, and they must cultivate these relationships.

Moral Leadership

The organizational head is expected to possess virtues such as humanity, patience, integrity, compassion, and humility. In the Confucian context, a leader's authority is sanctioned by becoming worthy of respect and providing a good role model for subordinates. Chinese values emphasize self-effacing behavior and propriety that builds trust.

Harmony

Group endeavors, such as those of a family, proceed not according to formal rules and obligations but according to informal understandings of mutual responsibilities. The viability of the social family unit (work group, organization, or nation) is therefore commensurate with the harmony within the referent group. Chinese organizations certainly establish their own complicated brands of bureaucracy, but Chinese leaders are expected to build and maintain harmony within their groups to support social order and authority.

Conflict Avoidance

Confrontations, conflicts, expressions of anger, and other forms of behavior that seem to challenge authority threaten harmony. A Chinese leader is expected to diffuse any form of disruptive conduct and, like a family head, to infuse subordinates with standards for socially accepted behavior that will not prompt confrontations. Leaders often take extreme measures to stifle dissident behavior, yet even when forceful or coercive, these measures are socially sanctioned.

Social Distance

Chinese leaders are expected to maintain social distance between themselves and their subordinates. To a westerner, this condition may seem incongruous with the concepts of collectivism and values of harmony and personal relationships. Chinese people see no paradox, however, in requirements to create harmonious relationships and behave in benevolent ways while also retaining the power and privileges of authority. These leaders actively seek to maintain the dignity of their positions, perhaps inspiring awe (or fear, when conditions warrant threats) while also seeking to demonstrate wise and caring behavior. Researchers find that Chinese subordinates apparently understand the line beween relationships that enhance harmony and relationships that violate prerogatives of rank.[80]

Didactic Role

Chinese leadership assumes a mystique comparable to the concept of charisma, yet this element takes on a unique Confucian interpretation. Many Chinese leaders carry superlative titles such as *supreme leader* or *master.* These titles further celebrate the importance of group heads as paragons of exemplary qualities, perhaps supported by some mysterious source of power and influence. In practice, leaders in China protect their images by hoarding knowledge and information.[81] Their control over intellectual resources, expertise, and simple everyday information is a substantial resource for bolstering their power and maintaining subordinate dependency. A leader is likely to pass on only limited information, often purposely leaving employees in doubt about work expectations, performance, or company activities. Implicit and vague communication is a leadership skill, and Chinese officials carefully maintain noncommittal stances in most relationships.

Proper Dialogue

A benevolent leader is expected to be an effective communicator within the limits that govern shared information. In a Chinese organization, effective communication requires sensitivity to subordinate expectations and sufficient information to convey the intentions of superiors. However, this exchange is constrained by the need to maintain power distance and to selectively release information. A proper dialogue provides subordinates with sufficient direction to allow them to intuitively behave according to expectations and, when they err, to correct behavior in a way that prevents loss of face for everyone involved.[82]

Similar patterns of leadership emerge in other Asian societies where Confucian thought prevails, yet it would be highly inappropriate to generalize similar behavior to all Asians. Japan recognizes a significant role for Confucian values, yet its leadership structures have evolved quite differently from those in China. This section has emphasized Chinese leadership because it represents patterns of behavior common among more than one-quarter of the world's population. This description does not, however, imply that a universal style of management exists in Asia. China, Japan, Malaysia, Indonesia, Thailand, South Korea, and other societies exhibit distinctly different cultures with enormous differences in ethnicity, religion, social history, and ideology.[83]

Contrasts and Similarities in Leadership

The contrasts in leadership behavior among European, North American, and Asian countries described so far are examples of prevalent themes in management. Often they have spread from major nations to developing countries that emerged under colonial influence, prompting similar behavior. For example, the Latin European characteristics of authoritative relationships tempered by paternalism are comparable to those in Mexico, Argentina, Brazil, and other Latin American countries. Mexico has attracted particular attention from researchers as a result of cross-border alliances with U.S. partners and increased foreign investment by European and Asian firms. The Mexican management style, described in earlier chapters, involves autocratic and paternalistic elements, and workers there acquiesce to hierarchies and accept their stations in life as long as managers avoid abrasive or insensitive treatment. Mexican workers associate their positions in society with their personal honor, and they expect recognition for their contributions. No one expects equal treatment, and everyone gives proper deference to those in higher ranks. The Mexican profile, like management relations in other Latin cultures, shows interesting similarities to management relations in Confucian societies, but no apparent causal connection exists.[84]

Arab and Persian cultures constitute a cluster of Middle Eastern societies with leadership characteristics that sharply contrast with those of other regions. Although few studies exist about the Middle East, there are marked differences among the region's cultures, including absolute rule by monarchs and emirs that foster autocratic organizations or theocracies that institutionalize Islamic laws throughout all business enterprises. The democratic government Israel is unique to the region.[85] These ideologies underscore pervasive patterns of leadership behavior in each society. As described in the previous chapter, Israelis have cohesive organizations, and their leaders tend to be paternalistic, nurturing a sense of democratic decision-making within organizations and among networks of social groups. This behavior, however, is tempered by authoritative hierarchies that may reflect years of military strife and nation-building experience by leaders who have brought with them many Western European characteristics.

The Arab and Persian cultures developed apart from European colonization, and their religious foundations set them apart from Israel, from Asian cultures, and from western societies. Leadership favors strongly authoritarian practices, and a directive style of management results in detailed, unquestioned, and inflexible orders. Large power differences clearly separate people by social status, rank, birthright, gender, and ethnicity. Arab organizations can be extremely bureaucratic with tightly controlled central authority. Rank and status reflect Islamic beliefs about deterministic social roles with power often vested in individuals born to their positions. Decisions are made within the context of religious beliefs that also dictate superior-subordinate relationships, yet the personal influence of authority figures often supersedes rules and procedures. Personal affiliations determine who has authority, how it is exercised, and what protocols are appropriate in relationships. These cultural antecedents also determine relations with suppliers, customers, and foreign investors.

International managers often encounter serious challenges working in the Middle East. For example, Saudi Arabia recognizes virtually no equivalent of the concept of legal obligation. Under contract law (Sharia), a contractual obligation amounts to "care as a duty of conscience." In effect, any contract (joint venture agreement, bargain of sale, or even terms of employment) can be completely ignored if it is perceived that circumstances are incongruent with religious beliefs. The driving force of responsibility is an internal standard (conscience), not an external one (rights of others).[86] Consequently, outsiders see little evidence of paternalism, although each person's conscience dictates extremely strong loyalties to family and to members of the same social or religious order. Leadership follows clearly autocratic lines in this environment. Leaders accomplish tasks through strength of position and the perceived

GLOBAL VIEWPOINT

STRANGER IN SINGAPORE

When Monica Holtforster arrived in Singapore to take up a new post representing her firm, Deloitte & Touche, she stepped into a new world of behavior and expectations. Singapore is an outwardly western society with high-rise buildings, shopping plazas, and luxury cars. Exquisite shops sell brand-name goods from Paris, London, New York, and Tokyo, and people maintain a squeaky-clean environment. Failing to flush a public toilet can draw a fine of $150, and peddling chewing gum will set you back $10,000. Littering earns assignment to a public street-cleaning mission for community duty, and graffiti may result in a sentence of flogging! Purchase prices of simple apartments can run $200,000—and better ones rent at $60,000—but expatriates praise the low crime rate and the tiny republic's picture-perfect island landscape.

Beneath the glitter, however, Singapore is a Chinese society, and doing business there can be an adventure. As Holtforster found out, meetings with Chinese colleagues can be long, inconclusive, and frustrating affairs. Chinese businesspeople seldom respond with definite yes or no answers to any question; a maybe probably means no. Business deals often close over lunch or dinner, and no one does a deal on a single visit. The parties must create relationships first, and as Holtforster explains, the Chinese want to know everything about you, including the color of your grandmother's eyes.

Superstitions powerfully influence practices. Wearing a red tie or dress to a business meeting is good for prosperity. Concluding business at eight o'clock, or on the 8th of the month, or in an eight-story office is a good sign; four o'clock is a bad time,

and the fourth day is worse, so everyone avoids telephone numbers with four in conspicuous positions.

Protocol also dominates business exchanges. Watch where you sit, speak deferentially to superiors, tell no jokes, and ask questions only when answers have no meaning.

Singapore enjoys freedom of speech and open-ended competition, but newspapers never openly criticize government or the country's leaders. Business leaders do not criticize others, and society tolerates bad news only about those who have broken faith with society or the law. Laws are followed—period. Authority figures make decisions—period. But society ensures protection for those not in power, and expectations of social order prevail for everyone. Order is the key word in organizations or relationships. Even a janitor has an intuitive feel for his or her place and respect for the duties it entails. Secretaries occupy their own spaces and fulfill duties clearly understood without the formality of job description or directives, as do hotel doormen. No one treads on another's domain; to do so would "take away face"—the ultimate sin. Don't try to help, and don't meddle. Let the doorman open the door, the janitor clean, and the secretary control the office. They won't encroach on you, and they don't want you to encroach on them.

Singapore enforces simple rules: As a foreigner in a strange land, assume that whatever you think you know about proper behavior at home could get you in trouble in a Chinese society.

Sources: Adapted from Nattalia Lea, "Stranger in a Strange Land," *CA Magazine*, December 1994, 6–7; also see Alfred C. F. Fong, "My Face, Your Face," *Straits Times*, 12 July 1996, p. 8.

---

power of their connections. They do not always adopt abusive or harsh practices, however. In fact, abuse of power is a serious breach of ethics, while society honors the ability to foster trust and respect. To the western mind, these characteristics seem paradoxical and result in uneasy international relationships.[87]

Many other countries adopt variations on leadership behavior too vast to explore in detail. For most countries, analysis flounders with only rudimentary evidence of management practices elsewhere. This lack of research is a particular problem for managers who seek to understand leadership issues in less-developed countries.

Meanwhile, globalization is rapidly bringing change to both developed and developing nations through convergent practices.

CONVERGENCE AND INTEGRATION

The concept of **convergence** is primarily concerned with leadership. Those who see signs of convergence suggest that management practices are incrementally moving toward a common pattern of behavior. Those who deny this argument suggest that cultural and ideological differences will never permit universal standards to emerge. Although much of the debate has focused on theoretical premises, cross-cultural research has begun to evaluate the transferability of leadership behavior. Studies typically try to compare past behavior with current practices in a particular country, determining whether and what kinds of changes have occurred.

For example, some studies have looked for evidence about whether Japanese managers are adopting more U.S. practices than they observed before, and conversely, whether U.S. managers have adopted Japanese techniques. The results are always controversial because behavior is difficult to measure and almost impossible to monitor over time with comparable methods. Evidence of significant trends can be appreciated when the procedures become broadly integrated into company practices. Specifically, U.S. managers have increased their involvement in team-building efforts in an effort to replicate Japanese successes, and Japanese managers have adopted U.S. process techniques. Industrialization has followed technological trends in both countries, evolving from craft environments to mass production to process methods. Consequently, observers generally acknowledge transferability of techniques, strategies, structures, and processes, but arguments continue about whether leadership behaviors have shown significant changes.

Although most recent studies have focused on contrasts in Japanese and American behavior, with the demise of the Soviet Union and China's open-door policy, more research has begun to be directed toward Russian and Chinese behavior. Also, European studies have been concerned with internal EU exchanges, and studies have found relatively important effects of NAFTA on Latin cultures (Mexico in particular). Unfortunately, no conclusive evidence suggests that there is convergence toward one universal model of leadership.

Further, evidence of convergence is met with equally strong evidence of divergence as nation-states and ethnic societies strive to protect their customs and cultures. The truth probably lies somewhere between these extremes as managers adopt foreign concepts that do not threaten their cultures yet support practical needs in their organizations.[88]

Change does not always signal convergence or divergence, but as a Finnish observer said of emerging practices in the Baltic states, "These people are shedding archaic Soviet systems and reaching out for methods that work. . . . [T]hey don't know that JIT is a Japanese concept or that there is a Swedish approach to team work, only that the world has 'good ideas' to offer, and when possible, they will grab on to those things that work best. . . . [I]t's a matter of 'good management,' not Japanese or American or German."[89] This quest for the best practices certainly brings some convergence, but people in each society naturally tend to believe, ethnocentrically perhaps, that their methods of leadership are superior to others. Even when managers adopt foreign practices, they hesitate to admit borrowing from or imitating others.

International managers must therefore accept the need to manage in diverse cultures where norms often prevent implementation of good (if foreign) ideas. Multinational companies may transfer technology, process methods, and all sorts of ideas that can improve foreign operations, but similar attempts to infuse foreign subsidiaries with new patterns of behavior can result in disaster. Expatriates bring with them ingrained models of practices that they believe work best, and any deviation from that model is perceived as a compromise in the quality of leadership. Contingency theorists, and more specifically the proponents of transformational leadership, suggest that this perception is erroneous.[90] On a pragmatic level, the most effective practices in one environment are those that are most congruent with cultural expectations and norms in that society.

In conclusion, evidence supports the contentions made early in the chapter that no universal definition captures the full scope of leadership. International managers must build cultural awareness, create harmony rather than discord, and integrate diverse interests through relational skills. Their approaches to these responsibilities clearly reflect their cultural differences; but the next, and last, chapter will confirm that a pervasive movement toward greater participation is driving interactions among managers and employees. Teamwork is paying dividends as a fundamental force that not only alters motivational concepts but also influences how future leaders define behavior.

REVIEW QUESTIONS

1. Although the trait approach to leadership is criticized, what credible characteristics do effective leaders generally possess?
2. What primary difficulties complicate international applications of leadership theories such as System 4 and the managerial grid to cross-cultural management situations?
3. Why is a contingency approach especially acceptable to international managers, and how can the path-goal theory be useful to international managers?
4. Describe the concept of transformational leadership. What is the essential role of a transformational leader, and how do subordinates' expectations affect that role?
5. Compare the results of European leadership studies. What are the primary patterns of leadership behavior in Europe, and what problems do they present for European multinationals?
6. How does the Latin European concept of paternalism influence leadership behavior?
7. How do Central and Eastern Europe differ from Western Europe, and what problems do you envision for international managers in former Eastern bloc countries?
8. Describe the Russian leadership psyche and difficulties that western managers face when working in the former Soviet Union.
9. Why do Middle Eastern leadership practices seem paradoxical to western observers?
10. How do cultural expectations influence leadership roles and the decision-making process in Japanese companies?
11. Describe the Chinese characteristics of leadership and their relationship to Confucian principles. How do these conditions contrast with those in Japan?
12. Explain the process of convergence in leadership behavior, and argue for or against converging approaches to leadership for multinational corporations.

GLOSSARY OF KEY TERMS

Charismatic leadership role   The capability to provide vision and inspiration, as emphasized by transformational leadership concepts.

Contingency theory   The concept that no single leadership style works well in all situations, but managers can prosper in situations that suit their leadership styles and capabilities.

Convergence   International movement toward a common approach to leadership for universal application.

Instrumental leadership role   The capability to design effective organizational processes, control activities, and meet organizational objectives.

Leadership   The process of influencing other people to behave in preferred ways to accomplish organizational objectives.

Life cycle theory   A continuum of possible leadership behaviors based on the maturity of the employees being managed.

Managerial grid   A model of leadership behavior that plots behavior on relations-oriented and task-oriented dimensions.

New leadership   The process of influencing others through consciously developed charismatic and transformational roles.

Paternalism   Benevolent application of authority in which superiors maintain high power distance but protect their subordinates. In Confucian thought, this concept is expressed as headship, which creates relationships resembling parent-child responsibilities.

Path-goal theory   The concept, linked to expectancy theory, that managers adapt their behavior to subordinate needs and work situations in order to match styles with expectations to achieve goals.

Style approach   A presumption that leaders effectively influence others' behavior through considerate or task-oriented patterns in their own behavior.

System 4   A way of describing four modes of leadership distinguished by autocratic, controlling, consultative, or participative behavior patterns.

Trait approach   A presumption that good leaders are born with characteristics they need to attract and inspire admiration in followers.

Transformational leadership   A charismatic, inspired example that creates a vision of meaningful change and motivates performance to fulfill the vision; a way of thinking that reaches for high-order needs and objectives rather than transactional priorities.

EXERCISES

1. Identify four different situations in which you experienced a need for leadership. For example, you might have worked in a factory or a fast-food store or participated in a scouting organization. Perhaps you can identify options from social clubs, sports teams, or experiences drawn from your parents' experience. In each instance, explain your perception of the best approach to leadership and defend your rationale.

2. Gather as many responses as possible (at least 10) from students, faculty members, or businesspeople of foreign nationalities on two questions. Ask them to say if they "strongly disagree, disagree, agree, or strongly agree" with the following statements:
    a. The main reason for a hierarchical structure in an organization is so that everybody knows who has authority over whom.
    b. Managers need to supply precise information to subordinates about their work, and subordinates need to follow instructions.

    When you have your answers, draw up lists of respondents and how they answered the questions. What similarities or differences did you observe, and how do these responses compare with examples in the chapter?

3. In teams of three or four, identify two foreign leaders that you can describe from their public images. They should be recognizable to most class members or explained in the presentations (politicians, military figures, business leaders, coaches, or anyone else in leadership positions). Develop a profile of the individual from news articles or other research, and describe the person's leadership behavior. Does the person exhibit distinctive traits, charisma, vision, or unusual characteristics? Describe rationales for his or her leadership behavior based on leadership models. How are cultural factors likely to influence the person's leadership style?

ALL SCANDINAVIANS DO NOT AGREE ON TEAMS OR LEADERSHIP STYLES

Stanislaus (Stan) Linkerd had worked in the U.S. lumbering business for 16 years when he was assigned to an international project team for procuring future woodland resources in northern Europe. Linkerd had not been to Europe before, except on brief trips, and his experience with Weyerhauser Corporation had been rather narrow for someone chosen to jointly manage a foreign team. Most recently, he had worked at the company's U.S. headquarters on international woodland contracts. That had taken him to the Philippines for several months, where he was highly successful in negotiating a reforestation project with the Ministry of Agriculture. Before that, Linkerd had traveled as part of a lumber procurement team for several months to Costa Rica and Brazil. The European assignment, however, had a two-year planning horizon, and Linkerd and his family were moved to Stockholm, Sweden.

Before leaving for Stockholm, Linkerd was counseled by Weyerhauser staff about living and working in Europe. He was advised to learn as much as possible about different Scandinavian cultures before he left the United States. Consequently, he read what he could find in management literature that was largely focused on Sweden, and he accessed Internet country profiles on Sweden, Finland, and Norway. He also contacted several embassies and foreign trade commissions about Estonia (a newly emerging Baltic state from the old Soviet bloc), Russia, and Poland—three high-potential areas that Weyerhauser had targeted for future lumber sourcing. After arriving in Sweden, Linkerd contacted the American embassy and got in touch with several U.S. businessmen who had worked in Scandinavia, and he and his wife explored popular literature on the country and the region.

Linkerd's team developed around four key people. One was Swedish and the company's technical director for regional forestry and lumber operations in Europe. Another was from Finland and an agronomist who specialized in regional woods. He worked for a Finnish company that had a contract with Wey-erhauser for wood pulp production. A third team member was a business development specialist and American who had worked for several years in London and Copenhagen for Weyerhauser, largely focusing on contract administration. The fourth was an ethnic Estonian who had only recently been hired by the Swedish office from a marketing position with British Petroleum in London. The Estonian was hired mainly for his language and cultural expertise because the company wanted to develop business contacts in Estonia. The team members actually worked very independently, although they expected to travel together at times and, in many instances, coordinate their research or jointly negotiate with potential suppliers. Officially, the project team was headed by Linkerd and the Finn, who had been appointed to the post specifically to pursue regional business that Weyerhauser and the Finnish alliance partner wanted to cultivate.

Coming from Weyerhauser where team development had been a major management concern, Linkerd expected to find a "team" ready to accept the idea of a self-directed group. He did not expect the members to behave as isolated specialists; indeed, all that he had read on Scandinavian culture had prepared him for a Swedish style of egalitarianism. Those expectations were short lived. The Estonian was rather quiet, and although very nice, he was not content until the group had mapped out individual responsibilities. He was adamant that every person must understand how they were to communicate with one another. He clearly wanted a hierarchical arrangement with very clear guidelines, and he chose to report to Linkerd while cooperating with everyone else. The Finn was unusually quiet on almost all counts. He would respond to questions and engage in discussions, but did not often venture his own opinions. In contrast, the Swede was very open to joint work and became the de facto working partner of Linkerd at the office. The American business development specialist was almost always away from the office or tied up on the telephone. Linkerd put this down to the individualism of the American and the nature of his job, which required travel and meetings with potential investors, bankers, government officials, and many of the firm's existing clients.

During the first few weeks, these relationships began to become apparent to everyone, including the office staff—which was entirely Swedish. The office ran smoothly, with almost no direction from Linkerd, but it was more of a communication center than a business center. Linkerd and his team were rarely there for more than a few days at a time. Six months into the project, they had all visited at least 59 different woodland sites, met with forestry specialists in four countries, talked with several hundred corporate leaders in different lumber and forestry businesses, and trudged through snow, mud, and smoky pulp mills. Meanwhile, relationships became strained. The Finn had become more and more remote from the group. He deferred decisions to Linkerd and seldom talked to the Swede or to the American. The Finn and Estonian seemed to get along well, but in an odd "formal" manner. Both were extremely efficient, and both, on their own accord, irritated Linkerd with a certain way of always structuring conversation and decisions. They simply did not want to work in a team environment, and Linkerd, who had gone out of his way to be informal and friendly, felt as if both men put up psychological barriers to any personal relationships. On several occasions, Linkerd had become frustrated with the situation and had snapped at the Finn to "get with it." In fact, during a meeting when all five of the team members were trying to evaluate the feasibility of bidding on a contract, the Finn spent most of the time silent, except to present a long and detailed report on yield data. Linkerd had exploded, saying: "What the [expletive deleted] is this? Are you brain dead, or do you have an opinion on this contract other than [expletive deleted] numbers?" The Finn simply stared at Linkerd and then coolly said: "If there is something more that you want from me, you should learn to be specific in your requests, not emotional."

Things came to a head when the Finn was put in charge of a technical team from his home company with consultants from an agricultural research unit in Stockholm. They were sent to Helsinki to analyze the processing costs of lumber for pulp and paper from a large government forest track. Two days after the team had arrived in Helsinki, one consultant resigned, explaining that he had no intention of "running errands" for the Finns. Linkerd flew to Helsinki,

only to be told that he was out of line—that the particular assignment was not his concern, and that the Finns would take care of things. When he returned to Stockholm, he invited a professor to lunch to help, as he put it, to "unravel the mystery of the relationship thing." The professor was a social scientist specializing in Nordic culture, and he tried to enlighten Linkerd to a number of misconceptions he had about Scandinavians.

"You've missed several crucial clues," the professor said. "First, like many Americans, you have assumed that all Scandinavians are the same . . . or at least similar. That's not true. Second, you've assumed that people in western cultures will naturally embrace teamwork, and that's not true . . . regardless of all the grand research on culture and human behavior. And third, you've assumed that Swedes, Finns, and whoever, will like you if you draw them into a conciliatory relationship rather than a directive approach to management. That's entirely false."

"What's all this stuff about teamwork and the wonderful easygoing Swedish mentality, then?" asked Linkerd. "The office almost runs itself. The gals are all great. I haven't run into an angry Swede since I've been here—except maybe in a traffic jam—and you're telling me that I've got it all wrong?"

"Well, maybe not all," the professor said, "but a lot. Swedes do work well together. We have a very strong sense of community at home and at work, but the Finns definitely do not like to work that way. They are very structured people—very task oriented and independent. You give a Finn a job to do, and he will do it. You ask him a question, and he'll reply. But there is such a thing as the 'silent Finn.' We joke about it. Finns do not talk with juniors . . . no small talk or unnecessary social stuff. In fact, most Finnish organizations have an official 'information manager,' a specialist in bridging gaps between hierarchical ranks. You have no such thing in America, nor do we in Sweden. The Norwegians have something similar, a person trained in passing information up and down the company's channels. Crazy, huh? But this keeps everyone at a so-called 'proper distance.' When your friends saw you come to Helsinki, it was an intrusion, and when you met in teams or committees, it was to address some specific problem, not to drink coffee together or laugh at some joke. Things in Finland go up and down. People always report to someone, and they don't talk to them unless invited. Managers pass decisions down, and they don't ask for your advice or input in the process. Maybe it's not that black and white, but it's nothing like you find here in Stockholm."

"Well, what's this business about not liking me? What have I done that has kept us all at arm's length from one another? No, several of us are at war," Linkerd said.

"Now, come on, Stan," the professor laughed a bit. "They like you. That's not what I meant. It's just that they don't want the informality of relationships you expect. You can't lead them unless you can make very hard decisions and show who's in charge. Your friend from Estonia is coming from a lockstep Soviet style society. He may reject that ideology, but he's been conditioned like Pavlov's dog to expect direction and authority. You give him authority, and he will wield it like a broad ax on others too. You should see that. You have to control him, or he won't respect you. But then a little human kindness will help too. Just don't give in too much. Maybe you already have, and then it's too late. You and the American are okay?"

"Bill's single and on a roll. You know, he's flying high doing his 'networking.' But he gets involved and digs in. No problem. And BJ, my Swedish scientist, is a sweetheart of a guy. Tough as nails on work, but never a sour note. He does a lot to quiet me down in meetings and run interference with everyone else."

"Hey, Stan, we Swedes are not all nice guys, you know," said the professor. "But it is true that we learn early in life to 'throw balloons, not bricks' when we work with other people. It's a social thing for certain. The Finns won't be as kind. But they have their strengths and they are very proud people. They work very very hard . . . goal driven, for certain, and we could learn a thing or two. But I would not study their human relation skills for insights. What you must do now is take control of this situation. Maybe be very straight with them and try to put these issues on the table. But if you can't take a firm hand—and also, by the way, stay out of the other guy's way once he has the ball—then you maybe should ask your company to change the team."

QUESTIONS

1. How does Linkerd's leadership style compare with the models of European management presented in the chapter? What contrasts are apparent in terms of American leadership behavior?

2. Although little is written about Finland in western literature and relatively more about Sweden, there seems to be a serious debate about how the two cultures differ in their approach to management and to leadership expectations. How would you contrast these two cultures, and why might they be so different?

3. Weyerhauser management may be only remotely involved in setting up these short-term project teams, but the case implies that teams are probably formed through headquarters. What guidelines would you suggest for the company when forming teams and making overseas assignments? What are the issues for cultural diversity, leadership control, and managing foreign activities?

BIBLIOGRAPHY

Interview with Bill Givney, consultant to the Business Development Council, Tallin, Estonia, July 1996.

Interview with Stanislaus Linkerd, forestry specialist for Agricultural Cooperative Development International (ACDI), Washington, D.C., June 1997.

Nurmi, Raimo, and Raoul Uksavrav. "Estonian and Finnish Organizations: A Comparative Analysis." *International Journal of Management* 13, no. 1 (1996): 101–107.

CASE 15.2

NIKE: LEARNING TO ADAPT

The $9-billion-a-year giant in athletic shoes, Nike, has discovered that global business brings with it a variety of expectations for both performance and management responsibility. An "antiestablishment" company with a "hip" culture, Nike was founded by Philip Knight, who created Nike shoes by making them on a used waffle iron. Now CEO of a global company, Knight stays close to the "dressed down" informal image and very personal style of leadership that made him and his company famous. The company flaunts its disdain for the conventional, even to the point of putting the company's Oregon headquarters in the John McEnroe Building, a location set up like a college campus and named for the *enfant terrible* of tennis.

Knight has stretched to reinforce an unorthodox image in business, signing leading sports stars like Michael Jordan, Charles Barkley, and golfing sensation Tiger Woods to sponsorship contracts. On a global scene, he has also signed controversial Japanese sports stars and European "bad boys" of soccer. Nike ads have been called "in your face" challenges as the company seeks to dominate world football (soccer), and even has bought into the boardroom of the International Federation of Football Association (FIFA) by acquiring the Brazilian National Soccer Federation. At home, Nike has a lock-tight grip on U.S. sports shoes and accessories with a commensurate command of market share. Internationally, Nike is still an upstart compared to Adidas AG and Puma—both have strongholds in Europe, world soccer, rugby, international track and field, and foreign Olympic teams. Nevertheless, Nike is pursuing the world's markets with a loose-gun flair in much the same way that it conquered the United States.

The problem, however, is that foreign markets are not yet ready for the type of advertising and tactics used by an aggressive Nike team. For example, Nike took its new Brazilian soccer team on a world tour with an "American accent" of PR and glitzy play, including American-style management of the team and its coaches. For the effort, Brazilians labeled Nike as "carpetbagger" owners who were threatening the history and spirit of the national sport. In another instance, Nike's approach to negotiating with the Olympic Committee ended when the IAAF quickly wrapped up sponsorship with Adidas, and soon after, withdrew its support of a Nike-sponsored international track meet in Japan over "communications difficulties."

Nike's international sales and marketing office codistributes company products through alliance partners on three continents. The rebel image at home has become the bully image abroad, but now managers are learning how to adapt to diplomacy. Nike's approach to marketing is mirrored in management. Knight and his top guns control core decisions, but have tremendous personal loyalty from employees who are relatively free to innovate and control their own work, whether in teams or individually, as long as the job gets done. Everyone is encouraged to be provocative in their ideas for new products and new ways to market,

but Knight sets the pace with a rugged sense of individualism. However, management may be changing as structure and some rationality has come to Nike.

Nike corporate headquarters has more halls and walls, and more people in suits and ties than in the old days of open space and unfettered dress code. Overseas operations are beginning to structure office procedures and responsibilities with greater attention to controls and systems. Yet throughout the company, there is a strong sense of conciliatory management. The Nike culture of "hip" remains, but the boardroom revolutionary style of laid-back decisions and group freewheeling is being replaced by a more rational hierarchy of behavior, job descriptions, and individual responsibility. The Flanders operation, Nike's European headquarters, for example, reflects more French and Belgian formality than American go-for-broke informality. Business negotiations have a shirt-and-tie demeanor, but still with the corporate flair. Employees are encouraged to work in a more egalitarian environment, yet they are more comfortable with structure and a directive style of management. Consequently, Nike is toning down its one-for-all and all-for-one organization to achieve a somewhat relaxed profile of management behavior. Nevertheless, the company maintains distinct stratification of decision-making authority that is tempered to cultural expectations in European, Asian, and Latin American facilities.

The company's foreign commerce is in the hands of alliance partners in most instances; major foreign activities are directly controlled by Nike. But with its overseas contractors, Nike is connected with a number of controversial facilities and partners where host-country managers are often accused of running sweatshops or exploiting workers. This is a dimension of management that Nike was not entirely prepared for. Indeed, supervisory practices by foreign managers are getting Nike much unwanted attention. Nike, like most of its competitors, manufactures shoes and sports accessories in low-wage countries. Nike has heavy investments in Indonesia and China, and growing alliances in several Asian locations. In some instances, the factories are managed by third-country nationals contracted to run host activities. Nike is highly visible because of its outspoken support of ethical foreign business practices and a corporate code of conduct that strongly favors compliance with international guidelines on human rights. Unfortunately, some of its factories are under fire by human rights activists for allegedly mistreating employees and otherwise engaging in unacceptable management methods.

In 1999, when Nike Australia accepted the sponsorship for supplying uniforms for the Australian Olympic team, it also agreed to "abide by the SOCOG [Sydney Organising Committee for the Olympic Games] Code of Labor Practice." Under this code, Nike is required to "conform to the International Labor Organisation standards." Given the amount of attention already placed on Nike due to working condition allegations and its high visibility as a market leader, the company's actions will be watched closely by the Australian unions because Nike's merchandise is produced with the assistance of over a half-million people in Asia.

In all fairness to Nike, many of the allegations have not been substantiated, and Nike is not in direct management control of many of their foreign contractors. Whether or not Nike's factories are managed in compliance with international human rights laws and labor standards is also very difficult to judge. However, human rights activists, and officials at the International Labor Organization (ILO), say that Nike is ultimately responsible for leadership behavior among its contractors as well as company-invested foreign activities.

To counter the allegations, Nike hired Andrew Young, former ambassador to the United Nations, to inspect factories and investigate exploitation charges. Young is a highly credible consultant, and he did indeed tour the Asian factories; but his visits may spark additional debate, because he was able to spend only a few hours at each location. Nevertheless, Young issued a report in which he claimed that conditions in Nike's overseas plants were "comparable" to those in U.S. factories. Because Nike paid Mr. Young, the effort has been condemned as an effort to smother rumors, not to realistically evaluate actual conditions. Nike is being held accountable for all global operations in which the company has an interest, or where the company should be able to influence behavior through its contracts. Ironically, Nike is not a target of extreme activists. Instead, it is well respected in most quarters for its leadership acumen and support for humane causes. The point of contention, however, is that while Nike may be highly successful at home, and subsequently enjoy a fine reputation for leadership in the United States, it may still be adapting to the responsibilities of international management. Nevertheless, Nike's second-quarter earnings showed increases over last year's, and international sales were strong, especially in Asia and Europe.

QUESTIONS

1. Describe Knight's general approach to leadership, and the success he has had as an individual who has transformed the athletic shoe industry.
2. Could the Nike system of management be adapted overseas? How do third-country nationals and host-country supervisors and employees influence behavior in Nike's foreign operations?
3. The company's marketing strategies, including its lineup of super-sports personalities, reflects its approach to leadership in general. Explain this connection, and give your impression of Nike's culture.

BIBLIOGRAPHY

Carr, Robert E. "German Trade vs. Nike Corporate Culture." *Sporting Goods Business*, 24 February 1997, 50.

"Flanders Who?" *World Trade Magazine*, May 1996, 58–60.

Henrichs, Paul. *ABIX—Australasian Business Intelligence: The Sunday Age*, 19 December 1999, 3. [Retrieved 20 December 2000 from Dow Jones Interactive database.]

Heinrichs, Paul. "Spotlight on Labor Practices." *The Sunday Age*, 19 December 1999, 3. [Retrieved 20 December 2000 from Dow Jones Interactive database.]

Labich, Kenneth. "Nike vs. Reebok: A Battle for Hearts, Minds & Feet." *Fortune*, 18 September 1995, 90–106.

Manning, Jeff. "Nike Earnings Continue to Finish Strong." *Knight-Ridder Tribune Business News: The Oregonian*, 20 December 2000. [Retrieved 20 December 2000 from Dow Jones Interactive database.]

Thurow, Roger. "In Global Drive, Nike Finds Its Brash Ways Don't Always Pay Off." *Wall Street Journal*, 5 May 1997, pp. A1, A10.

Zachary, G. Pascal, and Samantha Marshall. "Nike Tries to Quell Exploitation Charges." *Wall Street Journal*, June 25, 1997, p. A16.

INTERNATIONAL TEAMS: THE EMERGING MANAGEMENT CHALLENGE

CHAPTER OBJECTIVES

Describe the roles for international teams and ways in which teams facilitate cross-border relationships.

Explain how teams differ from groups and the behavior required to encourage teamwork in a multinational.

Demonstrate the impact of multicultural diversity on team activities and the benefits of forming diverse teams in a multinational environment.

Differentiate between homogeneous teams and culturally diverse teams, and review the advantages and disadvantages of each.

Detail the process of team development and the stages through which a team passes to reach maturity.

Highlight the effect on managerial careers of international teamwork, and project significant differences between future careers and the current practice of specialized career tracking.

CHAPTER 16

Employees at Federal Express find themselves in an Orwellian environment of electronic networking, remote, wireless, and instantaneous communication, and a technostructure of *virtual teamwork*.[1] They are not alone. Many of the world's corporations, and in particular those involved in global commerce, are part of an information age where interactive networks are penetrating every domain of work and life. FedEx came into this era early, recognizing the benefits of rapid access and linked response to its worldwide hub-and-spoke parcel delivery system. The company introduced a system of *intranets* during the early 1990s, and by 1995, 60 of the company's major operations were part of one large interactive distribution network. By the end of the decade, global use of the Internet and the company's proprietary intranet system reached nearly every FedEx activity.

More important, Federal Express experienced an organizational transformation away from traditional hierarchical systems to team-based coordination centers. Unlike many industrial corporations, Federal Express made this transition relatively easily because its hubs and logistics distribution centers were already managed through team concepts. Information technology simply gave the company tools to integrate these functions while eliminating both time and distance as constraints on management. Today, Federal Express describes its management framework as a social system of virtual teams. This has a mysterious sound to it, much like George Orwell's descriptive novel about a futuristic world, *1984* (written, of course, decades earlier). Orwell's concept of a centrally controlled, electronically dominated world remains ominous and futuristic, yet at companies such as Federal Express, the concept is very close to reality.

Unlike Orwellian predictions of an autocratic empire that *centralizes* power and authority, virtual teams at Federal Express, General Electric, Digital Corporation, and Oracle, to name a few, *decentralize* management activities.[2] Power and authority have become divergent, not convergent, through empowered employee teams and pervasive internal corporate coordination systems. The virtual team process occurs at several levels in Federal Express. First, at the thousands of activity sites, parcels registered into the system for delivery feed into pick-up, tracking, logistics, and billing centers. Operational information is then instantly transmitted to all routing channels for a particular parcel, and actual activities are traced and updated in the system until the item is delivered. Teamwork at this level is seldom noticed, because employees and franchise agents do little more than work within an automated operations system. Still, company troubleshooters spend much of their time tracking parcels and resolving customer difficulties as members of these globally networked "teams." At another level, managers and activity supervisors spend much of their time communicating electronically with one another, sorting problems, tracking inquiries, or coordinating decisions that range from staff scheduling to aircraft loading logistics.

At regional and national management levels, the virtual teams behave more like traditional structures, in which middle managers are responsible for well-defined functional task or geographic operations. However, these middle and more senior managers are members of networks with accountability for team-based decisions. They "convene" much as committees convene to tackle planning, staffing, or marketing questions, yet they use technology—in the form of electronic communication—rather than holding formal, physical group meetings. Recent changes at Federal Express include use of desktop videoconferencing systems (DVCS) at management levels. DVCS extend the use of simple e-mail and telephonic systems to include real-time video communications among network members—who may be linked down the hallway from one another, or across the world. Digital Corporation has used DVCS for nearly a decade, yet it has had only limited use in the vast majority of organizations. Essentially, DVCS allows a "committee" meeting among participants with no regard for time, location, or distance from one another. Coupled with recent encryptic innovations, languages can now be instantly translated, further dissolving boundaries to communication among a diversified global enterprise. DVCS makes a virtual team possible through teleconferencing, management seminars, and distance-committee meetings. At Digital, DVCS teams actually cooperate to design products or services, implement marketing plans, facilitate international financial transactions, and manage the logistics systems. Federal Express has included more critical distribution activities in its interactive management network, particularly when human intervention is required for rapid-response decisions.[3]

Virtual teams are now moving into the wireless, mobile communications era in which the existing limitations of desktop telecommunications will soon be resolved. Some analysts predict that by 2004, the wireless (mobile) Internet will have more than 350 million users—exceeding the total number of world Internet users that existed in 2000. Indeed, observers question the survival of desktop PCs and workstations as wireless systems become cost effective and common.[4] Federal Express has already introduced wireless protocols for distribution networks, and recent start-up business-to-business (B2B) companies have avoided hard-wired systems at the outset, preferring cellular telephones, mobile data-linked procurement and marketing systems, and "VTM" (virtual team management).

What analysts do not yet know is the social effect on human organizations. Federal Express is concerned with the traditional benefits of personal team activities and human interaction. Distributed and impersonal communications systems are questioned as team-building tools. Individual characteristics of team members may be lost through the relatively lean and insulated nature of electronic media. With that said, organizational team processes occur through relatively unrestricted communications that existed only rarely a few years ago. Paradoxically, systems technology that allows pervasive disintegration of decision-making authority and operations also encourages pervasive integration of decisions, further encouraging interdependent operations and cooperation.

TEAM MANAGEMENT—A GLOBAL APPROACH

International managers confront a pervasive concern with group activities and teamwork. The fundamental idea of an *integrated company* affects any interdependent environment where cooperation is a critical determinant of success. Teamwork, of course, means much more than cooperation or integration, but these concepts are similar in their applications within international alliances and collaborative joint activities. A multinational corporation succeeds through teamwork, and many executives must meet expectations for developing group approaches to global tasks and encouraging international teamwork.

This final chapter focuses on team development and the establishment of international teams. The technological implications of the Internet, or the innovations of digital and wireless communications suggested by the opening profile, are not specifically addressed in this chapter. Instead, the chapter is concerned with the human dynamics of teamwork and international leadership in an era when emerging concepts such as virtual teams present enormous challenges to managers. The chapter begins by examining the nature of teams and describing how teamwork evolves in multicultural groups with diverse interests and responsibilities. These are contrasted for selected societies as a way of comparing differences in multinational teams. The chapter concludes with a discussion of the career implications of team leadership and management responsibilities in the coming century.

International Teams

International teams form either by design as deliberate management initiatives or as evolutionary consequences of global expansion. In either case, teams work primarily to help their companies achieve global efficiency. Bartlett and Ghoshal identify international teams as forms of strategic management that are essential for strengthening global efficiency.[5] Without the intense focus on establishing worldwide network relationships, the multinational enterprise (particularly in its more pervasive transnational configuration) could not function effectively. However, international teams are also created to empower local subsidiaries or regional groups to be more responsive to competitive pressure. This occurs because, by their nature, teams are empowered groups with some degree of self-directed decision-making authority. In an international company, teams are often structured to support interdependent activities among diverse operations. Specifically, a company's teams are significantly independent within their own subsystems, yet as network members, they are interdependent within a global system. The concept of a virtual team, one linked by telecommunications technology, significantly enhances an interdependent global system.

International teams also function as conduits for organizational learning. A team brings together individual members who share diverse interests and offer unique contributions to team activities. This sharing process creates a transfer of knowledge as team members interact, debate, and negotiate. Of course, diversity also increases the risk of conflict and misunderstanding, but proper management of diversity can both enrich the group members and benefit the organization with an enhanced framework of joint decision-making. The benefits of human interaction are apparent, but these benefits can be lost through the virtual team network. Ironically, the insulation that occurs in a networked global team can also reduce the downside risks of conflict.

Because groups can become chaotic, or because team efforts can become hostile when poorly managed, the risk of conflict or unproductive compromise is always present. Consequently, a critical success factor is effective team leadership. It is the ability of company executives to inspire team-based development that determines success. Managers are responsible for encouraging constructive group processes and ensuring that group members are part of an inclusive team process. Group leaders are therefore team facilitators who help individual members to become a collective decision-making body that can work toward meaningful objectives. When these processes are encapsulated at the local, regional, and strategic levels of a multinational, they represent a combined system of organizational collaboration. With this in mind, there are several different types of teams distinguished by their membership and purposes.

Transnational Teams

The **transnational team** is a work group composed of multinational members whose activities span multiple countries.[6] Unlike many other strategic teams, the transnational team exists in a highly complex environment where member executives may be drawn from worldwide operations. Indeed, they may not be in physical proximity to

Meetings aren't what they used to be. Today team meetings and group interactions span the globe through information technology and company-based virtual network systems. Time and distance are no longer constraints on communication, and teamwork is unified by information proximity as close as the nearest computer screen with video-conferencing.

one another, but instead function through information networks and periodic meetings punctuated by hectic travel agendas. Although communication may be difficult due to geographic separation of members, the team members can remain psychologically attuned if their strategic focus provides common and worthwhile objectives.

Transnational team processes are also complicated by the multicultural diversity of the team itself. Members are, by definition, representatives of different cultures. They bring to the group their own perspectives, biases, language characteristics, and behavior that both enrich the team activities and distract from team unity. Clearly, **diversity** has advantages but also presents special problems for management. Nevertheless, international teams are gaining stature as essential coordinating elements of global strategy in multinational systems. They contribute to decisions about a firm's total portfolio of transnational interests, global brands and products, organizational configurations (including optimal expansion programs for subsidiary interests), and global sourcing strategies. They also assume responsibility for leading and coordinating the activities of subordinate (regional or divisional) teams.

The executives on a strategic transnational team must carefully develop human resource systems and establish the teamwork required for success in all international activities. In effect, the members become facilitators and trainers within their own system of team development. In this way, they create the vital linkage for orchestrating company-wide activities. Figure 16.1 suggests these relationships.

Representative Teams

Regional or geographically defined teams are called **representative teams.** This term invokes the concept of a "representative head" of international operations.[7] Recall from earlier chapters that a representative head is a regional or corporate group manager who functions as a coordinator of regional or group activities. In this role, the individual does not wield hierarchical authority in the traditional sense, but supports a

FIGURE 16.1
Strategic Transnational
Teams

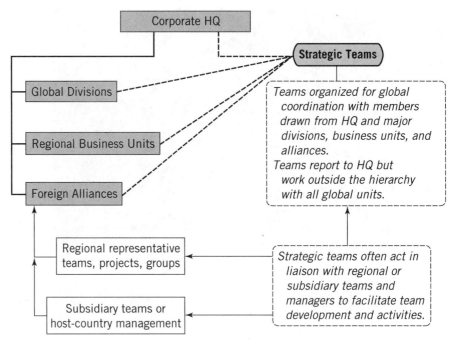

system of international teams within the region to be self-managed. Ideally, these teams will be primarily responsible for decisions within a framework of corporate objectives, and therefore accountable for interdependent operations. By implication, the representative team is an intermediate coordinating body that channels information and decisions between the strategic apex of the company and its regional or group subsidiaries. The facilitating executive concentrates on staff development rather than on directive top-down management to establish the team environment, encourage interaction among members, and, when necessary, reconcile differences among them. The team focuses on achieving operating efficiencies, allocating resources, optimizing priorities among regional subsidiaries, and harmonizing subsidiary or regional alliances.

Subsidiary Teams

The **subsidiary team** is a locally responsive operating unit concerned with operational performance. However, in the integrated environment of a multinational corporation, the subsidiary team has external accountability for products, services, or support operations within the corporate value chain. In this sense, the subsidiary team is not an isolated entity, but a linking pin within a system of operations. Consequently, many subsidiary teams include representatives from other subsidiaries who work in liaison with the host-country management team to coordinate performance objectives and operational activities.

Few companies actually have a complete team-based system that is structured as ideally as this scenario suggests. In most instances, subsidiaries are managed more traditionally through hierarchical systems and host-country enterprises rather than through systems of empowered teams. Nevertheless, host-country managers and their subsidiaries are nestled within the broader network of a corporate system where coordination of diverse interests is essential. In that sense, they are responsible to a relational network of international activities that require collaboration.

Team Systems and Processes

The three categories of teams just described suggest a hierarchical pattern similar to traditional concepts of top-down influence and stratified management. This is not, however, what international teamwork is about. The transnational teams are boundary-spanning groups that are neither stratified to replace existing managerial functions nor functionally limited to operate under a divisional structure. International teams are not simply group-oriented replacements for individual management activities. Instead, they are small consortia of people who work together to address broad ranges of issues or make better-informed decisions than the individuals could achieve on their own. A traditional CEO officially oversees Royal Dutch/Shell, for example. But in practice, the global corporation is managed through a strategic team called the *Committee of Managing Directors*, or CMD. Each of the six executives on this team acts as the equivalent of a CEO for one of Shell's worldwide business groups. They come from U.S. Shell, British Shell, the European headquarters in The Hague, and the world headquarters in London. Each person has substantial responsibilities for specific domains within Shell, but none of them could individually manage Shell's diverse global interests. The official CEO coordinates the CMD, which meets regularly to consider Shell's overall global strategy and to coordinate actions in their separate domains.[8]

A merger between U.S. and British multinationals created the giant pharmaceutical firm Glaxo-Wellcome, which doubled in size again by merging with Smith-Kline Beecham in October 2000. This organization brings together four strategic management teams from Europe and the United States, each with numbers of international teams within each division that cut across functional areas and literally operate outside the hierarchical framework of the company.[9] The company's International Quality Assurance Coordination Team (IQACT), for example, was officially established as an adjunct activity of a British research physician who had been an active proponent of quality assurance. The company built the team around his quality initiatives, and today team members come from 11 countries and speak a combined 38 different languages. Some participate on the team as part of their executive responsibilities for positions such as head of worldwide marketing and the regional head of European sales. Some are research scientists from the United States, Britain, and Belgium. Several are specialists from U.S., Swedish, and German universities who serve in advisory capacities. Several more were appointed from Glaxo-Wellcome's R&D, production, and global procurement sections.

The Glaxo-Wellcome team (IQACT) itself has institutional permanence, but team members are appointed on temporary terms that change with team projects and corporate priorities. IQACT has a mission of integrating Glaxo-Wellcome's worldwide quality assurance procedures under a global umbrella of standards and production methods designed and implemented by the IQACT group. The team members travel extensively, either individually or in smaller groups; work with foreign subsidiaries as well as with corporate executives; and make recommendations to corporate and board levels for changes that can affect the entire company. In this sense, the team does not have a hierarchical reporting channel and does not fit into a decision-making stratum. Its members do not report to a particular superior in their team capacity, and subsidiary or regional managers view them as intervention specialists. Nevertheless, the team has extraordinary power to influence the company's policies and operational procedures. The team itself is not identified with a particular country, group, or region, and has no specific headquarters. Members rotate team meetings at various national group facilities every month, and work with different team configurations on field projects.[10]

Regional or group teams seem to correspond to an intermediate level of management, but that description is not entirely accurate. As Figure 16.2 illustrates, these teams act in conjunction with line management to coordinate sector-specific interests; but they are not in a direct line of authority. Representative teams are coordinating bodies set up to tackle specific issues too small for the attention of global teams such as Shell's executive strategic body, the CMD, or Glaxo-Wellcome's quality assurance group.

For example, Heineken, the Dutch brewer with worldwide distribution, has established a representative team called the *European Production Task Force*. This 13-member group unites managers selected from Italy, France, Spain, and Holland to exercise strategic control over the company's European manufacturing and distribution systems. Several of the managers are assigned as permanent team members, but most serve on the team as part of their executive duties in national subsidiaries and Heineken's headquarters group. Their decisions cut across brewery and distribution facilities throughout Europe, and their primary purpose is to optimize Heineken's European configuration of activities while coordinating those operations with the company's global interests. The team decides where to expand breweries, where to locate distribution centers, how to source ingredients and other materials, and what resources to allocate to any particular subsidiary or operation. This responsibility extends to breweries in 20 countries and worldwide procurement systems. Thus the team plays an extremely influential role in the company's regional and corporate operations.[11]

In local operations, subsidiary teams act as cross-border coordinating groups. Members may come from only two neighboring facilities or as many as two dozen different countries. The teams usually consist of key managers from company units and autonomous subsidiaries who can orchestrate interdependent activities within a company's value chain. These international teams behave more like committees to address cross-border or multicultural problems that arise from the interdependence of their separate operations. IBM Europe, for example, forms intercultural teams to address marketing and distribution issues. The team meets monthly, rotating locations so that

FIGURE 16.2
Regional Representative Team

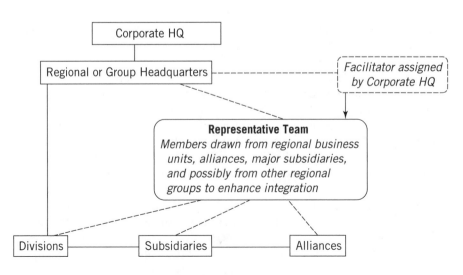

its members spend several days in local facilities, eventually becoming familiar with each subsidiary's operations and how they fit into the company's overall system. The members address coordination problems, expansion plans, human resource and staffing issues, vendor relationships, and European marketing.[12]

Each type of team—strategic, regional, or local—has a different mandate, and there are no prescribed models for membership or predetermined methods for pursuing team activities. Indeed, the nature of teamwork is to have self-managed activities. They may have a broad framework for their existence, such as Glaxo-Wellcome's quality assurance effort, or they may have a regional focus, such as Heineken's European production team. Many teams fulfill a coordination purpose, such as IBM's consortia approach that brings together operational managers for regular interdivisional and functional management decisions. The teams have no specific rules about how they will be formed or where they will be located, and in most instances the members determine their own priorities and how they will perform their tasks. A closer look at transnational teams and how they are established will be helpful in understanding the team process.

Establishing Strategic Teams

Most teams are deliberately created through strategic initiatives that determine a general framework for each group and the team's purpose. However, the process of team management has evolved almost capriciously as people within multinational companies have formed their own informal alliances over the years.[13] During the early 1980s, Xerox established alliances with the British Rank Organization and the Japanese Fuji Corporation in response to informal projects that engineers from each of the companies had been collaborating on. Formal alliances began to be created when British and American R&D engineers working together on a new photo redevelopment process realized that they needed help in specialized optics technology. They turned to Fuji Corporation, which had a reciprocal interest in working with Xerox. The Japanese sent a group of 15 engineers to New York to work in the consortium. Within a few months, the team had created the world photocopier, a breakthrough that had eluded the independent efforts of each company. The new product was the first in a line of innovations that helped Xerox to regain its market leadership in photo-reproduction equipment. More important, the advancement was recognized as a team effort, and three new alliances were established among Xerox, Rank, and Fuji for international R&D and marketing through multicultural teams strategically placed in the United States, Europe, and Japan.

In a similar way, marketing managers from IBM Latin America formed their own informal team in 1990 to establish an 11-country consortium for PC distribution systems. The IBM managers and staff acted entirely without authority to create a team-based marketing system, but it was so successful that IBM acknowledged the team's success and sanctioned it as a formal part of regional operations. The team now operates as an autonomous business unit for coordination of Latin American sales and distribution.

Formal teams are established specifically to address individual transnational problems that extend beyond national or geographic boundaries. For example, Eastman Kodak formed a team in 1991 to develop new consumer products based on CD technology. At the time, Kodak executives had only a vague idea of what the team might accomplish, but they knew that the company had to create a self-reliant team with the independence needed to challenge traditional limits on new product development. The team was established in London, far from the offices and research labs of the parent company. A team leader was selected, together with several core members who could attract international participants needed for the project. The result was a new photo CD system that brought together two key technologies and a global perspective for new consumer markets. The team took the product from inception to final worldwide marketing, launching it simultaneously in several European markets and then in North America and Asia. When the project began, the team consisted of a small product development group, then expanded to include marketing people, and finally evolved into an international project management team with technicians and support staff from many different domestic and foreign operations.

Much of the very limited research on international teams has focused on individual cases or incidents, but studies have revealed a pattern for team development, represented in Figure 16.3. Once a team is formally established, it enters a building stage. The team leader guides start-up activities such as searching for resources and creating an environment apart from the familiar bureaucracy to attract members who can work in a self-managed group. The team develops its own objectives, but it must link these priorities with the company's larger mission and strategic objectives. Members operate outside of so-called *normal channels*, so they must generate relational networks to support interactions with other organizational interests and alliance partners. During this shaky period of formation, little is known about the team. Indeed, the team members may not have a clear idea of what they will do or why they are working together. (A later section of the chapter explores this period of ambiguity, picturesquely called *storming* because team members usually must resolve conflicts and solidify disparate elements to nurture an effective team environment.)

To be successful, a team must transit through the start-up stage by demonstrating that it can make a contribution to corporate objectives. Consequently, team members must resolve their individual differences and learn to work together. The team then evolves into a second stage (or a third, if the period of storming constitutes a stage of its own). During this phase, individual team members differentiate their roles, refine their responsibilities within the team, and begin to work toward self-defined objectives. The team leader becomes a catalyst for team-based intervention, inspiring joint efforts and coordinating individual member activities. As the team gels, it becomes a mature entity with a strong sense of group commitment and well-understood integrative skills. Team members build consensus and coordinate problem-solving techniques, and they become focused on achieving closure of their projects.

FIGURE 16.3
A General Pattern of
Team Development

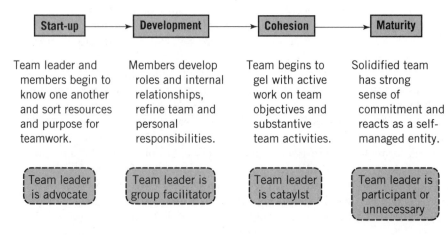

Once a team reaches this unified and mature status, the leader no longer relies heavily on the advocacy skills required during the start-up phase or the catalytic skills required in earlier stages to bring team members together. These team-building skills are still important, but the team leader's focus shifts toward managing the team's projects on behalf of its members. This responsibility requires astute integrative skills. The leader often must manage a complex multicultural group with diverse interests and provide an interface with external constituents and the company's own line units. As the demands of leadership change, a particular team may acknowledge different leaders during each stage. Further, as the group expands and changes its activities, its membership often changes.[14]

Many international teams become standing entities, as illustrated earlier for IBM's Latin American marketing consortium and Fuji-Xerox's R&D centers. Many others, however, limit their activities to short-lived projects and break up after they accomplish their objectives. This is the common model of project management through a matrix structure that draws team members from across an organization for temporary assignments on field teams. For example, the giant Swiss-Swedish AAB Group operates under a project system in which more than 2,000 field engineering operations exist at any one time.[15] The company has global procurement teams that service all field projects, and it has "standing teams" for engineering design projects and international marketing. However, ABB relies on a system of temporary *flying teams* that coordinate sector projects such as water development in Indonesia, transport systems in Thailand, and port facilities in Malaysia. ABB also activates R&D engineering teams, such as a North American group that was established to design and build a new form of rapid transit for airports. When a system is completed, the team members are reassigned, and their projects are transferred to operational line units.

Regional Integration and Teamwork

Perhaps the foremost problem facing multinational corporations is effective coordination of widely distributed activities. This activity involves not only integrating value-chain activities but also managing cross-functional specialization and reconciling alliance interests. Bartlett and Ghoshal argue that a "new management mentality" must emerge to suit the modern transnational corporation—a multinational that has expanded globally so completely that it has established a seamless worldwide operation. More to the point, a transnational must connect its resources, innovations, and activities through a unified stream of consciousness in which management itself is the catalyst for dealing with "complexity, diversity, and change."[16] This goal requires a mentality of integration through teamwork that provides the connections and liaison relationships needed to bring together regional, functional, and intercultural company activities. Companies with substantial foreign alliances, joint ventures, or cooperative agreements with other organizations must rely heavily on teamwork as a crucial aspect of international coordination.

The communicative dimension of team-based activities is an extremely important part of international management, because as companies expand, they must manage progressively complicated patterns of information. Indeed, managers rapidly face information overload, and information becomes ambiguous in a multicultural environment. Different patterns of language, often-conflicting cultural values, and a variety of interpersonal relationships contribute to this communicative ambiguity. The complexity of multinational companies and their networked associations seldom allows for familiar hierarchical patterns of channeled authority, and information patterns among dozens—often hundreds—of diversified activities can no longer be structured along hierarchical lines. Researchers on international communication problems have called this phenomenon *equivocality of information*. Problems with equivocal information do not allow managers to communicate through standard organizational channels or predetermined reporting systems; instead, managers rely on progressively intense interactions among smaller groups to communicate. These exchanges do not necessarily pass between formal groups set up as coordinating teams (although, as noted earlier, such team systems could evolve in ideal situations). Instead, communication relies on a pervasive team-building spirit through personal associations. In other words, people can manage the richness of information and its unstructured nature when they can interact. They can share perspectives and reconcile misunderstandings, therefore bridging cultural differences.

Thus, small groups working in a communicative team environment provide the forums for effective dialogue stifled by departmentalized chain-of-command organizations. These teams do not replace the command channels or impose decision-making priorities on departments or functional activities. Instead, they create the vital information links required to integrate disparate responsibilities. Of course, many teams are purposely endowed with decision-making authority at their creation. They essentially become organs in the international organization, but teams also need opportunities for spontaneous team efforts at every level, even though the organizational hierarchy does not officially sanction them.

More important, the process of team formation generates interpersonal relationships that digest and filter information from multifaceted interests. Teamwork, through formal efforts or through an atmosphere of spontaneous cooperation, provides a conduit made up of such associations. Team endeavors, therefore, help companies to make sense of their environments within their organizational cultures—much like the nervous system wires together functions of the human body.[17]

The importance of teamwork was emphasized in an earlier chapter through descriptions of international human resource management practices at companies such as General Electric, Compaq, Shell Oil, and AT&T. Each of these examples illustrated how management training and development focuses on building international team relationships. In almost every instance, management development and leadership training concentrate on building *interpersonal relationships* and *cross-cultural communications*. Earlier discussions also emphasized that team members must be carefully selected; in particular, team leaders must be recruited who can synthesize group activities. Companies often must select people who can work in self-directed team environments and adapt to multicultural environments. No one has yet clearly laid out methods for accomplishing this goal, and debates rage about whether firms should create well-diversified or homogeneous teams. The next section expands on this theme and related effects of multiculturalism and diversity in a team-based environment.

MULTICULTURALISM AND DIVERSITY

Presentations and examples throughout this book have emphasized that international organizations are composed of multicultural work groups, and that global enterprises can succeed only if they effectively integrate group activities on a worldwide scale. A work group, however, is not necessarily a team; it can be little more than a loose association of individuals. Indeed, a group can work in chaotic and dysfunctional processes. Teamwork assumes a collective and cooperative effort by individuals working together to achieve common goals in an environment of shared decision-making.

In an international organization, group behavior that leads to effective teamwork requires that members become acculturated to one another's values. Also, because multinational corporations by definition must deal with several (perhaps many) different cultural variables, their managers often face daunting tasks in team building and team leadership.

As noted earlier, often companies purposely establish **multicultural teams** in their efforts to integrate regional and strategic operations. Like Royal Dutch/Shell, companies can also create cross-functional international teams such as global procurement task forces; or like ABB, they can build a system of operational project teams coordinated through higher-level matrix teams. These types of teams require long-term programs of acculturation training and personal development, so that individuals can make the mental transformation required to be fully acclimated to a team environment. Acculturation is essential for managers of diversified organizations. Earlier discussions also emphasized that in some nations such as Japan, team development is strongly associated with ethnically homogeneous membership, which reduces the need to reconcile multicultural diversity. Teamwork evolves more easily in a culturally insular environment, and subsequently minimizes the risks associated with dysfunctional conflict that occurs in other, more ethnically diverse societies. However, homogeneous teams also face difficulties because team members share similar and often narrow values. Consequently, limited diversity constrains their viewpoints and opportunities.

During the early phases of a company's international expansion, it may well create teams oriented toward the parent company. Expatriate-led teams established through national headquarters are likely to head most international activities, and not surprisingly, they will consist of people with similar cultural roots. In the Japanese context, this effects a homogeneous team selection process that results in a strong sense of ethnic identity among team members. Research suggests that stability promotes effectiveness in these teams, especially since members share common cultural values. They work together more efficiently, and their cohesive character encourages rapid agreement on issues. On the other hand, they can also become so narrowly entrenched that the whole purpose of integrating the company's diversified interests is lost in the intransigence of the group itself.

Consensus and cohesion, characteristics often associated with homogeneous groups, do not necessarily equate to team effectiveness. In fact, research has shown that homogeneous teams are less likely than culturally diverse teams to generate highly effective decisions. At the same time, homogeneous teams are less likely to generate highly *in*effective decisions. The same research showed that ethnically homogeneous teams (i.e., those with members from a single ethnic background), made "average and relatively good" decisions, but they rarely came up with unusual or creative ideas. In contrast, culturally diverse teams were more creative and generated decisions that led to more productive results, yet they also often had disastrous results and internal team problems.[18] Put into perspective, the homogeneous teams held the middle ground with fewer notable successes and failures, while the culturally diverse teams had nearly equally outstanding successes and dramatic failures due to a higher risk profile and greater disparity of interests. Figure 16.4 emphasizes these differences.

Recent research on team effectiveness has determined that although patterns of team performance may sometimes follow the model described earlier, there are important distinctions in how multicultural groups perform. Specifically, teams that are at the polar extremes of heterogeneity and homogeneity tend to perform equally well, yet those falling between the extremes—teams with some ethnic or cultural diversity—struggle to work together or to perform well.[19] This does not invalidate earlier research, but instead amplifies the complexity of multicultural team environments.

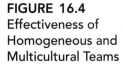

FIGURE 16.4
Effectiveness of
Homogeneous and
Multicultural Teams

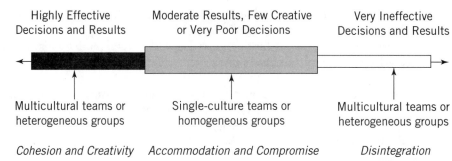

Indeed, the paradox of a curvilinear relationship in team performance was reinforced in a series of studies among Japanese and German joint ventures, and specifically for multicultural teams in multinational companies.[20] Teams with substantial cultural diversity were ultimately found to perform best in companies with pervasive international interests. This occurred because teams at all levels were comprised of members with such contrasting cultural values and management techniques that they formed extremely strong team alliances focused on substantive issues; personal idiosyncrasies, cultural differences, and ethnic distinctions added to the richness of decisions rather than detracted from team member relationships. At the same time, highly cohesive, ethnically or culturally homogeneous teams performed extremely well with little internal team strife. These homogeneous teams, however, could not coordinate their efforts well with diverse teams elsewhere in their corporations.[21]

There is little to conclude from these studies other than what the researchers themselves conclude: team structure and the effects of ethnic or cultural diversity on performance are far too complicated to reduce to simple models of team behavior. Nevertheless, the evidence points to success by companies when they purposely structure teams on a multicultural basis with members who have diversified interests and often substantially different cultural values. A company therefore will more likely benefit from group dynamics of diverse teams than from the cohesiveness of homogeneous teams. Ironically, the process of reaching agreement on a decision or coordinating a team activity in such diverse groups may be very difficult; but in the end, the result is a creative solution that has been thoroughly challenged. Indeed, conflict of interests may be an important feature of team contributions as individual members bring to the table a wide range of issues and a sense of advocacy for their particular corporate activities.[22]

Managing Diversity in the Work Group

Ultimately, team leadership is concerned with establishing a democratic climate of decision-making whereby employees are empowered to be active participants in team decisions and activities. Therefore, a team leader must have the ability to create participative patterns of group behavior, be able to reconcile conflicts in a constructive manner, and be a facilitator who teaches and supports team activities rather than directs them.[23] The team leader's responsibility is to assure that group members have an agenda, remain focused on performance objectives, and constructively take responsibility for decisions or resolving problems. In a culturally diverse group, this includes the responsibility for not only minimizing conflictual behavior among group members that can occur due to cultural differences but also encouraging the productive contribution of each member—specifically because each person brings to the team a unique and often very different perspective. This can be difficult, because the leader is expected to recognize differences among members and to encourage all members to honor those differences. During group meetings, this diversity brings out sharp contrasts in values and opens debates that would be uncommon in homogeneous groups; thus, team meetings are often sensitive, always bordering on potential conflict.[24]

Team success rests on a delicate balance of managing conflict in a way that constructively elicits individual differences while blocking behavior that threatens individuals or pits them against one another. Theorists have identified two types of conflict as bases for understanding how to manage group behavior. These are called *cognitive conflict* and *objective conflict*. One type of conflict can produce constructive effects, while the other usually exerts a debilitating influence. These are noted in Figure 16.5.

Cognitive Conflict

Some disagreements that occur among team members contribute to constructive debate of issues; these *substantive* arguments are collectively called **cognitive conflict.** Team members engaged in cognitive conflict may take strong, diametrically opposed viewpoints, become aggressive advocates for their interests or beliefs, and debate with intensity. But ideally, they focus on the issues before the group as part of its common interest in finding the best solution to a problem or making the best team decision. Cognitive conflict does not degenerate into personal battles or individual attacks. It targets the substance of the team's purpose, so no one feels personally threatened or disenfranchised by the group decision-making process. Indeed, such disagreements often strengthen team relationships, as the group collectively reaches beyond individual limitations and synergistically leverages contributions by individual members.

Affective Conflict

On the dark side, **affective conflict** results from provocation and individual animosity that detracts from team objectives. Instead, interactions degenerate into personal hostilities. Team members attack the values of others, cynically dismiss viewpoints different from their own, and personalize the anger that accompanies disagreements on issues. Consequently, the issues become lost in an interpersonal battleground full of individuals determined to win or lose; in the end, they may compromise to give the impression that the group had achieved a collective result.

Team leaders can manage cognitive and affective conflict by developing patterns of teamwork based on individual commitments to a consolidated group process.

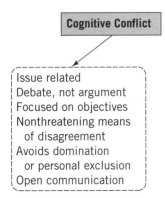

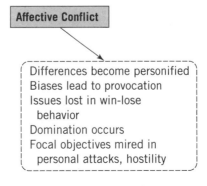

FIGURE 16.5
Contrast in Intragroup Conflict

Researchers have identified four goals that team members can pursue to forge this commitment, and effective team leaders keep these goals firmly at the forefront of all group processes:[25]

- *Maintaining a focused activity*. Effective groups stick close to the issues at hand and maintain a clear idea of the team's purpose and ultimate objective. A team leader can reinforce this behavior by helping to develop an agenda with **superordinate goals** that draw on the total team contribution, not individual capabilities or less important issues brought to the group by individuals. Trivial issues are not allowed to cloud the core issues that define a group's purpose for working together.
- *Encourage creativity*. Effective teams are encouraged to think beyond individual options and the limitations of each member's contribution. Instead, they consciously stretch options and build on the richness of individual differences to seek new, unexpected, and unknown solutions to problems. Creativity requires an ability to step beyond the mainstream, to venture beyond one's existing framework of knowledge to test new waters. Therefore, a team leader can help guide group behavior to accept differences of opinion and unusual viewpoints by individual members, and then build on them for new options that come from a shared experience.
- *Ensure open communications*. Effective teams enjoy a sense of freedom of expression that allows individuals to speak freely, challenge others on core issues, question flawed logic, and to put forward candid proposals without fear of threats. The team leader must ensure that individual team members do not resort to personal attacks or harbor resentment. This can be achieved when everyone is consciously aware of the importance for open dialogue and issue-based discussions. They must be prepared for the inevitability of disagreement as a natural (and necessary) component of teamwork. The crucial task is to encourage spontaneity of expression, but without self-serving or personalized behavior that creates defensive responses.
- *Nurture integration*. Members of effective teams firmly keep in mind the importance of nurturing the group's internal relationships, thus bringing each person into comparable balance as an active participant. In every group, particular members make larger contributions than others; some are more vocal, more involved, and perhaps more talented in participative behavior, but this difference need not prevent all members from contributing according to their capabilities. The team leader must facilitate this balance by drawing everyone into activities and protecting the team against domination by any one member.

Unfortunately, these guidelines are more complicated than they sound. In fact, teamwork requires a long-term commitment to developing new patterns of behavior and skillful leadership by individuals who have become adept at working in task-group environments. A company cannot turn on teamwork as easily as flicking a light switch, and an assignment as a team leader does not suddenly create the capabilities of a group facilitator—particularly in a multicultural environment with potentially dramatic contrasts in values. However, the drive to keep team goals firmly in focus is an important element of team evolution, and leaders can enhance team effectiveness in many other ways. Some research, for example, emphasizes the importance of selecting team members with comparable professional qualifications. People drawn from similar ranks or with comparable organizational standing are unlikely to dominate or to be dominated in a team setting with members of equal status. Diversity is achieved by selecting people from a broad range of activities or from representative cultures, ethnic groups, or personal backgrounds.

International team selection is enriched by equalizing power among members from different functional and cultural elements within the company. This precaution prevents formation of a team with a majority (or even a significant minority) of members from one cultural perspective. Depending on the nature of the team (a strategic team, regional coordinating team, or project group), selection criteria should promote a cross-sectional membership that can adequately represent a majority of the company's interests. Consequently, team members may bring to the group homogeneous ability levels but heterogeneous attitudes and values.[26]

Another useful suggestion for managing a diverse team is to establish a non-threatening learning environment in which team members can evolve toward a self-empowered pattern of behavior. This requires a team leader who is patient with change, which often occurs only gradually as members become accustomed to working together and taking responsibility for decisions that, in most instances, were made in a hierarchical system before the team was formed. The team leader is likely to face major behavior adjustments, giving up previously guarded rights to make decisions while also learning how to live with the inevitable conflict that arises in a group environment. Organizational development specialists can encourage this process by acting as intervention facilitators. An earlier chapter on human resource management described this process and several specific methods of intervention, but recall that effective consulting requires an intermediary capable of keeping the team and its leader on track with issues and away from tedious confrontations beyond the substantive boundaries of the team's purpose.[27]

A consistent theme of effective team building is to create a *team vision* or a clear purpose for the team members to work together. As noted earlier, this is often encapsulated in *superordinate goals*. A superordinate goal is one that transcends individual priorities. In a multicultural team, these goals prevail over individual differences.[28] It is a purpose, a vision, or an objective that ties members together in a concerted action leaving little room for individual or self-serving interests. In effect, the team identifies a "common enemy" (a common problem) that captures everyone's interest and focuses their energies. Superordinate goals require collaboration, which minimizes individual prejudices or preoccupations with trivial issues. More important, the team benefits collectively from the results, further enhancing integrative group behavior.[29]

Multicultural Behavior in Group Work

Cultural diversity complicates decisions and makes reaching agreement difficult, because people from different cultural backgrounds have fundamentally different patterns of behavior. Multicultural teams face three general categories of behavioral problems that must be managed effectively for the group to succeed. These are attitudinal problems, perceptual problems, and communication problems.[30]

Attitudinal Problems

In any group setting, individuals are drawn toward others with similar backgrounds, values, and ethnic characteristics. At the same time, people from different ethnic cultures tend to mistrust others, and in many instances they openly dislike individuals from other races or ethnic groups. By bringing people together from a variety of cultural backgrounds, companies purposely create diverse groups; but at the same time, companies can create very uncomfortable relationships. Even if the individuals selected have open minds and are eager to work together, their cultural biases are likely to remain intact. Given this limitation, team members can work together, yet they may remain guarded in their behavior. They will be cautious about what they say and protective of their own cultural values. Indeed, by definition, these situations will persist in a diverse team, yet the value of the team rests on its members' abilities to constructively bring different viewpoints and ideas to the group process.

Perceptual Problems

Individuals from high-status cultures and well-developed economies are stereotyped as being better educated, more technically sophisticated, having better professional experience, and possessing greater management acumen than individuals from low-status countries and underdeveloped economies. Consequently, team members behave toward one another with certain stereotypes that create group pecking orders and in-group role behavior. Whether these stereotypes are justified is not important; the unfortunate fact remains that each person's perceptions of others affect relationships and group behavior. In multicultural groups, for example, Americans and Europeans often enjoy deferential treatment; they are viewed as being better educated and more experienced, compared with team members from the Middle East, Latin America, Asia, and Africa. Whether this perception is true or not, team members from the other groups must prove themselves capable of working with Americans or Europeans as equals.

Communication Problems

Linguistically diverse teams always encounter fundamental difficulties in translating and interpreting both verbal and nonverbal messages. Written information may require several rounds of translation and patient explanation to convey accurate meanings. Discussions can quite innocently lead to misunderstandings or inaccurate interpretations. If meetings are held in one language, team members brought up with different languages or communication protocols often struggle to participate effectively. Even if these individuals have a reasonable understanding of the language being used, they may not be fully comfortable with the linguistic nuances. Instead of participating as group members, they often withdraw. In these situations, all team members must learn to patiently accommodate language capabilities and individual styles of communication, or effective teamwork may never be achieved.

These problems tend to occur among all multicultural teams. Often, the members can achieve little more than a tenuous accommodation; cohesion simply may not be possible. Indeed, a multicultural team may be little more than a group of individuals working in isolation, even though they appear to be collaborating.[31] On the other hand, the team members may remain socially and culturally distant from one another, yet contribute to the team a vast assortment of interesting perspectives that result in extraordinary results. In either situation, the diverse team is less likely to be trapped by problems that plague homogeneous groups, such as individual capitulation to group norms—or to a dominant member—in order to maintain group harmony.[32] Consequently, a diverse team is less likely than a homogenous team to engage in groupthink, which is an overly conforming mode of behavior.

Groupthink is associated with suboptimal decision-making and subordination of individual ideas to those that seem most common to the majority membership. Groupthink occurs in order to preserve the group's appearance of solidarity by not challenging issues or voicing dissenting opinions.[33] In effect, a group creates a consensus by proactively blocking expressions of new ideas or discouraging unusual suggestions that might disturb the group's sense of cohesive relationships. But the multicultural team has few, if any, predetermined relationships to protect, no subconscious expectations of group norms or conformity, and few culturally ingrained protocols that would prevent members from defending a variety of dissenting viewpoints.[34]

These are a few of the characteristics that make multicultural teams difficult to manage. They also foster a certain degree of enthusiasm among team members in a challenging work environment. All work groups—including teams, temporary task groups, and working alliances—share several distinct advantages and disadvantages. These are summarized in Table 16.1.

From an international perspective, teamwork can be very challenging. Prevailing attitudes in some societies may encourage teamwork, while those in other societies make it a very stressful experience. Teamwork itself takes on different dimensions in various societies, and managers must be able to adapt to different cultural expectations. The next section briefly examines contrasts in teamwork for selected cultural perspectives.

CONTRASTING CULTURES AND TEAMWORK

The concept of teamwork is fundamentally different among many world cultures. Consequently, assumptions about how to manage in team environments held by Americans and other westerners often flounder elsewhere. Concepts such as workplace empowerment, quality management, and productivity improvement through self-directed teams simply have no place in foreign autocracies or highly structured societies. Even the prevalent theme that effective management of a growing multinational enterprise depends on cross-cultural teams led by capable managers is often ridiculed abroad. Team integration, and the emerging concept of virtual teamwork

---

TABLE 16.1

ADVANTAGES AND DISADVANTAGES OF GROUP PROBLEM SOLVING

Advantages of Teams vs. Individuals
- Groups, particularly cohesive teams, bring a greater variety of perspectives to a problem than individuals, thus creating more alternatives to consider.
- Group members, particularly in multicultural teams, bring more knowledge and richer base of information to decisions than individuals.
- Group problem solving enhances successful implemention of decisions and changes by having wide participation and group advocacy for results.
- Group members understand the problem and decision and can effectively communicate with others in an organization, thus enhancing execution.

Disadvantages of Teams vs. Individuals
- Groups, particularly homogeneous teams, can satisfice and compromise, thus reaching suboptimal decisions too quickly to preserve group harmony.
- Group cohesion is difficult to achieve and teams are more likely to become dominated by strong formal and informal leaders, rendering group efforts ineffective or creating conflict and disintegration rather than effective results.
- Groups, particularly single-culture teams, can be trapped by "groupthink," where they fail to think critically or take either risky or responsible positions that might challenge a group leader or offend the group.

Sources: James A. F. Stoner and R. Edward Freeman, *Management*, 5th ed. (Englewood Cliffs, N.J.: Prentice Hall, 1992), 514–515. Also L. Richard Hoffman, "Applying Experimental Research on Group Problem Solving to Organizations," *Journal of Applied Behavioral Science* 15, no. 3 (1979): 382.

through network operations, are suspect ideas in many countries.[35] Relatively few organizations throughout the world have team-based activities; most remain entrenched in traditional decision-making behavior that is at least hierarchical if not autocratic.[36] The reason that more societies and international organizations do not embrace team processes is, to a great extent, the resilience of cultural values. That does not lessen the importance or the benefits of teamwork, but as explained in the following sections, international managers are often surprised by foreign attitudes toward concepts that affect teamwork, such as empowerment and managerial authority.

Individualistic Cultures

Cultures that embrace individualism, such as Anglo-influenced societies and much of Western Europe, may readily endorse team-based systems, but people generally work to achieve individual recognition, promotions, and monetary rewards. Indeed, most U.S. companies loudly sing the praises of teamwork, yet these same companies reward productivity almost entirely on an individual basis. Ironically, leading U.S. advocates for team-based leadership such as Disney, Coca-Cola, PepsiCo, and Merrill Lynch also pay the world's highest individual executive salaries and individual incentive premiums. A tendency to emphasize individual rewards and career competition for personal achievements pervades almost all western developed economies, and the focus on individualistic behavior runs throughout most organizations.[37]

These western societies also create generational transitions that reinforce individualistic values through competitive child development programs, schooling, sports, and recreation. Reason suggests that strongly individualistic cultures should be the least likely to develop consensus-based decision-making techniques and team-based management systems. This reasoning, however, presents a paradoxical situation. Although theories of team management and group behavior have evolved predominantly in North America and Western Europe, in practice, organizations more often reflect traditional hierarchical systems. Even when team development occurs, it often remains stratified with a certain chain-of-command approach to intergroup and team relationships.[38]

Team development, nevertheless, has followed a slow process of incremental change for many western companies. Managers are caught up in organizational development techniques and new concepts of organizational learning. They must unlearn many of the fundamental characteristics by which they and their predecessors have gained success. Multinational managers from these countries working abroad, as well as those working with multicultural groups, find teamwork a difficult process to accept. Research has shown that among the leading *Fortune 100* companies, executives talk the talk of teamwork, but they seldom walk the walk by actually accepting democratic leadership behavior or developing participative work environments.[39] In fact, among their most difficult problems of working abroad in collectivist societies, U.S. managers cite their own inability to share decision-making authority through collective group processes.[40]

Paternalistic Cultures

Managers in paternalistic societies seem capable of operating in pluralistic environments, where they can hold fast to rigorous status differentials and rank-based authority structures at the same time that they nurture somewhat collective work environments. These group-oriented environments reflect pervasive concepts of reciprocal loyalties and the patron or leader as head of an organizational family or protected referent group. Outwardly, paternalistic organizations, such as those in much of Latin America and East Asia, seem to favor extremely autocratic authority structures. Closer inspection reveals collective elements, including highly cohesive work groups and well-developed team environments. Really intimate involvement demonstrates the extremely narrow scope of cohesion within work groups, which often limit tolerance to members of the same ethnic groups and individuals with very close personal allegiances; teamwork almost never extends to shared decision-making. To the contrary, the paternalistic leader controls all decisions, and the collective involvement of cohesive groups often functions simply to ratify management prerogatives.[41]

Effective international teamwork can be extremely elusive in such countries, because subordinates simply do not expect to contribute to decisions, nor do they want the responsibilities that come with true team participation. Managers who participate in multicultural teams often find that they must relinquish their paternalistic tendencies in order to make meaningful contributions to team efforts. Managers from other cultures working with paternalistic leaders often find that they must patiently accommodate behavior that often seems arrogant and ritualized.[42] In effect, the meaning of *teamwork* changes in the transition from North America (and much of the theoretical literature) to a paternalistic society, where in-group loyalties and personal allegiances play more significant roles than collaboration and shared power for decision-making.

Collectivist Cultures

The Confucian model examined by Hofstede and Bond exemplifies the cohesive nature of nearly all group endeavors in collectivist cultures; however, teamwork is substantially different among these societies.[43] Japanese team management, for example, is the classic model put forward in contrast to western practices. The Japanese emphasize consensus, broad participation by all team members, patient and thorough deliberation of all issues, and total acceptance of final decisions with conformity expected by everyone involved. Perhaps this is an oversimplification, yet the Japanese proclivity for this approach to management is well known.

The Chinese and Japanese approaches to management *seem* to be similar, but they are not. Chinese loyalties run to family units, not to organizations, and teamwork does not take the form of collaboration with co-workers or with other organizational members as in Japan. Instead, the Chinese organization works through many paternalistic processes under the control of strong heads who wield autocratic power similar to that of the head of a family.

Business decisions in Japan evolve through systems of team recommendations that are reviewed and endorsed by managers; problematic recommendations are referred to the teams for further refinement. Japanese team leaders often fill teaching roles, but they also benefit from tremendous status and accept responsibility for guiding their teams in focused behavior. Team leaders in China often behave as "little emperors," imposing unilateral decisions or resolving issues on their own well apart from the work group. They then discretely involve team members, who have little recourse other than to accept effectively finalized decisions. Workers carefully avoid questioning issues, and they rarely behave in a confrontational manner. This style of decision-making in China has been called the *Chinese whisper*, suggesting a subtle, hidden power that really resolves issues apart from task groups and formal teams.[44]

International managers who find themselves working with Chinese or Japanese cross-cultural teams often struggle desperately to understand how decisions are actually made. Chinese teams establish elaborate protocols, formal agendas, and collections of information through processes that seem to empower team members.

Outsiders may then discover to their surprise that most of these arrangements are ceremonial gestures; the real decisions come down from autocratic leaders who expect unswerving conformity by rank-and-file employees.[45] Japanese teams work even more intensely to establish group protocols, and team meetings often involve lengthy and complicated interactions. However, unlike Chinese workers, Japanese team members *are empowered* to meaningfully influence company actions.[46] These differences in Japanese and Chinese behavior were emphasized in earlier chapters, but the main point here is that international managers operating in Asia will find few similarities between Japanese and Chinese organizations, or, indeed, among other Asian societies such as Malaysia, Korea, or the Philippines.

Autocratic Cultures

By definition, autocratic cultures do not embrace team concepts, yet most autocratic societies value pluralistic principles and ethnically cohesive social structures capable of supporting very close collaboration. Group harmony is expected, but only within the framework of a stratified society. Tribal cultures of East Africa, for example, consider individuality as a deviant human trait. Therefore, collective group support is vividly maintained, yet a tribal chief or head may wield extreme dictatorial power. Teamwork really has no meaning in situations apart from the ethnic group, and then only within the framework of the group leader's personal prerogatives.[47]

Most Islamic societies exhibit parallel patterns of group expectations, based in part on ethnicity but, more important, on religious codes that mandate social behavior. Relationships are defined by Islamic law and its prevailing interpretation in each culture. Teamwork is not part of the religious code and therefore not a significant consideration in leadership.[48] These practices do not make for an uncooperative or individualistic people, however. To the contrary, harmony is a highly regarded human value within the ethnic boundaries of Muslim societies, and a similar emphasis on strong family values keeps Islamic work groups extremely cohesive. Indeed, group discussions often become animated debates that border on hostile confrontations, yet in the end, the members present a united front. Unfortunately, this process can lead to exclusionary behavior that bars participation by anyone viewed as an outsider to a particular ethnic or religious group. Managers always experience teamwork in a Muslim state at arm's length and in relationships tempered by religious priorities and ethnicity.[49]

GROUP DEVELOPMENT AND TEAM PROCESSES

The contrasts in teamwork briefly described in the previous section should forewarn international managers that they cannot venture overseas with set models of team behavior in mind and expect to be received with open arms. A multinational company seeking to establish international teams with multicultural representation faces a complicated problem of reconciling how members from different cultures will fit into a team environment. Only after settling this question can management consider how to approach team activities. An IBM Latin American team will likely behave more paternalistically than an IBM European team that reflects western concepts of joint decision-making. Meanwhile, IBM's Japanese team may be a highly involved consensus-building group, while IBM staff in Malaysia or Saudi Arabia may work within autocratic styles tempered by religious tenets.[50] Consequently, development in each multicultural team setting requires a unique approach. The process of team formation, however, does reveal some similarities throughout the world, which are explored in the following sections.

Stages of Group Formation

Every team endeavor develops through several stages. Analysts typically highlight four stages, known in management literature as *forming, storming, norming,* and *performing,* as described in Figure 16.6. These labels may seem a bit flippant, but the following paragraphs will explain them in operational terms.[51]

Stage 1: Mutual Acceptance

As a team begins to form, members unfamiliar with one another begin to share information, test one another's opinions and values by discussing nonthreatening topics, and try to understand one another's expectations of teamwork. Often, a company can facilitate this stage and help members to reach mutual acceptance through simulation games and team-building exercises conducted by consultants. This activity represents a crucial stage of development for a multicultural team, because it prepares members for the attitudinal problems, perceptual differences, and communication constraints they must reconcile. A group facilitator therefore can provide valuable help in getting the group moving on the right track. This stage is also called *forming* to emphasize that the team accomplishes little substantive work; instead, the process emphasizes team behavior and mutual understanding of how members will work together.

Stage 2: Communication and Decision-Making

Once team members have begun to feel comfortable with one another, the group leader or intervention facilitator begins pushing the team to develop a statement of its initial purpose and to formulate objectives. This process often defines the group's structure and role expectations within the team. A self-directed group may complete a long process at this stage of development, as the team members carry out self-evaluations, establish their own agendas, and reconcile team-based priorities with individual interests. The process itself is an important aspect of team development, but it can be

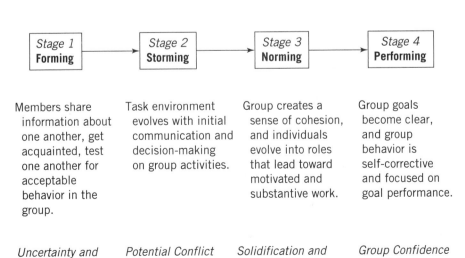

FIGURE 16.6
The Four Stages of Group Development

Sources: Gregory Moorhead and Ricky W. Griffin, *Organizational Behavior: Managing People and Organizations,* 4th ed. (Boston: Houghton Mifflin, 1995), 268–270; John P. Wamous, Arnon E. Reichers, and S. D. Malik, "Organizational Socialization and Group Development: Toward an Integrative Perspective," *Academy of Management Review* 9 (1984): 670–683.

stressful. Multicultural groups are particularly vulnerable to hostilities during this stage because effective communication requires significant adaptation of behavior. Nevertheless, as the group progresses, problems surface in a beneficial way that allows members to reconcile their differences. This stage is also called *storming*, because the process emphasizes brainstorming techniques and open communications to foster the team cohesion required to tackle more challenging work.

Stage 3: Motivation and Productivity

Also called *norming*, this stage begins as the group successfully resolves differences that become apparent in Stage 2. Ideally, this accommodation process creates a sufficiently cohesive team to pursue consensus on decisions. Members feel motivated to work together toward objectives that they have developed as a team. The members have reached a state of normalcy in their relations that leaves them comfortable with the entire team process and eager to achieve new and creative results as a team. At this stage, substantive goals surface, and the group finds that the sum of its collective efforts can yield far more effective accomplishments than individual contributions could produce. Of course, if the team has not evolved well enough in Stage 2, the motivation of team success fails to materialize, and the team may disintegrate.

Stage 4: Control and Organization

At this stage, a highly effective group demonstrates sufficient maturity to spontaneously adjust behavior to performance and team objectives. In effect, this level of activity is the work cycle of the team, and it is appropriately called the stage of *performing*. The team has evolved to a point where members understand their roles and expectations, and they can respond to group efforts without stressful attempts to consciously fit themselves into team relationships. In mature self-managed teams, the members report "feeling like family," and they can work together much like championship sports teams that have played together and understand one another's capabilities.

Homogeneous groups often advance very rapidly through the team development stages. Unlike diverse teams, they have few differences to resolve, and members already share an ingrained cultural identity on which to build later consensus. A multicultural group may take months, perhaps even years, to mature into a smoothly functioning Stage 4 team. Many teams never reach the point of self-control and effective performance. As discussed earlier, failure is nearly as prevalent as exceptional success among diverse teams, and team failure usually results from irreconcilable cultural differences among the members. Also, recall that *superordinate goals* represent one of the important factors for success. As the next section explains, these are integrated team objectives, or collective expectations for team performance.

Integrating Group Objectives

Superordinate goals transcend individual interests. They energize the entire group to achieve collective results greater than the sum of individual efforts could produce. Without these grand goals, team members resemble musicians in an orchestra warming up for a concert. Individually, they may be extremely talented players, but until they unite to play from a common score, they are attuned only to their own instruments. Once the concert begins, the collective contributions of the musicians create an entertainment experience.

Members of a work team need the same focal reason for contributing their talents and energy to a group endeavor. The primary objective does not have to articulate a dramatic advancement; perhaps it is little more than changing the way people think about their organizations and the value of their work. Indeed, this goal is an underpinning challenge for international managers working in Central and Eastern Europe, where workers have toiled for decades in a motivational vacuum. They have been told what to do, when to do it, and how much to do, but seldom why or how their efforts contribute to organizational plans. Under totalitarian regimes, all employees and managers amount to individual cogs in a mechanical production system, a premise that spreads to schools, public agencies, and services. Few people understand organizational operations, costs, sales (if any occur), customers, or, indeed, even jobs of nearby co-workers.[52]

Colgate-Palmolive company faced this situation several years ago when it moved into countries such as the Czech Republic, Romania, Poland, and the newly emerging states of the former Soviet Union.[53] Colgate entered into a number of joint ventures and co-distribution agreements throughout Central and Eastern Europe and immediately began to transform the nature of work by introducing *empowerment* programs for self-directed work. These were not fully articulated team efforts, since Colgate felt that moving suddenly into idealistic team practices would be a major jolt to workers accustomed to the communist factory systems. However, the company began by patiently soliciting ideas for work improvements from employees, and then formed small groups for operational projects and special tasks, later transforming many of these into focused teams.

The Colgate approach builds group confidence with training, open communication, mentoring for group work, and full access to company information. Employees are well informed about why they are working and what goals the company is trying to achieve. Some teams are given objectives, but most are provided with facilitating managers who assist them in establishing their own appropriate objectives. The company then further supports their efforts to develop the necessary work habits and work processes to get the job done. Incentives reward group activities and productivity. Creative ideas or innovations also are rewarded, generally on a team basis, and entire company work sites are organized for bonus systems and benefits under works-council agreements.

Colgate's model sets superordinate goals, particularly for Central and Eastern European enterprises, according to collective benefits that workers earn for their own joint endeavors. Two essential goals are to improve the quality of work and the value of human endeavor. The process of team building by itself serves to enhance these objectives, and workers are leveraging past results to launch themselves toward increasingly substantive issues, such as developing competitive marketing systems and high-quality production facilities.

Toward Group Effectiveness

Groups work effectively when they become teams rather than individuals working in proximity to one another. This distinction was made early in the chapter to emphasize the complex and time-consuming process involved in team building. Consequently, the techniques of team building are deeply embedded in organizational development, and these rather sophisticated interventions alter the fundamental value systems of work-related behavior among employees and managers. A full explanation of these techniques exceeds the scope of this book, yet it is important to note that team building needs more than good intentions by management to empower employees with self-directed responsibilities. Indeed, such a casual attitude toward team building may result in little more than ridicule. Deliberate intervention specifically for team building is usually the only effective means of achieving success, and this requirement is even more pronounced for multicultural groups.[54] Perhaps this caveat can be a jumping-off point for those who will soon launch their international management careers. The following section concludes this book by briefly describing several major career challenges international managers face in the near future.

CHALLENGES FOR THE TWENTY-FIRST CENTURY

It would be presumptuous to suggest what the most significant challenge is likely to be in the twenty-first century. There are no magic crystal balls to explain what is in store for management, yet clear evidence suggests that the fundamental nature of management is rapidly changing to reflect the characteristics of transnational enterprises. Management, like transnational organizations, will eventually disregard political or economic borders, creating a culturally transcendent leadership system of relational networks. The nature of organizations will therefore change to reflect a cybernetic knowledge base supported by global information exchanges. Transaction processes will no longer follow functional relationships, and diagrams of organizational authority will have little meaning. Instead they will reflect the results of integrated systems of activities. Management itself will be transformed from operating priorities of implementation to an entrepreneurial proclivity for change and innovation.[55]

These rather ambiguous concepts suggest a need for managers to prepare for chaos, and from that chaos to create feasible new systems of global organizations. On a practical level, tomorrow's managers must anticipate entirely new career expectations and prepare themselves psychologically to work in rapidly changing world enterprises. Organizations will become repositories of knowledge with integrated systems of team-based activities, and managers' careers will be defined according to their abilities to work in dynamic multicultural environments.

Management Careers in the New Millennium

The traditional concept of a career—one based on functional specialization, a clear promotional track, and distinct responsibilities—will eventually change toward a facilitating role of interfunctional coordination with no specific hierarchical definition. For the moment, traditional career accomplishments still depend critically on functional specialization, but they will soon reveal a growing emphasis on integrative skills and international management capabilities. Recent studies have shown that people in entrenched, narrowly defined careers are more at risk of losing their jobs than those who pursue challenging careers with diverse interests.[56]

More to the point, those who feel comfortable and safe in departmentalized positions may be a firm's most likely candidates for replacement. Downsizing has dramatically ended many careers in midstream, and companies are changing so rapidly that many technical and specialized occupations are becoming obsolete. Entirely new occupations are rapidly evolving, requiring new skills and unexpected qualifications. Many individuals can no longer keep abreast of changes in their fields, and if they have not become broadly trained or sufficiently educated to accept entirely new careers, they offer little value to a company. Thus, the concept of a career now entails constant learning and rapid evolution within a system of flexible specializations.

The organization itself is being redefined as a learning process, suggesting that structure evolves with knowledge and with rapid self-adjustment driven by the need

INTERNATIONAL DEVELOPMENT—UNCOMMON CAREER OPPORTUNITIES

At age 27, Jenny Orbach manages a multicultural staff of 18 employees, handles a $4 million budget, and affects the lives of more than 500 desperate families every year. She is project director for a remote branch activity in Azerbaijan under Mercy International, a government-funded foreign assistance organization supported by the U.S. Agency for International Development (USAID). Jenny, a young American on her fourth international assignment, in this instance has found herself in a little-known country on the Caspian Sea that regained its independence in the post-Soviet era.

Azerbaijan is a nation of roughly 5.5 million Moslem people, where families live on less than the equivalent of $600 a year, and more than 900,000 people are IDPs—internally displaced persons. IDPs are virtually homeless, most with little more than tents or stick shelters provided by international relief agencies such as the Red Cross or CARE. Many are refugees from recent wars with border countries to the north (Dagastan in the CIS), and to the south (Armenia). IDPs seldom have schools for their children, food other than that provided by relief organizations, and few jobs. Many barely survive on less than $1.00 a day, gained through farm labor or piecemeal work provided by government programs.

Jenny's organization tries to generate jobs in rural communities for IDPs, or tries to help families to become self-sufficient. For example, her staff trains IDP women to weave, supplies them with thread and yarn for making rugs and clothes, and then organizes ways to sell these goods into urban markets. She and her staff also purchase seeds and fertilizer, then help farm families establish small stands of crops. In some instances, Mercy International brings in sheep—two ewes and a ram—and then provides families with stock feed in an effort to establish a flock that might eventually generate income for the families. Unfortunately, so many people are desperately hungry that the stock animals are slaughtered (or stolen by other desperate people), and fledging crops are eaten before they mature. Her job, in short, is often demoralizing and difficult.

Jenny's staff includes only one other American, an agricultural consultant, and 17 Azerbaijanese. She also has access to assistance from other Mercy International volunteers and, on occasion, young American volunteers from the Peace Corps or European relief agencies. Her offices are decent; but heat is not always available during winter months, when temperatures can become frigid. There is no air conditioning, yet summers can be blistering. Her modest one-bedroom apartment is in a renovated building built during the Soviet era with little insulation and Victorian-age furniture. With a BA in economics and an MBA, in the United States Jenny could command a salary of twice what she earns at the USAID project.

Yet through all this, Jenny—together with hundreds of other young expatriate managers working in similar projects from the United States, Canada, and Europe—finds her career exhilarating. Indeed, Jenny describes her experience in Azerbaijan as "one of the most exciting and worthwhile things she has ever done." Her previous posts with different government-sponsored programs were equally exciting, and included assignments in Slovenia, Moldova, and Russia.

"I can't imagine any other career with so much to offer," she explains. "My first assignments were shocks. I was in tears more than once. My first Christmas alone and overseas was heartbreaking, but I also learned how fortunate I was when I first saw a child die of hunger. I learned at that moment that I had no right—ever again—to feel sorry for myself."

Jenny also explained how little most young people know about similar career opportunities. "Most of my friends who graduated with MBAs went straight toward the big companies and big bucks," she said. "Those with any kind of computer skills were scooped up immediately, grabbed huge stock options, and salaries to support a new BMW right away. I found myself on a meager stipend and a short contract headed for Russia because I had a couple of years of Russian language training. I was crazy, and I had lots of regrets, but no more. This is so satisfying that I can't imagine doing anything else."

Jenny is, indeed, an international manager. Her staff speaks three different languages and come from five different ethnic backgrounds. As a young woman, she is managing men who are almost all her elders in a society where male dominance is common and women are seldom found in leadership roles. She must deal with complicated international exchange, difficult budgets, and perplexing human resource issues among her staff as well as the hundreds of families that the agency assists. Jenny may find herself in the presence of the U.S. ambassador or an Azerbaijan senior minister, meet with a member of the UN or World Bank, yet share a meager bowl of soup with a refugee on her regular field trips.

Jenny is not a government employee, however. Her career has been with private contracting agencies funded through USAID or the World Bank, but these contractors have no direct connection with any government. They are so-called *nongovernmental organizations* (NGOs). Some are for-profit, international companies, with offices throughout the less-developed world and in transition economies such as Azerbaijan. They include, for example, PriceWaterhouseCoopers, Carana Corporation, Louis Berger International, and many others. Some are nonprofit organizations, such as the Eurasia Foundation, the Soros Group, or activities under the American Bar Association and Jenny's current contractor, Mercy International. Yet another type of contractor—called a *private volunteer organization* (PVO)—is established through private foundations or government grants. PVOs manage hundreds of overseas assistance projects, ranging from relief work in Kosovo to executive education programs in Cairo. More than 200 American, Canadian, British, Dutch, and German universities have formal business and economics programs contracted by the U.S. government in 140 foreign countries.

Jenny and several thousand other young men and women have found international development careers among these organizations. Their assignments may change often—some last a few months, some are contracted for several years—and most people in the development field work for a variety of contracting organizations. There also are many fast-track opportunities within the private organizations themselves, or with formal government agencies.

"I've already been offered positions with two major international foundations and every contractor that I've been with," Jenny said. "At the moment, I couldn't tell you where I will be in five or ten years, but I want to continue working in the field for awhile yet. Then I see very good opportunities with the UN or the World Bank—maybe even the OECD or a major European agency—but I have no plans to get into a State Department job or the Government. Many of my friends have gone that way because this work is a direct channel into very good positions."

When last seen, Jenny was climbing into her 4x4 with a local volunteer doctor, a translator, and two of her staff. They would be driving nine hours into the interior to help inoculate children in one of the many IDP encampments.

Source: Co-author David H. Holt's interviews during consulting assignments for Private Sector Development Evaluation under USAID, November 1999, Baku, Azerbaijan.

---

for adapting to new methods and human interactions.[57] Careers in the twenty-first century therefore will be defined by perpetual learning. Success will come to those who can accept the challenge of constant change and continuous learning. They will be judged by their contributions to their firms' knowledge bases—their value to their employers will depend on their contributions to the organizational repositories of knowledge and their companies' human capabilities.

In addition to the requirement of change through learning, managers must be able to accept the impermanence of organizations. Organizations change through restructuring and redefinition as a result of mergers, acquisitions, strategic alliances, and international agreements. In addition, information technology is changing the organizational processes and patterns of work. This was vividly illustrated in the opening profile of how Federal Express and many other companies have rapidly adapted to a *virtual organization* based on a globally networked system of *virtual teams*. Indeed, the concept of a virtual organization with its pervasive communication capabilities is tantalizing. Managers are no longer constrained by space or time, and throughout such an organization, the potential of infinite integration dramatically empowers everyone as organizational participants. *Empowerment* itself becomes more than a potent idea for team building; it is a mandate for management.[58]

Managers therefore must be fleet of foot and adept at moving into new transnational environments as their organizations evolve. At the same time, many positions offer only transitional and temporary security. Indeed, temporary employment, once considered a stopgap measure to fill low-skill vacancies, has become a pervasive aspect of organizational staffing for skilled workers, technicians, and even top executives. Impermanence pervades worldwide operations with thousands of projects employing tens of thousands of people, often in ad hoc teams. This trend has created a pattern of global employment based on permanent temporary workers. Even within their own companies, people fill temporary positions subject to periodic reassignments, but the "virtual age" accentuates these organizational patterns.[59]

Theorists in human resource development are beginning to explain career development in team-based terms. Individual careers that reflect functional specialization and prescribed career tracks are beginning to give way to team-based careers that depend on the success of integrated team projects and the evolution of work groups within organizational structures. Although cultural constraints in many parts of the world have slowed the development of teamwork, its popularity as a method of organizing work has begun to expand. This tendency is particularly important for international enterprises with complex integrated activities and a global structure with comprehensive information technologies. As a result, managers' careers now depend less on individual qualifications and initiative than in the past; in the future, their careers may not be defined apart from the team itself.[60]

CONCLUDING COMMENTS

This chapter has emphasized the nature of group activity and the importance of teamwork, particularly that of multicultural teams for international enterprises. The evolution of management toward a pervasive global orientation—based on team efforts and a multicultural organization that is itself in constant flux—suggests that managers must be prepared with new human relations skills. These will include the integrative skills and communicative abilities to work in a globally diverse environment with international teams. Managers must also be able to accommodate sociocultural values that differ from their own values and beliefs.

International managers will struggle with ethical dilemmas and differences in human values, and in the end, they must find ways to honor human differences while maintaining their own ethical standards of conduct. Finally, managers must rise to the challenge of creating the organizations, and integrating the diverse interests that civilized global commerce requires. They must take the initiative to create the future of global enterprise, rather than merely waiting for order to evolve from chaos. Managers and their enterprises will be defined through *cognitive transnationality*, which is the accumulated experience of global commerce and human integration.[61]

In conclusion, international managers of the twenty-first century face an exciting mandate of becoming *international transformational leaders*. Management as a discipline will no longer be culturally bound, nor will tomorrow's managers have defined roles or decision-making parameters. Indeed, management may soon have cosmic dimensions as it evolves from the archaic nation-bound beliefs prevalent only a few years ago, to the current threshold of a seamless world environment, and eventually to organizational leadership in the ethereal ambience of space.

REVIEW QUESTIONS

1. Describe how a strategic international team might function in a transnational corporation. How does it fit into the organizational hierarchy, and what types of problems might the team address?
2. What is the role of a representative team? How might such a team be organized for a U.S. multinational with joint alliances and multiple distribution offices in Europe?
3. What is multicultural diversity? What benefits will a firm gain by purposely developing a culturally diverse team?
4. What disadvantages does a firm risk when it creates a multicultural team? How can effective management reduce these problems?
5. What are the strengths and weaknesses of a homogeneous team?
6. If you were assigned to establish an international team to plan for expansion in Eastern Europe, would you establish a homogeneous team of experienced expatriates or a multicultural team? Explain why.
7. How can conflict benefit team building? How can it lead to disastrous group activities? Explain in terms of cognitive and affective conflict.
8. Describe the four-stage process of group development. What critical objectives arise during each stage, and what are the danger points in each stage?

GLOSSARY OF KEY TERMS

Affective conflict Group interactions that reflect individual animosity and provocation, leading to hostilities and win-lose relationships.

Cognitive conflict Constructive, issue-related disagreements among group members that ultimately benefit problem solving and teamwork.

Diversity Contrasting personal characteristics, usually associated with ethnicity but also including race, gender, age, religion, or other human differences.

Groupthink A suboptimal and ineffective group process that leads to compliant decisions or weak compromises in order to maintain an appearance of group solidarity.

Multicultural team A coordinated work group composed of members drawn from distinctly different cultures that represent the full range of a multinational corporation's interests and capabilities.

Representative team Regional or divisional work groups that perform intermediary coordination functions facilitating operational integration.

Subsidiary teams Locally responsive work groups that focus on host-country activities and provide external liaison links with other company subsidiaries or activities.

Superordinate goal A group goal that transcends personal priorities and prevails over individual differences to unify members' behavior in a common purpose, leaving little room for self-serving interests.

Transnational team A work group composed of multinational members whose activities span multiple countries.

EXERCISES

1. Envision a jigsaw puzzle made up of interlocking pieces and an interesting scenic picture with brilliant colors and a varied landscape. Individually, take about 10 minutes to make a list of the puzzle's attributes that are *similar* to the composition and operation of a highly effective team. On a separate sheet, list all the ways in which a puzzle *differs* from a highly effective team. Be prepared to present these lists in class. The instructor will summarize responses for the class to discuss.
2. As a team simulation, instead of summarizing responses generated in Exercise 1, form small teams and summarize within the teams. Each team should expand and develop the best

possible lists of similarities and differences for the exercise. How did individual and team results compare? What guidelines for group development might this metaphor suggest?

3. Form small teams to solve the following problem. Your student team has been entrusted with a $50,000 grant to devise an experimental course in international management. The money can fund any educational purpose, including equipment, new processes, student or faculty assistance, and creative new educational processes and research. The only constraint is that all students must benefit (and no vacation trips to Hawaii). Begin by individually listing how the money should be spent. Then, as a team, compile the responses, vote on the highest priorities, and try to reach a consensus, perhaps adding new ideas. Appoint a team representative to report the team findings.

TEAM BUILDING: THE "KILLER APP" OF PEOPLESOFT INC.

Information technology can either isolate people from one another or galvanize them into closely networked teams. Companies that entered the global race to become "connected" without preparing their people for the challenge of team-based management may suffer isolation more than benefit from network integration. This was the legacy of the multinationals during the last decade, and a critical element of human resource development was missing in most of the earlier information systems. An organization that recognized this flaw has subsequently become a billion-dollar public company, with more than half of the *Fortune 500* as clients and sales on five continents.

PeopleSoft Inc., a U.S. firm that was launched in 1987 to provide client-server network applications, came up with a "killer app" (industry shorthand for a killer application, such as the MS DOS phenomenon, Apple's user-friendly graphical user interface, and VisiCalc, the world's first spreadsheet). Only this time, the killer app was not software but an integrated approach to IT systems implementation through team training and human resource development programs. With nearly 8,000 employees and 2,400 consultants, the company now has more than 4,600 client organizations. PeopleSoft has created a virtual library of materials and learning resources, "knowledge centers" of staff and educational materials in 27 international locations, and its own corporate PeopleSoft University.

PeopleSoft applications are not exactly run-of-the-mill. They have won accolades in the industry and among client users for being able to integrate a global organization, accommodate multilingual interfaces in real-time information exchange, and automatically handle transactions that could reflect 20 or more different international accounting systems. In October 2000, PeopleSoft's Enterprise Performance Management program won the industry's top award for the best management software system. The company has a broad range of integration software, ranging from on-line manufacturing and materials handling to university distance-learning systems and health care administration. But the critical success factor is "implementation." PeopleSoft not only delivers software but also sets up a project implementation team with client employees, consultants, and PeopleSoft staff who are selected specifically for their team-building talents.

The team-building process is explained by Daniel Wymer, a project team leader from Siemens Automotive, a U.S. division of Siemens AG, Germany. "The corporation bought into PeopleSoft as a major change agent," Wymer explains. "Everyone liked the systems software on its own merits, but PeopleSoft had a detailed plan for bringing it on line that included training for our people, and a team facilitator to make it more of a technical system, but a human operation. This began with square one, as in 'What's a team, gang?' and then moved into a project team approach to actually building relationships among the members."

Wymer recalls the early weeks when the facilitator, a contracted consultant, began to bring the team together. "Many of the staff were apprehensive, even though most had worked together," Wymer said. "We had four technicians from systems and software design areas, a senior cost accountant, one plant engineer, and me, a product manager. Right away, on day one, the consultant screamed bloody [expletive deleted] at the company. The plan was to have a 'complete team,' he said, not just techies. 'Where are the maintenance people and the personnel and marketing folks? We need to see quality assurance, and this thing is not going a step further with me unless top management is not in the front row.' Well," said Wymer, "he got his way, and was he ever right. We had another 'first day' start a week later, and there were nearly 30 people in the room. We sat like school kids to hear lectures, watch videos, and do what seemed to be dumb little games. Everyone, including the head honcho, was there for about 16 intense hours of classroom-style team building."

Unlike many team-building programs, in which a small group is taken on wilderness treks or challenged to go through obstacle courses, this project was set up for decision-making exercises. Seven teams were organized, each with four or five people. Their first task was to have each person in every group individually list all the characteristics they could notice about a U.S. penny. Then, as a team, they did the same thing. Individually, the best score was from a personnel manager in one of the groups. She identified 13 attributes, such as a penny being round, copper colored, with President Lincoln's bust, a mint mark, and so on. Wymer admitted to seeing only nine characteristics. The personnel manager's team came up with 17 attributes of a penny, Wymer's team reported about 20, and the winning team described 34 items.

"It got the point across," Wymer said. "Team decisions can be dramatically superior. We did about twenty of these exercises combined with the lectures and inspiring videos over a two-week period, and an odd thing happened. We actually began to think together. Crazy, but at first we were just a mob. Then we progressed to individuals participating, sometimes reluctantly, with the appointed team. Then we become 'Dan and Meg and Ed and Mel' as one unit. But it was not always easy. Several teams went to war within their groups. One guy from production just couldn't get the hang of it. He had to make all the decisions. . . . He didn't stay with us. Several others quietly left too. They were either extreme extroverts trying to deal with extreme introverts, or vice versa. Anyway, they just could not get past the team expectations for group work."

As Wymer explained, it took four more weeks of incremental progress before the total group could address real business issues, and then not the actual implementation plan of PeopleSoft. "We learned processes, like how to make a decision, how to get everyone involved through structured brainstorming, sometimes a round-robin voting process, and so on. It didn't come easy. Then at some point, we were able to look back and see where we had been, and we knew we could tackle the systems project. That was phase one, and everyone including the top brass stayed with it until we reviewed the PeopleSoft project, collectively agreed to a time-line for benchmark activities, and defined the objectives. Once we got past that, the group was trimmed down to an implementation team of eight people, including two PeopleSoft consultants who literally moved in with us for the next seven months."

Wymer described the seven-month implementation plan as a progressive system of team meetings and sub-team activities. Each person came to accept a role in the project and a responsibility to the team goals. There were conflicts and misunderstandings, some cynicism, and much debate, but as a team, they had developed ways to short-circuit unproductive confrontations. For example, when things got heated, someone would loudly say, "Time Out!" and everyone knew the signal as time to go get a cup of coffee or to just cool down. Then they could get back together and address the issues without undue emotion. According to Wymer, all issues were phrased as questions, such as "could we do this or that," rather than statements such as "we should do this or that." This approach decoupled potential head-on disputes. The team had rules. No personal attacks, such as references to gender-related ideas or minority status. With two women, one African American, one ethnic Asian, and four Caucasian men, there was potential for value-loaded statements, so the rules were important. Still, there were difficulties. Two of the Caucasian men were higher-level managers, and older than two young IT specialists, and in Wymer's recollection, more friction existed between these pairings than among the men and women or ethnic minorities.

"We really had to learn some tough lessons," Wymer said. "I had to bite my tongue and back off several times, and hey, that isn't easy! Our Asian colleague had to learn to be a bit more forceful. He always took a back seat to discussions, rarely raised his voice, and never tested anyone. After several months, it was a different story. This guy would come to meetings armed for debate. He always had his ducks in a row, and he was ready to fight out any issue. That was good, because he never personalized things. He was always on the issue, and if you had a counterpoint, you had to have it backed up."

When the PeopleSoft team reached its primary implementation goal after seven months, the project team transferred operations to line management. "We remained involved, and even met as a team many times after that," Wymer said. "But the whole point was to put the system in place and to seed behavior among the line people to use it effectively. Seven months may seem long, but none of us expected to be up and running inside of a year, maybe even two years. Teamwork didn't end there either. All those people who were involved in the initial team-building process understood what we were about, and they were psychologically on board all the way. Teamwork seeds were planted from the board room to the shipping docks, and we are now sprouting new teams for almost everything."

The next challenge facing the company is to integrate its part of the PeopleSoft system with similar programs and teams in foreign locations. This team-building scenario was replicated, almost in unison, in nine countries and seven different languages. Ultimately, Siemens envisions a global network not only of integrated software systems, but of cooperative teams.

"We have begun this process," Wymer explains. "Phase one is behind us, and now it is up to the teams from Britain, Germany, Spain, Canada, and the U.S., among others, to pull the whole thing together. We can do it, and we know how it will work. The local teams are part of a family of teams now. We know what they went through and how their collective minds operate. We can walk into one of their meetings, and even when translators are needed, there is a gut understanding of the team process, the rules, and our expectations. Still, there are new challenges. We're from different cultures, and believe me, the Germans can get in your face in a hurry while the Spanish team can be frustrating. Our American good-ole-boy approach probably irritates the [expletive deleted] out of the Germans. And the Brits? Well, I haven't figured them out yet. Nice guys and gals, but they confuse me with too many adjectives."

QUESTIONS

1. Identify the stages of team development in the approach taken by the company to establish teamwork at its worldwide locations.
2. Although the company faces cultural differences in implementing a global information system, what other obstacles might it face when integrating teams from many different societies?
3. How might Siemens approach the task of introducing a global PeopleSoft process worldwide? How can the teams be brought together on a grand scale to tie together what they have achieved in each location?

BIBLIOGRAPHY

Bergunilles, Franz. "PeopleSoft and Siemens A.G. Team in Global License and Joint Development Agreements." *Business Wire Release*, Siemens AG, Munich, 12 December 1995, 1–5.

"PeopleSoft and Siemens A.G. Complete Successful Joint Development Project." *Business Wire*, 2 October 1996, p. 1.

PeopleSoft On Line, Worldwide Net, website <www.peoplesoft.com> [cited 10 November 2000]. History, development, product development, and client base information.

"Virtual Teamwork: Building Internal Bridges." *PeopleTalk Magazine*, October 2000, 4–5.

CASE 16.2

CAREER VISIONS: CEOS LOOK FOR LEADERSHIP FROM GLOBAL MANAGERS

At the World Economic Forum in Davos, Switzerland, hundreds of the world's top executives gathered in early 1997 to discuss changes in global competition and the future of world development. One of the notable panel discussions involved five CEOs of global corporations, who explored how business has changed and examined the concept of a "global manager" in the coming millennium. The discussion, "Driving Globalization: Lessons from the CEO," was led by James J. Schiro, chairman and senior partner of Price Waterhouse LLP (now PricewaterhouseCoopers). Other panelists included

- Rahul Bajaj, Chairman and Managing Director, Bajaj Auto Limited, India
- Percy Barnevik, Former Chairman, the ABB Group, Switzerland

- Cor A.J. Herkstroter, President, Royal Dutch/Shell Group, Netherlands
- Kenneth Lay, Chairman and CEO, Enron Corp., USA
- Heinrich von Pierer, President and CEO, Siemens AG, Germany

The panel members were unanimous in their conclusion that instilling a mentality of change within their organizations is one of their most important responsibilities. Although today's business climate is neither more nor less challenging or difficult than in the past, the panelists emphasized that it is vastly different. Schiro echoed the panelists' viewpoints when he said: "Global CEOs must possess an exceptional package of talents that enables them to foster cultural and functional unity while delivering superior business results. In my opinion, a passion to succeed is also vital in inspiring a global workforce."

Inspiring a global workforce was a crucial factor, according to Kenneth Lay from Enron. "You cannot do business without the ground support of people working at the roots of far-flung operations," Lay said. "It is teamwork and much more. It is a commitment to understanding the differences in our cultures, our foreign hosts, and our values. When people shed their yoke of nationality, they begin to appreciate the richness of the world's people. And in my opinion, that's when our organizations begin to function well."

Cor Herkstroter suggested that business had changed, and that organizations must accept a new age in which inspired leaders can introduce change in their companies. "At Shell, it wasn't obvious there was need for change, because people perceived we had a very successful group," Herkstroter said. "My first objective was to make clear to the organization why there had to be change, why performance had to be lifted. You're there as an organization for your customers, and customers need change all the time. Build the organization that serves your customers best." Herkstroter went on to say that the most important change would come in having globally minded managers able to integrate cultural expectations of both employees and customers, and then to be able to respond to very specific behavior and expectations in every activity.

Percy Barnevik from ABB added: "You have to have a vision for your company which is believable, and that you can communicate to people. I don't think it's enough to talk about volume, profit and shareholder value. To be proud of their company, employees must see some corporate purpose beyond performance figures." Barnevik said that as a new board member of General Motors, he had gained valuable insights about both good visions and poor visions of another of the world's major multinationals. In his opinion, many of GM's problems rest with an encrusted bureaucracy where executives cannot think in a global scope, yet GM also had global depth in a small but growing core of executives who could comprehend how world business had changed. GM was adapting to a "multidomestic" environment in which career managers would instigate change, and in due course, a new vision for GM that would reach people in the urban centers of the world as well as the remote village of even the poorest countries.

Heinrich von Pierer, Chairman of Siemens—perhaps one of world's most diversified multinationals—responded to the issues of leadership. He said, "I cannot use any proxies, I have to get personally involved with as many people as possible within our organization, which is a challenge with 400,000 employees." Von Pierer suggested that too many executives are too remote from the trenches, where thousands of innovative-minded young managers and employees from hundreds of different cultural backgrounds will find their own ways to live and work together. That is, if a company's leaders present them with the opportunity rather than impose a sanctioned way of managing.

Enron's chairman, Kenneth Lay, added: "The vision must be compelling, it must be reasonably simple and easily understood. It must be more overarching than just focused on making money. It must be something that individuals, including customers, not just employees, can relate to. You've got to communicate the vision, over and over every chance you get. It takes the personal involvement of the CEO, with the teams on the ground in virtually every region of the world, to demonstrate what the purpose of the organization really is."

Barnevik noted: "With the kind of global networks being built now, the idea of being domestic or foreign dissipates into thin air. But you need a strong corporate glue, an umbrella policy above national policies that holds it together and makes it stronger than if the various entities would go their separate ways."

Herkstroter commented: "If you want to call yourself a multinational, then you have to make certain that people of all nationalities in an organization get equal chances. An organization should not be dominated by just one or two nationalities, in the case of Shell, Dutch or British. That's vitally important to create a common purpose, a common objective." He also emphasized that Shell was virtually on a mission to erase this sense of having a national enclave of managers. In 10 years, he said, Shell will have no identity apart from the customers it serves. Managers will not even be called "international managers," but simply "managers"—with the understanding that they are citizens of the world.

"There is an urgent need for global managers, Barnevik said. "These managers are not born, you have to develop them. One of the best ways is to rotate people from their native country to another country when they're young, in their early 30s. Stay out a few years, and then you have picked up a language, you have a broader perspective, and are a more capable global manager. Out of our 25,000 managers, we need maybe five or six hundred who are truly global managers. Those people are really worth their weight in gold."

Lay replied: "We're in a fast-growth mode in terms of presence in the international marketplace. And when you're in that situation, you have to hire a lot of nationals, a lot of young people. You have to give them a lot of running room and latitude. You have to provide the system and controls as well as the vision and values for them. But they also become so valuable in their markets that it's almost impossible to rotate them around to different regions. Ideally we'd like to do that, but it's not practical at this time. We've still managed to go global and be reasonably successful at it." He added that, like ABB, Enron certainly needs an entire generation of internationally minded young managers, but that there is also value in diversity. In Lay's view, the richness of the corporate fabric can be found in the often-difficult contrasts between ethnic groups, gender-related values, and even gaps in age and skills. To his way of thinking, if you can manage these diverse interests without necessarily changing them, you answer the problem of having a global organization that can respond as a local enterprise.

Von Pierer said that at Siemens, his most valued asset is the local manager who knows how to energize teamwork and honor differences in his or her people. "The best global managers," he said, "are open minded, ready to learn and ready to listen. These are people who accept other people as they are and not how they should be."

The CEOs, and many participants at the conference, questioned the emphasis some speakers put on

"vision" and "teamwork." In one view, Lay's position of building strong local organizations through a method of coordinating individual differences was superior to a pervasive effort to make everyone think and behave as "world citizens," a view expressed by Shell's Herkstroter. Barnevik, meanwhile, is very charismatic and stresses "leading from the top," but with widely diversified authority and strong individual employee teams at the ground level. He and Von Pierer are famous for making hundreds of visits each year to their international projects, and then bringing a message of inspired self-management to local operations. In contrast, Lay and Herkstroter are not highly visible in their organizations but manage through executive teams and more structured systems. These executives seem to have different philosophies of management, yet they are adamant about developing a vision of multicultural management and borderless corporations. Each of these CEOs has been depicted as a transformational leader, and although the conference at which they spoke occurred several years ago, each of these executives is credited with significant contributions to a changing world business environment.

QUESTIONS

1. The CEOs are not entirely in agreement on what constitutes a *global manager*, but they agree on the idea of a "vision" of change and the crucial roles global managers will play in the future. From your viewpoint, what are the primary characteristics of a global manager, and what career aspirations might evolve for someone starting with Shell, ABB, Enron, Siemens, or PricewaterhouseCoopers?

2. Barnevik suggests a way to develop international managers, and although he makes it sound simple, a career would involve much more. Explain the critical challenges facing a young manager searching for the right career path in a major multinational organization.

3. Several points were raised by the panelists that suggested a concern for cultural sensitivity, managing diversity in foreign operations, and in particular, for creating a team spirit—a vision of integrated behavior—that would stretch from the boardroom to a company's multidomestic interests. In your view, what is this "vision" all about? What has given these CEOs reputations as transformational leaders?

BIBLIOGRAPHY

Excerpts from "Price Waterhouse CEO Panel Puts Emphasis on Change," a synopsis of the *World Economic Forum*, 4 February 1997. Retrieved from Price Waterhouse worldwide website <www.pw.com>.

Janet Guyon, "World Staffers: For ABB, Globalization is More than a Buzzword." *Asian Wall Street Journal*, 2 October 1996, p. 1.

A Transformational Role Model in Sri Lanka

Sri Lanka, known as Ceylon during British colonial rule, is a somewhat obscure nation of nearly 15 million just off the southeastern coast of India. The island civilization, which is literally in the center of the Indian Ocean, for centuries was the critical pivot point of navigation between the Middle East and Asia. Recorded history in Sri Lanka dates back 2,500 years, when its ancient civilization was as well known as that of the Greek city-states—and probably as well developed. Indeed, Sri Lanka (then recorded by the Egyptian geographer as "Taprobane") was the dominant culture bridging the Bay of Bengal and the Arabian Sea. In the fourth century B.C., Alexander's fleets were redesigned and harbored in Sri Lanka. There are trade records with Rome's Emperor Claudius for fruits, nuts, and rich spices. And second-century Arab writers dubbed the country as "Serendib," the root of our modern-day term *serendipity*, which captured a sense of "accidental paradise" that many found in Sri Lanka.

The Republic of Sri Lanka is a pearl-shaped island, about the size of New York state, Scotland, or a bit larger than Denmark. It is a land of distinct contrasts—with central mountains reaching more than 6,000 feet and major rivers, fed by picturesque waterfalls, that flow through mountainous tea plantations and farming plains. A dry zone to the north is home to antelope, elephants, and herding wildlife. To the south are lush jungles and hundreds of miles of palm forests stretching to expansive beaches. To the west lies the principal city of Colombo with natural anchorage, industrial shipping, and container ports. To the east are thousands of hilly plantations and teeming villages that harvest cashew nuts (a native nut of Sri Lanka), cocoa nuts, cinnamon (also native to the island), and dozens of unusual peppers, wild spices, and fruits of every kind. Throughout the country, there are pockets of gemstones. Indeed, Sri Lanka is the world's principal source of sapphires, rubies, and emeralds.

Today the country is engulfed in a long-running civil war, in which Tamil rebels seek an independent state in the north. The Tamils emigrated from India during the eighteenth and nineteenth centuries, many as forced labor on British, Dutch, and Portuguese plantations. The Sinhalese are the ancient tribal inhabitants of Sri Lanka, and they represent 80 percent of the nation's population. There are other ethnic minorities, including Arabs, Chinese, and an interesting assortment of Europeans. The Portuguese may have been the earliest Europeans to have a significant presence in Sri Lanka, dating back 400 years when they established colonial trading companies in Colombo. They also brought Christianity to the country, but never occupied Sri Lanka. Instead, they integrated into the society; still today, the surnames of many families reflect a kinship to Portugal. Dutch colonials arrived in the eighteenth century, bringing military and economic warfare to an otherwise peaceful nation. The Dutch easily ousted the Portuguese, taking by force the valuable colonial holdings in cinnamon, nutmeg, peppers, curry spices, cashew nuts, and many other varieties of exotic spices and nuts that the Portuguese had cultivated for European markets. At that time, Sri Lanka was known as the Spice Islands, or Serendib, names that prevailed for two centuries in European custom.

The British landed in several military waves during the years 1803–1817. They held Sri Lanka as a British colony for 150 years until 1947 when, in the aftermath of World War II, the Sri Lankans gained political independence. During the British rule, Ceylon became the undisputed leading source of commercial tea. Ceylon tea is still distinct, and it is exported worldwide to virtually every country on Earth, with the possible exception of Mongolia. With more than 12,000 villages and 2,800 tea plantations, tea production in Sri Lanka is exceeded only by the black fermented tea indigenous to China, and a ragged tea used in low-grade blends from India.

The tiny island nation is famous for exotic natural woods, still harvested in the rugged mountains using elephants. It is one of the finest commercial fishing centers in Southeast Asia, exporting hundreds of varieties of shellfish and ocean fish to markets ranging from Singapore to Tokyo. The capital city of Colombo is a natural seaport, and with five universities, major medical facilities, five-star hotels, and an efficient international airport, the city is an important center of commerce in the region. Unfortunately, 40 years of Soviet-style development has left the country far behind its Asian neighbors in infrastructure and trade. Sri Lanka became a political ally of the Soviet Union when Russians helped the nation win its independence from Britain. The Russians installed a strong communist government that was officially ousted in 1981, but only after 15 years of bitter struggles and armed skirmishes. The long battle for independence made few headlines, and Sri Lanka had little or no support from western powers. Indeed, Vietnam overshadowed events in the region, and there was little attention to Sri Lanka's difficulties. Today communism is gone, but a strong socialist sentiment remains. The turmoil of the past half-century has been economically debilitating, and the nation is only beginning to emerge with a sense of direction.

Every major foreign nation has an embassy and trade mission in Sri Lanka, and more than 6,000 foreign multinational corporations have business investments in the country. IBM, Unilever, Colgate-Palmolive, Hewlett-Packard, Sony, NEC, Caterpillar, Accenture (formerly Andersen Consulting), Ford, Bayer AG, Shell Oil, Procter & Gamble, and many other familiar companies have a strong presence in Colombo, and there are significant mineral and gemstone mining interests in the interior. Several high-rise buildings in the commercial district are evidence of international interests. American Express, Hong Kong & Shanghai Bank, and Fuji Bank are prominent. Visitors can rub elbows with a constant entourage of international investors at the Intercontinental Hotel, the Sheraton, or at one of the five-star beach resorts. These are in stark contrast to streets lined with impoverished people, small huts with no water or sewage, water buffalo that graze at night on fresh grass of modern divided highways, and the occasional elephant that appears in a hotel parking lot to push a stalled car. Elephants, the city's "wrecker ser-vice," are used by city services for maintenance and hauling.

Sri Lankan business leaders, many educated under the pro-Soviet regime and many more representing domestic industries that were expropriated from the colonial era, are capable executives and world travelers. The nation has more than 5,000 doctors, 3,200 engineers, and 2,700 executives who were educated at Sri Lankan universities and medical schools; many also attended European and Soviet programs. Nearly half of all professional people in Sri Lanka have second or third degrees; of those, two-thirds have graduate degrees earned in Britain, the Netherlands, Russia, or the United States. Virtually all speak English, a native language (Sinhala), and perhaps a second local tongue (Tamil or an Indian dialect). More than two-thirds speak Russian, a legacy of mandated language training in schools during the 1950s and 1960s. Half of those speak yet another Asian or European language. With more than 2,500 government-supported schools and mandatory education to age 15 (or to the point of achieving secondary school equivalency), Sri Lanka has a literacy rate second only to that of Japan, and higher than the United States, Britain, or France.

It is difficult to accurately profile Sri Lanka, except to summarize the contrasts. It is a beautiful country, some say a tropical paradise; yet the people are generally very poor, and their villages or urban quarters resemble something of an earlier century. Business executives, men and women alike, dress in the finest European fashions, work in glass-and-steel modern high-rises, and enjoy well-appointed homes, country clubs, and exquisite restaurants. Most people, however, still dress in simple saris, walk barefooted (even on the capital's main streets), and eat simple foods, often self-grown. Food and water is plentiful, and the population is well nourished and clean. Because the country has excellent social services, there are few problems with destitution or disease. Sri Lanka's commercial and industrial infrastructure is admittedly not comparable to those of most other Asian nations, yet a domestic and international banking system exists. The country has an active stock market, a strong central bank, stable currency, and reasonably low inflation. There are adequate means of public transportation (although somewhat archaic), including mini-buses, trains, taxis, too many cars for a growing urban population, and several forms of mini-scooters and three-wheelers used privately or for hire. Still, oxcarts are in abundance, even in the city center, and water buffalo are more prominent than tractors.

Indeed, Sri Lanka is a diverse culture from every perspective. The country has ample hydroelectric power and a system of irrigation that supports surplus agriculture, yet a third of the rural villages have neither home electricity nor running water. Many of the urban hut-like areas lack both; but in contrast, computers, telephones, television, and satellite communications are quite common. Leading business executives include many women. Sri Lanka has had two women as elected prime ministers since its struggle for independence began in the late 1960s. The two national chambers of commerce each have a membership that includes men and women executives, Sinhalese, Tamils, Arabs, Indians, Chinese, Japanese, mixed-ethnic groups of Dutch, Portuguese, and British heritages, Hindus, Buddhists, Muslims, and Christians.

From a management perspective, the country's leaders are challenged to develop a modern state from chaos, and one that must accommodate a multicultural, multilingual, and multifaceted population. One of those leaders, Moksevi Prelis, founding director and recently retired chairman of the Development Finance Corporation of Ceylon (DFCC), represents all these contrasting characteristics. He and his company reflect what Sri Lanka is all about, at the same time demonstrating the power of transformational leadership. The name "Moksevi" is a reflection of Soviet influence—a name that is clearly Russian, but with a tint of Sinhalese. Prelis—a surname of Portuguese influence—slipped into his family history in the seventeenth century when an ancestor was servant to a European planter. Prelis goes by the name of "Mahsi" (pronounced "Maxy"), and his family has no bloodlines in Portuguese or Russian. In fact, he can trace his Sinhala family tree back nearly 800 years. He is Buddhist, but it is not obvious. Educated at a local university with a BS in engineering, Mahsi won a scholarship to study at Birmingham University in Britain. After completing the British engineering course, he was assigned to a steel plant in Kiev—the heart of the industrial belt in the Ukraine, then part of the Soviet Union. This was in the early 1960s when the Eastern bloc countries were rapidly expanding inter-society trade, and when Russia exported industrial products and weaponry.

Mahsi had learned to speak Russian fluently, and he was educated both at home and abroad in English as his first tongue. Consequently, the Kiev authorities appointed him to an export trade and finance division where, for nearly eight years, he was in command of foreign commerce for the Soviet Union's fourth-largest integrated steel enterprise. When revolution occurred back home, he was transferred to a Sri Lankan government agency in Colombo for coordinating state industry. On his own accord, he left Sri Lanka and earned a Fullbright scholarship to Purdue University in the United States, where he completed graduate engineering studies and a graduate degree in business management. This led to an engineering post for a major U.S. steel company in Illinois, then to a financial trade specialist position with the Chicago Board of Trade.

On trips back to Sri Lanka, Mahsi met and married the daughter of a local plantation executive, and then returned to Illinois to pursue American citizenship. His plans were cut short by the successful bid for independence in Sri Lanka, and Mahsi returned home to head a new government-sponsored development bank. The bank, an extension of the new Sri Lanka Central Bank Authority, was charged with underwriting the country's mainstream infrastructure. During the first five years, through 1984, Mahsi utilized government loans and subsidies to establish the first stock exchange, and to register the first private brokerage firm in the new republic. He modeled both ventures on American systems, bringing in experts from the New York Stock Exchange and several Washington-based consultants to found the securities industry. DFCC was then spun off from government control and became one of the first four privately listed companies on the Sri Lankan exchange.

Mahsi set out to create an international vision for the corporation from the first day. His board represents members from the four major ethnic groups and the four primary religions in the country. He has subsequently participated in joint ventures with French, British, American, and German capital investment firms to establish a securities consortium of brokerages and licensed international trading houses. His development bank now has a venture capital investment division, a real estate development subsidiary, equity holdings in steel mills, power-generating companies, and a commodities board. In 1997, Mahsi engineered a joint venture with Morgan Grenfell of Germany, a consortium of American and Japanese investors, and DFCC to buy out the Sri Lankan telecommunications exchange, thus privatizing the nation's telephone system and satellite network. Along the way, DFCC has underwritten more than 200 Sri Lankan entrepreneurs, with projects ranging from small restaurants to beach resort complexes. Shortly after the millennium celebrations in 2000, DFCC launched a full international commercial bank division.

Mahsi also established the first commercial training institute for computers and IT systems, a pet initiative of his begun in the early 1990s. He called the school the Sri Lanka Business Institute, which he not only chaired but also supported financially through DFCC. Today, the institute is partially funded by the government with diploma and degree programs, with the City University of Dublin, and with a European consortium of universities.

Mahsi's vision also extended to international graduate education. In 1994, he attempted to establish the first graduate business school in Sri Lanka. Had it been successful, the school would have offered U.S. joint degrees from notable universities with faculty and student exchanges. He carried the proposal to the point of negotiating with Americans, including Babson College, James Madison University, the University of Texas, University of California at Berkeley, and Southern Methodist. Mahsi's son graduated from SMU in 1996 as one of the first resident students from Sri Lanka. His daughter graduated from JMU in 1997. Meanwhile, Mahsi's plans for a graduate school failed, partly due to flare-up battles between rebel Tamil forces and the government, and partly due to his own government's reluctance to help underwrite local student and faculty exchanges. DFCC was willing to put up $10 million in seed capital as a donation to launch the programs, and Mahsi had succeeded in getting the U.S. government to back matching funds for participating American universities.

Although he fell short of his goals for improving educational infrastructure, Mahsi generated a groundswell of interest by other business leaders. The interesting aspect, however, is that he accomplished this in a very quiet way. By creating multicultural teams of advisors and project teams drawn from Sri Lankan Chamber of Commerce members for every initiative that DFCC pursued, Mahsi built a reputation for being able to bridge cultural and ethnic gaps. Consequently, a Business Advisory Council has emerged to fund MBA programs in Sri Lanka, all with private money from individual business leaders. A series of training institutes have emerged as well, and an accounting society has become a focal organization for certification training and licensing. It is based on international standards (modeled generally on U.S. systems and with U.S. companies as members).

The team-based approach has been a critical success factor, and it has often involved Mahsi and DFCC in international alliances. Before his retirement in 2000, Mahsi served for nearly 10 years in adjunct roles with the World Bank on international finance and development committees in Washington D.C. He was a board member of four European investment associations, and he was jointly responsible under financing and lending agreements for managing funds generated through the Asian Development Bank, the International Monetary Fund, and the International Bank for Reconstruction and Development (IBRD). These, and various alliances through international development programs such as the United Nations mission in Sri Lanka and the U.S. Agency for International Development, put Mahsi squarely at the center of his nation's economic development. Yet he remained apart from politics and kept himself and DFCC separate from any party or political agenda. Today, Mahsi serves on the DFCC managing board of directors and has been adamant in keeping the company independent of any funds or projects with political strings, either in the country or with international interests. And he has structured DFCC entirely on a philosophy of private-enterprise development and western management methods.

In 1996 and again in 1999, DFCC was voted the "Best Managed Company in Asia" by the ASEAN committee on economic development. Mahsi was singled out at his 2000 retirement as a visionary leader who was changing the economic framework of private enterprise in Sri Lanka. In a typical reaction, Mahsi deferred the award and accepted the accolades of DFCC on behalf of his employees and his nation's business leaders who, he pointed out, were "Arab, Indian, Sinhala, Tamil, many Americans and Europeans, yet were individuals who worked together without national or ethnic interests." DFCC, he explained, was a "unity of purpose" that went beyond borders or personalities. "It was," he said, "a fabric woven of ideas from insightful human beings."

Today, DFCC is managed by self-directed teams in the subsidiaries and departments. Managers emulate Mahsi's approach to low-key leadership and consensus building. He claims to have no special vision, but many little visions that he expects his people to pursue—a foundation for business education, a network of professional societies that transcend national and ethnic interests, a financial environment that supports a securities and commodities industry, and an international trade economy that can attract and sustain foreign investment by leading multinationals. When DFCC was launched nearly 20 years ago as a small agency of government, the staff included Mahsi and two employees. When he went private several years later, there were barely 20 employees and an external board. Now, it is a multi-billion-dollar corporation with 206 alliances and infrastructure projects involving investors or companies from 18 other nations. Still, headquarters has fewer than 100 employees and only three levels of management; subsidiaries and alliance projects are self-directed under comanaged teams.

Mahsi's persona says even more about his leadership style, and in an important sense, the charisma that allows him to control without being "controlling." Mahsi and his wife live in a house that he built soon after they were married. It is sufficient, not large, and was extended to provide private rooms for his son and daughter as they grew up. They employ a housekeeper/cook, which is common in Sri Lanka and a small luxury. He drives a modest Toyota sedan and dresses conservatively in clothes purchased off the rack during visits to New York. His work keeps him airborne to the United States, Europe, Tokyo, and other parts of the world nearly 50 percent of the year, yet he flies economy class on most flights—business class on the long 20-hour trips to the United States. At work, his office is pleasant but not unusual, and there are no signs or plaques to say who he is or what he does; he is just "Maxy" to friends and associates. He never talks to anyone from behind his desk, but sits with guests or employees in casual chairs arranged for easy conversation. Mahsi could have become a wealthy man, but he never accepted a percentage salary increase greater than the average given to his company staff, and everyone shared in bonus systems.

Mahsi had several rules for business during his years as chief executive of DFCC. First, he believed that his day should not end if a client's call or question had not been answered. Even if he could not fully address a client's concern, he would respond or call before he left the office that day. Second, even if he could not resolve a question or concern by an employee, his responsibilities required that he address the problem or communicate with the employee. His busy schedule often kept him away from the office, but his rules were then passed on to his managers with equal expectations. Third, Mahsi evaluated his own decisions and all DFCC initiatives with one prevailing question in mind: "Will what I do here make a difference for my people?"

Mahsi Prelis remains an active senior member of DFCC and enjoys being a role model for younger staff managers. His daughter has returned from the United States to join DFCC as one of those younger managers. Mahsi regularly visits to lecture at the Business Institute that he founded, and he consults to the Sri Lankan Central Bank Authority. He also continues to work with the World Bank on new economic development initiatives for transition countries, and he is a roving ambassador for ASEAN development programs in Southeast Asia.

QUESTIONS

1. Explain the concept of transformational leadership and how Prelis demonstrates the important element of charisma as a manager.

2. Many people would argue that DFCC is a "domestic organization," not an international company, because it is focused on national commerce and internal growth. Yet others argue that DFCC is a multinational in the sense of integrated alliances and business investments brought to Sri Lanka from North America, Europe, and Asia. How would you argue the point; and if you were a member of DFCC's management team, how would you describe your role?

3. Sri Lanka is a very unusual country for its vast differences in ethnic groups, cultures, languages, and ideologies. What problems would you envision as a manager working there for a company like DFCC, or perhaps for a foreign multinational such as Unilever, IBM, or Caterpillar Corporation?

4. Mahsi Prelis and DFCC have had to overcome significant differences in this multicultural company, and certainly among its worldwide alliances, to implement a consensus approach to management. Based on teamwork with few authoritative differences in management ranks, bringing these diverse interests together would be a major challenge. Describe the principal success factors and potential pitfalls of building teamwork in the Sri Lankan business environment.

BIBLIOGRAPHY

DFCC Annual Report 2000. Development Finance Corporation of Ceylon, Colombo, Sri Lanka, pp. 2, 7.

Holt, David H., and M. R. Prelis. "A Strategic Initiative for Private Sector Development in Sri

Lanka." *Ministry of Industry, Science and Technology Report* (Colombo, Sri Lanka: Government of Sri Lanka, 1994).

Holt, David H. "Business Education in Sri Lanka: A Comprehensive Assessment of Strategic Needs." *U.S. Agency for International Development* (Washington, D.C.: USAID, 1995).

Prelis, Moksevi, and Ranjit Fernando. "Economic Diagnosis." *Lanka Monthly Digest*, September 1996, 5–10.

Zuber, Christian, and Senake Bandaranayake. *Sri Lanka: Island Civilisation* (Boulogne, France: Delroisse, 1992), 1–4, 16, 27–28.

ENDNOTES

CHAPTER 1

1. "Mr. Sony's Struggle," *Fortune*, 22 November 1999, 237–248.
2. Geoffrey Colvin, "The Ultimate Manager," *Fortune*, 22 November 1999, 185–187.
3. Richard J. Barnet and John Cavanagh, *Global Dreams: Imperial Corporations and the New World Order* (New York: Simon & Schuster, 1994), 13–14.
4. Bruce Barnard, "Corporate Europe's Love Affair with America," *Europe*, May 1999, 21–22.
5. "The World's View of Multinationals," *The Economist*, 29 January 2000, 21–22.
6. "Storm Over Globalization," *The Economist*, 27 November 1999, 15–16.
7. George S. Yip, *Total Global Strategy: Managing for Worldwide Competitive Advantage* (Englewood Cliffs, N.J.: Prentice Hall, 1995), 8.
8. Christopher A. Bartlett and Sumantra Ghoshal, *Transnational Management: Text, Cases, and Readings in Cross-Border Management*, 2nd ed. (Boston, Mass.: Irwin, 1995), 3.
9. Richard M. Hodgetts and Fred Luthans, *International Management*, 2nd ed. (New York: McGraw-Hill, 1994), 33.
10. Richard N. Farmer, "International Management," in Joseph W. McGuire (ed.), *Contemporary Management: Issues and Viewpoints* (Englewood Cliffs, N.J.: Prentice Hall, 1974), 300–301.
11. T. Quinn Spitzer and Benjamin Tregoe, "Thinking and Managing Beyond the Boundaries," *Business Horizons* (January–February 1993), 36–40.
12. Sean B. Eom, "Transnational Management Systems: An Emerging Tool for Global Strategic Management," *SAM Advanced Management Journal* (spring 1994): 22–27. Also see Robert Heller, "Survival of the Globally Adapted," *Management Today*, August 1994, 11–12.
13. Samuel Humes, *Managing the Multinational: Confronting the Global-Local Dilemma* (Hemel Hempstead: Prentice Hall International, 1993), 20.
14. Ibid., pp. 20–21.
15. Alfred D. Chandler, "The Multi-unit Enterprise: A Historical and International Comparative Analysis and Summary," in H. F. Williamson (ed.), *Evolution of International Management Structures* (Newark, N.J.: University of Delaware Press, 1975), 146.
16. A. Sampson, *The Seven Sisters* (London: Coronet, 1988), 43.
17. Alfred Chandler, *Scale and Scope* (Cambridge, Mass.: Harvard University Press, 1990), 52–53.
18. Thomas Watson Jr. and P. Petre, *Father, Son & Co., My Life at IBM and Beyond* (New York: Bantam Books, 1990), 34.
19. Humes, *Managing the Multinational*, 23–24.
20. Chandler, *Scale and Scope*, 611–612. Also see Ippei Yamazawa and F. C. Lo (eds.), *Evolution of Asia-Pacific Economies: International Trade and Direct Investment* (Kuala Lumpur: Asia and Pacific Development Centre, 1993), 6–10, 23, and appendices.
21. Lester Thurow, *Head to Head: The Coming Economic Battle Among Japan, Europe, and America* (New York: Warner Books, 1993), 30–33.
22. M. Ariff, "Dynamic Comparative Advantage, International Trading Rules and Their Implications for the Industrializing Countries," *EDI Working Papers* (Washington, D.C.: World Bank, 1990).
23. Humes, *Managing the Multinational*, 273–275.
24. T. W. Kang, *Is Korea the Next Japan?* (New York: The Free Press, 1989), 30–32.
25. Robert Lloyd George, *The East-West Pendulum* (Cambridge, U.K.: Woodhead-Faulkner, 1992), 6–7, 32, 37.
26. Joseph L. H. Tan and Luo Zhaohong (eds.), *ASEAN-China Economic Relations: Industrial Restructuring in ASEAN and China* (Singapore: Institute of Southeast Asian Studies, 1995), 13–17.
27. Y. C. Jao, "Hong Kong as an International Financial Centre: Evolution and Prospects," in Tzong-biau Lin and Chyau Tuan (eds.), *The Asian NIEs: Success and Challenge* (Hong Kong: Lo Fung Learned Society, 1993), 39–82.
28. A. A. Mclean, "Hong Kong's Economy—Past, Present and Future," in Lin and Tuan, *Asian NIEs*, 83–101.
29. James Clad, *Behind the Myth: Business, Money & Power in South East Asia* (London: Hyman Limited, 1989), 125–134. Also see George, *East-West Pendulum*, 82–83.
30. Humes, *Managing the Multinational*, 15–16.
31. William Pitt, *More Equal Than Others: A Director's Guide to EU Competition Policy* (Hemel Hempstead, U.K.: Simon & Schuster International, 1995), ii–x, 3–7.

32. Samuel Francis, "A Thousand Insults on the Way to Lost Sovereignty," *Washington Times*, 23 December 1994, p. A21.

33. David de Ferrant, Guillermo E. Perry, Indermit S. Gill, and Luis Serven, *Securing Our Future in a Global Economy* (Washington, D.C.: World Bank, 2000), 1–12.

34. "Canada and Chile Accelerate Free Trade," *World Trade*, February 2000, 14.

35. United Nations, *Restructuring the Developing Economies of Asia and the Pacific in the 1990s* (New York: UN Economic and Social Commission for Asia and the Pacific, 1993), 1–3, 16.

36. World Bank Development Research Center, *World Bank Development Report 1999–2000, Interim Edition* (Washington, D.C.: World Bank 2000), Social and Economic Indicators Summaries.

37. Thomas F. McGuire, "Marketing Moves from a Global to a Transnational Management Structure," *Euromarketing*, April 1995, 16–19.

38. Peter F. Drucker, "The New Productivity Challenge," *Harvard Business Review* 69, no. 6 (1991): 69–79; *People and Performance: The Best of Peter Drucker on Management* (New York: Harper & Row, 1977), 24–31, 77–78; and *Management: Tasks, Responsibilities, Practices* (New York: Harper & Row, 1974), 482–488.

39. Peter F. Drucker, "Peter Drucker's 1990s," *The Economist*, 21 October 1989, 22.

40. Tanya Gordrey, "Business Process Re-engineering," *International Management*, September 1994, 62.

41. Stewart Alsop, "E or Be Eaten," *Fortune*, 8 November 1999, 86–87; also see Eryn Brown, "Big Business Meets the E-World," *Fortune*, 8 November 1999, 88–98.

42. Bruce Elbert, "Satellite Communications: Instant Infrastructure for the New Millenium," *World Trade*, May 1999, 35–38.

43. Martha L. Celestino, "Pharmaceuticals, Medical, and Biotechnology: Hot Industries with a Global Focus," *World Trade*, May 1999, 98–102. Also see Peter Lynch, "The Upsizing of America," *Wall Street Journal*, 20 September 1996, p. A14.

44. Yip, *Total Global Strategy*, 165.

45. Ibid., p. 8.

46. Ibid., p. 166.

47. David H. Holt, "Procter & Gamble in China: Embracing Multicultural Management," *China Business Today*, March 1995, 37.

48. Robert P. Vecchio and Mario Sussman, "Choice of Influence Tactics: Individual and Organizational Determinants," *Journal of Organizational Behavior* (March 1991): 73–80.

49. Roland Calori, "Style of Stilted," *International Management*, June 1994, 51.

50. Denice Welch, "Determinants of International Human Resource Management Approaches and Activ-ities: A Suggested Framework," *Journal of Management Studies* 31, no. 2 (1994): 139–164.

51. N. Boyacigiller, "The Role of Expatriates in the Management of Interdependence, Complexity, and Risk in Multinational Corporations," *Journal of International Business Studies* 21, no. 3 (1990): 357–381. Also see I. Torbiorn, "The Structure of Managerial Roles in Cross-cultural Settings," *International Studies of Management and Organizations* 15, no. 1 (1985): 52–74.

52. Rosalie L. Tung, "Selection and Training Procedures of U.S., European, and Japanese Multinationals," *California Management Review* 25, no. 2 (1982): 57–71. Also see D. Eleanor Westney, "Sociological Approaches to the Pacific Region," in *The Pacific Region: Challenges to Policy and Theory* (Cambridge, Mass.: American Academy of Political & Social Science, 1989), 27.

53. Calori, "Style of Stilted," 51.

54. Deborah Lamb, "Expats Can Find Relief Offshore," *South China Business Post*, 28 April 1995, 1.

55. M. E. Mendenhall and G. Oddou, "The Dimensions of Expatriate Acculturation: A Review," *Academy of Management Review* 10, no. 1 (1985): 39–47.

56. Lori Ioannou, "Cultivating the New Expatriate Executive," *International Business*, July 1994, 40–46.

57. Michael E. Porter, "Changing Patterns of International Competition," *California Management Review* 28, no. 2 (1986): 9–40.

58. Humes, *Managing the Multinational*, 3. Also see Chandler, *Scale and Scope*, 16.

59. Peter F. Drucker, "The New World According to Drucker," *Business Month*, May 1989, 54.

CHAPTER 2

1. Steve Barth, "Peerless in Seattle," *Asia, Inc.*, June 1995, 56–58.

2. Ariane Sains, "Volvo: End of an Era," *Europe*, May 1999, 19–21.

3. *UNCTC World Investment Report* (New York: United Nations Center on Transnational Corporations, 1991), Executive Summary, i; also, *World Development Indicators* (Washington, D.C.: World Bank, 2000), CD-ROM, Economic Data Series.

4. "Kosovo: A Wasteland," *The Economist*, 15 May 1999, 52–53. Also see "Economic Fallout: The Balkans in the Wake of Diplomacy," *The Economist*, 9 June 1999, 47–48.

5. Ariane Sains, "Sweden a Country in Transition: Swedish Firms Seeking Shelter Abroad," *Europe*, May 1999, 17–18.

6. Discussions in this section are largely based on three sets of documents: *World Development Indicators* (Washington, D.C.: World Bank, 2000), Economic Time Series Tables; World Resources Institute, *World Resources 1996–97* (New York: WRI, 1996); and U.N. Department of Economic and Social Information and Policy

Analysis, *Monthly Bulletin of Statistics*, January 1999, Trade & Investment Summaries.

7. Allen J. Morrison, David A. Ricks, and Kendall Roth, "Globalization Versus Regionalization: Which Way for the Multinational?" in Rosalie L. Tung, *International Management* (Brookfield, Vt.: Dartmouth Publishing Company, 1994): 1–15.

8. Lara Sowinski, "Top Countries for Trade & Expansion," *World Trade*, June 2000, 38–46; also see Kenichi Ohmae, *The Borderless World* (New York: Harper Business, 1990): 1–5.

9. Kenichi Ohmae, "The Triad World View," *Journal of Business Strategy* (spring 1987): 8–17. Also see Kenichi Ohmae, *Beyond National Borders* (Homewood, Ill.: Dow Jones-Irwin, 1987).

10. H. Kwak, "Economic Consequences of Integration—The EU in 1992," *Harvard International Review* (spring 1989): 51–54, 63.

11. "What Is Europe? *The Economist*, 12 February 2000, 15–16; also see "Foreign Investment and the Triad," *The Economist*, 24 August 1991, 57.

12. "Europe: The Union Pause for Breath," *The Economist*, 12 February 2000, 49–51.

13. World Bank, *The Long March, A Reform Agenda for Latin America and the Caribbean in the Next Decade* (Washington, D.C.: World Bank Latin American and Caribbean Studies, 1999), 1–2, 14.

14. Daniel Lian and Lee Tsao Yuan, "Financial Development in ASEAN," in Joseph L. H. Tan and Luo Zhaohong (eds.), *ASEAN-China Economic Relations: Industrial Restructuring in ASEAN and China* (Singapore: Institute of Southeast Asian Studies, 1994), 240–272.

15. James Clad, *Behind the Myth: Business, Money & Power in South East Asia* (London: Unwin Hyman Ltd, 1989), 66–67. Also see "East Asia's Economic Growth 'Is No Miracle'," *South China Morning Business Post*, 16 May 1995, 12.

16. Stephen Haggard, Karim Shariff, and Steven Webb, *Politics, Inflation, and Stabilization in Middle Income Countries* (Washington, D.C.: World Bank, 1994).

17. Michael Schuman, "Free to Be," *Forbes*, 8 May 1995, 78, 80–81.

18. "War and Money—The Business of Conflict," *The Economist*, 4 March 2000, 46–48.

19. Andrew Dowell, "Growth in the Cross Hairs," *Business Monthly*, August 1999, 40–44.

20. Joe Studwell, "Economies: Clash of the Titans," *Asia, Inc.*, June 1995, 34–40.

21. Kim R. Holmes, Bryan T. Johnson, and Melanie Kirkpatrick (eds.), *1997 Index of Economic Freedom* (New York: Dow Jones & Company, Inc., 1997), Ranking Table, xxix–xxxi. Updated data cited here is from <www.wsj.com/reprints> on 7 September 2000.

22. Holmes, et al., *1997 Index of Economic Freedom*, 228–230. Also see U.S. Department of Commerce, *Country Commercial Guide, India* (Washington, D.C.: U.S. Government Printing Office, 1996), 14, 83.

23. Edwardo Boeninger, "Governance and Development: Issues and Constraints," *Proceedings of the World Bank Annual Conference on Development Economics*, (Washington, D.C.: The World Bank, 1992), 267–287.

24. Studwell, "Clash of the Titans," 36.

25. Moksevi R. Prelis, "Sri Lanka's Development Priorities for the Next Millennium," *Development Finance Corporation of Ceylon Bank Review*, no. 21 (January 2000): 2.

26. Alberto Alesina and Roberto Perotti, "The Political Economy of Growth: A Critical Survey of the Recent Literature," *World Bank Economic Review* 8, no. 3 (1994): 351–371.

27. Francisco H. G. Ferreira and Indermit Gill, "Weathering Storms: Households, Governments and Aggregate Income Shocks in Latin America," *World Bank Draft* (Washington, D.C.: World Bank, 2000), 6–9.

28. "The Americas: Brazil," *The Economist*, 15 May 1999, 38–39. Also see Ian Katz, "Brazil: Cardoso May Get the Time to Work His Magic," *Business Week*, 17 February 1997, 55.

29. World Bank, *World Development Indicators 2000*, CD-ROM, Economic Data Series.

30. Larry Luxner, "Knocking on NAFTA's Door: Region's Fastest-Growing Economy Forges Global Links," *Wall Street Journal*, 20 September 1996, p. B6.

31. Guillermo Le-Fort, "The Financial System and Macroeconomic Stability: The Chilean Experience," in Shakil Faruqi (ed.), *Financial Sector Reforms, Economic Growth, and Stability* (Washington, D.C.: Economic Development Institute of the World Bank, 1994), 113–138.

32. Reinaldo Penner, "Financial Liberalization in an Agrarian Economy: The Case of Paraguay," in Faruqi (ed.), *Financial Sector Reforms,* 153–178.

33. David de Ferranti, Guillermo E. Perry, Indermit S. Gill, and Luis Serven, *Securing Our Future in a Global Economy* (Washington, D.C.: World Bank, 2000), 6–11, 16–18.

34. Henry A. Kissinger, "The New Russian Question," *Newsweek*, 10 February 1992, 34–35.

35. "Less Poor, Less Democratic," *The Economist*, 22 April 1995, 62.

36. Sherrie E. Zhan, "Top Markets for Trade & Expansion," *World Trade*, June 1999, 38–44.

37. Shawn Tully, "Doing Business in One Germany," *Fortune*, 2 July 1990, 80–83. Also Richard Eccles, "Rules of Engagement," *International Management*, May 1994, 49–50.

38. "Executive Report: Business in the CEE," *International Trade & Business*, vol. 4 (1999), 31–40.

39. *The Global Competitiveness Report 1998*, (Geneva, Switzerland: World Economic Forum, 1998), x–xii and

trade statistics appendices for European Transition Economies; also see Alan Shipman, "Eurotrends: Shock Therapy has Yet to See Eastern Europe on the Way to Economic Recovery," *International Management*, March 1994, p. 8.

40. State Administration of Industry and Commerce, *China Statistics Yearbook* (Beijing, PRC: SAIC, 1998), Tables 3, 7; "More Competition Abroad from Chinese Companies," *World Trade*, May 1999, 22–25; and *World Development Indicators* (Washington, D.C.: World Bank, 2000), Social and Economic Tables on CD-ROM.

41. This section is drawn from Paul Romer, "Increased Returns and Long Run Growth," *Journal of Political Economy* 94 (1986): 1002–1037; and David Gould and Roy Ruffin, "What Determines Economic Growth?" *Economic Review* (Dallas, Tx.: Federal Reserve Bank of Dallas, 1993), 25–40.

42. Adam Smith, *An Inquiry into the Nature and Causes of the Wealth of Nations*, 5th ed. (Edinburgh: Adam and Charles Black, 1859).

43. Most of this section is drawn from several works: George S. Yip, *Total Global Strategy: Managing for Worldwide Competitive Advantage* (Englewood Cliffs, N.J.: Prentice Hall, 1995), 40–43; Richard R. Nelson and Nathan Rosenberg, "Technical Innovation and National Systems," in Richard R. Nelson (ed), *National Innovation Systems: A Comparative Analysis* (New York: Oxford University Press, 1993), 3–21; and Marquise R. Cvar, "Case Studies in Global Competition: Patterns of Success and Failure," in Michael E. Porter (ed.), *Competition in Global Industries* (Boston: Harvard Business School Press, 1986), 483–516.

44. Nelson (ed.), *National Innovation Systems*, 25–27.

45. David C. Mowery and Nathan Rosenberg, "The U.S. National Innovation System," in Nelson (ed.), *National Innovation Systems*, 29–75.

46. Timothy M. Collins and Thomas L. Doorley III, *Teaming Up for the 90s: A Guide to International Joint Ventures and Strategic Alliances* (Homewood, Ill.: Business One Irwin, 1991), 57–58.

47. A. A. McLean, "Hong Kong's Economy—Past, Present and Future," in Tzong-biau Lin and Chyau Tuan (eds.), *The Asian NIEs: Success and Challenge* (Hong Kong: Lo Fung Learned Society, 1993), 83–101.

48. Davis B. Goodman, "The WTO in Seattle: Did We Lose a Battle or the War?," *World Trade*, January 2000, 38–44.

49. James B. Teece, Kathleen Kerwin, and Heidi Dawley, "Ford: Alex Trotman's Daring Global Strategy," *Business Week*, 3 April 1995, 94–104.

50. Charles Edquist and Bengt-Ake Lundvall, "Comparing the Danish and Swedish Systems of Innovation," in Nelson (ed.), *National Innovation Systems*, 265–298.

51. Tawfik Jelassi, *Competing through Information Technology: Strategy and Implementation* (Hemel Hempstead, U.K.: Simon and Schuster International, 1994), 11–12.

52. M. D. Hopper, "Rattling SABRE: New Ways to Compete on Information," *Harvard Business Review*, May–June 1990, 118–125.

53. Sean B. Eom, "Transnational Management Systems: An Emerging Tool for Global Strategic Management," *SAM Advanced Management Journal* 59, no. 2 (spring 1994): 22–27.

54. Cora Daniels, "The Trauma of Rebirth," *Fortune*, 4 September 2000, 367–374; <www.dow.com> sites for reference, *Perspectives, Company History, Organization*; and W. J. Holstein, S. Reed, J. Kapstein, T. Vogel, and J. Weber, "The Stateless Corporation," *Business Week*, 14 May 1990, 98–105.

55. *World Development Report 1998/1999—Knowledge for Development* (New York: Oxford University Press, 1999), 63.

56. M. S. Scott Morton (ed.), *The Corporation of the 1990s: Information Technology and Organizational Transformation* (Oxford, U.K.: Oxford University Press, 1990), 3–23.

57. Susanne Schech and Jane Haggis, "Culture, Development, and the Information Revolution," in *Culture and Development* (Oxford, U.K.: Blackwell Publishers, 2000), 192–219.

58. Bruce Elbert, "Satellite Communications: Instant Infrastructure for the New Millennium," *World Trade*, May 1999, 34–38. Also see Bradley Johnson, "Surging IT Services' Battle Lines Take Shape: Companies in Hot Markets Line Pockets with Solutions," *Business Marketing*, 3 April 1995, p. T3.

59. Farok J. Contractor and V. K. Narayanan, "Technology Development in the Multinational Firm: A Framework for Planning and Strategy," *R&D Management* 20 (1990): 305–322.

60. Personal consulting and marketing results by the author for P&G (Guangzhou) 1988–1994.

61. "Reinventing the Future," *Industry Week*, 27 April 1995, 32.

62. Sumantra Ghoshal and Christopher A. Bartlett, "The Multinational Corporation as an Interorganizational Network," *Academy of Management Review* 15 (1990): 603–625.

63. Hugo Paemen, EU Ambassador to the United States, "EU-US Trade Relations on the Eve of the 21st Century," *World Trade Council Perspective*, July 1999, 2–4. Also Robert J. Guttman, "Charlene Barshefsky, U.S. Trade Representative: An Interview on the WTO and the EU's Banana Import Policy," *Europe*, May 1999, 11–13.

64. Douglas Appell, "Short-term Investors Fuel Gains in Malaysian Stocks," *Asian Wall Street Journal*, 2 June 1999, p. 13.

65. "Policies for Regional Trade Cooperation," *Proceedings of the Asian Trade Promotion Forum* (Tokyo: Japan External Trade Organization, 1995), 13–14.

66. Arthur Andersen Consulting, *Doing Business Abroad: A Guide to Foreign Investment* (Singapore: Arthur Andersen, 1996), 1, 15.

67. Gordon C. Anderson and K. C. Chan, "The MBA in South-East Asia: Dual Perspectives from the Provider and Customer," *Journal of Industrial and Commercial Training* 24, no. 2 (1992), 25–31. Also see "MBAs in Asia: Staying Close to Home," *Far Eastern Economic Review*, 31 March 1994, 42.

68. *Babson Abroad: A Guide to International MBA Programs* (Boston: Babson College, 1999).

69. J. Vickers and G. Yarrow, "Economic Perspectives on Privatization," *Journal of Economic Perspectives* 5, no. 2 (1991), 111–132.

70. N. Macro, "A Future History of Privatization, 1992–2022," *The Economist*, 3 January 1992, 15–18.

71. "BAA: The World's Most Successful Airports Group," *Asiaweek*, 31 March 1995, 31–34.

72. *Treuhandanstadt: Promoting the New Germany* (Berlin: Markt und Wirtschaft GmbH, 1994).

73. Louis Berger International and Checchi Consulting, *Evaluation of Private Enterprise Development in the ENI Region* (Washington, D.C.: United States Agency for International Development, 1998), Sec. 2, 28–32. Also see Frederick Studemann, "Treuhand's Closing-down Sale," *International Management*, September 1994, p .6.

74. David H. Holt, David A. Ralston, and Robert H. Terpstra, "Constraints on Capitalism in Russia: The Managerial Psyche, Social Infrastructure, and Ideology," *California Management Review* 36, no. 3 (1994), 31–45.

75. "Here Comes Reform, at a Price," *The Economist*, 9 March 1991, p. 17. Also see "Yelstin's Rival Warns of Ruin," *The Rossiskaya Gazeta*, 17 May 1993, p. 7; and D. S. L'Vov, "The Social and Economic Problems of Perestroika," *Communist Economies and Economic Transformation* 4, no. 1 (1992): 75–83.

76. Ira W. Lieberman, Stilpon S. Nestor, and Raj M. Desai, *Between State and Market: Mass Privatization in Transition Economies* (Washington, D.C.: The World Bank, 1997), 1–3, 44.

77. *Compendium: U.S. Nonprofit Assistance to Central and Eastern Europe and the Commonwealth of Independent States* (Washington, D.C.: CDC DataBank, 1994). Also "Evaluation of Assistance for Private Sector Development: The CIS, NIS, and Central Europe," *Transcript of Hearings by the House Foreign Affairs Committee, March 1995* (Washington, D.C.: United States Agency for International Development, 1995).

78. U.N. Department of Economic and Social Information and Policy Analysis, *Monthly Bulletin of Statistics*, December 1999, Employment Tables and Summaries.

79. Korn-Ferry International, *Board of Directors, Annual Study* (New York: Korn-Ferry International, Inc., 1999), 13–15.

80. Samuel Humes, *Managing the Multinational: Confronting the Global-Local Dilemma* (Hemel Hempstead, U.K.: Simon and Schuster International, 1993), 60–61.

81. Korn-Ferry International, *Board of Directors, Annual Study*, p. 14.

82. "On the Soon-to-Be Eastern Frontier," *The Economist*, 26 August 2000, 39. Also see "Europe's Migrants—Riding the Tide," *The Economist*, 5 August 2000, 49–50.

83. "U.S. Ambassador Talbott Sets Positive Trend for U.S.-Ukraine Relations," *Ukrainian Business Digest* 3, no. 5 (1993): 1, 3.

84. Pablo Fajnzylber and William F. Maloney, "Labor Demand and Trade Liberalization in Latin America," *Latin America and Caribbean Sector Management Unit for Poverty Reduction and Economic Management Mimeo* (Washington, D.C.: World Bank, 2000), reprint 1–22.

85. Nancy J. Adler, "Competitive Frontiers: Women Managing across Borders," *Journal of Management Development* 13, no. 2 (1994): 24–41.

86. Susanne Schech and Jane Haggis, "Feminism, Development, and Culture," *Culture and Development: A Critical Introduction* (Oxford, U.K.: Blackwell Publishers, 2000), 84–117. Also see Alan Shipman, "Eurotrends," *International Management* 49, no. 2, 1994, 8–9.

CHAPTER 3

1. Dean Foust, David Rocks, and Mark L. Clifford, "Is Douglas Daft the Real Thing?" *Business Week*, 20 December 1999. Also see <www.thecoca-colacompany.com> websites for "News," "History," and "Our Company" [cited 18 September 2000].

2. Mel Mandell, "Avoiding Overseas Crises," *World Trade*, October 1999, 44–46. Also see Coca-Cola's website "News@Coke," specifically issues dated 7 April 2000 and 7 September 2000, for the difficulties of CEO transition and official executive actions.

3. Thomas L. Brewer, "Politics, Risks, and International Business," in Thomas L. Brewer (ed.), *Political Risks in International Business: New Directions for Research, Management, and Public Policy* (New York: Praeger Publishers, 1985), 3–4.

4. Franklin R. Root, *Entry Strategies for International Markets* (Lexington, Mass.: D. C. Heath, 1987), 40–42, 77–78.

5. Shige Makino, "MITI Minister Kaoru Yosano on Reviving Japan's Competitive Advantage," *Academy of Management Executive* 13, no. 4 (1999): 9–11. Also see George Cabot Lodge, *Comparative Business-Government Relations* (Englewood Cliffs, N.J.: Prentice Hall, 1990), 14–16.

6. Geert Hofstede, "The Interaction between National and Organizational Value Systems," *Journal of Management Studies* 22, no. 4 (1985): 347–357.

7. F. Zapata, "Labor and Politics: The Mexican Paradox," in E. C. Epstein (ed.), *Labor Autonomy and the State in Latin America* (Boston: Unwin-Hyman Publishers, 1989), 178–187.

8. Richard Menger, "Japanese and American Negotiators: Overcoming Cultural Barriers to Understanding," *Academy of Management Executive* 13, no. 4 (1999): 100–101. Also see William J. Holstein, *The Japanese Power Game: What It Means for America* (New York: Plume Books, 1991), 150–153.

9. Hofstede, "Interaction between National and Organizational Value Systems," 347–357.

10. This section draws on George C. Lodge and Ezra F. Vogel (eds.), *Ideology and National Competitiveness* (Boston: Harvard Business School Press, 1987), Chapter 1; George Cabot Lodge, *Comparative Business-Government Relations* (Englewood Cliffs, N.J.: Prentice-Hall, 1990), 17–27; and John Zysman, *Governments, Markets and Growth* (Oxford, U.K.: Martin Robertson, 1983), 252–258.

11. Chalmers Johnson, *MITI and the Japanese Miracle: The Growth of Industrial Policy, 1925–1975* (Stanford, Calif.: Stanford University Press, 1982), 17–19.

12. Lodge, *Comparative Business-Government Relations*, 18–19.

13. Janice McCormick, "France: Ideological Divisions and the Global Reality," in Lodge and Vogel (eds.), *Ideology and National Competitiveness*, 56.

14. Ibid., p. 57.

15. Lodge, *Comparative Business-Government Relations*, 21.

16. U.S. Department of Commerce, *Index of Commercial Services: A Compendium and Review* (Washington, D.C.: Government Printing Office, 1996), 2.

17. Andrea Knox, "The World Trade Organization at a Crossroads," *World Trade*, October 1999, 34–38.

18. Lionel Barber, "Beef, Bananas, and Other Trade Skirmishes," *Europe*, May 1999, 10.

19. John Templeman, "A Troubling Barrage of Trade Sanctions from All Across America," *Business Week*, 24 February 1997, 59.

20. Lara L. Sowinski, "Top Markets for Trade & Expansion," *World Trade*, June 2000, 38–50.

21. "India and Pakistan: The Elephant and the Pekinese," *The Economist*, 18 March 2000, pp. 25–27.

22. UNCTAD, Division on Transnational Corporations and Investment, *World Investment Report 1993: Transnational Corporations and Integrated International Production* (New York: United Nations, 1993), Section 93, p. A14.

23. Christopher A. Bartlett and Sumantra Ghoshal, *Transnational Management: Text, Cases, and Readings in Cross-Border Management*, 2nd ed. (Boston: Irwin, 1995), 118–119.

24. Ibid., p. 119.

25. "France and the United States: Prickly Friends," *The Economist*, 19–25 October 1996, p. 56.

26. Michael E. Porter, "Competition in Global Industries: A Conceptual Framework," in Michael E. Porter (ed.), *Competition in Global Industries* (Boston: Harvard Business School Press, 1986), p. 39.

27. Lodge, *Comparative Business-Government Relations*, 13.

28. Michael R. Czinkota, Ilkka A. Ronkainen, Michael H. Moffett, and Eugene O. Moynihan, *Global Business* (Fort Worth: Dryden Press, 1995), 191–192.

29. John R. O'Neal, Frances O'Neal, Zeev Maoz, and Bruce Russett, "The Liberal Peace: Interdependence, Democracy, and International Conflict," *Journal of Peace Research* 33, no. 1 (1996): 11–29.

30. This section draws on Sam Wilkin, "Why Political Risk Is Important to You," *World Trade*, March 2000, 40–44; and Ralph H. Folsom, Michael Wallace Gordon, and John A. Spanogle, Jr., *International Business Transactions in a Nutshell* (St. Paul, MN: West Publishing Co., 1988), Chapter 8, 229–248, 253–254, and 277.

31. Gillian Flynn, "HR in Mexico: What You Should Know," *Personnel Journal* 73, no. 8 (1994): 34–44.

32. Leif Beck Fallesen, "Nordic Values a Source of Strength in the New Economy," *Europe*, December 1999/January 2000, 15–16. Also, Hugo Levi and Ake Sandberg, "Trade Unions and Workplace Technical Change in Europe," *Economic and Industrial Democracy* 12 (1991): 231–258.

33. U.S. State Department, "Advisory to U.S. Citizens: Travel in China," *Commercial Country Guide: China*, Attachment, January 2000, also on Internet at <http://www.travel.state.gov>.

34. Michael E. Porter, *The Competitive Advantage of Nations* (New York: The Free Press, 1990), 72–73.

35. Mel Mandell, "Safer Traveling: You Can Take Effective Precautions," *World Trade*, December 1999, 48–51. Also Czinkota et al., *Global Business*, 191–192.

36. Calvin Sims, "Peru's Leaders Cast Blame in Embassy Seizure," *International Herald Tribune*, 26 February 1997, p. 3. Also see Jathon Sapsford, "Tokyo Gets Rude Awakening in Peru," *Wall Street Journal*, 20 December 1996, p. A13.

37. Mandell, "Avoiding Overseas Crises: Nothing Beats Being Prepared," 44–48.

38. Brewer, "Politics, Risks, and International Business," 3–12.

39. Michael A. Hitt and Beverly B. Tyler, "Strategic Decision Models: Integrating Different Perspectives," *Strategic Management Journal* 12 (1991): 327–351.

40. Wilkin, "Why Political Risk Is Important to You," 41–44; David A. Schmidt, "Analyzing Political Risk," *Business Horizons*, July–August 1986, 43–50; "Of Mice and Men," *The Economist*, 25 November 1989, pp. 75–76.

41. Charles O. Bremmer, "The Rating Line on New Markets: Risks in Emerging Economies," *Executive Views*, January 1996, 33.

42. A. C. Shapiro, "Managing Political Risks: A Policy Assessment," *Columbia Journal of World Business* 16, no. 3 (1981): 63–69.

43. Joseph V. Miscallef, "Political Risk Assessment," *Columbia Journal of World Business* 16, no.2 (1981): 47–52.

44. Charles Piggot and Felix Salmon, "The Past Three Years," *Euromoney*, May 1996, 114–123.

45. "Forecasting Political Risk," *The Economist Intelligence Unit*, July 1999, 1–2 (reprint).

46. Jan Hatzius, "Foreign Direct Investment and Factor Demand Elasticities: Risk Associations and Methodologies," *European Economic Review* 44, no. 1 (2000): 117–143.

47. Frederick Stepenhurst, *Political Risk Analysis Around the North Atlantic* (New York: St. Martin's Press, 1992), xiv–xv.

48. Llewellyn D. Howell and Brad Chaddick, "Models of Political Risk for Foreign Investment and Trade: An Assessment of Three Approaches," *Columbia Journal of World Business* 29, no. 3 (1994): 70–83.

49. Llewellyn D. Howell, "Political Risk and Political Loss for Foreign Investment," *The International Executive* 34, no. 6 (1992): 496.

50. William Coplin and Michael K. O'Leary (eds.), *The Handbook of Country and Political Risk* (Syracuse, N.Y.: Political Risk Services, 1994), 173–274.

51. Howell and Chaddick, "Models of Political Risk for Foreign Investment and Trade," 70–83.

52. This section draws on Kent D. Miller, "A Framework for Integrated Management in International Business," *Journal of International Business Studies* 23, no. 2 (1992): 311–331. Also see Jeffrey D. Simon, "Political Risk Assessment: Past Trends and Future Prospects," *Columbia Journal of World Business* 17, no. 2 (1982): 62–71.

53. Paul W. Beamish, J. Peter Killing, Donald J. Lacraw, and Allen J. Morrison, *International Management: Text and Cases* (Boston: Irwin, 1994), 186–188.

54. Keith D. Brouthers, "The Influence of International Risk on Entry Mode Strategy in the Computer Software Industry," *Management International Review* 35, no. 1 (1995): 7–19.

55. Ibid., p. 9.

56. Mark L. Clifford, Nicole Harris, Dexter Roberts, and Manjeet Kripalani, "Coke Pours Into Asia," *Business Week*, 28 October 1996, 72–75.

57. "Sony Clips Ribbon on New Facility in KL," *Straits Times*, 16 March 1996, pp. 1, 8.

58. Jeffrey J. Reur and Michael J. Leiblein, "Downside Risk Implications of Multinationality and International Joint Ventures," *Academy of Management Journal* 43, no. 2 (2000): 203–214. Also see "Hedging the China Play," *South China Business Post*, 4 August 1996, p. B1.

59. George M. Taoka and Don R. Beeman, *International Business: Environments, Institutions, and Operations* (New York: Harper & Row, 1991), 239–240.

60. Clifford et al., "Coke Pours Into Asia," 72–75.

61. Mariah E. De Forest, "Thinking of a Plant in Mexico?" *Academy of Management Executive* 8, no. 1 (1994): 33–40.

CHAPTER 4

1. Fred R. Bleakley, "A Bastion of Paternalism Fights against Change," *Wall Street Journal*, 16 January 1997, pp. B1, B11.

2. Earnest W. Deavenport, "Doing the Right Thing," *Executive Excellence* 13, no. 5 (1996): 12–13.

3. John R. Boatright, "Ethics and the Role of the Manager," *Journal of Business Ethics* 7 (1988): 303–312.

4. Jacob Manakkalathil and Eric Rudolf, "Corporate Social Responsibility in a Globalizing Market," *SAM Advanced Management Journal* 60, no. 1 (1995): 29–32, 47.

5. David H. Holt, *Management Principles and Practices*, 3rd ed. (Englewood Cliffs, N.J.: Prentice Hall, 1993), 96.

6. Frederick B. Bird and James A. Waters, "The Moral Muteness of Managers," *California Management Review* 32, no. 3 (1989): 73–88.

7. Charles McCoy, "Exxon Corp.'s Settlement Gets Court Approval," *Wall Street Journal*, 9 October 1991, pp. A3, A10.

8. Manuel G. Velasquez, *Business Ethics: Concepts and Cases* (Englewood Cliffs, N.J.: Prentice Hall, 1992), 2–8; also see Subratra N. Chakravarty, "The Ghost Returns," *Forbes*, 10 December 1990, 108.

9. Steven H. Biondolillo, "The Father of Philanthropy," *Wall Street Journal*, 2 January 1997, p. A6.

10. William C. Frederick, "Corporate Social Responsibility and Business Ethics," in S. Prakash and Cecilia M. Falbe (eds.), *Business and Society* (Lexington, Mass.: Lexington Books, 1987), 142–161.

11. Kevin Thomas Jackson, "Jurisprudence and the Interpretation of Precepts for International Business," *Business Ethics Quarterly* 4, no. 3 (1994): 291–320.

12. Alex Taylor III, "Jac Nasser's Biggest Test," *Fortune*, 18 September 2000, 123–125. Also see R. Edward Freeman and Daniel R. Gilbert Jr., *Corporate Strategy and the Search for Ethics* (Englewood Cliffs, N.J.: Prentice Hall, 1988), 90–91.

13. Mark Methabane, "An Embargo That Backfires," *U.S. News & World Report*, 2 July 1990, 36.

14 Nelson Mandela's Address to the EIB on World Development, <www.eib.org>, "Development Initiatives" website [cited August 2000].

15. Charles Haddad, "Why Big Tobacco Can't Be Killed," *Business Week*, 24 April 2000, 68–71.

16. Carol Vinzant, "Smoke and Mirrors: Big Tobacco in the Crosshairs," *Fortune*, 18 September 2000, 298. For a summary of initial class-action lawsuits and the

tobacco industry's rejoinders, see Mike France, William C. Symonds, Monica Larner, and Dave Lindorff, "The World War on Tobacco," *Business Week*, 11 November 1996, 99–100.

17. Archie B. Carroll, "A Three-Dimensional Conceptual Model of Corporate Performance," *Academy of Management Review* 4, no. 3 (1979): 497–505.

18. Nicholas Stein, "The World's Most Admired Companies," *Fortune*, 2 October 2000, 182–196.

19. James A. F. Stoner and R. Edward Freeman, *Management*, 5th ed. (Englewood Cliffs, N.J.: Prentice Hall, 1992), 100–101.

20. Mark C. Bolino, "Citizenship and Impression Management: Good Soldiers or Good Actors?" *Academy of Management Review* 24, no. 1 (1999): 82–98.

21. Freeman and Gilbert, *Corporate Strategy*, 25–41.

22. Daniel J. Brass, Kenneth D. Butterfield, and Bruce C. Skaggs, "Relationships and Unethical Behavior: A Social Network Perspective, *Academy of Management Review* 23, no. 1 (1998): 14–31.

23. Robert Steiner, "Japan's Tax Man Leans on Foreign Firms," *Wall Street Journal*, 25 November 1996, p. A15.

24. Geert Hofstede, "The Cultural Relativity of Organizational Practices and Theories," *Journal of International Business Studies* 14 (1983): 75–89. Also see S. H. Schwartz, "Universals in Content and Structure of Values: Theoretical Advances and Empirical Tests in 20 Countries," in M. P. Zanna (ed.), *Advances in Experimental Social Psychology* (San Diego: Academic Press, 1992), 1–65.

25. Jonathan Friedland, "Bristol-Myers Aims to Boost Patent Laws as Argentine Unit Sells Pirate Drugs," *Wall Street Journal*, 23 September 1996, p. A17.

26. William Scheibal, "When Cultures Clash: Applying Title VII Abroad," *Business Horizons*, September–October 1995, 4–8.

27. Mariah E. de Forest, "Thinking of a Plant in Mexico?" *Academy of Management Executive* 8, no. 1 (1994): 33–40.

28. Geri Smith, "Mexico: Breaking the Curse," *Business Week*, 20 December 1999, 60–62. Also see "Mexico's Trade Unions Stick to the Same Old Tune," *The Economist*, 23 October 1999, 35–36.

29. Bruce Barnard, "Cross-Continental Convergences: In the Race to Go Global, Transatlantic Mergers Continue to Rise," *Europe*, September 2000, 32–34.

30. Norihiko Shirouzu, "Ex-Daiwa Trader Alleges 'Double-Cross'," *Wall Street Journal*, 8 January 1997, p. A18.

31. Bruce J. Klatsky, "Work Ethics," *Chief Executive*, June 1994, 28–31.

32. John Duerden, "'Walking the Walk' on Global Ethics," *Directors & Boards* 19, no. 3 (1995): 42–45.

33. David de Ferranti, Guillermo E. Perry, Indermit S. Gill, and Luis Serven, *Securing Our Future in a Global Economy* (Washington, D.C.: World Bank, 2000), 121–123. Also see "Why Wait for NAFTA?" *Business Week*, 5 December 1994, 54.

34. Helene Cooper, "Argentina Faces Sanctions by U.S. Over Drug Patents," *Wall Street Journal*, 16 January 1997, p. A11.

35. "China and the WTO: The Real Leap Forward," *The Economist*, 20 November 1999, 25–28.

36. "The Toppling of Helmut Kohl," *The Economist*, 8 January 2000, 45–47; Carol Matlack, "Why Jospin Is Squandering France's Chance for Reform," *Business Week*, 3 April 2000, 64; and Peter R. Kann, "A Report to the Wall Street Journal's Readers," *Wall Street Journal*, 8 January 1997, p. A23.

37. Scheibal, "When Cultures Clash," 4–8.

38. "Euroshambles," *The Economist*, 16 November 2000, 23–25. Also see Harry Costin, *Managing in the Global Economy: The European Union* (Fort Worth: Dryden Press, 1996), 43–48, 131–132.

39. Priscilla Elsass, "The Cost of Illegal Business Practices," *Academy of Management Executive* 12, no. 1 (1998): 87–88. Also see John L. Graham, "Foreign Corrupt Practices: A Manager's Guide," *Columbia Journal of World Business* 18, no. 3 (1983): 89–94.

40. Glenn A. Pitman and James P. Sanford, "The Foreign Corrupt Practices Act Revisited: Attempting to Regulate 'Ethical Bribes' in Global Business," *International Journal of Purchasing & Materials Management* 30, no. 3 (1994): 15–20.

41. Larry Ponemon, "Ethical Compliance at Tenneco Inc.," *Management Accounting*, August 1995, 59.

42. Eric W. K. Tsang, "Can Guanxi Be a Source of Sustained Competitive Advantage for Doing Business in China?" *Academy of Management Executive* 12, no. 2 (1998): 64–73. Also see "Commercial Corruption," *Wall Street Journal*, 2 January 1997, p. 6.

43. Pitman and Sanford, "Foreign Corrupt Practices Act Revisited," 16–17.

44. Ranjit Fernando, "Tariffs and Import Substitution: Protectionism Only Fuels Illicit Practices," *Lanka Monthly Digest* 3, no. 1 (1996): 10.

45. Graham, "Foreign Corruption Practices Act," 89–94.

46. "Vladimir Putin, Russia's Post–Cold War Warrior," *The Economist*, 8 January 2000, 51. Also see Vladimir Kvint, "Don't Give Up on Russia," *Harvard Business Review* 72, no. 2 (1994): 62–74.

47. "Commercial Corruption," *Wall Street Journal*, p. 6.

48. "Japan: Away with the Rogues," *The Economist*, 23 September 2000, 49–50.

49. "Trade Winds: Asia Pacific," *World Trade*, July 2000, 20–24. Also see Independent Commission against Corruption, *Legal Precedence and Corruption Enforcement in Asia: Progress Toward Unity of Purpose* (Hong Kong: ICAC, 1996), 3–5.

50. Joseph L. Badaracco, Jr., and Allen P. Webb, "Business Ethics: A View from the Trenches," *California Management Review* 37, no. 2 (1995): 8–28.

51. Nanette Byrnes, "The Smoke at General Electric: GE Continues to Struggle with an Ethics Program That's Not Producing Results," *Financial World*, 16 August 1994, 32–34.

52. John A. Byrne, "The Best & Worst Boards," *Business Week*, 24 January 2000, 142–151. Also see "Global Most Admired: GE Digs Into Asia," *Fortune*, 2 October 2000, 165–196.

53. John Rossant, "Old World, New Mandate," *Business Week*, 31 January 2000, 92.

54. "Commercial Corruption," *Wall Street Journal*, p. 6. Also see R. Michael Godfrey, "Negotiating Ethically to Reduce Conflict Costs in Transnational Firms," *International Journal of Management* 12, no. 2 (1995): 173–181.

55. Bodo B. Schlegelmilch and Diana C. Robertson, "The Influence of Country and Industry on Ethical Perceptions of Senior Executives in the U.S. and Europe," *Journal of International Business Studies* 26, no. 4 (1995): 859–881.

56. Carlo Mongardini, "Towards a European Sociology," in Birgitta Nedelmann and Piotr Sztompka (eds.), *Sociology in Europe: In Search of Identity* (New York: Walter de Gruyter, 1993), 67–77.

57. Dan Waters, *21st Century Management: Keeping Ahead of the Japanese and Chinese* (Singapore: Prentice Hall, 1991), 94–96.

58. Alan Richter and Cynthia Barnum, "When Values Clash," *HR Magazine*, September 1994, 42–45.

59. Velasquez, *Business Ethics*, 18–20.

60. Rosabeth Moss Kanter, "Transcending Business Boundaries: 12,000 World Managers View Change," *Harvard Business Review*, May–June 1991, 151–164.

61. Tom Peters, "Prometheus Barely Unbound," *Academy of Management Executive* 4, no. 4 (1990): 70–84.

62. Rosabeth Moss Kanter, "In Search of a Single Culture," *Business*, June 1991, 58–66.

63. Gillian Flynn, "HR in Mexico: What You Should Know," *Personnel Journal* 73, no. 8 (1994): 34–44.

64. Rochelle Kopp, "International Human Resource Policies and Practices in Japanese, European, and United States Multinationals," *Human Resource Management* 33, no. 4 (1994): 581–599.

65. Thomas A. Hemphill, "Beyond the Bottom Line: Putting Social Responsibility to Work for Your Business and the World," *Business & Society* 35, no. 1 (1996): 123–128.

66. Joel Makower, *Beyond the Bottom Line: Putting Social Responsibility to Work for Your Business and the World* (New York: Simon & Schuster, 1994), 12–13, 58, 117–124, 310–316.

67. Thomas E. Becker, "Integrity in Organizations: Beyond Honesty and Conscientiousness," *Academy of Management Review* 23, no. 1 (1998): 154–161.

68. Elizabeth Pond, Lionel Barber, Leif Beck Fallesen, and Barry D. Wood, "Europe in the New Century: 21st Century Views," *Europe*, December 1999/January 2000, 10–17. Also see Ferdinand Protzman, "Germany to Close Recycling Loop," *International Herald Tribune*, 6 July 1993, p. 4.

69. Scheibal, "When Cultures Clash," 4–8.

70. "Mirages and Classes in Middle East Business," *Financial Times*, 31 October 1995, p. 3.

71. Gary P. Ferraro, *The Cultural Dimension of International Business* (Englewood Cliffs, N.J.: Prentice Hall, 1990), 110–113.

72. Wendy Hardman and Jacqueline Heidelberg, "When Sexual Harassment Is a Foreign Affair," *Personnel Journal* 75, no. 4 (1996): 91–97.

PART 1 CASE

1. "Starting Up the Microsoft Man," *Precision Marketing*, 16 October 1995, 12–13.

2. "Microsoft and the Future," *The Economist*, 13 November 1999, 21–24.

3. *United States vs. Microsoft Corporation*, U.S. District Court, Civil Case No. 98—1232, 7 June 2000.

4. MSNBC, "Supreme Court Rejects Government Case, Sends Microsoft Appeal to Lower Court," Breaking News Digest at <www.msnbc.com> [cited September 26, 2000].

5. Charles Arthur, "Science: All Geek to Me," [Seattle] *Independent*, 15 October 1995, p. 74.

6. Pete Engardio and Dexter Roberts, "Microsoft's Long March," *Business Week*, 24 June 1996, p. 52.

7. "Help! I Need Somebody—Microsoft Talk," *Computing*, 20 March 1997, 34.

8. Jeffrey Parker, "Microsoft's Gates Gets Second Chance in China," *Reuters Business Report*, Beijing, 19 September 1995, 1, 17.

9. Engardio and Roberts, "Long March," 52.

10. "Microsoft Man," 12–13.

11. David Kirkpatrick, "He Wants *All* Your Business—and He's Starting to Get It," *Fortune*, 26 May 1997, 58–68.

12. Brent Schlender, "On the Road with Chairman Bill," *Fortune*, 26 May 1997, 72–78.

13. "Help!—Microsoft Talk," 34.

14. Sandra Sugawara, "Windows on a Huge New World," *Washington Post*, 25 July 1996, p. D14.

CHAPTER 5

1. Rahul Jacob, "The Resurrection of Michael Dell," *Fortune*, 18 September 1995, 117–128.

2. Dell Computers, Company Facts, "Who We Are," <www.dell.com> [cited 22 October 2000].

3. Betsy Morris, "Can Michael Dell Escape the Box?" *Fortune*, 16 October 2000 <www.fortune.com>.

4. Gary McWilliams, "Whirlwind on the Web," *Business Week*, 7 April 1997, 132–136.

5. Michael E. Porter, *The Competitive Advantage of Nations* (New York: Macmillan, 1990).

6. Alan M. Rugman (ed.), *International Business in Canada: Strategies for Management* (Scarborough, Ontario: Prentice-Hall, 1989). Also see A. Ryans, "Strategic Market Entry Factors and Market Share Achievement in Japan," *Journal of International Business Studies* 19, no. 3 (1988): 389–410.

7. Koh Sera, "Corporate Globalization: A New Trend," *Academy of Management Executive* 6, no. 1 (1992): 89–96.

8. Lester Thurow, *Head to Head: The Coming Economic Battle among Japan, Europe, and America* (New York: Warner Books, 1993), 3–7, 30, 128–130.

9. Michael E. Porter, "Changing Patterns of International Competition," *California Management Review* 27, no. 2 (1986): 9–40. Also see Alfred Chandler, *Scale and Scope* (Cambridge, Mass.: Harvard University Press, 1990), 50, 52–53.

10. Valerie Reitman and Bob Davis, "U.S., Japan Resuming Auto-Trade Talks," *Wall Street Journal*, 13 April 1995, p. A10. Also see "Power Gap—Who's Running the Show?" *The Economist*, 7 July 1995, 43.

11. Briance Mascarenhas, "International Industry Evolution Patterns," *International Business Review* 4, no. 4 (1995): 233–246.

12. Warren J. Keegan, *Global Marketing Management*, 4th ed. (Englewood Cliffs, N.J.: Prentice-Hall International, 1989), 123–124.

13. Porter, "Changing Patterns of Competition," 9–40.

14. Carl Menger, *Principles of Economics*, J. Dingwall and D. F. Hoselitz (trans.) (Glencoe, Ill.: Free Press, 1950), 56.

15. Michael E. Porter, *Competitive Advantage: Creating and Sustaining Superior Performance* (New York: Free Press, 1985).

16. Richard Normann and Rafael Ramirez, "From Value Chain to Value Constellation: Designing Interactive Strategy," *Harvard Business Review*, July–August 1993, 65–77.

17. Tracy Goss, Richard Pascale, and Anthony Athos, "The Reinvention Roller Coaster: Risking the Present for a Powerful Future," *Harvard Business Review*, November–December 1993, 97–108.

18. Porter, "Changing Patterns of Competition," 17.

19. Henry Mintzberg, *The Rise and Fall of Strategic Planning* (Englewood Cliffs, N.J.: Prentice-Hall, 1994), 81–82, 397. For a general background on strategic units and organizations, see H. I. Ansoff, *Implanting Strategic Management* (Englewood Cliffs, N.J.: Prentice-Hall, 1984). Also see Peter Wright, Charles D. Pringle, and Mark J. Kroll, *Strategic Management: Text and Cases* (Boston, Mass.: Allyn and Bacon, 1994), 84–88, 126–128.

20. Michael Cakrt, "Management Education in Eastern Europe: Toward Mutual Understanding," *Academy of Management Executive* 7, no. 4 (1993): 63–68. Also see

Vern Terpstra and Kenneth David, *The Cultural Environment of International Business* (Cincinnati: South-Western Publishing, 1985): 8–10.

21. Balaji S. Chakravarthy and Howard V. Perlmuter, "Strategic Planning for a Global Business," *Columbia Journal of World Business* 20, no. 2 (1985): 3–10.

22. Geert Hofstede, "Motivation, Leadership, and Organization: Do American Theories Apply Abroad?" *Organizational Dynamics* 8, no. 2 (1980): 42–63.

23. George S. Yip, *Total Global Strategy: Managing for Worldwide Competitive Advantage* (Englewood Cliffs, N.J.: Prentice-Hall, 1995), 103–104.

24. Yves L. Doz, "Government Policies and Global Industries," in Michael E. Porter (ed.), *Competition in Global Industries* (Boston: Harvard Business School Press, 1986), 225–266.

25. S. Gordon Redding, *The Spirit of Chinese Capitalism* (Berlin: Walter de Gruyter, 1990), 14, 76–78. Also see Lane Kelley, Arthur Whatley, and Reginald Worthley, "Self-Appraisal, Life Goals, and Rational Culture: An Asian-Western Comparison," *Asia Pacific Journal of Management* 7, no. 2 (1990): 41–58.

26. Yves L. Doz, "Strategic Management in Multinational Companies," *Sloan Management Review* (winter 1980): 27–46.

27. Michael E. Porter, *Competitive Strategy: Techniques for Analyzing Industries and Competitors* (New York: Free Press, 1980), 34–53.

28. Peng S. Chan and Anna Wong, "Global Strategic Alliances and Organizational Learning," *Leadership and Organization Development Journal* 15, no. 4 (1994): 31–36. Also see J. M. Juran, *Juran on Planning for Quality* (New York: Free Press, 1988), 4–8, 71–73.

29. Porter, *Competitive Strategy*, 37.

30. Kathleen Deveny, "Can Ms. Fashion Bounce Back?" *Business Week*, 16 January 1989, 64–70.

31. Robert Frank, "Coca-Cola Is Shedding Its Once-Stodgy Image with Swift Expansion," *Wall Street Journal*, 22 August 1995, pp. A1, A5. Also see H. Kent Bowen, Kim B. Clark, Charles A. Holloway, and Steven C. Wheelwright, "Development Projects: The Engine of Renewal," *Harvard Business Review*, September–October 1994, 110–120.

32. Laura Bird, "Saks, in Fifth Year under Bahrain Firm, Is Scrutinized," *Wall Street Journal*, 28 July 1995, p. B4. Also see Eric N. Berkowitz, Roger A. Kerin, Steven W. Hartley, and William Rudelius, *Marketing*, 3rd ed. (Homewood, Ill.: Richard D. Irwin, 1992), 382–384.

33. Porter, *Competitive Strategy*, 294–295.

34. Paulette Thomas, "Kimberly-Clark and P&G Face Global Warfare," *Wall Street Journal*, 18 July 1995, pp. B1, B4.

35. Kyle Pope, "High-Tech Firms Carry Jobs to Newcastle," *Wall Street Journal*, 21 August 1995, p. A5.

36. Matt Moffett, "Latin Nations Open Up to Long-Term Foreign Capital," *Wall Street Journal*, 23 June 1995, p.

A10. Also see "P&G Makes Strides in Guangzhou," *China Business Review*, September 1995, p. 14.

37. "Sprint Links with Euro-Giants for Global Reach," *Business Post*, 24 June 1995, p. 5.

38. Peter Waldman, "India Seeks to Open Huge Phone Market," *Wall Street Journal*, 25 July 1995, p. A9.

39. Bradley Johnson, "Surging IT Services' Battle Lines Take Shape: Companies in Hot Market Line Pockets with Solutions," *Business Marketing*, 3 April 1995, p. t-3.

40. Paul Lienert, "Ford Locks in Global Strategy: Lorain Plant Expected to Build Some Models Designed for World Car," *[Cleveland] Plain Dealer*, 18 June 1995, p. H1. Also see "Ford's Lofty Goal: Global Leadership," *Automotive News*, 29 May 1995, 29.

41. Porter, *Competitive Strategy*, 1–29.

42. Frank, "Coca-Cola Swift Expansion," pp. A1, A5.

43. James R. Healey, "Japanese Automakers Make Comeback," *USA Today*, 16 November 1995, p. 10B.

44. Daniel Simpson (ed.), "Planning in a Global Business," *Planning Review* 23, no. 2 (1995): 25–27.

45. Sugiura, "Honda Localizes Strategy," 77–82.

CHAPTER 6

1. James B. Treece, Kathleen Kerwin, and Heidi Dawley, "Ford: Alex Trotman's Daring Global Strategy," *Business Week*, 3 April 1995, 94–104. Also see Kathleen Kerwin, "Getting Two Big Elephants to Dance," *Business Week*, 18 November 1994, 83.

2. Christopher Tan, "Battle for the Top Spot," *Business Times* (Singapore), 20 July 2000, 28. [Retrieved 25 November 2000 from Dow Jones Interactive database.] Also see "Ford Misses Out Again: Making Cars in Asia: Ford Loses Out in Asia: Walking Away from Buying Bankrupt Daewoo Motors Leaves Ford Weaker Than Its Rivals in the Asian Market," *The Economist*, 23 September 2000. [Retrieved 22 November 2000 from Dow Jones Interactive database.]

3. Leonard Greenhalgh, "Ford Motor Company's CEO Jac Nasser on Transformational Change, E-Business, and Environmental Responsibility," *Academy of Management Executive*, 1 August 2000, 46. [Retrieved 28 February 2001 from Dow Jones Interactive database.] See also Richard Johnson, "Luxury Brand Management," *Automotive News Europe*, 12 February 2001, 15. [Retrieved 28 February 2001 from Dow Jones Interactive database.]

4. Charles R. Schwenk, "Strategic Decision Making," *Journal of Management* 21, no. 3 (1995): 471–493.

5. Personal interview with John Robertson, president, Robertson Marketing Group, 22 February 1997.

6. Ronald L. Schill, Roland G. Bertodo, and David N. McArthur, "Achieving Success in Technology Alliances: The Rover-Honda Strategic Collaboration," *R&D Management* 24, no. 3 (1994): 261–277.

7. C. T. Mahabharat, "IBM Plans Global Network in India," *Data Information Systems*, Bangalore, India, 21 April 1995, 1. Also see Vern Terpstra and Bernand L. Simonin, "Strategic Alliances in the Triad: An Exploratory Study," *Journal of International Marketing* 1, no. 1 (1993): 4–25.

8. Richard J. Babyak, "Strategic Imperative," *Appliance Manufacturer*, February 1995, 19–24.

9. Reinhilde Veugelers, "Strategic Incentives for Multinational Operations," *Managerial and Decision Economics* 16 (1995): 47–57.

10. Donal A. Dineen and Thomas N. Garavan, "Ireland: The Emerald Isle," *International Studies of Management & Organization* 24, no. 1–2 (1994): 137–164.

11. *Opportunities for the Coming Century* (Glasgow, U.K.: Scottish Development Board, 1994). Also see *Economic Perspectives for Eastern Europe* (Hong Kong: Trade Development Council, 1995); Alex Taylor III, "Driving for the Market's Heart," *Fortune*, 15 June 1992, 120–121; and Nancy J. Perry, "What's Powering Mexico's Success," *Fortune*, 10 February 1992, 109–115.

12. Ram Mudambi, "The MNE Investment Location Decision: Some Empirical Evidence," *Managerial and Decision Economics* 16 (1995): 249–257.

13. Saul Klein and Jehiel Zif, "Global versus Local Strategic Alliances," *Journal of Global Marketing* 8, no. 1 (1994): 51–71.

14. "Australian Tax Office Targets International Giants," *Xinhua News Agency*, 25 October 1995, 9.

15. Richard Westlund, "A New Focus," *Institutional Investor* 29, no. 6 (1995): 5–6.

16. Isaac Sonsino, "An Unlikely Tax Haven," *Corporate Finance*, May 1994, 30–31.

17. Harl Bedl, "Responsible for the World," *Asian Business*, July 1994, 16.

18. Liu Dongkai, "Australia Draws Overseas Business Headquarters," *Xinhua News Agency*, 10 September 1995, 9–10.

19. Peng S. Chan and Anna Wong, "Global Strategic Alliances and Organizational Learning," *Leadership and Organizational Development Journal* 15, no. 4 (1994): 31–36.

20. Joseph Duffey, "U.S. Competitiveness: Looking Back and Looking Ahead," in Martin K. Starr (ed.), *Global Competitiveness: Getting the U.S. Back on Track* (New York: W. W. Norton, 1988), 72–94.

21. U.S. Department of Commerce, *A Basic Guide to Exporting* (Washington, D.C.: U.S. Government Printing Office, 1994), 17–21.

22. Timothy M. Collins and Thomas L. Doorley III, *Teaming Up for the 90s: A Guide to International Joint Ventures and Strategic Alliances* (Homewood, Ill.: Business One Irwin, 1991), 8–9, 20–21.

23. Personal interview with John Zinkin, managing director of Gilman Office Supplies, 10 November 1993, Hong Kong.

24. *Annual Report 1995*, Boeing Company, 2–3. Also see "Selling American Medical Equipment in Japan," *Business Japan*, July 1995, 46, 61.

25. Commerce Dept., *Guide to Exporting*, 17–19.

26. "Foreign Trade Rights?" *Soviet Business & Trade* (Washington, D.C.: Welt Publishing, 1987), 2–3. Also see *Unraveling Border Mysteries with the CIS* (Washington, D.C.: U.S. Agency for International Development, 1994), 1.

27. U.S. Department of Commerce, *Export Trading Company Guidebook* (Washington, D.C.: U.S. Government Printing Office, 1988), 2.

28. *Toy Trade and Global Markets: Sales Trends in North American Markets* (Hong Kong: Trade Development Council, 1995), 2–3, Table 4.

29. Personal interview with Eric Yeung, managing director of Perfekta Toys, Macao, 11 November 1990.

30. Office of the U.S. Trade Representative, *U.S. Department of Commerce: Commercial Attaches* (Washington, D.C.: U.S. Government Printing Office, 1988).

31. China Business Forum, *U.S. Investment in China* (Washington, D.C., and Beijing: U.S.–China Business Council, 1995). Also see *Foreign Trade Relations, Donors, and Delegations: Roles and Activities* (Washington, D.C.: U.S. Agency for International Development, 1994).

32. U.S. Small Business Administration, *The World Is Your Market* (Washington, D.C.: SBA Office of International Trade, 1995), 55–77.

33. John Garland, Richard N. Farmer, and Marilyn Taylor, *International Dimensions of Business Policy and Strategy*, 2nd ed. (Boston: PWS-Kent, 1990), 105–107.

34. "Protection of U.S. Property Rights Remains Uncertain: Negotiators Face Difficulties in Trade Talks on All Fronts," *Asian Wall Street Journal*, 9 February 1996, pp. 1, 8.

35. Donald D. Boroian and Patrick J. Boroian, *The Franchising Advantage* (Schaumburg, Ill.: National Bestseller, 1989), 6–7.

36. Robert Neff and Kimberly Blanton, "You Can't Get Sushi at the Local 7-Eleven—Yet," *Business Week*, 12 November 1990, 59.

37. "Marketing Goes Global," *Business Europe*, 10 April 1995, 3.

38. Gareth Hewett, "Gordon's Golden Words Bring in the Millions," *South China Morning Business Post*, 21 February 1996, p. 18.

39. "Vietnam: MNCs Examine Risks and Strategies," *Crossborder Monitor*, 9 August 1995, p. 31; "Vietnam's Market: Can U.S. Firms Catch Up?" *Crossborder Monitor*, 23 February 1994, p. 1.

40. Janet Y. Murray, "Patterns in Domestic versus International Strategic Alliances: An Investigation of U.S. Multinational Firms," *Multinational Business Review* (fall 1995), 7–16.

41. Collins and Doorley, *Teaming Up*, 57–58.

42. Michael Denmead, "International Carriers Team Up for Global Reach," *Data Communications*, 21 November 1994, 85–88.

43. Peter Lorange and Johan Roos, "Why Some Strategic Alliances Succeed and Others Fail," *Journal of Business Strategy* 11, no. 2 (1990): 4–8.

44. Thomas W. Roehl and J. Frederick Truitt, "Stormy Open Marriages Are Better: Evidence from U.S., Japanese, and French Cooperative Ventures in Commercial Aircraft," *Columbia Journal of World Business* 11, no. 3 (1987): 87–95.

45. Jordan D. Lewis, "Making Strategic Alliances Work," *Research-Technology Management*, November–December 1990, 12–15.

46. Murray, "Patterns in Strategic Alliances," 7–16.

47. Keith D. Brouthers, Lance Eliot Brouthers, and Timothy J. Wilkinson, "Strategic Alliances: Choose Your Partners," *Long Range Planning* 28, no. 3 (1995): 18–25.

48. W. Chan Kim and Renee A. Mauborgne, "Procedural Justice, Attitudes, and Subsidiary Top Management Compliance with Multinationals' Corporate Strategic Decisions," *Academy of Management Journal* 36, no. 3 (1993): 502–526.

CHAPTER 7

1. Emily Nelson, "Rallying the Troops at P&G," *Wall Street Journal*, 31 August 2000. See also Damian Reece, "New CEO Seeks to Exorcise P&G's Woes: Procter and Gamble Has Been Bedevilled by Disaster," *Ottawa Citizen*, p. D6. [Retrieved 30 November 2000 from Lexis-Nexis database.]

2. Susan Jackson and Tim Smart, "Will the GE Magic Work at Stanley?" *Business Week*, 21 April 1997, 144–148. See also Barbara A. Nagy and Dan Haar, "Retooling Stanley a Wrenching Time for Manufacturer's Shareholders, Workers," *Hartford Courant*, 9 April 1999, p. D1. [Retrieved 26 November 2000 from Dow Jones Interactive database.]

3. Sumantra Ghoshal and N. Nohria, "Internal Differentiation within Multinational Corporations," *Strategic Management Journal* 10, no. 4 (1990): 323–338.

4. Gunnar Hedlund, "The First Theory of Hierarchy: Contemplation of Its Pervasiveness in Modern Business Life," Institute of International Business Research, Paper no. 88 (1988), 4.

5. Christopher A. Bartlett and Sumantra Ghoshal, *Managing across Borders: The Transnational Solution* (Boston: Harvard Business School Press, 1989), Chapter 2.

6. William H. Newman, *Constructive Control: Design and Use of Control Systems* (Englewood Cliffs, N.J.: Prentice-Hall, 1975), 44–49. Also see Terry Newell, "Applying a Consulting Model to Managerial Behavior," in J. William Pfeiffer (ed.), *The Annual 1988: Develop-*

ing Human Resources (San Diego, Calif.: University Associates, 1988), 229–243.

7. "Citigroup Simplifies Its Management Structure." Retrieved from Citigroup website <www.citigroup.com> (Press Room) [cited 25 July 2000]. See also Paul Beckett, "Citigroup New Power Structure Reflects Chairman's Old Style," *Wall Street Journal*, 7 August 2000, p. C1. [Retrieved 9 March 2001 from Dow Jones Interactive database.]

8. Michael E. Porter, "Changing Patterns of International Competition," *California Management Review* 28, no. 2 (1986): 9–40.

9. V. Reitman, "Rubbermaid Turns Up Plenty of Profit in the Mundane," *Wall Street Journal*, 27 March 1992, p. B3.

10. William G. Egelhoff, "Information-Processing Theory and the Multinational Corporation," in Sumantra Ghoshal and D. Eleanor Westney (eds.), *Organization Theory and the Multinational Corporation* (New York: St. Martin's Press, 1993), 182–210.

11. Andrew Kupfer, "AT&T: Ready to Run, Nowhere to Hide," *Fortune*, 29 April 1996, 66–71.

12. George Yip, *Total Global Strategy: Managing for Worldwide Competitive Advantage* (Englewood Cliffs, N.J.: Prentice-Hall, 1992), 148–151.

13. Nigel F. Piercy and David W. Cravens, "The Network Paradigm and the Marketing Organization: Developing a New Management Agenda," *European Journal of Marketing* 29, no. 3 (1995): 7–34.

14. Thomas Kamm and Matt Marshall, "Global Forces Push Europe's Firms Too, into a Merger Frenzy," *Wall Street Journal*, 8 April 1997, pp. A1, A4.

15. Pervez Ghauri, "New Structures in MNCs Based in Small Countries: A Network Approach," *European Management Journal* 10, no. 3 (1992): 357–364.

16. Yves Doz and C. K. Prahalad, "Managing DMNCs: A Search for a New Paradigm," in Ghoshal and Westney (eds.), *Organization Theory*, 24–50.

17. Christopher A. Bartlett and Sumantra Ghoshal, "Matrix Management: Not a Structure, a Frame of Mind," *Harvard Business Review*, July–August 1990, 138–145.

18. Bill Emmott, "Multinationals: The Non-Global Firm," *The Economist*, 27 March 1993, pp. SS10–14.

19. Lawrence Hrebiniak, "Implementing Global Strategies," *European Management Journal* 10, no. 4 (1992): 392–403.

20. William G. Egelhoff, "Information-Processing Theory and the Multinational Enterprise," in Heidi Vernon-Wortzel and Lawrence H. Wortzel (eds.), *Strategic Management in a Global Economy*, 3rd ed. (New York: John Wiley & Sons, 1997), 556–575.

21. Ibid., p. 568.

22. David B. Yoffie, *Strategic Management in Information Technology* (Englewood Cliffs, N.J.: Prentice Hall: 1994), 2–4.

23. Vijay K. Jolly and Kimberly A. Bechler, "Logitech: The Mouse that Roared," *Planning Review* 20, no. 6 (1992): 46–48.

24. Gunnar Hedlund, "Assumptions of Hierarchy and Heterarchy, with Applications to the Management of the Multinational Corporation," in Ghoshal and Westney (eds.), *Organization Theory*, 211–236.

25. Robert Wood and Albert Bandura, "Social Cognitive Theory of Organizational Management," *Academy of Management Review* 14, no. 2 (1989): 361–384. Also see Howard Perlmutter and Eric Trist, "Paradigms for Societal Transition," *Human Relations* 39, no. 1 (1986): 1–27.

26. Harl Bedl, "Responsible for the World," *Asian Business*, July 1994, 16.

27. K. P. Waran and Elaine Jeyakumar, "Electronics Giant to Manufacture Components Here for Factories Worldwide," *New Straits Times*, 22 March 1996, p. 1.

28. Mark W. Hordes, J. Anthony Clancy, and Julie Baddaley, "A Primer for Global Start-ups," *Academy of Management Executive* 9, no. 2 (1995): 7–11.

29. Samuel Humes, *Managing the Multinational: Confronting the Global-Local Dilemma* (Hemel Hempstead, U.K.: Prentice-Hall International, 1993), 348–349.

30. Bartlett and Ghoshal, *Managing across Borders*, 1–3, 22.

31. Carol Bower, "Amdahl, Fujitsu, and Peritas Form Strategic Alliance to Create Knowledge Pool," *Amdahl Corporation Business*, 22 February 1995, 1–2.

32. Sumantra Ghoshal and Christopher A. Bartlett, "The MNC as an Interorganizational Network," in Ghoshal and Westney (eds.), *Organization Theory*, 77–104.

33. Jeffrey R. Pfeffer and G. R. Salancik, *The External Control of Organizations: A Resource Dependency Perspective* (New York: Harper & Row, 1978). Also see Jeffrey R. Pfeffer, *Power in Organizations* (Boston: Pittman, 1981).

34. Ghoshal and Bartlett, "MNC as an Interorganizational Network," 88–89.

35. Sumantra Ghoshal and Christopher A. Bartlett, "The Multinational Corporation as an International Network," *Academy of Management Review* 15, no. 4 (1990): 603–625.

36. Humes, *Managing the Multinational*, 252–259.

37. Gregory G. Dess, Abdul M. A. Rasheed, Kevin J. McLaughlin, and Richard L. Priem, "The New Corporate Architecture," *Academy of Management Executive* 9, no. 3 (1995): 7–20.

38. Jim Rohwer, "GE Digs Into Asia," *Fortune*, 2 October 2000, 164+. Retrieved from *Fortune* website <www.fortune.com> [cited 28 October 2000].

39. Ibid. See also Thomas A. Stewart, "See Jack. See Jack Run Europe," *Fortune*, 27 September 1999, 124+.

40. Christopher A. Bartlett and Sumantra Ghoshal, *Transnational Management: Texts, Cases, and Readings in Cross-Border Management*, 2nd ed. (Boston: Richard D. Irwin, 1995), 472–473.

41. Steven H. Rhinesmith, John N. Williamson, David M. Ehlen, and Denise S. Maxwell, "Developing Leaders for the Global Enterprise," in Henry W. Lane and Joseph J. DiStefano (eds.), *International Management Behavior*, 2nd ed. (Boston: PWS-Kent, 1992), 73–84.

CHAPTER 8

1. Andrew Brown, "Hugo Boss: Better Suited for Good," *International Management*, September 1994, 34–37.

2. Hugo Boss, English Version websites: News, Company Profile, Group Management, and Investor Relations. Retrieved from website <www.hugoboss.com> [cited September 2000].

3. Susanne Schech and Jane Haggis, *Culture and Development: A Critical Introduction* (Oxford, U.K.: Blackwell Publishers Ltd., 2000), 20–26.

4. Gary P. Ferraro, *The Cultural Dimension of International Business* (Englewood Cliffs, N.J.: Prentice Hall, 1990), p. 18.

5. Fred Luthans, *Organizational Behavior*, 6th ed. (New York: McGraw–Hill, 1992), 26–27.

6. Ester Laushway, "Education in the EU: How Are Europe's Schools Challenging Children?" *Europe*, September 2000, 25–31. See also Susan Chira, "For Japanese Students, Club Spirit Outclasses Good Grades," *International Herald Tribune*, 30 June 1998, p. 4.

7. Edgar H. Schein, *The Corporate Culture Survival Guide: Sense and Nonsense about Culture Change* (San Francisco: Jossey-Bass Publishers, 1999), 3–5, 44–46.

8. David A. Ralston, Robert H. Terpstra, David H. Holt, and Yu Kai-ching, "The Impact of Culture and Ideology on Managerial Work Values: A Study of the United States, Russia, Japan, and China," *Academy of Management Best Papers 1995* (1995): 187–191.

9. This section draws on Karen C. Cash and George R. Gray, "A Framework for Accommodating Religion and Spirituality in the Workplace," *Academy of Management Executive* 14, no. 3 (2000): 124–133.

10. "Government Approved Feng Shui Chicken for Police," *South China Morning Post*, 14 October 1995, p. 21.

11. Ferraro, *Cultural Dimension of International Business*, p. 24.

12. David G. Myers, *Social Psychology*, 3rd ed. (New York: McGraw-Hill, Inc., 1990), 171–172.

13. Michael H. Bond and Kim Hwang, "The Social Psychology of Chinese People," in Michael H. Bond (ed.), *The Psychology of Chinese People* (New York: Oxford University Press, 1986), 213–266.

14. Ian Stewart, "National Day Motto Lost in War of Words," *South China Morning Post*, 1 June 1996, p. 12.

15. Richard Mead, *International Management: Cross-Cultural Dimensions* (Cambridge, Mass.: Blackwell Publishers, 1994), 390–391.

16. Ferraro, *Cultural Dimension of International Business*, 33–34.

17. James R. Lincoln, Harold R. Kerbo, and Elke Wittenhagen, "Japanese Companies in Germany: A Case Study in Cross-Cultural Management," *Industrial Relations* 34, no. 3 (1995): 417–440.

18. Mead, *International Management*, p. 7.

19. George W. England, "Personal Value Systems of American Managers," *Academy of Management Journal* (March 1967): 53–68.

20. "Desk-Bottom Diplomacy," *Wall Street Journal*, 3 April 1997, p. A1.

21. Thomas Weyr, "IBM Sees DM as Secret Weapon to Spur Global Sales Boom: Direct Marketing Revenues to Hit $13 Million in '97," *DM News*, 10 March 1997, International Supplement, p. 1.

22. "Ecuador Attempts to Regain Economic Stability at the Expense of the Short Term," *World Trade*, February 2000, p.16. Also see Thomas T. Vogel, Jr., "Oil in Ecuador: A Tale of Missed Opportunity," *Wall Street Journal*, 3 April 1997, p. A15.

23. Philip R. Harris and Robert T. Moran, *Managing Cultural Differences* (Houston: Gulf Publishing, 1991), 78–81.

24. Geert Hofstede, *Culture's Consequences: International Differences in Work-related Values* (Newbury Park, Calif.: Sage Publishing Co., 1980). The founding citation is Geert Hofstede, "Motivation, Leadership, and Organization: Do American Theories Apply Abroad?" *Organizational Dynamics* 9, no. 2 (1980): 42–63.

25. Geert Hofstede, "Dimensions of National Cultures in Fifty Countries and Three Regions," in J. B. Deregowski, S. Dziurawiec, and R. C. Annis (eds.), *Expiscations in Cross-Culture Psychology* (Lisse, Netherlands: Swets & Zeitlinger, 1983), 335–355. Geert Hofstede, "National Cultures in Four Dimensions: A Research-based Theory of Cultural Differences among Nations," *International Studies of Management & Organization* 13, no. 1 (1983): 46–74. Geert Hofstede, "The Cultural Relativity of Organizational Practices and Theories," *Journal of International Business Studies* 14, no. 3 (1983): 75–89. Geert Hofstede, "National Cultures Revisited," *Behavior Science Research* 18 (1983): 285–305. G. Hofstede, B. Neuijen, D. D. Ohayv, and G. Sanders, "Measuring Organizational Cultures: A Qualitative and Quantitative Study Across Twenty Cases," *Administrative Science Quarterly* 35 (1990): 286–316.

26. Geert Hofstede, *Cultures and Organizations: Software of the Mind* (London: McGraw-Hill Ltd., 1991), 251–252. Also Geert Hofstede and Michael H. Bond, "Hofstede's Cultural Dimensions: An Independent Validation Using Rokeach's Value Survey," *Journal of Cross-Cultural Psychology* 2 (1984): 221–243.

27. Hofstede, "National Cultures Revisited," 285–305. Also Hofstede et al., "Measuring Organizational Cultures," 286–316.

28. Hofstede, "Cultural Relativity of Organizational Practices and Theories."

29. Richard Menger, "Japanese and American Negotiators: Overcoming Cultural Barriers to Understanding," *Academy of Management Executive* 13, no. 4 (1999): 100–101. Also see George W. England, "National Work Meanings and Patterns: Constraints on Management Action," *European Management Journal* 4, no. 3 (1986): 176–184.

30. Christopher P. Earley, "East Meets West Meets Mideast: Further Explorations of Collectivistic and Individualistic Work Groups," *Academy of Management Journal* 36, no. 2 (1993): 319–348.

31. David H. Holt, David A. Ralston, and Robert H. Terpstra, "Constraints on Capitalism in Russia: The Managerial Psyche, Social Infrastructure and Ideology," *California Management Review* 36, no. 3 (1994): 124–141.

32. Ismail Serageldin, *Nurturing Development: Aid and Cooperation in Today's Changing World* (Washington, D.C.: The World Bank, 1995), 5–7.

33. Manuel Pastor Jr. and Jae Ho Sung, "Private Investment and Democracy in the Developing World," *Journal of Economic Issues* 29, no. 1 (1995): 223–243.

34. "The Case for Globalisation," *The Economist*, 23 September 2000, 19–21.

35. Mead, *International Management*, 434–454.

36. Harry C. Triandis, "Review of Culture's Consequences: International Differences in Work-Related Values," *Human Organisation* 41 (1982): 86–90. Also see K. H. Roberts and N. A. Boyacigiller, "Cross-national Organizational Research: The Grasp of the Blinded Men," *Organizational Behavior* 6 (1984): 425–475.

37. Hofstede, *Cultures and Organizations*, Chapter 7.

38. Robert G. Westwood and James E. Everett, "Culture's Consequences: A Methodology for Comparative Management Studies in Southeast Asia," *Asia Pacific Journal of Management* 4, no. 3 (1987): 187–202.

39. David A. Ralston, David J. Gustafson, Fanny Cheung, and Robert H. Terpstra, "Eastern Values: A Comparison of U.S., Hong Kong and PRC Managers," *Journal of Applied Psychology* 77 (1992): 664–671.

40. Checchi Consulting and Louis Berger International, *ENI Four-Country Study of Comparative Private Sector Development: Russia, Kazakhstan, Latvia, and Romania* (Washington, D.C.: United States Agency for International Development, 1999), 73–99.

41. Geert Hofstede and Michael H. Bond, "The Confucius Connection: From Cultural Roots to Economic Growth," *Organizational Dynamics* 16, no. 4 (1988): 4–21.

42. Michael H. Bond, "Chinese Values and Health: A Culture-level Examination," *Psychology and Health: An International Journal* 5 (1991): 137–152. Also see Michael Bond, *Beyond the Chinese Face: Insights from Psychology* (Hong Kong: Oxford University Press, 1991), 4–5, 28.

43. Hofstede and Bond, "The Confucius Connection." Also see Tzong-biau Lin and Chyau Tuyan (eds.), *The Asian NIEs: Success and Challenge* (Hong Kong: The Lo Fung Learned Society, 1993), 1–14.

44. Simcha Ronen and Allen I. Kraut, "Similarities among Countries Based on Employee Work Values and Attitudes," *Columbia Journal of World Business* (summer 1977): 83–97.

45. Simcha Ronen and Oded Shenkar, "Clustering Countries on Attitudinal Dimensions: A Review and Synthesis," *Academy of Management Journal* 10, no. 3 (1985): 435–454.

46. Evelyn Huber, Dietrich Rueschemeyer, and John D. Stephens, "The Impact of Economic Development on Democracy," *Journal of Economic Perspectives* 7, no. 3 (1993): 71–85.

47. Arvind V. Phatak, *International Dimensions of Management*, 4th ed. (Cincinnati: South-Western College Publishing, 1995), 66–73. Five of the formal labels were suggested in anthropological research by Melville J. Herskovits, *Man and His Works* (New York: Alfred A. Knopf, 1952), 17.

48. The author was a consultant to Procter & Gamble for several years during the China launch period in 1989–1992.

49. "Auction Brings Out High Numbers," *South China Morning Post*, 22 January 1996, p. 1.

50. Robert I. Westwood, "Culture, Cultural Differences, and Organisational Behaviour," in R. I. Westwood (ed.), *Organisational Behaviour: Southeast Asian Perspectives* (Hong Kong: The Longman Group, 1992), 47.

51. M. S. Noorzoy, "Islamic Laws on Riba (Interest) and Their Economic Implications," *International Journal of Middle East Studies* 14 (1982): 3–17.

52. Phatak, *International Dimensions of Management*, 72–73.

53. Nancy DeWolf Smith, "The Warriors Time Forgot," *Wall Street Journal*, 27 March 1997, p. A18.

54. Joyce S. Osland and Allan Bird, "Beyond Sophisticated Stereotyping: Cultural Sensemaking in Context," *Academy of Management Executive* 14, no. 1 (2000): 65–79.

55. Clifford Clarke and Mitchell R. Hammer, "Predictors of Japanese and American Managers Job Success, Personal Adjustment, and Intercultural Interaction Effectiveness," *Management International Review* 35, no. 2 (1995): 153–168.

56. J. Stewart Black, Hal B. Gregersen, and Mark E. Mendenhall, *Global Assignments: Successfully Expatriating and Repatriating International Managers* (San Francisco: Jossey-Bass, 1992), 4–16.

57. J. Stewart Black and Mark Mendenhall, "Cross-cultural Training Effectiveness: A Review and a Theoretical Framework for Future Research," *Academy of Management Review* 15, no. 1 (1990): 113–136.

58. Phatak, *International Dimensions of Management*, 56–68. Also see J. Stewart Black and Hal B. Gregersen,

"Expectations, Satisfactions, and Intention to Leave of American Expatriate Managers in Japan," *International Journal of Intercultural Relations* 14 (1990): 485–506.

59. Nancy Adler, *International Dimensions of Organizational Behavior* (Boston: PWS-Kent, 1991), 1–2, 40–47.

60. John Schermerhorn Jr. and Michael H. Bond, "Cross-Cultural Leadership Dynamics in Collectivism and High Power Distances Settings," *Leadership & Organization Development Journal* 18, no. 4 (1997): 187–193.

61. Sara Marley, "Learning Foreign Culture Is Critical," *Business Insurance* 29, no. 6 (1995): 51–52.

62. David A. Ricks, *Blunders in International Business* (Cambridge, Mass.: Blackwell Publishers, 1993).

CHAPTER 9

1. Sonja Sinclair, "The Best Revenge," *Canadian Business*, March 1994, 20–31.

2. Full company information about worldwide operations can be found at the Bata Group website <www.bata.com>; the website of the company's Czech division together with a profile of Eastern Europe's operations can be found at <www.bata.cz>. Information provided here reflects corporate reports as of October 2, 2000.

3. Richard Mead, *International Management: Cross-Cultural Dimensions* (Cambridge, Mass.: Blackwell Publishers, 1994), 56–60.

4. Edward T. Hall, *The Dance of Life* (New York: Anchor/Doubleday, 1983), 62–68. Also see Edward T. Hall, *Hidden Differences* (New York: Anchor/Doubleday, 1987), 128–129.

5. Lillian H. Chaney and Jeanette S. Martin, *Intercultural Business Communication* (Englewood Cliffs, N.J.: Prentice Hall Career and Technology, 1995), 6–10.

6. Robert Lloyd George, *The East-West Pendulum* (Cambridge, UK: Woodhead-Faulkner Ltd, 1992), 28–30.

7. Ibid., 31.

8. James R. Lincoln, Harold R. Kerbo, and Elke Wittenhagen, "Japanese Companies in Germany: A Case Study in Cross-Cultural Management," *Industrial Relations* 34, no. 3 (1995): 417–440.

9. Chris Yeung, "Lu Ping Defends Beijing's Stand on Rights," *South China Morning Post*, 6 June 1996, p. 1; Willy Wo-Lap Lam, "Preparatory Committee Muzzled by Beijing," *South China Morning Post*, 1 June 1996, p. 1; Tsang Yok-sing, "Alliance Free to Exit in SAR Rule," *South China Morning Post*, 4 June 1996, p. 2.

10. Christina Mungan, "Hong Kong Stock Prices Worry Some, Not Others," *Asian Wall Street Journal*, 9–10 July 1999, p. 13.

11. Kevin Cleaver and Gotz A. Schreiber, *Reversing the Spiral: The Population, Agriculture, and Environment Nexus in Sub-Saharan Africa* (Washington, D.C.: World Bank, 1994), 14–18.

12. Laurent Goater and Frederic Richer, "France," in Mariam Rothman, Dennis R. Briscoe, and Raoul C. D. Nacamulli (eds.), *Industrial Relations around the World* (New York: Walter de Gruyter, 1993), 111–125.

13. Deputy Prime Minister, Brigadier-General Lee Hsien Loong, "Singapore: Pragmatism and Success in ASEAN," address to the Sixth International Conference of the Eastern Academy of Management, Singapore, 12 June 1995; "Respect for Sovereign Law Crucial" *International Herald Tribune*, 10 November 1995, p. 1; and Lee Kuan Yew, "America in Asia, the Lee Strategy," *South China Morning Post*, 6 June 1996, p. 15.

14. Lim Chong-Yah, "Government and Development: The Case of Singapore," in Tzong-biau Lin and Chyau Tuan (eds.), *The Asian NIEs: Success and Challenge* (Hong Kong: Lo Fung Learned Society, 1993), 154.

15. S. Gordon Redding, *The Spirit of Chinese Capitalism* (Berlin/New York: Walter de Gruyter, 1990), 12–13, 127–130. Also K. K. Hwang, "Modernisation of the Chinese Family Business," *International Journal of Psychology* 25 (1990): 593–618.

16. Nancy Wilson Ross, *Buddhism: A Way of Life and Thought* (New York: Vintage Books, 1980), 71–76, 116–119.

17. Anita D. Bhappu, "The Japanese Family: An Institutional Logic for Japanese Corporate Networks and Japanese Management," *Academy of Management Review* 25 no. 2 (2000): 409–415.

18. Robert I. Westwood, "Culture, Cultural Differences, and Organisational Behaviour," in R. I. Westwood (ed.), *Organisational Behaviour: Southeast Asian Perspectives* (Hong Kong: The Longman Group, 1992), 50–53.

19. Arvind V. Phatak, *International Dimensions of Management*, 4th ed. (Cincinnati: South-Western, 1995), 60–62.

20. *The East Asian Miracle: Economic Growth and Public Policy* (Washington, D.C.: The International Bank for Reconstruction and Development/The World Bank, 1993), 43–47.

21. David H. Holt, David A. Ralston, and Robert H. Terpstra, "Constraints on Capitalism in Russia: The Managerial Psyche, Social Infrastructure, and Ideology," *California Management Review* 36, no. 3 (1994): 124–141.

22. David H. Holt, *Business Management Education: An International Assessment for Foreign Aid Strategies* (Washington, D.C.: U.S. Agency for International Development, 1995), 5–13.

23. Susan Chira, "For Japanese Students, Club Spirit Outclasses Good Grades," *International Herald Tribune*, 15 December 1988, p. 8.

24. UNESCO, *World Education Report* (Paris: United Nations Education, Scientific, and Cultural Organization, 1994), preface and tables. Also Paul W. Beamish and

Jonathan L. Calof, "International Business Education: A Corporate View," *Journal of International Business Studies* (Fall 1989): 553–564.

25. "Feminism, Development, and Culture," in Susanne Schech and Jane Haggis, *Culture and Development: A Critical Introduction* (Oxford, U.K.: Blackwell Publishers Ltd., 2000), 85–102.

26. Michael Harris Bond, *Beyond The Chinese Face: Insights from Psychology* (Hong Kong: Oxford University Press, 1991), 45.

27. Ibid., 46, 48–49.

28. Anecdote by Lorne Olsen, CEO; Technology for Private Sector, International Executive Service Corps, Sri Lanka, May 1995 interview.

29. Moskovi Prelis, "Guidelines for Office Relationships," *Development Finance Corporation of Ceylon*, Revised, June 1996, p. 3.

30. Young Yun Kim, *Communication and Cross-Cultural Adaptation* (Clevedon, U.K.: Multilingual Matters, 1988), 76–80.

31. Phatak, *International Dimensions of Management*, 60.

32. Boye DeMente, *Chinese Etiquette & Ethics* (London: NTC Business Book Books, 1989), 72, 81.

33. Martin Lockett, "Culture and Problems of Chinese Management," *Organization Studies* 4 (1988): 475–492.

34. Kim, *Communication and Cross-Cultural Adaptation*, 79.

35. Martin Rosch, "Communications: Focal Point of Culture," *Management International Review* 27, no. 4 (1987): 60. Also see Edward T. Hall, *Beyond Culture* (Garden City, N.Y.: Doubleday, 1976), 78–80.

36. Paul R. Timm, *Managerial Communications: A Finger on the Pulse* (Englewood Cliffs, N.J.: Prentice Hall, 1980), 4.

37. "Wired: Asian Enthusiasts Plug In, But Japanese Managers Lag," *South China Technology Post*, 20 March 1996, p. 2. See also A. Hatani, "Japanese Managers Face a New Challenge: The Computer," *South China Morning Post*, 18 January 1996, Business section, p. B1.

38. Peter F. Drucker, *Management: Tasks, Responsibilities, Practices* (New York: Harper & Row, 1974), 483.

39. Robert H. Lengel and Richard L. Daft, "The Selection of Communication Media as an Executive Skill," *Academy of Management Executive* 2, no. 3 (1988): 225–232.

40. "Yeltsin Searches for the Right Words in Rural Campaigns," *Straits Times*, 2 June 1996, p. 2.

41. T. K. Ann, *Cracking the Chinese Puzzles*, Vol. 1 (Hong Kong: Stockflow Publishers, 1982), iv–v.

42. Ibid., iii–xxv.

43. Ada Yau, "Do Your Homework Before You Pack," *Asian Business Review*, February 1996, p. 44.

44. Edward T. Hall, *The Hidden Dimension* (New York: Anchor/Doubleday, 1966), 107–118.

45. Abbas J. Ali, "The Islamic Work Ethic in Arabia," *Journal of Psychology* 26, no. 5 (1992): 507–519.

46. Jane Whitney Gibson and Richard M. Hodgetts, *Organizational Communication: A Managerial Perspective*, 2nd ed. (New York: Harper Collins, 1991), 124–129.

47. Conrad P. Kottak, *Anthropology: The Exploration of Human Diversity*, 4th ed. (New York: Random House, 1987), 209–212.

48. Ali, "Islamic Work Ethic in Arabia," 507–519.

49. Helmut Morsbach, "Aspects of Nonverbal Communication in Japan," in Larry Samovar and R. E. Porter (eds.), *Intercultural Communication: A Reader*, 3rd ed. (Belmont, Ca.: Wadsworth Publishers, 1982), 300–316.

50. Chaney and Martin, *Intercultural Business Communication*, 56.

51. John Condon and Fathi Yousef, *Introduction to Intercultural Communication* (Indianapolis: Bobbs-Merrill, 1975), 120–126. Also see Roger E. Axtell (ed.), *Dos and Taboos Around the World* (New York: John Wiley & Sons, 1991), Chapter 2.

52. Hall, *Hidden Dimension*, 141–144, 161–162.

53. Michael Argyle, *Bodily Communication* (New York: International University Press, 1975), 282–290.

54. Michael Harris Bond, *Beyond the Chinese Face: Insights from Psychology* (Hong Kong: Oxford University Press, 1991), 50–51.

55. Morsbach, "Nonverbal Communication in Japan," 307–309.

56. Kottak, *Anthropology: The Exploration of Human Diversity*, 210.

57. Morsbach, "Nonverbal Communication in Japan," 308. Also see Wee Chow Hou, Lee Khai Sheang, and Bambang Walujo Hidajat, *Sun Tzu: War and Management* (New York: Addison-Wesley, 1991), 3–6.

58. Nancy J. Adler, *International Dimensions of Organizational Behavior*, 2nd ed. (Boston: PWS-Kent, 1991), 228–229.

59. Adrian Woolridge, "Only Communicate," *The Economist*, 25 June 1995, SS18–19.

60. Diane St. John, "Old Competitors are New Co-conspirators," *Communication World* 13, no. 4 (1996): 20–23.

61. J. Stewart Black and Mark Mendenhall, "Cross-culture Training Effectiveness: A Review and Theoretical Framework for Future Research," *Academy of Management Review* 15, no. 3 (1990): 113–136.

62. Al Edge and Bernard Keys, "Cross-cultural Learning in a Multinational Business Environment," *Journal of Management Development* 9, no. 2 (1990): 43–49.

63. Gloria Chan, "The Cultural Context of Communication," *The Asian Manager*, February 1995, 1–8.

64. "How Not to Say What You Want to Communicate, but Do it Very Well," *Anecdotes for the Foreign Manager* (Manila, PI: Asian Institute of Management, 1995), 4.

65. Ferraro, *Cultural Dimension of International Business*, 61–63.

66. Charles Gancel, "ICM Management Training in Russia, Traps and Gaps," *Journal of Management Development* 14, no. 5 (1995): 15–26. Also see Holt et al., "Constraints on Capitalism in Russia," 124–141.

67. Gancel, "ICM Management Training in Russia," 15.

68. Ferraro, *Cultural Dimension of International Business*, 70–71.

69. "Computer Age Hits Japan at Long Last," *International Herald Tribune*, 28 March 1996, p. 22.

70. David A. Ricks, *Blunders in International Business* (Cambridge, Mass.: Blackwell Publishers, 1993), 22–30.

71. Interview with Jim Brice, manager for conventions, the Hong Kong Marriott, July 1996, Hong Kong.

72. J. Ramon Mendez, "Getting it Right—The Second Time," unpublished presentation to the Direct Marketing Association, Washington, D.C., 10 October 1996.

73. Edgar H. Schein, "Dialogue and Learning," *Executive Excellence* 12, no. 4 (1995): 3–4.

CHAPTER 10

1. "Coastal Port Development: Johor Port Authority," *Competitive Strategy for Johor Under the Corporatization Scheme*, PacRim Engineering, July 1993. Also interviews with PacRim principals and Johor Port Authority managers, March 1996.

2. Roy J. Lewicki, Joseph A. Litterer, John W. Minton, and David M. Saunders, *Negotiation*, 2nd ed. (Boston: Irwin, 1994), 1.

3. D. G. Pruitt and J. Z. Rubin, *Social Conflict: Escalation, Stalemate and Settlement* (New York: Random House, 1986), 4.

4. Jeswald W. Salacuse, "Making Deals in Strange Places: A Beginner's Guide to International Business Negotiations," *Negotiation Journal* 4 (1988): 5–13.

5. Farid Elashmawi and Philip R. Harris, *Multicultural Management: New Skills for Global Success* (Houston: Gulf Publishing Co., 1993), 26–28, 42–45.

6. Lewicki et al., *Negotiation*, 48–50, 80–84.

7. This section draws from the following: R. Michael Godfrey, "Negotiating Ethically to Reduce Conflict Costs in Transnational Firms," *International Journal of Management* 12, no. 2 (1995): 173–181; Lewicki et al., *Negotiation*, 48–60; and Robert T. Moran and William G. Stripp, *Dynamics of Successful International Business Negotiations* (Houston: Gulf Publishing Co., 1991), 91–98.

8. Jay Huber, "Here Come the 'No Money Down!' Guys," *San Diego Union*, 28 June 1995, p. 18.

9. Godfrey, "Negotiating Ethically to Reduce Conflict Costs," 173–181.

10. This section draws from the following: Lewicki et al., *Negotiation*, 80–96; Roger Fisher, William Ury, and B. Patton, *Getting to Yes: Negotiating Agreement without Giving In*, 2nd ed. (New York: Penguin Books, 1991), 1–11, 56–57, 90–93; and Moran and Stripp, *Dynamics of Successful International Business Negotiations*, 91–98.

11. Many interesting and personal examples can be found in John Gray, *Men Are from Mars, Women Are from Venus* (New York: Harper Collins, 1992).

12. Ibid., Gray, *Men Are from Mars, Women Are from Venus*, 171–205.

13. "China Opens Up," *The Economist*, 20 November 1999, 17–18. Also see Simon Beck, "The Door Is Ajar for Full Trade Privileges," *South China Morning Post*, 27 June 1996, p. 19.

14. Dexter Roberts, "WTO or Bust?" *Business Week*, 22 November 1999, 60–61. A perspective on earlier stages of talks is provided by Jasper Becker, "America Makes a Deal with Realism," *Sunday Morning Post*, Beijing, 23 June 1996, p. 11.

15. "China and the WTO: The Real Leap Forward," *The Economist*, 20 November 1999, 25–29. Also see "Barshefsky Proclaims 'Peace in Our Time' to End Sino-U.S. Stalemate—Where Have We Heard That Before?" *London Times*, 24 June 1996, p. 4.

16. Robert Gulbro and Paul Herbig, "Negotiating Successfully in Cross-Cultural Situations," *Industrial Marketing Management* 25 (1996): 235–241.

17. The stage models and discussions in this section draw on: Moran and Stripp, *Dynamics of Successful International Business Negotiations*, 91–92; Nancy J. Adler, Theodore Swartz Gehrke, and John L. Graham, "Business Negotiations in Canada, Mexico, and the United States," *Journal of Business Research* 15 (1987): 411–430; and John A. Graham, "Across the Negotiating Table from the Japanese," *International Marketing Review* (autumn 1986): 58–70.

18. Jeswald W. Salacuse, *Making Global Deals: Negotiating in the International Marketplace* (Boston: Houghton Mifflin, 1991), 1–12, 42–45.

19. David H. Holt, *Strategic Assessment of the Technology for Innovation Project, Sri Lanka* (Washington, D.C.: U.S. Agency for International Development, 1995), 32–34.

20. Gulbro and Herbig, "Negotiating Successfully in Cross-Cultural Situations," 235–241.

21. Robert T. Moran, Philip R. Harris, and William G. Stripp, *Developing the Global Organization* (Houston: Gulf Publishing Company, 1993), 227–229.

22. Richard Mead, *International Management: Cross-Cultural Dimensions* (Cambridge, Mass.: Blackwell Publishers, 1994), 260–261.

23. John L. Graham, "The Influence of Culture on the Process of Business Negotiations, an Exploratory Study," *Journal of International Business Studies* 16, no. 1 (1985): 81–96.

24. John Graham and Yoshihiro Sano, "The Japanese Negotiation Style," in Roy J. Lewicki, Joseph A. Litterer, David M. Saunders, and John W. Minton, *Negotiation: Readings, Exercises, and Cases*, 2nd ed. (Boston: Irwin, 1993), 541–552.

25. Nigel C. Campbell, John L. Graham, Alain Jolibert, and Hans Gunther Meissner, "Marketing Negotiations in France, Germany, the United Kingdom, and the United States," *Journal of Marketing* 52 (1988): 49–62.

26. Nancy J. Adler, *International Dimensions of Organizational Behavior*, 2nd ed. (Boston: PWS-Kent, 1991), 196–197.

27. David N. Burt, "Nuances of Negotiating Overseas," *Journal of Purchasing and Materials Management* 25 (1989): 56–64.

28. Dafna Izraeli and Yoram Zeira, "Women Managers in International Business: A Research Review and Appraisal," *Business & The Contemporary World* 5, no. 3 (1993): 35–46.

29. J. Soloman, "Woman, Minorities and Foreign Postings: Few Go Abroad, Many Challenge Reasons Why," *Wall Street Journal*, 2 June 1989, Section 2, p.1.

30. Mead, *International Management*, 254–255.

31. Paulson Ching, *Doing Business in East Asia* (Selangor Darul Ehsan, Malaysia: Pelanduk Publications, 1994), 9, 13, 42, 131.

32. Mead, *International Management*, 258–259.

33. Alan Goldman, "U.S.–Japanese Negotiating: An Intercultural Briefing," *International Business Communication* 2, no. 2 (1990): 3–7.

34. J. L. Johnson, Tomaki Sakano, and Naoto Onzo, "Behavioral Relations in Across-Culture Distribution Systems: Influence, Control and Conflict in U.S.–Japanese Marketing Channels," *Journal of International Business Studies* 21, no. 4 (1990): 639–655.

35. Peter Woo, CEO The Wharf Group, "Foreign Investment in the PRC," an unpublished presentation made to Chinese and American MBA students, Hong Kong, May 6, 1995.

36. Salacuse, "Making Deals in Strange Places," 5–13.

37. Mead, *International Management*, 264–265.

38. John Frankenstein, "Trends in Chinese Business Practice: Changes in the Beijing Wind," *California Management Review* 29, no. 1 (1986): 148–160.

39. Paul A. Herbig and Hugh E. Kramer, "Cross-Cultural Negotiations: Success through Understanding," *Management Decisions* 29 (1991): 19–31.

40. Dean Allen Foster, *Bargaining Across Borders: How to Negotiate Business Successfully Anywhere in the World* (New York: McGraw-Hill, 1992), 86, 106–107. Also see Adler, *International Dimensions of Organizational Behavior*, 197.

41. Marita van Oldenborgh, "Court With Care," *International Business*, April 1995, 20–22.

42. Lewicki et al., *Negotiation*, 83–84.

43. Ibid., p. 87.

44. Raymond Saner, Lichia Yiu, and Mikael Sondergaard, "Business Diplomacy Management: A Core Competency for Global Companies," *Academy of Management Executive* 14, no. 1 (2000): 80–92.

45. Terri R. Lituchy, "Cooperation and Competition in Negotiations: A Laboratory Study in the United States, Canada, and Mexico," *Managing in a Global Economy IV: Proceedings of the 6th International Conference*, June 1995, 21–25.

46. Graham, "Influence of Culture on the Process of Business Negotiations," 81–96.

47. Vincent Chi-Shing Heung, Daniel Kam-Tong Li, and TKP Leung, "Effective Negotiation in the People's Republic of China (PRC)," *International Conference on Global Business in Transition, Prospects for the Twenty First Century Proceedings* (1995), 293–299.

48. Mead, *International Management*, 268–271.

49. John H. Dunning, *Multinational Enterprise and the Global Economy* (New York: Addison-Wesley, 1995), 239–241. Also see J. Michael Geringer, "Strategic Determinants of Partner Selection Criteria in International Joint Ventures," *Journal of International Business Studies* 22, no. 1 (1991): 41–62.

50. Gulbro and Herbig, "Negotiating Successfully in Cross-Cultural Situations," 235–241.

51. Lewicki et al., *Negotiation*, 97–101.

52. Alan Goldman, "Litigation Isn't the Japanese Way: Nippon, Inc. and Raleigh, Ltd.," in Robert T. Moran, David O. Braaten, and John E. Walsh, Jr. (eds.), *International Business Case Studies* (Houston: Gulf Publishing Company, 1994), 186–194.

53. OECD, *More Equal Than Others: The EU In Transition* (Paris: Organisation for Economic Cooperation and Development, 1995), 16–18, Table XI.

54. Discussion is drawn from: Jack Denfeld Wood and Thomas R. Colosi, "Mastering Management: The Subtle Art of Negotiation," *Financial Times*, 5 January 1996, p. v; Lewicki et al., *Negotiation*, 78–80, 104–107, and 414–416; and Chong Ju Choi, "Contract Enforcement Across Cultures," *Organization Studies* 15, no. 5 (1994): 673–682.

55. Lewicki et al., *Negotiation*, 5–6.

56. Peter J. Pettibone, "Negotiating a Business Venture in the Soviet Union," *Journal of Business Strategy* (January/February 1991): 18–23.

57. Alfie Kohn, *No Contest: The Case Against Competition* (Boston: Houghton Mifflin, 1986), 11–24. Also see Richard Tanner Pascale, "The Renewal Factor: Constructive Contention," *Planning Review* 18 (1990): 4–13, 47–48.

58. Pamela L. Perrewe, Gerald R. Ferris, Dwight D. Frink, and William P. Anthony, "Political Skill: An Antidote for Workplace Stressors," *Academy of Management Executive* 14, no. 3 (2000): 115–123.

59. Stephen McKenna, "The Business Impact of Management Attitudes Towards Dealing with Conflict: A Cross-Cultural Assessment," *Journal of Managerial Psychology* 10, no. 7 (1995): 22–27.

60. Godfrey, "Negotiating Ethically to Reduce Conflict Costs," 173–181.

61. David H. Holt, *Management Principles and Practices*, 3rd ed. (Englewood Cliffs, N.J.: Prentice Hall, 1993), 494.

62. Mike France, Peter Burrows, Linda Himelstein, and Michael Moeller, "Does a Breakup Make Sense," *Business Week*, 22 November 1999, 38–41.

63. Rosalie L. Tung, "Handshakes Across the Sea: Cross-Cultural Negotiating for Business Success," *Organizational Dynamics* 19 (Winter 1991): 30–40.

64. Dan Waters, *21st Century Management: Keeping Ahead of the Japanese and Chinese* (Singapore: Simon & Schuster Pte Ltd., 1991), 100–101.

65. This discussion draws on the conceptual model by: Dean G. Pruitt and Jeffrey Z. Rubin, *Social Conflict: Escalation, Stalemate and Settlement* (New York: Random House, 1986), 24–30; Lewicki et al., *Negotiation*, 10–12; and McKenna, "Business Impact of Management Attitudes," 22–27.

66. Lionel Barber, "Food Scare," *Europe*, September 1999, 8–14.

67. David Ibison, "Textiles Talks Break Down," *South China Morning Post*, 5 July 1996, p. 1.

68. Nicolas C. Ulmer, "Bullet-Proofing Your International Arbitration," *World Trade*, July 2000, 70–72.

69. Ibid., p. 71.

70. Chong Ju Choi and D. Maldoom, "A Simple Model of Buybacks," *Economic Letters* 40 (1992): 77–82.

71. Choi, "Contract Enforcement Across Cultures," 673–682.

CHAPTER 11

1. "Eurotunnel—Binational Employee Relations?" *European Industrial Relations Review*, October 1994, 13–14.

2. Miguel Martinez Lucio and Syd Weston, "New Management Practices in a Multinational Corporation—The Restructuring of Worker Representation and Rights?" *Industrial Relations Journal* 25, no. 2 (1994): 110–121.

3. Michael E. Porter, *The Comparative Advantage of Nations* (New York: Macmillan, 1990), 14.

4. Mark Heinzl and Angelo B. Henderson, "GM Is Targeted by Canadian Auto Union," *Wall Street Journal*, 24 September 1996, p. A2. Also see "CAW Strike Has Ripple Effects in the U.S.," *Wall Street Journal*, 29 October 1996, p. A6.

5. Thomas A. Kochan and Robert B. McKerssie, "Human Resources, Organizational Governance, and Public Policy," in Thomas A. Kochan and Michael Useem (eds.), *Transforming Organizations* (New York: Oxford University Press, 1992), 169–186.

6. Peter F. Drucker, "Low Wages No Longer Give Competitive Edge," *Wall Street Journal*, 16 March 1988, p. A12.

7. Clark Kerr, John T. Dunlop, Frederick Harbison, and Charles A. Myers, *Industrialism and Industrial Man* (Cambridge, Mass.: Harvard University Press, 1960), 3–5, 141–143.

8. Richard Edwards, *Contested Terrain: The Transformation of the Workplace in the Twentieth Century* (London: Heinemann Publishers, 1979), 7–11, 86.

9. Richard M. Hodgetts and Fred Luthans, *International Management*, 2nd ed. (New York: McGraw–Hill, 1994), 322.

10. P. K. Edwards, *Conflict at Work: A Materialist Analysis of Workplace Relations* (Oxford, U.K.: Blackwell Publishers, 1986), 222–228.

11. P. K. Edwards, Jacques Belanger, and Larry Haiven, "The Workplace and Labor Regulation in Comparative Perspective," in Jacques Belanger, P. K. Edwards, and Larry Haiven (eds.), *Workplace Industrial Relations and the Global Challenge* (Ithaca, N.Y.: ILR Press, Cornell University, 1994), 6.

12. Hugh Collins, "Capitalist Discipline and Corporatist Law," *International Law Journal* 11 (1982): 164–178. Also see B. S. Klaas, "Managerial Decision Making about Employee Discipline: A Policy Capturing Approach," *Personnel Psychology* 43 (1990): 117–134.

13. Claudia L. Hale, Cathy Bast, and Betsy Gordon, "Communication within a Dispute Mediation: Interactants' Perceptions of the Process," *The International Journal of Conflict Management* 2, no. 2 (1991): 139–158.

14. Stuart Henry, "Disciplinary Pluralism: Four Models of Private Justice in the Workplace," *Sociological Review* 35 (1987): 279–319.

15. Richard Mead, *International Management: Cross-Cultural Dimensions* (Cambridge, Mass.: Blackwell Publishers, 1994), 226–236.

16. Larry Haiven, "Past Practice and Custom and Practice: Adjustment and Industrial Conflict in North America and the United Kingdom," *Comparative Labour Law Journal* 12 (1991): 300–334.

17. Rebecca Blumenstein, Nichole M. Christian, and Oscar Suris, "Work Force Guarantee in Ford's UAW Accord Puts Pressure on GM," *Wall Street Journal*, 18 September 1996, pp. A1, A6.

18. Michael Burawoy and Janos Lukacs, "Mythologies of Work," *American Sociological Review* 50 (1985): 723–737.

19. Roy J. Lewicki, Joseph A. Litterer, John W. Minton, and David M. Saunders, *Negotiation*, 2nd ed. (Burr Ridge, Ill.: Richard D. Irwin, 1995), 350–353.

20. Stephen A. Herzenberg, "Whither Social Unionism? Labor and Restructuring in the U.S. Auto Industry,"

in Jane Jenson and Rianne Mahon (eds.), *The Challenge of Restructuring: North American Labor Movements Respond* (Philadelphia: Temple University Press, 1993), 314–336.

21. Robert Rogrow, "Canada," in Mariam Rothman, Dennis R. Briscoe, and Raoul C. D. Nacamulli (eds.), *Industrial Relations Around the World* (New York: Walter de Gruyter, 1993), 67–86.

22. Tim Shorrock, "GE, Honeywell Are Focus of NAFTA Labor Complaints," *Journal of Commerce* (15 February 1994): 1–3.

23. Sue Greenfeld and Harold Dyck, "Free Trade in the Americas: The Debate Heats Up," *Business Forum*, Fall 1992, 17–21.

24. Sudhir K. Chawla, Dinesh S. Dave, and Peter B. Barr, "Problems of United States Maquiladora Firms Operating in Mexico: An Empirical Study," *International Journal of Management* 11, no. 2 (1994): 713–719.

25. Richard A. Morales, "Mexico," in Rothman, Briscoe, and Nacamulli (eds.), *Industrial Relations Around the World*, 285–295.

26. F. Zapata, "Labor and Politics: The Mexican Paradox," in E. C. Epstein (ed.), *Labor Autonomy and the State in Latin America* (Boston: Unwin–Hyman Publishers, 1989), 178–187.

27. Global Forecasting Service for Mexico (London: The Economist, 1990), 22–54.

28. Harley Shaiken, "The New International Division of Labor and Its Impact on Unions: A Case Study of High–Tech Mexican Export Production," in Belanger et al. (eds.), *Workplace Industrial Relations*, 224–239.

29. Larry Haiven, "Workplace Discipline in International Comparative Perspective," in Belanger et al. (eds.), *Workplace Industrial Relations*, 70–102.

30. P. K. Edwards, "The Pattern of Collective Industrial Action," in George S. Bain (ed.), *Industrial Relations in Britain* (Oxford: Blackwell Publishers, 1983), 16–31.

31. Graham Hollinshead, "Great Britain," in Rothman et al. (eds.), *Industrial Relations Around the World*, 151–171.

32. Hugo Levi and Ake Sandberg, "Trade Unions and Workplace Technical Change in Europe," *Economic and Industrial Democracy* 12 (1991): 231–258.

33. Marc Maurice, Arndt Sorge, and Malcolm Warner, "Societal Differences in Organizing Manufacturing Units: A Comparison of France, West Germany, and Great Britain," *Organizational Studies* 1, no. 1 (1980): 59–86.

34. Wolfgang Streeck, "The Federal Republic of Germany," in Rothman et al. (eds.), *Industrial Relations Around the World*, 127–149.

35. Michele Tallard, "Bargaining over New Technology: A Comparison of France and West Germany," in Richard Hyman and Wolfgang Streeck (eds.), *New Technology and Industrial Relations* (Oxford, U.K.: Blackwell Publishers, 1988), 284–296.

36. Keith Sisson, *The Management of Collective Bargaining* (Oxford, U.K.: Blackwell Publishers, 1987), 27–28.

37. Michael Burawoy, *The Politics of Production* (London: Verso Publications, 1985), 146–148.

38. "European Social Legislation: Union Comeback," *The Economist*, 23 November 1991, 81.

39. P. K. Edwards, "A Comparison of National Regimes of Labor Regulation and the Problem of the Workplace," in Belanger et al. (eds.), *Workplace Industrial Relations*, 23–42.

40. Anthony E. Smith, "New Technology and the Process of Labor Regulation: An International Perspective," in Belanger et al. (eds.), *Workplace Industrial Relations*, 157–189.

41. Koji Taira, "Japan," in Rothman et al. (eds.), *Industrial Relations Around the World*, 217–233.

42. Boye DeMente, *The Japanese Way of Doing Business* (Englewood Cliffs, N.J.: Prentice–Hall, 1981), 86.

43. Taira, "Japan," 219–220.

44. Koji Taira, "Labor Federation in Japan," *Current History* 87 (1988): 161–164, 177–178.

45. John H. Coll, "The People's Republic of China," in Rothman (eds.), *Industrial Relations Around the World*, 87–98.

46. J. S. Henley and Mee Kau Nyaw, "Introducing Market Forces into Managerial Decision-Making in Chinese Industrial Enterprises," *Journal of Management Studies* 23, no. 6 (1986): 635–656.

47. Dave Lindorff, "Raised Fists in the Developing World," *Business Week*, 18 November 1994, 130–132.

48. "Workers Rub Beijing the Wrong Way and Pay," *Asia Week*, 9–15 January 1995, p. 11.

49. David A. Ralston, David J. Gustafson, Robert H. Terpstra, and David H. Holt, "Pre–Post Tiananmen Square: Changing Values of Chinese Managers," *Asia Pacific Journal of Management* 12, no. 1 (1995): 1–20.

50. Connie J. L. Fang, "Factory Collapse Latest in Saga of Guangdong Disasters—Beijing Promises Action against Safety Offenders," *South China Morning Post*, 18 March 1995, pp. 1, 8. Also see Lindorff, "Raised Fists," 131.

51. "China to Unionize Foreign Firms," *Wall Street Journal*, 1 May 1994, p. A8.

52. Coll, "China," 87–98.

53. Virginia Trigo, "Chinese Entrepreneurs: The Case of Tian He Industrial Development Zone," *Journal of Management EuroAsia* 9, no. 1 (1995): 5–21.

54. David A. Ralston, David H. Holt, Robert H. Terpstra, and Yu Kai–Cheng, "The Impact of Culture and Ideology on Managerial Work Values: A Study of the United States, Russia, Japan, and China," *Academy of Management Best Papers* (1995), 187–192.

55. Laurent Goater and Frederic Richer, "France," in Rothman (eds.), *Industrial Relations Around the World*, 111–125.

56. Russell E. Smith, "Brazil," in Rothman et al. (eds.), *Industrial Relations Around the World*, 47–65.

57. Edward M. Davis, "The 1989 ACTU Congress: Seeking Change Within," *Journal of Industrial Relations* 32, no. 1 (1990): 100–110.

68. Greg J. Bamber, "Flexible Work Organization: Inferences from Britain and Australia," *Asia-Pacific Human Resources Management* 28, no. 3 (1990): 28–44.

69. Hem Jain, "Human Resource Management in Selected Japanese Firms, Their Foreign Subsidiaries, and Locally Owned Companies," *International Labor Review* 129 (1990): 73–89. Also see Eric Fong, "Workers in Jakarta Clash over Right to Demonstrate," *Straits Times*, 5 August 1995, pp. 1, 12.

70. Stephen Frenkel, "Patterns of Workplace Relations in the Global Corporation: Toward Convergence?" in Belanger et al. (eds.), *Workplace Industrial Relations*, 240–274.

71. Ross H. Webber, "Convergence or Divergence," *Columbia Journal of World Business* 4, no. 3 (1969): 75–83.

72. Ralston et al., "Impact of Culture and Ideology," 43–47.

73. "War of the Worlds," *The Economist*, 1 October 1994, 3–6.

74. "Industrial Relations: A Spanner in Europe's Works?" *The Economist*, 2 December 1995, 85.

75. Nicholas Bray, "European Labor Scorns Single Currency," *Wall Street Journal*, 10 October 1996, p. A14.

76. Wigbert Winkler, "Austria and the European Union," in Harry Costin, *Managing the Global Economy: The European Union* (Fort Worth: The Dryden Press, 1996), 255–263.

77. Ibid., 42.

78. "Reluctant to Bear the Burden," *Financial Times*, 13 August 1996, p. 11.

79. Costin, *Managing in the Global Economy*, 44–46.

80. "Adapt or Die," 56–57.

81. Geert Hofstede, *Culture's Consequences: International Differences in Work-Related Values* (Newbury Park, Calif.: Sage Publishing, 1980). Also see Geert Hofstede, *Cultures and Organizations: Software of the Mind* (London: McGraw–Hill, 1991), 251–252.

82. Gary S. Fields, "Changing Labor Market Conditions and Economic Development in Hong Kong, the Republic of Korea, Singapore, Taiwan, and China," *World Bank Economic Review* 8, no. 3 (1994): 395–414. Also see Lindorff, "Raised Fists," 130–132.

83. James R. Lincoln, Harold R. Kerbo, and Elke Wittenhagen, "Japanese Companies in Germany: A Case Study in Cross-Cultural Management," *Industrial Relations* 34, no. 3 (1995): 417–440.

CHAPTER 12

1. "Making It in Asia—with a Few Twists," *The Montpelier*, James Madison University, 1992, pp. 8–10. Also, personal interview with Elizabeth McDougall, Hong Kong, March 1996.

2. Nancy J. Adler, *International Dimensions of Organizational Behavior*, 2nd ed. (Boston: PWS-Kent, 1991), 225–226.

3. Mark Mendenhall and Gary Oddou (eds.), *International Human Resource Management* (Boston: PWS-Kent, 1991), 177–204.

4. Mark M. Mendenhall and Gary Oddou, "The Dimensions of Expatriate Acculturation: A Review," *Academy of Management Review* 10, no. 2 (1985): 39–47. Also see Mark E. Mendenhall and Gary Oddou, "Acculturation Profiles of Expatriate Managers: Implications for Cross-Cultural Training Programs," *Columbia Journal of World Business* 21, no. 3 (1986): 73–79.

5. Vanessa Houlder, "Foreign Culture Shocks," *Financial Times*, 22 March 1996, p. 12. Also see H. Scullion, "Why Companies Prefer to Use Expatriates," *Personnel Management*, November 1991, 32–35.

6. David C. Thomas and Brian Toyne, "Subordinates' Responses to Cultural Adaptation by Japanese Expatriate Managers," *Journal of Business Research* 32, no. 1 (1995): 1–10.

7. Rochelle Kopp, "International Human Resource Policies and Practices in Japanese, European, and United States Multinationals," *Human Resource Management* 33, no. 4 (1994): 581–599.

8. Denice Welch, "Determinants of International Human Resource Management Approaches and Activities: A Suggested Framework," *Journal of Management Studies* 31, no. 2 (1994): 139–164.

9. Nancy J. Adler and S. Bartholomew, "Managing Globally Competent People," *Academy of Management Executive* 6, no. 3 (1992): 52–65. Also see Mendenhall and Oddou, "Acculturation Profiles," 73–79; and Rosalie L. Tung, "Career Issues in International Assignments," *Academy of Management Executive* 2, no. 2 (1988): 241–244.

10. Adler, *International Dimensions*, 226–238.

11. Helen Deresky, *International Management: Managing Across Borders and Cultures*, 2nd ed. (Reading, Mass.: Addison-Wesley, 1997), 296.

12. J. Stewart Black, Hal B. Gregersen, and Mark E. Mendenhall, *Global Assignments: Successfully Expatriating and Repatriating International Managers* (San Francisco: Jossey-Bass, 1992), 4–16, 38–44. Also see Adler and Bartholomew, "Managing Competent People," 52–65; and Welch, "Determinants of Approaches," 139–164.

13. J. Stewart Black and Hal B. Gregersen, "The Other Half of the Picture: Antecedents of Spouse Cross-

Cultural Adjustment," *Journal of International Business Studies* 23, no. 3 (1992): 461–477.

14. M. G. Harvey, "Repatriation of Corporate Executives: An Empirical Study," *Journal of International Business Studies* 20, no. 1 (1989): 131–144.

15. Mendenhall and Oddou, "Acculturation Profiles," 73–79.

16. J. Stewart Black and Mark E. Mendenhall, "Cross-Cultural Training Effectiveness: A Review and Theoretical Framework for Future Research," *Academy of Management Review* 15, no. 1 (1990): 113–136.

17. T. F. O'Boyle, "Little Benefit to Careers Seen in Foreign Stints," *Wall Street Journal*, 11 December 1989, p. A4. Also see R. Pascoe, "Employers Ignore Expatriate Wives at Their Own Peril," *Wall Street Journal*, 29 March 1992, p. B1; and Tung, "Career Issues," 241–244.

18. Kuniyasu Sakai, "The Feudal World of Japanese Manufacturing," *Harvard Business Review*, November–December 1990, 38–49.

19. Christopher A. Bartlett and Sumantra Ghoshal, *Transnational Management: Text, Cases, and Readings in Cross-Border Management* (Boston: Richard D. Irwin, 1995), 73–74. Also see Mary S. Taylor, "American Managers in Japanese Subsidiaries: How Cultural Differences Are Affecting the Work Place," *Human Resources Planning* 14 (1991): 43–49; and H. C. Jain, "Human Resource Management in Selected Japanese Firms, the Foreign Subsidiaries, and Locally Owned Counterparts," *International Labour Review* 129, no. 1 (1990): 73–84.

20. Bartlett and Ghoshal, *Transnational Management*, 78–83. Also see Kopp, "International Policies and Practices," 581–599; and Rosalie L. Tung, "Selection and Training Procedures of U.S., European, and Japanese Multinationals," *California Management Review* 25, no. 1 (1982): 57–71.

21. Adler and Bartholomew, "Managing Competent People," 52–65. Also see S. J. Kobrin, "Expatriate Reduction and Strategic Control in American Multinational Corporations," *Human Resource Management* 27, no. 1 (1988): 63–75.

22. Much of this section is based on Rosalie L. Tung, "Selection and Training of Personnel for Overseas Assignments," *Columbia Journal of World Business* 16, no. 1 (1981): 68–78.

23. Ingemar Torbiorn, "The Structure of Managerial Roles in Cross-Cultural Settings," *International Studies of Management and Organization* 15, no. 1 (1985): 52–74.

24. Bartlett and Ghoshal, *Transnational Management*, 474–475.

25. Kopp, "International Policies and Practices," 581–599.

26. Harvey W. Wallender III and Vincent Bozzone, *International Joint and Coventures: Improving Competitiveness of U.S. and Developing Country Enterprises* (Stamford, Conn.: International Executive Service Corps Research, 1989), 24–30.

27. *Liberalization of Sino-Foreign Joint Ventures in Five Special Economic Zones*, Bulletin No. 4 (1995), China Council for the Promotion of International Trade, Beijing, p. 2.

28. Based on author's contracted consulting work with Procter & Gamble for strategic development of its Guangzhou joint venture manufacturing facility, 1988–1992.

29. U. Srinivasa Rangan and Christopher A. Bartlett, *Caterpillar Tractor Co.* (Boston: Harvard Business School, 1985), 1–19. Also see "An Interview with Caterpillar Chairman & CEO, Donald V. Fites," *Inter-Business Issues*, March 1994, 40–41, 47.

30. Personal interview with Dr. Sam Black, Caterpillar Director of Quality Assurance, January 1996.

31. Daniel Weeks, *Recruiting and Selecting International Managers* (New York: Conference Board, 1992), 2–4.

32. Mark E. Mendenhall, Edward Dunbar, and Gary R. Oddou, "Expatriate Selection, Training, and Career-Pathing: A Review and Critique," *Human Resource Management* 26, no. 3 (1987): 331–345. Also see Mendenhall and Oddou, "Acculturation Profiles," 73–79; and Tung, "Selection and Training," 68–78.

33. Chris Hendry, *Human Resource Strategies for International Growth* (New York: Routledge, 1994), 91–95.

34. Welch, "Determinants of Approaches," 139–164.

35. Hendry, *Human Resource Strategies*, 94–95. Also see M. C. Gertsen, "Intercultural Competence and Expatriates," *International Journal of Human Resource Development* 1, no. 3 (1990): 341–362.

36. Nancy J. Adler, "Women in International Management: Where Are They?" *California Management Review* 26, no. 4 (1984): 122–132.

37. Adler, *International Dimensions*, 258–259.

38. Gillian Flynn, "Lilly Prepares Its People to Take on the World," *Personnel Journal* 75, no. 1 (1996): 58. Also see Charlene Marmer Solomon, "Repatriation: Up, Down, or Out?" *Personnel Journal* 74, no. 1 (1995): 28–30; and Rosalie L. Tung, "Expatriate Assignments: Enhancing Success and Minimizing Failure," *Academy of Management Executive* 1, no. 2 (1987): 117–126.

39. Tung, "Expatriate Assignments," 117.

40. Reyer A. Swaak, "Expatriate Management: The Search for Best Practices," *Compensation and Benefits Review* 27, no. 2 (1995): 21–29.

41. Anne P. Copeland, "Helping Foreign Nationals Adapt to the U.S.," *Personnel Journal* 74, no. 2 (1995): 83–87; Jean-Marie Hiltrop, Charles Despres, and Paul Sparrow, "The Changing Role of HR Managers in Europe," *European Management Journal* 13, no. 1 (1995): 91–98.

42. Mendenhall, Dunbar, and Oddou, "Expatriate Selection," 331–345.

43. Ibid., p. 338.

44. Philip R. Harris and Robert T. Moran, *Managing Cultural Differences* (Houston: Gulf Publishing, 1987). Also see Mendenhall, Dunbar, and Oddou, "Expatriate Selection," 331.

45. John K. Kukuda and Priscilla Chu, "Wrestling with Expatriate Family Problems: Japanese Experience in East Asia," *International Studies of Management & Organization* 24, no. 3 (1994): 36–47. Also see Hendry, *Human Resource Strategies*, 96–97.

46. Mendenhall and Oddou, "Acculturation Profiles," 73–79.

47. Jennifer J. Laabs, "Eyeing Future HR Concerns," *Personnel Journal* 75, no. 1 (1996): 28–37. Also see Tung, "Selection and Training," 68–78.

48. Copeland, "Helping Foreign Nationals," 83–87.

49. Mendenhall, Dunbar, and Oddou, "Expatriate Selection," 331–345. Also see Mendenhall and Oddou, "Acculturation Profiles," 73–79.

50. Kerry Hannon, "The Fast Track Now Leads Overseas," *U.S. News & World Report*, 31 October 1994, 94, 98.

51. Timothy Aeppel, "Westinghouse Now Is Charting an Uncertain Course," *Wall Street Journal*, 13 November 1996, p. B4. Also see *Citibank—China Then and Now* (Hong Kong: Citibank HK, 1995), 2; and Stratford P. Sherman, "The Mind of Jack Welch," *Fortune*, 17 March 1989, 39–50.

52. Samuel Humes, *Managing the Multinational: Confronting the Global-Local Dilemma* (Hemel Hempstead, U.K.: Prentice-Hall International, 1993), 95–101.

53. Mendenhall, Dunbar, and Oddou, "Expatriate Selection," 331–345.

54. "Jack Welch Reinvents General Electric—Again," *The Economist*, 30 March 1991, 59–62.

55. Richard A. Guzzo, Katherine A. Noonan, and Efrat Elron, "Expatriate Managers and the Psychological Contract," *Journal of Applied Psychology* 79, no. 4 (1994): 617–626.

56. *A Study of the Repatriation of the American International Executive* (New York: Korn-Ferry International, 1981), 1, 22–23.

57. Rosalie L. Tung, "Human Resource Planning in Japanese Multinationals: A Model for U.S. Firms?" *Journal of International Business Studies* 15, no. 2 (1984): 139–149.

58. E. K. Briody and J. B. Chrisman, "Cultural Adaptation on Overseas Assignments," *Human Organization* 50, no. 3 (1992): 264–282.

59. Richard G. Linowes, "The Japanese Manager's Traumatic Entry into the United States: Understanding the American-Japanese Cultural Divide," *Academy of Management Executive* 7, no. 4 (1993): 21–40.

60. Nashika Kumaga, "Mitsui's Commitment to Foreign Staff Responsibilities," *Inside Business Japan*, November 1991, 31–32.

61. The presentation is largely based on Adler, *International Dimensions*, 225–232.

62. Ibid., p. 229.

63. Examples based on a roundtable discussion convened by the author and John Schermerhorn at the Eastern Academy of Management Biennial Conference, Managing in a Global Economy, Singapore, June 1995.

64. Personal interview with Mitchell A. Presnick, Warren Williams International Ltd., 12 May 1996, Hong Kong.

65. Shari Caudron, "Preparing Managers for Overseas Assignments," *World Executive Digest*, November 1992, 72–73.

66. Gary Oddou and Mark Mendenhall, "Succession Planning in the 21st Century: How Well Are We Grooming Our Future Business Leaders?" *Business Horizons* 34, no. 1 (1991): 26–34.

67. J. Stewart Black and Hal B. Gregerson, "When Yankee Comes Home: Factors Related to Expatriate and Spouse Repatriation Adjustment," *Journal of International Business Studies* 22, no. 4 (1991): 671–694.

68. Examples are drawn from the Doctoral Symposium on International Careers, the Eastern Academy of Management Conference, May 1996, Crystal City, Virginia.

69. Joann S. Lublin, "Warning to Expats: Maybe You Can't Go Home Again," *Asian Wall Street Journal*, 27–28 August 1993, pp. 1, 6.

70. J. Stewart Black, "Coming Home: The Relationship of Expatriate Expectations with Repatriate Adjustment and Job Performance," *Human Relations* 45, no. 2 (1992): 188.

71. Black, Gregersen, and Mendenhall, *Global Assignments*, 238–250.

72. Black and Gregerson, "When Yankee Comes Home," 671–694. Also see Welch, "Determinants of Approaches," 139–164.

73. Kopp, "International Policies and Practices," 581–599. Also see Tung, "Planning in Japanese Multinationals," 139–149.

74. Catherine Hodges, "Planning Is Key to Successful Expatriation," *People Management*, March 5, 1995, 18.

75. Nancy K. Napier and Richard B. Peterson, "Expatriate Re-entry: What Do Expatriates Have to Say?" *Human Resource Planning* 14, no. 1 (1991): 19–28. Also see Humes, *Managing the Multinational*, 98–99, 244.

76. Michael K. C. Lau (ed.), *Contractual Expenditures and Private Company Practices in Foreign Postings: A Comparative Summary* (Hong Kong: Oxford University Press, 1993), 18–19.

77. Solomon, "Repatriation," 28–30.

78. Richard M. Hodgetts and Fred Luthans, "U.S. Multinationals' Expatriate Compensation Strategies," *Compensation and Benefits Review*, January–February 1993, 57–62.

79. John H. Dunning, *Multinational Enterprises and the Global Economy* (Reading, Mass.: Addison-Wesley, 1993), 375–376.

80. *Guidelines for Foreign Contracts under 1986 Federal Tax Adjustment Act* (Tokyo: Price Waterhouse Asia, 1989), 1, 7.

81. *Foreign Affairs Advisory C-14/1: Recommendations for U.S. Travel to Sri Lanka* (Colombo: U.S. Agency for International Development, 1995).

82. Ingemar Torbiorn, *Living Abroad* (New York: John Wiley & Sons, 1982), 90–92, 97.

83. Personal interview with Kanji Haitani and family, July 1995, New York.

84. Nancy J. Adler, "Pacific Basin Managers: A Gaijin, Not a Woman," *Human Resource Management* 26, no. 2 (1987): 169–192.

85. Nancy J. Adler, "Expecting International Success: Female Managers Overseas," *Columbia Journal of World Business* 19, no. 3 (1984): 79–85.

86. M. Jelinek and Nancy J. Adler, "Women: World Class Managers for Global Competition," *Academy of Management Executive* 2, no. 1 (1988): 11–19.

87. Nancy J. Adler, "Woman Managers in a Global Economy," *Training & Development*, April 1994, 31–36.

88. R. I. Westwood and S. M. Leung, "The Female Expatriate Manager Experience: Coping with Gender and Culture," *International Studies of Management & Organization* 24, no. 3 (1994): 64–85.

89. Susan C. Schneider and Kazuhiro Asakawa, "American and Japanese Expatriate Adjustment: A Psychoanalytic Perspective," *Human Relations* 48, no. 10 (1995): 1109–1127.

CHAPTER 13

1. J. P. Donlon, "An Iconoclast in a Cutthroat World: Interview with Gillette Chairman and CEO Alfred M. Zeien," *Chief Executive*, March 1996, 34–39. Also see Rosabeth Moss Kanter and Thomas D. Dretler, "Global Strategy and Its Impact on Local Operations: Lessons from Gillette Singapore," *Academy of Management Executives* 12, no. 4 (1998): 60–69.

2. Samuel Humes, *Managing the Multinational: Confronting the Global-Local Dilemma* (Hemel Hempstead, U.K.: Prentice-Hall International, 1993), 84–85.

3. Jennifer J. Laabs, "Eyeing Future HR Concerns," *Personnel Journal* 75, no. 1 (1996): 28–37.

4. Shaun Tyson and Alan Fell, "A Focus on Skills, Not Organizations," *People Management* 1, no. 21 (1995): 42–45.

5. Humes, *Managing the Multinational*, 85.

6. *The Canon Story* (Tokyo: Canon Electronics, 1989), 21–22.

7. William B. Werther Jr., Jefferey M. Wachtel, and David J. Veale, "Global Deployment of Executive Talent," *Human Resource Planning* 18, no. 1 (1995): 20–29.

8. Emily Nelson, "Kodak's Carp Is Widely Seen as Next CEO," *Wall Street Journal*, 6 December 1996, pp. B1, B6.

9. Kathryn Harris, "Mr. Sony Confronts Hollywood," *Fortune*, 23 December 1996, 36. Also see Humes, *Managing the Multinational*, 88.

10. Humes, *Managing the Multinational*, 91–92.

11. "Communities of Interest: Survey of International Finance," *The Economist*, 27 April 1991, 40–42. Also see David Halberstam, "Reflections on Japan Inc.," *Business Month*, February 1989, 45–49.

12. Nelson, "Kodak's Next CEO," pp. B1, B6.

13. Kathleen Kerwin, "Getting Two Big Elephants to Dance," *Business Week*, 18 November 1994, 83. Also see Joyce Conor, "57 Varieties of Charm," *Investors Chronicle*, 14 October 1994, p. 19.

14. Kerwin, "Two Big Elephants," 83.

15. Humes, *Managing the Multinational*, 174–177.

16. Ibid., 244–245.

17. Bela Gold, "Strengthening the International Competitiveness of Industries: The Multi-functional Development of Executives in Japanese Industries," *International Journal of Technology Management* 9, no. 5/6/7 (1994): 516–528.

18. Ibid., 524–525. Also see O. P. Kharabanda and E. A. Stallworthy, "Let's Learn from Japan," *Management Accounting*, March 1991, 34, 37.

19. Werther, Wachtel, and Veale, "Global Deployment," 20–29.

20. Kalburgi M. Srinivas, "Globalization of Business and the Third World: Challenge of Expanding the Mindsets," *Journal of Management Development* 14, no. 3 (1995): 26–49.

21. Cecil G. Howard, "Profile of the 21st-Century Expatriate Manager," *HR Magazine* 37, no. 6 (1992): 93–99.

22. Kathy Jackson, "Chrysler Ships More Future Leaders Overseas," *Automotive News*, 18 March 1996, p. 6.

23. Mark Owen, "Chrysler Finds a Global Platform in Daimler-Benz That It Could Not Create Itself," *Financial Times*, 9 November 1999, pp. 1, 7. Also see Mark E. Mendenhall, Edward Dunbar, and Gary R. Oddou, "Expatriate Selection, Training, and Career-Pathing: A Review and Critique," *Human Resource Management* 26, no. 3 (1987): 331–345.

24. Daniel Weeks, *Recruiting and Selecting International Managers* (New York: Conference Board, 1992), 2–4, 6, 11–12.

25. Rosalie L. Tung, "Selection and Training Procedures of U.S., European, and Japanese Multinationals," *California Management Review* 25, no. 1 (1982): 57–71.

26. Rochelle Kopp, "International Human Resource Policies and Practices in Japanese, European, and United States Multinationals," *Human Resource Management* 33, no. 4 (1994): 581–599.

27. Personal interview with Edward V. Yang, president, Electronic Data Systems (HK) Ltd., and Steven P. Leakey, director, Marketing and Business Development, EDS Asia/Pacific Group, Hong Kong, July 1995.

28. Leonard Greenhalgh, "Ford Motor Company's CEO Jac Nasser on Transformational Change, E-Business, and Environmental Responsibility," *Academy of Management Executive* 14, no. 3 (2000): 46–51. Also see Bob Gibbs, "From Action to Integrity," *Training Tomorrow,* March–April 1995, 34–35.

29. *Ernst & Young Resources Global Expatriate Support Services* (Dallas: Ernst & Young Resources, 1996), 1–3.

30. Richard Mead, *International Management: Cross-Cultural Dimensions* (Cambridge, Mass.: Blackwell Publishers, 1994), 362–363.

31. Cynthia Pavett and Tom Morris, "Management Styles within a Multinational Corporation: A Five Country Comparative Study," *Human Relations* 48, no. 10 (1995): 1171–1191.

32. "Guest Briefing: Mexico Talent Competition," *Business Latin America* (Washington, D.C.: The Economist Intelligence Unit, 1994), 15–16.

33. Mariah E. De Forest, "Thinking of a Plant in Mexico?" *Academy of Management Executive* 8, no. 1 (1994): 33–40.

34. Fred Cannon, "Business-Driven Management Development: Developing Competencies Which Drive Business Performance," *Journal of European Industrial Training* 19, no. 2 (1995): 26–31.

35. David H. Holt, *An Educational Assessment of Business Schools and a Strategic Outline for U.S. Assistance* (Washington, D.C.: U.S. Agency for International Development, 1995).

36. Charlotte Crystal, "Making Russian Managers," *International Business* 7, no. 2 (1994): 26–28.

37. "Start 'em Young," *Business Asia,* 7 November 1994, p. 7.

38. Ismail Serageldin, *Nurturing Development: Aid and Cooperation in Today's Changing World* (Washington, D.C.: World Bank, 1995), 38–60.

39. P. K. Edwards, Jacques Belanger, and Larry Haiven, "The Workplace and Labor Regulation in Comparative Perspective," in Jacques Belanger, P. K. Edwards, and Larry Haiven (eds.), *Workplace Industrial Relations and the Global Challenge* (Ithaca, N.Y.: ILR Press, Cornell University, 1994), 6–8.

40. Charles Sweet, *Foreign Country Job Diplomacy: A Brief on Management Requirements for U.S. Sustainable Development in Southeast Asia* (Washington, D.C.: Development Associates, 1988), 1, 7–8, 11.

41. Mariah E. De Forest, "When in Mexico . . . ," *Business Mexico,* May 1991, 38–40.

42. Lim F. Chen, "Balancing Employee Needs: Managing in a Multicultural Environment," *Johor Management Symposia,* March 1995, 1, 7–8.

43. Michael Riff, "How to Combat Anti-Western Attitudes," *Journal of European Business* (January–February 1994): 12–15.

44. Riff, "Anti-Western Attitudes," 12–15.

45. Margaret Kaeter, "International Development," *Training* 32, no. 5 (1995): S23–S29.

46. Ibid., S27–S28.

47. Martha H. Peak, "Employees Are Our Greatest Asset and Worst Headache!" *Management Review* 84, no. 11 (1995): 47–51.

48. "German Educational Tracking Leads to Portable Credentials," *Purchasing and Supply Management,* January 1994, 33.

49. John Dykeman, "HR Takes an Active Role in Selecting Global IT Staff," *Managing Office Technology* 40, no. 4 (1995): 43–44.

50. Paul A. L. Evans, "Management Development as Glue Technology: Integration of Subsidiary Firms," *Human Resource Planning* 15, no. 1 (1992): 85–102.

51. Janet Guyon, "ABB Fuses Units with One Set of Values," *Wall Street Journal,* 2 October 1996, p. A15. Also see James B. Teece, Kathleen Kerwin, and Heidi Dawley, "Ford: Alex Trotman's Daring Global Strategy," *Business Week,* 3 April 1995, 94–104; and S. W. Quickel, "Welch on Welch," *Financial World,* 3 April 1990, 62–67.

52. Evans, "Management Development," 85–102.

53. Ibid., 86.

54. Mark Mendenhall, Betty Jane Punnett, and David Ricks, *Global Management* (Cambridge, Mass.: Blackwell Publishers, 1995), 443–444.

55. Fred E. Fiedler, Terence Mitchell, and Harry C. Triandis, "The Culture Assimilator: An Approach to Cross-Culture Training," *Journal of Applied Psychology* (April 1971): 88–102.

56. "Artz Sees Team Players as P&G's Next Generation Leaders," *International Forum on Global Change* (Washington, D.C.: World Affairs Council, 1991), 13.

57. Mary Cianni and Donna Wnuck, "Individual Growth and Team Enhancement: Moving Toward a New Model of Career Development," *Academy of Management Executive* 11, no. 1 (1997): 105–115.

58. Evans, "Management Development," 85–102.

59. Peak, "Employees Are Our Greatest Asset and Worst Headache!" 47–51.

CHAPTER 14

1. Personal interview and co-author David H. Holt's consulting work with Dan Westford and PolyChem Inc.,

March 1993, summer 1994, and May 1996. PolyChem is a privately held international company headquartered in Colorado, with activities in Britain, Italy, Israel, and Mexico.

2. David H. Holt, *Management Principles and Practices*, 3rd ed. (Englewood Cliffs, N.J.: Prentice Hall, 1993), 410.

3. Leonard Sayles, "A 'Primer' on Cultural Dimensions," *Issues and Observations of the Center for Creative Leadership* 9 (1989): 8–9. Also see John Child, "Culture, Contingency, and Capitalism in the Cross-National Study of Organizations," in Larry L. Cummings and Barry M. Staw (eds.), *Research in Organizational Behavior* (Greenwich, Conn.: JAI Press, 1981), 303–356.

4. Gary A. Yukl, *Leadership in Organizations*, 3rd ed. (Englewood Cliffs, N.J.: Prentice Hall), 89–90, 310–311.

5. Joseph Blasi, *The Communal Experience of the Kibbutz* (New Brunswick, N.J.: Transaction Books, 1986), 111–112.

6. Peter J. Dowling and Randall S. Schuler, *International Dimensions of Human Resource Management* (Boston: PWS-Kent, 1990), 163–164.

7. Geert Hofstede, *Culture's Consequences: International Differences in Work-Related Values* (Newbury Park, Calif.: Sage Publishing, 1980). The founding citation is Geert Hofstede, "Motivation, Leadership, and Organization: Do American Theories Apply Abroad?" *Organizational Dynamics* 9, no. 2 (1980): 42–63.

8. Geert Hofstede, "National Cultures in Four Dimensions: A Research-Based Theory of Cultural Differences among Nations," *International Studies of Management & Organization* 13, no. 1 (1983): 46–74. Also see Geert Hofstede, "The Cultural Relativity of Organizational Practices and Theories," *Journal of International Business Studies* 14 (1983): 75–89.

9. Dianne H. B. Welsh, Fred Luthans, and Steven Sommer, "Managing Russian Factory Workers: The Impact of U.S.-Based Behavioral and Participative Techniques," *Academy of Management Journal* 36, no. 3 (1993): 58–79.

10. Rhysong Yeh, "Values of American, Japanese, and Taiwanese Managers in Taiwan: A Test of Hofstede's Framework," *Academy of Management Proceedings* (1988): 106–110.

11. Simcha Ronen, "Personal Values: A Basis for Work Motivational Set and Work Attitudes," *Organizational Behavior and Human Performance* 21 (1978): 80–107.

12. Abbas J. Ali, "The Islamic Work Ethic in Arabia," *Journal of Psychology* 126, no. 5 (1992): 507–519. Also see J. R. Baum, J. D. Olian, M. Erez, E. R. Schnell, K. G. Smith, H. P. Sims, J. S. Scully, and K. A. Smith, "Nationality and Work Role Interactions: A Cultural Contrast of Israeli and U.S. Entrepreneurs' versus Managers' Needs," *Journal of Business Venturing* 8, no. 1 (1993): 499–512.

13. George W. England, "National Work Meanings and Patterns: Constraints on Management Action," *European Management Journal* 4, no. 3 (1986): 176–184.

14. MOW International Research Team, *The Meaning of Working: An International Perspective* (London: Academic Press, 1985).

15. James R. Lincoln, "Employee Work Attitudes and Management Practice in the U.S. and Japan: Evidence from a Large Comparative Survey," *California Management Review* 32, no. 1 (1989): 89–106.

16. "Stress Takes Toll on Japanese," *Wall Street Journal*, February 1992, p. A11.

17. Abbas J. Ali, "Decision-Making Style, Individualism, and Attitude toward Risk of Arab Executives," *International Studies of Management and Organization* 23, no. 3 (1993): 53–74. Also see Abbas J. Ali, "A Comparative Study of Managerial Beliefs about Work in the Arab States," *Advances in International Comparative Management* 4 (1989): 95–112.

18. Abbas J. Ali, Shmed A. Azim, and Krish S. Krishnan, "Expatriates and Host Country Nationals: Managerial Values and Decision Styles," *Leadership & Organization Development Journal* 16, no. 6 (1995): 27–34.

19. Geert Hofstede, "Cultural Constraints in Management Theories," *Academy of Management Executive* 7, no. 1 (1993): 81–94.

20. Ibid., 83.

21. Andre Laurant, "The Cultural Diversity of Western Conceptions of Management," *International Studies of Management and Organization* 13 (1983): 75–96.

22. Hofstede, "Cultures in Four Dimensions," 46–74. Also see Geert Hofstede and Michael H. Bond, "The Confucius Connection: From Cultural Roots to Economic Growth," *Organizational Dynamics* 16, no. 4 (1988): 4–21.

23. Hofstede, "Cultural Constraints in Theories," 81–94.

24. David H. Holt, David A. Ralston, and Robert H. Terpstra, "Constraints on Capitalism in Russia: The Managerial Psyche, Social Infrastructure, and Ideology," *California Management Review* 36, no. 3, (1994): 124–141.

25. David A. Ralston, David J. Gustafson, Fanny Cheung, and Robert H. Terpstra, "Differences in Managerial Values: A Study of U.S., Hong Kong, and PRC Managers," *Journal of International Business Studies* 24, no. 2 (1993): 249–275.

26. Kenneth A. Kovach, "What Motivates Employees? Workers and Supervisors Give Different Answers," *Business Horizons*, September–October 1987, 58–65.

27. England, "National Work Meanings," 176–184.

28. David A. Ralston, David J. Gustafson, Robert H. Terpstra, and David H. Holt, "Pre-Post Tiananmen Square: Changing Values of Chinese Managers," *Asia Pacific Journal of Management* 12, no. 1 (1995): 1–20. Also see David A. Ralston, David H. Holt, Robert H.

Terpstra, and K. C. Yu, "The Impact of Culture and Ideology on Managerial Work Values: A Study of the U.S., Russia, Japan, and China," *Academy of Management Best Papers* (1995): 187–192.

29. Mason Haire, Edwin E. Ghiselli, and Lyman W. Porter, "Cultural Patterns in the Role of the Manager," *Industrial Relations* 12, no. 2 (1963): 95–117. A more comprehensive explanation of the research is found in Mason Haire, Edwin E. Ghiselli, and Lyman Porter, *Managerial Thinking: An International Study* (New York: John Wiley & Sons, 1966).

30. Robert I. Westwood, *Organisational Behaviour: Southeast Asian Perspectives* (Hong Kong: Longman Group, 1992), 291–293. Also see H. Joseph Reitz, *Behavior in Organizations* (Homewood, Ill.: Dorsey Press, 1981), 200–210; H. Joseph Reitz, "The Relative Importance of Five Categories of Needs among Industrial Workers in Eight Countries," *Academy of Management Proceedings* (1975), 270–273; and Edward E. Lawler III and J. Suttle, "A Causal Correlation Test of the Need-Hierarchy Concept," *Organizational Behavior and Human Performance* 7, no. 2 (1972): 265–287.

31. Simcha Ronen, *Comparative and Multicultural Management* (New York: John Wiley & Sons, 1986), 316–318.

32. S. Runglerkrengkrai and S. Engkaninan, "The Motivation and Need Satisfaction of the Thai Managerial Elite," *Asia Pacific Journal of Management* 3, no. 3 (1986): 194–197.

33. Michael H. Bond, *Beyond the Chinese Face: Insights from Psychology* (Oxford: Oxford University Press, 1991), 34–40, 53–56. Also see K. S. Yang and Michael H. Bond, "Exploring Implicit Personality Theories with Indigenous or Imported Constructs: The Chinese Case," *Journal of Personality and Social Psychology* 58 (1990): 1087–1095; and Bond and Hwang, "Chinese People," 213–266.

34. S. Gordon Redding and S. Richardson, "Participative Management and Its Varying Relevance in Hong Kong and Singapore," *Asia Pacific Journal of Management* 3, no. 2 (1986): 76–98. See also S. Gordon Redding, "Some Perceptions of Psychological Needs among Managers in South East Asia," in Y. H. Poortinga (ed.), *Basic Problems in Cross-Cultural Psychology* (Amsterdam: Swets and Zeitlinger, 1977), 338–343; S. Gordon Redding and T. A. Martyn-Johns, "Paradigm Differences and Their Relation to Management, with Reference to South-East Asia," in George W. England, Anant R. Neghandi, and B. Wilpert (eds.), *Organizational Functioning in a Cross-Cultural Perspective* (Kent, Ohio: Kent State University, 1979), 103–125.

35. Edward C. Nevis, "Cultural Assumptions and Productivity: The United States and China," *Sloan Management Review* 24, no. 3 (1983): 17–29.

36. Frederick Herzberg, "One More Time: How Do You Motivate Employees?" *Harvard Business Review* 87, no. 5 (1987): 109–117.

37. Frederick Herzberg, Bernard Mausner, and Barbara Snyderman, *The Motivation to Work* (New York: John Wiley & Sons, 1959), Chapters 2 and 3, in particular.

38. Rabindra N. Kanungo and Richard W. Wright, "A Cross-Cultural Comparative Study of Managerial Job Attitudes," *Journal of International Business Studies* 14, no. 3 (1983): 115–129.

39. Westwood, *Organisational Behaviour,* 302–303.

40. Mariah E. de Forest, "Thinking of a Plant in Mexico?" *Academy of Management Executive* 8, no. 1 (1994): 33–40.

41. Hofstede and Bond, "Confucius Connection," 4–21. Also see Redding and Richardson, "Participative Management," 76–98.

42. Henry Mintzberg, *Structure in Fives: Designing Effective Organizations* (Englewood Cliffs, N.J.: Prentice Hall, 1983), 28–29.

43. Rabindra N. Kanungo, "Work Alienation: A Pancultural Perspective," *International Studies in Management and Organization* 13 (1983): 119–138. Also see Oded Shenkar and Simcha Ronen, "Culture, Ideology, or Economy: A Comparative Exploration of Work Goal Importance among Managers in Chinese Societies," *Proceedings: Managing in a Global Economy III* (1989), 162–167.

44. Thomas J. Atchison, "The Employment Relationship: Un-tied or Re-tied?" *Academy of Management Executive* 5, no. 4 (1991): 52–62.

45. Richard Mead, *International Management: Cross-Cultural Dimensions* (Cambridge, Mass.: Blackwell Publishers, 1994), 218–219.

46. Stefan Wills and Kevin Barham, "Being an International Manager," *European Management Journal* 12, no. 1 (1994): 49–58.

47. David C. McClelland, "Toward a Theory of Motive Acquisition," *American Psychologist* 20, no. 5 (1965): 321–333.

48. John W. Atkinson, *An Introduction to Motivation* (New York: Van Nostrand, 1961).

49. Robert H. Brockhaus and Pamela S. Horwitz, "The Psychology of the Entrepreneur," in Donald L. Sexton and Raymond W. Smilor (eds.), *The Art and Science of Entrepreneurship* (Cambridge, Mass.: Ballinger, 1986), 25–48.

50. William B. Gartner, "A Conceptual Framework for Describing the Phenomenon of New Venture Creation," *Academy of Management Review* 10, no. 2 (1985): 696–706.

51. Ronen, *Comparative Management,* 151–153.

52. David C. McClelland, *The Achieving Society* (Princeton, N.J.: Van Nostrand, 1961), 263–264. Also see David C. McClelland, "Achievement Motivation Can Be Developed," *Harvard Business Review,* November–December 1965, 64–70.

53. Oded Shenkar and Simcha Ronen, "Structure and Importance of Work Goals among Managers in the

People's Republic of China," *Academy of Management Journal* 30, no. 4 (1987): 564–576. Also see Gillian Flynn, "HR in Mexico: What You Should Know," *Personnel Journal* 73, no. 8 (1994): 34–44; Kuo-shu Yang, "Chinese Personality and Its Change," in Bond, *Chinese People*, 86–99; and Redding and Martyn-Johns, "Paradigm Differences," 103–125.

54. Flynn, "HR in Mexico," 34–44. Also see Yang, "Chinese Personality," 86–99.

55. Per Thygesen Poulsen, "The Attuned Corporation: Experience from 18 Scandinavian Pioneering Corporations," *European Management Journal* 16, no. 3 (1988): 229–235.

56. Kalburgi M. Srinivas, "Globalization of Business and the Third World: Challenge of Expanding the Mindsets," *Journal of Management Development* 14, no. 3 (1995): 26–49.

57. Victor H. Vroom, *Work and Motivation* (New York: John Wiley & Sons, 1964). Also see Victor H. Vroom and Arthur G. Jago, *The New Leadership: Managing Participation in Organizations* (Englewood Cliffs, N.J.: Prentice Hall, 1988), 121–127.

58. Westwood, *Organisational Behaviour*, 308–309.

59. David A. Nadler and Edward E. Lawler III, "Motivation: A Diagnostic Approach," in J. Richard Hackman, Edward E. Lawler III, and Lyman W. Porter (eds.), *Perspectives on Behavior in Organizations* (New York: McGraw-Hill, 1983), 74–76.

60. Michael L. Wheeler, *Diversity: Business Rationale and Strategies* (New York: Conference Board, 1996).

61. Susan Caminiti, "Ralph Lauren: The Emperor Has Clothes," *Fortune*, 11 November 1996, 80–92.

62. Nancy L. Mueller, "Wisconsin Power and Light's Model Diversity Program," *Training & Development* 50, no. 3 (1996): 57–60.

63. Taylor H. Cox Jr. and Stacy Blake, "Managing Cultural Diversity: Implications for Organizational Competitiveness," *Academy of Management Executive* 5, no. 2 (1991): 45–56.

64. Lynn R. Anderson, "Management of the Mixed-Cultural Work Group," *Organization Behavior and Human Performance* 31, no. 3 (1983): 303–330. Also see M. E. Shaw, *Group Dynamics: The Psychology of Small Group Behavior* (New York: McGraw-Hill, 1983).

65. Y. Paul Huo and Richard M. Steers, "Cultural Influences on the Design of Incentive Systems: The Case of East Asia," *Asia Pacific Journal of Management* 10, no. 1 (1993): 71–85.

66. Richard M. Steers, "Organizational Science in a Global Environment: Future Directions," in Chimezie A. B. Osigweh Yg (ed.), *Organizational Science Abroad: Constraints and Perspectives* (New York: Plenum Press, 1989), 293–304.

67. Wagner and Hollenbeck, *Organizational Behavior*, 749.

68. Bond, *Chinese Face*, 40–42.

69. Henry W. Lane and Joseph J. DiStefano, *International Management Behavior*, 2nd ed. (Boston: PWS-Kent, 1992), 54–55.

70. Cox and Blake, "Managing Cultural Diversity," 45–56.

71. Andre Laurant, "The Cross-Cultural Puzzle of International Human Resource Management," *Human Resource Management* 25, no. 1 (1986): 91–102.

72. Lane and DiStefano, *International Management Behavior*, 58–59.

73. Philip M. Rosenzweig, "The New 'American Challenge': Foreign Multinationals in the United States," *California Management Review* 36, no. 3 (1994): 107–123.

74. "Brit Has Reality Check in BA and USAir Agreement," *Washington Post*, 12 December 1996, p. B3.

75. "Fewer Japanese Consider U.S. Assignments as Plums," *Wall Street Journal*, 25 July 1996, p. A8.

76. Jathon Sapsford, "Tokyo Gets a Rude Awakening in Peru," *Wall Street Journal*, 20 December 1996, p. A13.

CHAPTER 15

1. Tonia Shakespeare, "From Star to Team Player," *Black Enterprise*, January 1996, 50.

2. David P. Hamilton and Robert Steiner, "Sony's Idei Tightens Reins Again on Freewheeling U.S. Operations," *Wall Street Journal*, 24 January 1997, p. A10.

3. Gary Yukl, "Managerial Leadership: A Review of Theory and Research," *Journal of Management* 15, no. 2 (1989): 251–289.

4. Manfred F. R. Kets de Vries, "The Leadership Mystique," *Academy of Management Executive* 8, no. 3 (1994): 73–89.

5. Bernard M. Bass, "From Transactional to Transformational Leadership: Learning to Share the Vision," *Organizational Dynamics* 18 (1990): 19–31.

6. Max Weber, *Economy and Society*, G. Roth and C. Wittich (eds. and trans.), vol. 3 (New York: Bedminster, 1968). Originally published in 1925.

7. Victor H. Vroom and Arthur G. Jago, *The New Leadership: Managing Participation in Organizations* (Englewood Cliffs, N.J.: Prentice Hall, 1988), 49–77.

8. David A. Kenny and Stephen J. Zaccaro, "An Estimate of Variance Due to Traits in Leadership," *Journal of Applied Psychology* 8, no. 4 (1983): 678–685.

9. Ralph M. Stogdill, "Personal Factors Associated with Leadership: A Survey of the Literature," *Journal of Psychology* 25, no. 1 (1948): 35–71.

10. Bernard M. Bass, *Stogdill's Handbook of Leadership: A Survey of Theory and Research*, 3rd ed. (New York: Free Press, 1990), 84–88. Also see R. D. Mann, "A Review of the Relationships between Personality and Performance in Small Groups," *Psychological Bulletin* 56, no. 4 (1959): 241–270.

11. Owen Ullmann, "Why the Force Isn't with the 'Third Force,'" *Business Week*, 30 September 1996, 49.

12. Tim Smart, "Jack Welch's Encore," *Business Week*, 26 October 1996, 154–160.

13. Paul Hersey, *The Situational Leader* (Escondido, Calif.: Center for Leadership Studies, 1984), 13–14.

14. Philip R. Harris and Robert T. Moran, *Managing Cultural Differences*, 3rd ed. (Houston: Gulf Publishing, 1991), 8–12.

15. Ralph M. Stogdill and Alvin E. Coons (eds.), *Leader Behavior: Its Description and Measurement* (Columbus: Bureau of Business Research, Ohio State University, 1957).

16 Rensis Likert, *New Patterns of Management* (New York: McGraw-Hill, 1961).

17. Robert R. Blake and Jane S. Mouton, *The Versatile Manager: A Grid Profile* (Homewood, Ill.: Richard D. Irwin, 1981).

18. Alan Bryman, *Charisma & Leadership in Organizations* (London: Sage Publications, 1992), 7–8.

19. Martin M. Chemers, "The Social, Organizational, and Cultural Context of Effective Leadership," in Barbara Kellerman (ed.), *Leadership: Multidisciplinary Perspectives* (Englewood Cliffs, N.J.: Prentice Hall, 1985), 91–112.

20. Richard Kustin and Robert Jones, "The Influence of Corporate Headquarters on Leadership Styles in Japanese and U.S. Subsidiary Companies," *Leadership & Organization Development Journal* 16, no. 5 (1995): 11–15.

21. Harris and Moran, *Managing Cultural Differences*, 11.

22. Gillian Flynn, "HR in Mexico: What You Should Know," *Personnel Journal* 73, no. 8 (1994): 34–44. Also see Abbas J. Ali, "Decision-Making Style, Individualism and Attitude toward Risk of Arab Executives," *International Studies of Management and Organization* 23, no. 3 (1993): 53–74; and Andre Laurant, "The Cultural Diversity of Western Conceptions of Management," *International Studies of Management and Organization* 13, no. 1 (1983): 75–96.

23. Fred E. Fiedler, *A Theory of Leadership Effectiveness* (New York: McGraw-Hill, 1967).

24. Robert J. House, "A Path Goal Theory of Leader Effectiveness," *Administrative Science Quarterly* 16, no. 5 (1971): 321–328.

25. Robert J. House and Terence R. Mitchell, "Path-Goal Theory of Leadership," in Louis E. Boone and Donald D. Bowen (eds.), *The Great Writings in Management and Organizational Behavior* (New York: Random House, 1987), 216–238.

26. Victor H. Vroom and Phillip Yetton, *Leadership and Decision Making* (Pittsburgh: University of Pittsburgh Press, 1973).

27. Paul Hersey and Kenneth H. Blanchard, *Management of Organizational Behavior: Utilizing Human Resources*, 5th ed. (Englewood Cliffs, N.J.: Prentice Hall, 1988), 169–201.

28. Noel M. Tichy and David O. Ulrich, "The Leadership Challenge—A Call for the Transformational Leader," *Sloan Management Review* 26, no. 1 (1984): 59–68.

29. James McGregor Burns, *Leadership* (New York: Harper & Row, 1978), 19–20.

30. Bryman, *Charisma & Leadership*, 91–114. Also see Joseph Seltzer and Bernard M. Bass, "Transformational Leadership: Beyond Initiation and Consideration," *Journal of Management* 16, no. 12 (1990): 24–33.

31. Weber, *Economy and Society*, vol. 3: 1, 112.

32. Robert J. House, "A 1976 Theory of Charismatic Leadership," in James G. Hunt and Lars I. Larson (eds.), *Leadership: The Cutting Edge* (Carbondale: Southern Illinois University Press, 1977), 189–207.

33. Bernard M. Bass, "From Transactional to Transformational Leadership: Learning to Share the Vision," *Organizational Dynamics* 18, no. 3 (1990): 19–31. Also see Bernard M. Bass, "Leadership: Good, Better, Best," *Organizational Dynamics* 13, no. 3 (1985): 26–40.

34. Bruce Lloyd, "Leadership and Learning," *Leadership & Organizational Development Journal* 15, no. 4 (1994): 19–26.

35. Kets de Vries, "Leadership Mystique," 73–89. Also see Manfred F. R. Kets de Vries, "The Organizational Fool: Balancing a Leader's Hubris," *Human Relations* 43, no. 8 (1990): 751–770; Laurant, "Cultural Diversity," 75–96; and Geert Hofstede, "Cultural Constraints in Management Theories," *Academy of Management Executive* 7, no. 1 (1993): 81–94.

36. Lloyd, "Leadership and Learning," 20.

37. Bernard M. Bass and B. J. Avolio, "The Implications of Transactional and Transformational Leadership for Individual, Team, and Organizational Development," *Research in Organizational Change and Development* 4 (1990): 231–272. Also see Bryman, *Charisma & Leadership*, 95–98.

38. Richard J. Schonberger, "Human Resource Management Lessons from a Decade of Total Quality Management and Reengineering," *California Management Review* 36, no. 4 (1994): 109–123.

39. Smart, "Welch's Encore," 154–160. Also see Stratford P. Sherman, "The Mind of Jack Welch," *Fortune*, 17 March 1989, 39–50.

40. Noel M. Tichy and Mary Ann Devana, *The Transformational Leader* (New York: John Wiley & Sons, 1990). Also see Warren G. Gennis and B. Nanus, *Leaders: The Strategies for Taking Charge* (New York: Harper and Row, 1985), 173–176; and Bryman, *Charisma & Leadership*, 136–146.

41. Geert Hofstede, "Motivation, Leadership, and Organization: Do American Theories Apply Abroad?" *Organizational Dynamics* 9, no. 2 (1980): 42–63.

42. B. R. Wilson, *The Noble Savages: The Primitive Origins of Charisma and Its Contemporary Survival* (Berkeley: University of California Press, 1975), 7.

43. This section draws extensively from several works including Geert Hofstede, *Cultures and Organizations: Software of the Mind* (London: McGraw-Hill U.K., 1991), 52–55, 122–125, and 140–143; Geert Hofstede, "National Cultures in Four Dimensions: A Research-Based Theory of Cultural Differences among Nations," *International Studies of Management & Organization* 13, no. 1 (1983): 46–74; and Geert Hofstede, "The Cultural Relativity of Organizational Practices and Theories," *Journal of International Business Studies* 14 (1983): 75–89.

44. Geert Hofstede and Michael H. Bond, "Hofstede's Cultural Dimensions: An Independent Validation Using Rokeach's Value Survey," *Journal of Cross-Cultural Psychology* 12 (1984): 221–243. Also see Harry C. Triandis, "Review of Culture's Consequences: International Differences in Work-Related Values," *Human Organisation* 41 (1982): 86–90; and Simcha Ronen and Oded Shenkar, "Clustering Countries on Attitudinal Dimensions: A Review and Synthesis," *Academy of Management Journal* 10, no. 3 (1985): 435–454.

45. Harris and Moran, *Managing Cultural Differences*, 11–12, 78–81.

46. Geert Hofstede, "Dimensions of National Cultures in Fifty Countries and Three Regions," in J. B. Deregowski, S. Dziurawiec, and R. C. Annis (eds.), *Expiscations in Cross-Culture Psychology* (Lisse, Neth.: Swets & Zeitlinger, 1983), 335–355.

47. Kets de Vries, "Leadership Mystique," 73–74.

48. Ibid., 76. Also see Murray R. Barrisk and Michael K. Mount, "The Big Five Personality Dimensions and Job Performance: A Meta-Analysis," *Personnel Psychology* 44 (1991): 1–26.

49. Michael H. Bond, *Beyond the Chinese Face: Insights from Psychology* (Hong Kong: Oxford University Press, 1991), 70–71.

50. Stefan Wills, "European Leadership: Key Issues," *European Management Journal* 14, no. 1 (1996): 97.

51. Ibid., 90–97.

52. Mason Haire, Edwin E. Ghiselli, and Lyman W. Porter, *Managerial Thinking: An International Study* (New York: John Wiley & Sons, 1966), 18–21, 29.

53. Sumantra Ghoshal and Christopher A. Bartlett, "Changing the Role of Top Management: Beyond Structure to Processes," *Harvard Business Review*, January–February 1995, 86–96. Also see Paul C. Earley, "East Meets West Meets Midwest: Further Explorations of Collectivistic and Individualistic Work Groups," *Academy of Management Journal* 36, no. 2 (1993): 319–348.

54. Fons Trompenaars, *Riding the Waves of Culture* (Avon, U.K.: The Economist Books, 1993), Ch. 2, 3.

55. Andrew Myers, Andrew Kakabadse, Tim McMahon, and Gilles Spony, "Top Management Styles in Europe: Implications for Business and Cross-National Teams," *European Business Journal* 7, no. 1 (1995): 17–27.

56. Charles Sweet and David H. Holt, *A Strategic Evaluation of Private Sector Impact in Central and Eastern Europe* (Washington, D.C.: U.S. Agency for International Development, 1993), 9–11.

57. Victor Gligorov, "Justice and Privatization," *Communist Economies and Economic Transformation* 4, no. 1 (1992): 45–57.

58. John Channon and Adam Dakin, "Coming to Terms with Local People," *People Management* 1, no. 12 (1995): 24–29.

59. Bruno Grancelli, "Organizational Change: Towards a New East-West Comparison," *Organization Studies* 16, no. 1 (1995): 1–25. Also see Jone Pearce, "From Socialism to Capitalism: The Effects of Hungarian Human Resource Practice," *Academy of Management Executive* 4, no. 2 (1991): 75–88; and Max Boisot, *East-West Business Collaboration: The Challenge of Governance in Post-Socialist Enterprises* (London: Routledge, 1994), 18–22, 71–79.

60. Channon and Dakin, "Coming to Terms," 28–29.

61. David H. Holt, David A. Ralston, and Robert H. Terpstra, "Constraints on Capitalism in Russia: The Managerial Psyche, Social Infrastructure and Ideology," *California Management Review* 36, no. 3 (1994): 124–141.

62. Avaraham Shama, "Management under Fire: The Transformation of Managers in the Soviet Union and Eastern Europe," *Academy of Management Executive* 7, no. 1 (1993): 22–35.

63. Sheila M. Puffer, "Understanding the Bear: A Portrait of Russian Business Leaders," *Academy of Management Executive* 8, no. 1 (1994): 41–54.

64. Andrzej Kozminski, "Framework for Comparative Studies of Management in Post-Socialist Economies," *Studies in Comparative Communism* 4 (1991): 413–424.

65. Sheila M. Puffer, "Shedding the Legacy of the Red Executive: Leadership in Russian Enterprises," *International Business Review* 4, no. 2 (1995): 157–176.

66. Shama, "Management under Fire," 22–35.

67. Grancelli, "Organizational Change," 1–25. Also see Boisot, *East-West Collaboration*, 57–59, 72.

68. Mitsuru Misawa, "New Japanese-Style Management in a Changing Era," *Columbia Journal of World Business* 22, no. 2 (1987): 9–17.

69. Leonard H. Lynn and Hayagreeva Rao, "Failures of Intermediate Forms: A Study of the Suzuki Zaibatsu," *Organization Studies* 16, no. 1 (1995): 55–80.

70. James R. Lincoln, "Japanese Organization and Organization Theory," in Barry M. Staw and Larry L. Cummings (eds.), *Research in Organizational Behavior*, vol. 12 (Greenwich, Conn.: JAI Press, 1990), 255–294.

71. Richard Kustin and Robert Jones, "The Influence of Corporate Headquarters on Leadership Styles in Japanese and U.S. Subsidiary Companies," *Leadership & Organization Development Journal* 16, no. 5 (1995): 11–15.

72. Kuniyasu Sakai, "The Feudal World of Japanese Manufacturing," *Harvard Business Review*, November–December 1990, 38–47.

73. Misawa, "New Japanese-Style Management," 9–17.

74. Kenichi Ohmae, "Companyism and Do More Better," *Harvard Business Review*, January–February 1989, 125–132.

75. Richard J. Schmidt, "Japanese Management, Recession Style," *Business Horizons*, March–April 1996, 70–76.

76. Samuel Humes, *Managing the Multinational: Confronting the Global-Local Dilemma* (Englewood Cliffs, N.J.: Prentice Hall, 1993), 23–25.

77. Robert I. Westwood, *Organisational Behaviour: Southeast Asian Perspectives* (Hong Kong: Longman Group, 1992), 124–125. Also see C. R. Holloman, "'Headship' versus 'Leadership,'" *Business and Economic Review* 32, no. 2 (1986): 35–37.

78. This section draws extensively on Michael H. Bond, *Beyond the Chinese Face* (Hong Kong: Oxford University Press, 1991), 40–48, 70–73.

79. Simcha Ronen, *Comparative and Multinational Management* (New York: John Wiley & Sons, 1986), 224–226. Also see S. Gordon Redding, *The Spirit of Chinese Capitalism* (Berlin: Walter de Gruyter, 1990), 153–160; and Westwood, *Organisational Behaviour*, 134–137.

80. Michael H. Bond and K. K. Hwang, "The Social Psychology of the Chinese People," in M. H. Bond (ed.), *The Psychology of the Chinese People* (Hong Kong: Oxford University Press, 1986), 88–90.

81. Redding, *Chinese Capitalism*, 158–159.

82. David A. Ralston, David J. Gustafson, Robert H. Terpstra, and David H. Holt, "Pre-Post Tiananmen Square: Changing Values of Chinese Managers," *Asia Pacific Journal of Management* 12, no. 1 (1995): 1–20. Also see S. B. Fiechter and K. J. Krayer, "Variations in Dogmatism and Leader-Supplied Information: Determinants of Perceived Behavior in Task-Oriented Groups," *Group and Organisational Studies* 11 (1987): 403–418.

83. David Kwok Po Li, "Asia's Managers Must Meet Changes," *Asian Business* 32, no. 1 (1996): 36–38.

84. Gregory K. Stephens and Charles R. Greer, "Doing Business in Mexico: Understanding Cultural Differences," *Organizational Dynamics* 24, no. 1 (1995): 39–55.

85. Abbas J. Ali, Shmed A. Azim, and Krish S. Krishnan, "Expatriates and Host Country Nationals: Managerial Values and Decision Styles," *Leadership & Organization Development Journal* 16, no. 6 (1995): 27–34.

86. Ugur Yavas, Dogan Eroglu, and Sevgin Eroglu, "Sources and Management of Conflict: The Case of Saudi–U.S. Joint Ventures," *Journal of International Marketing* 2, no. 3 (1994): 61–82.

87. Ali, "Arab Executives," 53–74.

88. David A. Ralston, David H. Holt, Robert H. Terpstra, and K. C. Yu, "The Impact of Culture and Ideology on Managerial Work Values: A Study of the U.S., Russia, Japan, and China," *Academy of Management Best Papers* (1995): 187–192.

89. Raimo Nurmi and Raoul Üksävrav, "Estonian and Finnish Organizations: A Comparative Analysis," *International Journal of Management* 13, no. 1 (1996): 101–107.

90. Kevin Hall, "Worldwide Vision in the Workplace," *People Management* 1, no. 10 (1995): 20–22.

CHAPTER 16

1. Anthony M. Townsend, Samuel M. DeMarie, and Anthony R. Hendrickson, "Virtual Teams: Technology and the Workplace of the Future," *Academy of Management Executive* 12, no. 3 (1998): 17–29.

2. Greg L. Stewart and Murray R. Barrick, "Team Structure and Performance: Assessing the Mediating Role of Intrateam Process and the Moderating Role of Task Type," *Academy of Management Journal* 43, no. 2 (2000): 135–148.

3. Townsend et al., "Virtual Teams: Technology and the Workplace of the Future," 19.

4. Manuel Castells, "The Network Becomes the Social Structure of Everything," *Fortune*, 9 October 2000, 270–271.

5. Christopher A. Bartlett and Sumantra Ghoshal, *Transnational Management: Texts, Cases, and Readings in Cross-Border Management*, 2nd ed. (Boston: Irwin, 1995), 479–480.

6. Charles C. Snow, Scott A. Snell, Sue Canney Davison, and Donald C. Hambrick, "Use Transnational Teams to Globalize Your Company," *Organizational Dynamics* 30 (spring 1996): 50–67.

7. Gregory G. Dess, Abdul M. A. Rasheed, Kevin J. McLaughlin, and Richard L. Priem, "The New Corporate Architecture," *Academy of Management Executive* 9, no. 3 (1995): 7–20.

8. Janet Guyon, "Why Is the World's Most Profitable Company Turning Itself Inside Out?" *Fortune*, 4 August 1997, 120–125.

9. Lee Clifford, "Tyrannosaurus RX," *Fortune*, 30 October 2000, 140–151.

10. Snow et al., "Use Transnational Teams to Globalize Your Company," 50–67.

11. Ibid., 50–51.

12. Bradley Johnson, "Surging IT Services' Battle Lines Take Shape: Companies in Hot Market Line Pockets Profits with Solutions," *Business Marketing*, 3 April 1995, p. T3.

13. This section draws on Snow et al., "Use Transnational Teams," 50–67. Also see David P. Hamilton, "World Business; United It Stands—Fuji Xerox Is a Rarity in World Business: A Joint Venture That Works," *Asian Wall Street Journal*, 30 September 1996, p. S3.

14. Snow et al., "Use Transnational Teams," 50–67.

15. Janet Guyon, "World Staffers: For ABB, Globalization Is More Than a Buzzword," *Asian Wall Street Journal*, 2 October 1996 p. 1.

16. Christopher A. Bartlett and Sumantra Ghoshal, *Managing Across Borders: The Transnational Solution* (Boston: Harvard Business School Press, 1989), 198–199.

17. Chris Hendry, *Human Resource Strategies for International Growth* (London: Routledge, 1994), 10–12.

18. Nancy J. Adler, *International Dimensions of Organizational Behavior*, 2nd ed. (Boston: PWS-Kent, 1991), 134–135.

19. P. Christopher Earley and Elaine Mosakowski, "Creating Hybrid Team Cultures: An Empirical Test of Transnational Team Functioning," *Academy of Management Journal* 43, no. 1 (2000): 26–49.

20. Jane E. Salk and Mary Yoko Brannen, "National Culture, Networks, and Individual Influence in a Multinational Management Team," *Academy of Management Journal* 43, no. 2 (2000): 191–202.

21. Greg L. Stewart and Murray R. Barrick, "Team Structure and Performance: Assessing the Mediating Role of Intrateam Process and the Moderating Role of Task Type," *Academy of Management Journal* 43, no. 2 (2000): 135–148.

22. L. G. Bolman and T. E. Deal, "What Makes a Team Work?" *Organizational Dynamics* 21 (1992): 34–44.

23. John Dew, "Creating Team Leaders," *Journal for Quality & Participation* 18, no. 6 (1995): 50–54.

24. Allen C. Amason, Kenneth R. Thompson, Wayne A. Hochwarter, and Allison W. Harrison, "Conflict: An Important Dimension in Successful Management Teams," *Organizational Dynamics* 30 (spring 1996): 20–35.

25. Ibid., 29–32.

26. Adler, *International Dimensions of Organizational Behavior*, 139–140.

27. Dew, "Creating Team Leaders," 50–54.

28. Adler, *International Dimensions of Organizational Behavior*, 140.

29. Gregory Moorhead and Ricky W. Griffin, *Organizational Behavior: Managing People and Organizations*, 4th ed. (Boston: Houghton Mifflin Company, 1995), 227–228.

30. This section is drawn from Adler, *International Dimensions of Organizational Behavior*, 118–130, and Marceline B. R. Kroon, Paul 't Hart, and Dik van Kreveld, "Managing Group Decision Making Processes: Individual Versus Collective Accountability and Groupthink," *International Journal of Conflict Management* 2, no. 2 (1991): 91–115.

31. Adler, *International Dimensions of Organizational Behavior*, 132–133.

32. Marvin E. Shaw, *Group Dynamics: The Psychology of Small Group Behavior*, 3rd ed. (New York: McGraw-Hill, 1981), 68–76.

33. Gregory Moorhead and John R. Montanari, "Empirical Analysis of the Groupthink Phenomenon," *Human Relations* 39 (1986): 399–410.

34. Kroon et al., "Managing Group Decision Making Processes," 91–115.

35. Karen Roberts, Ellen Ernst Kossek, and Cynthia Ozeki, "Managing the Global Workforce: Challenges and Strategies," *Academy of Management Executive* 12, no. 4 (1998): 93–106. Also see Fred Luthans and Robert Kreitner, *Organizational Behavior Modification and Beyond* (Grandview, Ill.: Scott Foresman, 1985), 81–82.

36. Richard J. Schonberger, "Human Resource Management Lessons from a Decade of Total Quality Management and Reengineering," *California Management Review* 36, no. 4 (1994): 109–123.

37. Jennifer Reingold, "Management: An Options Plan Your CEO Hates," *Business Week*, 28 February 2000, 82–87. Also see Jennifer Reingold, "Executive Pay," *Business Week*, 21 April 1997, 58–66.

38. Ellen Hart, "Top Teams," *Management Review* 85, no. 2 (1996): 43–47.

39. Ibid., 44.

40. Christopher P. Early, "East Meets West Meets Mideast: Further Explorations of Collectivistic and Individualistic Work Groups," *Academy of Management Journal* 36, no. 2 (1993): 319–348.

41. Gillian Flynn, "HR in Mexico: What You Should Know," *Personnel Journal* 73, no. 8 (1994): 34–44. Also see Miguel Martinez and Syd Weston, "New Management Practices in a Multinational Corporation—The Restructuring of Worker Representation and Rights," *Industrial Relations Journal* 25, no. 2 (1994): 110–121.

42. Ibid., 114–115.

43. Geert Hofstede and Michael H. Bond, "The Confucius Connection: From Cultural Roots to Economic Growth," *Organizational Dynamics* 16, no. 4 (1988): 4–21.

44. Dan Waters, *21st Century Management: Keeping Ahead of the Japanese & Chinese* (Singapore: Simon & Schuster, 1991), 35–37, 49.

45. Ibid., 49–50.

46. Clifford Clarke and Mitchell R. Hammer, "Predictors of Japanese and American Managers' Job Success, Personal Adjustment, and Intercultural Interaction Effectiveness," *Management International Review* 35, no. 2 (1995): 153–168.

47. Susanne Schech and Jane Haggis, *Culture and Development: A Critical Introduction* (Oxford, U.K.: Blackwell Publishers Ltd, 2000), 123–126.

48. Abbas J. Ali, "The Islamic Work Ethic in Arabia," *Journal of Psychology* 126, no. 5 (1992): 507–519.

49. Abbas J. Ali, Shmed A. Azim, and Krish S. Krishnan, "Expatriates and Host Country Nationals: Managerial Values and Decision Styles," *Leadership & Organization Development Journal* 16, no. 6 (1995): 27–34.

50. Judith H. Dobrzniski, "Rethinking IBM," *Business Week*, 4 October 1993, 86–97.

51. This section is drawn from Moorhead and Griffin, *Organizational Behavior: Managing People and Organizations*, 268–270.

52. Elizabeth Wolfe Morrison and Frances J. Milliken, "Organizational Silence: A Barrier to Change and Development in a Pluralistic World," *Academy of Management Review* 25, no. 4 (2000): 706–725.

53. Shari Caudron, "Create an Empowering Environment," *Personnel Journal* 74, no. 9 (1995): 28–36.

54. Melville Cottrill, "Give Your Work Teams Time and Training," *Academy of Management Executive* 11, no. 3 (1997): 87–89. Also see John A. Wagner III and John R. Hollenbeck, *Management of Organizational Behavior* (Englewood Cliffs, N.J.: Prentice Hall, 1992), 392–398.

55. Bartlett and Ghoshal, *Transnational Management*, 806–807.

56. Kerry D. Carson and Paula Phillips Carson, "Career Entrenchment: A Quiet March Toward Occupational Death?" *Academy of Management Executive* 11, no. 1 (1997): 62–75.

57. Tuomo Peltonen, "Managerial Career Patterns in Transnational Corporations: An Organizational Capability Approach," *European Management Journal* 11, no. 2 (1993): 248–257.

58. Russ Forrester, "Empowerment: Rejuvenating a Potent Idea," *Academy of Management Executive* 14, no. 3 (2000): 67–80.

59. Courtney von Hippel, Stephen L. Mangum, David B. Greenberger, Robert L. Heneman, and Jeffrey D. Skoglind, "Temporary Employment: Can Organizations and Employees Both Win?" *Academy of Management Executive* 11, no. 1 (1997): 93–104.

60. Mary Cianni and Donna Wnuck, "Individual Growth and Team Enhancement: Moving Toward a New Model of Career Development," *Academy of Management Executive* 11, no. 1 (1997): 105–115.

61. Yves Doz and C. K. Prahalad, "Controlled Variety: A Challenge for Human Resource Management in the MNC," *Human Resource Management* 25, no. 1 (1986): 55–71.

CREDITS

NAME INDEX

COMPANY INDEX

SUBJECT INDEX